Adobe® Creative Suite 2 Bible

Ted Padova
Kelly Murdock

Adobe® Creative Suite 2 Bible

Published by
Wiley Publishing, Inc.
111 River Street

Hoboken, N.J. 07030-5774
www.wiley.com

Copyright © 2006 by Wiley Publishing, Inc., Indianapolis, Indiana

Published by Wiley Publishing, Inc., Indianapolis, Indiana

Published simultaneously in Canada

ISBN-13: 978-0-471-75476-3
ISBN-10: 0-471-75476-5

Manufactured in the United States of America

10 9 8 7 6 5 4 3 2 1

1O/RU/RS/QV/IN

No part of this publication may be reproduced, stored in a retrieval system or transmitted in any form or by any means, electronic, mechanical, photocopying, recording, scanning or otherwise, except as permitted under Sections 107 or 108 of the 1976 United States Copyright Act, without either the prior written permission of the Publisher, or authorization through payment of the appropriate per-copy fee to the Copyright Clearance Center, 222 Rosewood Drive, Danvers, MA 01923, (978) 750-8300, fax (978) 646-8600. Requests to the Publisher for permission should be addressed to the Legal Department, Wiley Publishing, Inc., 10475 Crosspoint Blvd., Indianapolis, IN 46256, (317) 572-3447, fax (317) 572-4355, E-Mail: http://www.wiley.com/go/permissions

LIMIT OF LIABILITY/DISCLAIMER OF WARRANTY: THE PUBLISHER AND THE AUTHOR MAKE NO REPRESENTATIONS OR WARRANTIES WITH RESPECT TO THE ACCURACY OR COMPLETENESS OF THE CONTENTS OF THIS WORK AND SPECIFICALLY DISCLAIM ALL WARRANTIES, INCLUDING WITHOUT LIMITATION WARRANTIES OF FITNESS FOR A PARTICULAR PURPOSE. NO WARRANTY MAY BE CREATED OR EXTENDED BY SALES OR PROMOTIONAL MATERIALS. THE ADVICE AND STRATEGIES CONTAINED HEREIN MAY NOT BE SUITABLE FOR EVERY SITUATION. THIS WORK IS SOLD WITH THE UNDERSTANDING THAT THE PUBLISHER IS NOT ENGAGED IN RENDERING LEGAL, ACCOUNTING, OR OTHER PROFESSIONAL SERVICES. IF PROFESSIONAL ASSISTANCE IS REQUIRED, THE SERVICES OF A COMPETENT PROFESSIONAL PERSON SHOULD BE SOUGHT. NEITHER THE PUBLISHER NOR THE AUTHOR SHALL BE LIABLE FOR DAMAGES ARISING HEREFROM. THE FACT THAT AN ORGANIZATION OR WEB SITE IS REFERRED TO IN THIS WORK AS A CITATION AND/OR A POTENTIAL SOURCE OF FURTHER INFORMATION DOES NOT MEAN THAT THE AUTHOR OR THE PUBLISHER ENDORSES THE INFORMATION THE ORGANIZATION OF WEB SITE MAY PROVIDE OR RECOMMENDATIONS IT MAY MAKE. FURTHER, READERS SHOULD BE AWARE THAT INTERNET WEB SITES LISTED IN THIS WORK MAY HAVE CHANGED OR DISAPPEARED BETWEEN WHEN THIS WORK WAS WRITTEN AND WHEN IT IS READ.

For general information on our other products and services or to obtain technical support, please contact our Customer Care Department within the U.S. at (800) 762-2974, outside the U.S. at (317) 572-3993 or fax (317) 572-4002.

Wiley also publishes its books in a variety of electronic formats. Some content that appears in print may not be available in electronic books.

Library of Congress Control Number: 2005935154

Trademarks: Wiley and the Wiley logo are trademarks or registered trademarks of John Wiley & Sons, Inc. and/or its affiliates. Adobe is a registered trademark of Adobe Systems Incorporated. All other trademarks are the property of their respective owners. Wiley Publishing, Inc. is not associated with any product or vendor mentioned in this book.

Ted Padova is the author of more than a dozen computer books, the most recent include: *Adobe Acrobat PDF Bible* (John Wiley & Sons) versions 4, 5, 6 & 7; *Adobe Acrobat 6 Complete Course*; *Creating Adobe Acrobat Forms*; *Illustrator Illuminated and Adobe Reader 7 Revealed (Peachpit/Adobe Press)*.

Ted has been involved in PostScript imaging over a decade and started a computer service bureau in 1990 in Ventura, California. He retired as CEO and managing partner of The Image Source Digital Imaging and Photo Finishing Centers of Thousand Oaks and Ventura, California, in 2004 and now spends his time writing and speaking nationally and internationally on digital imaging, Adobe Acrobat, and PDF.

Kelly Murdock has been authoring computer books for several years now and still gets immense enjoyment from the completed work. His book credits include various Web, graphics, and multimedia titles, including five editions of the book, *3ds max 7 Bible.* Other major accomplishments include *Master VISUALLY HTML and XHTML, Maya 6 Revealed, JavaScript Visual Blueprint, Adobe Atmosphere Bible, 3d Game Animation for Dummies,* and co-authoring duties on two editions of the *Illustrator Bible* (for versions 9 and 10).

With a background in engineering and computer graphics, Kelly has had many opportunities to flex his design muscles from Web site creation and design to freelance 3-D design projects. In his spare time, Kelly enjoys the outdoors while rock climbing, mountain biking, or skiing. He currently heads a design company with his brother, Chris, called Logical Paradox Design.

Credits

Acquisitions Editor
Tom Heine

Project Editor
Maureen Spears

Technical Editor
Adam Pratt

Copy Editor
Kim Heusel

Editorial Manager
Robyn Siesky

Vice President and Group Executive Publisher
Richard Swadley

Vice President and Executive Publisher
Bob Ipsen

Vice President and Executive Publisher
Barry Pruett

Project Coordinator
Michael Kruzil

Graphics and Production Specialists
Sean Decker
Carrie Foster
Mary Gillot
Lauren Goddard
Denny Hager
Jennifer Heleine
Barbara Moore
Lynsey Osborn
Alicia B. South

Quality Control Technician
John Greenough

Proofreading and Indexing
TECHBOOKS Production Services

From Ted Padova:

For Kensington Whittaker who shall remain alive in the hearts and minds of his parents — my good friends Brian and Lily.

From Kelly Murdock:

*I am an addict and I'm not alone.
And my hobby goes straight to the bone.
I am a runner and though both shoes have a hole,
The track is my home and first place is my goal.
Track and field is a lifelong sport,
That you can do whether you're tall or you're short.
Striving to go always farther, faster, and higher,
You can enjoy running well after you retire.
Whether hurdles, sprints, or distance,
Success comes from persistence.
Track has jumps of long, triple, and high,
And field events with discus and javelin that fly.
Track is unique because you race against time,
Instead of opponents who are in their prime.
Competitors become allies pushing you to run faster,
Helping you as your event you master.
Someday, when my bones grow weary,
I'll take up golf or chess to keep myself cheery,
But as long as I can run with good speed,
I'll keep on running and aim for the lead.
To Corey and Kenny, my brothers in speed, 2006*

Acknowledgments

The authors would like to thank Adam Pratt who did a great job technical editing the book. His insights into the software have proved extremely helpful time and time again. Thanks also to Tom Heine, Maureen Spears, Kim Heusel, and the many other editors at Wiley who are always so great to work with. Additionally we would like to thank the many individuals at Adobe Systems, far too numerous to mention, who have worked passionately on a terrific suite of programs to bring all of us the most advanced software applications developed to date for the creative professional.

From Ted Padova:

I'd like to thank my coauthor Kelly Murdock for his hard work and dedication to this project. A special thank you to Wendy Halderman who was not able to participate in this project due to time constraints, but who gave us great material in the first edition to embellish in this work.

From Kelly Murdock:

Writing books on computer graphics are interesting. Some books seem to write themselves and others are a task to finish. This book has elements of both, but even the hardest chapters would be impossible without the help of a key group of critical people. First and foremost, I would like to thank Ted. He's the driving force behind this book. It contains his vision and expertise and I'm once again honored to work alongside him.

Finally, I'd like to thank my family once again for putting up with me during this project. It's been a hectic couple of months for our family having changed jobs and moved into a new house, but thanks to the incredibly patient attitude of my sweet wife, Angie and my sons, Eric and Thomas, we've made it through. The next task is to find space for my ever-expanding library, remodel the basement, and reestablish the network. Hey, family, how about a vacation or two?

Contents at a Glance

Acknowledgments vi
Introduction xxvii

Part I: Getting to Know the Creative Suite 1
Chapter 1: Introducing the Creative Suite 3
Chapter 2: Taking a Tour of the Creative Suite 33
Chapter 3: Setting Preferences 79
Chapter 4: Understanding User Interfaces 129

Part II: Getting Started with Design Workflows 175
Chapter 5: Creating Production Workflows 177
Chapter 6: Creating Color-Managed Workflows 189
Chapter 7: Using Adobe Bridge 203
Chapter 8: Using Version Cue 275
Chapter 9: Managing Adobe PDF Files 297

Part III: Working with Objects and Images 305
Chapter 10: Creating, Selecting, and Editing Objects 307
Chapter 11: Acquiring and Correcting Images 381
Chapter 12: Transforming Objects and Images 413
Chapter 13: Applying Effects to Objects and Images 453
Chapter 14: Working with Layers 511
Chapter 15: Automating Tasks 591

Part IV: Working with Type 613
Chapter 16: Working with Fonts 615
Chapter 17: Working with Styles 637
Chapter 18: Working with Text Frames 687
Chapter 19: Working with Special Characters 715

Part V: Using Creative Suite and Microsoft Word Documents 725
Chapter 20: Importing Microsoft Word Documents 727
Chapter 21: Exporting Text to Microsoft Word 747
Chapter 22: Working with Tables 765
Chapter 23: Creating Charts and Graphs 789
Chapter 24: Microsoft Office and Professional Printing 815

Part VI: Working in Creative Design Workflows 837
Chapter 25: Creating Review Sessions 839
Chapter 26: Designing Layouts 883
Chapter 27: Modifying Layouts 907

Part VII: Document Repurposing. 917
Chapter 28: Exporting Designs for Web and Screen Viewing 919
Chapter 29: Preparing Documents for Distribution 951
Chapter 30: Working with XML 985

Part VIII: Creative Suite Document Delivery Workflows 1007
Chapter 31: Understanding Digital Rights Management 1009
Chapter 32: Creating Interactive Documents 1029
Chapter 33: Hosting Documents on the Web 1073
Chapter 34: Creating and Distributing PDFs on CDs/DVDs 1087
Chapter 35: Creating SWF and SVG Files 1109
Chapter 36: Creating Slide Presentations 1141

Part IX: Printing and Digital Prepress 1167
Chapter 37: Choosing Print Setups 1169
Chapter 38: Commercial Printing 1207

Index 1237

Contents

Acknowledgments vi

Introduction xxvii

Part I: Getting to Know the Creative Suite   1

Chapter 1: Introducing the Adobe Creative Suite 3

Why Creative Suite? 3
    Native file support 4
    Consistent user interface 4
    Versioning tools 5
    Consistent color management 5
    Dynamic object and image editing 6
    Visual file exchanges 6
    Support for PDF 6
Understanding the Creative Suite 7
    Adobe Bridge 7
    Adobe Photoshop CS2 9
    Adobe Illustrator CS2 12
    Adobe InDesign CS2 15
    Adobe GoLive CS2 20
    Adobe Acrobat Professional 7 24
    Version Cue CS2 28
    New Adobe Open and Save dialog boxes 28
OpenType Fonts 29
Summary 30

Chapter 2: Taking a Tour of the Creative Suite 33

Starting with a Sketch in Acrobat 33
    Scanning a sketch into Acrobat 33
    Submitting a sketch for e-mail review 35
    Adding comments to the PDF 37
    Collecting review comments 39
Editing Images in Photoshop 40
    Adjusting image properties 40
    Correcting distortions 42
    Cropping images 43
    Editing images 44
    Extracting images 45
Creating Illustrator Objects 48
    Using Live Trace 48
    Creating and filling objects 49
    Using effects 51
    Revolving a path 52

Versioning Files in Version Cue CS2 54
Using Adobe Bridge 56
Creating a Layout in InDesign 58
    Setting layout properties 59
    Importing content into InDesign 60
    Creating Master pages in InDesign 62
    Threading text 63
Preparing a Layout for Print 65
    Previewing separations 65
    Exporting to PDF for printing 66
Soft-Proofing in Adobe Acrobat 67
    Checking color in Acrobat 67
    Flattening transparency 68
    Creating a PDF/X file 69
Repurposing a Document for Web Hosting 71
    Using PDF Optimizer 71
    Packaging for GoLive 73
    Exporting packaged HTML using GoLive 75
Summary 76

Chapter 3: Setting Preferences 79

Getting to Know Common Preference Attributes 79
    Setting application-specific preferences 80
    Setting document-specific preferences 80
    Returning to default preferences 81
    Making dynamic preference adjustments 82
Setting the Program Preferences 82
    Adobe Bridge 82
    Illustrator CS2 preferences 87
    Photoshop CS2 preferences 99
    InDesign CS2 preferences 108
    Acrobat Professional preferences 125
    GoLive CS2 preferences 127
Summary 128

Chapter 4: Understanding User Interfaces 129

Accessing Tools 129
    Illustrator/InDesign/Photoshop common tools 132
    Illustrator/InDesign common tools 134
    Illustrator/Photoshop common tools 134
    Adobe Bridge tools 134
    Acrobat tools 134
    GoLive tools 135
Accessing Tool Options 136
    Illustrator tool options 137
    Photoshop tool options 144
    InDesign tool options 144
    Acrobat and GoLive tool options 147
Using Palettes and Workspaces 147
    Managing palettes 149
    Grouping palettes 154
    Saving workspaces 156

Some Common User-Interface Features 158
    Using context menus 158
    Getting help 159
Using Keyboard Shortcuts 162
    Customizing keyboard shortcuts in Illustrator 163
    Customizing keyboard shortcuts in Photoshop 167
    Customizing keyboard shortcuts in InDesign 170
    Customizing keyboard shortcuts in GoLive 172
    Working with keyboard shortcuts in Acrobat 173
Summary 174

Part II: Getting Started with Design Workflows   175

Chapter 5: Creating Production Workflows 177

Understanding Workflows 177
Workflows for Independent Artists 178
    Modifying designs 180
    Extending the workflow 180
Workflows for Studios and Production Houses 181
Document Repurposing 182
Setting Workflow Standards 184
    Set standards for the tools used in your workflow 184
    Use vendors who support the tools you use 184
    Devote time to ongoing training 185
    Develop a paradigm for managing your projects 185
Summary 187

Chapter 6: Creating Color-Managed Workflows 189

Understanding Profiling 189
    Profiles in workflows 190
    Calibrating color 190
    Acquiring profiles 191
    Profile embedding 192
    Profile mismatching 194
Color Management in the CS2 Applications 196
    Adjusting color settings 196
    Synchronizing color settings 199
    Swapping color settings 200
Printing with Profiles 200
Summary 202

Chapter 7: Using Adobe Bridge 203

Getting Familiar with the Bridge Workspace 203
    Using the Bridge Tools 205
    Saving Bridge workspaces 210
    Managing panes 212
    Managing windows 213
Organizing Files and Folders 214
    Creating new folders 214
    Adding files to folders 215
    Moving and copying files 215

Contents

Navigating folders 215
Deleting files 216
Labeling Files 216
Using context menus 218
Working with Collections 220
Adding Favorites 221
Batch renaming files 221
Working with Metadata 224
Metadata properties 224
Using XMP templates 226
Searching in the Bridge 230
Searching documents 231
Saving searches 238
Searching Stock Photos 238
Acquiring Adobe Stock Photos 240
Understanding terms of service 240
Getting an overview of ASPS 241
Downloading comps 243
Opening Camera Raw Files 246
Setting camera raw preferences 246
Using the Camera Raw plug-In 248
Applying settings in Bridge 253
Saving Camera Raw files 254
Synchronizing Color Across the CS2 Programs 256
Enabling Application Commands from the Bridge 257
Photoshop support 257
Illustrator support 264
InDesign support 264
Exploring Options in the Bridge Center 265
Using the RSS Reader 268
Using Adobe Studio 271
Viewing Slide Shows 271
Summary 272

Chapter 8: Using Version Cue 275

Setting Up the Version Cue Workspace 275
Setting Version Cue preferences 275
Specifying workspace folders 276
Exporting workspace data 277
Updating Version Cue 278
Enabling Version Cue within a CS2 application 280
Working with Adobe Dialog 281
Accessing Version Cue Files 284
Creating a Version Cue project 284
Accessing remote Version Cue projects 285
Opening Version Cue files 285
Saving Version Cue files 286
Understanding states 287
Adding files to a Version Cue project 288
Working with versions 288

Working with alternates 288
Deleting Version Cue files 290
Using the Version Cue CS2 Administration Web Pages 290
Adding and editing users 291
Managing projects 292
Using the Advanced features 294
Summary 296

Chapter 9: Managing Adobe PDF Files 297

Organizing Files 297
Using the Categories pane 298
Using the Files pane 300
Using the Pages pane 302
Bookmarking Web-hosted PDFs 303
Summary 304

Part III: Working with Objects and Images — 305

Chapter 10: Creating, Selecting, and Editing Objects 307

Creating Objects in Illustrator 307
Using the Pen tool 308
Using the Type tool 311
Creating lines and shapes 311
Using the Paintbrush and Pencil tools 312
Creating Objects in InDesign 314
Creating Objects in Photoshop 315
Specifying custom shapes 316
Creating paths 316
Painting with shapes 317
Creating and Editing Objects in Acrobat 317
Adding document-enhancement objects 318
Adding commenting objects 319
Creating Objects in GoLive 320
Selecting Objects 320
Using Illustrator and InDesign's Toolbox selection tools 321
Selecting objects with Illustrator's Layers palette 322
Using Illustrator's Select menu 323
Organizing Objects 323
Adding objects to layers 323
Grouping objects 324
Hiding and locking objects 324
Filling and Stroking Objects 325
Applying fill and stroke colors to objects in Illustrator and InDesign . . 325
Applying other stroke attributes 326
Using Illustrator's Live Paint 331
Filling and stroking a pixel selection 336
Filling and stroking a Photoshop path 337
Assigning Color 337
Learning the various color modes 338

　　　　Using the Color palette 341
　　　　Using the Color Picker 343
　　　　Using the Eyedropper tool 344
　　　　Managing color profiles and settings 346
　　Working with Gradients 347
　　　　Using the Gradient palette 347
　　　　Using the Gradient tool 349
　　　　Creating gradient meshes in Illustrator 352
　　Working with Patterns 353
　　　　Using patterns in Illustrator 354
　　　　Using patterns in Photoshop 355
　　Using Transparency 356
　　　　Applying transparency to objects and images 356
　　　　Using blending modes 357
　　　　Creating an opacity mask 358
　　Using Symbols, Graphic Styles, and Swatches 360
　　　　Working with symbols in Illustrator 360
　　　　Working with object styles in InDesign 363
　　　　Working with graphic styles in Illustrator and Photoshop 365
　　　　Working with swatches 365
　　　　Using the Library palette 367
　　　　Exporting snippets 368
　　　　Using Photoshop's Preset Manager 368
　　Editing Objects 369
　　　　Editing paths in Illustrator 369
　　　　Cutting objects 373
　　　　Creating compound paths and shapes in Illustrator 374
　　　　Blending objects in Illustrator 375
　　　　Creating a clipping mask in Illustrator 377
　　　　Distorting objects in Illustrator 377
　　Summary 380

Chapter 11: Acquiring and Correcting Images 381

　　Scanning Images in Photoshop 381
　　Acquiring Digital Camera Images 384
　　　　Using Camera Raw 384
　　　　Correcting Red Eye 385
　　　　Using the Lens Correction filter 385
　　Correcting Images 387
　　　　Using Levels 387
　　　　Using Curves 388
　　　　Using Auto adjustments 389
　　　　Editing 32-bit High Dynamic Range images 390
　　Painting Images 391
　　　　Painting images in Photoshop 391
　　　　Working with images in the other CS2 applications 395
　　Selecting Pixels in Photoshop 403
　　　　Using the Selection tools 403
　　　　Using the Select menu 406
　　　　Converting drawn paths into selections 408
　　Editing Images 408
　　　　Cropping images in Photoshop 408
　　　　Retouching images in Photoshop 409
　　　　Using the Spot Healing Brush 410

>   Distorting images 411
> Summary 412

Chapter 12: Transforming Objects and Images 413

>   Transforming Objects in Illustrator 413
>   Using the bounding box 414
>   Using the transform tools 418
>   Using the Transform menu 425
>   Using the Transform palette 432
>   Transforming Patterns and Fills 434
>   Transforming patterns in Illustrator 434
>   Transforming patterns in Photoshop 436
>   Transforming content in InDesign 438
>   Transforming Images in Photoshop 440
>   Translating a selection 440
>   Moving pixels 441
>   Using Free Transform 441
>   Using the Transform menu 442
>   Controlling perspective 442
>   Using Image Warp 443
>   Arranging Stacking Order 444
>   Controlling stacking order using layers 444
>   Changing stacking order with the Arrange menu 445
>   Changing stacking order with the Clipboard 446
>   Changing stacking order within a group 446
>   Changing Z-Index in GoLive 446
>   Aligning and Distributing Objects 446
>   Aligning objects 447
>   Distributing objects 447
>   Distributing spacing 447
>   Aligning and Distributing Image Layers in Photoshop 449
>   Aligning image layers 450
>   Distributing image layers 450
>   Using Smart Guides 450
>   Summary 451

Chapter 13: Applying Effects to Objects and Images 453

>   Using Photoshop Filters 453
>   Accessing the Filter Gallery 454
>   Using other filters 458
>   Using third-party filters 477
>   Using the Filter interfaces 477
>   Blending filters 490
>   Using Photoshop filters in Illustrator 490
>   Using Illustrator Filters 491
>   Using the Colors filters 491
>   Using the Create filters 492
>   Using the Distort filters 493
>   Using the Stylize filters 494
>   Using Illustrator Effects 495
>   Rasterizing effects 496
>   Creating 3-D objects 497
>   Using the Convert to Shapes effects 502

　　　　Applying standard Illustrator features as effects 502
　　　　Using the Stylize effects 503
　　　　Using the Warp effects 504
　Using Photoshop's Layer Effects and Styles 506
　Applying Effects in InDesign 507
　　　　Adding drop shadows 507
　　　　Feathering objects 507
　　　　Creating corner effects 508
　Summary 509

Chapter 14: Working with Layers 511

　Using the Layers Palette 512
　　　　Creating layers 513
　　　　Selecting and targeting layers 513
　　　　Hiding and locking layers 514
　　　　Rearranging layers 514
　　　　Copying objects between layers 514
　　　　Duplicating layers 515
　　　　Deleting layers 515
　　　　Merging layers 515
　Using Layers in InDesign 517
　　　　Condensing the Layers palette 517
　　　　Using guides 517
　　　　Suppressing text wrap on hidden layers 517
　　　　Reordering Master objects above layers 518
　　　　Importing layered files 520
　　　　Applying transparency and blending modes to a layer 520
　Using Layers in Illustrator 521
　　　　Changing the Layers palette view 522
　　　　Using sublayers 522
　　　　Printing and previewing layers 523
　　　　Creating layer templates 524
　　　　Releasing items to layers in Illustrator 527
　　　　Collecting layers and flattening artwork 527
　　　　Importing Photoshop layers and comps
　　　　　　into Illustrator and InDesign 527
　　　　Exporting CSS layers 528
　　　　Applying appearance attributes to layers in Illustrator 529
　　　　Creating clipping masks 535
　Using Layers in Photoshop 539
　　　　Working with a Background layer 541
　　　　Selecting and controlling multiple layers 541
　　　　Auto Selecting layers with the Move tool 542
　　　　Aligning and distributing image layers 542
　　　　Creating layer groups 542
　　　　Linking layers 543
　　　　Locking transparency, pixels, and position 547
　　　　Working with Type and Shape layers 548
　　　　Setting layer opacity and selecting a blending mode 553
　　　　Using layer effects 558
　　　　Using adjustment and fill layers 563
　　　　Masking with layers 564
　　　　Using layer comps 568
　　　　Placing layer comps in Illustrator and InDesign 570

Using Layers in GoLive 571
    Adding layers to a Web page 572
    Using the Layers palette 573
    Editing layer attributes 574
    Animating layers 578
    Importing layered Photoshop images 582
    Showing and hiding InDesign Layers 583
    Layer options and properties 585
    Making the Layers tab appear when a document is opened 587
    Adding interactive layer buttons 587
Summary 590

Chapter 15: Automating Tasks 591

Using the Actions Palette in Photoshop and Illustrator 591
    Playing an action 592
    Creating and saving a new action set 593
    Creating new actions 593
    Editing existing actions 596
    Batch-processing actions 597
    Creating a droplet 598
Using Scripts 600
Using Photoshop's Script Events Manager 601
Using Photoshop's Additional Automation Features 602
Working with Data-Driven Graphics 602
    Defining variables 603
    Binding variables to objects 604
    Capturing a data set 604
    Saving variables 604
Batch-Processing PDF Files 604
    Executing sequences 605
    Editing sequences 606
    Creating a new sequence 608
    Setting batch-processing preferences 608
    Creating batch sequences using JavaScripts 609
Summary 612

Part IV: Working with Type   613

Chapter 16: Working with Fonts 615

Understanding Fonts 615
    Font formats 615
    Advantages of OpenType fonts 617
    Font licenses 618
Managing Fonts 618
    Installing fonts in Mac OS X 618
    Installing fonts in Windows 619
    Organizing your fonts 619
    Using font-management tools 620
Creating Type Outlines and Special Effects 623
    Converting type to outlines in Illustrator 624
    Converting type to outlines in Photoshop 628

  Converting type to outlines in InDesign 631
 Summary 634

Chapter 17: Working with Styles 637

 Setting Type 637
  Setting type in Illustrator 638
  Setting type in Photoshop 650
  Setting type in InDesign 653
  Creating type on paths 663
 Creating Character Styles 665
  Using character styles in Illustrator 665
  Using styles in Photoshop 667
  Using character styles in InDesign 667
 Creating Paragraph Styles 668
  Using paragraph styles in Illustrator 668
  Using paragraph styles in InDesign 670
 Creating Nested Styles 671
 Using Graphic Styles 676
  Using graphic styles in Illustrator 676
  Using graphic styles in Photoshop 680
  Using graphic styles in InDesign 682
 Summary 686

Chapter 18: Working with Text Frames 687

 Creating Text Frames 687
  Working with text threads 687
  Adding new frames to a text thread 689
  Unthreading text frames 690
 Setting Text Frame Attributes 691
  Creating columns and insets 691
  Setting text attributes 695
 Creating Text Frames on Master Pages 696
  Creating manual text frames 697
  Creating master text frames 699
  Modifying master text frames 700
 Creating Text Wraps 702
  Wrapping text in Illustrator 702
  Wrapping text in InDesign 709
 Summary 714

Chapter 19: Working with Special Characters 715

 Working with Glyphs Palettes 715
 Using Special Typographic Characters 719
  Inserting special characters 719
  Inserting white space characters 722
  Inserting break characters 722
 Inserting Inline Graphics 723
 Summary 724

Part V: Using Creative Suite and Microsoft Word Documents — 725

Chapter 20: Importing Microsoft Word Documents 727

Using the Clipboard 727
    Maintaining formatting 728
    Missing fonts 729
Exporting Text from Word 731
Importing Text 731
    Opening Word documents in Illustrator 731
    Placing text documents in Illustrator 732
    Placing Word documents into InDesign 732
    Drag and drop text files 734
    Importing Word documents in Photoshop 735
    Formatting imported text in Photoshop 736
    Pasting Word text in Acrobat 736
    Pasting Word text into Acrobat notes and form fields 738
Importing Styles 738
    Editing imported styles 739
    Deleting imported styles 739
    Mapping Word styles to InDesign styles 740
Working with Imported Text 740
Moving Word Content to GoLive 744
    Using the Clipboard for Web page text 744
    Using the Paste Special command 744
    Opening text files 745
Summary 745

Chapter 21: Exporting Text to Microsoft Word 747

Exporting Text 747
    Recognizing the advantages of Word 748
    Identifying exporting methods 748
    Selecting text 748
    Exporting formatting 749
Using the Clipboard 749
    Moving Illustrator, Photoshop, and GoLive text into Word 749
    Moving InDesign text to Word 751
    Moving Acrobat text to Word 751
Using Export Menu Commands 752
    Exporting Illustrator text 752
    Exporting text from InDesign 753
    Exporting text from Acrobat 754
    Exporting comments from Acrobat 755
Dynamic Text Editing 758
Summary 764

Chapter 22: Working with Tables 765

Importing Tables 765
    Importing Microsoft Word tables 765
    Importing Microsoft Excel tables 769

Working with Tables in InDesign 771
    Creating tables 771
    Editing tables 773
    Formatting tables 775
    Formatting cells 776
    Exporting tagged tables from InDesign 778
Using Excel Spreadsheets in InDesign 778
Working with Tables in GoLive 783
    Creating GoLive tables 784
    Populating cells 784
    Importing tables 785
    Selecting cells 785
    Moving, adding, and deleting rows and columns 785
    Resizing cells 786
    Formatting cells 786
    Using styles 786
    Merging cells 786
Summary 787

Chapter 23: Creating Charts and Graphs 789

Knowing the Various Chart and Graph Types 789
Using Illustrator Graphs 792
    Using the Graph tool 792
    Entering data in the Graph Data window 793
    Formatting graphs 797
    Combining graph types 800
Customizing Illustrator Graphs 801
    Selecting graph parts 801
    Changing shading 801
    Changing text 801
    Using graph designs 801
Importing Excel and Word Charts 810
    Creating Excel charts 811
    Transporting Excel charts via the Clipboard 811
    Creating Word charts and diagrams 812
    Transporting Word diagrams via the Clipboard 812
Summary 813

Chapter 24: Microsoft Office and Professional Printing 815

Printing Microsoft Word Documents 815
    Converting standard page sizes to PDF 816
    Converting Word files with custom page sizes 819
    Printing converted Word files in Acrobat 824
Printing from PowerPoint 827
Preparing Excel Files 834
Summary 835

Part VI: Working in Creative Design Workflows — 837

Chapter 25: Creating Review Sessions — 839

- Setting Commenting Preferences — 839
- Using Commenting Tools — 842
    - Using the Note tool — 842
    - Using Text Edit tools — 851
    - Using the Stamp tool — 852
    - Managing stamps — 857
    - Paste Clipboard Image as Stamp tool — 858
    - Drawing Markup Tools — 859
- Using the Comments Pane — 859
    - Viewing comments — 860
    - Sorting comments — 861
    - Navigating comments — 862
    - Searching comments — 862
    - Printing comments — 862
    - Deleting comments — 862
    - Marking comments — 863
    - Setting comment status — 863
    - Editing comment pop-up notes — 863
- Enabling PDFs with Reader Extensions — 863
- Creating an E-Mail-Based Review — 866
- Using the Review Tracker — 869
    - Viewing documents in the Tracker — 870
    - Expand/Collapse — 871
- Exporting and Importing Comments — 872
    - Exporting comments to Microsoft Word — 872
    - Exporting comments to AutoCAD — 873
    - Exporting comments to files — 873
    - Exporting selected comments — 874
- Filtering Comments — 874
- Creating Comment Summaries — 875
- Comparing Documents — 878
- Summary — 880

Chapter 26: Designing Layouts — 883

- Establishing an InDesign Layout — 883
    - Creating new documents — 883
    - Creating a document preset — 886
    - Changing document settings — 888
    - Exporting CS2 documents to CS — 889
    - Converting Quark and PageMaker files — 889
- Working with Pages and Spreads — 889
    - Using the Pages palette — 889
    - Selecting and targeting pages and spreads — 891
    - Inserting and deleting and rearranging pages — 891
- Creating and Using Master Pages — 892

    Creating a Master 892
    Applying Masters 893
    Overriding, detaching, deleting, and hiding Master objects 894
Using Layers 894
    Creating new layers 894
    Positioning Master objects on top of document objects 895
Adding Page Numbering 896
    Adding auto page numbering 896
    Defining sections 896
Enhancing Layouts 897
    Using rulers 897
    Using grids 897
    Using guides 898
    Using frames 900
Importing Images and Objects 901
    Importing Photoshop artwork 902
    Importing Illustrator artwork and PDF files 902
    Dynamically updating content 903
Assembling a Layout 903
Summary 906

Chapter 27: Modifying Layouts 907

Using Artwork Versions 907
    Using the Links palette 907
    Setting the display quality 910
    Anchoring objects 911
Summary 916

Part VII: Document Repurposing   917

Chapter 28: Exporting Designs for Web and Screen Viewing 919

Setting Up a Site Window with the Site Wizard 919
    Using the New dialog box 920
    Creating a new site 920
    Adding pages to a site 924
    Updating pages 924
Creating Web pages in GoLive 924
    Building Web pages and using views 925
    Using the Web page tools 927
    Adding objects to Web pages 928
    Changing object properties 929
    Adding Web page text 930
    Linking Web pages 930
    Working with Basic Objects and images 931
Using Smart Objects 934
    Using the Save for Web dialog box 934
    Editing the Smart Objects image 936
    Cropping Smart Objects 936
Cascading Style Sheets 937
    Using the CSS Editor 938

                Defining styles 939
                Applying styles 939
                Creating an external style sheet 940
            Designing for Mobile Devices 940
                Creating new GoLive documents for Mobile Devices 941
                Converting existing documents to XHTML Mobile 942
            Packaging for GoLive 944
                Packaging an InDesign document 944
                Examining package contents 945
                Viewing the package in GoLive 946
                Dragging and dropping package assets 947
                Exporting to HTML 949
            Summary 950

Chapter 29: Preparing Documents for Distribution 951

            Repurposing Documents 951
                Reducing file size 952
                Using PDF Optimizer 953
            Setting Document Open Preferences 957
                Setting initial views 958
                Saving the initial view 961
            Using Acrobat Catalog 962
                Preparing PDFs for indexing 962
                Creating a new index file 966
                Saving index definitions 969
                Options 970
                Building the index 972
                Rebuilding an index 974
                Purging data 974
                Setting preferences 975
            Using Index Files 976
                Loading index files 976
                Disabling indexes 978
                Index information 979
                Searching an index 980
                Searching external devices 983
            Summary 984

Chapter 30: Working with XML 985

            Understanding XML 985
                XML and Creative Suite 986
                XML and SVG 986
            Using XML in InDesign 987
                Marking elements with XML tags 987
                Using the Structure pane 989
                Exporting XML 993
                Importing XML tagged content 995
            Using XML in Creative Workflows 996
                Creating InDesign Layouts 996
                Tagging an InDesign Document 997
                Export InDesign Files as XML 999
                Import XML in InDesign 1000
            Viewing and Editing XML Data in GoLive 1002

| Using the Outline Editor 1003
| Using the Source Code Editor 1004
| Splitting the editors 1005
| Saving Acrobat Files as XML Documents 1006
| Summary 1006

Part VIII: Creative Suite Document Delivery Workflows 1007

Chapter 31: Understanding Digital Rights Management 1009

Understanding Document Security 1009
    Permissions 1010
    Levels of encryption 1010
    Signature handlers 1010
Securing Documents 1011
    Adding security in Acrobat 1011
    Adding security in other CS Programs 1018
Securing Files with Attachments 1020
    Creating Security Policies 1020
    Using Secure PDF Delivery 1024
Summary 1027

Chapter 32: Creating Interactive Documents 1029

Creating Hyperlinks 1029
    Creating links and buttons in InDesign 1030
    Creating links and buttons in Acrobat 1033
Working with Animation 1043
    Animation and Adobe Illustrator 1043
    Animation and Adobe Photoshop 1043
    Animation in InDesign and Acrobat 1045
Using Multimedia in Designs 1048
    Importing multimedia in InDesign 1048
    Creating interactive multimedia buttons 1050
    Importing multimedia in Acrobat 1055
Hyperlinks and Publications 1060
    Bookmarks in InDesign 1060
    Bookmarks in Acrobat 1061
    Opening files using bookmarks 1061
Creating On Demand Documents 1065
    Understanding the code 1069
    Running the scripts 1069
Summary 1072

Chapter 33: Hosting Documents on the Web 1073

Preparing to Publish a Web Site 1073
    Setting up Internet access 1073
    Specifying a publish server 1075
    Adding and configuring sites 1076
Publishing a Web Site Using GoLive 1079
    Connecting to a server 1079
    Uploading, downloading, and synchronizing files .. 1080
    Using the FTP Browser to view files 1081
    Downloading a Web page 1082

Exporting a Web Site 1084
Summary 1085

Chapter 34: Creating and Distributing PDFs on CDs/DVDs 1087

Preparing PDF Documents 1087
    Working with Adobe PDF Settings 1088
    Creating PDFs from Adobe Photoshop 1098
    Converting to PDF using Acrobat 1102
    Acquiring PDFs from clients 1103
Writing PDFs to CD-ROMs and DVDs 1105
    Adding metadata to files 1105
    Organizing a collection of PDFs 1105
    Replicating CD-ROM/DVDs 1106
    Adding a Web page for updates 1106
    Creating a welcome file 1106
    Adding Adobe Reader 1107
Adding Security to CD-ROMs 1107
Summary 1108

Chapter 35: Creating SWF and SVG Files 1109

Creating SWF Files in Illustrator 1109
    Saving SWF files 1109
    Illustrator and SWF differences 1114
    Creating SWF animations with layers 1114
    Using symbols 1115
Creating SVG Files in Illustrator 1117
    Using SVG effects 1118
    Adding interactivity 1121
    Addressing exporting issues 1122
    Saving SVG files 1122
Using SWF and SVG Files in GoLive 1129
    Adding SWF and SVG objects to a Web page in GoLive 1129
    Using Illustrator Smart Objects 1131
Using SWF Files in Acrobat 1134
    Converting Web pages to PDF 1134
    Importing SWF files in PDF documents 1136
Summary 1139

Chapter 36: Creating Slide Presentations 1141

Converting Presentation Documents to PDF 1141
    Converting PowerPoint slides to PDF 1142
    Converting Apple Keynote slides to PDF (Mac) 1146
Creating Presentations in CS programs 1147
    Using InDesign as a presentation-authoring tool 1147
    Using Photoshop as an authoring tool 1154
    Using Illustrator as an authoring tool 1155
Using Layers with Presentations 1157
Adding Page Transitions 1159
Using Full Screen Views 1160
    Viewing slides in Acrobat 1161
    Setting Full Screen preferences 1162
    Scrolling pages 1163
    Creating interactivity in Full Screen mode 1163
Summary 1165

Part IX: Printing and Digital Prepress — 1167

Chapter 37: Choosing Print Setups — 1169

Selecting Desktop Printers — 1169
    Printer selection on the Mac — 1169
    Printer selection on Windows — 1172
Setting Print Options — 1175
    Setting print options in Illustrator — 1175
    Setting print options in Photoshop — 1186
    Setting print options in InDesign — 1191
    Setting print options in Acrobat — 1199
    Printing PDF files to PostScript devices — 1205
Summary — 1206

Chapter 38: Commercial Printing — 1207

Soft-Proofing Documents in the CS Programs — 1207
    Soft-proofing files in InDesign — 1208
    Soft-proofing files in Illustrator — 1212
Proofing and printing in Acrobat Professional — 1214
    Soft-proofing menu commands — 1214
    Soft-proofing tools — 1219
Preflighting PDF Files — 1225
    Preflighting a file — 1225
    Producing a PDF/X-compliant file — 1226
    Creating PDF/A-compliant files — 1228
    Creating a new profile — 1228
    Creating reports and comments — 1231
    Preflighting batches of files — 1231
Packaging Documents for Commercial Printing — 1232
    PDF creation in Illustrator — 1232
    PDF creation in InDesign — 1233
Printing PDF/X Files — 1234
Summary — 1235

Index — 1237

Introduction

Welcome to the Adobe Creative Suite 2 Bible — your comprehensive guide to working with the complete suite of Adobe's imaging programs. In this book, we make an effort to help you understand design and productivity features available from all the Creative Suite 2 (CS2) programs and how the documents you create from the individual applications work together to help you create and publish content for print, Web hosting, and CD-ROM replication.

So why would we spend time covering subjects that are individually treated in other Wiley Bible publications? This is a good question and the answer should be clear to you before you walk out of your local bookstore with this sizeable volume. It's true that there is a Wiley Bible covering each of the individual programs mentioned in this book. These other works are comprehensive and teach you just about every tool and feature related to the specific programs.

This book is much different than the other Bibles. Our primary focus is to cover workflow solutions for independent designers and members of design teams working in agencies, publication houses, and any firm related to publishing for screen, print, and Web. Therefore, we won't go into minute detail on each program, and often we point you to one of the other fine Wiley publications to amplify your learning.

We assume you have some experience in at least one of the programs covered in this book. You may be a designer who works religiously with Adobe Photoshop, QuarkXPress, and Macromedia (Adobe) FreeHand. Or you may work with Adobe Illustrator and Adobe Photoshop, but know little about page-layout programs. What you need to know are essential methods for integrating application documents among the CS2 programs. Perhaps you don't need to know every aspect of Adobe InDesign, but you want to create sophisticated layouts using many outstanding type features and want to know how to import images in your designs.

If you're switching from another program or you want to add one of the CS2 applications to your design toolbox, this book helps you understand the relationships among programs and how to seamlessly integrate files among the most sophisticated suite of software applications ever developed for creative professionals.

As we said, the focus is on workflow solutions. In this book, you learn how to set up the CS2 applications for workflow environments, step through the creative workflow process, and get to productivity without having to master every feature in a program. The tools and tasks related to office workers and business professionals have been left out. Rather, the emphasis is on a complete coverage of tools and workflows to help creative professionals get up to speed fast.

How to Read This Book

The *Adobe Creative Suite 2 Bible* is made up of 38 chapters in nine parts. Unlike other comprehensive computer publications that target beginning users, reading this volume assumes you have some basic knowledge of at least one imaging program like Photoshop, an illustration program, or a layout program. We further assume you know something about user interfaces common to imaging programs that use palettes, menus, and tools. And, we make the assumption you know some aspects of the professional printing market for commercial prepress and printing.

Because you have some knowledge of computer programs similar to those found in the Creative Suite, you can jump in anywhere and learn about any feature set. In most chapters, we include a discussion concerning the integration of the CS2 programs. Therefore, a chapter dealing with text includes text handling not only in InDesign, but Illustrator, Photoshop, GoLive, and Acrobat. Rather than think of the programs you want to learn about, search more for the techniques and features you want to learn.

To give you a broad idea of how the programs work together, we recommend you look over Chapter 2, where we provide steps you can replicate to produce a design piece using the CS2 programs. Chapter 2 helps you understand the interoperability of the CS2 programs.

We also recommend you look over Chapter 7, which covers the new Adobe Bridge program. As the central heart of the Adobe Creative Suite, Adobe Bridge is where you start and end most of your design workflows. This extraordinary addition to the Creative Suite applications is something you'll use each time you launch one or more CS2 programs.

Apart from Chapter 2 and Chapter 7 and the specific features you want to learn, keep in mind that this book, like other Wiley Bible publications, is a reference work. Keep it handy as you work in the CS2 applications, and refer to the index and contents when you need help working on a task or trying to further understand one of the programs.

Icons

What would a Bible be without icons? The use of icons throughout the book offers you an at-a-glance hint of what content is being addressed. You can jump to the text adjacent to these symbols to help you get a little more information, warn you of a potential problem, or amplify the concept being addressed in the text. In this book you'll find the following icons:

A caution icon alerts you to a potential problem in using one of the CS applications, any tools or menus, or any issues related to exchanging files between programs. Pay close attention to these caution messages to avoid some problems.

A note icon signifies a message that may add more clarity or help you deal with a feature more effectively.

Tips help you find shortcuts to produce results or work through a series of steps to complete a task. Some tips provide you with information that may not be documented in the Help files accompanying each of the CS programs.

Walking you through steps and techniques in a linear fashion is almost impossible for a suite of programs. The applications have so many interrelated features that covering all aspects of a single feature in one part of a book just doesn't work. Therefore, some common features for commands, tools, actions, or tasks may be spread out and discussed in different chapters. When the information is divided among different parts of the book, you'll find a Cross-Reference icon that refers you to another part of the book covering related information.

We marked new CS2 features with a special icon so you can easily see a new program feature not available in earlier editions of each application. Pay particular attention to the new features to see how the engineers at Adobe Systems refined the interoperability of working among these programs.

The Book Contents

To simplify your journey through the Creative Suite applications, the book is broken up into nine separate parts. There are a total of 38 chapters that address features common to creative production workflows. These parts are covered in the following sections.

Part I: Getting to Know the Creative Suite

To start off, we offer some basic information related to the Creative Suite Premium Edition. You're given a tour of the programs in the form of steps to produce design pieces and learn how these applications work together to help you publish your content. You learn how to set up the work environments in all the programs and set preference options for standardizing workflows.

Part II: Getting Started in Design Workflows

Design workflow is a broad term and may mean different things to different people. This part clarifies the meaning of workflow solutions as they apply to creative professionals and the CS applications, as well as introduces you to new tools for versioning documents and creating consistent color across the CS programs. We added a chapter on using Adobe Bridge and another chapter on using Acrobat's Organizer in this section. These tools are used throughout the remaining chapters in the book.

Part III: Working with Objects and Images

You have basically three elements used to communicate messages in artwork. Images, objects, and type constitute the content of your products. In this part, we focus on objects you might create in Illustrator, InDesign, and Photoshop, as well as images that are edited in Photoshop and imported into other CS2 programs.

Part IV: Working with Type

Setting type and working with type as text and objects are standard design practices everyone uses. With many features for setting type in the CS2 applications, this part offers you a glimpse into how you can use the programs to implement these impressive features.

Part V: Using the Creative Suite and Microsoft Office

Whether Microsoft Office is part of your design toolbox or you acquire files from clients who provide you with Office documents, it's hard to talk about layout and design without introducing Office files. This part covers working with files that originate in Office programs and end up in one or more of the CS2 applications.

Part VI: Working in Creative Design Workflows

The CS2 applications offer you more than tools to create artwork. You can set up review sessions where you and your colleagues or clients mark up documents in a review session for collaboration. With the introduction of enabling PDF documents with Adobe Reader usage rights, you can extend comment and review to all your clients and coworkers who use the free Adobe Reader program. Add to comment and review, the use of templates and models for design pieces, you can minimize duplication and learn to work faster. This part covers aspects of both collaboration and working efficiently.

Part VII: Document Repurposing

When you create documents for one output purpose and need to modify files for other output results, you're engaged in document repurposing. Rather than start anew each time a modification needs to be made for delivering files for alternative content, you can save time by reworking existing documents suited for a variety of purposes. This part covers various aspects of document repurposing. We also simplified working with XML and provide a series of steps to help you understand how you can accomplish document repurposing with XML in terms that creative professionals can understand.

Part VIII: Creative Suite Document Delivery Workflows

Issues related to Digital Rights Management, archiving documents, delivering files for Web hosting, and replicating CD-ROMs are but some of the delivery workflows you're likely to experience. This part covers preparing files for delivery in various forms.

Part IX: Printing and Digital Prepress

Printing files is still a major function of every creative professional's workflow. This part covers printing to composite printers and preparing files for commercial printing.

Staying Connected

Adobe Systems maintains a comprehensive Web site where you can find information on product upgrades, conferences and seminars, aftermarket books, help and technical support, as well as tips and techniques. Visit Adobe's Web site at www.adobe.com for the latest news related to all the CS2 applications. Be certain to look over Chapter 7 where you can find easy access to Adobe's Web pages carrying tips and techniques from within Adobe Bridge.

Registration

Regardless of whether you purchase the Creative Suite or individual applications, Adobe Systems has made it possible to register the product. You can register on the World Wide Web or mail a registration form to Adobe. You'll find great advantages in being a registered user. First, update information will be sent to you, so you'll know when a product revision occurs. Secondly, information can be distributed to help you achieve the most out of using all the Creative Suite programs. By all means, complete the registration. It will be to your benefit.

Contacting Us

If, after reviewing this publication, you feel some important information was overlooked or you have any questions concerning the Creative Suite programs, you can contact us and let us know your views, opinions, hoorahs, complaints, or provide information that might get included in the next revision. If it's good enough, you might even get a credit line in the acknowledgments. By all means, send a note. E-mail inquiries can be sent to:

Ted at ted@west.net

Kelly at kmurdock@sfcn.org

Getting to Know the Creative Suite

PART

I

In This Part

Chapter 1
Introducing the Adobe Creative Suite

Chapter 2
Taking a Tour of Creative Suite

Chapter 3
Setting Preferences

Chapter 4
Understanding User Interfaces

Introducing the Adobe Creative Suite

CHAPTER 1

✦ ✦ ✦ ✦

In This Chapter

Understanding why Adobe developed the Creative Suite

Knowing the Creative Suite applications

Working with OpenType fonts

✦ ✦ ✦ ✦

The Adobe Premium Creative Suite is composed of several programs designed to work together to accomplish all your publishing needs for output to print, screen viewing, and Web hosting. Instead of marketing the individual program components of the Creative Suite, Adobe Systems has spent much of its marketing effort targeting the entire Creative Suite to design professionals.

This chapter offers a description of the Creative Suite programs and gives you an idea of how they work together. In this chapter, you learn about the purpose of each program and the relationship each program has with other members of the Creative Suite team. In addition, you receive a brief summary of new features contained in the latest releases of the individual programs.

Why Creative Suite?

Each program in the Creative Suite version 2 is an upgrade from the CS1 applications, and each is available for upgrades individually. So, why is Adobe Systems spending so much marketing effort informing users about the benefits of the Creative Suite? And why talk about the Creative Suite as a single entity when users are likely to upgrade the individual software programs in their design studios? These may be the first questions on your mind as you see the advertising for Adobe imaging product upgrades.

The answer is that Creative Suite is a single design solution where the whole is greater than its parts. For years, Adobe Systems built applications on programs like Adobe Illustrator and Adobe InDesign with core PDF technology. These programs evolved with common elements so that you, the creative professional, could easily exchange files among Adobe programs.

Rather than rely on a single program to perform tasks such as illustration, layout, and printing, Adobe offers you several applications, each a tool designed for a specific purpose to help you become more efficient in your creative process. These tools seamlessly integrate into the greater toolbox called Adobe Creative Suite. After working in individual programs, you can collect the creative elements together using Adobe Bridge and Adobe InDesign CS2 as the tool to perform layout assembly. You can then travel to output by exporting files to PDF documents in Adobe Acrobat, or you can host parts of your layout on a Web site using Adobe GoLive CS2.

Note Adobe Bridge is a separate executable application introduced in the Creative Suite version 2. Adobe Bridge is included when you purchase any of the CS2 stand-alone products but is not available for purchase as a separate product. For more information on Adobe Bridge, see the section "Adobe Bridge" later in this chapter.

As stand-alone programs, Adobe Creative Suite 2 offers many new marvelous tools with enhanced features to create, design, and express your ideas. Collectively, these tools build upon the integration and interoperability introduced in the first version of the Creative Suite.

Native file support

The strongest argument for using Adobe Photoshop CS2, Adobe Illustrator CS2, Adobe InDesign CS2, and Adobe GoLive CS2 together is that native file formats are easily transported between the CS programs. You no longer need to decide about saving Photoshop files as TIFF, EPS, GIF, PNG, or JPEG. Rather, you can import a native Photoshop PSD or Illustrator AI file into Adobe InDesign CS2 complete with layers and transparency. You can also import native Illustrator and Photoshop files directly in Adobe GoLive CS. The native file format import feature alone can save you space on your hard drive, because you need to save only a single file. Additionally, you save time in importing the correct file because only a single file is saved from the host application and used in your page layout or Web design. You can also directly open native Illustrator CS files in any Adobe Acrobat viewer, and you can open PDF documents in Illustrator and import them into InDesign and GoLive.

New Feature With the CS2 release, things just got better. Not only can you import native layered files in Adobe InDesign; you can also turn layers on or off when importing Photoshop and Acrobat PDF files in InDesign CS2.

Cross-Reference For information on importing native file formats across programs, see Part III.

Consistent user interface

Programs that creative professionals use today are sophisticated and complicated. One of the major problems facing many designers is the long learning curve necessary to become productive in a computer program. When you use several programs from several different computer-software manufacturers, your learning curve increases. Application-software companies develop software according to standards each company sets forth in the design of the user interface. One company may make extensive use of context-sensitive menus, while another company may avoid them. One company may use palettes and panes liberally, while another company relies on menu commands and dialog boxes. Add to these differences the extended use of keyboard shortcuts; program differences require you to spend a lot of time learning shortcuts. Additionally, the confusion of remembering one key sequence in one program invokes a different command than the same key sequence in another program.

In workflow environments, consistency is crucial. Time is money, and the time required to train your staff cuts into your productivity and your profits. When you use tools all developed by a single software manufacturer, you become more consistent in the design of the user interface and the keyboard shortcuts that access menus, tools, and commands. Adobe has taken the user interface design one step further by offering customizable keyboard shortcuts and custom workspaces in all CS2 programs.

Having a consistent look and feel in the user interface enables you to develop an intuitive sense for how to use a particular program to create a design project. The more you learn about a manufacturer's products, the faster you can become productive. In some cases, you can jump into a new program, poke around, and understand many features without reading exhaustive manuals and books.

For information on customizing workspaces and keyboard shortcuts, see Chapter 4.

Versioning tools

How many times have you created a tight comp and had a client tell you that he or she likes another version of the layout? You may create duotone images in Photoshop, offer a proof print to your client, and have the client tell you he wants another spot color in the Photoshop images. You offer a second proof and the client informs you the first proof print is really the one that best fits his or her campaign. You're back at your design studio scrambling through your hard drive looking for the first versions, locating the files and importing or relinking them back into the layout.

The Creative Suite lets you easily revisit earlier versions of illustrations, photo images, layouts, and Web pages. Along with the stand-alone programs in the Creative Suite, you also receive Version Cue, a marvelous utility that permits you to save multiple versions of a design in the same file. You decide what version to promote to the current look, and the linked file in your InDesign CS document dynamically updates. In workflow environments, nothing more easily tracks the current version of a design and quickly gets you to final output with the correct version.

In addition to saving versions of documents, the CS2 programs now support saving an alternate version of a document. You may have a Photoshop file saved with different versions and have an alternate Illustrator document of the same design. Version Cue helps you manage your versions and your alternates.

For more information on installing and using Version Cue and working with versions and alternates, see Chapter 8.

Consistent color management

Have you ever created an illustration, dropped it into a layout program, and seen a completely different color rendered in the layout? How about scanned images appearing with one color in Adobe Photoshop and different color values in the layout program? With the Adobe Creative Suite, you can access the same color engine and color-management policies among the design programs and Adobe Acrobat. Now in Creative Suite 2 you can manage color across all programs using Adobe Bridge. You assign color profiles in Photoshop or Illustrator, and all applications can conform to the same color management settings.

For more information on managing color across the Creative Suite programs, see Chapter 6. For more information on using Adobe Bridge, see Chapter 7.

Dynamic object and image editing

Ever have last-minute changes that you need to make before the last FedEx pickup of the day? A layout is complete, but you must quickly change an illustration or a photo image. In programs like Adobe InDesign CS, or even with embedded objects and images in PDF files, a double-click of the mouse button or the selection of a menu command launches the editing program that created the object or image and opens the file in a document window. You make your edits, save the file, and the edited version is dynamically updated in InDesign CS or Acrobat Professional. This kind of quick editing keeps you from having to find the original object or image, make edits, save back to another file format, update the link, and re-create a PDF file.

For more information on dynamic object and image editing, see Chapter 26.

Visual file exchanges

Let's face it; creative people are more visual and often work best in situations where they can first see a document before importing it in another program. More than ever before, Adobe has created a visually friendly workplace for you. You can easily drag and drop objects and images between document windows from one program to another, drag files from the desktop to open document windows, and copy and paste objects and images between documents.

Now with Adobe Bridge you can see all your files with thumbnail previews and drag and drop files into different application documents. You can also drag and drop Microsoft Office files into Adobe InDesign CS2 directly from the Bridge window.

For more information on importing and exchanging documents among programs, see Part III. For information on using Adobe Bridge, see Chapter 7.

Support for PDF

With InDesign CS as the central core of your Creative Suite programs for design purposes, PDF is the central file format for file exchanges and printing. All the Adobe CS programs support PDF imports and exports and all CS2 applications now use the same Adobe PDF Settings. In Creative Suite 2, PDF exports and imports are easier. InDesign CS2, as well as Photoshop CS2 and Illustrator CS2, supports exports to PDF/X format, which is a reliable document format used for commercial printing. Photoshop CS2 supports the creation of PDF slideshows; Illustrator CS2 and InDesign CS2 support PDF creation with Adobe PDF Layers; and GoLive CS2 supports PDF imports as smart objects, PDF previews, and PDF exports. InDesign CS2 now supports importing layered PDF documents and toggling layered views directly from within InDesign. You can also apply the same layer views to layered Photoshop CS2 documents. InDesign CS2 also supports multipage PDF file imports. Additionally, you can import media such as movie clips and sound files in InDesign CS and export them to PDF. Because PDF is the reliable standard for on-screen document viewing and output to professional printing devices, the CS2 programs take advantage of core PDF architecture.

 For more information on PDF/X and commercial printing, see Chapter 38. For more information on PDFs and multimedia, see Chapter 32.

Understanding the Creative Suite

There are two versions of the Adobe Creative Suite:

- **Adobe Standard Creative Suite 2:** This includes Adobe Bridge, Adobe Photoshop CS2, Adobe Illustrator CS2, Adobe InDesign CS2, and Version Cue.
- **Adobe Premium Creative Suite 2:** This includes the same programs with the addition of Adobe Acrobat Professional 7 and Adobe GoLive CS 2.

We cover all the premium edition programs in the other chapters in this book. In addition to the programs, you also get more than 100 OpenType faces with the Creative Suite editions. For a complete list of type, go to: www.adobe.com/products/creativesuite/type.html.

 Although the programs typically referred to as the CS applications include those mentioned in the preceding paragraph, you also find the addition of Adobe ImageReady CS2. The CS2 version is also a new upgrade to ImageReady CS1, which shipped with Photoshop CS1.

Each of the programs is an upgrade from previous CS versions of the software along with the introduction of Adobe Bridge, and Adobe Systems intends to upgrade the products in tandem for all future versions. Therefore, you can be confident that the next upgrade of a program like Photoshop CS will also include upgrades to Illustrator CS, InDesign CS, and GoLive CS.

Adobe Bridge

Adobe Bridge (see Figure 1-1) is a new executable application introduced in the Creative Suite version 2. If you launch Photoshop CS2 and become alarmed when you no longer find Photoshop's File Browser, worry no more. The Photoshop File Browser has been eliminated and replaced by a new more powerful type of file browser called Adobe Bridge. With Adobe Bridge, you can view document thumbnail previews for all Adobe applications as well as many non-Adobe applications.

 For information on using Adobe Bridge, see Chapter 7.

Figure 1-1: The Adobe Bridge is the central navigation tool for all CS2 applications.

You can use Adobe Bridge, which is your central navigation tool, to manage document assets and attributes. For example, using Adobe Bridge, you can assign common color management settings to all your CS applications, as well as add metadata to all your documents and run keyword searches on that the metadata. Some of the features available with Adobe Bridge include:

- ✦ **Bridge Center:** Adobe Bridge contains Bridge Center when used with the Creative Suite. The Bridge Center is the dashboard of the Creative Suite where you can view RSS feeds, view your most recent activities, read about tips and techniques for using Adobe software, save groups of files, and much more.

- ✦ **Camera Raw:** You can open and edit camera raw images from Adobe Bridge and save them in Photoshop CS2-compatible file formats. (Note that opening camera raw images in Bridge requires you to have Photoshop CS2 installed on your computer). You can edit camera raw settings in Adobe Bridge before opening files in Adobe Photoshop CS2.

- ✦ **Color Management:** Using Adobe Bridge you can synchronize color management settings across all applications to insure consistent color in all your CS application documents. You can import and export color settings for sharing among service providers and workgroups.

- ✦ **File Browsing:** As a file browser, Adobe Bridge is similar to the File Browser contained in earlier versions of Adobe Photoshop. Using Adobe Bridge as a file browser enables you to view thumbnail images of all Adobe application files and many other files created in other authoring programs. You can view page thumbnails from InDesign and Acrobat PDF documents. You can also view hidden files that your operating system uses on your computer. You can organize, sort files, create new folders, and move and delete files. You can edit metadata, rotate images, and run batch commands and automation scripts.

- **Launching Adobe Bridge:** You can launch Adobe Bridge as a separate executable program. You can also launch the Bridge directly from within Adobe Photoshop CS2, Adobe Illustrator CS2, Adobe InDesign CS2, and Adobe GoLive CS2.
- **Stock Photos:** From the Favorites pane in Adobe Bridge, a button links you to leading Web sites that host the leading royalty-free stock photo libraries. You can download low-resolution images to use as FPO (for position only) images when creating designs. When you decide which images to use in final comps, you can purchase high-resolution images via links from Adobe Bridge.
- **Version Cue:** In addition to launching all the CS2 applications from within Adobe Bridge, you can also access Adobe Version Cue CS2. You can create versions of documents, create alternates, apply document security, organize files into Version Cue private and shared project folders, and many other Version Cue-related tasks.

Adobe Photoshop CS2

If you're a creative professional, chances are you're no stranger to Adobe Photoshop. Adobe's flagship image-editing program is now in version 9 with the CS2 upgrade. As a stand-alone product, Photoshop has some very nice additions to an already feature-rich program. New enhancements to Photoshop add tools and options specific to interests by graphic designers, photographers, and Web designers. Adobe Photoshop CS2 offers you more integration with the other CS applications and some unique new editing tools. This version of Photoshop adds more polish to the program and enhancements that are likely to become favorites for creative professionals.

Among some of the more impressive additions to the program you'll find:

Cross-Reference

For information related to new features in Adobe Photoshop, see Part III.

- **Adobe Bridge:** Choose File ⇨ Browse and Adobe Bridge launches directly from within Adobe Photoshop. Close files and open Adobe Bridge from a Photoshop menu command. For information related to Adobe Bridge, see the section "Adobe Bridge" earlier in this chapter.
- **Animation:** Create animated GIF images in Photoshop like you do in ImageReady.
- **Color Swatch exchanges:** Export color swatch libraries and import libraries to and from Adobe Illustrator, Adobe InDesign, and Adobe GoLive.
- **Filters:** In Photoshop CS2 you'll find some nifty new filters added to the rich set of filters found in the last version of Photoshop. The new filters include:
  - **Blur:** New Blur filters include Box Blur, Shape Blur, and Surface Blur. For examples of results of these blur effects, see Chapter 13.
  - **Distort:** Lens Correction is a new filter in the Distort filters submenu. Lens Correction enables you to correct for photo aberrations such as barrel and pincushion distortion. *Barrel distortion* appears like a bloated photo and *pincushion distortion* appears as though a photo is pinched. You can easily correct images for perspective control using the grid in the Lens Correction window, shown in Figure 1-2.

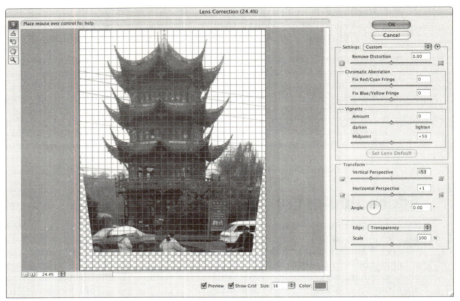

Figure 1-2: Lens Correction enables you to correct distorted images and correct image perspective.

- **Sharpen:** Smart Sharpen has been added to the Sharpen filters submenu. This filter introduces new algorithms for better edge detection and reduced sharpening halos. You can control the amount of sharpening you apply to highlights and shadows independent of each other.
- **Noise:** Reduce noise has been added to the Noise filters submenu. Reduce noise has the opposite effect of Add Noise that was part of Photoshop CS1.
- **Vanishing Point:** At the top of the Filter menu the new Vanishing Point filter has been added to Photoshop CS2. Vanishing Point is a marvelous tool that enables you to paste, clone, and paint image elements that automatically match the perspective of an image.

✦ **High Dynamic Range (HDR):** You can work with 32-bits-per-channel images with an extended dynamic range. You edit in 32-bit mode for brightness controls and other edits applied in Photoshop before reducing the mode to 24-bit for final output. You can capture the full dynamic range of a scene with multiple exposures, edit in 32-bit mode, and merge the files to obtain maximum detail in highlights, shadows, and a continuous range of midtones.

✦ **Image Processor:** You can batch process files and save them in multiple file formats.

✦ **Image Warp:** You can wrap, stretch, curl, and blend images around shapes for package designs.

- **Menu customization:** In addition to customizing workspaces and keyboard shortcuts, you can customize menus. You can show just the menu items you use in Photoshop by hiding menu commands and palette menu commands. You can save your menu settings, which you can select from a drop-down menu, or you can select preset menu configurations, which are available when you install Photoshop. You can also temporarily access all menus using a keyboard shortcut. Add color to menus or turn off colors in the General Preferences pane.

- **Multi-image Camera Raw:** You can batch process a group of Camera Raw images captured from multiple digital cameras. You can automatically adjust settings for multiple images, convert to universal Digital Negative (DNG) format, and apply nondestructive edits to batches of images.

- **Multiple layer control:** This allows you to work with layers as objects. You can select multiple layers and move, group, align, and transform them.

- **Shadow/Highlight:** You can apply Shadow/Highlight adjustments on CMYK images.

- **PDF Engine:** This allows you to save files as Photoshop PDF and use the same settings and controls as are available when you distill PostScript files or export to PDF from all other CS2 applications. You can create PDF settings in any CS2 application, and the settings are accessible to all CS2 applications.

- **Preserve vector data:** This feature retains vector attributes with placed vector images. You can save your Photoshop PSD files and return to layers containing vector objects. You can size and transform objects without losing the vector attributes.

- **Red-eye correction with one click:** You can correct red-eye with a single mouse click. You have options for adjusting pupil size and darkening amounts.

- **Script and action event manager:** Using the script and action event manager, you can write JavaScripts and Photoshop Actions that are invoked on user definable Photoshop events.

- **Smart Guides:** Allows you to align elements to guides, which appear only when you need them.

- **Smart Objects:** You can perform nondestructive transformations of embedded vector and pixel data. You can create multiple instances of embedded data and update all instances at once.

- **Spot Healing tool:** You can eliminate spots and artifacts quickly without selecting a source in the image.

- **UI Font size customization:** This allows you to customize the size of fonts in the Options bar, palettes, and Layer Styles.

- **Variables:** You can create data-driven graphics the same as when you use ImageReady.

- **Video preview:** You can display documents on a video monitor using a FireWire link.

- **Web Photo Gallery improvements:** This allows you to create Web Photo Galleries using Macromedia Flash content in Web Photo Galleries.

Adobe Illustrator CS2

Tried and true Adobe Illustrator is the premier illustration program for designers and artists. Many people still use Macromedia FreeHand because they know the program well and because they enjoy having multiple pages with different page sizes together in the same document. However, the advantages for using illustration programs together with other applications in the Creative Suite are significantly in favor of Adobe Illustrator. With Adobe's pending acquisition of Macromedia, FreeHand may be discontinued.

In the current version of Illustrator CS2, you can now save workspaces like you can in Adobe Photoshop, Adobe InDesign, and Adobe GoLive. New impressive tools have been added to Illustrator as well as some polish on editing features.

For more information on using Adobe Illustrator CS2 and some of its new features, see Part III.

Among the new features in Illustrator CS2, you'll find:

+ **Expanded support for Wacom tablets:** Adobe extends support for pressure tips and eraser, tilt two side switches, barrel rotation, and large felt-marker-shaped nib.
+ **Live Trace:** Live Trace is like having a new, improved Adobe Streamline program built into Illustrator. Much more detailed and much faster than Streamline, Live Trace renders beautifully designed vector drawings from raster images, as shown in Figures 1-3 and 1-4.

Figure 1-3: A raster image is placed in Illustrator.

Figure 1-4: Using Live Trace, you can trace a raster image as a vector object. You can size and scale the resultant image without any image degradation.

✦ **Live Paint:** Live Paint polishes your vector drawings by automatically detecting and correcting edge gaps that can result in printed artwork with gaps between objects.

✦ **Offset a stroke on its path:** You can control where a stroke on a path appears relative to the path. You can center strokes on a path, or place them inside or outside a path.

- **PDF Options:** Like the new PDF options in Adobe Photoshop CS2, Adobe Illustrator offers you the same export options previously available only in Adobe InDesign and Acrobat Distiller.
- **Place Photoshop Layer Comps:** You can control visibility of placed images from Photoshop Layer Comps and toggle views for the different layers.
- **Spot colors enhanced support:** Support for spot color from raster images is now available in Illustrator. You can apply spot colors to raster-based images, colorize embedded grayscale images with one spot color or process color, and preserve spot colors in your artwork when saving to AI, EPS, or PDF file formats.
- **SVG and SWF options:** New options have been added for saving SVG and SWF files. You can save in SVG-Tiny format that is optimized for mobile devices and incorporate the graphics into designs for viewing on mobile devices.
- **Templates:** Illustrator provides a host of new professionally designed template files easily accessible by choosing File ⇨ New From Template. You can use a variety of templates that are installed with the program to start a design project. When you open a template file, it opens as an Untitled document, as shown in Figure 1-5. Make your edits and save the file while Illustrator preserves the original template.

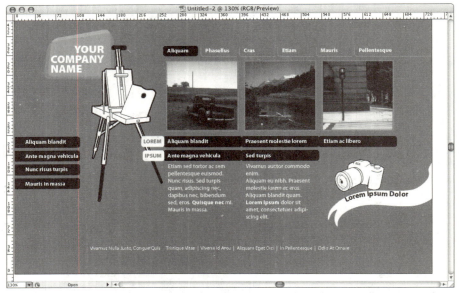

Figure 1-5: You can easily access an abundance of template files from Illustrator's File menu.

- **Type enhancements:** You can apply underline and strikethrough in the Character palette.
- **Workspace management:** Adobe Illustrator CS2 now comes in line with Adobe Photoshop and Adobe GoLive in terms of workspace management. You can now save your workspaces with palettes positioned according to your personal choices.

Adobe InDesign CS2

InDesign is the central hub of your creative workflow. You bring together the images and objects that you create in Adobe Photoshop CS2 and Adobe Illustrator CS2. You either import type created in a word-processing program, import from Adobe's InCopy, or you set type in the InDesign Story Editor. With InDesign's free-form ease of page layout, you can lay out a design for publication. You can then export the InDesign document as a PDF file suited for print, Web hosting, electronic file exchanges, or CD/DVD-ROM replication. If you want to include your design as HTML files for Web hosting, you can package the document for GoLive CS2. As you can see, InDesign's role among the Creative Suite programs is the anchor where files are imported to assemble a design and ultimately export for final output.

InDesign CS2 builds on the major upgrade that appeared in the first release of InDesign CS. All the wonderful features you had available in the previous version are still there along with some new enhancements introduced in InDesign CS2 (version 4 of Adobe InDesign). Among the more significant new additions are:

- **Assignments:** In collaborative environments you can assign selected frames, spreads, and documents to other users. Those users can observe their assignments in Adobe InCopy CS2 and make text edits to the same document you're editing at the same time.
- **Anchored objects:** You can anchor callouts, pull quotes, art, sidebars, and other objects respective to text and control their position. You can apply text wraps to anchored objects.
- **Library palette enhancements:** You can add items on a page as separate objects to the Library palette and easily update the library items. You can preserve the XML structure in nested elements.
- **Fill content proportionally:** You can resize an object to fit a frame and eliminate all white space.
- **Frame level baseline grids:** You can set baseline grids at the frame level for easy text alignment. You can rotate frames and snap text to the baseline grid assigned to the frame.
- **Metadata in documents:** Document-level metadata is supported much like Photoshop. You can embed information about fonts, color swatches, copyright information, author, keywords, and similar metadata. The metadata is available for viewing when you preview files in Adobe Bridge.
- **MS Word import enhancements:** You can map Word styles to InDesign styles, remove styles, remove styles from text and tables, and more (see Figure 1-6). You can preserve anchored objects and footnotes. You can save style mappings and other import options as a Word import preset.

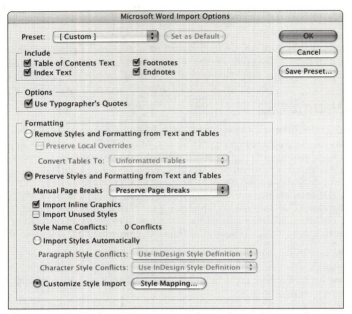

Figure 1-6: InDesign CS2 supports a host of new features for managing styles imported from MS Word.

- **Drop shadow noise and spread controls:** You can add noise to a layout to create an effect similar to using Photoshop's Add Noise filter. You can spread a drop shadow out to reduce the radius of the blur.

- **Style enhancement:** InDesign's wonderful treatment for style sheets introduced in InDesign CS is further developed in InDesign CS2. Among new styles and working with them you have:

  • **Object styles:** You can apply object formatting to multiple objects and define a style that you can apply to additional objects introduced in your layouts. Object styles work similar to character and paragraph styles and the options are contained in a style palette (see Figure 1-7).

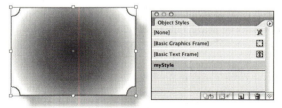

Figure 1-7: You can define and apply object styles in the Object Styles palette.

- **Selective loading of Styles:** You can selectively load styles including Object Styles from other InDesign projects.
- **Quick apply styles:** You can type a style name in one of the style palettes and quickly apply the style to a body of text or objects.
- **Apply Next Style:** Using Apply Next Style, you can quickly apply multiple styles to a single body of text. For example, you can apply a headline, subhead, drop cap, body copy, bullet points, and end style with one click.
- **Reset to base:** You can reset any style you apply to text or objects to the base style.
- **Automatically replace deleted styles:** When you delete a style you can specify a replacement style.

✦ **Packaging enhancements for GoLive:** You can select a page range or group of objects for packaging for GoLive. You can include linked objects on hidden layers in your package for GoLive. You can open InDesign packages in GoLive and export them to XHTML.

✦ **Pathfinder enhancements:** You can convert shapes into different shapes using the Pathfinder palette. For example, you can convert a rectangle to a rounded rectangle.

✦ **PDF integration:** All Adobe PDF Settings that you create in Acrobat Distiller are now visible in InDesign. You can create PDF settings in any CS2 application and the presets become visible in all applications.

✦ **Place PSD and PDF layers:** You can place Photoshop-layered PSD files and Adobe Acrobat-layered PDF files in InDesign and toggle the layer views (see Figure 1-8).

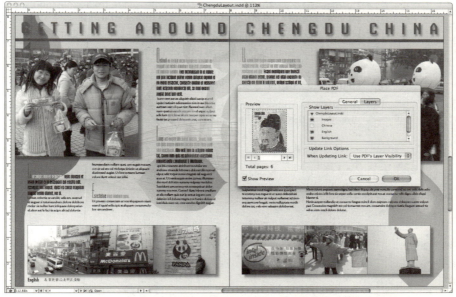

Figure 1-8: You can turn on and off different layers from Photoshop and Acrobat PDF-layered files placed in InDesign.

✦ **Place PDF multiple pages:** You can place all pages in a PDF document in InDesign CS2. Select a file to place and the cursor is loaded. You can manually place pages across InDesign pages or autoflow the pages much like autoflowing text.

✦ **Save backwards:** You can save InDesign CS2 documents backward to InDesign CS1 format.

✦ **Snippets:** You can drag and drop a group of objects into Adobe Bridge, onto your desktop, into the InDesign Library palette, or an e-mail message window. InDesign saves the objects as a Snippet that you can share with other users.

✦ **Swatch sharing:** You can export color swatches from InDesign for other CS2 applications to use. You can import swatch libraries from other CS2 applications into an InDesign file.

✦ **Text processing:** Several improvements to text handling have been added to InDesign CS2. These include:

- **Drag and drop text:** You can open MS Word and InDesign concurrently with both document windows in view. Select text in MS Word and drag it to the InDesign window. When you drop the text on an InDesign page, a text frame is automatically created with the selected text appearing in the frame. From the desktop you can drag a Word document to an InDesign document page and the text is imported the same as when using the Place command. You can drag and drop MS Excel worksheets to an InDesign page, then convert the text to a table. You can drag and drop Word and Excel files from the Find dialog box.

- **Footnotes:** You can create footnotes in InDesign or import them from MS Word documents and Rich Text Format (RTF) files. You can edit footnote numbering, formatting, and layout.

- **Unformatted paste:** You can automatically paste text while ignoring the original style and apply the style assigned to an InDesign frame.

- **Dynamic spell-checking and automatic text correction:** You can spell check while typing in InDesign much like you can in MS Word.

- **Dictionary management:** You can create and link to multiple dictionaries and share your custom dictionaries with other users.

- **WYSIWIG font management:** You can see font style previews (see Figure 1-9) directly in the Font menu and the Character and Control palettes.

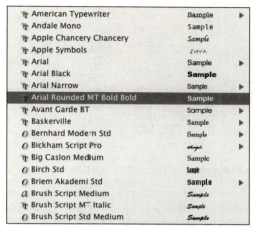

Figure 1-9: Font styles are displayed in the Font menu.

- **Story editor enhancements:** You can view overset text while working in the Story Editor. You can display a vertical ruler in the Story Editor to measure vertical placement of text. Additionally, you can anti-alias text for a better visual display.

✦ **Transform Again:** Much like Illustrator's Transform Again command, you can repeat and duplicate transformations.

✦ **Transform tools for PageMaker users:** You can convert PageMaker 6.0-7.0 documents and automatically impose pages into printer's spreads using InBooklet Special Edition.

✦ **XML and GoLive integration:** Enhancements have been made for XML tagging and integrating InDesign files with Adobe GoLive CS2. These include:

- **XML tagging of tables:** You can tag tables, table cells, and content within table cells. You can export and reimport tables while retaining table structure.

- **Smart XML import:** You can automatically clone matching elements from imported XML files to preserve styling. You can delete unmatched existing elements and their structure. You can omit unmatched imported elements or whitespace-only elements.

- **Linked XML files:** You can link to XML files upon importing them and easily update content when you edit and change the linked file.

Cross-Reference

For more information on using new features in InDesign CS2, look over the chapters in Parts III and IV.

Adobe GoLive CS2

Adobe GoLive CS2, now in version 8, is a Web authoring and site management program. As a stand-alone product, GoLive has suffered in sales because many Web designers favor other applications by several competing vendors. Because GoLive has had a major upgrade in the first CS version and continues with many new features now found in GoLive CS2, you should consider it for your Web design needs if you use the other CS applications. As a participant in the Creative Suite, GoLive CS2 has many benefits for handling file imports and exports similar to options in other CS programs. As a stand-alone editor, GoLive has reached a level of sophistication equal to or greater than other HTML editing programs competing for the same market.

 For more information on using new features in GoLive CS2, see Chapter 28.

Some of the features available in GoLive include importing native file formats from other CS applications much like you have available in InDesign (including Photoshop layered files, smart objects, and smart tracing made from cutouts in other CS native files); complete integration with InDesign CS2 where paragraph, character, and inline text styles are translated in GoLive documents; consistent color management using the Adobe Color Engine and Adobe Bridge; PDF previews of Web pages; visual CSS (Cascading Style Sheets) authoring and previewing; and much more. Some of the new feature highlights include:

- **Automatic style conversion:** Replace HTML styles with CSS styles.
- **Color management:** You can use the Adobe Color Picker in GoLive CS2 and choose the same color management settings as you use in all other CS applications.
- **Cropped components:** You can customize text components for different viewing circumstances.
- **CSS site management:** You can update CSS class and ID names throughout a site and view referenced HTML files.
- **Default CSS files:** You can apply a default style sheet to all new files you create.
- **Dynamic collections:** You can attach queries to collections.
- **Enhanced CSS editor:** You can view source code and check syntax while you edit style sheets.
- **Export to HTML:** You can optimize InDesign layouts for HTML and apply templates to linked exported pages.

- ✦ **Favorites:** You can quickly access frequently used documents in a favorites list.
- ✦ **Help:** The Adobe Help Center (see Figure 1-10) supports help documentation for GoLive CS2 and all other Adobe CS applications.
- ✦ **Import layers:** You can show and hide InDesign layers in GoLive's Layers palette (see Figure 1-11).

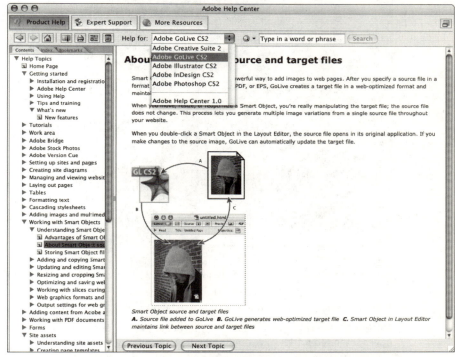

Figure 1-10: The Adobe Help Center gives you help for all the CS2 applications.

Figure 1-11: You can hide or show InDesign layers in GoLive's Layers palette.

✦ **Liquid layouts:** You can create flexible CSS layouts or use the redesigned CSS layout grid.

✦ **Mobile device support:** GoLive CS2 sports a number of new features for creating Web pages intended for viewing on mobile devices. Among them are:

- **Mobile workspaces:** You can automatically configure a workspace for mobile formats when you create a new document.
- **Small screen rendering:** GoLive CS2 has LiveRendering browser where you can preview files designed for mobile devices.
- **CSS Integration:** You can create flexible designs for dual purposes for mobile and screen viewing.
- **MMS messages:** You can create impressive multimedia messages for mobile devices.
- **Convert HTML to XHTML:** You can create mobile-compatible copies of Web pages.
- **SVG previews:** You can edit SVG files and add JavaScript interactivity using a visual user interface.

- **Nested page templates:** You can create complex designs by inserting page templates into template regions.
- **New downloadable extensions:** You can add GoLive extensions made available from the Adobe Studio Exchange at: http://share.studio.adobe.com.
- **Organize assets:** You can view text and image thumbnails, or categorize assets with XML tags.
- **PDF presets:** You can create a PDF preset in GoLive the same as all other CS2 applications. Once created in GoLive, the presets are available to all programs and presets created in other CS2 applications are accessible in GoLive.
- **Previews and descriptions:** A more intuitive New dialog box (see Figure 1-12) offers options for the type of site or documents you want to create. The Options pane offers previews for sites, Web pages, mobile, and scripting documents. Short descriptions provide you information about the type of document you can create.

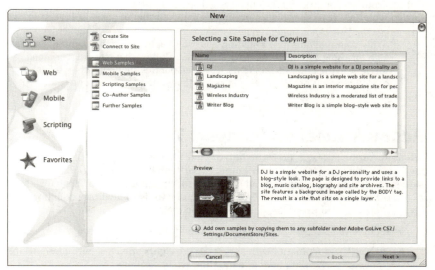

Figure 1-12: The New dialog box has previews and descriptions for the type of document you want to create.

- **Quick search:** You can search for files directly from the Site window.
- **Samples:** A number of different sample files are available for viewing from the New dialog box. You can see previews and descriptions for the sample files.
- **Secure FTP:** You can transfer files via the Secure Sockets Layer (SSL) or the Secure Sockets Shell (SSH).
- **Smart Favorite icons:** You can automatically optimize page icons for the Favorites and Bookmarks menus in Browser windows.

- **Streamlined workflow:** You can optimize text and images with one click. You can customize formatting in the CSS editor.

- **Swatches:** You can manage swatches and exchange them just like the other CS2 applications. Export or import swatch libraries to and from the other CS2 programs.

- **Tools:** New tools identical to the other CS2 applications include the Hand, Zoom, and Eyedropper tools. In addition, unique GoLive CS2 tools include the object Selection and Layer tools optimized for Web page layout.

- **Updated, preinstalled SDK:** The Adobe Software Development Kit (SDK) is installed on your hard drive with GoLive CS2. You can create new GoLive features using JavaScript.

- **Version control:** Adobe Version Cue is supported with GoLive CS2. You can easily collaborate and share files among GoLive workgroups.

GoLive supports a long list of new features and is enhanced in many ways over the last version of the program. If you're a graphic designer focused on print, perhaps the exports to GoLive from within InDesign is where you'll spend most of your time. If your work is Web site design, you'll want to spend a lot of time learning all the features GoLive offers you.

In this book, we offer you a starting point in Chapter 28 where you can glean some knowledge for using GoLive to create a Web site. In other chapters, we cover the integration of GoLive with the other CS programs. However, our treatment of GoLive is light and you'll need to acquire some other guides and publications in order to become proficient in using the program.

Adobe Acrobat Professional 7

Whereas Adobe InDesign CS is the hub of your creative satellite, PDF is at the center of the file-format universe. All the CS programs export and import PDF documents, and the expansion for PDF support is found in all the new product upgrades. For design workflows, Adobe Acrobat Professional in version 7 offers you many tools to facilitate collaboration with colleagues, clients, and prepress technicians. You can:

- Set up e-mail–based reviews for markup and approval of design concepts and proofs

- Enable PDF documents with special usage rights so users of the free Adobe Reader program can participate in comment and review sessions

- Export comments and corrections directly to Microsoft Word text documents (on Windows XP with Office XP only)

- Prepare files for electronic exchanges, Web hosting, and screen viewing complete with embedded graphics and fonts

- Prepare files for digital prepress and printing

- Authenticate and secure documents

- Develop media shows and slide presentations for kiosks, meetings, and presentations

- Design forms for point-of-sale purchases hosted on Web sites or distributed on CD/DVD-ROMs

- Organize your design environment and catalog design campaigns embedding native files in PDFs for an organized storage system
- Search for content contained on CDs, DVDs, network servers, and Web sites
- Create accessible documents for clients needing compliance with U.S. law governing document accessibility

All in all, Acrobat Professional has a significant place in your design workflow.

 As of this writing, Adobe Acrobat Professional and Adobe Reader are in version 7.0.5. Mac users are encouraged to upgrade to this version. All versions on the Mac prior to 7.0.5 don't display video or play sounds in PDF documents.

Acrobat Professional was released several months earlier than the other CS2 programs and is not on the same development cycle as the other CS programs. Part of the reason for the early release of Acrobat was the necessity to develop the PDF 1.6 specifications used by all the other CS programs. With PDF version 1.6 and Acrobat 7 compatibility, you can enjoy features like enabling PDF documents for Adobe Reader users and taking advantage of all the new Print Production tools.

Adobe Acrobat is unlike the other CS programs in that the application is designed to serve many different office professionals. Acrobat might be used by engineers, legal professionals, business office workers, government workers, school districts, and just about anyone in any industry working on a computer today. Therefore, there are a number of tools you, as a creative professional, may not use in Acrobat just because those tools may not serve your needs. The following are the additions to the new version of Acrobat that are most suited for design and publishing workflows:

- **Autosaving files:** You can set preference options for autosaving files.
- **Attaching files:** A new Attach File command offers an alternative to attaching files as comments. You can extract file attachments in Adobe Reader. When files are attached with the Attach File command, you do not need to enable the PDF with Reader usage rights.
- **Browser-based reviews on Mac:** Browser-based reviews are now supported on the Macintosh.
- **Enable PDF documents with Adobe Reader usage rights:** You can add special features to PDF documents such as enabling a PDF for comment and review for Adobe Reader users. When you open these files in the free Adobe Reader, all the comment and drawing markup tools are available (see Figure 1-13). Your clients, using Adobe Reader, can mark up and comment on PDF files in review sessions and send their comments back to you. Adobe Reader users can save the commented PDFs when usage rights are enabled.
- **Fast Launch:** One of the most frequent complaints from users of previous versions of Acrobat and Reader was the long time it took to launch the programs. In version 7, both Acrobat and Adobe Reader have been improved and now launch as fast as any MS Office application.
- **Forms:** On Windows, Adobe has introduced Adobe Designer. Designer is a separate executable application engineered for creating Adobe PDF forms. Adobe Designer is a tool that simplifies database connections to PDF documents and offers many new features for creating sophisticated forms.

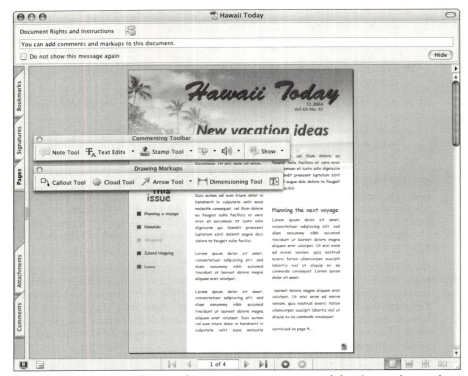

Figure 1-13: Adobe Reader users have access to comment and drawing markup tools when a PDF document is enabled with Adobe Reader usage rights.

- ✦ **JavaScript:** The JavaScript dialog box offers new features to help debugging, an XML parser with full DOM and Xpath support, XSLT for XML transformations, and a much-improved SOAP implementation.

- ✦ **Layers:** Multimedia placed on a separate layer is now editable only when that layer remains in view. Acrobat treats media placed on a layer specific to that layer as opposed to making the video accessible when viewing other layers.

- ✦ **Organizer:** Acrobat's Organizer is a junior cousin to Adobe Bridge. With the Organizer you can create collections, add to favorites, view thumbnail previews of PDF documents, scroll through all pages in a PDF file without opening the document, sort on metadata, initiate reviews, and open and delete files.

- ✦ **New Comment tools:** New tools have been added to the exhaustive list of comment and markup tools. A special Callout tool and Dimension tool have been added to the Commenting toolbar. These tools and all other comment and markup tools are available to users of Adobe Reader when PDFs are enabled with usage rights.

- ✦ **PDF Optimizer:** The PDF Optimizer has been improved and now provides transparency flattening, optimization of scanned images, and selective image compression based on color content. Discarding objects and cleanup have been separated into two panes.

✦ **PDF Standards:** Support for PDF/A (archival format) and new versions of PDF/X are added to version 7.

✦ **Prepress and Printing:** A host of new print production tools (see Figure 1-14) have been added to Acrobat Professional for soft-proofing color and commercial printing. Cropping files is much better, and the following features have been added: trap presets, JDF job definitions, a more simplified Preflight tool, and fixing hairlines. In addition, transparency flattening is now available before printing a file.

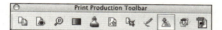

Figure 1-14: The new Print Production toolbar offers new tools for soft-proofing color and commercial printing.

✦ **Secure ePaper Mail:** You can use one of several templates for eEnvelopes (see Figure 1-15) that you can attach a file and secure the PDF. Users of the free Adobe Reader software can open the document when you provide them with the password and extract the file attachment. Note that you can attach a file of any type to a PDF document.

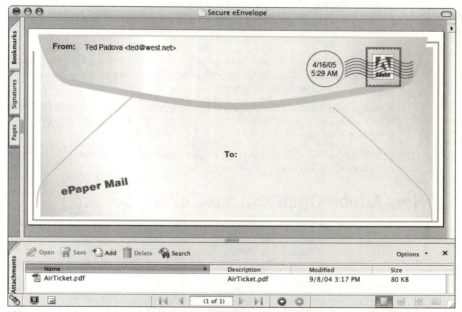

Figure 1-15: You can easily send secure PDF documents with file attachments using the Secure PDF Delivery menu command. Adobe Reader users can extract file attachments.

- **Security policies:** Security and digital signatures have been completely revised in Acrobat 7. You can now create a security policy and reuse the policy whenever you want to encrypt files using the same attributes. Security policies are like adding style sheets to security handling.
- **Version Cue Support:** Support for Version Cue has been added to version 7 of Acrobat Professional.
- **Watermarks and backgrounds:** The Watermarks and Backgrounds dialog box now supports adding custom text.
- **Web browser support:** Acrobat 7 offers more support for Web browsers. Safari users on Macintosh can view PDF files as inline views in Safari.

Version Cue CS2

You'll find the new enhancements to Version Cue another step toward complete integration of the Adobe CS applications. Together with Adobe Bridge this release of the Creative Suite helps you easily manage documents and revisions. Adobe Version Cue is now in version CS2 like the other CS applications. Some of the new features added to Version Cue include:

- **Adobe Bridge Integration:** Between Adobe Bridge and Version Cue you have two great tools to manage and revise all your artwork and projects. From Adobe Bridge you can search for and view all Version Cue files without opening individual CS2 components. You can manipulate files directly in Adobe Bridge to avoid delays as files open or as components start up.
- **Alternates:** You can create alternate work projects where an original document remains intact and an alternate to the project is modified. You can use alternates in addition to versions to manage your projects.
- **Manage non-Adobe files:** You can store other file types such as MS Word documents, MS Excel Spreadsheets, and various vertical market application program documents in a Version Cue project.
- **PDF Review:** You can initiate PDF reviews from within Version Cue and store the review comments in a Version Cue project.

New Adobe Open and Save dialog boxes

A number of features included in the CS2 applications are available in all or several of the CS2 programs. As such, most of these were discussed in the previous pages that covered the individual programs. One particular feature that deserves special attention, and that is used by Photoshop, Illustrator, and InDesign, is the new Adobe Open and Save dialog boxes.

When you choose File ➪ Open (or File ➪ Save/Save As), you have a choice to use your OS (operating system) dialog box to open or save any file from any application. Alternatively, you can use a new modified Open (or Save) dialog box developed by Adobe Systems. Adobe modified these dialog boxes to take advantage of how Adobe Bridge and Adobe Version Cue work together.

Click Use Adobe Dialog and the interface changes as you see in Figure 1-16. As shown in the figure, you can open drop-down menus, which have options for revealing a file in Bridge, creating a new Version Cue project, sharing a project, versioning a file, creating an alternate, closing a connection, synchronizing connections, and more. Click Use OS Dialog and you go to the familiar dialog box you use when opening (or saving) files.

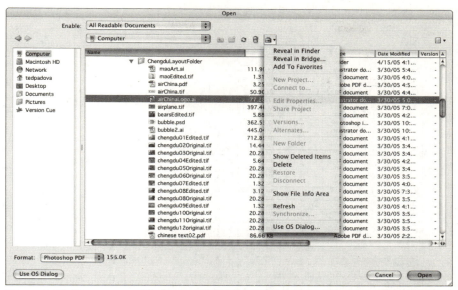

Figure 1-16: The new modified Open dialog box offers many options for working with Adobe Bridge and Version Cue.

OpenType Fonts

In addition to the programs contained in the Creative Suite, you can also find more than 180 installed OpenType fonts after completing your CS2 applications installation. OpenType fonts are a new font technology developed by Adobe Systems and Microsoft. OpenType fonts offer you new type-handling features among many of the CS2 applications. Starting to convert your type library to OpenType fonts as soon as possible is a good idea. The kind of benefits you derive from using OpenType fonts include:

- **Cross-platform support:** OpenType fonts are completely cross-platform. You can copy the same font to either Mac OS or Windows. Obviously, licensing restrictions do apply, so be certain to check these restrictions before installing fonts on multiple computers.

- **Reliability:** If you experience font problems when you print, be certain to first reevaluate your font sets. Off-brand fonts, especially many of a TrueType nature, can prevent embedding problems. Furthermore, some quality fonts carry licensing restrictions that prevent font embedding. If you create PDF files with font embedding, be certain to review the licensing restrictions on your fonts and check whether font embedding is prohibited. Many quality fonts offer you complete embedding permissions that help prevent problems when it comes time to print your creations. Good-quality fonts that permit font embedding include those found in the Adobe type library of OpenType fonts.

- **More glyphs:** A *glyph* is an individual font character. TrueType fonts and all earlier PostScript fonts contain a maximum 256 glyphs. The new OpenType fonts can contain more than 65,000 glyphs. These additional characters offer you many discretionary options for kerning pairs and expanded ligatures as well as special characters, precisely proportioned fractions, and foreign-language character alternatives. A portion of a glyph set for an OpenType font installed with the Creative Suite is shown in Figure 1-17.

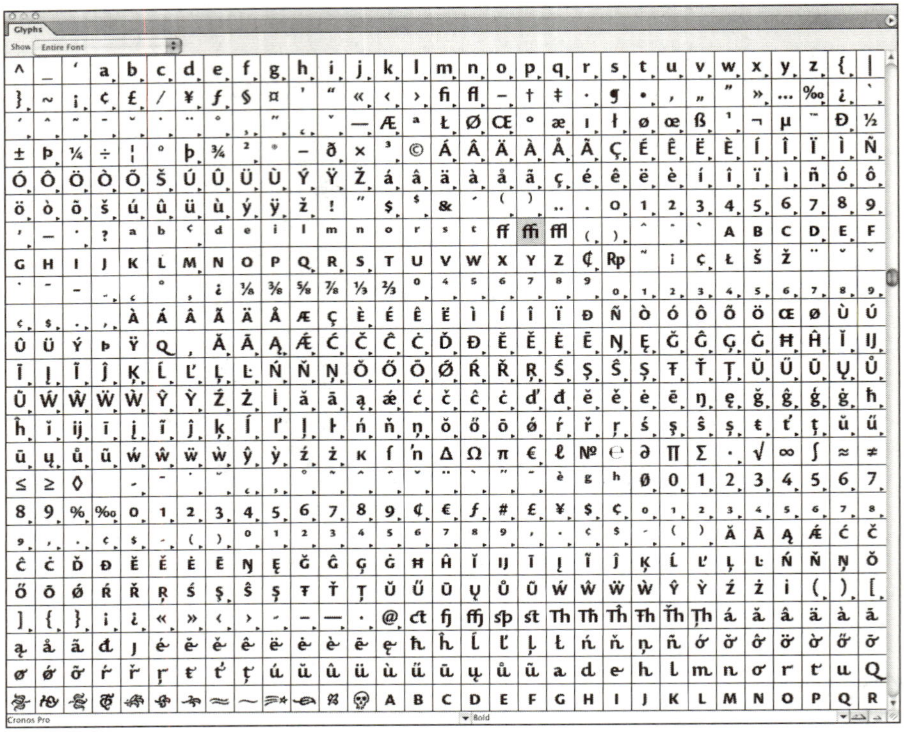

Figure 1-17: OpenType fonts offer you more than 65,000 characters.

- **Multi-language support:** All the OpenType Pro fonts contain characters needed for multiple-language typesetting.

- **Easier font management:** OpenType fonts contain only a single file for font viewing on-screen and fonts used for printing. Unlike PostScript fonts containing separate files for screen views and each face in a font set contained in a separate file, OpenType fonts are built in a single file, thereby providing you more ease in keeping track of fonts, installing them, and locating them.

Several CS2 applications support a Glyphs palette where you can view an entire font in a scrollable window. You can insert a character at the insertion point by double-clicking a glyph in the palette. You no longer need to open a utility to view all characters in a given font set when you use programs like Adobe InDesign CS and Adobe Illustrator CS.

Summary

- The Creative Suite is a collection of imaging applications offering professional designers complete integration for print, Web design, and screen viewing.

- Programs from a single software vendor provide consistent user interfaces and similar menu and tool functions, which reduce learning curves for new hires.

- Adobe Bridge is a central navigation tool offering features for viewing, editing, and managing Adobe CS application documents and non-Adobe files.

- Adobe Photoshop CS2 (version 9) offers new filters for lens correction, vanishing point, and other new editing methods. Photoshop CS2 now supports PDF presets consistent with Adobe InDesign and Acrobat Distiller. New features for Camera Raw support, HDR editing, preserving vector data, additions for brightness controls, introduction of multimedia and Web images support add to Photoshop's impressive arsenal of tools and features.

- Adobe Illustrator CS2 (version 12) offers new tools for tracing and painting images. Together with tighter type controls, saving workspaces, exchanging swatch libraries, and PDF settings control, Illustrator CS2 is more integrated in the Creative Suite.

- Adobe InDesign CS2 (version 4) offers new type-handling features. Building upon the impressive set of features introduced with InDesign CS1, the CS2 version adds more polish to the premier layout program available for creative professionals.

- Adobe GoLive CS2 (version 8) offers a host of new features for creating Web sites and support for mobile devices.

- Adobe Acrobat 7 Professional offers the creative professional tools for reviewing comps, soft-proofing color, preflighting documents, PDF/X compliance, and an option for creating PDFs with special features so your clients using the free Adobe Reader software can mark up and comment on proofs.

- Version Cue CS2 is a utility that supports saving files from Adobe Photoshop CS2, Adobe Illustrator CS2, Adobe InDesign CS2, and Adobe GoLive CS2, and Adobe Acrobat 7 Professional in different document versions and alternates. Changing versions dynamically updates linked files in the other CS2 programs. New features help manage non-Adobe documents, integrate versions with Adobe Bridge, create alternate designs, and initiate review sessions.

- The new Adobe Open and Save dialog boxes offer options for working with Adobe Bridge and Version Cue.

- The Creative Suite Premium Edition provides you with more than 180 OpenType fonts. OpenType fonts can contain more than 65,000 glyphs, offering you more choices for ligatures, discretionary ligatures, foreign-language characters, proportional fractions, and special characters.

✦ ✦ ✦

Taking a Tour of the Creative Suite

In This Chapter

Starting with a sketch in Acrobat

Editing images in Photoshop

Creating Illustrator objects

Versioning files in Version Cue

Accessing Adobe Bridge

Creating a layout in InDesign

Preparing a layout for print

Soft-proofing in Acrobat

Repurposing a document for Web hosting

Packaging for GoLive

The best way to understand the possibilities that the various Creative Suite applications offer is to walk through an example workflow that takes a project through each of the various applications. This tour starts out with Acrobat, where you can create a PDF file of an initial sketch that you can e-mail to all members of the creative team for review. The reviewers' feedback return is in the form of comments compiled within a single PDF file. This cycle continues until all members of the creative team approve the design.

With an approved design, you can use Photoshop and Illustrator to create and edit images and objects for the project. You can then import all this content into InDesign, where you lay them out with text. The final layout is then exported back to Acrobat, where you can print it or repurpose it for use on the Web using GoLive.

Starting with a Sketch in Acrobat

When a project first starts, you typically want to get input from several individuals on the creative team before the design is approved. Calling a meeting where all members of the creative team meet to discuss the design would accomplish the goal, but Acrobat makes another solution possible.

Using Acrobat, you can scan a rough design sketch into Acrobat where it is converted to a PDF file. Then you can e-mail this PDF file to members of the creative team. Each member of the team makes his comments into the PDF file and e-mails the document back to its owner. All the comments are then compiled into a single PDF document that provides feedback. This cycle can then be iterated until all involved approve the design.

 You can find complete coverage on e-mail review sessions in Chapter 26.

Scanning a sketch into Acrobat

Projects always start with an idea, but to share these ideas with others, you usually sketch them out roughly. You may then scan these rough sketches into a digital format where you can more easily distribute them. Using a scanner or a digital camera, you can directly sketches or scan images into Acrobat.

STEPS: Scanning a Sketch into Acrobat

1. **Initiate a scan in Acrobat.** Within Acrobat, choose File ⇨ Create PDF ⇨ From Scanner. This command opens the Create PDF From Scanner dialog box, shown in Figure 2-1. In the Scanner drop-down list, select the attached scanner and specify New Document as the Destination. You can also disable the Recognize Text Using OCR option, and click Scan.

Figure 2-1: The Create PDF From Scanner dialog box

2. **Set the scanner preferences.** After you click Scan, a dialog box for your scanner appears, like the one shown in Figure 2-2. Select the options appropriate for your sketched image and click Preview to check the scanning options. If you're comfortable with the preview, click Scan.

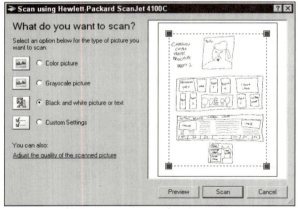

Figure 2-2: Each scanner has a similar dialog box to set scanning options.

3. **Save the PDF file.** After the scanned file is loaded into Acrobat, as shown in Figure 2-3, you need to save the file before you redistribute it. To save the scanned image, choose File ⇨ Save As. This command opens a file dialog box where you can name the file and specify a folder where you want to save the file.

Figure 2-3: A scanned and rotated image in Acrobat

Submitting a sketch for e-mail review

With a sketch scanned into Acrobat, you can send the PDF file out for review using e-mail or using a browser. These steps walk you through an e-mail review cycle. In actual projects, this review cycle may be repeated many times as needed.

STEPS: Submitting a Sketch for E-mail Review

1. **Send a PDF file for e-mail review.** To send the selected PDF file out for e-mail review, choose File ➪ Send for Review ➪ Send by Email for Review. The Send by Email for Review wizard starts and the first page of the wizard, shown in Figure 2-4, opens. Here, you specify the PDF file to send out for review. The default file is the current open file. You can edit your current profile and e-mail address at a future time using the Identity panel of the Preferences dialog box (Acrobat/Edit ➪ Preferences).

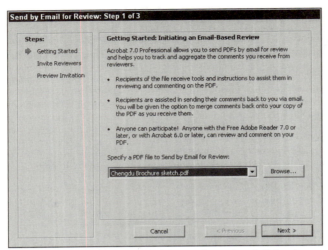

Figure 2-4: The Send by Email for Review wizard dialog box

2. **Specify the reviewers' e-mail addresses.** The next step in the Send by Email for Review wizard, shown in Figure 2-5, lets you enter the e-mail addresses of the individuals you want to review the attached PDF document. The Address Book button opens a contact manager where you can enter lists of individuals. Clicking the Customize Review Options opens a dialog box where you can type an e-mail address where reviewers automatically return their comments. By default this e-mail address is the initiator's email.

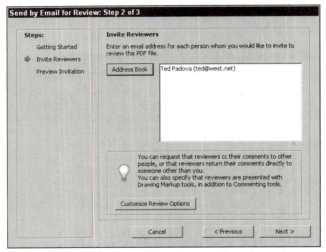

Figure 2-5: The second step lets you specify reviewers' e-mail addresses.

Chapter 2 ✦ Taking a Tour of the Creative Suite

3. **Extending a review invitation.** The final step of the Send by Email for Review wizard automatically composes the e-mail subject and message body text for you, as shown in Figure 2-6, but you can edit the email text as desired. When the e-mail addresses and message are completed, click Send Invitation. Acrobat delivers the e-mail message to your system's default e-mail application. If your e-mail system is set to automatically send out e-mails, the e-mail is sent automatically. But if not, you need to send out the e-mails manually.

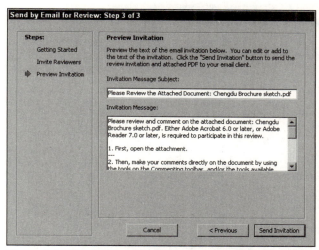

Figure 2-6: The third step lets you compose the e-mail that is sent to the reviewers.

Adding comments to the PDF

When a reviewer receives an e-mail requesting feedback, he can double-click on the attached file to open it in Acrobat or Adobe Reader 7. Within Acrobat, the Commenting toolbar may be used to add notes and comments to the sketch.

STEPS: Adding Comments to an E-mail PDF File

1. **Open an e-mail that you have received and you want to review.** Using your system e-mail client, the review request is sent out with the PDF file attached. Figure 2-7 shows what the resulting e-mail looks like.

E-mail reviews can mix comments from Macintosh and Windows platforms without any issues.

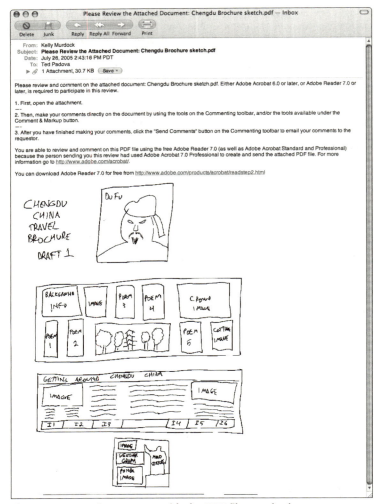

Figure 2-7: A review request with the PDF file attached

2. **Open the attached PDF in Acrobat.** If you double-click the attached PDF file, it opens within Acrobat. Comments are added to the document using the Commenting toolbar, which opens automatically when a review-enabled PDF is opened. The Commenting toolbar may also be accessed by choosing Tools ➪ Commenting ➪ Show Commenting Toolbar.

3. **Add review comments to the PDF.** Click on the Note Tool button in the Commenting toolbar. Click in the document where you want the note to be positioned. A note text area appears where you can type your message. Figure 2-8 shows the sketch document with some review comments added.

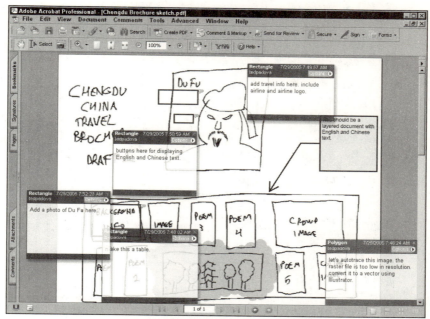

Figure 2-8: A sketch with comments attached

4. **Return comments.** After you've finished making comments, choose File ➪ Send Comments or click the Send Comments button in the Commenting toolbar. The PDF with its comments is sent back to the original sender.

Collecting review comments

When the reviewed documents are returned to the original sender, the comments are merged into the original document. These comments may then be summarized and printed.

STEPS: Collecting Review Comments

1. **Merge comments with the original document.** When a review PDF file is returned, it can also be double-clicked within the e-mail message to open it within Acrobat. Acrobat recognizes the document as one that was sent out for review and incorporates the comments into the original document. When this happens, a message dialog box appears.

2. **View and print a list of comments.** After a reviewed document is merged into the original PDF file, you open the list of comments by clicking on the Comments tab to the left. All comments in the PDF file appear at the bottom of the document (Figure 2-9).

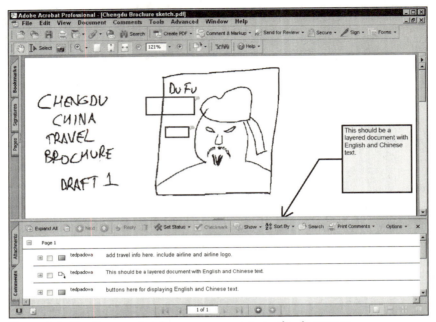

Figure 2-9: The Comments tab opens comments on the document.

3. **Sort comments.** The buttons along the top of the comments list let you set the status of comments and sort them by type, page, author, date, color, or check mark status.

4. **Print comments.** To print the comments, click the Print button at the top of the Comments list or choose File ⇨ Print with Comments Summary.

Editing Images in Photoshop

When you have a good idea of the content that needs to be in the final document, you can use Photoshop to edit and prepare the images to be included. These edits can include altering the image properties to adjust the image levels, color balance, brightness, and contrast. Another common way to edit images is to crop the image to the relevant portion. For images that aren't rectangular, you may need to extract a portion of an image. For images that appear on top of other page elements, you'll want to add transparency. All these tasks may be completed in Photoshop.

Many Photoshop editing features are covered in Chapter 11.

Adjusting image properties

After all the images for the project have been identified, Photoshop's image adjustment features may be used to change the image levels or its brightness and contrast. Adequate contrast is essential for objects that are to be combined with text.

STEPS: Adjusting Image Levels and Contrast

1. **Open an image in Photoshop.** Within Photoshop, choose File ⇨ Open and select an image to load. Because these images are to be used within a brochure, the levels and contrast need to be adjusted in order for the text that comes on top of the images to be legible. Figure 2-10 shows the original image.

Figure 2-10: This figure shows the original image before any adjustments.

2. **Auto-adjust the image levels.** With the image selected, choose Image ⇨ Adjustments ⇨ Levels. The Levels dialog box, shown in Figure 2-11, opens. This dialog box shows the Shadows, Midtones, and Highlights of the image. To auto-correct the balance of these levels, click Auto. The levels are evenly spaced and the image is adjusted.

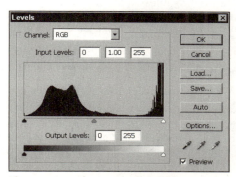

Figure 2-11: The Levels dialog box

3. **Adjust the brightness and contrast.** To change the brightness and contrast of the image, choose Image ➪ Adjustments ➪ Brightness/Contrast. This opens a simple dialog box with sliders for the Brightness and Contrast values. Set the Brightness value to –15 and the Contrast value to 10; then enable the Preview option to see the changes in the original image. This provides ample contrast for the text that is to appear on top of the image. Click OK to close the dialog box. Figure 2-12 shows the resulting image.

Figure 2-12: The image has sufficient contrast to make the text readable.

4. **Save the image.** Choose File ➪ Save to save the image with its changes.

Correcting distortions

In addition to color anomalies such as levels, brightness, and contrast, images captured with digital cameras and scanners often have lens flaws that make the image misaligned. A skewed image can throw off a good design, but Photoshop includes the Lens Correction filter to fix these types of problems.

STEPS: Using Lens Correction

1. **Open an image in Photoshop.** Within Photoshop, choose File ➪ Open and select an image that you want to fix.
2. **Open the Lens Correction filter.** With the image selected, choose the Filter ➪ Distort ➪ Lens Correction menu command. This opens the Lens Correction dialog box, shown in Figure 2-13, with a grid over the top of the image. This grid can be used to align the image objects to the image borders.

Figure 2-13: The Lens Correction dialog box lets you fix lens flaws.

3. **Zoom in the flawed area.** Click the Zoom tool in the upper-left corner of the dialog box and click image to zoom in. Then select the Hand tool and drag the affected area into the center of the preview pane.

4. **Use the Straighten tool.** Select the Straighten tool from the upper-left corner of the dialog box and drag along the left edge of the picture frame to align the image's picture with the image's borders. Click OK.

Cropping images

Although the levels and the contrast of the image look good, the image contains too many trees on either side of the pagoda. These unwanted details are easily removed using Photoshop's Crop tool.

STEPS: Cropping an Image

1. **Open an image in Photoshop.** Within Photoshop, choose File ➪ Open and select an image that you want to crop.

2. **Use the Crop tool.** Click on the Crop tool in the toolbar and drag within the interior of the image. This places a marquee with handles on each edge and corner. Click and drag the handles to precisely position the cropping marquee, as shown in Figure 2-14. Double-click within the cropping marquee to complete the crop.

3. **Save the image.** Choose File ➪ Save to save the image with its changes.

Figure 2-14: The marquee shows where the image is to be cropped.

Editing images

Photoshop includes many different tools for editing an existing image, but some of the most useful are the Clone and Healing Brushes. With these brushes you can remove unwanted details and generally cleanup an otherwise unusable image. In the following steps, the unwanted detail is the reflection off the glass of the cabinet in which the statue sits.

STEPS: Using the Spot Healing Tool

1. **Open an image in Photoshop.** Within Photoshop, choose File ➪ Open and select an image that you want to fix.

2. **Select the Spot Healing tool from the Toolbox.** With the Spot Healing tool selected, drag over the areas that you want to fix. In the example, you drag over the lighted portions of the image where the light is reflecting off the glass. The Spot Healing brush uses surrounding pixels to color over the spots. Figure 2-15 shows the image after the spots have been removed.

3. **Save the image.** Choose File ➪ Save to save the image with its changes.

Figure 2-15: You can use the Spot Healing Brush to remove problems from the image.

Extracting images

Not all images included in a design need to be rectangular. Using Photoshop's Extract filter, you can separate objects from their background, replacing the background with a transparent area. These images can later be used to wrap text in a layout.

Extracting image objects using the Extract filter is covered in Chapter 13.

STEPS: Extracting an Object from an Image

1. **Open an image in Photoshop.** Within Photoshop, choose File ⇨ Open and select an image that includes an object that you want to extract, such as the one in Figure 2-16.

2. **Increase the contrast between the object and its background.** Objects that have a clear contrast between the object and the background are much easier to extract. To increase the contrast for this image, choose Image ⇨ Adjustments ⇨ Auto Contrast.

3. **Open the Extract interface.** Choose Filter ⇨ Extract to open the Extract filter interface, as shown in Figure 2-17.

Figure 2-16: This object should be easy to extract because the line between the object and its background has a high contrast.

Figure 2-17: The Extract interface has all its tools along the left edge.

4. **Highlight the object edges.** Click the Edge Highlighting tool to the left, increase the Brush Size to 40, and enable the Smart Highlighting option on the right. Then drag over the edges of the object. Be sure to overlap the background.

5. **Fill the areas to keep.** Select the Fill tool and click within the object to mark it as the object to keep. The filled area is shaded with a blue highlight (Figure 2-18). If you have some gaps in the highlighted edge, the blue fill leaks into the background area. If this happens, select the Edge Highlighter tool again, close the gap, and refill the area you want to keep.

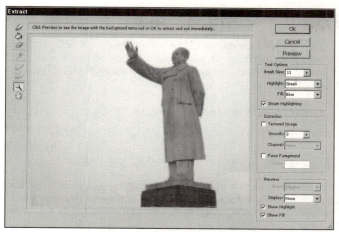

Figure 2-18: Use the Fill tool to mark the object that you want to keep.

6. **Preview the extraction.** With the object to keep marked, the Preview button becomes active. Click Preview to see the extracted object. The resulting extracted object is shown in Figure 2-19.

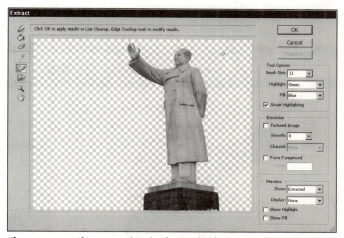

Figure 2-19: The extraction is shown in the Preview pane.

7. **Clean up the edges.** Click the Edge Touchup tool and drag on the edges that aren't extracted correctly. To erase part of the background that remains, use the Cleanup tool. Click OK when you're finished.

8. **Save the image.** Choose File ⇨ Save to save the image with its changes.

Creating Illustrator Objects

Images included in a design are best edited in Photoshop, but your design might also call for vector-based objects such as logos, maps, and shapes. These objects are easiest to create in Illustrator. For this example, we trace images into objects using the Live Trace feature and create some background objects.

Many Illustrator editing features are covered in Chapter 10.

Using Live Trace

Illustrated elements can add a lot to a design and Illustrator's new Live Trace feature make tracing bitmap images into objects easy. You can define and reuse the Live Trace presets to create unique looks such as cartoons, rough sketches, and technical illustrations.

STEPS: Tracing Bitmap Images with Live Trace

1. **Open a raster image in Illustrator.** Within Illustrator, choose File ➪ Place and place an image that you want to trace.

2. **Create a Live Trace object.** With the bitmap image selected, click the Live Trace button in the Options bar. This applies the default Live Trace preset. From the Options bar, choose the Color 6 preset. Figure 2-20 shows the results of applying Live Trace to the bitmap image.

Figure 2-20: Live Trace converts bitmap images into objects.

3. **Expand the Live Trace object.** To convert the traced image into actual objects that you can edit, choose the Object ⇨ Live Trace ⇨ Expand menu command. This makes the traced objects editable.

4. **Save the image.** Choose File ⇨ Save to save the image with its changes.

Creating and filling objects

Illustrator's Toolbox includes many tools for creating objects. These objects may be freehand lines drawn with the Pen, Pencil, or Paintbrush tools; straight lines; text; or various shapes, including rectangles, ellipses, polygons, stars, arcs, spirals, and grids.

After you create an object by dragging it in the art board, you can select a fill color or define the width and color of its outline, called a *stroke*.

STEPS: Creating a Background Object

1. **Open Illustrator.** Within Illustrator, choose File ⇨ New and create a new image.

2. **Create an object profile curve.** Click the Pen tool in the Toolbox. Then click and drag in the art board to create a profile curve. Select the Group Selection tool and drag the tangent handles to make the profile curve smooth, as shown in Figure 2-21.

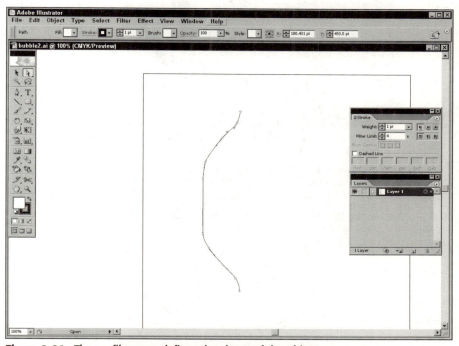

Figure 2-21: The profile curve defines the shape of the object.

3. **Add fill and stroke colors.** Click the Fill box in the Toolbox. Then select the light blue swatch in the Swatches palette to color this object light blue. Then, click the Stroke box in the Toolbox; then select the None color to remove the stroke color.

4. **Reflect the object.** Select the Object ⇨ Transform ⇨ Reflect menu command to open the Reflect dialog box. Select the Vertical option and click the Copy button. Then click OK.
5. **Align the two halves.** With the Selection tool, select and drag one of the halves until the midlines are aligned to each other, as shown in Figure 2-22.

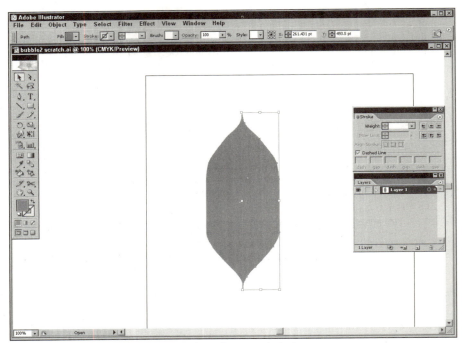

Figure 2-22: Two filled objects are aligned to match their centers.

6. **Add a gradient mesh.** Click the Mesh tool and select a point on the top half of the object where the light is shining and change its color to a lighter blue. Figure 2-23 shows the final bubble ready to be used as part of the background.
7. **Save the file.** Choose File ⇨ Save to save the file.

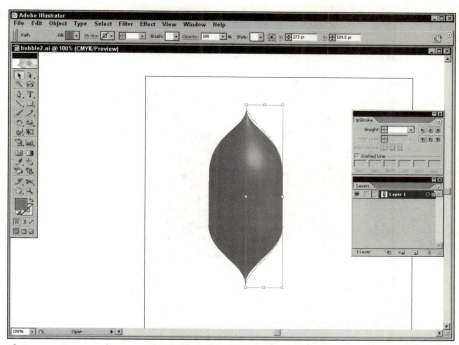

Figure 2-23: A gradient mesh adds some depth to the object.

Using effects

One common way to distort objects in Illustrator is with effects. Effects are applied to objects in memory, allowing you to edit or remove them anytime using the Appearance palette. A large variety of effects are available in the Effect menu.

Cross-Reference

Applying Illustrator effects is covered in Chapter 14.

STEPS: Extruding an Object

1. **Open Illustrator and select a file.** Within Illustrator, choose File ➪ Open and select a file that you want to apply an effect to.

2. **Group the objects.** Before you can apply an effect to separate objects, you'll need to group them together so the effect applies to them as a group. With all objects selected, choose Object ➪ Group. This groups the Chinese character in the example into a single object.

3. **Extrude the object.** With the grouped object selected, choose Effect ➪ 3D ➪ Extrude and Bevel. The 3D Extrude and Bevel dialog box opens. Select the Off-Axis Front option from the Position drop-down list and set the Extrude Depth to 20 pt. Then click OK. An extrude effect is applied to the Chinese character, as shown in Figure 2-24.

4. **Save the file.** Choose File ➪ Save to save the file.

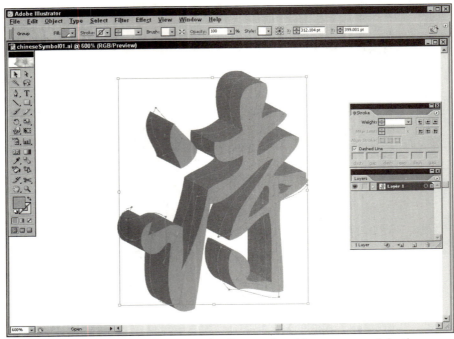

Figure 2-24: You can use the 3-D extrude effect to give objects a sense of depth.

Revolving a path

In addition to 3-D extrusions, the 3-D effect also includes the ability to create unique objects by rotating a path about an axis.

Using the 3-D effects found in Illustrator is covered in Chapter 13.

STEPS: Using a 3D Revolve Effect

1. **Open Illustrator.** Within Illustrator, choose File ➪ New to open a new file.
2. **Create a profile path.** Select the Paintbrush tool and draw a simple path that forms the profile of the revolved object. Be sure to include smooth corners for the path.
3. **Apply the 3D Revolve effect.** With the path selected, choose Effect ➪ 3D ➪ Revolve. This opens the 3D Revolve Options dialog box, shown in Figure 2-25. In the 3D Revolve Options dialog box, select the Off-Axis Front option in the Position field and set the Revolve Angle to 360. This creates a full revolution about the path's leftmost point.
4. **Enable wireframe rendering.** In the 3D Revolve Options dialog box, select the Wireframe option for the Surface setting. This changes the shading for the revolved path to be wireframe instead of solid, which is a good choice if you want to see the entire object and not just the front side of the solid object. After clicking OK, the finished object looks like the one in Figure 2-26.
5. **Save the file.** Choose File ➪ Save to save the file.

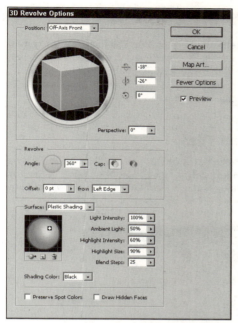

Figure 2-25: The 3D Revolve Options dialog box

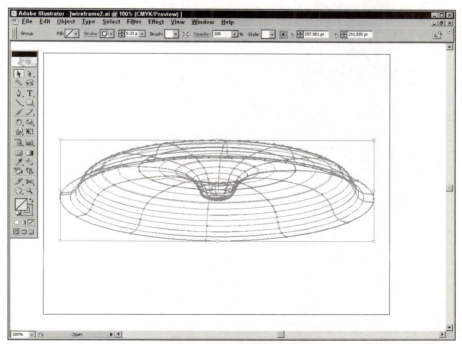

Figure 2-26: Revolving a path and shading it as a wireframe creates a unique object.

Versioning Files in Version Cue CS2

As you make changes to project content, the Version Cue CS2 features are helpful in maintaining versions. Version Cue is enabled automatically when CS2 is installed. The Version Cue interface may be accessed using any of the standard file dialog boxes.

Cross-Reference

Version Cue is covered in more detail in Chapter 8.

STEPS: Versioning Project Files

1. **Access the Adobe Dialog.** Within Illustrator, choose File ➪ Save As. This opens the Save As dialog box, shown in Figure 2-27. Click Use Adobe Dialog in the lower left of the Save As dialog box. This changes the look of the file dialog box, as shown in Figure 2-28.

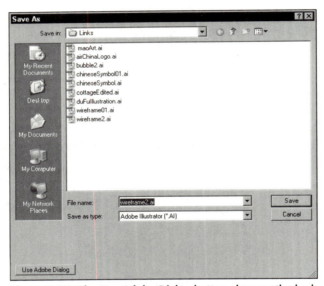

Figure 2-27: The Use Adobe Dialog button changes the look of the file dialog box.

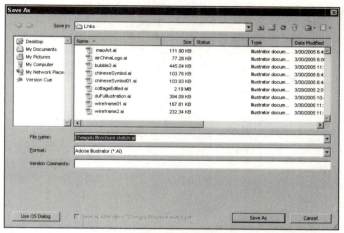

Figure 2-28: The Adobe Dialog file dialog box includes additional features.

2. At the top-right corner of the Adobe Dialog box, click the Project Tools icon and select the New Project option from the pop-up menu. The New Project dialog box, shown in Figure 2-29 appears, where you can enter the Project Name and Description. Enable the Share this project with others option and click OK.

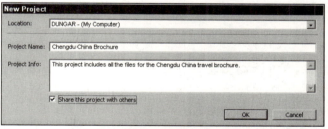

Figure 2-29: The New Project dialog box lets you name the new project and type a description for the project.

3. **Save the file in Version Cue.** Once a new project is created, the Version Cue option is selected from the left pane in the Adobe Dialog showing all the available projects, as shown in Figure 2-30. Double-click the new project folder to view the contents of the folder. Then name the file to save it. You can add a comment about the current version and click Save As.

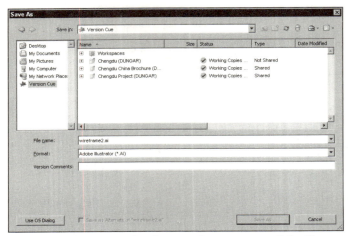

Figure 2-30: Once a project is created, you can see all the files within the project using the Adobe Dialog.

4. **Save a version.** To update the last saved file, choose File ➪ Save a Version. A dialog box, shown in Figure 2-31, appears, in which you can enter a comment for this version.

Figure 2-31: You can quickly save a new version of the current file.

Using Adobe Bridge

Version Cue makes shared project files accessible through the Adobe Dialog interface, but accessing project really isn't the purpose of Version Cue. Version Cue allows you to retain and catalog multiple versions of assets. It also enables the project team to access a single set of resources.

The real tool to access the volumes of content available in a project is Adobe Bridge. You open Adobe Bridge using the Go To Bridge icon in the upper-right corner of all the CS2 applications.

Adobe Bridge is covered in more detail in Chapter 7.

Once you create a new project, you can easily add files to the project without having to open Adobe Dialog for every file. Simply drag and drop the files from their current location into the Project folder in Adobe Bridge.

STEPS: Adding Files to a Version Cue Project using Adobe Bridge

1. **Collect the files to add to the project.** With Windows Explorer or Macintosh Finder, locate all the files that you want to add to the project.

2. **Locate the project folder.** Open Adobe Bridge by clicking on the button in the upper-right corner of any of the CS2 applications. This button causes the Adobe Bridge interface to open. Then click on the Version Cue option in the Favorites pane to display the available project folders. Double click on the folder that is named the same as the new project name and drag all the files that you want to add to the project into this folder from Windows Explorer or the Macintosh Finder.

3. **View the folder within Adobe Dialog.** Within Illustrator, select the File ➪ Open menu command and double click the project folder in Adobe Dialog. All the various files added to the project folder are now visible, as shown in Figure 2-32.

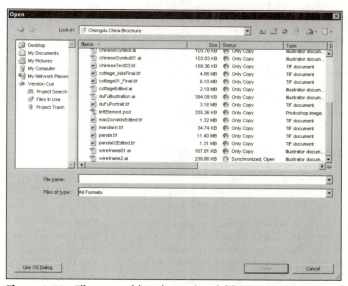

Figure 2-32: Files you add to the project folder appear in Adobe Dialog.

STEPS: Accessing Project Files using Adobe Bridge

1. **Open Adobe Bridge.** From within Illustrator, click on the Go to Bridge button in the upper-right corner of the interface. This opens the Adobe Bridge interface.

2. **Locate the project folder.** Within Adobe Bridge, select the Version Cue option from the pane on the left and double click the project folder to open it. Thumbnails for all files within the project folder display within Adobe Bridge, as shown in Figure 2-33.

Figure 2-33: Adobe Bridge displays thumbnails for all files in the project file.

3. **Open a file to work with.** Select a file within the project file and right-click the file thumbnail. A pop-up menu appears. Select the Open With option. The submenu lists all the various CS2 applications. You can also drag thumbnails directly to the different CS2 applications.

Creating a Layout in InDesign

After you create all the content for the project using Photoshop and Illustrator, you can use InDesign to lay out the project in preparation for printing. Each object within InDesign is contained within a frame. These frames are easily moved and resized.

Images and objects placed within frames in a layout aren't embedded within the layout but instead are only links to the actual image and object files. This allows the representative images to be updated quickly. When the layout is exported or printed, InDesign looks at content referenced as links and loads the actual linked files into the exported or printed document.

Cross-Reference Creating a layout and using master pages are covered in Chapter 26.

Setting layout properties

Before the content is placed on the pages, creating a document lets you create all the pages and spreads contained in the project. You can also specify the number of pages as well as the page dimensions, margins, and columns.

STEPS: Creating an InDesign Layout

1. **Create a new InDesign document.** Within InDesign, choose File ➪ New ➪ Document. In the New Document dialog box, shown in Figure 2-34, set the number of pages to 6 and enable the Facing Pages option. Set the Width to 7 inches, the Height to 10 inches, and click the Portrait Orientation button. Then set all the margins to 0.5 inches and the columns to 1, with a gutter of 0.

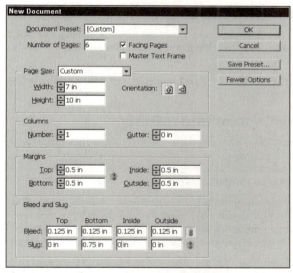

Figure 2-34: The New Document dialog box

2. **Set the bleed and slug dimensions.** While you're still in the New Document dialog box, click on More Options to reveal the fields for setting the bleed and slug dimensions. Set the Top Bleed value to 0.125 inches and click the Make All Settings the Same button to the right of the Bleed fields. Then set the Bottom Slug value to 0.75 inches and click OK.

3. **View the layout pages.** To see the layout pages, open the Pages palette by choosing Window ➪ Pages. The Pages palette is shown in Figure 2-35.

4. **Save the file.** Choose File ➪ Save to save the layout.

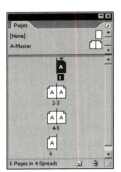

Figure 2-35: The Pages palette lets you view and select pages in a layout.

Importing content into InDesign

With a layout created, you can begin to import content into the InDesign layout by choosing File ➪ Place. Imported objects appear within frames that allow them to be easily moved about the layout.

Another easy way to import content is to select multiple files in the Adobe Bridge interface and simply drag them into InDesign.

STEPS: Importing Content into InDesign

1. **Create a layout frame.** Before importing an image into the InDesign layout, click the Rectangle Frame tool and drag in the layout to create a frame that is the same size as the page marked by black lines, as shown in Figure 2-36. The frame you create is marked with diagonal lines through its center.

2. **Place images from Photoshop.** With the image frame created, choose File ➪ Place. The Place dialog box (shown in Figure 2-37) looks like the Open file dialog box, except it lets you select a much large number of file types. Select the image file to place in the layout and click Open. The image is automatically loaded and sized to fit the frame.

3. **Place objects from Illustrator.** You can also use the File ➪ Place menu command to place objects created in Illustrator. For Illustrator objects, enable the Show Import Options check box in the Place dialog box. This causes the Place PDF dialog box, shown in Figure 2-38, to appear. In the Crop To drop-down list, select the Bounding Box option; enable the Transparent Background check box. Then click OK. The object to be placed appears on the cursor. Click in the upper-left section of the image to place the object.

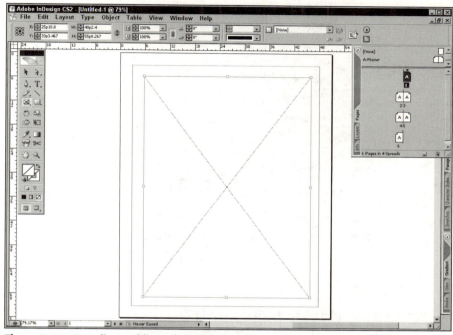

Figure 2-36: Two diagonal lines denote frames.

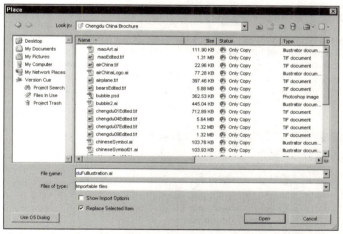

Figure 2-37: The Place dialog box opens a variety of different file formats.

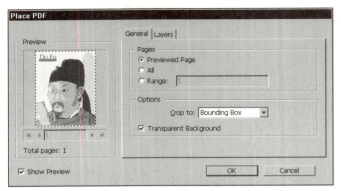

Figure 2-38: The Place PDF dialog box defines how objects are cropped.

4. **Resize the placed object.** The placed object appears within a frame. By dragging the handles, you can resize the frame, but the placed object's size doesn't change until you choose Object ⇨ Fitting ⇨ Fit Content to Frame Proportionally.

5. **Save the file.** Choose File ⇨ Save to save the layout.

Creating Master pages in InDesign

Using Master pages, you can place objects such as page numbers that appear on every page of the document. Master pages are created and accessed using the Pages palette.

STEPS: Using Master Pages

1. **Create a new Master spread.** Master pages are defined using the Pages palette. Using the palette menu (which can be accessed by clicking on the small right-pointing arrow icon in the upper right corner of the palette), select the New Master palette menu command. In the New Master dialog box, shown in Figure 2-39, type a prefix and a name for the master. Then type **2** as the number of pages and click OK. The Master appears in the top of the Pages palette.

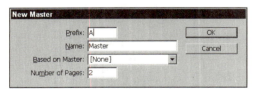

Figure 2-39: The New Master dialog box

2. **Apply the Master to pages.** With the new Master spread selected in the Pages palette, select the Apply Master to Pages palette menu command. In the Apply Master dialog box that appears, type the page numbers to which you want to apply the Master spread. The Pages palette is updated with the Prefix for the Master spread, as shown in Figure 2-40.

Figure 2-40: Master pages are displayed at the top of the Pages palette.

3. **Add page numbers to the Master spread.** Select the Type tool and drag within the Master pages where you want the page numbers to appear. With the text cursor blinking in the text object, choose Type ➪ Insert Special Character ➪ Auto Page Number. The Prefix for the Master spread is listed in the text object. However, when you view a page that uses the Master page, the correct page number displays.

4. **Save the file.** Choose File ➪ Save to save the layout.

Threading text

You can make text flow continuously from one text frame to another. This process is called threading text. You accomplish it by clicking the small plus icon in the lower right corner of the text frame. This icon turns red when some overflowing text exists.

STEPS: Threading Text Across Multiple Text Frames

1. **Create a text frame.** Text frames hold text. Using the In and Out ports, you can specify how text threads between multiple frames. To create a text frame, click the Type tool and drag in the layout where you want the frames to be located, as shown in Figure 2-41.

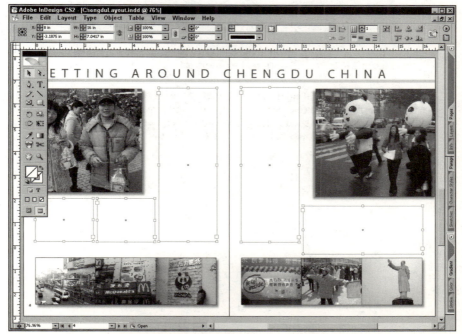

Figure 2-41: The Type tool creates a text frame.

2. **Add text to the text frame.** With the text cursor blinking in the text frame, type the text into the first text frame. (Or you can select the text that you want to paste from another application like a Word Processor and copy it to the Clipboard. Then, within InDesign, choose Edit ⇨ Paste.) The text appears, as shown in Figure 2-42, using the font and size specified in the Type menu. Notice how all the text doesn't fit in the first text frame so the Out port is colored red.

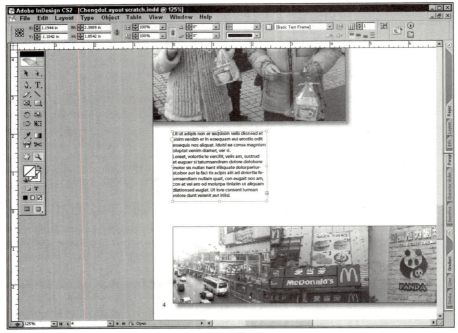

Figure 2-42: You can add text to a text frame by copying and pasting.

3. **Click the red Out port for the first text frame.** The cursor changes to a link icon. Then click the second text frame and the text spills over into the second text frame. Click the Out port for the second text frame and link it to the third text frame until all five text frames are linked, as shown in Figure 2-43.

4. **Save the file.** Choose File ⇨ Save to save the layout.

Figure 2-43: Text runs from text frame to text frame naturally when frames are threaded.

Preparing a Layout for Print

When the document layout is complete, InDesign includes some useful features that are helpful as you prepare the document to be printed such as previewing separations and exporting the document as a PDF file.

See Part IX for more on printing using the Creative Suite applications.

Previewing separations

When InDesign documents are printed, they are split into four different passes called separations, one for each color representing Cyan, Magenta, Yellow, and Black (CMYK). These separations are then combined to overlaid to create the finished print. Often, previewing a document's separations prior to printing can help identify potential problems, allowing you to fix these problems before a costly print run. Separations for the current document may be viewed using the Separations Preview palette.

STEPS: Previewing Separations

1. **Open the Separations Preview palette.** To open the Separations Preview palette, shown in Figure 2-44, choose Window ➪ Output ➪ Separations Preview. Select the Separations option in the View field to see a list of each of the separations.

Figure 2-44: The Separations Preview lists a document's separations.

2. **View a separation.** To see a separation in the layout, click on the Visibility icon for the separations that you want to see, and the document is updated to show those selected separations, as shown in Figure 2-45.

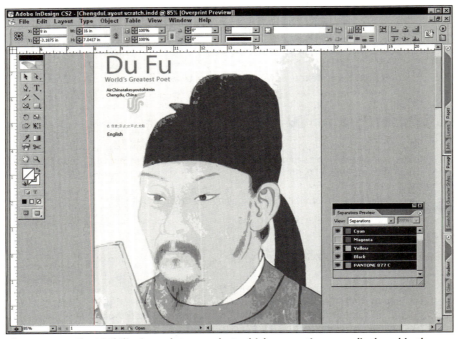

Figure 2-45: The Visibility icons let you select which separations are displayed in the layout.

Exporting to PDF for printing

When exporting the layout to PDF, InDesign includes several export presets that you can use to configure the document for a specific destination. One of these presets is for print.

STEPS: Exporting to PDF

1. **Export to PDF using the Print preset.** Choose File ➪ PDF Export Presets ➪ High Quality Print. This opens a file dialog box where you can name the file to be exported. After you click the Save, the Export Adobe PDF dialog box, shown in Figure 2-46, opens.

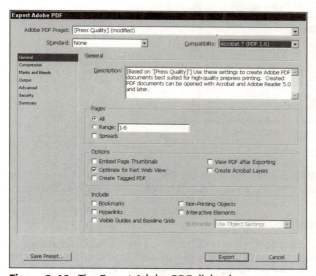

Figure 2-46: The Export Adobe PDF dialog box

2. **Open the PDF within Acrobat.** In the General panel of the Export Adobe PDF dialog box, enable the View PDF after Exporting option to have the document open in Acrobat after it's exported. Then click Export.

Soft-Proofing in Adobe Acrobat

Once a print file is exported to the PDF format, you can use Acrobat to soft-proof the print before it is sent the print house. Acrobat 7 includes some powerful print tools that can detect potential print errors before they occur. These print production tools are located in the Tools ➪ Print Production menu.

Checking color in Acrobat

You use the Output Preview tool to check the colors within the current PDF document. Selecting this menu option opens the Output Preview dialog box, shown in Figure 2-47. This dialog box offers options to preview the color Separations and any Color Warnings caused by Overprinting and Rich Black.

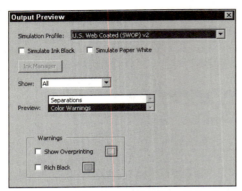

Figure 2-47: The Output Preview dialog box lets you preview color separations and Color Warnings.

The Convert Colors tool is used to convert RGB, CMYK, and Grayscale color definitions to the target color space. It also lets you embed the color profile within the PDF document.

Flattening transparency

The Transparency Flattening tool opens a Flattener Preview window, as shown in Figure 2-48, where you can quickly get a view of the transparent objects in the PDF file. You can also set the resolution for objects that get rasterized and view with updates the effect on the document objects.

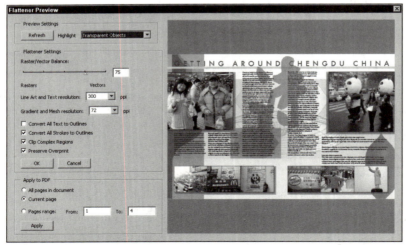

Figure 2-48: The Flattener Preview dialog box lets you preview the effect of flattening transparent objects.

Creating a PDF/X file

Adobe is a contributor and supporter of several ISO defined standards for high-resolution print formats. The most aggressive format is the PDF/X format. In order for a document to meet this standard, it must past a rigorous battery of tests. You can check a document for PDF/X compliance using the Preflight tool, which is accessed using the Tools ⇨ Print Production ⇨ Preflight menu command. This command opens the Preflight dialog box, shown in Figure 2-49.

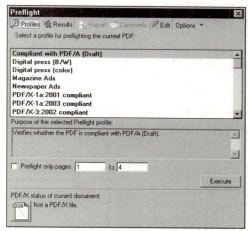

Figure 2-49: The Preflight dialog box is used to check the current document for PDF/X compatibility.

The Preflight dialog box lists the potential errors being checked. Clicking Execute tests the document and displays all noncompliant errors in the Results tab. To convert the current document to PDF/X format, click the Convert Current PDF to PDF/X button at the bottom of the dialog box.

STEPS: Checking a PDF Document for Errors

1. **Open Adobe Acrobat.** Locate the exported InDesign PDF print document and open it within Acrobat.

2. **View the Output Preview.** Choose Tools ⇨ Print Production ⇨ Output Preview. This opens the Output Preview dialog box. In the Output Preview dialog box, enable the Show Overprinting option to view all overprinting in the current document, as shown in Figure 2-50. Close the Output Preview dialog box.

3. **Check the transparency flattening.** Choose Tools ⇨ Print Production ⇨ Transparency Flattening. This opens the Flattener Preview window. Drop the Raster/Vector Balance slider to 75, click Refresh and select the Transparent Objects option from the top drop-down list. If the highlighted objects look fine, as shown in Figure 2-51, click Apply.

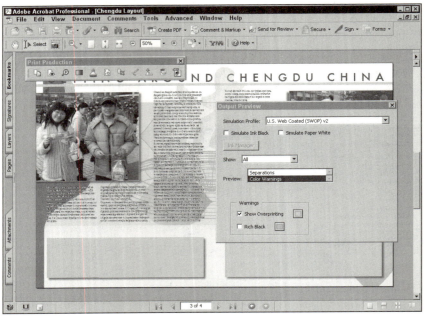

Figure 2-50: You can view Overprinting using the Output Preview dialog box.

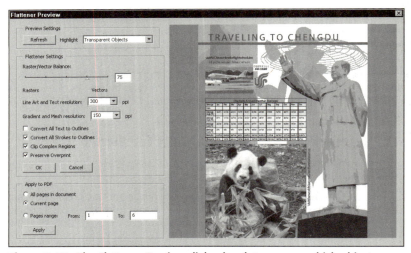

Figure 2-51: The Flattener Preview dialog box lets you see which objects are to be flattened.

4. **Checking the document against the PDF/X format.** Choose Tools ⇨ Print Production ⇨ Preflight to open the Preflight dialog box. Click Execute to perform the error checking. The Results tab opens to display the errors with this file, as shown in Figure 2-52.

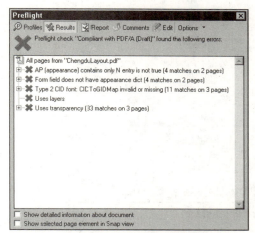

Figure 2-52: The Preflight dialog box checks for errors not compliant with the PDF/X format.

Repurposing a Document for Web Hosting

Completed print projects may be easily repurposed and used on the pages of a Web site. By doing this, you won't have to re-create designs specific to the Web. But Web pages require that the elements be optimized to reduce their file sizes.

Creative Suite 2 offers two ways to repurpose designs for delivery on the Web. Acrobat files may be posted online and viewed using an Acrobat Reader plug-in, but before posting existing PDF files, Acrobat's PDF Optimizer feature may be used to reduce the size of the PDF file before posting it online.

In addition to PDF files, InDesign includes a feature that packages all content elements included in a layout and delivers it to GoLive where the elements may be reused in a Web page.

Using PDF Optimizer

The PDF Optimizer interface in Acrobat includes many settings to downsample images, unembed fonts and provide several cleanup options.

Cross-Reference   The PDF Optimizer is covered in Chapter 29.

STEPS: Using the PDF Optimizer

1. **Open the PDF Optimizer.** With the file that you want to optimize open in Acrobat, choose Advanced ⇨ PDF Optimizer. The PDF Optimizer interface, shown in Figure 2-53, includes multiple panes.

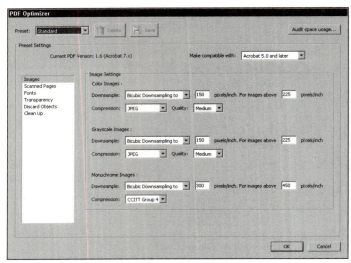

Figure 2-53: The PDF Optimizer interface

2. **Audit space usage.** Before changing any of the options, click Audit Space Usage at the top of the dialog box. Acrobat computes the size of all the various objects found in the PDF file and reports them in a Space Audit dialog box, shown in Figure 2-54.

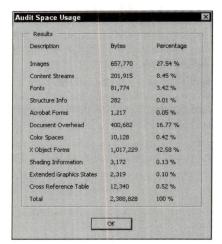

Figure 2-54: The Audit Space Usage dialog box

3. **Configure image downsampling.** In the Images panel, select the Bicubic Downsampling option of 72 pixels/inch for all image above 72 pixels/inch. Then enable JPEG Compression with a Medium quality setting.

4. **Specify cleanup options.** Select the Clean Up panel, shown in Figure 2-55, and enable all the Remove and Discard options, making sure the Optimize the PDF for Fast Web View check box is enabled. Then click OK. In the file dialog box that opens, give the file a name and click OK.

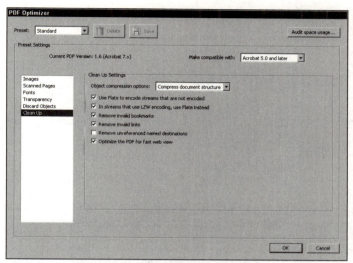

Figure 2-55: The Clean Up panel of the PDF Optimizer dialog box

Packaging for GoLive

InDesign documents may be packaged and delivered for use in GoLive. This can make all images and objects in the design be downsampled and compressed and moved into a folder where GoLive can reference them. How the images are optimized is customizable.

Cross-Reference

More details on packaging for GoLive are covered in Chapter 28.

STEPS: Packaging an InDesign Layout for GoLive

1. **Open an InDesign document.** Choose File ➪ Open and locate the file that you want to package.

2. **Specify a package folder.** Choose File ➪ Package for GoLive. This command opens a file dialog box where you can name the folder where the packaged layout is placed.

3. **Set packaging options.** After a folder is selected, the Package for GoLive dialog box, shown in Figure 2-56, appears. Enable the View Package when Complete check box.

4. **Choose the images to package.** The Package for GoLive dialog box gives you the option of packaging all the Original Images, the Formatted Images, and the Movies and Sounds together with the package. For this example, select only the Formatted Images option. Then click Package.

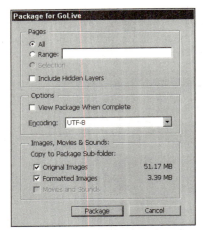

Figure 2-56: The Package for GoLive dialog box

5. **View the package in GoLive.** After you click Package, all the elements used in the layout are copied to the designated package folder and the packaged PDF is opened within GoLive, as shown in Figure 2-57.

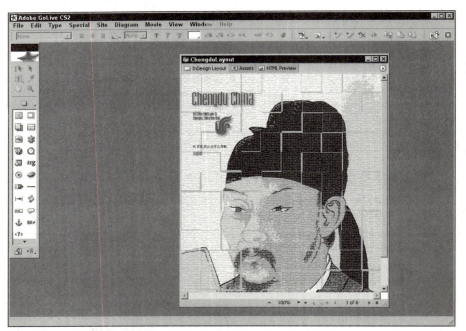

Figure 2-57: Once the packaged InDesign file is opened in GoLive, you can drag elements to a Web page from the packaged window.

Exporting packaged HTML using GoLive

Packaged InDesign layouts appear in GoLive in a separate window. You can drag elements directly from this window onto Web pages in GoLive, but you can convert the entire layout to HTML using the Export as HTML palette menu. Selecting this command opens the Export as HTML dialog box, shown in Figure 2-58. This dialog box lets you export only the current page, all pages or a selection of pages.

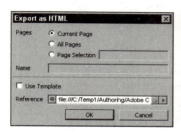

Figure 2-58: The Export as HTML dialog box can export the Current Page, All Pages, or a selection of pages.

STEPS: Exporting a Packaged Layout to HTML

1. **Open a packaged document in GoLive.** The Package for GoLive menu command opens the packaged file in GoLive automatically if the open option is enabled. If not, you can open the saved package file in GoLive using the File ⇨ Open menu command.

2. **Export the packaged file to HTML.** With the package preview window open in GoLive, choose the Export as HTML palette menu command. In the Export as HTML dialog box, select the All Pages option and click OK. All pages of the layout are converted to HTML and saved in the designated location. A status dialog box, shown in Figure 2-59, appears when the export is complete.

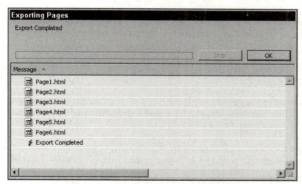

Figure 2-59: A status of the export activity appears when the exporting is completed.

3. **Open the exported HTML pages.** Once the export is completed, you can open the HTML pages within GoLive. Be aware that laying objects out in InDesign is much different from doing so in HTML, but the exported pages give you a good starting point, as shown in Figure 2-60.

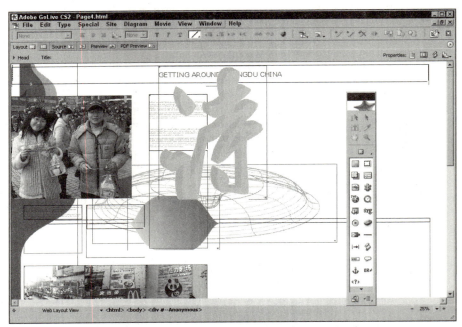

Figure 2-60: Exported HTML pages look different than the InDesign layout.

Summary

- Sketched ideas may be scanned directly into Acrobat and saved as a PDF file.
- PDF files may be submitted to reviewers by using e-mail. Reviewers can use Acrobat to enter comments into the PDF file and those comments are returned to the original sender.
- Photoshop is useful for editing images including adjusting image properties, cropping, extracting, and editing images.
- Illustrator objects are also useful for enhancing a design. Using Illustrator's features such as Live Trace, fills, strokes, effects, and 3-D extruding and revolving, many interesting objects may be created.
- Version Cue enables Creative Suite users to save multiple versions of a file. It also enables workgroups of users to share and work on a project without interfering with one another.
- Adobe Bridge provides direct access to project assets including thumbnails.
- Content from multiple sources may be compiled and laid out in InDesign in preparation for printing and exporting.
- InDesign's Master pages let you place common elements that appear on multiple pages.

- Acrobat's print production tools are useful for soft-proofing documents.
- Using the PDF Optimizer found in Acrobat, complex PDF files may be significantly reduced in size.
- InDesign files may be packaged for use in GoLive making it possible to repurpose layouts for use on the Web.

✦ ✦ ✦

Setting Preferences

CHAPTER 3

In your Creative Suite production workflow, you have eight different programs to work with: Adobe Bridge, Illustrator CS2, Photoshop CS2, ImageReady CS2, InDesign CS2, Acrobat 7 Professional, GoLive CS2, and Version Cue CS2. Fortunately, a single software publisher developed the programs, and the publisher uses a similar user interface among the programs. This alone helps you to develop an intuitive feel for how a program works and how to easily access commands that open tools and menus.

Taking the common user interface a step further, many of the CS2 programs offer you options for customizing your workplace and saving settings for preferences, creating custom workplace environments, and defining your own custom keyboard shortcuts to open menus and tools. In this chapter, you learn how to simplify your workflow by integrating common settings between programs that reduce confusion and the learning curve to master the program environments. All the CS2 programs are covered in this chapter; Version Cue CS2 is covered in Chapter 8.

Getting to Know Common Preference Attributes

As stated in Chapter 1, this information is intended for people who have at least some experience with one of the CS2 applications in an earlier version. If you have such experience, you no doubt are familiar with preferences choices and options settings you make in preferences dialog boxes to help you customize a program to suit your work habits.

When creating a workflow either for yourself or for a group of production artists, you'll want to make preference choices in each of the programs to help you work effectively in a given program and, where possible, to help bring preference choices in parity between the programs.

If your workflow includes several other workers, and in particular if other workers use your computer in different shifts or at times when you're away from your desk, spend a little time talking with the people in your organization about the choices you'll make not only for preferences but also for the other items discussed in this chapter related to workspaces and keyboard shortcuts.

✦ ✦ ✦ ✦

In This Chapter

Understanding preference settings

Setting individual program preferences

✦ ✦ ✦ ✦

To begin our coverage on preferences, we start by addressing each application and offer a description of choices available respective to each program. The following is not intended to be exhaustive as far as preference options are concerned, but it does highlight some of the key points related to making adjustments for a Creative Suite workflow.

Opening the Preferences dialog box in all the CS2 programs can be handled with a keyboard shortcut. Fortunately, the shortcut is identical for all programs. Your first keyboard shortcut to commit to memory is ⌘/Ctrl+K. This shortcut opens the Preferences dialog box no matter what CS2 program you use, including the new Adobe Bridge. If you elect to use a menu command, Preferences are located under the application menu on the Mac (for example, the Illustrator menu to the right of the Apple logo/menu when using Adobe Illustrator CS2) and under the Edit menu on Windows.

In all the programs, when you open the Preferences dialog box, a series of tabs or a list is made available for selecting categorical areas where specific options choices are found. In Illustrator and Photoshop, the categories are selected by opening a pull-down menu or clicking the Next/Previous buttons to change categories. Adobe Bridge, InDesign, GoLive, and Acrobat use a list in the left pane of the Preferences dialog box to address specific categories. InDesign and Photoshop have a common function in that you can press ⌘/Ctrl+1, 2, 3, and so on, to toggle between the categories. When you first access a Preferences dialog box, General Preferences are selected in each program. If you select a category other than the General category in Adobe Bridge, GoLive or Acrobat Professional, the next time you return to the Preferences dialog box, the category remains selected. The other programs default back to showing the options for the General Preferences.

Setting application-specific preferences

You can open the Preferences dialog box with or without a document open in the application window. If you open preferences and make choices for some settings in some of the programs before you open a document, the preference options you enable or disable apply to all new documents you create. Some examples of application-specific preferences include setting the default page size in Adobe InDesign each time you create a new document. If your work most often involves a portrait U.S. letter–size page, you can set the preferences in InDesign to a standard portrait-size page. The same holds true for many other options like the units of measurement (inches, millimeters, picas, and so on).

In GoLive, you have options for viewing your document pages in a Layout mode, a Preview mode, a PDF preview, and several other choices. If you make a preference choice in GoLive before opening any document, the preferences apply to all subsequent files you view in GoLive.

In programs like Adobe Acrobat, almost all the preference choices you make are application-specific preferences and apply to all documents you subsequently open in Acrobat. Photoshop treats preferences similarly to Acrobat — preferences apply to all documents and most of the preferences you make in Illustrator CS2 behave similarly.

Setting document-specific preferences

In some cases, you can make a preference choice that applies only to an open document. This feature applies most often to InDesign. In InDesign, you can make a choice for the display performance of an open document or change the units of measure that apply to the open document. If you create a new document, you return to your default preferences. If you want to override defaults, close all open files and make your preference changes.

Tip At times, you may be confused as to whether a preference setting is applied to a document or to the application. If you're not certain, make a preference choice with a document open in the application window. Save the file and close it. Create a new document and test the results. For example, check a font selection or a unit of measure in your new document if either choice was adjusted in your preferences. If the new document registers the same option as your old document, you'll know that the preference selection has been made as an application preference setting and will remain in effect until you change it.

Returning to default preferences

All the CS2 programs save preference changes to a file on your hard disk. If you want to return to the original preference settings (the ones in place when your CS2 programs were first installed), you can delete preference files from your hard disk. Preferences are much more complex in many CS2 programs and, often, you find many different preference settings that affect the behavior of a program. If you do intend to delete preferences, make a note for the location of a preference file and copy the file to another location on your hard disk. If you trash a file and the preferences are rebuilt or appear different than you expected, you can replace the new file with your copy. For specific locations of the preference files, use the online help in each CS2 program found under the Help menu. Follow the directions detailed in the help files to remove preferences manually.

In Adobe Bridge, Photoshop, and InDesign, you can use a keyboard shortcut to delete preference files. In any of these programs, double-click the program icon or click a program alias in the Dock (Mac) or Start menu (Windows) and immediately press Shift+⌘+Option+Control (Mac) or Shift+Ctrl+Alt (Windows). A dialog box relative to the program you open asks you to confirm deletion of the preference file, as shown in Figure 3-1, when the keyboard shortcut is used. In this example, the key modifiers were used while opening Adobe Bridge.

Caution Using the Shift key alone or in combination with any other keys when you open Acrobat disables all commenting functions and hides the Comments menu. Preferences are not set to defaults.

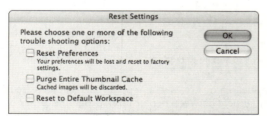

Figure 3-1: Select the Reset Preferences check box and click OK in the dialog box to reset preferences to defaults.

Illustrator and GoLive (and all other CS2 applications) write a new preference file upon program launch if the preference file has been deleted. You can restore factory defaults by deleting preferences. On the Macintosh, the directory path to the Illustrator preference file is found at `Mac OS X/Users/[username]/Library/Preferences/Adobe Illustrator CS2 Settings`. **On Windows the file is located at** `(Windows) Documents and Settings/[username]/Application Data/Adobe/Adobe Illustrator CS2/Settings/AIPrefs`.

GoLive is found at the same directory paths (use GoLive instead of Adobe Illustrator) for Mac and Windows. Delete the Main, FileMappings, and UserAgentProfiles to delete all preference settings. Relaunch the respective program, and new preference files are built upon program launch.

Making dynamic preference adjustments

When you change a preference setting, the change is dynamically applied to the application or a document for most settings in all the CS2 programs. You don't need to quit the program and relaunch it in order for the preference setting to be active. In a few cases, however, you need to restart a program in order to have new preference choices take effect. In Illustrator and Photoshop, changing the preferences for the plug-ins and scratch-disk locations requires you to restart the program before new locations for these items can be used.

Typically, you change the scratch partitions in these programs to a hard-drive hierarchy you want to use. For example, if you have two hard disks attached to your computer, you can set the primary scratch partition to the hard disk not containing your operating system and program files. The secondary partition is set to the drive containing your operating system and program files. When a choice like this is made, Illustrator and Photoshop first use the drive in the primary order as an extension of memory when a program eats up your available RAM. If more memory is needed, the partition in the second order is used, and so on. GoLive also has a scratch volume setting for QuickTime video editing.

With all other preferences, you can continue working in your program without relaunching it. The preferences remain in effect until you make another change in the Preferences dialog box. However, if you experience a program crash after making a new preference choice, the setting is not reflected when you relaunch the program, because preference settings are saved when quitting a program.

Tip

If you have many preference settings to change, make all your changes in the Preferences dialog box and then quit the program. Relaunch the program and all your preferences are intact. Preferences are written to disk when you quit a program. If you make a lot of preference changes and you experience a program crash, your new settings are lost. Quitting a program after making new preference choices insures you that the new settings are rewritten to disk.

Setting the Program Preferences

Each of the CS2 applications has individual dialog boxes where preference choices are made. In some cases, preference options are identical between two or more programs; other choices are unique to each specific program. Some of the common options choices you'll want to understand are listed in the following sections where preferences are covered for each individual program.

Adobe Bridge

The Bridge is used primarily for file management and organization and therefore doesn't have many common preferences to the authoring programs. Nevertheless, you'll want to address the Preferences dialog box when you first install Bridge to set your own custom working environment.

Chapter 3 ✦ Setting Preferences

 New Feature Adobe Bridge is a new feature in the Creative Suite2. For more on using Adobe Bridge, see Chapter 7.

General Preferences

Open the Bridge and press Command/Control+K to open the Bridge Preferences dialog box shown in Figure 3-2. By default, the General Preferences are selected in the left pane. Choices you have in the right pane include:

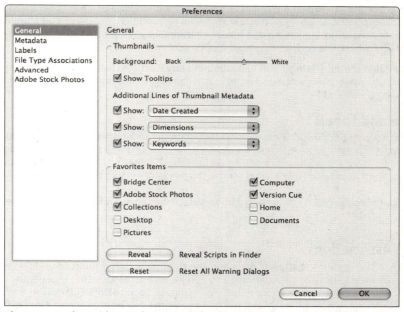

Figure 3-2: The Bridge Preferences dialog box allows you to view General Preference options.

- ✦ **Thumbnails:** Move the slider left or right to change the gray color of the background content area. You can change the neutral gray default to a lighter or darker color if you have images that closely match the background and want to add more contrast between the content area background and the thumbnail images.

- ✦ **Show Tooltips:** As you move the cursor over all objects, buttons, links, and so on, in the Bridge window, a tooltip appears below the cursor. If tooltips become distracting, deselect the box.

- ✦ **Additional Lines of Metadata:** You can show up to three lines of metadata below document thumbnails in the Bridge content area. If the three check boxes are selected, data are shown according to adjacent pull-down menus. You have many options for the data you want to view. Rather than show the common items like file name, creation date, and file size, you may want to show other options such as color mode, bit depth, and color profile used. These and many more options are available from the pull-down menus. A nice feature in the Bridge is that the metadata items you change in the dialog box are dynamically reflected in the Bridge window. You can show the metadata you want to see for general use, but for a glance you may want to view Exposure settings for Camera Raw files. You can open the General Preferences and view Exposures while in the dialog box. Click Cancel and you return to the defaults you prefer when viewing all files.

✦ **Favorite Items:** The Favorites tab displays items according to what you select in this area in the General Preferences. Your selections are shown as Favorites in the Favorites tab. These choices are also dynamic. You can view the Bridge window and notice the Favorites tab includes the items you select and excludes items you have not selected.

✦ **Reveal Scripts in Finder:** A number of JavaScripts are added to a folder installed with the CS2 applications. Many of these scripts can be modified. Be aware you should have sophisticated scripting knowledge before changing any scripts. When you click Reveal, the folder where the scripts are located opens on your desktop.

✦ **Reset All Warning Dialogs:** You can eliminate any warning dialog boxes, which appear by default, when you exercise an action. You can restore your setting to the original defaults by clicking Reset.

Metadata and Labels

The Metadata pane offers options for viewing metadata in the Metadata tab. You can choose to display or hide a number of different metadata items from view in the tab. Labels offers you options for selecting label colors and changing label names. You can select any thumbnail in the content area and apply a label for the purposes of sorting files.

For a complete description of working with Metadata and Labels Preferences, see Chapter 7.

File Type Associations

Click File Type Associations in the left pane and the right pane lists a number of different file formats from a wide variety of applications. You can change an association by opening the pull-down menu adjacent to a program name. For example, to associate QuarkXPress files with Adobe InDesign, where InDesign is launched each time you double click a QuarkXPress document in the Bridge, locate QuarkXPress QXP or QXT files. From the pull-down menu shown in Figure 3-3, select Adobe InDesign CS2. Each time you open a QuarkXPress document from the Bridge, InDesign launches and converts the file to an InDesign document. Note that this file association feature only affects documents opened from within Adobe Bridge.

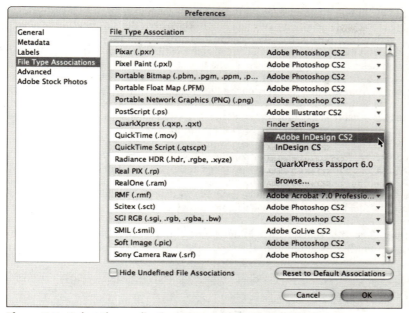

Figure 3-3: Select the application to associate with the file type.

Advanced

The Advanced settings, shown in Figure 3-4, offer options for some miscellaneous options choices and adjustments for the Bridge cache files. The options include:

- **Do not process files larger than:** The value in the field box by default is 200. When the Bridge encounters a file over 200MB, the image thumbnail is not created in the Content area. You can lower the value in the text box and significantly improve Bridge performance.

- **Number of Recently Viewed Folders to Display in the Look In Popup:** Acceptable values in the text box are from 0 to 30. The Look In menu appears at the top left of the Bridge window. When you open the menu, it displays the most recently visited favorites and folders. You can increase or decrease the number of items displayed in the menu. By default, 10 items appear for the Favorites list and 10 items appear in the Recent Folders list.

- **Double-click edits Camera Raw settings in Bridge:** When you open a camera raw file the Camera Raw Settings window opens where you can adjust many brightness and color options before opening the file in Photoshop. The Camera Raw Settings window is opened from a plug-in from Photoshop or the Bridge. If this check box is selected, the window opens from the Bridge. You might use this option when making adjustments for camera raw images to open and edit later in Photoshop.

✦ **Cache:** When you make choices for display performance such as processing images, adding metadata, and similar settings, the Bridge saves this information to a cache (a file saved to your hard drive). Two cache files are built for each folder you view in the Bridge. If the files are located in a centralized location, you can easily find the cache files and delete or copy them. If the cache files are stored in distributed locations, they are saved to the folders from which the cache was created. This option provides you with an easy method for copying cache files when writing folders of files to a CD or DVD-ROM. If the cache files are copied to other media sources, the Bridge viewing those files on another computer won't need to build a cache. This ultimately results in faster viewing and scrolling images in the content area.

Tip

Cache files are hidden files on your computer. If you want to copy a cache file to a CD or DVD-ROM, open the View menu in the Bridge and select Hidden Files. All hidden files are displayed in the Bridge window. (The files are not visible when you return to the desktop view; they are only visible in the Bridge window.) You can click and drag files from the Bridge window to a folder or media storage volume to copy it.

✦ **Choose:** Click Choose to locate a folder where you want to save the cache files if you want to identify a location other than the default folder.

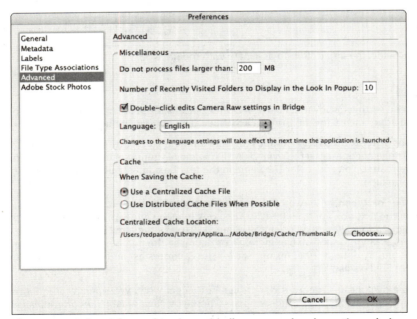

Figure 3-4: Select Advanced to view miscellaneous and cache options choices.

Adobe Stock Photos

Click Adobe Stock Photos in the left pane and the right pane displays settings for working with Adobe Stock Photos, as shown in Figure 3-5. Adobe Stock Photo options include:

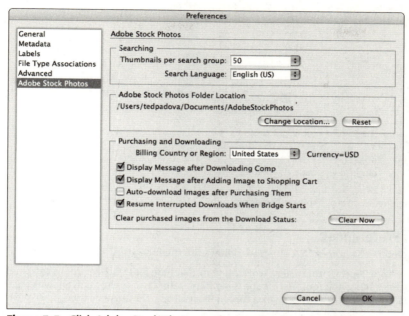

Figure 3-5: Click Adobe Stock Photos to view settings for using the Adobe Stock Photo Service.

- **Searching:** From the pull-down menu, you have fixed choices for the number of thumbnails to display for each search group. The default is 50. The Search Language menu offers choices for one of eight different languages to use for the search.

- **Adobe Stock Photos Folder Location:** The default location to which stock photos are saved is reported in the Preferences dialog box. You can choose another location by clicking Change Location. In design workflows, you may want to identify a network server location where all members of the workgroup have access to the photos. Click Reset to change back to the default folder location.

- **Purchasing and Downloading:** The options should be self-explanatory. Be certain to identify the Billing Country or Region appropriate for your area. Click Clear Now to clear the list in the Download Status pane.

Cross-Reference

For more information regarding acquiring and using the Adobe Stock Photos Service (ASPS), see Chapter 7.

Illustrator CS2 preferences

When you press ⌘/Ctrl+K to open the Preferences dialog box in Adobe Illustrator CS2, the default panel shows you the General Preferences, as shown in Figure 3-6. In the General panel, you'll find a number of options that change the view of elements on the Illustrator page and some settings that relate to the behavior of objects. Not all these settings need to be coordinated and agreed upon by members of your workgroup. Some settings have an impact on your workflow with other artists and service providers, while other settings can be made according to users' personal preferences.

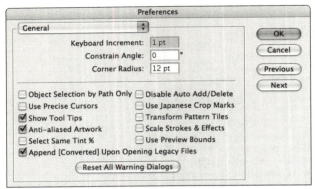

Figure 3-6: The Illustrator Preferences dialog box

General Preferences

Among preferences choices that affect workflows are the following:

Tip

- **Show Tool Tips:** If other users work on your machine and they're not up to speed in Illustrator, showing tool tips can be a big help. A tool tip opens in a yellow rectangle when you place the cursor over a tool in Illustrator's Toolbox.

  At the top of the General Preferences is a setting for Keyboard Increment. This setting is a personal preference and not significant to workflows with other users. However, it is a personal choice you'll want to adjust from time to time. The setting in the adjacent field box relates to the amount an object moves when you strike an arrow key to nudge objects. If you work with a unit of measure like inches, setting the field box to a fraction of an inch is merely guesswork. A better adjustment might be to make these increments adjustable in points. If you want to quickly change the distance to half a point for example, type **0p.5** (translating to 0 picas 0.5 points). This unit of measure works the same as when adjusting type sizes and leading distances.

- **Anti-aliased Artwork:** The display of your vector objects is improved on-screen and may be helpful to other users to ensure they know the images are likely to print without jagged edges. Turning off this option has no effect on the printing of the image or porting it to other CS2 programs.

- **Append [Converted] Upon Opening Legacy Files:** This setting can have an impact on other users in your workflow. If the check box is enabled (checked or turned on) and you open an earlier version of an Illustrator document, the word *[Converted]* along with the brackets appears in the filename. If you save a converted file without changing the filename, the file appears with *[Converted]* contained in the name. If other users disable the check box, their converted files are saved with a default *not* including *[Converted]* in the filename. For the sake of consistency, be certain to agree upon how to set this option with your workflow colleagues.

✦ **Use Japanese Crop Marks:** This option is important for studios producing files that are printed in Japan. Japanese crop marks appear similar to crop marks printed from Adobe PageMaker. When you choose Filter ➪ Create ➪ Crop Marks with this option enabled, Japanese crop marks are created.

Other settings in the General Preferences help you work with Illustrator objects and views. You should become familiar with all the preference settings to help advance your knowledge of Illustrator CS2, but the other settings have less impact on workflows in production studios. Therefore, we'll leave the remaining descriptions to what you can find in the *Adobe Illustrator CS2 Bible* by Ted and Jen Alspach (published by Wiley).

Converting legacy files in Illustrator CS2

When you open a *legacy* Illustrator file (any file created in any version of Illustrator prior to the CS1 version), a dialog box appears, as shown in the following figure, informing you that the file was created in a previous version of Illustrator and asking you if you want to update the file.

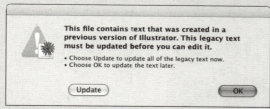

The legacy dialog box

This dialog box appears because the type engine in Illustrator CS1 was completely revamped, and all the type in the document needs to be updated. This dialog box also opens if no type exists in your legacy files.

To dismiss the dialog box, you have two choices. Click Update, in which case all type is updated in the document, or click OK. The default selection is OK, which is what happens if you press the Return/Enter key on your keyboard. The reason the default is set to OK is because your type may float on the page and lose many different paragraph attributes if you update the type in your document. Often, you'll find it better to *not* update all the type when you open a legacy file, particularly if you want to try to preserve the look of the original file.

Updating does occur when you click the Type tool in a block of text. Therefore, you can open the legacy file without performing a global update to the type and individually update different text blocks as you work on the document. You may find this option to be a better choice when working on legacy files with a lot of type.

Type

Click Next in the Preferences dialog box, and you arrive at the Type preferences, as shown in Figure 3-7. If you used Illustrator CS1 you'll notice the Type preferences have changed from Type and Auto Tracing to just type preferences.

Illustrator no longer has an Auto Trace tool. The Auto Trace tool has been replaced by the Live Trace command, and options settings are handled in a dialog box.

For information on using Live Trace, see Chapter 11.

Choices you make for Type preferences are for individual personal choices and how you want to handle type on your computer. Some attention should be paid to the following:

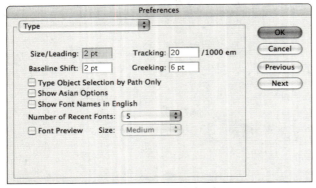

Figure 3-7: The Type preferences dialog box

- ✦ **Size/Leading:** The Size/Leading adjustment can be performed using keyboard equivalents. To raise a point size in type, you press Shift+⌘+> (Mac) or Shift+Ctrl+> (Windows). Conversely, to lower point sizes, you press Shift+⌘+< (Mac) or Shift+Ctrl+< (Windows). For leading changes, you can use keyboard shortcuts Option/Alt+Down Arrow to increase leading and Option/Alt+Up Arrow to decrease leading. If you change the amount of the jump in points specified in the Size/Leading field box, users sharing your computer may immediately see unexpected results. If you want to change this option in multiple-user workflows, discussing it with your colleagues is best.

- ✦ **Baseline Shift:** The Baseline Shift setting is also accessible with keyboard shortcuts (Shift+Option/Alt+Up Arrow moves the baseline one increment up and Shift+Option/Alt+Down Arrow moves the baseline one increment down). Likewise, you may want to leave the Baseline Shift at default values.

- ✦ **Tracking:** Tracking affects the amount of space between characters. This type option can also be adjusted by using keyboard shortcuts (⌘/Ctrl+Right Arrow increases text tracking, and ⌘/Ctrl+Left Arrow tracks text more tightly). Once again, to prevent unexpected results from users, you may find the defaults to be adequate.

✦ **Type Object Selection by Path Only:** This preference option is important if InDesign users are sharing your computer. Essentially, when the check box is enabled, text can be selected only when you click either the Selection tool or the Direct Selection tool on the path (usually at the baseline of a line of text). A handy feature in both InDesign CS2 and Illustrator CS2 is when you double-click the Selection tool or the Direct Selection tool anywhere on a text block, the tool changes to the Type tool, where you can edit text in the block. If you enable this preference, InDesign CS2 users who know less about Illustrator will likely become confused. In multiple-user workflow environments, leaving the check box disabled is best.

Units and Display Performance

Click Next or select the pull-down menu and choose Units and Display Performance. The options choices for Units and Display Performance are shown in Figure 3-8.

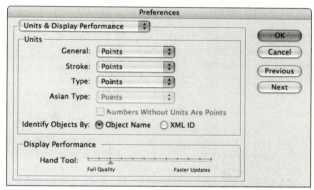

Figure 3-8: The Units & Display Performance preferences dialog box

✦ **General:** If you consistently design pieces in a unit of measure such as millimeters or inches, you should make the appropriate adjustment from choices you make in the General pull-down menu. This setting affects your personal workflow and your work in design production workgroups. The other settings for strokes and type are almost universally set to points, so leave these at their defaults.

✦ **Identify Objects By:** The default is set to Object Name, which is okay unless your workflow involves working with XML objects. If you do work with XML, you'll want to periodically change this preference setting. To understand completely how this option works, open the Window menu and click on Variables.

Cross-Reference

For more information on XML, see Chapter 30.

✦ Using XML objects requires you to adhere to strict naming conventions. If you save an Illustrator CS2 document as SVG (Scalable Vector Graphics) format for use with other Adobe CS2 programs, the names must conform to naming conventions permitted by XML. For example, you must begin an object name with a letter, an underscore, or a colon. Object names with spaces are not permitted. When you change the preference setting in the Units and Display Performance to view XML IDs, Illustrator shows the ID that will be exported when the file is saved. You can view the names in the Visibility palette and edit the names as long as you adhere to conventions acceptable to XML. In Figure 3-9, you can see the Visibility palette as it is shown when Object Name shows objects in the left palette and by XML ID in the right palette.

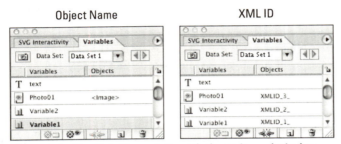

Figure 3-9: The Variables palette with the Units and Display Performance preferences enabled for Identify Objects by Object Name (left). On the right, the preference for Identify Objects By is changed to XML ID.

Guides and Grid

At first glance, the Guides and Grid may not seem important to you. However, the preference choices you make here can impact your work in the other Adobe CS2 applications or in workflows with multiple users. If you work with a grid, it will be beneficial to bring the grid size and style to identical views across all the CS2 programs supporting grids. Click Next or open the pull-down menu and choose Guides and Grid from the menu options to open the Guides & Grid preference options. A few key points to address in the dialog box shown in Figure 3-10 include the following:

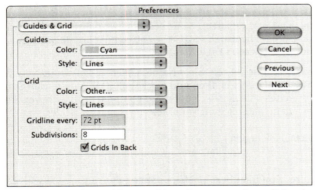

Figure 3-10: The Guides & Grid preference options dialog box

- **Guide Color:** Guides are drawn from the ruler wells, while grids are created on the pasteboard from attributes you set in the Guide and Grid preferences dialog box. The default Guides color is cyan in Illustrator CS2 and the same color value is used in Photoshop CS2. In Acrobat, the Guides color is light blue. InDesign goes much farther in offering you options for individually changing guide attributes for margins, columns, bleeds, slugs, and background; none of the default colors match the other programs (see "InDesign preferences" later in this chapter). GoLive CS2 does not support a grid and guide preference option; however the layout grid added to a GoLive page is also light blue. Illustrator CS2 makes the only distinction between the colors of Guides and Grids in the default settings. While Guides are cyan, the Grid color defaults to a light gray. To avoid confusion when working between programs, you may want to change all grids and guides in all programs to the same value. Either a light blue or a cyan color intuitively suggests to users that the lines belong to either a grid or a guide.

- **Guide Style:** Illustrator CS2 and Photoshop CS2 offer you options between using lines or dots (Illustrator) and dashed lines (Photoshop). Because the other programs support lines only, you can leave the Style option set to the default Lines value.

- **Grid Color:** Illustrator CS2 and InDesign CS2 use a light gray as the default Grid color while Photoshop uses a darker gray color. Acrobat and GoLive CS2 use blue for grid colors.

- **Grid Style:** The Style is the same as noted in the preceding bullet for Guide Style. Photoshop CS2 offers three options for lines, dashed lines, and dots. As a general rule, you might want to leave the Lines style at the default.

- **Gridline Every:** This unit is the major gridline measurement. If you are coordinating grids between programs, you'll want to set the same value in the other CS2 applications.

- **Subdivisions:** This item is the minor gridlines. Again, set this value the same across all programs. Both the major and minor gridlines are volatile and are likely to change according to your designs. You may want to decide on a color to be consistent across applications for guides and grid, but you're likely to make frequent changes to the major and minor divisions. Keep in mind that if you do so, you should review these settings when starting new designs. If you want to coordinate a grid between Illustrator or InDesign and Adobe Acrobat for creating a PDF form and you decide to use a layout grid, it will be best to check the grid settings before beginning your work. At times, you may also want to change the grid color if you need to see the grid while working on a background color similar to the grid color. This condition may also vary between projects, so you'll want to revisit these preferences often.

- **Grids in Back:** Illustrator CS2 offers you an option to position the grid behind all objects when the Grids In Back check box is enabled. InDesign CS2 offers separate settings for positioning the grids and guides in back while Photoshop CS2 automatically keeps all grids and guides in front of images. Acrobat is completely different — the grid is automatically placed on top of the background content and some elements you add in Acrobat such as form fields. Other items like note windows appear on top of grids and guides. Guides appear on top of the background content but behind some elements such as form fields you create in Acrobat. The positioning of grids and guides is not customizable in either Photoshop or Acrobat. Therefore, your only decision is to adjust grids in back between Illustrator and InDesign. Regardless of where you place the grid, try to keep it consistent between the programs.

Tip Setting major and minor gridline distances in the CS2 applications offers you proportional spacing without the ability to create more custom grid designs. If you want to create a design grid not achievable in the Preferences dialog box, draw lines in Illustrator CS2 and use the Blend tool to set up spacing equidistant between the lines. Save the file as PDF. You can import the PDF document in InDesign and place the file on a background layer to use as your custom grid. You can open the PDF document in Acrobat and position elements created in Acrobat, such as form fields, and copy/paste them to your form design.

Adding custom colors to the Preferences dialog box on the Mac

To change colors to a custom color for preference options in any of the CS2 programs — except Photoshop, where you use the Adobe Color Picker — double click a color swatch like the one shown in the following figure. On Windows, you can make color choices from the Windows color palette and add custom colors by adjusting RGB values. However, on the Mac, with OS X Panther or Tiger, you have many more capabilities for defining custom colors.

After double clicking the color swatch, the Colors palette opens as shown in the following figure. In GoLive you must option-click. Click on the Color Palettes icon positioned third from the top-left in the Colors dialog box. From the List pull-down menu, you have menu choices for selecting different color palettes, and you also have an option for creating your own custom color palette. Select New from the pull-down menu and name your palette. In the following figure, we created a palette and named it CustomColors.

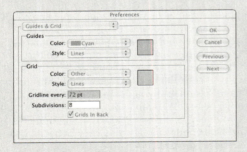

Creating a palette with custom colors

At this point you can select any color on your document page or pick a color from the Swatches palette to add to your custom color palette. Click the magnifying glass icon in the palette and position it over a color on a document page or position the magnifying glass over a color in the Swatches palette. Click the mouse button, and the color is added to the color bar adjacent to the magnifying glass in the Colors dialog box.

When you see a color in the color bar (as shown in the following figure), you can click in the color bar and drag the color to the list window. The color is listed with a default name that includes your palette name (in this example, CustomColors–1) as shown in the following figure. Adding a second color creates a name CustomColors–2, and so on. You can also add the color to the swatches at the bottom of the dialog box and add colors from different palettes. Click in the color bar and drag to one of the squares at the bottom of the dialog box to add the color to the swatches.

Illustrator lists a default name for your custom color.

As you change palettes from selections in the pull-down menu, the list changes to reflect all colors added to the list. However, colors added to the palette squares appear visible regardless of what color palette is selected from the pull-down menu.

Smart Guides and Slices

The most important thing to remember when using Smart Guides is the keyboard shortcut to turn them on and off. ⌘/Ctrl+U toggles the on/off switch for Smart Guides. When the guides are turned on with all the default display options checked, as shown in Figure 3-11, you see temporary guidelines at 90-degree and 45-degree angles. These guidelines can get in the way when users want to draw freeform objects. Accessing a keyboard shortcut to turn them off is the best solution for hiding the guides. In workflow situations where many users work with Illustrator, they expect to have the guides turned off when striking the default keyboard shortcut. Be certain not to change this key sequence when assigning new keyboard shortcuts.

Cross-Reference For more information on customizing keyboard shortcuts, see Chapter 4.

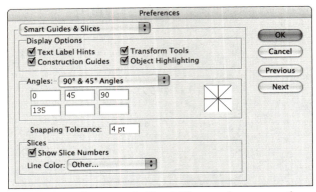

Figure 3-11: The Smart Guides & Slices preferences options dialog box

Hyphenation

The Hyphenation preferences enable you to add custom exceptions for hyphenations. When you add an exception by typing a word in the New Entry field box, as shown in Figure 3-12, and click Add, the word is added to the Exceptions list window. When a word is added to the list, Illustrator won't hyphenate the word.

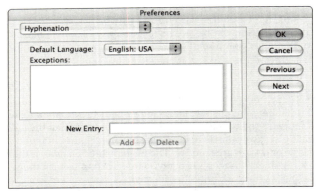

Figure 3-12: The Hyphenation preferences options dialog box

If you create multiple-language documents, you'll want to change the Default Language option in the Preferences dialog box's Hyphenation sheet. Be certain to make the appropriate language choice from the options available in the pull-down menu when laying out a design in a specific language. Be certain to change the defaults back to the most commonly used language in your workflow before quitting Illustrator.

> **Note** InDesign has an impressive means for handling words for spelling and hyphenation. However, the dictionary and hyphenation editing occurs in a separate dialog box instead of the preference settings. To integrate hyphenation exceptions between the programs, you need to address preferences in Illustrator and separately address hyphenation exceptions in the Dictionary dialog box in InDesign.

Plug-ins & Scratch Disks

The Plug-ins & Scratch Disks preferences work the same in Photoshop and Illustrator. GoLive also supports one scratch disk for QuickTime editing. Scratch disks are used to store temporary files and the extension of memory when your physical RAM runs out. Ideally, scratch partitions are best used on secondary hard disks for primary scratch disk locations. For example, if you have a second hard drive attached to your computer, use the drive not containing your operating system and application files as the primary scratch disk. Your secondary scratch disk would be your boot drive containing your operating system.

As shown in Figure 3-13, Illustrator supports assigning two scratch disks. Photoshop supports up to four scratch disks. All hard drives and partitions connected to your computer appear from pull-down menus.

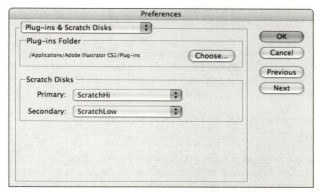

Figure 3-13: Illustrator supports up to two selections for scratch disks.

In workflow environments, one of the first tasks to perform after installing the CS2 programs is to visit the Plug-ins & Scratch preferences and identify what disks are used for primary and secondary scratch partitions. When you make choices for these preferences in either Illustrator or Photoshop, you need to quit the program and relaunch it before the preferences take effect.

Caution

When assigning scratch disk locations, be certain not to use slow devices such as USB hard disks, external Zip drives, memory cartridges, and so on. You can use external FireWire drives with satisfaction; however, the slower drives actually decrease performance when working with programs supporting scratch disks.

File Handling & Clipboard

There are two important considerations to make in the File Handling & Clipboard preferences dialog box, shown in Figure 3-14, with regard to workflow situations. These include handling Version Cue and the way you want to copy and paste Illustrator data.

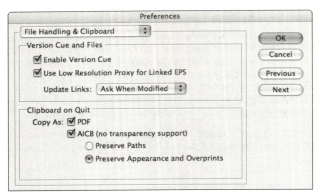

Figure 3-14: File Handling & Clipboard preferences

✦ **Enable Version Cue:** All the Creative Suite programs support Version Cue. By default Version Cue is enabled upon installation of the CS2 applications. Inactivation of Version Cue is handled in this dialog box or your system preferences dialog box (Mac) or Control Panels (Windows).

For more information on using Version Cue, see Chapter 8.

✦ **Clipboard on Quit:** The description in this section of the File Handling and Clipboard dialog box is a bit misleading, because it implies that selections you make are handled when quitting Illustrator. In reality, you have to make your choice regardless of whether Clipboard data are converted upon quitting Illustrator or when copying and pasting data between Illustrator and InDesign. If you enable PDF as an option, the data pasted from Illustrator to an InDesign page is imported as a grouped object and uneditable. If you disable the PDF option and click on AICB (no transparency support), all pasted objects are individually selectable and editable in Adobe InDesign. You need to make a choice as to whether you want to have InDesign users edit objects in InDesign or restrict the object editing to Illustrator. For independent artists creating your own workflows, it's a good idea to enable the option for AICB so you can quickly access individual objects where you may want to change an object's color, move an individual object, or reshape an object.

AICB stands for Adobe Illustrator Clip Board.

Appearance of Black

With Illustrator CS2, you now have the option of changing the appearance of the black that you see on screen and when you print. In the Appearance of Black preferences shown in Figure 3-15, you have choices in the two menus. These menus allow you to choose a rich black for display and for printing. Rich black results is a deeper more crisp black color when viewing on screen and on printed documents. As a matter of default, be certain Rich Black is selected for all printing.

The Appearance of Black is a new preference setting in Illustrator. By default, the preferences are set to view and print Rich Black. Be certain to leave the settings at the default for viewing and printing rich black. As you can see in the dialog box, rich black results in a solid black appearance, while 100 percent black appears dull and muddy.

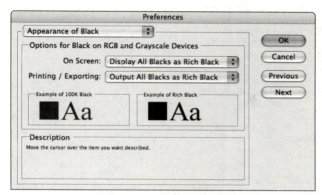

Figure 3-15: Appearance of Black preferences

Photoshop CS2 preferences

Adobe Photoshop preference settings are accessed by pressing ⌘/Ctrl+K or by choosing Preferences from the Application menu (Mac) or from the Edit menu (Windows). The Preferences dialog box has nine panes that are accessed by opening the pull-down menu or by pressing the ⌘/Ctrl+1 through 9 keys when the Preferences dialog box is open. All the settings you make in Photoshop relate to tool and menu features apart from color settings options. For Color Settings, you need to access a different dialog box.

For color preference settings, see Chapter 6.

Among the preference options most applicable to workflow environments are those covered in the following sections.

General Preferences

Most of the options in the General Preferences are the same as Photoshop CS1 (see Figure 3-16). A few new added items help you with your personal preferences when working with Photoshop and an option to help you in workflow environments.

The Show Menu Colors, Resize Image During Paste/Place, Automatically Launch Bridge, and Zoom with Scroll Wheel are all new features with Photoshop CS2. Automatically Launch Bridge and Zoom with Scroll Wheel are self-explanatory. Show Menu Colors helps you customize your workspace; Resize Image During Paste/Place eliminates a need to resize placed or pasted data to the size of the Photoshop canvas area.

Changes in the General preferences in Photoshop include:

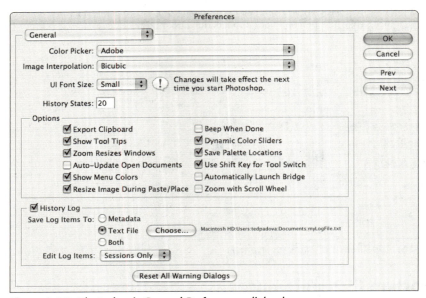

Figure 3-16: Photoshop's General Preferences dialog box

✦ **Show Menu Colors:** You can add colors to menu commands from the top-level menus by selecting the check box for Show Menu Colors in the General Preferences. To assign menu colors to menu items, choose Edit ➪ Menus and the Keyboard Shortcuts and Menus dialog box appears. Select menu commands from the Application Menu Command list and click on None appearing in the Color column. A pop-up menu provides choices from a list of custom colors. You can export your Keyboard Shortcuts and Menu Colors choices as a file, which other members of your workgroup can load.

Tip

To see an example of using menu colors, open the Actions palette in Photoshop. Open the Default Actions set and select What's New in CS2 Workspaces. Click Play Selection in the Actions palette. The workspace containing menu colors for all new Photoshop CS2 menu commands is loaded. Open the top-level menus and you can see the new commands highlighted with a color.

✦ **Resize Image During Paste/Place:** If you create a document in Photoshop at a 4-x-5-inch size and place an Illustrator file of 8 x 10 inches (or paste data from the clipboard), the pasted data retain the original object/image size. If you select the Resize Image During Paste/Place check box and place the same 8-x-10-inch Illustrator file in Photoshop, the pasted data fits within the size of the open document.

Tip

To place a document in Photoshop (or Illustrator or InDesign or GoLive), select the document in Adobe Bridge and choose File ➪ Place ➪ In Photoshop (or In Illustrator, In InDesign, or In GoLive). You must have a document page open in the target program or the Bridge can't place the document.

♦ **Automatically Launch Bridge:** Select the check box and when you launch Photoshop, the Bridge also launches. Photoshop opens first, followed by the Bridge. When the Bridge opens, the last view appearing in the Content area is the default view.

♦ **Zoom with Scroll Wheel:** This preference choice applies to users having a mouse with a scroll wheel. When you select the check box, moving the scroll wheel on the mouse zooms in and out of the canvas area.

♦ **History Log:** The History Log item in the dialog box shown is not new to Photoshop CS2, but the way history logs are viewed is handled differently. The History Log file is a recorded history of a Photoshop session that can be reported in a text file or as XML metadata. The difference between the two files is that a text file records your steps in a Photoshop session and saves the steps to a text file apart from the edited image. When using metadata, the history steps are included in the file and you can view them in the File Info dialog box (File ⇨ File Info), which you can access either through the Bridge or Photoshop. In Photoshop CS1, the history steps were viewed in either Photoshop or the File Browser.

Recording metadata can be important in design workflows. Settings you make to files, brightness and color adjustments, and other editing steps can be helpful information when collaborating on projects. To understand how you can add metadata to Photoshop files and how to review the editing history, follow these steps:

STEPS: Adding and Viewing Metadata in Photoshop Files

1. **Launch Photoshop and set the General Preferences. Open the General Preferences dialog box by pressing Command/Control+K.** Select the History Log check box. Select the Both radio button to record the metadata in Photoshop and a log file. From the Edit log Items pull-down menu select Detailed. The Detailed option records all your steps in Photoshop. Note that a file does not need to be open in Photoshop to make settings adjustments in the Preferences dialog box. Click OK to accept the new Preferences.

2. **Launch Adobe Bridge.** If you don't have the Automatically Launch Bridge check box selected and the Bridge didn't open after launching Photoshop, double-click the Bridge application icon or icon alias from your desktop.

3. **Locate a file to open in Photoshop in the Bridge window.** Use the Bridge to navigate your hard drive and locate a camera raw image if you have one. If you don't have a camera raw image, use any image you can open in Photoshop.

For a detailed description for working with Adobe Bridge and camera raw images, see Chapter 7.

4. **Open a file from the Bridge window.** Select a file in the Content area of the Bridge window and open a context menu (Control+click on Macintosh or right-click on Windows). Choose Open from the menu commands.

If you double-click a camera raw image in Adobe Bridge, the Bridge Camera Raw plug-in is used. When you open a context menu and select Open, the Photoshop Camera Raw plug-in is used. Because Photoshop is recording your steps, you want to open the camera raw image using Photoshop's plug-in. If you are not using a camera raw image, you can double-click the image in the Bridge window and it opens in Photoshop.

5. **Apply settings for opening the image in Photoshop.** If you are using a camera raw image, you make settings adjustments with the camera raw plug-in before opening the file in Photoshop. Inasmuch as the Photoshop camera raw plug-in is used, certain attributes can be selected for how the image is opened in Photoshop. Make your settings adjustments and click Open in the Camera Raw Settings dialog box.

 6. **Edit the Photoshop file.** Apply any adjustments you want to make for brightness, color correction, changing color modes, applying filters, and so on. Use your own discretion for making some edits in Photoshop.

 7. **Save the file.** Choose File ⇨ Save As. If you opened a Photoshop image not in camera raw format, be certain to select Save As to write a different version of the file. After naming the file and finding a target location for the saved image, select Save.

 8. **View the edit history.** Return to Adobe Bridge. Select the saved file and examine the Metadata tab in the Bridge window. If you need to expand the metadata pane, click and drag the separator bars to the right and up. In Figure 3-17, the Edit History reports all the settings used to open the camera raw image and the edits made in Photoshop.

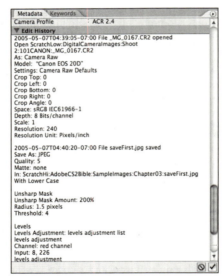

Figure 3-17: Scroll the Metadata pane to view Edit History.

 9. **Open the File Info dialog box.** The Metadata pane provides you a view of the detailed editing history. You can also view the editing history in the File Info dialog box. This dialog box can be opened from either the Bridge or from Photoshop using the same menu commands. In the Bridge, choose File ⇨ File Info. Click History in the left pane and you see a view of the edit history (see Figure 3-18) reporting the same information you see in the Bridge Metadata pane.

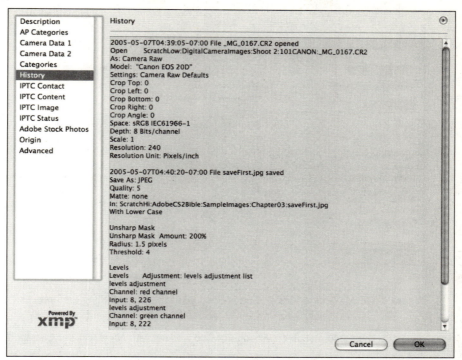

Figure 3-18: Choose File ⇨ File Info in either the Bridge or Photoshop to open the File Info dialog box.

File Handling

Among the most important preference settings in a workflow is the setting for enabling Version Cue. The traditional settings for File Saving Options are included in the File Handling preferences as well as the option for enabling Version Cue, as shown in Figure 3-19. By default, Version Cue is enabled. If the check box is not checked, be certain to select the Enable Version Cue Workgroup File Management check box.

Version Cue offers you options for saving different file edits that are not available when you create different layers. For example, to change the color mode of an image, you can't create a layer to accept a different color mode while maintaining other layers in another color mode. However, with Version Cue, you can convert modes and save different versions of the same file.

New Feature: In addition to saving different versions, Photoshop CS2 enables you to save Alternates. Alternates might be files that you create where Version Cue can't be used to create a different document view. You might want to use a Photoshop image of a rasterized Illustrator file with edits applied in Photoshop and save it as an alternate. Because you can't use Illustrator to apply the same Photoshop edits, you save the Photoshop file as an Alternate and manage the files in Adobe Bridge.

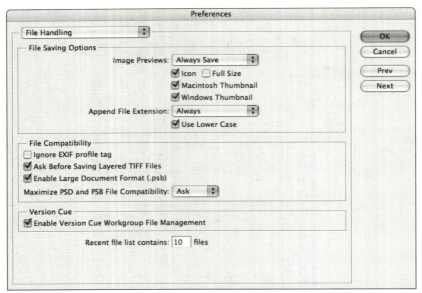

Figure 3-19: Make sure Version Cue is checked in the File Handling preferences.

For more information on Version Cue and working with Alternates, see Chapter 8.

Display & Cursors

Display & Cursors offer you options for different channel displays, cursor shapes for painting tools, and cursor displays for the non-painting tools, as shown in Figure 3-20. About the most important preference setting is to use the default Painting Cursor shape for a Brush Size, because most Photoshop users expect this cursor behavior when working in Photoshop. Another option common to many users is to leave the default for other Cursors at the Standard option that displays the tool icon for a selected tool in the Photoshop Toolbox and to let users activate Precise cursors by pressing the Caps Lock key. In workflow situations, you'll want to keep these defaults intact if the behavior is familiar to the workgroup members.

New options in the Display & Cursors preferences include Normal Brush Tip, Full Size Brush Tip, and Show Crosshair in Brush Tip. Normal Brush Tip is the same Brush Size option you had in Photoshop CS1. The size of the brush tip conforms to the size of the marks made with the tip. Full Size Brush Tip displays a cursor at actual size of a brush when the hardness is set to 100%. If the brush tip has a soft edge, the tip may appear smaller than the actual brush size. Show Crosshairs in Brush Tip displays a tiny crosshair in the center of the cursor. This feature is handy because it shows the center point of the tips, so you know exactly where the painting will fall inside and outside the center point.

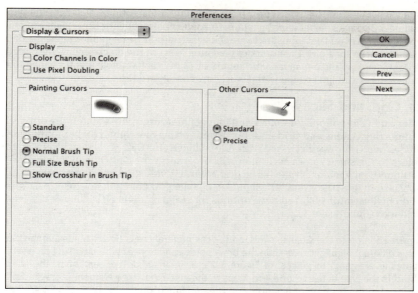

Figure 3-20: The Display & Cursors preferences dialog box

Transparency & Gamut

Users are accustomed to viewing transparency displayed as a grid with alternating white and gray squares. If you change the preferences in Photoshop, InDesign users may become confused. As a rule, keep intact the default settings.

Units & Rulers

Units of measurement are specified in the Units & Rulers preferences. When you show rulers in Photoshop (press ⌘/Ctrl+R), the ruler units are derived from the dialog box. If your workflow consistently uses a particular unit of measure, you'll want to change the ruler units by accessing the desired unit of measurement from pull-down menu choices for Rulers. The default unit is inches.

Columns and gutter sizes apply specifically to the file you are editing. Because users change column sizes according to an editing job, you don't have to worry about setting any particular default value.

Tip

When adjusting some options where values are changed in field boxes, you'll notice the hand cursor change shape to an extended index finger with opposing arrows, as shown in Figure 3-21. Whenever you see the cursor change to this shape, you can click and drag horizontally to change values in the adjacent field box.

Figure 3-21: The hand cursor changes shape when you can change a value.

Document Preset Resolutions are set for print and screen resolutions. The defaults typically work in most workflows. What's important is to keep consistent with other users in your workflow and be certain that all users leave these settings at the default values. Additionally, the same holds true for Point/Pica units of measure. Most of the electronic design world is fixed on PostScript point-to-pica measurements of 72 points to a pica. If you change to traditional values, be certain everyone in the workflow changes to the same units.

Guides, Grid, and Slices

The Guides and Grid options for colors and units of measure should match the other CS2 programs supporting Guides and Grid preference options. As mentioned earlier in this chapter when Guides and Grid was discussed with Adobe Illustrator CS2, you'll want to bring the guide colors to the same values across the CS2 programs especially in multiple-user workflows. Although not a major problem, the grid color in Photoshop is a darker gray than the grid color used in Illustrator and InDesign. You change grid colors in Photoshop CS2 the same way you do in Illustrator CS2. You have options for major gridlines (Gridline Every) and minor gridlines (Subdivisions).

A new addition to the Guides, Grids, and Slices preferences is Smart Guides. Smart Guides use a different highlight color than the other guides and appear when working on layers and snapping elements to guides. In Figure 3-22, a Smart guide appears when the left-most object in the type in the second line snaps to the guideline. If the element is dragged slightly left to snap the first line of type to the guide, the Smart Guide does not appear. In order to view Smart Guides you need to choose View ⇨ Show ⇨ Smart Guides.

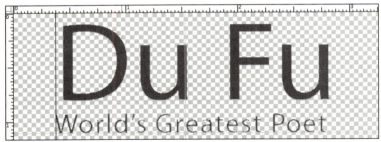

Figure 3-22: Smart Guides dynamically show objects and elements snapping to guidelines with a different highlight color.

For information on changing guide colors and grid values, see the section "Guides and Grid."

Slices are used when creating graphics for Web pages where an image may be divided in parts to optimize download speeds. When slicing images and objects, the sliced parts are represented with a keyline border. You have choices for the display of the keyline border colors in Photoshop CS2, Illustrator CS2, and ImageReady CS2. Borders default to black in GoLive, and ImageReady slices default to a dark blue. Illustrator and Photoshop default to a light blue. You may find it unnecessary to bring the slice colors consistent between the CS2 programs, because each slice is also represented with a small icon in the top left corner denoting the number of the slice. This visual representation of slices may be enough to clearly show you when an image or object has been sliced. If you change default colors, again, the most important thing to do is keep consistent among other designers in your workflow.

Plug-Ins & Scratch Disks

You have as many as four different scratch disks that can be identified in Photoshop CS2. Because Photoshop is the most memory-hungry application in the Creative Suite, Scratch Disks options enable you to extend memory to multiple hard drives and partitions.

Additionally, Photoshop enables you to identify a second Plug-Ins folder where third-party plug-ins can be stored in a folder apart from the application plug-ins. If you use custom plug-ins to extend Photoshop features, keep your third-party plug-ins in a separate folder. To identify a second Plug-Ins folder, check the box for Additional Plug-Ins Folder. The Choose an Additional Plug-Ins Folder dialog box opens immediately the first time you check the box. Navigate your hard drive and select the folder containing your plug-ins. If you want to change the locations of plug-ins, click Choose and the same dialog box opens where you can locate another folder.

A feature found in Photoshop that you don't find in Illustrator's Plug-in & Scratch Disks preferences is a field box where you can add a legacy Photoshop serial number. This preference option is handy when updating Photoshop to newer versions.

Memory & Image Cache

These preference options are more individual and don't necessarily require consistency among other users in your workflow. Adjusting these settings depends on the physical attributes of the machine where Photoshop CS2 is installed. If memory is limited, try to reduce the cache level from the default value of 4 to a lower number. If all your work is performed in Photoshop, you can change the Maximum Used by Photoshop percentage of total memory allocated to Photoshop to a higher value than the default 50 percent figure. If using InDesign CS2, Illustrator CS2, and Adobe Acrobat and/or GoLive, leave the default maximum memory allocated to Photoshop at 50 percent to provide sufficient memory to the other programs.

Type

The last preference pane in Photoshop CS1 was the File Browser preferences. Because the Photoshop File Browser was replaced by Adobe Bridge, some room was left to add a new set of preference choices. The Type preferences shown in Figure 3-23 address text handling and some new features in Photoshop CS2.

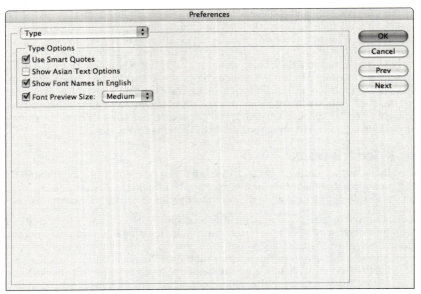

Figure 3-23: Type preferences are contained in a new pane in Photoshop CS2.

 Some of the items in this pane are self-explanatory. The Font Size Preview check box and pull-down menu relate to the change in the Font menu display. When you open the Font menu, the font names are listed with previews of the respective fonts. You can choose to display the font previews in three sizes. Choose Small, Medium, or Large from the pull-down menu. Figure 3-24 shows the font samples displayed in the Large size.

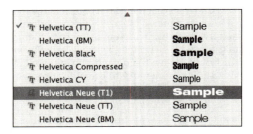

Figure 3-24: Choose a display size for font previews in the Type preferences and the font menu shows samples of the listed fonts at the respective size.

InDesign CS2 preferences

Adobe InDesign supports an elaborate set of preferences as well as options settings in a vast number of dialog boxes. On some occasions, you may expect to see a control in the Preferences dialog box and not find the option choice you want. If this is the case, poke around the dialog boxes and palettes and you're most likely to find a setting suited for a particular task. The first order of business when you begin using InDesign is to become familiar with all the preference choices.

One thing to keep in mind when you use Adobe InDesign CS2 is that preference choices can be enabled or disabled with or without a document open in the InDesign window. In many cases, changing a preference setting when no document is in view in the InDesign window changes the preference for all subsequent documents you create. If preferences are changed when a document is in view, often the preference change applies only to the open document. Therefore, you have a choice between setting application-level preferences and document-level preferences. Try to keep this in mind when you make changes in the Preferences dialog box as you customize the InDesign environment for your workflow.

In InDesign CS2, you'll find the addition of new preference choices and a good number of preferences have been moved around the panes in the Preferences dialog box.

General

The General preferences are shown each time you choose InDesign ➪ Preferences (Mac) or Edit ➪ Preferences (Windows) or press ⌘/Ctrl+K. General preferences, as shown in Figure 3-25, offer you options for page displays, handling the InDesign toolbar, printing options, and handling Clipboard data.

Among the more important preference options for you to consider in workflow environments are the following:

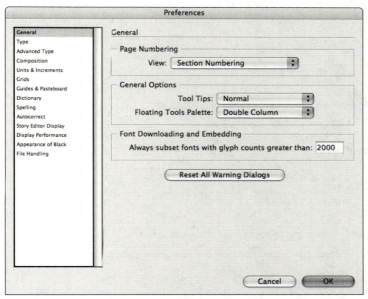

Figure 3-25: The General preference pane

✦ **Page Numbering:** You have choices between viewing pages with Absolute Numbering (disregarding sections and numbering in a linear fashion throughout a document) or Section Numbering. The page number display is recorded in the Pages tab. It has no effect on the actual pages in the document.

+ **General Options:** Choices in the General Options relate to the display of the InDesign toolbar that can be changed to view the palette as a single column, a two-column display, or an option for displaying the toolbar as a row for easy placement below the control palette at the top of the InDesign window. This personal preference affects single-user workflows but should be a standard you employ when multiple users access your machine. Other users working on the same machine should agree upon whatever display you choose.

+ **Font Downloading and Embedding:** The default is set to subset fonts with *glyphs* (the number of characters in a font set) fewer than 2,000. This default applies to OpenType fonts where the number of glyphs can be more than 65,000. PostScript fonts contain a maximum of 256 glyphs. Instead of embedding fonts in files exported to PDF with all 65,000 characters in an OpenType font, the default is set to subset the fonts and embed only the characters used in the document if the glyph count is greater than 2,000. By default, you can leave this setting alone and readjust it for special circumstances if an entire OpenType font needs to be embedded in a PDF document.

Type

Some new items have been added to what used to be called the Text pane in the Preferences dialog box. Now in the Type pane, in addition to the type options you had available in InDesign CS1, you now have options settings for dragging and dropping text and working with pasted text (see Figure 3-26).

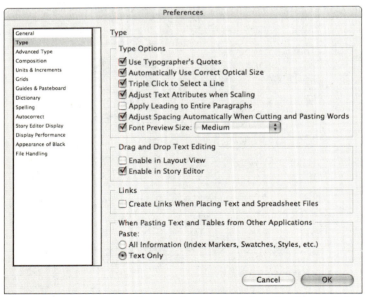

Figure 3-26: The Type preferences have new options for drag-and-drop text and pasting tables.

+ **Drag and Drop Text Editing:** You can select text in one frame, drag it to another, and when you release the mouse button the text is dropped into the target frame. You make preference choices for moving text between frames or from the Story Editor to a text frame. Select the check box for the respective item in the Preferences dialog box. In Figure 3-27, text is dragged from the Story Editor to a new text frame.

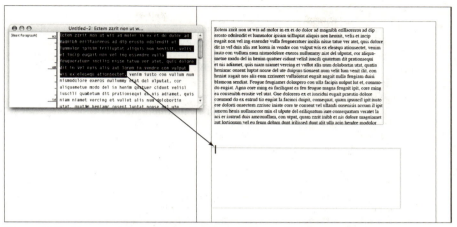

Figure 3-27: You can drag text from the Story Editor to the document page.

✦ **When Pasting Text and Tables from Other Applications:** The impressive introduction of table formatting in InDesign CS1 has been built upon in InDesign CS2. You can paste table data originating in other programs as a table without formatting or with formatting including index markers, swatches, styles, and so on. In Figure 3-28, a table was copied (top) with the All Information (Index Markers, Swatches, Styles, and so on) check box selected in the Type preferences. The second table was pasted with the Text Only check box selected in the Type preferences. Be aware that if you have a problem pasting text from Microsoft Excel, you should paste Excel data in Microsoft Word first, and then copy the table from the Word document. When you return to InDesign, choose Edit ➪ Paste.

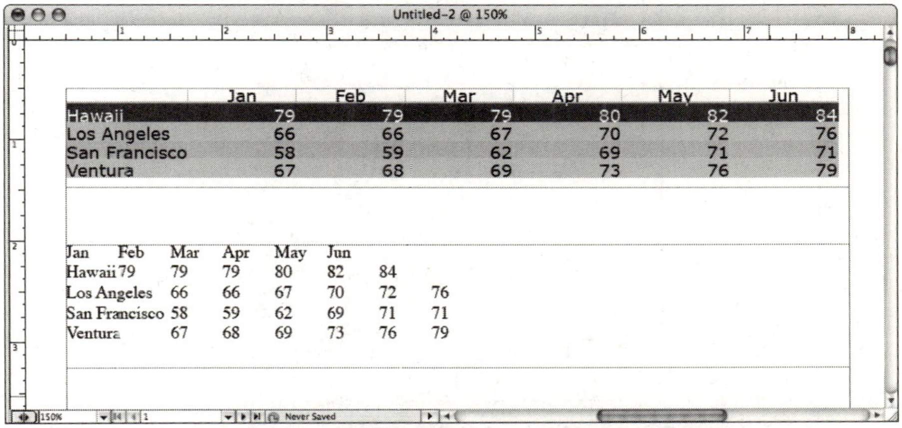

Figure 3-28: Data from Microsoft Word are pasted with and without formatting according to options choices in the Type preferences.

Advanced Type

All the options in the Advanced Type preferences are the same as you had available in InDesign CS1. What's changed is that the options for Character Settings and Input Method have been removed from the Type (formerly Text) preferences to their own preference pane. Here you have choices for superscript, subscript, and small caps attributes.

Composition

Composition preferences provide options for highlighting H&J violations, font substitution, custom tracking/kerning, substituted glyphs, and text wrap options such as justifying text to the next objects, skip wraps by leading, and wrap to objects above the text. These settings are all the same as was introduced in InDesign CS1.

Units & Increments

Similar settings are available in Adobe Illustrator for ruler units, and some of these option settings relate to individual user preferences. One important set of options to change is the Ruler Units items (see Figure 3-29). If most of your work is, for example, in millimeters, you should make a change for the Horizontal and Vertical ruler units by clicking the respective pull-down menu and selecting millimeters. This is one setting you may want to address before opening a document or creating a new document. This is because changing any units preference change to units, with no open document in the InDesign window, creates an application default.

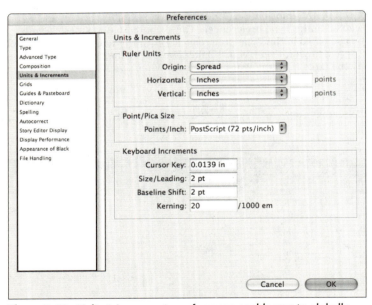

Figure 3-29: Units & Increments preferences enable you to globally change the unit of measure in your design layout.

New Feature Point/Pica Size offers options for selecting between traditional points to inches of 72.27 or PostScript ratios of 72 points to an inch.

Another setting, one that's more of a personal preference, is the Cursor Key distance. The default is 1 point. When an object is selected and you press an arrow key on your keyboard, the object moves in the direction of the arrow key the distance specified in this field box. If a 1-point increment is too much when you nudge objects, you may want to change the value to 0.5 (one-half point) or a unit you can comfortably use.

Tip Nudging objects with the arrow keys moves a selected object the distance specified in the Units & Increments preferences for Cursor Key distance. If you press Shift and press an arrow key, the object moves the preference distance times ten. That is to say, if 1 point is used for the Cursor Key distance and you press Shift while pressing an arrow key, a selected object moves 10 points. If you change the Cursor Key distance to something like 2 points, pressing Shift while pressing an arrow key moves a selected object 20 points. If you need to occasionally nudge objects in larger increments, you can open the Units & Increments preferences dialog box and change the Cursor Key distance repeatedly throughout a design session.

Grids

Changes for grids are the same as changing the Grid item in Adobe Illustrator. InDesign and Illustrator have consistent views for grid and guide colors. If you want to bring the other CS2 application grid appearances together, you might want to change grid colors in Photoshop and Acrobat. In the preferences dialog box, you have separate panes for grids and guides. Because InDesign is more elaborate with guide settings, it segregates the two categories into two separate preference dialog boxes.

An important item to note in the preference dialog box shown in Figure 3-30 is the last check box for Grids in Back. When the check box is enabled, a visible grid appears behind all text and objects. As a default, it's a good idea to leave this setting alone. Grids in front of your artwork can appear distracting. During an editing session, you may toggle the views, but at the end of a session in workflow environments you may want to return to defaults.

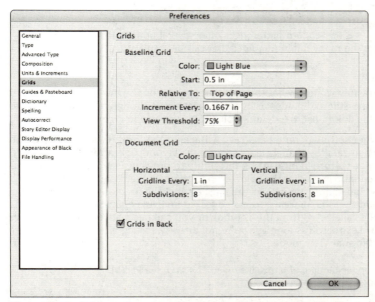

Figure 3-30: Grids preferences offer options for changing the grid appearances.

Guides & Pasteboard

InDesign offers you more options for viewing different types of guides than any of the other CS2 applications; understandably, the attribute choices offer more options. In Figure 3-31, you can see the default colors assigned to items like Margins, Columns, Bleed Area, and Slug Area. Colors are changed for any item by selecting from preset color values in the pull-down menus adjacent to the guide names or by selecting Custom from the bottom of the preset color list in the menu.

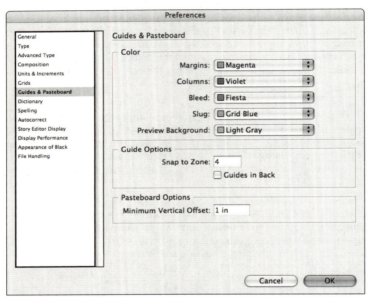

Figure 3-31: Guides & Pasteboard preferences offer several options for changing colors for the many different guides that can be displayed in a layout.

At first glance, you may wonder what the guides represent on the InDesign layout. In Figure 3-32, you can see the different guides assigned to a layout. Although the image in this figure is grayscale, the guide colors use the default color values shown in Figure 3-32.

You'll notice another setting denoted as Preview Background for the Color options. The default color is a neutral gray that appears around the layout page when you show a document preview. A nice feature in InDesign is the ability to preview a layout much like you would see a document trimmed at the print shop to the document page edge. The preview hides the slug and bleed area and shows the page against the preview background color without any visible guides, grids, margins, frame edges, or invisible characters as shown in Figure 3-33. Preview mode is selected from the Toolbox or you can use a keyboard shortcut. Press the W key on your keyboard (as long as you're not already editing type) to toggle from Preview mode to Normal View mode.

Cross-Reference For a better understanding of terms like *bleed* and *slug,* see Part VI.

Chapter 3 ✦ **Setting Preferences** 115

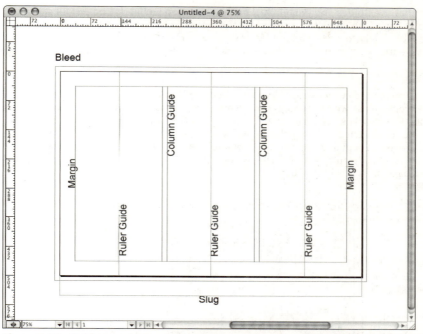

Figure 3-32: Guides are set for margins, bleeds, columns, ruler guides, and slug area.

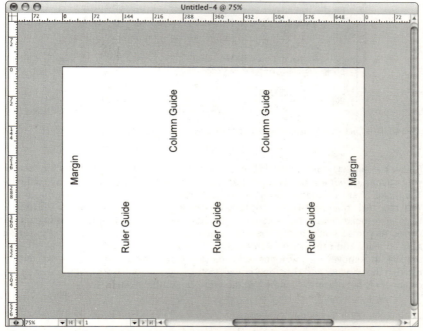

Figure 3-33: When Preview is selected, you see the document page against the preview background color.

Notice that the Guides and Pasteboard preferences also include an option for showing ruler guides in back. The default is set to show the guides in front of text and objects, because you're more likely to work with guides appearing in the foreground. If you need to temporarily change the position of ruler guides, check the box to display the guides in the background.

Dictionary

The Dictionary preferences enable you to choose a language for spell-checking and hyphenation exceptions as well as typographic symbols such as quotes you may want to use as defaults. Figure 3-34 shows a language choice from the Language pull-down menu for the language dictionary used for spell-checking. If you work with layouts in several languages, you'll want to revisit this dialog box and make changes as you check spelling and use hyphenation exceptions. As a default in your workflow, be certain to choose the language dictionary for the language used most often in your designs.

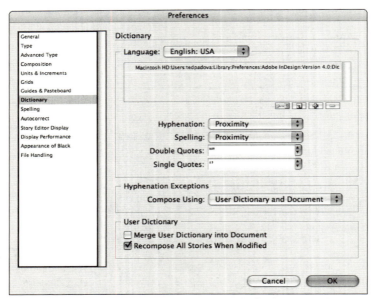

Figure 3-34: The Dictionary preferences specify the language dictionary.

New Feature Below the language dictionary, InDesign has new items. A window displays the location of your custom dictionary. Below the window are four tools for working with user dictionaries. The Relink User Dictionary tool on the far left, helps you recover lost links to your dictionary. You can click the New Dictionary tool to create a new user dictionary. The Add User Dictionary tool, which appears as a plus (+) icon, enables you to add multiple user dictionaries. As you add dictionaries, they are listed in the window where the default user dictionary appears. You can use the Remove User Dictionary tool, which appears as a minus (-) symbol, to remove user dictionaries. To remove a dictionary, first select a user dictionary listed in the window and click the Remove User Dictionary tool. Note that the default master dictionary is not a user dictionary and therefore cannot be deleted.

Below the user dictionary tools, you find options for special character assignments. The default is set to use smart quotes for single- and double-quote characters. You also have choices from pull-down menu options for several quote characters including straight quotes and chevron symbols. You might change the quote symbols when typing programming code in a body of text. However, in most cases you'll want to use smart quotes for better-looking typography.

Spelling

Spelling preferences offer options for either including or excluding word instances, as shown in Figure 3-35. By default, all options are enabled. If you want to spell-check a document and exclude one of the items, uncheck the item to be excluded.

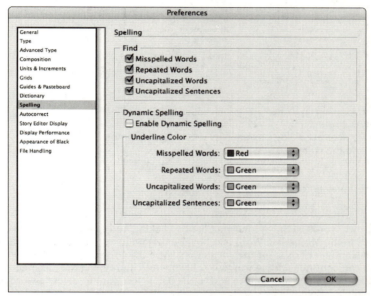

Figure 3-35: Spelling preferences offer four choices for items to be included or excluded in your spell check.

InDesign CS2 has new options for dynamic spell checking. As you type in either layout mode or the story editor, you can check spelling dynamically — which is generally what a word processing programs does. You can select the Enable Dynamic Spelling check box to view instances of misspelled words, which appear with underlines in colors associated with the preference options. You can change the color for each of the four instances from preset colors in the pull-down menus or select a custom color from the same menu.

Autocorrect

While in either layout mode or the Story Editor, you can enable auto-correction in the Autocorrect dialog box shown in Figure 3-36. A second check box provides options for case-sensitive errors. InDesign starts you off with a list of some common errors that, when detected, are dynamically corrected as you type providing you have selected the Enable Autocorrect check box.

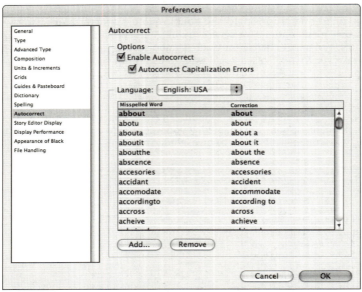

Figure 3-36: The Autocorrect dialog box enables you to add common misspelled words and the corrected versions.

 The Autocorrect preference is new in InDesign CS2.

You can add your own words to the autocorrect list by clicking Add and typing a word you commonly misspell in the Misspelled Word text box. Be certain to correctly misspell the word as you type. The second text box is for the correction. Type the correct word here as you see in Figure 3-37. You can continue adding words by clicking Add and typing the misspelled word and correct word for each item you want to add to the list. If you want to delete a word, select it in the list box and click Remove.

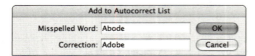

Figure 3-37: Type the correction and click OK.

Story Editor Display

InDesign supports use of an impressive Story Editor where type is created in a window apart from the layout. Taking off from Adobe PageMaker's Story Editor, the InDesign Story Editor offers you a customizable display. You can view type in any color against any background color you want to use. In the Story Editor Display preferences, you make color choices from pull-down menus, as shown in Figure 3-38.

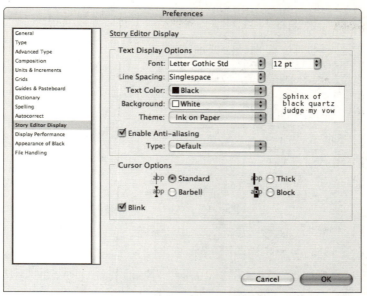

Figure 3-38: Story Editor Display preferences offer options settings for changing the display of the Story Editor.

New Feature

Selecting the Enable Anti-aliasing option smoothes text appearances, particularly at larger point sizes. A new feature in InDesign CS2 offers options for the kind of monitor you are using to view anti-aliased text. From the Type pull-down menu, choose Default, LCD Optimized, or Soft. Additional options offer you choices for cursor appearances while in Story Editor mode.

Display Performance

Perhaps nothing affects the speed of InDesign more than the display performance settings. You have choices in the Display Performance preferences (shown in Figure 3-39) for the quality appearances of objects and images. Obviously, the better the display, the slower the response you'll see from InDesign.

The default view is set to view all graphics at a Typical setting. The Typical option uses an image proxy of your placed artwork and displays the images and objects at low resolution with obvious degradation in viewing quality. The upside to using the default settings is that your editing session moves more quickly with faster screen redraws, faster object editing, faster text formatting, and just about any other kind of edits you make to your layout.

InDesign supports individually changing display performance on an object-by-object basis when working on a document. Therefore, you might leave the default views alone as a standard mode of operation. If you don't like the jagged preview of vector objects, you can move the slider for Vector Graphics to the far right while leaving the Raster and Transparency settings at the default values.

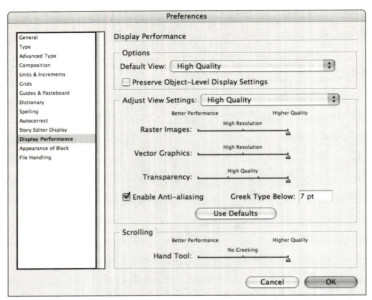

Figure 3-39: Display Performance preferences provide options for the quality of the displays for objects and images.

Another setting worth looking at is Greek Type Below. If you use a large display monitor, you might want to see text in smaller point sizes. When the text is *greeked,* it appears as gray bars in zoomed views when the point size falls below this setting. Change the value as needed for the kind of display you want to use.

Tip

If you create technical publications where detail in screen shots need to be clear, set the Greek Type Below box to 0 (zero) points. When zoomed out of a view, you can see the type characters no matter what zoom level you use.

New Feature

The Scrolling section in the Display Performance preferences is a new feature in InDesign CS2. You can adjust the slider to show type Greeked as you use the Hand tool to move a document page around the InDesign window. As you move the slider left, the performance is faster, but the type appears in Greek text. When you stop moving the page, the screen refreshes. The same options for the Appearance of Black found in Adobe Illustrator CS2 are also available in InDesign CS2. For information related to Appearance of Black preference settings, see the section "Illustrator CS2 Preferences."

File Handling

Click Choose in the File Handling preferences (see Figure 3-40) to identify a folder where recovery files are created. If your InDesign program crashes during an editing session, you may be able to recover the file up to the last edits you made. If you're converting documents like QuarkXPress files and you suffer an application crash, you can often recover files that haven't been saved in InDesign format without going through document conversions all over again.

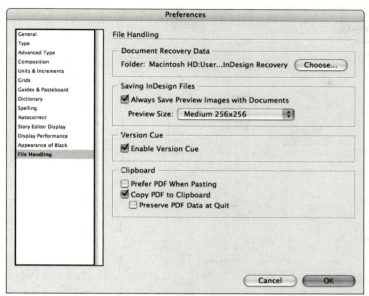

Figure 3-40: File Handling preferences offer options for recovering data, saving thumbnail previews, and enabling Version Cue.

The Save Document Preview Image option is handy if you use a file-management tool to organize your files. If you don't use such a tool, you may want to enable the preference setting and save your files with image previews for later cataloging in a program supporting image previews. Even if you use no tool for organizing files, you can quickly see a thumbnail image of the first page in an InDesign file in Bridge and in the Adobe Open dialog box when you choose File ⇨ Open. The Adobe Open dialog box displays a thumbnail image of InDesign documents, as shown in Figure 3-41, when this preference setting is enabled. If the preference option is disabled, no thumbnail preview appears in the Open dialog box.

Cross-Reference
A new feature in all the CS2 applications is an option to use a custom Open, Save, and Save As dialog box developed by Adobe. If you view InDesign thumbnails in the OS dialog boxes, you won't see thumbnail images for InDesign files. Only the Adobe dialog boxes offer you the option for viewing the thumbnails. For details on using the new dialog boxes, see Chapter 8.

New Feature
In InDesign CS2, you have choices for the size of the thumbnail to save with the file. From the Preview Size pull-down menu, select the size you want to apply to the thumbnail. The only time you can see different thumbnail sizes is when you view selected files in the Bridge window Preview tab. Thumbnail sizes don't have any effect on viewing the previews in the Adobe Open dialog box.

Following the options for saving page thumbnails (see Figure 3-40) is an option for enabling Version Cue. Be certain this check box is selected when you want to save document versions to the Version Cue workspace.

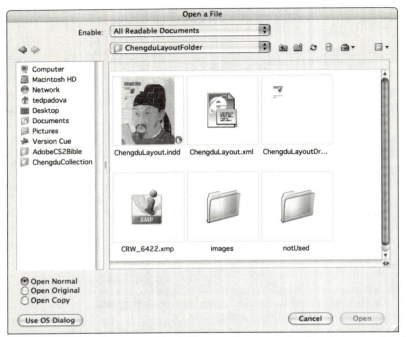

Figure 3-41: When you save files with Save Document Preview Image enabled, a thumbnail preview displays in the Open dialog box when you select the file.

 Cross-Reference For information on using Version Cue, see Chapter 8.

The last section handles options for the Clipboard preferences. These options relate to copying data in InDesign and then pasting it into other CS2 programs, or pasting other CS2 application data into InDesign. These settings offer choices for file format while copying and pasting and whether text attributes are preserved. The choices you make here are important for exchanging data between CS2 applications as well as sending your InDesign files or other CS2 application files containing pasted InDesign data to other users. Essentially, you must consider two things: what file format to use when you copy InDesign data, and the attributes to assign when you paste data from other CS2 applications into an InDesign document.

If you select the Preserve PDF when Pasting option when you copy data from Illustrator, transparency, blends, patterns, and similar effects are preserved when you apply them in Illustrator. If you elect not to use pasting PDF data, many of these effects are lost.

The Copy PDF to Clipboard option has no effect on copying and pasting data from an InDesign page back into the same or a different InDesign file. Regardless of whether this option is selected, the copy/paste feature within InDesign behaves as you would expect in any program. When you deselect the Copy PDF to Clipboard option and you copy data from InDesign and then paste it into another CS2 application, the data are not pasted. You must select the check box for Copy PDF to Clipboard in order to copy/paste or drag and drop data between InDesign and Photoshop and Illustrator.

Note You can copy and paste text between InDesign and GoLive and Acrobat, but you can't drag and drop text between the applications. You must either see a text insertion cursor in GoLive or create an insertion cursor using Acrobat's TouchUp Text tool unless you intend to paste in objects such as form fields or comment pop-up note windows. For pasting in form fields and comment notes be certain the Hand tool is selected.

When you copy data from InDesign into Photoshop CS2, all type that you copy from a frame selection using either the Selection or Direct Selection tool is pasted into Photoshop as a vector object and is rasterized when you press Enter to accept the data. If you want to paste editable text in Photoshop, first click the Type Tool in a document window, then choose Edit ➪ Paste. Type that you paste in Illustrator CS2 is recognized as type regardless of whether the text is selected with the Type tool or with the Selection tool or Direct Selection tool.

The last option (Preserve PDF Data at Quit) converts copied data in InDesign to PDF data when you quit the program. Select the check box and you can paste as PDF data after quitting InDesign.

Copying and pasting text on a path

InDesign CS2 supports the creation of type on a path. You use the Pen tool to draw a path. You then click the Type tool in the InDesign Toolbox and hold the mouse button down until you see the Type on a Path tool. Select the tool and click on the path. The insertion point defaults to the left side of the line for left-justified text. When you type a sentence, you see the type following the path.

If you decide to copy type on a path from InDesign and paste the data into an Illustrator, the type is broken up in into single-character text blocks. Type that you copy from InDesign into Photoshop is pasted as an object and rasterized, and therefore it loses type-editing attributes. If you create an insertion cursor in either program, you can paste the type at the insertion point but the type follows a straight horizontal line and loses the path attributes. You can create a path in either Illustrator or Photoshop and paste type on a path, but this requires you to precisely draw the same path in Illustrator or Photoshop as you draw in InDesign.

If you want to preserve the original path when you copy and paste type on a path from InDesign to Illustrator, you do have a workaround. First, create a path in InDesign and add type similar to what's shown in the following figure. Be certain that you enable the preference option for Copy PDF to Clipboard, and copy the text and path.

Continued

Continued

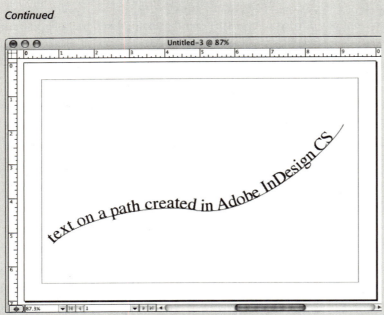

Create a path in InDesign and add type

In Adobe Illustrator, paste the data and you'll notice the text block is broken up. As shown in the following figure, you can see small anchor points adjacent to each character indicating the line of text is broken. Selecting all the text in the line immediately demonstrates that only individual characters are selectable with the Type tool.

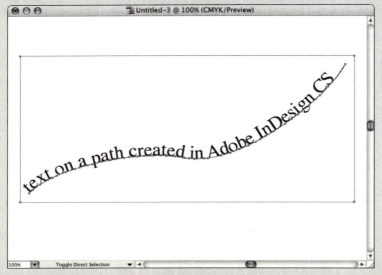

Small anchor points next to each character indicate a broken line of text

Notice the pasted text also contains a bounding box, as shown in the preceding figure by the lines at all sides around the text. To reform the paragraph, you must delete the bounding box and either hide the path or lock it. With the Selection tool, select only the text characters — selecting only text should be easy without the bounding box.

Choose Edit ➪ Cut to cut the text and either unhide the path or unlock it so it's selectable. With the Type tool, click the path to create an insertion point. Choose Edit ➪ Paste and the text is reformed into a single body of type, as shown in the following figure.

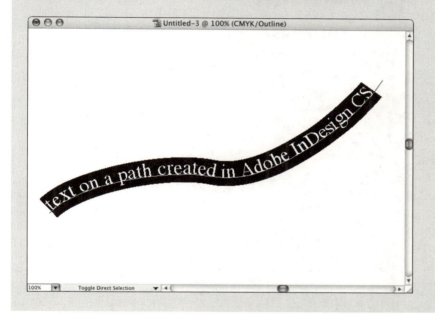

Updates

In InDesign CS2, you had another preference option for Updates. Updates were used to check Adobe's Web site for program updates. This feature has been removed from the Preferences in InDesign CS2 and has been moved to the Help menu. Consistent with other Adobe CS2 programs, choose Help ➪ Updates to check for maintenance upgrades.

Acrobat Professional preferences

Adobe Acrobat is a unique application among the Creative Suite programs. Whereas all other programs are designed for a specific role in your design workflow, Acrobat is a program that can perform many different roles in a good number of different workflows. For example, Photoshop is known as an image-editing program, Illustrator is an illustration program, InDesign is a layout application, and GoLive is a Web construction application. Acrobat, on the other hand, cannot be identified as a tool for a specific role in the design process. Acrobat is an application that can be used by creative professionals; e-book authors; technical writers; prepress professionals; forms authors; content providers; multimedia specialists; Web designers; engineering professionals; legal professionals, and more.

Because Acrobat serves so many professionals in many different industries, all the tools and menu commands relate to more than what you use in a creative design workflow. Likewise, the extraordinary number of preference options relate to work other than you might perform as an artist.

Take a peek at the Preferences dialog box shown in Figure 3-42 by pressing ⌘/Ctrl+K, and you see options for 3D followed by a number of different category choices in the left pane continuing to the bottom where Web Capture is shown. Click on any one of the categories in the alphabetical list of preference categories and the options settings in the right pane change to reflect specific options for a selected category.

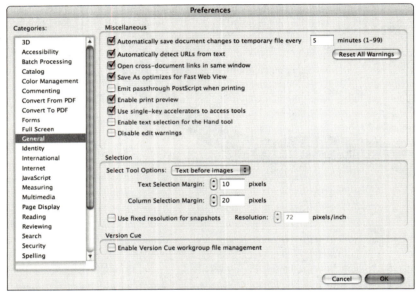

Figure 3-42: Acrobat Professional preference options are made by first selecting a category in the left pane and then changing settings in the right pane.

For your initial setup after installing the CS2 applications, you needn't be concerned with making changes to Acrobat's preferences. Unlike the other CS2 programs, Acrobat doesn't create new files from within the program. Files are created in the other CS2 applications and converted to PDF where the PDFs are opened in Acrobat. Therefore, coordinating preferences between Acrobat and the other CS2 programs during the design phase of your work is not relevant. Most often you'll use the commenting tools in your workflow, and you may at times visit the commenting preferences.

 For more information on setting commenting preferences in Acrobat, see Chapter 25.

Rather than discuss Commenting and other preferences specific to Adobe Acrobat now, we'll cover preference settings you'll want to make in chapters later in this book that deal with Acrobat and its role in the Creative Suite.

GoLive CS2 preferences

As with its other CS2 counterparts, the GoLive preference dialog box is accessed with the keystroke shortcut ⌘/Ctrl+K, or through the Application menu (Mac) or the Edit menu (Windows). Given that GoLive is designed for Web development rather than for the creation of print collateral, most of its preference settings are unique among the CS2 applications.

As shown in Figure 3-43, the preferences are listed by category on the left of the preferences window with a detail pane displayed to the right. When the preferences window is initially opened, you'll notice a right-pointing arrow (Macintosh) or a plus sign (Windows) displayed next to the preference categories. Click the arrow/plus sign to expose and expand a list of subcategory options, each having a corresponding detail pane on the right. Collapse the subcategory list again by clicking the minus sign. On the Macintosh platform, GoLive uses OS X-style reveal triangles to show the subcategories of preferences.

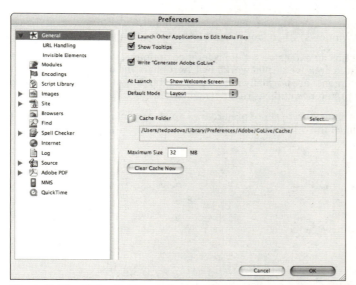

Figure 3-43: All the GoLive preference categories and subcategories

As noted in Chapter 1, this book deals with GoLive in a rather limited fashion and, therefore, a comprehensive discussion on preferences is not within the scope of this book. For individual preference choices as they relate to converting documents to GoLive HTML files and for creating Web sites in GoLive, preferences are described in later chapters.

Cross-Reference For more information related to GoLive preferences, see Chapter 28.

Summary

- Preference settings are adjusted in the Preferences dialog box for each Creative Suite program. You can open the Preferences dialog box in each program through a menu command or by using the keyboard shortcut ⌘/Ctrl+K.

- Some preference settings apply to individual documents, while other preferences apply globally to an application's settings. You can usually make application-preferences changes while no document is open in the application window.

- Each of the Creative Suite programs has an elaborate set of preferences that help you customize your work environment to suit your personal choice for the way you want to work. When participating in production design workgroups, it's a good idea to discuss various preference settings and agree on choices with other members of your workgroup.

- You can return to default preferences by pressing Shift+⌘+Option+Control (Mac) or Shift+Ctrl+Alt (Windows) when launching Adobe Bridge, Photoshop, and InDesign.

- Adobe Acrobat has an extensive set of preference options, many of which are not necessary to adjust in creative design workflows. Acrobat is the only CS2 application where new documents are normally not created in the program, therefore eliminating a need for many preference choices that pertain to new document designs.

- GoLive CS2 has an elaborate set of preferences appearing in a dialog box similar to dialogs found in all the other CS2 applications.

✦ ✦ ✦

Understanding User Interfaces

In This Chapter

Understanding tools

Working with palettes and workspaces

Identifying common user-interface features

Using keyboard shortcuts

✦ ✦ ✦ ✦

Working with several programs developed by a single software manufacturer has great advantages: The programs support a common user interface, and access to tools, menus, palettes, and preferences is handled similarly among the programs. Even if you've never used a particular program in the Creative Suite, you can explore a program that's new to you with an intuitive sense of knowing how to perform one function or another based on your experiences with other CS applications. The common user interface, knowing where to look for tools and commands to execute actions, and familiarity with the methods help shorten your learning curve.

Each of the Creative Suite programs obviously has unique features, but many aspects are exactly the same from one program to the next. In some cases, you can customize a program to suit your individual needs or a standard implemented for your workgroup. In this chapter, we cover tools, menus, commands, and customizing options to bring the programs close together.

Accessing Tools

Certainly, anyone who opens one of the Creative Suite applications is aware of how to use tools nested in the Tools palettes. Illustrator, Photoshop, and InDesign have many tools in common. GoLive and Acrobat have fewer tools in common with these three programs, and Adobe Bridge has its own set of unique tools.

Figures 4-1, 4-2, and 4-3 show the Toolboxes from Illustrator, Photoshop, and InDesign, respectively. Tools listed in bold type are tools common among two or all of the programs. Notice that the keyboard shortcuts used to access the tools are common in most cases among the programs (the shortcut you use to select the Pen tool in Photoshop is the same shortcut you use to select the Pen tool in InDesign, for example). The character in parentheses is used to select a tool in the Toolbox.

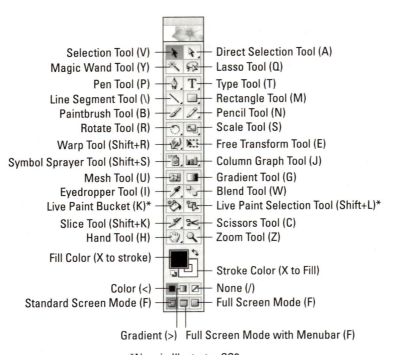

Figure 4-1: Adobe Illustrator Toolbox

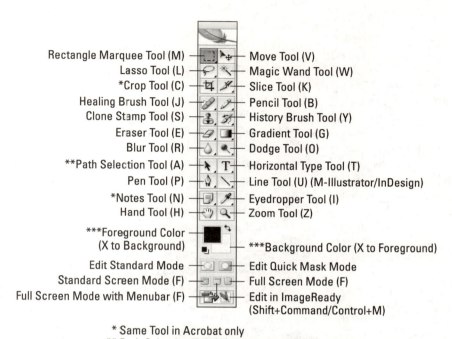

Figure 4-2: Adobe Photoshop Toolbox

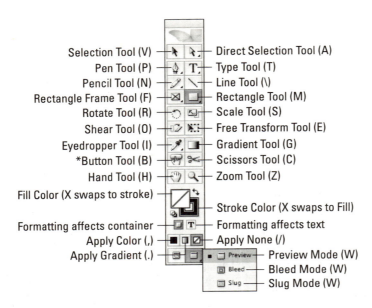

* Button Tool (B) - From Field Button in Acrobat only

Figure 4-3: Adobe InDesign Toolbox

Illustrator/InDesign/Photoshop common tools

The tools common to Illustrator, Photoshop, and InDesign include the following:

- **Selection tool (V):** Notice that the Move tool in Photoshop behaves like the Selection tool used in the other programs. The Move tool in Photoshop uses the same keyboard shortcut (V). Additionally, Photoshop has a Path Selection tool used for selecting vector objects. The Path Selection tool works similar to the selection tools in Illustrator and InDesign. In InDesign, you use the Selection tool to move objects and crop object and type frames.

- **Direct Selection tool (A):** The Direct Selection tool is used to reshape objects. In Photoshop, you access the Direct Selection tool by clicking on the Selection tool and holding down the mouse button. A pop-up toolbar opens from which you can select the Direct Selection tool.

    When you click on an object with the Direct Selection tool, the anchor points are shown deselected. Clicking a single anchor point or a path segment moves just that point or segment, thereby reshaping the object. In all programs, you reshape paths using the Direct Selection tool. In InDesign, you also use the Direct Selection tool to move objects around a placeholder frame or select the content to clear it from the frame.

- **Pen tool (P):** The familiar Pen tool that originated in Adobe Illustrator is found in Photoshop and InDesign alike. The Pen tool is used to draw free-form paths in all the programs.

- **Type tool (T):** As the name implies, the Type tool is used for typing text. In each program, you find additional options for the Type tool by holding down the mouse button on the Type tool and selecting other type tools from the pop-up toolbars.

- **Line/Line Segment tool (\ in Illustrator and InDesign; U in Photoshop):** Drawing straight lines is handled with the Line tool (Photoshop and InDesign) or Line Segment tool (Illustrator). In Photoshop, you access the Line tool by clicking on the Rectangle tool and opening the pop-up toolbar or by pressing Shift+U several times until the Line tool appears in the Toolbox.

- **Rectangle tool (M in Illustrator and InDesign; U in Photoshop):** The Rectangle tool appears at the top level in the Toolbox. In each program, click and hold down the mouse button to open a pop-up toolbar where you can select other tools like the Ellipse tool, Polygon tools, and other special vector-shape tools. In Photoshop, the objects you draw with these tools remain vector shapes until they are *rasterized* (the process of converting vector objects to raster images). In InDesign, the tools are used for artwork where you apply fills and strokes; however, the shapes can take the same form as the Frame tools and act as containers for text and placed graphics.

For more information on rasterizing objects, see Part III.

- **Pencil tool (N in Illustrator and InDesign; B in Photoshop):** Used for free-form drawing, much like you would use a pencil for an analog drawing.

- **Eyedropper tool (I):** The Eyedropper tool is used most often for color sampling in all three programs. In Adobe Bridge, you use this tool to work in the Camera Raw settings dialog box. In InDesign, the use broadens to sample certain styles such as type formatting.

- **Gradient tool (G):** Use the Gradient tool for drawing linear and radial gradients applied to shapes and selections.

- **Hand tool (H):** The Hand tool is used to move a document page around the monitor window.

- **Zoom tool (Z):** Click with the Zoom tool to zoom in on a document page. Press the Option/Alt key with the Zoom tool selected, and click to zoom out of the document page.

- **Fill/Stroke or Foreground/Background Color (D, X):** Press D to return colors to default values. Press X to switch between Foreground/Background and Stroke/Fill. In Illustrator and InDesign, the tools are used for assigning strokes and fills to objects. In Photoshop, the colors are used for foreground and background colors. A change of color from the Colors palette, the color wheel, or the Swatches palette is reflected in the tools in the Toolbox.

Illustrator/InDesign common tools

Tools that are common to InDesign and Illustrator but that don't appear in the Photoshop Toolbox include the following:

- **Rotate tool (R):** Rotates objects by selecting and dragging or supplying numeric values in a dialog box.
- **Scale tool (S):** Scales objects by selecting and dragging or supplying numeric values in a dialog box.
- **Shear tool (O in InDesign; no equivalent in Illustrator):** Shears objects by dragging with the tool or entering numeric values in a dialog box. In Illustrator, the tool is accessed by holding down the mouse on the Scale tool and selecting the Shear tool from the pop-up toolbar.
- **Free Transform tool (E):** Transforms objects (scaling, rotating, distorting) by clicking and dragging a selected object.
- **Scissors tool (C):** Used to cut a path drawn with the geometric tools or the Pen tool.

Illustrator/Photoshop common tools

Tools common to Illustrator and Photoshop but not found in InDesign include the following:

- **Lasso tool (L in Photoshop; Q in Illustrator):** Used to select pixels in Photoshop and objects in Illustrator.
- **Magic Wand tool (W):** In Photoshop, selects colors of common color values within a user-specified tolerance range. In Illustrator, selects objects of common color values.
- **Slice tool (K):** Used for slicing images/objects for Web hosting.

In addition to tools common between the programs, each application has a few unique tools. Photoshop has various tools for changing brightness values along with a Note tool (also found in Acrobat), cloning tools, and the History Brush tool. The Blend tool, Mesh tool, Graph tools, Warp tools, and Symbol Sprayer tools are unique to Illustrator. In InDesign, you find a Button tool similar to the Button Form Field tool in Acrobat.

Adobe Bridge tools

Adobe Bridge has a few tools located in the Bridge window. Most actions you perform in Bridge are handled with menu commands. As an application, you don't edit documents using tools. The edits made from within Bridge are generally applied to an entire document or initiating an edit that ultimately takes place in one of the other CS programs.

Cross-Reference For a detailed description of Bridge tools, see Chapter 7.

Acrobat tools

Because the tools in Acrobat are so different from the tools in Illustrator, InDesign, and Photoshop, it makes more sense to list them apart from the other programs. Acrobat is a program serving many different business professionals, and some of the tools you find in Acrobat may not be used in your work as a creative professional. The more common tools used in Acrobat by creative professionals include:

+ **Commenting tools:** Shown in Figure 4-4, the Commenting tools are used for adding comments to PDF files and participating in review sessions.

Figure 4-4: Commenting tools

+ **Drawing Markups tools:** The Drawing Markups tools (Figure 4-5) are also used for comment and review.

Figure 4-5: Drawing Markups tools

+ **Print Production tools:** Commercial printers use the Print Production tools (Figure 4-6) to preview, prepare, and print PDF documents that are intended to print on commercial printing devices.

Figure 4-6: Print Production tools

Cross-Reference

For information on using the Commenting and Drawing Markups tools, see Chapter 25. For information on using the Print Production tools, see Chapter 38.

Tools in Acrobat appear in separate toolbars. Unlike the other CS programs, the default position for the toolbars is horizontal across the top of the Acrobat window. Individual toolbars are docked in the Toolbar Well. You can open toolbars and dock them in the Toolbar Well or remove them from the Toolbar Well and place them anywhere in the Acrobat window as floating toolbars. Access toolbars by choosing View ⇨ Toolbars and choosing the toolbar you want to see, or by opening a context menu on the Toolbar Well and selecting a toolbar to open as a floating toolbar. After a toolbar is opened in the Acrobat window, the toolbar can be docked in the Toolbar Well by dragging it to the Toolbar Well or selecting Dock All Toolbars from a context menu.

GoLive tools

GoLive CS has a Toolbox similar to other CS2 programs, but selecting tools is a little different in GoLive. The Toolbox is divided vertically in two parts. The top half represents tools, while the lower half of the Toolbox displays categories of objects that you can add to a Web page or Web site. Click on a tool in the top half of the Toolbox and the tools change in the lower half of the Toolbox. What looks like a Toolbox in GoLive CS2 is actually called the Objects palette shown in Figure 4-7. Because much of the page building in GoLive is done via drag and drop, you don't use all the tools in the same manner as tools you find in the other CS2 programs.

Figure 4-7: Click the Basic tools group in the top-left corner of the Toolbox, and the tools change in the lower half of the Toolbox to tools used in laying out a Web page.

 For information on using tools in GoLive, see Chapter 28.

Accessing Tool Options

In Illustrator and InDesign, you have some option choices for certain tools that are controlled in accompanying dialog boxes. Not all tools have associated dialog boxes, so you need to either poke around or become familiar with tools offering these extended option choices. In Illustrator or InDesign, double-click the mouse button on tools in the Toolbox, and you'll see a dialog box similar to Figure 4-8 for tools supporting further options in dialog boxes.

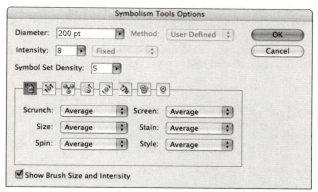

Figure 4-8: Double-clicking one of the Symbol tools in the Illustrator Toolbox opens the Symbolism Tools Options dialog box.

Illustrator tool options

Most often, double-clicking a tool opens an options dialog box typically not accessible other than by double-clicking a given tool. In some cases, double-clicking a tool opens a palette, a dialog box accessible through other commands, or a preference setting. Here's what happens when you double-click tools in Illustrator:

Selection tools: You need to have an object selected in the document window in order to open a dialog box when clicking either the Selection tool or the Direct Selection tool. When an object is selected and you double-click either tool, the Move dialog box shown in Figure 4-9 appears. You have options for moving objects and patterns at fixed distances. Like all dialog boxes that have a Preview check box, check the box and the view is dynamically rendered as you work in the dialog box.

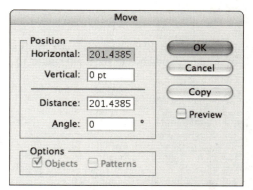

Figure 4-9: Double-click using the Selection tool or the Direct Selection tool on an object to open the Move dialog box.

Segment tools: A dialog box respective to the selected tool opens where you can make choices about options. You can also access the same dialog box by selecting a tool and single-clicking on the document page. The Segment tools include the Line Segment tool, the Arc Segment tool, the Spiral tool, the Rectangular Grid tool, and the Polar Grid tool. As shown in Figures 4-10 and 4-11, double-clicking different tools opens dialog boxes respective to the tool options.

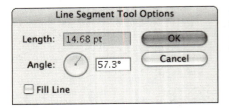

Figure 4-10: Double-click the Line Segment tool, and options associated with line segments are available in the Line Segment Tool Options dialog box.

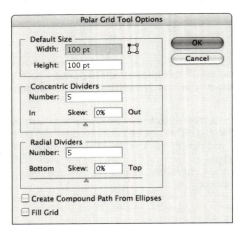

Figure 4-11: Double-click another Segment tool, and options respective to that tool appear in another dialog box. In this example, the Polar Grid tool was double-clicked.

Shape tools: The only tool in this group that opens a dialog box when you double-click the tool is the Flare tool. The Flare Tool Options dialog box is shown in Figure 4-12.

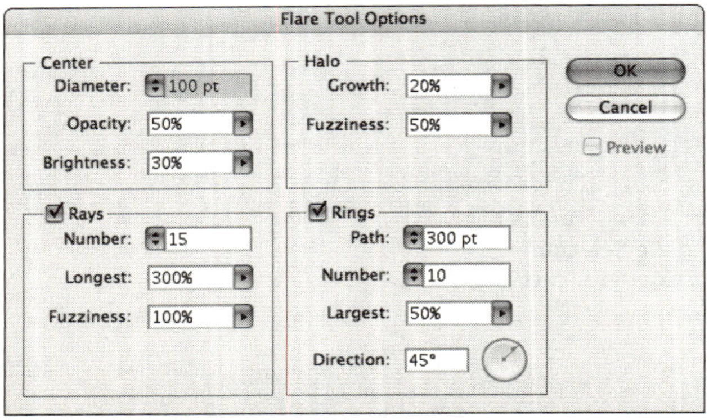

Figure 4-12: Double-click the Flare tool to open a dialog box.

Paintbrush tool: Doubling-click the tool opens the Paintbrush Tool Preferences dialog box, shown in Figure 4-13.

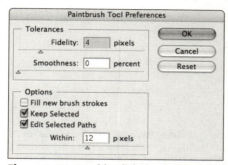

Figure 4-13: Double-click the Paintbrush tool and the Paintbrush Tool Preferences dialog box opens.

Pencil tool/Smooth tool: Although the toolbar for the Pencil tool contains three tools (Pencil, Smooth, and Erase), only the Pencil tool and the Smooth tool use a dialog box where you can make options choices. Double-click on either tool, and a dialog box opens specific to the options for the selected tool. Figure 4-14 shows options choices for the Pencil tool.

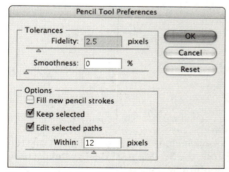

Figure 4-14: Double-click on the Pencil tool and the Pencil Tool Preferences dialog box appears.

Rotate/Reflect tools: Double-clicking on either tool opens a dialog box with options specific to the selected tool. In Figure 4-15, the Rotate dialog box appears after clicking on the Rotate tool.

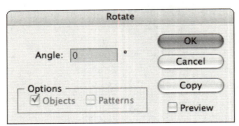

Figure 4-15: Double-click on the Rotate tool to open the Rotate dialog box.

Scale/Shear/Reshape tools: The Scale and Shear tools use dialog boxes for options settings. Note that double-clicking on the Reshape tool does not open a dialog box; no options are available for this tool. Double-click on either of the two other tools, and the options respective to that tool appear in a dialog box. Figure 4-16 shows the result of double-clicking the Scale tool.

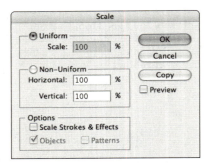

Figure 4-16: Double-click on the either the Scale or Shear tool to open a dialog box where you can make options choices.

Warp tools: The Warp tools include the Warp tool, the Twirl tool, the Pucker tool, the Bloat tool, the Scallop tool, the Crystallize tool, and the Wrinkle tool. Selecting a different tool and double-clicking on the selected tool opens a dialog box with options associated with that tool. In Figure 4-17, the Wrinkle tool options are shown.

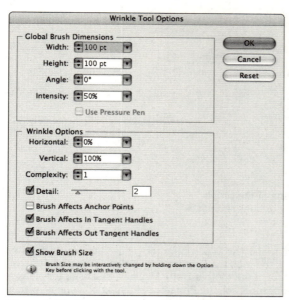

Figure 4-17: Double-click on the Wrinkle tool and the Wrinkle Tool Options dialog box appears.

Symbolism tools: The Symbolism tools — Symbol Sprayer, Symbol Shifter, Symbol Scruncher, Symbol Sizer, Symbol Spinner, Symbol Stainer, Symbol Screener, and Symbol Styler — have one advantage over other tools with respect to selecting tools and adjusting attributes: As was shown earlier in Figure 4-8, you can select any of the eight Symbolism tools directly in the Symbolism Tool Options dialog box. Therefore, you don't need to leave the dialog box, select another tool, and then reopen the dialog box to make adjustments respective to the selected tool. Double-clicking any of the Symbolism tools offers you options for selecting different tools and making options choices for a selected tool.

Graph tools: The Graph tools include the Column Graph tool, the Stacked Column Graph tool, the Bar Graph tool, the Stacked Bar Graph tool, the Line Graph tool, the Area Graph tool, the Scatter Graph tool, the Pie Graph tool, and the Radar Graph tool. Double-clicking on any tool in this group opens the Graph Type dialog box, shown in Figure 4-18. Like the Symbol tools, among the Graph tools options is the ability to select the tools in the Graph Type dialog box and make attribute changes for any one of the tools in the same dialog box. Double-click on any tool and you can make settings choices for the respective tool.

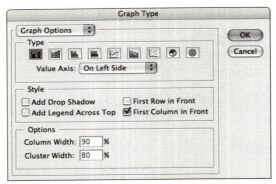

Figure 4-18: Double-click on any one of the Graph tools and you can make changes for options settings respective to that tool.

Eyedropper/Measure tools: The Eyedropper tool is used to assess color values. When you double-click the tool, the Eyedropper Options dialog box opens, as shown in Figure 4-19. The second tool in the toolbar is the Measure tool used for measuring distances. If you double-click the Measure tool, the Preferences dialog box opens, which allows you to change Guide and Grid colors.

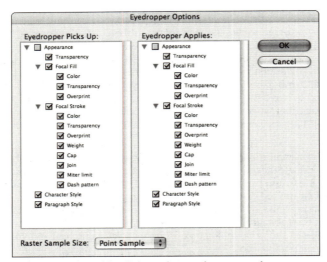

Figure 4-19: Double-click on the Eyedropper tool to open the Eyedropper Options dialog box.

Blend tool: Double-click on the Blend tool to open the Blend Options dialog box, shown in Figure 4-20. Notice that you can also open the same dialog box by clicking the Blend tool on one option and then pressing the Option/Alt key when clicking on the second object to be included in the blend.

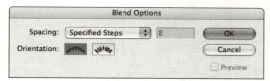

Figure 4-20: Double-click the Blend tool and the Blend Options dialog box appears.

Notice the absence of the Auto Trace tool. In earlier versions of Illustrator, the Auto Trace tool was contained in the same toolbar as the Blend tool. Illustrator CS2 no longer has an Auto Trace tool. A new feature that replaces Auto Trace is Live Trace, which you access from a menu command. Choose Object ⇨ Live Trace and a number of submenu commands offer many options for auto tracing artwork.

Cross-Reference   For information on using Live Trace, see Part III.

Live Paint Bucket/Live Paint Selection tools: The Paint Bucket tool has been replaced with the Live Paint Bucket tool. Additionally you find the Live Paint Selection tool. You use the Live Paint Bucket tool to apply a color, pattern, or gradient to a live paint group. You select multiple objects and click with the Live Paint Bucket tool to create a Live Paint Group. The Live Paint Selection tool can select edges of a Live Paint Group that can be painted with the Live Paint Bucket tool. Double-click either tool and the same set of options appears for changing paint fills, paint strokes, and highlight colors (Figure 4-21).

Figure 4-21: Double-clicking the Live Paint Bucket tool brings up a set of options.

Hand tool: Double-clicking the Hand tool sets the page view to a fit-in-window view. This view is also acquired in all CS applications by pressing ⌘/Ctrl+0 (zero).

Zoom tool: Double-click the Zoom tool to show the document window in an actual-size view (100 percent view).

Fill/Stroke tools: Double-clicking the Fill or Stroke tool opens the system Color Picker, shown in Figure 4-22. Note that programs like Photoshop open the Color Picker with a single click, while Illustrator requires you to double-click either tool.

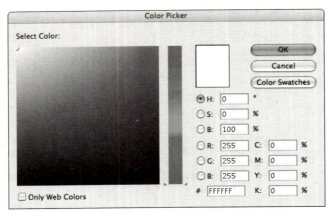

Figure 4-22: Double-click either the Fill or Stroke tool to open the Color Picker.

Photoshop tool options

In Photoshop, double-clicking tools produces an effect with only the Hand tool and the Zoom tool. Double-click the Hand tool, and you see the active document window zoomed to a Fit on Screen view. This view is similar to Fit Window view in other CS applications. Double-click the Zoom tool, and the window zooms to Actual Size view.

Remaining options for tools are addressed in Photoshop's options bar. Click a tool and the options bar changes to reflect choices pertaining to the selected tool. In Figure 4-23, the Rectangular Marquee tool was selected.

Figure 4-23: When you click a tool in the Photoshop Toolbox, the options bar changes options respective to the active tool.

InDesign tool options

InDesign is like a mixture of the UI (user interface) between Illustrator and Photoshop. In Illustrator, most tools have associated options dialogs accessed by double-clicking a tool in the Toolbox. Likewise, some of InDesign's tools also have similar options dialog boxes accessed the same way as in Illustrator. In Photoshop, tools don't have pop-up dialog boxes opened by double-clicking a tool; Photoshop uses an options bar that changes options settings each time a different tool is accessed. Likewise, in InDesign, you have a Control palette where many options settings are made respective to the currently selected tool. Tools in InDesign that support dialog boxes for options settings include the following:

Note Accessing some dialog boxes when double-clicking on a tool in the InDesign Toolbox requires you first to select an object in the document window.

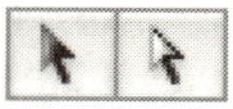

Selection/Direct Selection tools: The same Move dialog box opens in InDesign as you find in Illustrator when double-clicking on one of the Selection tools. Note that to open the Move dialog box, an object must be selected in the document window before you double-click on either tool. Notice that the options for the Move dialog box are almost always the same in the various programs, but the items that can be moved do vary a little. In Illustrator, either Objects or Patterns are targeted for movement. In InDesign, the only option is to move the content of the selected object, as shown in Figure 4-24.

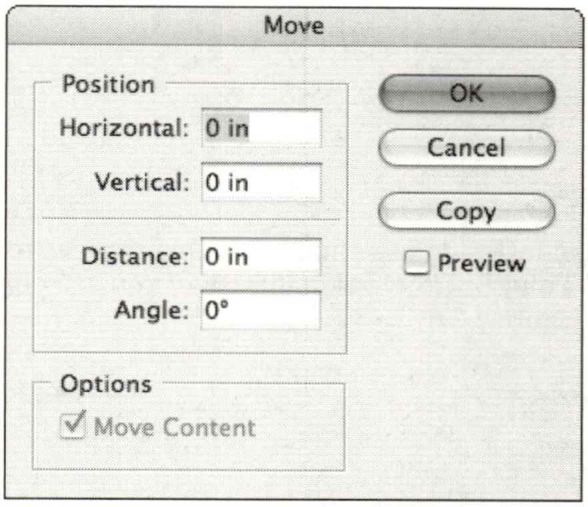

Figure 4-24: InDesign's Move dialog box is almost identical to Adobe Illustrator's Move dialog box with the exception of the Options choices.

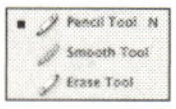

Pencil/Smooth tool: The Pencil tool options are identical in Illustrator and InDesign. The Smooth tool options vary slightly between Illustrator and InDesign. InDesign supports an additional option for keeping objects selected, as shown in Figure 4-25.

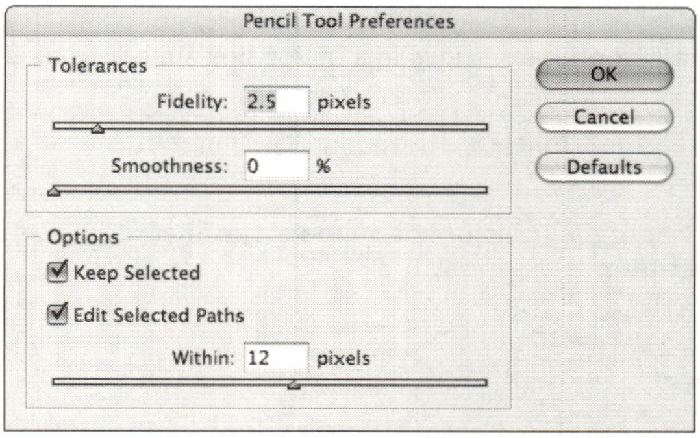

Figure 4-25: InDesign's Pencil Tool Preferences dialog box offers similar options to those in Illustrator.

Polygon tool: Double-click the Polygon tool to open the Polygon Settings dialog box, shown in Figure 4-26. A similar dialog box opens in Illustrator when you select the Polygon tool and click in the document window.

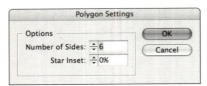

Figure 4-26: Double-click the Polygon tool to open the Polygon Settings dialog box.

Eyedropper tool: The Eyedropper tool in InDesign has similar options choices to those found in Illustrator. Because there is no Paint Bucket tool in InDesign, you see only options for the Eyedropper tool, as shown in Figure 4-27.

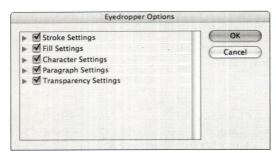

Figure 4-27: Double-click the Eyedropper tool to open the Eyedropper Options dialog box.

Rotate tool: The Rotate tool offers options settings in a dialog box similar to those found in Illustrator.

Scale tool: The Scale tool options are similar to those found in Illustrator.

Shear tool: Rounding out the last of the transformation tools, the Shear tool also has options choices similar to Illustrator.

Hand tool: The same effect takes place when you double-click the Hand tool in InDesign as you have in Illustrator. A Fit Page view is the result of double-clicking the tool in the Toolbox.

Zoom tool: Likewise, double-clicking the Zoom tool is the same as in Illustrator, where an Actual Size view is displayed in the document window.

Acrobat and GoLive tool options

Acrobat and GoLive make use of extended tools. Neither program supports options settings in dialog boxes that open from double-clicking a tool. Options choices are contained in palettes, preferences, and properties dialog boxes.

Using Palettes and Workspaces

A common characteristic among all Adobe products is an extensive set of palettes. Palettes offer you options choices for various tool uses, menu commands, and extended features not available through the selection of a tool or menu command. For the most part, palettes are accessed and used in all the CS programs similarly.

To open a palette, click the Window menu and select the palette you want to open. If a palette name appears with a check mark in the Window menu, the palette is already open in the application window. In Figure 4-28, you can see a comparison of the Window menu from Illustrator, Photoshop, InDesign, and GoLive, respectively.

 Palettes are always listed alphabetically.

Acrobat also makes use of palettes; however, accessing the palettes is handled from a different menu. To open palettes in Acrobat, choose View ⇨ Navigation Tabs and choose the palette to open from the submenu, as shown in Figure 4-29.

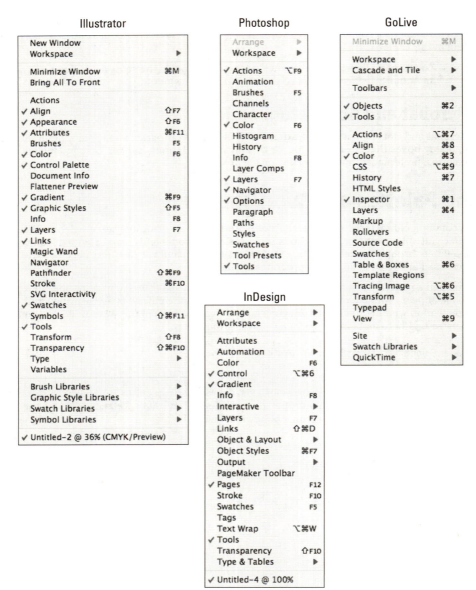

Figure 4-28: The Window menus for Illustrator, Photoshop, InDesign, and GoLive

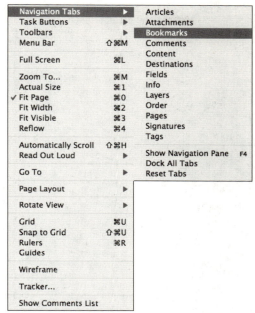

Figure 4-29: Acrobat palettes are accessed from a submenu by choosing View ⇨ Navigation Tabs.

Managing palettes

The extraordinary use of palettes in all the CS applications requires you to spend a little time managing palettes, showing only the palettes you need for any given editing job. Opening all the palettes at once in any program reduces a lot of screen space that you'll need to work on your documents. Fortunately, the programs have methods for docking palettes in wells or beside the application window.

Illustrator palettes

Of the CS programs, Illustrator has the least impressive means for managing palettes. Illustrator palettes are placed along the right side of the document window by default, as shown in Figure 4-30. When you open a new palette by selecting the Window menu and then selecting a palette name appearing without a check mark, the palette opens in the application window as a *floating palette*. To move a palette in Illustrator, drag the palette by the title bar (the topmost horizontal bar running across the top of a palette) to any side of the application window. When you drag to the edge of the application window in any direction, the palette snaps into position. If you're dragging to the right side of the application window, the palette snaps to the right side but moves freely up and down.

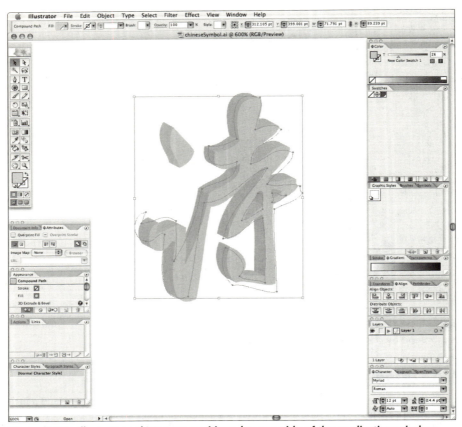

Figure 4-30: Illustrator palettes are positioned to any side of the application window.

Photoshop palettes

Photoshop goes one step farther than Illustrator when it comes to palette management, but it's still not quite as good as the docking options in InDesign and GoLive. In Photoshop, by default, palettes are docked along the right side of the application window, much like you find in Illustrator. Photoshop also has a docking well where you can dock palettes and tuck them away, similar to the way InDesign and GoLive stash palettes. On the top right of the options bar, you notice a horizontal gray bar, the Palette Well. Click and drag a palette tab to the gray bar, and release the mouse button. The palette is docked in the well. Drag additional palettes, and you can add them to the well. When you want to gain access to a palette's options settings, click the tab, as shown in Figure 4-31.

Caution   If you don't see the Palette Well in Photoshop, your monitor resolution is not sufficient to show it. The availability of the palette is dependent on a monitor resolution greater than 800 pixels wide.

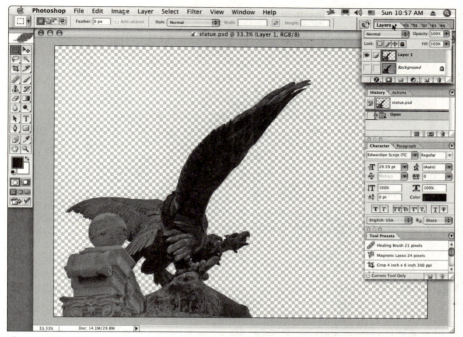

Figure 4-31: Photoshop also has a Palette Well where palettes are added and tucked away to provide you more room for editing your Photoshop documents.

InDesign and GoLive palettes

InDesign and GoLive share the same features for palette management, with a much more impressive means for arranging palettes in the application window than any other CS program.

You access invisible palettes the same as you do in Illustrator and Photoshop: by opening the Window menu and selecting the palette you want to open. The palette opens as a floating palette. Stashing the palette is where you see a big difference between InDesign/GoLive and Illustrator.

Each palette has a tab; when the palette is opened as a floating palette, you see a single tab denoting the palette name. Click the tab and drag to either the left or right side of the application window. The palette snaps when you move the palette to the edge of your screen. Unlike Illustrator and Photoshop, the palettes don't snap vertically to the top or bottom of your screen.

Note GoLive does snap to top and bottom, but they do not snap top and bottom in InDesign.

When palettes are stashed in InDesign or GoLive, the palette names and tabs rotate, providing you more screen real estate to work on your projects. When you need access to palette options, click the tab name, and the palette expands horizontally, providing you access to all the palette settings. In Figure 4-32, InDesign palettes are stashed on the right side of the screen with the Swatches palette expanded.

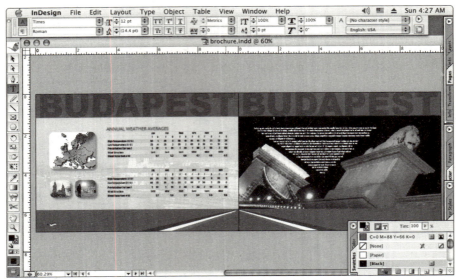

Figure 4-32: Palettes stashed to the right side of the application window where the tabs are rotated. Clicking a tab expands the palette to the left horizontally.

GoLive palettes are handled in the same manner as InDesign. Notice that in Figure 4-33 the Inspector palette is expanded to provide access to the attribute choices in that palette.

 Tip Option/Alt-click on the tab of a stashed palette to hide or reveal all collapsed palettes at the same time.

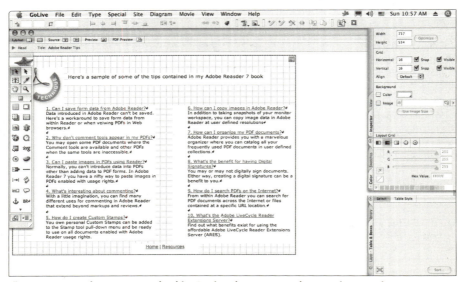

Figure 4-33: Palettes are stashed in GoLive the same as they are in InDesign.

Acrobat palettes

Acrobat uses a slightly different metaphor from the other CS applications. If you talk about palettes in Acrobat, you also need to consider toolbars. Unlike the other CS programs, not all of Acrobat's tools are visible when you launch the program. Therefore, tools, as well as palettes, need to be loaded in Acrobat for various different editing tasks.

When you launch Acrobat, the default tool set appears at the top of the application window, as shown in Figure 4-34. Individual tools are contained within toolbars that are docked in the Toolbar Well.

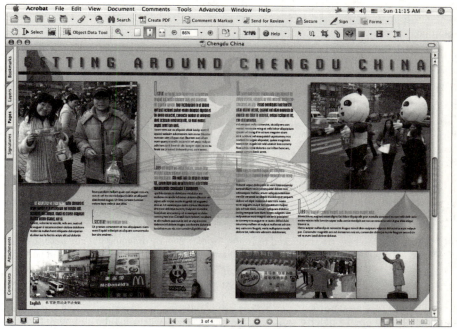

Figure 4-34: By default, a handful of tools appear docked in the Toolbar Well when you first launch Acrobat.

The default tools can be removed from the Toolbar Well and hidden from view or used as a floating toolbar, or additional tools can be added to the Toolbar Well. To gain access to additional toolbars, choose View ⇨ Toolbars and select the toolbar you want to open from the submenu list. An easier method for accessing tools in Acrobat is to open a contextual menu. Control+click (Mac) or right-click (Windows) on the Acrobat Toolbar Well to open a context menu, as shown in Figure 4-35.

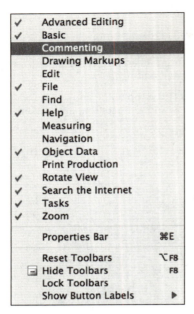

Figure 4-35: Open a context menu on the Toolbar Well, and select the toolbar you want to open.

If you want to return the Toolbar Well view to defaults, open a context menu and select Reset Toolbars. Also, when toolbars appear as floating toolbars in the Document pane, you can easily dock the toolbars by selecting Dock All Toolbars from the same context menu.

Note   Acrobat's toolbars are undocked from the Toolbar Well by dragging the separator bar on the left side of the toolbar. Look for a vertical embossed line appearing to the left of some tools. Clicking and dragging on the separator bar is the only way to move toolbars around the Document pane.

In addition to toolbars, Acrobat also makes use of palettes, as described for all the other CS applications. To open a palette, you need to access the Navigation Tabs submenu (refer to Figure 4-29). When a palette is selected in the Navigation Tabs submenu, it opens as a floating palette. Docking palettes in Acrobat appears similar to GoLive and InDesign; however, the palettes need to be docked in one specific place called the Navigation pane. Notice that palettes in Acrobat are not docked on the left or right side of the application window, but rather within the Navigation pane appearing on the left side of the document window. To dock a palette in the Navigation pane, click on any tab in the pane to expand the window, or press F6 on your keyboard. Click on the tab in a floating palette and drag it to the Navigation pane.

Tip   Palettes can also be dropped in the Navigation pane without expanding the pane. Just drag a tab to the left of the vertical bar separating the tabs from the Document pane or on top of any tab in the closed pane.

Grouping palettes

Palettes can be nested in groups in all the CS applications. When using floating palettes, you can group palettes together that give the appearance of a single palette with multiple tabs. Open any palette, and drag the tab from another open palette to the destination palette.

When the cursor appears over the tab area in the target palette, release the mouse button and the target palette accepts the new addition. In Figure 4-36, you can see the Layers palette in InDesign being moved to a palette containing several tabs.

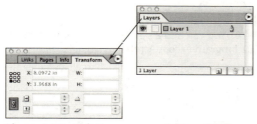

Figure 4-36: Palettes are grouped together by dragging tabs from one palette to another.

To ungroup a tab from a palette, click and drag the tab away from the palette. When you release the mouse button, the tab appears in its own palette.

Grouping palettes also occurs at another level in InDesign and GoLive. In InDesign and GoLive, drag a palette tab to a collapsed palette at one of the vertical edges of the application window. When the palette tab snaps into position and appears rotated, you can drag another palette tab to the stashed palette. Add as many tabs to a stashed palette as you like, but keep in mind they need to be grouped and ungrouped one palette at a time. In Figure 4-37, you can see several palettes docked together in InDesign and another palette to be added to the group by dragging the tab to the stashed palettes.

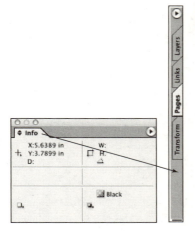

Figure 4-37: To add a palette to a stashed group, click and drag the palette tab to the tab well in the docked palette group.

In Illustrator, Photoshop, and Acrobat, you don't have an option for nesting palettes in the docking well. Photoshop and Acrobat offer you the opportunity to dock individual palettes in the docking areas (referred to as the Palette Well in Photoshop and the Navigation pane in Acrobat). However, stashing palettes together is permitted only in InDesign and GoLive. Illustrator unfortunately provides no palette well for collapsed palettes.

Palettes can also be docked in a hierarchy in all CS programs except Acrobat. If you want palettes in view without docking them on the sides of the application window, you can dock several palettes together and move them around the application window as a grouped object. In any CS2 program except Acrobat, you can add a palette below another palette. Simply click a palette tab and drag it to the base of the target palette. When the horizontal black line appears at the base of the target palette, release the mouse button drag one palette tab to the bottom of another palette, as shown in Figure 4-38.

Figure 4-38: You can add a palette below another palette in any CS2 program except Acrobat.

Be certain to drag a palette by the tab and move the cursor to the base of the target palette. When you see a horizontal black line at the base of the target palette, release the mouse button and the palettes are docked as shown in Figure 4-39. When you drag the title bar on the top of the palette, both palettes move together as a group. If you need to undock a palette, click on the palette tab for the palette to be moved and drag away from the group.

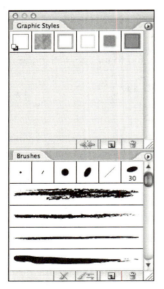

Figure 4-39: When palettes are docked, you can move them together by dragging the palette title bar.

Saving workspaces

Palettes offer you many options for addressing features and techniques available in the CS applications. They're essential program components and you'll rarely edit without making use of options contained in at least one palette. Those palettes you use most frequently are ones you'll want to keep open and have accessible every time you launch your program of choice.

Fortunately, all the CS2 applications remember the organization of your workspace each time you quit a program and relaunch it. If you move palettes around and rearrange them, then quit the editing program; the next time you open the program all the palette views are displayed according to the last view from the last editing session.

In Acrobat, not only do the palettes in the Navigation pane keep their last position, but all the toolbars you loaded are also placed in position exactly the same as the last Acrobat editing session. The same holds true for Illustrator, Photoshop, InDesign, and GoLive with respect to palette positions. However, Illustrator, Photoshop, InDesign, and GoLive have an additional benefit not found in Acrobat: options to save custom workspaces.

New Feature Saving Workspaces has finally been added to Adobe Illustrator. This feature was left out of Illustrator CS1. However, with the introduction of Illustrator CS2, you have the same options for saving workspaces as you have with Photoshop, InDesign, and GoLive.

In workflow environments where computers may be shared, the ability to save workspaces is a true benefit. You can customize your work environment to suit your own personal choices for palette positions, and save the palette views as your personal workspace. Notice that in Figure 4-40 the InDesign workspace includes several palettes nested and docked along the right edge of the application window. To capture the position of the palettes, choose Window ⇨ Workspace ⇨ Save Workspace. The Save Workspace dialog box opens prompting you for a workspace name. Type a name for your workspace and click Save. The new workspace is accessed in InDesign by choosing Window ⇨ Workspace ⇨ *workspace name* (where *workspace name* is the name you added). Each time you add a new workspace, the new workspace name is added to the Workspace submenu. Therefore, multiple users can save their own workspace preferences on the same computer.

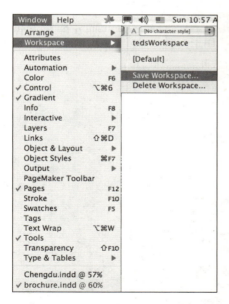

Figure 4-40: To save a workspace in InDesign, first arrange your palettes exactly as you want them to appear when you open the application.

Illustrator's, Photoshop's, and GoLive's treatment in regard to saving workspaces is the same as you find with InDesign. The menu command is identical and the same dialog box opens to prompt you for a workspace name.

Inasmuch as saving a workspace in both Illustrator and Photoshop uses the same menu command as InDesign and GoLive, the workspace includes the open palettes docked to the right of the application window and those tabs docked in the Palette Well. Because Photoshop does not support nested palettes in the Palette Well, you're limited to the view you can create in Photoshop and saving that view as a workspace.

The one thing to remember when adjusting workspaces is that all CS programs remember the last view you had before quitting the program. Therefore, if you save a workspace, then move palettes out of their docked positions and rearrange them differently from the saved workspace, after quitting the program and relaunching it, the last view you created becomes the new default. To regain your workspace view, choose Window ➪ Workspace ➪ *workspace name* (where *workspace name* is the name you used when you saved the workspace).

Some Common User-Interface Features

The inclusion of tools, palettes, and menus in all the CS programs makes for a common user interface where you can more easily discover new tools and editing techniques when first learning a program. Just as these features behave similarly across the CS programs, you also have some additional features consistent among programs that help reduce the learning curve when picking up a new Adobe CS program. Some of the most advantageous of the common user-interface items found in all CS programs include context menus and help documents.

Using context menus

If at any time you have difficulty finding a tool or menu command for a given task, first try to open a context menu. In all CS applications, context menus are used and the menu choices change according to the tool you select in the Toolbox or toolbar. Context menus are opened by Control+clicking (Mac) or right-clicking (Windows). The context menu pops up at the cursor location, as shown in Adobe Bridge in Figure 4-41.

Figure 4-41: Control+click (Mac) or right-click (Windows) to open a context menu.

Context menus are not limited to document pages. You can also open context menus in some palettes in Adobe Bridge, Photoshop, InDesign, GoLive, and Acrobat. In Figure 4-42 you see a context menu opened in the Preview palette in Adobe Bridge.

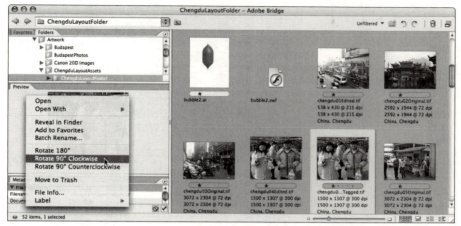

Figure 4-42: A context menu is opened on the Preview palette in Adobe Bridge.

 Tip As you work in the CS applications, try to get in the habit of opening a context menu when you want to apply an edit to an object, page, or function. The only way to determine whether a context menu offers a menu option is to poke around and try. As you become familiar with menu options, you'll begin to work much faster.

Getting help

You might think that with a purchase as substantial (both in terms of program features and the money you spent) as Creative Suite, you would get a hefty library of documentation. When you open the box for the CS installer CDs, you quickly learn that accompanying documentation is not offered in printed form. Instead of providing printed user manuals, Adobe created several different types of help information files accessible as you work in the CS programs.

Help files

In terms of user guides and documentation, what Adobe CS2 offers is an elaborate form of help files that you access from the Help menu in all CS2 programs. While you're working in a program, and when you need to meet tight deadlines, the online help files should be a welcome addition to the CS features. In all programs but Acrobat the help files are HTML documents. In Acrobat, the help file is a PDF document with a custom user interface.

From any CS2 program, open the Help menu and select *program name* Help (where *program name* is the name of the program you're currently using). For example, in Adobe InDesign, choose Help ⇨ InDesign Help; in Photoshop, it's Help ⇨ Photoshop Help; and so on.

After you access the Help command, the Adobe Help Center opens as shown in Figure 4-43. Note that the *Help for* pull-down menu can take you to help for a specific CS2 program. When you want help for Adobe Bridge, use the Help menu in the Bridge window.

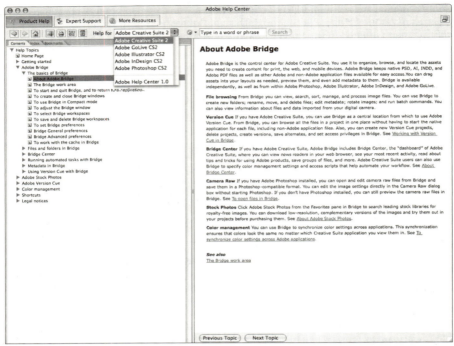

Figure 4-43: Select Help for any Adobe CS program, including the Bridge, and the Adobe Help Center opens.

Tip

When you type a word in the Help menu text box and click Search, the default returned results report findings for all the CS programs. If you want to narrow your search to a specific program, open the pull-down menu aside the magnifying glass icon and select *Search Current Product*. The returned results report findings specific to the product selected in the Help for pull-down menu.

In Acrobat, you access a PDF file either by using the Help menu or by using the How To pane, shown in Figure 4-44. By default, the How To pane opens on the right side of the Document pane when you first install Acrobat. Click on any of the listed items in the How To pane and help information respective to the selected item appears. Adobe designed the Acrobat user interface to help users quickly find help information on selected topics commonly used by Acrobat users. Design professionals will find quick access to Print Production and Review & Comment (two How To topics) helpful when working in Acrobat.

There's also a button in the Acrobat How To pane that allows you to access the Complete Acrobat 7.0 Help document. Click on this link in the How To pane and the Acrobat Help document opens. Although the file is a PDF document, you'll find items such as Contents, an Index, and a Search feature to be the same as the HTML help files.

Tip

Regardless of what CS application you work in, be sure to frequent the Help menus when you can't find a solution for working with tools and menus.

Figure 4-44: Acrobat has a How To menu that enables you to find help information on selected topics when you first launch the program.

Note: Although the Complete Acrobat 7.0 Help document is a PDF file, it was designed by Adobe engineers with a custom user interface and appears not quite the same as PDF files to which you may be accustomed. When the file opens, it appears on *top* of the Document pane, not contained *within* the Document pane as you would expect to view a PDF document. Furthermore, if a foreground PDF file appears in front of the Help document, you won't find it listed in the Window menu as you find with all open PDF files. Therefore, navigating the Help file can be a little awkward, and you might prefer using a standard PDF file that conforms more to the behavior you expect when viewing PDFs in Acrobat. If this is the case, open your Adobe Acrobat 7.0 Professional folder in your Applications folder (Mac) or Programs folder (Windows) and find the Help subfolder. Inside this subfolder, you'll find the ACROHELP.PDF file. Open the file and you find a comprehensive help document in standard PDF format. (Note: Mac users need to select the Program icon and open a context menu. From the menu options select Show Package Contents. The Contents folder opens. Nested in this folder you'll find the Help document.)

Online help

The Adobe online help offers you helpful tips and techniques posted online at Adobe's Web site. You can find many useful tips and techniques hosted as Web pages, video downloads, and PDF documents. There are descriptions for new program features, plug-ins and add-ons for different CS programs, upgrade information, and links to customer-support pages.

You can access online help in all the CS programs under the Help menu and listed as *program name* Online, where *program name* is the name of the CS application you're currently using (for example, Help ⇨ Photoshop Online).

Because these help files are hosted online, you obviously need an Internet connection to access them. Be sure your Web browser is operational, and click on the Online menu command in any CS program to open Web pages on Adobe's Web site.

Tip   For access to tips and techniques using the CS programs, open Adobe Bride and click Bridge Center in the Favorites pane. Scroll the RSS Reader pane and click on Adobe Studio and Tutorials. Scroll the list in the next pane to the right and click an item of interest. Your default Web browser opens and takes you to a related tip or technique hosted on Adobe's Web site. For more information on using the Bridge Center, see Chapter 7.

Updates

All the CS programs have the Help ⇨ Updates menu command. When you select Updates from the Help menu, the program from which the menu command was selected searches Adobe's Web site for update information. If an update exists, you're prompted for a download. Using the Updates menu command is an easy way to stay current with program upgrades and maintenance fixes. This is a command you should frequently use, because maintenance upgrades often repair bugs and programming errors in the applications. You can always expect an upgrade shortly after the release of each new program version.

Using Keyboard Shortcuts

Keyboard shortcuts are another item that could be listed as a common user-interface feature. We cover them here as a separate topic to elaborate a little bit more about the aspects of using keyboard shortcuts in the CS programs and customizing shortcuts for your personal workflow.

If you want a comprehensive list of keyboard shortcuts, consult the program help files. Obviously, you don't want to spend a lot of time memorizing the shortcuts, but you'll want to take advantage of using shortcuts common among the CS programs to perform identical tasks. One great advantage of using the CS programs is that, because the applications are developed by a single software manufacturer, the keyboard shortcuts from one program to the next are often the same. In some cases, however, you also find inconsistency between the programs or perhaps some features that could use a keyboard shortcut where one doesn't exist. Fortunately, several CS programs offer you an option to edit and redefine keyboard shortcuts.

There are some differences between the CS applications in handling custom keyboard shortcuts and features available in one program versus another. The following sections describe working with keyboard shortcuts and customizing them to suit your workflow according to each CS program.

Customizing keyboard shortcuts in Illustrator

Illustrator was the first of the CS programs developed by Adobe Systems and has a long tradition of assigned keyboard shortcuts to access tools and menu commands. As new programs have been developed, Adobe Systems has modified many keyboard shortcuts in Illustrator to match equivalent actions in other programs, such as Photoshop. If you want to return to a familiar keyboard shortcut in Illustrator, you can customize keyboard shortcuts.

Tip If you work in a production environment and share your computer with others, it's a good idea to settle on agreed changes if they deviate from defaults used by other users. If you use your computer exclusively, you'll want to give a little thought to customizing keyboard shortcuts that are consistent between the CS programs. The more consistent you make your shortcuts, the less confusion you'll experience.

To customize a keyboard shortcut, choose Edit ⇨ Keyboard Shortcuts. The Keyboard Shortcuts dialog box opens, as shown in Figure 4-45. In this dialog box, you can add a new keyboard shortcut for a menu command or tool selection, or change existing keyboard shortcuts to other keystrokes you want to use.

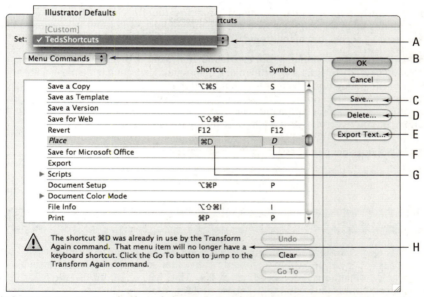

Figure 4-45: Custom keyboard shortcuts are defined in the Keyboard Shortcuts dialog box.

In the Keyboard Shortcuts dialog box, you have several options for creating a new shortcut or modifying an existing one. The options to understand in this dialog box include the following:

✦ **Set pull-down menu (A):** By default, the menu option is Illustrator Defaults. This menu choice remains listed in the pull-down menu so you can return to the Illustrator defaults at any time. When you assign a new keyboard shortcut or modify an existing one, the menu item changes to Custom. When you save your modified set, you're prompted to name the set. After saving, the name you use to identify your custom set is added to the pull-down menu.

- **Menu Commands/Tools (B):** Select from either Menu Commands or Tools to change shortcuts that invoke menu commands or select tools.
- **Save (C):** After changing the shortcuts to your personal liking, click Save to save your changes. The name you use for your set is added to the Set pull-down menu.
- **Delete (D):** The Delete button enables you to delete custom sets you add to the pull-down menu. To delete a set, first select the set to be deleted in the pull-down menu and then click Delete.
- **Export Text (E):** When you click Export Text, all your keyboard shortcuts are saved in a text file. You can use the text file to share with other workgroup members. For more information on custom keystrokes in workgroup environments, see the "Custom shortcuts for workgroups" sidebar in this chapter.
- **Shortcut edits (F):** To change a shortcut, first click in the Shortcuts column in the row for the item you want to change. For example, if you want to reassign the keystroke for accessing the Type tool, click the cursor in the Shortcut column where the Type row appears.
- **Symbol (G):** The keyboard shortcut to access a tool or invoke an action is defined in the Shortcut column. Adjacent to the Shortcut column is the Symbol column. The characters you add here appear in a menu list and/or tool tip. Notice that when you view the menus in all CS programs, you see the menu name and often the keys used for the shortcut to access the menu item.
- **Warning (H):** If you define a tool or a menu command with a key combination that is already used to select a tool or invoke a command, a warning is displayed at the bottom of the dialog box. If you don't want to interfere with an existing shortcut, click Undo. If you're overriding a preexisting shortcut, you can edit the shortcut used by another tool or menu command. Click Go To and you're taken to the item using the shortcut you overrode. Add a new shortcut if you so desire.

Note   Mac OS X does not permit assigning ⌘+Option modifiers.

Custom shortcuts for workgroups

If you make changes with keyboard shortcuts and want to share your custom set with other users, you can easily copy your custom keyboard set to other computers. When you save a custom set, the new definitions are saved to a file. This file is stored in the user logon Library/Preferences/Adobe Illustrator CS2 Settings folder (Mac) or Documents and Settings\username\Application Data\Adobe\Adobe Illustrator CS2 Settings folder on Windows. To find the files on Windows you need to turn on the ability to view hidden files and folders within the Tools>Folder Options>View>Advanced Settings>Files and Folders>Hidden Files and Folders> Show Hidden Files and Folders option. I know that's a mouthful, but that's where to find them and how to turn them on. Copy the file from one computer to the same folder on the other computers, and the keyboard-shortcuts set is added to the Illustrator Set pull-down menu.

If you make changes to the keyboard shortcuts either in an isolated environment or when working as part of a group, it's handy to have a template or guide that you can refer to in order to refresh your memory on changes made to the shortcut keys. When you create a custom set and click Export Text, all features that can accept keyboard shortcuts are exported along with all those features assigned a keyboard shortcut. The file is a text file with the items and keyboard shortcuts listed with tabs and carriage returns. You can easily convert the text file to a table in a program like Microsoft Word.

Tables are supported in Adobe InDesign; however, the text file exported from Illustrator cannot be imported directly into InDesign. In order to import the file in InDesign, you need to open it in Word and save the file from Word. Rather than performing two steps for saving from Word and creating the table in InDesign, you can create the table in Word and use the Convert to Adobe PDF macro button to create a PDF file.

When you open the exported file in Microsoft Word, the text appears as shown in the following figure. Tabs separate the item description from the keystroke used as the shortcut.

Continued

Continued

To convert the text to a table in Microsoft Word, select all the text in the document by pressing ⌘+A (Mac) or Ctrl+A (Windows). Choose Table ⇨ Convert ⇨ Text to Table. The Convert Text to Table dialog box opens, as shown in the following figure. Be certain to click the radio button for Tabs in the bottom-left corner of the dialog box. Word recognizes the columns to be created when you identify the separator.

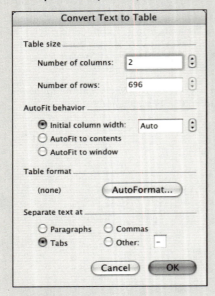

Click OK and Word creates the table for you. With a Word document, you can host the file on a server or print the file and distribute it among users in your workgroup. For a more accessible document (for users who don't have Microsoft Word installed on their computers), use the PDFMaker Macro in Word and create a PDF document. The PDF file (shown in the following figure) can be viewed in any Acrobat viewer.

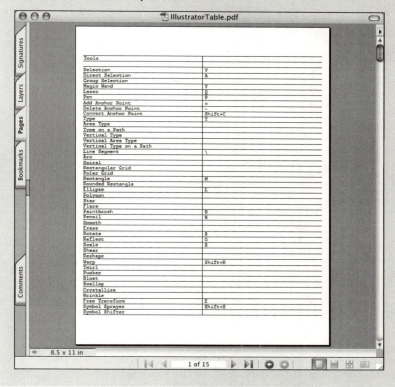

For more information on using the PDFMaker and converting Microsoft Word files to PDF, see Part V of this book.

Customizing keyboard shortcuts in Photoshop

Have you ever wondered why ⌘+I (Mac)/Ctrl+I (Windows) in Adobe Photoshop inverts an image when a much more functional use of the shortcut might be to open the Image Size dialog box? Well, the good news for Photoshop users is that Photoshop CS supports creating custom keyboard shortcuts just like Illustrator CS. You can assign new keyboard shortcuts or remap existing keyboard shortcuts to menus and tools.

To change keyboard shortcuts, choose Edit ⇨ Keyboard Shortcuts. The Keyboard Shortcuts and Menus dialog box opens, as shown in Figure 4-46.

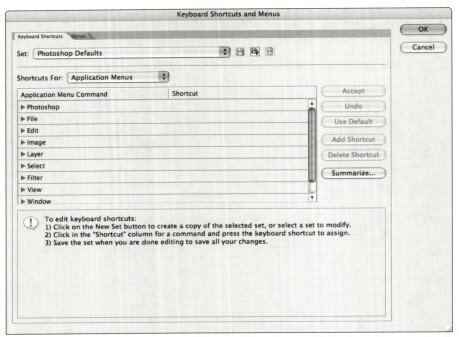

Figure 4-46: The Photoshop Keyboard Shortcuts and Menus dialog box offers very similar options to those found in the Illustrator Keyboard Shortcuts dialog box.

As you can see in Figure 4-46, the dialog box offers very similar options to the ones you find using the Illustrator Keyboard Shortcuts dialog box. The Set pull-down menu provides choices for using the default keyboard shortcuts or custom sets you create and save, much like those options discussed with Illustrator in the preceding section. From the Shortcuts For pull-down menu, you can choose to edit application menu commands, palette menus, or tools. When you select one of the categories from the Shortcuts For pull-down menu, the options change in the list below the pull-down menu. For Application Menus and Palette Menus, each menu is listed with a right-pointing arrow adjacent to the menu name. Click the right-pointing arrow symbol, and the menu expands where each individual command is exposed. In Figure 4-47, you can see the Palette Menus selected from the Shortcuts For pull-down menu and the Layers palette expanded where all palette menu commands are listed. Notice that, by default, only three commands have shortcut-key equivalents.

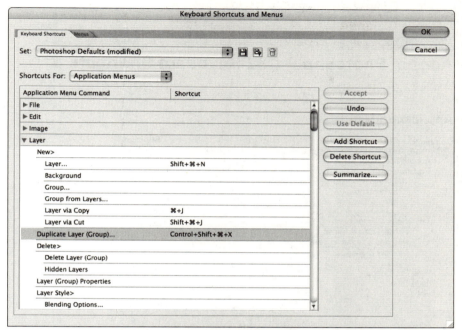

Figure 4-47: Select the category you want from the Shortcuts For pull-down menu and expand the menu or palette by clicking on the symbol adjacent to a palette name.

Most of the same options exist for creating, changing, and deleting keyboard shortcuts in Photoshop as you find in Illustrator. Photoshop enables you to export a list of all the assigned keyboard shortcuts; however, unlike the text-file export in Illustrator, Photoshop's export is in the form of an HTML file. Click Summarize in the Keyboard Shortcuts dialog box, and the Save dialog box opens, allowing you to navigate your hard drive and locate a folder destination for your file. After saving the file, you can view the list of shortcuts in your Web browser, as shown in Figure 4-48.

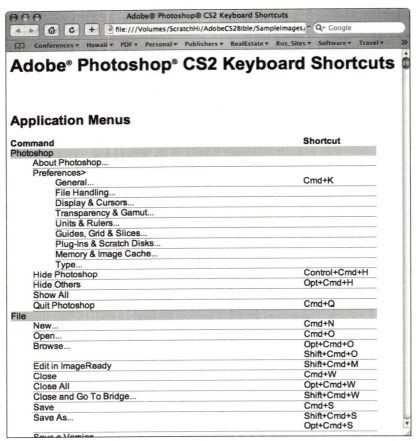

Figure 4-48: Open the exported list of keyboard shortcuts in your default Web browser to view a list of the assigned shortcuts.

Customizing keyboard shortcuts in InDesign

Fortunately, the Keyboard Shortcuts dialog box in all the CS applications that allow you to customize shortcuts is accessed with the same menu command. Select Edit ➪ Keyboard Shortcuts in InDesign, and the InDesign Keyboard Shortcuts dialog box opens. From a pull-down menu listed as Product Area, you see an extensive list of categories where keyboard shortcuts are assigned, as shown in Figure 4-49.

You select an option from the Product Area pull-down menu and click on a command in the Commands list box. From this point, you have another option where you can narrow the assignment of the keyboard shortcut to one of five categories listed in the Context pull-down menu. For example, if you want to assign a keyboard shortcut to Fill with Placeholder text, you start by selecting Type Menu in the Product Area. In the Commands list, you select Fill with Placeholder Text. Then click in the New Shortcut field box and press the keys to create the new shortcut. In Figure 4-50, you can see an example for assigning a keyboard shortcut to Fill with Placeholder Text.

Chapter 4 ✦ **Understanding User Interfaces** 171

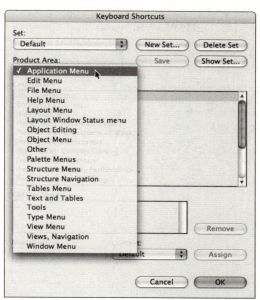

Figure 4-49: The Keyboard Shortcuts dialog box in InDesign contains an extensive set of categories from the Product Area pull-down menu.

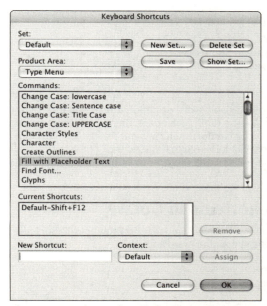

Figure 4-50: The Keyboard Shortcuts dialog box shown with selections to assign a shortcut to Fill with Placeholder Text

You handle the basic options for creating new sets, saving a set, and selecting custom sets from the Set pull-down menu in a similar to the way to how you handle these operations in Illustrator and Photoshop. As an added benefit for users who are former QuarkXPress users, InDesign provides a QuarkXPress-equivalent set of shortcuts accessible from the Set pull-down menu. A PageMaker set is also available for users familiar with Adobe PageMaker shortcuts.

If you want to create a table describing the key shortcuts created for a custom set, click Show Set. Like Adobe Illustrator, the list of assigned keys and those commands where no assignment has been made are all listed in a text file. When you click Show Set, the list appears in your default text editor, as shown in Figure 4-51.

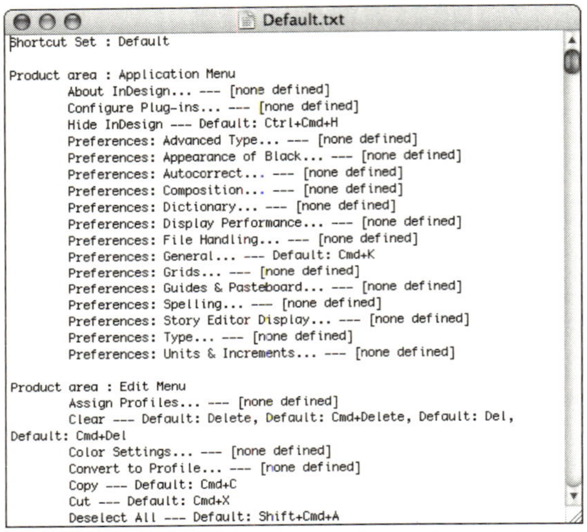

```
Default.txt
Shortcut Set : Default

Product area : Application Menu
        About InDesign... --- [none defined]
        Configure Plug-ins... --- [none defined]
        Hide InDesign --- Default: Ctrl+Cmd+H
        Preferences: Advanced Type... --- [none defined]
        Preferences: Appearance of Black... --- [none defined]
        Preferences: Autocorrect... --- [none defined]
        Preferences: Composition... --- [none defined]
        Preferences: Dictionary... --- [none defined]
        Preferences: Display Performance... --- [none defined]
        Preferences: File Handling... --- [none defined]
        Preferences: General... --- Default: Cmd+K
        Preferences: Grids... --- [none defined]
        Preferences: Guides & Pasteboard... --- [none defined]
        Preferences: Spelling... --- [none defined]
        Preferences: Story Editor Display... --- [none defined]
        Preferences: Type... --- [none defined]
        Preferences: Units & Increments... --- [none defined]

Product area : Edit Menu
        Assign Profiles... --- [none defined]
        Clear --- Default: Delete, Default: Cmd+Delete, Default: Del,
Default: Cmd+Del
        Color Settings... --- [none defined]
        Convert to Profile... --- [none defined]
        Copy --- Default: Cmd+C
        Cut --- Default: Cmd+X
        Deselect All --- Default: Shift+Cmd+A
```

Figure 4-51: Click Show Set in the Keyboard Shortcuts dialog box, and the list of keyboard shortcuts is listed in a text file.

You can save the text file and open it in Microsoft Word or import the text in InDesign where you can convert the text file to a table like the table conversion described when converting Illustrator text files. The text file for InDesign, unfortunately, is not as well formatted as the text file you have available in Illustrator. The InDesign text file doesn't convert to a table as cleanly as Illustrator's table conversion, so you may have to do a little editing to make a table guide for your workgroup.

Customizing keyboard shortcuts in GoLive

Keyboard shortcuts can also be assigned in GoLive. Choose Edit ⇨ Keyboard Shortcuts to open the Keyboard Shortcuts dialog box shown in Figure 4-52.

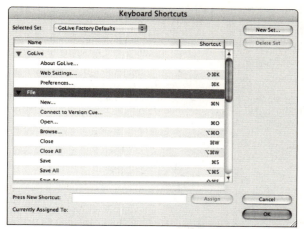

Figure 4-52 The Keyboard Shortcuts dialog box in GoLive

GoLive supports a list of commands in a list box that is expanded by clicking on a symbol adjacent to the menu name. On the Mac, a right-pointing arrow appears adjacent to the menu name; on Windows, the symbol is a plus sign. When expanded, the symbols change to a down-pointing arrow and minus sign, respectively.

As you scroll the list of commands in the list box, notice that the commands are nested in groups. Click on the symbol adjacent to a menu command and the list expands. In Figure 4-51, the Edit menu was expanded; then the Find command expanded to expand the nested group.

GoLive does not support saving a text file or creating an HTML file for a list of commands you can use as a guide.

Working with keyboard shortcuts in Acrobat

Acrobat is the only program in the Creative Suite that doesn't support creation of custom keystrokes for shortcuts. However, while discussing keyboard shortcuts, there is one thing important to point out when working in Acrobat: By default, accessing tools with keystrokes is not enabled. Users of earlier versions of Acrobat soon find that pressing the H key and expecting to select the Hand tool doesn't produce a result when they first launch Acrobat. In order to use key modifiers to access tools, you need to change a preference setting.

Open the Preferences dialog box by choosing Acrobat ➪ Preferences (Mac) or Edit ➪ Preferences (Windows). The Preferences dialog box opens by default to show the General preferences. If General is not selected in the left pane, as shown in Figure 4-53, click General and the right pane changes to reflect the options available for the General preferences.

Be certain that Use Single-Key Accelerators to Access Tools is selected. If the check box is unchecked, pressing a key on your keyboard to access a tool won't work. By default, when you first load Acrobat, this check box is unchecked.

Unfortunately, you cannot change any keyboard shortcuts in Acrobat.

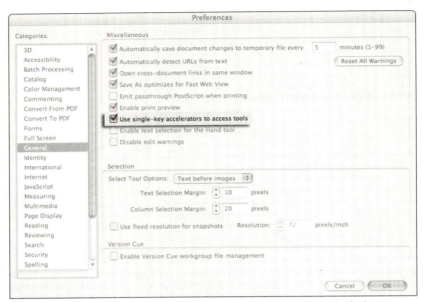

Figure 4-53: Open the General preferences and select the Use single-key accelerators to access tools check box.

Summary

- Several CS programs have some common tools. The vast majority of common tools exist among Illustrator, Photoshop, and InDesign. The tools work similarly in the programs that use them. Accessing the tools using keystrokes is also common between the programs.

- Acrobat uses a variety of toolbars that can be opened and docked in the top-level Toolbar Well. Context menus help greatly in accessing tools in Acrobat.

- Some tool options are accessible in some CS programs by double-clicking a tool in the program's Toolbox. Corresponding dialog boxes open where attributes are assigned for a given tool.

- Illustrator, Photoshop, InDesign, and GoLive offer options for saving workspaces. Workspaces involve arrangement of tools and palettes and the overall look of a program's editing environment.

- All the CS programs have some common user-interface features. Among the more popular are context menus and access to help documents.

- All CS programs with the exception of Acrobat offer you options for customizing keyboard shortcuts.

✦ ✦ ✦

Getting Started with Design Workflows

P A R T

II

In This Part

Chapter 5
Creating Production Workflows

Chapter 6
Creating Color Managed Workflows

Chapter 7
Using Adobe Bridge

Chapter 8
Using Version Cue

Chapter 9
Managing Adobe PDF Files

Creating Production Workflows

CHAPTER 5

In This Chapter

Understanding workflow concepts

Setting up workflows for independent designers

Creating workflows for workgroups

Repurposing files

Setting up your workflow

The Adobe Creative Suite is built around the concept of facilitating design production in workflow environments. Designers and production artists create workflows either as independent workers or as participants in workflow groups. A workflow helps you perform your work quickly and intelligently, often by streamlining redundant tasks. Workflows are designed to dramatically reduce the time you need to perform your work and reduce the time required to train new workers.

This chapter covers the initial development of production workflows as they relate to using the Adobe Creative Suite 2 Premium Edition. With all the tools at hand, you'll gain an understanding of how to use the CS2 applications in workflows and how you can save time producing artwork.

Understanding Workflows

Workflows as they pertain to the Adobe Creative Suite can be divided into several groups. As a graphic designer, you may be primarily concerned with production workflows where artwork creations originate in programs like Adobe Illustrator CS2 and Adobe Photoshop CS2. Document assembly may be performed in Adobe InDesign CS2 and from InDesign CS2 you may export files to Adobe PDF or package files for Adobe GoLive CS2. Furthermore, you may integrate your native Illustrator and Photoshop files along with PDF in Adobe GoLive. From creation to final output, you have a workflow focused on production.

You may also be concerned with a color-management workflow to insure the color is consistent among all the applications you use to produce your artwork. This workflow might be a subset of your production workflow. The color-management workflow might extend beyond your office and continue to the print shop or service center. In this regard, you need to work together with service technicians working outside your environment.

Cross-Reference For information related to creating color-management workflows, see Chapter 6.

Yet another workflow that affects your final results when you prepare documents for print is the production center printing your jobs. Printers and service bureaus develop workflows to run their production lines from digital file to final output. The bridge between you and the service center might include color management and file preparation to meet the standards set forth by your vendors. If you design files for print, you need to understand that the production center is part of your workflow and there is a great benefit to working together with your vendors to ensure your workflow is efficient and your product is delivered on time.

For more information on prepress and printing, see Chapter 38.

If you design files for Web hosting, you can include your Internet Service Provider (ISP) or your client's ISP in your workflow if your designs end up hosted on a site other than your own ISP. Working with ISP vendors is as important as working with print vendors. It is, therefore, equally important for you to include professionals at an ISP in your workflow.

For more information on Web hosting, see Chapter 33.

Regardless of whether you design files for print or for the Web, realize that you have two kinds of workflows with which you'll continually interact. Your internal workflow where you produce your artwork is something over which you have complete control. The workflows that extend to your print shop or ISP are something over which you don't have complete control, so you need to negotiate standards with the vendors to develop consistent reliable output.

In this chapter, we look at workflows you create in your office for design production and understanding workflow concepts as they apply to the Adobe Creative Suite. In several later chapters in this book, we address how to set up the CS2 programs to suit your production workflow.

Workflows for Independent Artists

If you're an independent designer working in a one-person shop, you have some advantages in that you can customize and work with the Creative Suite applications as you see fit. You don't need to concern yourself with setting up your environment to suit the needs of multiple users. The advantage is having it all your way; the disadvantage is you have to do everything yourself — acting as the creative director, artist, image editor, layout artist, Web designer, and office manager.

As someone who works with all the CS2 programs, you'll want to take a little time to plan your workflow and take more time to become productive in using all the CS2 applications. An example of a workflow for an independent graphic designer is illustrated in Figure 5-1.

In the example workflow, you begin an assignment with a client meeting either personally or through e-mail or telephone calls. As you develop a concept and after interviewing your client, you prepare sketches or comps that are sent back to the client in an e-mail review using Adobe Acrobat Professional. If more than one person is part of a committee that ultimately approves your commission, each committee member receives your draft via e-mail for review. When the final comp is approved you begin your work on the project.

When you prepare a PDF document for a review with your clients, be certain to enable the PDF with usage rights for Adobe Reader. Any member of a review team who doesn't use Acrobat Professional can use the free Adobe Reader 7 program to participate in a review. For more information on enabling PDF documents, see Chapter 25.

Chapter 5 ✦ Creating Production Workflows

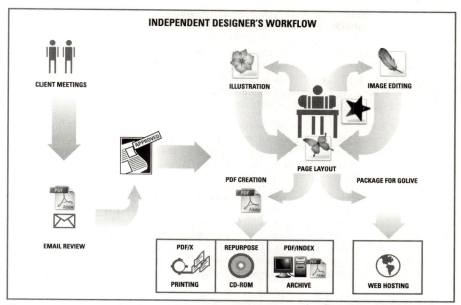

Figure 5-1: An example of a production workflow for an independent designer

You may start your project by creating a new Collection in Adobe Bridge where all the assets for a client job are maintained. If you need illustrated art as well as photo images, you may spend some time in Adobe Illustrator CS2 and Adobe Photoshop CS2, where you create artwork. Document files are saved to the folder or subfolders you created with Adobe Bridge and the files are managed in the Bridge window. All layers are preserved in the documents, and you save your files in native formats.

If the copy is developed in a word processor foreign to you and not compatible with your text editors, you might ask your client to send you an RTF (Rich Text Format) file, from which you import it into Adobe InDesign CS2. You import the illustrations and images into Adobe InDesign, and fit the copy to the design.

You export the InDesign CS2 document as Adobe PDF and open the file in Adobe Acrobat Professional. You soft-proof the file to ensure all colors will print as you expect and then repurpose the file for online delivery by reducing image resolution to create a smaller file. You may need to save this file as a copy with password security, which prevents your client from extracting data or printing the document. You enable the file with Adobe Reader usage rights and e-mail the enabled file to the client, who signs off on the design in a comment note and e-mails the file back to you. When you receive approval from your client, you e-mail or FTP the high-resolution PDF document to your printer.

Cross-Reference For information on enabling PDFs with usage rights, see Chapter 25. For information on soft-proofing color, see Chapter 38. For information on repurposing files, see the section on document repurposing later in this chapter.

If Web design is part of your work, you return to Adobe InDesign CS2 and package the file for GoLive. You integrate the InDesign CS2 document in the Web site design and use repurposed PDFs designed for Web hosting and CD-ROM replication. If point-of-sale order forms are part of your commission, you create the form designs in InDesign CS2 or Adobe Illustrator CS2 and export/save to PDF. You use Acrobat Professional to add form fields and JavaScripts to create interactive forms. If you are a Windows user, you have the option for using Adobe Designer to create the PDF form. You return to GoLive and add hyperlinks to the PDF forms and upload the forms via GoLive to the client's Web site.

At the end of your job, you write all the files to a CD-ROM where PDFs contain attachments to quickly open the original application documents. You create a search index that you include on the CD to help you search PDF content. Metadata are supplied for files to permit searches and quick access to files. You collect your money and take a vacation, because you have an efficient workflow that saved you time.

As an independent designer, you benefit from knowing how to work effectively in the CS2 applications. You also derive extra benefits for keeping files reduced to a minimum by using only native file formats and using Version Cue if you need to create multiple versions or alternates of files. If you need to return to a project, having fewer files that are well documented throughout the design process helps you easily revise content and create new designs for the same client. Because you add your files to organized collections, you can use Adobe Bridge to return to the client's files and easily modify designs with alternates or new versions.

Modifying designs

You may think that the workflow described in the preceding section doesn't require all the CS2 programs to perform the same steps. It's true, if all there were to creating a design piece was following the same steps in a linear fashion, you could substitute the use of an illustration program and/or use another layout program. You would miss the packaging for GoLive if you don't use InDesign CS2, but some layout programs do support exporting to HTML. What's not mentioned in the workflow is handling design modifications. Design modifications may occur during the design process where you need to nudge and move objects to create the look you want or when your client requests changes to objects, images, colors, type fonts, and so on.

The advantage of using the Creative Suite is more obvious when making changes to designs. As you change files, you can save different versions of the same file with Version Cue or you can use Version Cue to create alternates for files. If you need to change back to an earlier version, this tool alone will save you a lot of time. If you need to move or nudge objects, having files imported from native formats opens up your freedom for moving design elements without affecting underlying objects.

For information on using Version Cue and creating alternates, see Chapter 8.

Extending the workflow

Another advantage of using the Creative Suite is the easy portability of assets that can help you prepare files properly for vendors. When designing for print, you can acquire color profiles prepared by your vendor, designed for output on their devices.

For information on creating color-management workflows, see Chapters 6 and 7.

In addition to color management, you want to check your files for potential errors. When documents are *preflighted*, your files are analyzed for potential printing problems. Adobe Acrobat Professional contains a sophisticated preflight tool using built-in and/or custom preflight profiles. You can acquire preflight profiles from your service provider to use in Adobe Acrobat for checking files for proper printing. You can acquire preflight profiles from vendor Web sites or have them e-mailed directly to you.

Cross-Reference For understanding more about preflight and information on importing and exporting preflight profiles, see Chapter 38.

Workflows for Studios and Production Houses

If you work in a larger studio with coworkers participating in design projects, you need to be more concerned about the steps involved in your workflow and be consistent in all your tasks. Many studios that evolved with computer illustration and design often let employees determine what application software to use and what methods for creating designs to employ. The unknowing creative directors, who at times were computer illiterate, paid little attention to what tools were used and only focused on the final artwork. Today, some firms spend a lot of time updating documents from a variety of programs that their current staff no longer uses.

The first step in developing an efficient workflow is to begin with standards that all employees in a firm use. Deciding what application software to use, setting standards for file naming conventions, determining what archiving methods to use, and developing policies for updating documents are all preliminary steps that you should integrate in a workflow schema before engaging in production tasks. The time spent on management is insignificant when you compare it to the time it takes to train current employees and hire new ones.

As an example of a studio or production-center workflow, Figure 5-2 shows how creative production personnel participate in a design project. After a project is approved, artists working in Adobe Illustrator CS2 and image editors working in Adobe Photoshop CS2 save files to a server. Copy editors save files to the server for the page layout artists to acquire. The page layout artists retrieve files, complete the designs, and save the completed designs back to the server. All the files are viewed and managed in Adobe Bridge where all users can view the same collection; PDFs are exported from InDesign CS2 for print, Web hosting, CD-ROM replication, porting to handheld devices and tablets, and document archiving. Web designers retrieve InDesign files and package them for GoLive. PDFs are retrieved from the server for documents included on the Web site.

In this facility, it's easy to see how developing standards is critical for the workflow environment. When new employees are hired, they need to quickly fit into the workflow. Training new staff is a much easier task when following standards. If individual artists determine their own methods and use different programs to produce artwork, getting new employees up to speed is likely to take more time than you can afford.

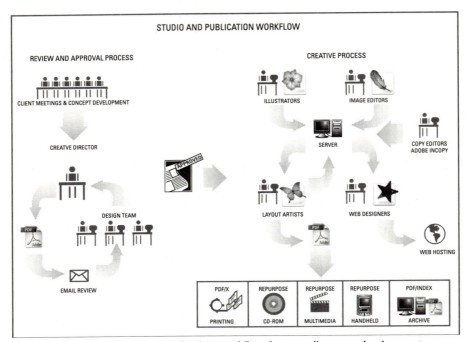

Figure 5-2: An example of a production workflow for a studio or production center

Document Repurposing

Document repurposing is taking a file suited for one output purpose and optimizing it for another output purpose. In regard to the Adobe Creative Suite, Acrobat is the application best suited for document repurposing.

If you design a piece for print in InDesign CS2, you have some options you can employ to repurpose a file. Because exporting to PDF is something you can do for printing, you can return to the InDesign file and export a second PDF document more suitable for Web hosting or screen displays. What goes on in InDesign CS2 is simply a matter of choosing the Adobe PDF settings most desirable for your output needs. To select the correct settings, follow these steps:

STEPS: Select the Correct Output Settings

1. **Choose File ⇨ Export in Adobe InDesign CS2.** The Export dialog box opens.
2. **From the Format pull-down menu, choose Adobe PDF.**
3. **Supply a name for the file in the Save As field and click Save.** A second dialog box opens where you set the attributes for the PDF file.

4. **From the top-level Preset pull-down menu, choose the Adobe PDF setting you want to use.** (See Figure 5-3.) Note that if you created presets either in InDesign CS2 or any other CS2 application, the preset appears in the Adobe PDF Preset pull-down menu. In Figure 5-3, a preset that was developed in Adobe Illustrator is selected from the menu list.

5. **Export to PDF.** Click Export to complete the file export to PDF.

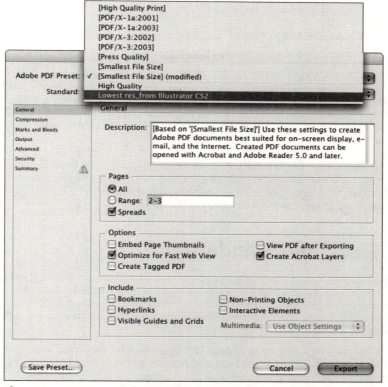

Figure 5-3: PDF presets that you develop in any CS2 application appear in the Adobe PDF Preset menu when you export to PDF.

In InDesign CS2 and all the other CS2 applications, any preset developed in Acrobat Distiller or any other CS2 application is available to all CS2 applications including Adobe Acrobat Professional and Acrobat Distiller for the purpose of creating PDF files.

When you choose a setting that contains options for downsampling images, the resultant PDF document becomes a smaller file than when you create PDFs with settings where you apply no downsampling.

Cross-Reference   To learn more about exporting to PDF from Adobe InDesign CS2, see Chapter 38.

Another method you have for repurposing PDF documents lies in Adobe Acrobat Professional. You can open a PDF in Acrobat and select the Advanced ➪ PDF Optimizer menu command. The PDF Optimizer provides you with options for downsampling images as well as any other options for reducing file sizes. In addition to using the PDF Optimizer, you can also set up a Batch Sequence to optimize a collection of PDF files together using the same amounts of downsampling and applying other attribute choices.

Cross-Reference   To learn more about PDF Optimizer and creating Batch Sequences, see Chapter 29.

Repurposing documents is one of the true benefits of an efficient workflow. If you relied on other methods to repurpose a document from print to Web hosting, you must open files in Adobe Photoshop CS2, downsample files, and save them as new files to disk. After downsampling the images, you must open your layout application and relink all the image links. Obviously, using PDF as your output format provides you with a much more efficient alternative when you need to repurpose documents.

Note   Downsampling an image is the process of reducing file size by lowering the image's resolution (for example, taking a 300 ppi [pixels per inch] image and lowering the resolution to 72 ppi). You can downsample images in Adobe Photoshop and Adobe Acrobat, as well as use methods for downsampling from within Adobe GoLive.

Setting Workflow Standards

Whether you're an independent designer or you own or manage an agency, there are some considerations you should think about when designing your workflow. Too often, individuals or managers become subordinates to vendors, contracting professionals, or production personnel instead of taking control of their environment and encouraging others to fit within their workflow schema.

Instead of having others dictate or impose standards on you, try to give some thought to the way you want to work and how you want others to fit into your workflow. The following sections offer some suggestions you may want to consider.

Set standards for the tools used in your workflow

When hiring employees or working with contract artists, ask people to use the same tools you use in your workflow. If you use all the programs in the Adobe Creative Suite, be certain to hire employees skilled in these tools and make it a necessary condition for all your contracting artists and professionals to use the same tools. The time to train people who fit in your workflow is dramatically reduced if they're skilled in using the same tools.

Use vendors who support the tools you use

We often hear design professionals complain, "My print shop or vendor doesn't like to print from InDesign" (or another product). Having your vendor dictate what tools you use to perform your work is like the tail wagging the dog. After all, who is paying whom the money?

If your vendor doesn't support one of the tools you use, and you produce even a moderate amount of work, tell your vendor that if they don't support your selection of software, you'll be forced to use the competitor across the street. Try this on for size and see how many vendors turn you down.

Devote time to ongoing training

Creative professionals today are in a category similar to other professionals like medical workers, legal workers, psychologists, educators, and people in all kinds of professions that deal with government regulations. All these professions require continuing education units (CEU) to sustain licensure or maintain compliance with changing laws. As a design professional, you work in an ever-changing world of high technology. The world of the creative professional in some ways changes more rapidly today than that of almost any other occupation. New software upgrades are occurring every 18 months. This rapid change related to the tools you use requires you and your staff to engage in ongoing training and education.

To help you work more effectively in your workflow, try to set up training sessions that you can provide in-house or with your vendors. You might approach a vendor and ask them to sponsor an evening session to introduce a new product upgrade. You can find many Adobe professionals working in cities throughout the world who are willing and able to make visits to communities for speaking sessions without charging any fees. You can also ask local community colleges and universities to sponsor similar events and hold workshops and classes on products you use in your workflow. In large agencies, you can employ policies and provide time off for production artists to take classes and workshops benefiting your workflow.

Develop a paradigm for managing your projects

Sometimes locating files and making file edits takes more time than designing a new piece from scratch. To avoid time lost due to searching for files, converting old files to newer versions, and locating fonts and assets contained in design projects, try to spend some time managing your artwork in an effective manner. With the CS2 programs, you can use Adobe Bridge to organize all files located on hard drives and networked servers. For archived files as well as the files you manage in Bridge, use Adobe Acrobat and create data sheets using form fields. You can use the form template to fill in new forms for each project as well as the source and location for the files. Try to complete a form for every project and supply all pertinent information on the data sheet related to personnel involved in the project and all related software used to create the project designs. Figure 5-4 illustrates a sample form created in Adobe Illustrator CS2 and opened in Adobe Acrobat where form fields were added.

Tip Files saved from Adobe Illustrator CS2 as a native AI file with the Create PDF Compatible File option selected in the Illustrator Options dialog box can be opened directly in any Adobe Acrobat viewer including Adobe Reader.

As you can see in Figure 5-4, the agency personnel and contracting vendors are all listed by name. A separate document contains all the contact information for the contractors and vendors. The software and version numbers of the applications used in the project are listed, as well as design specifics such as fonts and colors. The fields in the lower-right corner describe the location of CD-ROMs and DVDs where the completed files are stored. You can store PDF forms like this on a network server and use Acrobat Search to search for them or you can create a collection where forms are searched using Adobe Bridge. In a matter of minutes, any employee in a company including new employees can locate the files for any given project.

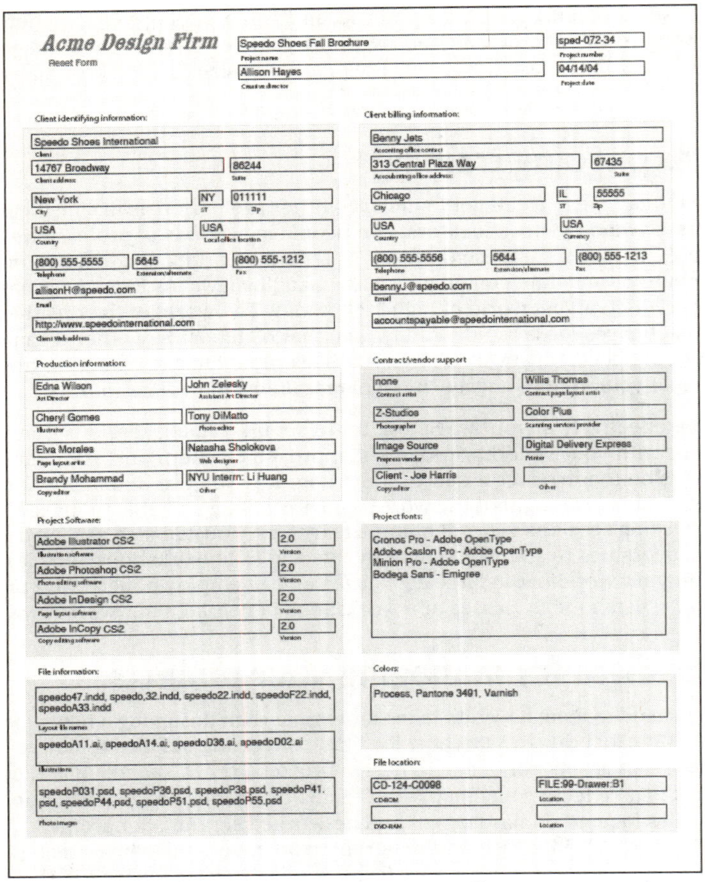

Acme Design Firm
Reset Form

Speedo Shoes Fall Brochure — Project name
sped-072-34 — Project number
Allison Hayes — Creative director
04/14/04 — Project date

Client identifying information:

Speedo Shoes International — Client
14767 Broadway — Client address; 86244 — Suite
New York — City; NY — ST; 011111 — Zip
USA — Country; USA — Local office location
(800) 555-5555 — Telephone; 5645 — Extension/alternate; (800) 555-1212 — Fax
allisonH@speedo.com — Email
http://www.speedointernational.com — Client Web address

Client billing information:

Benny Jets — Accounting office contact
313 Central Plaza Way — Accounting office address; 67435 — Suite
Chicago — City; IL — ST; 55555 — Zip
USA — Country; USA — Currency
(800) 555-5556 — Telephone; 5644 — Extension/alternate; (800) 555-1213 — Fax
bennyJ@speedo.com — Email
accountspayable@speedointernational.com

Production information:

Edna Wilson — Art Director; John Zelesky — Assistant Art Director
Cheryl Gomes — Illustrator; Tony DiMatto — Photo editor
Elva Morales — Page layout artist; Natasha Sholokova — Web designer
Brandy Mohammad — Copy editor; NYU Intern: Li Huang — Other

Contract/vendor support:

none — Contract artist; Willis Thomas — Contract page layout artist
Z-Studios — Photographer; Color Plus — Scanning services provider
Image Source — Prepress vendor; Digital Delivery Express — Printer
Client - Joe Harris — Copy editor; Other

Project Software:

Adobe Illustrator CS2 — Illustration software; 2.0 — Version
Adobe Photoshop CS2 — Photo editing software; 2.0 — Version
Adobe InDesign CS2 — Page layout software; 2.0 — Version
Adobe InCopy CS2 — Copy editing software; 2.0 — Version

Project fonts:

Cronos Pro - Adobe OpenType
Adobe Caslon Pro - Adobe OpenType
Minion Pro - Adobe OpenType
Bodega Sans - Emigree

File information:

speedo47.indd, speedo,32.indd, speedo22.indd, speedoF22.indd, speedoA33.indd — Layout file names
speedoA11.ai, speedoA14.ai, speedoD36.ai, speedoD02.ai — Illustrations
speedoP031.psd, speedoP36.psd, speedoP38.psd, speedoP41.psd, speedoP44.psd, speedoP51.psd, speedoP55.psd — Photo images

Colors:

Process, Pantone 3491, Varnish

File location:

CD-124-C0098 — CD-ROM; FILE:99-Drawer:B1 — Location
DVD-RAM; Location

Figure 5-4: A sample form created in Adobe Illustrator CS2 and opened in Adobe Acrobat where form fields were added

Cross-Reference

For more information on using Adobe Bridge, see Chapter 7. For information on searching PDF documents, see Chapter 34.

You may find other helpful ideas that can assist you in managing your workflow and you may find other relevant information to add to data sheets. The most important issue at hand is realizing that a little time spent in managing and organizing your work always saves you more time when you need to rework files or produce new pieces for the same client.

Summary

- Efficient workflows help you work quickly and intelligently by reducing redundancy. Workflow standards can help you reduce time in training new workers.

- You have complete control over your internal workflow and what tools to use. Your workflow extends beyond your internal workflow and includes contractors and vendors.

- Adobe Creative Suite 2 is a complete workflow solution for creative professionals, whereby all document files are fully integrated throughout the programs. Applications help you update files, change design elements, and create different design versions.

- You use document repurposing when a file is designed for one output need and you're reworking the same file suited for a different output need.

- Independent design professionals and creative art department managers are advantaged when planning workflows and attracting others to conform to standards set by an individual or agency.

- When working with contract artists and vendors, you'll find it best to attract people who fit into your workflow rather than have others fit you into their workflow.

- Keeping accurate data sheets on client projects helps you save time in relocating files and provides quick access for revisiting projects from the same clients. You can manage your data sheets using Adobe Bridge or Acrobat Search.

- Continuing education is a necessary ingredient in a creative professional's work life. You can solicit help from vendors to support training sessions and utilize Adobe field specialists to help you stay abreast of new software upgrades.

✦ ✦ ✦

Creating Color-Managed Workflows

In This Chapter

Getting familiar with color profiles

Working with color in CS2 applications

Using profiles

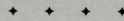

Perhaps the greatest challenge to design professionals is getting color on printed output to look like the color displayed on computer monitors. Artists can easily overcome common design dilemmas such as working around font problems, learning functional aspects of applications software, avoiding pitfalls related to image handling, and a host of other nuisances that hinder progress. But when it comes to color matching, the problems are more complicated and the solutions are often misunderstood and obscure.

Fortunately, Adobe has been working for several years on creating a common color engine that can be shared among imaging applications. The result of Adobe's efforts is exemplified in the CS2 applications. All the CS2 programs share the same Adobe Color Engine (ACE) that takes you one step closer to reliable color-matching among application documents, your computer monitor, and the output devices you use. In addition, once you set up your color-viewing workspace and color profiles you can use Adobe Bridge to synchronize the same color settings among all the CS2 applications. In this chapter, we cover some fundamental information related to color management among the Adobe CS2 applications.

Color management is a complex topic. An accurate description for identifying all the variables related to rendering reliable color is well beyond the scope of this chapter. For more-sophisticated descriptions, look for books written specifically to help you understand and manage color on computers and output devices.

 Cross-Reference For more information on managing color, see Deke McClelland's Wiley publication, *Adobe Photoshop CS2 Bible*. For information on synchronizing color among the CS2 applications, see Chapter 7.

Understanding Profiling

Color profiles provide the necessary information for the acquisition, display, and output of your images/documents. A color profile might be one you create through the use of calibration devices or ones you acquire from various equipment manufacturers. Color profiles interpret your images and documents in terms of display and output. Often, using a color profile can mean the difference between a printed image using the colors you expect on output and a rendered image with incorrect colors.

Tip

Color management is a complex issue. Fully comprehending the managing of color on computer systems and how color is reproduced on printing devices takes a lot of research and study. To learn more about color management, open Acrobat, click on the Search tool in the Acrobat toolbar, and type **color management** as your search criteria. Click on Search PDFs on the Internet in the Search pane, and the Yahoo.com search engine reports all PDF documents on the Internet where color management is found. You can download many PDF documents that offer you definitions of terms and thoroughly explain color management.

Profiles in workflows

The design of production pieces can make use of several different color profiles. You may have one profile developed for your scanner when acquiring an image through the scanning process. A calibrated profile converts the reflective artwork on your scanner platen to digital form, which captures and translates color the best it can, creating a digital file that is a close rendition of the print you scanned. When you open your scanned image in a program like Photoshop, you use a calibrated profile for your monitor. The scanned image color space is converted to the monitor working space. This conversion is a temporary preview condition and does not change the data in your image. When you finish your editing session, you convert the monitor color to the output color using yet another profile for your output device. The converted color ideally translates the color space from what you see on your monitor to the color space of your printer; the color range you see on your monitor fits as close as possible to within the color space of your output device. Throughout the color-management workflow, you're converting color from one space to another using color profiles.

Calibrating color

Software applications provide you with simplistic tools for calibrating color. You have tools such as Adobe Gamma installed on Windows to calibrate your monitor for white balance, gamma, black point, and so on. On Mac OS X (Panther and Tiger), the operating system provides you with tools to calibrate your monitor. On a more sophisticated level, you can purchase calibration systems that create monitor color profiles and output profiles for you printing devices. Using hardware devices for calibrating color is much more sophisticated than relying on the software tools that Adobe and Apple provide.

In some circumstances, you can use profiles that come with the installation of the CS2 applications. Profiles designed for four-color process printing on coated stock are generic and often do a reasonable job matching color from screen to press. As the lowest cost option, you can use simple software monitor-calibration tools and get fairly close to the kind of output you want on four-color process printing. However, if you're particular about color, and if your output varies to a range of devices including composite color printers, then you may want to invest in calibration equipment suited to create monitor and printer profiles for your workflow.

"But I don't want to spend $3,000 for that kind of equipment!" is often the cry we hear from creative professionals. Here's an analogy to help drive home the point. Ted wants a Mercedes. Kelly wants a Ferrari. However, neither of us has enough in our bank accounts to purchase the vehicles. Hence, we don't get what we want. To bring this home to you, if you're struggling with color and you haven't purchased a calibration system, don't complain; you're not going to get what you want — it's just that simple!

Acquiring profiles

If the thought of spending thousands of dollars to calibrate your system doesn't sit well with you, you have some alternatives. In large production centers, you can use a single calibration system to calibrate all the hardware in your environment. With this method, you need only a single calibration tool to create profiles for all the monitors and in-house output devices. Calibration tools are not like software, where you need to license the tool for each user.

Independent graphic designers can solicit assistance from their service centers. Most print shops and service bureaus have calibration devices on hand. You can ask technicians to visit you to calibrate your monitor and provide you with the profiles they created for their equipment.

When you acquire profiles for output devices, you must install the profiles in the proper location on your hard drive. For Mac users, copy the profiles to `Hard Drive/<user name>/Library/Application Support/Adobe/Color/Profiles/Recommended`. On Windows XP and 2000, copy acquired profiles or profiles you create as a result of your calibration system to `C:\Windows\System32\Spool\Drivers\Color`. When you install profiles in these locations, the profiles are accessible from all the CS2 programs. In Figure 6-1, you can see a profile accessed in the Photoshop CS2 Print dialog box.

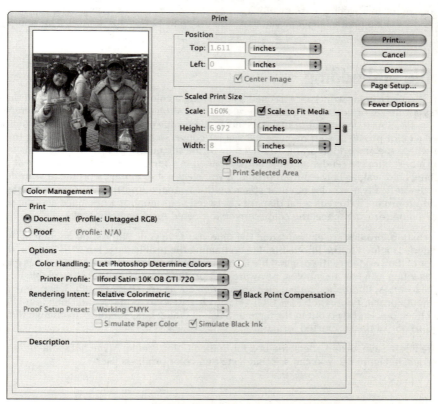

Figure 6-1: When placed in the proper location on your hard drive, the profile is accessible from all the CS2 applications.

> ### Using online profile development resources
>
> Discover a problem and someone is likely to provide a solution — for a fee, of course. If your problem is color profiling, then there are some online solution providers who can help by providing you a color profile to use both with in-house equipment and when using service centers. Some of the lowest cost centers such as Costco, Sam's Club, Office Depot, and others are providing photographic prints at incredibly low costs. Many of these mega-outlets can offer you photographic prints for less money than the cost of ink and paper for your desktop color printers. These stores use high-end photographic digital lab equipment like Fuji Frontier, Noritsu, Agfa D-Lab, Lightjet, Durst, and Chromira to name a few.
>
> At $.19 a print or less, you wouldn't expect to see a high-end service technician editing your Photoshop files to get the color right, But what you can find is a service center that has developed color profiles for most professional photographic printing systems and services clients worldwide. You can acquire color profiles for a huge range of systems and paper stocks by logging on to www.drycreekphoto.com. On the Dry Creek Web site you can download free color profiles custom developed for the most common equipment and paper stock.
>
> If you need a custom profile developed for your own printing equipment or for equipment and stock not within its current library, you can commission Dry Creek Photo to develop a custom profile for you. As of this writing, custom profiles are created for $50 for a single profile with no updates and $99 for a printer/paper profile that includes up to 12 updates at no cost for one year.

Profile embedding

When you use a color workspace defined by selecting a color profile, you can embed the profile in your image or document. As a general rule, you should opt for profile embedding whenever possible. As a document prints, it assumes the profile of the printing device. When you embed a color profile in your documents, a color conversion takes place, translating the color within the embedded profile to the color within the output profile. In effect, this translation is a best effort to render all the color contained in your document with the closest matching color values in the output profile. If you elect not to embed a profile in your document, theoretically, the color monitor space on the system outputting your file converts to the output profile. If there is great disparity between your monitor workspace and the service center's monitor workspace, the color conversion could result in color shifts.

In Photoshop, profiles are embedded at the time you save your Photoshop document. A little bit of code is added to the Photoshop file containing the profile data. For RGB images, the amount of data added to the original file is minimal. With CMYK images, the file sizes can grow as much as a few megabytes. Be aware that profile embedding is only available for certain file formats. Photoshop native files are supported, as are TIFF, EPS, JPEG, Large Document Format, Photoshop PDF, PICT (Mac), PICT Resource (Mac), and DCS (1 and 2) files. If the check box is grayed out in the Save or Save As dialog box, you need to change the file format to one of the supported formats.

Choose File ⇨ Save As and check the box for Embed Color Profile: *Name of Profile to Be Embedded*. In Figure 6-2, you can see that a custom color profile is used.

Figure 6-2: Check the box to embed a profile for all image formats supporting color profile embedding.

In Illustrator and InDesign, you assign profiles from a menu command. In both programs, choose Edit ➪ Assign Profile(s), and the Assign Profile(s) dialog box opens. In Figure 6-3, you can see that, in Illustrator, the choices are limited to three options. Choose Don't Color Manage This Document when you want color management turned off for the current file. Choose Working CMYK to assign the monitor working space. Choose Profile to select one of the installed color profiles used by your output devices.

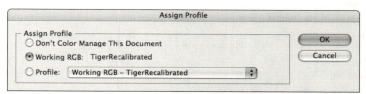

Figure 6-3: The Assign Profile dialog box, where profile assignment is made

In InDesign, you have more options for assigning profiles, as well as a preview check box where you can preview the results of profile assignment. Use the same Edit ➪ Assign Profiles menu command, and the Assign Profiles dialog box, shown in Figure 6-4, opens.

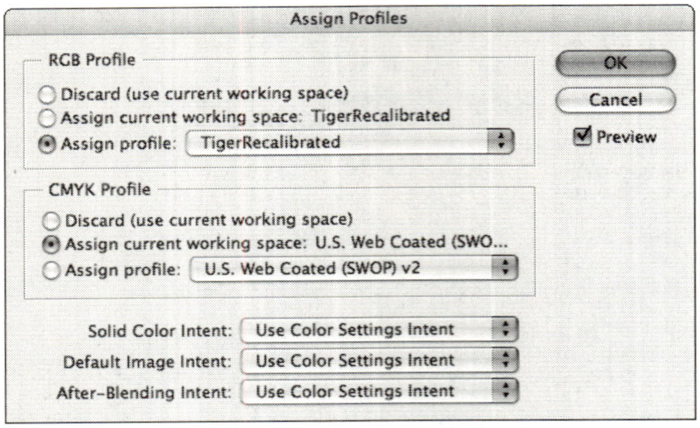

Part II ✦ Getting Started with Design Workflows

Figure 6-4: InDesign's Assign Profiles dialog box

InDesign enables you to assign a working profile (RGB Profile) and an output Profile (CMYK Profile). In addition, you can also make choices for the rendering intent. Finally, check the Preview check box, and the document pages behind the dialog box dynamically reflect the color profile you select in the Assign Profiles dialog box.

In the case of both Illustrator and InDesign, when you save the documents, the assigned profiles are saved with the file.

Profile mismatching

When you embed or assign a color profile to a document and your document is opened on a computer using another profile, there is a profile mismatch. When such mismatches occur, Illustrator, InDesign, and Photoshop all open dialog boxes to offer you some options on how to handle the mismatches. In Figure 6-5, you can see a file opening in Photoshop where a profile mismatch occurs.

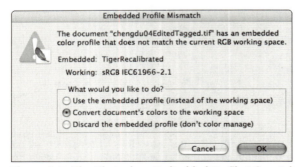

Figure 6-5: The Photoshop Embedded Profile Mismatch dialog box

The options available in the Missing Profile dialog box include the following:

+ **Leave as is (don't color manage):** The option description is self-explanatory. Selecting this option leaves the image alone without converting color.

+ **Assign working RGB:** This option assigns the current RGB workspace you've identified in your color settings. Adjacent to the description, you can see the current RGB workspace listed. In Figure 6-5, the workspace is sRGB IEC61966-2.1.

+ **Assign profile:** From the pull-down menu, select from the installed profiles on your system.

What to do when the Missing Profile dialog box opens is confusing to most people. As a general rule, the best option in a color-managed workflow is to convert color to calibrated systems. Therefore, when you know your RGB workspace is calibrated or you use the generic Adobe RGB (1998) profile, choose the Assign working RGB option. This choice converts the color embedded in the Photoshop image to the working space you use. In essence, all the color potentially assigned in the original image converts to the best representation that your current monitor space can assume.

In Illustrator, a similar dialog box used for color-profile assignment opens as a warning dialog box, informing you of the color mismatch. In Figure 6-6, Illustrator's Missing Profile dialog box opens as a warning when a color mismatch is encountered. Notice the similarities between the Mismatch Profile and the Assign Profile dialog boxes. The options choices are self-explanatory.

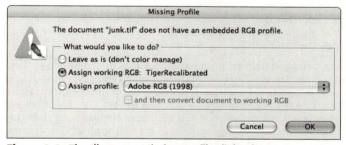

Figure 6-6: The Illustrator Missing Profile dialog box

If you open a file that was saved with an embedded profile different than your current working space, there is an embedded profile mismatch. The Embedded Profile Mismatch dialog box handles your monitor workspace if a mismatch occurs. When an embedded profile mismatch occurs, you have a choice for using the embedded profile instead of your current working space, convert colors from the embedded profile to your current working space, or discard the profile and not color manage the document. If you have your monitor calibrated and work in a color-managed workflow, your choice when you see the dialog box in Figure 6-7 should always be to convert the color to your current workspace.

After making a decision for your monitor workspace and clicking OK, another dialog box, almost identical to the previous dialog box, opens and asks about the CMYK workspace. Make a choice, click OK, and the document opens, either discarding color profiles or converting color per your choices in the dialog boxes.

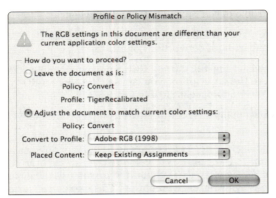

Figure 6-7: When a profile mismatch occurs in InDesign, the first warning dialog box addresses mismatches in RGB color.

Color Management in the CS2 Applications

When you want to manage color among the CS2 applications, you can benefit greatly from Adobe's Common Color Architecture. The profile management and assignment is similar among all the Adobe CS2 programs, and when you understand how to manage color in one program, you can easily apply the same settings across all the programs. Each of the applications begins by addressing the color settings via menu commands.

With the CS2 applications, you need only set up the color settings in one program, then use the Bridge to synchronize color among the remaining programs. Typically, Photoshop is the tool you most often use for adjusting color settings, but because of the consistency among programs, you can use any one of the CS2 programs to adjust the settings. Color settings are identical in Photoshop, Illustrator, and InDesign. A few variances occur among these programs and Acrobat and GoLive. To adjust color settings in the CS2 applications, choose Edit ➪ Color Settings. Acrobat's color settings are adjusted in the Preferences dialog box.

Adjusting color settings

You can address Photoshop color settings by choosing Edit ➪ Color Settings. The Color Settings dialog box shown in Figure 6-8 opens. Click More Options and the dialog box expands to offer additional settings. After you click More Options, it changes to Fewer Options. The options choices you have for managing color in any CS2 application include the following:

The first item you encounter that is new to the CS2 applications is a message at the top of the Color Settings dialog box. If you make color settings in one CS2 application and different color settings in another CS2 application, the colors are unsynchronized. When colors are or are not synchronized the message at the top of the Color Settings dialog box informs you of the synchronization status. In Figure 6-8 you can see the message reported as Unsynchronized.

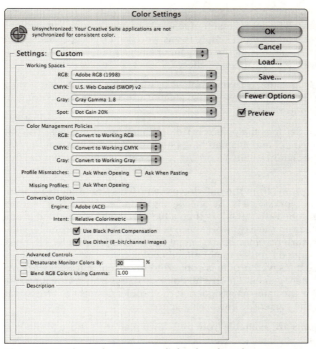

Figure 6-8: The Color Settings dialog box has the same appearance in Photoshop, Illustrator, and InDesign.

The first group is the Working Spaces where you select a color working space for your monitor. Ideally you want your monitor color to be as close to the color produced on a printing device. The four adjustments to make for your working space include:

- **RGB:** The RGB space defines what you see on your computer monitor. This space is commonly referred to as your *working space*. Because you perform most of your image editing on RGB images, you work in this color space before eventually converting to CMYK color for commercial printing. In some cases, you may leave images in RGB mode or not convert them to CMYK if the output device is an RGB device. Certain large-format inkjet printers, photo printers such as Fuji Frontier, and film recorders are best imaged from RGB files. If you have a calibrated monitor, use the profile created by your calibration equipment. If you plan on designing files for commercial output to imagesetters, platesetters, or press, use the Adobe RGB (1998) profile if your monitor is not calibrated. If your output is designed for screen and Web viewing, use sRGB IEC61966-2.1 as your monitor space.

- **CMYK:** This profile is used for the output device — typically a CMYK printing device for composite printing and press. If you are designing artwork for press, use the U.S. Web Coated (SWOP) v2 for printing in the U.S. If printing outside the U.S., use the model common to the area where you print your files. For example, use the Japan Color 2001 Coated when printing on coated stock in Japan. The settings you choose in this pull-down menu affect your color conversion when you convert color in Photoshop. If you prepare CMYK files for direct output or importing in other applications via the Image ⇨ Mode ⇨ CMYK Color menu command, Photoshop characterizes the color according to the output profile.

- **Gray:** The pull-down menu choices affect grayscale images only in terms of dot gain and gamma adjustments. The actual result of making changes among the available settings affects the dot gain on press. In simple terms, you can target grayscale images to print darker or lighter. By increasing the dot gain or the gamma, you darken the images. Decreasing the amounts has the opposite effects.

- **Spot:** The choices here are similar to the choices available for Gray, because the spot color separations are printed like gray plates. Making adjustments to the dot gain also results in darker and lighter images.

The next section in the Color Settings dialog box is Color-management policies. The choices here affect the profile management and mismatching behavior. You can instruct Photoshop to react to profile mismatches or ignore them according to the settings made from the pull-down menus:

- **RGB:** You have three options from the pull-down menu. This first item deals with the RGB workspace. If your workspace is the one we suggested earlier in this section in "the RGB section — Adobe RGB (1998) — then a file saved with embedded profiles using any other profile from the RGB workspace is a mismatch. Accordingly, you can instruct Photoshop to turn off color management for working spaces by selecting Off, choose Preserve Embedded Profiles to not affect a color conversion, or select Convert to Working RGB where the saved profile is converted to the current RGB working profile. Turning off color management ignores all color profiling. Preserving Embedded Profiles keeps the color the same as assigned in the profile. Convert to Working RGB converts the color to the current RGB working space.

- **CMYK:** The same options are available from pull-down menus as those found in the RGB pull-down menus.

- **Gray:** The same options are available from the same kinds of pull-down menus.

- **Profile Mismatches: Ask When Opening:** When you select this check box, a dialog box prompts you when a mismatch occurs. For workflow environments, it's a good idea to check the box so you know when a color conversion is about to take place.

- **Profile Mismatches: Ask When Pasting:** If you copy data from one file and paste it into another file, you can copy an image with one embedded profile and paste the data into a document with another identified profile. Checking this box opens a dialog box alerting you to the color conversion.

- **Missing Profiles:** If you open legacy files or files that were not color-managed or have no profile assignment, you can instruct Photoshop to offer you an option for managing color in the opened files. A dialog box opens where you can assign profiles as the documents open in the Photoshop window.

- **Conversion Options:** You have choices for using the Adobe Color Engine (ACE) or color engines that your operating system supplies. For handling color among the CS2 applications, use the Adobe Color Engine.

- **Intent:** There are four standard options related to color intent. *Intent* refers to what happens when color is converted, specifically in terms of white points and color equivalents. The options choices for intent include the following:

  - **Perceptual:** Perceptual preserves the overall color appearance through the process of changing colors in the source color space so they fit inside the destination color space. This option is a particularly good choice when you have a number of colors that reside outside the destination color space. The color equivalents are matched as close as possible.

- **Saturation:** As the name implies, Saturation tries to preserve the most vivid colors from the source space to the destination space. You might select this option when you want to convert PowerPoint slides, Excel graphs and charts, and other documents where vivid colors are apparent.

- **Relative Colormetric:** This option tries to closely match the white point in the destination space with the same whites in the source space. After converting white, the other colors are matched as closely as possible. If you're pondering what space to use between Perceptual and Relative, use this option, because the whites are more likely to be reproduced accurately.

- **Absolute Colormetric:** This option is an effort to simulate the color including white point for one output device to a second device. If a white in the source document is a bluish white and the destination is a yellowish white, the conversion adds more cyan to simulate the cooler white, thus rendering a closer approximation of the original image.

♦ **Use Black Point Compensation:** As the intents take care of the whites in converting color from source images to destination images, the separate option for black point compensation takes care of black ink conversion. Without compensating for black when converting colors, you can end up with muddy non-rich blacks. As a matter of default, keep this check box checked.

♦ **Use Dither (8-bit/channel images):** 8-bit channel images are 24-bit color images (8-bits per channel for 3 channels). If color transitions are stepped or crude, you may need to smooth them out. This check box does just that. Keep the check box enabled for all color conversion.

♦ **Desaturate Monitor Colors By:** By default, some bright colors tend to appear somewhat flat on your computer monitor when using the Adobe RGB workspace. To render the images more true to appearance and prevent any misleading representations, keep this check box enabled.

♦ **Blend RGB Colors Using Gamma:** When colors are blended in Photoshop like image data appearing on one layer over another layer, the blending of the colors can show visible problems in shadows and on the edges of the layers. If you see visible problems like this, check this box.

After you make your settings adjustments, click Save. The Save dialog box opens and the proper folder on your hard drive is targeted for the saved file. Type a name for the color-management setting and click Save. This color-management setting is then recognized by all the other CS2 applications and Adobe Bridge.

Synchronizing color settings

After adjusting settings in Photoshop, Illustrator, or InDesign, open the Bridge. Regardless of which program you use to make settings adjustments, choose File ➪ Browse to open the Bridge window.

In Adobe Bridge, choose Edit ➪ Creative Suite Color Settings. The Suite Color Settings dialog box shown in Figure 6-9 appears. At the top of the dialog box you can see of the color settings are synchronized. If they are not synchronized, select the color-management setting you saved after making the settings adjustments and click Apply. Settings are now identical in all the CS2 applications.

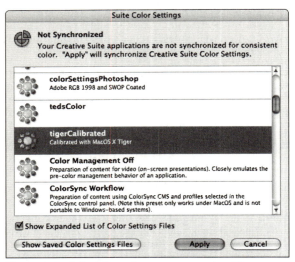

Figure 6-9: Select the color-management setting you want to use and click Apply to synchronize settings across all CS2 applications.

 For more information on working with Adobe Bridge, see Chapter 7.

Swapping color settings

If you create a settings file and click Save, the file is accessible to all the CS2 applications and to other users when you provide them with the profile. You can post a color-management setting on your network server, e-mail the file, or copy it to a media disk. Other users in your workflow can copy the file to the folder on their computers where all other color settings are saved. See the section "Acquiring Profiles" for the precise location where profiles are saved on the Macintosh and Windows. Once added to the proper folder, other users need only open Adobe Bridge and synchronize the color as explained in the section "Synchronizing Settings."

Printing with Profiles

All the information related to profiling and managing color is fine in a theoretical environment, but when it comes to the real world, you must implement all the work you do in setting up your environment and observe the results. Ideally, you would have a color-calibration device and calibrate your computer monitor and the output device for precise results.

When you use a color-calibration system, you calibrate your monitor and the output device and measure colors as they lay down on the substrate you use for your prints. You develop the profile for a given printer and a given paper. Once you develop the profiles, you edit your images according to the monitor working space so the color values on your monitor come within a predictable range on your output. In essence, the monitor and output device are in parity in terms of color.

To print an image from a program like Photoshop, you would follow these steps after calibrating your system:

STEPS: Printing Composite Color Using Calibrated Profiles

1. **Adjust the color settings.** Set up your color settings according to the calibrations you performed. Be certain to choose the monitor working space you used to calibrate your monitor.

2. **Print with Preview.** With your document open in Photoshop, choose File ➪ Print with Preview.

3. **Target the print for color management.** From the Printer Profile pull-down menu select Color Management from the menu options. Refer to Figure 6-1 to see the Print dialog box accessed when selecting Print with Preview.

4. **Select the color profile created for the printer and paper.** In the Profile pull-down menu, select the profile created for the paper.

5. **Select the intent.** Select the intent from the menu options for Intent.

6. **Select print options for the target printer.** If you're printing to composite color devices, you have options for your printer via the print driver, as shown in Figure 6-10. Various color settings, paper types, speed for printing, and so on are options choices in the Print dialog box. Choose the options from the Print Settings (Mac) or Properties (Windows).

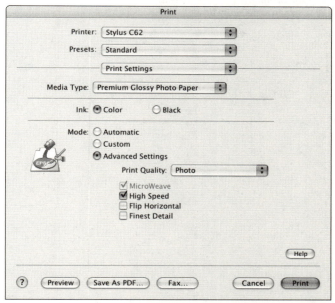

Figure 6-10: Set the print options from available settings defined by your print driver.

If you don't have a calibration system, you can run experiments using software tools to calibrate your monitor and test the output results. If you use this method, be ready to run tests many times before settling on a profile that works consistently for your printer.

Cross-Reference For more information on printing from Photoshop and the other CS2 applications, see Chapters 37 and 38.

Summary

- ✦ You can use color profiles to consistently reproduce color in your workflow among input devices, your viewing space, and your output equipment.
- ✦ Color calibration is optimum when using special tools to calibrate your computer monitor and output devices.
- ✦ You can acquire output profiles from service providers and install them on your computer.
- ✦ When profiles don't match, it's best to convert color to your calibrated workspace.
- ✦ The Creative Suite applications use a common color engine developed by Adobe Systems.
- ✦ You apply color synchronization in Adobe Bridge.
- ✦ You can share color profiles and color settings that you developed in one CS2 application with other users in your workflow.

✦ ✦ ✦

Using Adobe Bridge

In Adobe CS2, the Adobe Photoshop File Browser is no longer available. What used to be the File Browser in Photoshop has been reengineered as an enhanced File Browser for all Adobe CS2 programs and documents now called Adobe Bridge. With the Adobe Bridge you can organize all CS2 documents, version documents, learn tips and techniques on all the CS2 applications, and convert multiple camera raw images with different settings for saving and editing in Adobe Photoshop. You can also download stock photos from the Internet, and synchronize color management settings across all the CS2 programs, including GoLive CS2 documents. In short, the Adobe Bridge is the center of the CS2 universe from where you control, manage, and maintain all your applications documents as well as enjoy some nifty new features.

 Adobe Bridge is new in the Creative Suite 2 applications therefore all the following material in this chapter deals with brand new features.

Getting Familiar with the Bridge Workspace

If you are a Photoshop user, you are certainly familiar with the Photoshop File Browser. The Bridge is a tool much like the File Browser, but it is not dependent on any application running when you open the Bridge. It's really another program installed with your Creative Suite applications.

Adobe Bridge comes with both the Standard and Premium editions of the Creative Suite as well as with an individual copy of Photoshop CS2, Illustrator CS2, or InDesign CS2. Adobe Bridge is not included when you purchase a single copy of Acrobat Professional.

 Adobe Acrobat Professional 7 includes the Organizer tool that works in some ways similar to the Bridge. Acrobat's Organizer is built into the program and is used exclusively for managing PDF documents in Acrobat. For more information on Acrobat's Organizer, see Chapter 9.

✦ ✦ ✦ ✦

In This Chapter

Understanding the Bridge environment

Managing application documents

Using metadata

Using the Bridge search engine

Acquiring Stock Photos

Working with Version Cue

Using application services

Editing camera raw images

Managing color in Adobe Bridge

Using the Bridge Center

Running slide shows in Bridge

✦ ✦ ✦ ✦

To open the Bridge, follow these steps:

STEPS: Launch the Bridge

1. **Double-click the program icon.** Locate the Adobe Bridge program icon or the program alias and double-click to launch the Bridge. Note that this method of launch is necessary when you work in Acrobat Professional or when you work without any other CS2 application open.

2. **Use a menu command in a CS2 program.** If you have Adobe Photoshop, Adobe Illustrator, Adobe InDesign or Adobe GoLive open, select File ➪ Browse. The Bridge opens in the foreground while the application from which the Bridge was launched remains open in the background. Using either method (step 1 or step 2) for launching the Bridge opens the Bridge window as shown in Figure 7-1.

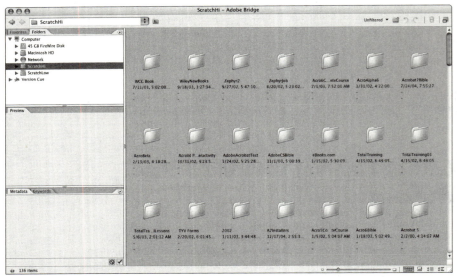

Figure 7-1: You can launch the Bridge from the program icon or from any CS2 program except Adobe Acrobat.

Why does Acrobat have a different organization tool?

Adobe Acrobat is the odd animal on the CS farm. Acrobat was developed and released before the CS programs. If you permit us to speculate a moment, it is our belief that the development teams sometimes don't work in tandem when they upgrade the programs. Inasmuch as this release of the Creative Suite brings together more consistent interoperability between the programs than ever before, there still remain some areas that can be fine-tuned — such as Acrobat supporting the Bridge.

A second reason for the difference between Acrobat's support for the Bridge compared to the other CS programs is that Acrobat is the one program more often sold apart from other Adobe imaging applications. Adobe implemented the Organizer in Acrobat to provide a file browser type utility for those users working with business programs who are not likely to purchase any of the CS programs.

As the CS programs evolve you may see Acrobat supporting the Bridge from a menu command like the other CS programs. Apart from launch from within the program, the Bridge does support organizing, viewing, and editing metadata in PDF files.

Cross-Reference

For information on editing metadata, see the section "Working with metadata."

Using the Bridge Tools

The Bridge has a number of tools and menu commands to perform all the tasks contained from within the Bridge environment. On the left side of the Bridge window you see the main components as shown in Figure 7-2.

206   Part II ✦ **Getting Started with Design Workflows**

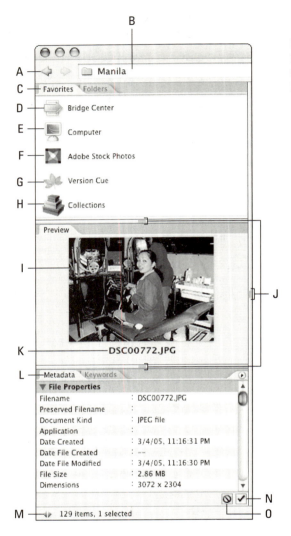

Figure 7-2: The left side of the Bridge offers many tools and options for working with Bridge tasks.

The Bridge components contained in the left panel include:

A Navigation arrows: As you view different folders, you can click the left arrow to view the previously viewed folder or the right arrow to trace your steps forward. Note that the right arrow becomes active only when you have first visited a previous folder by clicking the left arrow.

B Look In menu: The Look In menu is a pull-down menu that offers you quick navigation on your hard drive hierarchy, items in the favorites tab, and a history of recently viewed folders.

C **Favorites/Folders:** Two tabs appear at the top of the left pane. The Favorites items include the items detailed in D through H below. When you click the Folders tab, you can navigate your hard drive by opening folders viewed in a hierarchy containing root and nested folders.

The Bridge General Preferences determine what appears in the Favorites tab. You press ⌘/Ctrl+K to open Bridge preferences and click General in the left pane. Look for the section in the right called Favorite Items. The check boxes determine what is shown in the Favorites tab.

D **Bridge Center:** Bridge Center provides quick access to recently viewed files, tips on working with the CS programs, options for synchronizing color, RSS viewing of news-feeds and Adobe Studio information, and access to help documents.

E **Computer (My Computer):** Click the icon and you navigate to the root location where your boot drive, external drives, CD drives, and network places are accessed.

F **Adobe Stock Photos:** Click the Adobe Stock Photos and the pane changes to offer options where you can select and search more than 230,000 royalty free stock photos. You can download low-resolution images to prepare comps. You can return to purchase the images later in high resolution that you intend to use in your final layout.

G **Version Cue:** You can start a new Version Cue project directly from within the Bridge.

H **Collections:** Collections are designed to contain custom folders you create where you can copy all the assets for a project to a given folder and easily locate the folder from within the Collections list.

I **Preview:** Click an image in the content area to the right of the left pane and then selected document appears in the Preview pane. Note that previews for documents are provided for all CS application documents but not for non-Adobe files.

J **Separator bars:** You can drag the three separator bars to resize the panes. Resizing the Preview pane shows a larger thumbnail preview of the document before you open it.

K **Document title:** The filename is reported for the current selected file. You cannot edit he filename in the Preview pane.

L **Metadata:** Metadata is information that an authoring application automatically supplies. This information includes the creation and modification date as well as the custom data you can add to the file, such as copyright information or author name. The metadata are displayed for the current selected file in the content area.

M **Show/hide panels:** The two opposing arrows toggle views for showing and hiding the left side of the Bridge window. You can collapse the pane on the left to create more area to view in the content area, where the thumbnail views are contained. To the right of the Show/hide panel buttons is a description of the total number of files contained in the selected folder and the total number of files currently selected in the content area.

N **Apply:** Click the Apply checkmark to apply an edit made in the Bridge to a file's metadata.

O **Cancel:** Click Cancel if you edit metadata in a document and want to cancel all changes you made in the Metadata pane.

The right side of the Bridge window (content area shown in Figure 7-3) occupies more space by default. You use it to view thumbnail images of all CS2 application documents and PDF files. Non-Adobe documents are shown in the window, but previews are not shown. The viewing options and tools in the content area include:

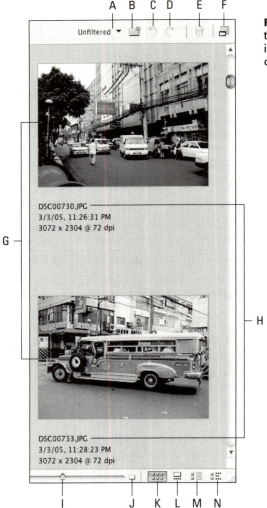

Figure 7-3: The content area contains thumbnail images and tools for viewing image previews of the CS2 application documents.

A **Filter menu:** From the menu, you have options for sorting files viewed in the Content area by no rating or by any one of five different ratings (identified as stars) that you can individually assign to files. Additionally, you can sort files by labels that are also individually user defined. When a document thumbnail is selected in the content area, five tiny stars appear below the thumbnail. Click a tiny star and the icon becomes larger as shown in Figure 7-4. In the figure you can see several documents tagged with different stars and one image with the default rating.

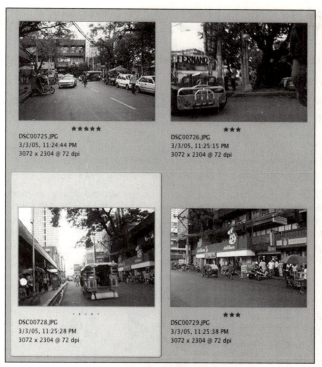

Figure 7-4: Four files are rated. At the top left are 5 stars, top right 3 stars, bottom left is the default rating, and bottom right with 3 stars.

- B **Create new folder:** As the icon implies, clicking on it creates a new folder. If you have a folder open, the new folder is created within the current active folder.

- C **Rotate left:** Select a thumbnail in the content area and click the Rotate Left tool. The image is rotated left.

- D **Rotate Right:** Rotates the selected thumbnail right.

- E **Delete:** The familiar trash icon denotes deleting a file when you click it. First select an image in the content area, a range of images, or a folder, and then click the trash icon.

- F **Switch to Compact Mode:** Compact mode is like minimizing a document window. Click the icon and the Bridge window reduces in size and nests itself in the lower left corner of your monitor. Click the icon again and the window expands to the last view.

- G **Document thumbnails:** The content area displays thumbnail images for all Adobe CS application documents. A description for each file is reported below the thumbnail image for filename, creation date and time, and resolution for the number of pixels and dpi (dots per inch).

- H **Filenames:** The filenames are editable in the content area. Click a filename and wait a moment for the I-beam cursor to appear.

- **I Zoom slider:** Move the slider to the left to zoom out of the thumbnail view and to the right to zoom in. Click the opposing icons to view the smallest (hidden in the figure) and largest (J) sizes respectively.
- **J Largest thumbnail size:** Zooms to the largest thumbnail size.
- **K Thumbnails view:** Displays the thumbnail view as shown in Figure 7-3.
- **L Filmstrip view:** Shows the thumbnails at the bottom of the content area in a horizontal row like a filmstrip while the selected thumbnail appears above the filmstrip in a larger size.
- **M Details view:** The thumbnails are shown in a vertical single column with detail information such as file size; document format, modified date; and with photos — data associated with the camera settings are displayed.
- **N Versions and Alternates view:** Displays all versions and alternates adjacent to a column list like the Details view. Click the Alternates tab at the top of the file list to display the Alternate view. In Alternate view you can create alternate groups containing files from different folders. Click Version View at the top of the file list to display files with the versions appearing in thumbnail views. Version thumbnails are shown in the right column as shown in Figure 7-5.

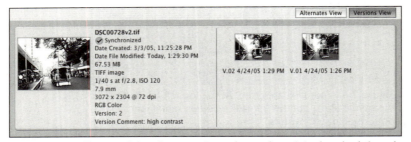

Figure 7-5: A file containing three versions shows the original at the left and two version thumbnails in the right pane. The Versions tab is selected at the top of the Bridge window.

Saving Bridge workspaces

When you practice a little using the Bridge to view files and mark documents with stars, you can easily understand simple methods for sorting and organizing all the content you use for a given project. When you create certain views such as navigating to a folder and sorting documents by stars and/or labels, you may want to return to the last view obtained in the Bridge. Fortunately, Adobe anticipated such needs and offers you a method of saving workspaces much like you save workspaces in other CS applications. To gain some understanding for viewing, sorting, and saving workspaces, look over the following steps:

STEPS: Saving a Custom Workspace

1. **Launch the Bridge.** Open the Bridge from the application icon or from the Browse menu command in the File menu in any CS2 program.
2. **Open a folder containing assets for a job.** If you have an InDesign project where all your linked files are contained in the same folder, select the folder or use a folder of

Photoshop images. In the left pane in the Bridge, click the Folders tab and open the folder you want to use.

3. **Mark files with stars.** Click on a thumbnail image in the content area and click on one of the tiny stars appearing below the document thumbnail. If you want to rate multiple files at once, click a thumbnail and Shift+click a second thumbnail away from the first to select files in a contiguous group. Use the Command/Control key and click to select files in a noncontiguous group. When multiple files are selected, click a tiny star to rate all selected files with the same rating. As you rate documents with stars, keep in mind that when you sort the files you can sort according to all files with a given rating plus files with a higher rating. For example, you can sort according to two or more starts whereby all documents rated with two, three, four, and five starts are shown in the content area. Any documents rated below two stars are hidden when you select the menu command.

4. **Sort the rated documents.** Open the Filter pull-down menu and select a rating of your choice. Be certain that you have marked files with the rating equal to or greater than the rating you choose. In Figure 7-6, you can see files in a folder sorted according to one or more stars.

Figure 7-6: Files are sorted according to star ratings. Files that you do not mark are temporarily hidden from view in the content area.

5. **Size and position the Bridge window.** You can size the Bridge window by dragging the lower right corner of the window in to reduce the size or out to size the window larger. After sizing, click and drag the Bridge title bar to a location of your liking. When you save a workspace you can also save the window position.

6. **Save the Workspace.** From the top-level menu above the Bridge, choose Window ⇨ Workspace ⇨ Save Workspace. The Save Workspace dialog box shown in Figure 7-7 opens. Type a name for your workspace in the Name text box. From the pull-down menu select a Keyboard Shortcut. Your options are assigning F keys from F6 through F12. Note that the shortcut is ⌘/Ctrl+F. As shortcuts are used, they become grayed out when adding new workspaces. If you want the floating Window fixed to your current view, check the box for Save Window Location as Part of Workspace. Click Save when finished setting the attributes.

Figure 7-7: The Save Workspace dialog box offers options for saving the window position and assigning a keyboard shortcut to open your custom workspace.

7. **Return to defaults.** As you use the Bridge, you may want to leave your saved workspace and browse your hard drive for different files. You can return to the default workspace by choosing Window ⇨ Workspace ⇨ Reset to Default Workspace or press Command/Control+F1.

8. **Open your custom workspace.** You can either quit the Bridge or return to the default workspace, then open the Window menu and choose Workspace ⇨ <name of your custom workspace> or press the F key you assigned to the workspace. You should see the window position return to the area where you saved the workspace and all the rated files should be visible in the content area.

Managing panes

You can manage tabs in the Bridge much like you can with other CS applications to customize the workspace. In the Bridge, the tabs are always docked in the Bridge window, but you can move and mix them in the left panel. If you want to add more room for displaying metadata, drag the Preview tab down to the Metadata/Preview pane and drop the tab to the right of the Preview tab. You can then toggle views between the Metadata, Keywords, and Preview tabs as shown in Figure 7-8.

Because you can size thumbnails in the content area, you may find little need for viewing a separate thumbnail view in the preview tab, especially when you view the Bridge in Thumbnails view. The extra space for displaying metadata is helpful when you need to edit metadata in a number of different files.

Cross-Reference For information on adding and editing metadata, see the section "Editing metadata," later in this chapter.

If you move your tabs around and you want to change the arrangement back to the original look, choose Window ⇨ Workspace ⇨ Reset to Default Workspace.

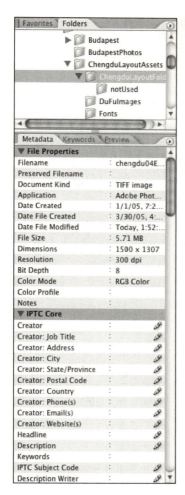

Figure 7-8: To provide more viewing room for metadata, drag the Preview tab down to the right of the Keywords tab.

Managing windows

You can open multiple windows in the Bridge and work back and forth between windows much like when you work with multiple file folders on your desktop. To open another window, choose File ⇨ New Window. The new window opens as an exact duplicate of the active window showing the same file location and window dimensions. You can then change folder locations and manage different tab views in different windows.

If you want to copy or move files between folders, open two windows and view the source and destination folders in separate windows. To copy a file from one folder to another, hold the Option/Alt key down and drag from the source folder to the destination folder as shown in Figure 7-9.

Figure 7-9: To copy files from one folder to another, press Option/Alt and drag a file from one window to another.

If you want to move a file from a source folder to a destination folder, click and drag a file without using a modifier key.

As you work with the CS applications and the Bridge, you may lose a window view while toggling back and forth between document views and Bridge views. To show all Bridge windows when multiple windows are open, choose Window ➪ Bring All to Front.

To close a window, click the close box or press ⌘/Ctrl+W.

Organizing Files and Folders

Just like you have many options for file organization on your computer desktop, the Bridge offers you many of the same options and more. When you work with the Creative Suite, you don't have to leave the Bridge to organize or edit any documents and you can move and arrange files and folders all within the Bridge window.

Creating new folders

New folders are created in the Bridge window. At the top of the Bridge window click the New Folder icon and a new *untitled folder* is added to the workspace in view. The text is highlighted when a new folder is added. Just type a name for your folder and press the Return/Enter or Num Pad Enter key to register the name.

You can locate new folders by dragging them around the content area. The content area behaves similarly to a slide sorter where you can organize documents and folders according to personal preferences. Click and drag a folder or document around the content pane. When you see a vertical black separator bar appear, Bridge informs you that when you release the mouse button, the folder (or document) will be dropped to the right of the separator bar.

Adding files to folders

To create subfolders within folders and place files within folders, first add a new folder as described in *Creating new folders*. Name your new folder. Select a group of files by Shift+clicking or ⌘/Ctrl+clicking. Drag the selected documents (and folders to nest the folders) to the new folder added in the Bridge. Release the mouse button and all your files/folders are added to the subfolder.

You can also add files and folders to folders by dragging and dropping from the desktop to the Bridge window. The Bridge is smart; when you drag a file from within an open folder in desktop view to the Bridge window and release the mouse button, Adobe Bridge drops the file in the respective folder. The Bridge view subsequently changes to the folder where the file is placed. In other words, your desktop view is completely mirrored in the Bridge window and file locations are preserved when you drag to and from the Bridge window.

Moving and copying files

You can easily drag and drop files between folders in the Bridge window to relocate them. The relocation of files in the Bridge window is mirrored on your desktop. If you drag a file from the Bridge window to your desktop or another folder you likewise relocate the file on your desktop and the action is mirrored in the Bridge window.

If you have two hard drives or an external media device attached to your computer and you drag a file from the Bridge window to a secondary drive, the file is copied to the target drive. To delete a file from a folder and ultimately from the Bridge window, press the ⌘/Ctrl key down and click and drag from one media source to another. The file is copied to another drive while deleted from the source drive.

To copy a file from one folder to another folder on the same drive, press Option/Alt and drag and drop a file.

Navigating folders

When browsing your hard drive to find files, you'll want to view the Folders tab in the Bridge window. The Folders tab displays your computer hard drive and all drives attached to your computer. Double click a drive or folder to access files contained therein or click the arrows adjacent to drives and folders to display nested folders.

You can easily return to last viewed folders by opening the Look In menu located above the Folders tab (see Figure 7-10). Clicking the folder icon adjacent to the Look In menu moves you up one level while clicking on the left and right arrows helps navigate to previous and next views.

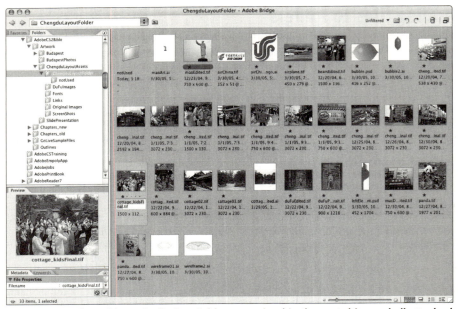

Figure 7-10: The Folders tab displays folders contained in the root drive and all attached media devices.

Deleting files

You can remove files and folders from your hard drive directly within the Bridge window. To delete a file or folder select the item(s) to delete and press Delete/Backspace or Del. Likewise, you can select files/folders to delete and click the Trash icon in the Bridge window. When you delete files using the Bridge, the files are moved to the trashcan on your desktop. If you change your mind and want to retain files, move them out of the trashcan in desktop view to the desired folder.

Labeling Files

In addition to rating files with stars, you can also label files with color codes. Labeling files with colors is an easy way to mark a number of files imported from digital cameras, CDs, external media cartridges, or other sources used to copy files to your hard drive. As files are reviewed you can mark them with one of five different colors. You can customize color names in the Preferences dialog box. Although you cannot change the colors, you can identify a color with a specific name. For example, you can use labels to identify files according to status in a workflow.

To change the color names open the Preferences dialog box. On the Macintosh choose Bridge ⇨ Preferences. On Windows, choose Edit ⇨ Preferences. Alternately, you can press ⌘/Ctrl+K. The Preferences dialog box opens. In the left panel, click Labels and the right panel changes to show the Label options as shown in Figure 7-11.

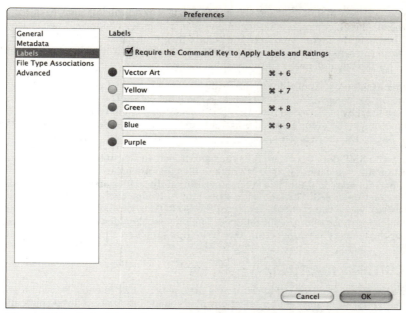

Figure 7-11: Open the Preferences dialog box and click Labels to change label options.

As shown in Figure 7-11, you can change the label name to a custom name by typing in the text box adjacent to any color. Changing labels should be something you do for your own personal file organization. If you change label names and share files with other users in your workgroup, the other users won't see the same label names.

> **Note** XMP (eXtensible Metadata Platform) Metadata is an Adobe-specific set of data that provides information about a file and its use by Adobe applications. In order to store XMP data, a file must be XMP write capable. File types such as BMP (bitmap format), DCS (desktop color separation format), PICT (Macintosh Picture format), and Photoshop 6 PDFs (Portable Document Format), are not XMP write capable.

After you label files, you can then sort and/or view according to label like sorting and viewing files according to stars. When you rate a file with a star rating and identify a document with a label you can sort and/or view nested labels. For example, you can rate images with 1, 2, 3, or 4 stars, and label the same documents with different colors. You can then choose to display only red files with three or more stars, hence narrowing the number of displayed documents to those you specifically identify with a given identity.

You can view metadata you add in the Bridge when you work with the CS2 applications. If you label a Photoshop document in the Bridge with a label name, the name is visible when you open the file in Photoshop and select File ➪ File Info. When the File Info dialog box opens, select Advanced in the left pane. In the right pane you see a list of XMP and XML data. Click XMP Core Properties and open the nested list by clicking the right pointing arrow. Down the list you find xap:Label. The label name you supplied in the Bridge is identified with the same name you added in the Bridge.

Likewise, you can view metadata when you import photos in Adobe InDesign. In InDesign, don't use the File menu command. Rather, open the Info palette (Window ⇨ Info). Select the Photoshop image in the layout, and from the palette fly-out menu, select File Info. A dialog box opens with the same options as you find in Photoshop. Click Advanced and view the XMP Core Data. The xap:Label displays the same label name.

Be aware that assigning a label color in the Bridge is just a means of visually identifying documents in the Bridge window. What's important is the label name. The name is written to the XMP data and thereby is visible to the other CS applications. When using labels in the Bridge, be certain to not use the color names if you want label names to be written to the XMP data. Descriptive names are more meaningful in your workgroup than color names.

You cannot write XMP data to certain file types mentioned earlier in this section on "Labeling Files." Additionally, you cannot write XMP data to files that are locked such as files you open from CD-ROMs. You may find that the label names for all these files are retained in the Bridge window, but don't be fooled. The labels are stored in the Bridge cache (a memory location on your hard drive). When the cache is cleared or the CD-ROM is viewed on a different machine, the label names for these files are not retained. The only label names retained are within the metadata for those file types supporting XMP write that aren't on a read-only storage device.

Using context menus

Like all the CS applications, the Bridge supports the use of context menus. Depending on the file type, menu options change. If you select any file type including non-Adobe application documents with the exception of Photoshop files, and open a context menu on a file in the content area, the menu choices are as shown in Figure 7-12. You open context menus by right-clicking the mouse. On Macintosh with a one-button mouse, press the Ctrl key and click to open a context menu.

Figure 7-12: Select any file type except a Photoshop file and open a context menu.

Menu options for all files except Photoshop documents include:

- **Open:** Select a file and choose open results in the same operation as double clicking a file in the content or Preview pane. The default editing application opens the file.

- **Open With:** From the submenu you have a list of programs from which to choose. You might have a PDF file that by default opens in Adobe Acrobat. If you want to open the file in Adobe Reader, use Open With and choose Adobe Reader from the menu options.

- **Reveal in Finder:** This menu choice is also available under the File menu. If you want to find a file in a desktop view, select this menu command.

- **Add to Favorites:** You can add a file to your Favorite list. For more information about using Favorites, see the section "Adding Favorites" later in this chapter.

- **Batch Rename:** You can rename a folder of files in a batch sequence. For more information on creating batch sequences, see the section "Batch processing with actions" later in this chapter.

- **Move to Trash:** Removes a file from a folder and deposits it in the Trash can on the desktop. Choosing this menu command performs the same operation as selecting a file and clicking on the Trash icon in the Bridge window or pressing the Delete/Backspace or Del keys.

- **File Info:** Select File Info and the same dialog box you open in the CS programs opens in the Bridge. You can add metadata in the File Info dialog box.

- **Label:** From the submenu you have choices the same as when using the label section in the Label menu. You cannot choose ratings from this submenu but you can assign labels to selected documents.

If you open a context menu on a Photoshop file, you have some additional menu choices all related to rotating images. These choices are the same as you have available from the tools appearing at the top of the Bridge window. Note that the 180-degree rotation is not available in the Bridge window and can only be selected using a context menu or a menu command in the Edit menu. The menu shown in Figure 7-13 appears when you open a context menu from a Photoshop document.

Figure 7-13: When you open a context menu on a Photoshop document, you find additional commands used for rotating images.

The context menu includes these additional commands:

- **Rotate 180°:** Flops an image 180 degrees.

- **Rotate 90° Clockwise:** Rotates right 90 degrees in a clockwise direction.

- **Rotate 90° Counterclockwise:** Rotates left 90 degrees in a counterclockwise direction.

When you rotate Photoshop images in the Bridge, the rotation is temporary. You can quit the Bridge after rotating an image and you may still see the rotation you applied. The cache retains the rotations made in the Bridge. However when the cache is cleared, the file reverts to the original view. Furthermore, users in your workgroup will always see the document as it was last saved. In order to register the rotation, click the Apply check mark below the metadata pane. When you click the check mark the rotation is saved.

Working with Collections

Collections are folders of documents you can create for easy and quick access to files used for a project under construction or frequently visited files. You create a new collection which is essentially a new folder contained within the Collections category. Additionally, you can save searches as a Collection and easily retrieve files having met a given set of search criteria.

Working with Collections is, in our opinion, one of the weaker aspects of the Bridge if used strictly as an organization tool. Collections in the Favorites pane cannot be displayed in a hierarchy list like collections viewed in Acrobat. Additionally, there is no menu command, context or otherwise, to add files to a collection, also like you can do in Adobe Acrobat. Where Collections are beneficial is when sorting files and saving the sort results as a collection. This feature saves you much time when returning to search results.

Cross-Reference   For information on using Acrobat's Organizer, see Chapter 9.

Creating a Collection

To create a new Collection, click Collections in the Favorites pane. From either a context menu (shown in Figure 7-14) or the File menu select New Folder. An *untitled folder* is created in the Collections content area. Likewise, you can click the New Folder icon in the Bridge window. Type a name for the folder and it's ready to store files.

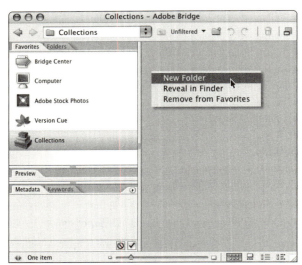

Figure 7-14: Click Collections and open a context menu in the content area to create a new Collections folder.

Collections are stored on your boot drive in a specific location. You can easily find where collections are stored by clicking Collections in the Favorites folder and open a context menu in the content area. Choose Reveal in Finder from the menu commands and the Bridge folder opens. Within the Bridge folder is the Collections folder. All Collections are stored here.

Adding files to a Collection

What would be nice would be a context menu with a command *Add Files* like Adobe Acrobat's Organizer. A dialog box opens and you navigate your hard drive to find a folder of files to add to your collection. However, the Bridge has no such menu command. The easiest way to add files to a collection is to open a second Bridge window and drag files from a folder in one Bridge window to the open Collections folder in another Bridge window. See the section "Adding files to folders" for more information.

You can open a folder and drag files to Collections in the Favorites pane; however, Bridge makes no provision for depositing your files in a given folder. You would need to open the Collections and select files to drag and drop to a folder. It's a two-step process so be certain to use the method for dragging and dropping files between two Bridge windows.

Adding Favorites

You can add files and folders to the Favorites pane. Open a folder in the Bridge and select a file or folder. From a context menu select Add to Favorites. Likewise, you can select a file or folder and choose File ⇨ Add to Favorites. Either command adds your file or folder to the list of Favorites and provides easy quick access to the files.

When you add files and folders to the Favorites pane, you are not copying files or moving them from one location to another. The Favorites are like document aliases or shortcuts and require very little storage space. When you delete a Favorite either by selecting it and clicking the Trash icon, use a key on your keyboard, or use a context menu, the Favorite is removed from the list, but your files remain in their original location.

Caution

Adding many files to the Favorites defeats part of the purpose for the Bridge — which is essentially to help you organize and manage your program documents. If you have a long list of Favorites and need to scroll the pane to find files, your organization becomes messy and unorganized. Be selective when you add files and try to use folders where files for a current project are stored. Be certain to perform cleanup and remove files and folders routinely from the Favorites list after you complete projects or no longer use the files.

Batch renaming files

If you use a digital camera, you may want to take the cryptic names the camera uses to save your files and change the names to more descriptive file names. Bridge lets you add names and extensions to files in a snap. You can add names that give a better clue for what the contents of images are rather than names like P1010273 or CRW_6062.

To rename files using a batch command, look over the following steps:

STEPS: Using Batch Rename

1. **Open a folder of files in the Bridge that you want to rename.** If you have digital camera files, use them for the following steps. If not, use any folder of photos. The original files won't be disturbed if you follow these steps.

2. **Select the files you want to rename.** Typically, you will rename an entire folder of files. When renaming all files in a folder press ⌘/Ctrl+A to select all the images. If you want to select certain files for renaming, Shift+click or ⌘/Ctrl+click to select contiguous or noncontiguous groups.

Tip If you have files in different folders and you want to rename files from the different folders, first perform a search. You need some form of metadata common to all the files. Your search results are reported in a new Bridge window, even though the files are stored in different folders. Select all the files you want to rename and save the results to either the source folder or a new folder. For more information on searching metadata, see the section "Searching in the Bridge" later in this chapter.

3. **Create a folder for the destination files.** You can choose to rewrite the existing file names or write copies of the files to a different folder. The new folder will contain the renamed files. For these steps, use a second folder where the files are to be copied. You can create a new folder in the Bridge window where you view the files to rename.

4. **Select the Batch Rename command.** Open the Tools menu and select the command or open a context menu on one of the selected images and choose Batch Rename. The Batch Rename dialog box opens as shown in Figure 7-15.

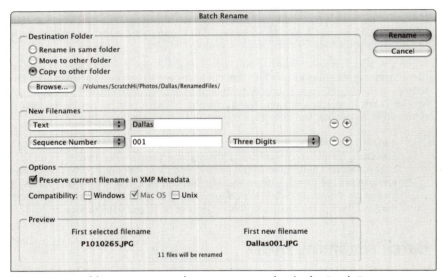

Figure 7-15: Add a root name and a sequence number in the Batch Rename dialog box.

5. **Choose a destination folder.** Select the radio button for Copy to other folder. This option copies the files to another folder while leaving the original images unedited. To specify the target folder for the copied images, click Browse. The Browse for Folder dialog box opens and you can navigate to your hard drive and identify the target folder. Select the folder you want to use and click Choose.

6. **Add a root name.** The default New Filename is the root name. The pull-down menu defaults to Text and the name you want to use is typed in the text box on the right. If you stop here and process the batch, your filenames will appear as photo (1), photo (2), photo (3), where photo is used as the root name. Add a name to the text box, but don't click Rename yet.

7. **Add a Sequence Number.** Rather than have your filenames appear as name+(1), and so on, you can add a sequence number so the name appears as photo001, photo002, photo003, etc. To do so, you need to add another option in the New Filenames section of the Batch Process dialog box. Click the plus (+) symbol to the right of the text box and the dialog box expands to reveal more options you can use for filenames. Open the second pull-down menu and select Sequence Number from the menu commands. In the text box to the right of the menu choice, add "001" as shown in Figure 7-15. Note the example of the file name shown at the bottom of the dialog box under the *First new filename* label.

Tip

Depending where you view files such as desktop views, dialog boxes, applications windows, etc., filenames do not always appear in dictionary order. A file labeled as *image9* may appear after *image89* in some windows or dialog boxes. To insure proper reading order in all windows and dialog boxes, be certain to add leading zeros sufficient enough to accommodate the number of files you want to rename. For example, a single leading zero and two digits for files numbered up to 99, two leading zeros and three digits to accommodate files numbered up to 999, and so on.

8. **Process the batch.** Select the check box to preserve XMP Metadata and click Rename in the top-right corner. After the Bridge processes the files, open the target folder and view the results. In Figure 7-16 the files were changed to a root name of "Dallas" — where the files were shot — and a sequence number beginning with 001.

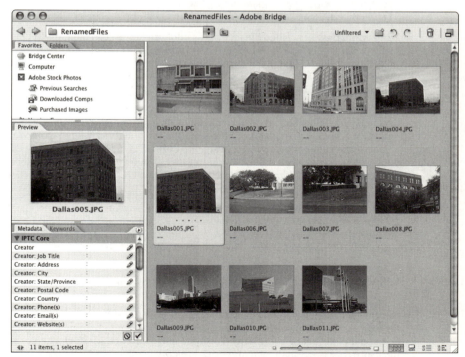

Figure 7-16: After running the Batch Rename command, the files are renamed and saved to the target folder.

Working with Metadata

Metadata are data that can be used to describe your file. The information can be sorted, viewed in other applications, searched upon, describe copyright information, identify files, and archive documents. With regards to user-supplied information, if you had to manually enter rows of field data in each and every file, metadata would be a useless tool. However, Adobe makes it much easier for you by providing a means for creating a template and using that template to apply common metadata to gigabytes of documents.

Metadata properties

The Bridge lets you see document metadata at a glance in the Metadata panel. The Bridge Metadata Preferences determine which fields are displayed in the panel. You caught a glimpse of the Metadata Preferences in the section "Labeling Files" earlier in the chapter. Label data is metadata, but the edits you made for label names occur in a separate preference pane than the Metadata pane. You cannot add metadata in the preferences; the Metadata Preferences are used to display and hide the categories shown in the Metadata panel in the Bridge window. Therefore, your first task is to open the Preferences and select which fields you want to view and ultimately edit when you work in the Metadata panel.

Open the Preferences dialog box and click Metadata in the left pane. Metadata are divided into several categories in the Bridge. Some of these categories are single items and others contain a nested group of fields expandable when you click the right pointing arrow to expand (and collapse) the category. The categories include:

- **File Properties:** Describes file attributes and most often the data are imposed automatically when you create files. Items like file size, creation date, modification date, resolution, bit depth, dimensions, etc. are all part of the File Properties and you cannot edit these items. Non-editable items do not provide field boxes for text entries in the Metadata pane in the Bridge.

- **IPTC (IIM, legacy):** These data are editable in the Metadata pane. You can add information here for things like copyright information, captions, document title, author, keywords, and location. By default, however, this set of data is hidden from view. You can also add the same information to the IPTC Core. IPTC Core is a newer specification and you should use it for all data you add to current documents. The IPTC (IIK legacy) data appears from legacy files created before October 2004.

- **IPTC Core:** Like IPTC (IIM, legacy) all the data here is editable. As a new specification developed by the International Press Telecommunications Council (IPTC) in October 2004, you should use it with all your current documents. The same field data are available in the IPTC Core fields where you find identifying information as described above with IPTC (IIM legacy).

- **Fonts:** Fonts are applicable only to Adobe InDesign files. All the fonts used in an InDesign document are displayed below the font heading when you select an InDesign file. When any other file type is selected, the Fonts category disappears.

- **Swatches:** Like Fonts, Swatches are visible only with Adobe InDesign files and likewise disappear when you select file types other than InDesign documents. In Figure 7-17 you can see the metadata information for fonts and swatches when you select an InDesign file. Note that the remaining categories are collapsed in the Metadata pane.

Figure 7-17: Fonts and Swatches only display when you select InDesign documents.

- **Camera Data (Exif):** This information is not editable. The data are derived from digital cameras and provide information related to the settings applied when the photograph was taken. Notice in Figure 7-18 all the information displayed with a photo taken from a digital camera. Exchangeable image file (Exif) data are written when files are saved from digital cameras in JPEG format and can also be embedded in TIFF-formatted files.

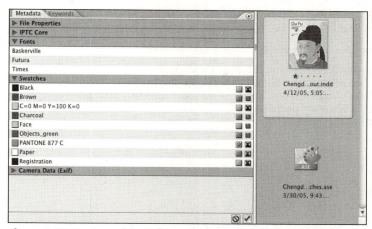

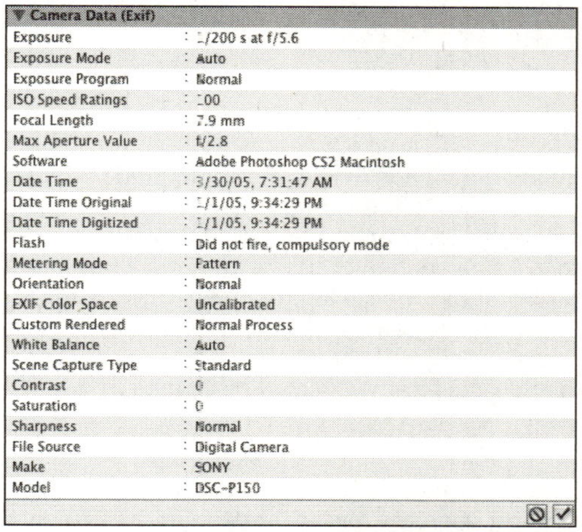

Figure 7-18: Camera Data (Exif) are reported for photos taken with digital cameras.

- **GPS:** Global Positioning System (GPS) data are only applied to files containing a GPS system on the digital camera. If your camera does not have a GPS, then the data fields are left blank.

- **Camera Raw:** Camera Raw information describes the settings that Photoshop uses when you open a file and certain information about your camera and the settings used to shoot a photo.

- **Edit History:** Edit History is like a log file that can keep track of editing history made in Adobe Photoshop.
- **Version Cue:** Version Cue information and comments are listed for Version Cue documents.
- **Adobe Stock Photos:** You can acquire Adobe Stock Photos using the Bridge (see the section "Acquiring Adobe Stock Photos" later in this chapter). All the metadata supplied for the stock photos are displayed in a separate category. For example, low-resolution (comp) photos are downloaded typically before you purchase a high-resolution image. The comp information is one of the items displayed as you can see in Figure 7-19.

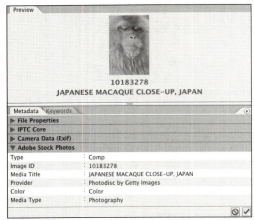

Figure 7-19: Metadata shown with an Adobe comp image downloaded from the Adobe Stock Photo library

- **Viewing relevant data:** The many data fields available for metadata inclusion result in a long list. There are many different fields and categories you are likely not to use in any given editing session. Explore all the preference choices you have in the Metadata Preferences and check off those items you never use or won't use for a collection of files. After disabling items you won't use, be certain to check the box for Hide Empty Fields. When you return to the Metadata pane in the Bridge window only the fields you have checked are visible. This makes scrolling the list much easier and you'll have an easier time when you need to add data to any given editable field.

Using XMP templates

If you want to edit a field, select a file and open the Metadata pane in the Bridge window and view the fields in the categories you have visible. On the right side of the pane you can see a pencil icon for all fields that are editable. If the icon is not present, you can't add data to the field. Click in a field and the text box becomes active for any field marked with a pencil icon. In Figure 7-20, note the Creator: Emails(s) field edited and the field boxes outlined among the IPTC Core fields.

Figure 7-20: Look for fields containing a pencil icon and click the field to make the text box active. Type the data you want to add to the document metadata.

Obviously, if you have hundreds of files and many fields to edit, the process of manually typing data in fields is laborious and you're not likely to add data to every image you take with a digital camera or use in a layout. Fortunately, you can supply common information to document metadata using templates.

Creating a template

You may be a photographer who shoots weddings, commercial, product, or other types of photography. If you perform a photo shoot and take the equivalent of several rolls or hundreds of digital photos, you are likely to use some common information in the metadata for your images on a given assignment. Typically you'll use your personal identifying information as well as information unique to the assignment such as location, client, project, and so on. All this information is common among the files and does not require you to add unique data for each file.

When you want to add common data to a group of images, you can easily create a metadata template and import the metadata into hundreds of photos with one click of the mouse. To see how a template is created, follow the steps detailed below:

STEPS: Creating a Metadata Template

1. **Select a Photoshop image in the Bridge.** You can use another CS application document, but for many artists the more common files you are likely to use more often are Photoshop documents.

2. **Open the File Info dialog box.** Be certain an image is selected and choose File ⇨ File Info.

3. **Add data to the field boxes.** There are several categories listed on the left in the File Info dialog box. The first pane you view is the Description data. Be certain to supply information that is common among all files. For example, for a given image, Author might be you or a professional photographer and thus you would add the same common data to a large collection of files. Additionally you might have some description information and keywords common among a group of files. However, the Document Title is typically a field that is unique among a group of images. Leave all unique fields blank. As an example, look over Figure 7-21 where metadata are added to a file.

4. **Add IPTC information.** The fields where you find the most editable text boxes are contained in the four IPTC items listed in the File Info dialog box. Select IPTC Contact and add your personal contact information or the information of the photographer used for the photo shoot. Continue adding information relevant to your job in each of the four IPTC categories.

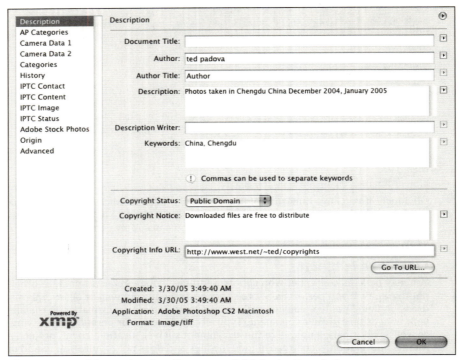

Figure 7-21: Add metadata for all common fields in the Description pane.

5. **Save a Metadata Template.** Click the arrow in the top right corner of the File Info dialog box to open a flyout menu. From the menu choices select Save Metadata Template.

6. **Name the template.** The Save Metadata Template dialog box opens. Note that you don't have an option to choose a destination folder. You need to save Metadata templates in a specific folder that the Bridge handles for you. Add a name in the dialog box and click Save. The template is saved to the proper location and it's ready for use.

Appending and replacing data

After you create a Metadata template it's time to add the template data to files. You have two choices. You can choose to replace data or append data. When you choose Replace Metadata the existing properties are replaced with the template data. When you Append Metadata the data from the template is added to fields only when non-existing data match the same fields. As a matter of rule, if you want the data to be identical in your files and the template data is current and correct, use the Replace Metadata command. To see how replacing (or appending) metadata is handled, follow these steps:

STEPS: Use a Metadata Template to Replace Data

1. **Select Files in the Bridge window.** You identify files to replace (or append) the template data by selecting them in the Bridge window. If you have a folder where you want all files to be replaced with the template data, press ⌘/Ctrl+A to select all files in the window. To select individual files in a folder use Shift+click or ⌘/Ctrl+click to make multiple selections.

Tip

To select most files in a folder with several files unselected, select the fewer files first. Open the Edit menu and select Invert Selection or press ⌘/Ctrl+Shift+I. The few files become deselected as the remaining files become selected.

2. **Open the Metadata palette menu.** Click the tiny right pointing arrow in the top right corner of the Metadata tab to open the fly-out menu.

3. **Select the template to use to replace the data.** Select Replace Metadata from the menu options in the fly-out menu and select the template name you want to use in the submenu (see Figure 7-22). If you have created only one template, you have only one choice in the submenu.

Figure 7-22: Select Replace (or Append) Metadata and select a template name appearing in the submenu.

4. **Click OK in the warning dialog box.** An application alert dialog box opens asking you if you want to proceed. Click Yes in the dialog box.

5. **Pause to let the Bridge import the metadata.** In the lower left corner of the Bridge window you can see the status of the file updates. Be certain to wait until the Bridge completes its work. When finished, you can view the metadata on the selected files as shown in the example in Figure 7-23. If you divided a photo shoot into several folders, open each folder, select files, and use the Replace Metadata and your template to repeat updating the files.

IPTC Core	
Creator	ted padova
Creator: Job Title	Author
Creator: Address	
Creator: City	Ventura
Creator: State/Province	CA
Creator: Postal Code	93003
Creator: Country	USA
Creator: Phone(s)	
Creator: Email(s)	ted@west.net
Creator: Website(s)	http://www.west.net/~ted
Headline	
Description	Photos taken in Chengdu China December 2004, January 2005
Keywords	China; Chengdu
IPTC Subject Code	
Description Writer	
Date Created	
Intellectual Genre	
IPTC Scene	
Location	
City	Chengdu
State/Province	Sichuan Providence
Country	China
ISO Country Code	86
Title	
Job Identifier	Adobe Creative Suite 2 Bible
Instructions	use for Chengdu layout
Provider	ted padova
Source	
Copyright Notice	Downloaded files are free to distribute
Rights Usage Terms	Public domain

Figure 7-23: Review the selected files and you can see the metadata from the template added to the respective fields in each file.

Deleting templates

Templates are stored as files on your hard drive. The Bridge doesn't have a command for you to delete a template after you create one, but it knows where the template files are located. To find the folder where the template files are saved, select any file in the content area of the Bridge window. From a context menu select File Info. Open the fly-out menu in the top right corner of the Bridge window and select Show templates. A folder opens on your desktop and a subfolder titled *XMP* is selected. Double-click this folder to open it where two subfolders are contained therein. Open the folder labeled *Metadata Templates*. The template files are viewed inside the folder. Select any template you want to delete and move it to the trash. The File Info dialog box dynamically updates to show a list of only the remaining templates in the Metadata Templates folder.

Searching in the Bridge

The Bridge provides you a powerful search engine where you can quickly search your hard drive, network server, and external media for files based on a large range of criteria. In addition, you can search for Adobe Stock Photos. The exercises you performed earlier in this chapter for assigning labels to files (see the section "Labeling files") and adding metadata (see the section "Working with metadata") become more meaningful when you use the labels and metadata information to search for documents. Not only the metadata such as file name, creation date, file size, and so on is searchable. You can search on all metadata you add to your documents.

You can narrow searches by adding multiple criteria and conditions as well as search on Boolean expressions. After you create a search in the Bridge you can save your search results as a new Collection. Just double click a Collection and all the results of a search are displayed in a Bridge window.

Searching documents

To search for files in the Bridge you use the Find command. Open the Edit menu and select Find and the Find dialog box opens as shown in Figure 7-24. At first glance, the dialog box appears limited in providing you with many search options. Don't be fooled. You can dynamically expand the dialog box to provide you with an elaborate set of criteria and conditions.

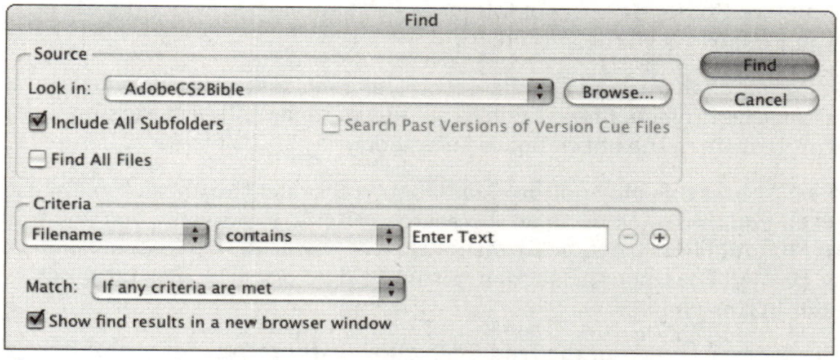

Figure 7-24: Choose Edit ⇨ Find to open the Find dialog box.

Before you perform a search, take a moment to look over all the options you have in the Find dialog box. These include:

- ✦ **Look in:** The pull-down menu contains four categories (shown in Figure 7-25) from which you can select a location where you want to search for documents. The categories include:

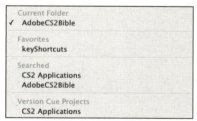

Figure 7-25: Four categories appear in the Look in pull-down menu.

- **Current Folder:** The current content area displays documents found in the current folder. You can change the current folder by clicking Browse to the right of the Look in pull-down menu. The Browse for Folder dialog box opens and you can navigate to your hard drive and select a folder. Searching the current folder reports results found only in this folder.

- **Favorites:** Favorites are grayed out unless you have identified documents or folders and added them to your Favorites. If you have several folders added to your Favorites, the search reports results from all folders that meet the search criteria. If you have, for example, five folders added to your Favorites and one file in each of the five different folders meet your search criteria, the five files display in a single Bridge window.

- **Searched:** The Searched category lists the recently searched locations. If you search different folders and want to return to a given folder it's often easier to select from the Searched category than to Browse your hard drive to find the folder again.
- **Version Cue Projects:** All current Version Cue Projects are listed in this category.

✦ **Include All Subfolders:** When you search a folder from any of the Look in areas, you can search the root folder or the root folder and all subfolders. Select the check box when you want to search all the subfolders.

✦ **Search Past Versions of Version Cue Projects:** This item is grayed out unless you choose Version Cue Projects in the Look in pull-down menu. All past Version Cue projects are searched when the check box is selected.

✦ **Find All Files:** At first this may not be clear when you select the check box. When this box is checked you loose access to all the search criteria. However, when you perform a search for Find All Files, you quickly discover how powerful this feature is. To understand using Find All Files, see the section "Using Bridge to search files for quick cleanup" later in this chapter.

✦ **Criteria:** The criteria section of the Find dialog box is where you determine precisely what you want to search. Several items are available to help narrow your search. These include:

- **Filename:** Filename is the default. Click Filename and you find a list of metadata items to search as shown in Figure 7-26. All of the items are self-explanatory. To sue All Metadata at the bottom of the list, see the section "Searching metadata."

Figure 7-26: Click Filename and a pull-down menu displays the metadata items you can search.

- **Conditions:** The menu shown in Figure 7-27 shows the different conditions that need to be met to return results. **contains**: reports any text you type to the right of the Conditions menu. **does not contain**: reports all data not containing the text you search. **is**: the searched data must equal what you search for. **starts with**: you can type a character, several characters, a word, several words, and the results are reported for data starting with what you add to the text box. **ends with**: same as starts with, but results are reported for text matching the end of a data string. This item is frequently used for file extensions such as .jpg, .indd, .ai, and so on.

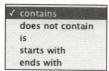
Figure 7-27: Search conditions that must be met to return results.

- **Text box:** You type the items you want to search in this box. Text is typed for all items except Rating. When you select Rating, the text box changes to a pull down menu where you can choose between 1 and 5 stars or No Rating. Some items require adhering to special formats. File size requires you to type numeric values to express the number of kilobytes and dates require using date formats.

- **Minus (-) and Plus (+):** Click the plus (+) symbol and you add a new line of criteria. To see how additional criteria helps your search, see the section "Searching metadata." Click the minus (-) symbol to eliminate a row of criteria.

✦ **Match:** You have two options in the Match pull-down menu. Choosing **if any criteria are met** reports results for any text in a string matching the metadata or any text from two criteria. This option is similar to using Boolean OR. Choosing **if all criteria are met** requires all text in a string or all text in all criteria to match the metadata. This option is similar to using Boolean AND. For an example in using the Match items, see the section "Searching metadata."

✦ **Show find results in a new browser window:** By default, results are reported in the current content area. If you want to keep the current content window active and view results in a separate Bridge window, select this check box.

One special item to note when you use the Find dialog box is that any criteria you type in the text box is not case sensitive. Additionally, there is no switch to enable case sensitivity.

Searching metadata

After familiarizing yourself with the search options available to you in the Bridge, the best way to get up to speed is to start searching for files. A little practice here goes a long way in helping you master some of the power the Bridge provides you when searching for documents. To acquaint yourself with the search options, try to work through the following steps:

STEPS: Searching Metadata in Adobe Bridge

1. **Open a folder in the Bridge window.** When you perform a search using the Find command, you need to have a Bridge window open. If no window is open, the Find command is grayed out.

2. **Chose Edit ⇨ Find.** The Find dialog box opens.

3. **Target a location to search.** Open the Look in pull-down menu to locate a recent folder. If the folder you want to search does not appear in the menu, click Browse and navigate your hard drive to locate a target folder to search. Note that you can choose a root folder with many subfolders and search all nested folders.

4. **Add the first line of criteria.** You can choose any one of the items in the first pull-down menu where you see the default name Filename. If you know a filename contains a text string, use Filename. The second pull-down menu is a condition. If you know a word or some characters are contained in a filename, use Contains or select another option that more closely meets your requirements. Type the text string to search in the text box. From the Match pull-down menu, select if any criteria are met.

5. **Add a second line of criteria.** Click the plus (+) symbol to the right of the first row of criteria. A second row appears offering you the same options. In this line select Filename again in the first pull-down menu. Select Contains, and type another text string in the text box. Make sure the same Match option is selected here the same as in step four above. When you choose the same item to search and choose *if any criteria are met* from the Match pull-down menu, you are using Boolean OR to report your search results. In other words you're asking Bridge to report the first text string OR the second text string to be contained in your search results. If you choose *if all criteria are met*, you are using Boolean AND where the results are reported only when the first text string AND the second text string are contained in the search results.

6. **Add a third line of criteria.** From the first pull-down menu, select All Metadata and likewise select *contains* in the second pull-down menu. In the text box, type one of the metadata items you added in a template when you performed steps earlier in this chapter in the section "Appending and replacing metadata." In this example, I'll use data supplied for author name. In the Match pull-down menu change the option to the "if all criteria are met" option. As a final item, check the checkbox for "Show find results in a new browser window." The Find dialog box at this point should look like Figure 7-28.

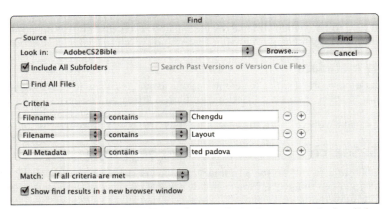

Figure 7-28: As you add additional rows of criteria to a search, the dialog box expands.

7. **Click Find in the top-right corner of the Find dialog box.** The results are reported in a new Bridge window as shown in Figure 7-29.

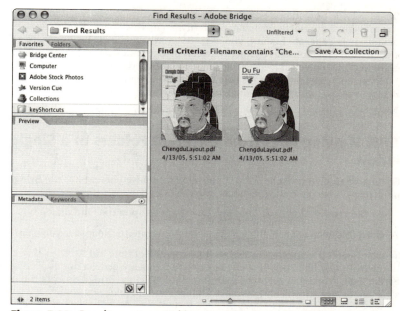

Figure 7-29: Results are reported in a new window when the *Show find results in a new browser window* is selected.

Tip

The criteria of your search are easily examined in the Bridge window after clicking Find. Look at the top of the Bridge window and the criteria are reported in a line of text.

Take a moment to review what occurred in this example. If you duplicated the steps, here you are asking the Bridge to report results when a filename contains one text string AND a second text string AND the metadata contains a third text string. All conditions must be true for any results to be reported in a new Bridge window.

Tip

If you want to narrow a search and the Find dialog box does not provide you all the options you need on the first pass, you can first report results in a new Bridge window. Next, perform a second search with additional criteria and use the Current Folder option from the Look in pull-down menu.

Using Bridge to search files for quick cleanup

Suppose you work on a project and you create multiple folders to contain different assets. Assume for a moment you have a folder for your layout and you copied links to this folder from other folders you created when you began a project. You may have a folder for original Photoshop images, another folder for edited Photoshop images, another for Illustrator images, maybe a folder containing text files, or other folders for different files related to the same project.

Your folders may be nested below a root folder with several levels of subfolders. In some cases you may have duplicate files unnecessarily occupying space. If you use the Bridge to view documents in separate folders, you need to create new Bridge windows to show the contents of each individual folder. Toggling between Bridge windows to compare file contents becomes difficult when you have several Bridge windows open. Wouldn't it be nice if you could compare and delete redundant files while viewing all the files from different folders in a single Bridge window? Fortunately, the Find command lets you do just that.

To view files from different folders in a single Bridge window, follow these steps:

STEPS: Viewing Files from Different Folders in a Single Bridge Window

1. **Open a Bridge window.** It doesn't matter what folder you view in the Bridge, you first need to have an open window to access the Find command.

2. **Open the Find dialog box.** Choose Edit ⇨ Find to open the Find dialog box.

3. **Select a folder to search.** Click Browse and navigate to the folder you want to search.

4. **Search for all files nested in the root folder.** Select the Find All Files check box. Note that when you check this box all the Criteria items are grayed out as you can see in Figure 7-30. When you invoke a search to Find All Files, Bridge reports the results irrespective of any criteria and displays all files from all folders.

Figure 7-30: When Find All Files is selected, the Criteria options are grayed out.

5. **Display the results in a new Bridge window.** Select the Show find results in a new browser window check box.

6. **View the results.** If you want to delete redundant files note that the files are sorted by default according to filenames as shown in Figure 7-31. You can easily compare files and delete duplicate documents.

Chapter 7 ✦ **Using Adobe Bridge** 237

Figure 7-31: When you check Find, all files from nested folders are reported in a new browser window and sorted according to filename.

Tip

If you have files scattered around your hard drive and not nested in a single folder, you can search an entire drive. The first step is to be certain you add some common identification to all files within a given work project. You can use a file naming convention where all files in a given project have some common text in the file name, or add one item in the metadata common to all files related to a given project — something like text added to a Description field. When you click Browse, select the drive where your files are contained. Additionally, set the criteria to search a string on a filename or All Metadata and use the common identifier in the text box. When you click Find, all files from different folders are reported in a Bridge window. If you want to narrow the search to common file types, use another criteria item and search using a file extension.

Caution

If you invoke a search on your hard drive, Bridge takes a long time to report your results — an extraordinary long time on large hard drives. You cannot bail out of the search short of force quitting the program or shutting your computer down. If you perform such searches, be prepared to wait some time for the search to complete.

Saving searches

If you add an elaborate set of criteria and conditions to perform a search, you may want to save the settings so you can easily return to the results. After you complete a search, the Bridge window contains a button labeled *Save as Collection*. Click the button and your search criteria are saved as a Collection.

When you want to return to the search results, click the Favorites tab in the Bridge window and click Collections. Find the Collection created from the search and double-click it. A Bridge window opens showing the results from the search. This option is a direct link to the results and does not require performing another search. If you searched a hard drive and the time to complete the search was inordinately long, you can quickly return to the results by saving as a Collection and opening the Collection each time you want to view the results.

Searching Stock Photos

Another form of search is related to the Adobe Stock Photos options you have available in the Bridge. For information regarding Stock Photos, see the section "Acquiring Adobe Stock Photos." For the moment, don't be concerned about how the stock photos feature in Bridge works — that's all explained in the next section. For now, look at the options you have for searching stock photos.

Searching the stock libraries

Click the Favorites tab in the Bridge window and click Adobe Stock Photos in the tab. The Bridge displays the Adobe Stock Photos pane as shown in Figure 7-32.

Figure 7-32: Click Adobe Stock Photos in the Favorites tab and the Adobe Stock Photos pane opens in the Bridge window.

To the right of the text box at the top of the pane you have three icons appearing as binoculars that are used for searching stock photos.

+ **The Search tool:** First of the three icons, this icon invokes a search according to the text you add in the text box to the left of the icon. The Adobe Stock Photos are detailed with an elaborate set of metadata enabling you to search on criteria to help narrow searches. You might type "one woman AND face AND mask" in the text box and click the search tool. The text box supports Boolean AND, OR, and NOT. The results are reported in the content area and derived from all the photo libraries contained in the Adobe Stock Photo Collection.

+ **Advanced Search:** Clicking the second icon (binoculars with a plus (+) symbol) produces the Advanced Search window. Click the Advanced Search tool and the Advanced Search dialog box opens as shown in Figure 7-33.

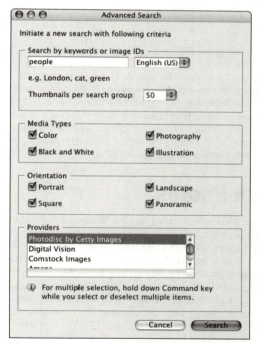

Figure 7-33: Click the Advanced Search tool to open the Advanced Search dialog box.

Advanced searches enable you to define how the thumbnails are displayed in the content area, the kinds of media types to be returned, image orientation, and returning images from specific provider libraries. As you can see in Figure 7-33, the categories are self-explanatory. Supply your search criteria, check the boxes for the items to be searched and click Search. The results are then returned as thumbnail views in the content area.

+ **Search Tips tool:** Click this tool and the Adobe Help Center opens where you can gain some information related to tips in regard to refining your searches.

Searching online services

The third search button in the Adobe Stock Photos pane is used to search the Adobe Photographers Directory. This service is an online search. Click the tool and your default Web browser opens the Adobe Photographers Web page. On the Web page you can search for participating photographers who best match your needs for a given campaign or design assignment. Among the search criteria are geographic locations, areas of specialty (product, advertising, portraiture, sports, and so on.). Additionally, you can search on names of photographers.

The caveat in using this search option is you need to know the name of the photographer you want to research. Adobe's Web site doesn't have an available, global list of regions and categories to search for multiple photographers. After you try searching the Web page and wind up with 10 instances of no results, you're more likely to reach out to the Web and use Google or Yahoo to find photographers in your area. Although the service is young, it's likely to grow in representation and gain more elaborate search features, so be certain to visit the Web site periodically.

Additional search options

If you take a moment and refer back to Figure 7-32, notice the icons on the top right side of the Stock Photo pane. The first icon is a link to the Adobe Stock Photos Service Home page. The Home page is where you are when looking at the figure. The icon to the right of the Home icon is another search tool. Click the tool labeled "More ways to find images" and your default Web browser is launched. The Web page placed in view in your Web browser is the Adobe Stock Photos Web page, where you can find links to a huge directory of service providers. Among the providers is the Hulton Archive that claims a library of more than 40 million images. If you don't find what you're looking for searching in the Bridge, you can go online and find images within libraries containing millions of files.

Acquiring Adobe Stock Photos

If you looked over the last section related to searching images in the Adobe Stock Photo library, you caught a glimpse of what is certain to be a great benefit for creative professionals. Many creative pro people would agree that the most time consuming aspect of an advertising campaign or design project is acquiring the right artwork. If you work with photo shoots you know that scheduling photographers, models, directing a shoot and then having transparencies scanned or obtaining digital photos is costly and takes the lion share of the time to create a design. If you use stock photos, you know that searching through volumes of stock photo books or online services is equally time consuming. After you have all the necessary artwork, the time required to layout a design is sometimes a fraction of what you invest in obtaining the artwork to use in your design.

Most creative professionals will immediately notice the advantages in using the Adobe Stock Photo options. You can easily search for the images you want to include in a campaign, design comps, and get your client approvals all with less time invested than when using more traditional methods. Furthermore, you won't spend any money until it comes time to purchase the final images. All in all, the Adobe Stock Photo options are one more feature in the Creative Suite that helps you become more efficient in your work.

Understanding terms of service

The first stop in using the Adobe Stock Photo Services (ASPS) options is to understand the usage rights. You want to be clear about what you can and can't do with ASPS before you invest any time in searching for images.

When you open the ASPS pane in the Bridge, notice the link at the bottom of the pane titled: Terms of Service. Click this link and the pane changes to offer you a detailed description of the service and usage rights. Additionally, a PDF document is available to download from within the pane that provides you the same information in a PDF file.

Without detailing all the aspects of your usage rights, in short, you cannot do anything with the images you download except use them as comps. The images you download are 72 ppi images to be used as comps to show your client. If you and your client agree to using images from the ASPS library, you need to go online and pay for the high-resolution images. This means that you cannot legally use comps for Web designs, use them with Illustrator's Live Trace for final artwork, share the images with anyone, or distribute them through any means, electronic or otherwise. Be certain you understand the terms of service before you invest any time in searching and acquiring files.

Getting an overview of ASPS

After reading the terms of service, your next stop is to browse the Overview pane. Click the button at the top of the Bridge window below the text box used to search for ASPS images and the Overview pane opens as shown in Figure 7-34.

Figure 7-34: Click the Overview tab to access a pane that provides information in using the ASPS.

The Overview pane is like a guide for using the service and provides you with some information related to terms of use, searching for photos, definitions of "comp" so you're clear on usage rights, purchasing, managing an account, and return policies. Click the links and look over the information hyperlinked to the Overview pane to familiarize yourself with using the service.

Provider libraries

As of the introduction of ASPS, there are more than 230,000 images accessible through the service. Providers such as Getty's Photodisc images, Digital Vision, Amana, Comstock Images, and Imageshop are among the providers introduced with the service. As new and additional providers become available, the ASPS service will update and provide access to more images.

If you like the images offered by one provider over others, you can confine searches to report results from any given provider. Additionally, you can browse the individual provider libraries as well as all images from multiple providers according to given categories.

Browsing images

Click Browse in the ASPS pane of the Bridge and the pane changes to display categorical listings of images you can view in thumbnail sizes before you download any comps. When you click a category in the Browse pane shown in Figure 7-35, the pane changes to the content area thumbnail view where image thumbnails from all providers are displayed.

Figure 7-35: The Browse pane provides links to thumbnail views of images from all providers.

When you visit the browse results where the thumbnails are shown in the content area, you see buttons that enable you to get prices, download comp images, and order high-resolution images (see Figure 7-36).

Figure 7-36: The Results pane offers options for pricing, acquiring comps, and ordering high-resolution images.

Getting news and offers

The last button on the top of the ASPS pane takes you to the News & Offers pane. This area of ASPS is designed for future services. As more content is added to the service, you'll see news and information displayed here as well as promotional offers and discounts. Be certain to check this pane routinely, as it is likely to be one of the most updated areas within the Bridge.

Downloading comps

To reiterate, comps in ASPS terms refers to a low-resolution image you download free and use exclusively to develop a creative concept. The file you acquire is not intended, nor do you have permission to, use the file for final artwork.

After you become familiar with all the ASPS has to offer, you're no doubt anxious to begin exploring the photos and the service. For a real worldview on using ASPS, look over the steps below that illustrate how you might search for images, acquire a comp, and eventually purchase the high-resolution commercial image.

STEPS: Acquiring and Using Comps

1. **Open the ASPS pane.** The first step in the process of acquiring a comp to use in a job is to search for an image. With the elaborate means for searching files, you can narrow your search criteria to fit the right kind of image that fits your design. Open a Bridge window and click Adobe Stock Photos. You need the ASPS pane in view in order to search the photos.

2. **Search for a photo.** Presume for a moment you want to design an ad campaign for a sports shoe manufacturer. You want a photo to build into a design of a woman jumping in the air with her tennis shoes highly visible. In the text box at the top of the ASPS pane, type: *woman AND jump AND shoes*. Click the Search tool.

Note Typing AND does not require uppercase. Boolean operators are typed in uppercase in this chapter to distinguish the operators from the keywords. To use the words AND, OR, or NOT as part of your search keywords, place the words within quote marks. ASPS perceives "and," "or," and "not" as Boolean expressions if you don't enclose these words in quotes.

3. **Open an image.** The search results display the found occurrences in the content area in thumbnail views as shown in Figure 7-37. Downloading an image and opening it in Photoshop is handled the same as if the file already exists on your hard drive and you view it in a Bridge window. Just double-click the desired image and it opens in Photoshop. When you double-click an image or click Download in the ASPS pane, the file is downloaded to a Comps folder created by the Bridge when you installed the Creative Suite.

Figure 7-37: The results are displayed in the content area as thumbnails.

4. **Get pricing information.** Select the image you want and click Get Price and Keywords in the results pane shown in Figure 7-37.

5. **View the Get Price & Keywords dialog box.** Take a moment and look over the Get Price & Keywords dialog box shown in Figure 7-38. This dialog box opens after you click Get Price & Keywords. Prices for different resolution sizes are reported in the dialog box as well as an option to search again. Notice that keywords used for the image are reported. You can click the check marks for keywords that best describe the image you want and search for similar files. Check some boxes that describe an image you want and click Search Again.

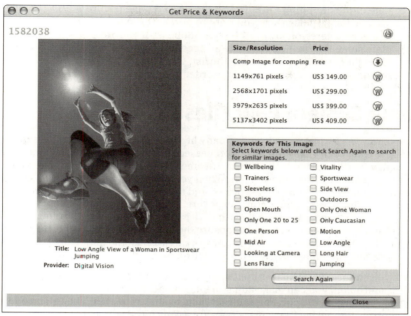

Figure 7-38: The Get Price & Keywords dialog box provides pricing information and options to search again.

6. **Order an image.** Don't worry. You aren't going to incur any charges by following along. Select the image you want and click Add to Cart.

7. **Proceed to check out.** A dialog box opens after you add an image to the shopping cart (see Figure 7-39). You have choices for View Shopping Cart or click OK. If you click OK, you can continue shopping. Click View Shopping Cart and you move to the checkout pane.

Figure 7-39: The Shopping Cart lists the files you are about to order and the estimated total price.

8. **Cancel the Shopping Cart.** The Shopping Cart pane (Figure 7-39) again offers the options for the image size you want to purchase. If you click Check Out, you are taken to a page where you log in with your Adobe ID. If you are a new user, you need to complete some information to create an account. To cancel the order, click the trash icon to the right of the item selected in the list. Click the left arrow at the top of the pane to revisit the previous view and your order is canceled.

Opening Camera Raw Files

Camera raw is a format supported by many higher end amateur and professional digital cameras. The camera raw file contains unprocessed data from the digital camera's image sensor. As such, you are working with a maximum amount of data and you're not relying on the camera to process any image information. When you open a camera raw image, you have control over how you want the image interpreted and thus you can make adjustments for lighting, brightness, sharpness, temperature, exposure, saturation, and more. Think of the camera raw format like a film negative while JPEG and TIFF images are like photo prints. You can make prints from a negative and control exposure times for the prints, dodge, burn, and so on. If you make a print from a print, you're not working with all the data you had when the negative was made and therefore have much less control over lighting, exposure, contrast, and so on.

When you shoot several images containing similar content, lighting conditions, brightness values, and so on, you can make adjustments on one image for the proper processing and then use the Bridge to apply the same settings to similar images. The Bridge offers you several controls for making the camera raw processing more automated that can significantly speed up the process of opening the files.

Setting camera raw preferences

Camera raw has its own set of preferences apart from the Bridge preference settings. On the Macintosh choose Bridge ➪ Camera Raw Preferences. On Windows choose Edit ➪ Camera Raw Preferences to open the Camera Raw Preferences dialog box as shown in Figure 7-40.

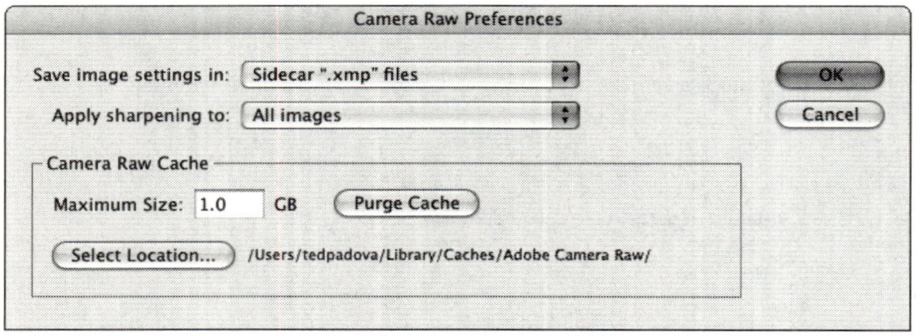

Figure 7-40: The Camera Raw Preferences are contained in an individual dialog box apart from the other Bridge Preferences.

The Camera Raw Preferences offer a few options for working specifically with these file types. The options include:

✦ **Save image settings in:** A pull-down menu offers two options for where Camera Raw settings are saved. This is an important adjustment when working with Camera Raw images and you'll want to visit the preference options regularly to be certain you know where the settings are saved. The choices include:

- **Sidecar XMP files:** This option is the best for collaborative workflow environments and for archiving images. The settings you apply to an image are saved in an XMP file in the same folder where the image resides. The filename uses the same base name as your image file with an .xmp extension. The XMP files can store IPTC metadata and other metadata associated with the file (see Working with Metadata earlier in this chapter). In Bridge, XMP sidecar files are hidden by default, but they are visible in the Macintosh Finder or Windows Explorer. When you copy, move, and delete camera raw images in the Bridge, the XMP sidecar files are moved along with their corresponding images. You can make the XMP sidecar files visible by choosing View ⇨ Show Hidden Files in the Bridge. Be certain to copy these files when you store Camera Raw files on CDs and other kinds of external media.

- **Camera Raw Database:** If you choose this option from the pull-down menu, the settings are stored in a Camera Raw database file on your local hard drive. On the Macintosh, the files are stored in the user's Preferences folder located at: Users/user name//Library/Preferences (Macintosh) or the user's Application Data folder located at: Documents and Settings/user name/Application Data/Adobe/CameraRaw (Windows). The filename where the preferences are stored is Adobe Camera Raw Database. The database file is indexed by file content. Therefore, if you move or rename camera raw files, the settings in the Camera Raw database stay connected with the images. It should be obvious that this method for saving settings is less desirable for collaborative workflow environments as the settings are not available to other users when retrieving files from offline media storage.

✦ **Apply sharpening to:** The Camera Raw plug-in can apply sharpening to camera raw images. If you want to use the plug-in to apply sharpening to the actual images select *All Images* from the pull-down menu. If you select the Preview Images Only option from the pull-down menu, sharpening is applied only to the preview image leaving the camera raw file intact.

✦ **Camera Raw Cache:** When working with camera raw files you have two cache files to deal with. The Bridge has its own cache where the processing of image thumbnails, previews, and metadata are stored. When files are saved to the cache, your computer speed increases so you can view items more quickly. The camera raw cache increases the speed of loading the Camera Raw dialog box and recalculating camera raw image previews after you make settings changes. This section of the Camera Raw Preferences dialog box handles the related camera raw cache.

- **Maximum Size:** The default is 1GB. You can increase the cache size by editing the value in the text box. You can process about 200 images per gigabyte. If you are working on significantly more images, open the preferences and increase the cache size.

- **Purge Cache:** The cache occupies storage space on your hard drive. If you want to free up some room on your hard drive, click Purge Cache. Be aware that when you return to the Camera Raw dialog box, the time to view previews and settings will take longer as a new cache file is built.

- **Select Location:** The default location where the cache file is saved appears in the dialog box. This location is your boot drive. If you want to change the cache location, click Change Location and navigate to the folder where you want the cache saved. If you use secondary hard drives for scratch data, you can change the cache location to your data drive.

Using the Camera Raw plug-In

The Camera Raw dialog box appears in Bridge and Photoshop because of a plug-in. Camera raw features are not hard coded in either program. Adobe created a plug-in to work with camera raw images because the plug-in requires some frequent updating. Camera manufacturers who support writing to the camera raw format all use a different flavor of camera raw. It's like Beta, VHS, and Super VHS, or cassette and 8-track. It's all tape, but the formats are different. As new cameras are made, newer camera raw formats are created. In order to regularly upgrade the camera raw features in Bridge and Photoshop, Adobe offers plug-in upgrades routinely so you can download and install them easily to keep your programs updated.

Adobe has been trying to get camera manufacturers to support the Adobe-developed format DNG (Digital Negative) so we can all experience consistency when saving and opening files from our digital cameras. Unfortunately the battle does not look too promising. After all, we're dealing with the hardheaded companies that battled over Beta versus VHS or 8-track versus cassette. Granted, the battles of Beta versus VHS were eventually won, but there were only two major players in those battles. With camera raw the number of players are significantly more and the likelihood that every manufacturer will support DNG is unlikely. We wish Adobe luck in their efforts, but don't hold your breath.

When you open a camera raw image, it opens in the Camera Raw dialog box. You have two choices for where the Camera Raw dialog box appears. If you select an image and choose File ➪ Open, use a context menu and select Open, or use a keyboard shortcut and press ⌘/Ctrl+O, the Bridge switches to Photoshop and the Camera Raw plug-in from Photoshop is used. If you select an image and choose File ➪ Open in Camera Raw or use a context menu and select the same menu command, the Camera Raw plug-in from the Bridge opens the file in the Camera Raw dialog box. You process the image regardless of where the Camera Raw dialog box appears and when you finish making adjustments, you click Done or Open (Image). When you click Done, your settings are changed from the original default to adjustments made in the Camera Raw dialog box. You are returned to the Bridge window or to Photoshop but the file(s) does not open. If you click Open in the Camera Raw dialog box (or Open Image when multiple files are opened in the dialog box), the file opens in Photoshop regardless of which plug-in you use. Your original camera raw image remains unaffected when you open a file in Photoshop and you can return to it to apply different settings to open again in Photoshop. If you apply settings without opening a file, you can return to defaults and the original image data are again available for making new settings adjustments.

You can also process multiple images. In the Bridge, Shift+click to make a contiguous selection or ⌘/Ctrl+click for a non-contiguous selection. From a context menu select Open or press ⌘/Ctrl+O to open with Photoshop's Camera Raw plug-in or select Open in Camera Raw from either the File menu or context menu to open using the Bridge plug-in. All files selected in the Bridge window open in the respective Camera Raw dialog box, where they appear listed in a Filmstrip along the left side of the dialog box.

When you open a camera raw photo in either Bridge or Photoshop, the camera raw plug-in opens the Camera Raw dialog box shown in Figure 7-41. There's a lot to the options in the Camera Raw dialog box, so be certain to look over the descriptions of the following settings:

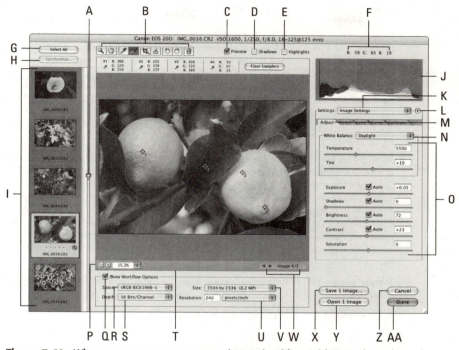

Figure 7-41: When you open a camera raw image in either Bridge or Photoshop, the Camera Raw plug-in opens the Camera Raw dialog box.

- **A Separator bar:** Drag the separator bar to size the Filmstrip (I) and Preview (T). As the Filmstrip is sized up, the Preview is sized down and vice versa. Double click the separator bar and the Filmstrip hides from view offering more area to preview the image.

- **B Tools:** Nine tools appear at the top of the window. The tools include:

  - **Zoom tool:** Click in the preview to zoom in. Press the Option/Alt key and click the Zoom tool to zoom out. Click and drag open a marquee to zoom into a defined area. Press the ⌘/Ctrl key to toggle the Zoom tool to the Hand tool.

  - **Hand tool:** Click and drag to move the document around the preview area when zoomed in. Press the ⌘/Ctrl key to toggle the tool to the Zoom tool.

  - **White Balance tool:** Click the White Balance tool in the image area to sample an area and set the white balance. If you click in an area too bright, a dialog box informs you that you cannot remap the white point to the sampled area.

  - **Color Sampler tool:** Move the tool around the image area and the RGB color values are reported in the RGB values (F). Click to plot a sampler point. Click again and another point is sampled. You can plot as many as four different color samples. Each sample's RGB values are reported below the tools area in the dialog box. When you click with the Color Sampler, a button appears. Click Clear Samples to delete all the sampled points.

- **Crop tool:** You can use the Crop tool to target an area you want to isolate to apply exposure controls. If you find the crop area to snap to proportions and you want to crop an image disproportionately, open a context menu (or the pull-down menu in the Crop tool icon) and select Normal from the menu commands. If you want fixed ratios, return to the context menu and select a fixed size that matches your needs. If you crop an area in the image preview and click done, you haven't changed the original raw image. Open the image again in the Camera Raw dialog box and open a context menu using the Crop tool. Select Clear Crop from the menu commands. Note that use of the Crop tool in the Camera Raw dialog box is much more limiting than using the Photoshop Crop tool. If you want to crop images, do it in Photoshop.

- **Straighten tool:** This tool is used for straightening crooked images. For example, if a series of shots is taken on a tripod that's slightly crooked, you can fix all the images with a single swipe of the Straighten tool. It gives the user the same results as straightening in Photoshop, except the Straighten tool has these benefits: doesn't require a two-step measurement *and* a rotation process as in Photoshop, is a live adjustment that can be changed on the fly, is stored in metadata and can be reverted or changed at any time without calculations, combines rotation and cropping into one step and is much easier to apply to multiple images.

- **Rotate image 90° counterclockwise:** Rotates the image left in a counterclockwise direction.

- **Rotate image 90° clockwise:** Rotates the image right in a clockwise direction.

- **Toggle mark for delete tool:** Select an image in the filmstrip and click the trash icon. The file is marked for deletion. Files are not trashed in the Camera Raw dialog box until you first mark them and then click Done. Files are moved to the trash on your desktop. If you want to move them out of the trash and back to a folder, be certain to bring back both the CRW file and XMP file if saving your settings in sidecar files.

C **Preview:** The Preview dynamically updates as you change settings. If you zoom in and out of the preview image and want to return to a fit page view, press ⌘/Ctrl+0 (zero). The keyboard shortcut is the same in all Adobe programs to fit in window or fit page. If the preview has a yellow ! icon over it that indicates the preview is being updated and is not accurate until the icon goes away.

D **Shadows:** When checked, the image shows clipped shadows appearing in blue highlights. Clipping indicates all areas where some color remapping will occur.

E **Highlights:** Clipped highlights are shown in Red.

F **RGB values:** The values reported here are derived from the position of the Color Sampler tool. As you move the tool around the Preview area, the color values change to report the values of the pixels beneath the tool. When you click in the Preview with the Color Sampler, the values for the plotted area are reported in the RGB values and duplicated below the tools.

G **Select All:** Select All selects all the images in the filmstrip. You can select all images and globally apply the same settings to the selected images. You can also Shift+click or ⌘/Ctrl+click in the filmstrip to select multiple images in a contiguous or non-contiguous group.

H Synchronize: When you open multiple files in the Camera Raw dialog box, you can apply settings to one image, then use Select All or individually select multiple images and synchronize the settings. When you select Synchronize, the Synchronize dialog box opens. You can use this dialog box to choose which settings to apply to the selected image. This dialog box offers the same options as the Paste Camera Raw Settings dialog box shown later in this chapter in Figure 7-43. See the section "Applying settings in Bridge" later in this chapter for more information.

I Filmstrip: The filmstrip shows a thumbnail preview for all files opened in the camera raw dialog box. You can click a thumbnail and the image appears in the Preview area as well as the filmstrip. The file in the Preview area is the one targeted for editing. Note that if you only open one Camera Raw image at a time, the filmstrip becomes unavailable in the Camera Raw dialog.

J Histogram: The histogram displays the total range of the image data. As you make settings adjustments in the Camera Raw dialog box, the histogram dynamically updates to display a graph showing the data changes.

K Settings: The Settings pull-down menu offers four options. Choose Image Settings to apply settings for processed images, choose Camera Raw Defaults to return to the original default settings when the photo was taken, choose Previous Conversion to apply the last conversion settings made, the menu command Custom changes automatically when you make an adjustment.

L Fly-out menu: Click the right pointing arrow to open the menu. Menu commands are available for saving and loading settings, exporting settings, deleting settings, setting new defaults and opening the Camera Raw Preferences dialog box.

M Tabs: The individual tabs change the default Adjust pane to provide you with more editing options. The tabs include:

- **Adjust:** Adjust is the default tab and the view you see in Figure 7-41. Use the sliders to adjust the image for proper white balance, temperature, and exposure settings.

- **Detail:** Use this tab to adjust sharpening and luminance smoothing or color noise reduction.

- **Lens:** Lens corrections are made for Chromatic Aberration and Vignetting that you might find apparent in digital camera images.

New Feature

For more control over correcting aberrations created from digital cameras, see the new Lens Correction filter in Photoshop CS2 in Chapter 11.

- **Curve:** The curve settings are similar to what you find in Photoshop's Curves dialog box. You can adjust highlights, midtones, and shadows in this tab.

- **Calibrate:** You may experience colorcasts and tint differences in shadows and non-neutral colors between the color profile used for your camera and the Camera Raw's built-in profile. Use this tab to compensate for the differences.

N White Balance: White balance sets the color balance of an image to reflect the lighting conditions under which the photo was taken. Here you'll find compensation for such items as sunlight, shade, flash, fluorescent, and tungsten lighting. You also have a Custom choice where the pull-down menu reflects custom if you change either the temperature or the tint.

O **Adjustment sliders:** The adjustment sliders affect the image brightness values. When one of the sliders is moved the Preview image dynamically changes to reflect the new setting. You see a preview of each setting made with the adjustment sliders and can choose settings that best produce the image detail and color balance.

P **Zoom settings:** In addition to using the zoom tool you can click on the minus (-) symbol to zoom out or the plus (+) symbol to zoom in. From the pull-down menu you can select fixed zoom sizes. Note that the text appearing between the symbols and the arrows used to open the pull-down menu is not an editable item. The readout is used for information only to show the zoom level in relation to actual size.

Q **Show Workflow Options:** Workflow options are the items appearing below the checkbox for Space, Depth, Size, and Resolution. When you uncheck the box, these four items disappear from the dialog box. If you need to make adjustments for these settings, click the checkbox.

R **Color Space:** Select from four options for your color working space. The default is Adobe RGB (1998). If you are processing files for Web hosting, you may want to change the color space to sRGB IEC61966-1.

S **Bit Depth:** Choose from 8-bit or 16-bit. If you have a camera that supports 16-bit images, leave them at 16-bit. High bit images can edited in Photoshop and preferred when adjusting Sharpening, Levels, Curves, or any other color or brightness controls.

T **Image Preview:** Displays the current image selected in the filmstrip. If only one image is open, the image appears in the preview area. The preview image is targeted for the adjustments you make for all the other settings in the dialog box.

U **Resolution:** The current image resolution is reported in the text box. You can change image resolution by adding a new value in the text box. You can choose to view either pixels/inch or pixels/cm from the pull-down menu to the right of the text box. As a matter of rule, you are best served by changing resolution in Photoshop. You can use this option when you have a number of files you want to process at the same resolution and size.

V **Size:** From the pull-down menu, you can select different physical sizes for your image. Resizing the image by selecting a menu item does not affect image sampling.

W **Image selection:** Use the left and right arrows to scroll images in the filmstrip up or down respectively. The readout to the right of the arrows displays the current image in the Preview window and the total number of images opened in the Camera Raw dialog box.

X **Save image:** Click Save Image to save the settings applied to the image(s). If you want to return to defaults, open the image and select Camera Raw Defaults from the Settings (K) pull-down menu.

Y **Open image:** Click Open Image to open the Preview image in Photoshop with the applied settings.

Z **Cancel:** Click Cancel to dismiss the dialog box without applying any settings. You can also press Esc to cancel out of the dialog box. Press the Option/Control and Cancel changes to Reset. Click Reset and all the settings made in your editing session are dismissed and return you to the same appearance as when you opened the file(s) in the Camera Raw dialog box.

AA **Done:** When you click Done, the settings you made apply to the image. The Camera Raw dialog box closes, but the file(s) do not open in Photoshop.

You can save any adjustments you make as settings or use them as new defaults. From the fly-out menu you open by clicking the right pointing arrow adjacent to the Settings pull-down menu, you have a number of choices as shown in Figure 7-42.

Figure 7-42: Open the fly-out menu to save settings or create new defaults.

The default setting is Auto Adjustments. You can change the settings by saving and loading settings or apply settings you make as a new default. When you want to return to the image as it was taken, select Reset Camera Raw Defaults.

Applying settings in Bridge

In addition to options available in the flyaway menu in the Camera Raw dialog box, you have similar menu commands when you choose Edit ⇨ Apply Camera Raw Settings or when you open a context menu on a selected image. The submenu commands offer the following options:

- **Camera Raw Defaults:** This option is the same as selecting Reset Camera Raw Defaults in the flyaway menu.

- **Previous Conversion:** If you convert an image and want to apply the same conversion setting, select an image or multiple images in the Bridge and choose Edit ⇨ Apply Camera Raw Settings ⇨ Previous Conversion.

- **Copy camera Raw Settings:** Assume you made some conversion settings changes on an image and click Done in the Camera Raw dialog box. The settings are applied to your image. You can select the image and choose Edit ⇨ Apply Camera Raw Settings ⇨ Copy Camera Raw Settings. The settings are now available for pasting into another image.

- **Paste Camera Raw Settings:** After copying settings choose Edit ⇨ Apply Camera Raw Settings ⇨ Paste Camera Raw Settings. This option offers you discretionary selection for what settings to apply. Rather than paste all the settings changes into the selected image, the Paste Camera Raw Settings dialog box shown in Figure 7-43 opens. As you can see in the dialog box, you can check the different settings you want to paste. Note that the options in this dialog box are the same as when clicking Synchronize in the Camera Raw dialog box.

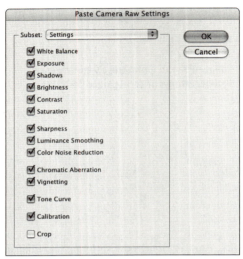

Figure 7-43: When you paste camera raw settings, the Paste Camera Raw Settings dialog box opens where you can selectively choose which settings to paste.

- **Clear Camera Raw Settings:** This command clears the settings that you applied to a camera raw file. Select a file in the Bridge and choose Edit ➪ Apply Camera Raw Settings ➪ Clear Camera Raw Settings. The settings are dumped from the file and the image returns to the defaults at the time it was shot. Note that clearing settings has nothing to do with the copy/paste features. If you clear settings, you can still paste settings on another image as the copied information was not disturbed when selecting Clear Camera Raw Settings.

Saving Camera Raw files

If you make settings changes and click Open in the Camera Raw Settings dialog box, the file opens in Photoshop. From Photoshop you can save files in a variety of different formats. But Photoshop won't let you save back to camera raw. Photoshop does support a Photoshop Raw format but it's not the same as camera raw. Camera raw saves uncompressed bits from a camera's CCD or CMOS. Photoshop Raw is a flexible file format designed for transferring images between applications and computer platforms.

If you want to adjust settings and save the adjusted images as a new file while preserving your settings and the camera raw format, click Save in the Camera Raw dialog box. When you click Save in the dialog box, the Save Options dialog box appears, as shown in Figure 7-44.

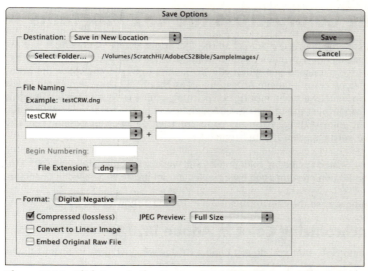

Figure 7-44: Click Save in the Camera Raw dialog box and the Save Options dialog box opens.

Attribute choices for your saved image from the Camera Raw Save option include:

- **Destination:** Click Select Folder to navigate your hard drive and find a new location to save your file.

- **File Naming:** Supply a name for your file in the text box on the left and an extension on the right. If you have multiple files open in the Camera Raw dialog box you can add additional names by clicking the plus (+) symbol to add more field boxes. You do not need to add or change extensions because the dialog box automatically supplies an extension in the File Extension pull-down menu when you change the format in the Format pull-down menu.

- **Format:** If you want to save back to raw format, you can choose Adobe's Digital Negative (DNG) format. The file is saved as a camera raw file. When you open the file it opens in the Camera Raw dialog box. However, the file you save as DNG does not retain all the original raw information obtained from the file you first opened in the Camera Raw dialog box. The new settings prevail and you can't return to original defaults. If you want to retain all data as the image was first taken with your camera, check the box at the bottom of the dialog box for Embed Original Raw File.

The remaining options in the Save Options dialog box for DNG files offer you choices for image compression, JPEG previews (only when DNG format is chosen), Convert to Linear Image (stores the data in an interpolated format). Other formats for JPEG, TIFF, and Photoshop all have different attribute choices for their respective formats. These attribute choices are the same as you are familiar with when saving files from Photoshop.

Synchronizing Color Across the CS2 Programs

In Bridge you can synchronize color across all the CS2 applications. Bridge does not provide you options for creating color profiles or embedding profiles in application documents. Rather, you use Bridge to ensure that when you work with a given color space in Photoshop, you work with the same color space in InDesign and all other CS2 programs. Synchronizing color in Bridge ensures that a given monitor or printing profile in Photoshop or Illustrator is maintained when you import the images in InDesign. If you have one color setting in one program and a different color setting in another program, the Color Settings dialog box alerts you that your color settings are not synchronized.

Cross-Reference For information related to creating color profiles and working in color-managed workflows, see Chapter 6. This section presumes you have created a color profile as detailed in Chapter 6.

To synchronize color across the CS2 applications in Bridge, follow these steps:

STEPS: Synchronizing Color in Adobe Bridge

1. **Launch Bridge.** Note that you do not need a Bridge window open in order to synchronize color.
2. **Open the Suite Color Settings.** Choose Edit ➪ Color Settings. The Suite Color Settings dialog box opens.
3. **Expand the list of color management settings.** By default, Bridge displays a short list of color management settings. Select the Show Expanded List of Color Settings Files check box, as shown in Figure 7-45.

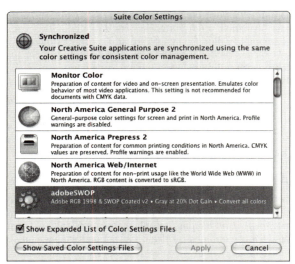

Figure 7-45: Select the Show Expanded List of Color Settings Files check box to view all color settings accessible to the CS2 programs.

4. **Select a color setting.** Color settings are created in other programs such as Adobe Photoshop or made available to you from service providers or other users in your workflow. If you have color settings installed properly on your computer, they are visible in the Suite Color Settings dialog box. Scroll the list of settings and select the setting used in your workflow.

5. **Apply a color setting to synchronize color.** Click Apply after selecting the setting of your choice. Your color settings are now synchronized across the CS2 applications. If you open Photoshop, Illustrator, InDesign, or GoLive and choose Edit ⇨ Color Settings, you'll find the same color settings applied to each application. In Acrobat, you need to choose Acrobat ⇨ Preferences (Macintosh) or Edit ⇨ Preferences (Windows), and click Color Management in the left pane. You should plan on double-checking Acrobat to be certain the color settings are applied. Acrobat is the one program where synchronizing color in Bridge may fail. If your color settings do not match the other CS2 applications, open the Settings pull-down menu and select the same setting you selected in Bridge.

Synchronizing color settings is of particular benefit for creative professionals who work on design projects for both print and Web. When you begin a new project, be certain to visit the Bridge Suite Color Settings dialog box and synchronize your color. As you switch between print and Web designs, change your color settings accordingly. Bridge makes it easy for you to be certain you work in the same color space in each CS2 application.

For information on using color settings for print and Web, see Chapter 6.

Enabling Application Commands from the Bridge

Some of the automated features in several CS applications have been added as menu commands in the Bridge. You can execute actions and commands in the Bridge without leaving the window or opening any one of the other CS programs. Actually, the Bridge opens the applications for you when actions and internal program features are used. Photoshop, Illustrator and InDesign are all supported with one or more features you are likely to use frequently.

Photoshop support

Among the automated features and commands integrated between the Bridge and the CS2 programs, Photoshop supports the most options. You can activate Photoshop online services as well as many of the automated features found in Photoshop CS1.

Photoshop services

Two Photoshop online services are accessible in the Bridge. You can order prints online using Kodak EasyShare. First select JPEG images as JPEG is the only file format supported by the service. After selecting the images, choose Tools ⇨ Photoshop Services ⇨ Photo Prints. A window opens where you set up an account to order prints online. The first 10 prints are provided free as a trial service.

The companion Photoshop service is Photoshare. Rather than order prints online the service is used for file sharing. If you have an account you can log on and upload files to your account folder. To access Photoshare, choose Tools ⇨ Photoshop Services ⇨ Photo Sharing.

A third option is available in the Photoshop Services submenu. Select Choose location to identify the country where you live. If you select Japan, Germany, or France, the services appear in the respective language.

Batch processing with Actions

The Photoshop Batch command is supported from within Bridge. When you choose Tools ➪ Photoshop ➪ Batch, Bridge opens Photoshop and the Batch dialog box opens just like you see when executing a Batch from within Photoshop.

Before you run a Batch sequence in Photoshop, you should visit the Actions palette and load actions you use in your workflow. Photoshop CS2 defaults to a new set of actions that are used to change workspace appearances. Many of the familiar actions found in earlier versions of Photoshop are left out of the Default Actions set. If you need one of the actions formerly included in the default set, you need to load a saved actions file. See the section "Loading Actions" later in the chapter for more information.

One of the new default actions that you may want to look at when you first install Photoshop CS2 is the What's New in CS2 workspaces action. Open the Actions palette, click this action and click Play Selection at the bottom of the Actions palette. A warning dialog box opens informing you that you are about to modify your menus and keyboard shortcuts. Click Yes in the dialog box and the action runs. When you open menus in Photoshop you'll see menu items for all commands with new features color highlighted. In Figure 7-46 you can see the Image menu as it appears after running the What's New in CS2 workspaces action. Note the highlights for several menu commands.

Figure 7-46: Running the What's New in CS2 workspaces action changes menus where new commands are color highlighted.

After you explore some of the actions sets loaded by default, you may find these new default actions somewhat useless in your design work. The familiar actions you have used in earlier versions of Photoshop are installed with Photoshop CS2, you just need to load them to make them available in the Actions palette.

Loading Actions

In the Actions palette, you can load actions files, save actions files, and replace actions files. Loading actions appends a new action set to the palette. Replacing an action set removes the former actions and adds the new action set you load. If you haven't worked with loading actions in earlier versions of Photoshop, look over the following steps to see how action sets are loaded.

STEPS: Loading Actions

1. **Open the Actions palette.** By default the Actions palette is visible when you launch Photoshop CS2. If the palette is not visible, choose Window ➪ Actions.

2. **Open the Load dialog box.** Click the right pointing arrow in the top right corner of the Actions palette to open a palette menu. Scroll down the menu options and select Load Actions. The Load dialog box opens as shown in Figure 7-47.

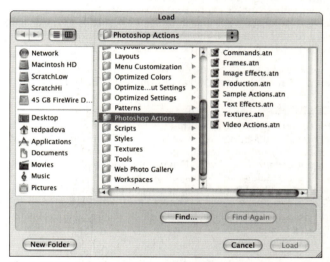

Figure 7-47: Select an Action set to load in the Load dialog box.

3. **Load an Action Set.** When you select Load Actions in the Actions palette menu, Photoshop opens the Photoshop Actions folder where all actions sets are saved. Select one of the sets and click Load. If you want to load actions that match the default actions in Photoshop CS1, select Sample Actions.atn and click Load. You can click to select a set and shift or ⌘/Ctrl+click to select multiple sets and load them all together. Look over the sets and load those preconfigured actions you use in your workflow. As was the case in Photoshop CS1, you still have the opportunity to create custom actions. If you have custom actions you created in Photoshop CS1, you can navigate to your Photoshop CS1 folder and load custom actions sets from the Photoshop Actions folder in the Photoshop CS1:Presets folder.

Running actions from the Bridge

If all you can do in the Bridge were run an action on a folder of files, there would be no benefit to running the action from Bridge or from Photoshop. However, the Bridge offers you one option that Photoshop doesn't. In Photoshop, you run actions on open files or on a folder of files. Photoshop does not offer you discretionary selection of images you want to affect with an action. Bridge, on the other hand, let's you individually select files in the content area and apply actions to a selected group. If you use Bridge search and find files from different folders meeting your search criteria, the files are loaded in a new Bridge window. Subsequently, you can run an action on files from different folders — something you can't do in Photoshop's Batch dialog box.

Cross-Reference For information on searching files in Bridge and adding results to a new Bridge window, see the steps in the section "Viewing Files from Different Folders in a Single Bridge Window."

When you have the files in view in a Bridge window, choose Tools ➪ Photoshop ➪ Batch. The Bridge immediately opens Photoshop (if not open) or switches to Photoshop and opens the Batch dialog box. You apply the same settings in the batch dialog box for the action you want to use, where you want to save your files, and the naming conventions you want to use. When you click OK, the action steps are applied to the selected Bridge files.

Note that when you load action sets or create custom actions, all the actions are available in the Batch dialog box and can be run from Bridge or from within Photoshop.

Creating contact sheets

The same benefits for running actions from within the Bridge also apply to creating contact sheets. Using the Contact Sheet II automation feature in Photoshop you can create user defined contact sheets where your selected Bridge files are automatically size and placed on individual Photoshop documents. The size and quantity of images on a single sheet are determined in the Contact Sheet II dialog box. When you select files from the Bridge and choose Tools ➪ Photoshop ➪ Contact Sheet II, Bridge switches to Photoshop the same as when applying actions to selected Bridge files. When the Contact Sheet II dialog box opens, the Use pull-down menu shows the Selected Images from Bridge option (Figure 7-48). Adjust settings in the Contact Sheet II dialog box and click OK. Your selected Bridge files are then added to Photoshop contact sheet documents.

Using Image Processor

A new feature in Photoshop CS2 is the Image Processor. You can select images in the Bridge and choose Tools ➪ Photoshop ➪ Image Processor to open Photoshop's Image Processor dialog box as shown in Figure 7-49.

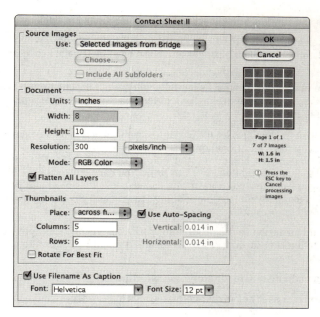

Figure 7-48: The Use pull-down menu shows you that the contact sheet Photoshop will create uses source images selected from the Bridge.

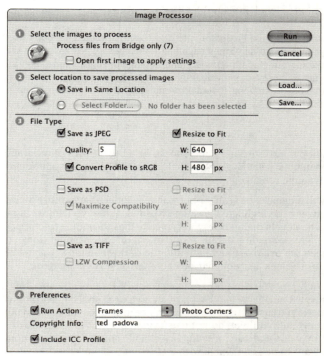

Figure 7-49: You can launch the new Image Processor in Photoshop CS2 from the Bridge.

Using the Image Processor is like running several actions at once. Options include:

- **Select Files:** You can select files from the Bridge or from within Photoshop. When you select Bridge files, the number of files to process is reported in the Image Processor dialog box.
- **Select location to save processed images:** Essentially you have the same option here as you do with actions. You can overwrite the processed images or save the processed files as copies to another folder.
- **File Type:** You can choose to save files as JPEG, Photoshop (PSD), or TIFF images. If you save files as JPEG, you have additional options for adjusting file compression (Quality text box), resizing images, and converting color profiles to sRGB. You might have used TIFF images in a layout that you want to print. You can repurpose the files for Web hosting when you use the JPEG option. You can size PSD files to fit and you can flatten the images by checking Maximize Compatibility. Saving as TIFF also offers resizing and you can use LZW compression.
- **Run Action:** You can add an action to the processing attributes. As one example, you might convert images to another format, resize them, and then add an action to convert images to grayscale.
- **Copyright Info:** You can add metadata for copyright information.
- **Include ICC Profile:** You can use the current color settings in Photoshop and embed an ICC profile.

When you finish setting attributes, click Run and the files are processed.

Note If all you want to do with the Image Processor is to add copyright metadata, don't use the Image Processor. The Image Processor opens each file in Photoshop, processes the image, and saves the results. Using a metadata template and adding copyright information in the Bridge works much faster because individual files are not opened and saved from Photoshop. For information on creating metadata templates, see the section "Creating a Template" earlier in this chapter.

Merge to HDR

This new feature in Photoshop is extraordinary and should be a big hit with photographers and designers alike. To understand what High Dynamic Range (HDR) does, you first need to understand a little about dynamic range.

When you shoot a scene with a camera or scan a photo on a scanner, you capture a range of gray values somewhere between the highlights and the shadows. When you adjust brightness values in Photoshop using the Levels dialog box, you typically make a choice to compensate for some of the loss of highlight or shadow detail. Your camera or your scanner doesn't quite capture all the range between the brightest highlight and the darkest shadow. Using Merge to HDR you can compensate for the loss and achieve a total range of grays in images.

If you can control the photography you can prepare images for HDR Merge by shooting a scene with different exposures. Use one or two EV (exposure values) steps apart (equivalent to one or two f stops). Be certain to use a tripod so you do not introduce motion to your photographic scenes. Also, be certain that if you do not use flash in one photo, that you do the same for the others. Keep the same aperture opening but change shutter speeds to control your exposures. You don't want to use one image with an f-stop at f16 and another with an f-stop at f2.8.

Take three or four images of the same scene with different exposure values and select them in the Bridge. Choose Tools ⇨ Photoshop ⇨ HDR Merge. Photoshop then takes control and merges the images together to create a 32-bit image with a higher dynamic range. Theoretically you can capture the complete dynamic range of a shot that captures all 256 levels of gray.

When Photoshop completes the merge, the Merge to HDR dialog box opens. You can adjust the bit depth by making selections from a pull-down menu. The default is 32-bit, which you should leave alone until after you save the image. Additionally the Merge to HDR dialog box has a slider, which lets you adjust the white point in the image.

You can also use Merge to HDR for abstract images and special effects. You can take three different images and merge them together creating a final image that looks like it may have passed through some Photoshop filters. In Figure 7-50 you can see such an image composed in the Merge to HDR dialog box.

Figure 7-50: Merging different images using Merge to HDR produces an abstract image.

PDF Presentation

PDF Presentation was available in Photoshop CS1. You can select a number of different files in the Bridge and create a multi-page document or a PDF Presentation. The files are converted to PDF and saved as a multi-page PDF file. The multi-page options just save the file as a multi-page document. Selecting Presentation in the PDF Presentation dialog box saves the file, also as a multi-page document, but opens automatically in Acrobat in Full Screen mode with transitions. In the Bridge, choose Tools ⇨ Photoshop ⇨ PDF Presentation.

Photomerge

Photomerge was also available in Photoshop CS1. This feature combines images to create a panoramic view. You can select the images in the Bridge of a scene shot at different angles and merge them into a panoramic image by choosing Tools ⇨ Photoshop ⇨ Photomerge.

Picture Package

Another feature in Photoshop CS1 is Picture Package. Now you can create a Picture Package from within the Bridge by selecting Tools ➪ Photoshop ➪ Picture Package. Picture Package takes the same image and duplicates it on the same page in user definable sizes — something like you might order at a photofinishing center. You can select one file or several files to process from the Bridge. Photoshop is opened and individual documents are created for each selected image.

Web Photo Gallery

The last menu command in the Photoshop submenu in the Bridge also performs a task that was available in Photoshop CS1. Use Web Photo Gallery to create images used for Web page display. Multiple images are selected in the Bridge and the final composition creates thumbnails and large images displayed from mouse clicks. The file can be exported as HTML and opened in GoLive to create a Web page of a photo gallery.

Illustrator support

Two features are supported in Bridge for Illustrator files. You can select a Photoshop image in the Bridge and choose Tools ➪ Illustrator ➪ Live Trace. Live trace is like having Adobe Streamline built into Adobe Illustrator. Live trace is no less than amazing in producing vector art images from raster image files. When launched from the Bridge, Illustrator opens and the Live Trace dialog box appears where you can choose from an abundant number of attributes to create the vector art.

For information on using Live Trace, see Chapter 11.

The other Illustrator command from the Illustrator submenu in the Bridge offers options for exporting Illustrator art to Flash SWF files. You can select a single layered Illustrator file or multiple Illustrator documents and choose from two options for exporting to SWF. Choose Quick Export to convert to SWF without having an opportunity to set attributes in the resultant SWF file. Choose Custom Export and the Illustrator Export to Flash dialog box opens where you select from many attributes before creating the SWF export.

For more information on converting Illustrator files to Flash SWF files, see Chapter 35.

InDesign support

A single option is available from within the Bridge for working with InDesign files. Choose Tools ➪ InDesign ➪ Create InDesign Contact Sheet. This option is only executable from the Bridge. InDesign does not support a menu command for creating a contact sheet, therefore you need to run the command from the Bridge.

Create InDesign Contact Sheet is similar to Contact Sheet II in Photoshop. When you choose the menu command in the Bridge, the Contact Sheet dialog box opens. The InDesign Contact Sheet dialog box offers you the same options for identifying the number of rows and columns you can specify in Photoshop, but additional features such as more control over caption placement, support for auto-rotations, ability to use an InDesign Template, and direct export to PDF give you more options than found in Photoshop. Photoshop does have one advantage over InDesign in that a thumbnail preview appears in the Photoshop Contact Sheet II dialog box and not in InDesign's dialog box.

Additional advantages for using InDesign over Photoshop are several. You can create contact sheets with smaller file sizes than with Photoshop. You can create tables in InDesign from the images. You can export the InDesign file as XML and have complete control over image replacement, and files are created as multiple pages instead of Photoshop's single pages.

When you process an InDesign contact sheet, the document appears as shown in Figure 7-51 when three columns and four rows are selected.

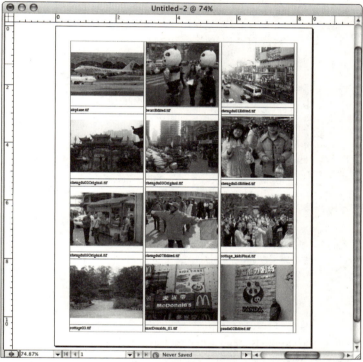

Figure 7-51: Contact sheets from InDesign offer some advantages over contact sheets created from Photoshop.

Exploring Options in the Bridge Center

The Bridge Center is like the dashboard on the Bridge vehicle. From the Bridge Center you can manage files, search for photos in the Adobe Stock Photo Service, connect to RSS news feeds and services, explore tips and techniques in using the Creative Suite programs, create a new Version Cue project, check your color management synchronization, and open the Creative Suite Help documents.

Note   Adobe Bridge Center is available with Creative Suite only. Individual copies of the other CS programs do not include Bridge Center in the Bridge application accompanying individual products.

The Bridge Center has several compartments that contain links to the supported features listed above. These separate areas of the Bridge Center include:

✦ **Saved File Groups:** Open files in any of the CS programs. Click the item denoted as "Save open files into a file group" and a dialog box opens where you type a name for the group. The group is then added in the scrollable window. Note in Figure 7-52 you can see a group that contains three files labeled *ChengduLayoutGroup*.

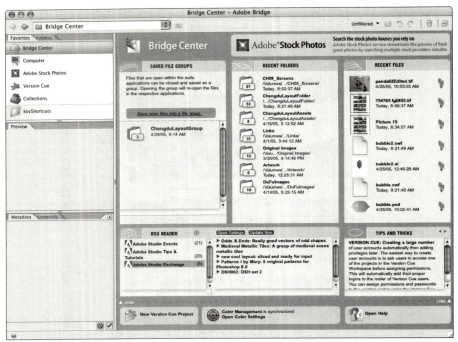

Figure 7-52: File groups in the Bridge Center are listed in the Saved File Groups compartment. Groups display the number of the files in the group, the group's name, and the date the group was created.

To delete a saved group, don't look at the Trash icon at the top of the Bridge Center window. It remains grayed out and inaccessible in the Bridge Center. Instead, select the group you want to delete and click the button appearing at the bottom of the window as shown in Figure 7-53.

Figure 7-53: To delete a saved group, select the group and click the Delete the selected file group button.

- **Adobe Stock Photos Link:** Click Adobe Stock Photos and the ASPS pane opens. For more information on using ASPS, see the section "Acquiring Adobe Stock Photos" earlier in this chapter.

- **Recent Folders:** Folders you visit in the Bridge content area are listed in the Recent Folders list. The folder icons indicate the number of files in each folder, the location of the folder on your hard drive, and the date the folder was last visited in the Bridge. Click a folder and the content area changes to display the folder contents.

- **Recent Files:** The most recent files are listed in the Recent Files list according to filename, date and time last viewing in one of the CS programs. Click a file and it opens in the authoring program. Documents from any program are listed. Clicking on a document opens the file in non-Adobe programs as well as the CS applications.

- **RSS Reader:** The RSS Reader contains links to RSS feeds. The preinstalled URL links to RSS feeds open Adobe's Web site where you can view information on tips and techniques and acquire files through the Adobe Studio Exchange. For information on using the RSS Reader and adding new feeds, see the section "Using the RSS Reader" later in this chapter.

- **Tips and Tricks:** Click one of the Reader links in the RSS Reader and the right side of the window lists the contents. In figure 8-53 you can see the five links to the Adobe Studio Exchange.

- **Create New Version Cue Project:** Click New Version Cue Project and the New Project dialog box opens. You can add a project name and project information. Click OK and a new Version Cue project folder is created.

- **Color Management Synchronization Access:** Click the Color Management item to the right of the New Version Cue Project button and the Bridge Color Settings dialog box opens. The current status of the CS color settings is reported in the Bridge Center before you open the Color Settings dialog box, therefore you only need to click the button when color is not synchronized or when you want to change color settings.

- **Help Files Access:** Click Open Help and the Adobe Help Center opens. The default view is the help document for the Bridge. From a pull-down menu at the top of the Help Center you can select other CS programs help information.

Using the RSS Reader

RSS is an acronym for Really Simple Syndication or Rich Site Summary — the former definition is more popular. RSS is an XML-based format for content distribution. The RSS v1 specification originated in 1999 as a lightweight, multipurpose extensible metadata description and syndication format. RSS is an XML application and is extensible via XML. The purpose of RSS is for delivering updates to Web-based content.

To view RSS content in XML format, you need an RSS reader. Using your Web browser displays a bunch of gibberish code unless you're an XML geek. Adobe Bridge contains such a reader where you can explore some of the URL links installed with the Bridge and you can add your own links to RSS feeds for news headlines, news services, and a growing line of support sites hosting new RSS feeds.

Notice in the Bridge Center you have the RSS Reader files appearing in a scrollable window. The preinstalled feeds link you to Adobe's Web site where you can explore information that is updated routinely on the CS applications, events, tutorials, and a place where file sharing is hosted.

RSS viewing in Web browsers

If you open a Web browser like Microsoft Internet Explorer and navigate to a URL where the Web page is written in XML, the view you see is the XML code. In the following figure, you can see an RSS feed that was opened in Microsoft Internet Explorer from Windows.

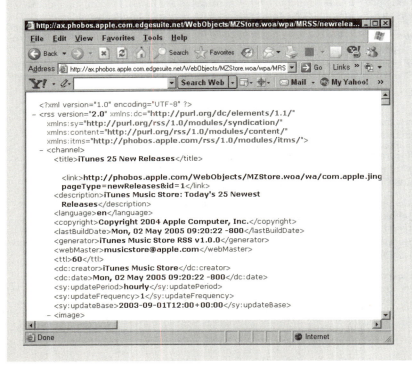

If you use a Mac and you upgraded to Mac OS X Tiger and Safari 2.0, you can see RSS feeds and XML code displayed more like a Web page. Apple introduced a lot of support for RSS viewing when OS X Tiger was released. The same Web page shown in the previous figure is shown in Apple Safari 2.0 in the following figure.

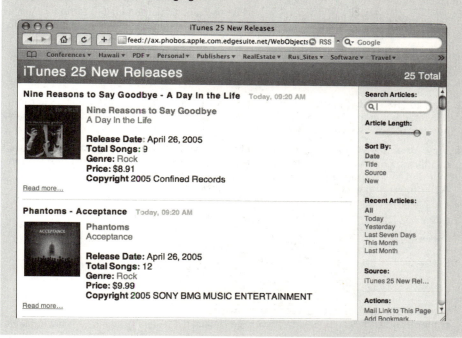

In addition to the preinstalled links to RSS feeds you can add your own links to feeds you want to monitor. For example, you can add a feed to a news service and view updated headlines in the window to the right of the Reader window. Click a headline to expand it and you see a short introduction to a news event or information from some service. At the bottom of the description, you see a More... button. Click More and your default Web browser is launched and takes you to the Web site where you can view the content in HTML in your Web browser. The benefit of the RSS feed is that you can determine intervals for updating information and see a short description (when provided by the host) before you launch your Web browser.

Adding a new RSS feed to the Bridge Center is easy, but you must first know the URL for the feed you want to monitor. You can often obtain this information by searching in your Web browser for free RSS feeds. To understand more fully how a feed is added to the Bridge Center, follow the step below to add a new feed:

STEPS: Adding an RSS Feed to the Bridge Center

1. **Open the Bridge Center.** Open the Bridge, click Favorites, and click the Bridge Center button.

2. **Add a URL.** Click the plus (+) symbol in the RSS Reader window. The Adobe Bridge dialog box opens. In this dialog box type the URL for the feed you want to add, as shown

in Figure 7-54. In this example, the URL added is: `http://www.rss-specifications.com/article-feed.xml`. This URL is handy to keep in the Bridge. The Web site hosts information about RSS and the RSS specification. There are links to free RSS feeds and informative Web pages to help you further understand RSS.

Figure 7-54: Click the plus (+) symbol in the RSS Reader window and type or paste a URL in the Adobe Bridge dialog box.

3. **View the RSS link.** Click OK in the Adobe Bridge. The title of the feed appears in the RSS Reader window as "RSS and News Feed Articles." Adjacent to the title you can see a number that shows you how many articles are currently in the feed.

4. **View an Article.** Click the link and scroll the right window to view the different article headlines. Click an article to expand the contents and you can see a short description followed by a More... button, as shown in Figure 7-55. Click More... and your default Web browser opens the Web page associated with the article.

Figure 7-55: Click an article headline to expand the content, and click More... to view Web pages linked to the article.

Setting update intervals

The beauty of RSS feeds is that they dynamically update according to the interval you want. On the other end, a system administrator can easily edit the XML text when headlines change and the content changes. Essentially, the information you see in the right window is XML-based and easily edited.

To edit the update interval, select a feed in the left window. Click the Open Settings button above the right window. The Adobe Bridge dialog box opens and the current refresh interval is reported in the dialog box as shown in Figure 7-56.

Figure 7-56: Select a feed and click Open Settings to view the current refresh interval.

If you want the feed refreshed at a different interval, type a value in the Adobe Bridge dialog box. The minimum you can add is 1 hour. The maximum is more than a hundred quadrillion (a much higher value than you'll ever use).

If you leave the default setting of 4 hours to refresh the interval and you want to have a look at the current update, click Update Now and the feed is updated to the moment.

Using Adobe Studio

The preinstalled feeds you find in the Bridge Center are direct links to Adobe's Web site. Here you find events such as fairs, conferences, seminars, training, and so on. As your feed is updated you are constantly aware of Adobe sponsored events and participation. Click the Adobe Studio Events and expand the items in the second window. Click More and your Web browser may take you to Adobe's Web site or a site hosting an event.

The second of the three Adobe Studio feeds is Adobe Studio Tips and Tutorials. Click the feed in the left window and a list of tips and tutorials appear in the second scrollable window. When you click More in the second window, your Web browser takes you to Adobe's Web site where you see a tip or tutorial related to the headline. In some cases you need to have an Adobe ID to log on. If you don't have an ID, you are prompted to create one with a user ID and password. The service is free, so be certain to create an ID and you can browse the tutorials. As you work with the Bridge Center, make a habit of reviewing this feed and you can learn some very good tips for using the CS2 programs.

The third feed is for the Adobe Studio Exchange. This part of Adobe's Web site hosts contributions from the user community. You can download files that work with the CS2 programs such as brushes for Photoshop, patterns and textures, and more.

Viewing Slide Shows

A nice feature of the bridge that rounds out this chapter is viewing slide shows directly in Bridge. The slide show feature is not like creating a permanent slide show that you can when exporting to a PDF Presentation from Bridge or Photoshop. The slide show feature in Bridge is a temporary viewing option. You might have a collection of images you want to use in a design campaign and quickly preview the images you're contemplating using in your artwork. The slide show feature in Bridge displays all Photoshop, Illustrator, InDesign, Acrobat PDFs, and Camera Raw images. GoLive pages are not supported with previews.

To view a slide show in Bridge, open a folder containing the images you want to preview. Choose View ➪ Slide Show or press ⌘/Ctrl+L. Note the keyboard shortcut is the same as the one you view in Full Screen mode in Acrobat. The first image is opened in Adobe Bridge Slide Show.

You can access a quick help menu when viewing the slide show. Press H and the help screen shown in Figure 7-57 appears. The help screen appears on top of the current slide in view.

You can use various keyboard shortcuts to control slide show viewing. You can even make some edits to the files as you view them in Slide Show. Note that you can change labels and ratings while in Adobe Bridge Slide Show. Most of the keyboard shortcuts are self explanatory when it comes to changing slides, opening a previous or next document, rotating images, pausing and playing, and so on.

When you press D on your keyboard, the display mode changes. You can view the slide show centered on your monitor screen, in a full screen mode, scale window, and fill window. The D key controls the window views according to the size of the window. To size the window press W.

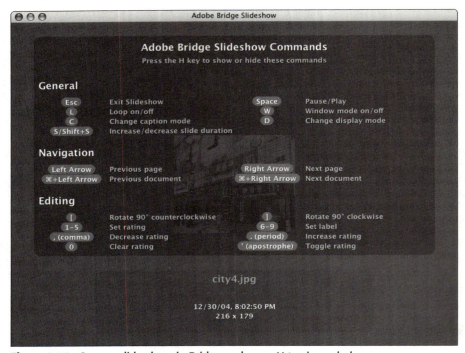

Figure 7-57: Open a slide show in Bridge and press H to view a help screen.

When you view images in Adobe Bridge Slide Show, just remember to use the H key and call upon help while viewing a show. If you want to compare documents, you can open multiple slide shows. Use the Bridge to open a folder and press ⌘/Ctrl+L. Keep the slide show open and select the Bridge window. Navigate to a new folder and press ⌘/Ctrl+L again. The two slide shows can be run aside each other.

Summary

- ✦ The Bridge is a stand-alone executable application similar to the File Browser found in earlier versions of Photoshop. The Bridge is the center of the CS2 applications from which all document launching and organization can be accomplished.
- ✦ The Bridge supports saving workspaces. You can open multiple windows and work between Bridge windows for file management and organization.
- ✦ You can manage, resize and nest tabs in Bridge.
- ✦ You can create Collections of files and add files and folders to a Favorites area for quick access.
- ✦ You can mark files with ratings and labels and sort documents according to ratings and label identify.

✦ You can batch rename files in Bridge.

 ✦ You can edit document metadata in Bridge.

 ✦ Bridge supports the creation of XMP metadata templates. You can apply metadata from a template to folders of files.

 ✦ You can search files on metadata in folders, nested folders, and different folder locations.

 ✦ You can save searches as collections and you can retrieve the results easily from the collections.

 ✦ The Adobe Stock Photo Service can be searched based on extensive metadata to help you find stock photo images quickly.

 ✦ You can download Stock Photo comps for free. Stock photos use in final project designs need to be purchased through the ASPS service.

 ✦ Bridge enables you to create Version Cue projects, open Version Cue files, Alternate files, promote versions, and promote primary members of alternate groups.

 ✦ You can open camera raw images using the Bridge camera raw plug-in. You can copy settings and paste settings into additional camera raw images in the Bridge window. You can return camera raw images to defaults in the Bridge window.

 ✦ You can synchronize color settings in the Bridge for all the CS applications.

 ✦ You can execute application automation commands in the Bridge for Photoshop, Illustrator and InDesign.

 ✦ You can execute new automated tasks from the Bridge. Tasks include Merge to HDR in Photoshop, Live Trace in Illustrator, and create InDesign contact sheets.

 ✦ You can execute Photoshop's Batch commands from the Bridge.

 ✦ The Bridge Center enables you to view and open recent files, create groups of commonly used images, access RSS news feeds and create links to new RSS feeds.

✦ ✦ ✦

Using Version Cue

CHAPTER 8

Version Cue is a file-versioning system that is tightly integrated into all the CS2 version applications. Its key benefit is that it lets you set up projects for sharing over a network. All files within these projects are version-controlled, allowing members of the team to access the very latest versions of each file. The versioning features also ensure that team members don't accidentally save changes over the top of other changes.

Version Cue is accessed from within all the standard file dialog boxes. Using the Version Cue Workspace Administration utility, you can control all aspects of Version Cue from an administration interface. This interface lets you create and edit the access and authentication for users, create and define project properties, and lock files.

♦ ♦ ♦ ♦

Setting up the Version Cue workspace

Working with Version Cue files

Using the Version Cue Workspace Administration utility

♦ ♦ ♦ ♦

Setting Up the Version Cue Workspace

When CS2 is installed, Version Cue is also installed and enabled by default, but it can be disabled using the Preferences dialog for the various CS2 applications.

Version Cue comes only as part of Creative Suite. If you purchased a license for only a single CS2 application, it won't include Version Cue, but the application can work with Version Cue if somebody else on your network has it installed.

Setting Version Cue preferences

Version Cue is enabled by simply installing CS2. Version Cue preferences are set using the Version Cue Preferences dialog box. To access this dialog box, shown in Figure 8-1, double-click the Version Cue icon. The Version Cue icon is found within the System Preferences (on the Mac) or in the Control Panel (in Windows). In the Version Cue Preferences dialog box, you can turn Version Cue on and off. You can also opt to turn Version Cue on when the computer starts.

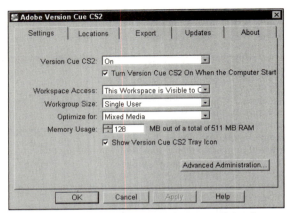

Figure 8-1: The Version Cue Preferences dialog box

The Workspace Access field lets you make the workspace shared or private. The two options are This Workspace Is Visible to Others and This Workspace Is Private.

You can use the next three preferences to optimize the workspace and to specify the type of files that you are versioning. You can set Workspace Size to Single User, Small (2–4 People), Medium (5–10 People), or Large (10+ People). By specifying the workspace size, Version Cue can make more connections available so users don't have to wait as long to gain access to the files. The Optimize For field lets you select the type of media files you'll most often be saving. The options include Print Media (which are typically fewer in number, but much larger), Web Media (which includes a large number of smaller files), and Mixed Media.

The Memory Usage field lets you specify the amount of memory on your local machine or on the network that is available for Version Cue to use. Increasing this value enables you to retrieve files very quickly but leaves less memory available for the other applications. For Windows systems, there is also an option to Show Version Cue CS2 Tray Icon, which makes the Version Cue CS2 icon visible in the system tray located in the lower right corner of the interface. Mac users have an option to Show Version Cue CS2 Status in Menu Bar, which makes Version Cue in the Macintosh menu bar.

Specifying workspace folders

When Version Cue is first enabled, two folders are created on your local system. The `Version Cue` folder is located in the `Documents` folder (on the Mac) or in the `My Projects` folder (in Windows). This folder holds temporary working copies of the files that you're currently editing.

The other folders are located by default in a folder where the Creative Suite applications were installed. These folders, consisting of folders named `Adobe Version Cue\data` and `Adobe Version Cue\backups`, hold the actual versioned files and are referenced in the Locations panel of the Version Cue Preferences dialog box, shown in Figure 8-2.

Caution

If you look at the files located in the `data` and `backups` folders, you won't be able to find any recognizable file formats. Do not manually move or edit any of these files; if you do, Version Cue won't work properly.

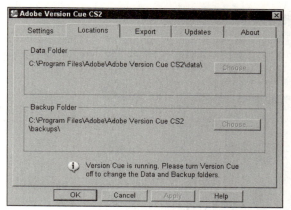

Figure 8-2: The Locations panel of the Version Cue Preferences dialog box lets you specify the location of data and backup folders.

If you want to change the `data` and `backups` folder locations, you must turn Version Cue off and click Apply before the Choose button in the Locations panel becomes active. After the Choose button is active, you can click it to select a new directory.

Exporting workspace data

The Export panel of the Version Cue Preferences dialog box, shown in Figure 8-3, lets you export all the existing project files to a specified directory or to export the Current Versions Only.

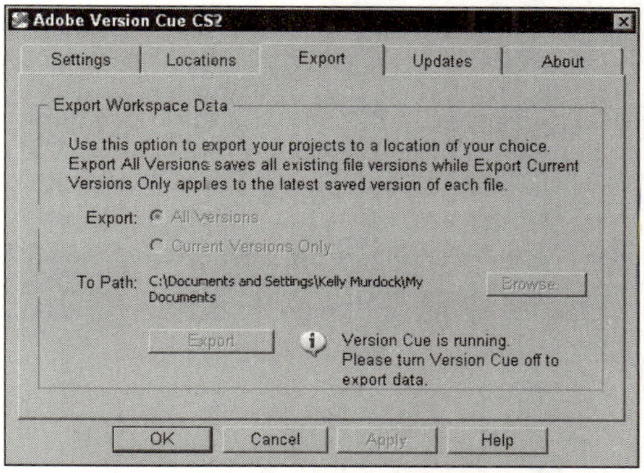

Figure 8-3: The Export panel of the Version Cue Preferences dialog box

This option is only available when Version Cue is turned off. Select a directory for the exported file using the Browse button and click Export to begin the export process.

Updating Version Cue

The Updates panel of the Version Cue Preferences dialog box, shown in Figure 8-4, includes a single button that lets you check for updates to the Version Cue. You computer needs to be connected to the Internet in order for this button to work.

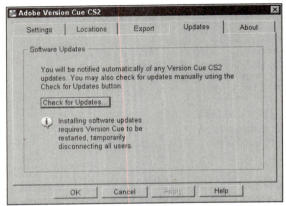

Figure 8-4: The Updates panel of the Version Cue Preferences dialog box checks the Adobe Web site for any CS updates.

New Feature

Software updaters aren't new to Adobe applications, but having a centralized Updater located within Version Cue is new to CS2.

If any software updates are found, the Adobe Updater, shown in Figure 8-5, appears. The Adobe Updater lists any updates that are available. If you select the check box to the left of the update filename in the All Available Updates section, the size of the download and the time required to download the update are displayed at the bottom of the Updater. The Download Updates button also becomes active. Clicking this button begins the update process. If you select any of the updates listed, a description of the update is listed in the Description text field.

The Preferences button opens a dialog box, shown in Figure 8-6, where you set the Adobe Updater to automatically check for updates every month. You can also specify a directory to save the downloads.

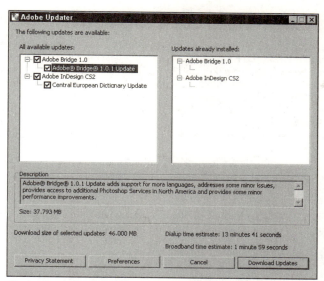

Figure 8-5: The Adobe Updater displays all updates available for download.

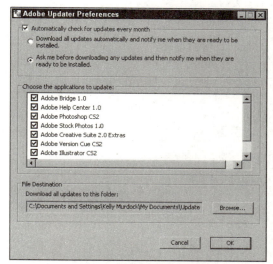

Figure 8-6: The Adobe Updater Preferences dialog box includes an option to automatically check for updates once a month.

Enabling Version Cue within a CS2 application

Although CS2 is enabled and turned on by default, each individual CS2 application can use its own preferences to turn off Version Cue. The setting for enabling Version Cue for each separate CS2 app is found in the File Handling panel of the Preferences dialog box. For example, to enable or disable Version Cue for Photoshop, Illustrator, InCopy, and InDesign, open the Preferences dialog box (found in the application-name menu on the Mac or in the Edit menu in Windows) and select the File Handling panel (within Illustrator, the option is located in the File Handling & Clipboard panel). The option for enabling Version Cue for Acrobat 7 is found in the General panel of the Preferences dialog box which you can access by choosing Edit ⇨ Preferences.

Note   Version Cue also works with InCopy.

Within the File Handling panel of the Preferences dialog box, shown in Figure 8-7, is a Use Version Cue option. Enabling this option makes Version Cue available for that application.

Note   GoLive and Bridge don't offer any method for disabling Version Cue.

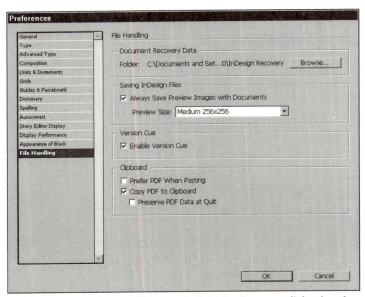

Figure 8-7: The File Handling panel of the Preferences dialog box for the various CS2 applications includes an Enable Version Cue option.

Working with Adobe Dialog

When Version Cue is turned on and enabled for the working application, a simple button titled Use Adobe Dialog, appears at the lower left corner of all file dialog boxes accessed by choosing the Open, Import, Place, Export, Save and Save As menu commands, as shown in Figure 8-8. If you click this button, the file dialog box changes, as shown in Figure 8-9, to reveal many additional features including Version Cue. You can return to the default file dialog box style by the clicking Use OS Dialog button, which replaces the Use Adobe Dialog button.

Once you click Use Adobe Dialog for an application, Adobe continues to use Adobe Dialogs for all future file dialog boxes for that application until you change back them to OS Dialog.

Figure 8-8: The Use Adobe Dialog button located at the bottom of each file dialog box lets you access a file dialog box with more features including Version Cue.

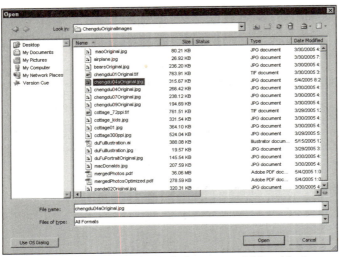

Figure 8-9: The Adobe Dialog includes many additional features.

The Adobe Dialog file interface, shown for InDesign's File ⇨ Open menu command in Figure 8-10, resembles a typical file dialog box with access to folders and files. If you double-click a folder, all the subfolders and files contained within that folder display. The Adobe Dialog interface contains the following:

- **File list columns:** Along the top of the file list are several information columns including Name, Size, Status, Type, Date Modified, Version, Comment, Alternate, and Location. Clicking any of the columns in the Version Cue interface sorts the files by the selected column. For example, you can quickly see the largest file in a project by clicking on the Size column title. Clicking a second time on the column title reverses the sorting order.

- **Favorites panel:** To the left of the file list is the Favorites panel that provides quick links to favorite folder locations. You can add folders to this panel by right clicking the folder in the file list and selecting the Add to Favorites menu command. As you browse through folders, you can click the Back and Forward buttons to navigate through previously and recently viewed folders.

- **Icon buttons:** The icon buttons in the upper-right corner let you move up one level, create new folders, refresh the current folder, delete the selected file or folder, access the Project Tools and change the folder view. Clicking the Up One Level button opens the folder above the current one. The View menu includes options for viewing files in details, as icons, as thumbnails, or as tiles. The Project Tools icon includes a menu of options for working with Version Cue. Figure 8-11 shows the Thumbnail view of the Adobe Dialog file interface for the File ⇨ Open menu command in InDesign.

Holding the mouse over a file displays a pop-up pane of information that includes the file's title, type, size, version number, last updated date, status, and project, as shown in Figure 8-12.

Chapter 8 ✦ **Using Version Cue** 283

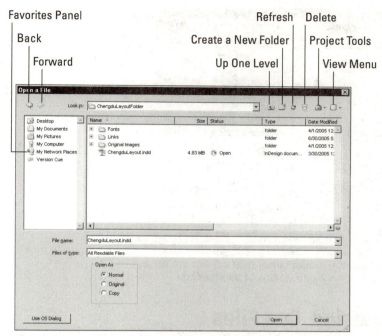

Figure 8-10: Double-clicking a folder in the Adobe Dialog interface opens the folder and displays all the files within the folder.

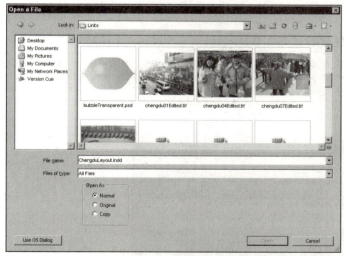

Figure 8-11: The Thumbnail view lets you visually select the file that you want to open.

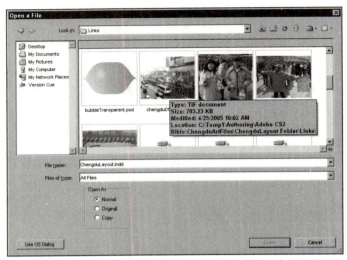

Figure 8-12: Holding the mouse cursor over a file in the Version Cue file interface displays a pop-up box of information.

Accessing Version Cue Files

If you click Version Cue in the Favorites panel of the Adobe Dialog interface, all Version Cue projects and files display. You must create projects before they appear within Version Cue. Once a new project is created, you can open, save, add and delete files in the project folder. You can also view details about the file including its state, size and alternates.

Creating a Version Cue project

To create a new project, select the top-level workspace folder in the Adobe Dialog, click the Project Tools button in the Version Cue interface, and select the New Project menu command. This command opens a dialog box, shown in Figure 8-13, where you can name the project and enter a description for it. To make the project viewable to other users, enable the Share This Project with Others option.

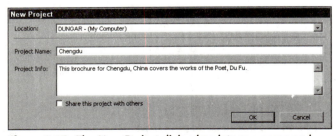

Figure 8-13: The New Project dialog box lets you name and describe the project as well as to share this project with others.

After a Version Cue project is created, files and folders can be added to the project folder as needed. Version Cue projects can include any type of file.

A new feature to Version Cue 2 is the ability to store any type of file in the project file. Non-Adobe files can be opened using Adobe Bridge and versioned in Bridge using the Tools ⇨ Version Cue ⇨ Save a Version menu command.

If you ever need to change a project's name or other properties, you can select the project folder and choose the Edit Properties menu command from the Project Tools pop-up menu in the Adobe Dialog. The Project Tools pop-up menu also includes a Share/Unshare Project menu command that you can use to quickly change the project's share status and the location of the project's local files.

Accessing remote Version Cue projects

To access remote Version Cue projects using the Adobe Dialog interface, select the Connect To menu command from the Project Tools pop-up menu. This opens a simple dialog box, shown in Figure 8-14, where you can type in the address for the remote workspace. The remote address can be any Version Cue project that is accessible over the Internet and not just on your current network. This makes it possible for groups to work on projects across the globe. Clicking OK displays a dialog box of available remote workspaces at the specified remote address.

If you are trying to connect to an existing shared Version Cue project, it is easier to simply browse to the project folder by selecting the Version Cue option from the Favorites pane in Adobe Dialog.

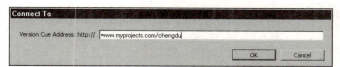

Figure 8-14: The Connect To dialog box lets you specify a Web address that includes remote Version Cue projects.

Opening Version Cue files

When a Version Cue file is opened, a copy of the latest version goes to your local working directory, which you can find within the project folder in the Documents/Version Cue folder (on the Mac) or the My Documents/Version Cue folder (in Windows).

When you choose File ⇨ Place in one of the CS2 applications, click the Version Cue option in the Favorites panel, and double click a Version Cue project, three new links appear beneath Version Cue in the Favorites panel. These links are at the top of the dialog box — Project Search, Files in Use, and Project Trash:

✦ **Project Search:** This lets you navigate the project folders by keyword. Clicking the Search tab opens a panel, shown in Figure 8-15, where you can enter a keyword for which to search. After you click Search, all files that match the search keyword display.

✦ **Files in Use:** This displays all files that each user has opened.

✦ **Project Trash:** This shows all project files that have been deleted.

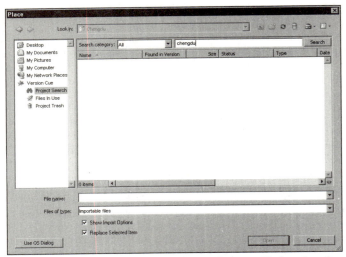

Figure 8-15: The Search panel of the Version Cue file interface is available when you choose File ⇨ Open.

Saving Version Cue files

When you save Version Cue files by choosing File ⇨ Save, the working copy updates, but the actual versioned copy isn't updated until you choose File ⇨ Save As or File ⇨ Save a Version.

When you're ready to save a new version of the edited file to the Version Cue repository, choose File ⇨ Save a Version. This command opens a simple dialog box, shown in Figure 8-16, where you can quickly type a version comment and save the file. The version comment that you enter appears in the Version Cue file interface when you select the file.

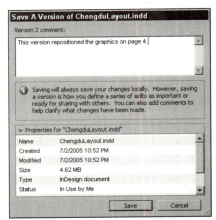

Figure 8-16: Choosing File ⇨ Save a Version lets you enter comments for the file.

When you choose File ➪ Save As, the Adobe Dialog file interface opens. The file interface, shown in Figure 8-17, includes fields for naming the file, selecting a format, and entering version comments. If you choose to save the file using the same filename, a warning dialog box asks if you want to save these changes as a new version. If you select to save the file as a file with a new name, a whole new branch is created. This new branch has its own versions that are separate from the original file.

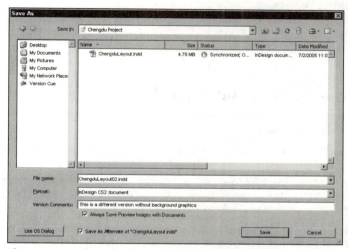

Figure 8-17: When the file interface opens with the File ➪ Save As menu command, you may choose to save the file using a different name.

Understanding states

Each file saved is given a status that defines the state of the file. The available statuses include the following:

✦ **Available:** Indicates that the file is available for you to select and edit.

✦ **Ready for Download:** Indicates that the file is available for you to copy to your local working file.

✦ **In Use By Me:** Indicates that you are currently editing this file.

✦ **In Use By Me Elsewhere:** Indicates that you're editing this file on a different computer.

✦ **In Use By User:** Indicates that another user is currently editing the file. The user's name is listed.

✦ **Offline:** Indicates that the file is unavailable because Version Cue has been turned off.

For files opened using the Version Cue interface, the status of the file displays along the bottom edge of the document, as shown in Figure 8-18.

Figure 8-18: When the Version Cue file is opened, the status of the file displays along the bottom edge of the document.

Adding files to a Version Cue project

You can add single files, multiple files, or synchronize files to a Version Cue project or you can drag and drop files into a Version Cue project using Adobe Bridge:

✦ **Singe file:** Choose File ➪ Save As or File ➪ Save a Version to add single files to a Version Cue project.

✦ **Multiple files:** To add multiple files to a project, copy all the files into their correct folders of the working project file located in the `Documents/Version Cue` folder (on the Mac) or in the `My Projects` folder (in Windows).

✦ **Synchronize files:** With the files added to the working directory, select the Synchronize menu command from the Project Tools pop-up menu. This command copies all the files from the working directory to the Version Cue repository so that all users can access them.

✦ **Drag and drop files into Bridge:** Locate the project folder in Adobe Bridge and select and drag the files into Bridge from Windows Explorer or Macintosh's Finder and drop them in Bridge's Version Cue folder.

The Project Tool menu includes an option to Reveal in Bridge that makes the selected file visible within the Bridge interface. The Bridge interface is covered in detail in Chapter 7.

Working with versions

When a versioned file is opened within one of the CS2 applications, you can gain access to the various versions by choosing the file and selecting the Versions option from the Project Tools menu. This command opens a dialog box, shown in Figure 8-19, where all the versions of the open file are listed along with their thumbnails, version numbers, and version comments.

Using this dialog box, you can select a version, delete a version, open a version, or promote a selected version to the current version.

Working with alternates

Alternates are different from versions because they represent a shift in direction for the art asset. This could be a new direction or a different approach altogether. You save alternates without altering the original file in any way. You add all alternates to a group that you or a client can quickly compare as needed.

New Feature Alternates are new to CS2.

To create an alternate, simply save the file by choosing File ➪ Save As and selecting the Save As Alternate option at the bottom of the file dialog box.

If you select the Alternate option from the Project Tools menu, a dialog box, shown in Figure 8-20, opens displaying all the various alternates. This dialog box lets you remove, open, or make the selected alternate the primary file.

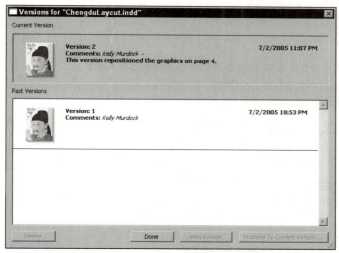

Figure 8-19: All the versions for an open file are accessible by choosing Versions from the Project Tools menu.

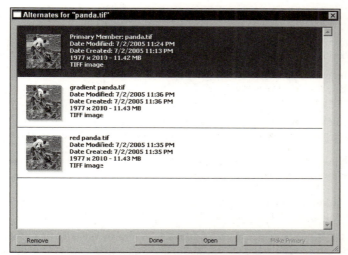

Figure 8-20: All the alternate versions for a file are accessible by choosing Alternates from the Project Tools menu.

Deleting Version Cue files

To delete a Version Cue-managed file, you select the Version Cue file in the Adobe Dialog interface and choose the Delete menu command from the Project Tools pop-up menu. This moves the file to the Project Trash link.

Tip   You can also select the Delete menu command from a pop-up menu that appears by right clicking on the file.

To restore a deleted file that appears in the Deleted Files tab, select the file, and choose the Restore menu command in the Project Tools pop-up menu. Selecting the Delete menu command for a file in the Deleted Files tab permanently deletes the file.

STEPS: Opening and Saving Files in Version Cue

1. **Verify Version Cue.** Open the Version Cue Preferences dialog box and make sure that Version Cue is turned on.
2. **Open a Version Cue file.** Within Photoshop, choose File ➪ Open. In the Open dialog box that appears, click Use Adobe Dialog to access the Adobe Dialog file interface. Click on the Version Cue option in the Favorites pane; then double-click the project folder that includes the file you want to edit. Select the file and click Open.
3. **Edit the file.** Use the Photoshop tools to edit the file that you opened.
4. **Save a version.** When the edits are complete, choose File ➪ Save a Version. The Format Options dialog box appears for the file. Click OK and a Save Version dialog box opens where you can add a comment for the recent edits.

Using the Version Cue CS2 Administration Web Pages

You can complete many Version Cue administrative tasks — including creating, deleting, backing up and editing projects, locking files, editing user access rights, and viewing logs and reports — using the Version Cue CS2 Administration Web pages.

You access this utility by clicking Advanced Administration in the Version Cue Preferences dialog box, or by selecting the Edit Properties menu command from the Project Tools pop-up menu and clicking Advanced Administration.

When you first access the Version Cue CS2 Administration Web pages, a Change System Account Figure Web page appears, asking you to enter your username and password.

Note   All users on the system are given access to this utility, but only the user with the System Administrator username and password may set the rights of the other users.

The Version Cue CS2 Administration utility opens within a Web browser. After you create an account, you need to log in every time you access the utility using a login page.

After you've logged in, the home page of the utility appears, as shown in Figure 8-21. This home page includes four page links on the left — Home, Users, Projects, and Advanced. The home page also includes several common tasks that you may perform using this utility.

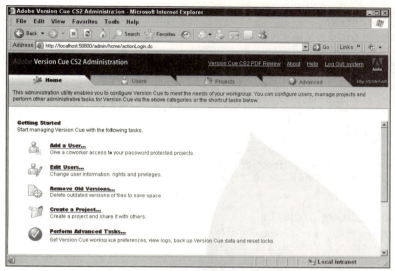

Figure 8-21: The Version Cue CS2 Administration utility home page includes links to several different utility pages and several basic tasks.

Adding and editing users

Clicking the Users link in the Version Cue CS2 Administration utility opens the page shown in Figure 8-22. This page lists all the users and their information and allows you to create, edit, duplicate, and delete users who have access to the workspace.

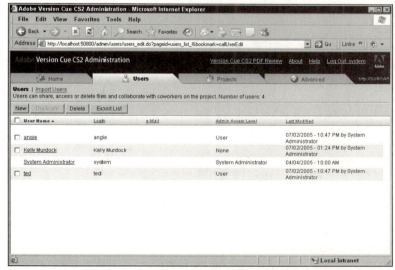

Figure 8-22: The Users page of the Version Cue Workspace Administration Utility.

To add a new user, click New and a New User page opens where you can enter the information for a new user including his username, login, password, phone number, and e-mail address, as well as comments about that user. You can also specify the user's privileges as None, User, Project Creator, or System Administrator.

Clicking a user's name in the User page opens the Edit User page, shown in Figure 8-23. The Edit User page is similar to the New User page. The Edit User page is where you can edit a user's information. This page also lets you specify the user's access to the various projects.

Managing projects

The Projects page in the Version Cue CS2 Administration utility opens a page, shown in Figure 8-24, that lists all the available projects. From within this page, you can click New to create a new project. Using the buttons in the page, you can also duplicate, back up, export, and delete the selected projects.

Creating and editing projects

Clicking New in the Projects page opens the New Project page, shown in Figure 8-25. Here, you can select to create a blank project, import from a folder, import from an FTP server, or import from a WebDAV server. Each of these options walks you through the steps to create and define the properties for the project. Clicking Next moves to the next page.

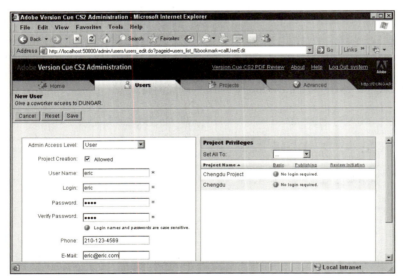

Figure 8-23: The Edit User page lets you change the user's rights to each project.

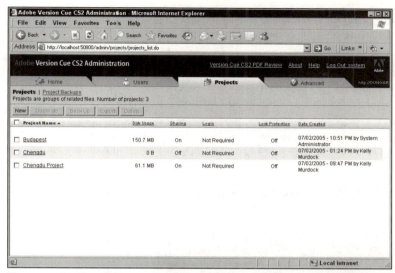

Figure 8-24: The Projects page of the Version Cue Workspace Administration Utility lets you manage projects in the current workspace.

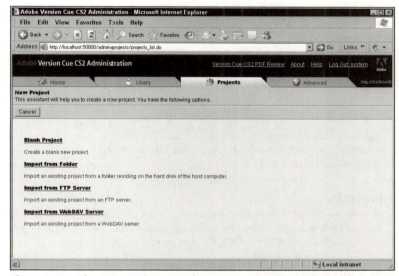

Figure 8-25: The New Project page lets you create new projects using several different options.

Clicking a project name in the Projects page opens an editing page, shown in Figure 8-26, that lists the properties for this project, its assigned users, and any project backups. The properties for each project that you may set include:

✦ **Share the Project with Others:** enables sharing this project with other users, so other users with rights to this project can view and access its files.

✦ **Require Login for this Project:** Users need to log in with their usernames and passwords before they can access files in the Version Cue project.

✦ **Enable Lock Protection:** Only one user can update the version of that file. Other users can open the file, but they're prevented from saving the file as a version of the original file. They may make changes and save the file with a different filename but not as a version of the original file.

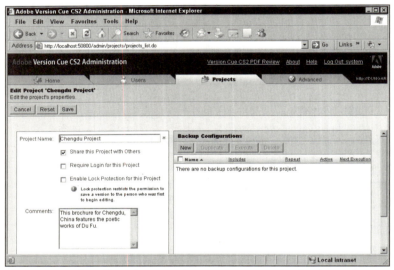

Figure 8-26: The Edit Project page lets you set properties for the project, such as sharing, authentication, and locking.

Backing up projects

If you click Back Up on the Projects page for a selected project, then a page, shown in Figure 8-27, appears. This is where you can verify the name that is used for the backup as well as which items are backed up. Clicking Save starts the backup process.

Back on the Projects page, the Backup List button opens a page that lists all the available backups. Selecting a backed-up project from the list opens a page with a Restore button that you may use to restore the backed up project.

Using the Advanced features

Clicking the Advanced tab (located to the right of the Projects tab) opens a Web page with options to set Preferences, Import Version Cue 1.0 workspaces, schedule maintenance and set logs and reports. This page is shown in Figure 8-28:

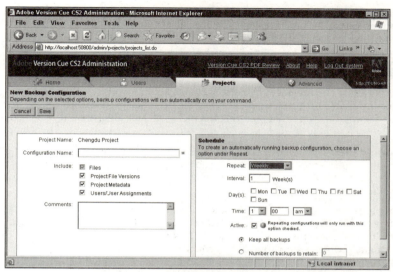

Figure 8-27: Clicking Back Up opens a page where you can select to back up the current project.

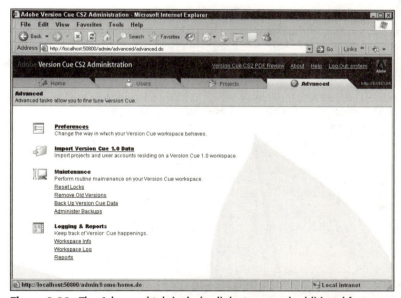

Figure 8-28: The Advanced tab includes links to several additional features.

- **Setting Preferences:** The Preferences link opens a page of preferences including the Workspace Name, the Log Level and Log Size, an option to Compress the log file, and ports for the FTP and HTTP Proxies.
- **Importing CS1 Data:** The Import Version Cue 1.0 Data lets you quickly import all projects and user accounts saved with the previous version of CS.
- **Unlocking files:** The Advanced tab also includes an option to Reset Locks. You may find this invaluable for times when a critical file becomes permanently locked so no one can view it. Be aware that resetting the locks will kick all users out of their opened files.
- **Purging old files:** The Remove Old Files option gives you a page where you can delete all files older than a certain date, or you can specify that only a given number of versions are kept. This is a quick way to clean up a project to free some network disc space if needed.
- **Viewing logs and reports:** The Workspace Log is a simple text file that keeps track of all system events. Every time a file is loaded and saved into a project an entry is logged into the log file. Using this tool can help you find where a file is. It can also help troubleshoot any problems that appear. You can schedule reports to run regularly and to report any errors for a project. Regularly reading these generated reports will help keep your projects in tune and running smooth.

Summary

- You may access the Adobe Dialog file interface by using any of the file dialog boxes used to open, save, place, import, and export files.
- The Version Cue file interface lets you create new projects, search for files, sort files, view thumbnails, and view deleted files.
- The Version Cue CS2 Administration utility may be accessed from the Version Cue Preferences dialog box. This browser-based tool is used to create and edit users and projects, back up and restore projects, and view project reports.

✦ ✦ ✦

Managing Adobe PDF Files

In This Chapter

Managing PDF files in the Organizer

Creating Web links to PDF documents hosted on the Web

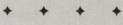

Acrobat has its own form of File Browser for viewing and organizing PDF documents. When Acrobat 7 Professional was developed, Adobe CS2 developers were still working on the Bridge. Since Acrobat 7 was released much sooner than the CS2 applications, inclusion for Bridge support was not possible in the latest release. Most of the time you'll find yourself using the Bridge to organize and manage PDF documents as well as all the other CS2 documents.

 Acrobat's Organizer is new in Acrobat 7 Professional.

The Organizer is like a junior cousin to the Bridge. Many Bridge tools and features are not included in the Organizer, but there are a few unique tools and features you can accomplish with the Organizer that you can't do with the Bridge. If PDF authoring is a major part of your workflow, perhaps you'll find working in the Organizer to be a better tool than using the Bridge. One obvious advantage is that when you work with Acrobat's Organizer you don't need to leave the program. When using the Bridge you need to toggle back and forth between the Bridge and Acrobat. It all depends on the kind of work you do and where you spend most of your time. If you are a casual user in Acrobat, then perhaps you might want to glance over the information contained in this chapter and note some of the unique features the Organizer has that the Bridge doesn't support.

 Working in Acrobat's Organizer also provides another benefit. The Organizer is much faster than working in the Bridge. During the initial release of Adobe Bridge, one disadvantage is that the Bridge runs slow, particularly when you view folders with many image files. Hopefully, future upgrades will take care of the performance problems and we will eventually see a more improved product.

For information related to working with the Bridge, see Chapter 7.

Organizing Files

To open the Organizer, choose File ⇨ Organizer ⇨ Open Organizer or click the Organizer tool in the File toolbar. (On Windows you can also choose File ⇨ History ⇨ Open Organizer.) When you select any of the options, the Organizer, shown in Figure 9-1, opens.

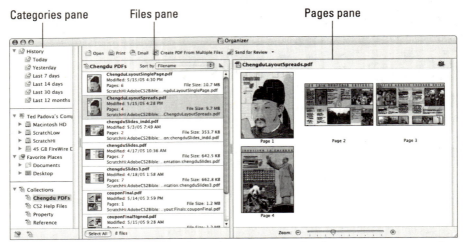

Figure 9-1: Click the Organizer tool or select Open Organizer from a menu command to open the Organizer window in Acrobat.

 Note You can view PDF-only files in the Organizer. Unlike the Bridge where all files are viewed in the Content area, the Organizer supports only PDF documents.

The Organizer window contains three panes, a number of tools, and menu commands that you select from context menus. When you first open the Organizer, you find three panes in the Organizer window divided by two separator bars. On the left side of the window is the Categories pane. In the center you find the Files pane and the right side holds the Pages pane. You can adjust the size of the panes by clicking a separator bar and dragging it to the left or right. As one pane is sized down, the adjacent pane is sized up. You can adjust the size of the Organizer window by dragging the lower-right corner of the window.

Using the Categories pane

The Categories pane in the Organizer contains three types of categories. At the top of the pane is History followed by My Computer (or your computer name) and at the bottom you find Collections:

- ✦ **The History category:** Offers you the same choices for viewing history as you find in the File menu where you can see a list of recently opened files. As you click one of the History options, the files listed in the Files pane reflect the history period you choose.

- ✦ **The My Computer (your computer name) category:** Shows you a view of your hard drive and all servers and drives connected to your computer, similar to the Files tab in the Bridge. You can select a folder, and all PDFs within that folder are listed in the Files pane regardless of whether they appear in the view history. Below your accessible hard drives and servers you find Favorite Places. If you keep documents within folders you frequently access, right-click (Windows) or Control+click (Macintosh) to open a context menu over Favorite Places or click Add Favorite Place at the bottom of the Categories pane. The Browse For Folder dialog box, shown in Figure 9-2, opens (Windows) or the Select a folder to add to your favorite places dialog box opens on the Macintosh. Adding Favorites in this fashion is similar to adding Favorites in the Bridge.

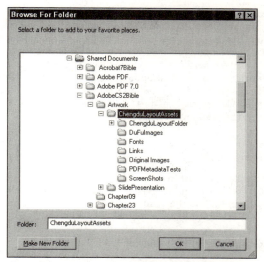

Figure 9-2: Open a context menu on Favorite Places in the Open Files category and a dialog box opens where you target a folder to add as a favorite place.

After you select a folder and click OK, the folder you selected appears at the bottom of the Favorite Places list.

✦ **The Collections category:** Works similarly to Favorite Places, except that instead of adding folders to a list, you can select individual files and add them to a collection. This feature in the Organizer is much easier than adding files to collections in the Bridge. The Bridge requires you to open two Bridge windows (something you can't do in the Organizer) and drag files from a folder in one Bridge window to a Collection in another Bridge window. You can add files to collections from different folders on your hard drive. By default, Acrobat offers you three collections: Collection 1, Collection 2, and Collection 3.

You manage collections through the use of a context menu. Open a context menu from any collection name in the Collections category and the menu options appear as shown in Figure 9-3.

Figure 9-3: To manage collections, open a context menu on any collection name.

The menu selections should be self-explanatory. Select Create a New Collection to add another collection to the list. Select Rename Collection to rename a collection. Select Delete Collection to remove the collection. Note that when a collection is deleted files on your hard drive are not deleted. Click Add Files to add documents to your collection. After you add documents to a collection and click the collection name, all files added to the collection appear in the Files pane.

Tip After installing Acrobat you may want to rename the default collection names to more descriptive names used in your workflow. Open a context menu on each collection name and select Rename Collection. The collection name is highlighted and ready for you to type a new name. One of the first collections you may want to create is one where you add Acrobat help documents such as the help guide, the Acrobat JavaScript Specification manual, the PDFMark Reference Manual, and so on. Most of these documents are contained inside the Help folder residing inside the Acrobat folder. On the Macintosh you need to expand the Acrobat 7 Professional package to locate the help files (open a context menu on the Acrobat Professional 7 program icon and select Show Package Contents).

Using the Files pane

The Files pane contains a list of all files derived from the choice you made in the Categories pane. For example, click a History category, and all files viewed within the selected history timeframe appear in a list sorted by metadata that you select from the Sort by pull-down menu.

For information related to sorting metadata, see Chapter 7.

Beginning with the tools at the top of the pane, you find:

- ✦ **Open:** By default, the first file in the pane is selected. Click the Open tool to open the selected file. If no file is selected in the pane, the Open tool, as well as all other tools, are grayed out. A condition where you might not have a file selected is when you click a collection that contains no file in the collection folder or when you view a folder that contains no PDF documents. Otherwise, the first file, by default, is always selected when files are shown in the list.

- ✦ **Print:** Click a file in the list and click the Print tool to print the file. When you click Print, the PDF document opens and the Print dialog box opens in the foreground. Make your print attribute choices in the Print dialog box and click Print to print the file.

- ✦ **Email:** Select a file in the list and click the Email tool, and your default e-mail application opens with the selected file attached to a new e-mail message.

- ✦ **Create PDF From Multiple Files:** Click this tool to open the Create PDF From Multiple Documents dialog box. In the dialog box you can select PDF documents to combine into a single file or select a variety of different file formats that can be converted to a PDF. The tool works the same as selecting the From Multiple Files command from the Create PDF Task Button pull-down menu.

To learn how to convert files to PDF with the Create PDF From Multiple Files command, see Chapter 34.

- ✦ **Send for Review:** Select a file in the list and choose from the pull-down menu options to Send By Email for Review, or Upload for Browser-Based Review.

Browser based reviews are not accessible to Adobe Reader users working with PDFs enabled with usage rights from Adobe Acrobat 7 Professional. In order for Adobe Reader users to participate in browser-based reviews, the PDFs must be enabled with usage rights using the Adobe LiveCycle Reader Extensions Server (LRES). For information on LRES, log on to Adobe's Web site at: www.adobe.com/products/server/readerextensions.

Cross-Reference   To learn how to enable files with Adobe Reader usage rights and send files for reviews and approval, see Chapter 25.

Below the tools is a pull-down menu used for sorting files. You can sort files on metadata contained within the file. From the pull-down menu, shown in Figure 9-4, you have several choices for sorting files. Advantages the Bridge has over the Organizer are that you can search more metadata and you can save the search results.

Figure 9-4: Open the Sort by pull-down menu to sort files according to file metadata.

Sorting by Filename is the default and lists files in an alphabetical ascending order. The Title, Subject, Author, and Keywords items are part of the Document Properties Description that you supply at the time of PDF creation from some authoring programs or that you later add in Acrobat. Creator and Producer are part of the Document Description supplied by Acrobat and relate to the original authoring program and the application producing the PDF file. Number of Pages, File Size, and Modified Date are data that Acrobat adds to the Document Properties derived from the structure of the file. The Last Opened Date sorts the files according to the last time you viewed them in Acrobat with the most recent file listed first and in descending order.

Cross-Reference   To learn more about Document Descriptions and Document Properties, see Chapter 29.

You can also manage files from a context menu opened on a file in the list. This menu has commands to perform the same tasks handled by the tools at the top of the pane. In Figure 9-5 you can see the top portion of the menu, duplicating the tools' functions, such as Open, Print, Email, Create PDF From Multiple Files, and Send for Review.

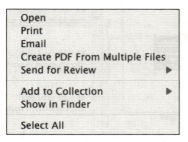

Figure 9-5: Open a context menu on a file listed in the Files pane and the menu options offer additional commands for managing files.

The Add to Collection menu item contains a submenu that lists all the collections in the Categories pane. As you add new collections to the Categories, they dynamically appear in the Add to Collection submenu. After you add a file to a collection, the context menu changes and displays a few more menu commands. In Figure 9-6, note the addition of Move to Collection and Remove from 'Collection 1.' The item within the single quotes denotes the collection name where a file has been added.

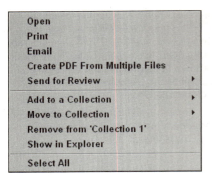

Figure 9-6: After you add a file to a collection, opening a context menu on a filename displays additional options for moving a file to another collection and deleting a file from a collection.

Select Move to Collection and the submenu displays all your collection names. Select a collection and the file is moved to the collection you choose in the submenu. Select Remove from '*n*' (where *n* represents the name of a collection) and a dialog box opens prompting you to confirm the deletion. When you delete a file from a collection, the file is deleted from the collection list but is not deleted from your hard drive.

The last menu item, Show in Explorer (Windows) or Show in Finder (Macintosh) takes you to Windows Explorer (Windows) or switches to Finder view (Macintosh) and opens the folder where the file is located.

Using the Pages pane

By default, the Pages pane displays the first page in a PDF document of a file selected in the Files pane — something like the Preview in Adobe Bridge. One of the great features of the Organizer is that it shows multiple pages in the Pages pane for all files containing more than one page (see Figure 9-1). This feature is an advantage over the Bridge where only the cover pages are shown in the Content area and you need to manually scroll pages in the Preview pane to see additional pages in a document. When you select a multi-page document, all pages are displayed in thumbnail view in the Pages pane before you open the file. At the bottom of the pane is a zoom slider. Drag the slider left to display smaller thumbnails and to the right to make the thumbnail views larger. The minus and plus buttons display thumbnails smaller and larger, respectively, in zoom increments.

As you view multi-page documents in the Pages pane, you can double-click any page thumbnail to open the respective page in Acrobat. Select a page thumbnail and open a context menu, and a single menu command appears, enabling you to open that page.

Another nice feature in the Pages pane is the display of a Document Status icon that appears when you save files that have a special status or special feature — another advantage over viewing files in Adobe Bridge. Such features might include a document saved with layers, a file status related to a commenting review session, or a certified document. In addition to the Document Status icon, some files may display a security key representing files that have been password secured. When you see an icon to the right of a filename in the Pages pane, click the file to see what special features are contained within the file before you open it. In Figure 9-7, a context menu is opened displaying a message window for a file containing layers.

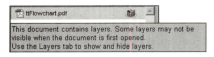

Figure 9-7: Select an icon to the right of a filename in the Pages pane to open a window reporting special features contained within the document.

Bookmarking Web-hosted PDFs

Acrobat is well integrated with many different Web services and support. The new Organizer is no exception when it comes to supporting Web-related services. You can add anything you can view in Acrobat as a PDF document to your Organizer. When you add a document to a collection from a Web-hosted PDF, the link is made to where the file is hosted. In this particular case, it's a link to a URL that you can create as easily as adding files from your hard drive to your collections. This is yet another feature you won't find in Adobe Bridge.

The first step is to view a PDF document as an inline view in a Web browser. Both Apple Safari and Microsoft Internet Explorer are supported. When you view a PDF in a Web browser, many Acrobat tools appear below your browser's tools. In Figure 9-8 you can see the Organizer tool adjacent to the Print tool inside Apple Safari. When you click the Organizer tool, the Add to Favorites dialog box opens. Click a collection and click OK to add the link to your collection.

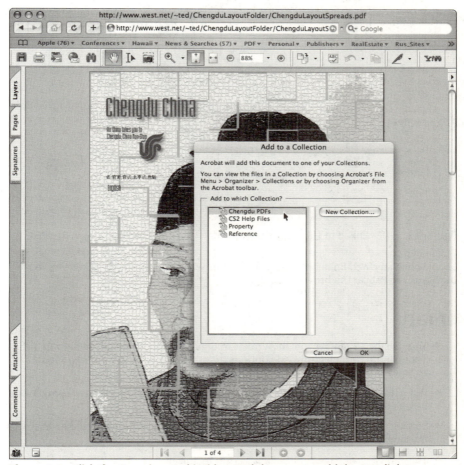

Figure 9-8: Click the Organizer tool inside a Web browser to add the URL link to a collection.

When you return to Acrobat, you can view the URL link in the respective collection. Open the Organizer and click the collection name where you added the link. In the Files pane, you see all the documents you have added to the collection. Those files added from Web URLs appear with a different icon than standard PDF documents in the Pages pane, as you can see in Figure 9-9. You can add files from PDFs on your hard drive and view them from within a Web browser (something you might do when working with browser-based reviews), or from URL addresses on the Web. In the Files pane, you see the URL address from where the document was retrieved appearing below the number of pages reported for the document.

Cross-Reference For more information related to browser-based reviews, see Chapter 25.

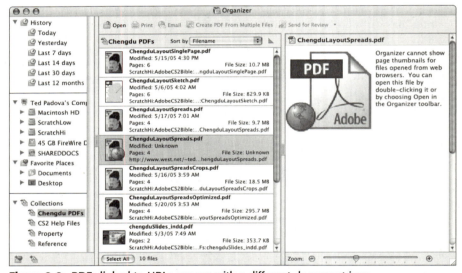

Figure 9-9: PDFs linked to URLs appear with a different document icon.

Double-click any Web-linked file and your default Web browser opens, takes you to the URL, and loads the PDF in the browser window.

Summary

✦ You use the Organizer tool in Acrobat to organize, sort, manage, and group PDF files. Tools in the Organizer provide options for creating PDF documents and initiating review sessions.

✦ PDF files are grouped in Collections where PDF documents are added using a single menu command.

✦ Sorting files on metadata in the Organizer is much more limited than sorting files in Adobe Bridge.

✦ You can view all pages in PDF files in the Organizer in the Pages pane.

✦ You can add Web links to PDF documents in the Organizer.

✦ ✦ ✦

Working with Objects and Images

P A R T

In This Part

Chapter 10
Creating, Selecting, and Editing Objects and Images

Chapter 11
Acquiring and Correcting Images

Chapter 12
Transforming Objects and Images

Chapter 13
Applying Effects to Objects and Layers

Chapter 14
Working with Layers

Chapter 15
Automating Tasks

Creating, Selecting, and Editing Objects

In This Chapter

Creating objects

Selecting objects

Organizing objects

Filling and stroking objects

Assigning color, gradients, and patterns

Working with transparency

Working with symbols, styles, and swatches

Editing objects

Creative Suite 2 documents have two groups of items: *objects,* which are editable and which include paths, shapes, type, and even multimedia elements, and *images,* which are pictures composed of an array of colored pixels. Although you have some crossover, you generally use Photoshop to work with images and Illustrator to work with objects. Most designs combine both of these items. Although all Creative Suite 2 applications use both objects and images and have similar tools, this chapter focuses mainly on Illustrator objects. Images in Photoshop are covered in the next chapter. The other CS2 applications of InDesign, GoLive and Acrobat have some of the same features for working with objects and images that are found in these two applications.

Several topics apply equally to both objects and images such as color, gradients and transparency. Although these topics are covered in this chapter on objects, they apply equally to images covered in the next chapter.

This chapter covers a lot of ground, including creating objects, the tools used to select them, and a sampling of the features used to edit them. The tools used to edit objects are as diverse as the tools and commands used to create and select them.

Creating Objects in Illustrator

The most common Illustrator objects are created using the various Drawing tools. These tools are the second section of tools located in the Toolbox directly under the Selection tools, as shown in Figure 10-1. They consist of the Pen tool, the Type tool, the Line Segment tool, the Rectangle tool, the Paintbrush tool, and the Pencil tool. Each of these tools also has several additional fly-out tools that you can use to create objects.

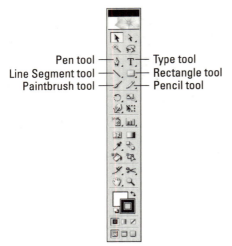

Figure 10-1: The Illustrator drawing tools

Drawing in the workspace with any of these tools creates a line that Illustrator calls a *path*, which is identified as an object. When you select an object, its path and the points that make up its path are highlighted using the layer color.

In addition to the objects presented in this section, Illustrator includes some other tools that create objects, such as the Symbol and Graph tools.

You can find information on Illustrator graphs in Chapter 23.

Using the Pen tool

You use the Pen tool to draw several connected lines by simply clicking once where you want the first anchor point and clicking again for each successive connected line.

But the power of the Pen tool isn't in creating straight lines. When you click with the Pen tool to place an anchor point, you can drag to extend a direction line that lies tangent to the curve. At the end of each direction line are direction points that may be moved to alter the curvature at the point. Figure 10-2 shows a path created with the Pen tool.

If you hold down the Shift key while dragging to create a direction line, the direction line is constrained to 45-degree increments.

Figure 10-2: The Pen tool can include straight and curved segments.

You can also use the Pen tool to do the following:

- **End a path:** Hold down the ⌘/Ctrl key when clicking to create the last anchor point. You can also end a path by selecting another tool.

- **Create a closed object:** Here, the first and last anchor points are the same. Position the last anchor point over the top of the first anchor point until a small circle appears as part of the cursor; then click.

- **Select individual points on a line:** Points created with the Pen tool can be selected with the Direct Selection or Lasso tools. If the point includes a direction line, the direction line and its points appear. When a direction line and its points are visible, you can drag them to alter the curvature around the point.

- **Add, delete, and convert anchor points on a line.** You can perform these tasks by using the Add or Delete Anchor Point tools, which are Pen tool fly-out tools. Another fly-out tool, the Convert Anchor Point tool, changes points without any direction lines to a smooth curve point. You simply click on the point and drag out a direction line. This tool also changes smooth anchor points to hard points without a direction line when you click on the anchor points. Holding down the Option/Alt key changes the cursor to the Convert Anchor Point tool.

- **Add or delete point on a path:** With the Pen tool selected, move the cursor over the top of the selected path. A small plus sign appears as part of the cursor when you're over the path; a small minus sign appears as part of the cursor when you're over a point that you may want to delete.

The Pen, Add Anchor Point, Delete Anchor Point, and Convert Anchor Point tools are found in Illustrator, Photoshop, and InDesign.

STEPS: Drawing with the Pen Tool

1. **Open an Illustrator document.** Choose File ➪ New to create a new document.

2. **Enable a snapping grid.** Choose View ➪ Show Grid to make a grid appear. Then choose View ➪ Snap to Grid. This enables snapping so all points snap to the visible grid.

3. **Draw straight lines.** Click on the Pen tool and click several times to create an anchor point every time you click.

4. **Close the shape.** To close the shape, move the cursor until it's on top of the first anchor point and click. A small circle appears as part of the cursor when it's over the first anchor point. Figure 10-3 shows the simple shape made from straight lines using the Pen tool.

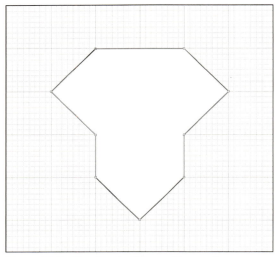

Figure 10-3: The Pen tool is used to create straight-line shapes.

5. **Draw curved segments.** With the Pen tool still selected, click to create the same shape beneath the first one, but after clicking each point, drag to pull a direction line out from the point before you release the mouse button. This direction line defines the curvature of the corner. Continue to click around the shape until the shape is closed.

6. **Edit the path points.** Select the Direct Selection tool, drag over each anchor point, and compare it to the anchor point across from it. Drag the direction points to make them similar to their opposite corner to make the object symmetrical. Figure 10-4 shows the resulting shapes.

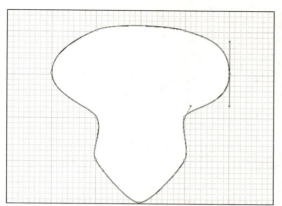

Figure 10-4: The Pen tool is also used to create curves.

Using the Type tool

You use the Type tool to create text objects. Clicking with the Type tool creates a Point text object, which you typically you use for a single line of text, such as a heading. You create a text-area object by clicking and dragging in the art board with the Type tool. All text that you type within a text area wraps to fit within the text object area.

Type and all the type tools are covered in detail in Part IV.

Text objects aren't limited to a rectangular area created by dragging with the Type tool. Using the fly-out tools available under the Type tool, you can add text to a selected area or have text follow a path. There are also tools for creating text that runs vertically instead of horizontally.

Type objects you create with the Type tool are a unique type of object. You edit them using the Type tool; you can select them in a similar manner as other objects by dragging over them with the Selection tool.

Creating lines and shapes

You use the Line Segment tool to create simple straight lines by clicking and dragging on the art board. If you double-click with the Line Segment tool, a dialog box, shown in Figure 10-5, opens where you can specify the line's length and angle. Holding down the Shift key while dragging constrains the line to 45-degree increments; holding down the Option/Alt key while dragging extends the line in both directions from the clicked first point; and holding down the Spacebar lets you move the line by dragging.

Figure 10-5: The Line Segment Tool Options dialog box

As fly-outs under the Line Segment tool, Illustrator includes tools for creating arcs, spirals, rectangular grids, and polar grids.

The Rectangle tool creates rectangle objects by dragging in the art board. Clicking without dragging opens a simple dialog box where you can enter precise Width and Height values. Holding down the Shift key creates a perfect square when you drag; holding down the Option/Alt key while dragging creates the rectangle from the center outward; and holding down the Spacebar lets you move and position the rectangle as you draw it out.

As fly-out tools under the Rectangle tool, you can find the Rounded Rectangle, Ellipse, and Polygon tools. Dragging the Ellipse tool with the Shift key held down creates a perfect circle. Clicking with the Polygon tool opens a dialog box where you can specify a radius and the number of sides to include in the polygon.

 Illustrator also includes tools for creating pointed stars and flares as fly-outs under the Rectangle tool.

Using the Paintbrush and Pencil tools

You can use both the Paintbrush and Pencil tools to draw freehand curves. The difference is that the Paintbrush tool applies a stroke to the resulting path. To draw with either the Paintbrush or Pencil tools, click and drag in the art board.

If you press the Option/Alt key and hold it down after starting a path, a small circle appears as part of the cursor, indicating that you're creating a closed path. When you release the mouse, regardless of where it's located, a line is drawn back to the first anchor point, creating a closed object.

If you double-click on either tool in the Toolbox, a dialog box of preferences for the selected tool appears, such as the Paintbrush Tool Preferences dialog box, shown in Figure 10-6. In this dialog box, you can set Fidelity and Smoothness values as well as other options:

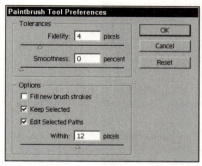

Figure 10-6: The Paintbrush Tool Preferences dialog box

✦ **Fidelity:** The Fidelity value determines how far the cursor can stray before a new anchor point is created. Increasing this value causes small changes in the path to be ignored. Figure 10-7 shows three curves drawn with the Paintbrush tool with different Fidelity settings. Notice how the curve with the lowest Fidelity value has the most anchor points.

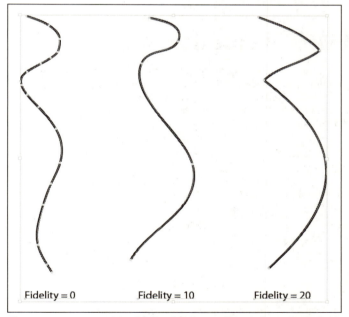

Figure 10-7: Increasing Fidelity decreases the total number of anchor points.

- **Smoothness:** The Smoothness value can range from 0 to 100 and sets the smoothness of the resulting path.
- **Fill New Brush Strokes option:** Only available for the Paintbrush tool, this option allows you to apply a fill to the path. If the path isn't closed, an imaginary line is drawn between the first and endpoints of the path, and the interior portion is colored with the fill color.
- **Keep Selected option:** Causes the path to remain selected after you release the mouse button.
- **Edit Selected Paths option:** Enables you to redraw portions of the path using the selected tool when the cursor is within the specified number of pixels. With this option, you can move the tool over the top of the selected path. If a small x displays as part of the cursor, a new path is created; if the small x disappears, you can drag over the path and replace that portion of the path with the new dragged path.

The fly-out tools under the Pencil tool are the Smooth and Erase tools. You can drag the Smooth tool over the top of a selected path to reduce the number of anchor points and smooth the line. You can use the Erase tool to delete the path section that you drag over. You must select the path to use the Erase tool.

Tip

You can temporarily enable the Smooth tool when you have the Paintbrush or Pencil tool selected by holding down the Option/Alt key.

Creating Objects in InDesign

InDesign, like Illustrator, relies heavily on the concept of objects. Almost everything placed in an InDesign document is an object. Objects are created in InDesign using the tools found in the second section of the Toolbox, shown in Figure 10-8, including the Pen tool, the Type tool, the Pencil tool, the Line tool, the Rectangle Frame tool, and the Rectangle tool along with the additional tools available as fly-outs.

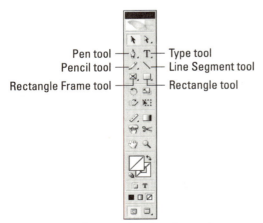

Figure 10-8: The InDesign drawing tools

All these tools include features that are similar to the Illustrator tools, but InDesign includes one additional object type created with the Frame tools. These frames offer a way to create an image placeholder.

Creating Objects in Photoshop

Although Photoshop's forte is working with images, you can also use Photoshop to create *shapes*. The tools used to create objects in Photoshop are located in the third section of tools in the Toolbox, as shown in Figure 10-9. They include a Type tool, a Pen tool, and a Rectangle tool, along with several additional tools available as fly-outs.

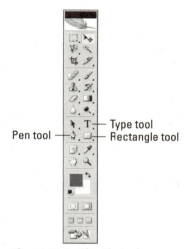

Figure 10-9: The Photoshop drawing tools

When you select one of these drawing tools, the Options bar, shown in Figure 10-10, displays all the drawing tools. Selecting a drawing tool and clicking the arrow to the right of the tools opens a pop-up menu of settings for the selected tool. These pop-up menus of settings let you enter precise Width and Height values for the shapes.

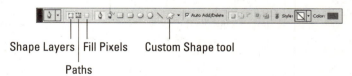

Figure 10-10: The Options bar displays all the different drawing tools.

Photoshop also includes a Freeform Pen tool, as a fly-out under the Pen tool that acts like Illustrator's Pencil tool. It lets you draw freehand paths. If you enable the Magnetic option in the Options bar, the Freeform Pen tool detects areas of contrast and snaps the line to follow a pixel image behind it.

Specifying custom shapes

The Photoshop object tools (referred to in Photoshop as Drawing tools) also work just like their Illustrator counterparts. Among these tools is a unique tool called the Custom Shape tool, which is a fly-out under the Rectangle tool.

The Custom Shape tool lets you select a custom shape from a pop-up menu in the Options palette, shown in Figure 10-11. You add the selected shape to the document by dragging with the tool. Add new shapes to the pop-up menu by choosing Edit ⇨ Define Custom Shape.

Figure 10-11: This pop-up palette lets you add Custom Shapes to the document.

Photoshop custom shapes are similar to Illustrator's symbols.

Cross-Reference

Symbols are covered in the "Using Symbols, Styles, and Swatches" section later in this chapter.

Creating paths

If you select the Paths option in the Options bar, select a drawing tool, and then create a shape, Photoshop adds the shape to the Paths palette, shown in Figure 10-12. You can then use these paths to mask areas or define a clipping path. You can also convert them into a selection.

You can also export paths to Illustrator by choosing File ⇨ Export ⇨ Paths to Illustrator.

Cross-Reference

Using paths as clipping masks is covered in the "Creating a clipping mask in Illustrator," section later in this chapter.

Paths drawn on an image are temporary and appear with the name Work Path in the Paths palette. If you deselect the Work Path in the Paths palette and draw another path, then the new path replaces the first path. Because paths placed in the Paths palette are temporary, you can save them using the Save Path palette menu command. This opens a simple dialog box where you can name the saved path. The saved path then appears permanently in the Paths palette where it can be selected and reused.

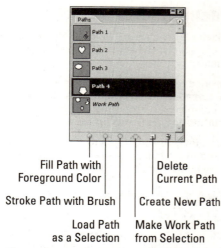

Figure 10-12: The Paths palette lets you store several different paths.

Painting with shapes

All shapes drawn in Photoshop as objects are contained within special layers called *shape layers*. If a single shape layer includes multiple shapes, you can use the Pathfinder buttons to add, subtract, intersect, or exclude the overlapping areas.

 Cross-Reference More on the Pathfinder commands is covered in the section "Using Pathfinder features."

If you select the Fill Pixels option in the Options bar when drawing a shape in Photoshop, the shape becomes rasterized and becomes part of the pixel layer. For these painted shapes, you can select a blending mode and an opacity. You can also rasterize existing shapes by choosing Layer ⇨ Rasterize ⇨ Shape.

Creating and Editing Objects in Acrobat

All items in an Acrobat document are objects. Most of these objects are created from the original document when it's converted into a PDF file, but Acrobat also lets you create several objects that you can use to enhance the Acrobat document or to add review comments.

You select most Acrobat objects by choosing Tools ⇨ Advanced Editing ⇨ Select Object. When selected, the object highlights and you can move it by dragging it to a new location. If you right-click on the object, a pop-up menu appears with commands to edit, align, center, distribute, and size the object. Most objects also include a pop-up menu option to access their Properties dialog box.

Adding document-enhancement objects

Objects used to enhance a PDF document — including the Article tool, the Movie tool, the Sound tool, the TouchUp Text and TouchUp Object tools, and several Form object tools — are located in the Tools ⇨ Advanced Editing menu:

- **Article tool:** Use this to add several threaded text areas to the document. To create an article object, drag to create each of the threaded text areas and press the Enter key to complete the article. After the article is completed, a Properties dialog box appears, where you can enter the title, subject, author, and keywords for the article.

- **Movie and Sound tools:** Use these to add movie or sound files to an existing PDF document. After selecting either of these tools and dragging in the document, a dialog box opens where you can browse to the desired movie or sound file.

Cross-Reference

The details of using movie and sound files within an Acrobat document are covered in Chapter 35.

- **TouchUp Text tool:** Use this to add a new text object to the existing document. Selecting the Text TouchUp tool and clicking in the document with the ⌘/Ctrl key held down opens a dialog box where you can select the font and mode for the new text.

- **Form object tools:** The Tools ⇨ Advanced Editing ⇨ Forms menu includes several form objects that you can easily add to an Acrobat document. After selecting a form object from the menu, you can drag with the mouse to specify the form object's size. These form object tools include a Button tool, a Check Box tool, a Combo Box tool, a List Box tool, a Radio Button tool, a Text Field tool, and a Digital Signature tool. When you create a form object, a Properties dialog box (Figure 10-13) opens, where you can specify all the settings for the form object. For example, the Button Properties dialog box includes four panels — General, Appearance, Options, and Actions, but other form objects include more panels.

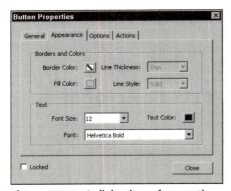

Figure 10-13: A dialog box of properties helps define the object's appearance.

Adding commenting objects

All the commenting objects for reviewing a document are included in the Tools ⇨ Commenting menu and Tools ⇨ Advanced Commenting menu. The Commenting menu includes the Note tool. Dragging with the Note tool in the document creates a Note object, which includes the name of the person making the comments, along with the date and time and a text area where the comments may be added.

The Commenting menu also includes the Stamps submenu, which is used to add stamped image objects to the document. The Stamps submenu includes many different default stamps choices, including stamps that say Approved, Confidential, Void, and so on. There is also a category of dynamic stamps that include the applier's name and date. Figure 10-14 shows several Acrobat objects including some note boxes and an Author stamp.

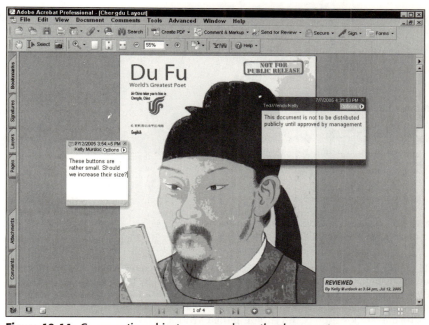

Figure 10-14: Commenting objects appear above the document.

To add more attention to a comment, you may select to use one of the tools found in the Tools ⇨ Drawing Markups menu. These tools include a collection of drawing tools, including tools for creating rectangles, ovals, arrows, lines, clouds, polygons, and polygon line objects. The Drawing Markups menu also includes a Text Box tool that creates highlighted text area objects, the Pencil tools, which lets you draw freehand objects, and the Pencil Eraser tool, which erases lines drawn with the Pencil tool. In addition, the Attach File tool opens a dialog box where you can select a file to attach to the document. After you've selected the file, the File Attachment Properties dialog box appears; here, you can define how the attachment looks in the PDF document. The Attach Sound tool opens a Sound Recorder, where you can record a simple audio message or select a sound file to attach to the document.

Creating Objects in GoLive

GoLive also uses objects extensively to lay out Web pages. All the objects that you can add to a Web page are available in different categories in the Objects palette. The various categories can be selected from the top of the Toolbox, and selecting a category displays all the available objects as icons in the lower half of the Objects palette. Figure 10-15 shows many of the objects in the Basic Objects category.

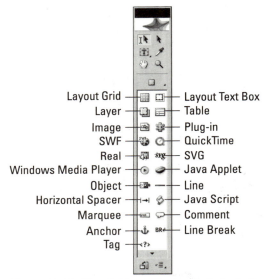

Figure 10-15: The GoLive Objects palette includes dozens of objects in several different categories.

Objects are added to a Web page by dragging its icon and dropping it on the Web page in the location in the Layout Editor where you want it to appear. The properties for the selected object are adjusted in the Inspector palette. You can also drag and drop object into the Source and Outline views. Double clicking on an object in the Objects palette adds it to the page at the current location of the cursor in the Layout Editor.

Cross-Reference: You can learn more about working with GoLive objects in Chapter 28.

Selecting Objects

Before the properties of an object are displayed, you need to select the object that you want to change. Selecting an object is as easy as clicking on it with the Selection Tool. When selected, the object is surrounding with a bounding box. An object's bounding box may be used to transform the object.

Cross-Reference Transforming objects is covered in Chapter 12.

The core Selection tools — including the Selection and Direct Selection tools found in Illustrator, Photoshop, and InDesign — all work the same.

Using Illustrator and InDesign's Toolbox selection tools

Both the Illustrator and InDesign Toolboxes include several tools for selecting objects and parts of objects. These tools are located at the top of the Toolbox, as shown in Figure 10-16 for Illustrator include the Selection tool, Direct Selection tool, the Magic Wand tool and the Lasso tool. InDesign includes the Selection and Direct Selection tools.

 Figure 10-16: The Illustrator selection tools

+ **Selection tool:** The simplest way to select objects is to click on them with the Selection tool. You can also select multiple objects by dragging over them with the Selection tool. All objects that are at least partially included within the area that is dragged over are selected. You may also select multiple objects by holding down the Shift key while clicking on each object.

 Tip You can access the Selection tool in Illustrator regardless of the current tool by holding down the ⌘/Ctrl key. This allows you to select an object quickly at any time. In Photoshop, the ⌘/Ctrl key accesses the Move tool; in InDesign, the ⌘/Ctrl key accesses the Direct Selection tool.

+ **Direct Selection tool:** Use this to select individual points or segments on a path. When a path point is selected, it appears solid; unselected path points appear hollow. When the Direct Selection tool is over the top of a line segment, a small line appears as part of the cursor; if the Direct Selection tool is over an anchor point, a small hollow square appears as part of the cursor.

 Note Even if only a single path point is selected with the Direct Selection tool, the entire object is also selected and may be transformed.

Using Illustrator's other selection tools

Illustrator's Group Selection tool (available as a fly-out under the Direct Selection tool) may be used to select a single object that is part of a group. Double-clicking on a grouped set of objects selects the object and the group it belongs to. Each successive click adds another group level.

Illustrator's Magic Wand tool (Y) is used to select all objects that have a similar fill color, but using the Magic Wand palette, shown in Figure 10-17, you can choose to have the Magic Wand tool select all objects with a similar fill color, stroke color, stroke weight, opacity, and blending mode. For each of these (except for blending mode), you can specify a Tolerance value. The Tolerance value determines how loose the selected attribute may be while still being selected.

Selecting by path only

By default, you can select objects by clicking on their fill, but this isn't your only option. If you have several overlapping objects, this option might lead to some frustration. The General panel of the Preferences dialog box (opened with the Illustrator/Edit ➪ Preferences ➪ General menu command) includes an Object Selection by Path Only option. With this option enabled, objects are only selected with the Selection tool when you click or drag over their path and not their fill.

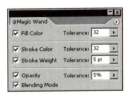

Figure 10-17: The Magic Wand palette lets you select which attributes to select.

Illustrator's Lasso tool (Q) may also be used to select multiple path points on multiple objects. Every object that has a point encircled by the Lasso tool is selected. Holding down the Shift key lets you add to the current selection; holding down the Option/Alt key subtracts from the current selection.

Note

You cannot select objects that are locked or hidden. To unlock all objects, choose Object ➪ Unlock All (Alt+Ctrl+3 in Windows; Option+⌘+3 on the Mac). To show all hidden objects, choose Object ➪ Show All (Alt+Ctrl+3 in Windows; Option+⌘+3 on the Mac).

Using Photoshop's other selection tools

Although you use most of Photoshop's selection tools to make pixel selections, Photoshop also includes Selection and Direct Selection tools specifically for selecting objects. When you select a layer containing images in the Layers palette, you can use Photoshop's Marquee, Lasso, or Magic Wand tools to select a pixel area. You move pixel selections using the Move tool, but the Move tool is also used to move objects when an object is selected.

When objects are created in Photoshop, each object resides on its own layer. Photoshop CS2 lets you select multiple layers by holding down the Shift key. Once multiple layers are selected, they can be moved and altered as needed.

New Feature

The ability to select multiple layers is new to Photoshop CS2.

Selecting objects with Illustrator's Layers palette

You can use the Layers palette to select all objects contained on a layer or individual objects within that layer. To the right of the layer name in the Layers palette is a circle button used to target objects. Clicking on this target button for a given layer selects all objects on that layer. If you expand a layer, you can select the individual objects that make up the layer.

Cross-Reference

Layers are covered in detail in Chapter 14.

Using Illustrator's Select menu

In addition to the Toolbox tools, there are many selection-menu commands available in the Select menu. Choose Select ⇨ All (⌘/Ctrl+A) to select all objects in the scene. Choose Select ⇨ Deselect (Shift+⌘/Ctrl+A) to deselect all objects in the document so that no objects are selected. Choose Select ⇨ Reselect to select again all objects that were previously selected.

Photoshop also includes a Select menu, but all these menu commands apply to the pixel selection tools.

Choosing Select ⇨ Inverse selects all objects that weren't selected and deselects all objects currently selected.

Objects can also be selected using their stacking order. Choosing Select ⇨ Next Object Above (Alt+Ctrl+] in Windows; Option+⌘+] on the Mac) selects the object immediately above the current object in the stacking order. Choosing Select ⇨ Next Object Below (Alt+Ctrl+[in Windows; Option+⌘+[on the Mac) selects the object immediately below the current object in the stacking order. If the topmost or bottommost objects are selected when these commands are used, the current object remains selected.

The First Object Above, Next Object Above, Next Object Below, and Last Object Below menu commands are found in InDesign's Object ⇨ Select menu.

The Select ⇨ Same menu includes several options for choosing all objects that have similar properties. The options include Blending Mode, Fill & Stroke, Fill Color, Opacity, Stroke Color, Stroke Weight, Style, Symbol Instance, and Link Block Series.

The Select ⇨ Object menu includes several subobjects that you may select for the selected object. These options include All on Same Layers, Direction Handles, Brush Strokes, Clipping Masks, Stray Points, and Text Objects.

The Select ⇨ Save Selection menu command lets you name and save the current selection of objects. The Save selections may be recalled at any time by selecting the selection name from the bottom of the Select menu. Choosing Select ⇨ Edit Selection opens a dialog box where you can rename or delete a selection.

Organizing Objects

Illustrator and InDesign both include several ways to organize objects. Chief among these is the Layers palette, which lets you place objects on separate layers. Other organization features are contained within the Object menu; these features help in grouping and preventing unwanted edits by locking and hiding objects.

The Object menu includes many other commands, such as commands to transform and arrange objects. These commands are covered in Chapter 12.

Adding objects to layers

All the CS2 applications have layers accessed through a Layers palette. You create new layers by selecting the New Layer palette menu command or by clicking on the New Layer icon button at the bottom of the palette. All new objects are added to the selected layer, and objects may be moved between layers.

Note Although Acrobat doesn't have a Layers palette, layers can be imported from other CS2 applications and be viewed in Acrobat using the Layers interface.

The first two columns of the Layers palette let you hide or lock layers by clicking in the column boxes. Locked and hidden layers cannot be selected or edited.

 Cross-Reference Turn to Chapter 14 for much more information on layers.

Grouping objects

You may group together several selected objects by choosing Object ⇨ Group (⌘/Ctrl+G). Groups may also be nested. When a single object that is part of a group is selected with the Selection tool, the entire group is selected, but individual objects that are part of a group may be selected using the Group Selection tool in Illustrator. Choose Object ⇨ Ungroup (Shift+Ctrl+G in Windows; Shift+⌘+G on the Mac) to ungroup a grouped set of objects.

Hiding and locking objects

To prevent set objects from accidentally being selected or edited, you can lock and hide objects in Illustrator by choosing Object ⇨ Lock and by choosing Objects ⇨ Hide. Both of these menus let you lock (or hide) the current selection (⌘/Ctrl+2), all artwork above, or other layers. You cannot select objects you lock or hide. InDesign only includes the menu commands Object ⇨ Lock Position (⌘/Ctrl+L) and Object ⇨ Unlock Position (Alt+Ctrl+L in Windows; Option+⌘+L on the Mac).

Objects or layers that are locked have a small lock icon displayed in the second column of the Layers palette, as shown in Figure 10-18, and objects or layers that are hidden have no eye icon in the first column of the Layers palette. The Layers palette provides another way to quickly hide and lock objects by clicking on the palette's columns.

 Note You can also lock or hide layers in Photoshop using the Layers palette: Select the layer and click the Lock Position or Lock All icons at the top of the Layers palette. When locked, a small lock icon appears to the right of the Layer name. You hide layers in Photoshop clicking the eye icon in the first column of the Layers palette.

Hidden layer

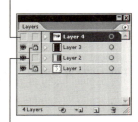

Figure 10-18: The Layers palette allows you to lock or hide layer objects.

Locked layers

Filling and Stroking Objects

The two properties probably most common for objects are the object's fill and stroke. An object's *fill* is the color, gradient, or pattern that fills the interior portion of an object, and an object's *stroke* is the line or outline that makes up the object. Fills and strokes may be any color or they may be set to no color. Fills may also be added with a gradient or a pattern.

Applying fill and stroke colors to objects in Illustrator and InDesign

Fill and stroke colors are applied to objects using the colors for each that are identified in the Fill and Stroke boxes located at the bottom of the Toolbox, as shown in Figure 10-19. The Fill box looks like a filled colored square; the Stroke box looks like a thick outlined square. The Fill box is active by default, but you can click on the Stroke box to select it.

Tip   The X key toggles between the Fill and Stroke color swatches in the Toolbox.

Figure 10-19: The Fill and Stroke boxes appear at the bottom of the Toolbox.

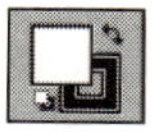

With either the Fill or Stroke box in the Toolbox active, you can change the box's color by selecting a new color from the Color or Swatches palette, or you can double-click on the box to access a Color Picker dialog box.

The double-headed arrow that appears above and to the right of the Fill and Stroke boxes swaps the colors, so the Fill color becomes the Stroke color and vice versa. The small icon to the lower left of the Fill and Stroke boxes set the Fill and Stroke colors to their defaults, which are a white fill and a black stroke.

Tip   The keyboard shortcut to swap the Fill and Stroke colors is Shift+X; the keyboard shortcut for setting the fill and stroke colors to their defaults is D.

Below the Fill and Stroke boxes in the Toolbox are three simple icons, shown in Figure 10-20. These icons are used to set the active Fill or Stroke box to hold a Color (<), a Gradient (>), or None (/). When the None icon is clicked for either box, a red diagonal line appears in the box.

Caution   Gradients may be applied only to a Fill, not to a Stroke, in Illustrator. If the Gradient button in Illustrator is clicked for a stroke, a gradient is added to the Fill box. InDesign can add gradients to strokes.

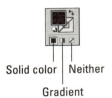

Figure 10-20: The icons under the Fill and Stroke boxes can fill the selected object with a color, a gradient, or neither.

If the fill and stroke colors are changed without any objects selected, the selected colors are applied to the next objects created.

The Color palette also includes Fill and Stroke boxes that match those in the Toolbox, as shown in Figure 10-21.

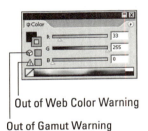

Figure 10-21: The Color palette also includes Fill and Stroke boxes.

One other place that may be used to change fill and stroke colors is the Attribute palette. Using the Attribute palette, shown in Figure 10-22, you can change the stacking order for fills and strokes. Attributes listed in the Appearance palette are applied to an object from front to back in the order that they appear in the Appearance palette.

Figure 10-22: The Appearance palette shows all an object's attributes.

By dragging the fill above the stroke, the fill appears above the stroke, making any portion of the stroke that overlaps the fill hidden behind the fill.

Applying other stroke attributes

Although the only attribute that may be applied to a fill is a color, gradient, or pattern, strokes include several additional attributes. These attributes are applied using the Stroke palette, shown in Figure 10-23.

The stroke weight defines how thick the stroke is. By default, half of the weight thickness appears on either side of the object path marked in the object's layer color when the object is selected. Stroke weights ranging from 0.25 points to 100 points may be selected from the pop-up menu to the right of the Weight field, or you may enter a custom weight value in the Weight field.

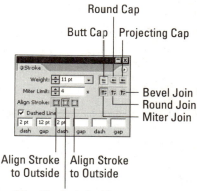

Figure 10-23: The Stroke palette includes additional stroke attributes.

Note Entering a Weight value of 0 sets the stroke to None.

Selecting the Show Options palette menu command causes several additional stroke attributes to appear at the bottom of the Stroke palette.

The row of icons that appears to the right of the Weight field lets you select from three different cap styles that are applied to the end of the stroke. The three options are Butt Cap, Round Cap, and Projecting Cap. Butt Cap squares the ends of a stroke, Round Cap applies half a circle to the stroke ends, and Projecting Cap applies a square end that is extended half a line width beyond the end of the stroke.

Note Selecting a cap style for a closed object such as a rectangle has no effect.

Beneath the three cap style buttons are three Join options. These buttons define how the corners of an object appear. The Join options are Miter Join, Round Join, and Bevel Join. Miter Join draws the corners as sharp squares, Round Join rounds the corners, and Bevel Join replaces the corners with diagonal lines. The Miter Limit sets a limit for the corner point as a number times the weight when Miter Joins are automatically switched to Bevel Joins.

The Align Stroke options let you move a stroke so its thickness is centered on the objects boundary, so the stroke's thickness is inside the object or so it is outside the object. Setting the stroke align option to Outside causes the stroke to be completely free of the fill color, but setting the alignment to Inside causes the stroke to conceal a portion of the fill color. Figure 10-24 shows each of these alignment options.

New Feature The stroke alignment options are new to the Stroke palette in Illustrator CS2.

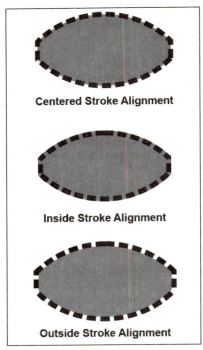

Figure 10-24: The Stroke palette includes options for specifying how the stroke is aligned.

If the Dashed Line option is selected, you can enter the Dash and Gap values for three separate dashes, enabling you to create many unique dashed lines. Not all the Dash and Gap values need to be filled in. Whatever values are entered are repeated around the entire object.

Figure 10-25 shows several stroke samples of various weights, cap types, and dashed lines.

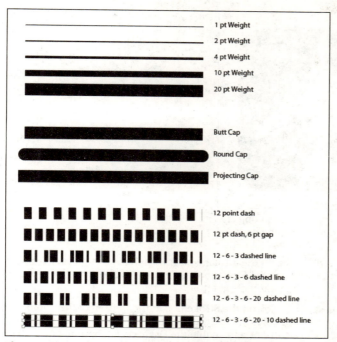

Figure 10-25: Altering the settings in the Stroke palette changes the attributes for the stroked path.

STEPS: Applying Fills and Strokes

1. **Open an Illustrator document.** With Illustrator open, choose File ➪ New to create a new document. Choose Window ➪ Symbol Libraries ➪ Maps to open a palette of map symbols. Select and drag one of the symbols to the art board. The symbol is fairly small. Select a corner handle and drag it away from the symbol while holding down the Shift key uniformly scales the symbol.

2. **Expand and ungroup the symbol.** With the symbol selected, choose Object ➪ Expand. In the Expand dialog box, select to expand both the Object and the Fill and click OK. Next choose Object ➪ Ungroup three times to ungroup all the objects. The object now consists of two objects — a rounded black square and an airplane path — as shown in Figure 10-26.

Figure 10-26: You can select an object after expanding and ungrouping it.

3. **Select and apply a fill.** Click on the airplane path with the Selection tool. Notice that the Fill box is set to white and the Stroke box is set to None. With the Fill box selected, click on a blue color in the Swatches palette.

4. **Select and apply a stroke.** Click on the Stroke box at the bottom of the Toolbox to select it. Then choose a red color in the Swatches palette. In the Stroke palette, increase the Weight value to 10 pt and enable the Dashed Line option. Enter **20 pt** in the first dashed line field and **2 pt** in the second field. The stroke is updated as you change the Stroke settings in the Stroke palette. The resulting fill and stroke are shown in Figure 10-27.

Figure 10-27: After applying a stroke and fill to the interior shape, the design is altered dramatically with a few simple changes.

5. **Copy the style to the Graphic Styles palette.** Choose Window ⇨ Appearance to open the Appearance palette. Drag the Appearance icon to the left of the Path title in the Appearance palette to the Graphic Styles palette (or just drag the object itself to the Graphic Styles palette). This copies the created style to the Graphic Styles palette where it's applied to other objects.

6. **Apply the copied style to the background object.** Select the background rounded square object and drag the copied style from the Graphic Styles palette to the background object. This applied the same fill and stroke attributes to the square object, as shown in Figure 10-28.

Figure 10-28: Styles copied to the Graphic Styles palette may be easily applied to other objects.

Using Illustrator's Live Paint

If you create and fill a circle in Illustrator and overlap that circle with another circle object that is also filled and stroked, changing the color of the overlapped section becomes difficult. This is because the colors are inherited from each separate object. Illustrator's new Live Paint feature overcomes these difficulties by splitting the overlapping objects into a series of edges and faces. You can fill each face independent of the other faces much like a simple coloring book.

 New Feature Live Paint is a new feature in Illustrator CS2.

Converting objects to Live Paint

You can convert selected objects to Live Paint objects by choosing the Object ⇨ Live Paint ⇨ Make menu command. Once converted, each independent path changes to an edge and each separate area converts to a face. This allows you to color each face independent of the others. Figure 10-29 shows two simple circle objects that are overlapped before and after they are converted to Live Paint objects.

Caution Live Paint objects have several limitations that you need to keep in mind. In particular, Live Paint objects can't use transparency, effects, symbols, blends, clipping masks, or pathfinder.

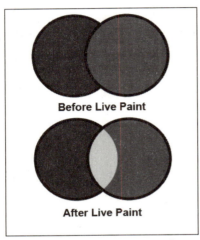

Figure 10-29: You can convert objects to Live Paint objects using the Object ⇨ Live Paint ⇨ Make menu command.

You cannot convert some object types, such as type and brushes, to Live Paint objects directly, but if you first convert them to paths using the Type ⇨ Create Outlines or the Object ⇨ Expand menu commands, then you can perform the conversion to Live Paint with the Object ⇨ Live Paint ⇨ Make menu command.

 Cross-Reference You can also convert bitmap images to Live Paint objects by first using the Live Trace feature. Simply select the bitmap image and choose the Object ⇨ Live Trace ⇨ Convert to Live Paint menu command. More on Live Trace is covered in Chapter 13.

Using the Live Paint tools

Once converted, you can fill faces using the Live Paint Bucket tool (shortcut, K) and select them with the Live Paint Selection tool (Shift+L). Moving the mouse over a face with either tool highlights the face boundaries in red. Double clicking either tool opens a dialog box of options, as shown in Figure 10-30. With these options, you can select to apply only Paint Fills, only Paint Strokes, or both. You can also change the highlight color and width. You can also use the Live Paint Bucket and Live Paint Selection tools to convert the selected objects to Live Paint objects.

If you double click a Live Paint face with the Live Paint Bucket tool, all adjacent faces are filled across an unstroked edge. A triple click will change all faces to the current fill. Holding down the Shift key switches the current settings in the Live Paint Bucket Options dialog box. For example, if you select Paint Fills, the Shift key causes the Paint Strokes option to be selected.

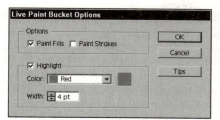

Figure 10-30: The Live Paint Bucket Options dialog box lets you choose to apply fills or strokes.

Adding paths to a Live Paint object

If you want to add more paths to the existing objects to divide it into even more faces, simply double-click the face where you want to add another path to isolate the face. Then draw the path using one of the drawing tools and double click the art board again with the Selection tool (not the Live Paint Selection tool, just the normal Selection tool). The new path is added to the Live Paint objects and new faces are created.

You can also add new paths to an existing Live Paint group using the Object ⇨ Live Paint ⇨ Add Paths menu command or by dragging the path to the Live Paint group in the Layers palette. Figure 10-31 shows a simple line segment added to the existing overlapping circles. The new face is filled a different color.

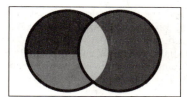

Figure 10-31: You can add new paths to an existing Live Paint object.

Editing Live Paint paths

Perhaps the coolest feature of a Live Paint object is that you can edit it and all the filled faces readjust to maintain their filled colors. Figure 10-32 shows the same two overlapping circles where the points have been selected and moved. Live Paint is smart enough to adjust the objects so that the faces remained filled.

Figure 10-32: Editing a Live Paint object readjusts the filled faces so they stay consistent.

Releasing and expanding a Live Paint group

If you need to apply a feature that Live Paint can't handle such as transparency, you can dissolve the Live Paint group using the Object ⇨ Live Paint ⇨ Release menu command. This command converts the Live Paint group back into regular paths without any fills and a 0.5 black stroke.

Expanding a Live Paint group maintains the current fills and strokes but separates each edge and face into a separate object. Figure 10-33 shows an expanded Live Paint group, which has had each edge and face moved using the Group Selection tool.

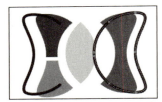

Figure 10-33: You can expand Live Paint groups into separate objects.

Managing fill gaps

If two paths don't exactly meet in the Live Paint group, a fill could spill over into the next face when you click with the Live Paint Bucket tool. To prevent this, you can manually edit all paths to eliminate existing gaps. To see any gaps in the current Live Paint group, choose View ⇨ Show Live Paint Gaps. Gap Detection is enabled through the Gap Options dialog box, shown in Figure 10-34. You can access the Gap Options dialog box using the Objects ⇨ Live Paint ⇨ Gap Options menu command. You can now set paint to stop at Small (3 pt), Medium (6 pt), or Large (12 pt) gaps or select the Custom option and set your own gap size. You can also set the Gap Preview color and choose to automatically close all gaps in the Live Paint group with the Close Gaps with Paths button.

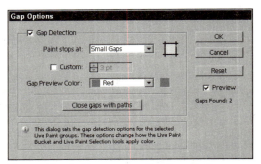

Figure 10-34: You can use the Gap Options dialog box to close any gaps in the current Live Paint group.

Chapter 10 ✦ **Creating, Selecting, and Editing Objects** 335

STEPS: Working with Live Paint

1. **Open an Illustrator document.** With Illustrator open, choose File ➪ Open to open a document that includes several overlapping objects.

2. **Create a Live Paint group.** Select all the overlapping objects and choose the Object ➪ Live Paint ➪ Make menu command. A new Live Paint Group layer is added to the Layers palette and the entire group is selected and highlighted.

3. **Fill the Live Paint faces.** Select the Live Paint Bucket tool from the Toolbox and change the fill color to blue. Then click the square backgrounds. Then change the fill color to yellow and click the elliptical portions of the kite. You can speed the coloring of each portion by double clicking on the area that needs to be filled. This automatically fills each face where a stroke doesn't exist. The resulting kite is shown in Figure 10-35.

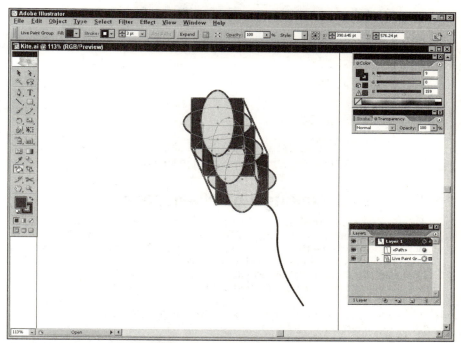

Figure 10-35: You can easily fill this Live Paint group using the Live Paint Bucket tool.

4. **Add a path to the Live Paint group.** Click and hold the Rectangle tool fly-out until the Star tool is selected. Then drag in the art board to create a simple 5-pointed star object. Drag the star object with the Selection tool to the center of the top kite circle. Drag over the entire kite object and choose the Object ➪ Live Paint ➪ Add Paths menu command. Then change the fill color to red and double click on the star object to color it red, as shown in Figure 10-36.

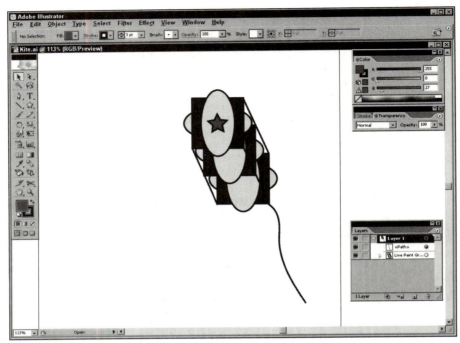

Figure 10-36: New paths can be added to an existing Live Paint group.

Filling and stroking a pixel selection

Although fills and strokes are mainly applied to objects, they may also be applied to a pixel selection in Photoshop using the Edit ➪ Fill (Shift+F5) and Edit ➪ Stroke menu commands. Both of these commands open a dialog box, shown in Figure 10-37, where you can select the color to use. The color options include Foreground Color, Background Color, Color (which opens a Color Picker), Pattern, History, Black, 50% Gray, and White. You can also select a blending mode, an opacity, and whether to preserve transparency.

Note If the Edit ➪ Fill menu command is used with no selection, the entire canvas is filled with the selected color.

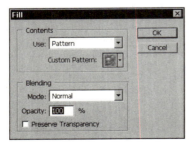

Figure 10-37: The Fill dialog box lets you select the color or pattern.

The Stroke dialog box, shown in Figure 10-38, also includes options to specify the width and color of the stroke and whether to place the stroke inside, in the center, or outside of the selection.

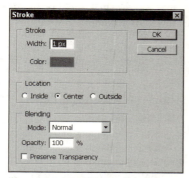

Figure 10-38: The Stroke dialog box lets you specify a width, a color, and whether the stroke appears inside, centered, or outside the selection.

Filling and stroking a Photoshop path

Paths in the Paths palette in Photoshop may also be filled and stroked using the Fill Path and Stroke Path palette menu commands. The Fill Path dialog box includes the same settings used to fill a selection along with a Feather Radius value and an Anti-aliased option.

The Stroke Path dialog box, on the other hand, includes a single option to select the Tool that is used to stroke the path, as shown in Figure 10-39. The options include all the various drawing and editing tools including Pencil, Brush, Eraser, Clone Stamp, Smudge, and so on.

Figure 10-39: The Stroke Path dialog box lets you select a tool to use to stroke the path.

Assigning Color

Color plays an important part in any design, and the color features found in the Creative Suite applications are amazingly diverse. Whether your documents are designed for print, CD-ROM, or a Web site, colors are easily selected and manipulated. You add colors to objects using fills and strokes, and you paint images using an assortment of tools.

Learning the various color modes

Color is a major part of any design, and in the CS2 applications, you can access several different color models, including RGB, Web Safe RGB, CMYK, HSB, and Grayscale. Which color model you use depends on where you intend the artwork to end up. For example, the RGB color mode works well if you intend your design to be viewed on a computer monitor via a CD-ROM. However, if the design is going to be placed on a Web site, you'll want to consider using the Web Safe RGB color mode. For designs that are to be printed, the CMYK color mode is appropriate. The good news is that you can switch among these different color modes at any time using the Color palette menu.

Tip

Holding down the Shift key while clicking on the color bar in the Color palette toggles through the different color modes.

RGB color mode

This color mode is used to display colors on a computer monitor. Inside each computer monitor (or television) are thousands of tiny red, green, and blue phosphorous guns that project beams of red, green, or blue light, one for each pixel. By changing the intensity of each gun, you can control the resulting color of each pixel. The RGB color mode produces colors by mixing together red, green, and blue. The amount of each color determines the final color. Figure 10-40 shows the Color palette with the RGB color mode selected.

Figure 10-40: The Color palette for the RGB color mode includes separate sliders for Red, Green, and Blue values.

Note

The RGB color system is *additive,* meaning that the colors combine to make white. This is different from the *subtractive* color system used by the CMYK color mode, in which the colors are created by mixing inks.

Within Photoshop and Illustrator, you can create colors by specifying the amount of each color to use. The values range from 0, which includes none of that color, to 255, which includes a full amount. A separate value is listed for red, green, and blue. By altering these color values, 16.7 million different colors are possible.

For example, a color that includes a value of 255 for red, 0 for green, and 0 for blue would be pure red. Amounts of 255 of each color produce white, and amounts of 0 of each color produces black. Equal amounts of each of the three colors produces gray. Mixing red and green produces yellow, mixing green and blue produces cyan, and mixing red and blue produces magenta.

Web Safe color mode

The Web Safe color mode is a subset of the RGB color mode that includes a limited palette of colors displayed more consistently without dithering on a browser regardless of the system used to view the design. Figure 10-41 shows the Color palette with the Web Safe color mode selected. Notice how the color values are displayed as hexadecimal numbers.

Common RGB colors

One of the easiest ways to learn how to use the RGB color values is to examine the relationships between the various RGB values and their resulting colors. Consider the following table of colors and RGB values.

Color	R value	G value	B value
Bright red	255	0	0
Medium red	192	0	0
Dark red	128	0	0
Bright green	0	255	0
Bright blue	0	0	255
White	255	255	255
Black	0	0	0
Light gray	192	192	192
Medium gray	128	128	128
Dark gray	64	64	64
Yellow	255	255	0
Cyan	0	255	255
Magenta	255	0	255

Figure 10-41: The Color palette for the Web Safe color mode.

Because of the difference between system color sets on Mac and Windows systems, some Web-page colors viewed on one system look dramatically different from the same Web page viewed on a different system. To fix this problem, a 216-color palette that includes colors that are common between Windows and Mac systems has been defined as a Web Safe palette. Using these colors ensures that the colors are consistent between different systems.

Note Although systems that only display 256 colors are rare with the modern monitors and video cards, but Web-safe colors are important for insuring that specific colors such as logos are consistent across all systems.

HTML code refers to Web colors using the hexadecimal (base-16) numbering system. The results are two-digit numbers instead of three, but the value is still the same. The hexadecimal equivalents to the RGB numbers are displayed in the Color Picker dialog box.

> ## Understanding hexadecimal numbers
>
> Understanding the hexadecimal numbering system isn't that difficult. Our current numbering system is *base 10*, meaning that the numbers range from 0 to 9 before another digit is added. But the hexadecimal numbering system is *base 16*, meaning that the numbers range from 0 to 15 before adding another digit.
>
> The characters used to represent the numbers 10 through 15 in the hexadecimal system are the letters A through F. So, counting in hexadecimal would be 00, 01, 02, 03, 04, 05, 06, 07, 08, 09, 0A, 0B, 0C, 0D, 0E, 0F, followed by 10.
>
> For Web pages, the three hexadecimal values for red, green, and blue are combined into a single number that begins with a number sign such as #FF9910. If you know a few hexadecimal values, you'll be able to approximate color values listed in HTML code. Full color is denoted as FF, no color is 00, half color is 80, so #20FF31 is a green tint and #0C8091 is a darker-cyan color.
>
> The advantage that hexadecimal numbers have for Web pages is that an RGB color is represented by seven digits. If the base-10 numbering system was used, then 10 digits would be needed. Although saving three digits for each color doesn't seem like much, if you multiply that times the total number of pixels included in an image, the result makes a huge difference in the file size.

HSB color mode

The HSB color mode defines colors using the common physical properties of hue, saturation, and brightness. This color mode is useful if you need to change the brightness or a color without changing its hue. Hue is measured as a position on a circular color wheel, which ranges from 0 to 360 degrees. Red is found at 0 (and 360) degrees, yellow at 60 degrees, green at 120 degrees, cyan at 180 degrees, blue at 240 degrees, and magenta at 300 degrees. Figure 10-42 shows the Color palette with the HSB color mode selected.

Figure 10-42: The HSB color mode displays its values as percentages.

Colors found in between are a mixture of the primary colors. For example, orange is represented by 48 degrees between red and yellow. Colors on the opposite side of the color wheel are inverted pairs — red and cyan, yellow and blue, and green and magenta.

The Saturation value determines the purity of the color. This value can range from 0 to 100 percent. Reducing a color Saturation value is analogous to mixing the color with white. Colors with a 0 percent Saturation value are displayed as pure white, regardless of the Hue value.

Brightness is the opposite of saturation. It ranges from 0 to 100 percent and measures the amount of black that is mixed with the color. Reducing the brightness makes the color darker. HSB colors with a Brightness value of 0 are pure black.

Note The Brightness value takes precedence over the Saturation value. An HSB color with a Saturation value of 0 still appears black if its Brightness value is 0.

CMYK color mode

The CMYK color mode is based on cyan, magenta, and yellow inks that are mixed to create colors. The *K* stands for black. This color mode is used for designs that you print. Figure 10-43 shows the Color palette with the CMYK color mode selected.

 Note The letter *B* typically represents the color blue, so *K* represents black. Although you can create black by mixing full equal portions of cyan, magenta, and yellow inks, the actual result from mixing these inks is a muddy brown, so true black is printed using black ink.

Figure 10-43: When the CMYK color mode is selected, the out-of-gamut warning icon appears for all colors that are out of the CMYK gamut.

You specify CMYK colors by providing a percentage between 0 and 100 percent for each color. Digital printers typically print CMYK documents using a four-color process where the sheets are run once for each color.

Grayscale color mode

The Grayscale color mode converts all colors to grayscale values. This color mode is used for black and white images. Grayscale values are represented by a single brightness value that ranges from 0 to 100 percent with 0 percent being white and 100 percent being black. When colors are converted to grayscale, the color's luminosity value determines its grayscale value. Figure 10-44 shows the Color palette with the Grayscale color mode selected.

Figure 10-44: The Grayscale color mode includes a single value for brightness only.

 Note Photoshop actually includes an additional color mode called the Lab color mode. The *L* stands for lightness, the *a* for the green-red color wheel axis, and the *b* for the blue-yellow color wheel axis. This color mode makes it intuitive to work with the luminance of an image.

Using the Color palette

Colors may be applied to an object's fill or stroke using the Fill and Stroke boxes in the Toolbox. Fill and Stroke boxes are also found in the Color palette (Figure 10-45) for convenience, which lets you specify specific colors using color values or select a color by simply clicking on the color bar.

Understanding spot versus process colors

For colors saved to the Swatches palette, you can select the Color Type as a spot color or as a process color. These types correspond to different types of ink that are used to print the colors. Spot colors are printed using premixed inks, and process colors are mixed on the spot using CMYK values.

Spot colors require a separate printing plate for each spot color that is used in a document, but process colors can represent a wide range of colors using only four printing plates. So a document that has only one or two spot colors may be less expensive than a document with all process colors. Another advantage of spot colors is that they're used to print colors that are out-of-gamut for the CMYK color method.

Spot colors are identified in the Swatches palette by a small black dot that appears in the lower-right corner of the swatch. You can switch between spot and process colors in the Color palette by clicking on the spot or process color icons.

Note To see the Fill and Stroke boxes and the color values for the selected color mode in the Color palette, select the Show Options palette menu command.

When the mouse is moved over the top of the color bar, the cursor changes to an eyedropper. Clicking on the color bar changes the color for either the Fill or Stroke box, whichever is active.

Tip If you drag one of the color value sliders with the Shift key held down, all color values scale along with the selected color. This works for all color modes except for the HSV and Grayscale.

Beneath the Fill and Stroke boxes in the Color palette are two icons that randomly appear as you drag about the color bar. The top icon is the Web Safe color warning. This icon looks like a simple cube and informs you that the current color is not a Web Safe color. The color swatch next to the icon displays the nearest Web Safe color and clicking on it changes the current color to the nearest Web Safe color.

Beneath the Web Safe color icon, another icon may appear that looks like a yellow triangle with an exclamation point inside it. This icon appears when the current color is out-of-gamut and is not available in the CMYK color mode. The color swatch next to it is the nearest color available in the CMYK color mode, which means it may be printed.

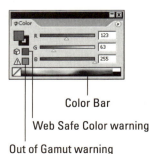

Figure 10-45: The Web Safe color warning icon and the Out-of-Gamut color warning icon both appear within the Color palette.

Color Bar
Web Safe Color warning
Out of Gamut warning

Understanding gamut

Color models are based on theoretical values, but in real life all the colors that are defined mathematically aren't always possible. The actual range of colors possible for a certain color space or device is called its *gamut*. Any color that falls outside of its gamut is called *out-of-gamut* and may cause a problem for the device.

The Color palette menu in Illustrator also includes two commands (Inverse and Complementary) for quickly locating the inverse or complementary color to the current color. An *inverse color* is opposite the current color in the color wheel for the current color model; a *complementary color* offers a decent amount of contrast to the original color.

Using the Color Picker

If you double-click on the Fill box in the Toolbox, a Color Picker, shown in Figure 10-46, appears. Using the Color Picker, you may select any color by manipulating the color values or by selecting a color from the color spectrum.

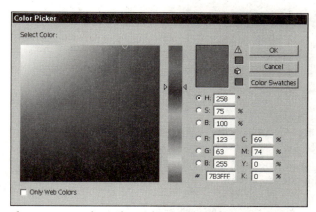

Figure 10-46: The Color Picker lets you select color, and it shows the color values.

The color values for several color modes are displayed in the Color Picker. These values are linked to one another, so a change in one value impacts the other values. Toward the top of the Color Picker dialog box, the Web Safe and Out-of-Gamut icons randomly appear just like the Color palette along with color swatches that you can click to reset the color. The Only Web Colors option in the lower-left corner limits the colors in the color spectrum so only Web-safe colors are displayed. Figure 10-47 shows the Color Picker with this option enabled.

The Color Swatches button (called Color Libraries in Photoshop) opens a dialog box of distinct named colors that coordinate to the color swatches available in the Swatches palette. In Photoshop, you can choose from a specific color book at the top of the dialog box. These color books include several Pantone specific color libraries like the one shown in Figure 10-48.

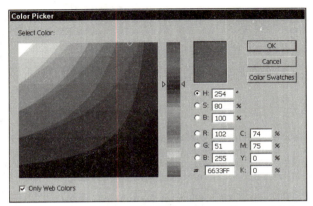

Figure 10-47: With the Only Web Colors option enabled, the total number of colors is severely limited.

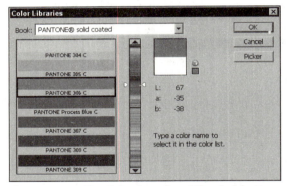

Figure 10-48: The Color Swatches (Libraries) button in the Color Picker opens a specific list of color swatches or libraries.

Using the Eyedropper tool

In addition to using the Color Picker, you can select colors from within the image using the Eyedropper tool. The Eyedropper tool works differently in Photoshop and Illustrator. The tool in Photoshop and GoLive is used to get only color. But in Illustrator and InDesign, the Eyedropper tool can retrieve appearance attributes, character style, and paragraph style.

Using Photoshop's Eyedropper tool

Dragging over an image with the Eyedropper tool changes the Foreground color. In the Options bar, you can use the color of the point directly under the tool or to sample a 3-x-3 or a 5-x-5 grid around the cursor. Holding down the Option/Alt key while dragging in the image with the Eyedropper tool changes the Background color.

> **Tip**
> The Eyedropper tool may be temporarily selected while using one of the painting tools by holding down the Option/Alt key.

The Color Sampler tool is available as a fly-out under the Eyedropper tool. Using this tool, you can click on four different points in the image and the color values for those points are displayed in the Info palette. Only four color sample points may be placed in an image, but you can drag these points to new locations as needed or clear them all using the Clear button in the Options bar.

Using Illustrator's Eyedropper tool

You can use Illustrator's Eyedropper tool to gather property values from one object and apply them to another object. The specific properties that are gathered by the Eyedropper tool is set using the Eyedropper Options dialog box, shown in Figure 10-49, which is opened by double-clicking on the Eyedropper tool.

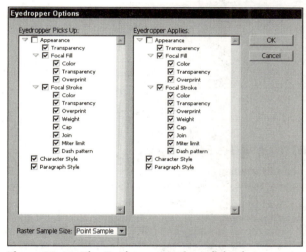

Figure 10-49: The Eyedropper Options dialog box

The attributes that are picked up by the Eyedropper tool are immediately applied to the selected object. These attributes may include Appearance attributes such as Transparency, Fill Color, Stroke Color, Stroke Weight, Cap and Join Type, and even Character and Paragraph Style. If you hold down the Shift key, then only the color attribute is gathered. You can also gather color from the computer's desktop using the Eyedropper tool by clicking and holding in the Illustrator document window and then dragging around the desktop.

The Eyedropper Options dialog box also lets you sample raster images using a point sample, a 3-x-3-pixel sample or a 5-x-5-pixel sample.

Using InDesign's Eyedropper tool

The Eyedropper tool in InDesign works the same as the one in Illustrator. It is used to both gather and apply selected attributes. Double-clicking on the Eyedropper tool opens a dialog box of options, shown in Figure 10-50, that may be gathered using the Eyedropper tool.

Clicking on an object gathers all the attributes for that object, and the cursor changes so the eyedropper is pointing in the opposite direction and appears to be filled. Clicking on another object applies the attributes. You can click on multiple objects while the Eyedropper is filled. To fill the Eyedropper with new attributes, hold down the Option/Alt key while clicking on another object.

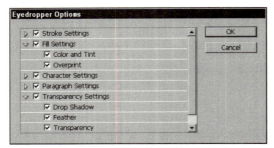

Figure 10-50: The Eyedropper Options dialog box in InDesign

Managing color profiles and settings

Adobe understands all the issues surrounding color and has endowed the CS2 applications with color-management methods including a Color Settings dialog box accessed under the Edit menu.

This dialog box, shown for Photoshop in Figure 10-51, lets you select from several different color setting profiles. Using the same profile, settings and color management policies for all applications produces consistent color output regardless of the application or system. Some of these color setting profiles include North America General Purpose Defaults, U.S. Prepress Defaults, Web Graphics Defaults, as well as profiles for Europe and Japan.

The Color Settings dialog box also lets you define a custom color setting. Custom setting may be saved and loaded for use across applications.

Cross-Reference

The Color Management features found in the various CS2 applications are covered in Chapter 6.

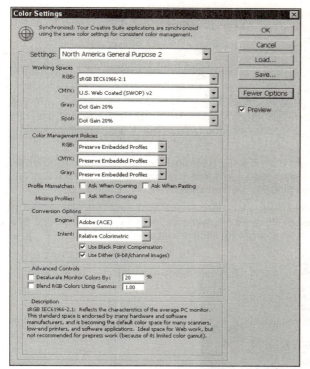

Figure 10-51: The Color Settings dialog box lets you select a default color profile.

Working with Gradients

When a light source shines on an object, the point closest to the light is usually the brightest and the light intensity gradually decreases the further you get away from the light. This decrease in light intensity over distance is called *attenuation,* and it's common for most light sources (the Sun being an exception to this principle).

Simple light attenuation may be simulated in Illustrator, InDesign, and Photoshop using gradients. Gradients let you specify two or more colors, and the gradient interpolates between these two colors by gradually changing between the specified colors.

Using the Gradient palette

In addition to color, gradients may be applied as an object fill by clicking on the Gradient button in the Toolbox or by clicking on the gradient in the Gradient palette. The Gradient palette, shown in Figure 10-52, includes controls for specifying gradient colors and behavior.

Figure 10-52: The Gradient palette lets you create custom gradients.

You can expand the Gradient palette in Illustrator and InDesign to show some additional controls including a Type drop-down list, which includes two gradient Types including Linear and Radial. Photoshop goes even further offering Linear, Radial, Angle, Reflected, and Diamond gradient options.

Linear gradients run in a straight line from the color specified at one end of the gradient to the color specified at the other end. For Linear gradients, you can specify an Angle value, which determines the direction that the gradient runs.

Radial gradients place the gradient color specified at one end of the Gradient palette at a specified point and the changing colors are displayed as concentric circles around this designated point. Figure 10-53 shows an example of a linear and a radial gradient.

Linear gradient

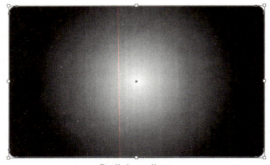

Radial gradient

Figure 10-53: Linear and radial gradients are uniquely different from each other.

The color bar at the bottom of the Gradient palette lets you specify gradient colors and the midpoints between those colors. The color stop icons appear below the gradient bar; the midpoint markers appear as diamond icons above the gradient bar. To change the position of either of these icons, drag them to the left or right. The position of the icon is displayed in the Location field as a percentage of the entire gradient.

To change the color of a color stop, select the color stop and choose a new color from the Color palette. When a color stop is selected, the small arrow above it turns black.

 You can select a color swatch to use in the gradient color stop by holding down the Option/Alt key while clicking on a color swatch, or you can drag swatch colors to the gradient color stops. But if you select a gradient color stop and click on a color swatch, the color in the swatch is selected and the gradient goes away.

To add new color stops to a gradient, click below the gradient bar where you want to position the new color stop, drag a color swatch from the Swatches palette to the gradient bar, or hold down the Option/Alt key and drag an existing color stop to the side. A new midpoint icon is added for each new color stop that is added.

Using the Gradient tool

Although the Angle may be specified for Linear gradients in the Gradient palette, the Gradient tool (found in the Toolbox) is useful for interactively specifying the gradient angle. With the gradient tool selected, click on a selected object where you want to position the leftmost gradient color and drag to where you want to place the rightmost gradient color. This lets you control precisely how the gradient runs across an object.

If the line that is dragged with the gradient tool lies at an angle, the Angle value is set accordingly. Holding down the Shift key while dragging constrains the angle to 45-degree increments.

The Gradient tool may also be used to cause a single gradient to span multiple objects. To do this, select all the objects and apply a gradient fill to them, then drag with the Gradient tool across the selected objects.

STEPS: Creating and Applying a Custom Gradient

1. **Open an Illustrator document.** With Illustrator open, choose File ➪ New to create a new document. Select the Star tool and drag in the art board to create a star object.

2. **Apply a radial gradient.** With the star selected, click on the Gradient button at the bottom of the Toolbox. Then in the Gradient palette, select the Radial type. The star is filled with a radial gradient, as shown in Figure 10-54.

3. **Change the gradient colors.** With the Swatches palette and the Gradient palette opened at the same time, drag a bright yellow color swatch from the Swatches palette to the first color stop at the left end of the gradient bar in the Gradient palette. Then drag a red color swatch from the Swatches palette to the last color stop at the right end of the gradient bar in the Gradient palette. The colors are immediately applied to the star, as shown in Figure 10-55.

Figure 10-54: Selecting the Radial type applies a radial gradient to the object using its center as an endpoint for the gradient.

Figure 10-55: Dragging colors from the Swatches palette to the gradient bar color stops changes the colors applied to the gradient.

Chapter 10 ✦ Creating, Selecting, and Editing Objects

4. **Add a new gradient color stop.** Click under the middle of the gradient bar to create a new color stop. This new color stop uses the intermediate color from the gradient bar. Drag a black color swatch from the Swatches palette to the new color stop in the Gradient palette. The new color stop changes the color applied to the star dramatically, as shown in Figure 10-56.

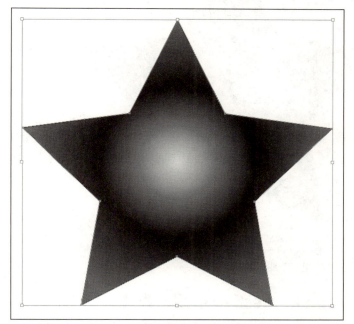

Figure 10-56: Clicking under the gradient bar adds a new color stop to the gradient bar.

5. **Reduce the black color stop spread.** To reduce the spreading color of the black color stop, select the midpoint icons above the gradient bar on either side of the black color stop and drag them toward the black color stop. This limits the spread of the black color within the gradient, as shown in Figure 10-57.

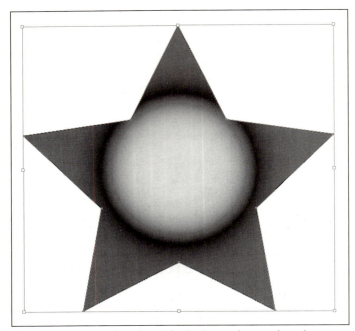

Figure 10-57: Dragging the midpoint icons changes how far a gradient color stop can spread its color.

Creating gradient meshes in Illustrator

You can change vector objects within Illustrator to mesh objects using the Mesh tool or the Object ⇨ Create Gradient Mesh menu command. Mesh objects are divided into rows and columns with editable points located at each intersection. A gradient color stop may also be positioned at each intersecting point. Choosing Object ⇨ Create Gradient Mesh opens a dialog box, shown in Figure 10-58, where you can specify the number of rows and columns to divide the object into.

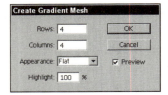

Figure 10-58: The Create Gradient Mesh dialog box

The Appearance drop-down list includes Flat, To Center, and To Edge options. The Flat option colors the entire object with a single fill color. The To Center option adds a white highlight at the center of the object that gradually changes to the fill color at the edges. The To Edge places a white highlight at the object's edges that gradually changes to the object's fill color at its center. The Highlight percentage sets how white the highlight color is.

Caution Mesh objects in Illustrator take up a lot of system resources and can greatly slow down your system if they're overly complex. It's best to keep mesh objects simple if you experience performance problems.

Figure 10-59 shows three simple rectangles that have been converted to meshes by choosing Object ➪ Create Gradient Mesh. The top mesh object uses the Flat appearance option, the middle one uses the To Center appearance option, and the bottom one uses the To Edges appearance option.

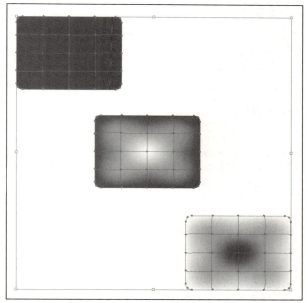

Figure 10-59: The Gradient Mesh feature creates some interesting objects.

The Mesh tool is used to place the intersecting mesh points within an object. After clicking to place an intersecting point on an object, you can choose a color from the Color palette to apply as a gradient color for the new intersecting point. Clicking again on the object with the Mesh tool creates another new intersecting mesh point. Holding down the Shift key while clicking on an object creates an intersecting mesh point without changing its fill color.

Objects that have a gradient fill applied to them may be expanded to a gradient mesh object with the Object ➪ Expand menu command. This opens a dialog box where you can select to expand the gradient to a Gradient Mesh object. Mesh object points may be selected and moved using the Direct Selection tool. You can change mesh point colors by dragging a color to a mesh point or apply a color using the Eyedropper tool.

Working with Patterns

In addition to colors and gradients, Photoshop and Illustrator can use patterns to fill objects or paint onto images. Patterns are used differently in both these applications.

Using patterns in Illustrator

Patterns may be selected from the Swatches palette and applied as an object fill. Any artwork may be used as a new pattern by simply dragging the artwork to the Swatches palette or by selecting the artwork and choosing Edit ⇨ Define Pattern. This opens a dialog box, shown in Figure 10-60, where you can name the pattern.

Figure 10-60: Choosing Edit ⇨ Define Pattern creates a new swatch.

To add some spacing behind the pattern, drag a rectangle with its fill and stroke colors set to None, arrange this object as the backmost object, and include it as part of the pattern.

If the pattern fills an object that is larger than the pattern, then the pattern is tiled to fill the entire shape.

STEPS: Creating a Custom Pattern in Illustrator

1. **Open an Illustrator document.** With Illustrator open, choose File ⇨ New to create a new document.
2. **Create a background area.** Select the Rectangle tool and drag in the art board to create a rectangle object that is the size of the pattern that you want to create. With the background object selected, set its Fill and Stroke to None.
3. **Add shapes to the pattern area.** Select the Ellipse tool and drag several small circles within the background square with the Shift key held down to make them perfect circles. Set each circle to have a different fill color, as shown in Figure 10-61.

Figure 10-61: Patterns may be created using the Illustrator tools.

4. **Resize the background square.** After creating all the pattern objects, select the background square object and resize it to fit all the objects within it.

5. **Define the pattern.** Drag over all the objects including the background square and all the colored circles, and choose Edit ➪ Define Pattern. In the New Swatch dialog box, name the new swatch and click OK. The new pattern is added to the Swatches palette.

6. **Test the pattern.** Select the Rectangle tool and drag in the art board to create a rectangle that is larger than the pattern. Then click on the pattern swatch in the Swatches palette and the new pattern is applied to the rectangle, as shown in Figure 10-62.

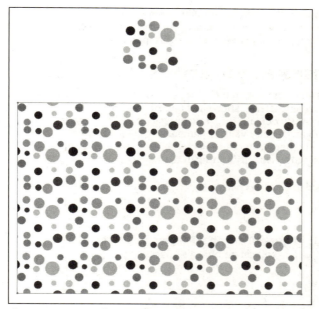

Figure 10-62: Apply new patterns to an object to see how the pattern tiles.

Using patterns in Photoshop

Patterns show up on the Options bar when the Paint Bucket, Pattern Stamp, Healing Brush, and Patch tools are selected. By clicking on the Pattern pop-up, you can access several default patterns, shown in Figure 10-63. The pop-up palette also includes a palette menu that you can use to create new patterns, load and save pattern sets, and access different pattern sets.

New patterns are created by selecting a portion of an image with the Rectangular Marquee tool and choosing Edit ➪ Define Pattern. This opens a dialog box where you can name the pattern. To apply a pattern to a selected area use the Edit ➪ Fill menu command and select the Pattern option in the Fill dialog box or use the Pattern Overlay layer style.

Patterns may also be created in Photoshop by choosing Filter ➪ Pattern Maker. This opens a window where you can select and preview patterns. This window and the other filters are covered in Chapter 13.

Figure 10-63: The Pattern pop-up palette displays the current library of loaded patterns.

Using Transparency

Another common property that may be applied to objects is transparency. When an object has some transparency applied to it, all objects underneath it are visible. For example, placing transparent text on top of an image lets the overlapped image show through the text.

Applying transparency to objects and images

Transparency is applied to the selected object in Illustrator and InDesign using the Opacity setting in the Transparency palette, shown in Figure 10-64. Open this palette by choosing Window ⇨ Transparency. By default, the Transparency palette includes only a drop-down list of blending modes and an Opacity value. Changing the Opacity value changes the transparency of the selected object using the selected blending mode. Transparency in Photoshop is applied to layers using the Opacity setting in the Layers palette.

Cross-Reference

Layers are covered in detail in Chapter 14.

Figure 10-64: The Transparency palette lets you set an object's opacity.

Changing the Opacity value in the Transparency palette applies transparency to the selected object's fill and stroke. This value is then listed at the bottom of the Appearance palette, but you can apply different transparency values to the fill and stroke by selecting each in the Appearance palette prior to changing the Opacity value in the Transparency palette. The Opacity value for the fill or stroke is listed under each in the Appearance palette.

Selecting the Show Thumbnails palette menu command expands the palette to reveal a thumbnail of the selected object. The Show Options palette menu command reveals some additional options at the bottom of the palette.

Using blending modes

When you apply transparency to an object, the colors of the object positioned underneath the object blend together. Choosing a blending mode defines how the blend color and the base color are blended together. The *blend color* is the color of the overlaid object; the *base color* is the color of the underlying object.

The blending modes alter the color of the selected object by:

- **Normal:** Using the blend color.
- **Darken:** Using either the base or blend color depending on which is darker. This is the opposite of the Lighten mode.
- **Multiply:** Multiplying the base and blend colors resulting in a darker color. Any color multiplied by white doesn't change the color and multiplying any color with black produces black. This is the opposite of the Screen mode.
- **Color Burn:** Darkening the base color. This is the opposite of the Color Dodge mode.
- **Lighten:** Using either the base or blend color depending on which is lighter. This is the opposite of the Darken mode.
- **Screen:** Multiplying the inverse of both the base and blend colors resulting in a lighter color. Any color screened with black doesn't change the color, and screening any color with white produces white. This is the opposite of the Multiply mode.
- **Color Dodge:** Lightening the base color. This is the opposite of the Color Burn mode.
- **Overlay:** Mixing the base color with the blend color to lighten the highlights and darken the shadows.
- **Soft Light:** Lightening the light areas of the blend color and darkening the dark areas.
- **Hard Light:** Screening the light areas of the blend color and multiplying the dark areas of the base color.
- **Difference:** Subtracting the lighter of the base or blend colors from the other.
- **Exclusion:** Removing all the light value of the base or blend colors from the other.
- **Hue:** Colors the object using the luminance and saturation values of the base color and the hue of the blend color.
- **Saturation:** Colors the object using the luminance and hue values of the base color and the saturation of the blend color.
- **Color:** Using the luminance of the base color and the hue and saturation of the blend color. This is the opposite of the Luminosity mode.
- **Luminosity:** Using the hue and saturation values of the base color and the luminance of the blend color. This is the opposite of the Color mode.

Note: Photoshop includes several additional blend modes not listed here.

Figure 10-65 shows examples of all the blending modes.

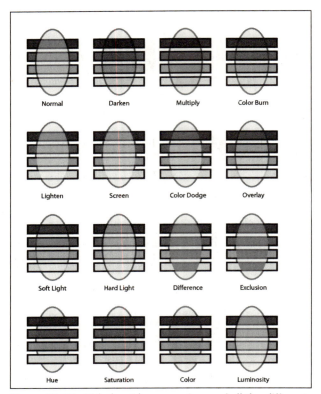

Figure 10-65: Side-by-side comparisons of all the different blending modes are helpful in understanding how they work.

Creating an opacity mask

An *opacity mask* is used to define how much transparency is applied to the objects on the linked layer. The white areas on the opacity mask have no transparency applied, but black areas are fully transparent. Gray areas are partially transparent.

To make an opacity mask, select two objects and choose the Make Opacity Mask palette menu command. The top object is used as the opacity mask, and the bottom objects are objects that are affected by the opacity mask.

In the thumbnail section of the Transparency palette, the objects that are affected by the opacity mask are displayed to the left, and the opacity mask is displayed to the right. The Clip option causes the opacity mask to act also as a clipping mask and the Invert Mask option inverts the opacity mask, making the transparent areas opaque and vice versa. Figure 10-66 shows an example of an opacity mask. The snapshots in the Transparency palette show the objects used to determine the transparency of the objects below.

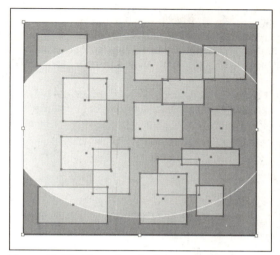

Figure 10-66: The colors in the opacity mask determine which objects are visible below.

STEPS: Creating an Opacity Mask

1. **Open an Illustrator document.** With Illustrator open, choose File ➪ New to create a new document.

2. **Create an object to mask.** Drag a symbol object on the art board from the Symbols palette and resize it to fit the art board. The resized object is shown in Figure 10-67.

Figure 10-67: This symbol is fully opaque with no transparency applied.

3. **Draw a mask object.** Select the Rectangle tool and drag it over the top of the symbol. With the fill box selected, choose the Gradient button in the Toolbox to apply a linear gradient to the rectangle. Make sure the rectangle is positioned above the symbol.

4. **Select all objects and create an opacity mask.** Drag over both objects with the Selection tool to select them. Open the Transparency palette and choose the Make Opacity Mask palette menu command. The symbol object and the gradient rectangle both show up as thumbnails in the Transparency palette; the black portions of the gradient mark where the underlying symbol is transparent, as shown in Figure 10-68.

Figure 10-68: Using the opacity mask, the butterfly gradually changes from transparent to opaque.

Using Symbols, Graphic Styles, and Swatches

All the CS2 applications make use of libraries. Open your favorite Creative Suite application, and you'll find libraries of symbols, styles, swatches, and brushes. Libraries are used to store any feature that has a lot of settings, allowing you to recall the settings at an instant without having to enter all the settings again. Across the various CS2 applications, creating and using library items are consistent whether you're dealing with brushes, styles, symbols, or swatches.

Many of the CS2 applications include many default libraries that you can open and use. For example, Illustrator's Window menu includes submenus of brushes, styles, swatches, and symbol libraries, and Photoshop includes default libraries of swatches, styles, and brushes that may be selected from the various palette menus.

Working with symbols in Illustrator

Symbols in Illustrator are a special type of object with a key advantage — reuse. If you add a symbol to a document and then reuse elsewhere in the same document, a new copy isn't required, because the symbol references the first object. This makes symbols very convenient to work with because adding hundreds of symbols to a single document doesn't dramatically increase the overall file size.

Cross-Reference

Reference symbols are particularly useful for files viewed on the Web, such as SWF and SVG files. These file types are discussed in Chapter 35.

Accessing symbol libraries

Symbols are stored in libraries, and Illustrator includes several default symbol libraries that you may access by choosing Window ⇨ Symbol Libraries or the Open Symbol Library palette menu command off the Symbols palette. Symbol libraries appear in their own custom palette when opened. Selecting the Persistent palette menu option causes the palette to open automatically when Illustrator starts.

In addition to the symbol libraries, the Symbols palette, shown in Figure 10-69, includes several default symbols. All symbols that are included in the current document are displayed in the Symbols palette. These symbols are associated with the current document and are saved as part of the document.

Tip   To remove all symbols that aren't used in the current document from the Symbols palette, choose the Select All Unused palette menu command and then choose the Delete Symbol palette menu command.

Figure 10-69: The Symbol palette holds symbol instances used in the document.

You add symbols to the Symbols palette by using the Add to Symbols palette menu command or by dragging the symbol to the Symbols palette. Also, any symbols selected from a symbol library are automatically added to the Symbols palette. You delete symbols in the Symbols palette with the Delete Symbol palette menu command or the trashcan icon at the bottom of the palette. You can save all symbols in the Symbols palette to create a new symbol library using the Save Symbol Library palette menu command.

Inserting, editing, and creating symbols

From a symbol library or the Symbols palette, you can add a symbol to the current document by dragging it from the library to the art board or by selecting the symbol and choosing the Place Symbol Instance palette menu command. Any symbols that are duplicated using the Option/Alt drag or the copy and paste methods are still symbol instances.

You can edit symbol instances by using the transform tools or by changing its color and style while still maintaining its symbol status. If more drastic editing is required, you can unlink a symbol using the Break Link to Symbol palette menu command. This command causes the symbol to be expanded.

You may add Illustrator artwork to the Symbols palette as a new symbol by simply dragging the selected object or group to the Symbols palette. You can also create a new symbol by selecting the artwork and choosing the New Symbol palette menu command or by clicking on the New Symbol icon at the bottom of the Symbols palette. Symbols may include vector, raster and type objects. To rename the new symbol, double-click on it in the Symbols palette. A Symbols Options dialog box appears, shown in Figure 10-70; here, you can type a new name for the symbol.

Figure 10-70: The Symbol Options dialog box lets you rename symbols.

Using the Symbolism tools

You may use Illustrator's Symbolism tools to create a large number of symbols very quickly. The various tools let you alter specific object properties such as size, rotation, color, and style while creating a set of symbols.

The Symbolism tools include the following:

- **Symbol Sprayer:** Creates a set of symbols by dragging in the art board.
- **Symbol Shifter:** Moves symbols within a set relative to one another and to adjust the stacking order.
- **Symbol Scruncher:** Changes the density of symbols within a set by pushing them closer together or pushing them farther apart.
- **Symbol Sizer:** Increases or decreases the size of symbols within a set.
- **Symbol Spinner:** Rotates the symbols within a set.
- **Symbol Stainer:** Changes the colors of symbols within a set by adjusting their hue.
- **Symbol Screener:** Adjusts the transparency of symbols within a set.
- **Symbol Styler:** Applies a selected graphic style to symbols within a set.

With any of these tools selected, you can double-click on the tools to open the Symbolism Tools Options dialog box, shown in Figure 10-71. Using this dialog box, you can set the diameter, intensity, and symbol set density. The Options dialog box also shows any shortcut keys available for the various tools, such as holding down the Option/Alt key to reduce the size, coloring, transparency, and style that is applied.

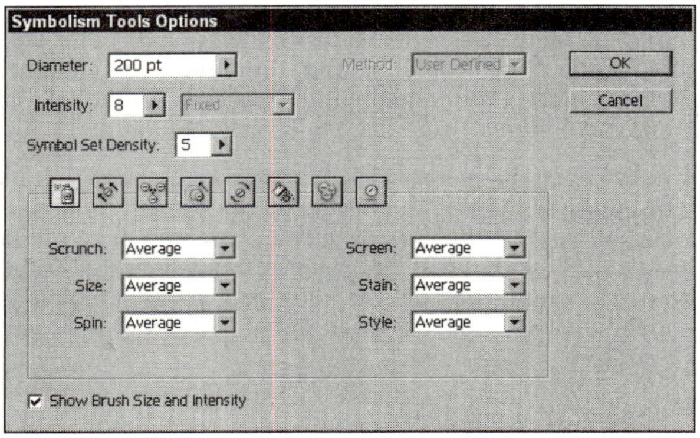

Figure 10-71: The Symbolism Tools Options dialog box

Figure 10-72 shows a simple example of the Symbol Sprayer tool created by selecting the fire symbol (the fire symbol is found in the Nature library) and dragging with the Symbol Sprayer over a path. After this set of symbols is created, you can use the other Symbolism tools to change the position, size, rotation, color, transparency, and style of the symbols in the set.

Figure 10-72: The Symbol Sprayer draws a path of symbol objects.

Working with object styles in InDesign

The concept of graphic styles apply equally well in InDesign. InDesign already has features for handling paragraph and character styles, but it can also handle graphical styles. Object styles are kept in the Object Styles palette, shown in Figure 10-73.

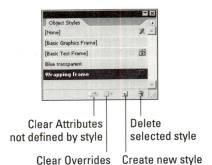

Figure 10-73: The Object Styles palette hold graphical attributes for InDesign objects.

You can add new object styles by selecting an object and choosing the New Object Style palette menu command or by clicking the Create New Style button at the bottom of the palette. This opens the Object Style Options dialog box, shown in Figure 10-74. Using this dialog box, you can select and alter any of the object attributes that are associated with the object including Fill, Stroke, transparency, corner effects, drop shadows, text wrap, and so on.

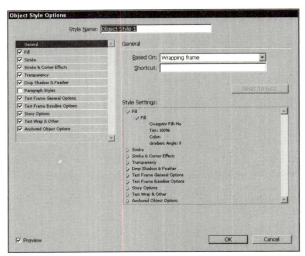

Figure 10-74: The Object Style Options dialog box includes settings for defining the object style.

Defined object styles can be applied to an object by dragging the style from the Object Styles palette and dropping it on the object, or an even easier method is to select objects and click the style name in the Object Styles palette.

Working with graphic styles in Illustrator and Photoshop

If you've tinkered with the appearance attributes applied to an object until it is perfect, you can save all these settings so they may be easily reapplied to other objects using styles. A *graphic style* is a collection of appearance settings stored within a library for easy recall. The Graphic Styles palette, shown in Figure 10-75, holds a library of default styles. These styles are applied to objects by simply dragging the style icon from the Graphic Styles palette and dropping it on an object.

Break Link to Graphic Style | Delete Graphic Style

Create Graphic Style

Figure 10-75: The Graphic Styles palette includes appearance attributes.

Illustrator includes, by default, several additional libraries of styles that you can access by choosing Window ➪ Graphic Style Libraries or by selecting the Open Graphic Style Library palette menu command in the Graphic Style palette. You may save the styles contained within the Graphic Styles palette as a new library using the Save Graphic Style Library palette menu command.

Photoshop also includes several default style libraries that are accessed from the Styles palette menu. To apply a style to the current canvas, simply click on the style in the Styles palette or drag it to the canvas. Opening a style library presents a dialog box where you can select to replace the current styles in the Styles palette with the new library or append them to the end of the palette.

Creating new styles

You add new styles to the Graphic Styles palette by selecting an object with a style that you want to add to the palette and choosing the New Graphic Style palette menu command or by clicking on the small New Graphic Style button at the bottom of the palette.

You can add custom styles to the Graphic Styles palette by dragging the Appearance icon at the top-left of the Appearance palette for the selected object to the Graphic Styles palette. Double-clicking on the style icon opens a dialog box where you can rename the style.

Working with swatches

If you've mixed and selected specific colors that you want to keep, you could write down the values for that color or you could add the color to the Swatches palette. Colors in the Swatches may be selected and applied to the Fill and Stroke boxes.

Note: Swatches palettes are found in all the various CS2 applications. Swatches in Photoshop and GoLive are mainly used to hold colors, but Illustrator and InDesign uses the Swatches palette to hold colors, gradients, and styles.

Using the Swatches palette

To add the current Fill or Stroke color to the Swatches palette, shown in Figure 10-76, simply drag the color from the Fill or Stroke box in the Toolbar to the Swatches palette or select the New Swatch palette menu command. If the New Swatch menu command is used, the New Swatch dialog box opens; here, you can name the new color swatch, specify the color type, and choose the color mode. The New Swatch dialog box also includes the values to specify a color depending on the selected color mode.

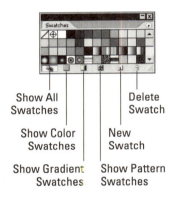

Figure 10-76: The Swatches palette holds colors, but in Illustrator it may also hold gradients and patterns.

Creating Custom Swatch libraries

Several default Swatch libraries are available by choosing Window ⇨ Swatch Libraries; new swatch libraries may be created and saved. To create a new swatch library, choose the Save Swatch Library palette menu command. This opens a file dialog box where you can name the swatch library file. Swatch libraries use the AI file format just like standard Illustrator documents.

Note: Although the discussion of palettes in this section focuses on colors, you can also add and store gradients and patterns within swatch libraries. You use the buttons at the bottom of the Swatches palette to show only a single category of swatches.

You can also drag colors from the various swatch library palettes and dropped on the Swatches palette. Colors in the Swatches palette may be saved as a new swatch library using the Save Swatch Library palette menu command.

Sharing swatches between CS2 applications

If you've spent some time establishing a set of color swatches for your design, you'll be happy to know that you can save color palettes in a format that you can open in the other CS2 applications. This unique format is the ASE format and you can select to save the current swatch palette in this format using the Save Swatches for Exchange palette menu command. You can find the Save Swatches for Exchange menu command in the Swatch palette in Photoshop, Illustrator, InDesign, and GoLive.

Cross-Reference Swatch palette exchange files can be easily shared between the various CS2 apps using Adobe Bridge. You can learn more about Adobe Bridge in Chapter 7.

Using the Library palette

To keep content organized, InDesign allows you to create libraries of content. To create a new library, which appears as a palette, simply select the File ➪ New ➪ Library menu command. This causes an empty library palette to appear. You can add items, including text frames and graphics, to the palette by dragging and dropping them on the empty palette, or you can add the selected item with the Create Library Item palette menu command. Figure 10-77 shows a new Library palette with several items added to it.

Note You can also find the Library palette in GoLive. The GoLive Library palette is divided into sections that hold Snippets, Components, Smart Objects, Stationery, Templates, and Documents.

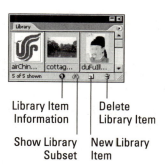

Figure 10-77: The Library palette can hold graphics, graphic frames, guides, and text frames that you can reuse as needed.

You can re-open saved library palettes using the File ➪ Open menu command. Library palettes are saved using the INDL file extension. You can place library items on the page by dragging them from the Library palette and dropping them on the current page or by using the Place Item palette menu command. If any item is selected in the Library palette, you can select the Item Information palette menu command to access a dialog box, shown in Figure 10-78, which includes information about the item and a field for entering a description.

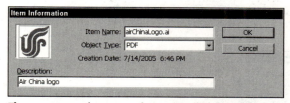

Figure 10-78: The Item Information dialog box includes information about the selected item and lets you enter a description.

The Show Subset palette menu command opens a dialog box, shown in Figure 10-79, which allows you to search for specific items using keywords. The palette menu also includes options to sort items by Name, Oldest, Newest, and Type.

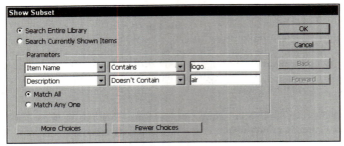

Figure 10-79: The Show Subset dialog box lets you search for specific items in the Library palette.

Exporting snippets

Snippets are XML-based content from InDesign that is saved as a separate file. You save snippets into a library or open them into another document. To export the selected items, simply select the item to export and then choose the File ⇨ Export menu command. In the file dialog box that appears, select the InDesign Snippet as the Save as Type. You can also create snippets by dragging items into the Bridge window to the system desktop. The file with the INDS file extension can then be loaded within other InDesign documents.

To place a snippet, use the File ⇨ Place menu command or drag it from the desktop directly into the document.

 Snippets are a new feature in InDesign CS2 and provide an easy way to reuse various elements.

Using Photoshop's Preset Manager

Photoshop includes a clever way to manage all the various presets and libraries using a special dialog box called the Preset Manager, shown in Figure 10-80. This dialog box may be opened from most of the palette menus that include presets or libraries or by choosing Edit ⇨ Preset Manager.

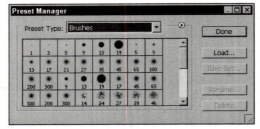

Figure 10-80: The Preset Manager dialog box in Photoshop

At the top of the dialog box is a drop-down list of the various preset types, including brushes, swatches, gradients, styles, patterns, contours, custom shapes, and tools. When a preset type is selected, its library of items is displayed. Using the palette menu, you can change how the items are displayed or choose one of the default libraries to open. The dialog box also includes buttons to load, save, rename, and delete the current sets.

Editing Objects

After you create objects, you have several ways to edit them. An object's position and orientation may be altered using the transformation tools, its properties may be changed using the various palettes such as Illustrator's Appearance palette, and filters and effects may be applied to change the object in many different ways.

Transformations are covered in Chapter 12. Applying filters and effects is covered in Chapter 13.

In addition to these editing methods, there are several other ways to edit objects including joining, slicing, and cutting paths; blending objects; distorting objects; and using the Pathfinder features.

Editing paths in Illustrator

Paths are created by dragging with tools such as the Pen, Paintbrush, Pencil, and Line Segment tools, but there are also several tools that you may use to edit paths.

Using the Smooth and Erase tools

Drawing freehand paths with the Pencil tool often results in jagged lines, but these lines are easily smoothed over with the Smooth tool. The Smooth tool is a fly-out under the Pencil tool. Dragging over a freehand line with the Smooth tool gradually removes all the sharp changes in the line and smoothes it. Double-clicking on the Smooth tool opens a dialog box where you can set the Fidelity and Smoothness values for the tool. The Erase tool, a fly-out under the Pencil tool, may be used to delete a portion of the selected path. By dragging over the selected path with the Erase tool, the section that is dragged over is deleted.

Figure 10-81 shows a rough line drawn with the Pencil tool. The second line has been smoothed with the Smooth tool, and the portions of the last line were erased using the Erase tool.

You can select the Smooth tool by holding down the Option/Alt key when the Paintbrush or Pencil tool is selected.

Figure 10-81: You use the Smooth and Erase tools to edit existing paths.

Using the Reshape tool

The Reshape tool (located as a fly-out under the Scale tool) lets you select an anchor point, several anchor points, or a line segment as part of a path and drag it while maintaining the overall shape of the path. This causes the entire path to move along with the selected portion. By comparison, anchor points and line segments selected with the Direct Selection tool are moved independent of the entire path; the Scale tool moves all points equally in the scaled direction.

To select anchor points or line segments with the Reshape tool, simply click or drag over the portions of the path that you want to select. The relative distance between the selected points won't change as you drag the path; adjacent anchor points move in proportion to the distance from the selected points.

Figure 10-82 shows three duplicate paths. The left line was drawn with the Pencil tool. The middle path is a duplicate that was scaled horizontally, and the right path is a duplicate that was modified using the Reshape tool. Notice how the scaled path is distorted, while the reshaped path maintains its path details.

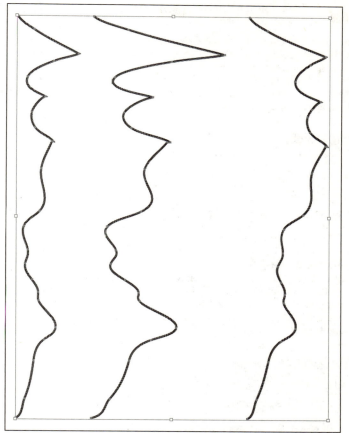

Figure 10-82: The Reshape tool can bend a path while maintaining its details.

Other methods to editing paths

The following is a list of other ways to edit paths:

- **Splitting paths:** You can use the Scissors tool to cut a path in two. You don't need to select the path to split it. The location where you click with the Scissors tool determines where the path is split.

- **Joining and averaging paths:** If the endpoints of two different paths are selected with the Direct Selection tool, you can make a straight line connect these two endpoints by choosing Object ⇨ Path ⇨ Join (⌘/Ctrl+J). The Object ⇨ Path ⇨ Average (Alt+Ctrl+J in Windows; Option+⌘+J on the Mac) menu command is also used to connect the endpoints of two paths, but instead of a straight line, this command opens a simple dialog box where you can select to move the endpoints to an average Horizontal, Vertical or Both position. After two paths are joined or averaged, they become a single closed shape.

- **Converting strokes to filled objects:** You can convert strokes into filled objects by choosing Object ⇨ Path ⇨ Outline Stroke.

- **Offsetting paths:** Choosing Object ⇨ Path ⇨ Offset Path opens a dialog box, shown in Figure 10-83, where you can specify an offset distance and a join type. The join types are the same as those in the Strokes palette, namely Miter (with a Miter Limit value), Round, and Bevel. This command may be used on open or closed paths. A positive Offset value offsets each point of the path outward; a negative Offset value offsets the path points for a closed shape inward.

Figure 10-83: The Offset Path dialog box

Simplifying and cleaning up paths

Cleaning up a document reduces the file size. Choosing Object ⇨ Path ⇨ Simplify opens a dialog box, shown in Figure 10-84, where you can specify settings that reduce the path's complexity by eliminating unneeded anchor points. The Curve Precision value sets the amount that the path may change during the simplification process. A value of 100% requires that the original path be fully maintained.

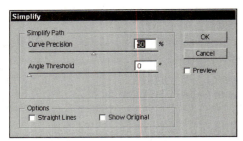

Figure 10-84: The Simplify dialog box lets you define how radically a path is simplified.

The Angle Threshold value determines the corner smoothness. If the angle of a corner point is less than the Angle Threshold value, the corner isn't smoothed.

Tip: When you enable the Preview option, the total number of points in the original and simplified curves is displayed.

The Straight Lines option simplifies the curve using only straight lines; the Show Original option displays the original line in the art board.

Choosing Object ⇨ Path ⇨ Clean Up opens a dialog box, shown in Figure 10-85, where you can select to eliminate stray points, unpainted objects, and empty text paths. Stray points can appear by clicking once with the Pen tool, which typically happens when you click to select on object when the Pen tool is selected instead of the Selection tool. Unpainted objects are objects with None set for both the fill and stroke. Empty text paths are created by clicking on the art board with the Type tool.

Figure 10-85: The Clean Up dialog box lets you select which cleanup objects to delete.

Splitting objects into grids

With a closed object selected, you can choose Object ⇨ Path ⇨ Split into Grids, which opens a dialog box, shown in Figure 10-86, where you can specify the number of rows and columns of a grid. You can also specify the height, width, gutter, and total dimensions of the grid cells. The Add Guides option creates guides for the top and bottom of each row and column, letting you change all the cells in a single row or column quickly.

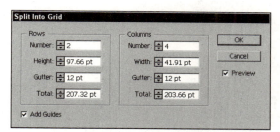

Figure 10-86: The Split into Grid dialog box divides a closed path into grid cells.

Cutting objects

Sometimes shape editing calls for removing or separating a portion of an object. There are several ways to split an object:

Note

You use the Slice tool to separate images and objects into slices. Each slice can hold vector or raster sections. By slicing documents, you can move them to the Web as separate files that work together.

♦ **Using the Knife tool:** The Knife tool (located as a fly-out tool under the Scissors tool) is a freehand tool that cuts through a selected object. Objects split where you drag the tool. Holding down the Option/Alt key drags a straight line.

♦ **Cutting holes in shapes:** You can use closed shapes as a cookie cutter to punch out the selected shape from all the objects beneath it. To do this, position the cutting object on top of the object that you want to cut, and choose Object ⇨ Path ⇨ Divide Object Below.

Creating compound paths and shapes in Illustrator

Compound objects are created when two or more selected paths or shapes are combined to create a single object. Compound objects are different from grouping objects. Objects within a group may have different attributes, but all the paths or shapes in a compound object share the same appearance attributes. Even though compound objects are combined to make a single object, the individual items may still be selected using the Direct Selection or Group Selection tools, just like groups. Compound objects may be restored to their original components using the Release menu command.

Creating compound paths

You can combine two or more paths into a compound path by choosing Object ⇨ Compound Path ⇨ Make (⌘/Ctrl+8). When paths are combined to create a compound path, the paths create a single path and a hole is left in the fill where the two paths were overlapped. Whenever paths are combined to create a compound path, the appearance attributes of the bottommost object are applied to the resulting path.

Using Pathfinder features

In addition to compound paths, Illustrator can create compound shapes using the Pathfinder palette, shown in Figure 10-87. Open this palette by choosing Window ⇨ Pathfinder (Shift+F9). Selected objects are made into a compound shape using the Make Compound Shape palette menu command. This eliminates all the interior paths and combines all the shapes into a single compound shape.

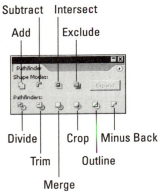

Figure 10-87: The Pathfinder palette includes shape modes.

In addition to the palette menu command, you can also use the icon buttons found in the Pathfinder palette to add to the shape area, subtract from the shape area, intersect shape areas, or exclude overlapping shape areas. The Subtract button removes from the first object all shape areas that overlap the first object. The Intersect button leaves only those areas that are common to all selected shapes. The Exclude button removes all areas of the objects that overlap another shape.

After a compound shape is created, you can change the shape mode for any of the objects that make up the compound shape by selecting it with the Direct Selection tool and choosing a new button in the Pathfinder palette.

Whenever objects are combined to create a compound shape, the appearance attributes of the topmost object are applied to the compound object.

Note Compound shapes use the appearance attributes of the topmost shape. Compound paths use the appearance attributes of the bottommost path.

Using InDesign's Pathfinder tools

In addition to Illustrator, InDesign's has a robust set of pathfinder features also that make it possible to create any type of shape. The top section of InDesign's Pathfinder palette, shown in Figure 10-88, includes the standard pathfinder features that work the same as Illustrators, but the lower section includes options for converting shapes. Using the Convert Shape features, you can change a frame into a Rectangle, Rounded Rectangle, Beveled Rectangle, Inverse Rounded Rectangle, Ellipse, Triangle, Polygon, Line or Horizontal or Vertical Line. There are also options to Open a Path, Close a Path, or Reverse a Path.

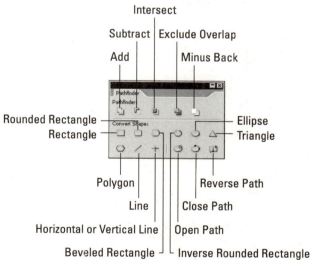

Figure 10-88: InDesign's Pathfinder palette includes Pathfinder and Convert Shape options.

Blending objects in Illustrator

The Blend tool (W) may be used to morph the shape, path, color, or style of one object to another. To use this tool, click on an object and then on a second object to blend to. Several intermediate objects appear between the two objects. Figure 10-89 shows a blend that moves between different shapes, strokes, and fills.

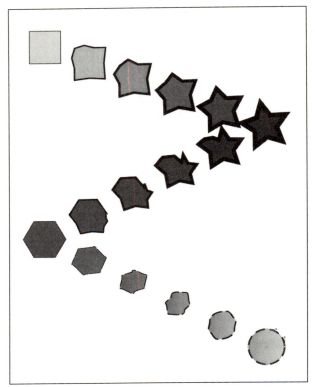

Figure 10-89: Blends can interpolate shapes, strokes, fills, and styles.

Blend objects are selected as a single object, but you may select individual objects that make up a blend object by using the Direct Selection tool. Changing a selected shape or color of either of the objects that make up the blend also updates the intermediate objects.

Double-clicking on the Blend tool opens the Blend Options dialog box, shown in Figure 10-90, where you can select a Spacing option of Smooth Color, Specified Steps, or Specified Distance. When the Smooth Color option is selected, Illustrator determines the number of steps needed to make a smooth color transition between the two blend objects. For the Specified Steps and Specified Distance options, you can enter the number of steps or the distance between each step.

Figure 10-90: The Blend Options dialog box lets you define the number of steps between each blend object.

The Blend Options dialog box also lets you set the Orientation to be either Align to Page or Align to Path. The Align to Page option orients all the blend objects relative to the art board; the Align to Path option orients the blend objects relative to the blend's spine path.

When a blend is made between two objects, a straight path connects the two objects. With the Direct Selection tool, you can select this path and add anchor points to it with the Add Anchor Point tool or by choosing Object ⇨ Path ⇨ Add Anchor Points. Dragging these new anchor points gives you control over how the path moves. As the path is altered, all the intermediate objects that are part of the blend follow the path.

In addition to the Blend tool, you can also blend two selected objects by choosing Object ⇨ Blend ⇨ Make (Alt+Ctrl+B in Windows; Option+⌘+B on the Mac). Blended objects may also be undone by choosing Object ⇨ Blend ⇨ Release (Alt+Shift+Ctrl+B in Windows; Option+Shift+⌘+B on the Mac). Choosing Object ⇨ Blend ⇨ Expand separates all the intermediate objects from the blend object and makes them independent, editable objects.

The line connecting two blend objects is called the *spine*. You may choose Object ⇨ Blend ⇨ Reverse Spine or choose Object ⇨ Blend ⇨ Reverse Front to Back to change the direction and stacking order of the blend objects. If a separate path is selected along with the blend, choosing Object ⇨ Blend ⇨ Replace Spine causes the blend to use the new selected path instead of the straight-line spine.

Creating a clipping mask in Illustrator

A clipping mask is a closed object positioned over the top of objects that are to be clipped. With all these objects selected, choosing Object ⇨ Clipping Mask ⇨ Make (⌘/Ctrl+7) causes the top object to hide all the objects underneath. The clipping mask may be undone by choosing Object ⇨ Clipping Mask ⇨ Release (Alt+Ctrl+7 in Windows; Option+⌘+7 on the Mac).

Distorting objects in Illustrator

There are several different ways to distort objects with the Liquify tools and with Envelope Distort commands.

Using the Liquify tools

Illustrator includes several tools that you may use to distort selected objects. You use these tools by dragging over the selected objects with the selected tool. The longer you drag with the selected tool, the greater the effect. Figure 10-91 shows a simple circle that has been distorted using each of these Liquify tools. These tools collectively are called the Liquify tools and include the following:

- **Warp tool (Shift+R):** Stretches object paths by pushing or pulling them.
- **Twirl tool:** Causes paths to be twirled.
- **Pucker tool:** Sucks paths towards the cursor.
- **Bloat tool:** Pushes path edges away from the cursor.
- **Scallop tool:** Adds arcs and barbs to a path edge.
- **Crystallize tool:** Adds spikes to path edges.
- **Wrinkle tool:** Wrinkles the edge paths with details.

Cross-Reference Most of the available Liquify tools may also be applied as filters and effects, which are covered in Chapter 13.

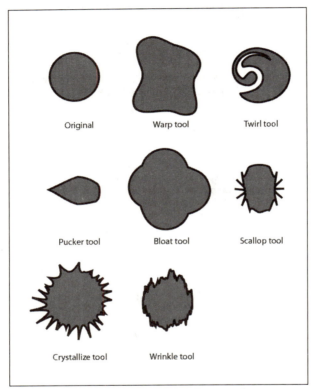

Figure 10-91: The Liquify tools provide several unique ways to distort objects.

Double-clicking a Liquify tool opens a dialog box of options, like the Pucker Tool Options dialog box, shown in Figure 10-92. Using this dialog box, you can set the Width, Height, Angle, and Intensity of the tool's brush. You can also set the individual settings for the selected tool. The Show Brush Size option changes the cursor to an outline of the brush.

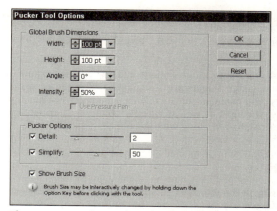

Figure 10-92: The settings for the various Liquify tools

Using the Envelope Distort command in Illustrator

Envelopes are preset or selected shapes into which object is distorted to fit inside. Choosing Object ⇨ Envelope Distort ⇨ Make with Warp (Alt+Shift+Ctrl+W in Windows; Option+Shift+⌘+W on the Mac) opens a dialog box of preset envelope shapes, shown in Figure 10-93, including Arc, Arc Lower, Arc Upper, Arch, Bulge, Shell Lower, Shell Upper, Flag, Wave, Fish, Rise, Fisheye, Inflate, Squeeze, and Twist.

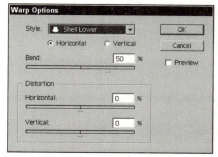

Figure 10-93: The Warp Options dialog box

Most of these preset envelope shapes are applied horizontally or vertically by a certain Bend amount. You can also specify the Horizontal and Vertical Distortion amounts.

You apply the envelope as an editable mesh by moving its points with the Direct Selection tool. To apply a mesh to the selected object with a specified number of rows and columns, choose Object ⇨ Envelope Distort ⇨ Make with Mesh (Alt+Ctrl+M in Windows; Option+⌘+M on the Mac). This opens a dialog box where you can enter the number of mesh rows and columns.

Choosing Object ⇨ Envelope Distort ⇨ Make with Top Object (Alt+Ctrl+C in Windows; Option+⌘+C on the Mac) causes the top selected object to act as the distortion envelope. Any selected distortion envelopes are released by choosing Object ⇨ Envelope Distort ⇨ Release.

Choosing Object ⇨ Envelope Distort ⇨ Envelope Options opens a dialog box of options. Using these options, you can specify whether raster objects are antialiased and whether to preserve clipping masks or transparency. You can also set the *fidelity*, which determines how well the selected object fits within its envelope, as well as whether an object's appearance, linear gradients and/or pattern fills are distorted along with the object.

Summary

- You can create and use objects in all the various CS2 applications. To create objects, tools and menu commands are used.

- Tools that create objects include the Pen, Type, Line Segment tools, and shape tools. You create freehand path objects with the Paintbrush and Pencil tools. The Paintbrush, Pencil, and Paint Bucket tools apply paint to the canvas in Photoshop.

- All CS2 applications include tools to select objects and images. These tools include shape tools like Photoshop's Marquee tools and freehand tools like the Lasso tool. Objects and images with similar areas are selected using the Magic Wand tool.

- Fills and strokes offer a way to add color to objects. Pixel selections may also be filled and stroked. Objects may also be filled with gradients and patterns as well as colors. Live Paint offers options for automatically filling discreet faces.

- Color is applied using the Color palette, the Color Picker, and color swatches.

- The CS2 applications deal with several different color models, including RGB, HSV, CMYK, Grayscale, and Web Safe RGB colors.

- Illustrator, InDesign and Photoshop can apply linear and radial gradients as fills and may be used to create custom patterns.

- Transparency is another common property that allows objects underneath overlapped objects to be partially visible.

- Often-used items are saved in libraries. Libraries include symbols, styles, swatches, and brushes.

- Symbols provide an efficient way to work with many duplicate objects.

- Each of the CS2 applications includes various tools and commands for editing objects and images, including tools and commands to combine objects and split and distort objects.

✦ ✦ ✦

Acquiring and Correcting Images

In This Chapter

Scanning images

Acquiring digital camera images

Correcting images

Painting images

Selecting pixels

Editing images

Retouching images

In addition to objects, images are another important design element. Although all applications handle images, Photoshop is the main tool for working with images. The first task is to load digital images. Photoshop includes a lot of features to not only scan and acquire digital photos but also to correct them.

Once you load images within Photoshop, you can edit them using Photoshop's vast array of features. You can then easily transport these images to the other CS2 applications using the clipboard, exported files or Adobe Bridge.

Scanning Images in Photoshop

One method for loading images into Photoshop is with a scanner. Several different manufacturers make scanners that employ several different drivers. Scanners almost always come with a CD-ROM of compatible drivers that you can install to interface with Photoshop or with their own proprietary software.

If your scanner includes Photoshop compatible drivers, then the scanner's name will appear in the File ⇨ Import menu. If the scanner's driver doesn't include a Photoshop driver, check the manufacturer's Web site for an updated driver.

If the scanner manufacturer doesn't have a Photoshop driver available, you can take advantage of a TWAIN compatible interface. The TWAIN compatible device is listed in the File ⇨ Import menu.

A third driver option is to scan images using the WIA (Windows Image Acquisition) Support driver. You also select this option using the File ⇨ Import ⇨ WIA Support menu. This menu opens the WIA Support dialog box, shown in Figure 11-1, where you can specify a Destination Folder and options to open the image after the scan has completed.

 WIA Support is only available for Windows XP computers. Macintosh computers use the Image Capture features to access scanning devices.

Part III ✦ Working with Objects and Images

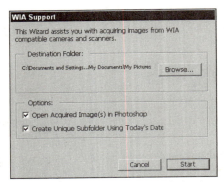

Figure 11-1: The WIA Support dialog box lets you access a scanner's software.

Clicking Start opens a dialog box, shown in Figure 11-2, where you can choose the Scanner and/or Digital Camera to access. Selecting a device and clicking OK, opens the device's software. The Properties button opens a dialog box of properties that let you define how the device can be used to scan directly into Photoshop.

Figure 11-2: The Select Device dialog box lets choose which scanning device to use.

STEPS: Setting up Photoshop Scanning

1. **Open Photoshop and select WIA Support.** With Photoshop open, choose File ➪ Import ➪ WIA Support to access the WIA Support dialog box.

2. **Set a Destination Folder.** Click Browse and select a destination folder where the scanned images are saved. Enable the Open Acquired Images in Photoshop option to view the images in Photoshop once they are scanned. Then click Start.

3. **Access the Scanner's Properties.** In the Select Device dialog box, choose the installed scanner and click Properties. This opens a dialog box of properties for the selected device.

4. **Set the Scan button to open Photoshop.** In the device Properties dialog box, shown in Figure 11-3, click the Events tab and select the Scan Button event. In the Actions section, choose the Start this Program option and choose Photoshop as the program to open. Then click OK.

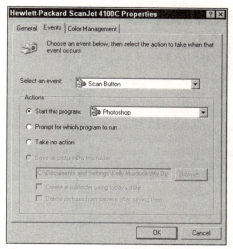

Figure 11-3: You can set Photoshop to open when you push the scan button on the scanner device.

After clicking OK in the Select Device dialog box, a Scan dialog box appears, shown in Figure 11-4. Options to scan the image include scanning as a Color Picture, a Grayscale Picture, or a Black and White Picture or Text. The Adjust the quality of the scanned Picture link opens another dialog box where you can adjust the Brightness, Contrast and Resolution of the scanned image. The Preview button shows the scanned image in the preview pane, where you can set its cropping using the corner handles.

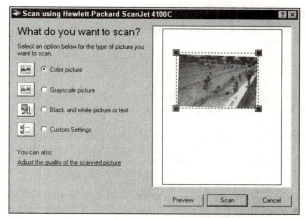

Figure 11-4: You can scan images as Color, Grayscale, or Black and white.

Acquiring Digital Camera Images

Digital cameras work the same as scanners. Images from a digital camera can be accessed using the File ⇨ Import menu command using the TWAIN driver, the WIA Support driver, or Mac's Image Capture feature.

Using Camera Raw

Most digital cameras have a varied assortment of configuration settings for controlling everything from brightness and aperture to contrast and digital noise. These settings are crucial for getting just the right picture, but they also include many of the same settings found in Photoshop. If you capture an image with the incorrect brightness setting while hanging halfway over a fence at the zoo, you don't need to throw away the image, you can simply take the pictures and download the raw camera data, which is the actual digital data captured by the camera's optical sensor. Then you can reclaim much of the image data in Photoshop at your leisure without having to revisit the zoo to take another shot.

Caution Not all cameras can record raw camera data. Check the Adobe.com site for a list of compatible cameras.

Raw camera data can be imported into Photoshop using the File ⇨ Open menu command. The file extension for this data may be different depending on the camera, but Photoshop can recognize a huge variety of raw formats. When you open a raw camera file, the Camera Raw plug-in opens.

Cross-Reference You can open the Camera Raw plug-in from within Photoshop or within Adobe Bridge. More details on this plug-in are covered in Chapter 7.

Understanding Digital Negative Specification

Working with raw camera data makes a lot sense, but there is a problem with the current raw camera formats. Each camera manufacturer uses a different format to output its raw camera data, which makes it difficult to standardize when you load the data in a program like Photoshop.

New Feature New additions to the Camera Raw plug-in include the ability to work on multiple images simultaneously and support for formats including the DNG format. These are all new to CS2.

Although CS2 supports a majority of the available raw camera formats, there are some less popular camera makers that aren't supported. To address this issue, Adobe has defined and made publicly available the Adobe Digital Negative (DNG) format. One advantage of this new format is that it also includes support for metadata that describes the images.

As of this printing, many camera manufacturers have announced support for this new raw camera format. Adobe has also made a Conversion utility available that converts many of the existing raw camera data formats to the DNG format. For more information on this format, see Adobe's Web site.

Correcting Red Eye

Attentive camera subjects looking directly at the camera typically have a red eyes when the digital camera's flash lights their eyes. This can quickly be fixed using the Red Eye tool, which is located as a flyout under the Healing Brush. To use the tool, simply drag it over an eye with this problem. Figure 11-5 shows an example where this tool was used. The right eye of each of these toddlers has been corrected using this tool. When this tool is selected, the Options bar includes settings for controlling Pupil Size and Darken Pupil.

 The Red Eye tool is new to Photoshop CS2.

Figure 11-5: The Red Eye tool can quickly fix images with red eyes.

Using the Lens Correction filter

Another common problem with images taken with a digital camera are lens flaws such as barrel and pincushion distortion. These flaws are similar to the corrections that you can make to you computer monitor. These are especially visible when the image includes many parallel straight lines.

 The Lens Correction filter is new to Photoshop CS2.

Lens flaws can be remedied in Photoshop using the Lens Correction filter located in Filter ⇨ Distort ⇨ Lens Correction. This filter opens the Lens Correction dialog box, shown in Figure 11-6.

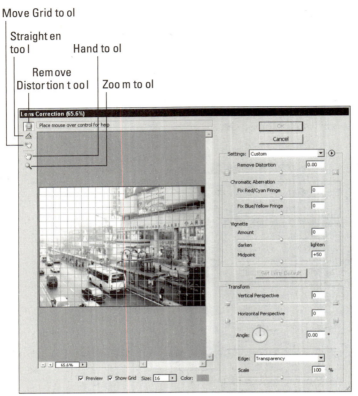

Figure 11-6: The Lens Correction filter can fix many lens flaws added by the digital camera.

The upper-left corner of the Lens Correction dialog box includes several tools. The Remove Distortion tool alternates the image between a pincushion and barrel settings. Dragging with the Straighten tool causes the image to reorient about the dragged line. This provides a way to recreate the horizontal and vertical axis for the image. Over the top of the image is a grid that can be turned on and off. The Move Grid tool is used to move and reposition this grid.

Cross-Reference

For additional coverage on Photoshop filters, see Chapter 13.

To the right of the preview pane are several sliders that can be used to further modify the image. The Remove Distortion slider associates a value to the distortion. The Chromatic Aberration values are used to change the colors located at the fringe of the lens. You can adjust for Red/Cyan and Blue/Yellow colored fringes. The Vignette value alters the brightness of the image about the lens center. The Vertical and Horizontal Perspective settings tilt the image to or away from the image center. You can also change the image's orientation Angle and Scale. The Edge setting determines how the edge is colored when the image's perspective, angle or scale is changed. The options include Edge Extension, Transparency, and Background.

Correcting Images

Once digital images are loaded into Photoshop, you have a lot of control in adjusting the images. This is the power of Photoshop — to correct images.

Cross-Reference
Image adjustments can also be applied to a specific layer using Adjustment Layers, which are covered in Chapter 14.

Using Levels

One of the first corrections you'll want to make to acquired digital images is to adjust the image's levels. This can be done in the Levels dialog box, shown in Figure 11-7, which is opened for the current image using the Image ⇨ Adjustment ⇨ Levels menu command. The Levels dialog box shows a histogram for the image, which is a graph showing the number of pixels for each color intensity level.

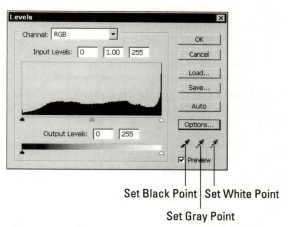

Figure 11-7: The Levels dialog box shows the tonal range for the image.

At the top of the Levels dialog box is the Channels drop-down list, where you can view the levels for All RGB Channels, or just the Red, Green or Blue channels. Level settings can be saved and restored using the Load and Save buttons.

The Input Level values are associated with the black and white color values in the shadows and highlights. The middle value represents the gamma setting for the image. The tonal range can be adjusted manually by changing the Input Level values, by dragging the markers under the level graph or by clicking Auto to automatically set the range. Dragging the middle gray marker under the levels graph alters the image's midtones. The Options button opens the Auto Color Correction Options dialog box, shown in Figure 11-8. Using these settings, you can set how the Auto button corrects the image.

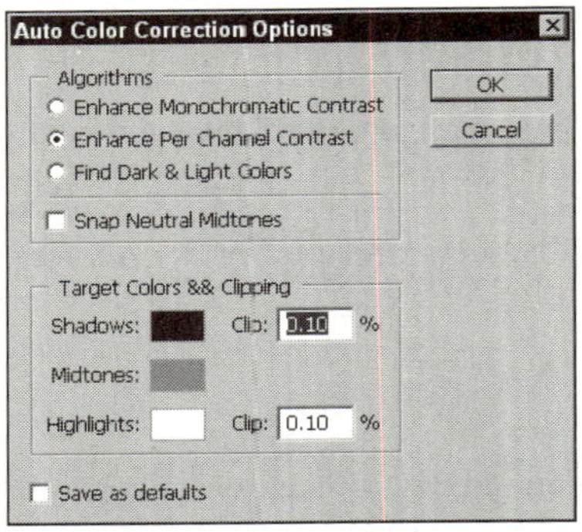

Figure 11-8: The Auto Color Correction Options dialog box lets you set how the Auto button works.

You can also correct colorcast in the Levels dialog box by double clicking the Set Black, Gray or White Point icons. You can then select the color in the Color Picker for the selected point and click in the image where that color point is located.

Using Curves

In addition to the Levels dialog box, the Curves dialog box, shown in Figure 11-9, can also be used to alter the tonal range of an image, but with more precision. The Curves dialog box shows the intensity for the entire image range from black's 0 value to white's 255 value.

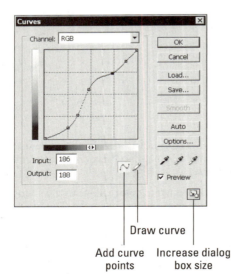

Draw curve
Add curve points
Increase dialog box size

Figure 11-9: The Curves dialog box offers a more precise way to change the tonal range of an image.

Most of the settings in this dialog box are identical to those in the Levels dialog box including viewing individual channels, loading and saving curves, the Auto and Options buttons and setting black, gray and white points.

The Curves dialog box can add up to 14 additional points to the curve, each of which you can move as needed by dragging with the cursor. You can remove points by dragging them off the curve or by selecting them and pressing the Delete key. You can also draw a curve using the Draw Curve tool. The Smooth button becomes enabled when a curve is drawn.

Using Auto adjustments

Within the Image ⇨ Adjustment menu are options for Auto Color, Auto Contrast and Auto Levels. These commands correspond to the algorithms found in the Auto Color Correction Options dialog box and selecting these menu commands is the same as selecting each in the Options dialog box and clicking Auto.

STEPS: Adjusting Shadows and Highlights

1. **Open Photoshop and select an image.** With Photoshop open, load an image that needs to have its shadows and highlights set. Figure 11-10 shows the image before any adjustments have been made.

Figure 11-10: This image needs to have its tonal range reset.

2. **Open the Levels dialog box.** With the image selected, choose the Image ⇨ Adjustment ⇨ Levels menu command. The image shows a lot of pixels in the lower third of the levels graph.

3. **Adjust the highlights.** Drag the highlights marker on the right end of the graph to the left until it is aligned with the right edge of the levels graph, as shown in Figure 11-11.

Figure 11-11: Dragging the right marker resets the highlights.

Editing 32-bit High Dynamic Range images

Even if you adjust the tonal range of an image, our eyes can detect a greater range than a computer monitor represents. Think of how your eyes react when you walk out in the bright sun. The range that makes everything seem to glow can't be represented using any of the existing image formats, but another format has been developed that captures this extended range and it actually allows the color range to change as needed. This new format is called High Dynamic Range (HDR) images.

New Feature   The ability to work with HDR images is new to Photoshop CS2.

HDR images are represented using 32-bit numbers instead of the standard 8 or 16-bit image formats. The extra numeric values are used to represent the luminance associated with each pixel in the image. HDR images are created by merging in multiple photographs of different exposures.

To merge several images of the same scene into a single HDR file, use the File ⇨ Automate ⇨ Merge to HDR menu command. This opens the Merge to HDR dialog box, shown in Figure 11-12, where you can select individual files using the Browse button, select a folder and choose to merge the existing open files. After clicking OK, the files are merged and you can save the file.

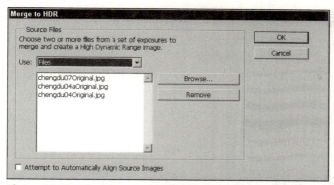

Figure 11-12: The Merge to HDR dialog box can combine multiple images into a single HDR image.

Painting Images

Unlike objects, which can be thought of as a group of items sitting on a shelf ready for you to place in a document, you create images by drawing them on a canvas or by loading an existing image file. All the CS2 applications also support images, but the first place to look is obviously Photoshop.

The process of creating objects within the CS2 applications is referred to as *drawing* and the process of creating images is called *painting*.

Painting images in Photoshop

The main tools used in Photoshop to paint images are the Paintbrush tool, the Pencil tool, and the Paint Bucket tool. All these tools apply the foreground color to the canvas.

Using the Paintbrush tool

The Paintbrush tool coupled with the Brushes palette offers unlimited flexibility and power in applying paint to the canvas. Selecting the Brush tool (B) in the Toolbox changes the cursor to match the shape of the selected brush. Dragging with this tool in the canvas paints a line using the properties set in the Brushes palette.

You may open the Brushes palette, shown in Figure 11-13, by choosing Window ➪ Brushes (F5) or by clicking on the Brushes tab on the right end of the Options bar. The Brushes palette includes many panels of properties that are opened by clicking on their panel name listed to the left of the palette. Most of these panels include a check box that lets you enable or disable the properties contained in the panel. The panels are as follows:

The Brushes palette is active only when one of the painting tools is selected.

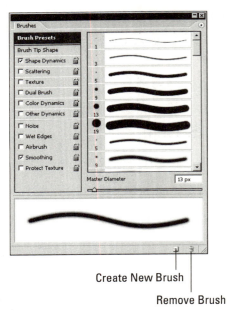

Create New Brush
Remove Brush

Figure 11-13: The Brushes palette includes many preset brushes to start with.

- **Brush Presets:** Lets you choose a brush from a long list of presets. To select a preset brush, just click on it and a preview of the selected brush appears at the bottom of the panel. You can also change the Master Diameter for the selected brush. In the Brush palette menu are several options for setting how the preset brushes are viewed, including Text Only, Small and Large Thumbnails, Small and Large Lists, and Stroke Thumbnail.

  The Brushes palette menu also includes a New Brush Preset option that is used to add a new preset to the Brush Preset panel. A set of brush presets may be saved to the local system using the Save Brushes palette menu command. The brush libraries are saved using an ABR file extension. Photoshop includes several brush libraries that may be loaded into the Brushes palette or selected from the bottom of the Brushes palette menu.

- **Brush Tip Shape panel:** Shown in Figure 11-14, this panel displays thumbnails of the brush tips for the respective brush presets listed in the Brush Presets panel. The brush tip properties let you change the tip's diameter and orientation using controls to flip the brush tip and set its angle and roundness. You can also alter its Angle and Roundness values by dragging in the diagram pane to the right of the Angle and Roundness values. The Hardness value sets the diameter of the brush's hard center, where no softening takes place. The Spacing value determines the distance between successive brush marks in a stroke. Low Spacing values causes the brush tip to overlap into a continuous path.

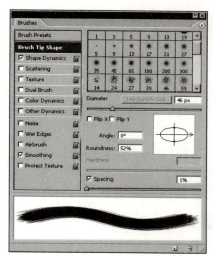

Figure 11-14: The Brush Tip Shape panel of the Brushes palette

- **Shape Dynamics panel:** Includes controls to add some randomness to the brush strokes, including the amount of jitter that is added. The Scattering panel is used to spread the brush tip over a given width with a specified density. The Texture panel lets you specify an underlying texture for the brush. The Dual Brush panel lets you select a secondary brush tip that is combined with the original brush tip to create a new unique pattern. The Color and Other Dynamics panels let you specify how the colors, transparency, and brightness change as the brush is painted.

The Noise, Wet Edges, Airbrush, Smoothing, and Protect Texture options don't open a panel of settings but may be enabled to change the characteristics of the selected brush.

When the Paintbrush tool is selected, the Options bar includes controls that let you select a tool preset or a brush tip. You can also select a blending mode to use and change the amount of opacity and flow that is applied to the brush.

STEPS: Painting with the Paintbrush Tool

1. **Open a Photoshop document.** With Photoshop open, choose File ⇨ New to create a new document.

2. **Select a Brush.** Click on the Paintbrush tool to select it. In the Options bar, click on the Brushes tab to open the Brushes palette. Click on the palette menu and select the Special Effect Brushes command. A dialog box opens asking if you want to replace the brush sets. Click OK. The new brush set is displayed in the Brush Presets panel, as shown in Figure 11-15. In the Brush Presets panel of the Brushes palette, select the first brush preset, called the Azalea brush.

Figure 11-15: The brushes in the Brush Presets panel

3. **Set the brush properties.** In the Swatches palette, select an orange color. This color becomes the new foreground color. Click on the Color Dynamics panel in the Brushes palette and drag the Hue Jitter over to 50%.

4. **Paint with a Preset brush.** Drag with the Paintbrush tool in the canvas. The Azalea brush paints a random assortment of colored flowers in the canvas, as shown in Figure 11-16.

Figure 11-16: By altering the Hue Jitter in the Color Dynamics palette, the color of the flowers is changed as you paint with the brush.

Using the Pencil and Paint Bucket tools

The Pencil tool works just like the Paintbrush tool, except it produces a hard edge instead of a smooth, soft edge. The Pencil tool uses all the same controls found in the Brushes palette for specifying its shape and characteristics.

The Paint Bucket tool, located as a fly-out under the Gradient tool, applies the selected foreground color or pattern to an area where all the contiguous pixels are the same or within the specified Tolerance. You can select the properties of the Paint Bucket tool in the Options bar when the Paint Bucket tool is selected. You can also select a blending mode and an opacity.

Working with images in the other CS2 applications

All the other CS2 applications can work with images, but these images are confined to an object or frame. This lets you transform the images within the work area and place them relative to the other objects, but Illustrator and InDesign don't include any tools that alter the pixels by painting. You can load images into Illustrator and InDesign using the File ➪ Place menu command. These loaded images appear within an object or frame.

You can also convert certain text and vector objects to their bitmap equivalents through a process called *rasterizing*. Raster images may be moved back to Photoshop using the Clipboard. When pasted into Photoshop, the images are contained within a frame that allows you to move the object, but when you select a different tool, a confirm dialog box asks if you want to place the object. Choosing to place the object permanently places it in the current image.

Illustrator also includes a Live Trace feature that works the opposite of rasterizing, allowing you to convert images into vectorized objects.

 Caution Rasterizing objects eliminates their resolution independence. Scaling a rasterized object reveals all the individual pixels.

Rasterizing objects

You can rasterize Illustrator objects by choosing Object ⇨ Rasterize. This opens the Rasterize dialog box, shown in Figure 11-17, where you can select a color model, a resolution, a background, an anti-aliasing option, and a clipping mask, as well as specify whether space is added to the object:

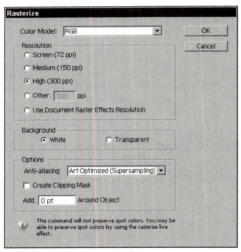

Figure 11-17: The Rasterize dialog box lets you specify a color model.

- ✦ **Color Model options:** Include RGB, CMYK, Grayscale, or Bitmap, depending on the color settings for the document.
- ✦ **Background options:** Define whether the object background are colored as white pixels or made transparent. Selecting the Transparent option causes an alpha channel to be saved with the document.
- ✦ **Anti-aliasing options:** These include None, Art Optimized (which is used for graphics), and Type Optimized (which is used for text).

✦ **Create Clipping Mask:** Creates a clipping mask that hides all the background pixels. It isn't needed if the Transparent Background option is selected.

✦ **Add field:** Lets you specify a distance that is added to every edge of the rasterized object.

You can define all these settings for the document using the Document Raster Effects Settings dialog box, shown in Figure 11-18, which you open by choosing Effect ➪ Document Raster Effects Settings. You use these settings for any effects that need to rasterize the object as the effect is being applied. The Document Raster Effects Settings dialog box also includes the Preserve Spot Colors where Possible option. This setting attempts to use spot colors where they can be used.

More on using effects is covered in Chapter 13.

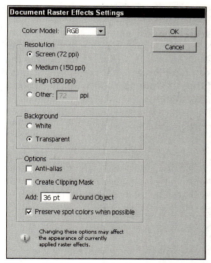

Figure 11-18: The Document Raster Effects Settings dialog box

STEPS: Rasterizing Objects

1. **Open an Illustrator document.** With Illustrator open, choose File ➪ New to create a new document. Select the RGB Color option in the New Document dialog box.

2. **Drag a symbol from the Symbols palette.** For a quick object that may be rasterized, drag a symbol from the Symbols palette onto the art board.

3. **Resize the object.** Because the object loses its resolution independence when it's rasterized, drag on the bounding-box handles of the symbol with the Shift key held down to maintain its aspect ratio until it is the size you want to use, as shown in Figure 11-19.

Figure 11-19: Sizing the object in Illustrator before rasterizing.

4. **Rasterize the symbol.** With the symbol selected, choose Object ➪ Rasterize. The Rasterize dialog box appears. Select the RGB Color Mode, and change the Resolution depending on how the raster image intends to be used. Use Screen for images that are viewed on a computer monitor and High for raster images that are to be printed. Select Transparent as the Background and select the Art Optimized Anti-Aliasing option. Then click OK. Figure 11-20 shows the rasterized symbol.

Figure 11-20: The rasterized object appears the same as the object version, but if you were to scale the raster image, you would see the individual pixels.

5. **Copy the raster image to the Clipboard.** With the rasterized symbol still selected, choose Edit ➪ Copy. This copies the raster image to the Clipboard.

6. **Paste the raster image into Photoshop.** With Photoshop open, choose File ➪ New. The New dialog box appears with the Clipboard preset selected. This preset has the exact dimensions of the raster image copied from Illustrator. Click OK to create a new canvas. Then choose Edit ➪ Paste. The raster image appears in the current open document within Photoshop inside a bounding box (see Figure 11-21). Drag the bounding box to the position where you want to place it, and click on the Selection tool. A simple confirmation dialog box appears, giving you the following options: Place, Cancel, or Don't Place. Click Place.

Figure 11-21: Raster images copied to Photoshop may be positioned before they're placed on the canvas.

Using Live Trace

Just as you can rasterize vector objects into pixel images, Illustrator also includes a feature that reverses the process. Illustrator's Live Trace takes raster images and traces them into editable objects. Figure 11-22 shows a simple airplane image that has been traced into black and white objects.

 The new Live Trace feature is new to Illustrator CS2.

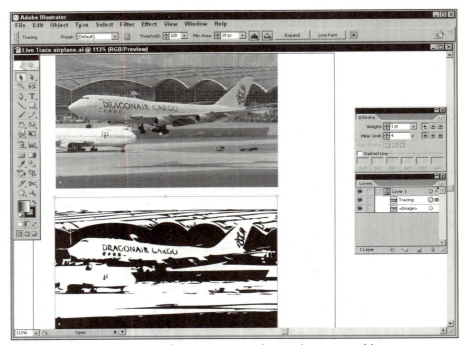

Figure 11-22: Live Trace is used to convert raster images into vector objects.

The Live Trace button appears in the Options bar anytime a bitmap image is selected in Illustrator. Once a bitmap image is traced, the Options bar displays a drop-down list of Presets that you can select. There is also a button on the Options bar to open the Tracing Options dialog box, shown in Figure 11-23. The Options bar also includes setting for controlling the Threshold and the Minimum Area. The Threshold value applies to the black and white tracing mode. All pixels in the trace area lighter than the Threshold value are converted to white and all pixels darker are converted to black. The Minimum Area setting control the size of the details considered during the trace pass. Details in pixel areas smaller than the Minimum Area value are ignored.

Live Trace can also be selected from the Object ⇨ Live Trace ⇨ Make menu and the Tracing Options dialog box is accessed using the Object ⇨ Live Trace ⇨ Tracing Options menu. Each traced image includes the original raster image along with the traced result. Using the black and gray up arrow icons on the Options bar, you can set what is visible. Options for the raster image include No Image, Original Image, Adjusted Image and Transparent Image. Options for the Vector traced image include No Tracing Result, Tracing Result, Outlines, and Outlines with Tracing.

You can remove the existing tracing using the Object ⇨ Live Trace ⇨ Release menu command.

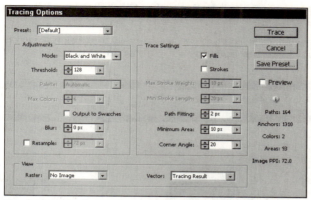

Figure 11-23: The Tracing Options dialog box lets you define new tracing presets.

STEPS: Using Live Trace

1. **Open an Illustrator document.** With Illustrator open, choose File ⇨ Open to open a document to trace that includes a raster image. Figure 11-24 shows the image before being traced.

Figure 11-24: This raster image is about to be traced.

2. **Select the bitmap image.** Choose the Selection tool and click the raster image in the center of the artboard.
3. **Use Live Trace.** With the image selected, click Live Trace on the Options bar at the top of the interface. This applies the default tracing preset, as shown in Figure 11-25.

Figure 11-25: The default trace preset traces using black and white.

4. **Open the Tracing Options dialog box.** Select the Object ⇨ Live Trace ⇨ Tracing Options menu command. In the Tracing Options dialog box, choose the Color 16 option, the reduce the Blur value to 0, the Path Fitting value to 6 px, and the Minimum Area value to 2 px. Then click OK.
5. **Expand the traced image.** With the traced image still selected, choose the Object ⇨ Live Trace ⇨ Expand menu command. This makes all the traced objects selectable. Figure 11-26 shows the final result.

Figure 11-26: The final traced image includes objects that can be selected and edited.

Selecting Pixels in Photoshop

Just as Illustrator and InDesign include several tools that select objects, Photoshop includes several tools that select specific pixels. The Selection tools are located at the top of Photoshop's Toolbox and include several Marquee tools, several Lasso tools and the Magic Wand tool, as shown in Figure 11-27.

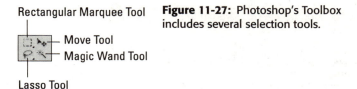

Figure 11-27: Photoshop's Toolbox includes several selection tools.

Using the Selection tools

When one of the Selection tools is selected, the Options bar displays four icon buttons that are used to create a new selection, add to the current selection, subtract from the current selection, and intersect with the current selection. These buttons let you continuously edit a selection until you have exactly what you want.

Holding down the Shift key while selecting an area adds to the current selection. Holding down the Option/Alt key subtracts from the current selection. Holding down the Shift+Option/Alt keys intersects the current selection.

The Options bar also lets you specify a feather amount and includes an option to enable anti-aliasing. Dragging with a selection tool in the canvas marks a selection with a blinking dashed line often called *marching ants*.

If a selection isn't visible, choose View ⇨ Show ⇨ Selection Edges.

You can only display one selection on the canvas at a time, but you may save and load selections by choosing Select ⇨ Save Selection and Select ⇨ Load Selection.

Using the Marquee selection tools

The Marquee selection tools included in Photoshop include the Rectangle Marquee tool, the Ellipse Marquee tool, the Single Row Marquee tool, and the Single Column Marquee tool. The difference among these tools is the shape of the selection they make.

In the Options bar, which appears directly under the menu at the top of the interface, shown in Figure 11-28, you can choose a selection Style as Normal, Fixed Aspect Ratio, and Fixed Size. If the Normal option is chosen, then a selection is made by clicking and dragging to specify the selection size. The Fixed Aspect Ratio option lets you specify Width and Height values. Dragging with this option produces a selection that maintains the specified aspect ratio. The Fixed Size option also lets you specify Width and Height values. Clicking and dragging with this option drags a selection of the specified dimensions in the image.

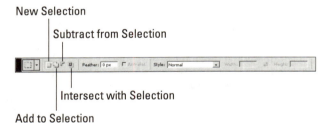

Figure 11-28: Selection tool options are displayed in the Options bar.

Holding down the Shift key while dragging with the Rectangle or Ellipse tools constrains the selection to a perfect square or circle. You can also hold down the Option/Alt key to drag from the center of the shape. Holding down the Spacebar lets you move the current selection as you make it. When you release the Spacebar, you can continue dragging to create the selection. The Single Row and Single Column Marquee tools let you click and drag to select a single row or column of pixels.

Using the Lasso selection tools

Photoshop actually includes three different Lasso tools:

- **Lasso tool:** You create a selection by drawing in the canvas. When you release the mouse, a straight line is drawn back to the point where you first clicked. If you hold down the Option/Alt key, you can click and drag to create straight lines. With the Option/Alt key held down, you can also press the Delete key to delete the last created straight line point or gradually delete the drawn path.

- **Polygonal Lasso tool:** This is the opposite of the Lasso tool. You create a selection by clicking at the endpoints of each successive straight line, but if you hold down the Option/Alt key, you can draw freehand. The Delete key also works to delete line segments. To close a selection created with the Polygonal Lasso tool, move the cursor near the starting point until a small circle appears as part of the cursor, and click or hold down the ⌘/Ctrl key and click or simply double-click and a straight line is created from the cursor's position to the starting point.

- **Magnetic Lasso tool:** This automatically creates selection anchor points based on the contrast of the image below. To use this tool, set the Width, Edge Contrast, and Frequency values in the Options bar. The Width value specifies how far around the cursor the Magnetic Lasso tool looks for contrasting pixels. The Edge Contrast value sets the amount of contrast required for an edge to be selected. The Frequency value determines the number of anchor points used to define the selection area.

Click on an image border that you want to trace with the Magnetic Lasso tool and drag along the image border. The tool places anchor points regularly along the path and connects them. If you click, you can manually place an anchor point as needed. The Delete key may be used to backtrack if needed and holding down the Option/Alt key changes the Magnetic Lasso tool to the normal Lasso tool for dragging or the Polygonal Lasso tool for clicking. Double-click or drag back to the first point again to close the selection.

Using the Magic Wand

The Magic Wand tool selects all areas with the same color or a color that is within the specified Tolerance value. The Tolerance value (found on the Options bar) can range between 0 and 255. Tolerance values of 0 require that the color values be exactly the same, and a Tolerance value of 255 is so forgiving that almost all colors are selected.

On the Options bar, the Contiguous option selects only those areas immediately connected to the selected color, but if the Contiguous option is deselected, all colors within the canvas that are within the Tolerance value are selected. The Use All Layers option makes selections from all layers but only from the selected layer if disabled.

STEPS: Building a Selection

1. **Open a Photoshop document.** With Photoshop open, choose File ⇨ New to create a new document. Fill the entire image with a pattern by choosing Edit ⇨ Fill. In the Fill dialog box that appears, select the Pattern option and choose one of the default patterns; then click OK.

2. **Choose an initial selection.** Click on the Rectangle Marquee tool and drag in the canvas to select a rectangular area.

3. **Subtract an interior section.** With the Rectangle Marquee tool still selected, click on the Subtract from Selection button in the Options bar. Then drag over an interior section of the current selection. The interior section is removed from the selection.

4. **Use the Ellipse Marquee tool.** Click and hold on the Rectangle Marquee tool to select the Ellipse Marquee tool from the fly-out menu. Click on the Add to Selection button in the Options bar. Then select the Fixed Size Style with Width and Height values of 64 pixels. Click and drag the circular selection so it's positioned on top of each of the corners of the current selection.

5. **Save the selection.** With the selection completed, choose Select ➪ Save Selection. In the Save Selection dialog box, give the selection a new name and click the OK.

6. **Fill the selection.** Choose Edit ➪ Fill and, in the Fill dialog box, select to fill with the white color and click OK. The selection is now clearly visible, as shown in Figure 11-29.

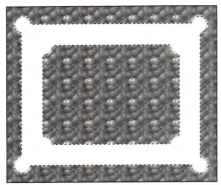

Figure 11-29: Filling the selection with a color makes it easy to see.

Using the Select menu

In addition to the Selection tools, Photoshop also includes a Select menu that holds many commands that are helpful for selecting pixels. Choose Select ➪ All (⌘/Ctrl+A) to select all canvas pixels; choose Select ➪ Deselect (⌘/Ctrl+D) to eliminate any selections. Choose Select ➪ Reselect (Shift+Ctrl+D in Windows; Shift+⌘+D on the Mac) to make the recent selection active again; choose Select ➪ Inverse (Shift+Ctrl+I in Windows; Shift+⌘+I on the Mac) to deselect the current selection and select all pixels that weren't selected.

Selecting a color range

Choosing Select ➪ Color Range opens a dialog box, shown in Figure 11-30, where you can select a range of colors in the image. With the dialog box open, the cursor changes to an eyedropper that you can use to click on the preview pane in the Color Range dialog box or within the actual canvas. The Preview pane is set to show the selection or the image, or you can use the ⌘/Ctrl key to switch between these two.

If a selection exists in the canvas, opening Photoshop's Color Range dialog box displays the selected area only. If no selection exists, the entire image displays in the Color Range dialog box.

Figure 11-30: The Color Range dialog box

Increasing the Fuzziness value increases the color range included in the selection, much like the Tolerance value for the Magic Wand.

To add more colors to the selection, click on the Add to Sample eyedropper; to remove colors, click on the Subtract from Sample eyedropper. You can also select the Add to Sample eyedropper by holding down the Shift key and the Subtract from Sample eyedropper by holding down the Option/Alt key. The Invert option switches the colors used in the Preview pane.

The Select drop-down list at the top of the dialog box lets you select from several default colors, including reds, yellows, greens, cyans, blues, magentas, highlights, midtones, shadows, and out of gamut. The Out of Gamut selection in particular is useful as a color check prior to printing.

The Selection Preview options at the bottom of the dialog box project the selection back into the canvas using None, Grayscale, Black Matte, White Matte, or Quick Mask. Color Range selections may be saved using the AXT file extension and reloaded again.

Modifying a selection

The Select ⇨ Modify menu includes several commands that change the current selection. Each of these menu commands opens a simple dialog box, shown in Figure 11-31, where you can specify a pixel value. The Border menu command turns the selection into a border as wide as the specified Width value. The Smooth command eliminates any stray or jagged pixels by smoothing the entire selection. The Expand command increases the selection by the designated number of pixels. The Contract command reduces the selection by the designated number of pixels.

Figure 11-31: You can select a pixel value to expand the current selection.

Choosing Select ⇨ Grow increases the selection step-by-step by gradually selecting similar adjoining colors. Choosing Select ⇨ Similar increases a selection by selecting all colors similar to the selected color through the entire image.

Transforming selections

Choosing Select ⇨ Transform Selection adds a bounding box to the current selection that lets you move, rotate, scale, shear, and change the perspective of the selection using the same bounding box controls used on objects. After all the transformations are made using the bounding box, confirm the transformation by clicking on the Commit Transform button in the Options bar. If you select another tool before committing the transform, a confirmation dialog box appears letting you Apply, Cancel, or Not Apply all the transformations. The Cancel option removes the confirmation dialog box letting you transform the selection some more, but the Not Apply option returns the selection to its last transformation state.

Converting drawn paths into selections

Paths that are saved in the Paths palette may be turned into a selection using the Make Selection palette menu command. This opens the Make Selection dialog box where you can select a Feather Radius value and whether the selection is anti-aliased. You can also choose that the selection is a New Selection, added to the existing selection, subtracted from the existing selection, or intersected with the existing selection.

Editing Images

Just as when editing objects, several tools and commands are useful when editing images.

Cropping images in Photoshop

Image sizes are set when a document is first created or loaded into Photoshop, but you can cut out a portion of the image using the Crop tool or the Crop and Trim commands found in the Image menu.

- **Using the Crop tool:** With the Crop tool (C), you can drag on the portion of an image that you want to keep. This selected area is marked with a bounding box that is moved, scaled, and rotated by dragging on the handles at their edges and corners. When the crop area is correctly positioned and oriented, double-click with the Crop tool within the selected area, click the Commit button on the Options bar or press the Return/Enter key, and the image is cropped to the selected area.

- **Cropping and trimming an image:** You may also crop an image using a selection made with one of the default selection tools with the Image ⇨ Crop menu command. Choosing Image ⇨ Trim opens a dialog box of trimming options, shown in Figure 11-32. This command is useful for editing scanned images or images taken with a digital camera that include a border of color that you want to trim.

Figure 11-32: The Trim dialog box lets you trim unneeded edges from the image.

The Transparent Pixels option trims all the transparent pixels along the image edges. The Top Left Pixel Color and Bottom Right Pixel Color options trim all pixels that match the color of the top-left or bottom-right pixels. You can also select to trim just along the top, bottom, left, or right of an image.

Retouching images in Photoshop

Photoshop includes many tools to retouch an image. Most of these tools redistribute pixels by moving or copying pixels to other places within the same image. The tools used to retouch images include the Clone Stamp tool, the Pattern Stamp tool, the Healing Brush tool, the Spot Healing tool, the Patch tool, and the Color Replacement tool.

Using the Stamp tools

Two different Stamp tools are available in Photoshop, including the Clone Stamp tool and the Pattern Stamp tool.

The Clone Stamp tool allows you to paint pixels copied from a selected area to another area in the image. With the Clone Stamp tool selected, you can choose a brush tip and blending mode to use in the Options bar. Then hold down the Option/Alt key and click in the image to mark the area that you want to clone pixels from and paint in the area where you want to clone the pixels to.

If the Aligned option is selected, the pixels relative to the marked area are copied for every painted stroke. If the Aligned option is disabled, every new stroke starts painting from the marked area.

The Pattern Stamp tool works just like the Clone Stamp tool, except it lets you paint with the pattern selected in the Options bar.

Using the Healing Brush and Patch tools

The Healing Brush tool, like the Clone Stamp tool, lets you select an area of pixels where the painted pixels are taken from using the Option/Alt key. But the Healing Brush tool matches the surrounding pixels where they're painted, making the pixels blend in with the image. This tool is great for removing small imperfections from a scanned image or a digital photo.

The Patch tool can also copy an area of pixels to another area in the image, and the moved pixels are blended into their new area matching the surrounding pixels. With the Patch tool, you can drag to select a freehand area like the Lasso tool. You can add to the selection by dragging with the Shift key held down or remove from the selection by dragging with the Option/Alt key held down. Holding down the Shift+Option/Alt keys while dragging over the selection keeps only the intersected selection. You can also change the selection area using the Add, Subtract, and Intersection buttons on the Options bar.

After a selection is made, you can choose the Source option in the Options bar and drag from within the selection. This projects the area under the cursor to the selected area, and if you release the mouse, the displayed pixels are copied to the selected area.

If the Destination option in the Options bar is enabled, then you can drag the selected area to the pixels that you want to cover. Each time the mouse is released, the dragged area is copied over the area that it's on top of. Dragging and releasing the mouse lets you replace many areas quickly.

Using the Spot Healing Brush

One drawback to the Healing Brush is that you need to take time to select an area where the painted pixels are taken, but the Spot Healing Brush doesn't require this step. The Spot Healing Brush is specifically made to replace spots in the image by sampling pixels around the area. It provides a quick clean way to remove spots from images without the fuss. Figure 11-33 shows an original image and the same image fixed with the Spot Healing Brush. Notice how the bright reflection off the glass has been removed without drastically altering the image.

New Feature The Spot Healing Brush is new to Photoshop CS2.

Figure 11-33: The Spot Healing Brush can quickly remove spots from an image by sampling the pixels surrounding the area.

Using the Color Replacement tool

The Color Replacement tool, located as a fly-out under the Brush tool, may be used to replace a selected color with the foreground color. The Mode options let you choose to replace pixels based on Hue, Saturation, Color, or Luminosity. The Sampling options let you replace the pixels continuously, just once, or using the background swatch color to replace the background color with the foreground color.

The Limits options include Discontiguous, which replaces any colors that you paint over; Contiguous, which only paints connected areas of color; and Find Edges, which also replaces only connected areas of color but keeps the edges sharp.

Using the Eraser tools

Photoshop includes three different eraser tools used to remove pixels. The Erase tool removes pixels revealing the background color underneath. The Mode options let you choose a smooth edged brush, a hard-edged pencil, or a square block, which is useful to get the sharp corner areas. You can also set the opacity and flow to use as you erase. The Erase to History option removes all changes applied to an image, leaving the base saved image when enabled.

The Background Eraser tool is used to replace the background of an image with transparency. When you drag with this tool, the color that is immediately under the center of the tool is sampled and removed from the areas where you paint, but the other colors and the edges of the images are retained.

The Magic Eraser tool works like the Magic Wand tool, letting you click on a background color that you want to erase. All connected pixels (if the Contiguous option is enabled) are erased, or all similar pixels in the entire image are deleted (if the Contiguous option is disabled).

Distorting images

Another useful way to edit images is to distort the pixels using the various distorting tools. These tools include the Smudge tool, the Blur tool, the Sharpen tool, the Dodge tool, the Burn tool, and the Sponge tool.

The effects of these pixel distortion tools may also be accomplished using the various Filters, which are covered in Chapter 13.

- **Smudge tool:** Used to smear the color of several pixels together like wiping wet paint across the canvas. This tool lets you choose from several different modes and a Strength value. The Finger Painting option uses the foreground color as you begin to smear the pixels.

- **The Blur and Sharpen tools:** Are the opposite of each other. The Blur tool softens hard edges and reduces details, and the Sharpen tool makes edges harder and more pronounced.

- **Dodge and Burn tools:** Used, respectively, to lighten and darken the pixels of an image. For each tool, you can set the Range to lighten or darken the highlights, the midtones, or the shadows.

- **Sponge tool:** Increase or decrease the saturation of pixels in the image. For this tool, you can select a brush tip, a Flow amount, and a Mode to be either Saturate or Desaturate.

- **History Brush and Art History tools:** As you make changes to an image, you may want to return to the original image, but only in one section. The History Brush lets you paint over pixels and replace the painted area with the pixel from the saved image file.

    The Art History brush, like the History Brush tool, replaces the painted pixels with pixels from the original saved image file, but it paints them using a specialized Style simulating various famous artistic painting methods. These styles include Tight Short, Tight Medium, Tight Long, Loose Medium, Loose Long, Dab, Tight Curl, Tight Curl Long, Loose Curl, and Loose Curl Long.

Summary

- Photoshop allows you to acquire images from scanners and digital cameras and includes tools to clean up problems such as red eye and lens flaws.

- Many of Photoshop's key features let you correct and adjust images. You can make tonal adjustments with the Levels and Curve dialog boxes.

- In addition to acquiring loaded images, Photoshop can also create custom images using the Painting tools and a robust set of paintbrushes.

- You can also obtain images by rasterizing vector objects from Illustrator, but the reverse is also possible with Illustrator's new Live Trace feature.

- Photoshop includes several tools for selecting pixels including the Marquee tools and freehand tools like the Lasso tool. Pixels with similar colors are selected using the Magic Wand tool.

- However you decide to obtain Photoshop images, you have many tools to edit it, including features such as Crop, the Stamp and Healing Brush tools.

✦ ✦ ✦

Transforming Objects and Images

CHAPTER 12

In This Chapter

Transforming objects, fills, and images

Arranging stacking order

Aligning and distributing objects and images

After you select objects, you can easily move them by clicking and dragging them to a new location. You can also move selected images using Photoshop's Move tool, but there is much more to transforming than just dragging an object or image to a new location.

The CS2 applications include many different ways to transform objects and images. You can also use the bounding box that surrounds a selection to rotate and scale an object. Understanding the visual cursor cues allows you to transform objects without bothering with tools or menus.

Within the Photoshop, Illustrator, and InDesign toolboxes are several tools that are used to transform objects, such as the Rotate tool, the Scale tool, the Reflect tool, the Shear tool, and the Free Transform tool. If you choose Object ⇨ Transform or go to the Transform palette in Illustrator and InDesign, you can find even more features that enable you to transform objects in multiple ways with a single action.

In addition to covering altering a selection's position and orientation, this chapter also discusses stacking order, alignment, and distribution, all of which are nothing more than special transformation cases.

Transforming Objects in Illustrator

Objects are found in all the CS2 applications. The various transformation methods let you place those objects into the precise location needed to create an appealing design. Acrobat is the oddball among the group. In Acrobat, you can rotate pages and you can move objects, but you have no options for transforming objects on a PDF page. The remaining CS2 applications offer you tools and methods for transforming objects.

A selected object or group is identified by a bounding box that surrounds the object. The color of this bounding box is the layer color. If multiple objects are selected, the bounding box encompasses all the selected objects, as shown in Figure 12-1.

Selecting objects is covered in Chapter 10.

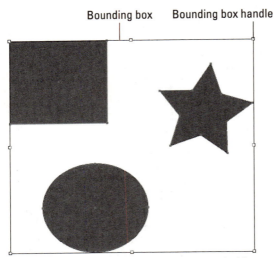

Figure 12-1: Selected objects are surrounded by a bounding box, which is the same color as the layer where the object appears.

You can move and scale even the simplest objects in all the CS2 applications using the bounding box. Clicking inside the bounding box and dragging moves the selected object. Dragging on one of the handles that surrounds the object scales its size. But these actions are common features, and the bounding-box features covered next enable a wider range of transformations.

Using the bounding box

Perhaps the easiest and certainly the quickest way to transform objects is to use the selection's bounding box. You can use bounding-box transformations in Illustrator, Photoshop, InDesign, and GoLive (except for rotate).

For all three of these applications, the bounding box is always rectangular and includes transformation handles at each corner and along each edge. By dragging these handles, you can scale or rotate an object using the Selection tool.

In Illustrator, you can hide the bounding box by choosing View ➪ Show/Hide Bounding Box (Shift+Ctrl+B in Windows; Shift+⌘+B on the Mac), or in Photoshop, by disabling the Show Bounding Box option in the Option bar when the Move tool is selected. If the bounding box isn't visible when an object is selected, check these options.

Moving objects

To move selected objects, you simply need to click on the object's path or fill and drag it to its new position. If you drag an object with the Option/Alt key held down, then a duplicate copy of the original object is moved and the original copy stays in its place. Holding down the Shift key while dragging an object constrains it to move along regular 45-degree angles.

In addition to dragging with the mouse, you can also move objects using the arrow keys. The distance that the object moves when pressing each arrow key is determined by the Keyboard Increment value set in the General panel of the Preferences dialog box, shown in Figure 12-2. The default is set to 1 point. Holding down the Shift key while pressing an arrow key moves the selected object ten times the increment value.

Cross-Reference For more information on adjusting preferences, see Chapter 3.

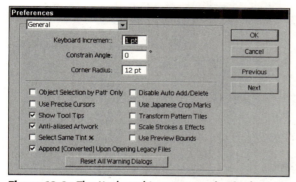

Figure 12-2: The Keyboard Increment value in the General panel of the Preferences dialog box determines the amount an object moves when you press the arrow keys.

Snapping objects

You can control where an object moves in Illustrator by choosing View ⇨ Snap to Grid (Shift+Ctrl+" in Windows; Shift+⌘+" on the Mac) and View ⇨ Snap to Point (Alt+Ctrl+" in Windows; Option+⌘+" on the Mac).

If the Snap to Grid option is enabled, the corner points of objects that are moved snap to align with the grid intersection points. This enables you to precisely position objects relative to one another. Make grids visible by choosing View ⇨ Show/Hide Grids. Set the grid size using the Guides & Grids panel in the Preferences dialog box.

The Snap to Point option aligns the point under the cursor when the selected object is clicked to the anchor point of another object or to a guideline. The cursor turns white when it's over a point to which it can snap.

Photoshop and InDesign also include snapping options. In Photoshop, you can select to snap to Guides, Grids, Slices, or Document Bounds using the View ⇨ Snap To menu command. Snapping functionality may be turned on and off using the View ⇨ Snap (Shift+⌘/Ctrl+;) menu command. InDesign includes commands in the View menu to Snap to Guides (Shift+⌘/Ctrl+;) and Snap to Document Grid (Shift+⌘/Ctrl+').

Rotating objects

When you move the Selection tool cursor near one of the bounding-box handles, the cursor changes. When the cursor looks like two small arrows and a curved line, you can drag the object to rotate it about its center point. Figure 12-3 shows three selected objects in Illustrator being rotated by dragging on its bounding box when the rotate cursor is visible.

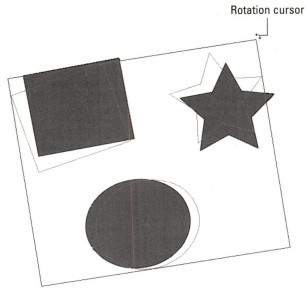

Figure 12-3: When the rotation cursor displays, you can rotate the selected object about its center point.

Rotating an object also rotates its bounding box. If you want to reset the bounding box in Illustrator, you can choose Object ⇨ Transform ⇨ Reset Bounding Box.

When objects are selected in Photoshop, a Reference Point is positioned within the center of the object. If the object is moved or scaled, the reference point remains in the center, but if you click and drag, you can reposition the reference point. This reference point is used to define the center about which the object is rotated. It can be positioned anywhere within the canvas.

Note

When an object is selected within InDesign, its bounding box doesn't enable rotation. InDesign objects can be rotated using the Object ⇨ Transform ⇨ Rotate menu command or with the Rotation tool, but not using its bounding box.

Scaling and reflecting objects

Positioning the cursor directly over one of the bounding-box handles changes it to a double-headed arrow, and dragging the object with this cursor scales the object, as shown in Figure 12-4. If you drag a corner, the object scales horizontally and vertically; if you drag on one of the segment midpoint handles, the object scales in a single dimension.

Holding down the Shift key while dragging one of the corner handles constrains the scaling to be uniform so that no distortion is introduced. Holding down the Option/Alt key while dragging scales the object about the center of the bounding box. Figure 12-5 shows an object that has been scaled with the Shift and Option/Alt keys held down. Notice how all objects have been scaled equally from the center outward.

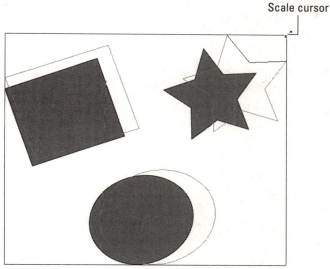

Figure 12-4: Dragging a selected object when the Scale cursor is displayed scales the object.

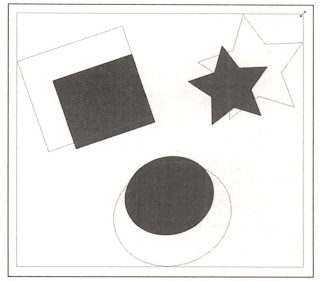

Figure 12-5: Scaling objects with the Shift key held down maintains the proportions of the object; with the Option/Alt key held down, it scales the objects about the selection center.

If you drag one of the handles through the object to its opposite side, the object is reflected about the bounding-box sides through which it was dragged.

Using the transform tools

The third section of tools in both the Illustrator Toolbox and the InDesign Toolbox includes several tools that you can use to transform objects. These tools include the Rotate, Scale, Reflect, Shear, and Free Transform tools, as shown in Figure 12-6.

Note   The Shear tool in Illustrator is located as a flyout under the Scale tool and the Reflect tool is a flyout under the Rotate tool. InDesign doesn't include a Reflect tool.

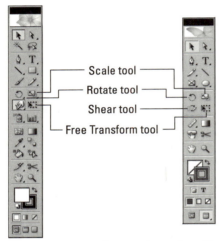

Figure 12-6: Transform tools are found in the Toolbox in Illustrator and in InDesign.

Double-clicking on any of these tools opens a dialog box where you may enter precise values.

Using the Rotate tool

When the Rotate tool is selected, the rotation center for the selected object, called the reference point, is positioned in the center of the object as indicated by a small circle icon with four small lines extending from it, as shown in Figure 12-7. Dragging in the art board rotates the selected object, but if you click in the art board with the Rotate tool, you can position the rotation center. Any dragging then rotates about the new rotation center. Holding down the Shift key rotates the selected object using 45-degree increments.

If you double-click on the Rotate tool or choose Object ⇨ Transform ⇨ Rotate command in Illustrator or InDesign, a simple dialog box opens, shown in Figure 12-8. Here, you can enter a precise Angle value. The Copy button rotates a duplicate copy of the object and leaves the original object in its place.

Figure 12-7: The rotation reference point marks the center about which the rotation takes place.

Figure 12-8: The Rotate dialog box

Using the Scale tool

The Scale tool works like the Rotate tool in that the scale point is positioned initially in the center of the selected object, but by clicking on the art board, you can place it in a different location. Dragging up and down scales the selected object in the vertical direction; dragging left and right scales the selected object in the horizontal direction about the scale point. Holding down the Shift key while dragging constrains the scaling, making it uniform or equal both horizontally and vertically.

Double-clicking on the Scale tool or choosing Object ⇨ Transform ⇨ Scale opens a dialog box, shown in Figure 12-9, where you can choose to scale the selected object uniformly or non-uniformly using precise values. The Copy button scales a duplicate copy using the scale values and leaving the original object in place. You can also enable the Scale Strokes & Effects option, which scales any strokes and effects added to the object along with the object. If disabled, the strokes and effects maintain their original size and only the path is scaled.

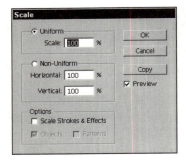

Figure 12-9: The Scale dialog box lets you scale an object in a uniform or non-uniform manner.

Using the Reflect tool

The Reflect tool allows you to flip the selected object about an axis. To select the axis about which to flip the selected object, click once to place one point of the axis line and click a second time to define the second point of the axis line. When you click a second time, the selected object is reflected about this line. Figure 12-10 shows several selected objects that have been reflected about an imaginary axis created by clicking two times in the art board.

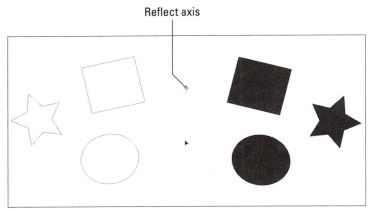

Figure 12-10: The Reflect tool mirrors the selected object on the opposite side of a designated axis.

If you hold down the Option/Alt key while clicking the second point, a copy of the original object is reflected. If you drag after clicking the second point, you can control the position of the reflected object; holding down the Shift key constrains the axis to 45-degree increments.

 The Reflect tool is only available in Illustrator, as a fly-out under the Rotate tool, but you can flip objects in InDesign and Photoshop using menu commands.

The Reflect dialog box, shown in Figure 12-11, opened by double-clicking on the Reflect tool or by choosing Object ⇨ Transform ⇨ Reflect, lets you reflect the selected object horizontally, vertically, or about a specified angle. The dialog box also includes a Copy button.

Figure 12-11: The Reflect dialog box lets you reflect the selected object horizontally, vertically, or about a designated angle.

Using the Shear tool

The Shear tool is a fly-out under the Scale tool in Illustrator. It lets you distort the selected object by moving the opposite bounding-box edges in opposite directions. Dragging up and down shears the object vertically; dragging left and right shears the object horizontally. Clicking twice in the art board lets you place a shear axis, just like the Reflect tool. If the shear axis is located below an object, the entire object slants in the same direction with portions farther from the shear axis being sheared to a greater extent. Holding down the Shift key maintains the height or width of the object as it's sheared. Figure 12-12 shows several objects that have been sheared to the right. The square background was added to make the shear effect more obvious.

Figure 12-12: Placing the shear axis below the object causes the entire object to be sheared in one direction.

The Shear dialog box, shown in Figure 12-13, lets you specify a shear angle and the shear axis as horizontal, vertical, or a specified angle.

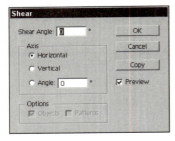

Figure 12-13: The Shear dialog box lets you specify the amount of shear with the shear angle and the axis about which the shear takes place.

Using the Free Transform tool

The Free Transform tool enables you to perform all the transformations with a single tool. In many ways, it works just like the bounding box, but it has some additional features built in. Moving, rotating, scaling, and reflecting work just like with the bounding box, but you can also shear an object by holding down Ctrl+Alt (⌘+Option on the Mac) while dragging sideways on one of the side handles.

 Note In Photoshop, you can enable free transformation of paths using the Edit ⇨ Free Transform Path (⌘/Ctrl+T) menu command.

Another unique feature of the Free Transform tool is that you can distort the selected object by moving a single bounding box corner without moving any of the other corner points. To do this, start dragging a corner handle and then press the ⌘/Ctrl key to move only the selected point. Figure 12-14 shows the selected objects in the process of being distorted in this way by dragging its upper-right corner handle.

Figure 12-14: You can distort the bounding box by moving a single corner handle by holding down the ⌘/Ctrl key and dragging with the Free Transform tool.

You can also use the Free Transform tool to alter perspective by moving two corner points at the same time. You can accomplish this by dragging a corner point and then holding down Shift+Ctrl+Alt (Shift+⌘+Option on the Mac) at the same time. Figure 12-15 shows an object whose perspective has been altered using the Free Transform tool.

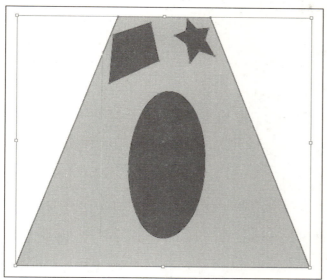

Figure 12-15: Dragging a bounding-box corner handle with the Free Transform tool while holding down Shift+Ctrl+Alt (Shift+⌘+Option on the Mac) alters an object's perspective.

Note   The Free Transform tool has no dialog box that opens when you double-click on the tool.

STEPS: Transforming in Illustrator

1. **Create a symbol.** Create a sample object in Illustrator or drag an object from the Symbols palette. The symbol for these steps comes from the Logos Symbol Library accessed by choosing Window ⇨ Symbol Libraries ⇨ Logo Elements.

2. **Select the object.** With the Selection tool, click on the symbol to select it. A bounding box surrounds the selected object.

3. **Create several duplicate copies.** Click on the symbol and begin to drag it downward. Then press and hold down the Shift and Option/Alt keys to create an aligned duplicate underneath the original. Repeat this step until six planets are aligned, as shown in Figure 12-16.

Figure 12-16: Dragging an object with the Option/Alt key held down moves a duplicate copy and keeps the original.

4. **Use the Rotate tool.** Select the second planet and double-click on the Rotate tool. In the Rotate dialog box, set the Angle value to 60 and click OK. The second planet is rotated so its rings are almost vertical.

5. **Use the Scale tool.** Select the third planet and double-click on the Scale tool. In the Scale dialog box, select the Non-Uniform option and set the Horizontal value to 60% and the Vertical value to 120%. Then click OK.

6. **Use the Reflect tool.** Select the fourth planet and click on the Scale tool. Click to the right of the planet and click again directly below the first click to form a vertical axis. Drag with the Option/Alt key held down to create a reflected duplicate of the planet to the right.

7. **Use the Shear tool.** Select the fifth planet and double-click on the Shear tool. In the Shear dialog box, enter **45** for the Shear Angle and choose the Horizontal axis. Then click OK. The planet is elongated by fitting it into a stretched bounding box.

8. **Use the Free Transform tool.** Select the sixth planet and choose the Free Transform tool. Drag the upper-right corner while holding down the Option/Alt key to scale the object about its center. Figure 12-17 shows all the resulting transformed planets.

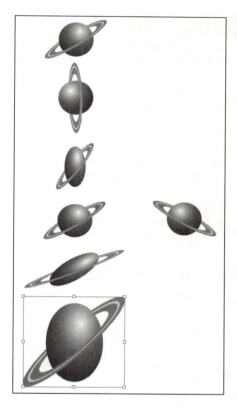

Figure 12-17: Each of these planets was transformed using a different transform tool.

Using the Transform menu

The Object ➪ Transform menu in Illustrator and InDesign includes several commands to open the dialog boxes for the various transform tools. You may access these same dialog boxes by double-clicking on the respective tool in the Toolbox, but the Transform menu in Illustrator also includes some additional commands such as Transform Again, Transform Each and Reset Bounding Box. In Illustrator, choosing Object ➪ Transform ➪ Move (Shift+Ctrl+M in Windows; Shift+⌘+M on the Mac) opens the Move dialog box, shown in Figure 12-18, where you can enter precise values to move an object. You can also move objects by selecting Angle and Distance values.

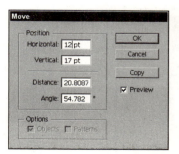

Figure 12-18: The Move dialog box lets you specify an object's horizontal and vertical position values or move an object a given distance along a specified angle.

Photoshop also includes several menu commands for transforming paths. These are located in the Edit ⇨ Transform Path menu and include commands such as Again, Scale, Rotate, Skew, Distort, Perspective, and several Rotate and Flip options. None of these menu commands open a dialog box, but they allow the path's bounding box to be transformed in a certain way. If the active layer includes pixels or text, they also can be transformed by choosing Edit ⇨ Transform.

Using Transform Again

Choosing Object ⇨ Transform ⇨ Transform Again (⌘/Ctrl+D) in Illustrator repeats the last transformation again. This enables you to quickly create multiple aligned copies of an object.

For example, if you select and move an object downward with the Shift and Option/Alt keys held down, the result is a duplicate copy of the object that is positioned directly under the first. After this is done, you can use the Transform Again menu command to quickly create a whole column of objects.

A similar command is found in Photoshop, Edit ⇨ Transform ⇨ Again (Shift+Ctrl+T in Windows; Shift+⌘+T on the Mac). This command repeats the last applied transformation, which may include multiple transformations, to the selected object.

STEPS: Creating an Array of Objects in Illustrator

1. **Create an object to duplicate.** Create or select an object that you want to duplicate many times in a repeating pattern. A simple symbol like this planet may be used.

2. **Select the object.** With the Selection tool, click on the symbol to select it. A bounding box surrounds the selected object.

3. **Create a single duplicate copy.** Click on the symbol and begin to drag the symbol downward, then press and hold down the Shift and Option/Alt keys to create an aligned duplicate underneath the original.

4. **Use the Transform Again command.** Choose Object ⇨ Transform Again (⌘/Ctrl+D) to repeat the transformation. This creates a third planet object that is moved the same distance as the first duplicate. Hold down the ⌘/Ctrl key and press the D key six more times to create a column of planets that are equally spaced, as shown in Figure 12-19.

Figure 12-19: You can choose Object ⇨ Transform ⇨ Transform Each to quickly and precisely repeat a transformation operation several times.

5. **Select the column of planets.** With the Selection tool, drag over the entire column of planets to select them all.

6. **Create a duplicate column.** Begin to drag the selected planets to the right, then press and hold down the Shift and Option/Alt keys to constrain the movements of the planets to the horizon, and the Option/Alt key creates a duplicate column of planets.

7. **Use the Transform Again command.** Choose Object ⇨ Transform Again (⌘/Ctrl+D) and press the ⌘/Ctrl+D keyboard shortcut four more times. The resulting array of planets, shown in Figure 12-20, was created fairly quickly.

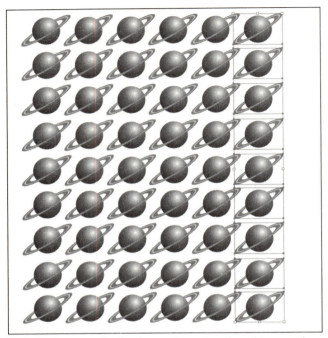

Figure 12-20: By duplicating and transforming objects and then using the Transform Again menu command, you can quickly and easily create an array of objects.

Using Transform Again in InDesign

The Transform Again feature is also found in InDesign. Every transformation applied to an object is remembered and can be reapplied to another selection using the Object ➪ Transform Again menu command. Transformations that are remembered include moving, scaling, rotating, resizing, reflecting, shearing and fitting.

 Transform Again is a new feature to InDesign CS2.

The Transform Again menu in InDesign includes four different options:

✦ **Transform Again:** This option applies the last single transformation to the selected object.

✦ **Transform Again Individually:** This option applies the last single transformation to all selected objects separately instead of as a group.

- **Transform Sequence Again:** This option applies the last sequence of transformations to the selected object.
- **Transform Sequence Again Individually:** This option applies the last sequence of transformations to all selected objects separately instead of as a group.

Using the Transform Each dialog box

In Illustrator, choosing Object ⇨ Transform ⇨ Transform Each (Alt+Shit+Ctrl+D in Windows; Option+Shift+⌘+D on the Mac) opens the Transform Each dialog box, shown in Figure 12-21. This dialog box combines several transformations into a single location and includes Scale, Move, and Rotate values. It also includes options to Reflect an object about the X or Y axis.

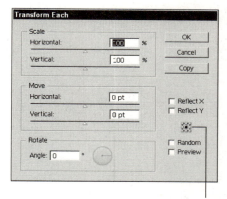

Reference point selector

Figure 12-21: The Transform Each dialog box combines the transformation values of several different transformations into a single dialog box.

The small icon underneath the Reflect options lets you select the point about which the selected object is transformed. The selected transformation point is marked black. You can click on any of these points to specify the transformation point, which could be the object center, any object corner, or any object side.

The Random option chooses a random value between the default value and the specified value and applies the transformation using these random values. To see some of the random possibilities, enable and disable the Preview option multiple times to see some of the random transformations. Figure 12-22 shows many random stars created using the Random option in the Transform Each dialog box.

Figure 12-22: Enabling the Random option in the Transform Each dialog box produced a varied assortment of stars.

STEPS: Creating a Flower in Illustrator

1. **Create a simple path.** Click on the Paintbrush tool and drag in the art board to create a simple, mostly vertical line. In the Stroke palette, set the Weight to 3 pt, select the Round Cap button, and set the color to a dark red, as shown in Figure 12-23.

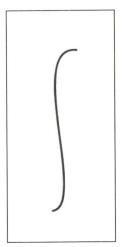

Figure 12-23: You can place the path near the middle of the document to create a simple path with the Paintbrush tool.

2. **Open the Transform Each dialog box.** Choose Object ➪ Transform ➪ Transform Each (Alt+Shift+Ctrl+D in Windows; Option+Shift+⌘+D on the Mac) to open the Transform Each dialog box. Set the Horizontal and Vertical Scale values to 100% and the Move values to 0. Then set the Rotate value to 360 degrees, select the center point as the reference point and enable the Random option. Then click Copy to close the dialog box and create a copy that is randomly rotated about its center point. Figure 12-24 shows the Transform Each dialog box after the values have been set.

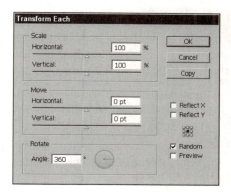

Figure 12-24: The Transform Each dialog box with the Random option enabled randomly rotates the selected object.

3. **Create duplicate objects.** With the duplicate selected, reopen the Transform Each dialog box using the Alt+Shift+Ctrl+D (Option+Shift+⌘+D keyboard shortcut, and click Copy again or simply press Command/Ctrl+D. Repeat this step until enough copies are created to fill in the flower.

4. **Add a flower center.** Create a simple circle with the Ellipse tool and set its fill color to a bright yellow. Then drag the circle to the center of the flower. The resulting flower is shown in Figure 12-25.

Figure 12-25: Using the Random option in the Transform Each dialog box and the Copy button, you can create a flower.

Rotating and flipping InDesign objects

You can quickly rotate and/or flip selected objects in InDesign using the popup up menu at the right end of the Options bar. The menu commands found there include Rotate 180 Degrees, Rotate 90 Degrees Clockwise, Rotate 90 Degrees Counterclockwise, Flip Horizontal, Flip Vertical, and Flip Both.

Rotating and flipping in Photoshop

Photoshop includes some menu commands found in the Edit ⇨ Transform Path menu to rotate and/or flip the selected object. The options include Rotate 180 Degrees, Rotate 90 Degrees CS, Rotate 90 Degrees CCW, Flip Horizontal and Flip Vertical. The commands apply to text and pixels also.

Photoshop also includes commands to rotate and flip the entire Canvas. These commands are useful if you need to transform all objects. The commands are located in the Image ⇨ Rotate Canvas menu and include 180 Degrees, 90 Degrees CW, 90 Degrees CCW, Arbitrary (which lets you select an Angle value), Flip Canvas Horizontal, and Flip Canvas Vertical.

Using the Transform palette

In addition to the bounding box, tools, and menus, several of the CS2 applications include a Transform palette including Illustrator, InDesign and GoLive.

Using the Transform palette in Illustrator and InDesign

Illustrator's Transform palette, shown in Figure 12-26 and which you can open by choosing Window ⇨ Transform, displays information about the object's position and size. By changing these values, you can transform the selected object. The Transform palette in InDesign looks and acts the same.

Figure 12-26: The Transform palette displays information about the position and dimensions of the selected object.

The X and Y values denote the horizontal and vertical positions of the reference point selected using the icon at the left of the Transform palette relative to the art board's lower-left corner. For example, if the object's center point is selected and the object is positioned on the page 100 points above the bottom of the art board and 50 points from the left edge, then the X and Y values in the Transform palette would be 100 pt and 50 pt. Changing the X and Y values in the Transform palette moves the selected object.

Note All of the same values found in the Transform palette are also displayed in the Options bar in InDesign.

The W and H values denote the object's Width and Height. Clicking the link icon to the right of these values links the values together, so that changing one automatically changes the other. Changing the W and H values in the Transform palette scales the selected object. If the link icon is enabled, changing the values causes the selected object to be scaled uniformly.

At the bottom of the Transform palette are Rotate and Shear values. Changing these values causes the selected object to be rotated or sheared the given amount. InDesign's Transform palette also includes values for the Scale X and Scale Y Percentage values. These values can be linked to stay equal.

Illustrator's Transform palette may also be used to reflect the selected object using the Flip Horizontal or Flip Vertical palette menu commands. The palette menu also includes an option to Scale Strokes & Effects and options to Transform the object only, the pattern only, or both.

The palette menu options for the Transform palette in InDesign are different than the options in Illustrator. Within InDesign, you can select options to Scale Text Attributes, Transform Group Content and Reset Scaling to 100%. There are also options to Rotate and Flip the selected object.

At the bottom of InDesign's Transform palette menu are several toggle options that can be enabled including Transform Content, Dimensions Include Stroke Weight, Transformations are Totals, Show Content Offset and Scale Strokes. The Transform Content option causes the content within the selected frame to be transformed along with the frame when enabled. The Dimensions Include Stroke Weight option changes the Width and Height displayed values to include the stroke weight.

The Transformations are Totals option causes the displayed transformation values to be absolute relative to the document. For example, if a selected image inside a rotated frame is also rotated even further, enabling the Transformation are Totals option would display the image's angle relative to the bottom of the document page and disabling the Transformations are Total option would display a rotation value that includes the rotation values of both the image and its frame.

The Show Content Offset option is used when content is selected within the frame. It displays the amount that the content is offset from the frame's reference point. When an offset value is displayed, two small plus signs appear next to the X and Y values, as shown in Figure 12-27.

Offset indicators

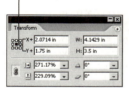

Figure 12-27: Two small plus signs appear in InDesign's Transform palette when the Show Content Offset option is enabled.

Using the GoLive Transform palette

GoLive also includes a Transform palette, shown in Figure 12-28, which displays the Position and Size values of the selected GoLive object, which may include a layer, objects on a Layout Grid, or image map hotspots. Using this palette, you can edit the position and size of the various elements relative to the upper-left corner of the Web page (for layers) or the upper-left corner of the Layout Grid.

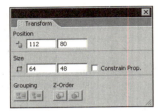

Figure 12-28: The Transform palette in GoLive displays Position and Size information for the selected object.

GoLive layers are quite a bit different from the layers used in the other CS2 applications. The GoLive layers stem from HTML code and refer to areas that can hold text and images that may be stacked one on top of another.

You can learn more about GoLive's layers in Chapter 14.

The stacking order for GoLive layers is determined by a Z-Index value, which is set in the Inspector palette when a layer object is selected.

Transforming Patterns and Fills

When an object is filled with a solid color, rotating the object has no affect on the fill color. However, if an object is filled with a gradient or a pattern, rotating an object may or may not impact the filled gradient or pattern depending on the setting in the Transform palette.

Transforming patterns in Illustrator

Using Illustrator's Transform palette menu, you can select to apply a transformation to the object only, the pattern only, or to both. When the Pattern Only option is selected, a small warning icon appears in the lower-left corner of the Transform palette, as shown in Figure 12-29, to remind you that any transformations are applied only to the pattern.

Selecting the Pattern Only option in the Transform palette applies only to transformations that are done using the Transform palette. Transformations completed using the transform tools or by choosing Object ⇨ Transform are determined by the respective transformation dialog boxes.

Figure 12-29: A small warning icon appears in the lower-left corner of the Transform palette when the Pattern Only option is selected.

To transform a pattern or gradient using one of the transform tools or the Object ⇨ Transform menu, you need to enable the Patterns option in the dialog box for the selected transformation. Each transform dialog box includes options for selecting objects and patterns. Enabling the Patterns option applies the transformation to the pattern.

STEPS: Rotating a Pattern in Illustrator

1. **Create a filled object.** Select the Ellipse tool and drag in the art board to create a simple ellipse object. In the Swatches palette, select a striped pattern as the fill. The stripes run horizontally across the ellipse object, as shown in Figure 12-30.

Figure 12-30: An ellipse object filled with a striped pattern that runs horizontally across the object

2. **Select and duplicate the object.** With the Selection tool, click on the ellipse object to select it. Then drag it downward with the Option/Alt key held down to create a duplicate copy.

3. **Create a single duplicate copy.** Then choose Object ⇨ Transform ⇨ Transform Again to duplicate another ellipse for a total of three.

4. **Enable the Transform Pattern Only option.** Choose Window ⇨ Transform to open the Transform palette. In the palette menu, select the Transform Pattern Only option. A warning icon appears in the bottom-left corner of the Transform palette.

5. **Rotate the pattern.** Select the second ellipse object and type **45** in the Rotate field of the Transform palette. The pattern within the ellipse is rotated.

6. **Enable the Transform Both option.** In the Transform palette menu, select the Transform Both option.

7. **Rotate the pattern.** Select the third ellipse object and type **90** in the Rotate field of the Transform palette. The pattern and the ellipse are both rotated. Figure 12-31 shows the resulting rotations.

Figure 12-31: Using the options available in the Transform palette, you can rotate just the object, just the pattern, or both.

Transforming patterns in Photoshop

When a path or shape is created in Photoshop, it is automatically filled with the Foreground color. This color of the selected object may be changed to a pattern or a fill using the Layer ⇨ Change Layer Content ⇨ Pattern menu command. Applying this menu command opens a dialog box, shown in Figure 12-32, where you can select a pattern from the available presets and set the Scale of the pattern. The Snap to Origin button realigns the pattern so the upper-left corner of the pattern corresponds to the upper-left corner of the object.

Figure 12-32: The Pattern Fill dialog box lets you scale the pattern used to fill an object. A similar scale setting is also available for Gradients.

Once a pattern or a gradient is applied to a path or shape, a fill thumbnail appears in the Layers palette next to the Vector Mask. Double-clicking this fill thumbnail in the Layers palette opens the Pattern Fill dialog box again where you can change the Scale value.

Cross-Reference

More on working with layers is covered in Chapter 14.

A pixel selection may also be filled with a pattern using the Layer ➪ New Fill Layer ➪ Pattern menu command. This menu command creates a new layer and opens a dialog box where you can name the layer, choose a layer color, and set the blending mode and Opacity value. The Pattern Fill dialog box then opens letting you select a pattern and set a scale value.

Another way to apply a pattern to a layer is with the Pattern Overlay layer effect. To apply a layer effect, select a layer in the Layers palette and choose the Layer ➪ Layer Style ➪ Pattern Overlay menu command. Layer effects may be applied to any layer and all pixels or objects on that layer are covered with the selected pattern. Using the Layer Style dialog box, shown in Figure 12-33, you can set the pattern's blending mode, Opacity and Scale.

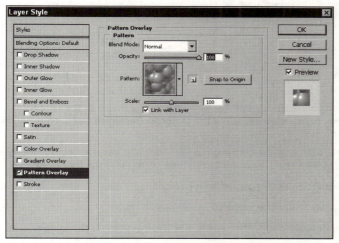

Figure 12-33: The Layer Style dialog box lets you overlay an object with a pattern. The pattern may also be scaled.

Note Although patterns may be scaled and repositioned in Photoshop, there isn't any way to rotate a pattern once it is applied. Gradients, however, include both Angle and Scale controls that allow you to rotate and scale applied gradients.

Transforming content in InDesign

InDesign is unique in how it handles content positioned within objects because all content in InDesign are placed within containers such as a frame or a drawn object. Images and drawings are added to a document using the File ⇨ Place menu command. InDesign lets you change the move, rotate, and scale a container and its content together or independently.

With a frame that holds some content selected, the Options bar lists the position and dimensions of the selected frame, as well as its Scale, Rotate, and Shear values. At the right end of the Options bar, shown in Figure 12-34, are two buttons that let you select the container, select the content, or select the previous or next object in a group. If you select the content then the values in the Options bar are updated, a new bounding box appears that shows the dimensions of the content and all transform tools may be used to transform the content independent of the container. These buttons are also available as menu commands in the Object ⇨ Select menu.

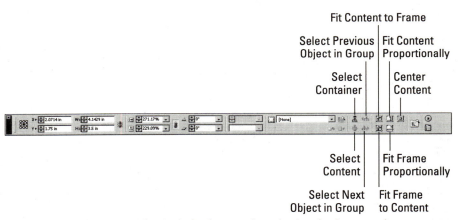

Figure 12-34: The Options bar includes buttons for selecting the frame or the content. Whichever is selected may be transformed using the Object ⇨ Transform menu commands.

When a filled container is selected, the Options bar also includes several buttons for synching the size of the content with the container. These buttons include the following:

✦ **Fit Content to Frame:** Scales the placed image to fit the frame.

✦ **Fit Frame to Content:** Scales the frame to fit the placed image.

✦ **Fill Frame Proportionally:** Proportionally scales the frame to fill the image.

✦ **Fit Content Proportionally:** Proportionally scales the placed image to fit within the frame.

✦ **Center Content:** Moves the placed image so its center matches the frame without scaling the image.

These buttons are also found in the Object ⇨ Fitting menu. The keyboard shortcuts are Fit Content to Frame (Option/Alt+⌘/Ctrl+E), Fit Frame to Content (Option/Alt+⌘/Ctrl+C), Fill Frame Proportionally (Shift+Option/Alt+⌘/Ctrl+C), Center Content (Shift+⌘/Ctrl+E), and Fit Content Proportionally (Option/Alt+Shift+⌘/Ctrl+E). Figure 12-35 shows each of these options applied to an image placed in a frame.

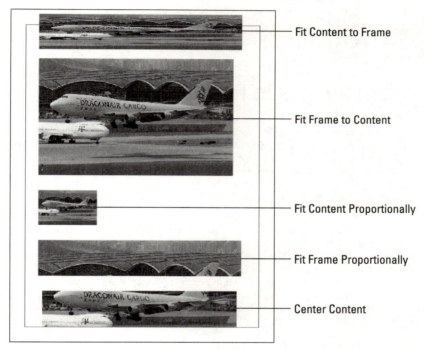

Figure 12-35: InDesign includes several methods for automatically scaling content and frames.

Each of the transform dialog boxes available from the Object ⇨ Transform menu, including Move, Rotate, Scale and Shear, includes a Transform Content option, such as the Shear Content option shown in Figure 12-36. If this option is enabled, then the specified transformation is applied to both the frame and the content. If this option is disabled, the transformation is applied only to the frame. If the content is selected, this option isn't available.

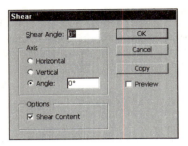

Figure 12-36: Each of the transform dialog boxes in InDesign includes an option to transform the content along with the frame.

Transforming Images in Photoshop

Images in Illustrator and InDesign are contained within objects and may not be selected or edited using pixel selections. But in Photoshop, pixel selections are very common, and they have several tricky aspects when dealing with transformations. One of the key differences between transforming objects and transforming images is that image selections are usually not rectangular, depending on the selection tool that was used. But if the Move tool is selected, a rectangular bounding box is placed about the selection. Using the bounding box, you can move, rotate and scale the selected pixels in a manner that is the same as that used for objects.

Another key aspect of transforming images is that every time you apply a transformation to pixel selection, you potentially alter the selection. Applying multiple successive transformations to a pixel selection distorts the pixels. To limit this effect, Photoshop keeps track of all the transformations that are made to a pixel selection at one time. Then when a different tool is selected, a confirmation dialog box, shown in Figure 12-37, appears asking if you want to apply the transformation with buttons for Apply, Cancel, and Don't Apply. By waiting until all the desired transformations are completed before applying them, the number of actual transformations is minimized and the fidelity of the pixel selection is maximized.

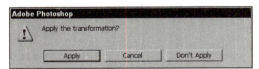

Figure 12-37: This confirmation dialog appears after several transformation operations have been combined within Photoshop.

Translating a selection

When a selection is made, marching ants surround the selection and show the selected area. If you choose the Select ⇨ Transform Selection menu command, then a bounding box surrounds the selection. Using this bounding box, the options in the Options bar or the Edit ⇨ Transform menu commands, you can transform the selection without altering the pixels within the selection.

Moving pixels

When an area of pixels is selected with one of the Marquee tools, dragging the selection with the Marquee tool has no impact on the pixels; instead, it moves only the selection. To move the selected pixels, you need to select the Move tool. With the Move tool selected, you can click within the selection and drag it to move the actual pixels. Figure 12-38 shows an image where a pixel selection has been moved using the Move tool.

Figure 12-38: Moving a pixel selection with the Move tool can abruptly alter the continuity of an image.

Holding down the Option/Alt key while dragging a pixel selection creates a duplicate copy of the pixels and leaves the original pixels in place. Holding down the Shift key while dragging a pixel selection constrains the movement to regular 45-degree angles.

Using Free Transform

Photoshop's Edit ⇨ Free Transform (⌘/Ctrl+T) menu command places a bounding box around the selection or encloses all objects on the current layer within a bounding box if there is no selection.

This bounding box works just like the bounding boxes used to transform objects. Clicking within the bounding box and dragging moves the selection. Dragging one of the corner or side handles scales the selection; moving the cursor near one of the handles until it changes to a rotation icon allows you to rotate the selection. You can also reflect an object by dragging it through its opposite side.

Holding down the Shift key while dragging a corner handle causes uniform scaling; holding down the Shift key while moving constrains the movements to 45-degree angles; and holding down the Shift key while rotating constrains the rotations to 15-degree increments.

To scale opposite handles relative to the reference point, hold down the Option/Alt key while dragging. To move a corner handle independent of the other corner handles, hold down the ⌘/Ctrl key while dragging. To shear the selection, hold down the Shift+Ctrl keys (Shift+⌘ on the Mac) while dragging a side handle. Finally, to alter perspective, drag with the Shift+Alt+Ctrl keys (Shift+Option+⌘ on the Mac) held down.

With the Free Transform command selected, the values for the various transformations appear on the Options bar, as shown in Figure 12-39. The Reference Point icon lets you select the position about which the transformations take place. The X and Y values denote the position of the reference point relative to the upper-left corner of the image. The W and H values denote the Width and Height of the selection's bounding box. The final three values are the rotation, horizontal, and vertical shear values.

 Note The link icon between the W and H values links the W and H values together so that altering one automatically alters the other. This causes all scaling to be uniform.

Figure 12-39: When the Free Transform command is selected, various transformation values appear in the Options bar.

Using the Transform menu

In Photoshop, choosing Edit ⇨ Transform ⇨ Again (Shift+Ctrl+T in Windows; Shift+⌘+T on the Mac) causes the last transformation to be repeated.

If remembering all the various keyboard keys to use for the various transformations is tricky, you can select the specific type of transformation that you want to apply to the object from the Edit ⇨ Transform menu. The options include Scale, Rotate, Skew, Distort, and Perspective.

The Edit ⇨ Transform menu also includes commands to rotate 180 degrees, rotate 90 degrees clockwise, rotate 90 degrees counterclockwise, flip horizontal, and flip vertical. The rotations and flipping takes place about the designated reference point.

Controlling perspective

Photoshop includes a transform feature for changing the perspective of an image selection. With a selection made, choose Edit ⇨ Transform ⇨ Perspective and the selection is surrounded with a handled box. Clicking and dragging any of the corner or edge handles changes the perspective for the selection. Figure 12-40 shows an example where a portion of an image has been altered in its perspective.

 Cross-Reference Photoshop includes a valuable feature for setting and painting in perspective view called Vanishing Point. This feature is covered in Chapter 13.

Figure 12-40: Choose Edit ⇨ Transform ⇨ Perspective to change the perspective of the selected area.

You can also set perspective using the Crop tool by enabling the Perspective option in the Control bar. This tool changes the perspective when the image is cropped.

Using Image Warp

In addition to the Free Transform mode, Photoshop includes another unique transformation method called Warp mode. Warp mode covers the current selection with a grid that you can modify by dragging its control points.

The ability to warp images in Photoshop is new to CS2.

To access Warp mode, choose Edit ⇨ Transform ⇨ Warp. This makes the Warp commands available in the Control bar at the top of the interface. The warp settings on the Control bar include a drop-down list of warp presets including Arc, Arc Lower, Arc Upper, Arch, Bulge, Shell Lower, Shell Upper, Flag, Wave, Fish, Rise, Fisheye, Inflate, Squeeze, and Twist. When a warp preset is selected, settings for controlling the amount of bend and vertical and horizontal distortion display to the left of the drop-down list in the Control bar. There is also a button for controlling the warp orientation.

If the warp presets look familiar, then you probably remember seeing them in Illustrator's Effects menu or in Photoshop's Type Warp presets. You can see examples of each in Chapter 13.

At the right end of the Control bar are buttons for switching between Warp and Free Transform modes, and canceling or committing the transform. Figure 12-41 shows an image warped with the Squeeze preset.

Figure 12-41: Using the Transform Warp Mode, you can bend, twist, and distort image selections.

Arranging Stacking Order

The order in which objects are displayed or printed is determined by the stacking order. This order places the object at the bottom of the stacking order on the document first and then stacks each additional object in order on the document up to the top object. If an object that is higher in the stacking order is placed on top of an existing object, and if the top object doesn't include any transparency, the lower object is obscured.

When objects are created, each new object is placed higher in the stacking order than those already created.

Controlling stacking order using layers

The easiest way to control stacking order is using layers. Layers at the top of the Layers palette have a higher stacking order and appear on top of all layers below it. By placing objects on a new higher layer, you may be assured that it appears above the objects on a lower layer.

Layers and the Layers palette are covered in more detail in Chapter 14.

Layers provide a way to control stacking order, but within a single layer, objects may be stacked on top of one another. If you expand a layer in Illustrator by clicking on the arrow button to the left of the layer name, all objects within the layer are visible, as shown in Figure 12-42. The expanded objects in the Layers palette are listed in their stacking order with the top objects toward the top of the Layers palette.

Figure 12-42: You can make all the objects contained on a single layer visible by expanding the layer.

If you select and drag an object in the Layers palette and drop it above another object, the stacking order is changed.

You can also reverse the order of several objects or layers using the Reverse Order palette menu command in the Layers palette. To use this command, select several adjacent objects or layers by selecting a layer and holding down the Shift key and clicking on the last sequential layer, then selecting the Reverse Order palette menu command.

Illustrator also includes the Object ➪ Arrange ➪ Send to Current Layer menu command, which moves the selected object to the current layer.

Changing stacking order with the Arrange menu

You can also control an object's position in the stacking order within a layer using the Object ➪ Arrange menu, found in Illustrator and InDesign.

The Object ➪ Arrange menu includes the following commands:

- Bring to Front (Shift+Ctrl+] in Windows; Shift+⌘+] on the Mac)
- Bring Forward (Ctrl+] in Windows; ⌘+] on the Mac)
- Send Backward (Ctrl+[in Windows; ⌘+[on the Mac)
- Send to Back (Shift+Ctrl+[in Windows; Shift+⌘+[on the Mac)

The Bring to Front and Send to Back menu commands move the selected object to the very top or very bottom of the stacking order, and the Bring Forward and Send Backward menu commands move the selected object forward or backward one place in the stacking order. With these commands, you can quickly arrange the objects within a layer.

Changing stacking order with the Clipboard

Another way to change the stacking order of objects in Illustrator is to copy and paste them using the Edit ⇨ Paste in Front (⌘/Ctrl+F) and the Edit ⇨ Paste in Back (⌘/Ctrl+B) menu commands. These commands paste the object in front of or behind the selected object.

If no object is selected or if the Edit ⇨ Paste (⌘/Ctrl+V) menu command is used, the object is pasted at the top of the stacking order for the selected layer.

Changing stacking order within a group

Objects within a group also have a stacking order. You can alter a group's stacking order by expanding the group in the Layers palette and dragging the one object above another, or by selecting an object within the group with the Group Selection tool and using the Object ⇨ Arrange menu commands to alter its order.

Changing Z-Index in GoLive

Most objects on a Web page cannot be stacked on top of one another. The exception to this rule is GoLive layers. The stacking order for GoLive layers is determined by a Z-Index value, which is set in the Inspector palette for the selected layer. Layers with a higher Z-Index value appear in front of layers with a lower value.

Aligning and Distributing Objects

To create aesthetic designs, there are times when you'll want to precisely orient two or more objects together. You can do this by recording the position values of the various objects and then changing those values for one of the objects to align it with the other one, but these can be time consuming if you have a lot of objects to align. Instead of a manual process, all of the CS2 applications include palettes and controls that make aligning and distributing objects easy.

Commands to align and distribute objects are contained on the Options bar and in the Align palette (shown in Figure 12-43) for Illustrator, InDesign, and GoLive. You can access this palette by choosing Window ⇨ Align (Shift+F7). The palette includes several icon buttons that align or distribute the selected objects to an edge or center.

Figure 12-43: The Align palette includes several rows of buttons used to align and distribute multiple objects.

Before you use an align or distribute icon button, you must select more than one object with the Selection tool. When you select one of the align or distribute icons, you can move all the selected objects to the match the edge or center of the selection boundary box. However, if you click on one of the objects after making the selection, that object becomes the Key Object and you must complete all alignment using the Key Object's center and edges.

If you select the wrong object as the Key Object, you can use the Cancel Key Object palette menu command to cancel the existing key object and select a new key object.

Note: The Align and Distribute buttons have no affect on objects that have been locked.

Aligning objects

To use the Align palette, select two or more objects that you want to align; then click on the align icon in the Align palette for the alignment that you want. The align options include Align Left Edges, Align Vertical Centers, Align Right Edges, Align Top Edges, Align Horizontal Center, Align Bottom Edges.

If you enable the Use Preview Bounds option in the Align palette menu, you can align the objects by their edges using the stroke width. If the Use Preview Bounds option is disabled, the objects are aligned by the path edge, denoted by the bounding box.

To align objects to the art-board edges, enable the Align to Artboard option in the Align palette menu. This option works for aligning objects to the center of the art board as well as the art-board edges.

Note: The Align palette found in GoLive includes an additional row of buttons that are used to align a child object to its parent. You need only to select the child object to use these buttons. For example, several images within a Layout Grid may be selected and aligned to the top edge of the Layout Grid using the Align to Parent button. The images would be the children and the Layout Grid, the parent.

Distributing objects

Distributing objects is different from aligning objects in that the distribution icons in the Align palette position the selected objects so that the distance between the selected edges or centers of the selected objects is equal. For example, if three objects are selected and the Distribute Horizontal Centers button is clicked, then the middle object is moved so that the distance between the center of the bottom object and the middle object is equal to the distance between the center of the top object and the middle object.

The Distribution icons available in the Align palette include Distribute Top Edges, Distribute Vertical Centers, Distribute Bottom Edges, Distribute Left Edges, Distribute Horizontal Centers, and Distribute Right Edges.

Distributing spacing

If the Show Options palette menu command is selected, the Distribute Spacing buttons for Distribute Vertical Space and Distribute Horizontal Space appear. Using these buttons and the spacing value, you can space all the selected objects from the Key Object by the specified space amount.

The drop-down field at the bottom of the Align palette also includes an Auto option that automatically spaces the objects using an average of their current position. The Auto option also doesn't require that a Key Object be selected.

STEPS: Aligning Objects in InDesign

1. **Open an InDesign document.** Choose File ➪ Open and open an InDesign file that includes several misaligned objects like the images shown in Figure 12-44.

Figure 12-44: You can easily align randomly placed objects using the Align palette.

2. **Select all the objects to align.** With the Selection tool, drag over the top of all the objects that you want to align or hold down the Shift key and click on each one individually.

3. **Aligning objects with the Align palette.** With the objects selected, choose Window ➪ Align to open the Align palette. Click on the Align Bottom Edges button in the Align palette. The bottom edges of all the image objects are aligned, as shown in Figure 12-45.

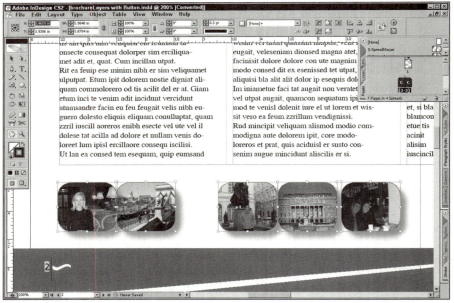

Figure 12-45: The Align palette enables you to align all these image objects using the Align Bottom Edges button in the Align palette.

4. **Distribute the image objects.** The alignment of the image objects looks good, but the spacing between the objects is still a problem. To fix this, use one of the Distribution buttons in the Align palette. With the image objects still selected, click the Distribute Right Edges button in the Align palette. This action evenly spaces the image objects, as shown in Figure 12-46.

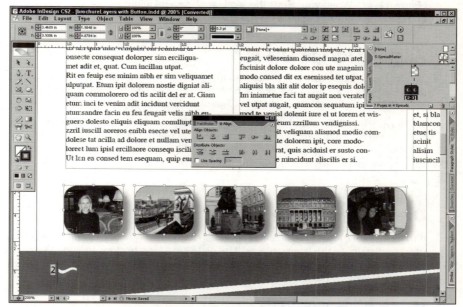

Figure 12-46: After distributing the image objects using their right edges, they line up perfectly spaced.

5. **Move the final objects.** As a final step, you'll want to drag the image objects upward slightly with the Selection tool. With all the objects selected and aligned, they move together, maintaining their alignment and spacing.

Cross-Reference

Once you've correctly aligned and positioned objects, you can lock them in place by clicking on the Lock icon in the Layers palette. More on locking layers is found in Chapter 14.

Aligning and Distributing Image Layers in Photoshop

Photoshop includes align buttons on the Options bar when the Move tool is selected. Using these buttons, you can align the current layer with the current selection. When three or more layers are selected, the distribution buttons become active on the Options bar.

Image selections may be aligned and distributed to a selected layer using the Move tool in Photoshop. With a selection made, click on the Move tool. Several align and distribute icon buttons appear on the Options bar, as shown in Figure 12-47.

Figure 12-47: When you select the Move tool, several align and distribute buttons appear on the Options bar.

Aligning image layers

To align a selection to a layer, make an image selection and choose a layer in the Layers palette, then click one of the align icon buttons in the Options bar. If multiple layers are linked together, each of the linked layers is aligned with the selection.

The align icon buttons include the following: Align Top Edges, Align Vertical Centers, Align Bottom Edges, Align Left Edges, Align Horizontal Center, and Align Right Edges.

Cross-Reference   More on aligning and distributing layers is covered in Chapter 14.

Distributing image layers

If three or more layers are selected, the distribute icon buttons become active and may be used to distribute the layer objects. The distribute icon buttons include Distribute Top Edges, Distribute Vertical Centers, Distribute Bottom Edges, Distribute Left Edges, Distribute Horizontal Centers, and Distribute Right Edges.

Using Smart Guides

Guides are helpful as you begin to move objects and image selections about a document, but Photoshop includes another incredibly useful feature — Smart Guides. You can enable Smart Guides by choosing View ➪ Show ➪ Smart Guides. When enabled, guides appear to align the moved object or selection to the edge and center of surrounding objects. Figure 12-48 shows an arrow symbol being moved. Smart Guides magically appear to align the top of the arrow to the top of the rounded rectangle and another Smart Guide appears to align the right edge of the arrow to the right edge of the text. Smart Guides are also found in Illustrator and GoLive.

New Feature   Smart Guides are new to Photoshop CS2.

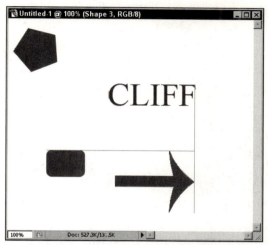

Figure 12-48: Smart Guides make aligning objects in Photoshop easy.

Summary

- The CS2 applications include many different ways to transform objects including the bounding box, transform tools, a Transform menu, and a Transform palette.
- The common transformation tools include Move, Rotate, Scale, Reflect, Shear, and Free Transform.
- The Transform Each dialog box lets you combine several transformations into a single operation.
- In addition to objects, patterns and gradients may also be transformed.
- Images may be transformed in many of the same ways as objects using the Photoshop tools.
- Stacking order determines which objects appear in front of other objects and is altered using layers and the commands in the Arrange menu.
- Aligning and distributing objects is accomplished using the Align palette or the Options bar in Photoshop.

✦ ✦ ✦

Applying Effects to Objects and Images

In This Chapter

Using Photoshop filters

Using Illustrator filters

Using Illustrator effects

Using Photoshop's layer effects and styles

Applying effects in InDesign

When Adobe first introduced the concept of filters in Photoshop, it was a risky move. To allow other developers to access the inner workings of the Photoshop graphics engine and develop their own filters to alter images was brilliant or a huge mistake. History has now validated that the move was, indeed, brilliant.

Filters are found mainly in Photoshop and Illustrator, but Illustrator has taken the concept one step further with the introduction of effects. Effects are essentially filters applied in memory, allowing them to be edited or even removed at any time from the Appearance palette without affecting the rest of the attributes. Both Photoshop and Illustrator include filters and effects.

The variety of filters and effects found in both Photoshop and Illustrator are quite diverse, covering everything from unique brush strokes and object distortion to color adjustment and even 3-D effects.

Many filters in Photoshop are moving into complex interfaces like the Filter Gallery that let you explore, preview, and apply many filters at once. Other common filter interfaces include the Extract, Liquify, and Pattern Maker interfaces.

Using Photoshop Filters

All the filters that may be applied to an image are contained within the Filter menu. Filters are applied to a selection or to the active layer if there is no selection. The top menu command in the Filter menu always lists the last filter command used. It includes a keyboard shortcut of ⌘/Ctrl+F, allowing it to be accessed quickly.

Some filters may be applied only to images with the RGB color mode selected and some filters may only be applied to an 8-bit image. Filters that cannot be applied to the current image are disabled. In Photoshop, choosing Image ➪ Mode lets you change these properties for the current image.

Accessing the Filter Gallery

The Filter Gallery lets you apply multiple filters at once or a single filter multiple times. To open the Filter Gallery, choose Filter ➪ Filter Gallery. The Filter Gallery, shown in Figure 13-1, includes a preview pane that shows the results of the applied filters.

All the filters listed in the Filter Gallery also include their own menu commands in the Filter menu. Selecting a filter menu command for a filter that is part of the Filter Gallery opens the Filter Gallery with the selected filter highlighted.

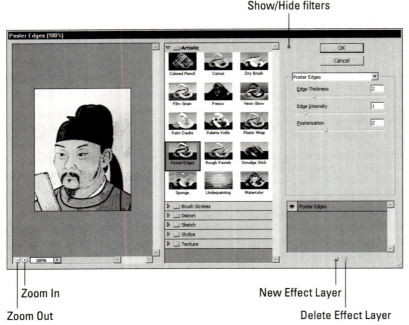

Figure 13-1: The Filter Gallery includes most of the Photoshop filters and lets you apply many filters at once.

The Filter Gallery interface is divided into three different panes. The left pane is the preview pane that displays the current layer or selection. The middle pane includes thumbnails of all the available filters. Clicking on a filter highlights it in gray and selects the filter. The right pane includes all the settings for the selected filter.

Although the Filter Gallery includes many filters, it doesn't include all filters available in Photoshop.

Using the Preview pane

Moving the mouse over the Preview pane changes the cursor to a hand. Dragging with this hand cursor pans the preview image within the pane. The buttons and popup menu at the bottom of the Preview pane are used to zoom in, zoom out, and select a specific zoom percentage. The pop-up menu also includes an Actual Pixels option, which displays the image at its actual size of 100%; a Fit in View option, which zooms the image so the entire image is visible in the Preview pane; and a Fit on Screen option, which maximizes the Filter Gallery to fill the entire screen.

Clicking the Show/Hide button in the top-left corner of the Settings pane hides the filter thumbnails and uses that space to increase the size of the Preview pane, as shown in Figure 13-2.

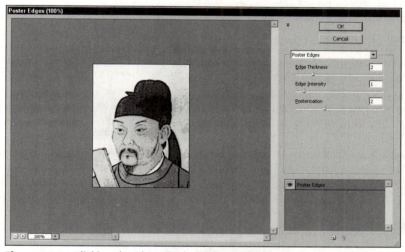

Figure 13-2: Clicking the Show/Hide button increases the size of the Preview pane by hiding all the filter thumbnails.

Using the Filter pane

The Filter pane is organized into several different categories of filters including Artistic, Brush Strokes, Distort, Sketch, Stylize, and Texture. Similar categories are found in the Filter menu. The category that includes the current selected filter is highlighted in bold.

Clicking on the small arrow to the left of the filter category name expands the category to reveal all the filters within that category. Clicking on a filter thumbnail selects the filter and displays all its settings in the Settings pane. The selected filter's name is displayed at the top of the interface along with the zoom percentage, and the background of its thumbnail is highlighted dark gray.

Using the Settings pane

The Settings pane includes a drop-down list of all the filters. Filters may be selected from this list when the filter thumbnails are hidden. Below this list, the settings for the current selected filter are displayed. Changing any of these settings alters the effects of the filter, and the Preview pane shows the changes.

At the bottom of the Settings pane is a list of filters applied to the preview listed in the order in which they are applied to the image. If you click on a new filter, it replaces the currently selected filter. To apply an additional filter to the image, click on the New Effect Layer button at the bottom of the Settings pane. This freezes the current selection and adds a new filter layer to the interface. The name of this filter layer is that of the filter that was applied.

If you click on the Visibility icon to the left of the filter layer name to toggle it off, the Preview pane is updated to show the image without the filter. Selecting the filter layer and clicking the Delete Effect Layer button at the bottom of the Settings pane deletes filter layers.

If multiple filter layers exist in the Filter Galley, you can rearrange them by dragging one layer above or below another. Changing the order in which filters are applied can drastically change the resulting image.

When you're satisfied with the resulting preview, click OK to apply the listed filter layers to the image. Click Cancel to exit the Filter Gallery without applying any filters.

STEPS: Using the Photoshop Filter Gallery

1. **Open an image in Photoshop.** Within Photoshop, choose File ⇨ Open to open an image to which you want to apply some filters. To apply the filter to the entire image, do not select any portion.

2. **Open the Filter Gallery.** Choose Filter ⇨ Filter Gallery to open the Filter Gallery interface. The image shows up in the Preview pane. Click and drag on the image in the Preview pane until an interesting portion of this image is visible.

3. **Select a filter.** Click on the Artistic category and select the Poster Edges filter. In the Settings pane, set the Edge Thickness to 2, the Edge Intensity to 1, and the Posterization to 2. Figure 13-3 shows the image with this single filter applied in the Filter Gallery.

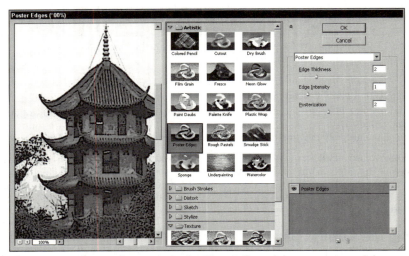

Figure 13-3: The Preview pane in the Filter Gallery shows a preview of the applied filter with its modified properties.

4. **Add another filter.** Click on the New Effect Layer button at the bottom of the Settings pane to add another filter to the image. Click on the Texture category and select the Texturizer filter. In the Settings pane, select the Canvas option from the Texture drop-down list. Set the Scaling value to 100%, the Relief value to 4 and the Light option to Top. Figure 13-4 shows the resulting image in the Preview pane.

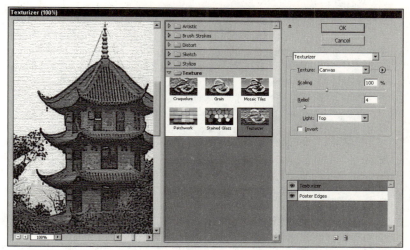

Figure 13-4: The Preview pane shows the resulting image after two filters are applied.

5. **Apply the selected filters.** Click OK to apply the two selected filters to the image. Figure 13-5 shows the resulting image with the filters applied.

Figure 13-5: Several filters may be applied to an image at one time using the Filter Gallery interface.

Using other filters

In addition to the filters included in the Filter Gallery interface, Photoshop has several other filters that are applied using the Filter menu.

Most of these filters have their own dialog boxes of settings that appear when the filter's menu command is selected. Some of the filters don't have any dialog boxes that open. The menu commands that have an ellipsis (. . .) following their menu command open a dialog box.

Most filter dialog boxes include a Preview option and a Preview pane, like the Gaussian Blur dialog box, shown in Figure 13-6. The Preview pane gives you an idea of what the filter effect is before it's applied to the entire image. By clicking and dragging on the image in the Preview pane, you can reposition the portion of the image that is displayed in the Preview pane. The plus and minus buttons underneath the Preview pane let you zoom in and out of the image. Enabling the Preview option applies the current filter settings to the entire image.

Caution — Applying some filters, even in Preview mode, can take some time depending on the calculations involved in the filter and the size of the image.

Figure 13-6: The Gaussian Blur dialog box, like most filter dialog boxes, includes a Preview pane.

Blurring an image

The Filter ➪ Blur menu includes several different filters used to blur an image or a selection by averaging local groups of pixels.

The first three Blur filters — Average, Blur, and Blur More — are applied without a dialog box. Average takes the average of all the selected colors and applies that average color to the entire selection. The Average filter is useful when used with the Magic Wand tool to create a single area with a single color.

The Blur filter removes any noise along hard edges by averaging the colors along these hard edges, resulting in a smoother overall image. The Blur More filter does the same but to a greater extent.

The Box Blur filter blurs the selected area by taking the average color value of pixels within a square area. The Radius value determines the size of the box.

 New Feature The Box Blur, Shape Blur, and Surface Blur filters are all new in Photoshop CS2.

The Gaussian Blur filter opens a dialog box where you can specify the amount of blur to add to the image. The Radius value determines the size of the groups of pixels that are averaged.

The Lens Blur filter opens a dialog box, shown in Figure 13-7, that lets you simulate a depth-of-field effect where the camera is focused on a particular point in the scene and all objects farther or nearer than that point are blurred in relationship to their distance from the focal point.

The Source field lets you base the focal point on the image's Transparency value or an included Depth Mask. The Iris Shape field lets you choose the shape of the defined averaged areas where the blur is applied as well as its Blade Curvature and Rotation. You can also specify values for Specular Highlights and Noise.

Figure 13-7: The Lens Blur dialog box includes a Preview pane.

The Motion and Radial Blur filters let you control the direction of the blur lines. The Motion Blur filter specifies an Angle and a Distance value to blur the image linearly, as shown in Figure 13-8. The Radial Blur filter blurs the image in concentric circles about a point that you can select in the Radial Blur dialog box, also shown in Figure 13-8.

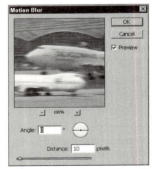 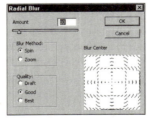

Figure 13-8: The Motion Blue and Radial Blur dialog boxes let you blur the image using linear or radial lines.

The Shape Blur filter blurs the image using a selected shape. The Shape Blur dialog box, shown in Figure 13-9, includes several default options, but you can load new shapes using the pop-up menu. The Radius setting determines the size of the shape that blurs the image. Notice in the figure how the circular shape causes details in the image to be blurred in circular patterns.

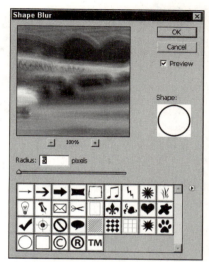

Figure 13-9: The Shape Blur dialog box blurs areas using a selected shape.

The Smart Blur filter is unique in that it lets you blur areas of similar colored pixels based on the Threshold value. The Mode may be set to Normal, Edge Only, or Overlay Edge. The Edge Only and Overlay Edge options color the edges white based on the Threshold value. Figure 13-10 shows the Smart Blur dialog box. In the Preview pane, similar areas have been blended together.

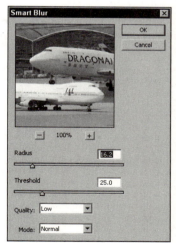

Figure 13-10: The Smart Blur dialog box blurs local areas of similar pixels.

You can use the Surface Blur filter to blur the image while preserving its edges. This has the effect of softening the entire image while maintaining the image details. The larger the Radius setting, the more that the pixels bleed into one another and the Threshold value sets the limit for edges that are blurred. Figure 13-11 shows the Surface Blur dialog box.

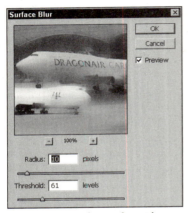

Figure 13-11: The Surface Blur dialog box blurs the image while preserving its edges.

STEPS: Blurring an Image's Background

1. **Open an image in Photoshop.** Within Photoshop, choose File ➪ Open and select an image that includes a background that you want to blur.

2. **Select the background.** Click the Magnetic Lasso tool and drag around the foreground objects to roughly select the background. After making an initial selection, hold down the Shift key and select the additional areas with the Magic Wand tool. Figure 13-12 shows the selected background area.

Figure 13-12: You can select the background, then apply the Lens Blur filter to make the background blurry.

3. **Apply the Lens Blur filter.** Choose Filter ➪ Blur ➪ Lens Blur. In the Lens Blur dialog box that opens, set the Radius value to 5 and zoom in on the Preview pane to see the applied blur, as shown in Figure 13-13. Then click OK.

Figure 13-13: The Lens Blur dialog box lets you control how blurry the background becomes.

Distorting an image

The Filter Gallery interface includes three filters in its Distort category, but the Filter ➪ Distort menu includes many more filters, including Displace, Lens Correction, Pinch, Polar Coordinates, Ripple, Shear, Spherize, Twirl, Wave, and ZigZag.

The Displace filter distorts the image based on a loaded displacement map. The displacement map defines how the pixels move, with black areas marking a negative displacement and white areas marking a positive displacement. Figure 13-14 shows a patterned image with the Displace filter applied using the simple displacement map.

Displacement maps must be saved using the PSD file format. Some sample displacement maps are found in the `plug-ins\displacement maps` directory.

The Lens Correction filter, found in the Filter ➪ Displace menu, is covered in Chapter 11.

The remaining Distort filters all open a dialog box where you can enter the amount of distortion to apply. Most of these dialog boxes, like the Twirl dialog box shown in Figure 13-15, include a graphical representation of what the distortion looks like. In some cases, such as for the Shear filter, the graphical representation may be manipulated to define the distortion.

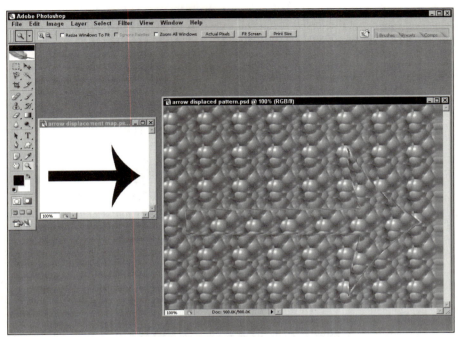

Figure 13-14: The Displace filter distorts images based on an externally loaded displacement map.

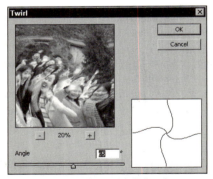

Figure 13-15: The Twirl dialog box includes a Preview pane and also a graphical representation of the distortion that is applied.

Of all the Distort filters, the Wave filter dialog box, shown in Figure 13-16, includes many unique settings for distorting the image such as selecting the Wave Type as Sine, Triangle, or Square, as well as a Randomize button.

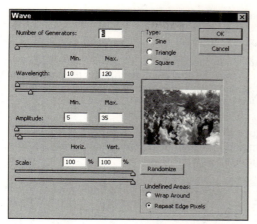

Figure 13-16: The Wave dialog box includes many settings for precisely controlling the distortion of an image.

Adding noise to an image

When noise is added to an image, it randomly alters the colors of many of the surrounding pixels, making the image grainy. But it can also be used to blend areas that have been retouched, making them appear more realistic. The Filter ➪ Noise menu includes several noise filters used to add and remove noise to an image or a selection.

The Add Noise filter opens a dialog box, shown in Figure 13-17, where you can specify the amount of noise to add to the image. The Uniform option randomly adds noise about the selected value, and the Gaussian option adds noise using a bell-shaped average curve. The Monochromatic option causes the noise to be black and white.

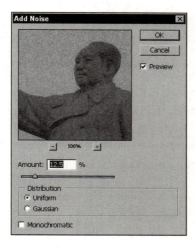

Figure 13-17: The Add Noise dialog box determines the amount of noise that you add to an image.

The Despeckle filter doesn't open a dialog box, but it removes noise from the image. It also detects edges to maintain the details of the image. The Median filter also removes noise from the image by replacing the brightest and darkest pixels with a median-colored pixel.

Most scratches and dust irregularities are small enough that they may be removed using the Dust & Scratches filter. This filter looks for small abrupt changes that are as small as the designated Radius value and with a given threshold. This filter applies a general blurring of the entire image. Figure 13-18 shows the dialog box for this filter.

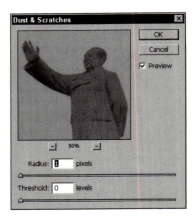

Figure 13-18: The Dust & Scratches dialog box eliminates irregular high-contrast dots and lines from an image.

Removing noise and JPEG artifacts

Adding noise to an image can soften an image by including a grainy feel, but having too much grain can affect image clarity. Some cameras can add film grain to an image and digital cameras add digital noise. Saving images to the JPEG format can also add unwanted noise and can reduce the image to the point that ugly artifacts and distortions appear. Photoshop includes a filter that can help remove noise from an image. It is also found in the Filter ⇨ Noise menu and is called Reduce Noise.

The Reduce Noise dialog box, shown in Figure 13-19, includes a preview pane along with several settings. You can save and recall settings using the Settings dialog box. You can also switch the dialog box between Basic and Advanced displays. The Basic display includes settings for Strength, Preserve Details, Reduce Color Noise and Sharpen Details. There is also an option to Remove JPEG Artifact:

- ✦ **Strength:** Removes luminance noise in all channels that cause the image to appear grainy.
- ✦ **Preserve Details:** Controls how aggressively the image edges and details are affected.
- ✦ **Reduce Color Noise:** Removes any random color pixels that exist in the image caused by noise.

✦ **Sharpen Details:** Increases the sharpness lost by noise reduction.
 ✦ **Remove JPEG Artifacts option:** Enables the filter to deal with the blocky artifacts caused by saving the image to the JPEG format. These artifacts appear because of the compression algorithm used by the JPEG format.

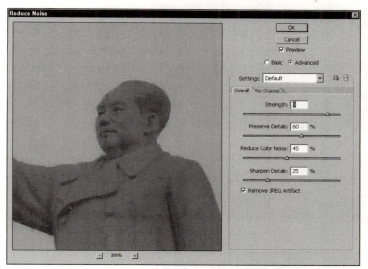

Figure 13-19: You can use the Reduce Noise dialog box to remove noise and artifacts from images.

If you determine that the luminance noise exists in only a single channel, you can switch to the Advanced display to make a Per Channel pane available. This pane displays the Red, Green and Blue channels and lets you set the Strength and Preserve Details for only the selected channel.

Using the Pixelate filters

The Filter ⇨ Pixelate filters are used to emphasize the pixel nature of an image by grouping several pixels together. The filters in this category include Color Halftone, Crystallize, Facet, Fragment, Mezzotint, Mosaic, and Pointillize. The Facet and Fragment filters apply the filter directly without opening a dialog box.

The shapes of the grouped pixels in each of these filters are slightly different, each creating a unique stylized look. For example, the Color Halftone filter changes each pixel group into a circle based on its brightness, the Crystallize filter changes groups of pixels into an irregular polygon shape, the Mosaic filter changes each grouping into a square, and the Pointillize filter groups pixels into solid dots. Figure 13-20 shows examples of several of these filters.

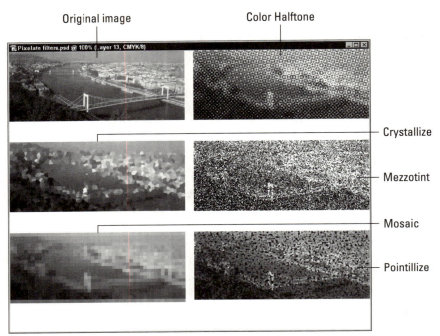

Figure 13-20: The Pixelate filters are used to alter an image by expanding the shape of specific pixel groups.

Using the Render filters

The process of rendering involves additional computations that alter the image in new and interesting ways. Using the filters in the Render category enables you to create clouds, fibers, and lighting effects like lens flares.

The Render filters include two filters for creating clouds — Clouds and Difference Clouds. The Clouds filter replaces the current image or selection with a random distribution of pixels using the Foreground and Background colors.

Tip Holding down the Option/Alt key while choosing Filter ➪ Render ➪ Clouds results in a cloud pattern that has a much higher contrast.

The Difference Clouds filter is similar, but instead of replacing the image, it blends the clouds with the image or the selection using a Difference blending mode, which inverts the colors of the image. Figure 13-21 shows an image where the Clouds filter has been applied to the left half, and the Difference Clouds filter has been applied to the right half.

Cross-Reference You can learn more about the various blending modes in Chapter 10.

Figure 13-21: The Clouds filter has been applied to the selection on the left of this image, and the Difference Clouds filter has been applied to the right half of the image.

The Render ⇨ Fibers filter replaces the current selection or image with threads of fibers created using the Foreground and Background colors. The Variance value controls how long fibers of a single color are, and the Strength value defines how stringy the fibers are. The Randomize button mixes these two values; this filter is excellent for creating textures that are used as hair. Figure 13-22 shows the Fibers dialog box.

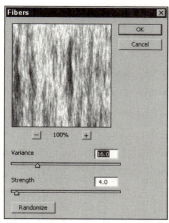

Figure 13-22: The Fibers dialog box creates long strands of fiber.

Lens flares are lighting anomalies that appear when you point a camera at a bright light. The Lens Flare filter opens a dialog box, shown in Figure 13-23, where you can click in the Preview pane to position the lens flare. You can also set the brightness of the lens flare and choose one of four lens types.

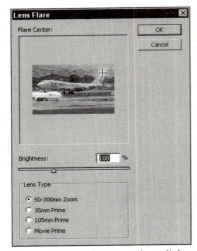

Figure 13-23: The Lens Flare dialog box lets you position the flare by dragging within the Preview pane.

Each of the various lens types creates a different pattern of streaks, rings, and glows. You can see results of each lens type in Figure 13-24.

Figure 13-24: Each of the lens types creates a unique lens flare.

Using the Lighting Effects filter

Of the various filters in the Render category, the Lighting Effects filter offers the most functionality. This filter may only be applied to RGB images using the Filter ➪ Render ➪ Lighting Effects menu command.

Caution The Lighting Effects filter requires a substantial amount of memory, and if your system doesn't have enough memory available, a warning dialog box appears. You can make more memory available using the Edit ➪ Purge menu command to free memory used by the Undo, Clipboard, and Histories features.

When the Lighting Effects filter is applied, the Lighting Effects dialog box, shown in Figure 13-25, is displayed. Using this dialog box, you can add multiple lights to shine upon the image shown in the Preview pane.

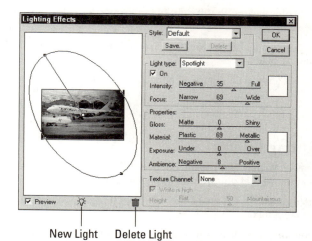

New Light   Delete Light

Figure 13-25: The Lighting Effects dialog box lets you position multiple lights around the image and change their settings.

To add a light to the image, click the Light icon at the bottom of the Preview pane and drag it into the Preview pane, or hold down the Option/Alt key and drag from an existing light to duplicate the light. All lights appear in the Preview pane as white dots. These lights may be repositioned by dragging the white dots to a new location.

When a light is selected in the Preview pane, an ellipse that represents the light's range is displayed. By dragging on its handles, you can change the light's range. Holding down the Shift key while dragging on these handles constrains the ellipse to change only a single dimension.

Lights are deleted by dragging their white dots to the Trash Can icon beneath the Preview pane.

The Light Type field lets you select from three different light types: Directional, Omni, and Spotlight. A Directional light shines light rays from a distant source, and all its rays are parallel much like the Sun. An ellipse represents a Spotlight and controls the Spotlight's angle and direction. A Spotlight decreases in intensity the further from its source it gets. An Omni light, represented by a circle, casts light equally in all directions, much like a light bulb.

Each light is enabled or disabled using the On option. Each light type also has an Intensity value, which may be positive or negative. A negative light value actually pulls light away from the image. Each light can also have a color, which is specified by the color swatch to the right of the Intensity setting. Click on the color swatch to open a Color Picker where you can change the light's color.

When the Spotlight type is selected, one end of the ellipse acts as the source and is the brightest point (or the darkest if the Intensity value is negative). The Focus value sets how much of the ellipse is filled with light.

The Properties values determine how the light interacts with the image surface. The Gloss value determines how shiny the surface is and how much the light reflects. The Material setting controls whether the light color (Plastic) or the image color (Metallic) gets reflected. The Exposure setting is a multiplier for the light, and the Ambience setting controls the background lighting in the image. The color swatch to the right of the Properties is for the ambient light color.

The Texture Channel field lets you select a channel and use it to emboss the image by raising the channel relative to the remaining pixels.

With all these controls, it may be difficult to configure an effective lighting setup. Photoshop includes several default Style settings that you can select from. These presets include a variety of settings, and you can save your own presets using the Save button at the top of the dialog box.

STEPS: Applying Lighting Effects

1. **Open an image in Photoshop.** Within Photoshop, choose File ⇨ Open and open an image that includes a background that you want to apply lighting effects to.

2. **Open the Lighting Effects dialog box.** Choose Filter ⇨ Render ⇨ Lighting Effects to open the Lighting Effects dialog box.

3. **Select a lighting style.** From the Style drop-down list at the top of the dialog box, select the Five Lights Down style. This adds several lights to the Preview pane, as shown in Figure 13-26.

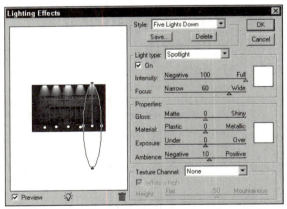

Figure 13-26: Selecting a lighting style automatically configures the Lighting Effects dialog box.

4. **Configure the lights.** Click on one of the white dots to select a light in the Preview pane. Notice that the Intensity value is already at maximum, but the lighting is still too dark. Drag the Ambience slider up to 25 to increase the overall light for the scene. Then click OK to apply the lighting to the image. Figure 13-27 shows the resulting image.

Figure 13-27: Applying a lighting effect to this image changes the image from a daytime image to a nighttime image.

Sharpening an image

The Sharpen filters are used to enhance the details of blurry images by increasing the contrast of edges. Choose Filter ⇨ Sharpen ⇨ Sharpen to apply a general sharpening over the entire image without a dialog box. The Sharpen More filter increases the sharpening effect, and the Sharpen Edges focuses specifically on the image edges.

The Unsharp Mask filter opens a dialog box, shown in Figure 13-28, that lets you adjust the amount of sharpness that is applied. This filter works by increasing the pixel contrast for areas where adjacent pixels have a value that is greater than the specified Threshold. The Radius value determines the size of the area where the pixel values are compared, and the Amount setting controls how much the contrast of adjacent pixels within the Threshold is increased.

Be warned that oversharpening an image adds halos to the image edges. Images that include particularly bright colors may be oversaturated by setting the Amount setting too high. Figure 13-29 shows an image with the Unsharp Mask filter applied to different sections. The left end of the palace image has a large Radius value and a low Threshold causing the contrast to be increased for the entire section. The right end of the image has been sharpened with a high Amount and Radius settings and a low Threshold settings, causing the section to be over-saturated. The middle section is unchanged.

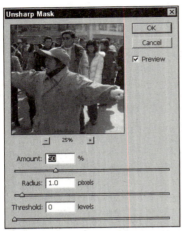

Figure 13-28: The Unsharp Mask dialog box lets you control the amount of sharpening applied to an image.

Figure 13-29: The Unsharp Mask filter has been applied to this image using different settings.

Using the Stylize filters

The Stylize filters apply a variety of unique effects that give an image a specific style. The filters in this category include the Diffuse, Emboss, Extrude, Find Edges, Glowing Edges, Solarize, Tiles, Trace Contour, and Wind.

The Diffuse filter moves pixels around to make the image appear unfocused. The options include Normal, Darken Only, Lighten Only, and Anisotropic. The Emboss filter colors the entire image gray and raises the image along its edges to form a relief. The Emboss dialog box lets you choose Angle, Height, and Amount values.

The Extrude filter divides the image into squares and colors each square to look like it is rising from the surface of the image. In the Extrude dialog box, you can select to use blocks or pyramids, set the size of the squares, and set the depth that they rise to.

The Find Edges and Solarize filters are applied without a dialog box. The Find Edges filter identifies all the edges in the image and displays them as dark borders on a white background. The Solarize filter combines the image with the image's negative to produce a darkened image with inverted colors.

The Tiles filter divides the entire image into square tiles and offsets each one slightly. In the Tiles dialog box, you can select the number of tiles and a maximum offset. The Trace Contour filter outlines the edges of the image, based on brightness, and displays them on a white background. The Wind filter spreads the edges of an image in different intensities as if something were dragged over the image when it was wet. Figure 13-30 shows a sampling of the Stylize filters applied to an image.

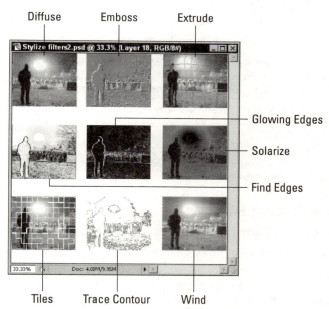

Figure 13-30: The Stylize filters may be used to create a number of unique effects.

Using the other filters

At the bottom of the Filter menu are two miscellaneous filter categories — Video and Other. The Video filters include De-Interlace, which is used to remove interlaced lines from images captured from a video source, and NTSC Colors, which limits the color palette to those used for broadcast television.

The Other category includes the Custom filter. This filter opens a dialog box, shown in Figure 13-31, that includes an array of value fields. Each text field represents the brightness value of the pixels that surround the pixel represented by the center text field. These brightness values can range from –999 to +999. The Scale value is used to divide the sum of all brightness values and the Offset value is added to the brightness values after scaling. By entering custom values into these text fields, you can create your own custom filter. These custom filters may be saved and reloaded as needed. The custom filters are saved with an ACF extension.

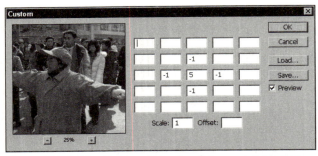

Figure 13-31: The Custom dialog box lets you create your own original filters.

The Other category also includes a High Pass filter, which highlights all the sharp color changing edges. The Minimum and Maximum filters look at a grouping of pixels defined by the Radius value and remove the brightest (or darkest) pixel from the group.

The Other category also includes the Offset filter. This filter offsets all the pixels in an image, making the image edges appear within the image interior. This filter is often used to mask the image edges to make an image tileable.

 Within Image Ready, the Other category includes a Tile Maker filter that may be used to create seamless background tiles that are tileable.

STEPS: Creating a Custom Filter

1. **Open an image in Photoshop.** Within Photoshop, choose File ⇨ Open and open an image.
2. **Open the Custom dialog box.** Choose Filter ⇨ Other ⇨ Custom menu command to open the Custom dialog box.
3. **Enter filter values.** Enter a value of **5** in each cell in the top and bottom rows of the Custom dialog box. Then set the Scale value to **50**, as shown in Figure 13-32.

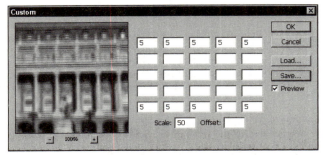

Figure 13-32: Entering values in these positions causes the image to blur.

4. **Save the custom filter.** Click the Save button and save the custom filter with the name **Double exposure**. The resulting image is shown in Figure 13-33.

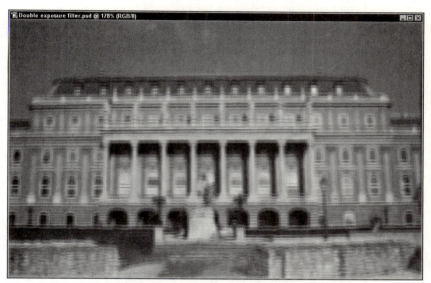

Figure 13-33: This double-exposure image has a custom filter applied to it.

Using third-party filters

At the bottom of the Filter menu is a separator line. All third-party filters installed appear below this line. Photoshop, by default, includes one third-party filter category. The Digimarc filters enable you to embed a digital watermark into an image to secure copyright information.

Using the Filter interfaces

At the top of the Filter menu, along with the Filter Gallery, are four interfaces that let you interactively filter an image or a selection. These interfaces include the Extract interface, the Liquify interface, the Pattern Maker interface, and the Vanishing Point filter.

Using the Extract interface

The Extract interface provides a way to separate foreground objects from the background of the image. Open the Extract interface, shown in Figure 13-34, by choosing Filter ⇨ Extract (Alt+Ctrl+X in Windows; Option+⌘+X on the Mac). The background objects are made transparent.

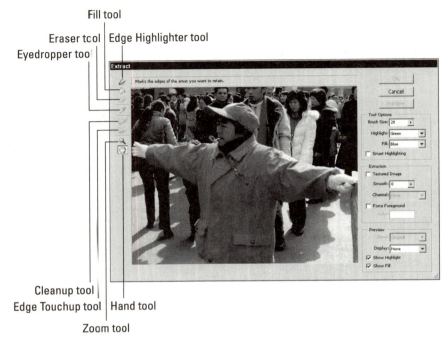

Figure 13-34: The Extract interface lets you separate objects from their background.

The first step in extracting foreground objects is to highlight all the edges of the object that you want to extract with the Edge Highlight tool. By default, the edges are highlighted in green, but you may change this color along with the Brush Size in the Tool Options section. You can enable the Smart Highlighting option to have the Edge Highlight tool follow the edge boundary closely. The highlighted edges should follow the edges fairly closely, but they should overlap the background. The Eraser tool may be used to erase part of the highlighted edges if you need to correct a mistake.

Cross-Reference   Editing tools such as the Eraser tool are covered in Chapter 10.

After the edges are highlighted, you can fill the objects that you want to keep with the Fill tool. These areas appear in blue, but their color can also be changed.

When the object is highlighted and the area to keep is filled, you can select from two different extraction methods. The Textured Image option is used when the image contains a lot of texture. The Smooth value sets how smooth the highlighted edges are. If the image includes an alpha channel, then you can select the alpha channel as a way to define the edges.

The Force Foreground extraction option lets you select an interior color that closely matches the tones of the object that you want to extract. You can select a color from the image using the Eyedropper tool.

With an extraction area defined, click the Preview button to see the resulting extraction, as shown in Figure 13-35. With the extraction visible, the Cleanup tool and the Edge Touchup tool become active. The Cleanup tool is used to erase any background areas that were accidentally extracted. The Edge Touchup tool adds details back into the extracted image.

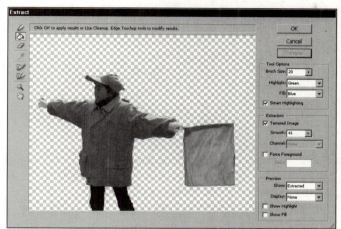

Figure 13-35: After an object is extracted, the background is made transparent.

In the Preview Show field, you can select to see the original image again and you can choose to display the extraction on a black, gray, or white matte, or on a custom color. Clicking OK in the Extract interface updates the selected layer with the extracted object on a transparent background.

STEPS: Extracting Foreground Objects

1. **Open an image in Photoshop.** Within Photoshop, choose File ➪ Open and open an image that includes a well-defined object that you want to extract.

2. **Open the Extract interface.** Choose Filter ➪ Extract to open the Extract interface. Click on the Zoom tool and zoom in on the object that you want to extract, as shown in Figure 13-36.

3. **Highlight the object.** Click on the Edge Highlighting tool. Then choose a Brush Size just large enough to overlap the edge that you want to extract and drag around the object with the Edge Highlighting tool. Be sure to overlap the background as you highlight the edges.

4. **Fill the object.** Click on the Fill tool and click within the object to fill the highlighted area. The filled area is shaded with a transparent blue, as shown in Figure 13-37.

Figure 13-36: The Extract interface includes Zoom and Hand tools to zoom in and focus on the object that you want to extract.

Figure 13-37: The edges of the object to be extracted are highlighted in green and the object interior is highlighted in blue.

5. **Preview the extraction.** With the object filled, the Preview button becomes active. Select the Textured Image option and click on the Preview button. Photoshop calculates the extraction and displays it in the interface, as shown in Figure 13-38. After being extracted, the background becomes transparent and is shown as a checkerboard pattern, but this can make it difficult to see the extraction. You can change the background color using the Display drop-down list in the lower-right corner of the interface. The Display options are None (checkerboard pattern), Black Matte, Gray Matte, White Matte or Other.

Chapter 13 ✦ Applying Effects to Objects and Images

Figure 13-38: After an object is extracted, the background is transparent, but choosing to show the background as a Black Matte makes it easier to see the extraction.

6. **Clean the extraction edges.** Click on the Cleanup tool, set the Brush Size to 20, and erase those portions around the object that need to be deleted. Finally, click on the Edge Touchup tool and refill those edges that weren't included in the extraction. Figure 13-39 shows the object after it has been cleaned up.

Figure 13-39: The extracted object may be cleaned up using the Cleanup and Edge Touchup tools.

Using the Liquify interface

The Liquify interface may be used to stretch and distort images and image selections as if they were placed on putty. To open the Liquify interface, shown in Figure 13-40, choose Filter ➪ Liquify (Shift+Ctrl+X in Windows; Shift+⌘+X on the Mac).

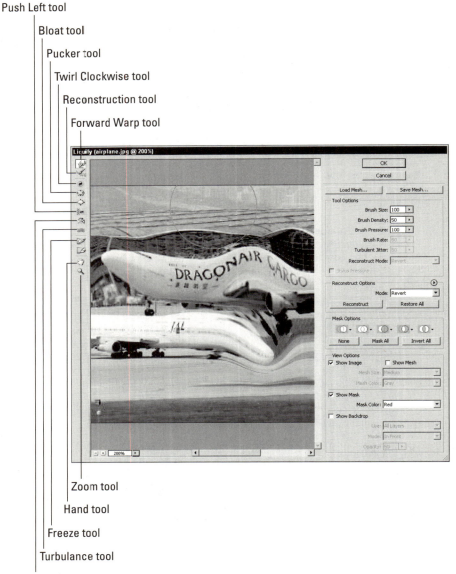

Figure 13-40: The Liquify interface lets you distort images by pushing and pulling pixel areas.

Moving the cursor over the Preview pane where the image is displayed reveals the outline of a brush. The brush options include its Size, Density, Pressure, Rate and Turbulence Jitter. Each of these options is set using the controls listed to the right.

The various liquify tools are displayed in a toolbar to the left of the Preview pane and include the following:

- **Forward Warp tool:** This tool is used to push pixels in a forward direction as you drag the mouse. Holding down the Shift key while dragging moves the mouse in a straight line.
- **Reconstruct tool:** This tool is used to remove any liquify effects from the image and restore the brushed area to its original look.
- **Twirl Clockwise tool:** This tool is used to rotate the pixels about the center of the mouse in a clockwise direction. Holding down the Option/Alt key while dragging rotates the pixels in the counterclockwise direction.
- **Pucker tool:** This tool is used to move the pixels toward the center of the brush.
- **Bloat tool:** This tool is used to move the pixels away from the center of the brush.
- **Push Left tool:** This tool is used to move the pixels to the left when you drag upward. Dragging the mouse downward moves the pixels to the right. Rotating the mouse in a clockwise direction increases the areas. Rotating in a counterclockwise direction reduces the area. Holding down the Option/Alt key forces the mouse to drag straight up or down.
- **Mirror tool:** This tool is used to copy the pixels being dragged over to the opposite side of the brush. Holding down the Option/Alt key while dragging flips the effect to the other side.
- **Turbulence tool:** This tool is used to randomly move pixels underneath the brush area.
- **Freeze Mask tool:** This tool is used to paint a mask layer onto the Preview pane.
- **Thaw Mask tool:** This tool is used to erase a mask layer onto the Preview pane.
- **Hand tool:** This tool is used to drag the Preview pane to reposition the visible portion of the image. Double-click to fit in window.
- **Zoom tool:** This tool is used to zoom in on the image in the Preview pane. Holding down the Option/Alt key lets you zoom out. You can also zoom in on the image using the small plus and minus icon buttons in the lower-left corner. Double-click to see 100%.

Dragging with any of the Liquify tools in the Preview pane distorts the image. These distortions may be undone using the Reconstruct tool. The Reconstruct tool has several modes including Revert, Rigid, Stiff, Smooth, and Loose. Each of these modes reconstructs the image in a different manner. Pressing the Restore All button returns the image to its original state.

At any time during the modifications, you can use a mask to lock an area from any changes. The Mask Options dialog box includes buttons to replace, add, subtract, intersect, or invert the current mask selection, transparency, or layer mask.

The View Options let you toggle on and off the image, the distortion mesh, the mask, and the backdrop. The *backdrop* is the faded version of the original image.

STEPS: Using the Liquify Interface

1. **Open an image in Photoshop.** Within Photoshop, choose File ➪ New and create a new image.
2. **Set the Foreground color.** Click on the Fill box in the Toolbox and select a light blue color from the Color palette.
3. **Apply the Fiber filter.** Choose Filter ➪ Render ➪ Fibers to apply the Fibers filter to the blank canvas. In the Fibers dialog box, set the Variance to 16 and the Strength to 4. Then click OK. The fibers appear running vertical on the canvas, as shown in Figure 13-41.

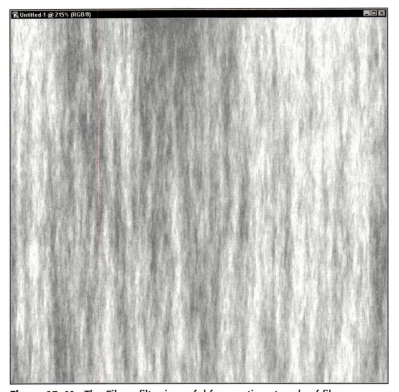

Figure 13-41: The Fibers filter is useful for creating strands of fiber.

Chapter 13 ✦ **Applying Effects to Objects and Images** 485

4. **Rotate the canvas.** Choose Image ➪ Rotate Canvas ➪ 90 degrees CW to rotate the canvas so the fibers run horizontally, as shown in Figure 13-42.

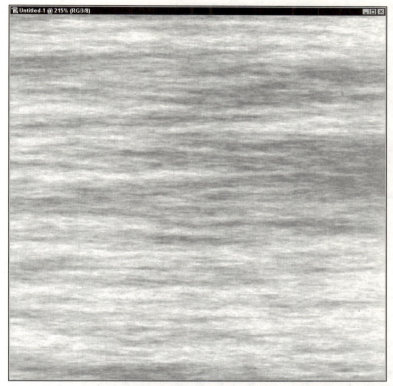

Figure 13-42: Rotating the canvas makes the fibers run horizontally.

5. **Use the Liquify interface.** Choose Filter ➪ Liquify to open the Liquify interface.

6. **Drag with the Liquify tools.** Select the Forward Warp tool and drag up and down throughout the image to create some ripples. Select the Bloat tool and drag small lines up and down to expand areas of the image. Finally, select the Turbulence tool and drag throughout the image to add some turbulence to the image. Figure 13-43 shows the final distorted image.

Figure 13-43: The Liquify interface allows you to add variety to the current image.

Creating patterns with Pattern Maker

Many designs make use of tileable background patterns. The opposite edges of the tileable patterns match perfectly so the background appears seamless. Creating seamless background patterns is manually possible with some help from the Filter ➪ Other ➪ Offset filter, but the Pattern Maker interface, shown in Figure 13-44, makes it quick and easy. Open the Pattern Maker interface by choosing Filter ➪ Pattern Maker (Alt+Shift+Ctrl+X in Windows; Option+Shift+⌘+X on the Mac).

Figure 13-44: The Pattern Maker interface allows you to quickly create seamless patterns from a selected image.

Within the Pattern Maker interface, use the Rectangle Marquee tool to mark the area in the image that you want to use to create the pattern. Using the Width and Height fields, you can specify the size of the pattern tile, or you could click the Use Image Size button to create a pattern the same size as the current image. The Offset field lets you specify to offset the pattern either Vertically or Horizontally a specified amount.

After an area has been selected, click the Generate button to create a pattern. The Smoothness value defines how smooth the pattern is, and the Sample Detail defines the size of the sample used to create the pattern. Figure 13-45 shows a sample pattern.

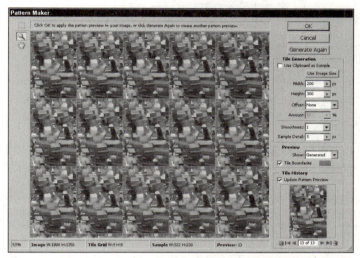

Figure 13-45: Generated patterns are displayed in the Preview pane and stored in the Tile History pane.

When a pattern is generated, the pattern is saved in the Tile History section. To see the original image again, select the Original option from the Show field. Several patterns may be generated and viewed in the Pattern Maker interface and saved using the Saves Preset Pattern button.

Controlling Vanishing Point

Painting walls in Photoshop is easy enough when the wall is a solid color, but if you're trying to add a patterned texture to the wall, it can be difficult to match the perspective view as you apply the paint. A work-around is to apply a Perspective transformation to the texture before applying the transformation, but you need to match the area exactly or apply it to a different layer that you can clean up later.

Photoshop CS2 has a new way of handling this complex problem. The Vanishing Point interface, under the Filter menu, has a dialog box that opens with the current image in its preview pane (Alt+Ctrl+V in Windows; Option+⌘+V on the Mac). The interface then expects you to click four points that mark the corners of the plane. From these selected points, Photoshop can create a perspective plane that aligns to the perspective view, as shown in Figure 13-46.

Figure 13-46: The Vanishing Point interface lets you define perspective planes by clicking the plane's four corner points.

Once you define a perspective plane, you can use the tools located in the upper left corner of the Vanishing Point interface to edit the perspective plane, paint, or transform selections. When a tool is selected, its settings appear in the Control Bar at the top of the interface. Each of these tools works the same and has the same keyboard shortcuts as the original interface.

STEPS: Using the Vanishing Point Interface

1. **Open an image in Photoshop.** Within Photoshop, choose File ⇨ Open and open an image that includes a well-defined perspective plane.

2. **Open the Vanishing Point interface.** With the image selected, choose Filter ⇨ Vanishing Point.

3. **Click each of the corners of the perspective plane.** When the Vanishing Point interface is first opened, the Create Plane Tool is selected. Click each of the four corners that make up the perspective plane. The plane is highlighted with a grid as shown in Figure 13-47.

Chapter 13 ✦ Applying Effects to Objects and Images

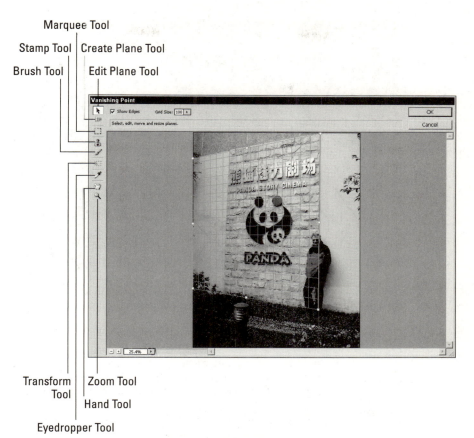

Figure 13-47: The perspective plane is highlighted with a grid.

4. **Select a paint area.** To control where the paint is applied, click the Marquee tool in the upper-left corner of the interface and drag over the left portion of the perspective plane where the gray wall is.

5. **Use the Stamp tool.** Select the Stamp tool and hold down the Alt/Option key while clicking the lower portion of the rock texture under the Panda sign. Then paint a new rock face in to the left of the Panda sign. Continue to reset the Stamp tool's origin and repaint the rest of the left gray wall. Figure 13-48 shows the new perspective painted rock wall.

Figure 13-48: With the Vanishing Point interface, the Stamp tool copies image portions while maintaining the perspective view.

Blending filters

Filters are applied with an Opacity value of 100%, making the filter take over the image completely. But you can make the applied filter effect transparent and even specify a blending mode by choosing Edit ➪ Fade (Shift+Ctrl+F in Windows; Shift+⌘+F on the Mac).

This command opens the Fade dialog box, shown in Figure 13-49, where you can specify an Opacity value and select a blending mode.

For more details on the various blending modes, see Chapter 10.

Figure 13-49: The Fade dialog box lets you blend the last applied filter by setting an Opacity value and selecting a blending mode.

Using Photoshop filters in Illustrator

Most of the default filters found in Photoshop are also available in Illustrator under the Filter menu. These filters are located at the bottom of the Filter menu underneath the Illustrator default filters.

These same Photoshop filters are also found in Illustrator in the Effect menu, allowing them to be applied as effects.

The Photoshop filters found in Illustrator may be applied only to raster images. If you select a vector object, these filters become disabled. But you can rasterize vector objects with the Edit ⇨ Rasterize menu command. However, this command eliminates the vector nature of the object.

Most Photoshop filters work only in RGB mode, not in CMYK mode.

Using Illustrator Filters

In addition to the Photoshop filters, Illustrator also includes several filters that are unique to Illustrator. These filters are found in the Filter menu and include the Colors, Create, Distort, and Stylize submenus.

You can apply all of these default Illustrator filters to vector-based objects.

At the top of the Filter menu are two menu commands based on the last filter used. The top menu command reapplies the last applied filter using the same settings. The second menu command re-opens the filter dialog box for the most recently used filter, allowing you to change the filter settings.

Using the Colors filters

Because Photoshop deals with pixels, it includes many controls to adjust colors. Object colors may be adjusted and converted between color modes in Illustrator using the filters found in the Filter ⇨ Colors menu. The filters included in this category include Adjust Colors, Blend Front to Back, Blend Horizontally, Blend Vertically, Convert to CMYK, Convert to RGB, Invert Colors, Overprint Black, and Saturate.

The Adjust Colors filter opens a dialog box where you can alter the color values for the fill and stroke colors. It also offers an option to convert between the various color modes. Another way to convert the selected object between color modes is with the several Convert filters found in this category.

The Blend filters are used to change the color of intermediate objects based on the colors of the two end objects. At least three objects must be selected to use any of these filters. If the Blend Front to Back filter is used, the middle object in the stacking order is changed. If the Blend Horizontally filter is used, the object between the leftmost and rightmost objects is changed. If the Blend Vertically filter is used, the middle object between the top and bottom objects is changed. Figure 13-50 shows a series of stacked rectangles before (on the left) and after (on the right) the Blend Front to Back filter was used.

This same effect may be created using the Blend tool, but the filter doesn't maintain a link between the two end objects, so any updates to the end object's color has no impact on the intermediate object's color.

The Invert Colors filter replaces all the object colors with their negative counterparts. The Overprint Black filter lets you apply an overprint black to the selected object's fill or stroke. Finally, the Saturate filter opens a dialog box where you can adjust the Saturation Intensity for the selected object.

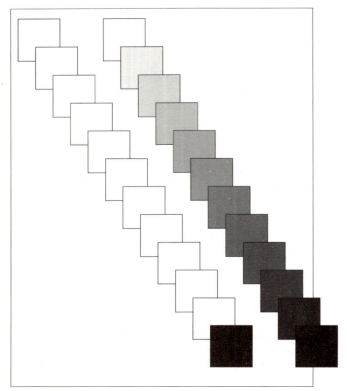

Figure 13-50: The Blend Front to Back filter changes the colors of all the intermediate objects.

Using the Create filters

The Create category includes the Crop Marks filter to add crop marks to the current document based on the objects in the art board.

The Object Mosaic filter is only enabled when a raster image is selected. It lets you turn the image into a mosaic of small squares where each square is a selectable object, as shown in Figure 13-51.

Figure 13-51: The Object Mosaic filter lets you change a raster image into many selectable square objects.

Using the Distort filters

The Distort filters let you distort object paths in a number of different ways, including Free Distort, Pucker & Bloat, Roughen, Tweak, Twist, and Zig Zag. Each of these filters opens a dialog box where you can control the settings for the distortion.

These filters may only be applied to object paths, not to raster images, symbols, or text objects.

The Free Distort filter lets you distort a path by dragging the corner points of its bounding box. Figure 13-52 shows this dialog box.

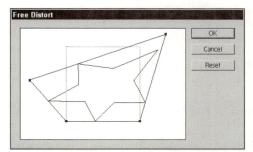

Figure 13-52: The Free Distort dialog box lets you distort an object path by dragging the corners of its bounding box.

The Pucker & Bloat filter is used to push the center of each segment toward the object center (Pucker) or away from the object center (Bloat).

The Roughen filter may be used to add small random changes to the path as if someone scribbled with a pen. The Tweak filter also applies randomness to a path by bending each segment inward or outward. The Twist filter lets you specify an Angle value that defines how much the path is twisted about its center. The Zig Zag causes the path to be angled back and forth in a regular pattern.

Figure 13-53 shows each of the Distort filters applied to a simple rectangle.

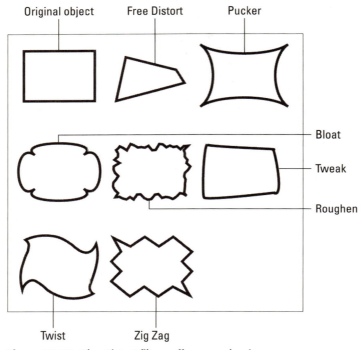

Figure 13-53: The Distort filters offer several unique ways to alter Illustrator paths.

Using the Stylize filters

There are only three Illustrator Stylize filters — Add Arrowheads, Drop Shadow, and Round Corners.

The Add Arrowheads filter may only be applied to an open path. The Add Arrowheads dialog box, shown in Figure 13-54, lets you select from a library of arrowheads for the start and end of the path.

Figure 13-54: The Add Arrowheads dialog box lets you select the arrow type to use for the Start and End of a path.

The Drop Shadow filter adds a simple drop shadow to the selected object using the Drop Shadow dialog box, shown in Figure 13-55. For the drop shadow, you can select a blending mode, an opacity, offset distances, a blur amount, and a color.

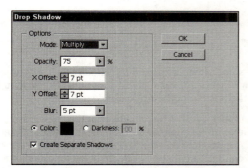

Figure 13-55: The Drop Shadow dialog box lets you control the look and position of the drop shadow.

The Round Corner filter opens a simple dialog box where you can specify a radius to use to round the corners of the selected path.

Using Illustrator Effects

If you compare the Filter and Effect menus in Illustrator, you'll see many of the same submenus. The key difference between applying a filter verses applying an effect is that effects show up in the Appearance palette, as shown in Figure 13-56, where they may be selected, edited, and removed at any time. Filters, on the hand, are permanently applied to an object and may only be removed using the Undo feature.

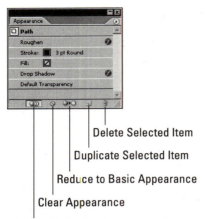

Figure 13-56: The Appearance palette lists all effects applied to the current selection.

Once an effect is applied to an object, the same effect is applied by default to all additional new objects that are created. To make new objects appear without these effects, click on the New Art Has Basic Appearance button at the bottom of the Appearance palette.

Effects can be removed from the selected object by selecting an effect in the Appearance palette and choosing the Remove Item palette menu command or by clicking on the Delete Selected Item button at the bottom of the Appearance palette. To remove all effects, click the Reduce to Basic Appearance button. This command causes all effects to be removed, but it doesn't change the stroke or fill settings. Clicking the Clear Appearance button removes all effects and sets the stroke and fill colors to None.

The drawback to using effects is that they take up valuable memory, and applying too many of them could significantly slow down the system, but if you have a lot of RAM, this shouldn't be a problem.

The Effect menu also includes many features that aren't found in the Filter menu. At the top of the Effect menu are two commands for instantly repeating the last applied effect and for recalling the dialog box used in the last applied effect.

Rasterizing effects

Many effects convert the object to a raster image before the effect is applied. Actually, the conversion doesn't happen until the file is saved or printed, but the object still maintains its vector outline. Choose Effect ⇨ Document Raster Effects Settings to open the dialog box shown in Figure 13-57. Here, you can set the global rasterization settings for all objects that are converted to raster images. The effects that require rasterization include all the SVG filters, all the Photoshop filters listed at the bottom of the Effect menu, and several of the Stylize effects.

SVG filters are covered in more detail in Chapter 34. The Document Raster Effects Settings dialog is covered in more detail in Chapters 11 and 37.

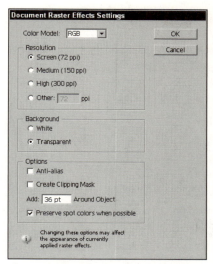

Figure 13-57: The Document Raster Effects Settings dialog box lets you specify the settings to use when an object is rasterized.

The Effect menu also includes a Rasterize menu command that opens up a dialog box with the same settings as the Document Raster Effects Settings dialog box. The settings in this dialog box are object-specific.

Creating 3-D objects

The 3-D category of effects lets you convert simple 2-D paths into simple 3-D objects. The 3-D menu includes three different effects — Extrude & Bevel, Revolve, and Rotate. For example, a simple square path can be made into a cube with the Extrude effect, and a half circle path may be revolved to create a sphere. 3-D objects in Illustrator created with these effects include shading using controllable lights.

Extruding objects

Extruding a 3-D path is simply the process of adding depth to the path. This is accomplished using the 3D Extrude & Bevel Options dialog box, shown in Figure 13-58.

The Position field at the top of the dialog box lets you select one of the default preset positions. Selecting a position preset automatically updates the X-axis, Y-axis, Z-axis, and Perspective values. If any of these values are changed, then the Custom Rotation preset is used. The default position presets include positions such as Front, Left, Top, Off-Axis Front, Off-Axis Top, Isometric Left, and so on. Isometric views are views where the Perspective value equals 0 and all parallel lines remain parallel.

Tip You can drag in the Preview pane, and the X-Axis, Y-Axis, and Z-Axis values are automatically updated.

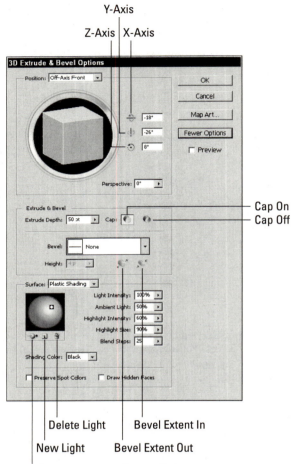

Figure 13-58: The 3D Extrude & Bevel Options dialog box lets you specify the direction and distance to extrude the selected path.

The Extrude Depth value determines how far the path is moved to create depth. The Cap On and Cap Off buttons determine whether the extruded object is hollow or capped on either end.

The Bevel pop-up menu lets you choose the type of bevel to apply to the object. Each bevel type shows a profile curve. This curve matches the extruded portion of the object, and the Height value sets the maximum distance from the edge of the path. The bevel profile curve may be applied outward or inward using the Bevel Extent In and Bevel Extent Out buttons.

The Surface options define how the extruded object is shaded. The options include Wireframe, No Shading, Diffuse Shading, and Plastic Shading. If you click on the More Options button, several lighting controls appear. Figure 13-59 shows several extrude, bevel, and shading options applied to an object.

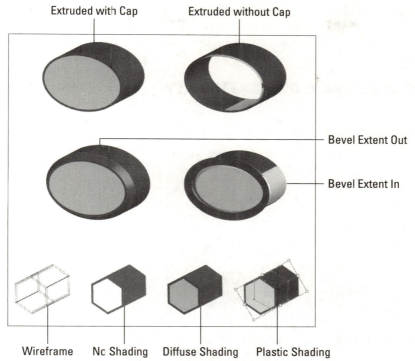

Figure 13-59: The Extrude & Bevel dialog box includes several different options for creating extruded 3-D objects.

The Wireframe option only draws the lines used to make up the 3D object. The No Shading option colors each face of the object using the selected fill and stroke colors. Neither the Wireframe nor No Shading options have any lighting settings.

The Diffuse Shading option colors each face a different shade depending on how the light is cast upon the object. For this option, you can specify the Light Intensity, the Ambient Light percentage, the number of Blend Steps to use, and the Shading Color.

The Plastic Shading option colors the object as if the light were shining on an object with the surface made of plastic. Plastic objects are highly reflective and include specular highlights. For this option, you also have settings for the Highlight Intensity and Size.

When either the Diffuse or Plastic Shading options are selected, you can position the precise location of the lights used to illuminate the object by dragging in the Lighting Preview pane. Using the buttons underneath the pane, you can move the selected light to the back of the object so it shines from behind, create new lights, or delete a selected light. Lights are represented by the small white dots, and a single object can have many lights.

The Light Intensity value determines the strength of the light, which is at 100% at the center of its highlight. The Ambient Light value determines how much background light is used to light the object. The Blend Steps defines the number of different colors that are used to blend colors from the highlight to the shadows. The Shading Color is the color reflected off the object away from the highlight.

Mapping artwork

Within the Extrude & Bevel dialog box, the Map Art button opens another dialog box, shown in Figure 13-60, where you can select a Symbol to map onto the various surfaces of the extruded object.

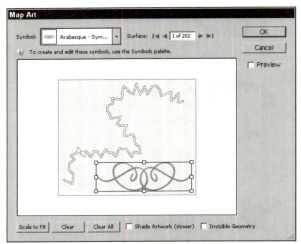

Figure 13-60: The Map Art dialog box lets you add symbols to the surfaces of the selected extruded object.

The Symbol pop-up menu lets you choose a Symbol from the active Symbol palette to apply to the selected surface. The Surface control includes arrows, which let you cycle through all the various surfaces that make up the extruded object. When a surface is selected, it is highlighted red in the art board.

Cross-Reference

Symbols and the Symbol palette are covered in Chapter 10.

The Scale to Fit button causes the selected symbol to be scaled to fit within the selected surface. The Clear button removes the mapped symbol from the selected surface and the Clear All button removes all mapped symbols from the entire object. The Shade Artwork option includes the mapped artwork as part of the shading calculations and the Invisible Geometry option may be selected to hide the geometry and show only the mapped artwork. Using the Invisible Geometry option is helpful to warp artwork along a 3-D surface.

Revolving objects

The Effect ⇨ 3D ⇨ Revolve menu command opens a dialog box, shown in Figure 13-61, which is very similar to the Extrude & Bevel dialog box.

Using the Revolve effect, you can revolve a path about an axis to create a 3-D object like the glass shown in Figure 13-62. The 3D Revolve Options dialog box lets you specify how much of an Angle to revolve about and whether the open ends are capped or not.

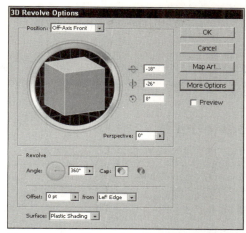

Figure 13-61: The 3D Revolve Options dialog box is similar to the dialog box for the Extrude & Bevel effect.

Figure 13-62: Revolving an open path about its left edge creates a 3-D revolved object.

The Offset lets you specify the location of the center axis about which the selected path is revolved. The Surface options are the same as those for the Extrude & Bevel effect.

Rotating objects

The final effect in the 3-D category is the Rotate effect. This effect lets you rotate and shade 2-D and 3-D objects and paths. The 3D Rotate Options dialog box includes the same position and shading controls as the other 3-D effects.

Using the Convert to Shapes effects

The Convert to Shapes effects let you change the shape of an object into a Rectangle, a Rounded Rectangle, or an Ellipse. Each effect opens a dialog box, like the one shown in Figure 13-63, where you can specify the dimensions of the new shape.

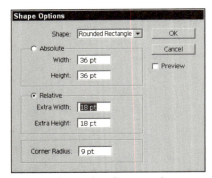

Figure 13-63: The Shape Options dialog box lets you convert shapes and bitmaps into a rectangle, a rounded rectangle, or an ellipse.

Applying standard Illustrator features as effects

Many of the effects found in the Effect menu offer the same functionality as features found elsewhere in Illustrator. For example, all the effects in the Distort & Transform category are exactly the same as those found in the Filter ⇨ Distort menu, except for the Transform effect, which is identical to the Object ⇨ Transform ⇨ Transform Each dialog box.

Applying transforms as an effect causes the effect to appear in the Appearance palette where you have the ability to edit or remove them as needed at a later time without affecting the other attributes.

Cross-Reference More details on the Appearance palette are covered in Chapter 10.

In addition to the Distort & Transform effects, the effects found in the Effect ⇨ Path menu are identical to the features found in the Object ⇨ Path menu. The Effect ⇨ Pathfinder features are also found in the Pathfinder palette.

Using the Stylize effects

Most of the effects in the Effect ⇨ Stylize menu are also found in the Filter ⇨ Stylize menu, but several Stylize effects are unique to the Effect menu.

The Feather effect opens a simple dialog box where you can enter a Feather Radius amount. The Inner and Outer Glow effects open a dialog box like the one in Figure 13-64, where you can select a blending mode, a glow color, an opacity, and blur values, as well as whether the glow emanates from the center or from the edges of the object.

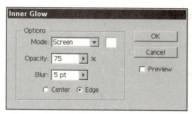

Figure 13-64: The Inner Glow dialog box lets you add a glow to the stroke of an object.

The Scribble effect opens a dialog box, shown in Figure 13-65, where you can make a path look like it was drawn using scribbled strokes. Although the resulting line looks like it was drawn freehand, the object is still a path and maintains it vector properties.

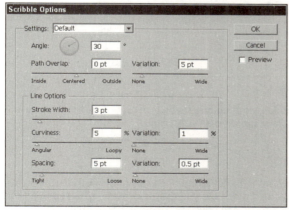

Figure 13-65: The Scribble Options dialog box lets you specify the options to create a rough scribbled look.

At the top of the Scribble Options dialog box is a drop-down list of presets. These presets lets you choose from several different setting configurations, including Childlike, Dense, Loose, Moire, Sharp, Sketch, Snarl, Swash, Tight, and Zig Zag.

The Angle setting defines the angle at which the strokes are aligned, and the Path Overlap defines how often a drawn path crosses itself. Most settings include a Variation setting that is used to specify how random the attribute is. You can also define the Stroke Width, Curviness, and Spacing of the scribble marks.

Figure 13-66 shows examples of the Inner and Outer Glow effects and the Scribble effect.

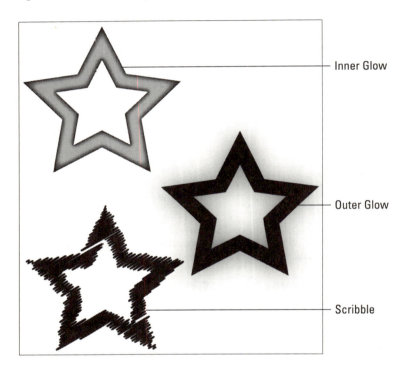

Figure 13-66: The Stylize effects offer some unique features that would be difficult or impossible to create manually.

Using the Warp effects

All the effects in the final category of the Effect menu open the same Warp Options dialog box, shown in Figure 13-67. Using this dialog box, you can deform the selected object into several different shapes including an Arc, Arc Lower, Arc Upper, Arch, Bulge, Shell Lower, Shell Upper, Flag, Wave, Fish, Rise, Fisheye, Inflate, Squeeze, and Twist.

The shape applied may be selected from the Style drop-down list at the top of the dialog box. For each shape, you can specify a Bend value, as well as Horizontal and Vertical Distortion values. The Bend value determines how closely the object matches the designated shape and the Distortion values skew the shape either vertically or horizontally.

Figure 13-68 shows each of the Warp styles found in the Effect ⇨ Warp menu applied to a simple rectangle.

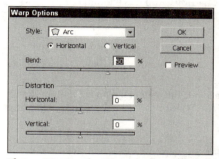

Figure 13-67: The Warp Options dialog box lets you choose the shape style to make the shape conform toward.

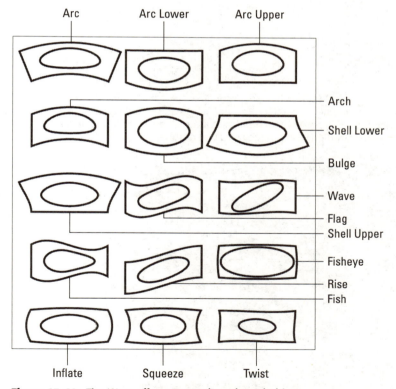

Figure 13-68: The Warp effects cause the selected object to warp to conform to the chosen shape.

Using Photoshop's Layer Effects and Styles

Although effects are typically found in Illustrator, Photoshop has a similar feature that may be applied to a layer called Layer Effects. A pop-up menu of Layer Effects is found at the bottom of the Layers palette.

 Cross-Reference Layers and the Layers palette are covered in detail in Chapter 14.

Not only can you apply these Layer Effects to a layer, but you can also store them as Styles in the Styles palette, shown in Figure 13-69. From the Styles palette, you can apply the Layer Effects to any image or selection.

Figure 13-69: The Styles palette holds all styles, which include Layer Effects.

All the Layer Effects found in the Layers palette open the same dialog box, shown in Figure 13-70. This Layer Style dialog box includes a panel for each of the Layer Effects including Blending Options; Drop Shadow; Inner Shadow; Outer Glow; Inner Glow; Bevel and Emboss; Satin; Color Overlay; Gradient Overlay; Pattern Overlay; and Stroke.

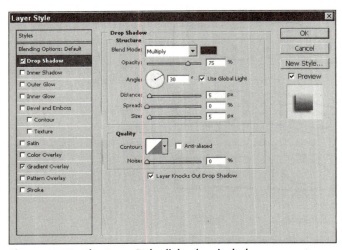

Figure 13-70: The Layer Style dialog box includes a separate panel for each Layer Effect.

Each Layer Effect may be turned on or off using the check box to the left of the effect name. To the right of the dialog box is a sample thumbnail of the defined style and a New Style button. Clicking the New Style button opens a dialog box where you can name the new style. Clicking OK adds the defined style to the Styles palette.

Each Layer Effect applied to a layer is listed in the Layers palette. Double-clicking on the effect in the Layers palette opens the Layer Style dialog box where you can edit the effects settings.

Applying Effects in InDesign

Although InDesign doesn't include support for graphic filters or effects, it does include several special effects that may be applied to objects including Drop Shadows, Feathering, and Corner Effects. Each of these features is found in the Object menu.

Adding drop shadows

Choosing Object ⇨ Drop Shadow opens a dialog box, shown in Figure 13-71, where you can set the properties of the drop shadow including a blending mode, an opacity, an X and Y offset, a blur, and a color. The bottom of the dialog box includes several swatches that you can select from.

Note For drop shadows, the default blending mode, Multiply, creates the most realistic shadow and is probably the most reliable blending mode for printing.

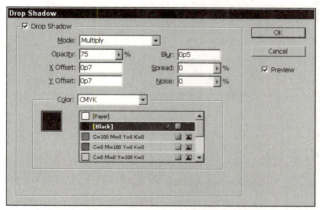

Figure 13-71: The Drop Shadow dialog box in InDesign lets you add drop shadows to any element.

Feathering objects

Choosing Object ⇨ Feather opens a simple dialog box where you can set the Feather Width and choose whether the corners stay sharp, rounded, or diffused.

Creating corner effects

Choosing Object ⇨ Corner Effects opens a simple dialog box where you can choose from the available effects. The options include None, Fancy, Bevel, Inset, Inverse Rounded, and Rounded. You can also set the size of the effect.

Figure 13-72 shows each of the corner effects available in InDesign.

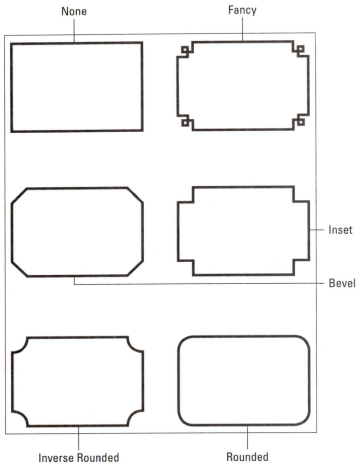

Figure 13-72: Using corner effects adds some flair to the rectangular frames.

Summary

- Most Photoshop filters are applied using the Filter Gallery interface. This interface includes a wide assortment of filters and allows you to preview and apply multiple filters at once.
- The Filter menu in Photoshop also includes many other filters that aren't part of the Filter Gallery. These filters are selected from the Filter menu.
- Photoshop includes three additional filter interfaces for working with images, including the Extract, Liquify, and Pattern Maker interfaces.
- Most of the Photoshop filters may also be applied to objects within Illustrator.
- In addition to the Photoshop filters, Illustrator also includes some filters that may only be used on vector objects. These filters are found at the top of the Filter menu.
- Effects used in Illustrator show up in the Appearance palette and may be edited or removed at any time.
- Layer Effects in Photoshop appear in the Layers palette and may be used to create a new style.
- InDesign includes a few effects in its Object menu.

✦ ✦ ✦

Working with Layers

CHAPTER 14

♦ ♦ ♦ ♦

In This Chapter

Using the Layers palette

Using layers in InDesign

Using layers in Illustrator

Using layers in Photoshop

Using layers in GoLive

Viewing layers in Acrobat

The real benefit of layers is their ability to organize a project into several easy-to-select sections. Previously, this was done with groups, but groups can be tricky to work with, requiring the Group Selection tool to work within a group. Layers are a much more convenient way to organize all the images and objects in a document.

Another benefit of layers is that you can quickly turn them on and off. If a project is sluggish because of its size and content, you could place these slow to refresh items on a layer and make them invisible so they don't slow down the rest of the project.

Layers may also be locked. You may want to lock parts of your completed project, so you don't accidentally select and move them.

You can also create several design ideas and keep them on several layers. Then you can quickly switch between the various designs using layers. This is a concept mastered by Photoshop with the Layer Comps feature.

Layers are available in Photoshop, Illustrator, InDesign, GoLive, and Acrobat, but the ways layers are used in each of these applications are very different. Layers in each of these applications include some basic concepts that are common for all applications:

- **InDesign:** Layers in InDesign use the most basic layer features, but even InDesign includes some specialized layer features.

- **Illustrator:** Illustrator expands on the layer basics with many additional layer features, including support for sublayers, layer templates, releasing items to layers, and clipping and opacity masks.

- **Photoshop:** Photoshop takes layer functionality to a whole new level with support for layer sets, linked layers, transparency, adjustment and fill layers, layer effects, masks, and layer comps.

- **Acrobat:** In Acrobat 7, you find support for Adobe PDF Layers. PDF documents containing layers must be authored in applications supporting layers and having the ability to export to the PDF 1.5 format. If you view a layered PDF document in earlier versions of Acrobat, the layers are flattened and viewed as a single layer document.

✦ **GoLive:** The layers found in GoLive are created with the Cascading Style Sheet (CSS) features for placing Web page content in stackable layers. This endows the GoLive layers with several unique features such as Web page placement, background colors and images, and animation capabilities.

In this chapter, we present these layer basics first, starting with InDesign. We then move on to the specific layer features for each individual application. In this chapter, we start by looking at the Layers palette's basic features found in InDesign. Finally, we show you how layered files exported to the PDF format can access layers in Acrobat.

Using the Layers Palette

Within the CS2 applications, layers for the current file and all the layer features are contained in the Layers palette, shown in Figure 14-1. Open this palette by choosing Window ⇨ Layers.

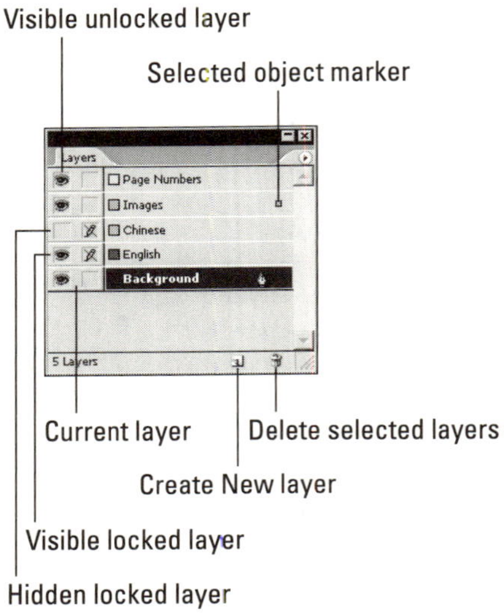

Figure 14-1: All layers for the current InDesign document display in the Layers palette.

All new projects created in Illustrator and InDesign include a default layer named Layer 1; a new layer added to the document is named Layer 2 by default. Double-clicking on a layer opens a dialog box where you can rename the layer and set the layer's properties.

Within the Layers palette are several visual icons that determine whether the selected layer is visible, locked, selected, or targeted. The eye icon in the first column to the left of the layer name determines layer visibility. The lock icon in the second column to the left of the layer name is used to show if a layer is locked.

Note   Actually, in Illustrator, it's a lock icon; in Photoshop, it's a lock icon at the top of the Layers palette; and in InDesign, it's a no-write icon. There are subtle differences among the different CS2 applications.

Other icons appear to the right of the layer name and are used to denote the targeted layer and any selected objects on that layer. The selected layer(s) are highlighted.

Creating layers

To create a new layer, select the New Layer palette menu command or click on the Create New Layer button at the bottom of the Layers palette. If you select the menu command, the Layer Options dialog box appears, shown in Figure 14-2. Here, you can name the new layer, select a layer color, and specify several layer properties. Clicking the Create New Layer button creates a new layer using default values without opening the Layer Options dialog box. To force the Layer Options dialog box to appear when you click Create New Layer, hold down the Option/Alt key when clicking.

Figure 14-2: The Layer Options dialog box

The layer properties that appear in the Layer Options dialog box set options such as whether the layer is visible or locked. You can open the Layer Options dialog box for any existing layer by double clicking on the layer.

Note: Other than layer name and color, the specific layer properties found in the Layer Options dialog box are unique for each CS2 application. For example, InDesign includes options to show guides, lock guides, and suppress text wrap when the layer is hidden; Illustrator includes options to make the layer a template, print, preview, and dim images to a percentage; and Photoshop includes options to use the previous layer to create a clipping mask, select a blending mode, and set an opacity.

If you double-click on a layer name or if you select a layer and choose the Layer Options palette menu command, the Layer Options dialog box reappears, letting you change the layer properties. Double-clicking the layer name in Photoshop or GoLive selects the name and lets you rename it within the Layers palette.

In InDesign, new layers always appear at the top of the Layers palette, but if you hold down the ⌘/Ctrl key while clicking on the Create New Layer button, the new layer appears directly above the selected layer. In Photoshop, you can make the new layer appear directly below the current layer by holding down the Option/Alt key. Creating a new layer in Illustrator or Photoshop places the new layer directly above the selected layer.

Selecting and targeting layers

Clicking on a layer name selects and targets a layer. To select multiple layers, hold down the ⌘/Ctrl key while clicking on each layer that you want to select, or hold down the Shift key and click on the first and last layers to select all layers between these two layers.

The targeted layer in InDesign is marked with a Pen icon to the right of the layer name. Targeted layers in Illustrator are marked with a small triangle in the upper-right corner; the targeted layer in Photoshop is the selected layer. All new objects that you add to the project, including all newly created objects and any imported, copied, or placed files, are placed on the active layer.

Caution If you lock the targeted layer, you can't create the new object, but a warning dialog box appears, informing you that the targeted layer is hidden or locked and asking if you want to unlock and show it.

Hiding and locking layers

The first column in the Layers palette holds the Visibility icon. If the eye icon is present, the layer is visible, but if the eye icon isn't present, the layer is hidden. You can toggle the eye icon by clicking on it. Hidden layers are not printed either, although you can print hidden layers in Illustrator if you select the Print option in the Layers Options dialog box.

The second column is the Lock icon. If the lock icon is present, the layer is locked and cannot be selected or edited, but if the lock icon isn't present, the layer is editable. You can also toggle the lock icon by clicking on it.

Note Within InDesign, the lock icon looks like a pencil icon with a red line through it; in Illustrator, the lock icon looks like a lock. Photoshop uses the second column for other purposes and allows layers to be locked using the Lock properties at the top of the palette. Photoshop includes the option to lock specific attributes; the lock icon is displayed to the right of the layer name. GoLive locks layers using the second column in the Layers palette.

To hide or lock multiple layers at once, choose the Hide Others or Lock Others palette menu commands, and all layers that aren't selected are hidden or locked. If at least one layer is hidden or locked, these menu commands change to Show All Layers or Unlock All Layers.

Rearranging layers

The order in which the layers are listed in the Layers palette determines the stacking order of objects on the page, with the layer listed at the top of the Layers palette appearing in front of all other objects in the document.

You can rearrange layers by selecting and dragging one layer above or below another. A dark black line appears between the two layers where the dragged layer is positioned if dropped.

Copying objects between layers

The Selection tool may be used to select any object on any layer that is not locked. A small square icon appears to the right of the layer name of each layer that includes a selected object in Illustrator and InDesign.

The bounding box of the selected object is colored using the layer color.

Tip To select all objects on a single layer, hold down the Option/Alt key while clicking on the layer name in the Layers palette. If the layer doesn't contain any objects, then you can't select it with the Option/Alt key held down.

To move a selected object to another layer, click and drag the small square icon to the layer that you want to move the object to. If you hold down the Option/Alt key while dragging the small square icon, a copy of the selected object moves to the selected layer. If you hold down Ctrl+Alt (Windows) or ⌘+Option (Mac) while dragging the small square icon, the selected object may be moved onto a hidden or locked layer.

You can choose Edit ➪ Cut, Edit ➪ Copy, or Edit ➪ Paste to move objects between layers and between documents. If you enable the Paste Remembers Layers option (only available in Illustrator and InDesign) in the palette menu, then the pasted objects are pasted in the same layers from which you copied them. If you paste the copied objects into a document without the same layer names, the layer names for the selected objects are added to the new document and the copied objects are pasted on these new layers.

Duplicating layers

You can use the Duplicate palette menu command to duplicate a layer and all the objects on that layer. The duplicated layer appears directly above the original layer. You can also duplicate a layer by dragging a layer to the Create New Layer button at the bottom of the palette. The duplicated layer appears with the same layer name with the word, *copy* after it, so duplicating a layer named "Sword" results in a layer named "Sword copy." Duplicating this layer again results in a layer named "Sword copy 2."

Deleting layers

You can use the Delete palette menu command to delete the selected layers, or you can click on the Delete Selected Layers button at the bottom of the Layers palette. If the layer contains any objects, a warning dialog box appears confirming that you want to delete the objects on the layer.

To delete any empty layers in the current document, select the Delete Unused Layers palette menu command. This removes any layers that don't contain any objects.

Merging layers

You use the Merge Layers palette menu command to combine all objects on the selected layers. The objects all appear on the targeted layer, and the other selected layers are deleted. Selecting all layers and choosing this command offers a way to flatten all layers to a single layer.

STEPS: Creating a Layered Document

1. **Create a new document.** Within Photoshop, Illustrator, or InDesign, choose File ➪ New to create a new document.

2. **Open the Layers palette.** Choose Window ➪ Layers to open the Layers palette. The default layer is listed as Layer 1.

3. **Add content to the layer.** Using the tools in the Toolbox, add some content to the existing layer.

4. **Create a new layer.** Before you being to add a new type of content, click the Create New Layer button at the bottom of the Layers palette to create a new layer. In the New Layer dialog box that appears, name the layer appropriately.

5. **Hide and lock the first layer.** To hide the content on the first layer so it isn't accidentally edited, click on the eye icon to the left of the first layer's name. This icon hides the layer. If you need to see the content in the first layer, but you don't want it edited, click the eye icon again to make the layer visible; then click the lock icon in the second column to lock the layer.

6. **Rearrange the layers.** The new layer appears in front of the first layer. To change this order, click and the drag the first layer above the new layer in the Layers palette. Placing the first layer above the other layer makes its content come to the front of the stacking order.

STEPS: Dividing an Existing Document into Layers

1. **Open a document in InDesign.** Within InDesign, select a document that you want to divide into layers for better organization.
2. **Open the Layers palette.** Choose Window ⇨ Layers to open the Layers palette.
3. **Create new layers.** Click on the Create New Layer button at the bottom of the Layers palette several times to create some new layers.
4. **Rename the layers.** Double-click on each of the new layers and, in the Layer Options dialog box that appears, type a new descriptive name for the layer such as Background, images, text, guides, etc.
5. **Move objects to their correct layer.** Move through each page in the document and select the objects on that page. Then drag the square selected icon in the Layers palette to the correct layer for that object. After an object is moved to its correct layer, its bounding box changes to the same color as its layer. Continue this step for all objects in the document. Figure 14-3 shows the layers created for this document.

Figure 14-3: After creating and naming the necessary layers, objects are easily placed on the correct layer.

Using Layers in InDesign

In addition to the basic features found in the Layers palette, InDesign also includes a couple of layer features that are unique to the application, including the ability to condense the layers list in the Layers palette, show and lock layer guides, suppress text wrap, and features for dealing with objects on Master pages.

Condensing the Layers palette

Within InDesign, the Layers palette may be condensed using the Small Palette Rows palette menu option. Figure 14-4 shows the Layers palette in InDesign with the Small Palette Rows option enabled.

Figure 14-4: The Small Palette Rows option condenses layer sizes.

Using guides

Guides in InDesign are especially useful for aligning and positioning elements; each layer may have its own set of guides. Guides are created for the selected layer by clicking on the Horizontal or Vertical rulers and dragging into the page. If the rulers aren't visible, you can choose View ➪ Grids & Guides ➪ Show Rulers to make them visible.

Guides appear as straight lines in the document and the selected guide has the same color as the selected layer.

The View ➪ Grids & Guides ➪ Show/Hide Guides menu command and the View ➪ Lock Guides menu command are used to show, hide, and lock all guides in the current document. But you can also select to show, hide, and lock guides on a specific layer using the Show Guides and Lock Guides options in the Layer Options dialog box. Double-clicking on a layer in the Layers palette opens this dialog box.

Suppressing text wrap on hidden layers

In an InDesign document, it's often helpful to separate text and graphics onto separate layers. By doing so, you can make the graphics hidden when you're proofreading the text, and you can hide the text when you're working on the graphics.

If the text object is set to wrap around a graphic, making either layer hidden affects the text wrapping. You can control whether the text is wrapped when the graphic layer is hidden using the Suppress Text Wrap When Hidden option in the Layer Options dialog box.

Figure 14-5 shows two similar documents that have separated the graphics and text onto two different layers. Although the text is set to wrap around the center graphic, the document on the left has the Suppress Text Wrap When Hidden option disabled in the Layer Options dialog box, so the text wrap is still visible; the document on the right has enabled this option, causing the text wrap to be suppressed.

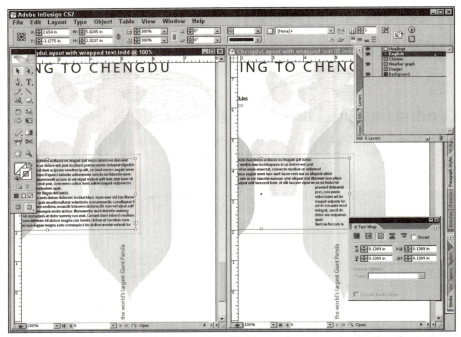

Figure 14-5: The Suppress Text Wrap When Hidden option controls whether the text wraps when the graphic layer is hidden.

Reordering Master objects above layers

By default, Master objects placed on the same layer as page objects appear behind those page objects. To make the Master object, such as auto page numbers, appear in front of the page objects, place the Master objects on a layer that is above the page object's layer.

STEPS: Making Page Numbers Appear in Front of Other Elements

1. **Open a document in InDesign.** Within InDesign, open a document that includes Master pages and auto page numbers.

2. **Add an element to the Master page.** In the Layers palette, select the Background layer. Then in the Pages palette, double-click on the master page you want to change to select them. Then click on the Rectangle tool and drag a rectangle over the top of the page number in the upper-right corner of the Master page. Change the rectangle's Fill color to red and its Stroke color to black with a Weight of 2 pt, as shown in Figure 14-6.

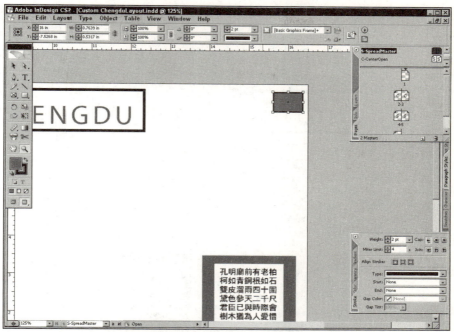

Figure 14-6: Adding an object onto the current layer places the object on top of the Master objects that appear on that page.

3. **Create a new layer for the Master page numbers.** In the Layers palette, click on the Create New Layer button at the bottom of the Layers palette. A new layer is added at the top of the Layers palette. Then double-click on the new layer, name the layer Master Page Numbers, and click OK.

4. **Move the Master Page Number element to the new layer.** Click the Visibility icon for the background layer to temporarily hide the background layer so you can see the page number element hidden behind the rectangle. Then select the page number element. In the Layers palette, drag the small rectangle to the right of the Master Objects layer to the Master Page Numbers layer to move the selected object to the new layer.

5. **Make all layers visible.** As a final step, click the eye icon for the background layer to show all layers. The results are shown in Figure 14-7, where the page number is positioned in front of the red rectangle.

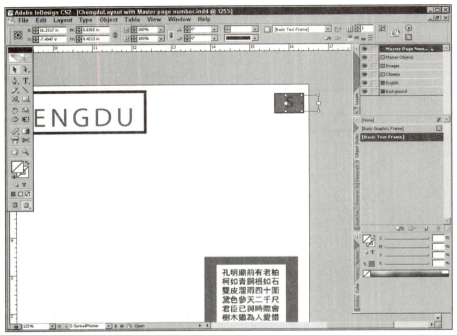

Figure 14-7: Moving the Master elements to a layer positioned above the layer with the obscuring object makes the Master elements visible.

Importing layered files

When layered files such as Photoshop, Illustrator, PDF, and TIFF images are placed within InDesign by choosing File ⇨ Place, InDesign flattens all layers. This flattening affects only the image within InDesign and does not affect the original image file or its layers.

If you need to edit the original file, you can select the file in the Links palette and choose the Edit Original palette menu command. This opens the image file in the application that was used to originally create the image or if you double click on the file in the Links palette with the Option/Alt key held down, the file is opened in its native app.

Cross-Reference

To learn more about working with the Links palette, see Chapter 27.

Applying transparency and blending modes to a layer

You use blending modes to define how the colors of two overlapping transparent objects are blended. Although InDesign doesn't include a way to apply transparency or blending mode to an InDesign document layer, you can quickly select all objects on a selected layer by holding down the Option/Alt key while clicking on the layer in the Layers palette. With all objects on a layer selected, you can set the layer's Opacity value and blending mode using the Transparency palette, shown in Figure 14-8.

Note Photoshop allows you to apply an Opacity value and blending mode to an entire layer.

Figure 14-8: The Transparency palette in InDesign

 Cross-Reference Details on using transparency and the blending modes are found in Chapter 10.

Using Layers in Illustrator

Layers in Illustrator have much more functionality than those found in InDesign, but the Layers palette still includes all the basic layer features already covered. One of the key benefits is that the Illustrator's Layers palette lets you drill down within layers to view and select the each individual item included in a layer.

The Layer options within Illustrator are also unique, offering options to specify whether the layer objects are shown in Preview or Outline mode and whether the layer objects are printed.

Layers in Illustrator are capable of holding appearance attributes. You can select and move these attributes between different layers. You can also apply graphic styles directly to a targeted layer from the Graphic Styles palette. Illustrator's Layers palette also includes a simple way to create clipping masks.

 Cross-Reference Using Graphic Styles and attributes is covered in Chapter 10.

Figure 14-9 shows the Layers palette in Illustrator. It includes additional palette buttons for creating sublayers and clipping masks.

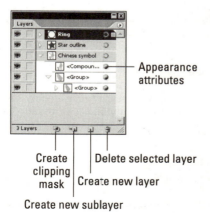

Figure 14-9: The Layers palette in Illustrator offers some additional features.

Changing the Layers palette view

Illustrator offers several different ways to view the Layers palette, as specified in the Layers Palette Options dialog box, shown in Figure 14-10. This dialog box is accessed using the Palette Options palette menu command.

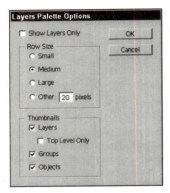

Figure 14-10: The Layers Palette Options dialog box

The Show Layers Only option hides all sublayers and displays only the top-level layer names.

The Row Size section lets you choose the size of the layer rows in the Layers palette from Small, Medium, Large, or Other, where you can set the row size in pixels. The Small option displays the layers without any thumbnails, similar to the Layers palette in InDesign when the Small Palette Rows option is enabled. The Medium option displays smaller thumbnails, as shown in Figure 14-9, and the Large option is shown in Figure 14-11.

Figure 14-11: The Large option increases the size of the layer thumbnails.

The Thumbnails section lets you display the thumbnails for layers, the top level only, groups, and/or objects. Selecting the Top Level Only option only shows thumbnails for the top level and hides the thumbnails for all sublayers.

Using sublayers

All layers that contain objects have a small arrow to the left of the layer name. Clicking this arrow changes the arrow's direction and expands the layer to reveal all the layer's sublayers or objects. Clicking on an expanded arrow icon collapses the layer again. If you hold down the Option/Alt key while clicking on an arrow, all sublayers expand.

You can create new sublayers in Illustrator just as new layers by selecting the New Sublayer palette menu command or by clicking on the Create New Sublayer button at the bottom of the Layers palette. Selecting this command or holding down the Option/Alt key while clicking the Create New Sublayer button causes the Layer Options dialog box to appear.

If you select the Top Layer Only option in the Palette Options dialog box, then thumbnails don't display for any sublayers.

Because layers and/or sublayers are rearranged by dragging them in the Layers palette, if you drop a layer when a layer name is highlighted, the dropped layer becomes a sublayer under the selected layer.

With all the layers and sublayers, it can become difficult to find objects in the Layers palette. To locate an object's layer using the object, just select the object in the art board and choose the Locate Object palette menu command; the object's sublayer is revealed and selected in the Layers palette.

Object groups created by choosing Object ⇨ Group show up in the Layers palette as a sublayer identified with the word *Group* listed in brackets. Expanding the Group sublayer reveals all the objects that are part of the group. If you create a group from several objects on different layers, all the objects move to the same layer as the frontmost object.

Printing and previewing layers

The Layer Options dialog box, shown in Figure 14-12, for layers in Illustrator includes Print and Preview options. These options determine whether the designated layer is printed and whether the layer is displayed in Preview or Outline mode.

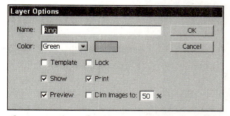

Figure 14-12: The Layer Options dialog box in Illustrator

Holding down the ⌘/Ctrl key while clicking on the Visibility icon toggles the selected layer between Preview and Outline mode. This changes the Visibility icon, as shown in Figure 14-13. Using the Outline Others palette menu command, or holding down Ctrl+Alt (Windows) or ⌘+Option (Mac) while clicking on the Visibility icon changes all layers except for the selected one to Outline mode.

The Layer Options dialog box also includes an option to dim images by a specific percentage. This is helpful if you're tracing images, as shown in Figure 14-14.

Disabling the Print option prevents the layer from printing when you choose File ⇨ Print, even if the layer objects are visible. If you disable the Preview option, the layer objects are viewed in Outline mode. This is a useful option if you have a complex object that takes a long time to redraw.

Layer in Outline mode

Figure 14-13: The eye icon shows what layers are in Outline mode.

Layer in Preview mode

Figure 14-14: The Dim Images By option makes tracing images easy.

Creating layer templates

The Layer Options dialog box also includes an option to make a layer into a template layer. You can also make a layer a template by selecting the Template palette menu command. The Visibility icon for templates changes as shown in Figure 14-15.

Note Layer templates are different from the Illustrator templates created by choosing File ➪ Save as Template. Illustrator templates have a different file extension (AIT), but layer templates may exist in any Illustrator document.

Normal layer

Figure 14-15: Template layers don't print or export with the rest of the layers.

Template layer

Template layers are unique because you cannot print or export them. You can also hide them by choosing View ➪ Show/Hide Template (Shift+Ctrl+W in Windows; Shift+⌘+W on the Mac).

When you choose File ➪ Place, the Place dialog box includes a Template option. If this option is selected, the placed image is put on a new template layer. This new layer is positioned directly below the selected layer. By default, this template layer is locked and the layer dims to 50 percent.

You may change template layers back to normal layers by disabling the Template option in the Layer Options dialog box.

STEPS: Tracing Layers in Illustrator

1. **Open a new document in Illustrator.** Within Illustrator, open a new document by choosing File ➪ New.

2. **Open an image to trace from.** Choose File ➪ Place. In the file dialog box that opens, select an image that you want to trace from and enable the Template option, as shown in Figure 14-16. Then click on the Place button. The image is placed on a new template layer and the Dim Layer to 50% option is enabled in the Layer Options dialog box.

3. **Trace the image.** Select a layer above the template layer and trace over the image with the Paintbrush tool, as shown in Figure 14-17.

4. **Hide the template layer.** After the sketch is complete, you can hide the template layer by clicking on the Visibility icon.

Cross-Reference Another approach is to use Illustrator's Live Trace feature, which is covered in Chapter 11.

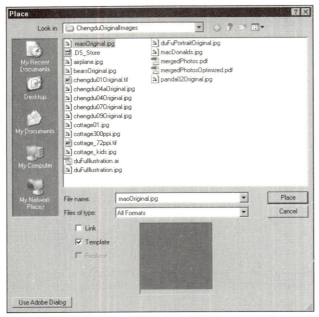

Figure 14-16: The Place dialog box includes a Template option.

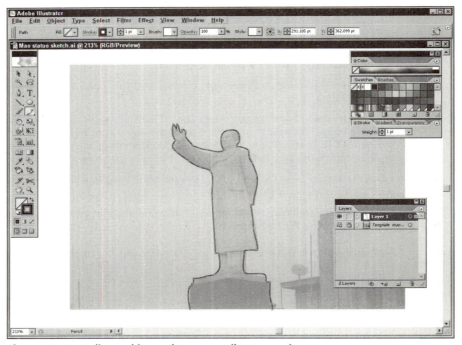

Figure 14-17: A dimmed image lets you easily trace an image.

Releasing items to layers in Illustrator

If a single layer has many different objects, you can use the Release to Layers palette menu commands to move (or copy) each successive object to its own layer.

Illustrator's Release to Layers menu commands are useful in building animation sequences that you can then export to the SWF format. More information on this format and using the Release to Layers commands to create animations is covered in Chapter 35.

There are actually two different Release to Layers menu commands. The Release to Layers (Sequence) palette menu command moves each object to its own layer, but the Release to Layers (Build) menu command copies and accumulates the objects to new layers where first object gets copied to a new layer, the second object along with the first gets copied to the second layer, and so on until the final layer has all objects.

When objects within a layer are released to layers, the objects are added to layers starting with the object farthest back in the stacking order and moving forward, so the front-most object is placed on the highest layer.

With several layers selected, you can select to reverse their order in the Layers palette by using the Reverse Order palette menu command.

Collecting layers and flattening artwork

Illustrator includes palette menu commands for merging, collecting, and flattening layers. Merging layers places all objects from several layers into the topmost layer. Collecting layers is similar to merging layers, but instead it collects the objects on several layers and moves them to a new layer while making the layers sublayers under the new layer. The Collect in New Layer palette menu command moves all objects on the selected layers to a new layer and deletes the old layers.

Illustrator also includes a Merge Selected menu command that merges the objects on all selected layers into the targeted layer.

The Layers palette only lets you select multiple layers within the same hierarchical level, so you cannot merge or collect layers at different levels within one another.

To merge all layers together, you could select all layers and use the Merge Selected palette menu command, or you could use the Flatten Artwork palette menu command. This merges all layers into one layer that includes all the objects in the file.

The Flatten Artwork palette menu command cannot include layers that are hidden or locked. If you try to use the Flatten Artwork palette menu command with a hidden layer, a warning dialog box appears, asking if you want to discard the hidden art. Clicking the Yes button throws away all objects on the hidden layer and combines the rest of the objects into a single layer.

Importing Photoshop layers and comps into Illustrator and InDesign

When you choose File ➪ Open or you choose File ➪ Place to open or place a layered Photoshop image into the current document, the Photoshop Import Options dialog box appears, shown in Figure 14-18. The Photoshop Import Options dialog box gives you the option to convert the Photoshop layers to objects or flatten the Photoshop layers.

Note The Photoshop Import Options dialog box also gives you the option to import image maps and/or slices if they exist in the Photoshop image.

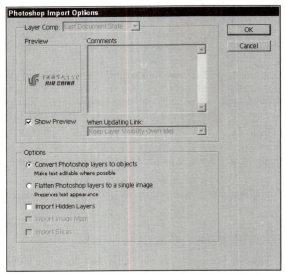

Figure 14-18: When you place layered Photoshop images in Illustrator, you can convert the layers to objects or flatten all the layers.

If you select to convert the layers to objects, Illustrator imports the Photoshop layers, as best it can, into the current selected layer. It also does it best to make any text in the Photoshop file editable. However, if the Photoshop layer includes features not supported in Illustrator such as Layer Effects, Adjustment or Fill layers are merged during the conversion process.

You can also select to import any hidden layers included in the Photoshop image, but if the hidden layer includes a feature that isn't supported, the layer is simply ignored.

New Feature The ability to select Photoshop layer comps in Illustrator is new to CS2.

If the layered Photoshop image includes any layer comps, then you can select which comp to import after viewing them in the Preview pane. If the layer comp has any comments, they are shown in the Comments field. The When Updating Link option includes two options–Keep Layer Visibility Overrides and Use Photoshop's Layer Visibility. This setting determines how the visibility of the file is determined for images that are linked into Illustrator or InDesign.

Exporting CSS layers

When exporting Illustrator artwork to a Web-based format using the File ➪ Save for Web menu command, you can choose to export the layers as Cascading Style Sheet (CSS) layers. These layers are recognized within GoLive and may be used to add animated effects on a Web page.

To export layers as CSS layers, select the Layers panel in the lower-right corner of the Save for Web dialog box, as shown in Figure 14-19, and enable the Export As CSS Layers option. The Layers panel also lets you select a specific layer and designate it as Visible, Hidden, or Do Not Export. If the Preview Only Selected Layer option is selected, only the layer selected in the Layer panel is visible in the Original panel.

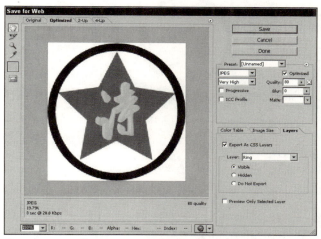

Figure 14-19: The Layers panel in the Save for Web dialog box

When you save the document, each layer is saved within a folder named `images` using the format designated in the Save for Web dialog box. The first layer is given the specified filename, and each additional layer has a sequential number following it. For example, if you save an Illustrator document with three layers as a GIF image with the name myFile, the first layer is named myFile.gif, the second layer becomes myFile01.gif, and the third layer becomes myFile02.gif.

If you select to have the Save for Web dialog box create an HTML page for you, then opening the HTML page in GoLive displays all layers as CSS layers in their same positions that were found in the Illustrator artwork, as shown in Figure 14-20. The layers are named Anonymous when opened within GoLive.

Note   CSS Layers are specified in the HTML page, so if you don't select to create an HTML page along with the graphics, the exported image won't include any layers.

Applying appearance attributes to layers in Illustrator

The column of circles to the right in the Layers palette allows appearance attributes to be set for all objects on the targeted layer or sublayer.

Clicking on the circle once targets that layer to receive any appearance changes, such as fill or stroke color, an effect, or a style from the Graphic Styles palette. When a layer is targeted, an additional circle surrounds the existing circle, as shown in Figure 14-21. You can target multiple layers at the same time by holding down the Shift key while clicking on the circle icon for several layers.

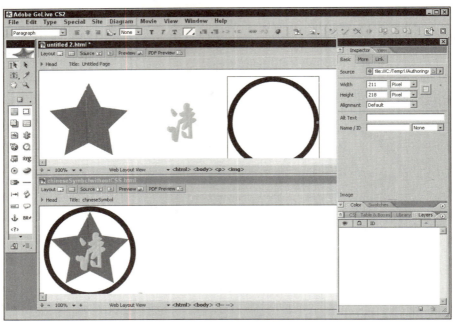

Figure 14-20: Opening the separated layers as images within a Web page (top) keeps all layer objects separate, but opening the HTML page places all layers in their original positions (bottom).

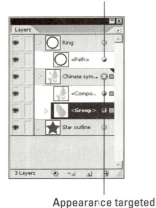

Additional Appearance exists

Appearance targeted

Figure 14-21: The circle target is circled again when a layer is targeted.

With a layer (or several layers) targeted, change an attribute setting such as the fill color, a stroke setting, or a style in the Graphic Styles palette, or apply an effect from the Effect menu, and all the objects on the targeted layers are changed.

If you move an object out of a layer that has certain appearance attributes applied, the moved object no longer has those attributes. Attributes that you assign to a layer stay with that layer, not with the objects.

When a layer includes any appearance attributes other than standard fill and stroke attributes, the appearance attribute circle in the Layers palette appears shaded solid.

You can move appearance attributes between layers by dragging the appearance attributes circle from one layer to another. Holding down the Option/Alt key while dragging an appearance attribute copies the attribute to the other layer. Dragging the appearance attribute circle to the Delete Selection icon button at the bottom of the Layers palette deletes the attributes from the layer, except for the fill and stroke colors, which remain.

More on using effects and styles is covered in Chapter 12.

STEPS: Tracing Layers in Illustrator

1. **Open a new document in Illustrator.** Within Illustrator, open a new document by choosing File ➪ New. In the New Document dialog box, click OK.

2. **Create a circle.** Select the Ellipse tool and drag in the center of the art board with the Option/Alt and Shift keys held down to create a perfect circle in the center of the art board. Set the Fill color to white and the Stroke color to black with a Stroke Width of 10.

3. **Scale down the circle.** Choose Object ➪ Transform ➪ Scale. In the Scale dialog box, set the Uniform Scale value to 80% and click the Copy button.

4. **Duplicate the scaling command.** With the inner circle selected, choose Object ➪ Transform ➪ Transform Again or use the ⌘/Ctrl+D keyboard shortcut to apply this transformation eight more times. This creates nine centered circles in the center of the art board on a single layer, as shown in Figure 14-22.

5. **Release the objects to separate layers.** With the layer that holds all these objects selected in the Layers palette, choose the Release to Layers (Sequence) palette menu command. This moves each object to its own layer. Although each object was selectable as a sublayer previously, releasing the objects to layers makes them easier to reference and work with.

6. **Apply a fill color to every other circle.** Within the Layers palette, hold down the Shift key and select the appearance attribute-targeting circle for every odd number layer starting with Layer 3. Then select a red color swatch from the Swatches palette. Every other circle is filled with this color, as shown in Figure 14-23.

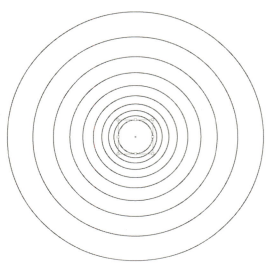

Figure 14-22: After scaling a duplicate object, you may use the Transform Again menu command to quickly create many additional copies.

Figure 14-23: Using the target circle in the Layers palette, you can selectively choose exactly which layers get a certain appearance attribute.

7. **Change the stroke weight for all layers.** In the Layers palette, click the appearance attribute target for the top layer named Layer 1 to select all objects. Then set the Weight value in the Strokes palette to 4 pt. This adds a darker ring to each object, as shown in Figure 14-24.

Figure 14-24: With all the sublayers conveniently located under a parent layer, you can easily target all layers.

8. **Apply an effect.** With the top layer still targeted, choose Effect ⇨ Distort & Transform ⇨ Pucker & Bloat. In the Pucker & Bloat dialog box that appears, set the Pucker/Bloat value to 50% and click OK. The result is shown in Figure 14-25. Notice how the appearance attribute target is now shaded for the top layer, indicating that an appearance attribute other than a fill and stroke has been applied.

9. **Increase the Bloat effect.** Just for fun, try reapplying the Bloat effect with a value of 200% by double-clicking on the effect in the Appearance palette. This pushes the edges of the circles through each other to create an interesting pattern, shown in Figure 14-26.

Figure 14-25: Even effects may be targeted and applied to specific layers.

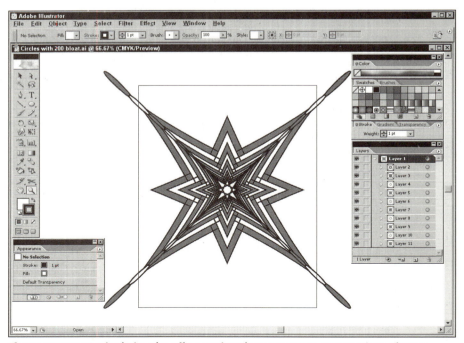

Figure 14-26: Manipulating the effect settings lets you create many unique shapes.

Creating clipping masks

Illustrator includes an Object ⇨ Clipping Mask ⇨ Make menu command for creating clipping masks. You can specify that an Opacity Mask is used as a clipping mask, but you can also create clipping masks using a layer or sublayer.

Standard Illustrator clipping masks and opacity masks are covered in Chapter 10.

When creating a clipping mask using a layer or sublayer, the topmost object in the layer becomes the clipping mask and it masks all objects in the layer underneath it. To create a clipping mask from a layer, select the layer and choose the Make Clipping Mask palette menu command, or click on the Make/Release Clipping Mask button at the bottom of the Layers palette. Figure 14-27 shows a sample clipping mask applied to a placed image.

You can only use vector objects as clipping masks in Illustrator. If you want to use a raster image as a clipping mask, use Photoshop.

The object used as the clipping mask loses its appearance attributes, and its stroke is changed to none. If you want to use the stroke or effect outline as part of the clipping mask, choose Object ⇨ Expand Appearance before making a clipping mask.

Figure 14-27: By placing an object above the placed image, you can use the Make Clipping Mask palette menu command in the Layers palette.

You can identify clipping masks in the Layers palette because they're separated from the objects that they mask by a dotted line. If you need to reposition the clipping mask or any of the objects that it masks, simply click on the target circle in the Layers palette and then click and drag the object or the mask to its new location. You can also choose Select ⇨ Object ⇨ Clipping Mask to select the clipping mask.

If you select a layer with a clipping mask, the palette menu changes to Release Clipping Mask, allowing you to remove a clipping mask.

STEPS: Creating a Clipping Mask

1. **Open a document in Illustrator.** Within Illustrator, choose File ⇨ Place and open an image to which you want to apply a clipping mask. Figure 14-28 shows an image placed within an Illustrator document.

2. **Add some text to the image.** Select the Type tool and drag a text area on top of the image. Then type the word **CHENGDU** (in all capitals). In the Character palette, change the Font to Cooper Black and the Size to 90 pt. The text, shown in Figure 14-29, doesn't cover much of the image, but this is easily fixed by stretching the text.

Figure 14-28: The File ⇨ Place menu command places an image within an Illustrator document.

Figure 14-29: Use the Type tool to add text to an Illustrator document.

3. **Converting the text to outlines.** Before the text can be stretched, it needs to be converted to outlines. Choose Type ➪ Create Outlines to complete the conversion.

4. **Scale and position the text.** With the text converted to outlines, you can drag on its lower edge to stretch the text vertically. Then drag the text until it covers most of the relevant image areas, as shown in Figure 14-30.

5. **Create a clipping mask.** In the Layers palette, click on the top layer and all other objects that you want to be affected by the mask, and select the Make Clipping Mask palette menu command. The area beneath the text object is clipped, as shown in Figure 14-31.

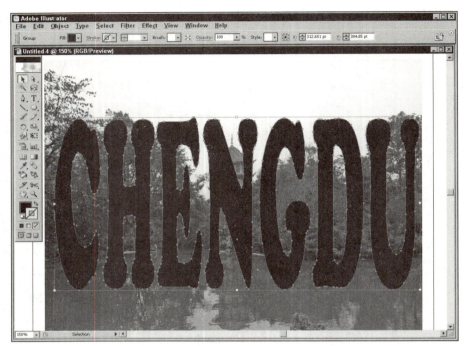

Figure 14-30: Converting text to outlines lets you stretch the text.

6. **Create a compound shape.** When the text is converted to outlines, all letters were grouped together and listed as a group in the Layers palette. This group contains compound paths, which confuses Illustrator when creating a clipping path. To get around this, select the text group and choose Object ⇨ Ungroup. Then, with all the letters selected, choose Object ⇨ Compound Path ⇨ Make. This combines all the separate letters into a single object.

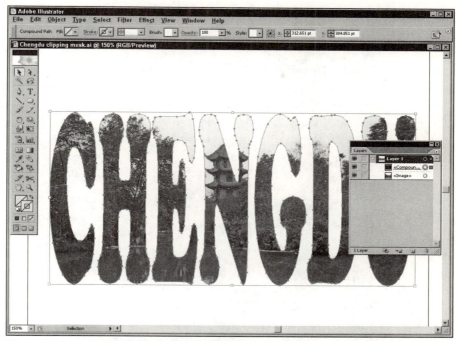

Figure 14-31: When all letters are combined into a single compound path, the object is used as a clipping path to the image underneath.

Using Layers in Photoshop

Layers in Photoshop are more advanced than any other CS2 applications, enabling many additional features including layer sets, linked layers, specialized type and shape layers, property-specific locking, an opacity setting, layer effects, adjustment and fill layers, layer masking, and layer comps. Figure 14-32 shows the Layers palette found in Photoshop.

Like Illustrator, Photoshop also includes a Layers Palette Options dialog box, shown in Figure 14-33, which lets you change the size of the thumbnails viewed in the Layers palette. You can also choose to have the layer thumbnail show the Layer Bounds or the Entire Document. There is also an option to Use Default Masks on Adjustments.

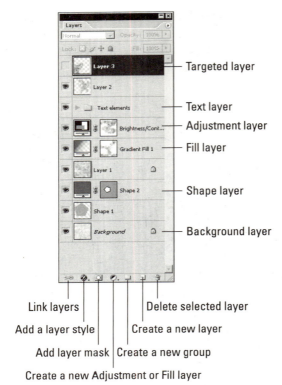

Figure 14-32: The Layers palette in Photoshop

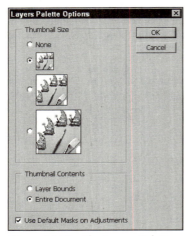

Figure 14-33: The Layers Palette Options dialog box

Working with a Background layer

When you create a new document in Photoshop, Photoshop creates a single layer named Background. You set the color of this background layer using the New dialog box. The choices are White, Background Color, or Transparent. If you select either the White or Background Color option, a background layer appears in the Layers palette. If Transparent is selected, then a gray and white checkerboard pattern appears denoting the transparent area.

The background layer by default is locked and cannot be moved, but you can paint and draw on the background layer. You also cannot change its opacity or blending mode. It's always the lowest layer. By choosing Layer ⇨ New ⇨ Layer from Background or by choosing Layer ⇨ New ⇨ Background from Layer, you can convert a background layer to a normal layer or a normal layer to a background layer.

When you choose Layer ⇨ New ⇨ Layer from Background, the New Layer dialog box appears, shown in Figure 14-34. Here, you can set the layer's options, including the layer name, the layer color, the blending mode, and the opacity.

Tip   Double-clicking on the Background layer opens the New Layer dialog box, allowing you to turn the Background layer into a normal layer.

Figure 14-34: The New Layer dialog box displays the layer options.

Selecting and controlling multiple layers

Photoshop allows you to select multiple layers. To select multiple layers, simply hold down the Ctrl (or Command) key and click on the layers to select in the Layers palette. To select multiple contiguous layers, click on the first and last layers with the Shift key held down and all layers in between the first and last selected layers are selected.

New Feature   The ability to select multiple layers is new to Photoshop CS2.

You can also select all layers using the Select ⇨ All Layers menu command or just layers that are similar to the current layer with the Select ⇨ Similar Layers menu command. The Select ⇨ Deselect Layers menu command will deselect all layers making the background layer the current layer.

Caution   Many common tools won't work with multiple layers selected including the various paint tools.

Auto Selecting layers with the Move tool

Photoshop allows you to select different layers with the Move tool. If the Auto Select Layer option in the Control bar is enabled, then clicking on the document selects the top-most layer under the cursor. You can also select the Auto Select Group option to click and select a layer group. Another way to select layers is to right click (Control-click on Mac) on the document with the Move tool and all layers underneath the cursor's position are shown in a pop-up menu where they can be selected.

Aligning and distributing image layers

When two or more layers are selected, the layers can be aligned and distributed using the Layer ⇨ Align to Selection and the Layer ⇨ Distribute menu commands. The various align and distribute commands let you align and distribute layers to their left, right, top and bottom edges, and to their horizontal and vertical centers. These commands are also available as icons in the Control bar when two or more layers are selected.

Selecting one of the distribute menu options moves the middle layers so that the space between the middle layer and the layers at either end are equal. For example, if you have five images that are horizontally aligned, you can equally space them by choosing to distribute them using their vertical centers.

Creating layer groups

Photoshop lets you create new layers just like the other applications, but you can also create layer groups. A layer group is a folder that includes several layers and, like Illustrator's sub-layers, it provides a way to bundle several layers together, as shown in Figure 14-35. Layer sets may be nested up to five levels deep and can contain any type of layer.

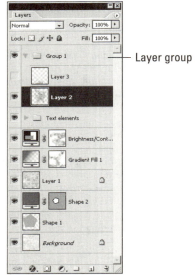

Figure 14-35: Layer sets are used to collect several layers together.

To create a layer group, select the New Group palette menu command or click on the Create a New Group button at the bottom of the Layers palette. You can also create a new layer group from the selected layers using the New Group from Layers palette menu command or simply press Command/Ctrl+G. A layer group appears as a folder icon in the Layers palette. Using the palette menu command or holding down the Option/Alt key while clicking on the Create a New Set button opens the New Layer Group dialog box, shown in Figure 14-36, where you can name the layer set, select a color, a blending mode, and an opacity.

Tip Holding down the ⌘/Ctrl key while creating a new layer or a new group adds the layer below the current selected layer.

Figure 14-36: The New Group dialog box lets you set the attributes for the layer group.

To add layers to a layer group, drag them in the Layers palette and drop them when the layer group is selected, or select the layer group folder before creating a new layer.

Selected layer groups can be deleted using the Delete Group palette menu command. This opens a dialog box that gives you the choice to delete the Group Only, the Group and Contents, or Cancel.

Linking layers

In addition to selecting multiple layers, you can also move the contents of multiple layers together by linking the layers together. To link a layer, select the layers that you want to link and choose the Link Layer palette menu command or click the small link icon at the bottom of the Layers palette. Linked layers have a bounding box in the canvas that surrounds all objects in both layers. A small link icon appears to the right of the layer name for all linked layers when one of the linked layers is selected.

Clicking on the link icon a second time unlinks the layer or you can choose the Unlink Layers palette menu command. Figure 14-37 shows both linked layers. To quickly select all linked layers, simply select one of the linked layers and choose Layer ⇨ Select Linked Layers.

Merging and flattening layers

When multiple Photoshop layers are selected at the same time the palette menu includes some additional menu commands for working with them.

The New Set from Linked palette menu command combines all linked layers into a separate layer set. This command opens a dialog box where you can name the layer set and choose a layer color, blending mode, and opacity value.

The Merge Layers (⌘/Ctrl+E) palette menu command merges all selected layers into the active selected layer. Merging layers decreases the size of your file. To reduce the file size even more, you can select the Merge Visible palette menu command. This causes all visible layers to be combined into the background layer. It is different from flattening an image in that it retains all hidden layers separately, where the Flatten Image command gives you the option of discarding hidden layers.

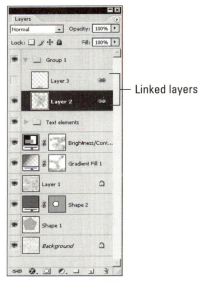

Figure 14-37: The link icon to the right of the layer name marks whether a layer is linked or unlinked.

STEPS: Distributing Images

1. **Open a new document in Photoshop.** Within Illustrator, open a new document by choosing File ➪ New. In the New dialog box, click OK.

2. **Open several images.** Choose File ➪ Open, and open several images within Photoshop.

3. **Create new layers.** In the Layers palette, click on the Create a New Layer button at the bottom of the Layers palette once for each opened image.

4. **Copy and paste the images.** Select the first layer and select an image. Choose Select ➪ All to select the entire image; then copy and paste the selected image into the new document. Repeat this until every open image is pasted onto a different layer, as shown in Figure 14-38.

Tip

These steps are accomplished quickly using keyboard shortcuts with ⌘/Ctrl+A to select the entire image, ⌘/Ctrl+C to copy the selected image to the Clipboard, and ⌘/Ctrl+V to paste the image into the new document.

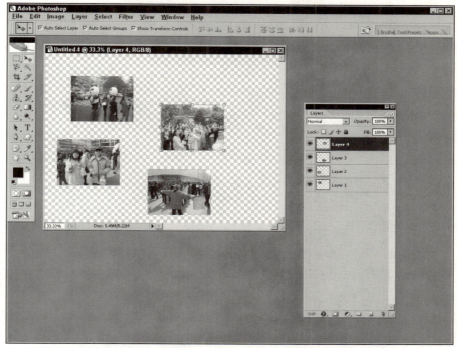

Figure 14-38: Placing each image on a separate layer makes it easy to align and distribute the images.

5. **Position the aligning image.** With the Move tool selected, move one of the images to its correct position.

6. **Align the images.** With the aligning image's layer selected, hold down the Ctrl (⌘) and select the other layers or choose the Select ⇨ All Layers menu command. Then choose Layer ⇨ Align ⇨ Left Edges. All the images are moved to align with the selected layer, as shown in Figure 14-39.

7. **Position the two end images.** Before distributing the images, select the images that are to appear on either end of the row of images and place them in their correct positions.

8. **Distribute the images.** With the layers all still selected, choose Layer ⇨ Distribute ⇨ Vertical Centers. This evenly spaces the aligned images, as shown in Figure 14-40.

Figure 14-39: All the layers are aligned with the selected layer by using the Layer ⇨ Align menu command.

Figure 14-40: When you distribute images, it equalizes the space between the layers.

Locking transparency, pixels, and position

You can lock each layer in Photoshop in a number of different ways using the Lock icon buttons at the top of the Layers palette, as shown in Figure 14-41. The Lock transparent pixels button prevents you from being able to paint on transparent areas. The Lock image pixels button won't let you paint on the image with any of the paint tools. The Lock position button prevents the selection from being moved. The Lock all button prevents any edits to the layer objects.

Lock transparent pixels
Lock image pixels
Lock position
Lock all

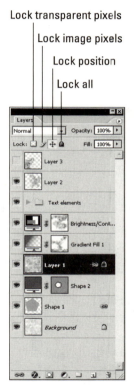

Figure 14-41: The Lock icon buttons are used to lock transparency, pixels, position, or all of these.

If the Lock Image Pixels button is enabled, the Lock Transparent Pixels button becomes disabled. If the Lock All button is enabled, all other locks are disabled.

When the Lock All button is selected, a black lock icon appears to the right of the layer name; when any of the other locks are selected, a white lock appears to the right of the layer name.

If the selected layer is part of a layer group, then you can choose the Lock All Layers in Group palette menu command to lock the entire group. This command is used to open a dialog box, shown in Figure 14-42, where you select which locks to apply to the group layers.

Figure 14-42: The Lock All Layers in Group dialog box

Working with Type and Shape layers

Type and Shape layers cannot be edited with any of the painting tools or filters because they hold vector-based data, but you can use the Layer ➪ Rasterize menu commands to convert these layers to pixel-based data. The options in the Rasterize menu include Type, Shape, Fill Content, Vector Mask, Layer, Linked Layer, and All Layers.

Creating a Type layer

When the Type tool is used to add type to an image, a Type layer is added to the Layers palette. Type layers are identified by a capital *T* in the thumbnail, as shown in Figure 14-43. Type layers automatically have both the Lock Transparent Pixels and Lock Image Pixels options disabled.

Cross-Reference

Working with Type is covered in detail in Part IV.

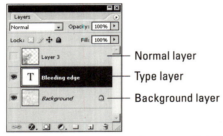

Figure 14-43: Type layers have a capital *T* in their thumbnail in the Layers palette.

The key benefit of a Type layer is that you can select the text with the Type tool and edit, delete, and add new text even after it has been manipulated. When a Type layer is selected in the Layers palette, several menu commands are available in the Layer ➪ Type menu.

Tip

If you double-click on the Type layer thumbnail, all the text is instantly selected.

Changing Type orientation and anti-aliasing

By default, text entered into a text layer appears horizontally from left to right, but you can change the text orientation so it runs vertically from top to bottom using the Layer ➪ Type ➪ Vertical menu command. You can use the Layer ➪ Type ➪ Horizontal menu command to reorient vertical text horizontally again.

Figure 14-44 shows two Type layers — one with a horizontal orientation and one with a vertical orientation.

The Layer ➪ Type menu also includes several anti-alias options that are applied to the Type layer. The options include None, Sharp, Crisp, Strong, and Smooth.

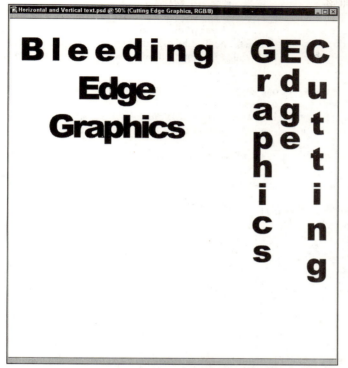

Figure 14-44: Type layers may be orientated horizontally or vertically.

Converting between paragraph and point text

If you click on the canvas with the Type tool, you create point text. Point text doesn't have a bounding box — the cursor just appears and lets you type without constraining the text flow to a certain area. Point text is typically used for headings or single lines of text.

If you click and drag on the canvas with the Type tool, you create Paragraph text. Paragraph text confines the text to the bounding box, so that any text that extends beyond the edge of the bounding box gets wrapped to the next line. This is useful for longer paragraphs of text, because the text is automatically wrapped to fit the designated area.

The Layer ⇨ Type menu includes commands to switch between these two types. When a layer containing point text is selected, the Convert to Paragraph Text menu command is available, and vice versa.

Caution

When you convert paragraph text to point text, all characters that overflow outside the bounding box are deleted. To avoid this, resize the bounding box before performing the conversion.

Warping text

When Type layers are rasterized, you can distort and manipulate them using all the standard Photoshop tools, but doing so makes them uneditable as text objects. However, there are several distortions that you can do to text while keeping it editable, such as transforming and warping the text.

To warp a selected Type layer, choose Layer ➪ Type ➪ Warp Text. This opens a dialog box, shown in Figure 14-45, where you can select from several different warp types: Arc; Arc Lower; Arc Upper; Arch; Bulge; Shell Lower; Shell Upper; Flag; Wave; Fish; Rise; Fisheye; Inflate; Squeeze; and Twist.

Cross-Reference

These warp types are the same as those available within Illustrator and are covered in Chapter 13.

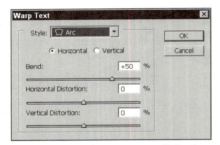

Figure 14-45: The Warp Text dialog box allows you to warp text objects in Photoshop the same way as text in Illustrator.

Creating a Shape layer

In addition to Type layers created with the Type tool, Photoshop's Toolbox includes the Pen tool and several shape tools for creating rectangles, rounded rectangles, ellipses, polygons, straight lines, and custom shapes. When these tools are selected, the Options bar includes three different modes for applying these shapes as Shape Layers, Paths, and Fill Pixels.

The Shape Layers mode creates a shape layer in the Layers palette, as shown in Figure 14-46, the Paths mode creates a temporary work path that appears in the Paths palette, and the Fill Pixels mode lets you create a raster-based shape when a normal layer is selected.

Cross-Reference

The Paths and Fill Pixels modes, along with the Pen and Shape tools, are covered in more detail in Chapter 10.

Shape layers are displayed in the Layers palette with two thumbnails. The first thumbnail is the fill applied to the shape, and the second thumbnail shows the shape as a layer mask called a vector mask. When the Vector Mask thumbnail is selected, you can move the shape. The link icon between the fill and layer mask thumbnails binds the layer mask to the layer. If you click the link icon to unlink the layer mask, you can no longer reposition.

Cross-Reference

Layer masks are covered in more detail later in this chapter.

Shape layer

Figure 14-46: Shape layers show up in the Layers palette with two thumbnails — one for the fill and one for the layer mask.

STEPS: Creating a simple logo

1. **Open a new document in Photoshop.** Within Photoshop, create a new document by choosing File ⇨ New. In the New dialog box, click OK.

2. **Create a Type layer.** Select the Type tool, click and drag in the center of the canvas, and type the text within the bounding box. The Type layer appears in the Layers palette.

3. **Change the text style and size.** Choose Window ⇨ Character to open the Character palette. Select the Type tool and drag over the text in the text layer to select it; then change the font to Croobie (or some other stylized font) and the size to 36 pt. In the Paragraph palette, select the Center Text button. The text should now look like Figure 14-47.

Figure 14-47: You can use the Type tool to select type, and the Character and Paragraph palettes to change the text settings.

4. **Warp the text.** With the Type layer selected, choose Layer ⇨ Type ⇨ Warp Text. In the Warp Text dialog box, select the Arc style and set the Bend value to 50%. Then click OK to apply the warp, as shown in Figure 14-48.

5. **Add a background rectangle.** Click on the Rectangle tool and select the Shape Layer button in the Options box. Change the foreground color to red and drag to create a rectangle that covers the text. This adds a shape layer to the Shapes palette. With the shape layer selected, choose Layer ⇨ Arrange ⇨ Send to Back. This moves the shape layer below the Type layer and moves the red rectangle behind the text, as shown in Figure 14-49.

Figure 14-48: Using the Warp Text dialog box, you can distort text in a number of different ways.

Figure 14-49: You can use the Rectangle tool to add shapes that you may move behind the text.

6. **Rasterize the Shape layer.** To add some details to the background rectangle with a filter, you'll need to rasterize the rectangle. With the Shape layer selected, choose Layer ⇨ Rasterize ⇨ Shape. This converts the Shape layer to a normal layer named Shape 1.

7. **Apply a filter to the background.** With the rectangle layer still selected, choose Filter ⇨ Distort ⇨ Ripple. This opens the Ripple dialog box. Set the amount to 150% and the size to Large; then click OK to ripple the edges of the background rectangle, as shown in Figure 14-50.

Figure 14-50: To add some details to the edges of the rectangle layer, the Ripple filter adds just what is needed.

Setting layer opacity and selecting a blending mode

Although you can set the opacity and blending mode when a layer is first created in the New Layer dialog box, the options may be changed at any time using the controls at the top of the Layers palette. The Opacity value and blending mode are applied to the entire layer.

Note   You cannot change the opacity or blending mode for the Background layer or for any locked layer.

To change the blending options, select a different blending mode from the list at the top of the Layers palette, or choose Layer ⇨ Layer Style ⇨ Blending Options, or double-click on one of the normal layers. This command opens the Blending Options panel of the Layer Style dialog box, shown in Figure 14-51.

Cross-Reference   More on transparency and blending modes is covered in Chapter 10.

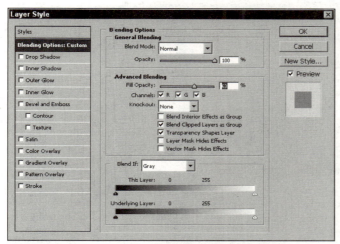

Figure 14-51: The Layer Style dialog box lets you set the blend mode for the layer.

Setting fill opacity

Directly beneath the Layer Opacity value is another value marked as Fill. This value is the Fill Opacity value. It is used to set the opacity for the layer pixels or shapes without affecting the opacity of any pixels added as layer effects, such as drop shadows or glows.

Creating a knockout

A knockout layer is used to remove, or knock out, a layer underneath it to reveal the Background layer or the bottom layer in a layer set. To create a knockout layer, simply place the knockout layer above the layer that you want to remove pixels from and choose one of the Knockout options in the Blending Options panel of the Layer Style dialog box.

The Knockout options include None, Shallow, and Deep. The Shallow option knocks out all layers to the bottom of the layer set that contains the knockout layer, but the Deep option knocks out all layers between the Knockout layer and the Background layer. If no Background layer exists, the knocked out area is made transparent.

You can control the amount of knockout using the Fill Opacity value. A Fill Opacity value of 0 knockouts all the in-between layers to reveal only the background and a Fill Opacity of 100 doesn't knockout any of the in-between layers. Figure 14-52 shows an arrow shape used as a Knockout layer, revealing a pattern in the Background layer.

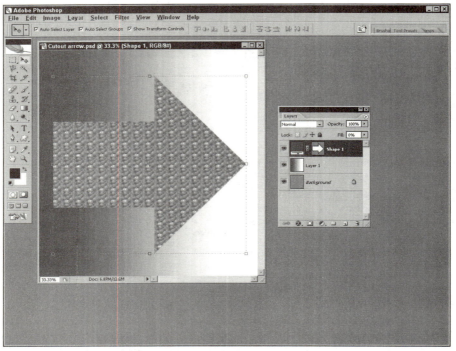

Figure 14-52: The arrow shape in the top layer is used as a knockout for the gradient layer, allowing the pattern on the Background layer to show through.

Using advanced blending options

In the Advanced Blending section of the Blending Options panel of the Layer Style dialog box are several additional options besides Fill Opacity and Knockout. The Channels check boxes let you apply the selected blending mode and options to specific channels only. Deselecting a channel causes it *not* to be included in the blending process. The availability of the channels depends on the color mode for the given image:

✦ **The Blend Interior Effects as Group option** treats any effects applied to the interior of the current layer as part of the layer and blends them with the layer pixels. Interior effects include Inner Glow, Satin, Color, and Gradient Overlay but not Inner Shadow.

✦ **The Select Blend Clipped Layers as Group option** applies the blending mode to all layers that are part of a clipping mask. If this option is deselected, then each clipping mask retains its original blending mode and options. This option is enabled by default.

✦ **The Select Transparency Shapes Layers option** prevents knockouts and layer effects from interfering with the layer's pixels. This option is also selected by default.

✦ **The Select Layer Mask Hides Effects and Select Vector Mask Hides Effects options** are used to confine layer effects to the area defined by the Layer or Vector Mask.

You can use the sliders at the bottom of the Blending Options panel of the Layer Style dialog box to target only a certain range of pixels for blending. The Blend If field lets you choose which color channel to blend. Select Gray for all channels. The This Layer slider lets you specify the bright- and dark-colored pixels to blend for the current layer, and the Underlying Layer slider lets you specify the pixels to blend for a layer under the current one.

Tip

If you hold down the Option/Alt key while dragging on the slider arrows, you can split the arrows in half to define a specific range of pixels.

Figure 14-53 shows a simple layer (top left) created with a stylized brush. The pixel-blending slider to the right has been moved to include all the bright pixels in the blending process, and the lower image shows the same document with all the dark pixels blended.

Figure 14-53: By manipulating the sliders in the Blending Options dialog box, you can select exactly which pixels are included in the blending operation.

STEPS: Creating a Knockout Border

1. **Open a document in Photoshop.** Within Photoshop, create a new document by choosing File ⇨ Open.

2. **Convert the image to a Background layer.** Select the Background layer and choose the Delete Layer palette menu command to remove the existing background. Then, with the image layer selected, choose Layer ⇨ New ⇨ Background From Layer. This converts the image layer to the Background layer.

3. **Create a new border layer.** Click on the Create a New Layer button at the bottom of the Layers palette. The new layer appears in the Layers palette. Change the Fill color to red, click the Paintbrush tool, and select the Scattered Leaves brush tip from the Brushes palette. Then drag over the entire layer to create a layer to use as a border, as shown in Figure 14-54.

4. **Create a Shape layer.** Select the Rectangle tool and make sure the Shape Layer mode is selected in the Options bar. Then drag in the canvas to create a rectangle that leaves a border around the image, as shown in Figure 14-55. This creates a new Shape layer in the Layers palette.

Chapter 14 ✦ **Working with Layers** 557

Figure 14-54: This layer, created with the scattered leaves, is used as a border for the image.

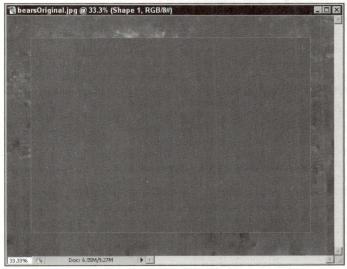

Figure 14-55: Shape layers are useful for selecting areas to be knocked out.

5. **Make the Shape layer a knockout.** Double-click on the Shape layer mask thumbnail to open the Blending Options panel of the Layer Style dialog box. Select the Deep option in the Knockout field and set the Fill Opacity value to 0%. Then click OK. Figure 14-56 shows the resulting image.

Figure 14-56: By knocking out the area defined in the Shape layer, the image has a nice border.

Using layer effects

You can add layer effects to the current layer by enabling an effect in the Layer Style dialog box. This dialog box is opened by selecting the Blending Options palette menu command, by selecting one of the Layer Effects from the Add a Layer Style button at the bottom of the Layers palette, or by double-clicking on the layer thumbnail. Figure 14-57 shows the Layer Style dialog box for the Drop Shadow effect.

Note   Layer effects may not be added to the Background layer or to a locked layer.

The available default Layer Effects include Drop Shadow, Inner Shadow, Outer Glow, Inner Glow, Bevel and Emboss, Satin, Color Overlay, Gradient Overlay, Pattern Overlay, and Stroke. Figure 14-57 shows each of these layer effects. Selecting any of these Layer Effects from the Add a Layer Style button opens the Layer Style dialog box and displays the settings for the selected effect.

Cross-Reference   Each of these layer effects is covered in Chapter 13.

Chapter 14 ✦ **Working with Layers** 559

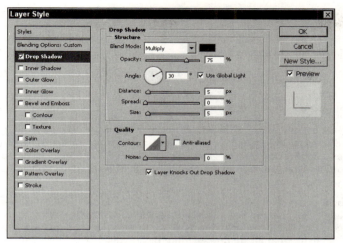

Figure 14-57: Each of the layer effects has its own panel in the Layer Style dialog box.

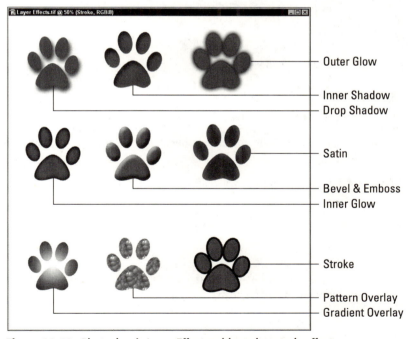

Figure 14-58: Photoshop's Layer Effects adds and controls effects.

When a Layer Effect has been applied to a layer, the Layer Effect icon appears to the right of the layer title. Clicking the arrow that appears next to this icon expands and displays the list of effects. Double-clicking on any of these listed effects opens the Layer Style dialog box again; here, you can edit the effect's settings.

To remove a layer effect, simply drag the effect to the Delete Selected button at the bottom of the Layers palette.

Adjusting global lighting

Several of the layer effects depend on a lighting effect to determine where the shadows are cast, including the Drop Shadow, Inner Shadow, and Bevel & Emboss layer effects. Although each of these effects has a setting that controls the light's Angle and Altitude, you can select the Use Global Light option. When this option is selected, the light settings are controlled using the Global Light settings.

To Access the Global Light settings, choose Layer ⇨ Layer Style ⇨ Global Light. This opens a dialog box, shown in Figure 14-59, where you can set the Angle and Altitude values. You can also drag the crosshairs within the light circle to reposition these values. Using the Global Light dialog box, you can ensure that all shadows within the document are consistent.

Figure 14-59: The Global Light dialog box

Scaling effects

Layer effects may be saved as styles and reapplied to other layers, but an effect that looks great on one layer may be too small or too big when applied to another layer. Instead of reconfiguring the settings for the effect, you can simply change its scale by choosing Layer ⇨ Layer Style ⇨ Scale Effect.

Cross-Reference

To learn more about working with styles and effects, see Chapter 10.

This command opens a simple dialog box with a slider for determining the scale of the effects applied to the current layer.

Turning effects into layers

You can separate effects from a layer by choosing Layer ⇨ Layer Style ⇨ Create Layers. This makes the layer effect an independent layer that you can manipulate and edit. Double-clicking on the new layer still opens the effect's settings in the Layer Style dialog box.

STEPS: Adding Layer Effects

1. **Open a document in Photoshop.** Within Photoshop, open a new document by choosing File ➪ Open.

2. **Add a Type layer.** Click on the Type tool and click in the lower center of the image. Choose Window ➪ Character to open the Character palette. Select the Myriad font with a bold face and set the size to 120 points with a color of white. Then type the word **CHENGDU**, as shown in Figure 14-60, in all capitals.

Figure 14-60: Text helps identify the location, but the type is harsh against the image.

3. **Add an Inner Glow layer effect.** With the Type layer selected, click on the Add a Layer Style button at the bottom of the Layers palette and select the Inner Glow effect. In the Layer Style dialog box, set the blend mode to normal, the color to black, and the size to 25 pixels. Click OK. The text should now look blurred and the layer effect is added beneath the Type layer in the Layers palette, as shown in Figure 14-61.

4. **Add an Outer Glow layer effect.** With the Type layer still selected, click on the Add a Layer Style button at the bottom of the Layers palette, and select the Outer Glow effect. In the Layer Style dialog box, click on the color swatch to open the Color Picker; then click on the Eyedropper tool and click in the image to select a light color from the image. Set the size to 25 pixels and click OK. The layer effects offset the text so it isn't so harsh, as shown in Figure 14-62.

Figure 14-61: Using the Inner Glow layer effect, the text is made to look somewhat blurred.

Figure 14-62: The Outer Glow layer effect smoothes the transition into the image using a color from the image.

Using adjustment and fill layers

Within Photoshop, the Image ⇨ Adjustment menu lets you adjust image properties such as contrast, color balance, and saturation, but applying the menu commands found in the Image ⇨ Adjustment menu permanently changes the image.

Using the Layers palette, you can apply an Adjustment layer to the image that holds the adjustment changes in a separate layer, so you can edit or even remove the adjustment changes at any time without affecting the image.

Fill layers are similar to adjustment layers. They're used to fill the canvas with a solid color, a gradient, or a pattern, but fill layers don't change the layers underneath them.

To add an adjustment layer, select one of the commands from the Layer ⇨ New Adjustment Layer menu or from the pop-up menu at the bottom of the Layers palette. The available adjustment layers include Levels, Curves, Color Balance, Brightness/Contrast, Hue/Saturation, Selection Color, Channel Mixer, Gradient Map, Photo Filter, Invert, Threshold, and Posterize. Figure 14-63 shows the Layers palette with an adjustment and a fill layer.

Cross-Reference You can learn more about these adjustment options in Chapter 11.

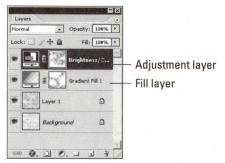

Figure 14-63: Adjustment and fill layers keep adjustments and fills separate from other layers.

To add a fill layer, select one of the commands from the Layer ⇨ New Fill Layer menu or from the pop-up menu available at the bottom of the Layers palette. The available fill layers include Solid Color, Gradient, and Pattern.

Selecting any of these layers opens the appropriate dialog box for the layer type that was selected. Figure 14-64 shows the Color Balance dialog box.

Figure 14-64: Each of the adjustment and fill layers opens a dialog box.

Masking with layers

Masks are used in Photoshop to hide areas of a layer. Photoshop creates masks out of pixel selections or shapes. When a mask is applied to a layer, it appears as an additional thumbnail in the Layers palette positioned to the right of the main thumbnail. The mask thumbnail shows all hidden areas as black, all visible areas as white, and all semitransparent areas as gray.

Creating a layer mask

To apply a mask to a layer, select the layer and choose Layer ➪ Add Layer Mask ➪ Reveal All to add a mask that displays the entire layer underneath, or click on the Add Layer Mask button at the bottom of the Layers palette. You can also choose Layer ➪ Add Layer Mask ➪ Hide All, or click on the Add Layer Mask button at the bottom of the Layers palette with the Option/Alt key held down to create a layer mask that hides the image underneath.

If a pixel selection exists, that selection may be used as the basis for the mask. To make the interior of the selection a mask, choose Layer ➪ Add Layer Mask ➪ Hide Selection. To make all but the interior selection a mask, choose Layer ➪ Add Layer Mask ➪ Reveal Selection. The Add Layer Mask button at the bottom of the Layers palette may also be used with a selection.

The link icon that appears between the thumbnails in the Layers palette is used to make the layer move with its mask. Clicking on the link icon unlinks the two and allows the mask to move independently of the layer.

Editing a layer mask

To edit a mask, click on its thumbnail in the Layers palette and use the paint tools to color the canvas using black, white, and grayscale colors. A mask thumbnail appears to the right in the Layers palette, as shown in Figure 14-65, when a mask is selected and the foreground and background colors change to black and white.

Mask layer

Figure 14-65: The mask icon is displayed in the second column of the selected layer when the Mask layer is selected.

To see the mask in black and white while editing it, hold down the Option/Alt key while clicking on the mask thumbnail in the Layers palette. To get back to the normal editing mode, click on the layer thumbnail.

If you click on the Layer Mask thumbnail with the Shift key held down, or if you choose Layer ⇨ Disable Layer Mask, the layer mask is disabled and a red X appears through the thumbnail. Clicking the mask thumbnail again makes the mask active again.

Creating vector masks

Vector objects such as paths, shapes, and text may also be used as masks. One benefit of vector masks is that you can move and edit them after they've been applied. To create a vector mask, choose Layer ⇨ Add Vector Mask ⇨ Reveal All or choose Layer ⇨ Add Vector Mask ⇨ Hide All, just like the layer mask.

To use a vector object as a mask, select the layer that you want to mask and then select the Paths option in the Options bar. This allows you to create a path without creating a new layer. Then choose Layer ⇨ Add Vector Mask ⇨ Current Path.

Vector masks may be converted to a normal layer mask by choosing Layer ⇨ Rasterize ⇨ Vector Mask. However, layer masks cannot be converted to vector masks.

Removing masks

To remove a layer mask, simply drag its thumbnail down to the Delete Selected button at the bottom of the Layers palette, or select the mask that you want to remove and choose Layer ⇨ Delete Layer/Vector Mask. When a mask is removed, a warning dialog box appears, giving you the option to apply, cancel, or discard the mask. If you choose to apply the mask, the layer assumes the results of the mask.

STEPS: Painting a Layer Mask

1. **Open a document in Photoshop.** Within Photoshop, open a new document by choosing File ⇨ Open.

2. **Add a layer mask.** With the image layer selected in the Layers palette, choose Layer ⇨ Add Layer Mask ⇨ Hide All. This command applies a white layer mask, and the entire layer mask appears black in the Layers palette.

3. **Paint on the layer mask.** Select the Paintbrush tool, select a wide spatter brush from the Brushes palette, and drag the paintbrush across the canvas to slowly reveal the image underneath. Figure 14-66 shows the results of painting on the layer mask with a stipple brush. It resembles looking through a foggy window.

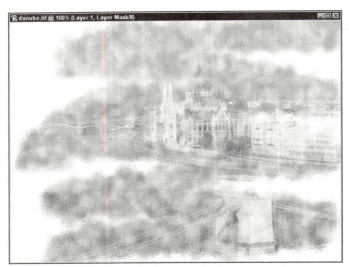

Figure 14-66: Painting on a layer mask with a spatter brush creates the effect of looking through a foggy window.

Using Smart Objects

Beside layer groups, Photoshop offers another way to combine several layers together. Smart Objects are a special object type that embeds the content of several layers into a single container. Smart Objects can include both raster and vector data and can be edited in a separate application while maintaining its links to Photoshop. For example, an Illustrator file can be placed within a Photoshop file as a Smart Object.

New Feature Smart Objects are new to Photoshop CS2.

To create a Smart Object, select several layers and choose the Group into New Smart Object palette menu command. This creates a new layer that is identified as a Smart Object by the small icon in the lower right corner of the thumbnail, as shown in Figure 14-67.

You can also create a Smart Objects by placing Illustrator, PSD, or Camera RAW files in the current document using the File ⇨ Place menu command or by copying and pasting Illustrator objects. When pasting an Illustrator object with the Edit ⇨ Paste command, a simple dialog box, shown in Figure 14-68, appears with the options to paste the object as a Smart Object, as Pixels, as a Path or as a Shape Layer. Smart Object layers can be copied to a new layer using the Layer ⇨ Smart Objects ⇨ Layer via Copy menu command.

Tip Smart Object layers can be linked together so that updating one automatically updates the other.

Figure 14-67: Smart Objects are identified by a small icon in the lower right of the thumbnail.

Figure 14-68: Smart Objects are also created by pasting Illustrator objects into the Photoshop document.

Double-clicking on a Smart Object layer or selecting the Edit Object palette menu command opens the Smart Object as a separate document in the original creator software, which may be Illustrator or Photoshop. When the command is first selected, a warning dialog box appears explaining that if you simply save the file being edited, then the changes are automatically updated in the Photoshop document.

Smart Objects can be exported independent of the document that contains them. To export a Smart Object layer, select the layer in the Layers palette and choose the Layer ⇨ Smart Objects ⇨ Export Contents menu command. This opens a file dialog box where the Smart Object can be saved using the format of its original software (AI for Illustrator, or PSB for Photoshop).

To update an existing Smart Object with new content, choose the Layer ⇨ Smart Objects ⇨ Replace Content menu command and a file dialog box opens where you can choose a new file to replace the current one. The new content assumes the size and position of the current Smart Object layer.

Smart Objects can be changed back into a normal layer with the Layer ⇨ Smart Objects ⇨ Convert to Layer. This rasterizes any vector data and eliminates the links to the original editing application.

Using layer comps

Layer compositions (or *comps,* for short) offer a way to display multiple versions of a Photoshop file. Stored in the Layers Comps palette, shown in Figure 14-69, layer comps record a snapshot of the Layers palette by keeping track of each layer's Visibility, Position, and Appearance.

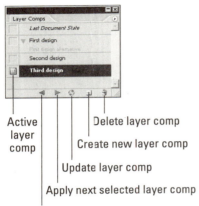

Figure 14-69: The Layer Comps palette holds snapshots of the visible layers.

To create a new layer comp, click the Create New Layer Comp button at the bottom of the Layer Comp palette. This opens a dialog box, shown in Figure 14-70, where you can name the new layer comp, specify which properties to record, and add a comment.

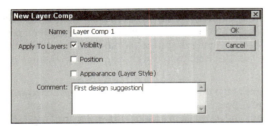

Figure 14-70: The New Layer Comp dialog box lets you name the layer comp and select which layer attributes to record.

If changes are made to a layer comp, you may update the comp by clicking on the Update Layer Comp button at the bottom of the Layer Comp palette.

The Apply Previous and Apply Next Layer Comp buttons at the bottom of the Layer Comps palette let you quickly cycle through the various layer comps.

To delete a layer comp, select it and click the Delete Layer Comp button at the bottom of the Layer Comps palette.

Note Deleting a layer comp deletes the memory of the layer configuration, but it doesn't delete the related layers in the file.

STEPS: Creating Several Layer Comps

1. **Open a document in Photoshop.** Within Photoshop, open a new document, such as the image with text and layer effects applied, by choosing File ➪ Open.

2. **Apply multiple layer effects.** Select the Type layer and apply each of the available layer effects to the Type layer. Figure 14-71 shows the image with the Pattern Overlay and Stroke layer effects applied.

3. **Creating new layer comps.** Experiment with the applied layer effects by enabling and disabling certain combinations. When you come across a design that is appealing, choose Window ➪ Layer Comps to open the Layer Comps palette, and click the Create New Layer Comp button at the bottom of the palette. In the New Layer Comp dialog box that appears, name the layer comp appropriately, select the Visibility and Appearance options, and click OK. Figure 14-72 shows the Layer Comps palette with several options.

Figure 14-71: Layer effects are displayed in the Layers palette where you can quickly hide or show them.

Figure 14-72: The Layer Comp palette lets you quickly cycle through a number of different design ideas.

4. **Preview the layer comps.** When you've finished creating a number of layer comps, click on the Apply Next Selected Layer Comp several times to cycle through the available layer comps.

Placing layer comps in Illustrator and InDesign

When Photoshop files that include layer comps are placed within Illustrator or InDesign, the Options dialog box, shown in Figure 14-73, includes a drop-down list of the available layer comps. Using the Preview pane and comments, you can select the exact layer comp that you want to open and place in the current document.

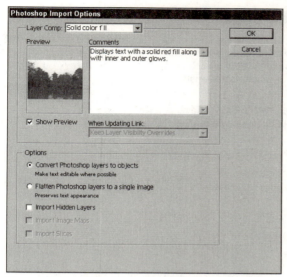

Figure 14-73: When Photoshop files containing comps are placed in Illustrator or InDesign, you can choose which comp to open.

Using Layers in GoLive

Layers in GoLive in some ways are similar to layers used in the other CS2 applications, but GoLive layers actually represent layers that are defined as part of the CSS specification, which makes them behave differently in many ways. CSS stands for Cascading Style Sheets, which is a specification for handling and defining styles for Web pages.

CSS layers work like the layers in the other CS2 applications in that they allow you to stack content on top of each other, but there are some differences that you need to be aware of, including the following:

- ✦ CSS layers are always rectangular.
- ✦ CSS layers are positioned relative to the Web page's upper-left corner or relative to the upper-left corner of other layers.
- ✦ CSS layers may inherit attributes from a CSS.
- ✦ CSS layers are contained within the HTML code inside a <DIV> tag.
- ✦ CSS layers are not supported on all browsers and may not appear correctly if a user has disabled CSS features for his browser.
- ✦ CSS layers may be connected to execute actions when certain mouse events occur.
- ✦ CSS layers may be used to create simple animations by changing layers positioned in the same place.

Adding layers to a Web page

Layers are added to a Web page by dragging the Layer icon from the Objects palette, shown in Figure 14-74, to the Web page, or by clicking on the Create New Layer button at the bottom of the Layers palette. This button inserts a layer at the cursor position in the Web page. A small yellow marker marks the layer placeholder position.

Layer icon

Figure 14-74: The GoLive Objects palette lets you add objects to a Web page by dragging the objects' icons.

When a layer is created, its name appears in the Layers palette, as shown in Figure 14-75. The Layers palette is opened by choosing Window ⇨ Layers (⌘/Ctrl+4). The default names for new layers are simply layer1, layer2, and so on. To rename a layer, double-click on its name in the Layer palette and type a new name. A layer's name is known within the HTML code as its ID, and this ID is used in JavaScript to refer to the layer for interactive effects.

Figure 14-75: The Layers palette lets you sort layers by clicking on the column headings.

When a layer is created, its dimensions appear in the upper-left corner, and each layer is given a number based on the order in which they were created. This number is displayed in the lower-right corner, as shown in Figure 14-76. These lower-right-corner numbers are also used in the Timeline Editor to animate the layers.

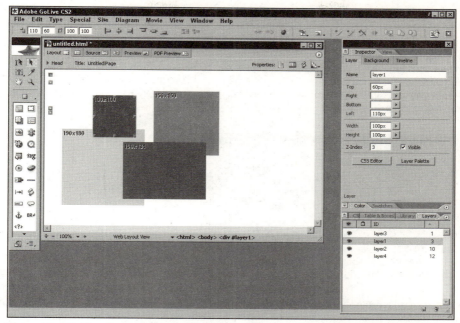

Figure 14-76: The dimensions of each layer are listed in the upper-left corner, and a sequential number is listed in the lower-right corner.

Layers are selected by clicking on their position marker, clicking the borders when the cursor changes to a hand icon or by clicking on its name in the Layers palette. When the hand icon appears when you click on a layer's border, you can move the layer by dragging it to a new position. Dragging on the layer handles lets you resize the layer.

Tip — When a layer is selected, you can move it by pressing the arrow keys. Holding down the Shift key while using the arrow keys lets you resize the layer; holding down the ⌘/Ctrl key lets you move the selected layer using grid spacing.

To delete a layer, just select it in the Layers palette and click the Remove Selected Layers button at the bottom of the Layers palette.

Using the Layers palette

The Layers palette includes some of the same layer features found in the other CS2 applications, including the eye and lock icons. Clicking on the first and second columns of the Layers palette, you can change the visibility of the selected layer or lock it in place.

To the right of the layer name is another column that lists the Z-Index value. Clicking on the Name or Z-Index column head lets you sort the layers by their name or Z-Index value.

Note — When a layer is selected, it's automatically brought to the front of the stacking order so the layer is visible. But when the layer is unselected, it returns to its correct position in the stacking order.

The palette menu includes two methods for viewing layers — hierarchic, which displays nested layers underneath their parents, and flat, which displays all layers at the same level.

Using layer grids

When working with layers, you can enable a grid to help position layers using the Layer Grid Settings palette menu command. This command opens a dialog box, shown in Figure 14-77, where you can set the horizontal and vertical spacing in pixels. You can also select to snap and make the grid visible while dragging.

Figure 14-77: The Layer Grid Settings dialog box lets you define the grid-spacing distance and whether objects snap to the grid.

The Prevent Overlapping option restricts objects from being positioned on top of other layers when enabled. When you disable this option, you can stack layers on top of one another.

Converting layers into layout grids

If you've gone to the effort to lay out a Web page using layers, only to discover that you need to abandon the layers design due to incompatible browser issues, you can use the Convert to Layout Grid palette menu command to create a new Web page where all layers and their content are converted to standard layout grids.

Caution

The Convert to Layout Grid palette menu command can only convert layers that aren't overlapped. If a Web page includes overlapped layers, the Convert to Layout Grid palette menu command is not available.

Editing layer attributes

When a layer is selected, its attributes display in the Inspector palette, shown in Figure 14-78. For layers, the Inspector palette includes three panels — Layer, Background, and Timeline.

Using the Layer panel

The Layer panel of the Inspector palette includes the Layer's Name in an editable field, its positions and/or dimensions, a Z-Index value, and a Visible check box. The layer's position values may be specified, or you can enter its Top and Left position values along with the Width and Height values. If all four position values and the Width and Height values are specified, the Width and Height values take precedence over the unneeded position values.

Any customized values included in the HTML code are highlighted in blue, and if a value is invalid, it's highlighted in orange. Unaltered fields stay black.

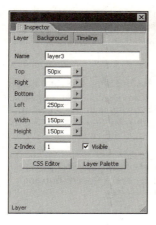

Figure 14-78: The Inspector palette changes depending on the selected object. When a layer is selected, the Inspector palette includes three different panels for Layer, Background, and Timeline.

The pop-up menu to the right of the Top, Right, Bottom, Left, Width, and Height fields lets you convert the current value between several different measurement systems including point, pica, pixel, em, ex, mm, cm, inch, and percentage of the total page.

The Z-Index value determines the stacking order of the layers with the higher values appearing on top of the lower values, so a layer with a Z-Index of 10 appears in front of a layer with a Z-Index of 2.

The Layer panel of the Inspector palette also includes buttons to open the CSS Editor and the Layer palette.

Using the Background panel

The Background panel, shown in Figure 14-79, lets you select a background color for the layer or load an image to be displayed within the layer. To change the background color, click on the lower-right corner of the color swatch and a pop-up color picker appears with Web-safe color swatches.

Figure 14-79: The Background panel of the Inspector palette lets you change the background color or image.

The Image option lets you fetch or browse for an image. If the image is larger than the available size, only the portion of the image that fits in the layer is displayed. If the image is smaller than the layer, the image is placed in the upper-left corner of the layer.

Using the Timeline panel

The Timeline panel, shown in Figure 14-80, includes controls for enabling layer animations. From the Animation field, you can select the animation type from None, Linear, Curve, and Random. The Key Color changes the colors used to represent the layer in the Timeline Editor, and the Record button lets you create Timeline keyframes by moving and positioning the layers in the Layout Editor.

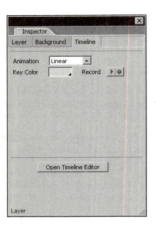

Figure 14-80: The Timeline panel of the Inspector palette includes several animation options and a Record button that lets you create animation keyframes.

Clicking the Open Timeline Editor button opens the Timeline Editor, where you can precisely control the animation.

STEPS: Creating Layers in GoLive

1. **Open a Web page in GoLive.** Within GoLive, open a new Web page with the File ⇨ New Page menu command.

2. **Drag the Layer icon onto the page.** Select and drag the Layer icon from the Objects palette onto the blank Web page. The layer appears as a 100-x-100-pixel square at the top of the Web page, and the layer name appears in the Layers palette, as shown in Figure 14-81.

3. **Resizing and positioning the layer.** Drag the mouse over the layer edge, and click when the mouse icon changes to a hand icon. Resize the layer by dragging its corner handles, and drag the layer edges to reposition the layer.

4. **Change the layer's background color.** In the Inspector palette, select the Background tab and enable the Color option. Then click and hold the lower-right corner of the color swatch to open a color palette, where you can select a new background color.

5. **Add an image to the layer.** Drag the image icon from the Objects panel onto the layer. In the Inspector palette, click on the Browse button and select an image to open. Then click on the Align Center button in the Toolbar to center the image within the layer, as shown in Figure 14-82.

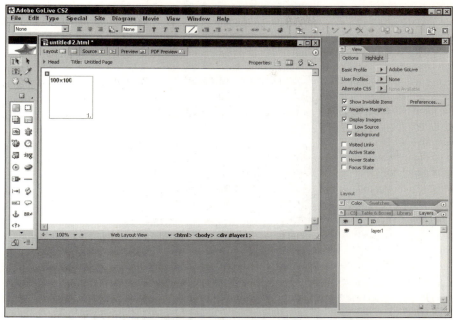

Figure 14-81: Layers are added to the Web page by dragging the Layer icon from the Objects palette to the Web page.

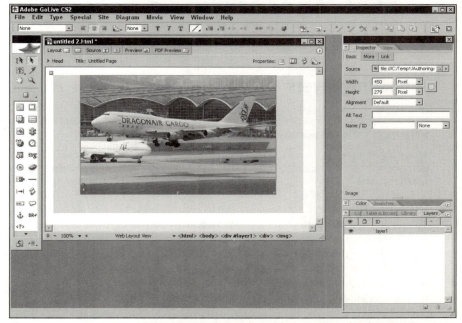

Figure 14-82: Content such as this image may be added to a layer by dragging items onto the layer from the Objects palette.

6. **Add text to the layer.** Click in the layer to have the text cursor appear. Use the arrow keys to move the cursor to the left side of the image and enter some text. Then drag over the text to select it, and choose the Header2 option from the toolbar, as shown in Figure 14-83.

Figure 14-83: Clicking in the layer positions the text cursor within the layer. You can then use the arrows to move the mouse cursor to either side of the image.

Animating layers

Animating layers in GoLive is made possible with the Timeline Editor, shown in Figure 14-84. Within this editor, a number represents each layer. Corresponding numbers are listed in the lower-right corner of the layers in the Layout Editor.

Along the top are the frames of the animation; the position of each layer is denoted by color-coordinated small rectangles called *keys*. If a key is dimmed out, the layer is hidden for that frame.

Creating new keys

To create a new key in the Timeline Editor, ⌘/Ctrl+click in the layer row at the time that you want to create a keyframe. To move a keyframe, position the cursor over the top of the keyframe and drag it to its new location. Holding down the Option/Alt key while dragging a keyframe creates a duplicate.

When a keyframe is selected in the Timeline Editor, it's highlighted in black and the properties for the respective layer are shown in the Inspector palette.

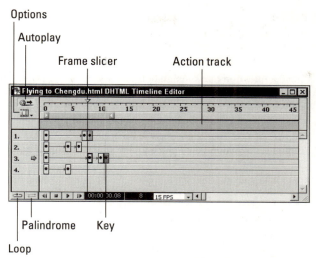

Figure 14-84: The Timeline Editor lets you place and position layer keyframes to define how the layer is animated.

Previewing animations

The buttons along the bottom of the Timeline Editor window include Loop and Palindrome toggle buttons, Backward, Stop, Play, and Forward. The Loop and Palindrome toggle buttons let the animation loop continuously through the total frames or play backward once the last frame is reached.

The time and frame number are also displayed along the bottom of the Timeline Editor. The FPS pop-up menu lets you specify the number of frames played per second. The options range from 1 FPS to 30 FPS. A setting of 1 FPS plays the frames very slowly, and a setting of 30 FPS plays all frames very fast.

Recording keyframes

Clicking the Record button in the Timeline panel of the Inspector palette causes all layer-position changes to automatically be recorded as keyframes that show up in the Timeline Editor. Depending on the Animation option selected in the Timeline panel, the dragged path is recorded as a straight line (Linear), a curved path (Curve), or as a random set of positions between the first and last spot (Random).

Creating a new animation scene

You can use the Timeline Editor to create several animation sequences called *scenes*. To create a new scene, click on the Option pop-up menu in the upper-left corner of the Timeline Editor and select the New Scene menu command. This opens a simple dialog box where you can name the new scene.

Add a Play Animation action

Actions are placed in the Action Track, which is positioned between the top timeline and layer tracks. To add an action to the current animation, hold down the ⌘/Ctrl key and click on the Action Track.

In the Timeline Editor, actions have a question mark inside of them. If you click on the Action icon in the Timeline Editor, a single button appears inside the Inspector palette titled Show Action Palette. Clicking this button makes the Actions palette appear, as shown in Figure 14-85.

Figure 14-85: The Rollovers & Actions palette lets you define what action takes place when an event is triggered.

To add an action to play an animation scene, click the Action button and select the Multimedia ⇨ Play Scene menu command in the pop-up menu. From the Scene field that appears, select the scene name that you want to play. After a specific action is selected, the question-mark icon in the Timeline Editor changes to a movie icon.

STEPS: Animating Layers

1. **Open a Web page in GoLive.** Within GoLive, open an existing Web page that includes a layer with the File ⇨ Open menu command.

2. **Open the Timeline Editor.** Select the layer object in the Web page by clicking on its edge. Select the Timeline tab in the Inspector palette and click the Open Timeline Editor button. The Timeline Editor appears in the window.

3. **Create new keys.** Within the Timeline Editor, hold down the ⌘/Ctrl key and click on frame 15 and frame 30 for the first layer to add new keyframes, as shown in Figure 14-86.

Figure 14-86: Clicking in the Timeline Editor with the ⌘/Ctrl key held down creates a new key for the selected layer.

4. **Set visibility.** With the keyframe at frame 1 selected, click the Layer tab in the Inspector palette and disable the Visible option. The keyframe turns white. This change causes the layer to be hidden until frame 15 and then to appear until frame 30.

5. **Add another layer.** Drag the Layer icon from the Objects palette and drop it on the Web page. Then drag the image icon onto the new layer. Click the Browse button in the Inspector palette, and add a new Chinese Symbol image to the layer. With the layer selected, in the Timeline panel of the Inspector palette, change the Key Color.

6. **Animate the new layer by dragging.** (In the Timeline panel, select the Curve Animation option and click the Record button.) Then drag the symbol in looping circles across the scene, as shown in Figure 14-87. Many new keyframes appear in the Timeline Editor.

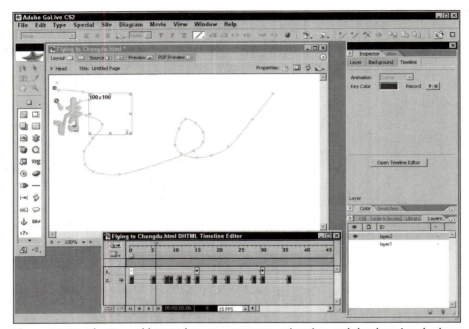

Figure 14-87: The Record button lets you create an animation path by dragging the layer object in the Web page.

7. **Preview the animation.** To see the animation in progress, click the Play button at the bottom of the Timeline Editor. Figure 14-88 shows the animation in progress.

Importing layered Photoshop images

You may import layered Photoshop images into GoLive by choosing File ➪ Import ➪ Photoshop Layers. After you select a layered Photoshop image to open, the Save for Web dialog box opens with the first layer. Clicking the Save button places this layer into a GoLive layer and adds the layer to the Layers palette. If you click the Cancel button, this layer is skipped and the next layer opens in the Save for Web dialog box. This continues until all layers have been added as layers or skipped.

Tip — If you hold down the ⌘/Ctrl button and click the Save All button, all layers are imported using the same settings.

If the imported layer name begins with a number, GoLive automatically changes it to something Web-compliant.

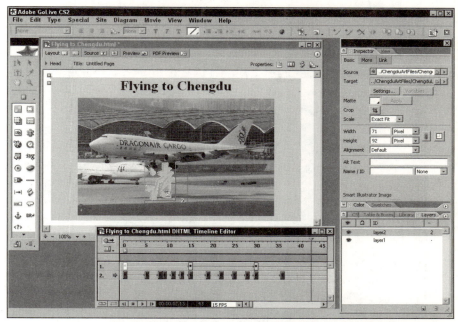

Figure 14-88: You can preview animations in the Web page by clicking the Play button at the bottom of the Timeline Editor.

Showing and hiding InDesign Layers

InDesign packages moved to GoLive have their layers exposed. This makes it easy to move between the different layers in GoLive.

Cross-Reference More on packaging InDesign layouts for GoLive is covered in Chapter 28.

Viewing Layers in AcrobatFiles that include layers that are saved or exported to the PDF file can maintain their layers when loaded within Acrobat. This not only includes documents created in the CS2 applications (except for Photoshop) but also other applications that use layers such as AutoCAD and Visio. The support for creating Adobe PDF layers requires an application supporting layers and supporting exports to Acrobat 5 compatibility. If you use other programs supporting layers and those programs do not export to the Acrobat 5–compatible PDF 1.4 format, the layers are not retained in the PDF document. You can access Adobe PDF layers using the Layers tab located to the left of the interface, as shown in Figure 14-89.

Note Viewing layers within Acrobat is available only for files that are exported using the PDF 1.4 (Acrobat 5.0–compatible) format. The layers of files that use previous format versions are flattened prior to being exported. When exporting documents to PDFs containing layers, the current layer view in the authoring document displays the same layer view in Acrobat. For example, if two layers are created and the background layer is hidden at the time of PDF export, the background layer is also hidden by default in the resultant PDF document.

Figure 14-89: The Layers tab in Acrobat shows all the layers present in the exported PDF file.

If the Layers tab isn't visible, you can make it visible by choosing View ➪ Navigation Tabs ➪ Layers. Within the Layers tab, you can click on the Visibility icon to show or hide the selected layer.

When a PDF file that includes layers is opened in Acrobat, a small layered-cake icon appears in the lower-left corner of the interface. This icon is a visual reminder that the current file has layers and that some of the layers may not be visible. If you click on the icon, the dialog box shown in Figure 14-90 opens with a reminder message visible.

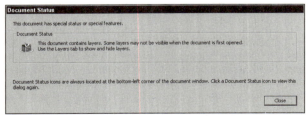

Figure 14-90: The Document Status dialog box opens when you click on the layered cake icon in the lower-left corner of the interface, reminding you that the current PDF file includes layers.

Layer options and properties

The Options pop-up menu at the top of the Layers tab includes the following options: List Layers for All Pages; List Layers for Current Page; Reset to Initial Visibility; Apply Print; Export and Layer Overrides; Merge Layers; Flatten Layers; and Layer Properties.

Listing layers

The list options let you choose to see all layers for the entire document or just the layers for the current page selected. If the latter option is selected, the layers listed in the Layers tab are updated when you switch among the different pages in the document.

Setting initial visibility

The initial visibility is determined by the layer's visibility when the document is exported to the PDF format. These initial states are remembered within the PDF file and may be recalled with the Reset to Initial Visibility option. The initial state of a layer is recorded as the Default State value in the Layer Properties dialog box. Changing this Default State value and saving the file with the File ⇨ Save menu command lets you change the initial visibility of the PDF file.

Merging and flattening layers

Selecting the Merge Layers menu command from the Options pop-up menu opens the dialog box shown in Figure 14-91. Using this dialog box, you can select layers to be merged together. The pane on the left includes all layers both visible and hidden.

Select all the layers that you want to merge in the pane on the left, and click the Add button to move them to the center pane. Using the pane on the right, you may select the name of the layer that the layers are merged into. After clicking OK, all the layers listed in the center pane are deleted (except if one of these layers is selected in the right pane as the target layer) and all the content on these layers is moved to the target layer.

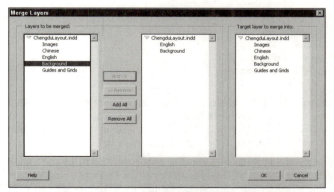

Figure 14-91: The Merge Layers dialog box lists all the layers in the left pane, lets you select which layers to merge in the center pane, and lets you select which layer to merge the content into in the right pane.

When the Flatten Layers menu command is selected in the Options pop-up menu, a warning dialog box opens explaining that this operation cannot be undone. The flattening operation merges the content on all visible layers together and deletes all layers. Any content contained on a hidden layer is deleted. Flattening a document reduces its file size.

Setting layer properties

The Layer Properties menu command opens a dialog box, shown in Figure 14-92, where you can change the layer's name, its default state, and its initial states, as well as view information about the application from which it came. The Layer Properties dialog box applies to the selected layer only.

Tip   The Layers panel also lets you rename layers by double-clicking on the layer name and typing the new name.

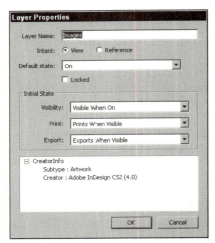

Figure 14-92: The Layer Properties dialog box lets you rename the layer and change its states.

The initial states may be set for a layer's visibility, print, and export options. The Visibility options include Visible When On, Never Visible, and Always Visible. The Visible When On option causes the layer's visibility to be determined by the eye icon in the Layers panel; the other two options cause the layer never to be visible or always to be visible.

You can also set states for when the PDF file is printed or exported. The Print and Export options include Prints (or Exports) When Visible, Never Prints (or Exports), and Always Prints (or Exports). Using these properties, you can control when a layer is printed with the document and when it's exported with the File ⇨ Save As menu.

The Options pop-up menu in the Layers panel includes three options for overriding the Visibility, Print, and Export states set in the Layer Properties dialog box. So, if a layer is set to Never Print, selecting the Apply Print Overrides option causes the layer to be printed regardless of the setting in the Layer Properties dialog box.

Making the Layers tab appear when a document is opened

You open the Document Properties dialog box, shown in Figure 14-93, by choosing File ⇨ Document Properties. If you click on the Initial View option in the pane on the left, you can set the Layers tab to appear when the document is first opened. In the Show field at the top of the dialog box, select the Layers Panel and Page option and save the PDF file. This option causes the Layers panel to appear when the PDF file is opened, revealing the available layers. Making the Layers panel visible when the PDF file opens is especially helpful for files that include hidden layers.

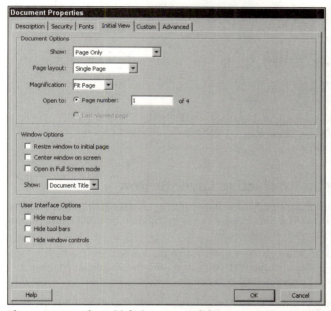

Figure 14-93: The Initial View pane of the Document Properties dialog box lets you set the Layers tab to appear when the document is opened.

Adding interactive layer buttons

When you choose Tools ⇨ Advanced Editing ⇨ Forms ⇨ Button Tool, you can create a button and set its action to control the layer visibility. Before you create the button, click on the Visibility icons for the layers that you want visible when the button is clicked, and then drag in the document to create the button.

In the Button Properties dialog box, shown in Figure 14-94, select the Actions panel. In the Select Action field, choose the Set Layer Visibility option, and click the Add button. The action is added to the Action pane of the dialog box. After clicking the Close button, you can test the button by selecting the Hand tool and clicking on the button.

Figure 14-94: The Button Properties dialog box lets you create a button with an action that controls which layers are visible.

STEPS: Creating an Interactive Layer Button

1. **Open a document in Illustrator.** Within Illustrator, open a file that includes layers that have been exported as a PDF file. Some of the layers should be hidden and others should be visible before exporting.

2. **Open the Layers panel.** Click on the Layers tab to the left to open the Layers panel. All the available layers in the document are displayed and the visible layers have an eye icon to the left of their name, as shown in Figure 14-95.

3. **Set the viewable layers.** Click on the eye icon for the layers that you want to be visible when the button is clicked.

4. **Create a button.** Choose Tools ➪ Advanced Editing ➪ Forms ➪ Button Tool, and drag over the Chinese text in the upper-left corner of the first page. This opens the Button Properties dialog box.

5. **Set the button properties.** In the Button Properties dialog box, click on the General tab and name the button Chinese. This is the text that appears on top of the button. Then select the Actions panel, select the Mouse Up option in the Select Trigger field, set the Select Action field to Set Layer Visibility, and click the Add button. Click the Close button to exit the dialog box.

6. **Reset layer visibility.** Click on the Options pop-up menu in the Layers panel and select the Reset to Initial Visibility menu command to restore the layer visibility to its initial state.

7. **Test the button.** Click on the Hand tool in the Acrobat toolbar and click on the newly created button. The selected layers should become visible, as shown in Figure 14-96. Notice how the poems are now displayed in Chinese.

Figure 14-95: The Layers panel is opened by clicking on the Layers tab to the left of the interface.

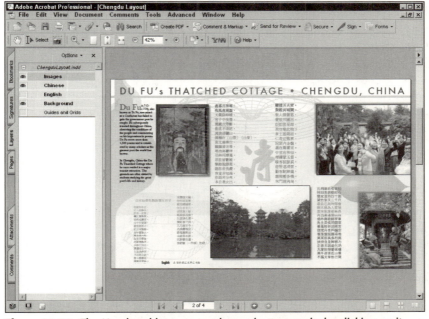

Figure 14-96: The Hand tool lets you test how a button works by clicking on it.

Summary

- Layers provide a way to organize objects into easy-to-select groups. These layers include properties such as visibility and locking that are enabled with a single click in the Layers palette.
- The Layers palette is used to create new layers, change the layer properties, move objects between layers, and manage layers.
- Layers may be used in all the CS2 applications, but the features available in each application are slightly different.
- Layers in Illustrator include the ability to work with sublayers, release layers, add styles to layers, and create clipping masks.
- Layers in Photoshop include layer sets, linked layers, transparency and blending modes, multiple locking attributes, adjustment and fill layers, type and shape layers, layer effects, and masks.
- The Layer Comps palette in Photoshop lets you take snapshots of different layer configurations and recall these snapshots quickly.
- Layers in GoLive enable you to place Web page content on top of other layers. The GoLive layers follow the CSS specification.
- GoLive layers may be animated using the DHTML Timeline Editor.
- Individual layers may be selected for a PDF file that includes layers within Acrobat using the Layers tab.

✦ ✦ ✦

Automating Tasks

CHAPTER 15

Suppose you've been asked to alter all the images in a 1,000-page travel Web site by applying a simple Drop Shadow filter. Using the Actions palette, you could quickly record all the steps required to alter the images and apply these steps to the images, thereby eliminating this repetitive and boring task.

Many of the CS2 applications include features that automate mundane, repetitive tasks. Chief among these features is the Actions palette, found in Illustrator and Photoshop, which lets you record a series of commands and play them back with a single mouse-click.

In addition to playing back an action, you can also save actions for use on other projects and batch-processed against a large number of files and/or folders. Scripts are supported by all the CS2 applications and provide a way to automate tasks that span several applications.

Photoshop includes many automated features that let you quickly perform such tasks as cropping and straightening scanned photos and create a page of thumbnails for printing. These features are found in Photoshop's File ⇨ Automate menu.

Illustrator and Photoshop include support for data-driven graphics. Data-driven graphics are document objects that are linked to variables and that an external program can read and alter to create numerous customized designs.

Finally, Acrobat includes an interface for batch-processing a series of commands called a *sequence*. Using the Batch Processing menu command, found in the Advanced menu, you may define your own sequences and execute them against a selection of files and/or folders.

If the goal is to get work done more quickly, automation is the name of the game and this chapter covers how to do it in the Creative Suite.

Using the Actions Palette in Photoshop and Illustrator

The Actions palette, shown in Figure 15-1, is used to create, manage, and execute actions within Illustrator and Photoshop. Access this palette by choosing Window ⇨ Actions. When the Actions palette is first opened, it contains several different default actions that you may select and use. These actions are all grouped in a folder called `Default Actions`.

In This Chapter

✦ ✦ ✦ ✦

Using actions in Illustrator and Photoshop

Using scripts

Using Photoshop's automation features

Working with data-driven graphics

Batch-processing PDF files

✦ ✦ ✦ ✦

Figure 15-1: All created actions are stored and accessed from the Actions palette.

You can view the Actions palette in two different ways. The default view lists all sets, actions, and commands in hierarchical order. By expanding and collapsing the names in the Actions palette, you can view or hide the individual commands that make up each action. The second view is Button mode, which you enable using the Button mode palette menu command. This mode displays all actions as single buttons. Clicking on one of these buttons executes the action. Figure 15-2 shows the Actions palette in Button mode.

Figure 15-2: When the Actions palette is in Button mode, all actions appear as buttons.

Playing an action

Actions within the Actions palette may be executed by selecting an action, then select an object in the document to receive the action commands and choose the Play palette menu command or click the Play Selection button at the bottom of the palette.

If you expand an action, the individual commands that are part of the action become visible. If you select a single command and click the Play Selection button, all commands from this selected command to the end of the action are executed. You can exclude any single command from an action by disabling the check box to its left.

Tip

Holding down the ⌘/Ctrl key while clicking the Play Selection button causes only the selected command within an action to execute.

By default, actions are set to execute as quickly as possible, but you can slow them down using the Playback Options dialog box, shown in Figure 15-3. Open this dialog box with the Playback Options palette menu command.

Figure 15-3: The Playback Options dialog box lets you choose the speed at which actions are executed.

The Playback Options dialog box includes settings for Accelerated, Step by Step, and Pause. The Accelerated option plays the actions as quickly as possible; this is the default setting. The Step By Step option executes each command and then redraws the screen before continuing. The Pause option lets you set the amount of time in seconds to wait after each command is executed.

Creating and saving a new action set

Actions may be organized into sets making it easier to locate a given action. To create a new action set, select the New Set palette menu command or click the Create New Set button at the bottom of the palette. This opens a simple dialog box where the set's name may be entered.

To add an existing action to the new set, select and drag the action and drop it when the new set's name is selected. The dropped action then appears as a child under the new set name.

You can save sets of actions using the Save Actions palette menu command. Action sets are saved using the AIA file extension in Illustrator and the ATN file extension in Photoshop.

Note   You can only save action sets. You cannot save individual actions.

You can reload saved action sets into the Actions palette with the Load Actions palette menu command. When new action sets are loaded into the Actions palette, they appear at the bottom of the Actions palette. To clear the Actions palette, select the Clear Actions palette menu command.

Creating new actions

New actions are created using the New Action palette menu command or by clicking the Create New Action button at the bottom of the palette. This command opens the New Action dialog box, shown in Figure 15-4. You use this dialog box to give the new action a name, to add the action to an existing set, and to assign the action a Function Key and a color. The color is used to color the action button when the Actions palette is in Button mode. Clicking the Record button starts the recording process.

Tip   Holding down the Option/Alt key while clicking the Create New Action button in the Actions palette instantly creates a new action named Action and a number and begins recording. To rename the action after recording has stopped, select the Action Options palette menu command.

During the recording process, each new command is added underneath the action's name in the Actions palette. To stop the recording process, select the Stop Recording palette menu command or click the Stop Playing/Recording button at the bottom of the palette.

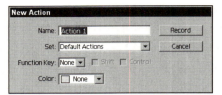

Figure 15-4: The New Action dialog box lets you name the new action.

Adding paths to an action

If a path is drawn as part of a recorded action, the path is typically not recorded as part of the action, but if you select the Insert Select Path from the Actions palette menu, the drawn path is included as part of the action and is redrawn in the same location when you execute the action.

Selecting objects as part of an action

When actions are executed, the commands are applied to any selected objects, but you may also select objects as part of the action using the Select Object palette menu command. This opens the Set Selection dialog box, shown in Figure 15-5, where you may enter the note text to search for and select. The Select Object command selects all objects that have a note with the same text as that entered in the Set Selection dialog box. The dialog box also includes options to match the whole word and to make the match case-sensitive.

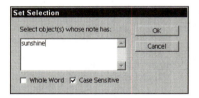

Figure 15-5: The Set Selection dialog box lets you select objects as part of an action by matching text to the text in the Note field of the Attributes palette.

To add text to an object's note, select the object and open the Attributes palette by choosing Window ⇨ Attributes (F11). In the Attributes palette menu, select the Show Note palette menu command. This reveals a text area, shown in Figure 15-6, where you may enter text.

Figure 15-6: The Attributes panel includes a Note text area where you can enter a keyword that allows the object to be selected as part of an action.

Inserting menu items

Although actions are fairly robust in what they can record, you cannot record several commands, including drawing with the Pen, Paintbrush, and Pencil tools (although you may add a drawn path to an action); changing tool options; any commands in the Effects and View menus; and setting preferences.

Although you cannot record these commands, you may still add them to an action using the Insert Menu Item palette menu command. This command opens a simple dialog box, shown in Figure 15-7, where you may enter a command, type part of the command and click Find, or select a menu item to have it appear in the dialog box. Clicking OK adds this menu command to the action.

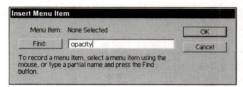

Figure 15-7: The Insert Menu Item dialog box lets you add unrecorded menu items to an action.

Adding a stop with comments

The Insert Stop palette menu command adds a stop to the action that suspends execution of the action allowing you to select new objects, check the progress of the action, or perform a task before continuing.

The Insert Stop palette menu command also opens a dialog box, shown in Figure 15-8, where you may type a message to appear when the stop point is reached. The Allow Continue option adds a Continue button to the stop point.

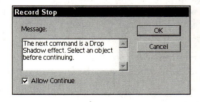

Figure 15-8: The Record Stop dialog box lets you enter a message that appears when execution of an action is halted.

Figure 15-9 shows the resulting message box that appears when the Stop command is encountered.

Figure 15-9: A dialog box like this one appears whenever a Stop command is encountered in an action.

Allowing dialog boxes to appear

The second column of the Actions palette, also shown in Figure 15-1, has several icons that represent a dialog box. If you disable this dialog box icon, the command settings remain the same as when you recorded the command. But if you enable the dialog box, the action stops and displays the dialog box for the selected command.

If you enable the dialog box for a set or an action, all dialog boxes for the entire set or the entire action are enabled. A red dialog box indicates that only some of the actions or commands have enabled dialog boxes.

Editing existing actions

You may change the options for a set using the Set or Action Options dialog boxes. These dialog boxes are opened for an existing set or action by double clicking on the item in the Actions palette or by selecting the Set Options or Action Option palette menu commands.

Rearranging actions and commands

Within the Actions palette, you can rearrange actions and commands by dragging the selected item above or below the other items. A line appears when dragging an action or a command to indicate where the dropped item is positioned. If an item is dropped on top of a selected set, then the item becomes a child of the selected item.

If you hold down the Option/Alt key while dropping a command or an action, the selected item is duplicated. You can also duplicate actions and commands using the Duplicate palette menu command.

Editing actions and commands

To add new commands to an existing action, select the action and click the Begin Recording button at the bottom of the Actions palette. Then complete the new commands. These new commands show up at the bottom of the current action.

If an action includes one command with a dialog box that isn't quite right, select the command in the Actions palette and choose the Record Again palette menu command. The command's dialog box, where you may change its values, opens. Double-clicking on a command also opens the dialog box.

Deleting actions and commands

You can delete actions and commands selected in the Actions palette using the Delete palette menu command or by clicking the Delete Selection button at the bottom of the palette.

Batch-processing actions

To execute an action on an entire folder of files, use the Batch palette menu command. This opens the Batch dialog box, shown in Figure 15-10.

Note Open the Batch dialog box in Photoshop by choosing File ➪ Automate ➪ Batch. The Batch dialog box in Photoshop offers three additional Source options (Import, Opened Files, and Bridge) and some additional options to suppress the File Open dialog boxes and Color Profile warnings.

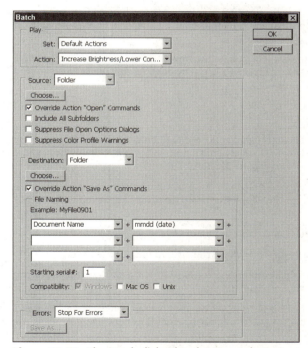

Figure 15-10: The Batch dialog box lets you select an action and execute it on all the files within a given folder.

The Batch dialog box lets you choose an action from all the sets and actions that are currently opened in the Actions palette:

- **Source options:** The Source field lets you choose to apply the selected action to all files in the folder or to apply the action to each data set in the current document. If the Folder option is selected, clicking Choose lets you select the folder to process. The Override Action Open Commands causes any commands in the action to open a file to be ignored because the folder and files are already designated. The Include All Subdirectories option causes all files in the folder and in its subsequence subdirectories to be processed.

- **Destination options:** These include None, Save and Close, and Folder. The None option leaves each document open in the application. The Save and Close option saves the files to the same folder after the changes are made. The Folder option lets you choose a new folder where the files are saved. If the action includes a save command, it can be disabled by enabling the Override Action Save Commands option. You may also select to export the altered file and select the Override Action Export Commands option.

- **FileName options:** If the Data Sets option is selected in the Source field, you may select to save the filename using the file and a number, the file and the data-set name, or just the data-set name.

- **Errors option:** The final option lets you define how to handle errors. The options include Stop for Errors and Log Errors to File. The Save As button lets you name and save the log file.

Creating a droplet

Photoshop includes an additional way to use actions called *droplets*. Droplets are created by choosing File ➪ Automate ➪ Create Droplet. This command opens a dialog box, shown in Figure 15-11. This dialog box looks similar to the Batch dialog box:

- **Choose button:** The top Choose button opens a file dialog box where you may name and specify a location where the droplet is saved. Droplets are saved with an EXE extension on Windows.

- **Play section:** Lets you select an action to include in the droplet.

- **Destination section:** Lets you select where the altered images are saved.

The options in both of the Play and Destination sections work the same as those for the Batch dialog box.

After you create a droplet, you can place it anywhere that is convenient. Image files and folders that are dropped onto the droplet automatically open in Photoshop and process using the specified action.

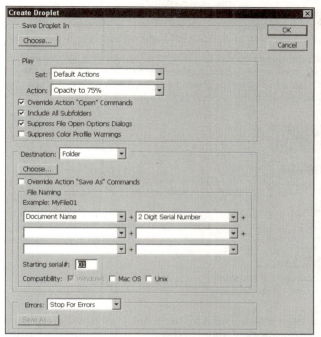

Figure 15-11: The Create Droplet dialog box lets you select where to save the droplet and which action to play to create the droplet.

STEPS: Creating an Action in Illustrator

1. **Open an Illustrator document.** With Illustrator open, choose File ⇨ New to open a new Illustrator document. Within the document, create and select a simple rectangle object.

2. **Create a new action set.** Choose Window ⇨ Actions to open the Actions palette. A set of default actions is listed. Select the New Set palette menu command. A simple dialog box opens. Type a name for the set and click OK. The new set is added to the Actions palette.

3. **Create a new action.** With the new set selected in the Actions palette, select the New Action palette menu command. In the New Action dialog box that appears, name the new action, "Random Shapes" and click the Record button. The new action is added to the Actions palette under the new set and the Record button at the bottom of the Actions palette turns red to indicate that the action is recording commands.

4. **Record commands.** With the Record button enabled, choose Object ⇨ Transform ⇨ Transform Each. The Transform Each dialog box opens. Drag the Horizontal and Vertical Scale sliders both to 0, drag the Horizontal and Vertical Move sliders both to 100, set the Angle value to 360, enable the Random option, and click Copy. The command appears in the Actions palette as part of the Random Shapes action. Click the Stop Playing/Recording button at the bottom of the palette.

5. **Add an object selection command.** Select the original rectangle object and, with the Transform Each command selected in the Actions palette, select the Insert Select Path palette menu command. This adds a Set Work Path command to the Actions palette.

6. **Rearrange the action commands.** Select and drag the Set Work Path command above the Transform Each menu command. Rearranging these commands causes the original object to be selected before the object is randomly transformed. Figure 15-12 shows the resulting Actions palette with the defined action expanded.

Figure 15-12: Each action and command may be expanded to reveal all its details.

7. **Duplicate commands.** Select all commands for the action just created in the Actions palette by holding down the Shift key while clicking on them. Then select the Duplicate palette menu command to duplicate the selected commands. Repeat this step nine more times until the commands appear ten times each.

8. **Disable the dialog boxes.** Locate the new action in the Actions palette and click on the dialog box icon in the column to the left of the action's name. This makes the action work without opening the Transform Each dialog box each time.

9. **Execute an action.** Select the new action in the Actions palette and click the Play Selection button at the bottom of the Actions palette. The selected object is duplicated ten times and randomly transformed, as shown in Figure 15-13.

Figure 15-13: Using an action, all these random rectangles were created with a single button click.

Using Scripts

Another way to automate tasks in Photoshop and Illustrator is with scripts. These scripts are authored using Microsoft's Visual Basic, Apple's AppleScript, or JavaScript. A key advantage that scripts have over actions is that scripts can automate tasks across different applications.

Scripts are loaded and executed in Photoshop or Illustrator by choosing File ⇨ Scripts ⇨ Browse.

Note InDesign and GoLive can also use scripts.

Both Photoshop and Illustrator include several default scripts. These scripts appear in the File ⇨ Scripts menu. For Photoshop, the scripts include Export Layers to Files, Image Processor, Layer Comps to Files, Layer Comps to PDF, and Layer Comps to WPG. For Illustrator, the scripts include Export Documents as Flash, LiveTrace, Save Open Documents as PDF, and Save Docs as SVG.

To add scripts to the File ⇨ Scripts menu, simply copy the script file into the `Presets/Scripts` folder where Illustrator or Photoshop is installed.

Using Photoshop's Script Events Manager

Scripts and actions are a great way to automate tasks in Photoshop, but they need to be executed before they can perform their magic. The Script Events Manager, shown in Figure 15-14, provides an alternate way to execute scripts and actions. Using this manager, you can define certain events and have these events trigger the designated script or action.

New Feature The Script Events Manager is new to Photoshop CS2.

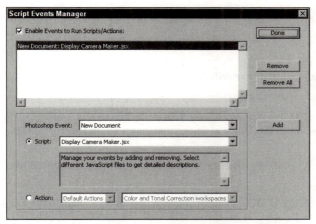

Figure 15-14: You can use the Script Events Manager to execute scripts and actions when an event is triggered.

To add an event, simply select one from the Photoshop Event drop-down list. Available default events include Start Application, Open, Save, Close, Print, and Export Document. There is also an option to Add an Event. If the Add an Event option is selected, then a simple dialog box appears where you can designate a new event name. Available event names are listed in the Scripting Reference.

Once an event is selected, you can choose the Script or Action to execute when the event takes place. The available default Scripts include Display Camera Maker, Resize, Save Extra

JPEG, Update File Info, Warn if RGB, and Welcome, or you can Browse to any script file with the .jsx extension. The available actions are the default actions or any actions that are defined in the Actions palette. After you select a script or action, click Add to add the action and its trigger to the queue.

Using Photoshop's Additional Automation Features

Photoshop includes support for actions, but it also includes several other valuable automation features available in the File ➪ Automate menu command. Using these features allows you to quickly perform complex Photoshop tasks using a simple dialog box.

The available automation tasks include the following:

- **Batch:** Lets you apply an action to an entire folder of image files in a single process.
- **PDF Presentation:** Lets you create a PDF slideshow using multiple selected files.
- **Create Droplet:** Lets you save an action as an executable file called a *droplet*, which processes files when they're dropped on top of it.
- **Conditional Mode Change:** Changes the color mode of the specified files.
- **Contact Sheet II:** Creates a page of thumbnail previews for the specified folder. This is useful for printing a catalog of images.
- **Crop and Straighten Photos:** Locates, separates, crops, and straightens multiple images from a scanned page.
- **Fit Image:** Resamples an image to a specified width and height.
- **Picture Package:** Creates and fits several copies of the selected image on a single page ready to be printed.
- **Web Photo Gallery:** Creates a Web page of thumbnail images with links to the full-sized images.
- **Photomerge:** Creates a panoramic image from several individual images that have overlapping sections.
- **Merge to HDR:** Combines three or more files from different exposures to create a High Dynamic Range image.

Working with Data-Driven Graphics

Suppose it's Christmastime and you've designed a nice Christmas card to send to all your family and friends. Using data-driven graphics, you can set a variable that loads the family name into the design or swaps the images for your friends who celebrate Hanukkah.

By automating the production of multiple designs based on data contained in a list, an arduous task becomes simple. Data-driven graphic features are available in Illustrator and Photoshop.

Data-driven graphics work a bit differently in Photoshop from the way they work in Illustrator. Within Photoshop, the variables are defined in the Layers palette, and the commands for creating variables and data sets are located in the Image ➪ Variables menu.

Defining variables

The first step in using data-driven graphics is to define variables. In Illustrator, variables are stored in the Variables palette, shown in Figure 15-15, which you can access by choosing Window ➪ Variables. Every object in the document that changes needs to have a variable assigned to it.

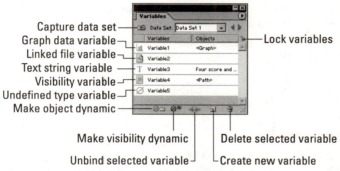

Figure 15-15: Variables are linked to the objects in the document that are changed.

Illustrator includes four different variable types. The type to select depends on the type of content that it represents. The four types are Graph Data, Linked File, Text String, and Visibility. Each variable type is identified by an icon to the left of the variable name in the Variables palette.

To create a new variable, select the New Variable palette menu command or click the Create New Variable button at the bottom of the palette. Creating a new variable opens the Variable Options dialog box, shown in Figure 15-16. In this dialog box, you can give the variable a name and select the variable type. Clicking the Create New Variable button or selecting the No Type option in the Variable Options dialog box creates an unbound variable.

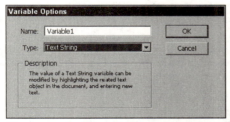

Figure 15-16: The Variable Options dialog box lets you name the variable and select a variable type.

Double-clicking on a variable in the Variables palette opens the Variable Option dialog box, where you can alter the variable's name and type.

When you have added all the variables to the Variables palette, clicking on the Lock Variables icon prevents variables from being deleted or changed.

Binding variables to objects

To link a variable to an object in the design, you should select the object when you create the variable. The selected object needs to match the variable type, except for the Visibility variable, which you can link to any type of object.

Unbound variables may be linked to a selected object in the art board using the Make Object Dynamic or Make Visibility Dynamic palette menu commands or by using one of the buttons at the bottom of the palette. The Make Object Dynamic button and palette menu command are only available if the selected object matches the selected variable's type.

Variables can also be unbound by selecting the variable and selecting the Unbind Variable palette menu command or by clicking the Unbind Variable button at the bottom of the palette.

If you click on a variable in the Variables palette with the Option/Alt key held down, the object linked to the variable is selected in the art board. You can also select linked objects using the Select Bound Object palette menu command.

Capturing a data set

Once a dynamic object has been added to the document, a data set is captured by selecting the Capture Data Set palette menu command or by clicking the Capture Data Set button. This saves all the attributes of the dynamic objects into a collection called a *data set*. Editing the dynamic objects and clicking the Capture Data Set button again creates a parallel set of data.

Each data set may have a different name and the various data sets may be selected from the list or by clicking on the arrow icons to the right of the data-set list.

Saving variables

Variables defined in the Variables palette may be saved to communicate the defined variables to a Web developer using the Save Variable Library palette menu command. This command opens a file dialog box where the variable library is named. The file is saved using the XML file format.

 More information about the XML format is presented in Chapter 30.

XML variable libraries may also be loaded into the Variables palette using the Load Variable Library menu command. This command opens a dialog box where you can select an XML file to load. The loaded variables are then displayed in the Variables palette.

Batch-Processing PDF Files

Acrobat enables automation using its Batch Processing dialog box, shown in Figure 15-17. You can access the Batch Processing dialog box by choosing Advanced ⇨ Batch Processing. The dialog box includes several default batch-processing sequences, including Create Page Thumbnails, Fast Web View, Open All, Print 1st Page of All, Print All, Remove File Attachments, Save All as RTF, and Set Security to No Changes.

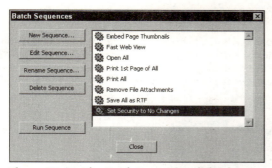

Figure 15-17: The Batch Processing dialog box lets you define new sequences, edit existing sequences, and run existing sequences.

Selecting one of these batch sequences, you can execute the sequence. This causes the steps of the sequence to run letting you select which files to apply the sequence steps to and where to save the changes. The dialog box also lets you edit the existing batch sequences and creating new sequences.

Executing sequences

To execute a sequence, simply select it from the list and click Run Sequence. A confirmation dialog box, like the one in Figure 15-18, appears, listing where the input is coming from, what commands are to be executed, and where the output is saved.

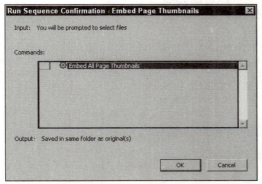

Figure 15-18: When you are executing a sequence, a confirmation dialog box appears explaining what is about to happen.

Editing sequences

You may edit existing sequences listed in the Batch Processing dialog box by selecting the sequence that you want to edit and clicking Edit Sequence. This button opens the Batch Edit Sequence dialog box, shown in Figure 15-19, where you can select new commands to add to the sequence, specify the files that the sequence is run against, and designate the output location.

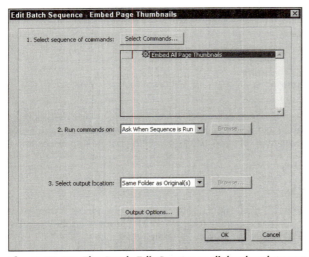

Figure 15-19: The Batch Edit Sequence dialog box lets you change the input, output, and commands for a sequence.

Clicking Select Commands opens the Edit Sequence dialog box, shown in Figure 15-20, which lists all the available Acrobat commands in the pane on the left and lists all the commands included in the current sequence in the pane on the right. Selecting a command in the left pane and clicking Add adds the command to the sequence pane on the right. The Remove button is used to remove commands from the sequence pane.

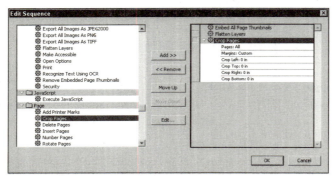

Figure 15-20: The Edit Sequence dialog box lets you pick commands to include in the sequence.

If the command includes settings, you can expand the command to reveal the settings. Clicking Edit opens the appropriate dialog box of editable settings. The sequence commands may also be selected and moved up and down in order. If the selected command has a dialog box associated with it, click on the first column to the left of the command name in the right pane to enable the settings dialog box. When enabled, the dialog box of settings appears when the command is executed, allowing you to change the settings as the sequence is being run.

The input options for the sequence include Selected Files, Selected Folders, Ask When Sequence Is Run, and Files Open in Acrobat. These are the files that the sequence is executed on. If the Selected Files or Selected Folders options are selected, the Browse button becomes active. For the Selected Folders option, another button appears that opens a dialog box, shown in Figure 15-21, that lets you select which file types to include along with the PDF files.

Figure 15-21: The Source File Options dialog box lets you select many additional file types to process in addition to PDF files. The list is different for Mac and Windows.

The Output options in the Batch Edit Sequence dialog box include Specific Folder, Ask When Sequence Is Run, Same Folder as Original, and Don't Save Changes. For the Specific Folder option, the Browse button becomes active, letting you specify a folder where the processed files are saved.

The Output Options button opens the Output Options dialog box, shown in Figure 15-22, which offers options for naming the processed files. You can save the file name with the same as the original or by appending a prefix or suffix to the filename with the Add to Original Base Name option. The Do Not Overwrite Existing Files option is a safeguard in case the new name of the file happens to be the same as a file in the folder.

The Output Format selection list lets you select the format used to save the processed files. The options include Adobe PDF Files, Encapsulated PostScript, HTML 3.2, HTML 4.01 with CSS 1.00, JPEG, JPEG2000, Microsoft Word Document, PNG, PostScript, Rich Text Format, TIFF, and XML. For the PDF file format, you may select the Fast Web View option, which optimizes the PDF file by reducing its file size and optimizing its images. The PDF Optimizer makes the Settings button active, which opens the PDF Optimizer dialog box.

 The PDF Optimizer is covered in Chapter 29.

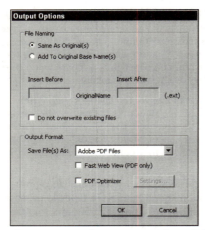

Figure 15-22: The Output Options dialog box lets you specify the filename and file format.

Creating a new sequence

The New Sequence button opens a simple dialog box where the new sequence is given a name. After you name a sequence, the Batch Edit Sequence dialog box opens; here, you select the commands to add to the sequence, determine the files to process, and define the output settings.

After the sequence is defined, the new sequence is displayed in the Batch Sequences dialog box, where you can select and execute it. To rename a sequence, simply select it and click Rename Sequence. To delete a sequence, simply select it and click Delete Sequence.

Setting batch-processing preferences

Within the Preferences dialog box, shown in Figure 15-23, which you open by choosing Acrobat ➪ Preferences (on the Mac) or Edit ➪ Preferences (in Windows), is a panel of settings for the Batch Processing dialog box.

The Show the Run Sequence Confirmation dialog option causes the confirmation dialog box to appear when a sequence is executed. If you choose not to see this confirmation, disable this option. As a sequence is run, you can save all warning and errors to a log file. If this option is enabled, you may click Choose Location to define where the error log is saved.

The Security Handler offers options for controlling the security of the sequences. The options include Do Not Ask for Password, Password Security, Certificate Security, and Adobe Policy Server.

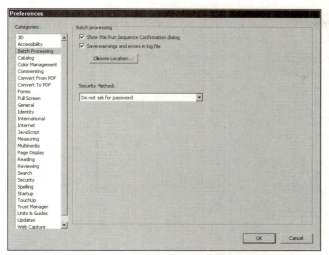

Figure 15-23: The Preferences dialog box includes some settings for the Batch Processing dialog box.

Creating batch sequences using JavaScripts

Acrobat can also use scripting to automate tasks with an implementation of JavaScript. With JavaScripts, you can extend beyond preset options, menu commands, and keyboard shortcuts to an infinite number of actions that you can perform using custom batch sequences created with JavaScripts.

If you're not a programmer, you'll want to become a little familiar with JavaScripting by examining code written by other users. You can acquire PDF documents containing scripts from many Web sites and copy and paste code into your own documents after a short review of how JavaScript is handled in Acrobat. In addition, the *Acrobat JavaScript Scripting Reference* is a complete manual shipped with Acrobat; you can find it on the installer CD. After reviewing this guide and with a little practice writing simple code, you can add more automation for PDF processing in many ways. As an example, suppose you have a collection of PDF documents you want to stamp for not releasing information to the public. Instead of opening each document, adding a stamp comment, adding a comment note, and saving and closing the file, you can write a JavaScript for a custom batch sequence and Acrobat does all the work for you. To see how this is accomplished and learn the code to exercise such a task, follow these steps:

STEPS: Creating a JavaScript Batch Sequence

1. **Create a New Batch Sequence.** Choose Advanced ➪ Batch Processing. In the Batch Sequences dialog box, select New Sequence. When the Name Sequence dialog box opens, type a name for the sequence. In this example, we use NotForDistribution. Click OK.

2. **Select Execute JavaScript and add it to the list of sequences to be executed.** In the Batch Edit Sequence dialog box, click on Select Commands to open the Edit Sequence dialog box. In the Edit Sequence dialog box, select Execute JavaScript from the list on the left and click Add to move the command to the right window.

3. **Add the JavaScript code to execute the action.** Select the command in the right window and click Edit. The JavaScript Editor dialog box opens. In the JavaScript Editor, type the following code (see Figure 15-24).

```
/* Add a Stamp comment to Page 1 in a PDF file */
var annot = this.addAnnot
({
  page:0,
  type: "Stamp",
  name: "NotForDistribution",
  strokeColor: color.blue,
  popupOpen: true,
  rect: [460, 450, 650, 500],
author: "Ted/Wendy/Kelly",
contents: "This document is not to be distributed publicly until approved by management",
AP: "NotForPublicRelease"
})
```

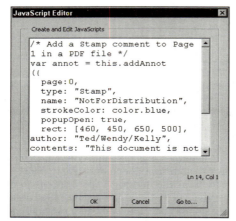

Figure 15-24: Type the code in the JavaScript Editor dialog box.

4. **Save the JavaScript.** Click OK in the JavaScript Editor dialog box. Click OK in the Edit Sequence dialog box to return to the Batch Edit Sequence dialog box. The script is saved when you exit the JavaScript Editor dialog box.

5. **Set the output options.** Leave Run commands on at the default for Ask When Sequence Is Run. In the Select Output Location pull-down menu, select the option you want to use for the saved files location. If you want to be prompted at the time the sequence is run, select Ask When Sequence Is Run. Click OK in the Batch Edit Sequence dialog box, and the sequence is added to the list of Batch Sequences.

6. **Run the sequence.** Select the Add Stamp sequence in the Batch Sequences dialog box and click on Run Sequence.

   Note: If you closed the Batch Sequences dialog box after the last step, choose Advanced ➪ Batch Processing to reopen the dialog box.

7. **Examine the results.** Select a single file to process when the Select Files to Process dialog box opens. You should see a stamp comment in the on the first page of the document page. The open pop-up note window displays the note contents, as shown in Figure 15-25.

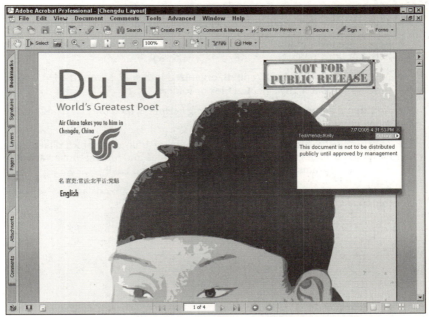

Figure 15-25: The stamp comment is added to the first page of all documents processed with the Add Stamp routine created in the JavaScript Editor.

The preceding steps create a stamp comment in line 2 (`var annot = this.addAnnot`) at the coordinates in line 9 (`rect: [460, 450, 650, 500],`). Note that the page size where the stamp is added is a custom landscape page measuring 10 by 7 inches. When using a Batch Sequence with multiple files, you need to run the sequence on PDF documents using the same page size to ensure the comment falls on the page. Note that JavaScript is zero based and line 4 (`page:0,`) targets the comment for page 1 in the file. In line 7 (`strokeColor: color.blue,`), the note pop-up window is set to blue and the pop-up window is opened after the Stamp is added to the page (`popupOpen: true,`). The content of the note pop-up is: *This document is not to be distributed publicly until approved by management* (line 11).

Line 10 (`author: "Ted/Wendy/Kelly",`) adds the author name (in this example, three author names were added). You can change the position of the note by editing the coordinates in line 9, changing the contents in line 11, or changing the stamp type in line 12 (`AP: "NotForPublicRelease"`). The code can be easily modified or you can copy and paste the code in the JavaScript Editor if you want to create other similar sequences.

Tip   If you're serious about scripting, the ExtendScript Toolkit is a valuable asset that you can access.

Summary

- Several of the CS2 applications include features for automating tasks.
- Repetitive tasks in Illustrator and Photoshop may be recorded and saved as an action in the Actions palette.
- Actions may be executed, edited, organized into sets, saved to a file, and run in a batch process against many selected files or folders.
- Additional automation is possible using scripts, which are run using the File ⇨ Scripts menu command.
- Another way to automate the creation of many unique graphics based on a template is with data-driven graphics. By defining variables and linking those variables to objects, external programs can modify designs quickly and easily.
- Acrobat includes support for Batch Processing commands against selected files and folders.

✦ ✦ ✦

Working with Type

PART IV

◆ ◆ ◆ ◆

In This Part

Chapter 16
Working with Fonts

Chapter 17
Working with Styles

Chapter 18
Working with Text Frames

Chapter 19
Working with Special Characters

◆ ◆ ◆ ◆

Working with Fonts

In This Chapter

Understanding fonts

Managing fonts

Creating type outlines and special effects

Understanding how to manage and utilize fonts for CS applications is essential for creating an efficient workflow environment. This can be a daunting task, however, because it typically requires keeping track of hundreds or even thousands of fonts, which come in a variety of formats such as Type 1 or OpenType. In addition, fonts may have varying degrees of functionality depending on the kind of computer and software you use.

Understanding Fonts

Typesetting on desktop computers has been around for more than 20 years. During this evolutionary era of digital page layout and design, there have been phenomenal changes in the tools and methods we use to produce our work. As rapid advances have been made in software development, so also has font technology evolved. And just as software packages are available that aren't suitable for current operating systems and design needs, there are also different font formats that aren't suitable for layout and imaging.

Fonts have been developed over the years using different technologies and categorized as different formats. Some font formats are obsolete today and won't work properly in some of the CS applications and with newer printing devices. Knowing what fonts are acceptable for use with the CS programs will help you prevent problems associated with printing and font embedding.

Font formats

With literally thousands upon thousands of fonts to choose from, it's important to know the different formats and which ones are best suited for your individual working environment. Ideally, you should have a thorough knowledge of all the fonts currently installed on your system.

The various font types are covered in the following sections.

✦ **Type 1:** The most popular PostScript font today. These fonts are single-byte fonts handled well by all PostScript printers. Type 1 fonts use a specialized subset of the PostScript language that has been optimized for performance. Type 1 fonts are reliable, and present the fewest problems when embedding and printing to PostScript devices.

Type 1 fonts were designed to be used with the Compact Font Format (CFF). CFF was designed for font embedding and substitution with Acrobat PDFs. As is the case with all PostScript fonts, you must install two files to view and print fonts properly. Screen fonts display a font on your monitor; printer fonts carry the PostScript code necessary to download to your printer. Each font in your layout needs an accompanying printer font. For example, if you use Adobe Garamond Bold, you need an Adobe Garamond Bold printer font. If you attempt to bold a font by using the "B" in a type formatting palette, the font may display properly on the monitor and may even print properly on your laser printer. But if you don't have the matching printer font, it typically does not print properly when printing to commercial devices.

Note When preparing files for output for commercial printing, Acrobat PDFs offer you an advantage, because the fonts used in a design piece can be embedded in the PDF file. (Be sure the font licensing agreement doesn't prohibit embedding.) This way, the fonts do not need to be supplied separately to your commercial printer.

✦ **Type 3:** Type 3 fonts are PostScript fonts that have often been used with type design and stylizing applications. These fonts can have special design attributes applied to them such as shading, patterns, exploding 3-D displays, and so on. Type 3 fonts can't be used with Adobe Type Manager (ATM), and they often present problems when printing to PostScript devices.

✦ **Type 4:** Type 4 was designed to create font characters from printer font cartridges for permanent storage on a printer's hard drive (usually attached by a SCSI port to the printer). PostScript Level 2 provided the same capability for Type 1 fonts and eventually made these font types obsolete.

✦ **Type 5:** This font type is similar to the Type 4 fonts but used the printer's ROM instead of the hard drive. PostScript Level 2 made this format obsolete.

✦ **Type 32:** Type 32 fonts are used for downloading bitmap fonts to a PostScript interpreter's font cache. By downloading directly to the printer cache, space is saved in the printer's memory.

✦ **Type 42:** Type 42 fonts are generated from the printer driver for TrueType fonts. A PostScript wrapper is created for the font, making the rasterization and interpretation more efficient and accurate. Type 42 fonts work well when printing to PostScript printers.

✦ **OpenType:** OpenType is a new standard for digital type fonts, developed jointly by Adobe and Microsoft. OpenType supersedes Microsoft's TrueType Open extensions to the TrueType format. OpenType fonts can contain either PostScript or TrueType outlines in a common wrapper. An OpenType font is a single file, which can be used on both Mac and Windows platforms without conversion. OpenType fonts have many advantages over previous font formats because they contain more glyphs, support more languages (OpenType uses the Unicode standard for character encoding), and support rich typographic features such as small caps, old style figures, and ligatures — all in a single font.

Beginning with Adobe InDesign and Adobe Photoshop 6.0, applications started supporting OpenType layout features. OpenType layout allows you to access features such as old style figures or true small caps by simply applying formatting to text. In most applications that don't actively support such features, OpenType fonts work just like other fonts, although the OpenType layout features are not accessible.

- **Compact Font Format:** Compact Font Format (CFF) is similar to the Type 1 format but offers much more compact encoding and optimization. It was designed to support Type 2 fonts but can be used with other types. CFF can be embedded in PDFs for all levels of PDF compatibility. Fonts supporting this format are converted by Acrobat Distiller during distillation to CFF/Type 2 fonts and embedded in the PDF. When viewed on-screen or printed, they're converted back to Type 1.

- **CID-keyed fonts:** This format was developed to take advantage of large character sets, particularly the Asian CJK (Chinese, Japanese, and Korean) fonts. The format is an extension of the Type 1 format and supports PostScript printing. Kerning and spacing for these character sets are better handled in the OpenType format.

- **TrueType:** TrueType is a standard for digital type fonts that was developed by Apple Computer and subsequently licensed to Microsoft Corporation. Each company has made independent extensions to TrueType, which is used in both Windows and Mac operating systems. Like Type 1, the TrueType format is available for development of new fonts.

Advantages of OpenType fonts

You can copy an OpenType font from Mac to Windows and vice versa. The OpenType format is supported for font embedding in Acrobat PDFs. Fonts produced with this technology are as reliable as you find with Type 1 and Type 42 fonts. In addition, OpenType offers a means for flagging the fonts for embedding permissions.

The OpenType format is an extension of the TrueType SFNT format that also can support Adobe PostScript font data and new typographic features. OpenType fonts containing PostScript data, such as those in the Adobe Type Library, have a filename extension of .otf, while TrueType-based OpenType fonts have a .ttf extension.

OpenType fonts can include an expanded character set and layout features, providing broader linguistic support and more precise typographic control. Feature-rich Adobe OpenType fonts can be identified by the word "Pro" in their name. OpenType fonts can be installed and used alongside PostScript Type 1 and TrueType fonts.

See Chapter 19 for more information on working with expanded character sets.

Creative Suite 1 came with 83 OpenType fonts that are installed as part of the Illustrator CS application. If you upgraded the Creative Suite you have these fonts available. In addition the Creative Suite 2 includes more than 180 bundled fonts — most of which are OpenType fonts. OpenType fonts offer you an extended set of characters where you find more *ligatures* (character combinations) and special characters and symbols. Whereas PostScript fonts offer you a maximum of 256 glyphs (individual characters), OpenType fonts can contain more than 65,000 glyphs. Look for the OpenType "Pro" fonts and you'll find extended character sets.

For a list of fonts that ship with each component product among the Creative Suite 2 applications, visit www.adobe.com/products/creativesuite/type.html.

As a standard of practice, you would be wise to replace your TrueType and PostScript fonts with OpenType fonts. This is likely to be an expensive proposition, but if you gradually begin to convert your font library and acquire new fonts in OpenType format, you'll benefit by having access to more characters, enhanced typographic features, and increased printing reliability.

Font licenses

Fonts generally carry licensing restrictions, and you need to be sure to honor them. This can be a confusing issue, however, because different font manufacturers impose different restrictions, and many licensing agreements are difficult to interpret. In order to provide font files to your service center or printer, developers often require you to get permission to distribute the font. Many developers prohibit such distribution altogether. In addition, some developers prohibit font embedding as you might do in programs like Acrobat. It's important to be aware of these limitations.

One possible way around font licensing issues is by converting any type not within your service provider's library to outlines in your documents before submitting them. In this way, the type becomes a graphic, and you don't need to copy your font files. This eliminates the transfer of the font's computer code, which is protected by copyright law. As a matter of practice, you should avoid converting large bodies of type to outlines, but in an emergency situation, it may mean the difference between getting the job out on time or not at all.

Managing Fonts

Font management has become more complicated for Mac OS X users. Prior to OS X, you could manage fonts easily using one of several different utilities, as well as by installing fonts in a single, logical location on your hard drive. With the introduction of Mac OS X, fonts are stored in several areas on your hard drive and, if not installed in the right folders, become inaccessible to your programs. In order to avoid complicated font installation procedures and ensure that fonts are accessible by CS applications, we highly recommend using a professional font-management utility. You'll find that this is a better solution than installing fonts in folders and letting your operating system handle the font management.

Installing fonts in Mac OS X

Mac OS X allows you to create accounts for multiple users, and you can choose to install fonts at the system level so all users of the computer have access to the same fonts, or you can store the fonts in individual users' Home folders to make them accessible only to a specific user.

Fonts for the Mac are installed in these locations:

- **Fonts accessible to all users of the computer:** Store them on the hard drive in Library/Fonts To install fonts in the system Library folder, open your hard drive and open the Library folder at the root level. Inside the Library folder, you'll find a Fonts folder. You can copy TrueType, PostScript, and OpenType fonts to this location.

- **User-specific fonts:** Store them in ~/Library/Fonts. (The tilde represents a user's Home folder.) Fonts stored here are available only to the owner of the active Home folder, which means different users may have access to different fonts. In case of font conflicts, fonts in this location take precedence over those in other folders.

✦ **System fonts:** The Mac OS X System folder also contains a Library folder. Once again, a Font folder resides inside the Library folder. As a default, Apple fonts required by the operating system are placed in this location. It's possible to add fonts here, but as a general rule, don't.

  ✦ **Mac OS 9:** For Classic applications, fonts are installed in the System Folder/Fonts location. Notice that the folder is titled System Folder, not System. Because all the CS applications run in native mode on OS X, you don't need to bother loading fonts here.

By default, system fonts are installed in one of the above four font locations. In addition, some fonts required by applications are also installed in these locations. However, for creative professionals who use fonts for design purposes where operating systems do not require the fonts, you should build a separate folder on your hard drive and copy all your fonts to the folder. Use a font management utility to load and unload fonts as needed for any given project.

Installing fonts in Windows

For Windows, like the Mac, you're best served by using a font utility. Follow these steps:

1. **Open the Settings menu from the Start menu.**

2. **From the Settings menu, select Control Panel and double-click on Fonts in the submenu.** The Fonts folder opens.

3. **From the File menu select Install New Font, as shown in Figure 16-1.** A navigation dialog box opens where you can search your hard drive and locate a font to install.

4. **Select the fonts you want to install and click OK.**

Figure 16-1: Open the Fonts dialog box and choose File ⇨ Install New Font to install TrueType fonts in Windows.

Fonts are also located in the PSFonts folder. On your boot drive (usually drive C:), open the folder and copy PostScript and OpenType fonts to this folder.

Organizing your fonts

Fonts play a crucial role in any designer's work. Thus, it's important to take some time to learn how to best organize your fonts to ensure maximum productivity. The amount of time you invest up front in organizing your fonts will more than pay off down the road, especially if you face an eleventh-hour deadline and can't afford for anything to go wrong at the last minute.

Check your computer's fonts on a regular basis to be sure they organized properly. Whenever you add, move, or delete fonts, there is a chance that something can go awry. Or, if you install a new operating system or font-management utility, you may need to reorganize your fonts, throw out obsolete formats, or replace existing formats to become more compatible with your current operating system and programs. If you continue to use old fonts that aren't optimized for current technology, you'll eventually experience problems.

On the other hand, if you use high-quality fonts designed to work with current software and output devices, you avoid annoying imaging problems. One of the more common font errors is the inability of the printing device to recognize the font information in the file. The printing device then automatically substitutes a default font for the one you specified, with the end result looking nothing like what you intended. Thus, choosing fonts that have a high degree of printing reliability may mean the difference between getting the job out on time and missing a critical deadline.

Using font-management tools

Font-management tools greatly facilitate font accessibility and usage. They also help prevent the installation of duplicate fonts, especially on the Mac. Mac OS X Panther and Tiger users have a utility that ships with the operating system called Font Book. Font Book 2.0 is installed with OS X Tiger. This is a good, basic utility that allows you to enable and disable fonts. It doesn't offer the convenience of auto-activation, however. You can also use third-party tools such as Extensis Font Reserve, Extensis Suitcase, or FontAgent Pro,

Using Font Book (Macintosh)

Like the other font management utilities, Font Book offers you an option for detecting corrupt fonts. If you use Font Book and you suspect a font may be corrupted, use the validation features in Font Book to be certain your font is usable.

Open Font Book, select a font appearing in the Font list, and select Validate Font from the pull-down menu in the top left corner of the Font Book dialog box. The Font Validation dialog box opens as shown in Figure 16-2. The dialog box displays the selected font with icons representing the validation results. A checkmark icon informs you the font passed validation.

Another nice feature in Font Book is the ability to easily size fonts for previews. Suitcase offers you the option to preview different sizes, but Font Book provides you a slider to size up and down the font preview. Rather than select fixed sizes or type a point size in a text box like you do in Suitcase, just drag the slider up or down to size the font and see the results dynamically in the preview area (see Figure 16-3).

Using FontAgent Pro (Macintosh)

Perhaps the most aggravating nightmare for creative professionals on Macintosh OS X is related to reliable font activation. You may have copied fonts to all of the system font locations (see the section "Installing Fonts on the Macintosh") and find one of the CS2 programs informing you a font is missing. You then uninstall the font from system font folders, attempt to load the font in another font management utility, and an alert dialog box opens informing you the font is already loaded by the system. Your aggravation continues as you poke around your hard drive trying to find a way to load the offending font and make it available to the CS2 programs.

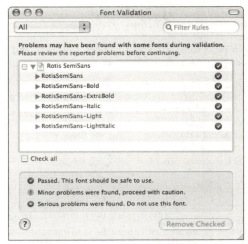

Figure 16-2: Select Validate Font from the Font Book pull-down menu and the validation results are reported for the selected font.

Figure 16-3: Drag the slider on the far right of the window to size the preview up or down.

If you're a designer who has experienced problems with alert dialog boxes informing you that a font is not available, we have a solution for you. FontAgent Pro from Insider Software (www.insidersoftware.com) solves annoying font-management problems. This $99 (as of this writing) utility is our personal choice for reliable font management on the Macintosh.

When you install FontAgent Pro (FAP), the first thing you encounter in the install wizard is a dialog box prompting you to import your fonts into a user-defined font folder FAP manages. During the import process, FAP isolates corrupt and duplicate fonts and stores them in folders apart from your font library where the reliable fonts are stored. Fonts are organized in folders and subfolders for each font family. With this feature in FAP, you don't need to use Font Book's validation options.

One very nice feature is that FAP automatically splits font suitcases into one font style per suitcase. This means you can activate only those fonts used in a design without loading the entire font family. When it comes time to send your files off to a service bureau or print shop, only the used fonts are packaged with the application document and file links.

 For information on packaging documents for service providers, see Chapter 38.

Auto-loading fonts

FontAgent Pro isn't stingy in supporting application programs with auto-loading features. Unlike other utilities that support only Illustrator CS2 and InDesign CS2 and that auto-load a font when the program launches an application document, FAP automatically loads a font from any application document you open. This could be your mail client, MS Office programs, text editors, or any document having a font not activated at the time of launch.

FontAgent Pro features

FontAgent Pro offers you an intuitive workspace where you can view and activate fonts, create new libraries and sets, share fonts in workgroups, and change the font display in the FAP window from lists to WYSIWYG (What You See Is What You Get) views (see Figure 16-4).

In addition to reliable font management, FAP also offers you some very nice options for viewing fonts in WYSIWYG style. From tools in the Font Player pane you can view a selected font character set and a sample sentence in the view window. Click the Display Paragraph tool and the display changes to paragraphs of text set in Greek type. Moving to the right side of the Font Player pane, you have buttons that offer you a slide show. Select a root folder containing sub folders of font families and click the "Auto play fonts forward" (or backward) button and the window shows you a slide show of the fonts displayed in WYSIWYG views in the Font Player display window. This option lets you quickly view all font families within a given face.

Try before you buy

Obviously, there are many more features available than in this short description of FontAgent Pro. To test the product, visit the Insider Software Web site (www.insidersoftware.com) and download the free trial version. Insider Software offers you a 30-day free trial option where you can freely try all features and access the free user guide available as a PDF document. If font activation is a problem for you on Mac OS X, we guarantee this product is likely to solve all your font-management nightmares.

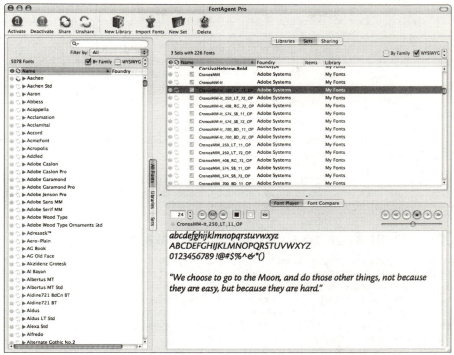

Figure 16-4: FontAgent Pro offers an intuitive workspace where you can easily manage your fonts.

Creating Type Outlines and Special Effects

Creating outlines from type has long been a common practice by graphic artists and imaging technicians. If a stubborn font problem is encountered, a workaround solution is to convert the text to outlines so the type is transformed into an object. This way, the font information doesn't need to be downloaded to the output device in order for the document to be imaged properly. When word got out that converting text to outlines eliminated font-imaging problems, many designers decided to convert text to outlines as a matter of practice.

One disadvantage in converting text to outlines is that the resulting file size can become quite large and thus take an inordinate amount of time to print. In some cases, the document is rendered unprintable. So, before you convert text to outlines, be certain that you use this option as a last resort.

Another disadvantage in converting text to outlines is that, unless you save a backup copy of your document, you lose the ability to access and edit your file utilizing the original font information. Say, for example, you create a half a dozen logotype variations for a client using different fonts. You then convert the type to outlines in order to apply special effects, and resave the document. You won't be able to go back into the Character palette to see which fonts you used, nor will you be able to edit any text if there are copy changes. The caveat here is always to save a separate copy of the document that contains the original font information when you choose to convert text to outlines. Fortunately, when using the CS applications, you can use Version Cue to save a different version of the same document or save an Alternate version. When you want to return to the document containing the original font information, promote that version to the top level in Version Cue or select the Alternate in the Bridge.

For information on using Version Cue and promoting versions, see Chapter 8. For information on using Alternates, see Chapters 7 and 8.

So, you may need to convert text to outlines either as a workaround for stubborn font printing issues, or when you want to apply certain type effects. The Create Outlines command is available in Illustrator, Photoshop, and InDesign.

Converting type to outlines in Illustrator

To convert type to outlines in Illustrator, select the type with either of the selection tools in the Tools palette. (Note that you cannot use the Type tool here as you can in InDesign.) Next, Choose Type ➪ Create Outlines or press Shift+⌘+O or Shift+Ctrl+O. As you can see in Figure 16-5, after creating outlines each character becomes a compound path, editable with either the Selection tool or the Direct Selection tool. To edit or move individual characters with the Selection tool, you'll need to first ungroup the object. Choose Object ➪ Ungroup, or press Shift+⌘+G or Shift+Ctrl+G.

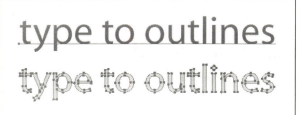

Figure 16-5: Type shown before and after converting to outlines. Each character becomes a compound path, which you can edit with the selection tools.

Creating type effects in Illustrator

The options are almost limitless when it comes to creating eye-catching type effects with Illustrator. You can apply custom gradients, transparency, meshes, shadows, lighting and shading, distortion, stylization, 3-D effects, and more. Figure 16-6 shows an example of the 3D type effects you can achieve quickly in Illustrator. For a more in-depth look at the ways you can use Illustrator to enhance your type, see the *Illustrator CS Bible* by Ted Alspach and Jennifer Alspach (published by Wiley).

Figure 16-6: In Illustrator, this 3-D effect was easily created using regular type (top) and then applying a stroke, gradient, extrude effect, warp effect, and drop shadow.

Creating type masks in Illustrator

Other interesting effects can be achieved by using type as a mask. Note that when creating type masks in Illustrator you can create a mask without converting the type to outlines.

Position the type in front of the artwork that will be masked. Select both the type and the item to be masked by drawing a marquee around the objects or by shift-clicking if necessary (two objects must be selected for this command to work). Then choose Object ➪ Clipping Mask ➪ Make, or press ⌘+7 or Ctrl+7. Areas of the background artwork that are outside the type mask disappear, and your type now appears filled with the portion of the artwork directly behind it (see Figure 16-7). You can move the background image or the type around to experiment with different mask positions.

Figure 16-7: You can create type masks in Illustrator without converting the text to outlines.

Converting raster type to vector type

You may have a need to re-create logos for clients where original artwork for the company logo is not available in digital form. If your client faxes you a copy of the company logo and you need to size it up for use in a large tradeshow display, a scan of the logo is likely to lose image quality. If you convert a logo to a vector object, you can then freely size the object without being concerned about losing image quality.

New Feature With Illustrator CS2, you can easily convert raster data to vector objects using Live Trace. The results of the Live Trace object will be as good as the scan you use, so be certain to obtain good-quality originals and scan at high resolutions. To see how easy it is to convert a scanned logo from a Photoshop image to a vector object in Illustrator using Live Trace, follow the steps below:

STEPS: Converting Raster Data to Vector Objects

1. **Scan the logo.** Scan a logo at a high resolution and save the file as a TIFF file from Adobe Photoshop.

2. **Create a new document in Adobe Illustrator.** Choose File ➪ New and supply the desired dimensions in the New Document dialog box. Click the Color mode you want to use and click OK to create a new blank document.

3. **Open Adobe Bridge.** Choose File ➪ Browse to open the Bridge window. The Illustrator document window remains open in the background. Locate the file you saved from Photoshop in the Bridge window and drag the file to the Illustrator art board. Alternately you can choose File ➪ Open in Illustrator or File ➪ Place and select the file to import. The image appears in Illustrator as an image (see Figure 16-8).

Cross-Reference For more information about using Adobe Bridge to manage files, see Chapter 7.

Figure 16-8: Drag and drop, open, or place the image in Illustrator.

4. **Adjust the trace settings.** Choose Object ➪ Live Trace ➪ Tracing Options. The Tracing Options dialog box appears, as shown in Figure 16-9. Set the Mode and Threshold options. Adjust Max Colors if your image is a color scan. If tracing a black-and-white logo, use the Black and White mode. Leave the remaining settings as you see in Figure 16-9. Click OK to register the settings.

Caution If you trace logos with gradients, be certain to set the maximum number of 255 for the Threshold. If scanning color logos with gradients, set the Max Colors setting to 256. If you don't set these values high, Live Trace may clip or posterize the image.

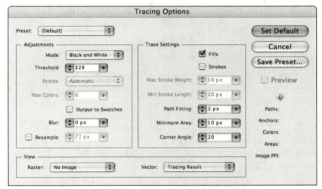

Figure 16-9: Open the Tracing Options dialog box and make settings choices for the type of image you intend to trace.

Cross-Reference For more information on using Live Trace, see Part III.

5. **Trace the object.** Choose Object ➪ Live Trace ➪ Make and Expand (or Make and Convert to Live Paint). If you have potential problems with overlapping colors, use the Make and Convert to Live Paint option. Otherwise use Make and Expand. Either choice expands the trace so the individual characters can be masked, edited, or used with a variety of effects. In Figure 16-10, the image is traced.

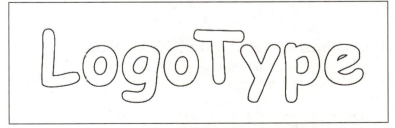

Figure 16-10: Live Trace renders the image as a vector object.

6. **Apply effects.** You may need to expand the object. Select Object ⇨ Expand and expand the strokes and fills. Use the Direct Selection tool and delete a background if one appears. Apply effects to create the look you want by selecting options from the Effect menu. In Figure 16-11, the type is masked, stroked, filled with a Graphic Style, warped, and has a drop shadow applied.

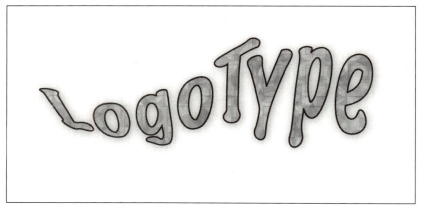

Figure 16-11: After converting to a vector object, you can mask the type and apply many different effects.

Converting type to outlines in Photoshop

If it's a matter of printing a font, Photoshop files can always be rasterized in order to convert the type object to pixels. When type is rasterized in Photoshop it loses all the type attributes and prints like any Photoshop image.

In Photoshop CS2, you can also convert type to outlines. If you want to mask type originally created in Photoshop in Illustrator, you can convert the type to outlines in Photoshop and then import the Photoshop file into Illustrator, where you can apply the mask. Of course, if your mask object is in Photoshop, you can also mask type in Photoshop. With the new Photoshop CS2 features, you have a choice for where you want to apply type masks.

Photoshop type converted to outlines is recognized only in Illustrator. If you import a Photoshop file with outline type in InDesign, the text is not recognized as a vector object. To experiment a little with type converted as outlines in Photoshop, follow these steps:

STEPS: Converting Type to Outlines in Photoshop

1. **Add type to a document in Photoshop.** Create a new file in Photoshop. Select the Horizontal Type tool and add some type to the document. Type is added on a new layer.
2. **Convert the type to outlines.** Open a context menu on the layer containing type and select Convert to Shape as shown in Figure 16-12. The Photoshop type is converted to outline type and remains a vector graphic.

Chapter 16 ✦ **Working with Fonts** 629

Figure 16-12: Open a context menu and select Convert to Shape.

3. **Copy the type in Photoshop.** Select the Direct Selection tool from the Pen tool pop-up toolbar in the Toolbox and drag a marquee around the type to select it. Choose Edit ⇨ Copy. When you select the type, you can see the paths around the type as shown in Figure 16-13.

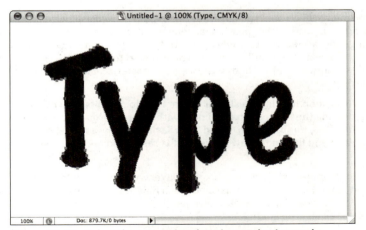

Figure 16-13: Select the type using the Direct Selection tool.

4. **Paste the type in Illustrator.** Create a new document in Illustrator. Choose Edit ⇨ Paste.

5. **Apply effects to the type.** You can size the type and apply effects from the Effect menu or from palettes such as the Graphic Styles palette. In Figure 16-14, the type was sized and a neon effect was added using a Neon Effects Graphic Style.

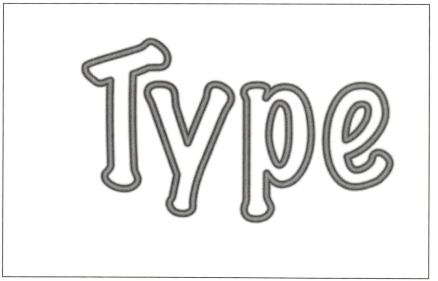

Figure 16-14: After pasting the Photoshop type in Illustrator, you can size the type and add effects.

You can create many effects for type masks in Photoshop as well as stylize type with shadows, embossing, filters, and brightness enhancements after rasterizing type. Photoshop's array of editing tools allows you to apply effects to type in the same way you apply them to images. When you create type in Photoshop, type is added to a separate layer and remains as a vector object until you either flatten the layers or rasterize a layer by choosing Layer ➪ Rasterize ➪ Type.

If you import Photoshop files in InDesign or create PDF documents, you can keep your type in vector form by saving the Photoshop document with layers. Formats that can preserve layers include the native PSD, Photoshop PDF, and TIFF. Saving with layers keeps type as text and it remains editable. If you flatten the layers, the text is rasterized and you lose the ability to edit your text.

If you open a Photoshop PDF file in Acrobat with layers and vector data preserved, the text is searchable and editable. If you open the same file in Illustrator, Illustrator automatically converts the type to outlines. The same file saved as a native Photoshop (PSD) file opened in Illustrator preserves all type editing.

The type effects you can create in Photoshop are mind-boggling. For a comprehensive coverage see the *Photoshop CS Bible* by Deke McClelland (Wiley, 2004).

Cross-Reference For more information on creating type effects in Photoshop, see Part III.

Converting type to outlines in InDesign

InDesign offers you the same option as Illustrator for converting type to outlines. With this feature, you can create many type effects directly in InDesign without having to create them in Illustrator and import them. After outlines have been created in InDesign, you have similar options as Illustrator for shaping text objects with the selection tools, as well as creating type masks.

To convert type to outlines in InDesign, select the characters you want to convert to outlines by highlighting them with the Type tool or by selecting the text frame with a selection tool. With the Type tool, you can select one character or a range of characters. If you want to convert your entire page to outlines as a workaround for font downloading problems or licensing issues, select all by choosing either of the selection tools in the Tools palette and then pressing ⌘/Ctrl+A. Next, choose Type ➪ Create Outlines or press ⌘+Shift+O or Ctrl+Shift+O.

Creating type effects in InDesign

Many type effects can be achieved in InDesign without converting the type to outlines. As demonstrated in Figure 16-15, you can create sophisticated type treatments with strokes, fills, gradients, and drop shadows and still be able to edit the text. This is a difficult or impossible feat in most other page-layout programs.

Figure 16-15: InDesign CS allows you to create sophisticated type effects without converting the type to outlines. The text remains fully editable.

A new feature introduced in InDesign CS1 is the Stroke style editor. You can create and save striped, dotted, and dashed stroke styles and apply them to type, as well as underlines, strikethroughs, lines, and paragraph rules.

Creating type masks in InDesign

Type masks are created a little differently than they are in Illustrator. Instead of placing type over artwork to be masked, the type is essentially turned into a graphics frame. You can then paste or import an image into the frame.

After you've converted your type to outlines, simply select it and choose File ➪ Place, or press ⌘/Ctrl+D, and navigate to the image you want to import. When selecting the type, you can use either the Selection tool or the Direct Selection tool. In Figure 16-16, type is converted to outlines and the text is selected with the Direct Selection tool.

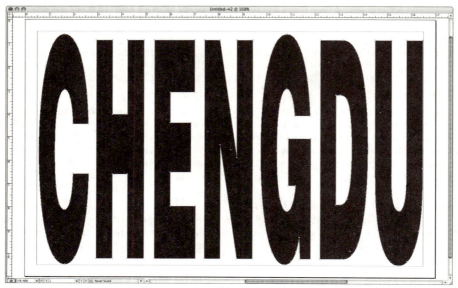

Figure 16-16: After converting type to outlines, select the type with either the Selection tool or the Direct Selection tool.

When the Place dialog box appears, be certain to select the check box for Replace Selected Item, as shown in Figure 16-17. If you don't check the box, the cursor is loaded with the graphic and InDesign expects you to place the file somewhere on the document page. When you select Replace Selected Item, the file is placed within the outlined type, resulting in a mask. If you want to place an item in a multi-page document, be certain to select the Show Import Options check box as shown in Figure 16-17.

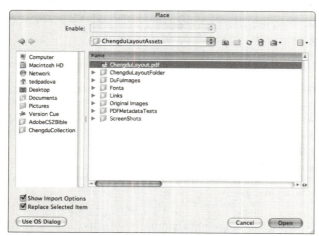

Figure 16-17: Be certain to select the check boxes for Replace Selected Item and Show Import Options in the Place dialog box.

When selecting Show Import Options, another dialog box appears. The type of dialog box and the options available are dependent on the file type you place. In Figure 16-18, the Place PDF dialog box opens because the file type being placed is a PDF. In the Preview window, you can navigate pages and see page thumbnails before committing to place the document.

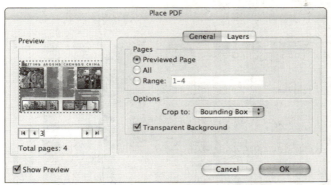

Figure 16-18: Be certain to Show Import Options when placing multiple-page PDF documents and layered files.

A new Feature in InDesign provides options for selecting layers when you place Photoshop and PDF files. Click the Layers tab in the Place PDF dialog box and the Layers pane opens with choices for selecting layers on a given page to place. You toggle layers on and off like you do in any of the CS programs. Click the right-pointing arrow to open the nested layers and click the eye icon to toggle layers on and off. The Layers pane in the dialog box displays a preview of the selected layers, as you can see in Figure 16-19.

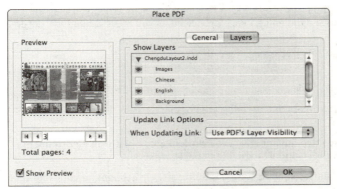

Figure 16-19: When you place layered Photoshop and layered PDF files, you can click the Layers tab and toggle layer views.

For more information on working with layers in the CS applications, see Chapter 14.

Click OK in the Place PDF dialog box and the layer view you see in the preview is placed inside the type, as shown in Figure 16-20. If you need to move the image within the mask, select the Direct Selection tool. When the cursor approaches the text, the cursor changes to a Hand tool, thus informing you that the image can be moved within the mask.

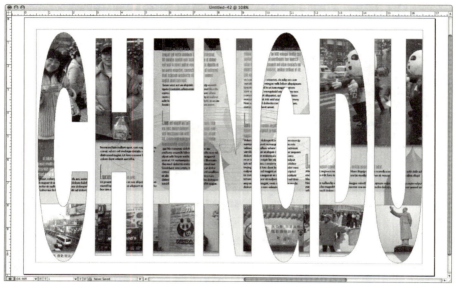

Figure 16-20: When the Replace Selected Item check box is selected, the image is placed within the selected object.

Tip   When you drag with the Hand tool, click and pause a moment. When you drag the cursor after pausing you can see the entire image previewed as you move around the document window.

Summary

✦ The three main font formats in use today are PostScript Type 1, TrueType, and OpenType.

✦ OpenType fonts have two advantages: they work in cross-platform environments (Mac and Windows), and they support expanded character sets.

✦ Font-management utilities such as Extensis Suitcase help streamline your font-management tasks.

✦ Converting all type to outlines in your documents is a way to circumvent font downloading problems, but this approach should be used as a last option.

✦ Special type effects are easy to achieve in Illustrator, Photoshop, or InDesign. Illustrator offers a sophisticated array of transformation tools, including extrusion (3-D) and lighting effects for type objects. Photoshop CS2 enables you to create type outlines. InDesign allows certain type effects to be applied without first converting the type to outlines.

✦ Photoshop provides virtually unlimited options for creating type effects. If you want your text to remain editable, however, be sure to keep the type in vector form by preserving layers when saving your file.

✦ ✦ ✦

Working with Styles

CHAPTER 17

In This Chapter

Formatting type

Working with character style sheets

Working with paragraph style sheets

Combining styles to create nested style sheets

Working with graphic styles

Adding type to a page is one of the more common tasks performed by creative professionals. Long gone are the days when we ordered type from a professional typesetter. Today's graphic artists are both artists and typographers. Fortunately, the typographic tools in the CS applications make your job easier when setting type.

For anyone who has set type for manuals, books, and other long documents, style sheets should be familiar tools. It's hard to imagine working with large bodies of text without the use of style sheets. Without them, your labors would be tenfold. You would have to manually set the styles for each body of text throughout a document, and any style changes would require the same laborious process.

Illustrator CS supports character and paragraph styles that make layouts much more flexible. Photoshop supports text styles for applying effects to type. In InDesign CS, you'll find impressive style sheet capabilities such as nested styles. In GoLive, you have abundant opportunities for adding styles to Web page designs as we describe in Chapter 27.

 Cross-Reference For information on working with styles in GoLive, see Chapter 28.

This chapter takes you through setting type in CS applications and creating character, paragraph, and graphic styles in Illustrator and InDesign, and text effect styles in Adobe Photoshop.

Setting Type

If you have type created in programs like Microsoft Word, you can import text into both Illustrator and InDesign, as described in Chapter 18. If you don't use a word-processing program to set type, you can add type in Illustrator, Photoshop, or InDesign with the Type tool. In Illustrator, setting type is a bit clumsy as compared to setting type in InDesign. Illustrator doesn't support the use of any special tools for typesetting such as InDesign's Story Editor. However, Illustrator adds some flexibility when setting type on irregular shapes and paths. Each program has its own strength in regard to typesetting, and it's worth your time to look at both programs so you know which one is best for a particular job.

Setting type in Illustrator

Illustrator has two kinds of type functions, both created with the Type tool. You create p*oint type* by clicking the cursor in the document window and type. The primary limitation of point type is that the type doesn't wrap or conform to a specific area. If you keep typing, the characters eventually go off the page, unless you add a carriage return at the end of each line.

The other kind of type in Illustrator is *area type*. Area type conforms to a specific boundary and the type wraps to the outside boundary. The type boundary is created by clicking and dragging open a rectangle with the Type tool or by clicking the cursor inside an object. Doing so binds the type to the shape of the object. The object can be a simple geometric shape, a polygon, or an irregular shape.

You also have tools for creating vertical type. Click on the Type tool and keep the mouse button depressed to expand the toolbar. There are two vertical type tools — one for point type and one for area type. The results of creating type with the type tools are shown in Figure 17-1.

Creating point type

To create point type, simply click on the Type tool in the Illustrator toolbox and click the cursor at the location where you want to begin typing. A blinking cursor appears.

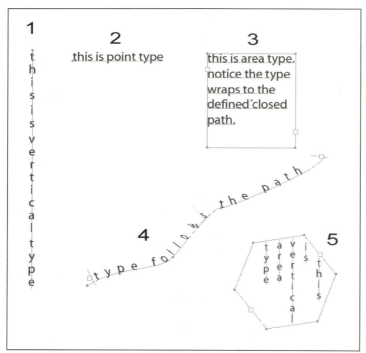

Figure 17-1: Type created in Illustrator can appear as (1) vertical point type, (2) point type, (3) area type, (4) type on a path, or (5) vertical area type.

After typing a line of text, you can use the Character palette or keyboard shortcuts to change type appearances. Choose Window ⇨ Type ⇨ Character or press ⌘/Ctrl+T to open the Character palette. The default view of the Character palette is collapsed. To expand the view and show more options, click on the right-pointing arrow to open the palette menu and select Show Options. In Figure 17-2, the palette view is shown with the options expanded.

Figure 17-2: The Character palette

The type control available in the Character palette includes the following:

A Font selection is made from the pull-down menu.

B Font style is selected from options in the pull-down menu.

C Type point size can be selected from fixed sixes in the pull-down menu or by typing values in the field box. The values range from 0.1 points to 1,296 points.

D Kerning type is handled by selecting from fixed sizes or by typing values in the field box.

E Horizontal scaling is defined from fixed values or by typing values in the field box.

F Baseline shifts move the baseline of the type up when positive values are entered and down when negative values are entered.

G Underline and strikethrough. Select type and click on either the underline option or the strikethrough option or both to apply the respective type effects.

H Language selection is made from the pull-down menu.

I Leading is controlled by selecting from fixed values or by typing values to $\frac{1}{100}$ of a point.

J Tracking amounts are specified in whole numbers ranging from –1,000 to 10,000 points.

K Vertical scaling of type can be adjusted in increments ranging from 1 percent to 10,000 percent.

L Characters can be rotated in increments as small as $\frac{1}{100}$ degree.

In addition to using the Character palette, you can perform several adjustments using keyboard shortcuts. To modify the type, use the following key combinations:

✦ **Alt+Right Arrow (Option+Right Arrow on the Mac):** Increases tracking. Select type characters for the characters of which you want to change tracking amounts.

- **Alt+Left Arrow (Option+Left Arrow on the Mac):** Decreases tracking. Select type characters for the characters of which you want to change tracking amounts.

- **Alt+Up Arrow (Option+Up Arrow on the Mac):** Increases leading. Affects only selected characters.

- **Alt+Down Arrow (Option+Down Arrow on the Mac):** Decreases leading. Affects only selected characters.

- **Alt+Shift+Up Arrow (Option+Shift+Up Arrow on the Mac):** Increases baseline shift. Affects only selected characters.

- **Alt+Shift+Down Arrow (Option+Shift+Down Arrow on the Mac):** Decreases baseline shift. Affects only selected characters.

- **Alt+Ctrl+Left Arrow (Option+⌘+Left Arrow on the Mac):** Tightens kerning on all selected characters. Clicking in a line of type tightens kerning between characters at the cursor position.

- **Alt+Ctrl+Right Arrow (Option+⌘+Right Arrow on the Mac):** Expands kerning. Clicking in a line of type expands kerning between characters at the cursor position.

Other options available in the Character palette are selected from the palette menu. Click the right-pointing arrow in the upper-right corner of the palette, and the palette menu opens as shown in Figure 17-3. The menu options include the following:

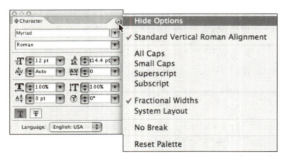

Figure 17-3: The right-pointing arrow opens the palette menu.

- **Standard Vertical Roman Alignment:** The direction of half-width characters such as Roman text or numbers changes in vertical alignment. When this option is checked, you can rotate selected individual characters within a block of text without affecting the rotation of the unselected characters.

- **All Caps:** Sets all selected characters to caps. (See Figure 17-4.)

- **Small Caps:** Sets all selected characters to small caps. (Refer to Figure 17-4.)

- **Superscript:** Selected characters appear as superscript above the baseline. (Refer to Figure 17-4.)

- **Subscript:** Selected characters are subscripted below the baseline. (Refer to Figure 17-4.)

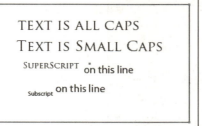

Figure 17-4: Type styles: All caps, small caps, superscript, and subscript

- **Fractional Widths:** As a default, leave this item checked because the type is displayed in the best appearance. The spacing between characters varies. If disabled, the characters are monospaced.

- **System Layout:** Characters are previewed using the operating system's default text handling. This option is particularly helpful when designing user-interface designs where you might create dialog boxes, palettes, and menus.

- **No Break:** Prevents you from creating line breaks. If you enable the option while using either point type or area type, after pressing the Return key, new type is set over the last line of type.

- **Reset Palette:** Restores the default character settings in the palette.

Creating area type

The Character palette by default is nested together with two other palettes. The Paragraph palette is used for paragraph formatting, and it makes sense to describe the options when discussing area type. The OpenType palette offers options for a number of different settings you can make when using OpenType fonts.

Cross-Reference

For more information on OpenType fonts, see Chapter 16.

Area type is created using the Type tool. Instead of clicking the cursor where point type is created, click the cursor and drag open a rectangle. By default, when you release the mouse button, a blinking I-beam cursor appears in the top-left corner of the rectangle. Area type can also be created within closed paths. Any object you draw in Illustrator can define the boundaries for area type. When adding area type to a closed path, simply click the cursor inside the path and the blinking I-beam informs you the object is ready to accept type. In Figure 17-5, you can see results of area type applied to different shapes.

In the Paragraph palette, you'll find options for paragraph formatting. Some of the options, such as paragraph alignment, can also apply to point type. However, indents and paragraph spacing are more likely to be applied to area type.

When you create area type and want to change paragraph formatting, click on the Paragraph tab to show the options. If the palette is not in view, choose Window ⇨ Type ⇨ Paragraph, and the palette shown in Figure 17-6 opens.

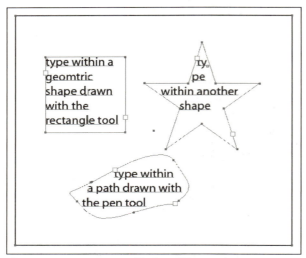

Figure 17-5: Area type added to different shapes

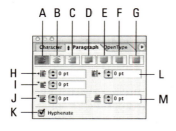

Figure 17-6: The paragraph palette has options for paragraph formatting.

As shown in Figure 17-6, the palette contains many options. These include the following:

A Align Left: Text alignment for the paragraph is aligned left.

B Align Center: Paragraph text is aligned centered.

C Align Right: Paragraph text is aligned right.

D Justify with Last Line Aligned Left: The paragraph is fully justified with the last line aligned left.

E Justify with Last Line Aligned Center: The paragraph is fully justified with the last line aligned center.

F Justify with Last Line Aligned Right: The paragraph is fully justified with the last line aligned right.

G Justify All Lines: All text is justified and the last line is justified. If you have only two words appearing in the last line of text, one word is aligned left and the other word is aligned right.

- **H Left Indent:** Text is indented from the left edge of the text block.
- **I First Line Left Indent:** The first line of text in the paragraph is indented left and the other lines are aligned left without indentation.
- **J Space Before Paragraph:** Adds space above the paragraph in amounts specified in the field box.
- **K Hyphenation:** When the check box is checked, hyphenation is applied to the paragraph.
- **L Right Indent:** Text is indented from the right edge of the text block.
- **M Space After Paragraph:** Adds space after a paragraph in amounts specified in the field box. Use the space after and space before paragraphs instead of using carriage returns.

The seven views of type formatted using the different paragraph formats are shown in Figure 17-7.

Using OpenType

As detailed in Chapter 16, OpenType fonts offer you many more glyphs than TrueType or PostScript fonts. With more glyphs available in an OpenType Pro font, you have alternate choices for the way you want to display characters. Because the number of characters can vary between OpenType fonts, be aware that all options are not available with every font. As you open the Character palette and view the tabs, the final tab is the OpenType tab. Click this tab, and the options shown in Figure 17-8 appear.

Figure 17-7: The seven different paragraph formats

Figure 17-8: The OpenType tab has options for OpenType fonts.

The palette displays two pull-down menus and a line of buttons. To have the menu commands and buttons active, you need to have an OpenType font selected. Not all options are available for all OpenType fonts. Depending on the number of characters and styles contained within an OpenType font, the options vary. From the Figure pull-down menu, the options include the following:

Note: If using Asian OpenType fonts (Chinese, Japanese, and Korean), you may have more options available in the OpenType palette.

+ **Default Figure:** Choose this option to use the default style for numbers appearing in the selected font.
+ **Tabular Lining:** Only when the OpenType characters are available, the full-height figures line up proportionally. You might use this option when setting type in tables and charts.
+ **Proportional Lining:** When characters are available, this option lines up characters with varying widths. You might use this option when setting type containing numbers and uppercase characters.
+ **Proportional Oldstyle:** When characters are available, use this option when you want a classic type appearance. It creates a more sophisticated look when using lowercase characters.
+ **Tabular Oldstyle:** Applies to varying height characters with fixed, equal widths. This option might be used when you want a classic appearance of old-style figures, but you want the characters to align in columns.

Another set of menu commands appears in the Position pull-down menu. The Position options offer choices for the placement of characters respective to the baseline. These options are particularly helpful when working with numbers and fractions. Again, these are available only if they are offered in the current OpenType font. The menu choices include the following:

+ **Default Position:** Keeps the default position of characters for the selected font.
+ **Superscript/Superior:** Raises characters above the baseline.
+ **Subscript/Inferior:** Lowers characters below the baseline.
+ **Numerator:** Applies to numerals designed as fractions. The fractional characters only are raised to appear as numerators.
+ **Denominator:** Applies to numerals designed as fractions. The fractional characters only are lowered to appear as denominators.

Figure 17-9 displays the various options choices when using the Cronos Pro OpenType font and applying the different position options to alpha and numeric characters.

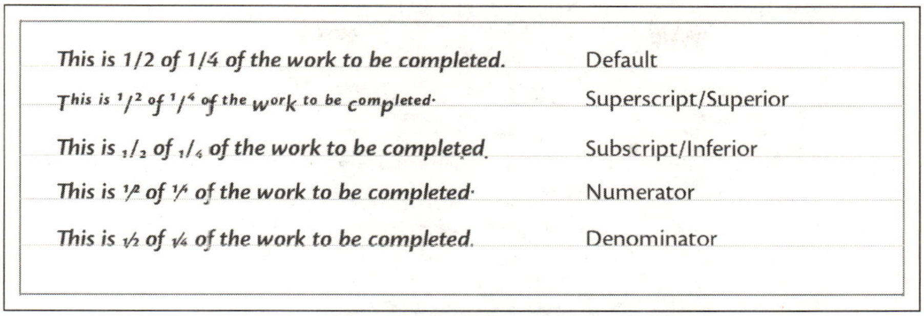

This is 1/2 of 1/4 of the work to be completed.	Default
This is ¹/² of ¹/⁴ of the work to be completed.	Superscript/Superior
This is ₁/₂ of ₁/₄ of the work to be completed.	Subscript/Inferior
This is ½ of ¼ of the work to be completed.	Numerator
This is ½ of ¼ of the work to be completed.	Denominator

Figure 17-9: The five different OpenType options for Position are applied to the OpenType font Cronos Pro.

Combining point type and area type

Many different types of documents can be opened and edited in Illustrator. Often, the objects appear to be translated without problems, but you may find that a lot of the original paragraph formatting is lost. Files you may want to convert to Illustrator documents — CAD drawings, page layouts from other programs, charts and graphs, and so on — typically open in Illustrator with broken type blocks. To convert the point type segmented throughout a document, look over the following steps to see how you can fix such problems.

STEPS: Converting Point Type to Area Type

1. **Open an EPS file in Illustrator.** For this example, we use a QuarkXPress document saved from XPress using the Save Page as EPS menu command. Notice that in Figure 17-10, when all the type is selected in Illustrator, you see point type on each line of text and broken along the lines of type. This copy would be difficult to edit in its present form.

2. **Cut the text from the art board.** Choose Edit ➪ Select All or press ⌘/Ctrl+A to select all the type. Be certain to have either the Selection tool or the Direct Selection tool selected in the Toolbox before selecting the type. If the Type tool is selected and the cursor is blinking in a line of type, only that segment of type will be selected. After selecting all the related type objects, choose Edit ➪ Cut to cut the text to the Clipboard.

3. **Paste the type.** Select the Type tool and drag open a rectangle to define the boundaries for the area type. Choose Edit ➪ Paste. The type is pasted from the blinking cursor and fills the area type boundary. When the type is pasted, all paragraph formatting is lost, as shown in Figure 17-11. However, the type is one contiguous body of text.

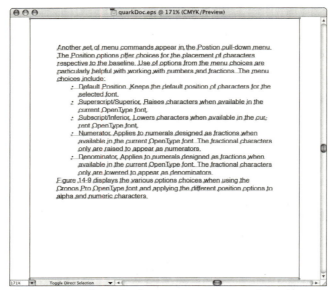

Figure 17-10: After selecting type, you can see where the type blocks are broken by observing the handles (small squares) on the baselines.

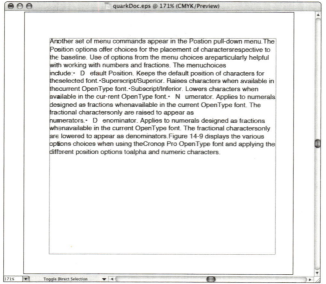

Figure 17-11: Although the paragraph formatting is lost, the text is pasted as one contiguous body of type.

4. **Format the type.** Add carriage returns and tabs where needed to create the paragraph format you want to apply to the body of text. Use the Paragraph palette to set type formats such as space before and after, as well as any alignment considerations you need, as shown in Figure 17-12.

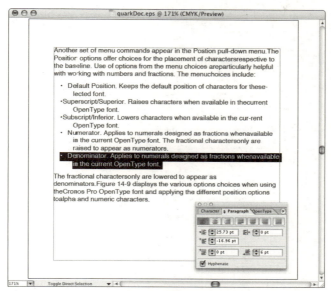

Figure 17-12: As a contiguous body of text, you can use the Paragraph palette to format the type.

For more-precise placement and sizing of the text block, you can use guides and create text frames according to guide positions. If you have legacy Illustrator files that were designed with point type where it makes more sense to use area type and paragraph formatting, you can cut the point type and paste it back into a type frame.

Updating type

The new additions to the type features in Illustrator CS required recoding the Illustrator type engine. The results of the update create some problems when opening legacy files in Illustrator CS. Any Illustrator document created from version 10 and prior uses a different type engine than Illustrator CS. When you open a legacy file in Illustrator CS, you first see an alert dialog box, as shown in Figure 17-13.

If you click Update, the text is updated to conform to the new type engine. The text is editable, but you may experience shifts in type appearance and position. If you click OK, the text is not updated, and the type appearance and position remain intact. The type is not editable, however. The type blocks appear within rectangular bounding boxes, as shown in Figure 17-14.

Figure 17-13: Opening legacy files in Illustrator CS prompts you to preserve the type appearance in the document or update the text.

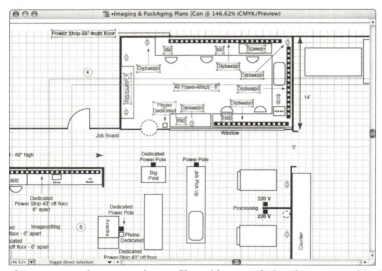

Figure 17-14: If you open legacy files without updating the text, text blocks appear within bounding boxes when the text is selected.

You can elect to update text on a block-by-block basis. If you click OK and don't update the type when opening a legacy file, you can individually update text blocks by clicking with the Type tool on a given body of text or by double-clicking on the type with the Selection tool. Illustrator then prompts you in another alert dialog box, offering you a few choices. In Figure 17-15, you can see the choices appearing for Copy Text Object and Update.

When you select Copy Text Object, a duplicate of the text block is placed behind the converted text. After copying the text, the foreground text is selected when you click with the Type tool. The other option for Updating the text accomplishes the same result as when you first open a legacy document and click Update, as shown in Figure 17-15.

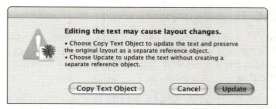

Figure 17-15: Clicking on any legacy text block with the Type tool opens a dialog box where you can decide how the type is updated.

If you want to update multiple items, options are available in a menu command. Choose Type ⇨ Legacy and a submenu offers options for handling legacy text. Note that the menu is grayed out unless you open a legacy file and do not update the text. If you click Update when opening a file, the Legacy submenu options are grayed out as they are when opening files originally authored in Illustrator CS.

In the Legacy submenu, the options include the following:

- **Update All Legacy Text:** If you open a legacy file and choose to not update the text, you can later select this option to update all the text in the file. This gives the same result as if you had opened a legacy file and clicked Update.

- **Update Selected Legacy Text:** You can select individual text blocks to update by using the Selection tool and pressing the Shift key as you continue clicking on additional text blocks. With a group of objects selected, choose this menu item and the selected text is updated.

- **Show/Hide Copies:** When clicking on Copy Text Object, as shown in Figure 17-15, copies of the original text are placed behind the updated text. If you click on Hide Copies, the copied text is hidden. Conversely, when clicking on Show Copies, all hidden text is shown. If you have a converted unedited text block in front of the original text, you won't see the copies hidden or shown. To see the original text, hide the foreground text by selecting it and choose Object ⇨ Hide ⇨ Selection (⌘/Ctrl+3).

- **Delete Copies:** Selecting this menu command deletes all copies.

- **Select Copies:** This menu command selects all copies.

It's best to keep copies of your artwork until your text conversions are made successfully. When updating text, you may encounter problems such as the following:

- **Character position and attribute changes:** Updating text may shift characters and change attributes such as leading, tracking, and kerning.

- **Word shifts:** Words may shift to the next line. The text within a bounding box may scroll past the bottom of the text frame thereby hiding one or more lines of text. Hyphenation may be altered.

- **Word overflows:** In linked text frames, words may overflow to the next thread.

As a matter of practice, you should carefully check the type conversions on legacy files. Before deleting copies, be certain that the text attributes and word flow follow your design intent.

Setting type in Photoshop

Setting type in Photoshop is a task you optimally perform only on small bodies of text and when creating headlines and stylizing type. We say *optimally* because Photoshop is not as well suited for setting type as are Illustrator and InDesign. Therefore, we won't spend much time talking about typesetting in Photoshop.

You create type in Photoshop by clicking on the Type tool in the Toolbox and then clicking the cursor in the document window. A blinking I-beam appears, and you are now ready to type. The default type tool is Horizontal Type. If you click and hold down the mouse button in the Toolbox, you can also choose the Vertical Type tool, the Horizontal Type Mask tool, or the Vertical Type Mask tool. The latter two are used to create type masks that essentially are selections that can be filled, painted, or used to capture underlying pixels.

Type in Photoshop changed from raster-based to vector-based back in version 6. When you set type in Photoshop, it appears on a separate layer and remains fully editable as long as the Photoshop image is not flattened or the layer is not rasterized. If you want to preserve the type on a layer and keep it editable, you need to save the file with layers intact. Saving as a Photoshop PSD or PDF (with layers) preserves the type on the layers and keeps it in vector form.

Tip If you prepare files for PDF viewing, leave the type on a layer and save as Photoshop PDF. When the PDF is opened in Acrobat, all the type is searchable with Acrobat Search.

For typesetting in Photoshop, you have attribute choices you can make in the Options Bar as well as two palettes where character and paragraph options choices are made.

Using the Options Bar

When you click on the Type tool in the Photoshop Toolbox, the Options Bar displays options for setting type. As shown in Figure 17-16, the choices extend from character attributes to paragraph options. The individual settings include the following:

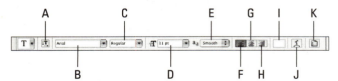

Figure 17-16: The Type tool changes its options to reflect attribute choices for setting type.

- **A Change Text Orientation:** Click the icon to change from horizontal to vertical and vice versa. If a block of text has been created on a layer, you can change type orientation by simply selecting the layer and applying the change.

- **B Font Family:** The pull-down menu lists all fonts available to your system. Photoshop reads installed fonts when you launch the program. Therefore, if you load a new font with a font-management tool, you need to quit Photoshop and relaunch it before the font is recognized in the menu.

C **Font Style:** You have choices for font style from pull-down menu commands. Choose from options such as Regular, Bold, Italic, and Bold Italic when the styles are available for a given font.

D **Font Size:** From the pull-down menu, you have choices for fixed point sizes, or you can enter a value in the field box. Sizes range from 0.01 to 1,296 points. Because the type is vector art, however, you can use the transformation tools to create any type size you want.

For more information on transforming objects, see Chapter 12.

E **Anti-Aliasing Method:** Antialiasing creates an illusion of smoothing objects. When you antialias objects, small partially transparent pixels are added to objects, giving the appearance of smoother edges. Photoshop offers you several choices for anti-aliasing, including the following:

- None: Applies no anti-aliasing.
- Sharp: Adds a slight amount of anti-aliasing, keeping the type sharp in contrast.
- Crisp: Similar to Sharp but adds a little more anti-aliasing, making the appearance slightly less sharp.
- Strong: Creates a slightly bold appearance to the type. If you anti-alias type and it appears to lose the normal type weight, add Strong to thicken the characters.
- Smooth: Adds more anti-aliasing. A good choice for type that may appear with strong jagged edges.

F **Align Left:** Aligns text left.

G **Align Center:** Aligns text centered.

H **Align Right:** Aligns text right.

I **Text Color:** Click on the color swatch and the Photoshop Color Picker opens. You can make choices for the type color from the Color Picker, from the Color and Swatches palettes, or from the Foreground Color tool in the Photoshop Toolbox.

J **Create Warped Text:** Photoshop offers you many options for applying effects to type from the Create Warped Text tool. Select the type you want to use to apply a new style, and the Warp Text dialog box opens as shown in Figure 17-17. When warping text, you can apply changes by either selecting the text with the Type tool or selecting the layer containing the text.

K **Toggle the Character and Paragraph Palettes:** This toggles the Character and Paragraph palettes open and closed.

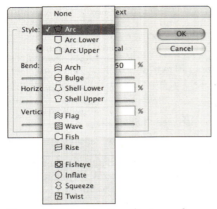

Figure 17-17: Selecting the type of warp effect you want

Using the Character palette

Some character attributes are the same in the Character palette as you find in the Options Bar. Choices for font family, font style, and anti-aliasing methods are duplicated in the Character palette. The palette also contains other options. When you open it, you'll notice the palette appears similar to the Character palette found in Illustrator. To open the palette, choose Window ➪ Character or click on the Toggle the Character and Paragraph Palettes icon in the Options Bar. The palette shown in Figure 17-18 opens.

Figure 17-18: The Photoshop Character palette

As you can see, the options are almost identical to those found in Illustrator. Notice that the horizontal and vertical scaling is flopped in the Photoshop Character palette, but the six attribute choices below the pull-down menus for font and style are identical to Illustrator.

Photoshop does offer additional choices that appear at the bottom of the palette. From the row of icons, reading left to right, you have the following choices:

✦ **Faux Bold:** Enables you to bold a font that does not have a bold equivalent with the chosen typeface

✦ **Faux Italic:** Enables you to italicize a font that does not have an italic equivalent

✦ **All Caps**

- **Small Caps**
- **Superscript**
- **Subscript**
- **Underline**
- **Strikethrough**

From the lower-left pull-down menu, you can choose from installed languages. The pull-down menu in the lower right is where anti-aliasing choices are made.

Using the Paragraph palette

When creating type in Photoshop, you press the Num Pad Enter key to complete the typesetting and signal Photoshop that you've ended your type edits. If you press the Return/Enter key, Photoshop adds a carriage return to the body of type. The ability to add carriage returns means Photoshop supports paragraph type. The attributes you can assign to paragraphs are, in part, located in the Options Bar, where you can choose from three justification methods. The remaining choices are located in the Paragraph palette. When the Character palette is open, click on the Paragraph tab to open the palette shown in Figure 17-19.

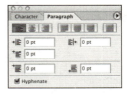

Figure 17-19: The Paragraph palette offers options for paragraph formatting.

As you can see in Figure 17-19, the Paragraph palette options in Photoshop are identical to those in Illustrator. As is the case with changing character attributes, you can select the text with the Type tool or simply click on the layer in the Layers palette. Changes you make in the Paragraph palette are applied to the text regardless of which selection you make.

Setting type in InDesign

In many design workflows, you're likely to be handed copy that has been composed in a word processing program. If you work with copywriters or obtain copy from clients, the files are usually Microsoft Word documents. And unless the author used style sheets you can import, you'll need to reformat the text in InDesign.

Cross-Reference

For more information on importing Microsoft Word documents, see Chapter 20.

For some creative professionals, using word-processing programs may not be as appealing as setting type in InDesign. Certainly, for single-page ads and smaller pieces, you may use InDesign for both creating copy and performing the layout tasks. Fortunately, InDesign does have some impressive tools if you decide to use the program for creating copy.

Using the Story Editor

InDesign's Story Editor is like having your own word processor built into the program. In order to use the Story Editor, you need to have a text frame created on a document page. If no text frame exists, the Story Editor is not accessible.

To open the Story Editor, select a text frame or several text frames and then choose Edit ⇨ Edit in Story Editor (⌘/Ctrl+Y). If you select noncontiguous text frames, each body of text opens in separate Story Editor windows as shown in Figure 17-20.

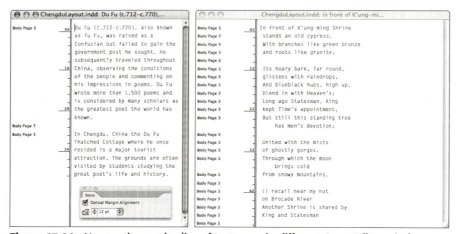

Figure 17-20: Noncontiguous bodies of text open in different Story Editor windows.

The Story Editor opens and appears in front of the document window. The Story Editor is dynamic in many ways. As you type in the Story Editor, the text is updated on the document page within the selected text frame. As its own document window, the Story Editor does not prevent you from using other tools and menus in InDesign that are needed for setting type. Palettes used for styles and text formatting are accessible to you while working in the Story Editor. In Figure 17-20, the Story Editor is open where text is added in the editor and displayed on the document page. The Paragraph Styles palette is used to select styles and apply them in the Story Editor.

New Feature

In Figure 17-20 notice the appearance of the vertical ruler. InDesign CS2 offers you a vertical depth ruler to measure the depth of text. Another feature new in InDesign CS2 is support for viewing overset text with markers. When you set type and your type frame is not large enough to display the type, the text is overset and hidden from view. You need to open the text frame to reveal the hidden text. In the Story Editor, the hidden text is marked with an Overset, as you see in Figure 17-21.

While working in the Story Editor, you can make choices from the Type menu and palettes where type attributes are selected, or you can make similar choices from a context menu. To open a context menu in the Story Editor, press the Control key and click (Mac) or right-click (Windows) and the context menu shown in Figure 17-22 opens.

When you want to return to the InDesign document window, click the close box in the Story Editor window, or select Edit in Layout from the context menu (or choose Edit ⇨ Edit in Layout).

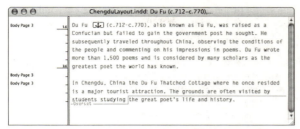

Figure 17-21: Overset text is marked with a line. The text falling below the line is hidden from view when you return to the Layout mode.

Figure 17-22: Context menus offer choices similar to the menu commands and palette options.

Using the Character palette

The Character palette in InDesign offers the same options as Illustrator, with the exception of the Skew option in place of the Rotate option. Below the Horizontal Scale setting, you see the Skew option (shown as a slanted *T*) as shown in Figure 17-23.

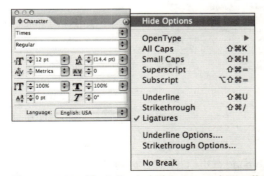

Figure 17-23: The InDesign Character palette offers almost identical options to those in the Illustrator Character palette.

From the palette menu, you can see some other options choices available only in InDesign. The underline and strikethrough options are listed in the palette, but each contains a companion Options menu where you can change attributes for underlines and strikethroughs, such as line weight, spacing, color, gaps, and so on. Select Underline Options and the dialog box opens as shown in Figure 17-24. The items in the dialog box should be self-explanatory. If you aren't certain what results are applied using a given setting, select the Preview option, and the changes you make to text are dynamically applied to the selected characters.

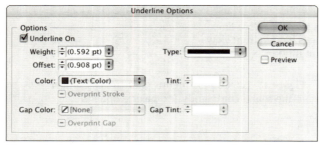

Figure 17-24: InDesign offers many options for setting underline attributes.

The options for strikethrough are similar to the options for underlining. Click on the Strikethrough Options menu command and a similar dialog box opens. Again, the options should be self-explanatory.

Another distinction you'll find between the Character palettes in Illustrator and InDesign are the options selections for OpenType fonts. In Illustrator, buttons appear in the bottom of the OpenType palette, and in InDesign you can see the submenu items in Figure 17-25 offering the same options.

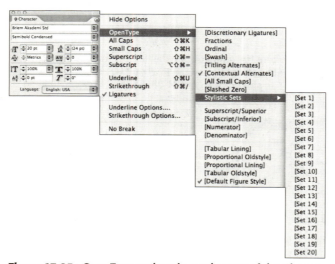

Figure 17-25: OpenType options in a submenu of the Character palette

New Feature A new feature added to InDesign CS2 is an option for selecting Stylistic Sets, as you see in Figure 17-25. OpenType fonts contain many alternate characters such as ligatures, fractions, swashes, ornaments, ordinals, titling, stylistic alternates, and so on. The OpenType palette lets you set up rules for using glyphs such as using ligatures, titling characters, and fractions for a given body of text. By using Stylistic Sets, you can apply alternates to a selected block of text without having to change each character individually.

Using the Control palette

Setting type in InDesign does not require you to access Character and Paragraph palettes to change attributes. The Control palette that appears by default at the top of the screen when you launch InDesign is one of the most frequently used tools favored by design professionals. Depending on the tool you select in the InDesign Toolbox, the palette changes to reflect options choices for the selected tool. In Figure 17-26, formatting options are shown for characters (top), paragraphs (middle), and objects (bottom).

Figure 17-26: When the Type tool is selected, you can toggle between formatting options for characters (top) and paragraphs (middle). When other tools are selected, options for transforming objects are displayed (bottom).

With the Type tool selected, you can toggle between character and paragraph options in the Control palette. Simply click on either the letter *A* or the paragraph symbol on the far left side of the palette. From there, you can make attribute choices by changing field box values and using pull-down menus. When using tools other than the Type tool, the palette displays options for applying attributes to objects, as shown in the last palette in Figure 17-26.

The Control palette is a handy place to select styles either for character or paragraph styles. From the pull-down menus, all the style sheets contained in your document are listed. When you add a new style, it's added to the appropriate pull-down menu.

Cross-Reference For information on creating style sheets, see the sections "Creating Character Styles" and "Creating Paragraph Styles."

Another menu is found when you click the right-pointing arrow. Depending on the palette shown, you'll see different menu items with additional choices for setting type or for working with objects. Many of the options choices you see in pull-down menus are the same options found in the palettes. You can choose among top-level menus, palettes, or the Control palette to apply the same edits. InDesign offers you this flexibility so you can make choices quickly and easily.

Using placeholder text

One nice distinction between InDesign and the other CS applications (except GoLive) is the ability to use dummy copy when preparing templates, creating styles, or creating comps for a new design project. Rather than search your hard drive for the *Lorem Ipsum* Greek text file you've probably used since the early days of PageMaker, you can now use InDesign's built-in support for filling text frames with placeholder text.

To use placeholder text, click in any text frame or any object where you want to convert the object to a text frame. When you see the I-beam cursor blink, choose Type ⇨ Fill with Placeholder Text. Greek text is added from the point of the blinking cursor to the end of the text thread, as shown in Figure 17-27.

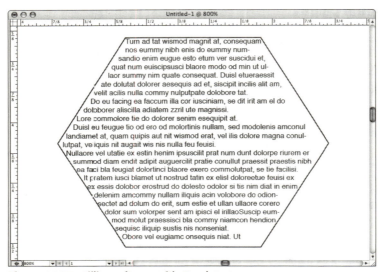

Figure 17-27: Filling a frame with Greek text

If you create comps and layouts where Greek type is used frequently, you may want to create a keyboard shortcut to access the menu command. Look over the steps that follow to see how you can assign a keyboard shortcut to access the Fill with Placeholder Text menu command.

STEPS: Using Placeholder Text

1. **Assign a keyboard shortcut to the Fill with Placeholder Text menu command.**
   Choose Edit ⇨ Keyboard Shortcuts. The Keyboard Shortcuts dialog box opens. Select Type Menu from the Product Area pull-down menu and click on Fill with Placeholder Text, as shown in Figure 17-28. With the menu command selected, press the shortcut keys you want to use to assign to the menu command. A good choice is to use Shift+F12. This keyboard shortcut is easily accessible and doesn't conflict with any existing InDesign keyboard shortcuts.

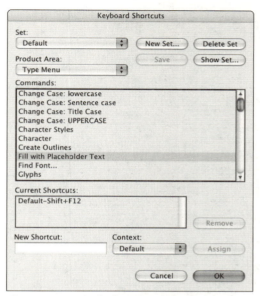

Figure 17-28: Assigning menu commands

2. **Create an object.** From the InDesign Toolbox, click on the Rectangle tool, the Ellipse tool, or the Polygon tool, and draw an object on the document page. For this example, we created an ellipse using the Ellipse tool.

3. **Convert the object to a text frame.** When you draw an object in InDesign, the object appears as an Unassigned object. You can convert the object to a text object or a graphic object via a menu command. For a quick and easy method, select the Type tool and position the cursor within the object. When the cursor shape changes to the Type tool, displayed with a marquee oval around the *T* character, click the mouse button. The I-beam cursor starts to blink, signifying the object is ready to accept type.

4. **Set the font attributes.** From the Control palette, select a font, point size, and other attributes you want displayed on the type. The type attributes you assign before filling the object with text are used when filling with placeholder text.

5. **Use your keyboard shortcut to fill with placeholder text.** Press the keyboard shortcut you assigned to the Fill with Placeholder Text command. The object is filled with text using the font attributes you selected in the Control palette. Figure 17-29 shows the results of filling an object with placeholder text.

Figure 17-29: Use your new keyboard shortcut to fill the object with text.

Using the Paragraph palette

The paragraph styles palette in InDesign offers many of the same options as found in Illustrator, with the exception of two icons used for defining drop caps in paragraphs. The last two icons, shown in Figure 17-30 as A and B at the bottom of the palette, contain an option for defining the height of a drop cap (A). Setting the value to 4, for example, creates a drop cap whose height is equivalent to the first four lines of the paragraph. On the lower-right side of the palette, you can specify the number of sequential characters you want to appear as drop caps (B).

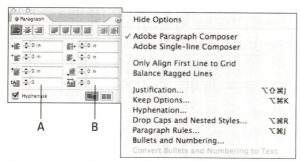

Figure 17-30: The last two field boxes offer options for choosing the number of lines a drop cap is applied to (A) and the number of characters to be used as drop caps (B).

You find more distinction between the Illustrator Paragraph palette and the InDesign Paragraph palette when opening the palette menus. InDesign offers some advanced formatting features not found in the other CS programs and some that are not found in any other layout and design program. When you open the palette menu, the options shown in Figure 17-30 appear. The menu commands include the following:

- **Adobe Paragraph Composer:** Break points are created to help prevent unattractive line breaks in paragraphs. Traditional methods for creating break points handled only one line at a time. The Adobe Paragraph Composer composes the breaks by taking into consideration the lines preceding and following the current line of text. This results in a more attractive paragraph (available in InDesign, Illustrator, and Photoshop).

- **Adobe Single-Line Composer:** This option uses the more traditional method of creating break points, taking into consideration only single lines of text (available in InDesign, Illustrator, and Photoshop).

- **Only Align First Line to Grid:** When aligning text to a grid, only the first line of text is aligned to the grid.

- **Balance Ragged Lines:** This option is helpful for headlines and pull quotes and when centering paragraphs. Multiple lines of type appear more balanced, as widow-type oversets at the end of the text block are eliminated. You must use Adobe Paragraph Composer to see any results with this menu command.

- **Keep Options:** Opens a dialog box where you can assign attributes to lines in paragraphs that you want to stay together when the paragraph flows to other frames and pages.

- **Hyphenation:** Offers similar options for controlling hyphenation as you find in Illustrator.

- **Drop Caps and Nested Styles:** One of the truly amazing features available for typesetting is the ability to create nested styles. When you are selecting the command, the Drop Caps and Nested Styles dialog box opens.

> **Cross-Reference:** For more information on nested styles, see the section "Creating Nested Styles."

- **Paragraph Rules:** The attributes for rules assigned to paragraphs are handled in the Paragraph Rules dialog box. Select this menu command to open the dialog box.

> **New Feature:** The Bullets and Numbering and the Convert Bullets and Numbering to Text menu commands are new to the Paragraph palette. Bullets and Numbering opens the Bullets and Numbering dialog box shown in Figure 17-31. You have choices for selecting from preset characters to use as bullet markers (or number styles), or click Add to display any character set loaded in your active system fonts. Attribute choices enable you to choose font, point size, style, color, indentation, and tab positions. To Convert Bullets and Numbering to Text, select a block of bulleted or numbered text and select this menu command. The bullets/numbers are cleared of formatting and the text returns to the current active style.

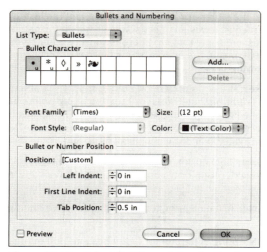

Figure 17-31: Select Bullets and Numbering from the Paragraph palette fly-out menu and the Bullets and Numbering palette opens.

Paragraph formatting can also be applied in the Control palette and via menu commands. One particular option not found in either the Control or Paragraph palettes is setting paragraphs for Optical Margin Alignment. When you choose Window ⇨ Type & Tables ⇨ Story, the Story palette opens, as shown in Figure 17-32. The palette contains only a single option.

Figure 17-32: The Story palette contains an option for selecting Optical Margin Alignment.

When you select the Optical Margin Alignment check box, paragraph alignment displays a different appearance. With traditional computer typesetting methods, paragraphs can appear misaligned, especially when punctuation marks and/or wide characters are used. In Figure 17-33, you can see where Optical Margin Alignment was applied to the bottom text block compared to the default margin alignment on the first text block. Because the punctuation hangs outside the text frame on the second block of text, the characters appear more aligned.

InDesign has so many different options for setting character and paragraph attributes that a complete coverage would take the space occupied by all the chapters in this book. We've highlighted some of the main features here and discussed the options found in the menus and palettes. For a comprehensive view of setting type in InDesign, see the *Adobe InDesign CS2 Bible* by Galen Gruman (Wiley, 2005).

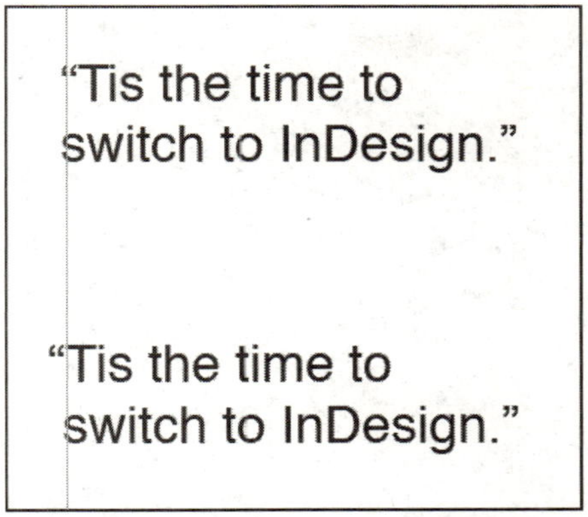

"Tis the time to
switch to InDesign."

"Tis the time to
switch to InDesign."

Figure 17-33: Optical Margin Alignment corrects misaligned characters.

Creating type on paths

Once the job of Illustrator, applying type to paths is now available in Photoshop and InDesign. Applying type to paths opens up worlds of possibilities for each application. With the capability for adding type to paths in Photoshop, you can use familiar methods for stylizing type with shadows, embossing, filter effects, and so on, and you don't need to rely on rasterizing type in Photoshop that was originally created in Illustrator.

Adding type to paths is a simple process in any of the CS programs where this feature is available. Basically, you create a path either with the Pen tool or use segments from paths created with other tools used for drawing objects. In Photoshop, select the Type tool, click on a path and begin typing. In Illustrator and InDesign, use the Type on a Path tool. Access the Type on a Path tool by pressing the mouse button down on the Type tool and selecting it from the pop-up menu.

To add type to freeform paths, click the mouse button on the path and begin typing. For closed paths in either Illustrator or InDesign, the type is added to the outside edge of the path by default. The respective program knows the distinction between adding type to a path and creating type inside a closed path. This is determined with the proper selection of the Type tool. When the Type on a Path tool is selected, the type conforms only to the path and not to the inside of a closed path.

In Photoshop, the task is a little different. When you have a closed path, placing the cursor on the path and clicking the mouse button enables you to type on the path. If you move the cursor inside the path, the cursor shape changes to the oval marquee around the letter *T*, signifying that type is to be added inside the path. The shape of the cursor informs you where the type will be placed.

In Figure 17-34, you can see type added to a path in Photoshop. When adding type to a path, be certain to check the paragraph attributes for alignment. If your type doesn't show up on the path, you may need to adjust the alignment from center-aligned to left-aligned or reduce the type size. After adding the type, you can change the alignment and other text attributes.

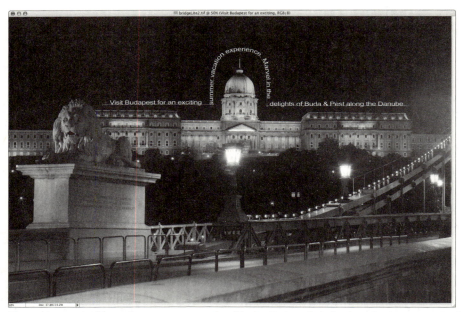

Figure 17-34: In Photoshop, create a path with the Pen tool and select the Type on a Path tool.

Both Illustrator and InDesign permit adjustments to type on paths in the same manner. When you add type to an open path, the type is added in a straightforward fashion. However, if you start with a closed object and then delete one side, type may be added to the shape flopped or upside-down. In each program, you can move type along a path or flop it by moving the centerline appearing within the type. In InDesign, the line is much less visible than in Illustrator, but it does exist. In Figures 17-35 and 17-36, you can see type added to a semicircle that began as an elliptical shape. The type is flopped. To move the type up where the type reads from left to right, drag the line at the center point upward.

Drag this line up/down or left/right to reposition type

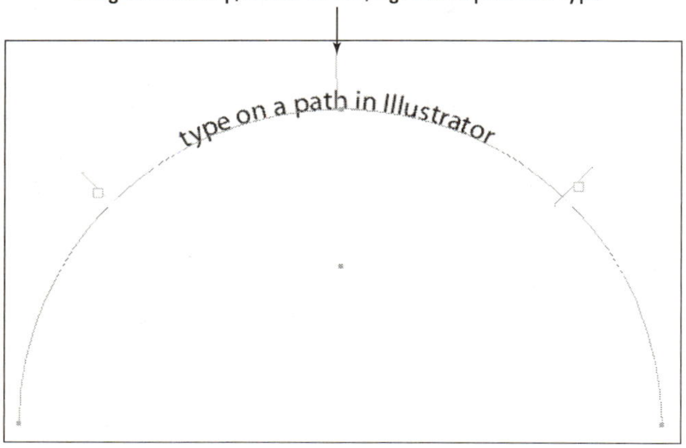

Figure 17-35: To align type on a path in Illustrator, drag the centerline left/right or upward.

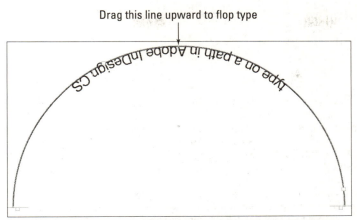

Figure 17-36: The same centerline appears in InDesign, but the line is less visible.

Creating Character Styles

In both InDesign and Illustrator, you have the ability to create style sheets at the character level. Using character styles allows you to specify formatting attributes for a selected range of text within your documents. For instance, you may want to use different character formatting for Web-site URLs and e-mail addresses that appear in your copy. Instead of changing type specs in the Character palette, or using tedious find-and-replace commands to alter attributes of single characters or a string of words within a document, you can apply global changes to characters quickly and easily by changing formatting options in the Character Styles palette. All text to which you've applied the specific style is changed automatically. Using both character and paragraph styles saves time and ensures that your documents have a consistent look.

Using character styles in Illustrator

In Illustrator, you can set up character styles from scratch or by designating preformatted text as the basis of the new style. You can also copy an existing style and make formatting variations in order to create a new style.

Creating new character styles

To create a new character style, open the Character Styles palette by choosing Window ⇨ Type ⇨ Character Styles. The palette lists all the styles that have been created for the document. If no custom styles have been created, the only style that appears is the default, Normal Character Style, as shown in Figure 17-37.

Figure 17-37: The Character Styles palette

To create a new style from scratch, click the Create New Style button in the lower-right portion of the palette. A new style with a default name automatically appears in the palette. An alternative way to create a new style is to select New Character Style from the palette menu. At this point, you're prompted to give the style a custom name. Either way, when the new style name appears in the list, double-click on it to edit its attributes with the Character Style Options box, shown in Figure 17-38.

Caution Double-clicking on a style in the Character Styles palette applies the style to any text you currently have selected in your document. If no text is selected, the style is applied to any new text you type. To keep either of these events from happening, press Shift+Ctrl (Shift+⌘ on the Mac) when you double-click the style name.

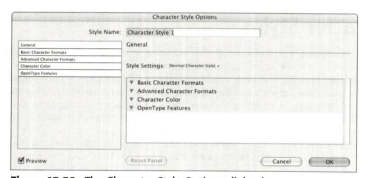

Figure 17-38: The Character Style Options dialog box

When the Character Style Options box opens, you see the name of the selected style at the top and five options to the left. The options include the following:

- **General:** This is the pane displayed when you first open the Character Style Options box. It's a summary of the remaining four settings, the style settings. You can view attributes of the separate style settings by toggling the gray arrows in the right side of the pane.

- **Basic Character Formats:** In this menu, you can specify font family, font style, size, leading, kerning, tracking, case, position (superscript or subscript), and whether or not you want Standard Vertical Roman Alignment.

- **Advanced Character Formats:** Here you can specify horizontal and vertical scale, baseline shift, character rotation, and desired language.

- **Character Color:** Choose your desired color, stroke, and overprint options here.

- **OpenType Features:** This panel allows you to set OpenType options just like those found in the OpenType palette (see the section "Using OpenType").

After you've set up your attributes the way you want them, simply click OK.

You can easily create copies of existing character styles by either dragging the style onto the Create New Style button, or by choosing Duplicate Character Style from the Character Styles palette menu. To delete styles, simply drag the style name to the trash icon, or select the style and choose Delete Character Style from the palette menu. You can also import styles from other Illustrator documents by using the Load Styles command.

Tip

You can easily create a new style sheet based on the formatting of existing text. This is handy if you're experimenting with different design options because it eliminates the need to manually type all the formatting details in the Character Style Options menus ahead of time. Simply select the text whose attributes you want to use, and click the Create New Style button.

Applying character styles

To apply character styles in Illustrator, first select the characters with the Type tool or a selection tool. If you're typing new characters, place the cursor where you want the style to begin. Then simply click the style name in the Character Styles palette. To designate a style to be used for any new type in the document, be sure to deselect all type objects first; then click the style name.

Using styles in Photoshop

Photoshop doesn't support the use of character or paragraph style palettes. Logically, you wouldn't use Photoshop for setting large bodies of type. However, Photoshop is often used when stylizing type where you may apply various effects and filters. The edits you make to type in Photoshop can be captured as graphic styles. To see how graphic styles and tool presets are used with Photoshop, see the section "Working with Graphic Styles."

Using character styles in InDesign

The process of setting up and using character styles in InDesign is very similar to Illustrator. InDesign does offer a few additional options for refining your typesetting capabilities, however.

Creating new character styles

Open the Character Styles palette by choosing Type ⇨ Character Styles, or Window ⇨ Type & Tables ⇨ Character Styles. As in Illustrator, the palette lists all the styles that have been created for the document. If no custom styles have been created, all you'll see is the default: No Character Style.

Creating a new style is the same procedure as in Illustrator: Click the Create New Style button in the lower-right portion of the palette or click the right arrow and select New Character Style. You can then specify attributes with the Character Style Options or New Character Style box. The options here are pretty much like Illustrator's, with a few minor differences. As shown in Figure 17-39, with InDesign you have the added ability to base styles on existing styles and create shortcuts. There are also advanced options for underlining, strikethroughs, and ligatures, as well as a no-break option and a skew option in place of Illustrator's rotation option.

Duplicating, editing, and deleting Character Styles is the same as in Illustrator. InDesign can import character styles from other InDesign documents using the Load Character Styles command.

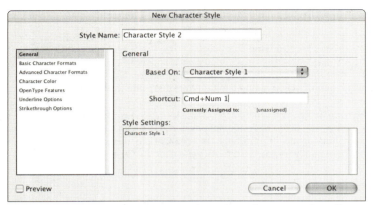

Figure 17-39: InDesign offers more character style options than Illustrator.

Applying character styles

There are four ways to apply a character style to selected text in InDesign. You can click the style name in the Character Styles palette, choose the style name from the pull-down menu in the Control palette, choose Edit ⇨ Quick Apply (Ctrl+Enter, Windows; Ctrl+Return, Mac) or use the keyboard shortcut you've assigned to the style.

Creating Paragraph Styles

Paragraph styles are especially helpful for managing large amounts of text in both InDesign and Illustrator. The one limitation you have with respect to both character and paragraph styles among the CS applications is that styles created in either Illustrator or InDesign cannot be imported across programs. You can import styles from application documents using the same application. For example, you can load character styles in Illustrator from another Illustrator document. However, you cannot load character styles in Illustrator from an InDesign document or vice versa. The same applies to paragraph styles. Furthermore, when you import Illustrator files containing style sheets in InDesign, or copy and paste text between programs, the style-sheet information is lost. In the next upgrade, maybe we'll see more interoperability between Illustrator and InDesign style-sheet usage.

Using paragraph styles in Illustrator

Just like with Character Styles, you can set up paragraph styles from scratch or by designating preformatted text as the basis of the new style. You can also copy an existing style and make formatting variations in order to create a new style.

Creating new paragraph styles

Open the Paragraph Styles palette by choosing Window ⇨ Type ⇨ Paragraph Styles (see Figure 17-40). You can change the display size of the palette items by choosing either Small List View or Large List View in the palette menu.

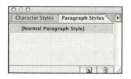

Figure 17-40: The Paragraph Styles palette

By default, every paragraph is assigned the Normal Paragraph Style. To create a new paragraph style, click the Create New Style button in the lower-right portion of the palette. A new style with a default name automatically appears in the palette. Or create a new style by selecting New Paragraph Style from the palette menu. At this point, you'll be prompted to give the style a custom name. Either way, when the new style name appears in the list, double-click on it to edit its attributes with the Paragraph Style Options box, shown in Figure 17-41.

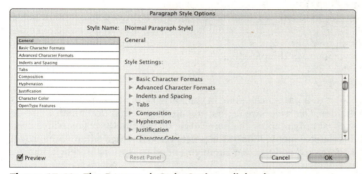

Figure 17-41: The Paragraph Style Options dialog box

When the Paragraph Style Options dialog box opens, you see the name of the selected style at the top and ten options to the left. These include the following:

✦ **General:** This pane is displayed when you first open the Paragraph Style Options box. It's a summary of the remaining nine settings, the style settings. You can view attributes of the separate style settings by toggling the gray arrows in the right side of the pane.

✦ **Basic Character Formats:** In this menu, you can specify font family, font style, size, leading, kerning, tracking, case, position (superscript or subscript), and whether or not you want Standard Vertical Roman Alignment.

✦ **Advanced Character Formats:** Here you can specify horizontal and vertical scale, baseline shift, character rotation, and desired language.

✦ **Indents and Spacing:** Specify alignment, left indent, first-line indent, right indent, space before, and space after.

✦ **Tabs:** Specify tab settings.

✦ **Composer:** Choose a composition method here.

✦ **Hyphenation:** Specify hyphenation preferences.

- **Justification:** Specify justification preferences.
- **Character Color:** Choose desired color, stroke, and overprint options.
- **OpenType Features:** This panel allows you to set OpenType options just like those found in the OpenType palette (see the "Using OpenType" section earlier in this chapter).

After you've set up your paragraph attributes the way you want them, click OK.

You can easily create copies of existing paragraph styles by either dragging the style onto the Create New Style button, or by choosing Duplicate Paragraph Style from the Paragraph Styles palette menu. To delete styles, simply drag the style name to the trash icon, or select Delete Paragraph Style from the palette menu. You can also import styles from other Illustrator documents by using the Load Paragraph Styles command in the palette menu.

Applying paragraph styles

To apply paragraph styles in Illustrator, insert the cursor in a single paragraph or select a range of paragraphs. Simply click the style name in the Paragraph Styles palette. To designate a style to be used for all new paragraphs in the document, be sure to deselect all type objects first; then click the style name in the palette.

About overrides

If you see a plus sign next to a paragraph style in the Paragraph Styles palette, it means the selected text has overrides. *Overrides* are formatting attributes that don't match the defined style. To clear overrides, simply reapply the same style or use the Clear Overrides command in the Paragraph Styles palette menu. Illustrator preserves overrides when you apply a different style to text with overrides, and to clear them you need to Option/Alt+click on the style name when you apply the style.

Using paragraph styles in InDesign

Just like with character styles, the process for setting up and using paragraph styles in InDesign is very similar to Illustrator. InDesign offers additional options here as well.

Creating new paragraph styles

Open the Character Styles palette by choosing Type ⇨ Paragraph Styles, or Window ⇨ Type & Tables ⇨ Paragraph Styles. As in Illustrator, the palette lists all the styles that have been created for the document. If no custom styles have been created, all you see is the default — No Paragraph Style.

Creating a new style is the same procedure as in Illustrator: click the Create New Style button in the lower-right corner of the palette or select New Paragraph Style from the palette menu. You can then specify attributes with the Paragraph Style Options or New Paragraph Style box. The options here are similar to Illustrator, with the addition of keyboard shortcuts, basing styles on other styles, paragraph rules, keeping lines together, drop caps, nested styles, and underline and strikethrough options. As shown in Figure 17-42, the many options for paragraph-style formatting are selected in the left pane where individual options appear on the right side of the dialog box.

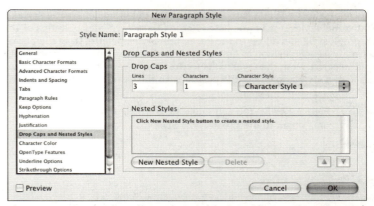

Figure 17-42: InDesign offers advanced features for creating paragraph styles.

Duplicating, editing, and deleting Paragraph Styles in InDesign is the same as in Illustrator. You can import Paragraph Styles from other InDesign documents using the Load Paragraph Styles command. This feature is particularly helpful in workflow environments where you can create layout templates with paragraph and character styles. All members of your workgroup can load styles from a master template and set type according to the styles defined for a particular project.

Applying paragraph styles

There are four ways to apply a paragraph style to selected text in InDesign. You can select the text and click the style name in the Paragraph Styles palette, choose the style name from the pull-down menu in the Control palette, use the Quick Apply method be selecting Edit ⇨ Quick Apply, or use the keyboard shortcut you've assigned to the style.

When you apply a paragraph style to text, it doesn't automatically remove any existing character formatting in the paragraph. A plus sign (+) appears next to the paragraph style in the Paragraph Styles palette if there is any formatting applied that doesn't match the current style. Even if you click No Paragraph Style, the formatting remains intact. If you want to remove all formatting, including the existing character styles, you must press Alt or Option and then click No Paragraph Style in the palette.

Creating Nested Styles

Nested styles enable you to apply complex formatting to text using one or more character styles. You may decide, for example, that multiple paragraphs in your layout need to include a custom drop cap, a special style treatment for the first sentence, and a third style for the remainder of the body copy. In this instance, you would create three separate character styles, capture all three as a nested style, and apply the nested style to other paragraphs in your composition. Each time the nested style is applied to a new paragraph, the drop cap, first sentence characters, and remaining body copy styles are applied automatically.

The easiest way to create a nested style is to first create the individual character styles required. These individual styles need to be listed in the Character Styles palette. For the body copy, create a paragraph style and add it to the Paragraph Styles palette. Drag the paragraph style name to the Create New Style icon to create a duplicate style. Notice in Figure 17-43 the style named *Body* is selected. Drag the style name to the Create New Style icon, as shown in the figure. The duplicated style appears in the palette with the word *copy* after the style name.

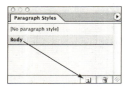

Figure 17-43: You can duplicate the style by dragging it to the Create New Style icon.

Double-click on the paragraph style copy to open the Paragraph Styles palette. In the Paragraph Style Options dialog box, scroll down the list and select Drop Caps and Nested Styles in the left pane, as shown in Figure 17-44. The options change to settings used for creating nested styles. To make this process a little more comprehensible, work through the following steps to see how a nested style is created and then applied to a body of text.

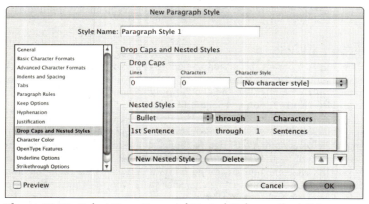

Figure 17-44: Select Drop Caps and Nested Styles on the left to access the attribute choices for creating nested styles.

STEPS: Creating and Applying Nested Styles

1. **Create a text passage in InDesign.** Import text from a text file or use placeholder text containing several paragraphs.

2. **Set type attributes for the body copy.** Select all the placed text and choose a font style and point size that represents the main body copy you intend to use.

3. **Define a new paragraph style.** Click the cursor anywhere in the placed text after setting the font attributes, and select New Paragraph Style from the Paragraph Styles palette menu. Provide a name for the style. In our example, we use *Body* for the style

name. After creating the style, select all the text by placing the cursor anywhere in the text body and press ⌘/Control+A to select all. Click on the Body style name in the Paragraph Styles palette to apply the style to the selected text.

4. **Select the first two words in the first paragraph and change the font attributes.** Change the selected text point size to a larger point size than the body copy. Add points to the type in the Control palette and change the font. Open the Color palette and assign a new color to the character.

5. **Create a character style for the first two words.** Select the first two words you changed in step 4 and select New Character Style from the Character Styles palette menu, shown in Figure 17-45. Name the style *1st two Words*.

6. **Create another style for the first sentence.** Select the first character in the third word through the last character in the first sentence. Change type attributes to a different font style as the style used for the body copy. Open the Character Styles palette menu and select New Character Style. Be certain the cursor appears within the sentence where you just changed the font attributes before opening the New Character Style dialog box. Provide a name for the style, such as *1st Sentence*, and click OK.

7. **Duplicate the Body text paragraph style.** Select Body in the Paragraph Styles palette and drag it to the Create New Paragraph Style icon. InDesign automatically names the new style *Body copy*.

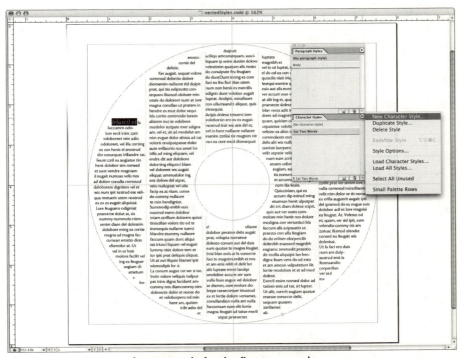

Figure 17-45: Create a character style for the first two words.

8. **Create a nested style.** Double-click on the Body copy style you created in the Paragraph Styles palette to open the Paragraph Style Options dialog box. Click Drop Caps and Nested Styles in the left pane. Click New Nested Style. In the Nested Styles window, the highlighted item appears as No Character Style. When you click the item, a pull-down menu shows all the character styles you created in the Character Styles palette. Select *1st Two Words* from the menu items. Select Words on the right side of the new nested style entry in the Nested Styles window, as shown in Figure 17-46. Select the default number 1 and type 2 in the field box.

9. **Add a second character style to the nested style.** Click New Nested Style. From the Character Style pull-down menu on the left, select *1st Sentence* (the second character style you created) as shown in Figure 17-47. Select Sentence in the last pull-down menu. Click OK when you're finished defining the style. Be certain to leave the value in the field box at the default 1 for one sentence.

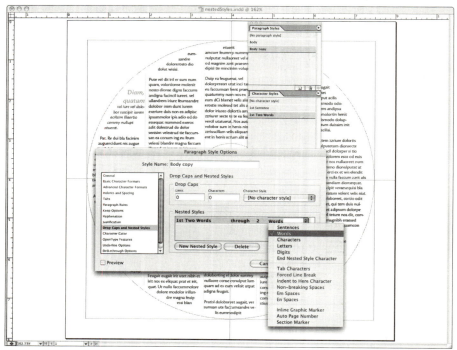

Figure 17-46: Create a new nested style and choose the style from the first pull-down menu. In the new entry added to the Nested Styles list, select Words from the last pull-down menu and change 1 to 2 for assigning the style to two words.

Chapter 17 ✦ Working with Styles   675

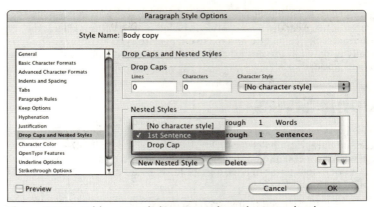

Figure 17-47: Add a second character style to the nested style.

10. **Apply the nested style to the copy.** Click the cursor in the text passage and press ⌘/Ctrl+A to select all the text. Click on the new nested style in the Paragraph Styles palette to apply it to all the selected paragraphs.

11. **Deselect the text.** Click the cursor anywhere on the page, and the text is deselected. The final styling appears as shown in Figure 17-48.

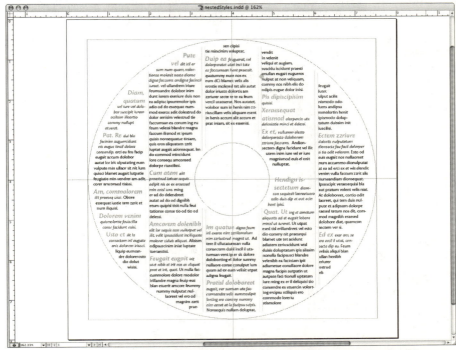

Figure 17-48: Deselect the text and examine the copy. All the paragraphs should appear with the assigned character styles.

Making changes to type attributes where nested styles have been assigned is easy. As is the case with paragraph styles, the nested style is based on the various character styles. You can revisit the Character Styles palette and make changes to type attributes. The type changes are dynamically updated in the nested style, which directly changes the type where the nested style was applied.

Using Graphic Styles

Graphic styles are used when you want to apply effects to type and objects. Instead of using the character and paragraph palettes, Illustrator, Photoshop, and InDesign offer you a graphic styles palette where effects applied to type can be captured as a style. When you add additional type to a document you can click a graphic style and all the effects associated with that style are applied to the selected type.

Graphic styles are not restricted to text. You can use graphic styles with objects as well as type. Just to stay consistent with the content in this chapter, we'll confine the discussion on graphic styles to applying them to type.

Using graphic styles in Illustrator

Illustrator provides you with a number of different graphic styles libraries you can load in the Graphic Styles palette. Choose Window ⇨ Graphic Styles or press Shift+F5 to open the palette. From the palette menu you have several menu commands used when creating and working with graphic styles. Select Open Graphic Style Library, and a submenu displays preset styles you can load in the palette as shown in Figure 17-49.

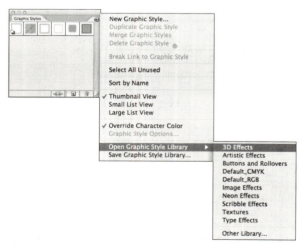

Figure 17-49: Choose Window ⇨ Graphic Styles to open the Graphic Styles palette, or press Shift+F5. Open the palette menu and select Open Graphic Style library to view the preset styles available to you in Illustrator.

In addition to applying preset styles, you can create custom styles and add them to your Graphic Styles palette. Graphic Styles are created much like character and paragraph styles. You first edit text or an object and then capture the edits as a new graphic style. To see how easy you can create graphic styles, follow the steps below:

STEPS: Creating Graphic Styles in Illustrator

1. **Create text.** Type a single character on a page. Use 72 points or more for the point size. You can create more than one text character; but if you decide to apply effects that take some time to render, everything will move faster when using a single character.

2. **Fill and stroke the character.** Use the Swatches or Color palette and the Stroke palette and select colors to add for the fill and stroke. Set the stroke value between 3 to 5 points.

3. **Apply a second stroke.** Open the Appearance palette and from the palette menu select Add New Stroke, as shown in Figure 17-50. While the new stroke is selected in the Appearance palette, change the stroke value to about one-half the size of the first stroke. In our example, we use a 4-point stroke for the first stroke and 1.5 for the second stroke. Click a contrasting color in the Swatches color palette to change the color of the stroke.

Figure 17-50: Open the Appearance palette and select Add New Stroke from the palette menu.

Tip

When you want to add multiple strokes to a path, always use the Appearance palette. You might want to illustrate a map with road paths where a white path appears above a larger black path to give the appearance of parallel lines. Rather than creating two strokes where the narrower white stroke appears above a larger black stoke, just use the appearance palette to add a second stroke. Your illustration will have fewer objects and it is much easier to edit the stroke sizes and colors using the Appearance palette.

4. **Apply an effect.** Select Type or Character in the Appearance palette and open the 3D Extrude & Bevel Options dialog box by choosing Effect ⇨ 3D ⇨ Extrude and Bevel. Edit the Extrude Depth to a lower value than the default 50 points. Select the Preview check box and you can see your results in the document window as you make changes to the extrude and bevel attributes (see Figure 17-51). Click OK when the extrusion appears as you like.

Caution Be certain you select the top-level name (default is Type) or Character in the Appearance palette before applying other effects. If you select one of the strokes or a fill in the palette, a new effect is applied only to the item selected.

5. **Apply a drop shadow.** Be certain the text character is selected and choose Effect ⇨ Stylize ⇨ Drop Shadow. Select Preview in the Drop Shadow dialog box so you can see the effect as you make settings adjustments in the dialog box. Move the sliders to create the effect you want and click OK. The Appearance palette should now look something like Figure 17-52.

Tip When you want to make changes to effects such as Extrude and Bevel, open the Appearance palette and double-click on 3D Extrude & Bevel. The 3D Extrude and Bevel Options dialog box opens where you can change the settings. If you attempt to use the 3D Extrude & Bevel menu command to edit a previous 3-D effect, you'll be applying another extrusion to an object that already has one 3-D effect applied to it.

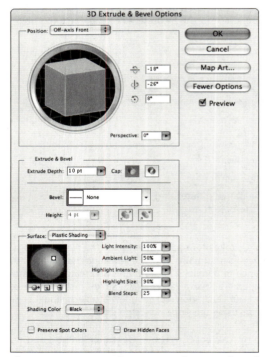

Figure 17-51: Open the 3D Extrude & Bevel Options dialog box and select the Preview check box to preview the changes in the document window.

Figure 17-52: The Appearance palette lists all the effects applied to an object.

6. **Create a new Graphic Style.** Place the Appearance palette adjacent to the Graphic Styles palette. Drag the item listed as *Type: Graphic Style 1* in the Appearance palette to the Graphic Styles palette as shown in Figure 17-53. The effects applied to the type are added as a new Graphic Style.

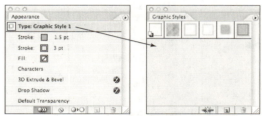

Figure 17-53: Drag the *Type: Graphic Style 1* item in the Appearance palette to the Graphic Styles palette to create a new Graphic Style.

7. **Name the style.** Double-click the new style in the Graphic Styles palette. The Graphic Styles Options dialog box appears. Type a name for the style and click OK.

8. **Apply the style to new type.** Type a word in the document window and click on the new style you added to the Graphic Styles palette. All the attributes assigned to the style are applied to your new type as shown in Figure 17-54.

Figure 17-54: The style is applied to new type.

Using graphic styles in Photoshop

Photoshop doesn't support character and paragraph styles, but you do have many options for creating and applying graphic styles to vector objects in Photoshop.

To open the Styles palette, choose Window ➪ Styles. From the palette menu shown in Figure 17-55 you can see a selection of preset styles available for loading. The items denoted as Abstract Styles through Web Styles offer you style libraries that can be loaded in the palette. When you select a style library, a dialog box appears offering choices for appending the selected library to the current library or replacing the open library with the selected library.

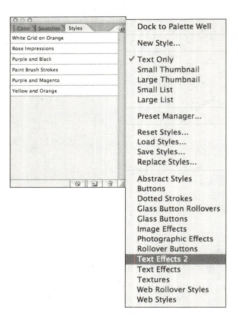

Figure 17-55: The Styles palette offers options for selecting style libraries you can load in the Styles palette.

In addition to the preset library styles, Photoshop offers you an option for creating your own custom style by selecting the New Style menu command. You can define style attributes for vector and raster artwork.

You apply styles from the library style options to selected layers or objects in Photoshop. Create any type characters in Photoshop and click a style in the Styles palette. In addition, you can create type and vector objects in Illustrator, copy the artwork and paste the artwork as a Smart Object in Photoshop.

When you choose Edit ➪ Paste in Photoshop, a dialog box appears offering you an option to paste the object as a Smart Object. This means you can apply all the type and object effects available in Illustrator such as using Live Trace, 3D Effects, and all other effects you can apply to vector objects. Copy the object, then paste in Photoshop and apply a style. In Figure 17-56, type was created in Illustrator. The Roughen effect was applied by choosing Effect ➪ Distort & Transform ➪ Roughen. The type was copied to the clipboard and pasted as a Smart Object in Photoshop. In Photoshop the Type Effects library was loaded in the Styles palette. With the new type layer selected, Brushed Metal was selected in the Style palette.

Figure 17-56: The Styles palette offers options for selecting style libraries you can load in the Styles palette.

Objects created as 3-D renditions in Illustrator lose the 3-D views when applying styles in Photoshop. When a 3-D object is pasted in Photoshop and you apply a style, the object appears as a 2-D object. In Figure 17-57, a simple object was drawn in Illustrator and the object was revolved in the 3D Revolve Options dialog box. When pasted in Photoshop where a Style was applied to the object, the end result produced a 2-D object, as you see on the right side of the figure.

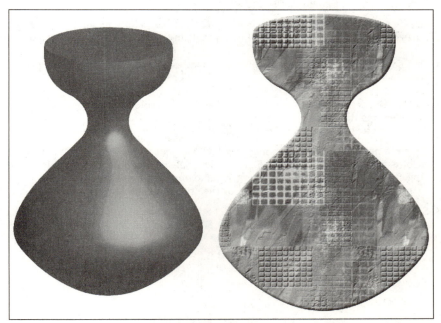

Figure 17-57: Illustrator 3-D objects lose the 3-D view when Styles are applied in Photoshop.

Using graphic styles in InDesign

 New Feature In addition to all the powerful features you have in creating and using character, paragraph, and nested styles in InDesign, the CS2 upgrade provides you with the new Object Styles palette. Object styles provide the same kind of options in InDesign for stylizing type and objects as you have available in Illustrator and Photoshop.

To open the Object Styles palette choose Window ⇨ Object Styles. The palette opens and appears similar to the graphic styles palettes you use in Illustrator and Photoshop. From a palette menu you have some similar menu commands that provide, among other choices, an option to Load Object Styles. Object Styles can be imported from other InDesign documents. Unfortunately, exchanging Object Styles with Graphic Styles from Illustrator and Photoshop is not available in this release of InDesign.

Graphic styles can be used with type or text frames or both. If you want to apply type attributes such as font style, color, character and paragraph formatting, and so on, you need to create a paragraph style for those attributes. You can then add additional effects in the Object Styles palette.

To understand how Object Styles are used in InDesign, follow these steps:

STEPS: Creating Object Styles in InDesign

1. **Add type to a document page.** Type a word on a new blank document.

2. **Set the type attributes.** Select a font and set the point size. Add color from the Swatches or Color palettes. Use a gradient color if you like.

3. **Create a Paragraph Style.** Open the Paragraph Styles palette menu and select New Paragraph Style. Type a name for the new style in the New Paragraph Styles dialog box.

 Cross-Reference For information on creating paragraph styles in InDesign, see the section "Using paragraph styles in InDesign."

4. **Apply effects to the text.** You can add fill and stroke colors to the text frame, add corner effects to the frame corners, add transparency, drop shadows, feather edges, set text wrap attributes, story options, and set anchored objects attributes.

5. **Create a new Object Style.** Choose Window ⇨ Object Styles to open the Object Styles palette. From the palette menu (Figure 17-58), select New Object Style. This opens the Object Style Options dialog box. Type a name for the style in the Style Name text box. In our example, we use *TypeGradient* for the style name, as shown in Figure 17-59.

6. **Set Fill and Stroke attributes.** The Object Style Options dialog box has a number of attribute categories in the left pane. Click Fill and you can set fill and stroke attributes as shown in Figure 17-60.

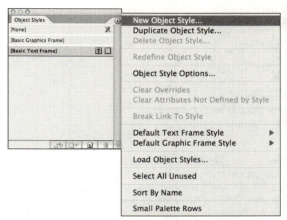

Figure 17-58: Select New Object Style from the Object Styles palette menu.

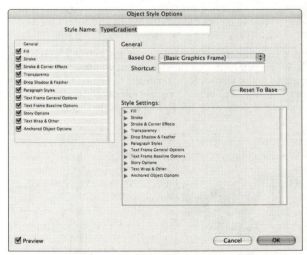

Figure 17-59: Open the Object Style Options dialog box and type a name for your new style.

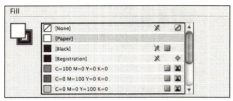

Figure 17-60: Click Fill in the left pane to adjust fill and stroke attributes in the right pane.

 The list of check boxes on the left side of the dialog box enables you to select the settings you want to apply to the Object Style. You can remove check marks for those items you want eliminated from your style. When using fills and strokes, you can click the Fill and Stroke tool in the dialog box to apply either when a Fill or Stroke is selected in the left pane. For example, you can add a stroke color when Fill is selected in the left pane by clicking on the Stroke tool in the right pane and selecting a color from the scrollable color list.

7. **Apply additional settings.** Click each of the items in the left pane to open attribute choices in the right pane for each respective item. The most important item to select is Paragraph Styles. Be certain to select Paragraph Styles and select the style you added for your type effect.

8. **Apply the Style.** Click OK when you finish adding all the settings in the Object Styles Options dialog box. When you return to the document window, add a new line of type and click the style name in the Object Styles palette. In Figure 17-61, we added a drop shadow, a stroke to the frame, and applied corner effects to the frame corners. The type is filled with a gradient defined in the Paragraph Style Options dialog box.

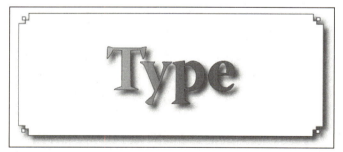

Figure 17-61: Create text and click the style name in the Object Styles palette.

If you want to reuse styles, save your InDesign document. Open a new document and select Load Object Styles from the Object Styles palette menu. The Open a File dialog box appears. Locate the file containing the style you want to load and select it in the Open a File dialog box. Notice in Figure 17-62 you can see a preview of styles contained in the file you select. Click OK and the Load Styles dialog box appears.

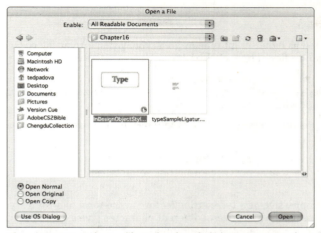

Figure 17-62: Select a file to load and click OK to open the Load Styles dialog box.

The Load Styles dialog box offers you options for selecting which styles you want to load in your new document as shown in Figure 17-63. The first two styles are defaults. These styles are added to each new document you create in InDesign. Deselect the styles and select the custom styles you want to load. Notice that the Load Styles dialog box offers you a description for a selected style in the dialog box and the style you are about to import. Click OK and the style is added to the Object Styles palette in your new document.

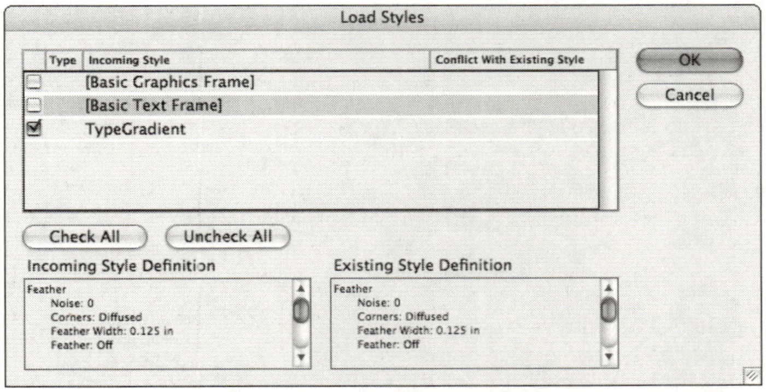

Figure 17-63: Select the styles you want to load and click OK to add the styles to your new document.

Summary

✦ Illustrator text is created as either point type or area type. When formatting paragraphs and working with larger bodies of text, click and drag the cursor to create area type.

✦ Legacy Illustrator files need to be updated to edit type in Illustrator CS2. You can update type when opening a legacy file in Illustrator CS or at a later time after a document has been opened without updating the type.

✦ OpenType fonts offer you many more sophisticated typesetting features as compared to PostScript and TrueType fonts.

✦ Both Illustrator and InDesign offer options for creating character and paragraph style sheets. Style sheets are used to apply type formatting when repeating format designs throughout a layout.

✦ InDesign provides an impressive new typesetting feature in the form of nested style sheets. Nested styles are used when several different character styles are applied to a paragraph and you want to duplicate the paragraph formatting throughout a passage of text.

✦ Illustrator, Photoshop, and InDesign have styles palettes you can use to create styles when applying graphic effects to text and objects. The styles are not transportable among the programs but you can import styles in new documents for styles created in the respective program.

✦ ✦ ✦

Working with Text Frames

In This Chapter

Adding text frames to documents

Managing text frames

Using master frames

Wrapping type around objects

Photoshop, Illustrator, and InDesign allow you to create type within bounding boxes. In Photoshop you can create multiple paragraphs within a bounding box and choose justification options, but you have no ability to link multiple blocks of text (known as text threading). When you set type in a bounding box in Illustrator, the box is called area type; in InDesign, it is referred to as a text frame. To make our discussion easier in this chapter, type bounding boxes in both InDesign and Illustrator are referred to as text frames.

Both Illustrator and InDesign offer advanced options for handling text blocks, including the ability to thread text, apply attributes to text frames, and wrap text around objects. Text frames can assume many different shapes and can appear as graphic objects or flow around objects and images. In both Illustrator and InDesign, text frames give you great flexibility when working with type.

Creating Text Frames

Text frames are created in the same manner in both Illustrator and InDesign. Simply click the Type tool and drag open a rectangle. A blinking cursor tells you the program is ready to accept type within the frame you created.

To resize a text frame, click and drag any one of the handles on the bounding box and reshape as desired. Any text within the frame conforms to the new size. If you start typing in a text frame and you want to quickly reshape the frame, press the ⌘/Ctrl key and you temporarily gain access to the frame handles. Drag the handles to reshape the frame, and when you release the keyboard modifier the Type tool is left uninterrupted, and you're ready to continue typing.

Working with text threads

You can add text to a frame either by typing it in directly from the keyboard or by importing it from another document. If the text oversets the frame (that is, the bounding box is not large enough to hold all the text) you will see a tiny red plus symbol (+) in a box at the bottom-right corner of the text frame. If you don't want the text to carry over to a new text frame, you need either to make the type size smaller or the text frame larger, until the plus sign disappears. However, if you want to create a text thread (that is, carry the text over to a new frame), click on the plus symbol with the Selection tool. This action "loads" the cursor with all the overset text. Click and drag open a new text frame and the overset text automatically flows into the new frame.

In Illustrator, when you select threaded text frames, you see a visible link between them, as shown in Figure 18-1. You can hide the text threads by choosing View ➪ Hide Text Threads.

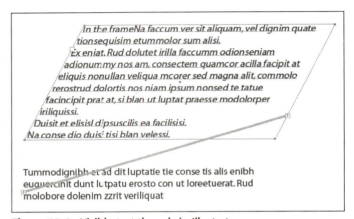

Figure 18-1: Visible text threads in Illustrator

InDesign's default setting hides the text threads, as shown in Figure 18-2. There is no visible indication that the text blocks are linked. If you want to view the text threads, choose View ➪ Show Text Threads.

Figure 18-2: InDesign's default setting keeps text threads hidden.

Adding new frames to a text thread

Text frames in both Illustrator and InDesign have *in ports* and *out ports* that enable linking to other text frames for continuation of a thread. The in port is a small square located in the top-left area of the text frame and the out port is located at the bottom-right. An empty port indicates that no text precedes or follows the text frame. A port containing a right arrow indicates that text is threaded from one frame to another. An out port with a plus (+) symbol indicates that more text is contained within the frame but has not yet been threaded and remains hidden. In Figure 18-3, you can see a thread where the symbols are placed.

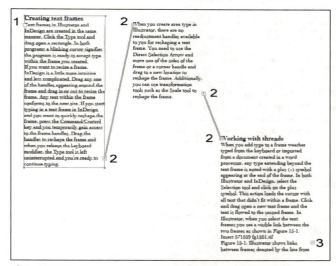

Figure 18-3: An empty port (1) indicates no text precedes the text in the frame. A port with a right arrow (2) indicates the thread flows from one frame to another. A plus (+) symbol in an out port (3) indicates there is overset text in the frame that has not yet flowed to another frame.

To flow overset text to a new text frame, simply click the plus symbol on the out port with the Selection tool. Click on a blank area of the document, or drag open a rectangle, and the overset text flows to the new frame.

If you need to add a new text frame between frames in an existing thread, use the Selection tool to click the out port preceding the frame where you want to add the new frame. Clicking on the out port loads the cursor with text following the selected frame. Click and drag open a new text frame, and the text is then threaded through it.

To make this process a little clearer, take a look at Figure 18-4. At the top, you see two linked text frames with overset text as indicated by the plus symbol (+) in the out port of the second text frame. To eliminate this overset, we want to create a new text frame in the second column and thread the text through it. To do this, we click on the out port at the bottom-right of the text frame in column one. The cursor changes to indicate that it is loaded with all the text following that frame. Then we click and drag to create a new text frame in column two. As you can see in the bottom example in Figure 18-4, the text thread now runs through the newly created text frame and is no longer overset in the third frame.

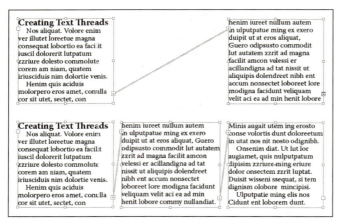

Figure 18-4: The top example shows an existing text thread with overset text in InDesign. The bottom example shows a new text frame added in the middle of the existing thread. The text now runs through the new frame, eliminating the overset text.

Unthreading text frames

Illustrator and InDesign differ a little when unthreading frames. In Illustrator, you can break a thread between two objects, release an object from a text thread, or cut the threads without changing the placement of the text. In InDesign, you have only two options: You can unthread frames that result in breaking the thread to all subsequent frames, or you can cut a frame from a thread. The methods for handling each of the three options in Illustrator and the two options in InDesign include the following:

+ **Breaking a thread in Illustrator:** Using the Selection tool, double-click on an out port to break the thread to the current object, double-click on an in port to break the thread to a previous object, or use a single click on an in or out port and move the cursor to another in or out port and click the cursor.

+ **Releasing an object from a text thread in Illustrator:** Click on the object you want to release from the thread with the Selection tool. Choose Type ➪ Threaded Text ➪ Release Selection.

+ **Cutting threads in Illustrator:** Select a linked text object with the Selection tool and choose Type ➪ Threaded Text ➪ Remove Threading.

+ **Breaking frames in InDesign:** To unthread or break frames in InDesign, start by clicking on an in or out port with the selection tool. The cursor loads with text. Move the cursor over an in or out port in another frame and double-click the mouse button. Note that when the cursor is loaded and positioned over an in or out port, the cursor shape changes to a broken-chain-link symbol informing you that the thread will be broken.

+ **Cutting frames in InDesign:** To cut a frame in InDesign, start by selecting one or more frames in a thread with the Selection tool. For multiple frame selection where you want to cut several frames, use Shift+click. Choose Edit ➪ Cut. The frames are cut from the thread, but text is not lost — it flows from the frame preceding the cut frame(s) to the next frame in the thread order.

Setting Text Frame Attributes

Text frame attributes include options for creating columns, creating offsets, setting type, adjusting baselines, and so on. The ability to change text frame attributes is a time-saver because it allows you to make text formatting and/or layout changes quickly and easily. For example, if you need to change the type style and column width of multiple text frames, you can make these changes simply by selecting the text frames and applying the desired attributes. In both Illustrator and InDesign, dialog boxes offer options for setting attributes of text frames.

Creating columns and insets

When you create layouts in InDesign, you can specify the number of columns applied to pages. You can create threaded text frames within individual columns and flow the text through multi-columned pages. Likewise, in Illustrator, you can create several text frames and link the frames to create a single thread. As an alternative to creating multiple frames, you can create single text frames and divide the single frames into multiple columns. You can create multicolumn text frames in either Illustrator or InDesign.

In Illustrator, create an area type frame by selecting the Type tool and dragging open a rectangle. From the Type menu, select Area Type Options, and the Area Type Options dialog box opens, shown in Figure 18-5.

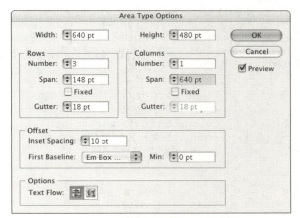

Figure 18-5: You can apply Area Type attributes in Illustrator.

In Illustrator's Area Type Options dialog box, you can specify overall width and height, define rows, columns, and offset values, and select a text flow method. When experimenting with different attributes, place a check mark in the Preview box to dynamically preview the results.

InDesign has a similar dialog box for setting text frame attributes. In InDesign, choose Object ⇨ Text Frame Options, and the Text Frame Options dialog box opens. Notice there are two panes in the Text Frame Options dialog box. The dialog opens with the General pane selected, as shown in Figure 18-6.

New Feature The Text Frame Options dialog box offers you a Preview check box. This new InDesign CS2 feature enables you to preview settings made in the Text Frame Options dialog box dynamically in the page layout as you make settings adjustments.

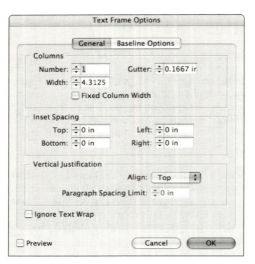

Figure 18-6: By default, the General tab is active when you open the dialog box.

InDesign CS2 provides you additional settings for baseline adjustments. You can now set up baselines for frames instead of the entire document. Click the Baseline Options tab in the Text Frame Options dialog box and the options choices for baseline settings appear, as shown in Figure 18-7. The new choices for using a custom baseline include defining a start point (off-setting from the layout grid); setting the baseline relative to the page, page margin, frame or inset; increment values (normally this setting is equal to the body text leading); and displaying a user-defined color for the grid lines.

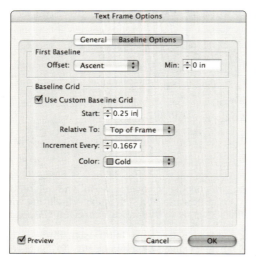

Figure 18-7: To apply baseline settings on a frame, select the Use Custom Baseline Grid check box and make settings choices for the Offset, Relative to, and a gridline color.

The following steps show how you might apply options for text frame attributes using the Text Frame Options dialog box in InDesign.

STEPS: Setting Text Frame Options in InDesign

1. **Create a new document.** Open InDesign and choose File ⇨ New Document. In the New Document dialog box, set the page size to 6 inches by 6 inches and uncheck Facing Pages.

2. **Create a frame object.** Drag guidelines from the ruler wells to the 3-inch vertical and horizontal ruler marks. The guidelines intersect at the center point of the document. Select the Ellipse Frame tool and position the cursor at the center point. Hold the Option/Alt key, and press Shift to drag from center and constrain the angle to create a perfect circle. Click and drag from the center out toward the outside guidelines to create a circle. The default margin guides appear at 0.5 inches around the inside of the document page, as shown in Figure 18-8.

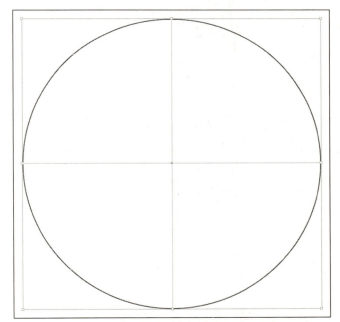

Figure 18-8: The Ellipse Frame tool creates a circle from the center point to the outside guidelines.

3. **Convert the object to a text frame.** Select the object and choose Object ⇨ Content ⇨ Text or click inside the object with the Type tool. The object becomes a text frame.

4. **Set the text frame options.** Select the text frame and choose Object ⇨ Text Frame Options. The Text Frame Options dialog box opens. In the Columns section, set Number to **5**, and Gutter to **6** points. If your unit of measure is currently set to inches and you want to specify point measurements instead, you can apply point units to the field boxes using 0p*n* — where 0 is picas, *p* stands for points, and *n* is the number of points. In the example shown in Figure 18-9, 0p6 is used in the Gutter field box. When you tab out of the field box, the value is translated to the defined unit of measure. In this example, 6 points translates to 0.833 inches. In the Inset Spacing section, type **0p8** for the Inset. This will inset the text 8 points from the outer edge of the frame.

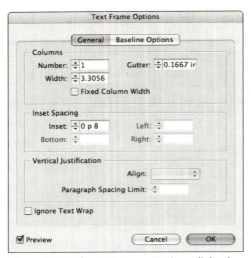

Figure 18-9: The Text Frame Options dialog box

5. **View the text frame edges.** By default, you may not be able to see the column and inset spacing guidelines. If the guidelines are not shown, choose View ⇨ Show Frame Edges. When the guidelines are visible, you should see an object similar to Figure 18-10.

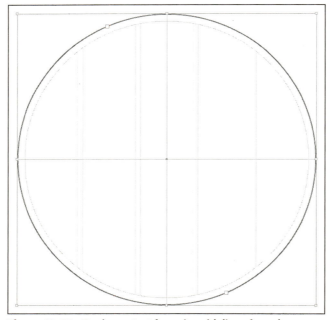

Figure 18-10: To view a text frame's guidelines for columns and inset spacing in InDesign, select Show Frame Edges from the View menu.

6. **Set the text attributes.** From the Control palette, select the font and point size for your type. In Figure 18-11, Kabel Book was selected from the Font drop-down list and the type size was set to 8 points.

7. **Fill with placeholder text.** If you created a keyboard shortcut for filling with placeholder text as discussed in Chapter 17, click the cursor in the first column and press Shift+F12. If you didn't create a keyboard shortcut, click the cursor in the first column and choose Type ⇨ Fill with Placeholder Text. The final result should appear similar to Figure 18-11.

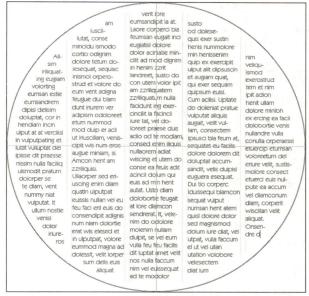

Figure 18-11: After setting font attributes, fill the columns with text.

Setting text attributes

You can set text attributes via the Control palette for options such as typeface, font size, leading, kerning, and tracking. In addition, you have a couple of text formatting options in the Text Frame Options dialog box. They include First Baseline positioning and Vertical Justification options.

In the Text Frame Options dialog box (see Figure 18-7), the First Baseline pane allows you to choose a first baseline offset method from a pull-down menu, and also lets you specify a minimum value for first baseline offset. The following explains these items in more detail:

✦ **Ascent:** With this setting, the first baseline is calculated so that the top edges of characters with ascenders (such as *d* and *b*) fall just below the top inset of the text frame.

✦ **Cap Height:** With this option, the top edges of uppercase letters touch the top inset of the text frame.

✦ **Leading:** This setting uses the text's leading value as the distance between the baseline of the first line of text and the top inset of the frame.

- **x Height:** Calculates the first baseline whereby the top of the *x* character falls just below the top inset of the text frame.
- **Fixed:** Allows you to specify the distance between the baseline of the first line of text and the top inset of the frame.
- **Minimum:** The field box to the right of the Offset pull-down menu is where you can specify a minimum value for the first baseline offset.

Vertical Justification in the General pane allows you to specify how text is aligned vertically within a text frame. When you choose Top, Center, or Bottom from the Align menu, the text retains its specified paragraph leading and paragraph spacing values. When you choose Justify as the vertical alignment option, the lines are spaced evenly to fill the frame, regardless of the specified leading and paragraph spacing values. Figure 18-12 shows examples of the four vertical justification options available in InDesign.

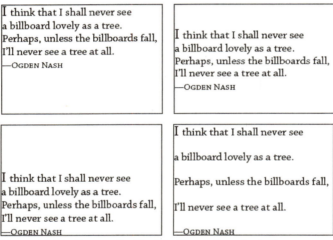

Figure 18-12: Four vertical justification options for text are available in InDesign. Shown clockwise from top, they are Top, Center, Bottom, and Justify.

Creating Text Frames on Master Pages

One big advantage of using layout programs is the ability to use *master pages*. Elements placed on the master page automatically appear on all subsequent pages where the master page is applied. The use of master pages eliminates repetitive keystrokes, ensures greater design consistency, speeds up the editing process, and conserves memory because objects are applied on a single page and referenced on all other pages. Master pages are only available in InDesign. Since Illustrator is limited to creating single-page designs, there is no need for master pages.

Illustrator CS2 permits you to create multiple-page documents when tiling pages and saving as PDF documents. For more information on creating multiple pages from Illustrator, see Chapter 32.

You can add a text frame on a master page and define the type attributes for the frame. On all subsequent pages where a given master page is applied, the text frame is positioned and ready for use. You can either type text in the frame or import text from another document. The text will automatically pick up the attributes you established on the master page.

Cross-Reference For a more comprehensive view on creating master pages, see Chapter 26.

Creating manual text frames

You create text frames on master pages in the same way you create them on regular pages. Use either the Type tool or convert objects to text frames. To set text attributes, styles, and other options, click the cursor inside the frame. While the cursor is blinking, set the attributes using the various palettes and menu options used for type, such as the Control palette, the Character palette, and the Paragraph palette. In Figure 18-13, you can see a master page containing two separate text frames, a stroke below the second frame, and the folio. You set text attributes for the separate frames by clicking in each frame and then setting options.

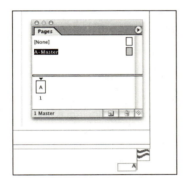

Figure 18-13: On a master page, add the objects and text frames.

When you have one or more frames created on a master page and you apply the master page to document pages, you can type in the frames or import text. Selecting the Type tool and clicking on a frame, however, does not access the frame. Neither the Type tool nor the selection tools alone can activate a text frame from a master page. You need to use ⌘/Ctrl+Shift and double-click on a frame. It doesn't matter what tool you select in the toolbox; pressing the ⌘/Ctrl key temporarily activates the Selection tool. Add the Shift key, double-click, and the I-beam cursor starts blinking in the text frame. At this point, you can type text or import text into the frame. In Figure 18-14, you can see two text frames with different text attributes. Both text frames were created on a master page.

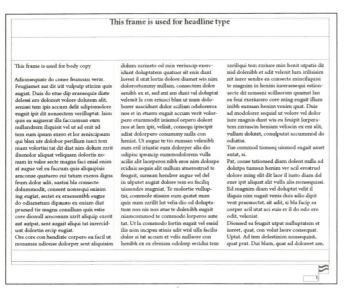

Figure 18-14: Assigning different type attributes to different frames on a master page

All the options you have for creating text threads, autoflowing text, and assigning attributes are available to you when creating frames on master pages. If you create frame threads on master pages, you can flow text through the frames, as shown in Figure 18-15. The frames in Figure 18-15 were drawn on the master page, and text was placed on a document page based on the master page. Notice that the frame threads show the direction of the text flow.

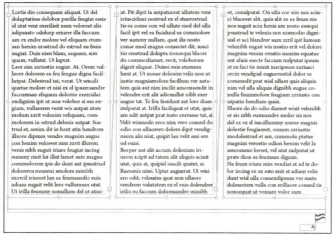

Figure 18-15: Frame threads on master pages can be applied to document pages keeping the thread order.

Creating master text frames

When you want to flow text through a document using InDesign's text autoflow feature, you need to create a master frame. Unlike manual frames, master frames are created at the time you set up your document. You add the master frame in the New Document dialog box, and InDesign automatically creates an indefinite thread when you place text within the frame using autoflow features. To understand more completely how this works, follow these steps.

STEPS: Autoflowing Text in Master Frames

1. **Create a new document.** Open InDesign and choose File ⇨ New ⇨ Document. In the New Document dialog box, check the box for Master Text Frame, as shown in Figure 18-16. Set attributes for the number of columns and margin distances.

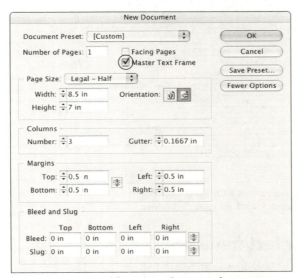

Figure 18-16: To add a master frame to the master page, select the Master Text Frame check box.

Note If you don't see the Bleed and Slug area in the New Document dialog box, click More Options.

2. **Import text.** Choose File ⇨ Place. The Place dialog box opens. Locate a text file you want to import, select the file, and then click Open. You can also double-click the file to be placed, but be certain not to triple-click the mouse button. The third click adds the text to the page.

3. **Autoflow the text.** When you double-click a filename or select a file in the Place dialog box and click Open, the cursor is loaded with text from the selected file. To place the text, you simply click the cursor to place text in an existing frame or click and drag the cursor to place text within a new frame. However, when placing text within a master frame, where you want to flow the text through many pages in your document, press the Shift key and you see the cursor change shape. Click the mouse button with the Shift

key depressed, and the text flows through the master text frame. If more text is placed than can fit within the current frame, InDesign adds new pages with new master frames and threads the text. More new pages are created with frames until the end of the passage of text is reached. In Figure 18-17, we added text to a master frame in a one-page document and InDesign created an additional nine pages to accommodate the text file.

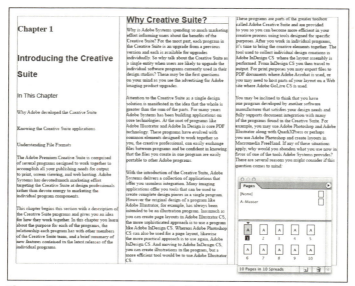

Figure 18-17: InDesign automatically adds new pages to accommodate text placement when using autoflow.

Modifying master text frames

When you create a master text frame, you can return to it and modify its attributes. Changes made on the master frame are reflected on all pages where the frame is used. Manual text frames placed on master pages, however, don't offer the same flexibility. If you create manual frames and link them on a master page, and then make changes to the frame attributes, the changes are not reflected on placed text within the frames in the document.

To modify a master frame, double-click on the master page in the Pages palette where the frame is positioned. Select the frame with a Selection tool and either open a context menu and select Text Frame Options or select the Object menu and select Text Frame Options. The Text Frame Options dialog box opens. You can make changes to the number of columns, gutter spacing, inset spacing, baseline shifts, and vertical justification the same as when you make changes to frames drawn manually on individual pages. Likewise, you can also apply attribute choices for text styles and transformations to the master frames.

After making adjustments on the master frame, all text within a master frame thread is readjusted to the changes made to the frame on the master page. In Figure 18-18, text was placed on a page in a single column. The text was placed within a frame created from a master frame on the master page. By adjusting the Text Frame Options and changing the frame from one column to three columns, all the text in the document using the master frame adjusts automatically, as shown in Figure 18-19.

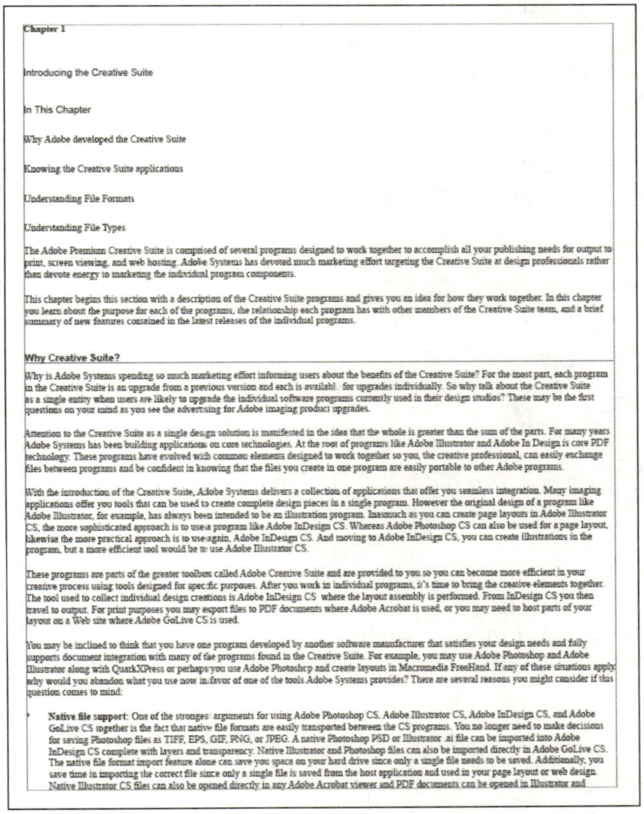

Chapter 1

Introducing the Creative Suite

In This Chapter

Why Adobe developed the Creative Suite

Knowing the Creative Suite applications

Understanding File Formats

Understanding File Types

The Adobe Premium Creative Suite is comprised of several programs designed to work together to accomplish all your publishing needs for output to print, screen viewing, and web hosting. Adobe Systems has devoted much marketing effort targeting the Creative Suite at design professionals rather than devote energy to marketing the individual program components.

This chapter begins this section with a description of the Creative Suite programs and gives you an idea for how they work together. In this chapter you learn about the purpose for each of the programs, the relationship each program has with other members of the Creative Suite team, and a brief summary of new features contained in the latest releases of the individual programs.

Why Creative Suite?

Why is Adobe Systems spending so much marketing effort informing users about the benefits of the Creative Suite? For the most part, each program in the Creative Suite is an upgrade from a previous version and each is availabl for upgrades individually. So why talk about the Creative Suite as a single entity when users are likely to upgrade the individual software programs currently used in their design studios? These may be the first questions on your mind as you see the advertising for Adobe imaging product upgrades.

Attention to the Creative Suite as a single design solution is manifested in the idea that the whole is greater than the sum of the parts. For many years Adobe Systems has been building applications on core technologies. At the root of programs like Adobe Illustrator and Adobe In Design is core PDF technology. These programs have evolved with common elements designed to work together so you, the creative professional, can easily exchange files between programs and be confident in knowing that the files you create in one program are easily portable to other Adobe programs.

With the introduction of the Creative Suite, Adobe Systems delivers a collection of applications that offer you seamless integration. Many imaging applications offer you tools that can be used to create complete design pieces in a single program. However the original design of a program like Adobe Illustrator, for example, has always been intended to be an illustration program. Inasmuch as you can create page layouts in Adobe Illustrator CS, the more sophisticated approach is to use a program like Adobe InDesign CS. Whereas Adobe Photoshop CS can also be used for a page layout, likewise the more practical approach is to use again, Adobe InDesign CS. And moving to Adobe InDesign CS, you can create illustrations in the program, but a more efficient tool would be to use Adobe Illustrator CS.

These programs are parts of the greater toolbox called Adobe Creative Suite and are provided to you so you can become more efficient in your creative process using tools designed for specific purposes. After you work in individual programs, it's time to bring the creative elements together. The tool used to collect individual design creations is Adobe InDesign CS where the layout assembly is performed. From InDesign CS you then travel to output. For print purposes you may export files to PDF documents where Adobe Acrobat is used, or you may need to host parts of your layout on a Web site where Adobe GoLive CS is used.

You may be inclined to think that you have one program developed by another software manufacturer that satisfies your design needs and fully supports document integration with many of the programs found in the Creative Suite. For example, you may use Adobe Photoshop and Adobe Illustrator along with QuarkXPress or perhaps you use Adobe Photoshop and create layouts in Macromedia FreeHand. If any of these situations apply, why would you abandon what you use now in favor of one of the tools Adobe Systems provides? There are several reasons you might consider if this question comes to mind:

- **Native file support:** One of the strongest arguments for using Adobe Photoshop CS, Adobe Illustrator CS, Adobe InDesign CS, and Adobe GoLive CS together is the fact that native file formats are easily transported between the CS programs. You no longer need to make decisions for saving Photoshop files as TIFF, EPS, GIF, PNG, or JPEG. A native Photoshop PSD or Illustrator .ai file can be imported into Adobe InDesign CS complete with layers and transparency. Native Illustrator and Photoshop files can also be imported directly in Adobe GoLive CS. The native file format import feature alone can save you space on your hard drive since only a single file needs to be saved. Additionally, you save time in importing the correct file since only a single file is saved from the host application and used in your page layout or web design. Native Illustrator CS files can also be opened directly in any Adobe Acrobat viewer and PDF documents can be opened in Illustrator and

Figure 18-18: Text placed in a master frame where the frame attributes are set to one column

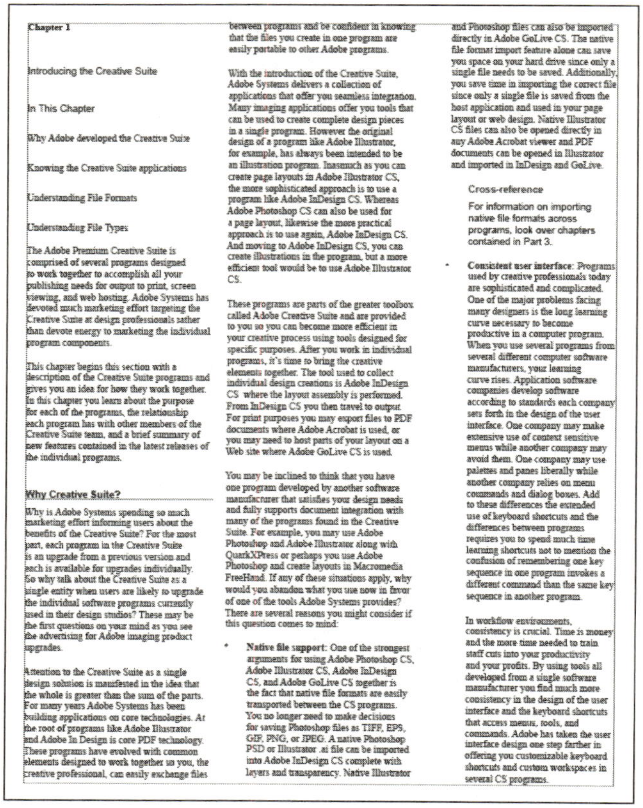

Chapter 1

Introducing the Creative Suite

In This Chapter

Why Adobe developed the Creative Suite

Knowing the Creative Suite applications

Understanding File Formats

Understanding File Types

The Adobe Premium Creative Suite is comprised of several programs designed to work together to accomplish all your publishing needs for output to print, screen viewing, and web hosting. Adobe Systems has devoted much marketing effort targeting the Creative Suite at design professionals rather than devote energy to marketing the individual program components.

This chapter begins this section with a description of the Creative Suite programs and gives you an idea for how they work together. In this chapter you learn about the purpose for each of the programs, the relationship each program has with other members of the Creative Suite team, and a brief summary of new features contained in the latest releases of the individual programs.

Why Creative Suite?

Why is Adobe Systems spending so much marketing effort informing users about the benefits of the Creative Suite? For the most part, each program in the Creative Suite is an upgrade from a previous version and each is available for upgrades individually. So why talk about the Creative Suite as a single entity when users are likely to upgrade the individual software programs currently used in their design studios? These may be the first questions on your mind as you see the advertising for Adobe imaging product upgrades.

Attention to the Creative Suite as a single design solution is manifested in the idea that the whole is greater than the sum of the parts. For many years Adobe Systems has been building applications on core technologies. At the root of programs like Adobe Illustrator and Adobe In Design is core PDF technology. These programs have evolved with common elements designed to work together so you, the creative professional, can easily exchange files between programs and be confident in knowing that the files you create in one program are easily portable to other Adobe programs.

With the introduction of the Creative Suite, Adobe Systems delivers a collection of applications that offer you seamless integration. Many imaging applications offer you tools that can be used to create complete design pieces in a single program. However the original design of a program like Adobe Illustrator, for example, has always been intended to be an illustration program. Inasmuch as you can create page layouts in Adobe Illustrator CS, the more sophisticated approach is to use a program like Adobe InDesign CS. Whereas Adobe Photoshop CS can also be used for a page layout, likewise the more practical approach is to use again, Adobe InDesign CS. And moving to Adobe InDesign CS, you can create illustrations in the program, but a more efficient tool would be to use Adobe Illustrator CS.

These programs are parts of the greater toolbox called Adobe Creative Suite and are provided to you so you can become more efficient in your creative process using tools designed for specific purposes. After you work in individual programs, it's time to bring the creative elements together. The tool used to collect individual design creations is Adobe InDesign CS where the layout assembly is performed. From InDesign CS you then travel to output. For print purposes you may export files to PDF documents where Adobe Acrobat is used, or you may need to host parts of your layout on a Web site where Adobe GoLive CS is used.

You may be inclined to think that you have one program developed by another software manufacturer that satisfies your design needs and fully supports document integration with many of the programs found in the Creative Suite. For example, you may use Adobe Photoshop and Adobe Illustrator along with QuarkXPress or perhaps you use Adobe Photoshop and create layouts in Macromedia FreeHand. If any of these situations apply, why would you abandon what you use now in favor of one of the tools Adobe Systems provides? There are several reasons you might consider if this question comes to mind:

- **Native file support**: One of the strongest arguments for using Adobe Photoshop CS, Adobe Illustrator CS, Adobe InDesign CS, and Adobe GoLive CS together is the fact that native file formats are easily transported between the CS programs. You no longer need to make decisions for saving Photoshop files as TIFF, EPS, GIF, PNG, or JPEG. A native Photoshop PSD or Illustrator .ai file can be imported into Adobe InDesign CS complete with layers and transparency. Native Illustrator and Photoshop files can also be imported directly in Adobe GoLive CS. The native file format import feature alone can save you space on your hard drive since only a single file needs to be saved. Additionally, you save time in importing the correct file since only a single file is saved from the host application and used in your page layout or web design. Native Illustrator CS files can also be opened directly in any Adobe Acrobat viewer and PDF documents can be opened in Illustrator and imported in InDesign and GoLive.

Cross-reference

For information on importing native file formats across programs, look over chapters contained in Part 3.

- **Consistent user interface**: Programs used by creative professionals today are sophisticated and complicated. One of the major problems facing many designers is the long learning curve necessary to become productive in a computer program. When you use several programs from several different computer software manufacturers, your learning curve rises. Application software companies develop software according to standards each company sets forth in the design of the user interface. One company may make extensive use of context sensitive menus while another company may avoid them. One company may use palettes and panes liberally while another company relies on menu commands and dialog boxes. Add to these differences the extended use of keyboard shortcuts and the differences between programs requires you to spend much time learning shortcuts not to mention the confusion of remembering one key sequence in one program invokes a different command than the same key sequence in another program.

In workflow environments, consistency is crucial. Time is money and the more time needed to train staff cuts into your productivity and your profits. By using tools all developed from a single software manufacturer you find much more consistency in the design of the user interface and the keyboard shortcuts that access menus, tools, and commands. Adobe has taken the user interface design one step farther in offering you customizable keyboard shortcuts and custom workspaces in several CS programs.

Figure 18-19: By changing the master text frame attributes from one column to three columns, all text using the frame is adjusted automatically.

Creating Text Wraps

Wrapping text around graphic elements in your design layouts can add greater visual appeal to your document. If you must manually set type around objects to create a text wrap, your job could become tedious and time-consuming. Fortunately, both Illustrator and InDesign offer you many different options for wrapping text around objects and images.

Wrapping text in Illustrator

You can wrap text around any placed object, around type objects, imported images, and objects you draw in Illustrator. If you save files as bitmaps from Photoshop with transparency, Illustrator can wrap text while ignoring transparent pixels. In Figure 18-20, you can see a text wrap around a Photoshop bitmap image with transparency.

Figure 18-20: Illustrator can wrap type around objects as well as images with transparency, clipping paths, and transparent layers.

Wrapping graphic objects

To understand how to wrap text around graphic objects, look over the following steps.

STEPS: Applying Text Wraps to Objects in Illustrator

1. **Create area type.** Create a text block by selecting the Type tool and dragging open a rectangle where you want the text to appear. You can import text or type text in the text block.

Tip

If you want to use Greek text in Illustrator, open InDesign and use the Fill with Placeholder Text command to add Greek text to a text frame. Click the cursor inside the frame and choose Edit ⇨ Select All or press ⌘/Ctrl+A. Copy and paste the text in Illustrator.

2. **Place a graphic you want to use for the text wrap.** You can place an object created in another program or use objects created in Illustrator. If you don't have an object handy, use the Symbols palette and drag an object to the document window. Use the transformation tools to size the object as desired. In Figure 18-21, an object from the Symbols palette was sized and placed on top of the text. Be certain the object to be wrapped is on the same layer as the text and that it appears in front of the text.

Figure 18-21: Objects to be wrapped need to be placed on the same layer as the text and appear in front of the text used for the wrap.

3. **Assign a text wrap to the object.** Objects are assigned attributes for a text wrap. Select the object with one of the selection tools and choose Object ⇨ Text Wrap ⇨ Make Text Wrap. The Text Wrap Options dialog box opens, as shown in Figure 18-22. Click the Preview check box and the text wraps in the document window, showing you the results of the wrap and offset. To adjust the offset amount, change the value in the Offset field box. Click OK when the wrap appears the way you want.

Figure 18-22: Select the Preview check box in the Text Wrap Options dialog box, and the background document window displays the results of the text wrap. To change the distance between the object and the text, edit the value in the Offset field box.

In the Text Wrap Options dialog box, an option appears for inversing a wrap. Check the box and click Preview to see the results of an inverse wrap. This option is used for containing text within objects, as shown in Figure 18-23.

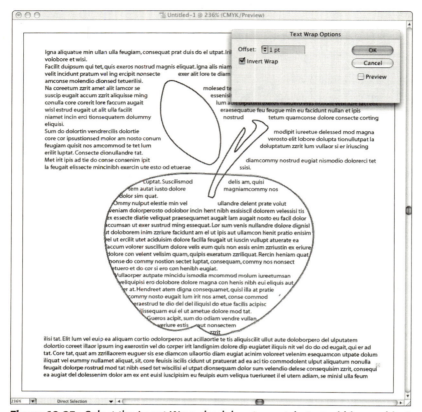

Figure 18-23: Select the Invert Wrap check box to contain text within an object.

Wrapping text objects

You can also wrap text around type objects. You can use the text frame as the object, or you can create outlines and wrap text around the outlined type. Follow the same procedures for applying text wraps to graphic objects. In Figure 18-24, you can see the effects of wrapping text around a text frame (top) and text converted to outlines (bottom).

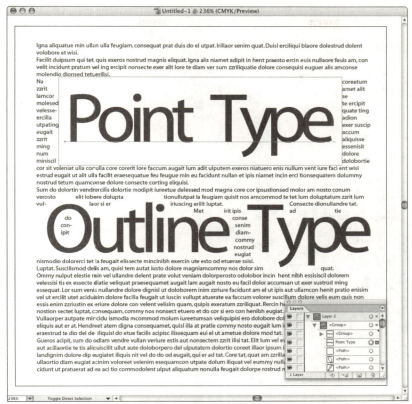

Figure 18-24: Text frames and type converted to outlines can be assigned text wrap attributes.

Wrapping images

Images from Photoshop can be assigned text wraps. Follow the same steps as mentioned previously for applying text wraps to graphic objects. Be certain the placed Photoshop file is contained in the same group as the text that wraps the object. If a Photoshop file contains a mask or transparency, be certain to create a clipping path and save the file with the path in either Photoshop native format or EPS. In Figure 18-25, a clipping path is added to the image. Notice that the transparency is not enough to create the wrap around the object in Illustrator to properly designate the path. The clipping path is needed to mask the object so the text wrap falls around the image.

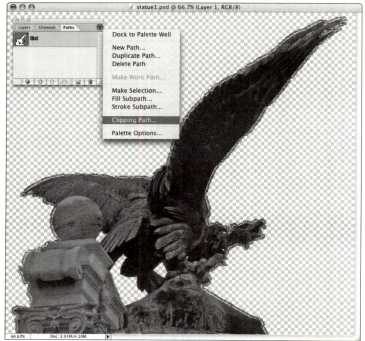

Figure 18-25: Create and save a clipping path in a Photoshop file when you want to mask an image. Save the document in Photoshop native format (PSD) or as an EPS.

Notice that the text neatly wraps the image (see Figure 18-26) at the offset distance defined in the Text Wrap Options dialog box.

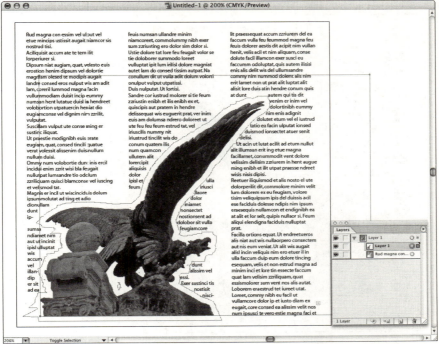

Figure 18-26: Text will wrap around the clipping path assigned in a Photoshop document.

Wrapping text in InDesign

InDesign offers the same options for wrapping text that you find in Illustrator, as well as some additional options for setting the text-wrap and path attributes. You can adjust clipping paths and path tolerances in InDesign, as well as set the same options found in Illustrator's Text Wrap Options dialog box.

Importing text wraps into InDesign

If you have an Illustrator document that needs to be imported into InDesign, you can create text wraps and complete the layout in Illustrator. When the file is imported into InDesign, the text wraps and layout appearance are preserved in InDesign when you place the file. In Figure 18-27, you can see the results of importing a native Illustrator document with a text wrap into InDesign.

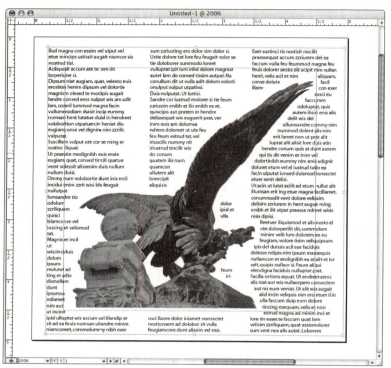

Figure 18-27: Text wraps created in Illustrator are preserved when placed in InDesign. Save the Illustrator files in native Illustrator Document (AI) format and import directly by choosing File ⇨ Place in InDesign.

InDesign offers you options for adjusting the clipping path on placed objects and also on objects placed in Illustrator and imported into InDesign. The path defined in Photoshop is the default path used in Illustrator and ultimately appears in the InDesign view.

You may have situations where artifacts appear around the edges of an image to which you have assigned a clipping path. If you need to adjust the tolerance so more of the path edge is cut off or the edge is pushed out to show more image and less mask, you can make the adjustments in InDesign. With the placed object selected, choose Object ⇨ Clipping Path. The Clipping Path dialog box opens and here you can make adjustments to a path.

From the Type drop-down list, select Detect Edges. The Threshold and Tolerance sliders enable you to adjust the path. In Figure 18-28, you can see the results of changing the Tolerance and Threshold on the same image used in Figure 18-26.

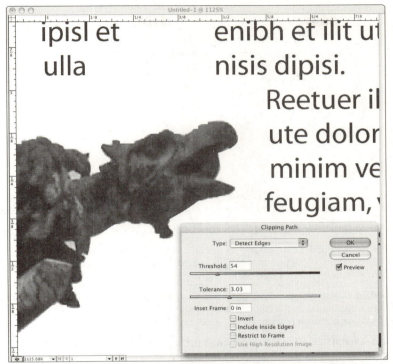

Figure 18-28: Open the Clipping Path dialog box to adjust the path edge. This dialog box lets you clip more of the image or reduce the mask to show more of the image.

Using InDesign text-wrap options

InDesign offers you a more elaborate set of options for wrapping text than you find in Illustrator. InDesign's Text Wrap palette lets you specify wrap options for a selected object in the foreground, as well as specify how the text behind the object is wrapped. In Figure 18-29, the Text Wrap palette is opened by choosing Window ⇨ Type and Tables ⇨ Text Wrap. As you learn from viewing the Text Wrap palette, you have many different options for controlling the text-wrap attributes.

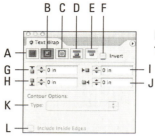

Figure 18-29: Choose Window ⇨ Type and Tables ⇨ Text Wrap to open the Text Wrap palette.

In the Text Wrap palette, you see five icons across the top of the palette, some field boxes, and drop-down lists, all used to adjust text-wrap options. The items include the following:

A **No Text Wrap icon:** The first icon in the top row turns off text wrap.

B **Wrap Around Bounding Box icon:** The second icon sets the text wrap around the bounding box of the imported image. The bounding box represents the periphery of the farthest elements to the edge of the object.

C **Wrap Around Object Shape icon:** This icon wraps the shape of objects and can include images with clipping paths. When this icon is selected, the drop-down lists for the Contour Options become active.

D **Jump Object icon:** Selecting this icon stops the wrap at the top of the image and starts it again at the bottom of the image. In essence, the wrap jumps over the object/image.

E **Jump to Next Column icon:** When you want the text to stop at the top of the image and continue below the image, select this icon. In essence, the wrap offset is used for the top of the image only, without regard to the sides or bottom of the image.

F **Invert check box:** This option is the same as you find in Illustrator. It is used to invert the text wrap and wrap text inside objects.

G **Top Offset field:** Controls the offset distance on the top edge of the object/image. Edit the field box or click the up/down arrows to adjust the offset distance. Note: When contour options are selected (see below), Top Offset is the only available field and applies to the entire contour, not just the top of the object.

H **Bottom Offset field:** Same as Top Offset but controls the bottom offset distance.

I **Left Offset field:** The same offset options controlling the left side of the object/image.

J **Right Offset field:** Controls the offset for the right side of the object/image.

K **Contour Options drop-down list:** From the Contour Options Type drop-down list, you have options that are used when you select the Wrap Around Object Shape icon. The options in the menu include the following:

- **Bounding Box:** Choose this option when you want to place the wrap around the frame where the outside edges appear.

- **Detect Edges:** InDesign can automatically detect edges in objects and images with paths. To enable auto-detection of edges, use this option.

- **Alpha Channel:** Use this option when a Photoshop image contains an Alpha Channel or transparency and you want the image masked. InDesign interprets layered Photoshop files with transparency the same as when creating a clipping path. All the transparency is masked when you select this option.

- **Photoshop Path:** The same as Alpha Channel, except you need a path created in the image. InDesign clips the image to the path saved in Photoshop.

- **Graphic Frame:** The frame holding an object or image can be larger or smaller than the imported item. When you select this option, the wrap forms around the frame, ignoring the frame contents.

- **Same As Clipping:** The same as Photoshop Path when a clipping path has been saved. You can import native PSD files as well as EPS files saved with clipping paths.

L **Include Inside Edges check box:** If you have an object with a cutout inside the object and want text to wrap around the outside and fill the inside cutout, select this option.

As is the case with Illustrator, you can adjust the text-frame options and change frames from single to multiple columns. In multiple-column frames, text wraps apply to all columns interacting with the object, as shown in Figure 18-30. If you create multiple frames on a page and either link the frames or keep them isolated as independent frames, the text wraps likewise occur for all text interacting with the object/image.

Figure 18-30: Text wraps are applied to multiple column frames and linked frames.

Summary

✦ Text is typed or imported into text frames in Illustrator and InDesign.

✦ When text is extended from one frame to another, the text follows a thread. Text frames in threads can be linked, unthreaded, or cut. New frames can be added between existing threaded frames.

✦ Text frames in Illustrator and InDesign can be assigned different properties. You can specify number of columns, inset spacing, column gutter widths, and font attributes.

✦ Frames created on master pages in InDesign can be used for autoflowing text.

✦ Text can be wrapped around graphic objects, text objects, and images in both Illustrator and InDesign.

✦ Text wraps can be applied to paths, transparencies, and clipping paths of Photoshop images placed in InDesign.

✦ ✦ ✦

CHAPTER 19

Working with Special Characters

In This Chapter

Understanding glyphs

Accessing special characters

Working with inline graphics

Both Illustrator and InDesign allow you to handle typography like a master, especially when working in conjunction with the OpenType fonts that offer you thousands of character selections. InDesign, in particular, with its abundant set of menu commands and palette options, is the most powerful typesetting tool developed to date for desktop computers. With it, you have the ability to set high-quality type that rivals the output from professional typesetting machines used before the computer revolution.

Older PostScript fonts give you a maximum of 256 different characters, or glyphs. With the OpenType fonts, however, you get as many as 65,000 glyphs per font. These additional characters offer you many more options for pairing characters in ligatures, customizing fractions, accessing foreign language characters, and working with a wide variety of symbols and special characters that can be used as type or graphic elements.

Working with Glyphs Palettes

Both Illustrator and InDesign have a Glyphs palette that shows you, at a glance, the different characters available in any given font. It's much like the old Keycaps control panel available in earlier Mac operating systems. In addition to viewing glyphs in a scrollable palette, you can also create custom glyph sets in InDesign and you can view different special characters by selecting menu options in the palettes.

In Illustrator, choose Type ➪ Glyphs to open the Glyphs palette shown in Figure 19-1. The palette contains several menus, scrollbars to view any hidden characters, font selection menus, and zoom tools.

The default selection in the Show menu at the top is Entire Font. All characters in a given font are displayed in the scrollable palette. In the Show menu, you also have the option to show Alternates for Current Selection. Note in Figure 19-1 that when you press the mouse button on a particular character with a flag in the lower-right corner, a pop-up bar shows alternate characters. When you select the menu command, the alternate characters are displayed in the palette. Other options you have from the menu choices include many of the same options found in the Character palette.

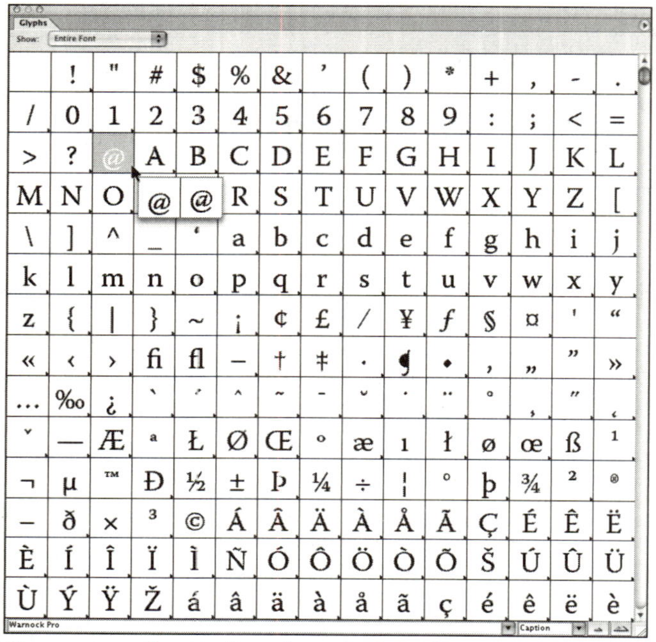

[Figure: Glyphs palette showing all characters in the Warnock Pro font]

Figure 19-1: The Glyphs palette displays all characters in a given font.

Cross-Reference For more information on using the Character palette, see Chapter 17.

To use glyphs, and particularly to use alternate characters in Illustrator, you can easily access the palette and select characters for insertion in text as you type. For character insertions, follow these steps.

STEPS: Inserting Special Characters in Text Using the Glyphs Palette

1. **Begin by typing a body of text.** Add some area type to a page in Illustrator. Select an OpenType Pro font you want to use by choosing Type ⇨ Font. Next, drag open a rectangle with the Type tool, and begin to type.

2. **Open the Glyphs palette.** Choose Type ⇨ Glyphs to open the Glyphs palette.

3. **Locate the character you want to insert.** The Glyphs palette opens with the current selected font displayed in the palette. Scroll the palette and find a character to insert. In our example, we use a ligature for combining the *f* and *l* characters into a single character.

4. **Insert the character.** When you find the character in the Glyphs palette, double-click on the character. The character is inserted at the cursor location. In Figure 19-2, the inserted character is highlighted.

Figure 19-2: Double-clicking on a character inserts it at the cursor.

In addition to the different displays in the palette for showing various combinations of characters via the Show menu, you can make font selections from the pull-down menu at the bottom of the palette. If you're searching for a special character or want to view a specific font, use the menu to select fonts without disturbing your text editing. You can select a font family from the pull-down menu at the bottom-left side of the palette; you select the font style from the second pull-down menu at the bottom of the palette. In Figure 19-1, the selected font family is Warnock Pro and the selected style is Caption.

To the right of the Style pull-down menu, zoom buttons offer different zoom views. Click on the smaller mountain symbols to zoom out and click on the larger symbol to zoom in on the characters in the palette.

In InDesign, you have a few more style combinations that you can view in the Show menu, but the main distinction between Illustrator and InDesign exists with the fly-out menu commands accessible via the arrow at the top right of the Glyphs palette. In Illustrator, the only option available here is resetting the palette to the default view. But in InDesign there are options for working with glyph sets. Click on the right pointing arrow to open the fly-out menu and the options shown in Figure 19-3 appear.

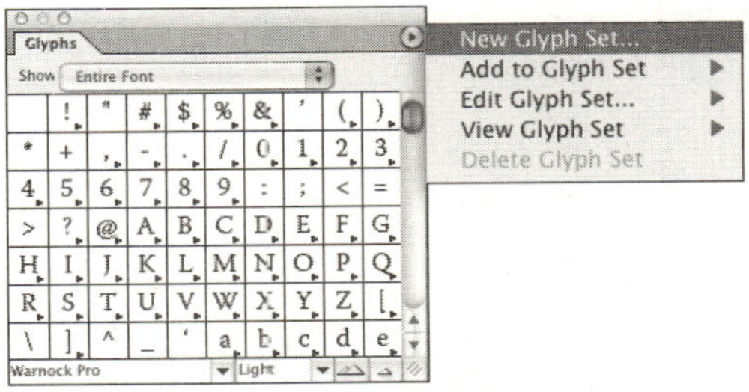

Figure 19-3: InDesign supports several menu commands unavailable in Illustrator.

The menu commands available from the fly-out menu enable you to create and edit custom glyph sets. This feature can be a time-saver when you need to access special characters or alternatives while typesetting in InDesign. To understand how custom sets are created and used, follow these steps.

STEPS: Working with Custom Glyph Sets in InDesign

1. **Open the Glyphs palette in InDesign.** Choose Type ➪ Glyphs to open the Glyphs palette.

2. **Create a new glyph set.** You can use the Glyphs palette with or without a document open in the InDesign application window. You can temporarily ignore the current font selected. When you create a new set and add characters to your custom set, you can add characters from different fonts. From the fly-out menu select New Glyph Set.

3. **Name the new glyph set.** The New Glyph Set dialog box opens. Type a name in the field box for the name you want to use for your custom set. In our example, we use myGlyphs for the set name. You can view your new glyph set by choosing it from the Show menu or via View Glyph Set in the fly-out menu. Currently the palette includes no characters.

4. **Select a font family and font style.** Be sure the Show option is set to Entire Font. At this point, you can view all your installed fonts and available styles by making selections in the pull-down menus at the bottom of the Glyphs palette. Select a font family and the font style you want to view.

5. **Add a character to the custom glyph set.** When you find a character you want to add to the set, click on it to highlight it. Open the fly-out menu and choose Add to Glyph Set. A submenu opens where you should see your new custom set listed. If you create several sets, select the one you want to edit. In our case, we select myGlyphs from the submenu.

6. **Add additional characters to the custom glyph set.** Continue selecting and adding characters to the glyph set with the Add to Glyph Set command in the fly-out menu. When you want to use the custom set, select it from the Show menu at the top of the Glyphs palette or by choosing View Glyph Set in the fly-out menu. The characters you added to the set appear in the Glyphs palette, as shown in Figure 19-4. When you want to access a character from the set while you are typing in InDesign, simply open the set and double-click the desired character. It will automatically be inserted at the cursor location.

Figure 19-4: You can add a custom glyph set to the Glyphs palette.

7. **Delete a character from your custom glyph set.** If you want to delete a character from your glyph set, select the set in the Show menu. In the fly-out menu, select Edit Glyph Set. The Edit Glyph Set dialog box opens, as shown in Figure 19-5. Select the character you want to delete, and click Delete from Set. In addition to deleting characters, the Edit Glyph Set dialog box also enables you to change the font and style of individual characters included in the set.

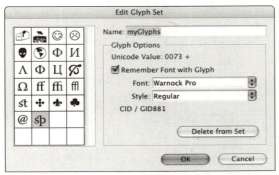

Figure 19-5: To delete a character, click Delete from Set.

Using Special Typographic Characters

A number of advanced typographic features are available to you in InDesign. By using simple menu commands, you can easily achieve special effects that are popular with layout artists and typographers. In the Type menu, you will find several options for handling special characters. Three of these options provide an even wider selection of options in submenus. They include Insert Special Character, Insert White Space, and Insert Break Character.

Inserting special characters

When you choose Type ⇨ Insert Special Character, a submenu opens where a number of options provide you with features for handling special characters, as shown in Figure 19-6.

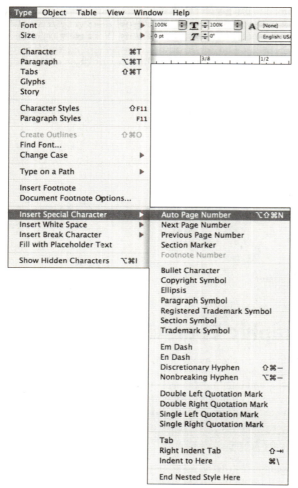

Figure 19-6: You find numerous special typographic features via the Type menu.

The submenu items available for Insert Special Character include the following:

✦ **Auto Page Number:** The keyboard shortcut for automatic page numbering is Alt+Shift+Ctrl+N (Windows) or Option+Shift+⌘+N (Mac). If you don't want to memorize the keyboard shortcut, you can use a menu command. To use the Auto Page Number command, open a master page, select a font and font style, and create a text frame. With the cursor blinking in the text frame, select the menu command. Automatic numbering is then applied to all pages associated with the master page. Although you often apply Auto Page Number to master pages, you aren't required to use it on master pages exclusively. You can also use it on regular document pages to number them individually.

✦ **Next Page Number:** The Next Page Number and Previous Page Number (see Previous Page Number below) commands are helpful when you have blocks of text that start on one page and then continue on another page in your document (also known as "story jumps"). Where the text ends on one page, for example, you would want to inform the reader that it continues on another page with a "Continued on page X" notation (also known as a "jump line.") To do this, create a separate text frame that overlaps the text frame of the story you are jumping. Be sure to group these two text frames together so if you move the story, the jump line stays with it. Type **Continued on page**; then choose Type ⇨ Insert Special Character ⇨ Next Page Number. InDesign automatically inserts the "continued to" page number.

✦ **Previous Page Number:** This option works like Next Page Number, but instead of using a "continued to" page number, you use a "continued from" page number. Again, create a separate text frame that overlaps the text frame of the jumped part of the story. Type "Continued from page," then choose Type ⇨ Insert Special Character ⇨ Previous Page Number. InDesign automatically inserts the "continued from" page number. Again, you should group the text frames so the page reference stays with the story if you decide to move it.

✦ **Section Marker:** You can divide documents into sections using the Layout ⇨ Numbering and Section Options menu command. Once you create sections within a document, inserting the Section Marker inserts the number of the section at the cursor position.

New Feature

A new InDesign feature permits creating footnotes directly and importing them from Microsoft Word and RTF (Rich Text Format). Inserting a Footnote Number inserts the number in the footnote text. Notice the item is grayed out unless your cursor appears in a footnote (see Figure 19-6).

✦ **Bullet Character:** The ability to insert special symbols with a menu command is particularly helpful to people who work in cross-platform environments and don't know the key combinations for certain characters. The bullet character inserts a bullet at the cursor insertion point.

✦ **Copyright Symbol (©):** Inserts the copyright symbol.

✦ **Ellipsis (. . .):** Inserts an ellipsis.

✦ **Paragraph Symbol (¶):** Inserts a paragraph symbol.

✦ **Registered Trademark Symbol (®):** Inserts a registered trademark symbol.

✦ **Section Symbol (§):** Inserts a symbol representing a new section.

✦ **Trademark Symbol (™):** Inserts a trademark symbol.

✦ **Em Dash (—):** Inserts an em dash.

✦ **En Dash (–):** Inserts an en dash.

✦ **Discretionary Hyphen:** Add a hyphen as desired by using this option.

✦ **Nonbreaking Hyphen:** Select this option when you don't want a hyphenated word to break to the next line.

✦ **Double Left Quotation Mark ("):** Inserts a double left quotation mark.

✦ **Double Right Quotation Mark ("):** Inserts a double right quotation mark.

- **Single Left Quotation Mark ('):** Inserts a single left quotation mark.
- **Single Right Quotation Mark ('):** Inserts a single right quotation mark.
- **Tab:** Has the same effect as pressing the Tab key.
- **Right Indent Tab:** Adds a tab indented from the right side of the text line.
- **Indent to Here:** Indents to the cursor position.
- **End Nested Style Here:** Ends a nested style at the cursor position.

Inserting white space characters

The next set of typographic controls you find in the Type menu are the spacing options. When you choose Type ➪ Insert White Space, a submenu offers commands for adding space between characters and words. The commands include the following:

- **Em Space:** Em spaces are equal in horizontal width to the vertical point size for a font. For example, in 18-point type, the em space is 18 points wide.
- **En Space:** En spaces are exactly one-half the width of an em space.
- **Flush Space:** You apply this option to fully justified paragraphs. A variable amount of space is added to the last line in a paragraph and justifies the last line of text.
- **Hair Space:** This option adds the smallest space between characters. It's $\frac{1}{24}$ the width of an em space.
- **Nonbreaking Space:** This option adds space equal to that of the Spacebar, but prevents the line from being broken at that point.
- **Thin Space:** One-eighth the width of an em space.
- **Figure Space:** The same space used for a numeric character in a font. This option is helpful when aligning numbers in columns.
- **Punctuation Space:** The same amount of space used for other punctuation marks such as commas, periods, colons, and exclamation marks.

Inserting break characters

Rounding out the options for using special typographic characters, you'll find a selection in the Type menu that controls line breaks. Choose Type ➪ Insert Break Character and the submenu items include the following:

- **Column Break:** When inserting a column break, text following the break flows to the next column in a multiple-column text frame. If text is set to a single-column frame, the text flows to the next frame in the thread.
- **Frame Break:** Flows text to the next frame in the text thread. If text is set to multiple columns and you insert a frame break in column 1, the text is flowed to the next frame thread, ignoring columns 2 and 3.
- **Page Break:** Flows text to the next page when text is threaded across pages.
- **Odd Page Break:** Flows text to the next odd-numbered page when following a thread.

- **Even Page Break:** Flows text to the next even-numbered page when following a thread.
- **Forced Line Break:** Forces a line break (same as pressing Shift+Enter/Return).
- **Paragraph Return:** Inserts a paragraph return (same as pressing Enter/Return).

Inserting Inline Graphics

You can automatically scroll text to separate columns, threads, and pages. Graphics placed in your layout in image frames do not follow the threading behavior of the text. This is a problem if you reformat your text and you need the graphics to stay connected to specific parts of the copy. Normally, you would have to move the graphic elements separately each time your text reflowed. However, if you use inline graphics, the graphic is interpreted similarly to the way text is interpreted and maintains its respective position within a given line of text.

Creating an inline graphic is easy. You simply select an object or image, cut it from a page, and paste the graphic back into a text frame with the cursor blinking at the spot where you want the object to appear. To see an example of this process, look over the following steps.

STEPS: Creating an Inline Graphic

1. **Place type within a frame.** Either place a body of text from a file or type a few lines of text.
2. **Cut a graphic from the document page.** Use an object imported from Illustrator, use the Glyphs palette, select a character and convert the character to outlines, or draw an object in InDesign. Select the object and choose Edit ➪ Cut.
3. **Identify the insertion point in the text.** Place the cursor at the point where you want to insert the inline graphic in the text frame. Use the Type tool and wait for the blinking I-beam cursor to appear.
4. **Paste the graphic.** Choose Edit ➪ Paste. The graphic is now part of the text block and follows the same scrolling behavior as the line of text where it resides. Figure 19-7 shows the results of pasting a graphic in a line of text.

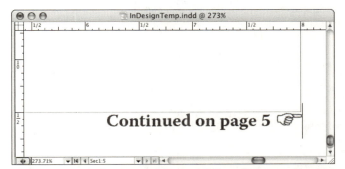

Figure 19-7: To place a graphic as an inline object, cut the object and click in a text block. Choose Edit ➪ Paste and the object is pasted at the cursor position.

Summary

✦ OpenType fonts support more than 65,000 glyphs in a given font. Opening the Glyphs palette in Illustrator or InDesign displays examples of all the glyphs contained within a selected font.

✦ InDesign allows you to create custom glyph sets where you can access frequently used characters in a single palette.

✦ InDesign has numerous options for accessing special typographic characters and functions. These include symbols, punctuation, white space options, line breaks, automatic page numbering, tab settings, and more.

✦ Inline graphics are inserted in text frames and scroll with the text as it is flowed through a frame or frame thread.

✦ ✦ ✦

Using Creative Suite and Microsoft Word Documents

PART

V

In This Part

Chapter 20
Importing Microsoft Word Documents

Chapter 21
Exporting Text to Microsoft Office Applications

Chapter 22
Working with Tables

Chapter 23
Creating Charts and Graphs

Chapter 24
Microsoft Office and Professional Printing

Importing Microsoft Word Documents

In This Chapter

Moving text via the Clipboard

Exporting text from Microsoft Word

Importing text into Illustrator and InDesign

Importing styles

Importing text into GoLive

✦ ✦ ✦ ✦

Whether it is copy for an InDesign layout, product descriptions for a GoLive Web page, or a marketing line you want to manipulate in Illustrator, you create most text in a word processor like Microsoft Word and import it into the CS2 applications. Although the CS2 applications handle type very well, they aren't designed to handle type from an editorial standpoint.

This chapter covers the crucial workflow step of importing text. Although several different word processors are available, Microsoft Word is the most popular word processor available today, and it is used for all the examples in this chapter.

There are essentially two methods for importing text from Microsoft Word. One method uses the Clipboard and the Cut, Copy, and Paste features. The other method exports (or saves the Word document) in a format that you can easily import into the CS2 applications. Both Illustrator and InDesign open or place Word documents saved in the Word (DOC) format. After you import the text, you can easily move among any of the CS2 applications using the PDF format.

Importing a Word document into InDesign or Illustrator, not only moves text, but can also import the text styles.

Using the Clipboard

In Microsoft Word, you copy selected text to the Clipboard by choosing Edit ⇨ Cut (⌘/Ctrl+X) or Edit ⇨ Copy (⌘/Ctrl+C). You can then paste the text into the various CS2 applications by choosing Edit ⇨ Paste (⌘/Ctrl+V). Text pasted into Illustrator and InDesign appears within a newly created text object, like that shown in Figure 20-1.

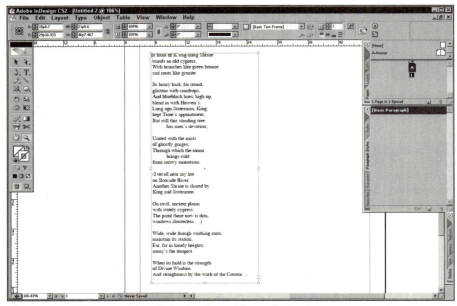

Figure 20-1: Text pasted into InDesign from Microsoft Word

In addition to the standard Edit ⇨ Paste menu command, Illustrator also includes Paste in Front (⌘/Ctrl+F) and Paste in Back (⌘/Ctrl+B) commands. These commands place the pasted text on top of (or behind) the currently selected object.

InDesign includes Paste Into (Alt+Ctrl+V on Windows; Option+⌘+V on the Mac) and Paste in Place (Alt+Shift+Ctrl+V on Windows; Option+Shift+⌘+V on the Mac) commands. You use the Paste Into command to mask an image by pasting into a converted outline. You cannot use this command on imported text. The Paste in Place command pastes the text in the same place as the original text object.

Cross-Reference   Masking images in InDesign using a converted outline is covered in Part III.

Text pasted into Illustrator and InDesign appears within a newly created text object unless you previously selected some text using the Type tool. If you selected text, the pasted text replaces the selected text.

In addition to transporting text using the Clipboard, text that you select in Word and drag and drop in an Illustrator or InDesign document moves the text into the target application.

Maintaining formatting

Although text pasted into Illustrator maintains formatting, text pasted into InDesign gives you the options to paste All Information or Text Only. This is set in a Preference setting found in the Type panel of the Preferences dialog box. The InDesign Preferences dialog box is opened by choosing InDesign/Edit ⇨ Preferences ⇨ Type, as shown in Figure 20-2.

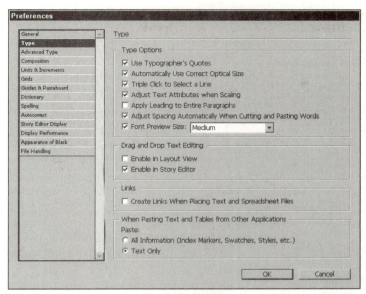

Figure 20-2: The InDesign Preferences dialog box lets you choose how text is pasted into the application.

Text pasted into GoLive from Microsoft Word also maintains formatting.

Missing fonts

If the text that you paste into Illustrator or InDesign from Microsoft Word is missing a font, a warning dialog box, like the one in Figure 20-3, appears listing the offending font. In addition to the warning dialog box, both applications list the missing font in brackets in the Control palette, and highlight the text that uses this font in pink, as shown in Figure 20-4.

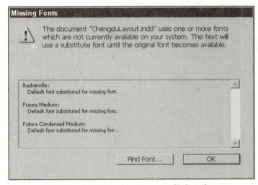

Figure 20-3: The Missing Fonts dialog box

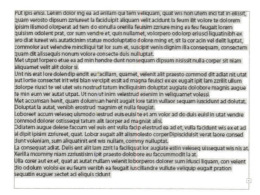

Figure 20-4: Pink highlighting identifies missing fonts.

If you choose Type ⇨ Font, you'll find a Missing category that lists all missing font faces and styles.

You can choose to have Illustrator highlight all Substituted Fonts and all Substituted Glyphs using the Type panel of the Document Setup dialog box, shown in Figure 20-5. You open this dialog box by choosing File ⇨ Document Setup (Alt+Ctrl+P on Windows; Option+⌘+P on the Mac). The Highlight Substituted Fonts and Highlight Substituted Glyphs options cause all text that uses a missing font to be highlighted pink.

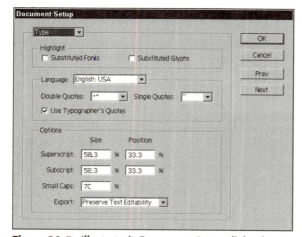

Figure 20-5: Illustrator's Document Setup dialog box

Cross-Reference For more information on glyphs, see Chapter 19. Installing and locating missing fonts is covered in Chapter 16.

Exporting Text from Word

Part IV covers in-depth how to create text in the CS2 applications, but if you already have the text available in a Word documents, the easy workflow path is to export it from Word and import it into the CS2 applications.

Word doesn't include a File ➪ Export menu command, but you use the File ➪ Save As menu command to save the file into one of several different formats, including Rich Text Format (RTF) and Plain Text (TXT). In addition to these formats that are imported into most CS2 applications, Illustrator can open and place native Word (DOC) files and InDesign can place native Word files.

Caution Although Word includes a File ➪ Save as Web Page menu command, Word adds some markup to the Web page content that might confuse GoLive and some Web browsers. The best approach is to import the Web-page text into GoLive using the Rich Text Format or the Plain Text format and let GoLive add the Web-page markup.

The difference between the Rich Text Format and Plain Text is that the former maintains any formatting within the text and the latter strips all formatting out.

Importing Text

Importing text into the various CS2 applications happens by opening a file saved from within Word into a CS2 application. The two most useful CS2 applications for doing this are Illustrator and InDesign. Both can use native Word documents (DOC), as well as files saved using the Rich Text Format (RTF) and Plain Text (TXT) formats. Illustrator can open these files using the File ➪ Open menu command and InDesign can import these files using the File ➪ Place menu command.

Cross-Reference Working with fonts and text is covered in Part IV.

Opening Word documents in Illustrator

You open Word documents natively within Illustrator by choosing File ➪ Open (⌘/Ctrl+O). In the file dialog box that appears, select the Microsoft Word (DOC) file type. This format includes support for files created using Word 97, 98, 2000, and 2002. All formatting in the Word document is maintained as the file is imported into Illustrator.

After you select and open a file, another dialog box of options opens, as shown in Figure 20-6. This dialog box lets you specify whether to import the Table of Contents Text, Footnotes/Endnotes, and Index Text. You can also select Remove Text Formatting.

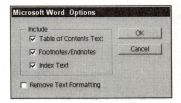

Figure 20-6: The Microsoft Word Options dialog box

If the fonts used in the Word document are not available to Illustrator, a Font Problems dialog box opens, shown in Figure 20-7, listing the fonts in question.

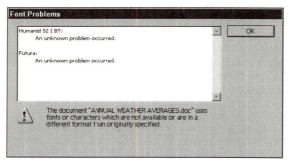

Figure 20-7: The Font Problems dialog box

Placing text documents in Illustrator

Text files saved using the Rich Text Format (RTF) and Plain Text (TXT) formats are also opened in Illustrator with the File ➪ Open menu command. Rich Text Format files use the same Options dialog box as the Word (DOC) files, but Plain Text files present a different dialog box of Options, as shown in Figure 20-8.

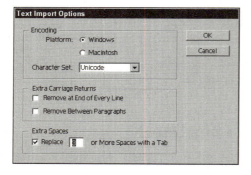

Figure 20-8: The Text Import Options dialog box

The Text Import Options dialog box lets you specify the encoding platform as Windows or Mac and which Character Set to use. The dialog box also has options to select how to handle extra carriage returns and to replace a specified number of spaces with a tab.

If you want to import a Word document into an existing Illustrator document, choose File ➪ Place. This command opens the Word or text document into the current Illustrator document.

Placing Word documents into InDesign

The File ➪ Place (⌘/Ctrl+D) menu command in InDesign opens a file dialog box where you select Microsoft Word and Excel files that you want to open and place into the current document. Once you select a file and click Place, the mouse cursor changes to indicate that it is holding the imported text. To place the imported text, you need to click the location in the document where you want to place the upper-left corner of the imported text.

Cross-Reference Importing Excel data as tables is covered in Chapter 22.

The Place dialog box, shown in Figure 20-9, includes a Show Import Options check box and a Replace Selected Item check box. Holding down the Shift key while clicking the Open button forces the Options dialog box to appear.

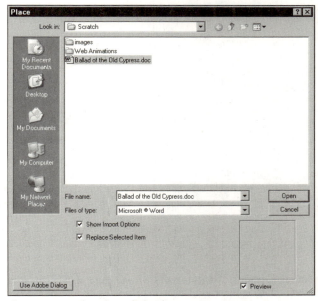

Figure 20-9: The Place dialog box

 Note You use only the Preview option to show previews of images and PDF files. You cannot preview text files with this option.

The Microsoft Word Import Options dialog box, shown in Figure 20-10, includes the same features as mentioned previously for Illustrator including the ability to specify the inclusion of table of contents text, footnotes and endnotes, and index text. It also offers the Use Typographer's Quotes check box.

This Word Import Options dialog box includes several options for handling formatting. You can select to Remove Styles and Formatting from Text and Tables or preserve the same. If you select to remove styles and formatting, the Preserve Local Overrides options become available along with options to Convert Tables to Unformatted Tables or Unformatted Tabbed Text. If you select to preserve styles and formatting, several additional options become available including handling Manual Page Breaks. The options include Preserve Page Breaks, Convert to Column Breaks, or No Breaks. You can also select to Import Inline Graphics and Import any Unused Styles. The dialog box also shows the number of Style Name Conflicts that exist between the current InDesign file and the imported Word document. For Paragraph and Character Style Conflicts, you can choose to automatically import styles with options to Use the InDesign Style Definition, Redefine the InDesign Style, or Auto Rename; or you could Customize the Style Import by defining a style mapping between the two documents. Defined options can be saved as a preset for easy recall. For RTF files, the same options are available.

The improved Word import options found in InDesign are new to CS2.

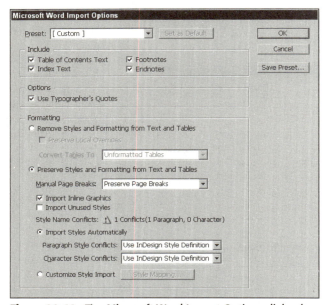

Figure 20-10: The Microsoft Word Import Options dialog box

Plain Text files open the Text Import Options dialog box, shown in Figure 20-11. This dialog box lets you select a character set, platform, and dictionary. It also offers options for handling extra carriage returns, replacing spaces with tabs, and using typographer's quotes.

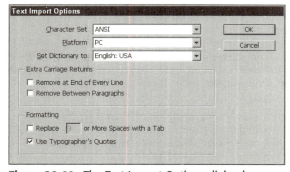

Figure 20-11: The Text Import Options dialog box

Drag and drop text files

Dragging and dropping Word files from the Finder (Mac) or from Windows Explorer also opens text into Illustrator, InDesign, or GoLive.

Importing Word documents in Photoshop

Of all the Creative Suite applications, Photoshop is one of the more popular. Many designers are so comfortable with Photoshop that they choose to create layouts including the extensive use of text in Photoshop rather than InDesign or Illustrator. For these designers, this section covers importing Microsoft Word into Photoshop.

If you copy and paste text from Word into Photoshop, it appears as a graphic image with all its formatting in place. This is fine, but it requires that you make all the edits in Word, which leaves you with only Word's design features.

A better way to handle the import process is to create a text layer in Photoshop by dragging a bounding box with the Type tool before pasting the Word text. With the text bounding box selected, the pasted text appears as editable text in the text bounding box. The drawback to this approach is that all the formatting is stripped from the Word text, but you can still use Photoshop's type formatting tools. Figure 20-12 shows some text that has been imported into a Photoshop text object from Word.

Tip   If you hold down the Option/Alt key while dragging with the Type tool, a dialog box appears where you can enter exact width and height values for the paragraph.

Figure 20-12: You can edit text from Word in a text object in Photoshop.

You can also import Word text into a Point text object. You create Point text objects by simply clicking in the document rather than dragging an area. Be warned that importing text into a Point text object won't limit the text within an area but places an entire line of text (up to a paragraph return) on a single line. All paragraph returns in the pasted text wraps the text to a new line.

More details on creating text layers and Point text objects are in Part IV.

Formatting imported text in Photoshop

When you import text into a Photoshop text layer, you use the Type tool to select and edit the text. Clicking once on the text object text with the Type tool selects the text layer. When the text layer is selected, you can drag with the mouse over the text to select words or characters. The selected text is highlighted. Clicking twice selects a word, clicking three times selects an entire line of text, clicking four times selects an entire paragraph, and clicking five times selects all the text in the text layer.

Pressing the Delete key deletes any selected text, and typing new text replaces the selected text with the newly typed text. Any characters that you add to the text use the same formatting as the existing text area.

Selected text is formatted using the Character palette, which is opened by choosing Window ➪ Character. With this palette, you can change the text font, style, size, leading, kerning, scale, color, and anti-aliasing.

Paragraph formatting such as text alignment, indentation, and paragraph spacing is set for the selected paragraph in the Paragraph palette, which is accessed by choosing Window ➪ Paragraph.

Pasting Word text in Acrobat

Acrobat is typically used to turn Word documents into PDF files by choosing File ➪ Create PDF. If you've converted a Word document to a PDF file and then found some minimal edits that need to be made, you can use the TouchUp Text tool to edit the PDF document. If major text edits are required, you should make the edits within Word and then you should regenerate the PDF document.

You can only edit text within a PDF file with the TouchUp Text tool if the font you used to create the PDF file is installed on your system or embedded within the PDF document.

When using the TouchUp Text tool, you can copy and paste text from within Word. To do this, choose Tools ➪ Advanced Editing ➪ TouchUp Text Tool to select the TouchUp Text tool. Then select the text that you want to edit and press Delete to delete the selected text, type new text to replace the selected text, or choose Edit ➪ Paste (⌘/Ctrl+V) to paste text copied from Word.

You can also use the TouchUp Text tool to add new portions of text to the existing PDF document. With the TouchUp Text tool selected, hold down the Option/Ctrl key and click the position where you want to place the new text. A dialog box appears, shown in Figure 20-13, letting you select a font face to use for the new text. Clicking OK creates a text object with "New Text" selected in it.

Figure 20-13: The New Text Font dialog box lets you select a font face.

With the new text object selected, you can type new text to replace this text or paste text from Word by choosing Edit ⇨ Paste. Text pasted from Word loses its formatting and uses the selected font face. The pasted text also loses all its line returns, but you can easily place these back in with the TouchUp Text tool. The line returns are easy to identify because they're replaced with a character (often just a simple square). Selecting each square character with the TouchUp Text tool and pressing the Enter key reformats the pasted text.

If you need to move the newly created text object, you can select the TouchUp Object tool by choosing Tools ⇨ Advanced Editing. This tool lets you select and move text objects by clicking and dragging with the mouse.

This process requires some additional work, but if you don't have the original document, then it's worth the trouble if you need to add some text. Figure 20-14 shows a PDF file where some new text has been pasted from Word using the Option/Ctrl+TouchUp Text tool. When the text was pasted, it all appeared on a single line.

Figure 20-14: You can paste new text into an existing PDF file using the TouchUp Text tool.

Pasting Word text into Acrobat notes and form fields

When reviewing and commenting a PDF file, you can create notes with the Note tool. Choose Tools ➪ Commenting ➪ Note Tool to select this tool and then click and drag at the location in the PDF document where you want to place a note. A note box appears that includes the creator's name and the time and date. Figure 20-15 shows a single commenting note. Typing enters the text for these note boxes, or you may paste the note text from Word by choosing Edit ➪ Paste.

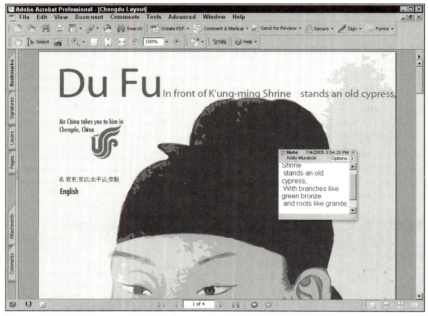

Figure 20-15: You can add Note boxes to a PDF document with the Note tool.

In addition to pasting text in note boxes, you can also paste Word text into form fields that appear within the PDF document. You can use Tab and Shift+Tab to move forward and backward between form fields on a page. When a form field is selected, you may type the text or paste text from Word.

Cross-Reference Text that is pasted into Acrobat can be edited with the TouchUp Text Tool. A good example of this tool is found in Chapter 20.

Importing Styles

When importing text files into InDesign, the styles are also imported as determined by the import settings. All imported styles from Microsoft Word appear in the Paragraph Styles palette using the same style name. The imported styles are also identified by a small disk icon to the right of the style's name, as shown in Figure 20-16.

Figure 20-16: Placing a Word document within InDesign automatically imports the Word styles into the Paragraph Styles palette.

Cross-Reference Using text styles in Illustrator and InDesign is covered in Chapter 17.

You can prevent the styles from being imported by enabling the Remove Styles and Formatting from Text and Tables option in the Microsoft Word Import Options dialog box. If the Preserve Styles and Formatting from Text and Tables option is enabled, styles are also imported when text is pasted from Word using the designated settings. The Import Options settings take precedence over the application preferences set in the Type panel of the Preferences dialog box.

Note If the imported style has the same name as an existing InDesign style, the style is not imported from Word, and the text is formatted using the InDesign style.

Editing imported styles

In the Paragraph Styles palette, click on a style to select it. Then choose Style Options from the palette menu (or you could right-click on the style and choose Edit from the pop-up menu). This action opens the Paragraph Style Options dialog box, shown in Figure 20-17. Using these options, you set the paragraph formatting style options.

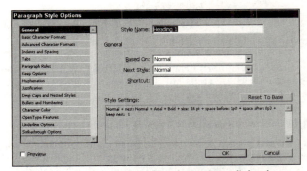

Figure 20-17: The Paragraph Style Options dialog box

Deleting imported styles

The Paragraph Styles palette menu includes several useful commands. When a layout is complete, use the Select All Unused menu command to instantly select all the styles that aren't referenced in the document. These styles, whether native or imported, are then deleted with the Delete Style menu command. Deleting unused styles is an easy way to clean up a document, especially if text has been imported from Word.

Mapping Word styles to InDesign styles

If you select the Custom Style Import option in the Microsoft Word Import Options dialog box, the Style Mapping button becomes active. Clicking this button opens the Style Mapping dialog box shown in Figure 20-18. The Style Mapping dialog box includes two lists of styles, one for the Word styles and one for the InDesign styles. For each imported Word style, you can select an InDesign style to map the Word style to.

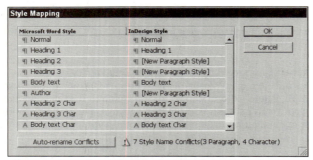

Figure 20-18: The Style Mapping dialog box

At the bottom of the Style Mapping dialog box is a count of the style name conflicts. Clicking the Auto-rename Conflicts automatically maps all the conflicted style names with the Auto Rename option. Once imported the auto rename styles are appended with "wrd_1" on the end of the style making them easy to identify and rename in the Paragraph Styles palette.

Once all the work to map styles has been completed, you can use the Save Preset button on the Microsoft Word Import Options dialog box to save the import options including the style mapping to a file that can be recalled for another file using the drop-down list at the top of the dialog box.

Working with Imported Text

As a final working example of the process of importing and using Microsoft Word documents, we'll walk you through the steps involved. These steps are similar for both Illustrator and InDesign, with only slight differences between the two.

STEPS: Importing Microsoft Word Text into InDesign

1. **Open the DOC document in Word.** Figure 20-19 shows a Word document that includes all the text for a poem. Using the features of Word, the document has been spell-checked and grammar-checked, and all edits are ready to be moved to InDesign.

Chapter 20 ✦ Importing Microsoft Word Documents

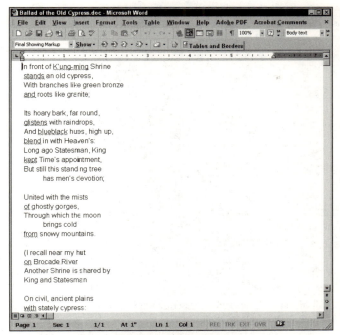

Figure 20-19: Open a Word document.

2. **Save the Word document.** Choose File ➪ Save As in Word and save the file using the default DOC file format. This format includes all the referenced styles. After you save the file, close the Word file by choosing File ➪ Close.

Caution

If you forget to close the Word document within Windows, InDesign opens an alert dialog box stating "This file is already in use by another application," when you try to place the Word document in InDesign. The same alert doesn't seem to happen on Macintosh systems.

3. **Open the current InDesign file.** If you already have a start on the layout, open the existing file in InDesign by choosing File ➪ Open.

4. **Place the text file in InDesign.** Choose File ➪ Place (⌘/Ctrl+D) to open the Place dialog box. Make sure Show Import Options is enabled; then select the Word document and click the Open button.

5. **Set the import options.** In the Microsoft Word Import Options dialog box, shown in Figure 20-20, you can disable the Table of Contents Text, Footnotes and Endnotes, and Index Text options because none of these elements are included in the original document. Also, make sure the Preserve Styles and Formatting from Text and Tables option is enabled. Notice how two paragraph style conflicts have been identified in the Import Options dialog box. Select the Import Styles Automatically option and set the Paragraph Style Conflicts setting to Auto Rename. Click OK to proceed.

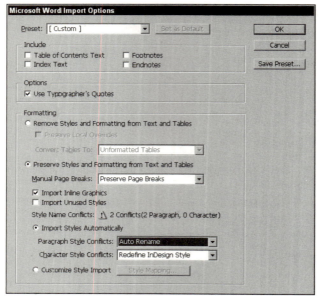

Figure 20-20: All of the Include options are disabled because they aren't included in the original document.

6. **Locate the missing fonts.** When the import options are set, the import process proceeds and a Missing Fonts dialog box appears, as shown in Figure 20-21. The dialog box lists all the fonts used in the Word document that aren't available to InDesign. Click the Find Font button to open the Find Font dialog box, shown in Figure 20-22. Using this dialog box, locate and change the missing fonts. The Find Next button locates the first instance of text in the InDesign document that uses the specified font. Click Done when you're finished.

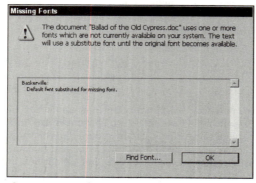

Figure 20-21: The Missing Fonts dialog box

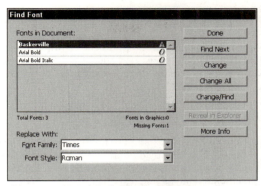

Figure 20-22: The Find Font dialog box

7. **Place the text into the InDesign document.** The cursor holds the imported text. Click at the location in the InDesign document where you want to place the imported text. Notice how the Word styles have been imported into InDesign and now appear in the Paragraph Styles palette, as shown in Figure 20-23.

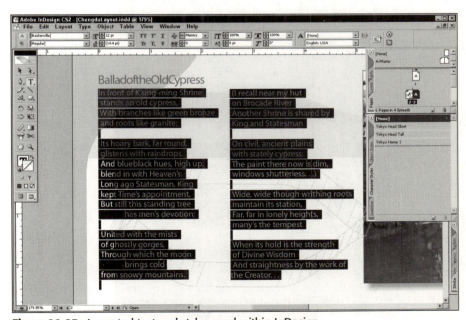

Figure 20-23: Imported text and styles used within InDesign

Moving Word Content to GoLive

Text for Web pages can start out in Word, but if you don't follow the right path, it could end up being a real mess. Although Microsoft Word can save text files as an HTML document, Word files saved using the HTML format include many unnecessary markup tags recognized only by Word.

Using the Clipboard for Web page text

The best way to move text from Word to GoLive is to use the Clipboard. Simply copy the selected text to the Clipboard by choosing Edit ⇨ Copy and choose Edit ⇨ Paste to paste it in its desired location in GoLive. For most cases, this is sufficient, but be aware that the text will flow around the existing Web page elements such as images.

Using the Paste Special command

If you need more control over the pasted text, you can choose Edit ⇨ Paste Special in GoLive. This opens the Paste Special dialog box shown in Figure 20-24. This dialog box gives you the options to paste the clipboard text as Plain Text, Unstyled Text, Styled Text, HTML, Cleared HTML, or as an Image. If the Plain Text option is selected, each line break can be specified as a Space, Line Break, or a Paragraph, and Two consecutive Line Breaks create a paragraph.

Figure 20-24: The Paste Special dialog box in GoLive

The Paste Special menu is only available in GoLive's Layout view and not in the Source view. Pasting with the HTML option converts simple styles such as bold and italics to their HTML equivalents, but it can add some unneeded markup depending on the formatting of the text. A better choice is to use the Cleared HTML option, which includes only the bare minimum markup to maintain the text styles. If you switch to the Source view in GoLive, you can see the markup that is added to the text.

Opening text files

GoLive can also import text files by choosing File ➪ Open. By changing the Files of Type setting in the Open Document dialog box, you can choose to open .HTML files and TXT files. HTML and TXT files open directly within the GoLive editor, but for TXT files the Layout, Source, Outline and Preview views are all the same, shown in Figure 20-25. From this viewer, you can copy and paste text into the open GoLive pages, but all formatting is lost when you do this.

Figure 20-25: Text files can be opened in the code editor.

Summary

✦ A word processor like Microsoft Word makes a good workflow piece for creating importable text.

✦ Text in Word may be easily copied and pasted into all of the CS2 applications.

✦ Illustrator can open and InDesign can place existing Word documents using Word's native DOC file format. The Rich Text Format (RTF) and Plain Text (TXT) file formats are also available.

✦ Text styles defined in Microsoft Word are also imported and show up in the Paragraph Styles palette in InDesign.

✦ GoLive also includes methods for opening text and HTML files from Word.

✦ ✦ ✦

Exporting Text to Microsoft Word

In This Chapter

Exporting text using the Clipboard

Exporting text using export commands

Exporting Acrobat comments to Word

Updating text in layouts

Although CS2 includes many programs that can work with type or text (which you can learn about in Part IV), a word processor is not included as part of the suite. Text for design purposes is very different from text produced with a word processor, but there are times in your design workflow when you want to export text from CS2 applications into a word processor.

Writing copy is often much easier in a word processor because its features focus on manipulating text rather than design. For example, Microsoft Word includes a grammar checker that benefits longer sections of text. You can take advantage of this feature by exporting text to a word processor, checking its grammar, and then importing it again.

Of the available word processors, Microsoft Word is the most popular. Most word processors available today have similar features, so we focus only on Word in this chapter. We also cover the text-export features found in the CS2 applications that enable you to move text to Microsoft Word and the other Office applications.

Exporting Text

The chapters in Part IV focused on creating text within the Creative Suite applications, and the last chapter covered importing text. This chapter completes the topic by discussing how to export text from the various CS2 applications to Microsoft Word.

Cross-Reference Part IV covers creating text within the CS2 applications. Importing text from Word is covered in Chapter 20.

Before we discuss the techniques used in exporting text, we need to discuss the purpose behind exporting text. The first question to ask yourself is this: With all the power found in Creative Suite, why would you want to export text to an application like Microsoft Word? The answer lies in Word's ability to do what it does best — create text documents.

Recognizing the advantages of Word

Many of the features found in Word are out of place in the Creative Suite applications. Here is a list of some of the Microsoft Word features of which you can take advantage when working with large portions of text:

+ **Outline mode:** Word can view documents in several different modes including Normal, Web Layout, Print Layout, and Outline. The layout modes are a far cry from the features found in Illustrator, Photoshop, and InDesign, but the Outline mode is very helpful for organizing a table of contents or a large structured list of items. In Word's Outline mode, you can quickly promote and demote headings and rearrange entire structures by dragging.

+ **Headers, footers, and footnotes:** Word's ability to automatically create and adjust headers, footers, and footnotes is much easier to use than anything you find in Creative Suite (although anchored text in InDesign works better for inline graphics and sidebars).

+ **AutoCorrect:** Word's AutoCorrect feature is very helpful as you type long sections of text. Because this feature can automatically capitalize the first letter of a sentence makes it worth the trouble to export the text into Word. With some fine-tuning, the AutoCorrect feature saves many keystrokes, allowing you to finish a document in less time.

+ **Interactive spelling and grammar check:** Word underlines all misspelled words in red and all grammatical errors in green as you type. This immediate feedback lets you fix the problems as you type, which offers a benefit over the spell-check features found in the CS2 applications.

 InDesign CS2 includes dynamic spell-check features.

This short list isn't exhaustive, nor does it do justice to the plethora of features found in Word, but it gives you a brief idea of the types of features that you can take advantage of by exporting to Word.

Identifying exporting methods

All the CS2 applications deal with text, and all can export text to Word. There are essentially three different methods for exporting text from the various CS2 applications and each of these methods has its advantages and disadvantages:

+ **Copy and paste to the Clipboard:** Most CS2 applications can take advantage of this feature. By selecting text objects or portions of text, you can cut (⌘/Ctrl+X) or copy (⌘/Ctrl+C) them to the system Clipboard and then paste (⌘/Ctrl+V) them into the Word document.

+ **Using an export command:** Several applications include a File ⇨ Export command that you can use to export the text from the source application to Word.

+ **Save to an importable file:** The final method is to save the text using a text-file format (such as TXT or RTF) that you can import into Word.

Selecting text

Before exporting any text to Word, you need to locate and select the text that you want to move. For most CS2 applications, you select text using the Type tool. To select text, just click the Type tool and drag over the text that you want to select. The selected text is highlighted.

Illustrator and InDesign use text objects. If a text object is selected with the Selection tool, the borders that make up the text object are highlighted using its layer color and all text contained within the text object is selected. If multiple text objects are selected, all text contained within the selected text objects is selected.

Exporting formatting

Through the exporting process, the text formatting is often lost. Some techniques maintain formatting and others do not. Copy and pasting via the Clipboard typically discards formatting. Exporting text using the TXT file format also discards formatting. If you need to keep the formatting intact, look to export the text using the Rich Text Format (RTF), which maintains the formatting during export.

Tip   If you lose your formatting during an export, keep track of the changes that you make to the text in Word, and manually enter those changes into the formatted text in the CS2 application.

In some cases, the export command offers you the chance to specify the font standard. If you have a choice, use the OpenType font standard, which has the same font file for both Windows and Mac computers. This lets you maintain your fonts as you export them, regardless of the system to which you export them.

Cross-Reference   You can learn more about the OpenType font standard in Chapter 16.

Using the Clipboard

The easiest way to export smaller pieces of text from the CS2 applications is to use the Clipboard. Although the Clipboard can handle large sections of text, it relies on the amount of available memory.

The Office Clipboard can copy many pieces of text to the Clipboard at a time (up to 24 by default). You can then select these different pieces from the Office Clipboard and paste them into the current Word document. You can make the Office Clipboard, shown at the right in Figure 21-1, appear by choosing Edit ⇨ Office Clipboard or by pressing ⌘/Ctrl+C twice. After you select text, simply click on it to paste it into the current document. Right-click on the text to reveal a pop-up menu with a Delete option.

Note   The Office Clipboard menu is a Windows-only feature.

Moving Illustrator, Photoshop, and GoLive text into Word

Selected text within Illustrator is copied to the Clipboard by choosing Edit ⇨ Cut (⌘/Ctrl+X) or Edit ⇨ Copy (⌘/Ctrl+X). This moves the selected text to the Clipboard. From the Clipboard, text is pasted into Word by choosing Edit ⇨ Paste (⌘/Ctrl+V).

Caution   You can only paste text that you cut or copy from an Illustrator document into Word as unformatted text. Text you copy from InDesign and Acrobat maintains its formatting.

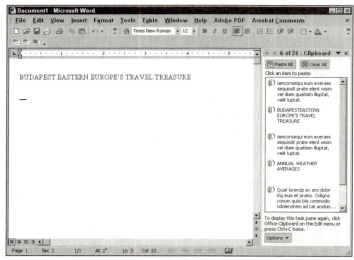

Figure 21-1: Items on the Office Clipboard are placed within Word simply by clicking on them.

Word also includes an Edit ⇨ Paste Special menu command that opens the dialog box shown in Figure 21-2. This dialog box identifies the source application and allows you to paste the Clipboard contents as unformatted text, several image formats, or unformatted Unicode text. Text that you save on the Clipboard cannot be saved as an image using the Paste Special command.

Caution

Be aware that any text that you export to Word loses its positional constraints, such as wrapping around images or type on a path.

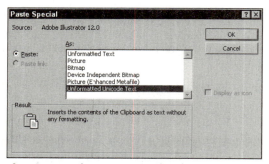

Figure 21-2: The Paste Special dialog box identifies the source application and offers several paste choices based on that application.

You move text in Photoshop to Word using the same Clipboard technique discussed for Illustrator in this section. The only exception is that you must select the text using Photoshop's Type tool. You also move text from GoLive using the Clipboard without formatting.

Moving InDesign text to Word

You move formatted text in InDesign to Microsoft Word using the Copy and Paste features. The standard Copy and Paste features retain the formatting created in InDesign.

Caution In order to copy text in InDesign to the Clipboard, you need to select the Type tool and drag over the text. You can't just select the text object as you can in Illustrator.

Within Word, you can also choose Edit ⇨ Paste Special. This action opens the Paste Special dialog box, shown in Figure 21-3, which includes the same options as those for Illustrator, except it can handle RTF text.

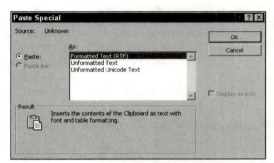

Figure 21-3: The Paste Special dialog box offers several options for pasting text as formatted text, unformatted text, or unformatted Unicode text.

Moving Acrobat text to Word

You select text in Acrobat using the Select Text tool. You can then cut or copy the selected text to the Clipboard by choosing Edit ⇨ Cut (⌘/Ctrl+X) or Edit ⇨ Copy (⌘/Ctrl+C). Acrobat also offers an option to copy an entire file to the Clipboard, Edit ⇨ Copy File to Clipboard.

The Edit ⇨ Paste Special command in Word opens the same dialog box as the one shown in Figure 21-3, including the option to paste as formatted text.

Object Linking and Embedding (Windows only)

Another exporting option is to create a link between the content created in a CS2 application and Microsoft Word using a technology known as Object Linking and Embedding (OLE). However, object linking works only with image content, not with text.

CS applications — including Photoshop, Illustrator, and InDesign — can act as an OLE 2.0 server. This allows you to copy and paste a piece of content into Word using the Paste Special menu command. This action causes the Paste Special dialog box to appear with a Paste Link option, which lets you paste an object as a recognized CS2 object. After you paste the object, you can double-click on the object in the Word document to load it within the native CS2 application for more editing. Changes made to the object are automatically forwarded back to the object in the Word document, thereby keeping the two in sync. You can force the documents to update by choosing File ⇨ Update.

Using Export Menu Commands

When it comes to moving entire documents, the Clipboard isn't the best choice. Instead, you should rely on the export menu commands, typically found in the File menu. These export commands let you save CS2 documents to a format that is easily imported into Word.

Caution Be aware that text in Photoshop is exported via the Clipboard only.

Exporting Illustrator text

You export text from Illustrator by choosing File ⇨ Export and using the TXT format, but be aware that you lose all formatting applied to the text in Illustrator. All text included in an Illustrator document is exported to a single text file by choosing File ⇨ Export. If you select a text object, multiple text objects, or text within a text object, only the selected text exports.

The File ⇨ Export menu command opens an Export dialog box, like the one shown in Figure 21-4. The Save as Type pull-down menu includes many different file formats that you can use to export the existing document, but only the TXT format makes the text editable within Word.

Figure 21-4: The Export dialog box

After clicking Export (Mac) or Save (Windows), another dialog box, shown in Figure 21-5, opens. This dialog box lets you specify the Platform as PC or Mac, as well as the Encoding standard to use. The Encoding options are Default Platform and Unicode. If the text you're exporting includes any foreign text or any special glyphs, use the Unicode Encoding option.

Note The File ⇨ Export command exports all visible text objects, even if the text within those text areas isn't visible. However, hidden text objects in the document are not exported.

Figure 21-5: The Text Export Options dialog box

When the exported text file is opened in Word, the File Conversion dialog box appears, shown in Figure 21-6, if an encoding standard other than the default platform is used. This dialog box includes a Preview window that shows the text before you open it.

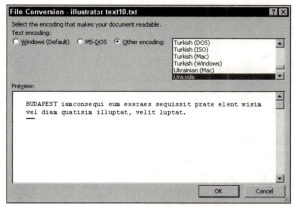

Figure 21-6: The File Conversion dialog box

Illustrator includes tight integration with Microsoft Office using the File ⇨ Save for Microsoft Office menu command. Be aware that this command saves the Illustrator document as a PNG image file that you can import into Word, but you can't edit any of the text.

Exporting text from InDesign

InDesign includes an Export command under the File menu that exports formatted text to a number of different formats. To export text, you must first select the text within a text object using the Type tool. If you don't select specific text, the Rich Text Format and Text Only options are not available as file types in the Export dialog box.

When exporting from InDesign, each story exports as a separate document.

Choosing File ⇨ Export in InDesign gives you the options to export the current file using the following formats: Adobe InDesign Tagged Text, Adobe PDF, EPS, InDesign Interchange, JPEG, Rich Text Format (RTF), SVG, SVG Compressed, Text Only, and XML. Note that only the RTF format and the Text Only format are used to import text into Word

If you export text from InDesign using a format other than RTF or Text Only, the file includes a lot of additional mark-up information that you probably don't want to see. For example, Figure 21-7 shows the File Conversion dialog box that opens in Word when an InDesign document exported using the SVG format is opened. Notice in the Preview pane how the XML syntax is visible. If you scroll down further in the document, you'll find a lot of gibberish that Word was unsuccessful in converting.

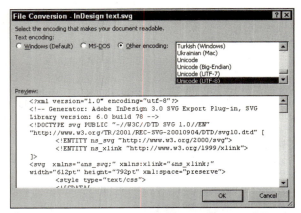

Figure 21-7: You can use Word to see the raw XML exported from InDesign.

Exporting text from Acrobat

Choosing File ➪ Save As from within Acrobat lets you save the current PDF file using a number of different formats, many of which are suitable for moving text to Word including Word's default format (DOC). The Rich Text Format (RTF) and Text Only (TXT) formats are options also.

Note
By default, any images contained within a PDF file that you save as a Word document is saved using the JPEG format. However, you can select the PNG format in the Settings dialog box if you prefer.

In Acrobat's file dialog box, you can click the Settings button, which opens the Save As Settings dialog box. The Save As DOC Settings dialog box is shown in Figure 21-8. The Settings dialog box for RTF is the same as that for the DOC format.

Figure 21-8: The Save As DOC Settings dialog box

Batch-converting files in Word

If you have a large number of documents that you've exported to Rich Text Format and that you want to convert to Word documents, you can use Word's Batch Conversion Wizard. To access this wizard in Word, choose File ➪ New (⌘/Ctrl+N), and click on the General Templates link. In the Templates dialog box that opens, select the Other Documents tab and double-click on the Batch Conversion Wizard icon.

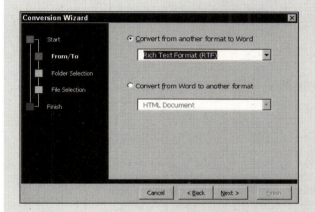

This action launches the Conversion Wizard, shown in the figure. Following the wizard steps, you can select the format to convert from and the format to convert to along with Source and Destination directories. The following figure shows the Conversion Wizard dialog box, which walks you through the batch-conversion process. The Conversion Wizard is available only in Word for Windows.

In the Settings dialog box, you can choose to include comments and/or images. The Settings dialog box also includes options to Retain Columns and Retain Page Size and Margin. You can also downsample the image resolutions, which is a good idea if you're exporting to Word to check just the text. You may also want to keep the text files small by specifying Grayscale as the Colorspace. PDF files that were saved in Acrobat using the RTF format that are subsequently imported into Word are easy to identify because each piece of content is separated from the others by a section break.

Exporting comments from Acrobat

In addition to moving text to Word, Acrobat also offers an option to export all comments in the Acrobat document to Word. Choosing Comments ➪ Export Comments ➪ to Word from within Acrobat causes an information dialog box, shown in Figure 21-9, to appear. This information dialog box explains the procedure for importing comments from a PDF file. Within the Export Comments menu are also options to export comments to AutoCAD and to File.

Exporting comments to Word is only available in Acrobat running on Windows XP with Office 2002 or greater installed. Comment exports to Word are not available on the Mac.

Batch-converting files in Acrobat

You can also use Acrobat to convert a large number of Acrobat files to Word or RTF files using the Batch Sequences dialog box. You can access this dialog box (which is available only within Acrobat Professional) by choosing Advanced ⇨ Batch Processing.

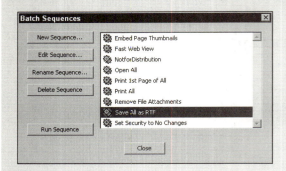

The Batch Sequences dialog box, shown in the figure, includes a predefined batch command called Save All as RTF. Selecting this command and clicking Run Sequence executes the command, allowing you to select the files you want to convert. The Batch Sequence dialog box includes a number of predefined commands, but you can also create a new sequence of commands or edit an existing one.

Clicking New Sequence or Edit Sequence lets you create a different set of commands for execution. For more information on using the Batch Sequence commands, see Chapter 15.

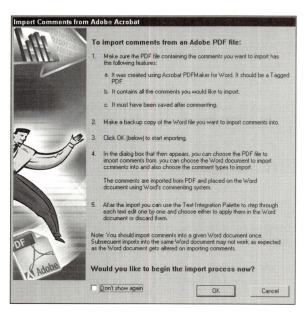

Figure 21-9: This information dialog box explains how to proceed with the import process.

Before you can export comments to Word, you must be certain to use the proper comment tools. The Text Edit tools are designed to mark text for insertions, deletions, underlines, strikethroughs, and so on that are exported to Word. If you know that you're going to export your comments to Word, be certain to inform all users in your workflow to use these tools. Inasmuch as Mac users can't export comments to Word, the Text Edit tools are available in Acrobat on the Mac and comments you make with these tools can be exported to Word from Acrobat running on Windows XP.

 Cross-Reference For more information on using commenting tools, including the Text Edit tools, see Chapter 25.

Using this menu command opens Word and presents the Import Comments from Adobe Acrobat dialog box, shown in Figure 21-10. Selecting a source PDF file and a destination DOC file and clicking Continue moves all the comments from the Acrobat file to the Word file. This dialog box also gives you options to export All Comments, All Comments with Checkmarks, or the Text Edits Only. The Text Edits Only option includes only the text that has been edited with the Commenting toolbar. You can also select to turn on Word's Track Changes feature.

Note The Exporting Comments to Word command can also be initiated from within Word using the Adobe Comments ⇨ Import Comments from Acrobat menu command. This command uses the same dialog boxes as the command in Acrobat.

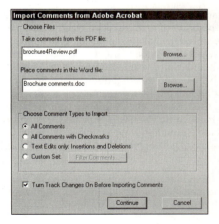

Figure 21-10: The Import Comments from Adobe Acrobat dialog box

The dialog box shown in Figure 21-11 appears if the import has been successful. It tells you the number of placed comments.

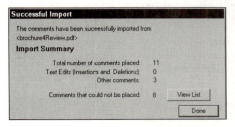

Figure 21-11: The Successful Import dialog box shows the results of the import.

After you move the comments to Word, you can use the Acrobat Comments menu to review the changes, accept or delete all changes, and enable the Reviewing toolbar.

Dynamic Text Editing

Exporting text from one of the CS2 programs is typically an exercise where you need to get copy back to Microsoft Word, create changes in the copy, and import the text back to your original design. The most likely candidates for this activity are Illustrator and InDesign. Unless you want to burden yourself with clumsy typesetting tools and extraordinary file sizes, you'll stay away from Photoshop.

Reintroducing type in an existing design can mean quite a bit of work. If the edits are extensive, you may need to delete long passages of text and then reformat pages in InDesign after importing the edited text. For Illustrator files, you have to deal only with single pages, but the complexity of the design could be quite complicated and take some time to rework the text.

Ideally, you're best bet is to recompose a layout when you need to make major edits. However, in some circumstances, you may have moderate to light modifications to make in layouts. If you exported documents to PDF and need to make text changes, you need to return to the original authoring program, make your edits, and re-create the PDF document. In some workflows, this is a simple task, especially if all the native files are easily accessible. However, if you have only a PDF document and don't have access to the native application document, you may want to use another method by editing text and let the text edits dynamically change the PDF file.

Dynamic text editing is handled in Adobe Illustrator when text is targeted for editing from within Acrobat. You start in Acrobat and select the body of text you want to edit with the TouchUp Object tool. Click on the text line to be edited or marquee a paragraph, multiple paragraphs, or an entire page. When the text is selected, open a context menu and choose Edit Object. Alternately, you can press Option/Alt and double-click on the selected objects. This action launches Illustrator CS2 and opens the selected text in a document window. Unfortunately, the text is broken up in Illustrator and all paragraph formatting including word wrap is lost. To reform the paragraphs, select all the text and click the Type tool in the document page at the same location where the first character in the first line of text was before you cut it. Then cut the text with the Edit ➪ Cut menu command. When the I-beam cursor starts blinking, choose Edit ➪ Paste. The text may need a little tweaking, but the paragraph formatting including word wrap is regained.

To update a PDF document after making such edits in Illustrator, choose File ➪ Save. Be certain you don't use Save As and write the file using a new filename. The current document has a link to the PDF file. When you choose Save and return to Acrobat, the text is dynamically updated.

Caution Be certain you have all the type fonts used in the original document loaded on your system before attempting to edit text externally in Illustrator. Also, check your work very carefully. Some edits may not be accurate, especially when you attempt to edit text with transparency and other forms of stylized fonts.

This process seems a little complicated, but after you've made a few text edits, you won't find it difficult to repeat. To illustrate the process further, look over the following steps where text is edited in Illustrator and dynamically updated in Acrobat.

STEPS: Dynamically Updating Text in PDF Documents

1. **Open a PDF document in Acrobat.** In Figure 21-12, a document is opened in Acrobat. The type on a path needs to be edited for text changes, eliminating the drop shadow, and changing the text color. You could try to edit the text in Acrobat, but with text on a path, the results can often be unsatisfactory. Furthermore, eliminating the drop shadow can't be accomplished using the TouchUp Text tool. A document like this needs to have the text edited in an external editor.

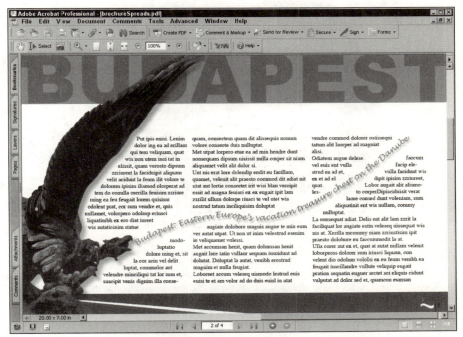

Figure 21-12: Open a document in Acrobat where you want to edit text.

2. **Select the text needing editing.** Selecting the text you want to edit can at times be a challenge. You can edit the entire page, but often you'll find it best to select just the text you want to edit. In this example, it makes sense to select the text columns and the text on a path together because it makes the task of selecting the text on a path much easier. To select the text shown in Figure 21-13, marquee through the text with the TouchUp Object tool. If you select other objects not needed for the edits, press the Shift key and click on selected objects to deselect them.

3. **Open the text in Illustrator.** From a context menu, open the selected text. Choose Edit Objects from the menu commands. Alternately, you can press Option/Alt and double-click the selected text. (Be certain the TouchUp Object tool is used with either the context menu or the double mouse click.) Acrobat initiates the Illustrator CS2 launch, and the selected text is opened in a new document window.

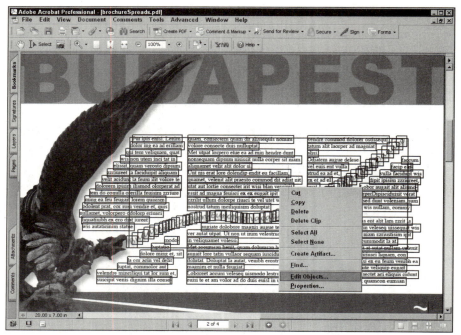

Figure 21-13: You select multiple objects with the TouchUp Object tool.

Depending on how your text was formatted, you may see some warning dialog boxes open, informing you that tags must be eliminated and the appearance of the page may appear different. Click Yes in the dialog boxes and the file eventually opens in Illustrator.

4. **Select all the text.** Press ⌘/Ctrl+A to select all. Notice the selected objects in Figure 21-14. For the text columns, the selected text is broken and Illustrator interprets each line of text as a separate paragraph. For the text on a path, the text is broken at each character, making the line of text very difficult to edit.

5. **Hide the text that won't be edited.** In this example, the text columns won't be edited. To eliminate the text from view so you can easily work with only the text you want to edit, click the text and press ⌘/Ctrl+3. The keyboard shortcut hides selected text. Continue selecting and hiding text until only the text to be edited remains in view.

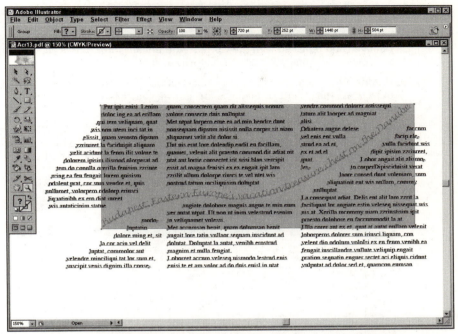

Figure 21-14: Select all objects and you can easily see where text is broken up.

6. **Lock the text in view.** Press ⌘/Ctrl+A to select all text and press ⌘/Ctrl+2 to lock the selected text. The text is temporarily locked so you won't disturb it while creating a path.

7. **Draw a new path to match the path of the existing text.** Select the Pen tool and draw a path following the same general path shape as the text along the path you want to edit.

Cross-Reference

Chapter 10 includes details on using Illustrator's Pen tool.

8. **Unlock the locked text and cut and paste it to the Clipboard.** Press Ctrl+Alt+2 (⌘+Option+2 on the Mac) to unlock text. As you unlock the text, the text is selected, while the stroke you just created is deselected. Choose Edit ➪ Cut or press ⌘/Ctrl+X to cut the selected text to the Clipboard.

9. **Paste and edit the text on a path.** Select the Type tool and click on the path. Press ⌘/Ctrl+V to paste the text. The text is pasted on the path and the line of text is unbroken, as shown in Figure 21-15. Edit the text as desired. In this example, the colon was removed and replaced with the word *is*. Additionally, the color is changed and the drop shadow was eliminated when the text was opened in Illustrator.

10. **Unhide all objects.** Press Ctrl+Alt+3 (⌘+Option+3 on the Mac) to show all hidden objects. As the other text columns are shown, you can see the new text on a path edited in relation to the other objects. See Figure 21-16 as an example.

11. **Save your edits.** Be certain to choose File ⇨ Save and not Save As. When you save the file, you update the temporary document, which is a link to the Acrobat PDF. Close Illustrator and your Acrobat view should show the updated file, as shown in Figure 21-17.

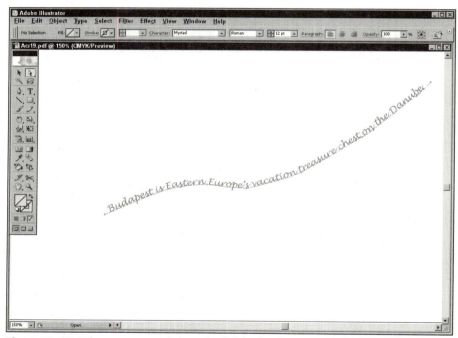

Figure 21-15: When you paste the text back into the Illustrator document, all the text is re-formed into a single paragraph. The former broken text at each character is pasted back as one object, making editing much easier.

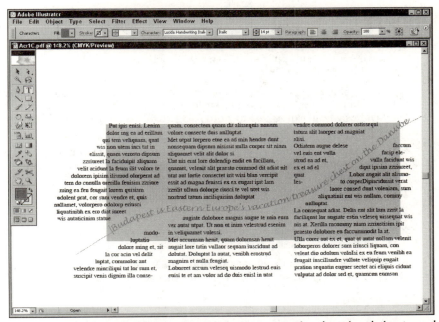

Figure 21-16: When all objects are in view, you can examine them in relation to each other. When everything looks fine, save the file.

Figure 21-17: After saving, maximize Acrobat or bring it into view, and the edited elements are dynamically updated in the open PDF file.

Summary

- Many Creative Suite applications can export text to Microsoft Word using several different methods. Some applications can export only the plain text, and others can export text with formatting intact.

- One common method for exporting text to Word is to use the Clipboard. Illustrator and Photoshop can export text to Word using the Clipboard without formatting, but Acrobat and InDesign can export text to Word using Rich Text Format (RTF) with formatting intact.

- Using export commands enables you to move text from Illustrator to Word without formatting, from InDesign to Word with formatting, and from Acrobat natively to the Word (DOC) format.

- You can export comments in Acrobat to Word directly using the File ⇨ Export Comments to Word menu command (Windows only).

- You can dynamically update text in Acrobat by selecting objects with the TouchUp Object tool and selecting Edit Objects from a context menu.

- Text object editing is handled in Illustrator CS2. When editing objects such as type from a PDF file, be certain to save the edits to dynamically update the PDF file.

✦ ✦ ✦

Working with Tables

CHAPTER 22

In This Chapter

Importing tables created in Microsoft Word and Excel

Creating and using InDesign tables

Creating and using GoLive tables

One common way to present data is in tabular format. Tables orient data into rows and columns. The intersection of each row and column is called a *cell*. Cells can hold text, images, or even another table. The format applied to a table is typically consistent across all the cells that make up the table.

Tables created in external applications such as Microsoft Word or Excel may be imported into CS2 applications such as InDesign, Illustrator, and GoLive. The Clipboard is often used to move tables between applications.

In addition to importing tables, InDesign supports tables and can create its own tables using a table object. InDesign includes table features for adding rows and columns, merging cells and creating a table from a tab-delimited text file. Individual cells are formatted in a number of ways including alignment, cell strokes and fills, and evenly distributed cells.

GoLive can also create tables based on HTML. Although most of the table-formatting options in GoLive are the same as tables in InDesign, there are some differences between the two.

Importing Tables

InDesign, Illustrator, and GoLive can create tables natively, but tables can also be imported from external packages like Microsoft Word and Microsoft Excel.

Importing Microsoft Word tables

Microsoft Word has a fairly robust table-creation feature allowing you to create tables by simply drawing them. Tables created in Word are moved into the CS2 applications by copying the table onto the Clipboard and pasting it into the target application.

Before a table is copied to the Clipboard, the cells that you want to move must be selected. Selecting table cells in Word is as easy as dragging over the cells with the mouse. All selected cells are highlighted, as shown in Figure 22-1.

Note The entire table is selected by clicking on the table-move icon located in the upper-left corner of the table when viewed in Print Layout mode. This selects the entire table and all its contents.

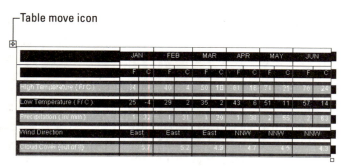

Figure 22-1: Table cells are highlighted when selected. Clicking the table-move icon selects the entire table.

After the cells are selected, choose Edit ➪ Cut (⌘/Ctrl+X) or Edit ➪ Copy (⌘/Ctrl+C) to copy the selected table cells to the Clipboard. From the Clipboard, choose Edit ➪ Paste (⌘/Ctrl+V) to paste the table into the CS2 application.

Using Word tables in InDesign

Table cells that are copied in Word and pasted into InDesign are recognized in InDesign as tables and are edited using InDesign's table features. All table and character formatting in Word is also pasted into InDesign.

Another way to import Word tables into InDesign is by choosing File ➪ Place. Microsoft Word is one of the importable file formats that InDesign supports. If you enable the Show Import Options check box in the Place dialog box (or if you hold down the Shift key while clicking the Open button), the Microsoft Word Import Options dialog box appears, shown in Figure 22-2.

Tables imported in this manner from Word appear in InDesign as editable tables, but if you want to remove the table formatting, you can select the Remove Styles and Formatting from Text and Tables option in the Microsoft Word Import Options dialog box. This makes the Convert Tables To drop-down list become active with options to convert as Unformatted Tables and Unformatted Tabbed Text.

Tip If you have any trouble with the imported tables, try to import the table as Unformatted Tabbed Text and use InDesign's Table ➪ Convert Text to Table menu command to create the table.

Using Word tables in Illustrator

Illustrator, like InDesign, can open native Microsoft Word documents; choose File ➪ Open (⌘/Ctrl+O). The File ➪ Place menu command is used to open the Word document into an existing Illustrator document. If the Word document includes a table, the table is imported into Illustrator.

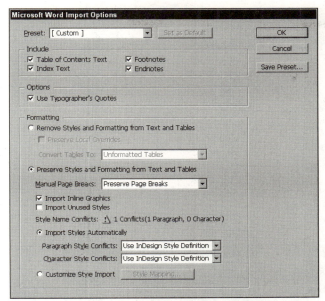

Figure 22-2: The Microsoft Word Import Options dialog box includes options for handling text formatting.

With the exception of graphs, Illustrator has no concept of a table and table formatting for the imported Word table is lost, but Illustrator recognizes the content as editable text objects. The Microsoft Word Options dialog box that appears when the Word document is opened offers a Remove Text Formatting option.

Table cells that are copied from Word and pasted into Illustrator include the cell borders and formatted table data, but the data is grouped with the formatted cells, making the text uneditable. Selecting the pasted table and choosing Object ⇨ Ungroup (Shift+Ctrl+G in Windows; Shift+⌘+G on the Mac) ungroups the table object, making the individual text objects editable with the Type tool.

Figure 22-3 shows a sample table that has been opened into Illustrator using the File ⇨ Open menu command and the same data beneath it copied and pasted into Illustrator using the Clipboard.

Although Illustrator thinks of tables as text surrounded by line objects, there is one feature in Illustrator that understands table data very well — the Graph Data window. Table data may be pasted directly into the Graph Data window, but to create a graph that makes sense, the table data must be fairly simple with no extra cells.

Cross-Reference
The graphing features found in Illustrator are covered in more detail in Chapter 23.

The Graph Data window, shown in Figure 22-4, opens automatically whenever one of the graph tools is used, but you can also open it by selecting a graph object and choosing Object ⇨ Graph ⇨ Data. One of the buttons in this window is for importing data.

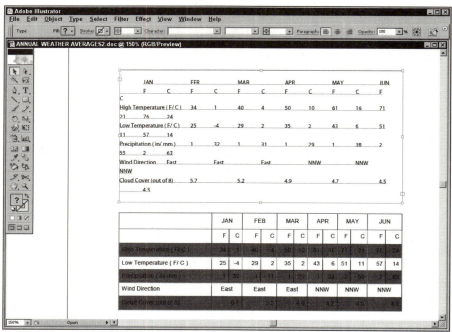

Figure 22-3: The top table sample is a Microsoft Word document that was opened in Illustrator, and the lower table is the same table copied and pasted into Illustrator using the Clipboard.

Import data button

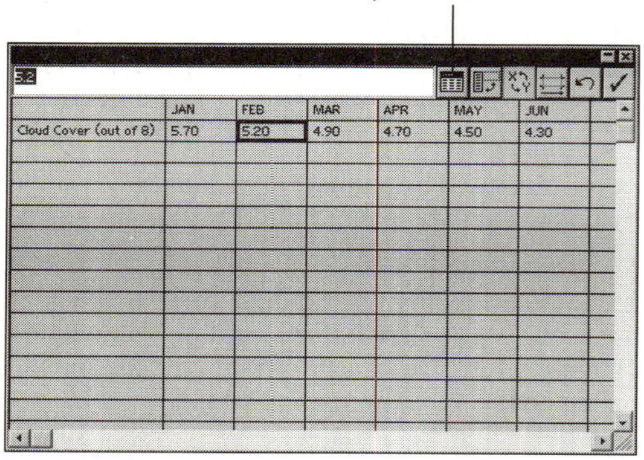

Figure 22-4: Table data copied in Word or Excel may be pasted directly into the Graph Data window for creating a graph.

The Import Data button opens a file dialog box where you can select a tab-separated file. You must separate each cell with a tab and each row with a paragraph return.

Using Word tables in GoLive

The HTML tables found in GoLive are copied and pasted from Word using the Clipboard. This maintains the text formatting, but most of the table formatting such as cell height is dropped in support of HTML tables.

When a table is established, a tab-separated text file may be imported to fill the existing table by choosing Special ⇨ Table ⇨ Import Tab-Delimited Text.

Importing Microsoft Excel tables

Although tables in Word are useful, the real king of tables among the Microsoft Office products is Excel. Excel tables include formulas that compute the value of a cell based on other cells. This is a powerful concept that saves countless hours of manual calculations. However, after an Excel table is imported into a CS2 application, all of its formulas and automatic calculations are lost.

Using the Clipboard

You can copy Excel spreadsheets to the Clipboard and paste them into InDesign, Illustrator, and GoLive by choosing Edit ⇨ Paste (⌘/Ctrl+V). When table cells are selected in Excel and copied to the Clipboard, a moving dashed line (known as marching ants) surround the copied cells. This is done to maintain the formulas within Excel.

Excel tables that are copied into InDesign are converted to an InDesign table, allowing them to be edited using the InDesign table features.

The data found in Excel tables, like Word tables, can also be copied and pasted into the Graph Data window for graphing in Illustrator.

Tip   Remember that Excel tables, like Word tables, that are copied and pasted into Illustrator must first be ungrouped before the table text may be edited within Illustrator.

The cell height of Excel tables that are pasted into GoLive is expanded so all the text for the cell is visible. Column width remains constant to the Excel tables.

Excel tables by default do not include cell borders. To have borders appear when a table is copied and pasted into a CS2 application, you need to make the cell borders visible in Excel. This is done in Excel by opening the Format Cells dialog box (Format ⇨ Cells). In the Format Cells dialog box, select the Border tab, shown in Figure 22-5, and click on the Outline and Inside buttons to add cell borders. This causes the Excel table cells to have borders when they're copied and pasted.

Placing Excel tables in InDesign

In addition to the Copy and Paste features, you can also place Excel documents within an InDesign document by choosing File ⇨ Place (⌘/Ctrl+D). With the Show Import Options check box enabled in the Place dialog box (or by holding down the Shift key when the Open button is clicked), the Microsoft Excel Import Options dialog box, shown in Figure 22-6, is opened.

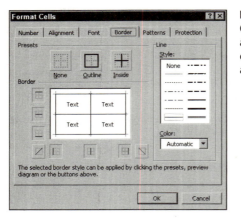

Figure 22-5: The Border tab of the Format Cells dialog box in Microsoft Excel is used to add cell-visible cell borders to tables being copied and pasted into the various CS2 applications.

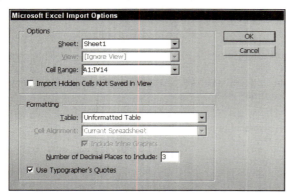

Figure 22-6: When you place a Microsoft Excel document within an InDesign document, this dialog box of options appears, letting you select which sheet and view to open and letting you specify how to format the tables.

Excel documents are divided into sheets, which are selected using tabs at the bottom of the Excel window. Large sheets of data can also be made up of customized views. Once you import data into InDesign, you can select which sheets and views to use. The Cell Range drop-down list displays the row and column numbers referenced in Excel; hidden cells can also be imported.

The formatting options include a formatted table, unformatted table, and unformatted tabbed text. Although the Formatted Table option works most of the time, if you encounter any trouble, select to format the table as Unformatted Tabbed Text and let InDesign's Table ⇨ Convert Text to Table menu command create the table.

The Cell Alignment options include Left, Center, Right, and Current Spreadsheet alignment.

Note After clicking OK to place an Excel spreadsheet, an Information dialog box appears if the Formatted Table option was selected. This dialog box instructs you that you can speed up the import process by choosing to import the table as an unformatted table.

Working with Tables in InDesign

Although several packages can import and use tables imported from external packages such as Microsoft Word and Microsoft Excel, only InDesign and GoLive deal natively with table objects. And of these two applications, GoLive tables are hindered by the restrictions that HTML requires.

Tables in InDesign, however, are very robust and offer a host of formatting and editing options. Tables can also be threaded to flow about the frames of an InDesign document.

Creating tables

Tables in InDesign are a specialized form of text object. To create a table, you must first create a text object using the Type tool or position the cursor within an existing text object at the place where the new table is located.

Choose Table ⇨ Insert Table (Alt+Shift+Ctrl+T in Windows; Option+Shift+⌘+T on the Mac) to open the Insert Table dialog box, shown in Figure 22-7. This dialog box lets you specify the number of body rows and columns to include in the new table. You can also select the number of header and footer rows.

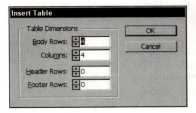

Figure 22-7: When you create a new table, the Insert Table dialog box specifies the number of rows and columns to include in the table.

The new table fills the width of the text frame that contains it with the specified number of columns. The cell height is determined initially by the size of the text contained in the text object. After the table is created, the container text frame has no control over the table's height and width. You alter the cell size by dragging on the cell borders using the Type tool. The cursor changes to show the directions that the cell can move.

 Tables cannot be added to type positioned along a path.

Populating tables

Once a table is created, you can populate it with data using the Type tool. Just click in a cell and type the data. Add graphics to a cell by choosing File ⇨ Place (⌘/Ctrl+D). You can also copy and paste text into the various table cells using the Type tool.

 Be aware that if a table created in Word, Excel, or even InDesign is copied and pasted into a table cell, the entire table is nested within the single table cell.

Moving between cells

Tab and Shift+Tab move the cursor between adjacent cells. Tab moves to the next cell and Shift+Tab moves to the previous one. If the next cell already has some data, that data is selected. Pressing the Tab key when the cursor is positioned in the last cell adds a new row to the table. The arrow keys can also be used to move between cells.

If you're dealing with a particularly long table, choose Table ⇨ Go to Row to jump to a specific Header, Body Row, or Footer using the dialog box, shown in Figure 22-8. This causes the entire row to be selected.

Figure 22-8: The Go to Row dialog box jumps to a specified table row.

Converting text into a table

Normal text is converted into a table using common delimiters such as tabs, commas, and paragraph returns. Before converting text to a table, make sure that you separate the text for each cell with a common separator and that you separate the end of each row is also separated with a different separator. For example, separate each text cell using a comma and each row using a paragraph return.

Select the text that you want to convert into a table with the Type tool and choose Table ⇨ Convert Text to Table. A dialog box opens, shown in Figure 22-9, letting you select the separators used for the columns and rows.

Figure 22-9: The Convert Text to Table dialog box lets you select the separator to use to delineate rows and columns. The options include Tab, Comma, Paragraph, and Other.

InDesign also includes a command to do the opposite — convert tables into text. During this process, you select the separators that are placed in the text for separating rows and columns. The menu command (Table ⇨ Convert Table to Text) is available only when the Type tool's cursor is placed within a table cell.

Running a table between frames

Longer tables are formatted to run between several different text frames. If the size of the table exceeds the text frame, the frame's out port has a red plus sign in it, as shown in Figure 22-10. If you create a new text frame, you can click on the out port for the first frame and then on the in port for the second frame to connect (or thread) the two frames. This causes the table data not visible in the first frame to be displayed in the second frame; if new rows or columns are added to the first frame's table, the table data is pushed down to the second frame.

 Cross-Reference Frame threading and in and out ports are covered in Chapter 18.

Using headers and footers

Tables that span several frames and/or pages benefit from using headers and footers. Headers and footers are specified when a table is created, but you can convert any row to a header or footer (or any header or footer to a body row) by choosing Table ⇨ Convert Rows ⇨ To Header, To Footer, or To Body.

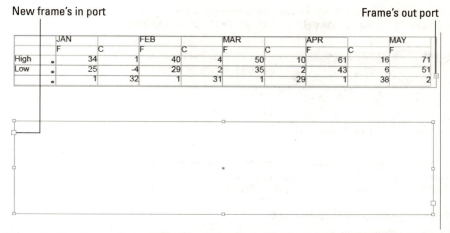

Figure 22-10: Connecting a frame's out port to another frame's in port threads the two frames together. Content in the first frame that isn't visible appears in the second frame.

Headers and Footers have an option to appear in every text Column, once per frame, or once per page. This makes tables that span multiple frames or pages easier to understand.

Editing tables

After an InDesign table is created, you have complete control over the size and number of cells. New rows and columns may be added or deleted and individual cells merged or split.

Selecting cells

You can easily select table cells using the Type tool. A single click on an empty cell positions the cursor within the cell and a double-click on a populated cell selects all the contents of that cell. Dragging a marquee over several cells selects multiple cells at once.

Moving the cursor over the top and/or left edge causes the cursor to change to an arrow. If you click when this arrow cursor is visible, then the entire column or row is selected. If you position the cursor in the upper-left corner, it changes into a diagonally pointing arrow. Clicking selects the entire table.

You also select table elements — including Cell (⌘/Ctrl+/), Row (⌘/Ctrl+3), Column (Option/Alt+⌘/Ctrl+3) and Table (Option/Alt+⌘/Ctrl+A) — by choosing Table ⇨ Select. You can also use the Table ⇨ Select menu to select header, footer, and body rows.

Inserting rows and columns

It is unnerving to find that you need a new row or column in the middle of a table that has already been formatted correctly. Luckily, InDesign offers an easy way to do this. Hold down the Option/Alt key while dragging to resize a row or a column and a new row or column is created.

Note To create a new row by dragging with the Option/Alt key held down, you must drag a distance at least equal to the height of the table's text.

You add multiple rows and/or columns to a table by choosing Table ⇨ Insert ⇨ Row (⌘/Ctrl+9) or Table ⇨ Insert ⇨ Column (Alt+Ctrl+9 in Windows; Option+⌘+9 on the Mac).

These menu commands, which are available only if the cursor is positioned within a table's cell, cause a dialog box, like the one shown in Figure 22-11, to appear.

Figure 22-11: The Insert Rows dialog box positions the new rows above or below the current selection.

The total number of rows and columns that make up a table are listed in the Table Options dialog box and in the Table palette. Entering a new value for either the Row or Table field adds or deletes rows or columns from the current table.

Deleting rows and columns

You can delete rows and columns by choosing Table ⇨ Delete ⇨ Row (⌘/Ctrl+Backspace) or Table ⇨ Delete ⇨ Column (Shift+Backspace). The Table ⇨ Delete menu also includes a command to delete the entire table. Deleting a row or a column also deletes all the content contained within its cells.

Note   When you select a single cell, a row, or a column, pressing the Delete key only clears the contents of the selected cells; it doesn't remove the cells.

Rows and columns also are deleted by dragging the bottom edge upward or the right edge leftward with the Option/Alt key held down.

Merging cells

Often, the first row or column of cells is used as a header to describe the data that follows. Because this single header applies to all cells, you can merge all the cells in the header to make a single cell that extends the entire width of the rows or columns. To merge several cells, just select them and choose Table ⇨ Merge Cells. This keeps the common dimension of the cells and extends the other dimension the extent of all the selected cells. Merged cells do not need to be a header or footer row. You can unmerge merged cells by choosing Table ⇨ Unmerge Cells. Figure 22-12 shows a sample table that has had a number of cells merged. Notice the title at the top of the table; all the cells in the first row have been merged, and the title has been centered in the first row.

Annual Weather Averages							
JAN		FEB		MAR		APR	
F	C	F	C	F	C	F	C
High 34	1	40	4	50	10	61	16
Low 25	-4	29	2	35	2	43	6
1	32	1	31	1	29	1	38
Wind Direction East		East		East		NNW	
Cloud Cover (out of 8)	5.7		5.2		4.9		4.7

Figure 22-12: Merged cells make more room for text such as titles to be displayed.

Splitting cells

You can split selected cells into two by choosing Table ⇨ Split Cell Horizontally or Table ⇨ Split Cell Vertically. These commands add another table border and split each selected cell into two equal cells.

Note   Splitting a row creates a new row that is half the size of the original row.

Formatting tables

Text and images contained within a table are formatted just as normal using the Control palette, but tables and table cells have several unique formatting options. You can set these options in the Table Options dialog box, shown in Figure 22-13; choose Table ⇨ Table Options ⇨ Table Setup (Alt+Shift+Ctrl+B in Windows; Option+Shift+⌘+B on the Mac).

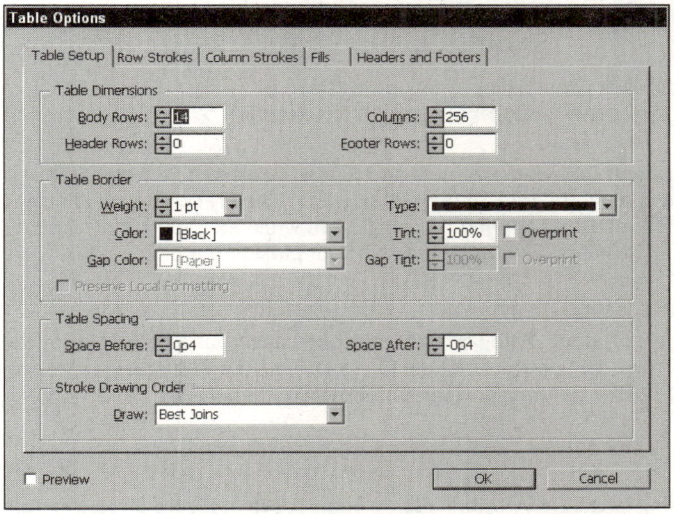

Figure 22-13: The Table Options dialog box is divided into several different panels for controlling the table settings, the row and column strokes, the background fills, and the headers and footers.

The Table Setup panel of the Table Options dialog box lists the total number of body rows, columns, header rows, and footer rows. Increasing or decreasing these values adds or deletes from the table. The Table Setup panel also includes controls for defining the table border and the spacing before and after the table. The Headers and Footers panel is used to specify the number of header and footer rows and where they're repeated for tables that span several frames or pages.

Alternating strokes

The strokes used to create the rows and column borders are changed using the Row and Column Strokes panels in the Table Options dialog box, shown in Figure 22-14. Access this panel by clicking on the Row Strokes tab or by choosing Table ⇨ Table Options ⇨ Alternating Row Strokes.

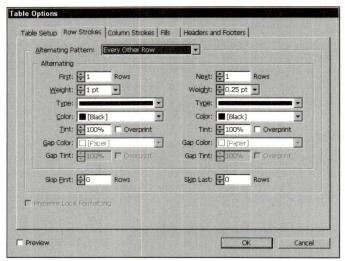

Figure 22-14: The Row Strokes panel defines the look of the row borders. The Column Strokes panel is similar but applies to columns.

Using the First and Next fields, you can establish any type of pattern. The Weight, Type, Color, and Tint settings let you control the look of the row borders. The Preserve Local Formatting check box keeps any cell formatting applied to a single cell when enabled. Using the Preview option lets you make changes and view the results without closing the dialog box.

Alternating fills

The Fills panel of the Table Options dialog box changes the background cell color for the specified alternating pattern. The options include Every Other Row/Column, Every Second Row/Column, Every Third Row/Column, and Custom Row/Column.

Formatting cells

You control cell formatting in the Cell Options dialog box, shown in Figure 22-15. Open this dialog box for the current cell by choosing Table ⇨ Cell Options ⇨ Text (Alt+Ctrl+B in Windows; Option+⌘+B on the Mac).

Changing row and column dimensions

You change row and column size by positioning the mouse cursor over a cell border and dragging to increase or decrease the row or column size. The mouse cursor changes to show the direction that the border can move, as shown in Figure 22-16. If the text entered into a cell exceeds the width of the column, the text is displayed as a red dot to indicate that the text exceeds the cell size.

Holding down the Shift key while dragging an internal row or column border changes the adjacent row or column at the expense of the other. Dragging the bottom or rightmost border with the Shift key held down proportionally sizes all the rows or columns at once.

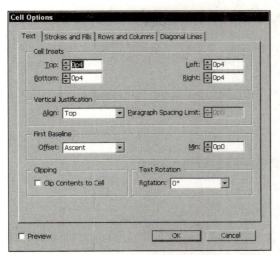

Figure 22-15: The Cell Options dialog box is also divided into several different panels for controlling the cell's alignment, strokes and fills, and cell dimensions, as well as for adding diagonal lines.

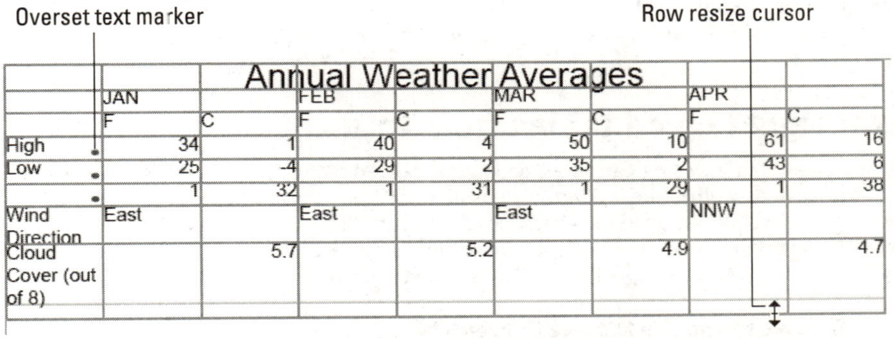

Figure 22-16: The cursor changes to show the directions that the cursor can move to resize the selected row. Overset text is marked with a red dot indicating that the text doesn't fit in the cell.

Initially, the row height is set based on the text size, and increasing the text size increases the row height. This is based on Row Height set to the At Least option. It can also be set to use the Exactly option, which makes the cell size consistent regardless of the text size. These controls are found in the Rows and Columns panel of the Cell Options dialog box.

Evenly distributing rows and columns

To make several rows and columns have the same dimensions, select the rows or columns that you want to distribute and choose Table ⇨ Distribute Rows Evenly or Table ⇨ Distribute Columns Evenly.

Aligning cell content

The Cell Inset values are the amount of space between the cell text and the cell border. A Cell Inset value of 0.0 causes the text to print on top of the cell border. The Vertical Justification options include Top, Center, Bottom, and Justify; the First Baseline options include Ascent, Cap Height, Leading, x Height, and Fixed.

The Text Rotation values include 0, 90, 180, and 270 degrees. This allows the text to be rotated and displayed vertically. Figure 22-17 shows a sample table where the text for the months has been rotated 90 degrees.

Annual Weather Averages

	JAN		FEB		MAR		APR	
	F	C	F	C	F	C	F	C
High Temperature (F/ C)	34	1	40	4	50	10	61	16
Low Temperature (F/ C)	25	-4	29	2	35	2	43	6
Precipitation (in/ mm)	1	32	1	31	1	29	1	38
Wind Direction	East		East		East		NNW	

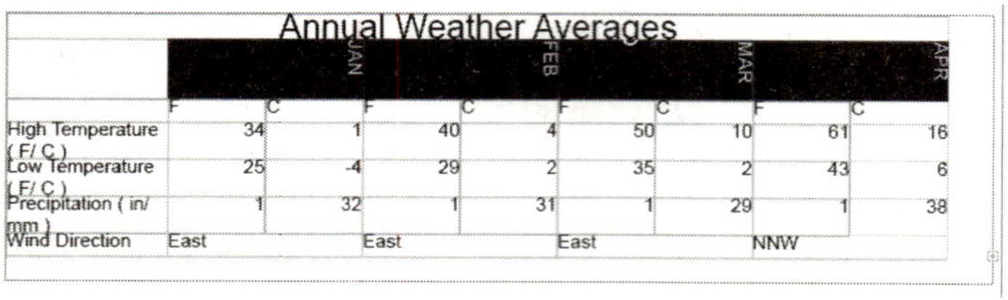

Figure 22-17: This sample table shows some text that has been rotated 90 degrees.

Altering cell strokes and fills

The Strokes and Fills panel of the Cell Options dialog box includes settings for defining the border stroke and fill for the selected cell. This is useful if you want to highlight a specific table value. The Diagonal Lines panel includes options to place a diagonal line through the selected cell.

Exporting tagged tables from InDesign

Tables created in InDesign can be tagged and exported using the XML format. Keep in mind that the table as well as the individual cells all need to be tagged in order to be exported. To see the applied tags, choose View ➪ Structure ➪ Show Structure to open the Structure pane. Tags can be applied from the Tags palette, which is opened by choosing Window ➪ Tags. Once tagged, the table can be exported by choosing File ➪ Export and selecting the XML file type.

Cross-Reference For more coverage on XML, see Chapter 30.

Using Excel Spreadsheets in InDesign

As a final working example of the process of importing and using a Microsoft Excel document in InDesign, we'll walk you through the steps involved. These steps are specific to the project at hand, but they're similar to the type of process that you follow.

STEPS: Importing a Microsoft Excel table into InDesign

1. **Open the document in Excel.** Figure 22-18 shows the data for the annual weather averages in an Excel document. Notice that the table data has been split into two separate six-month periods with duplicate titles. This formatting makes it easy to thread the data between two text frames. Before importing the Excel file, make a note of the cell range, which for this file extends from cell A1 to cell M14.

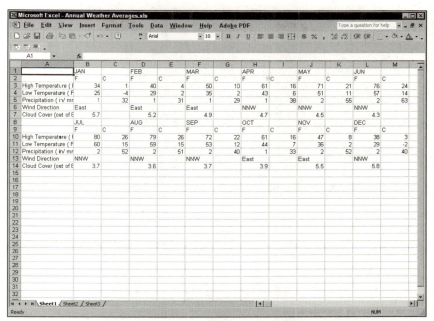

Figure 22-18: Open an Excel document that includes all the tables and data that you want to import into InDesign.

2. **Add cell borders.** During the import process, adding cell borders helps make each of the table cells visible, so we'll add them to the table in the Excel document. Drag over all the cells that make up the table in the Excel document, then choose Format ⇨ Cells to access the Format Cells dialog box. Select the Border tab and click on the Outline and Inside buttons to add cell borders. Click OK to exit the dialog box.

3. **Save the Excel document.** Choose File ⇨ Save As in Excel and save the file using the default XLS file format. After the file is saved, close the Excel document by choosing File ⇨ Close. If you forget to close the Excel document on a Windows system, InDesign opens an alert dialog box stating "This file is already in use by another application" when you try to place the Excel document in InDesign.

4. **Open the current InDesign file.** If you already have a start on the layout, open the existing file in InDesign by choosing File ⇨ Open.

5. **Place the Excel file in InDesign.** Choose File ⇨ Place (⌘/Ctrl+D) to open the Place dialog box. Make sure the Show Import Options check box is enabled; then select the Excel document and click Open.

6. **Set the Import Options.** In the Microsoft Excel Import Options dialog box, shown in Figure 22-19, type **A1:M14** in the Cell Range field. In the Table drop-down list, select Formatted Table. Click OK to proceed.

Note The Microsoft Excel Import Options dialog box automatically sets the Cell Range field to include the entire table, but you can use this field to limit the range.

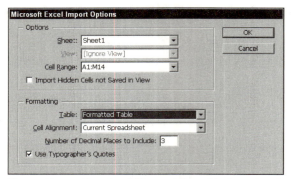

Figure 22-19: You should import the table from Excel as a formatted table.

7. **Resize the text frame.** The table text is imported into the cursor. Click and drag to create a text frame where the imported table appears. After importing the Excel table, select and position the text frame on the page. Notice how the text frame's out port changes to a red plus sign if the table text doesn't fit within the text frame.

8. **Create and position a new text frame.** Click on the Type tool and drag to create a new text frame underneath the existing one, as shown in Figure 22-20.

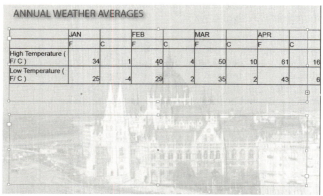

Figure 22-20: The two text frames are in place, selected, and ready to be threaded.

9. **Threading the text frames.** Click on the out port for the top text frame, the cursor changes to show that it's holding frame text. Then move the cursor over the top of the in port for the second frame. The cursor changes to a link icon. Click to thread the two frames. This makes some of the table text appear in the lower text frame, as shown in Figure 22-21.

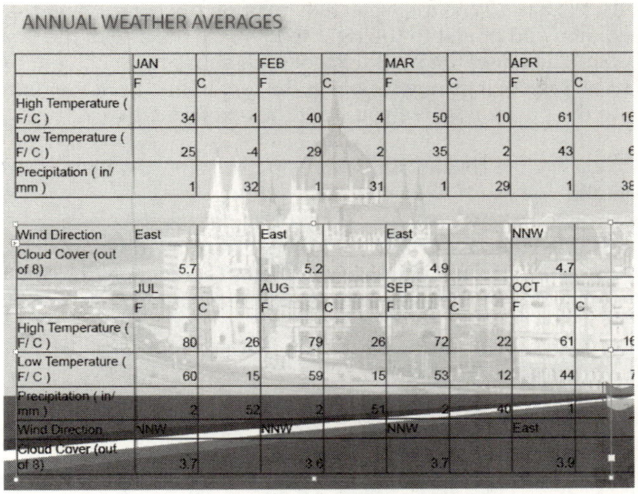

ANNUAL WEATHER AVERAGES

	JAN		FEB		MAR		APR	
	F	C	F	C	F	C	F	C
High Temperature (F/ C)	34	1	40	4	50	10	61	16
Low Temperature (F/ C)	25	-4	29	2	35	2	43	6
Precipitation (in/ mm)	1	32	1	31	1	29	1	38
Wind Direction	East		East		East		NNW	
Cloud Cover (out of 8)		5.7		5.2		4.9		4.7
	JUL		AUG		SEP		OCT	
	F	C	F	C	F	C	F	C
High Temperature (F/ C)	80	26	79	26	72	22	61	16
Low Temperature (F/ C)	60	15	59	15	53	12	44	7
Precipitation (in/ mm)	2	52	2	51	2	40	1	
Wind Direction	NNW		NNW		NNW		East	
Cloud Cover (out of 8)		3.7		3.6		3.7		3.9

Figure 22-21: After the two text frames are threaded, some of the text from the first text frame spills over into the second frame.

10. **Select all table rows.** The next step is to apply some textual formatting to the table data so it is easily read. Select the Type tool and position it over the left edge of the first row. When the cursor changes into an arrow, drag downward to select the content of all rows.

11. **Format table data.** With all table cells selected, choose the Impact font in the Control palette with a type size of 9 points. This changes the style of the table data, as shown in Figure 22-22.

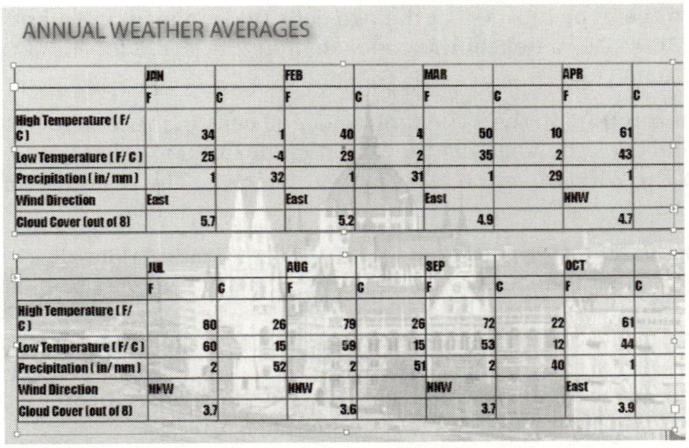

ANNUAL WEATHER AVERAGES

	JAN		FEB		MAR		APR	
	F	C	F	C	F	C	F	C
High Temperature (F/ C)	34	1	40	4	50	10	61	
Low Temperature (F/ C)	25	-4	29	2	35	2	43	
Precipitation (in/ mm)	1	32	1	31	1	29	1	
Wind Direction	East		East		East		NNW	
Cloud Cover (out of 8)		5.7		5.2		4.9		4.7

	JUL		AUG		SEP		OCT	
	F	C	F	C	F	C	F	C
High Temperature (F/ C)	80	26	79	26	72	22	61	
Low Temperature (F/ C)	60	15	59	15	53	12	44	
Precipitation (in/ mm)	2	52	2	51	2	40	1	
Wind Direction	NNW		NNW		NNW		East	
Cloud Cover (out of 8)		3.7		3.6		3.7		3.9

Figure 22-22: After selecting all the table cells, you can quickly change the font, style, and color for the table data.

12. **Resize table cells.** With the Type tool selected, position the cursor over the right border of the first column and drag it to the right to increase the size of the first column so all its text is visible. Then drag the right edge of each subsequent column to the left to reduce its size so all the columns are visible in the text frame. Drag the right edge of the last column to the position where you want the text frame to end.

Note

When you drag to change the column size in the top text frame, the bottom text frame is changed automatically.

13. **Evenly distribute table columns.** With the Type tool selected, drag over the top edge of all the columns except for the first one to select them. Then choose Table ➪ Distribute Columns Evenly. All the columns are equally spaced, as shown in Figure 22-23.

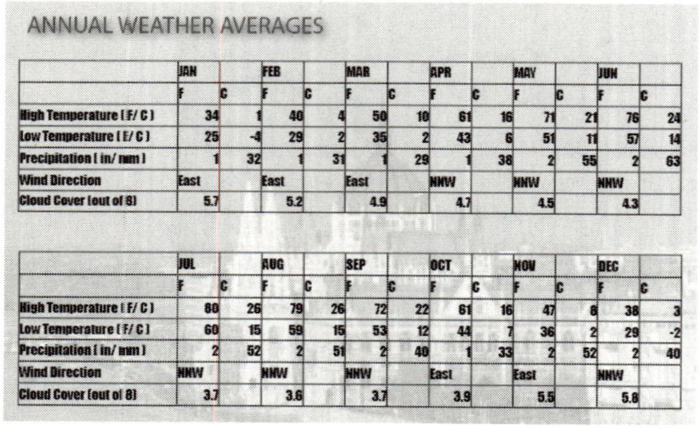

ANNUAL WEATHER AVERAGES

	JAN		FEB		MAR		APR		MAY		JUN	
	F	C	F	C	F	C	F	C	F	C	F	C
High Temperature (F/ C)	34	1	40	4	50	10	61	16	71	21	76	24
Low Temperature (F/ C)	25	-4	29	2	35	2	43	6	51	11	57	14
Precipitation (in/ mm)	1	32	1	31	1	29	1	38	2	55	2	63
Wind Direction	East		East		East		NNW		NNW		NNW	
Cloud Cover (out of 8)	5.7		5.2		4.9		4.7		4.5		4.3	

	JUL		AUG		SEP		OCT		NOV		DEC	
	F	C	F	C	F	C	F	C	F	C	F	C
High Temperature (F/ C)	80	26	79	26	72	22	61	16	47	8	38	3
Low Temperature (F/ C)	60	15	59	15	53	12	44	7	36	2	29	-2
Precipitation (in/ mm)	2	52	2	51	2	40	1	33	2	52	2	40
Wind Direction	NNW		NNW		NNW		East		East		NNW	
Cloud Cover (out of 8)	3.7		3.6		3.7		3.9		5.5		5.8	

Figure 22-23: After resizing the columns and evenly distributing them, the table data is correctly lined up.

14. **Merge cells.** With the Type tool, select the two cells that make up the month title and choose Table ➪ Merge Cells. Repeat this for each month title and for the Wind Direction and Cloud Cover data cells.

15. **Align text within a cell.** With the Type tool, select all cells in the first two rows of the first text frame and click the Align Center button in the Control palette. Repeat this for the data cells for the Wind Direction and Cloud Cover cells. The resulting formatting is shown in Figure 22-24.

16. **Change Cell Inset values.** If you look closely at the temperature data, you'll notice that the right edge of the text touches the cell border. Changing the Cell Inset values puts some space between the text and the cell border. Open the Cell Options dialog box by choosing Table ➪ Cell Options ➪ Text (Alt+Ctrl+B in Windows; Option+⌘+B on the Mac). Select all the temperature cells and change the Left and Right Cell Inset values to 0.05 in. With the Preview option enabled, you can see the changes before closing the dialog box. Repeat this for the text in the second frame.

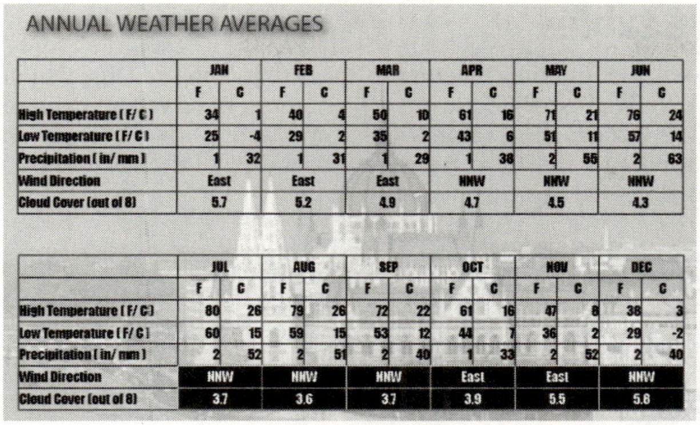

ANNUAL WEATHER AVERAGES

	JAN		FEB		MAR		APR		MAY		JUN	
	F	C	F	C	F	C	F	C	F	C	F	C
High Temperature (F/ C)	34	1	40	4	50	10	61	16	71	21	76	24
Low Temperature (F/ C)	25	-4	29	2	35	2	43	6	51	11	57	14
Precipitation (in/ mm)	1	32	1	31	1	29	1	38	2	55	2	63
Wind Direction	East		East		East		NNW		NNW		NNW	
Cloud Cover (out of 8)	5.7		5.2		4.9		4.7		4.5		4.3	

	JUL		AUG		SEP		OCT		NOV		DEC	
	F	C	F	C	F	C	F	C	F	C	F	C
High Temperature (F/ C)	80	26	79	26	72	22	61	16	47	8	38	3
Low Temperature (F/ C)	60	15	59	15	53	12	44	7	36	2	29	-2
Precipitation (in/ mm)	2	52	2	51	2	40	1	33	2	52	2	40
Wind Direction	NNW		NNW		NNW		East		East		NNW	
Cloud Cover (out of 8)	3.7		3.6		3.7		3.9		5.5		5.8	

Figure 22-24: After merging cells and centering the text in several cells, the data looks much cleaner.

17. **Enable Alternating Fills.** To make each alternating row a different color, open the Fills panel in the Table Options dialog box with the Table ➪ Table Options ➪ Alternating Fills menu command. Select Every Other Row as the Alternating Pattern option. Then select a light-blue color for the first row and set the Skip First Row value to 1. Figure 22-25 shows the resulting table with inset values and alternating fills.

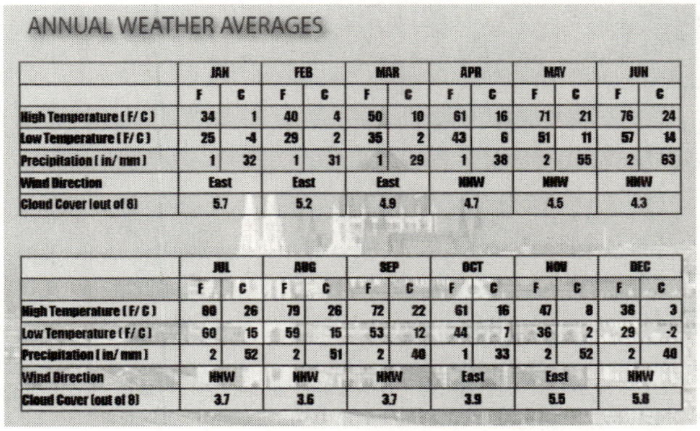

ANNUAL WEATHER AVERAGES

	JAN		FEB		MAR		APR		MAY		JUN	
	F	C	F	C	F	C	F	C	F	C	F	C
High Temperature (F/ C)	34	1	40	4	50	10	61	16	71	21	76	24
Low Temperature (F/ C)	25	-4	29	2	35	2	43	6	51	11	57	14
Precipitation (in/ mm)	1	32	1	31	1	29	1	38	2	55	2	63
Wind Direction	East		East		East		NNW		NNW		NNW	
Cloud Cover (out of 8)	5.7		5.2		4.9		4.7		4.5		4.3	

	JUL		AUG		SEP		OCT		NOV		DEC	
	F	C	F	C	F	C	F	C	F	C	F	C
High Temperature (F/ C)	80	26	79	26	72	22	61	16	47	8	38	3
Low Temperature (F/ C)	60	15	59	15	53	12	44	7	36	2	29	-2
Precipitation (in/ mm)	2	52	2	51	2	40	1	33	2	52	2	40
Wind Direction	NNW		NNW		NNW		East		East		NNW	
Cloud Cover (out of 8)	3.7		3.6		3.7		3.9		5.5		5.8	

Figure 22-25: Setting a table to have alternating fills makes the table easier to read.

Working with Tables in GoLive

The other CS2 application that can create and work with tables is GoLive. GoLive tables are based on the HTML language, which imposes some constraints on the tables. Tables in the HTML world are used for more than just presenting data in rows and columns. Web-page tables are frequently used to position objects, since they offer control of the placement of objects within a Web page.

Creating GoLive tables

To create a table in GoLive, just double-click on the Table object in the Objects palette or drag the table object onto a Web-page document. The number of rows and columns in the table is determined by the values in the Table Inspector palette, shown in Figure 22-26. In addition to the Inspector palette, the Table palette holds a view of the current table for simple selection and application of styles.

Figure 22-26: The Table Inspector palette includes the various settings for the selected table, and the Table palette includes a panel where you can select rows, columns, and cells.

If you hold down the ⌘/Ctrl key while dragging the Table object to a page, you can interactively select the number of rows and columns that the table has.

Populating cells

Once a table is created, you can add text to a table cell by clicking on the table cell and typing the text. In addition to text, most objects included in the Objects palette may be dragged and dropped in a table cell, such as images, multimedia, and even other tables.

The cell size is determined by the content entered in the table cell. If a single line of text fills the table cell, the table width is automatically increased to hold the text. Figure 22-27 shows a sample table that has been pasted from a Word document. Notice how the cell size is just large enough to hold the text.

	JAN		FEB		MAR		APR		MAY		JUN	
	F	C	F	C	F	C	F	C	F	C	F	C
High Temperature (F/ C)	34	1	40	4	50	10	61	16	71	21	76	24
Low Temperature (F/ C)	25	-4	29	2	35	2	43	6	51	11	57	14
Precipitation (in/ mm)	1	32	1	31	1	29	1	38	2	55	2	63
Wind Direction	East		East		East		NNW		NNW		NNW	
Cloud Cover (out of 8)	5.7		5.2		4.9		4.7		4.5		4.3	

Figure 22-27: The default setting for tables is to resize the cell size just large enough for the text to fit.

Importing tables

The easiest way to import a table from Word or Excel into GoLive is to use the Clipboard. Tables imported in this manner retain the individual cell content and structure. However, you cannot use this method to import cells into an existing table. If you copy a table from Word, select a single cell in GoLive and perform a paste operation, the entire table and all its cells would be pasted into the single selected GoLive cell.

Selecting cells

Dragging between cells selects multiple cells. All the selected cells are highlighted with a black border, as shown in Figure 22-28. Moving the mouse over the top or left edge enables you to select an entire column or row. The cursor changes to an arrow when an entire row or column is selected. This works the same as tables in InDesign.

Tip

Selecting nested tables can be tricky, but the Table palette includes some helpful tools. If you move the mouse over a nested table, the cursor changes to a small grid with arrows extending from each corner. This is the Child Zoom tool. Clicking on the nested table selects it and makes the Parent Zoom tool in the lower-left corner of the Table palette active. Clicking the Parent Zoom button selects the parent table. Table cells are also selected using the Select panel in the Table palette.

	JAN		FEB		MAR		APR		MAY		JUN	
	F	C	F	C	F	C	F	C	F	C	F	C
High Temperature (F/ C)	34	1	40	4	50	10	61	16	71	21	76	24
Low Temperature (F/ C)	25	-4	29	2	35	2	43	6	51	11	57	14
Precipitation (in/ mm)	1	32	1	31	1	29	1	38	2	55	2	63
Wind Direction	East		East		East		NNW		NNW		NNW	
Cloud Cover (out of 8)	5.7		5.2		4.9		4.7		4.5		4.3	

Figure 22-28: Selected cells are outlined in black.

Moving, adding, and deleting rows and columns

With a cell, row, or column selected, a black square appears in the upper-left corner of the selected object. Moving the cursor over the top of this black square changes the cursor to a hand icon. Dragging the hand icon moves the selected object.

Rows and columns are added above, below, left, or right of the current selected cell using the Special ➪ Table ➪ Insert Column or Insert Row menu commands. There are also buttons to add and remove rows and columns in the Cell panel of the Table Inspector palette.

Resizing cells

By default, the size of each cell is determined by the contents of the cell, but HTML allows you to specify the exact size of a cell in pixels or as a percentage of the entire Web page.

The size of each cell is set to be a specific number of pixels, a percentage of the Web page, or Auto, which automatically size the cell to fit the content contained therein. These options are selected in the Cell panel of the Table Inspector.

Formatting cells

Each cell, row, or column is formatted using the controls found in the Inspector palette. These controls include border size, background color, cell padding and spacing, and alignment options. Many of these controls work the same as they do in InDesign tables.

Using styles

Although each cell is formatted individually, GoLive includes several default styles that may be applied to a table. These styles are listed in the Style panel of the Table palette. To apply a style, just select it from the drop-down list and click Apply. Figure 22-29 shows a simple style applied to a sample table.

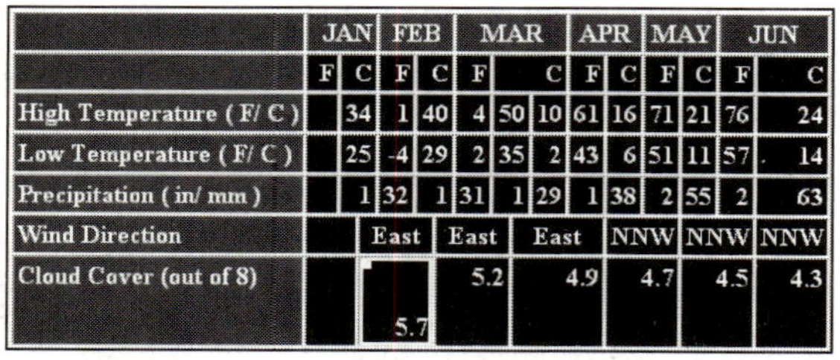

	JAN		FEB		MAR		APR		MAY		JUN	
	F	C	F	C	F	C	F	C	F	C	F	C
High Temperature (F/ C)		34	1	40	4	50	10	61	16	71	21	76	24
Low Temperature (F/ C)		25	-4	29	2	35	2	43	6	51	11	57	14
Precipitation (in/ mm)		1	32	1	31	1	29	1	38	2	55	2	63
Wind Direction		East		East		East		NNW		NNW		NNW	
Cloud Cover (out of 8)		5.7		5.2		4.9		4.7		4.5		4.3	

Figure 22-29: Table styles applied to the selected table change its look automatically.

Merging cells

Web designers frequently use tables to create a simple layout and for these layouts it is often helpful to merge cells together to create a single cell that spans the entire row or column. Cells can span several rows or columns using the Row Span and Column Span values in the Cell panel of the Inspector palette.

By default, all cells have Row and Column Span values of 1, but increasing either of these values causes the selected cell to be merged with the other row or column cells. Figure 22-30 shows a simple table with several row and column spanned cells.

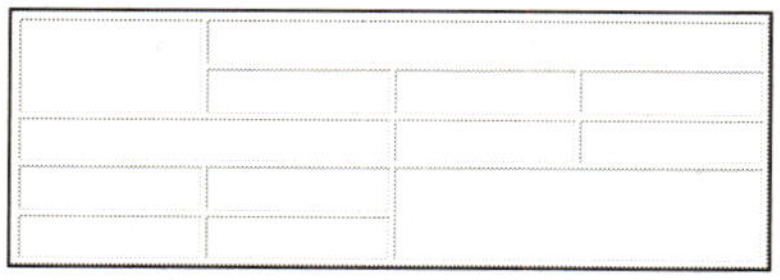

Figure 22-30: Table cells may span multiple rows and/or columns.

If multiple cells are selected, you can merge them with the Special ⇨ Table ⇨ Merge Cells menu command or split a merged cell into separate cells with the Special ⇨ Table ⇨ Split Cells menu command.

Tip Selected cells can be merged with adjacent cells by holding down the Shift key and pressing one of the arrow keys.

Summary

- Tables created in Microsoft Word may be imported into InDesign, Illustrator, and GoLive using the Clipboard.
- Tables copied from Word or Excel may be pasted into Illustrator's Graph Data window.
- Tables created in Microsoft Word and Excel may be imported directly into InDesign.
- InDesign can create, edit, and format tables.
- GoLive tables are based on HTML and are often used to position objects on a Web page.

✦ ✦ ✦

Creating Charts and Graphs

In This Chapter

Learning the various graph, chart, and diagram types

Designing graphs in Illustrator

Customizing Illustrator graphs

Importing charts created in Microsoft Excel

Importing diagrams created in Microsoft Word

Using Photoshop, Illustrator, InDesign, and even GoLive with a little ingenuity enables you to not only manually create an endless number of charts and graphs but to create a graph from a set of numerical data requires specialized features. With Creative Suite 2, these features are only found in Illustrator.

Using Illustrator's graphing features, graphs are generated automatically from the data that you enter into a spreadsheet-like window. After they're created, you can change the graph by changing its underlying data. Illustrator also offers many different formatting options, but the real benefit of Illustrator graphing is the ability to customize the graphs.

Although Illustrator's graphing features are first-rate, the real king of graphing data is Microsoft Excel. Excel, as a spreadsheet program, is a powerful piece of software, and its graphing features enable you to create any type of graph and formatting with a host of different features.

In addition to Excel, Microsoft Word includes several different charts and diagrams that may prove helpful, including organizational charts and Venn diagrams.

You can easily export the graphs, charts, and diagrams you create in Excel and Word to the various CS2 applications using the Clipboard and the other importing features.

Knowing the Various Chart and Graph Types

Many different types of graphs are available. To familiarize you with the various types, we start with a list of graphs that Illustrator can create. This list isn't comprehensive, but it covers the most basic graph types. Illustrator can create the following types of graphs:

- ✦ **Column:** Column graphs are used to compare values where the length of each column is proportional to its value. High or low values are easy to find because they're separated from the other columns.

- ✦ **Stacked column:** Stacked column graphs are used to show how a value makes up part of the whole. In this graph, columns are stacked on top of each other.

- **Bar:** Bar graphs are similar to column graphs, except their rectangles are oriented horizontally.
- **Stacked bar:** Stacked bar graphs are similar to stacked column graphs, except their rectangles are oriented horizontally.
- **Line:** Line graphs plot each value and then connect all these values with a line. These graphs are used to show trends in the data set.
- **Area:** Area graphs are similar to line graphs, except the total area under the line is also computed.
- **Scatter:** Scatter graphs plot two sets of values side-by-side and are used to look for groupings of data points.
- **Pie:** Pie graphs are drawn as wedges and show the amount that each slice contributes to the whole.
- **Radar:** Radar graphs are similar to line graphs, except they run along a circular path with larger values spread farther from the center.

Figure 23-1 shows a sampling of the Illustrator graphs.

In addition to the graphs created using Illustrator, Excel uses the following:

- **Doughnut:** Doughnut charts in Excel are similar to pie graphs, except they include multiple concentric layers.
- **Surface:** Surface charts in Excel are created by adding depth to several combined line graphs.
- **Bubble:** Bubble charts in Excel are similar to a scatter graph, except a third value sets the size of the bubble for each region.
- **Stock:** Stock charts in Excel plot three sets of data in a single column representing High, Low, and Close values.

Figure 23-2 shows the first step of Excel's Chart Wizard, where you select the chart type. It includes a list of the available Excel charts. The Custom Types tab includes an additional list of specific charts, including many combination charts like column-area, line-column, and logarithmic.

Microsoft Word offers several additional charts and diagrams, including the following:

- **Organizational chart:** Organizational charts show the relationships of a hierarchy, with each object represented as a rectangle and the hierarchy shown with connection lines.
- **Cycle diagram:** Cycle diagrams in Word show a process with several steps that repeat.
- **Radial diagram:** Radial diagrams in Word are used to show the relationship of many items to a core object.
- **Pyramid diagram:** Pyramid diagrams in Word show a series of steps that are based on one another.
- **Venn diagram:** Venn diagrams in Word are used to show the overlapping relationships among several groups.
- **Target diagram:** Target diagrams in Word show the steps as concentric circles required to meet a goal.

Chapter 23 ✦ **Creating Charts and Graphs**   791

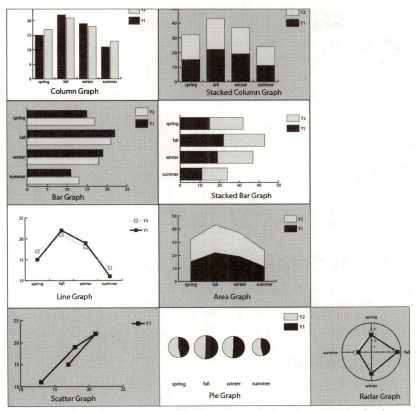

Figure 23-1: Graph types created in Illustrator include column, stacked column, bar, stacked bar, line, area, scatter, pie, and radar.

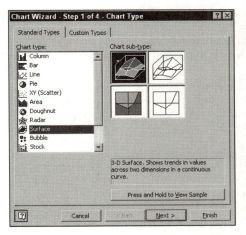

Figure 23-2: Excel chart types include the same graphs found in Illustrator, plus some additional charts.

Figure 23-3 shows the Diagram Gallery found in Microsoft Word.

Figure 23-3: Using Word's Diagram Gallery, you can choose from several unique diagram types.

Graphs, charts, and diagrams created in external packages like Word and Excel are moved to the CS2 applications using the Clipboard and import features.

Using Illustrator Graphs

The graphing features in Illustrator are often considered out of place, but considering Creative Suite as a whole, Illustrator is the only CS2 application that has any kind of graphing features. This makes Illustrator's graphing features not only a valuable timesaver but also a means to create unique customized graphs and charts.

Using the Graph tool

Graphs are created in Illustrator using the Graph tool. This tool includes fly-out buttons for each of the supported graph types, as shown in Figure 23-4.

 Regardless of the graph type selected when the graph is first created, the Graph Type dialog box, accessed by double clicking on any of the graph tools, lets you change among the various graph types.

Figure 23-4: The Graph Tool fly-out includes a button for each of the nine graph types supported by Illustrator.

With the graph type that you want to use selected, click with the Graph tool and drag between opposite corners in the document to specify the dimensions of the graph. Or click on the art board and a simple Graph dialog box, shown in Figure 23-5, appears where you type the width and height values of the graph.

 If you hold down the Shift key while dragging to create a graph, a square graph is created. And if you hold down the Option/Alt key while dragging, the graph is created from its center outward.

Figure 23-5: Clicking in the document with the Graph tool opens the Graph dialog box.

Entering data in the Graph Data window

After the graph is created, the Graph Data window, shown in Figure 23-6, appears. This simple window is like a spreadsheet; data entered herein is plotted in the associated graph. The Graph Data window is a simple spreadsheet of rows and columns where you enter the data to be graphed. It can include headers such as axis titles and legend data, as well as numerical data. You can reopen the Graph Data window for the selected graph by choosing Object ➪ Graph ➪ Data.

 The Graph Data window doesn't hold focus when opened. This lets you work with the Illustrator document while the Graph Data window stays open. The window closes only when the Close button is clicked.

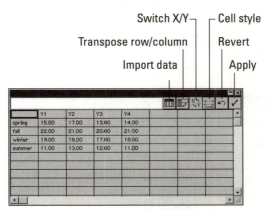

Figure 23-6: The Graph Data window lets you enter or import the data you want to graph.

Entering data

To populate the Graph Data window, just click in a cell and type the value. The current cell is highlighted with a black border, and the value in that cell is displayed in the white field at the top of the window. Pressing the Tab key moves to the next cell in the current row, and pressing the Enter key moves the cursor to the next cell in the current column. The arrow keys can also be used to move about the Graph Data window cells.

Pressing the Delete key deletes the contents of the current cell only, but you can remove the data from multiple selected cells at once by choosing Edit ➪ Clear.

 After using the Clear command, the text is still visible; however, if you select a different cell, the cleared cells are cleared.

Importing data

In addition to manually entering data, Illustrator's Import Data button is used to import a *tab-delimited* text file. To import a data file, click Import Data. A file dialog box opens and lets you choose the file to import. Several files may be imported in a single session.

Note   Illustrator's Import Data feature is fairly forgiving. It can open any file type and tries to extract what it can from the file. If the file doesn't have any data that Illustrator can use, a warning dialog box appears stating, "Some data values were out of range."

Tab-delimited text files must have a tab between each separate value and each row must end with a paragraph return. From within Microsoft Excel, you can create a tab-delimited text from an open spreadsheet by choosing File ⇨ Save As and selecting the Text (Tab delimited, .txt) file type.

In addition to data, labels may also be entered into the Graph Data window and appear as part of the graph. For example, data (or labels) entered in the first column of the Graph Data window for most graph types is used as the Category Axis (X axis or horizontal axis), and data entered in the first row (except for the first cell) is used as Legend data. The Value Axis (Y axis or vertical axis) is determined by the numeric values. Figure 23-7 shows the Graph Data window and its graph. Notice the position in the Graph Data window of the Category and Value Axes.

Note   The upper-left cell of the Graph Data window needs to be left blank in order to create Legend text. Also, if any data cells are left blank or contain a non-digit character, a warning dialog box appears complaining that it cannot create the graph.

All numbers entered in the Graph Data window are interpreted as numeric values. To make a number a label, enclose it in quotes. For example, "2004" is used as a label and not a number. Line breaks can also be added to a label using the vertical bar (|) character.

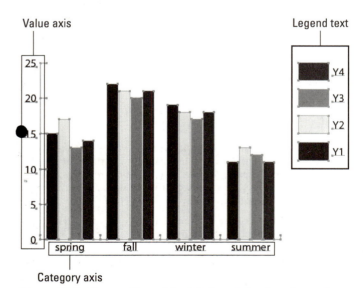

Figure 23-7: The position of the labels and the data determines the Category Axis and legend text.

Scatter graphs are unique because values are measured along both axes and there aren't any categories. To create legend text for a scatter graph, enter each legend item at the top of every other column. The first column contains the vertical-axis data, and the second column contains the horizontal-axis data. Figure 23-8 shows an example of a scatter graph.

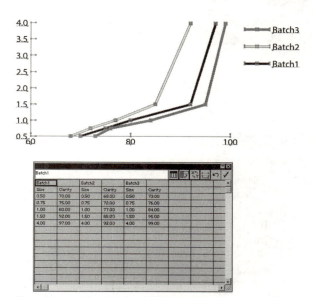

Figure 23-8: The label positions for the scatter-graph type are a little different from the other graphs.

Pie graphs are also handled a little differently from the other graph types. For pie graphs, each row in the Graph Data window creates a separate pie graph. Legend text for the pie graph is placed in the first row (including the first cell if only one graph is created); a category label for each different pie graph is placed in the first column. Figure 23-9 shows an example of a pie graph.

Positioning data

The data's location in the Graph Data window determines how the graph looks. If you mistakenly enter the rows as columns or vice versa, the Transpose Data button switches the rows with columns. To use this feature, just select the cells that you want to transpose and click the Transpose row/column button.

Another common error when entering data is to switch two columns of data. The Switch X/Y button transposes two selected columns. Just like the Transpose row/column button, you use this feature by selecting the two columns or data and clicking the Switch X/Y button.

Note The Switch X/Y button is used only with the Scatter graph type.

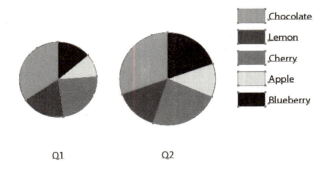

Figure 23-9: The legend labels for the pie graph type are positioned in the first row.

Increasing column width

The Cell Style button opens a simple dialog box, shown in Figure 23-10, where you enter the number of decimals and the column width. Positioning the cursor over a column border in the Graph Data window and dragging the column edge changes column width. The cursor changes to a double arrow when it's over a column that may be changed. Changing column width has no affect on the graph but only supplies more room to view the Graph Data window.

Figure 23-10: The Cell Style dialog box lets you alter the column width for the Graph Data window and specify the number of decimals to use.

Applying data changes

The Apply button, at the right edge of the Graph Data window, applies any changes made to the graph. The Revert button returns the data in the Graph Data window to its last generated state.

Formatting graphs

For the selected graph, the Graph Type dialog box, shown in Figure 23-11, includes settings for formatting the graph. The drop-down list at the top of the dialog box lets you switch among three different panels of settings — Graph Options, Value Axis, and Category Axis — for most graph types. Open the Graph Type dialog box by choosing Object ⇨ Graph ⇨ Type.

Tip You can also open the Graph Type dialog box by double-clicking on the Graph tool.

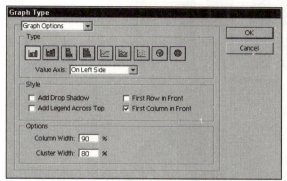

Figure 23-11: The Graph Type dialog box lets you change the graph type for the selected graph.

Changing graph type

In the Graph Options panel of the Graph Type dialog box, you select a different graph type by clicking on the graph buttons. The Value Axis option sets the position of the Value Axis. The options are On Left Side, On Right Side, and On Both Sides, except for bar graphs, which offer options to place the Value Axis On Top Side, On Bottom Side, or On Both Sides.

Note If the Value Axis is assigned to be on both sides of a graph, you can change the scale of one graph. This is explained in the "Combining graph types" section later in this chapter.

Changing graph options

The Style section of the Graph Options panel includes several options. These options are consistent for all graph types and include adding a drop shadow, positioning the legend (to the right or above the graph), and making the first row or the first column in front. Figure 23-12 shows two examples of graphs that include a drop shadow. The drop shadow is added only to the graphed portion.

The last set of options changes depending on the selected graph type. The Column Width and Cluster Width values determine the width of the column or bar used for column and bar graphs. A Column Width value less than 100 percent makes some space appear between adjacent columns or bars. If the Column Width value is greater than 100 percent, the First Row in Front option becomes important, because it defines which column (or row) appears in front when the columns overlap.

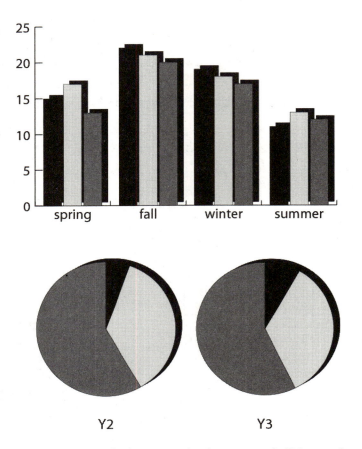

Figure 23-12: Drop shadows are a simple way to embellish a graph.

Figure 23-13 shows an example where the Column Width value is greater than 100 percent. For this example, the Column Width has been set to 130 percent, which causes the columns within each cluster to be overlapped. The First Column in Front option has also been disabled, making the last column in each cluster appear in front of the other columns.

For Line, Scatter, and Radar graph types, the Options section includes Mark Data Points, Edge-to-Edge Lines, Connect Data Points, and Draw Filled Lines with a specified Line Width. The Mark Data Points option places a small square where each data point is located. The Edge-to-Edge Lines option extends the graph lines all the way to the edge of the graph. The Connect Data Points option draws a line between the data points. If the Connect Data Points option is enabled, the Draw Filled Lines becomes active. If that option is enabled, you can specify a Line Width for the lines that connect the data points.

Caution If you disable both the Mark Data Points and Connect Data Points options, nothing is graphed.

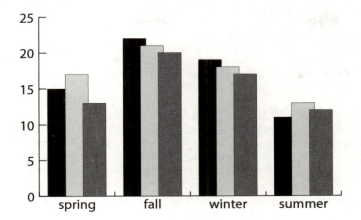

Figure 23-13: By setting the Column Width value over 100 percent, the columns overlap.

For pie graphs, the options include the position of the legend (which may be placed within the pie wedges), how multiple pie graphs are displayed (proportionally, even, or stacked), and how the wedges are sorted. Area graphs have no additional options.

Setting Value and Category Axes

The Value Axis panel of the Graph Type dialog box, shown in Figure 23-14, lets you manually set the tick values for the Value Axis. These tick marks may be set to None, Short, or Full Width and the Value Axis labels can receive a prefix and/or suffix. For example, a dollar sign ($) would make a good prefix, and a measurement value like centimeters (cm) would make a good suffix. Be sure to include a space to separate the prefix or suffix from the number value. Tick marks can also be specified for the Category Axis.

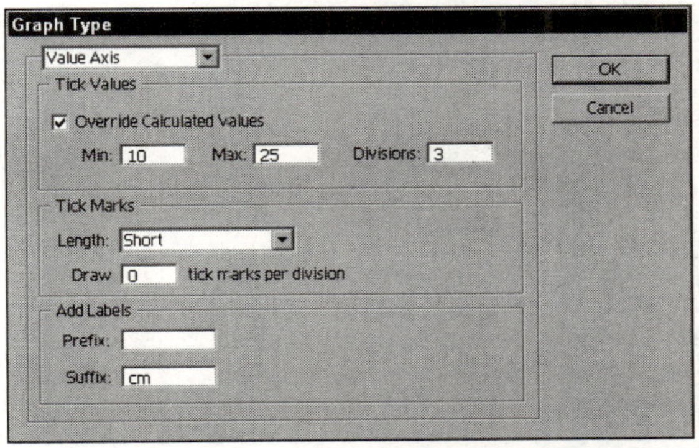

Figure 23-14: The Value Axis panel of the Graph Type dialog box includes options for setting where the tick values appear.

Combining graph types

In some cases, you'll want to combine several graphs into one. For example, suppose you want to represent sale values for different categories as a column graph and include the totals in the same graph. The size of the column for the totals exceeds all the other columns, thereby skewing the graph. By applying the totals as a line graph that is superimposed on top of the column graph, you'll be able to see both sets of values.

Assigning a data set to a different graph type

To combine different graph types together, you first need to enter all the data for both graphs in the Graph Data window. After the graph is created, click away from the graph so no part of the graph is selected. Then, with the Group Selection tool, double-click the legend item for the data set that you want to apply a different graph type to. This selects the graphed portion along with the legend item.

With the graphed portion selected, simply open the Graph Type dialog box and select a different graph type. The newly selected graph type is overlaid on the existing graph.

 Caution   Scatter graphs cannot be combined with other graph types.

Changing Value Axis scale

With two graph types combined into a single graph, you can have two Value Axes displayed by enabling the On Both Sides option for the Value Axis. Each axis can then be set to a different scale.

When you first select to use Value Axis on both sides, both axes are set to the same scale, but you can change either one. Click away from the graph so it isn't selected and then double-click on the legend item for the data set that you want to change. The graphed portion is selected. Open the Graph Type dialog box and select the Value Axis that you want to change. Select the Value Axis panel from the top drop-down list and enable the Override Calculated Values option. Then enter the Min, Max, and Divisions values for the selected axis. The selected graphed portion is re-scaled to match the new Value Axis scale.

Figure 23-15 shows a graph that has combined the column and line graph types. Notice also that the Value Axis on each side is set to a different scale.

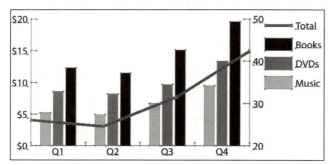

Figure 23-15: By combining two graph types into a single graph, you can represent a data set that would otherwise have values too small to see.

Customizing Illustrator Graphs

The value of having graphs in Illustrator is that you can customize them. Every aspect of the default graphs is customizable, including the graphed columns, bars and lines, the text, the legend, and even the tick marks. This makes it possible to create some original graphs.

Caution If the data in the Graph Data window changes after a graph has been customized, the graph data is regenerated and all customization is lost.

Selecting graph parts

Before the graph is customized, you need to be able to select the various graph parts. When a graph is created, all the parts are grouped together. Individual graph parts are selected using the Group Selection or the Direct Selection tools.

Caution Do not ungroup any portion of graph or you won't be able to work with the graph anymore.

When selecting graph parts, it's helpful to understand how the graph is grouped. Individual columns of data are grouped by categories that in turn are grouped to its legend item. So, clicking on a single column with the Group Selection tool selects the single column. Clicking again on the column selects all the columns in that data set and clicking a third time selects the corresponding item in the legend.

Changing shading

With a graphed portion selected with the Group Selection tool, you can change its stroke and/or fill by selecting new colors from the Swatches palette or the Toolbox.

Changing text

When a graph is first created, all text including the category labels, the legend, and the Value Axis values use the default font and text styling settings, but these settings may be changed. Individual text items are selected by clicking on them once with the Group Selection tool. Clicking twice selects all text items in the axis, category, or legend. Clicking three times on any text item selects all graph text.

When it's selected, you can edit the text using the Type tool or change its style settings using the Paragraph or Character palettes. Figure 23-16 shows a sample graph with a new font and the columns are shaded with gradients.

Using graph designs

Although the default graphs are composed of simple rectangles, lines, and pie wedges, you can replace those elements with custom designs. These designs may be any logo, symbol, or drawing created in Illustrator.

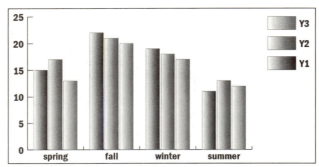

Figure 23-16: Selecting graph parts and changing their properties changes the style of the graph.

Adding new designs

All designs used within a graph are held in the Graph Design dialog box, shown in Figure 23-17. To add a new design to the Graph Design dialog box, create and select the design you want to use and choose Object ➪ Graph ➪ Design to open the Graph Design dialog box. Click New Design and the selected design is added to the list and displayed in the Preview pane. With the New Design selected in the list, click Rename and give the design a new name.

Figure 23-17: The Graph Design dialog box holds all the designs that may be selected to replace a graph's column, bar, or markers.

Using this dialog box, you can add new designs to the list, rename designs, delete and paste selected designs, and select all unused designs.

Applying designs to a graph

Before you can apply a design element to a graph, you need to select the graph element that you want to replace. Click on the graph part with the Group Selection tool (or click twice to select the entire data set and three times to select the data set and its legend); then choose Object ➪ Graph ➪ Column to open the Graph Column dialog box, shown in Figure 23-18.

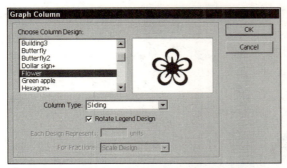

Figure 23-18: The Graph Column dialog box includes many different designs used to replace a graph's plain columns.

The Graph Column dialog box includes many new and interesting design options, including all the designs added to the Graph Design dialog box. Selecting a design item displays a preview next to the design list.

All column designs may be applied using four different methods specified in the Column Type drop-down list:

- ✦ **Vertically Scaled:** This option scales the design item vertically to match the value of the column.

- ✦ **Uniformly Scaled:** This option scales the design item uniformly to match the value of the column causing the design item's width to increase proportionally with its height.

- ✦ **Repeating:** This option repeats the design item for a designated number of units. For example, if the design item is a wheel and each design represents 5 units, a column with a value of 30 would display 6 wheels vertically stacked. For this option, you can also select that fractional portions get Scaled or Chopped. For the previous example, a value of 33 would display the entire wheel scaled vertically three-fifths for the Scale Design option and only three-fifths of the wheel displayed for the Chop Design option.

- ✦ **Sliding:** This option displays the top portion of the design at the top of the column and scales the bottom portion to fill the remaining column height.

Figure 23-19 shows two simple graphs. The buildings in the top graph use the Vertically Scaled option, and the buildings in the lower graph use the Uniformly Scaled option. Notice also that the Rotate Legend Design option has been disabled so the design in the legend is oriented the same as the graphs.

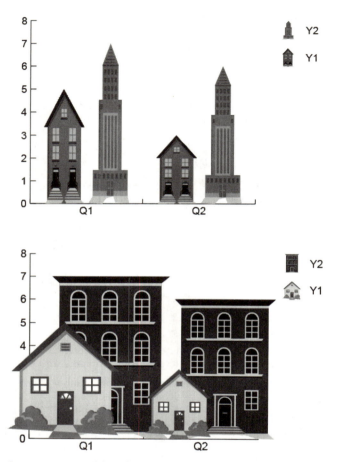

Figure 23-19: Building designs replace the columns. The top graph uses the Vertically Scaled option, and the bottom graph uses the Uniformly Scaled option.

Figure 23-20 shows the same two simple graphs with the Repeating option enabled. Each design item is set to represent 2 units. The top graph has the Scale Design option selected, so the partial butterflies get scaled to half size. The bottom graph has the Chop Design option selection, so the partial leaves get cut in half.

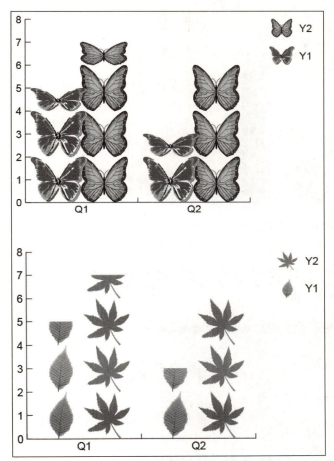

Figure 23-20: Graphs that use the Repeating option may be set to scale or chop the partial designs.

Finally, Figure 23-21 shows an example of the Sliding option. Notice the horizontal line on both designs. This is the line that tells where the sliding should take place.

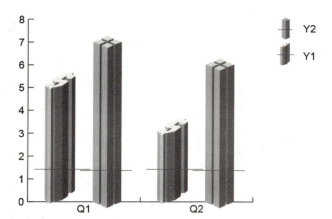

Figure 23-21: This graph uses the Sliding option to replace the normal columns.

In addition to columns, markers found within Line, Scatter, and Radar graphs may be replaced using the Graph Marker dialog box, shown in Figure 23-22. This dialog box uses the same designs as the Graph Column dialog box.

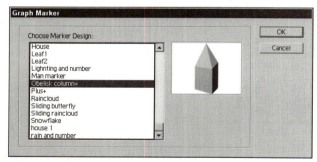

Figure 23-22: In addition to columns, markers can also be replaced using the Graph Marker dialog box.

Creating graph designs

Any design may be used as a graph design, but before it's added to the Graph Design dialog box, it should include a background rectangle object that defines the design's boundaries, and all parts of the design should be grouped together.

Tip Symbol libraries are a good place to find many designs that are used to enhance graphs.

For designs that are to use the Sliding option, add a horizontal line to the design with the Pen tool at a position where the design can stretch. For example, if the design is a pencil, then a horizontal line through the middle of the pencil lets the design be stretched making the middle section of the design as long or as short as needed.

After grouping the design (including the horizontal line), select the horizontal line with the Group Selection tool and choose View ➪ Guides ➪ Make Guides. Make sure the View ➪ Guides ➪ Lock Guides option is not enabled.

Designs can also be made to include the numeric value of the column it represents. To add this text, as shown in Figure 23-23, use the Type tool to create some text that is grouped with the rest of the design. The text should include a percent sign (%) followed by two digits. These two digits represent the number of digits that should appear before the decimal and the number of digits that should appear after the decimal point. For example, the text "%32" would display 3 digits followed by a decimal and two more digits, such as 123.45.

Caution   Any text that is part of a design is scaled along with the design. This can cause problems if the Vertically or Uniformly Scaled options are selected.

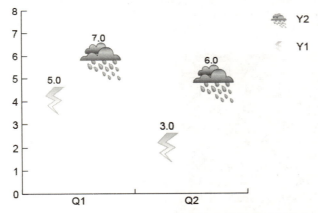

Figure 23-23: Value labels added to graph designs highlight the value of each column.

As a working example of creating an Illustrator graph, this example walks you through the steps to create a standard graph, and a second set of steps shows how to customize an Illustrator graph.

STEPS: Creating an Illustrator graph

1. **Open the data document in Excel.** It is often easier to manipulate data using a spreadsheet such as Excel. With the data file open in Excel, move the data so each row has an equal number of cells and add category and legend labels. Figure 23-24 shows the resulting data set in Excel after it has been manipulated.

2. **Create a graph in Illustrator.** Open a new document in Illustrator and click on the Graph tool in the Toolbox. Drag diagonally with the Graph tool to create a new graph object. This makes the Graph Data window open automatically.

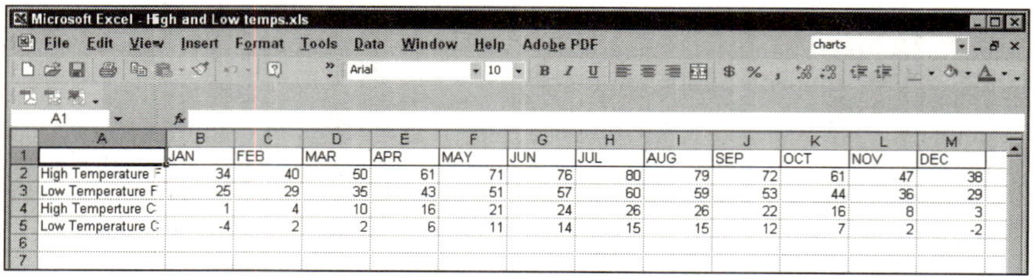

	A	B	C	D	E	F	G	H	I	J	K	L	M
1		JAN	FEB	MAR	APR	MAY	JUN	JUL	AUG	SEP	OCT	NOV	DEC
2	High Temperature F	34	40	50	61	71	76	80	79	72	61	47	38
3	Low Temperature F	25	29	35	43	51	57	60	59	53	44	36	29
4	High Temperture C	1	4	10	16	21	24	26	26	22	16	8	3
5	Low Temperature C	-4	2	2	6	11	14	15	15	12	7	2	-2

Figure 23-24: Data in Excel ready to be moved to the Graph Data window in Illustrator has an equal number of cells in each row.

3. **Import Excel data to Illustrator's Graph Data window.** In Excel, select the graph data and save it as a Tab-delimited Text file. Then click the Import Graph Data button in the Graph Data window in Illustrator. Then select the saved Tab-delimited Text file in the file dialog box to import the data into Illustrator. All the Excel data is moved into Illustrator's Graph Data window, as shown in Figure 23-25.

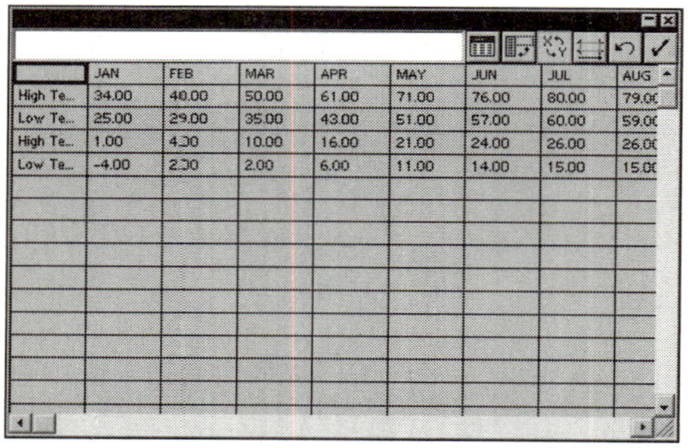

	JAN	FEB	MAR	APR	MAY	JUN	JUL	AUG
High Te...	34.00	40.00	50.00	61.00	71.00	76.00	80.00	79.0
Low Te...	25.00	29.00	35.00	43.00	51.00	57.00	60.00	59.0
High Te...	1.00	4.00	10.00	16.00	21.00	24.00	26.00	26.0
Low Te...	-4.00	2.00	2.00	6.00	11.00	14.00	15.00	15.0

Figure 23-25: Importing data from Excel is perhaps the easiest way to populate the Graph Data window.

4. **Generate the graph.** Click Apply in the Graph Data window to generate the graph. From the graph that is created, it appears that the months have been listed as the legend and the temperature titles are listed along the Category Axis. This is easily fixed in the Graph Data window.

5. **Transpose the data.** Drag over all the data in the Graph Data window and click the Transpose Row/Column button. This makes all the rows into columns and vice versa, which places the months along the Category Axis and the temperatures into the legend. Click Apply to update the graph. Then close the Graph Data window.

6. **Format the graph.** With the graph selected, choose Object ⇨ Graph ⇨ Type to open the Graph Type dialog box. In the Graph Type dialog box, click the Line graph button and set the Value Axis to appear on both sides. Then, enable the Mark Data Points, Edge-to-Edge Lines, and Connect Data Points options, but disable the Draw Filled Lines option.

7. **Change the text font and size.** With the entire graph selected, choose the Impact font by choosing Type ⇨ Font. Change the font size in the Character palette to 18 pt. This affects all the text in the entire graph. With the Type tool, select the legend text and reduce the word to "Temp" for each of the items. Figure 23-26 shows the resulting graph.

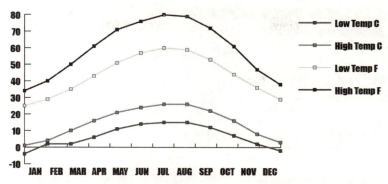

Figure 23-26: This simple graph was created completely within Illustrator.

STEPS: Customizing an Illustrator graph

1. **Create a graph in Illustrator.** Follow the steps in the previous example to create a Column graph using a unique set of Excel data.

2. **Format the Value Axis.** With the graph selected, choose Object ➪ Graph ➪ Type to open the Graph Type dialog box. In the top drop-down list, select the Value Axis option. This action opens the Value Axis settings. In the Add Labels section, enter a space and the text mm for the Suffix field. This denotes the units as millimeters. Figure 23-27 shows the graph at this stage.

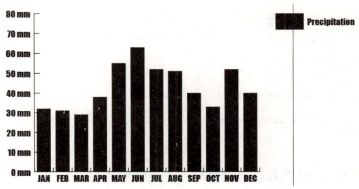

Figure 23-27: Before customizing the column design, the column graph is fairly simple.

3. **Add marker design elements.** Next we'll access the symbol libraries to find some symbols that we can use as Marker designs. Choose Window ➪ Symbol Libraries ➪ Weather to open one of the symbol libraries. Drag a rain-cloud symbol onto the art board. With the rain-cloud symbol selected, choose Object ➪ Graph ➪ Design. In the Graph Design dialog box, click New Design. This action adds the rain-cloud symbol to the preview pane, as shown in Figure 23-28. Click Rename and name the marker "Rain cloud."

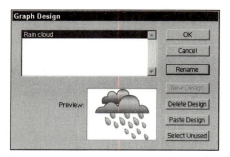

Figure 23-28: Design elements are held in the Graph Design dialog box.

4. **Assign design elements to the graph.** Click on the Group Selection tool and click away from the graph to deselect everything. Then click twice on the Precipitation legend item. This selects all the columns for this data set. Choose Object ⇨ Graph ⇨ Column. In the Graph Column dialog box, select the rain-cloud design, choose the Repeating Column Type, disable the Rotate Legend Design option, set each design to represent 10 units, choose the Chop Design option for fractions, and click OK. Figure 23-29 shows the resulting graph.

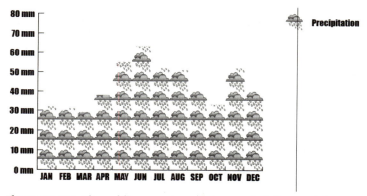

Figure 23-29: After adding a custom design symbol, the graph is improved.

Importing Excel and Word Charts

One of the key limitations of the Illustrator graphs is that the data entered into the Graph Data window must conform to a strict format with an equal number of cells per row. Excel, on the other hand, doesn't have these limitations. Excel offers many additional charting features that aren't found in Illustrator, including many more chart types.

Another key difference is that Excel calls them charts, while Illustrator calls them graphs.

Creating Excel charts

To create a chart in Excel, you need to select the spreadsheet data that you want to graph and then choose Insert ⇨ Chart. This launches the Chart Wizard, which consists of only four steps. The first step of the Chart Wizard, shown in Figure 23-30, lets you choose the chart type. Excel organizes charts into types and sub-types. The available chart types include: Column; Bar; Line; Pie; XY (Scatter); Area; Doughnut; Radar; Surface; Bubble; Stock; Cylinder; Cone; and Pyramid. The sub-types are the same graphs with different formatting options.

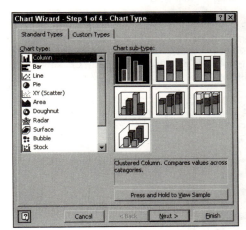

Figure 23-30: Use Excel's Chart Wizard to select a chart type and sub-type.

Note It's important to complete all chart formatting before exporting the chart from Excel. After it's exported, the ability to edit the chart automatically is significantly reduced.

Transporting Excel charts via the Clipboard

Selected Excel charts may be copied and pasted into most of the CS2 applications. To select the Excel chart, click on the chart's background or select Chart Area from the Chart toolbar. This selects all the chart objects including the legend, titles, and axes.

With the entire chart selected, choose Edit ⇨ Cut or Edit ⇨ Copy in Excel to copy the chart to the Clipboard. The copied chart is then pasted into the CS2 applications using the Edit ⇨ Paste (⌘/Ctrl+V) menu command.

Excel charts that are pasted into Photoshop, InDesign, and GoLive are imported as images. Excel charts that are pasted into Illustrator are editable. After an Excel chart is pasted into Illustrator, you can edit the text labels when the chart is ungrouped with the Object ⇨ Ungroup (Shift+Ctrl+G in Windows; Shift+⌘+G on the Mac) menu command.

Note Although the File ⇨ Place command in InDesign supports the placing of Excel spreadsheets within an InDesign document, this feature cannot be used to place an Excel chart.

Creating Word charts and diagrams

In addition to the charts found in Excel, several specialized charts and diagrams are also found in Microsoft Word. These charts and diagrams are accessed by choosing Insert ⇨ Diagram in Word. This opens the Diagram Gallery dialog box, which presents the following six diagram types: Organizational Chart, Cycle Diagram, Radial Diagram, Pyramid Diagram, Venn Diagram, and Target Diagram.

Note A different set of diagrams is available in Word for Macintosh.

Each of these chart and diagram types may be created manually in Photoshop or Illustrator, but creating these items in Word is quick and easy. After selecting one of these types, like the Venn diagram in Figure 23-31, Word places text labels around the diagram. Clicking on these text labels selects the label and lets you edit the text.

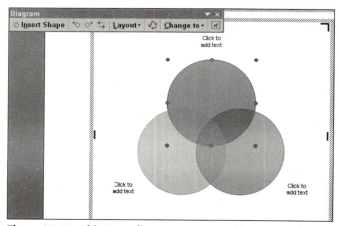

Figure 23-31: This Venn diagram was created in Word with a single menu command and is easily edited using the Diagram toolbar.

After a diagram is created, the Diagram toolbar is used to insert additional shapes, change the diagram layout, or change the diagram type.

Transporting Word diagrams via the Clipboard

Charts and diagrams created in Word are easily moved to the CS2 applications using the Clipboard. To copy the object to the Clipboard in Word, just select the object and use Word's Edit ⇨ Cut or Edit ⇨ Copy menu commands. Then open the CS2 application and choose Edit ⇨ Paste to paste the diagram.

Word diagrams that are pasted into Photoshop, InDesign, and GoLive appear as standard images, but diagrams that are pasted into Illustrator may be edited using the Illustrator tools, after the object is ungrouped by choosing Object ⇨ Ungroup (Shift+Ctrl+G in Windows; Shift+⌘+G on the Mac).

Summary

- Among the features found in Illustrator, Excel, and Word, many different types of graphs, charts, and diagrams can be created.
- Graphs created within Illustrator using the Graph tool and by entering data in Illustrator's Graph Data window.
- You can customize all Illustrator graphs by replacing the graph columns or markers with design elements.
- Charts created in Excel may be imported into Photoshop, InDesign, and GoLive as images using the Clipboard. Excel charts pasted into Illustrator may be edited within Illustrator.
- Diagrams created in Word can also be imported into the various CS2 applications using the Clipboard and edited in Illustrator.

✦ ✦ ✦

Microsoft Office and Professional Printing

CHAPTER 24

In This Chapter

Special printing considerations for Microsoft Word documents

Using PowerPoint presentations

Working with Excel documents

As a professional designer, you wouldn't dream of using Microsoft Office documents for professional output and commercial printing. If all your work is limited to the design pieces you create without using Office documents collected from colleagues or clients, this chapter won't mean much to you. However, if you do receive documents from clients that you need to output to print or to host on Web sites, you'll want to look over some of the more common issues discussed in this chapter that you can potentially face when serving your customers who supply you with Microsoft Office files.

At times, you may need to output an Office file "as is" without reworking the documents by importing text from Word or charts and tables from Excel into InDesign. As stand-alone applications, Microsoft Office programs fall short of features needed for professional output. A book you create in Word can't be printed directly to most high-end devices due to a lack of print controls for screening, printer's marks, and other features needed to print to commercial printing equipment. Excel charts can't be color-separated from Excel. And PowerPoint's Print dialog box lacks attribute settings to successfully print slides to commercial printing devices.

As a design professional or printing technician, you can be certain that on occasion you'll be called upon to take your clients' Office files and prepare them for output to commercial printing devices. In this chapter, you learn how to prepare Office documents for printing on professional equipment.

Printing Microsoft Word Documents

If Word documents are designed to be taken from your clients without modifying them, you can choose one of two options to prepare the documents for professional output — either import the Word document in InDesign and then print from InDesign or print the Word file via Acrobat. Assuming you have a file like a book, manual, story, or other long publication primarily comprised of text, the labor involved in importing the file in InDesign and formatting pages with proper page breaks is going to take you much more time than if you find a way to print the existing document without reformatting it. The problem you encounter when printing Word files to high-end imaging devices is that the Microsoft Word Print dialog box doesn't give you options for selecting commercial print controls. Options such as printer's marks and setting halftone frequency are not available in the Word Print dialog box.

Cross-Reference

For more information on controlling halftone frequency, see Chapter 37.

In order to print a Word file utilizing commercial print options, you need to get the Word document into a program capable of printing with these options or convert the file to Adobe PDF where the PDF can be printed from Acrobat. The method requiring the least amount of effort is converting the file to PDF.

Converting standard page sizes to PDF

For Word documents using standard page sizes, you can simply convert the Word file to PDF without fussing around with special page handling options. Conversion to PDF from all Microsoft Office programs is best achieved with the PDFMaker macro.

 When you install Acrobat, Acrobat tools (two tools on the Mac, three tools in Windows) are added to the Word toolbar:

Note

In earlier versions of Acrobat it was essential that you install Office applications before installing Acrobat in order to see the PDFMaker tools. With Acrobat 7, you no longer need to be concerned about the order of installation. The PDFMaker is installed easily in applications by selecting the Help menu and choosing Detect and Repair in Acrobat. Acrobat searches your hard drive and installs the PDFMaker in all applications supporting the tool if not currently installed.

✦ **Convert to PDF tool:** The first tool on the left in the Acrobat toolbar is the Convert to PDF tool. Clicking this tool opens the Save dialog box, where you supply a filename and choose a destination for the resultant PDF file.

✦ **Convert to Adobe PDF and Email tool:** The second tool is the Convert to Adobe PDF and Email tool. Using this tool converts the Word document to PDF and adds the resultant PDF as a file attachment to a new e-mail message in your default e-mail program.

✦ **Convert to PDF and Send for Review tool:** A third tool available only in Acrobat running on Windows is the Convert to PDF and Send for Review tool. This tool is designed to convert Word documents and set up a review session.

Cross-Reference

For more information on setting up review sessions, see Chapter 25.

In addition to the two Acrobat tools installed by Acrobat is the Adobe PDF menu available only in Microsoft Word running in Windows. In Office XP, you also have the addition of the Acrobat Comments menu. The Adobe PDF menu contains a menu option for changing PDF conversion settings. Choose Adobe PDF ⇨ Change Conversion Settings, and the Acrobat PDFMaker dialog box opens, as shown in Figure 24-1. The Acrobat PDFMaker dialog box is available only to Windows users.

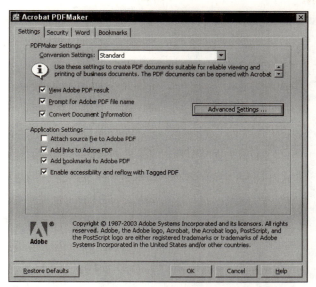

Figure 24-1: In Windows, you can change conversion settings here.

A variety of options exist in the Acrobat PDFMaker dialog box in addition to the Adobe PDF settings adjustments you can make after clicking the Advanced Settings button. The Adobe PDF settings relate to the options choices made for Acrobat Distiller. Mac users need to open Acrobat Distiller and make settings adjustments in the Adobe PDF Settings dialog box. From the Edit Adobe PDF Settings menu command in Acrobat Distiller on the Mac or after clicking the Advanced Settings button in the Adobe PDFMaker dialog box, the Adobe PDF Settings dialog box opens, shown in Figure 24-2. Through the series of tabs at the top of the dialog box, you make choices for a variety of attribute settings that control PDF conversion when Acrobat Distiller is used. When using the PDFMaker macro on either the Mac or Windows, Distiller is used in the background to produce the resultant PDF file.

In almost all circumstances, you'll want to visit the Page Setup dialog box before executing the Convert to Adobe PDF command by clicking the tool in either Mac OS or Windows. You can adjust conversion settings before or after making choices for your page setup. To access the Page Setup dialog box, shown in Figure 24-3, choose File ⇨ Page Setup.

Be certain you choose the proper page size and orientation in the Page Setup dialog box before converting to PDF. If paper orientation is incorrect, the page will be clipped or cut off. If you don't visit the dialog box and choose settings according to the page layout used in the current Word file, you run the risk of having to re-create PDFs.

After making choices for either the Adobe PDF Settings in Acrobat Distiller (Mac) or in the Adobe PDFMaker dialog box (Windows — accessible by selecting Change Conversion Settings) and choosing page-layout attributes in the Page Setup dialog box, click on the Convert to Adobe PDF tool. Word pauses as the PDF conversion is made. Be certain to wait until the conversion is completed before attempting to perform other tasks in Word.

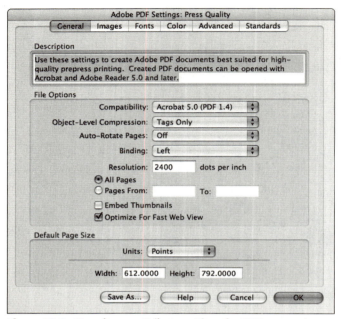

Figure 24-2: You change attribute settings for PDF conversion here.

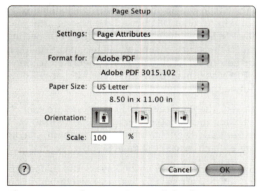

Figure 24-3: The Page Setup dialog box

Tip

PDF conversion with the PDFMaker is painfully slow on the Mac. If you plan to convert many Word documents to PDF and you don't experience problems with font management across computer platforms, you'll find PDF conversion in all Office applications greatly superior on Windows. If you have access to a Windows machine running Acrobat, try to convert to PDF with the PDFMaker on Windows for all your Office files.

Converting Word files with custom page sizes

PDF conversion from Microsoft Word using the PDFMaker tool for standard page sizes is straightforward and requires little preparation. For documents that use custom page sizes, you need to prepare your printer driver and create any custom page sizes that are not part of the default set of page sizes.

Creating custom page sizes can be performed on both Mac OS X and Windows. The results are the same, but the means for achieving the results vary a little.

Creating custom page sizes on the Mac

Custom page sizes on the Mac are handled a little different when using Mac OS X Tiger than when using Mac OS X Panther and below. There have been a few minor changes to dialog boxes when using Page Setup; however, if you haven't upgraded to Mac OS X Tiger, you can follow the steps below and poke around a little in the dialog boxes to figure it out. On Mac OS X Tiger, do the following to create a custom page size in MS Word:

STEPS: Creating Custom Page Sizes in Word on Mac OS X Tiger

1. **Open the Page Setup dialog box.** While in Word, you need to have a document open to access the Page Setup dialog box. You can open a blank document and create a new custom page size or use an existing document to create the custom page size. If using an existing document, the Word file will reform to the new page size after you create it. To begin, open the Page Setup dialog box by choosing File ➪ Page Setup. In the Page Setup dialog box, open the Paper Size pull-down menu and select Manage Custom Sizes, as shown in Figure 24-4.

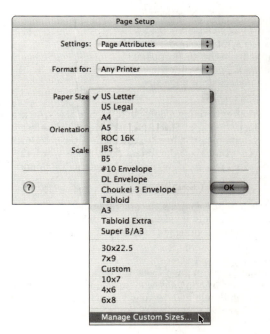

Figure 24-4: Choose Paper Size ➪ Manage Custom Sizes to open the Custom Page Sizes dialog box where new custom page sizes are created.

2. **Set the page size attributes.** Type the width and height for your new custom page size in the Width and Height text boxes. Below the Printer Margins pull-down menu, edit the margins in the four text boxes.

3. **Add the new size to the list of available sizes.** Click the plus (+) symbol on the left side of the dialog box. The attributes defined in the text boxes are added as a new custom page size.

4. **Name the new custom page size.** When you click the plus (+) symbol your new custom page is added with an *Untitled* label. Double-click Untitled and type a name for your new page size. Use a descriptive name for the page such as simply using the page dimensions as a name. In Figure 24-5, you can see several custom page sizes all labeled with the page dimensions.

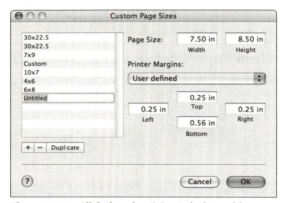

Figure 24-5: Click the plus (+) symbol to add a new page size. When the size appears in the custom page sizes list, it is labeled as *Untitled*. Double-click the text and type a name for the new custom page size.

5. **Select the page size.** Click OK after defining a new custom page size. You are returned to the Page Setup dialog box. Open the Paper Size pull-down menu and select your new custom page size. The size is dynamically added to the menu after creating it in the Custom Page Sizes dialog box. If you have a document open in MS Word, the file reforms to the new page size and margins. You are now ready to create a PDF document suitable for commercial printing.

Caution If the Word file you use to convert to PDF contains any graphic images you'll need to lay out the final document in InDesign. Your clients are likely to use graphic formats not suitable for commercial printing. Steps noted here are designed to assist you when needing to print text-only documents.

In all CS applications, when you create custom page sizes, it's important to remember to return to the Page Setup dialog box after creating a new custom page size. When you first create the page size, you haven't set the document to the new size. Choose File ⇨ Page Setup and select the new page size from the Paper Size pull-down menu. A readout below the page name in the pull-down menu shows what size appears, as you can see in Figure 24-6. This readout helps you identify page sizes in the event that the name you gave the new custom page is obscure.

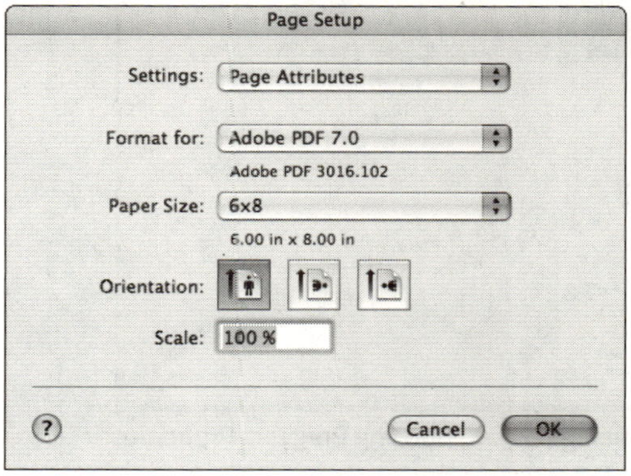

Figure 24-6: Return to the Page Setup dialog box and select a new page size.

If you're using Microsoft Word, your document conforms to the page size. You may need to readjust margins and examine a file if you're changing page sizes in documents that you have created at another page size. After examining the file for correct page setup, you can use the PDFMaker, and the new PDF document is created with the page margins adhering to the page size you selected in the Page Setup dialog box.

Creating custom page sizes on Windows

Windows users follow a similar path as Mac users when creating custom page sizes. On Windows, your first task is to go to the Desktop and open the Start menu. Choose Settings ➪ Printers and Faxes ➪ *a PostScript printer*. You can choose to select either a target printer or the Adobe PDF printer that is installed when you install Acrobat. If selecting a target printer, be certain to select a PostScript printer.

There are several settings you need to make on Windows to create a custom page size for your printer. To understand the process more clearly, Windows users should look over the following steps:

STEPS: Creating PDFs from Word Files Using Nonstandard Page Sizes

1. **Open the Adobe PDF Printer (or a PostScript printer you've installed on your system).** When you create a Word document with a nonstandard page size, you need to add the custom page size to the printer driver you intend to use to create the PDF document. Use the Start menu and choose Settings ➪ Printers and Faxes ➪ Adobe PDF (or *your printer*). For this example, the Adobe PDF Printer is used. If you use another printer, replace your printer name where you see Adobe PDF Printer addressed in the remaining steps.

2. **Open the printer properties.** Select the Adobe PDF Printer, and choose Printer ➪ Properties, as shown in Figure 24-7. The Adobe PDF Properties dialog box appears.

Figure 24-7: Open the Properties dialog box by choosing Printer ⇨ Properties.

3. **Open the Printing Preferences.** In the Adobe PDF Properties dialog box, shown in Figure 24-8, click Printing Preferences.

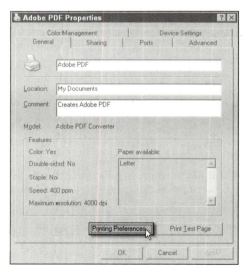

Figure 24-8: Click Printing Preferences in the Adobe PDF Properties dialog box.

4. **Create a custom page.** In the Adobe PDF Printing Preferences dialog box, you'll see a button titled Add. Click the button to open the Add Custom Paper Size dialog box, where the page sizes are defined.

5. **Set the paper size attributes.** In the Add Custom Paper Size dialog box, supply a name in the Paper Names field. It's important to add a new name because overwriting fixed

paper sizes is not permitted. Add the values for the Width and Height. In Figure 24-9, we created a custom page size for 7 inches x 9 inches.

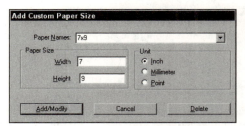

Figure 24-9: Add a name for the new paper size, type the page size values, and click Add/Modify.

6. **Add the page.** Click Add/Modify in the Add Custom Paper Size dialog box, and click OK through the dialog boxes until you arrive at the original Adobe PDF Printer dialog box. Close the window and open Word.

7. **Select the new page size.** In Word, choose File ⇨ Page Setup. From the pull-down menu for Paper Size, select the new paper size you added to the Adobe PDF Printer. In Figure 24-10, you can see the 7-x-9-inch page we added to the Adobe PDF printer. After a custom page size has been created, you can begin a new document or open an existing document and re-form the pages to the new page size.

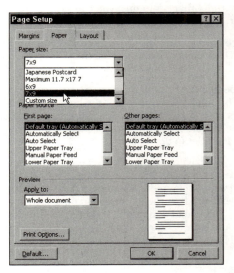

Figure 24-10: In Microsoft Word, choose File ⇨ Page Setup and choose the new paper size in the Paper Size pull-down menu.

8. **Convert to Adobe PDF.** Click on the Convert to Adobe PDF tool in the Word Toolbar Well. If you enabled View Adobe PDF Result in the Adobe PDFMaker Settings tab, the resulting PDF opens in Acrobat.

Note Creating custom page sizes is particularly important for programs like Photoshop CS, Illustrator CS, and the Microsoft Office applications where you want to print oversized color documents for trade-show panels, display prints, and similar output. When converting files to PDF, always be certain you have the proper page size defined for the Adobe PDF Printer before attempting to convert to PDF. Acrobat supports a page size of up to 200 inches square.

Printing converted Word files in Acrobat

If you print a lot of Word files with different sizes or you don't want to set up custom pages in Word or any other program, you have an alternative in Acrobat for printing files with trim marks. If a page size large enough to accommodate trim marks using your printer's PPD is not available to you, you can use Acrobat to create a size large enough to print the marks on your output device.

To understand how to apply trim marks and create larger page sizes to accommodate the marks in Acrobat, follow these steps:

STEPS: Applying Trim and Crops in Acrobat

1. **Convert a Word file to PDF.** Use a standard letter-size page and convert to PDF using the PDFMaker. Note that the steps here can be applied to any document converted to PDF. If your client sends you files from other programs, you can print using the same steps.

2. **Open the file in Acrobat.** After conversion to PDF, launch Acrobat and open the file or open the Bridge and locate the PDF document. Double-click the PDF in the Bridge to open the file in Acrobat.

3. **Adjust the Page Setup.** Before opening the Print dialog box, be certain to double-check the Page Setup for page size and orientation. Acrobat has a nasty habit of always defaulting to U.S. letter-size pages with Portrait orientation rather than defaulting to the document's page size and orientation. If printing a landscape page, be certain to make the proper selection in the Page Setup dialog box.

4. **Open the Print Production tools.** Open a context menu on the Acrobat Toolbar Well by right-clicking (Windows) or Control + click (Macintosh with a one-button mouse) and select Print Production from the menu commands. Alternately, you can select View ⇨ Toolbars ⇨ Print Production. Accessing either menu command opens the Print Production toolbar. The two tools you use to add marks and increase the page size to accommodate the marks are the Add Printer Marks and Crop Pages tools shown highlighted respectively in Figure 24-11.

Figure 24-11: Open the Print Production toolbar from a context menu on the Toolbar Well or select View ⇨ Toolbars ⇨ Print Production.

5. **Add printer marks.** Click the Add Printer Marks tool in the Print Production toolbar. The Add Printer Marks dialog box appears.

6. **Set the printer marks attributes.** If you want all printer marks options provided in Acrobat, select the All Marks check box. If you want selective marks, select the check boxes for the marks you want to appear on the printed page. If you have a multipage document, be certain to select the check box for All under the Page Range category, as shown in Figure 24-12.

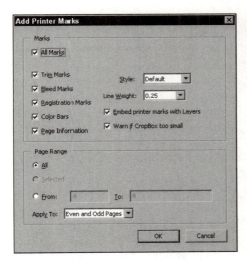

Figure 24-12: Select the check boxes for the marks you want to appear in the printed document, and select the All option in the Page Range section when printing multiple pages.

7. **Apply the marks.** Click OK in the Add Printer Marks dialog box. The marks are applied to the page. If you selected the Warn if CropBox too small check box, a warning dialog box opens informing you that you may need to expand the crop box using the Crop dialog box. Click OK in the warning dialog box to proceed.

8. **Open the Crop Box.** If you applied crops to a page size equal to the page size you have selected in the Page Setup dialog box, you won't see the crop marks on the page in the Document pane. The marks are there, but you need to expand the page size in order to see the marks. To add more page area to accommodate the marks, you begin by opening the Crop Box. Click the Crop Pages tool in the Print Production toolbar and the Crop Pages dialog box opens.

9. **Define a custom size.** Select the Custom radio button and add the width and height dimensions to accommodate the trim marks. Add one-half inch to the existing page size in the Width and Height text boxes.

10. **Select the page range.** If you want all pages to print with marks, select All in the Page Range area of the Crop Pages dialog box. Custom page ranges can be selected by selecting the From radio button and typing the page ranges in the two adjacent text boxes.

11. **Preview the results.** Observe the thumbnail preview and note the new page size reported below the page preview. Adjustments in our example are shown in Figure 24-13 for a standard letter-sized page cropped to 9.5 inches x 12 inches.

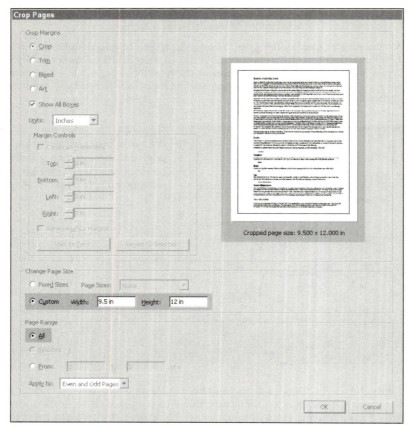

Figure 24-13: Add a custom page size, check the page range, and view the preview in the Crop Pages dialog box.

12. **Apply the crop settings.** Click OK to return to the Document pane.
13. **Preview the results.** When you return to the Document pane view the current page to be certain all printer marks appear on the page as shown in Figure 24-14. The file is now ready to print.
14. **Adjust the Page Setup.** Before opening the Print dialog box, be certain to double-check the Page Setup for page size and orientation. If printing a landscape page, be certain to make the proper selection in the Page Setup dialog box.

Tip

If you want to create client proofs for custom page sizes on your desktop color printer, you can use the same steps outlined here. Crop marks can be added to a PDF file created from any authoring program. Add the printer marks and crop the pages. Print the file to your desktop printer and trim the pages to the crop marks for a client proof. If creating standard U.S. letter or larger pages with bleeds, you can print to oversized paper (like tabloid) and trim to the bleed edges.

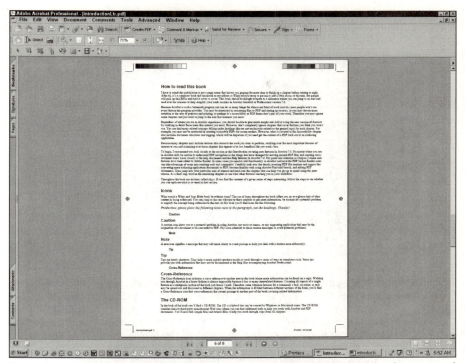

Figure 24-14: Printer's marks are displayed on a new page sized in Acrobat large enough to accommodate the marks.

For more information on printing PDF files to commercial printing devices, see Chapter 38.

Printing from PowerPoint

In design workflows, it's very common to receive PowerPoint files from clients who want to print to large-format color printers for display posters and trade-show panels. PowerPoint is a primary application used for graphics representations by business workers for everything from slide presentations to large prints. When you need to print slides to desktop color printers, you don't need any CS application interventions. However, when you want to output a PowerPoint slide to large-format devices and commercial printing equipment, you need to get the PowerPoint slides to CS applications to access features such as oversized printing, printing with crop marks, setting halftone frequencies, and so on.

To export a PowerPoint file for oversized printing, you use the Print dialog box and set the page size to your output size in the printer Properties dialog box. To begin setting up an oversized print, choose File ➪ Print. The Print dialog box opens, shown in Figure 24-15. From the Name pull-down menu, select Adobe PDF for your printer. If you have large-format inkjet printers on your network, be certain to not use the device printer driver. In many cases, the page sizes for custom pages don't work. Your best solution is to use the Adobe PDF Printer.

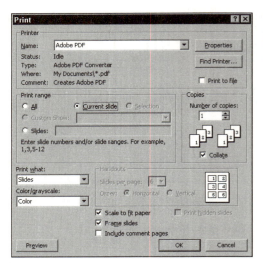

Figure 24-15: In the Print dialog box, you make choices for the printer driver by selecting options from the Name (Windows) pull-down menu.

To adjust the page properties, click Properties, and the Adobe PDF Document Properties dialog box opens (see Figure 24-16). From the Adobe PDF Page Size drop-down list, select a fixed page size as close to your final output size as possible. If you try to set up a custom page size, PowerPoint may produce some unexpected results and the actual output size may be clipped. After selecting a page size, be certain to deselect the box Do Not Send Fonts to "Adobe PDF" Check box." If the box is left selected, you're warned in a dialog box that you need to deselect the check box in order to produce a file using the Adobe PDF Printer.

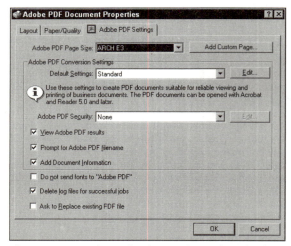

Figure 24-16: Select a fixed page size and uncheck the box for Do Not Send Fonts to "Adobe PDF."

Click OK after making adjustments, and you're returned to the Print dialog box. Select the Scale to Fit Paper check box and click OK. The Save dialog box opens, prompting you to name the resultant PDF document and target a location on your hard drive. Click Save and the PowerPoint slide is exported to PDF.

New Feature If you don't find an exact fit for a page size in the Adobe PDF Document Properties dialog box, you can open the PDF document in Photoshop and size to final dimensions. When you open a PDF document in Photoshop, where the PDF was created from any other source but Photoshop, the Import PDF dialog box opens, as shown in Figure 24-17.

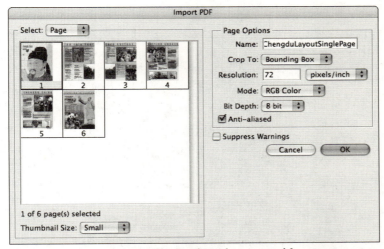

Figure 24-17: Opening PDF files in Photoshop created from any program but Photoshop opens the Import PDF dialog box.

In this dialog box, you can specify the resolution of the file to *rasterize* it. If you need a file sized 300 percent, be certain to select a resolution that accommodates a 300 percent size at the target resolution for the printing device. For example, suppose you have an 8-x-10-inch document that needs to be sized 400 percent to produce a final image size of 32 inches x 40 inches. If the required resolution for the printing device is 150 dpi, you need to set the resolution in Photoshop's import dialog box to 600 ppi (pixels per inch). As you decrease the resolution, the physical size proportionately changes.

Note Rasterizing data in Photoshop is the process of converting objects, such as drawing objects and text to pixels. As objects, the elements contain no resolution and always print at the resolution of the printing device. Raster images that are pixel based have fixed resolutions. Through the process of rasterizing vector objects and text, you can determine what resolution you want the final file.

To understand more about opening PowerPoint files converted to PDF and rasterizing the file in Adobe Photoshop CS2, follow these steps:

STEPS: Rasterizing PDFs in Adobe Photoshop

1. **Open a PDF in Photoshop.** Open the Bridge and locate the PDF file you want to open in Photoshop. If you need to convert a PowerPoint document to PDF, follow the directions outlined at the beginning of this section. From the Bridge, open a context menu on a document thumbnail and select Open With. From the submenu, select Photoshop CS2 as shown in Figure 24-18. Alternately, you can select File ⇨ Open With in the Bridge, drag a PDF document on your desktop to the Photoshop CS2 application icon or an application icon alias, or from within Photoshop chose File ⇨ Open.

Cross-Reference For more information about opening files from Adobe Bridge, see Chapter 7.

Figure 24-18: From the Bridge, select a PDF to open in Photoshop and open a context menu. Choose Open With ⇨ Adobe Photoshop CS2.

2. **Select a page to open.** Photoshop's former PDF Page Selector dialog box has been replaced in Photoshop CS2 with the Import PDF dialog box. The Import PDF dialog box offers all the options you need to rasterize a PDF in Photoshop in a single dialog box. As was the case in Photoshop CS1, you have an option for selecting any page in a multipage PDF document to rasterize. From the Thumbnail Size pull-down menu, select Large if you need to see a larger thumbnail view. Click a page thumbnail to select it for opening in Photoshop. In Figure 24-19, the large thumbnails are viewed and Page 2 is selected.

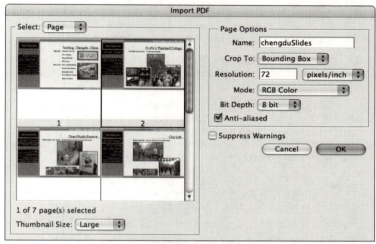

Figure 24-19: Select a page to open in the Import PDF dialog box by clicking on a page thumbnail.

Tip

If you want to rasterize multiple pages, you can Shift + click or Command + click to select a contiguous or noncontiguous range of pages, respectively. When you click OK, all pages are opened in Photoshop as separate documents. The document titles are named according to the filename or name you add to the Name field in the Import PDF dialog box. Each page is identified with a number corresponding to the original page number in the PDF document. For example, if you add the name Slide in the Name field and select pages 3, 5, and 9 in a PDF document, the document names Photoshop adds to the resultant open files are Slide-3, Slide-5, and Slide-9.

3. **Select the resolution to rasterize the file.** Type in the field box the resolution you want for the final file size while considering how much you need to increase or decrease the file dimensions. Where you see Bounding Box selected in the Crop To pull-down menu, be certain to leave the menu choice at the default. A Bounding Box selection opens the file at full size without cropping the page(es).

Caution

If the resolution for images imported into PowerPoint is not sufficiently sized for a larger output size than the image resolution can support, the final file may show significant image degradation. For example, if you import a Photoshop image in PowerPoint at 72 ppi to fit on a 10-x-7½-inch slide and output the slide for a 40-x-30-inch print (a 400 percent increase in size), the Photoshop image is reduced to an effective resolution of 18 ppi (25 percent of the original size). If you open the PDF file in Photoshop and add resolution to the file, the resolution is interpolated and will noticeably degrade the image.

4. **Select the color mode.** If using the final image for Web use, leave the default selection as sRGB. If using the file for print, select RGB for the color mode. Be aware that if you intend to print the file on large format color printers, the preferred color mode is RGB. Do not use CMYK.

5. **Set the Bit depth and anti-aliasing.** Under most circumstances, 8-bit images are fine. You typically won't achieve any better options when rasterizing PowerPoint slides, especially when the slides contain photos. However, if rasterizing vector art, select 16-bit from the Bit Depth pull-down menu. You can make some adjustments in Photoshop in 16-bit mode that won't destroy some precious data. Be certain also to select the Anti-aliased check box especially when you have type on the slides. Anti-aliased type rasterized at the recommended device resolution will print much better.

6. **Open the slide in Photoshop.** Click OK and the slide is rasterized and opens in Photoshop. If you add 300 ppi or more to the resolution, you may need to wait a few minutes for Photoshop to complete its work and open the file.

7. **Change the image size to the desired output size.** Choose Image ⇨ Image Size to open the Image Size dialog box shown in Figure 24-20. Be certain the Resample Image check box is deselected so you don't lose image data when resizing. Type the output resolution in the Resolution text box, and the Width and Height dimensions adjust automatically. Click OK to change to the new image size and resolution.

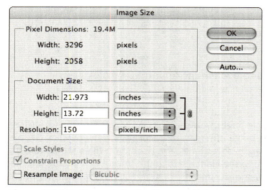

Figure 24-20: Be certain the Resample Image check box is deselected when you change resolution.

8. **Add a new layer to the Photoshop file.** If you submit files to imaging centers for output to large format devices, the files are typically not printed from a Print dialog box, and as such, won't be printed with trim marks. Quite often, large-format color prints in TIFF format are submitted direct to the device RIP (Raster Image Processor) for output while bypassing printing from an application program. If you have any white space on the image, particularly at any corner, it will be difficult to accurately cut the print to final size. To be certain your file is trimmed properly at a service center, add your own trim marks in Photoshop. To begin, create a new layer in Photoshop by clicking the New Layer tool in Photoshop's Layers palette. Drag the new layer down in the Layers palette so the new layer is behind the image layer.

Chapter 24 ✦ **Microsoft Office and Professional Printing** 833

9. **Change the canvas size.** Choose Image ➪ Canvas Size. The Canvas Size dialog box opens. Be certain the unit of measure is in inches, and click the cursor in the Width field and press the up arrow on your keyboard. The width dimensions are sized up approximately 30 pixels. Click the cursor in the Height text box and press the up-arrow key to size the height up the same value.

10. **Add a trim color.** Click the empty layer (first layer in the Layers palette, as shown in Figure 24-21) and fill the layer with Black. (Press D to return to the default colors of black foreground and white background. Press Option/Alt+Delete/Backspace to fill with the foreground black color). If the edges or your image area is black, use another color for the trim color. Any contrasting color will work, but don't select white.

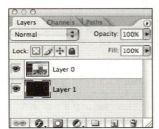

Figure 24-21: Add a new layer below the content layer and fill it with black after resizing the canvas.

Caution

If you have transparency inside the image area, you need to add a white layer between the content layer and the new layer you fill with black.

11. **Flatten and save.** Flatten the layers in the Layers palette and choose File ➪ Save As. Select Tiff for your output format and save the file. The final file is ready for output to a service center. In Figure 24-22, you can see a PowerPoint file rasterized in Photoshop with the trim line added to the file.

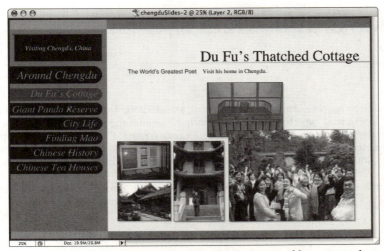

Figure 24-22: Flatten layers and save in the format used by your service center.

For more information on using Layers in Photoshop, see Chapter 14.

Preparing Excel Files

With Microsoft Excel, you find the same lack of support for commercial printing devices as you have with Word and PowerPoint. No support for color separations, printer's marks, or specification of halftone frequency is available in the Microsoft Excel Print dialog box. The process for conversion to PDF is the same in Excel as you find in Word. Use the PDFMaker in Excel, and the Excel worksheet is exported to PDF.

 If you want to use more sophisticated typesetting features when formatting tables, import the Excel files in InDesign. InDesign offers you much more advanced type features in a layout view that provides a print preview while laying out the table.

If an Excel chart is something you want to introduce in a design for print, you can import the PDF file in InDesign. If you need to rework the file and make edits to type, you can convert to PDF and use Acrobat's Copy Table command to copy text in a table, then paste the text in InDesign.

 For more information on working with type from Microsoft Excel, see Chapter 22.

If you have charts you want to edit and prepare them for output to commercial printing devices, you can convert to PDF and open the PDF document in Adobe Illustrator CS. You most likely need to change fonts and re-form paragraphs for editing. Illustrator will open the PDF document generated from Excel and almost every other program with broken lines of text. In Figure 24-23 you can see how Illustrator sees type after opening a PDF file created in a program other than Illustrator. When selecting the type, you can see that each line is broken into separate characters — indicated by the multiple anchor points on each line of type.

Figure 24-23: Illustrator doesn't maintain paragraph formatting when opening PDFs generated from any program but Illustrator.

If you need to re-form a paragraph in Illustrator, select all the text and copy it to the clipboard. Select the Horizontal Type tool and drag a marquee around the area approximately at the same boundaries as the original text occupied. Choose Edit ⇨ Paste, and the text is pasted as a single paragraph, as shown in Figure 24-24. You may need to do some formatting, but formatting text in Illustrator in paragraphs enables you to better control the text placement.

 For more information on working with type in Illustrator and creating area type, see Chapter 18.

Figure 24-24: To re-form text into paragraphs, cut the text and paste it back into Illustrator as area type.

Summary

✦ Microsoft Word documents that you want to print to commercial printing equipment are made print-ready by converting to PDF.

✦ You can create PDF documents from Word files with nonstandard pages sizes by adding custom page sizes to your printer driver.

✦ You can add printer marks to a PDF document in Acrobat and add more page size to accommodate the marks.

✦ You can export PowerPoint files to PDFs for printing large display prints. To crop and size files, open the PDFs exported from PowerPoint in Photoshop.

✦ When you open PDF files in Photoshop that were not originally created in Photoshop, all vector objects and type are rasterized.

✦ You can export Excel files as PDFs and edited in Illustrator.

✦ To reform text blocks to regain paragraph formatting in Illustrator, select text with the Direct Selection tool, cut the text, and paste it back into the document.

✦ ✦ ✦

Working in Creative Design Workflows

PART VI

In This Part

Chapter 25
Creating Review Sessions

Chapter 26
Designing Layouts

Chapter 27
Modifying Layouts

Creating Review Sessions

CHAPTER 25

♦ ♦ ♦ ♦

In This Chapter

Setting commenting preferences

Working with commenting tools

Working with the Comments pane

Adding special features for Adobe Reader users

Working in review sessions

Tracking reviews

Exporting and importing comments

Viewing filtered comments

Summarizing comments in new PDF files

Viewing document comparisons

♦ ♦ ♦ ♦

Adobe Acrobat is the best of the CS programs when you want to engage in workgroup collaboration. With sophisticated tool sets and a number of menu options, Acrobat provides you the ability to comment, mark up, and annotate PDF documents and share your annotations with users through file exchanges on servers or via e-mail. You can mark up documents, send your comments to a group of colleagues or clients, ask for return comments, and track the review history. When PDF documents grow, you can export comments to smaller data files or summarize them and create new PDF documents from comment summaries. You can send these summaries to members of your workgroup or clients for final job approval. Additionally, you can compare documents for changes, comment status, and errors and omissions.

New Feature

In Acrobat 7 Professional you can create PDF documents with special features that permit users with the free Adobe Reader to comment on PDFs, save the comments, and e-mail them back to you. This new feature in Acrobat is perhaps the single best addition to the program for creative professionals.

You can create PDF documents from any of the other CS programs and begin a commenting session with colleagues or clients. Whether your designs are illustrated drawings, Web sites, or graphics designed for print, the commenting tools and features in Acrobat help you facilitate collaborative work efforts where you need to seek opinions or gain approval from others including your clients who may only have the free Adobe Reader program. In this chapter, you learn how to use Acrobat's review and commenting features related to comment markups, e-mail-based reviews, and how to enable PDFs with Adobe Reader usage rights.

Setting Commenting Preferences

Acrobat provides an elaborate set of preference options that enable you to control comment views and behavior. As you draw comments on PDF pages, you may see pop-up windows, connector lines across a page, changes in page views, and a host of other strange behaviors that might confuse you. Before you begin a commenting session, familiarize yourself with the comment preferences and plan to return to the preference settings several times to completely understand how you control comment behavior in Acrobat.

Open the preference settings by pressing ⌘/Ctrl+K or choosing Acrobat ➪ Preferences (Mac) or Edit ➪ Preferences (Windows). In the left pane, select Commenting. In the right pane, you see a long list of preference settings, as shown in Figure 25-1. Take a moment to review these settings before you begin a commenting session.

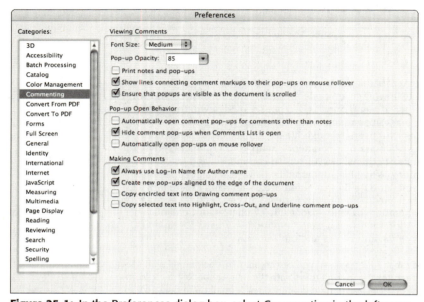

Figure 25-1: In the Preferences dialog box, select Commenting in the left pane.

For the most part, you need only to address the preference settings for Commenting in the right pane once. All subsequent editing sessions in Acrobat use the preference options you made the last time you changed an item in the Preferences dialog box. The individual preference options include the following:

- **Font:** Most tools have associated pop-up notes where you type remarks in a note window. By default, the font used for the note text is Arial. To change the font, select another font from the pull-down menu. All fonts loaded in your system are available from the menu choices. The fonts you use aren't embedded in the file. If you exchange PDFs containing comment notes with other users, the fonts default to another user's preference settings.

- **Font Size:** Font point sizes range from 4 points to 144 points. You can type a number between these values in the field box or select from the preset point sizes from the pull-down menu.

- **Pop-Up Opacity:** By default, a pop-up note background color is white with 85 percent opacity. At 100 percent, the note is opaque and hides underlying data. You can change the opacity so users can see the background data when a pop-up note window opens. You adjust transparency by typing a value in the field box or selecting one from the preset choices in the pull-down menu.

- **Print notes and pop-ups:** Enabling this check box prints the pop-up note contents for all pop-up note windows regardless of whether they are opened or collapsed.

- **Show lines connecting comment markups to their pop-ups on mouse rollover:** When you roll the mouse pointer over a comment markup (such as highlighting or a note icon), the shaded connector line between the comment and the open pop-up window appears as shown in Figure 25-2.

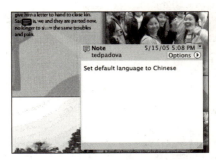

Figure 25-2: Connector lines extend from a comment note to the comment icon.

- **Ensure that pop-ups are visible as the document is scrolled:** If a comment note extends beyond one page in a continuous page view, the note is visible when scrolling pages.

- **Automatically open comment pop-ups for comments other than notes:** As you create comments with drawing tools, the Text Box tool, or Pencil tool, the pop-up note windows are collapsed by default. If you want a pop-up note window opened and ready to accept type when creating comments with these tools, check the box.

- **Hide comment pop-ups when Comments List is opened:** The Comments List is contained in the Comments pane. When you open the Comments pane, the list shows expanded comment notes with the content displayed in the pane. To hide the pop-ups in the Document pane when the Comments pane is opened, enable the check box. If you set this item as a default, you can expand comments in the Comments pane by clicking icons to see the content of the pop-ups.

- **Automatically open pop-ups on mouse rollover:** Pop-up note windows can be opened or closed. Double-clicking a collapsed pop-up note window opens the window. If you want to have a pop-up note window open automatically as the cursor is placed over a comment icon, enable this check box.

- **Always Use Log-In Name for Author Name:** Another set of preferences appears when you click on Identity in the left pane. The login name specified in the Identity preferences is used for the author name on all comments when you enable this check box. If you're a single user on a workstation, setting the Identity preferences and enabling this check box saves you time creating comments when you want to add your name as the author name.

- **Create new pop-ups aligned to the edge of the document:** By default, the top-left corner of a pop-up note window is aligned to the top-left corner of the comment icon. If you enable this check box, no matter where you create the note icon, the pop-up note aligns to the right edge of the document.

- **Copy encircled text into Drawing comment pop-ups.** When proofreading a document and using the Text Edit tools, you might add strikethrough to text, highlight text, or mark it for replacement, or you may use drawing tools to encircle passages of text. When you select the text for editing or encircle text with a drawing tool, the text selection automatically appears in the note pop-up window when you select this option. You might use this option to show the author of the PDF document how the old text appears and follow up with your recommendations to change the text. In essence, the PDF author can see a before/after comparison.

✦ **Copy selected text into Highlight, Cross-Out, and Underline comment pop-ups:** This enables the text selected with tools in the Highlighting toolbar to automatically appear in the pop-up note window.

As you can see, there are many different preference settings. The options you set in the Commenting preferences influence how you view comments and the methods you use for review and comments. Take some time to play with these settings as you use the tools discussed in this chapter.

Using Commenting Tools

Users of either Acrobat Professional or Acrobat Standard can access the Commenting tools. Acrobat refers to these tools simply as Commenting tools; however, there are two other sets of commenting tools that include Drawing Markup and Measuring tools.

The Commenting tools are intended for use by anyone reviewing and marking up documents. Much like you might use a highlighter on paper documents, the commenting tools enable you to electronically comment and mark up PDF documents. A variety of tools with different icon symbols offer you an extensive library of tools that can help you facilitate a review process. For most creative design workflows these tools are sufficient for engaging in review sessions.

Many comment tools, among any group, have a symbol or icon that appears where the comment is created. They also have a note pop-up window where you add text to clarify a meaning associated with the mark you add to a document. These pop-up note windows have identical attributes. How you manage note pop-ups and change the properties works the same regardless of the comment mark you create, with the exception of the Callout and Text Box tools. The Note tool is covered here in detail. Any other comment tool you use that supports a pop-up note window has attributes identical to the Note tool.

Using the Note tool

The Note tool is the most common commenting tool used in Acrobat. To create a comment note, select the Note tool in the Commenting toolbar and drag open a note window. When you release the mouse button, the note pop-up aligns to the top-left corner of the note icon.

Tip You can also add notes to a page via menu commands. To add a note to a page, choose Comments ⇨ Add a Note or select the Hand tool and open a context menu on a page. From the menu choices, select Add Note.

Alternately, you can click without dragging. When you release the mouse button, a pop-up note window is created at a fixed size according to your monitor resolution. The higher you set your monitor resolution the smaller the pop-up note window appears. On an 800 × 600 display, the window size defaults to 360 × 266 pixels.

To add text to the pop-up note, begin typing. Acrobat places an I-beam cursor inside the pop-up note window immediately after creating the note. For font selection and font sizing, you need to address the Comment preference settings discussed in the section "Setting Commenting Preferences" earlier in this chapter.

Managing notes

The color of a note pop-up and the note icon is yellow by default. At the top of the note pop-up, the title bar is yellow and the area where you add the contents is white. The title bar contains information supplied by Acrobat that includes the subject of the note, the author, and the date and time the note is created. You can move a note pop-up independently of the note icon by clicking and dragging the title bar.

Cross-Reference The Subject of a note by default is titled *Note*. The default Author name is derived from either your computer log-on name or your Identity depending on how your preferences are established. For information on how to change the Subject and Author in the title bar, see "Note tool properties" later in this chapter.

You delete note pop-up windows and note icons either by selecting the note icon and pressing the Delete/Backspace or Del key on your keyboard or through a context menu selection. If you use a keystroke to delete a note, you must be certain to select the icon; then press the Delete/Backspace or Del key. Selecting the title bar in a note pop-up and using the same keys won't delete the note.

To resize a note pop-up window grab the lower-right corner of the window and drag in or out to resize smaller or larger, respectively. Note pop-ups containing more text that can be viewed in the current window size use elevator bars so you can scroll the window much like you would use when viewing pages in the Document pane. Only vertical elevator bars are shown in the pop-up windows. As you type text in the window, text wraps to the horizontal width, thereby eliminating a need for horizontal scroll bars. As you size a note pop-up window horizontally, the text rewraps to conform to the horizontal width.

You open context menus from either the note icon or the note pop-up window. When opening a context menu from the note pop-up window, you have two choices: open the context menu from the title bar or open the context menu from inside the note window (below the title bar). Depending on where you open the context menu, the menu selections are different. Opening a context menu from the title bar or from the note icon shows identical menu options. You can also use the Options menu to open the same menu as when opening a context menu inside the note window. Click the right-pointing arrow adjacent to Options and the menu opens.

In Figure 25-3, a context menu is opened from the title bar on a pop-up note window. The menu options are the same as if the note was opened from the context menu on the note icon. In Figure 25-4, a context menu is opened from inside the note pop-up window. Depending on edits you make in the note window and whether you have text selected, menu options change. In Figure 25-4, text was edited in the note window, which adds the Undo command to the context menu. Additionally, text is selected which adds several other commands for cut, copy, and adding the selected text to a dictionary. In both menus, you can select Delete Comment to remove the note pop-up menu and the note icon.

Figure 25-3: This context menu is opened from the note pop-up window title bar. From the menu options, select Delete to remove the note icon and the note pop-up menu.

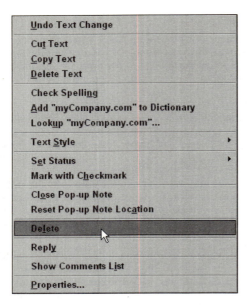

Figure 25-4: When you open a context menu from the note pop-up window below the title bar, menu options change. If you select text in the note window, additional commands are added to the context menu.

The context menus are similar and most commands existing in the smaller menu are the same as those found in the larger menu. If two notes are selected, additional menu commands appear in a context menu. From menu options you have a command to Group notes.

To group notes together, you need to select the Hand tool and Control/Command+click each note icon to include in a selection. From a context menu opened on any note title icon and select Group. If you open the Comments list by clicking on the Comments tab, you see the note icon change for grouped notes as shown in Figure 25-5.

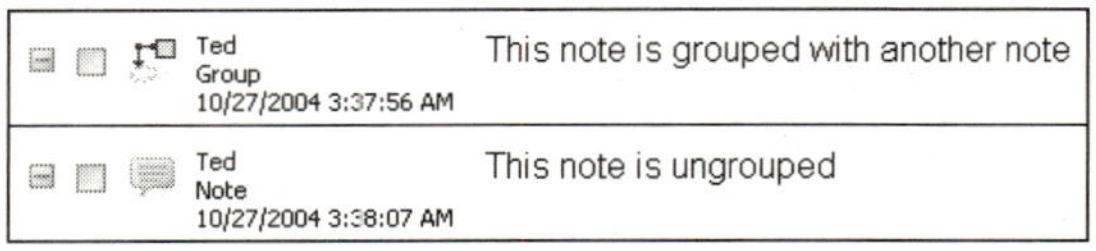

Figure 25-5: Grouped notes appear in the Comments list with a different icon than ungrouped notes.

In Figure 25-4, you see a long list of menu commands. Let's take a look at these commands; the same commands found in the context menu shown in Figure 25-5 operate the same way.

- ✦ **Undo Text Change:** When you type text in the pop-up menu and delete it, you can select the Undo Text Change command to regain your text. Deleting a comment note can also be undone. However, because deleting a comment note eliminates an opportunity to open a context menu from the note pop-up window, you need to choose Edit ➪ Undo. If text was added to a pop-up note window and you delete the note, choosing Edit ➪ Undo returns the note and the text in the note pop-up window.

- ✦ **Redo Text Change:** If you type a block of text and select Undo, you can later select Redo and bring the text back.

✦ **Cut Text/Copy Text:** These items work as you might assume from using any text editor or word processor. The commands relate to typing text in the note pop-up window. You can also highlight text and use key modifiers (Ctrl/⌘+C for Copy; Ctrl/⌘+X for Cut; Ctrl/⌘+V for Paste).

✦ **Delete Text:** Select text and choose Delete Text. The selected text is deleted.

✦ **Check Spelling:** When you select Check Spelling in the note pop-up menu, the Check Spelling dialog box opens, as shown in Figure 25-6. When the dialog box opens, click the Start button and Acrobat checks the spelling for all the text typed in the note pop-up. When Acrobat finds a word it thinks is misspelled, the word is highlighted and a list of suggestions that closely match the spelling are shown in the lower window. Select a word with the correct spelling and click Change.

Figure 25-6: Select Check Spelling from a context menu and the Check Spelling dialog box opens. Click Start and Acrobat checks the spelling for the note pop-up contents. You can choose a replacement for the misspelled word(s) from a list of suggestions in the dialog box.

✦ **Add "..." to Dictionary:** Select text and the selected text appears within the quote marks. When you choose the menu command the selected text is added to your custom dictionary used when spell checking. If the word already exists in your custom dictionary, the menu command appears as *Remove "..." from Dictionary*.

✦ **Remove "..." from Dictionary:** This menu item is active only when you have a word selected in the note pop-up window and that note is contained in your custom dictionary. It's a nifty little feature in Acrobat 7.0. Because Acrobat automatically spell-checks text you type in the comment note pop-up window by matching your words to those found in its dictionary, words not found by Acrobat as a match in its dictionary are underlined in red with a wavy line like you might see in programs like Microsoft Word. If you want to have Acrobat flag you whenever you type a specific word, remove that word from the dictionary. Then Acrobat displays the word with a red underline each time you use it.

When would you use this feature? Assume for a moment that you want to use a generic reference to users as opposed to a masculine or feminine reference. Highlight the word *he* or *she* and open a context menu from the note pop-up window. Select Remove "*he*" from Dictionary. Each time you type the word *he*, Acrobat underlines the word because it can't find a match in the dictionary. When you review your notes, you might substitute *s/he* for the word *he*.

✦ **Look Up "...":** The default menu command is *Look Up Definition*. When a word is selected, the menu command changes to Look Up *selected word*. For example, if you select a word like *reply*, the menu command changes to Look Up "reply." Select the menu command and your Web browser launches and the Dictionary.com Web site opens in your Web browser where the word is searched and a definition is displayed on the Web page.

Users of Mac OS X Tiger can use the dictionary and thesaurus in the Dashboard or the Dictionary application for faster results than opening the Dictionary.com Web page.

✦ **Text Style:** From a submenu select from (Bold/Italic/Underline/Superscript/Subscript/Clear Formatting). Select any one of the formatting options to apply to selected text. You can combine format changes by selecting text and a format option, then return to the context menu and select another option, and so on.

✦ **Set Status:** You as a PDF author may share a document for review with others. As comments are collected you may decide to determine a status for comments among your workgroup. You may want to mark a comment as *Accepted, Rejected,* or *Cancelled,* or mark a comment thread as *Completed*. You select these options from the submenu that appears when you select the Set Status command. By default, a status is set to *None* when you begin a session. A second submenu appears for Migration where you have choices for None, Not Confirmed, and Confirmed.

✦ **Mark with Checkmark:** Whereas the Set Status items are communicated to others, a check mark you add to a comment is for your own purposes. You can mark a comment as checked to denote any comments that need attention or are completed and require no further annotation. Check marks are visible in the Comments pane and can be toggled on or off in the pane as well as the context menu. Check marks can be added to comments with or without your participation in a review session. You can choose to have your comments sorted by those with checkmarks and those without checkmarks.

✦ **Close Pop-up Note:** Closes the note pop-up window.

✦ **Reset Pop-up Note Location:** If you move a note pop-up window, selecting this menu command returns the note pop-up to the default position.

✦ **Delete:** Deletes the comment pop-up note and the note icon.

✦ **Reply:** When participating in a review, you select the Reply command to reply to comments made from other users. A new window opens in which you type a reply message. From the pop-up bar you can review a thread and click the Reply button to send your comments to others via e-mail, to a network server, or to a Web-hosted server.

✦ **Show Comments List:** Selecting this item opens the Comments pane. Any comments in the open document are expanded in a list view in the Comments pane. When the Comments pane is open, this option toggles to Hide Comments List.

✦ **Properties:** Opens the Properties dialog box.

Note tool properties

Each comment created from either the Commenting tools or the Drawing Markup tools has properties that you can change in a properties dialog box. Properties changes are generally applied to note pop-up windows and icon shapes for a particular tool. In addition, a variety of properties are specific to different tools that offer you many options for viewing and displaying comments and tracking the history of the comments made on a document.

With respect to note pop-ups and those properties assigned to the Note tool, you have choices for changing the default color, opacity, author name, and a few other options. Keep in mind that not all property changes are contained in the properties dialog box. Attributes such as font selection and point sizes are globally applied to note pop-ups in the Comment preferences.

Cross-Reference For information about Commenting preferences, see the section "Creating an E-Mail-Based Review."

You open the properties dialog box from a context menu. Be certain to place the cursor on a pop-up note title bar or the note icon before opening a context menu. Select Properties from the menu choices and the Note Properties dialog box shown in Figure 25-7 opens.

Tip To keep a comment tool selected without returning to the Hand tool after creating a comment, check the box in the Properties bar for Keep tool selected.

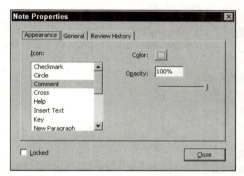

Figure 25-7: Open a context menu from a pop-up note title bar and select Properties.

The Note Properties dialog box contains three tabs. Select a tab and make choices for the items contained in the dialog box. For pop-up note properties the items you can change include the following:

✦ **Appearance:** Options in the Appearance tab relate to the note icon appearances and the pop-up note window appearance.

- **Icon:** From the scrollable list, select an item that changes the Note icon appearance. Selections you make in this list are dynamic and change the appearance of the icon in the Document pane as you click on a name in the list. If you move the Note Properties dialog box out of the view of the note icon, you can see the appearance changes as you make selections in the list. Fifteen different icons are available to choose from as shown in Figure 25-8.

- **Color:** Click the color swatch to open the pop-up color palette shown in Figure 25-9. You select a preset colors from the swatches in the palette. You add custom colors by selecting the Other Color item in the palette, which opens the system color palette. In the system color palette, make color choices and the new custom color is applied to the note.

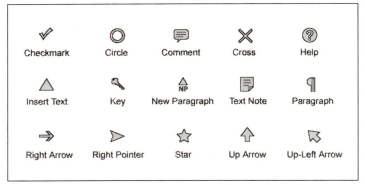

Figure 25-8: You select icon shapes from the Icon list in the Appearance tab in the Note Properties dialog box. You can choose from 15 different shapes.

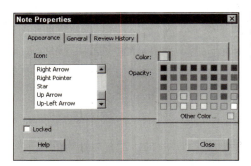

Figure 25-9: Click the color swatch to select from preset colors or select Other Color to open the system color palette where you select custom colors.

Changing color in the Appearance properties affects both the color of the note icon and the pop-up note title bar. If you mark up and review documents in workgroups, different colors assigned to different participants can help you ascertain at a glance which participant made a given comment.

- **Opacity:** Global opacity settings are applied in the Comment Preferences dialog box. You can override the default opacity setting in the Appearance properties for any given note pop-up window.

- **Locked:** Select the Locked check box to lock a note. When notes are locked, the position of the note icon is fixed to the Document pane and cannot be moved when you leave the Note Properties dialog box. All other options in the Note Properties dialog box are grayed out, preventing you from making any further attribute changes. If you lock a note, you can move the pop-up window and resize it. The note contents however, are locked and no changes to the text in the pop-up note window can be made. If you want to make changes to the properties or the pop-up note contents, return to the Note Properties dialog box and uncheck the Locked check box.

✦ **General:** Click the General tab to make changes for items appearing in the note pop-up title bar. Two editable fields are available as shown in Figure 25-10. The changes you make in the Author and Subject fields are dynamic and are reflected in the Document pane when you edit a field and tab to the next field. You can see the changes you make here before leaving the Note Properties dialog box.

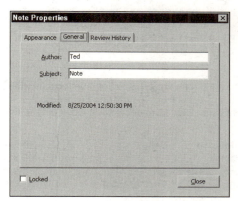

Figure 25-10: Make changes to the Author name and the pop-up note Subject in the General preferences.

- **Author:** The Author name is supplied by default according to how you set your Comment preferences. If you use the Identity preferences, the Author name is supplied from the information added in the Identity preferences (see "Setting Commenting Preferences" earlier in this chapter). If you don't use Identity for the Author title, the name is derived from your computer log-on name. You might see names like Owner, Administrator, or a specific name you used in setting up your operating system.

  If you want to change the Author name and override the preferences, select the General tab and edit the Author name. The name edited in the General preferences is applied to the selected note. All other notes are left undisturbed. One reason you might change author name is when engaging in review sessions where other members in the review have the same first name. If your default name is your first name only, you may want to change the author name in some reviews to include both first and last name.

- **Subject:** By default, the Subject of a note is titled *Note* appearing in the top-left corner of the pop-up note title bar. You can change the subject in the General properties by typing text in the Subject line. You can add long text descriptions for the Subject; however, the text remains on a single line in the pop-up note properties dialog box. Text won't scroll to a second line. The amount of text shown for the Subject field relates to the horizontal width of the note window. As you expand the width, more text is visible in the title bar if you add a long Subject name. As you size down the width, text is clipped to accommodate the note size.

- **Modified:** This item is informational and supplied automatically by Acrobat from your system clock. The field is not editable. The readout displays the date and time the note was modified.

✦ **Review History:** The Review History lists all comment and status changes in a scrollable list. The list is informational and not editable.

After making changes in the Note Properties dialog box, click Close to apply the changes. Clicking on the close box or pressing the Esc key also applies the changes you make in the Note properties dialog box.

Tip   The Properties dialog boxes for all Comment tools are dynamic and enable you to work in the Document pane or the dialog box when the dialog is open. Make adjustments to properties and move the dialog box out of the way of your view of an object you edit. The updates are made when you tab out of fields in the dialog box. You have complete access to menu commands and other tools while the Properties dialog box remains open.

Using the Properties bar

If you set up your work environment to view the Properties bar while working in a review session, you can address several properties options from it. Options for note color, icon type, and fixed opacity changes in 20 percent increments are accessible without opening the Properties dialog box.

As shown in Figure 25-11, from a pull-down menu on the Properties bar, you can select the different note icons when the Note tool is selected. Clicking the color swatch opens the same color selection pop-up window as it does in the Properties dialog box. The checkerboard to the right of the icon menu is the opacity selection. Click the down arrow to see a list of preset opacity choices.

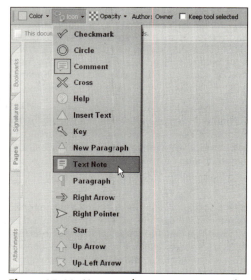

Figure 25-11: You can change some properties options in the Properties bar. To open the toolbar, open a context menu on the Toolbar Well and select Properties bar.

Notice the Author name appears in the Properties bar; however, the name is not editable and you need to open the Properties dialog box to make an author name change. The last item in the Properties bar is a check box. Click this box if you want to keep the Note tool selected. Disabling the check box causes the Hand tool to be selected each time a note is created.

When you select a different comment tool from either the basic Commenting toolbar or the Advanced Commenting toolbar, the Properties bar changes to reflect choices available for the selected tool.

Tip With some tools you see a *More* button on the Properties bar. Clicking More opens the Properties dialog box.

Adding a note to a page

You can add notes to a page either inside a page in the Document pane or outside the page boundary. Use the Note tool to add notes or add a note while browsing pages with the Hand tool selected. Open a context menu with the Hand tool and the menu options include Add Note.

The new note is added at the cursor position. You can use the Hand tool to browse pages by selecting the Next Page and Previous Page context menu commands and add a note when you want to comment on a page without changing tools.

The Add Note command is also available from the Comments menu. Choose Comments ➪ Add a Note and the note is added to the center of the page.

Tip If you're proofreading a document and you think terms might be expressed better using different words and you want to find word definitions or access a thesaurus, open a context menu with the Hand tool and select Add Note. Type a word in the note pop-up window and highlight the word. Open a context menu from the highlighted word and select LookUp "...." The Dictionary.com Web site opens in your Web browser, with the word definition on the open Web page.

Using Text Edit tools

Adjacent the Note tool in the basic Comments toolbar is an item labeled Text Edits. Text Edits in and of itself is not a tool. The tools are available from menu selections made from the pull-down menu shown in Figure 25-12.

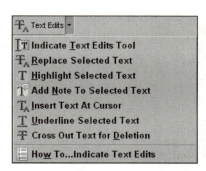

Figure 25-12: Select the Text Edit tools from a pull-down menu.

Text Edit tools are designed primarily for use with Microsoft Word where you convert a Word file to PDF, mark up the PDF in a review session, and export the Text Edit comments directly to the original Word document. Unfortunately, exporting comments from Acrobat back to Word is only available on Acrobat running under Windows XP and with Microsoft Word 2002 or above. You can use the comment tools to mark up documents on Windows 2000 and Mac OS X, but you can't export the comments from Acrobat to Word.

In workflow environments where your clients or colleagues use Word running on Windows, you can simplify major editing jobs using a Windows machine and exporting comments like text deletions, replacements, and insertions back to original Word files. You can then import the edited Word file(s) in InDesign without having to perform major copyediting while creating the layout.

Select text with the Select tool and apply one of the Text edits to the selected text. You can mark text for replacing text, highlighting text, add a note to selected text, insert text at the cursor, underline text, and cross out text.

To the right of the Stamp tool is another set of highlighting tools. In almost all review sessions, avoid using these tools. The Text Edit tools provide the same options. If someone receives a document you marked up and the document originated in MS Word, the PDF author can integrate the comments in the original Word document. The highlighting tools don't provide an option to export comments to Word.

Using the Stamp tool

The Stamp tool is part of the basic commenting tools, but it differs greatly from the other tools found in the Commenting toolbar. Instead of marking data on a PDF page and adding notes to the marks, stamps enable you to apply icons of your own choosing to express statements about a document's status or add custom icons and symbols for communicating messages. Stamps offer you a wide range of flexibility for marking documents similar to analog stamps you might use for stamping approvals, drafts, confidentiality, and so on. You can use one of a number of different icons supplied by Acrobat when you install the program, or you can create your own custom icons tailored to your workflow or company needs.

Whether you use a preset stamp provided by Acrobat or create a custom stamp, each stamp has an associated note pop-up window where you can add comments. You select stamps from menu options in the Stamp pull-down menu where stamps are organized by categories. Add a stamp to a page by clicking the Stamp tool after selecting a stamp from a category; or you can click and drag the Stamp tool to size the icon. After creating a stamp, you access Stamp Properties the same as when using the Note comments.

Selecting stamps

Using a stamp begins with selecting from among many different stamp images found in submenus from the Stamp tool pull-down menu. Click the down arrow and the first three menu commands list categories for stamps installed with Acrobat. Selecting one of these three menu items opens a submenu where specific stamps are selected from the respective category, as shown in Figure 25-13.

Adding a stamp to a page

The stamp name you select in the menu becomes the new default stamp. When you click the Stamp tool or click and drag open a rectangle with the Stamp tool, the default stamp is added to the document page. Stamps are created by default with the pop-up note window collapsed. To open the pop-up note window, double-click the mouse button on the stamp image. The pop-up note opens and appears the same as other pop-up note windows for other Comment tools.

If you want to resize a stamp after creating it on a page, select the Hand tool and click on the stamp icon to select it. Move the cursor to a corner handle, shown in Figure 25-14, and drag in or out to resize the stamp.

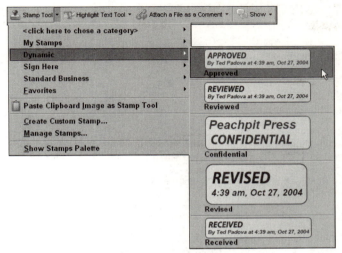

Figure 25-13: Selecting a default stamp

 Stamps are always proportionately sized when dragging any one of the corner handles. You don't need to drag handles while pressing the Shift key to proportionately size the image.

Figure 25-14: To resize a stamp, drag a corner handle on the selection marquee.

Acrobat offers an assortment of stamps you can select from the category submenus in the Stamp tool pull-down menu. These stamps are created for general office uses, and you'll find many common stamp types among the sets. The three categories of stamps and their respective types and icons are shown in Figure 25-15.

You should think of these stamps as a starter set and use them for some traditional office markups when the need arises. The real power of stamps, however, is creating custom stamps that use virtually any illustration or photo image.

 For learning how to create custom stamps, see the section "Creating custom stamps."

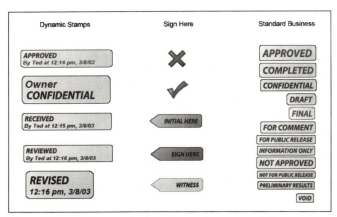

Figure 25-15: You can choose stamps from one of three categories.

Stamp properties

You change stamp properties in the Stamp Properties dialog box, where you have the same options as those found in the Note Properties dialog box, with one exception. In the Note Properties dialog box, you make choices for the icon appearance from a list in the dialog box. Because stamps have appearances determined before you create the stamp, no options are available for changing properties.

If you want to change the appearance of a stamp, you need to delete the stamp and create a new stamp after selecting the category and stamp name from the category submenu. You delete stamps by opening a context menu and choosing Delete or by selecting the stamp icon and pressing the Backspace/Delete or Del key.

You make stamp icons opacity adjustments in the Stamp Properties dialog box and you can change opacity for stamps created from either vector art or raster art. Open the Stamp Properties dialog box and move the slider below the Opacity field box or edit the field box to change the level of opacity.

Creating custom stamps

You add custom stamps from the Stamp tool pull-down menu. Click the down arrow on the menu and choose Create Custom Stamp or choose Tools ➪ Commenting ➪ Stamps ➪ Create Custom Stamp. The Select Image for Custom Stamp dialog box opens, as shown in Figure 25-16.

Click Browse to open the Open dialog box. Select an image for the custom stamp in the Open dialog box and click Select. The Create Custom Stamp dialog box opens as shown in Figure 25-17. Type a Category name and a Name for the stamp and click OK. The new category and stamp now appear listed in the Stamp pull-down menu.

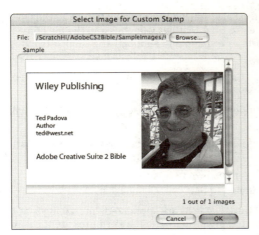

Figure 25-16: In the Select Image for Custom Stamp dialog box, click Browse to locate a file you want to use for a new custom stamp.

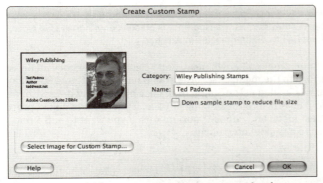

Figure 25-17: Add a category and stamp name for the new custom stamp.

Acrobat permits importing file types for custom stamps from the following file formats:

- ✦ **PDF:** You can use all PDF documents as Stamp icons; however, you can only import single pages as a stamp. PDFs containing transparency are supported. Any PDF document you import as a custom stamp can have opacity applied in the Stamp Properties dialog box.

- ✦ **AI (Adobe Illustrator native files):** Acrobat supports native AI files. Illustrator art can be layered and can have transparent elements. Importing Illustrator images with transparency displays transparent effects in Acrobat. All vector art, including transparent objects, can have transparency applied in Acrobat by making opacity adjustments in the Stamp Properties dialog box. Illustrator AI files aren't listed as a file type in the Open dialog box on Windows. In order to recognize Illustrator native files, type ***.*** in the File Name field box in the Open dialog box.

- ✦ **BMP (Bitmap):** You can import 1-bit line art to 24-bit color images saved as BMP as a custom stamp. BMP files can be adjusted for opacity in the Stamp Properties dialog box.

+ **EPS:** You can select an EPS file in the Select dialog box and subsequently the Open dialog box. When you open an EPS file, Acrobat Distiller launches and the file converts to PDF. The resultant PDF then imports as a stamp and supports the same attributes as PDFs, earlier in this list.

+ **GIF:** GIF files, including transparent GIFs, are supported. GIF files can be adjusted for opacity in the Stamp Properties dialog box.

+ **JPEG/JPEG2000:** JPEG files are supported with the same options as GIFs and BMPs, mentioned earlier.

+ **PCX:** PCX files are supported. The file attributes are the same as those found with BMPs and GIFs, mentioned earlier.

+ **PICT (Mac only):** You can import PICT (Picture Format) files from Mac OS. The attributes are the same as those applied to BMP and GIF images.

+ **PNG:** PNG files and files saved as interlaced PNG are supported. Interlacing is not applied to the image once it's imported in Acrobat. The file attributes are the same as those found with BMPs and GIFs, mentioned earlier.

Note   Although several file formats are supported for importing layered files, the layers are flattened when imported as custom stamps. Transparency is preserved with these file types, but you can't have stamps applied to different layers in Acrobat.

To use the stamp, open the Stamp tool pull-down menu and select your category name. Acrobat automatically adds the category to the menu. Select the stamp name (see Figure 25-18) from the submenu and your new stamp is loaded in the Stamp tool. Click or click and drag with the Stamp tool and the new stamp inserts into the document page. If you want to adjust properties such as opacity, open a context menu and choose your options. If you want to add a note, double-click the stamp icon and a pop-up note opens.

Figure 25-18: Select your new category and the stamp image is shown in a submenu. Select the stamp and it's ready to use.

Tip   If you aren't in a review and markup session and you don't have the commenting tools open, you can apply a stamp from the top-level menus. Choose Tools ⇨ Commenting ⇨ Stamps and select the desired category and stamp. All the stamp categories and stamps added to a favorite list are accessible from submenu choices.

Managing stamps

Acrobat offers you various options for handling stamps and making them easily accessible. The second half of the Stamp tool pull-down menu offers menu choices for managing stamps where you can append and delete stamps.

Using the Manage Stamps command

You may have some icon or symbol used frequently on PDF documents (for example, a logo, address, signature, or watermark). If you use other Acrobat features such as adding watermarks and backgrounds, copying and pasting images, or importing PDF documents, you're required to know the location of these files. If you want to easily access an icon or symbol, you can create a custom stamp and the stamp icon is always accessible without your having to navigate your hard drive. For those frequently used images, you can add a list of favorites to the Stamp pull-down menu to further simplify easy access.

To add a favorite to the Stamp pull-down menu, select a stamp from a category and make it active in the Stamp tool. From the Stamp pull-down menu, select Add Current Stamp to Favorites. The stamp name is added to the top of the menu. When you add a stamp listed in a submenu, the stamp still resides in the submenu as well as the location at the top of the menu.

If you want to add more stamps to your favorites, follow the same procedures and new stamp names are added to the menu. To delete a stamp from the favorite list, you must first select the stamp and make it active in the Stamp tool. Return to the Stamp pull-down menu and select Remove Current Stamp From Favorites.

Managing stamp libraries

You may want to edit category names, edit stamp names, or delete stamps after adding them to a category. To make edits like these, select Manage Stamps from the Stamp tool pull-down menu. The Manage Custom Stamps dialog box opens, shown in Figure 25-19.

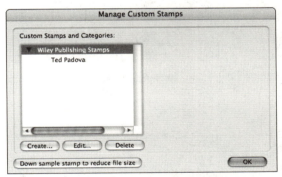

Figure 25-19: To edit stamps, use the Manage Custom Stamps dialog box.

Exchanging stamp libraries

If you work in an environment where you want to share custom stamp libraries, you can copy files created on any computer and export them across computers of the same or different platforms. The stamp files must be located in a folder where Acrobat can recognize the documents as stamps.

On Windows XP, stamp files are saved to the My Documents/Adobe/Acrobat/Stamps folder. On Mac OS X, stamps are located in the Library/Acrobat User Data/Stamps folder. Locate the file you want to send to other computer users and copy the file across your network or e-mail the file to a colleague. The user on the other end needs to copy the file to the same folder.

When you add a stamp file to the Stamps folder on either platform, or you append the file using page templates, you may need to quit Acrobat and relaunch the program. If at first you don't see new stamps, be certain to relaunch Acrobat.

Paste Clipboard Image as Stamp tool

The Paste Clipboard Image as Stamp tool is a great new addition to the comment tools in Acrobat 6.0. To use this tool, you copy an image in another authoring application like Adobe Photoshop or Adobe Illustrator and paste the image in a PDF as a comment. As a comment, you have all the options for properties changes and review tracking. Keep in mind that pasting with this tool is much different than pasting data using menu and context-menu commands.

In Figure 25-20, a screen shot of a dialog box was copied to the Clipboard. The Paste Clipboard tool was used to bring the Clipboard data into the document as a comment. When you double-click the image with the Hand tool, a pop-up note window opens where a text description is added.

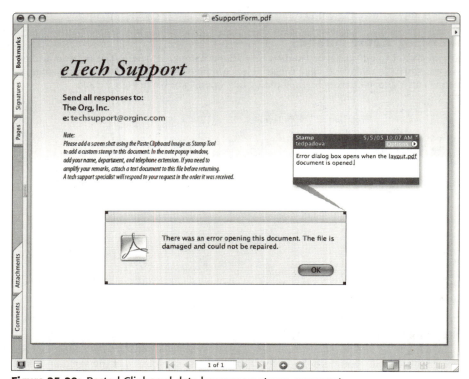

Figure 25-20: Pasted Clipboard data becomes a stamp comment.

Pasting data with the Paste Clipboard Image tool requires you to copy image data. If you copy a passage of text, Acrobat doesn't recognize the text on the Clipboard for use with the Clipboard tool. The tool is grayed out unless an image is copied to the Clipboard.

Tip   Select the Hand tool and press Command/Ctrl+V and the data on the clipboard is pasted as a clipboard image.

Drawing Markup Tools

The Drawing Markup tools offer you more options for marking up documents, attaching files, importing sound comments, and copying/pasting data to add as a comment. The Advanced Commenting tools are an extension of the basic Commenting tools but they're only available to Acrobat Professional users. Many of these tools also have associated note pop-up windows where you can use descriptions for markups, and they all have various options in a properties dialog box.

New Feature   The Callout tool is new to Acrobat 7. Use the tool to create callouts in the document. Click the tool and draw a rectangle. You type text in the rectangle shape and a line with an arrowhead can be moved to position where you want to reference the callout. The Callout does not have an associated popup note window. You add text inside the box for your note comments.

You use the Cloud tool to draw polygon shapes that appear like the outline of a cloud. In the pull-down menu aside the Arrow tool you have several other tools for drawing lines, geometric, and free-form shapes. The properties for these tools offer options for arrowheads, fills, opacity settings, inline text, and so on. Open the Properties dialog box to set attributes for the shapes.

New Feature   The Dimensioning tool is also new in Acrobat 7. Use the Dimensioning tool to mark an area where you want to note a distance — something like the dimensions of a door opening on an architectural drawing. The dimensions can be typed over the line extending between the start and stop points.

The Text Box tool is used to create a box shape where you add text. Like the callout tool, there is no associated note popup window.

Using the Comments Pane

The Comments palette conveniently contains many tools and options for managing comments. By default, the Comments palette opens horizontally across the bottom of the Acrobat window and lists all the comments created in a PDF document. If you toggle views between several PDF files, the Comments palette dynamically updates the list of Comments to reflect comments on the file active in the Document pane.

Depending on the size of your monitor, you'll find that viewing the palette occupies substantial space in the Acrobat window. If you're working on a small monitor, the amount of room left over for viewing pages, after loading toolbars in the Toolbar Well and expanding the Comment palette, can be very skimpy. Fortunately, you can view the palette docked in the Navigation pane and control the size of the palette by dragging the horizontal bar at the top of the palette down to reduce the size.

You also have a choice for floating the palette by undocking it from the Navigation pane and resizing the palette. To undock the Comments palette, click on the tab and drag the tab to the Document pane. You can resize the palette by dragging the lower-right corner in or out to reduce or expand the size.

Whichever way you choose to view the Comments palette, you'll find using it to be a great asset when reviewing documents and participating in review sessions. At first, it may be a struggle to find the right size and location for the palette, but with a little practice you'll find the many tools contained in the palette much easier to access than using menu commands.

Viewing comments

The Comments palette lists all the comments contained in the active document. By default, the comments are listed by page. In a multi-page document, you'll see Page 1, Page 2, Page 3, and so on displayed in the list on the left side of the palette.

You can view the list of comments expanded or collapsed. In Figure 25-21, the list is collapsed. Expanded lists show comments in a hierarchy like bookmarks are shown in the Bookmarks palette. You can expand individual pages where comments are contained by clicking on the plus (+) symbol (Windows) or the right-pointing arrow (Mac). To expand all comments, click on the Expand All button in the Comments palette toolbar Conversely, you can collapse all comments by clicking on the Collapse All button.

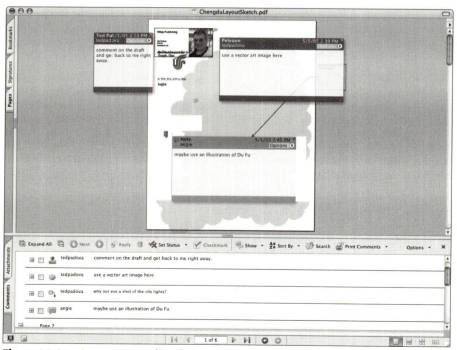

Figure 25-21: Comments are listed in a collapsed view.

Comments are listed in a hierarchical order. If you have several comments on a page and you click on the icon to the left of the comment to expand the page comments, you see the Comment icon, author, and content of a note pop-up. You can further expand each comment in the expanded list by clicking on the plus (+) symbol (Windows) or right-pointing arrow (Mac). When further expanded, the comment subject and the creation date display in the palette. Figure 25-22 shows comments expanded.

Figure 25-22: Comments are listed in an expanded view.

Sorting comments

Also shown in Figure 25-22 is the pull-down menu that allows you to change how comments are sorted. You can change the default-page sorting to any of the following:

✦ **Type:** Comments are sorted together by the type of comment contained on pages. All note comments appear together, highlight comments together, stamps together, and so on.

✦ **Page:** The default. Comments are listed together successively by page.

✦ **Author:** If a document has comments from several different authors, the comments are listed by author and sorted in alphabetical order by author name.

✦ **Date:** The creation date is the sort order with the most recent date appearing first in the list.

✦ **Color:** Comments are sorted according to the color settings made in the comment properties dialog box.

✦ **Checkmark Status:** You can check a comment for your own personal method of flagging a comment. You may create checking comments to alert yourself to review comments, perhaps mark them for deletion, or to spend more time in a later editing session reviewing the comments made by others. The choice for what the check mark signals is a personal choice. When you view comments according to Checkmark Status, all unchecked Comments (Unmarked) are listed first, followed by comments marked with a check mark.

✦ **Status by Person:** The menu option includes a submenu where you can select an author. Select an author name from the submenu and comments are sorted with the comments for the selected author appearing first. The unchecked comments are listed next by author name. You must have Status set on at least one comment to activate this command.

Navigating comments

The up and down arrows in the Comments toolbar enable you to move back and forth between comments. Click the down-pointing arrow to move to the next comment in the list. Click the up-pointing arrow to navigate to a previous comment. The arrow tools are grayed out when comments are collapsed. In order to use the tools, you need to have one or more groups of comments expanded and have a comment selected.

Double-clicking on a comment in the list takes you to the page where the comment appears. When you double-click on the comment in the Comments palette, an associated pop-up note also opens.

Searching comments

The contents of comment pop-up notes can be searched. To find a word in a pop-up note, click on the Search Comments tool. Enter the search criteria and click Search Comments. You can also open the Search pane and select the Search in Comments check box. The Search pane offers you the same search options used for searching open PDF documents. You can match case, search for whole words only, and use other search criteria. The results of your search, however, return words found in the document as well as words found in comment pop-up notes.

When a word is found in a comment pop-up note, the page where the note appears opens and the pop-up note opens with the found word highlighted.

Printing comments

The Print Comments tool does more than print the comments in a document to your printer. When you select the Print Comments tool, a pull-down menu opens where you can choose from three menu options. These menu commands include the following:

- ✦ **Print Comments Summary:** Use this command to create a summary page as a new PDF file and print the summarized comments to your default printer. The comment summary is a temporary file that Acrobat creates while you print the summarized comments. After printing, Acrobat deletes the summary.

- ✦ **Create PDF of Comments Summary:** Use this command to create a new PDF document that summarizes the comments in your document, instead of printing a file to your printer. You can save this file and keep it around to review a summary of the comments. This document is created with a Continuous-Facing page layout.

- ✦ **More Options:** This option opens a dialog box where you can choose from a number of different attributes for the way the comment summary is created. After making options choices in the Summarize Options dialog box, click OK. A PDF file is created according to the options you select in the dialog box.

From each of the menu commands, Acrobat handles comments with summarized pages. If you want to print pages with comments, choose File ➪ Print with Comments.

Deleting comments

In addition to the context menus used when creating comments, you can delete them from within the Comments palette. Select a comment in the palette and click on the Trash icon to delete the selected comment. After deleting a comment, you have one level of undo available to you. If you change your mind after deleting a comment, choose Edit ➪ Undo.

Selecting multiple comments and clicking on the Trash icon can also be undone. Choose Edit ➪ Undo Multiple Deletes if you change your mind after deleting multiple comments. In the event you lose the Undo command, you need to choose File ➪ Revert to bring back the comment. The Revert command reverts back to the last saved version of the file.

Marking comments

You use the Mark the Current Comment with a Checkmark tool to flag comments for a special purpose. You can select a comment in the Comments list in the palette and click on the tool to checkmark the current selection. Check marks are also applied to comments by clicking in the open check-mark box when a comment is expanded. Between the expand/collapse icon and the comment icon is a check box. Click the box to checkmark a comment. Comments do not need to be selected to mark the check boxes when viewing an expanded list.

Setting comment status

Marking a comment with a check mark, described in the preceding section, is a method for you to keep track of comments for your own purposes. The Set the Comment Status tool is used to mark a comment's current status; it's intended for use in comment reviews and in sharing comments with other users. From the tool pull-down menu, you have several options for marking the status of a comment.

When you mark comments for status and view the comments sorted according to Status by Person, the comments are sorted according to the status groups. Beginning with Rejected, comments are listed for an author for all rejected comments appearing first in the list. Next, the same author's completed comments are listed, followed by the cancelled comments. Comments marked as None are listed last for each author. (The order is: Rejected, Completed, Cancelled, Accepted, None.)

Editing comment pop-up notes

A very handy feature available to you when viewing comments in an expanded list is the ability to edit note pop-up text. Instead of navigating to each page containing a comment and opening the associated note pop-up window to make your edits, you can delete, change, or modify text listed in the Comments palette.

When you select the note pop-up text in the Comments palette, the note pop-up window opens in the Document pane. As you make changes in the Comments palette, changes are reflected in the pop-up note window. If you edit text in the pop-up note window, the text edits are reflected in the Comments palette. To enable the dynamic viewing between the pop-up notes and the Comments palette, be certain to disable the check box in the Comment preferences for Hide Comment Pop-Ups when Comments List Is Open.

Enabling PDFs with Reader Extensions

Perhaps the most exciting new feature for creative professionals in Adobe Acrobat 7 Professional is a simple menu command used for enabling PDFs with Adobe Reader extensions. When you enable a PDF document with Reader extensions, users of the free Adobe Reader 7 (and newer) software can use the commenting features discussed in all the previous pages of this chapter. Reader users can use all the comment and markup tools, create custom stamp comments, paste clipboard data as stamp comments, sort and mark comments, and save their edits.

You can provide enabled PDF documents to clients and coworkers who need to review, approve, or sign off on files. Using an electronic review process eliminates needs for overnight express mail and faxes. The review process can be handled quickly and you can archive electronic records of all participant notes and comments solicited for a given assignment or campaign. One thing to note, however, is that you cannot enable PDF documents with form fields and have Reader users fill in form data or electronically sign a document enabled with Reader usage rights from Acrobat 7. PDF forms enabled with usage rights discards the form fields.

Cross-Reference

PDF documents can be enabled with the Adobe LiveCycle Reader Extensions Server (LRES) permitting Adobe Reader users of Reader 7 and lower to save form data, digitally sign documents, add comments using Reader versions below version 7, participate in Browser-based reviews, and more. To learn more about LRES, log on to Adobe's Web page at: www.adobe.com/products/server/readerextensions/.

To understand how PDF files are enabled with Reader usage rights, follow these steps:

STEPS: Enabling PDFs with Reader Extensions

1. **Open a PDF document in Acrobat Professional.** Launch the Bridge or Organizer and locate a PDF file to open in Acrobat. Double-click a PDF document you want to share with an Adobe Reader 7 user. Note that in order for Reader users to comment on PDFs enabled with Acrobat 7 Professional, they must use Adobe Reader 7 or greater.

2. **Add a comment.** If you want to add a stamp comment or any other edits you want to make to the PDF, be certain to do it before enabling the document. In Figure 25-23, a stamp comment is added with a note asking users to make comments and return the file to the author.

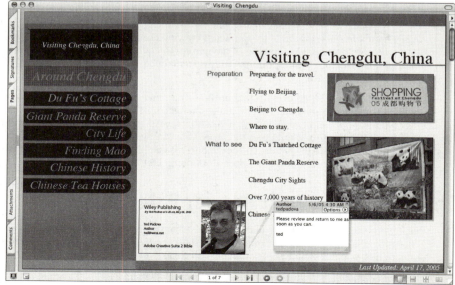

Figure 25-23: A comment is added to a file before enabling the document with Reader extensions.

3. **Enable the PDF document.** Choose Comments ⇨ Enable for Commenting in Adobe Reader. With this single menu command, you add the special features, providing Adobe Reader users all that is needed to comment and mark up the PDF document. You are prompted to save the file in a Save As dialog box. Type a new name for the file and click Save.

4. **Open the Document Properties.** Press Command/Ctrl+D to open the Document Properties dialog box. Click the Description tab at the top of the dialog box. Notice that all the data fields are grayed out. You cannot edit the PDF document once you have enabled it. Click Cancel in the Document Properties. Open the File menu and notice you have a Save a Copy command. If you want to make any edits on the file, you need to save a copy, make your edits, and then return to the Enable for Commenting in Adobe Reader command.

5. **Open the PDF in Adobe Reader.** Quit Acrobat and open Adobe Reader 7 or greater. Click the Open tool and open the document you enabled with Reader extensions.

6. **Open the commenting and markup tools.** If you don't see the comment tools appear when the file is opened, open a context menu on the Toolbar Well and select Commenting. Return to the context menu and select Drawing Markups. Return a third time and select Dock All Toolbars. Notice at the top of the Document pane a message reports that you can add comments and markups to the document. Figure 25-24 shows the file enabled in step 2 opened in Adobe Reader with the toolbars docked in the Toolbar Well.

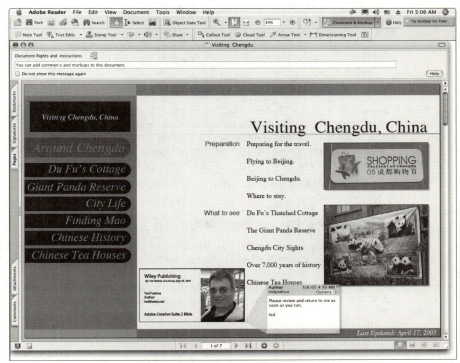

Figure 25-24: The enabled PDF document is opened in Adobe Reader where the Commenting and Drawing Markup tools are docked in the Toolbar Well.

In addition to enabling documents for Reader users to add comments on PDF files, you can also invite Adobe Reader users to participate in review sessions. All the options you have for both commenting and reviews are available to Reader users when the PDFs have been enabled with usage rights.

Creating an E-Mail-Based Review

Acrobat 7 supports two kinds of review options. You can send files for an E-mail-based review or a Browser-based review. Any Acrobat user can initiate e-mail-based reviews and the review participants can be other Acrobat users as well as Adobe Reader users when files have been enabled with usage rights. E-mail-based reviews are easy to initiate, and no special requirements are needed to begin a review.

Browser-based reviews are performed online from within a Web browser. Comments are uploaded and downloaded by review participants. To engage in Browser-based reviews, there are some additional requirements and restrictions over e-mail-based reviews. In order to initiate an online Browser-based review, you need to have a properly configured Web server requiring some configuration by your system administrator. Also, Adobe Reader 7 users cannot participate in online reviews even when PDFs are enabled with Reader extensions in Acrobat Professional.

Enabling PDF form fill-in, commenting privileges, digital signatures, and Browser-based reviews can be achieved with the Adobe LiveCycle Reader Extensions Server (LCRE) software available from Adobe Systems. For more information on LCRE, visit www.adobe.com/products/server/readerextensions. Third-party solutions offer you opportunities for form fill-in and online commenting using Adobe Reader. For working with Adobe PDF forms, take a look at www.formrouter.com/services/. For online commenting solutions, take a look at Rosebud PLM at www.rosebudplm.com.

Most independent creative professionals and advertising agencies are more likely to use an e-mail-based review with clients. The advantages for using e-mail-based reviews are less costly and clients won't need anything other than an e-mail account to participate. If you are interested in learning more about Browser-based reviews, see the Acrobat Help document or look at the *Adobe Acrobat 7 PDF Bible* (Wiley Publishing).

To understand how an e-mail-based review is initiated and how to participate in a review, look over the following steps.

STEPS: Setting Up an E-mail-Based Review

1. **Initiate a review.** From the Send for Review task button in the Toolbar Well open the pull-down menu and select Send by Email for Review, as shown in Figure 25-25.

When using the wizard to send an email review, you don't need to first enable a PDF document with Reader Extensions. Steps in the wizard take care of adding the Reader Usage rights.

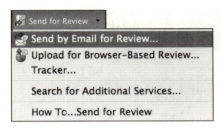

Figure 25-25: Select Send by Email for Review from the Send for Review task button in the Toolbar Well.

2. **Identify the document to send.** The Send by Email for Review wizard opens. If you have a document open in the Document pane, the current active document is identified as the file to send for review. If you want to select a file on your hard drive other than an open document, click Choose as shown in Figure 25-26. A dialog box opens where you can navigate your hard drive and select a file to send for review. After identifying the file to send for review, click Next.

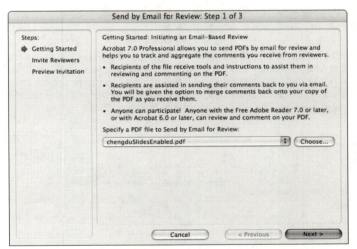

Figure 25-26: Identify a PDF document to send for review in the Send by Email for Review wizard.

3. **Identify recipients.** In the Invite Reviewers pane shown in Figure 25-27, add recipients to the list window by typing the recipients' e-mail addresses. If you have a list prepared in your e-mail program, click Customize Review Options. Another dialog box opens where you can select your address book and choose from a recipient list. The address book is the same address data used in Microsoft Outlook (Windows) and Address Book (Mac OSX).

4. **Send the invitation.** Click Next and review the message information. By default, Acrobat supplies a message for your e-mail. You can leave the message providing recipients instructions for participating in reviews or edit the message. After review and/or appending the message information, click Send Invitation.

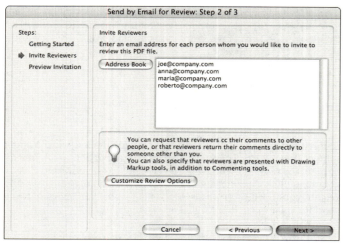

Figure 25-27: Add recipient e-mail addresses.

5. **E-mail the invitation to recipients.** The PDF identified for the review is attached to a new e-mail message window in your default e-mail application. If your default e-mail program is not launched by Acrobat, you need to launch the program. The e-mail message is automatically added as a new message together with the list of recipients added to your message To text box, as shown in Figure 25-28.

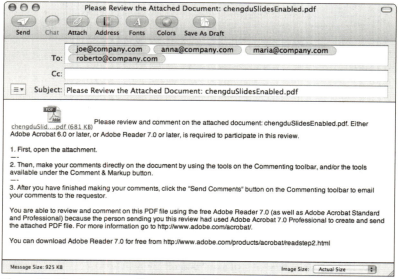

Figure 25-28: A new e-mail message window opens with the list of recipients added to the To text box.

6. **Send the message.** Click Send and the message and PDF file attachment are sent to the list of recipients.

When recipients receive your message, they double-click the attachment and it opens in the user's default Acrobat viewer. If only Adobe Reader is installed on the end user's computer, the file opens in Reader. The How To pane opens on the right side of the Acrobat window where step-by-step help information is provided to the review participant. Recipients then make comments and click the Send Comments button in the Commenting toolbar. When files are received for review, the Send Comments button is automatically added to the Commenting toolbar by Acrobat, as seen in Figure 25-29.

Mac users will see a PDF document open in review by default. If double-clicking a PDF file opens in Preview, open the PDF from within an Acrobat viewer.

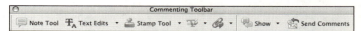

Figure 25-29: PDF documents sent for review are opened with a Send Comments button added to the Commenting toolbar.

As comments are returned to you, they are attached to e-mail messages. Either a PDF document or an FDF (Form Data File) is returned as an attachment in an e-mail message. Double-click the attachment and the recipient's comments are appended to your original PDF file. As additional reviewers send back comments you double-click the e-mail attachments and the comments are integrated in the original PDF file.

Either a PDF document or a data file containing only comment information is returned to you. The determination for whether a PDF or an FDF file is returned is handled in the Reviewing preferences dialog box. Open Preferences (command/Ctrl+K) and click on Reviewing. Note the *Send comments as FDF for files greater than* text box. The value typed in the field box determines when a PDF is sent and when an FDF file is sent. For example, if you type **5** in the text box, all PDF files of 5MB and lower are returned to you as PDF files. For all files larger than 5MB, an FDF file is returned. Regardless of the file format, double-clicking the e-mail attachment populates your original PDF with participant comments.

Using the Review Tracker

The Tracker is a separate window that opens on top of the Acrobat window where you find menu commands to help manage e-mail-based reviews and Browser-based reviews. To open the Tracker, select Tracker from the Comment & Markup Task Button, choose Comments ➪ Tracker, or from the Options pull-down menu in the Comments pane select Tracker. All three menu items open the Tracker, which is shown in Figure 25-30.

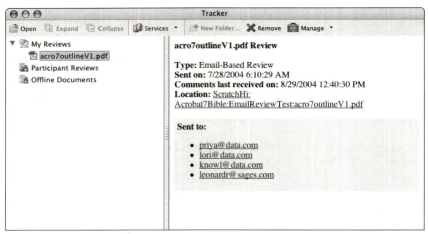

Figure 25-30: The Tracker is a pane that provides menu commands for helping you manage e-mail– and Browser-based reviews.

Viewing documents in the Tracker

The left pane in the Tracker lists all documents you have in review. From the list, select a filename and click the Open tool in the Tracker. The respective file opens in the Document pane.

Three categories appear in the left pane. All reviews you initiate are listed in the My Reviews list. Expand the list to see reviews by filename. The Participant Reviews contain all reviews sent to you by another review initiator. Offline comments include Browser-based reviews where you have saved files for offline commenting.

When a document is viewed in an expanded list, you can select additional menu commands by opening a context menu from a file in the list. The menu commands include:

✦ **Open:** Opens the selected file the same as clicking the Open tool.

✦ **Email All Reviewers:** Select this option and your default e-mail application is opened with the To field populated with all review participants. Type a message and click the Send button and you can send a message to the reviewers.

✦ **Send Review Reminder:** This option also launches your default e-mail application with the To field populated with the addresses of the review participants. An automated message appears in the message window to remind reviewers to comment on the document in review. This option is only available to review initiators and does not appear in a context menu when selecting a file in the Participant Reviews context menus.

- **Invite Additional Reviewers:** Also launches your default e-mail application with an automated message to invite other reviewers. The selected PDF file used for initiating the original review is added as a file attachment.
- **Remove:** Removes the selected file from the review category the same as clicking the Remove tool.
- **Send To Folder:** From the submenu you can create a new folder that is added to the menu. When you return to the Send To Folder command, the submenu shows a list of folders where you can nest reviews to organize the documents in a hierarchical order.

Expand/Collapse

Click the Expand tool to expand a list. A collapsed list is marked with a plus (+) symbol. If a list is collapsed, the Expand button is active. If a list is already expanded, the Expand button is grayed out.

Click the Collapse tool when a list is expanded. Collapsing lists can help you manage more reviews in the list.

Expand and Collapse appear active for any one of the three groups when you select that group. For example, selecting Participant Reviews when the list is expanded activates the Collapse tool. Selecting a file in the expanded list from any category displays the name of the PDF document used in the review, the date the review was sent, and a list of participants that were invited to the review in the right pane.

Services

Whereas you have an impressive set of features for monitoring RSS (Really Simple Syndication) feeds in Adobe Bridge, Acrobat offers you options for accessing RSS feeds in the Tracker window. This option is handy for users who have purchased Acrobat and not the Creative Suite. As a CS2 user, you'll find the Bridge features for working with RSS feeds much better and more intuitive in the Bridge compared to using the Tracker services.

If you opt to use RSS feeds in Acrobat, select from the first two menu commands for additional services. The first command is Subscribe. Select Subscribe and a dialog box opens where you type a URL to subscribe to an online service. In Figure 25-31, you can see news services listed in the Tracker window. These services were subscribed to using the Subscribe command in the Services pull-down menu. The Tracker can be used as a news subscription service just like you have available with Adobe Bridge. Additional services can include news broadcast services, music channels, and any other services using the RSS feed.

The second command is Search for Additional Services. The Search for Acrobat Services dialog box opens and lists additional services if they are available. If nothing appears in the dialog box, no additional services are available for the respective review.

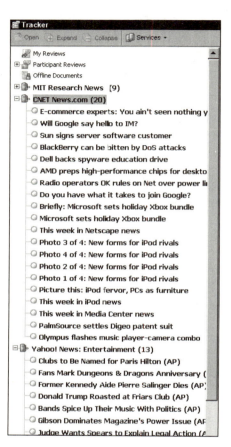

Figure 25-31: After subscribing to an RSS subscription service, services are listed in the Tracker window.

Exporting and Importing Comments

If you ask a colleague to comment on a document, you can bypass the e-mail and Browser-based reviews by having a reviewer export comments and e-mail the exported file to you. When you export comments from a PDF document the data are exported as an FDF or XFDF file. The data file results in much smaller file sizes than PDF documents and can easily be imported back into the original PDF or a copy of the original PDF document.

To export comments from a PDF document, choose Comments ➪ Export Comments. From a submenu you have three options. Select from To Word, To AutoCAD, and To File.

Exporting comments to Microsoft Word

If you create PDFs from Microsoft Word and use comments in Word and Acrobat, it may be easier to export comments directly back to your Word document. In order to take advantage of this feature you must be running Windows XP Service Pack 1 or above and you must be using Word 2002 or above. The feature is not supported on Macintosh OS X or in Windows 2000.

Be certain to use the Export Comments to Word feature on files that are not changed while importing or exporting comments. If you edit a Word document after creating the PDF file, or you edit the PDF document by inserting, deleting, or performing other page-editing functions, the import/export operations may not work properly.

Comments that are exported from Acrobat to a Word document appear as comment bubbles in Word. Marking text for deletion and insertion are also supported in Word and will appear as integrated comments in the Word text.

You can either start this process from within Acrobat with Export Comments To Word, or you can start this process from within Word with Import Comments from Acrobat under the Acrobat Comments menu. In both cases, the Import Comments from Acrobat dialog box is launched. If you start from Word, the Word file is filled in and the PDF file is blank. If you start from Acrobat, the PDF file is filled in and the Word file is blank.

To export comments to a Word document from Acrobat, choose from one of several menu commands, such as Comments ⇨ Export Comments ⇨ To Word, or use the Comments pane Options pull-down menu and select Export Comments To Word.

To import the exported comments in a Word document, in Word 2002 on Windows XP open the Word file that you converted to PDF. In Word, choose Acrobat Comments ⇨ Import Comments from Acrobat. The Import Comments from Adobe Acrobat dialog box opens. You can select the comments you want to import and choose from All Comments, All Comments with Checkmarks, and Text edits only: Insertions and Deletions. For a specific set of comments, select Custom Set and choose the filter options to filter the comments.

 For information on comment filtering, see the section "Filtering Comments."

If you import text edit comments, Word prompts you for confirmation as each comment is imported. Be certain to track changes in Word or you won't see the dialog box appear. As you are prompted to accept changes, you can choose to apply changes or discard them as the comments are imported.

Exporting comments to AutoCAD

You can export comments to an AutoDesk AutoCAD file. The menu options and process are very similar to exporting comments to Microsoft Word. You need the original source document in order to export the comments to the DWG file.

Exporting comments to files

When you export comments to a file the Export Comments dialog box opens. The dialog box behaves similarly to a Save As dialog box where you select a destination folder, provide a filename, and click Save. Acrobat provides a default name by using the PDF filename with an .fdf extension. You can use the default name or change the name in the File Name field. From the Save as Type (Windows) or Format (Macintosh) pull-down menu you can select between FDF formatted files and XFDF (XML-based FDF file). The default is FDF.

Click Save in the Export Comments dialog box. The resulting file can be exported to a user who has the same PDF document from which the FDF file was created. If you receive an FDF file and want to load the comments, choose Comments ⇨ Import Comments. The Import Comments dialog box opens. Navigate to the location where the data file is located and select it. Click Select and the comments are imported into the open PDF document.

Note You have three file format options — not only FDF and XFDF for export, but also PDF. If someone sends you not just the comments but the whole PDF with the comments, you can import those comments directly to your version without having to export them from your reviewer's copy and then import into your copy.

When you import comments in a PDF document, all the comments are imported in the exact location where they were originally created. If you delete a page in a PDF file and import comments, Acrobat ignores comments where it can't find matching pages. Note pop-ups and icons are matched with the way they appear in the file from which the comments were exported.

Exporting selected comments

You can select comments and choose to export only the selected comments to an FDF file. Open the Comments pane and select comments according to the sort order listed in the Comments pane. The default is by page. Select a page in the list and open the Options pull-down menu from the Comments pane toolbar. Select Export Selected Comments from the menu options, as shown in Figure 25-32.

Figure 25-32: Select comments in the Comments pane and select Export Selected Comments from the Options pull-down menu. In the Export Comments dialog box, provide a filename and click Save.

The Export Comments dialog box opens. Navigate your hard drive to find the folder where you want to save the FDF or XFDF file, provide a name for the file, and click Save.

 Tip When exporting all comments leave the filename for the FDF or XFDF exported file at the default provided by Acrobat. When exporting Selected Comments, be certain to edit the filename. By default, Acrobat uses the same name. If you elect to export all comments and then want to export selected comments, you might mistakenly overwrite files with the same filename. By getting into a habit of being consistent when naming files, you'll prevent potential mistakes.

Filtering Comments

You can further enhance the features available to you for review and markup, exporting and importing comments, and viewing comments in the Comments pane, by filtering comments in groups. Filtering comments temporarily hides comments you don't want to use at the moment. You can choose to display all comments by an author, a date, a reviewer, and a range of other criteria. When comments are filtered, exporting comments or creating comment summaries (explained in the next section) is applied only to those comments currently viewed. Any hidden comments are excluded from the task at hand.

You manage the comment filter through the Show pull-down menu. The options in the Show pull-down menu in the Toolbar Well are identical to the menu options in the Show tool pull-down menu in the Comments pane.

To understand more about the Show menu options, see the section "Using the Show menu."

If you know ahead of time that you want to export edits back to Microsoft Word, you can mark only those comments received from reviewers that you intend to export to Word. When the review session is complete, choose Show ⇨ Hide All Comments. Open the menu again and choose Show by Type ⇨ Text Editing Markups. Return to the menu and choose Show by Checked State ⇨ Checked. Export the comments, and only the Text Edit comments with the items you checked during the review are exported to Word.

The remaining menu options include nonfiltering menu choices such as opening/closing note pop-ups, showing connector lines, aligning icons and pop-up notes, and accessing the Comment preferences. You can also make these menu selections from other tools and menus as described earlier in this chapter.

Creating Comment Summaries

If you create an extensive review from many participants over a period of time, the number of comments may become too many to comfortably manage in the Comments pane or on the document pages. Or you may have a need to create a comment summary you want to distribute to users after filtering out comments that you don't want included in a summary. Furthermore, you may want to print a hard copy of comments that show the PDF pages with connector lines to a summary description. You can accomplish all these tasks and more when you create comment summaries.

To create a comment summary, you need to have a PDF document open in the Document pane and comments in view in the Comments pane. The pane can be open or collapsed. Comments can be filtered according to the sorts and filtering you want to apply, but at least one comment with the criteria must exist for a summary report to contain comment information.

If the Comments pane is collapsed, you create a comment summary by opening the Comment & Markup Task Button pull-down menu and select Summarize Comments. If the Comments pane is open, you can choose the menu command from the Options menu.

When you select Summarize Comments from either menu command, the Summarize Options dialog box opens, as shown in Figure 25-33.

The first four radio buttons in the dialog box offer you choices for the way the summary pages are created and the page layout view, which may contain single-page views or Continuous – Facing Pages views. The resulting summaries are created as separate PDF documents.

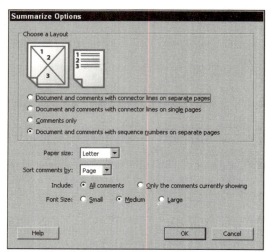

Figure 25-33: Select Summarize Comments from the Comments menu or a context menu in the Comments pane to open the Summarize Options dialog box.

Choices for creating a comment summary in the Summarize Options dialog box include:

+ **Document and comments with connector lines on separate pages:** This option creates a comment summary with each summary page aside the respective document page with connector lines from each comment on a page to the summarized item in a new summary. When the summary is created, Acrobat automatically switches to a Continuous – Facing Pages layout, as shown in Figure 25-34.

+ **Document and comments with connector lines on single pages:** The summary is similar to the preceding option; however, the PDF document and the summary are created together on a single landscape page as shown in Figure 25-35. The size of the paper is determined by the setting specified in the Paper size drop-down menu. One advantage for this summary view compared to the preceding summary is the comments, connector lines, and summary data require a little less room on your monitor to view the original file and the summary information. Furthermore, if you export summaries for other users, the summarized information and original file are assembled together in a single document.

+ **Comments only:** This summary option is similar to summaries created in earlier versions of Acrobat. Only the summarized data are assembled together on single pages. The comment summaries are shown in a hierarchy according to the sort order you select in this dialog box. The page layout is a single-page view.

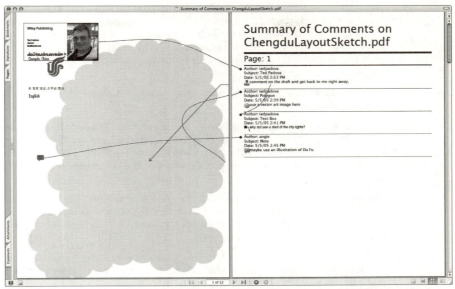

Figure 25-34: Summarized comments are shown with connector lines from original PDF pages and comments. Summary pages are created for each page in the PDF.

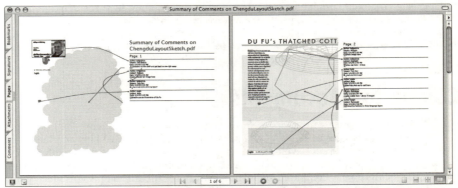

Figure 25-35: This summary is similar to the one created in the preceding figure, but the PDF page and summary are created on new pages in a single document.

- **Document and comments with sequence numbers on separate pages:** Summaries are created similarly to the method described in the preceding bullet, but with the addition of sequence numbers assigned to each comment according to the sort order and the order in which the comments were created. The page layout view is Continuous – Facing Pages, which shows the comments with sequence numbers and the resulting summary in the opposing page view.

- **Paper size:** From the pull-down menu, select a paper size according to the sizes available for your selected printer.

- **Sort comments by:** From the pull-down menu you can choose from four different options. The default is a sort according to Page. If you want another sort order, choose from Author, Type, or Date from the pull-down menu options. The sort order selected in the Summarize Options dialog box supercedes the sort order selected in the Comments pane.

- **Include:** All comments summarizes all comments on the PDF pages regardless of whether the comments are in view or hidden. The Only the comments currently showing option creates a comment summary from the comments visible in the Comments pane.

- **Font Size:** Applies to the font used in the comment summary description on the newly created pages. Depending on the size selected, the summary pages may be fewer (Small) or more pages (Large). The point size for small is 7.5 points, for medium 10 points, and for large 13.33 points.

Comment summaries are particularly useful when sending PDF documents to Adobe Reader users. Although Reader users can see comments you create in a PDF document, they cannot create comment summaries. Additionally, newer comment features in later versions of Acrobat are not visible to users of earlier versions of Reader. When you summarize the comments, all users of all versions of Reader can see all the comments. You can create a summary for a Reader user and append the new document to the existing PDF file, then send the file to other members in your workgroup.

Comparing Documents

If you set up a review for users to provide feedback on a document, you may incorporate recommended changes in a file. As you work on modifying files, you may end up with several documents in different development stages. If you aren't quite certain which document contains your finished edits, you may have a need to compare files to check for the most recent updates. Acrobat's Compare Documents feature (Acrobat Pro only) provides you a method for analyzing two files and reporting all differences between them.

To compare two documents choose Document ⇨ Compare Documents. The Compare Documents dialog box opens. You can open the dialog box without any file open in the Document pane or open both files to compare and then select the menu command. In Figure 25-36, two files titled graph.pdf and grapha.pdf are compared. Because these two files have similar names, it's not certain which document contains revisions. Therefore, the documents are selected for comparison to check the differences.

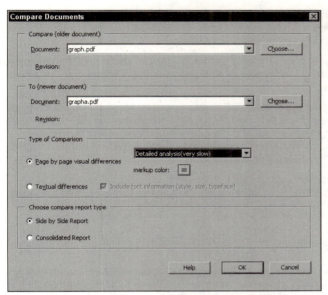

Figure 25-36: Choose Document ➪ Compare Documents to open the Compare Documents dialog box.

The Compare Documents dialog box contains the following options:

+ **Document:** The first two items are used to identify the documents for comparison. If no files are open in the Document pane, click Choose and select a file in the Open dialog box that appears. Click Choose to open a second file. If you have the two documents to be compared open in the Document pane before opening the Compare Documents dialog box, the pull-down menus show both open files. Select one file in the top pull-down menu and the second file in the next pull-down menu.

+ **Page by page visual differences:** Three options are available from pull-down menu choices. Depending on which item you choose, the reports are more or less detailed and the speed in which the documents are compared relates to how much detail you want to analyze. A detailed analysis takes more time than the other two options. Choose from Detailed analysis, Normal analysis, and Coarse analysis from the menu. Small visual differences between documents are reported when choosing the Detailed analysis (very slow) option. The resulting report shows differences in very small graphics. The Coarse analysis ignores small graphics that may appear on one document or another, and the Normal option falls somewhere in between the other two.

+ **Textual differences:** Selecting this option deselects the preceding radio button selection. Use this option if your only interest is in comparing text in the document while ignoring graphics and the layout or reading order. If you want to compare fonts between documents, select the Include font information (style, size, typeface) check box. This option is very handy for reviews where you have moved chunks of text around in a document, but have not really changed the words. It's good for legal documents, chapters, articles, and so on.

- **Markup color:** A report is created with markups. You can choose what color is used for the markups by clicking on the color swatch and selecting a preset color or a custom color.

- **Choose compare report type:** After comparing two files, Acrobat creates a report. The type of report can be either a Side by Side Report with the two documents displayed in a Continuous – Facing Page layout and comparison marks showing the differences, or a Consolidated Report where differences are marked with comment notes in a single PDF document. Choose the report type and click OK.

Acrobat compares the documents according to the attributes selected in the Compare Documents dialog box. When the comparison is finished, the report is created according to the report type selected in the Compare Documents dialog box.

Summary

- Acrobat provides an extensive set of Comment preferences. Before beginning any review session, you should review the preference settings by choosing Edit ⇨ Preferences and clicking on Commenting in the left pane.

- Two toolbars exist with commenting tools in Acrobat Professional — the Commenting toolbar and the Drawing Markups toolbar.

- Most comments created in Acrobat have associated note pop-up windows where you can type comments.

- You access comment properties by opening context menus from a note icon or pop-up note title bar.

- You can create custom stamps in Acrobat from a variety of different file formats.

- The Paste Clipboard Image as Stamp comment tool enables you to copy images to the Clipboard and use the pasted image as a comment with an associated comment note.

- The Comments palette lists all comments in a PDF document. Additional tools are available in the Comments palette, where you can mark status changes in comments, check comment status, and filter comments.

- You can enable PDF documents in Acrobat Professional with Reader extensions permitting Adobe Reader 7 users options for commenting on PDFs.

- Anyone with an e-mail address can participate in an e-mail review. A PDF author sends a PDF document to selected members of a review team who comment on the document and send the comment data back to the PDF author.

- All active documents under review are listed in the Review Tracker pane. You can select from a number of ways to communicate with reviewers from menu options in the Review Tracker.

✦ Comments can be filtered and sorted to isolate authors, types, dates, and other criteria. When exporting comments, only the sorted comments in view in the Comments palette are exported.

✦ Comments exported from a document can be imported in a matching PDF file. The comment data is saved as an FDF and results in smaller file sizes.

✦ Comments can be exported directly to Microsoft Word files on Windows XP with Word 2002.

✦ Comment summaries are displayed in one of four different report styles. When a summary is created, it can be sorted upon creation and saved as a separate PDF file.

✦ The Compare Documents command enables you to locate differences in text and images between two PDF documents. Reports are generated with comments describing the found differences.

✦ ✦ ✦

Designing Layouts

CHAPTER

In This Chapter

Creating a new layout document

Modifying layout settings

Working with pages and spreads

Creating Master pages

Using layers

Adding auto numbering

Using rulers, grids, guides, and frames

Importing artwork

Imagine the process of creating a sidewalk. The first step is to create the forms that define the edges of the sidewalk. If you create these before you mix the cement, the cement easily flows into the right location and the job is completed rather quickly. However, if the forms are not straight or secure, the cement flows outside the bounds and finished work won't be smooth and straight. Similarly, if you complete the layout design beforehand, the text and images flow easily into the document in the correct positions.

This chapter covers the basics of creating a useful layout in InDesign. The initial settings for a layout document are set when you create a new document. You can use the Pages palette to add and delete pages, rearrange pages, and create spreads and Master pages. Master pages provide a convenient way to update similar content on many pages at once. Several other useful layout objects include rulers, grids, guides, and frames. Using these objects, you can quickly lay out all the objects that are included in a page before the content is ready. The content can then be easily placed within these frames when it's ready.

Establishing an InDesign Layout

You establish layouts in InDesign when you create a new document. The New Document dialog box that opens when you create a new document includes settings for defining the number of pages, the page size, the orientation, the margins and columns, and the bleed and slug areas. You can save these settings and reuse them to create other new documents. You can also change settings at any time using the Document Setup dialog box.

Creating new documents

You initially specify basic layout design in InDesign when you first create a new document. Choose File ⇨ New (⌘/Ctrl+N) and the New Document dialog box opens, shown in Figure 26-1. The settings specified in this dialog box determine the initial document layout.

Using the New Document dialog box, you can specify the total number of pages that make up the layout. The Facing Pages option causes left and right pages to face one another. If this option is disabled, each page stands alone. The Master Text Frame option causes a text frame to be added to the Master.

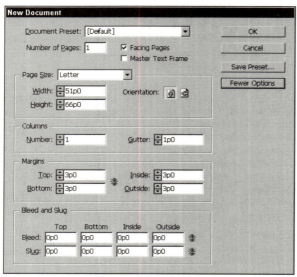

Figure 26-1: The New Document dialog box includes settings for initial layout.

The following options on the New Document dialog box control the page layout of your new document:

- **Page Size options:** The Page Size drop-down list includes several common paper-size options including Letter, Legal, Tabloid, Letter – Half, Legal – Half, A4, A3, A5, B5, Compact Disc, and Custom. Selecting any of these sizes automatically adjusts the Width and Height settings. The Custom option lets you manually set the Width and Height values.

Tip   You can add your own options to the Page Size menu by editing the `New Doc Sizes.txt` file located in the `InDesign\Presets` folder. Just follow the same format used by the other entries in this text file.

Pages versus spreads

The seemingly simple Facing Pages option in the New Document dialog box defines the differences between pages and spreads. If the Facing Pages option is disabled, each page is separate from the others and displays on its own art board. If you enable the Facing Pages option, then adjacent pages are combined together to create a spread.

To understand a spread, open a book or a magazine and notice how two pages are viewed at once with one page on each side. Together these pages make up a spread. Spreads in InDesign are displayed together on a single art board.

When you create a spread, you always place odd-numbered pages on the right (the *recto*) and even-numbered pages on the left (the *verso*). The first page (numbered page 1 by default) appears by itself. Each successive even-and-odd-page pair is a spread.

The Orientation icon buttons include Portrait and Landscape options. A Portrait orientation has a height greater than its width, and a Landscape orientation has a larger width than height. Clicking the unselected icon button swaps the Width and Height values. Figure 26-2 shows two new Letter-sized documents. The left one has a Portrait orientation, and the right one has a Landscape orientation.

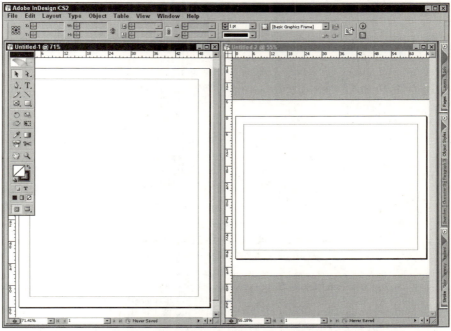

Figure 26-2: You orient new documents with a Portrait (left) or a Landscape setting (right).

- ✦ **Column options:** The Columns section of the New Document dialog box lets you specify the number of text columns on all pages in the layout. The gutter is the space between each column. Figure 26-3 shows two new layouts. The left layout has two columns and the right layout has three columns with a wider gutter.

- ✦ **Margins options:** *Margins* are the space between the edge of the paper and the page content. Guides, which appear where you specify margins, denote this space. You have four margin values correlating to each edge of the page — Top, Bottom, Left, and Right. If you select the Facing Pages option, the Left and Right margins become the Inside and Outside margins. Between the margin values is an icon button with an image of a link on it. Clicking this button sets all settings to equal values.

- ✦ **Bleed and Slug:** Clicking More Options expands the dialog box to reveal Bleed and Slug settings. The Bleed and Slug areas of a page extend beyond the edges of the page. The *Bleed* tells the printer how far to extend a color or image beyond the edge of the page in order to ensure that the color or image runs all the way to the paper edge after trimming. The *Slug* area displays printer instructions and other information that isn't intended to be part of the printed page. Bleed and Slug values include settings for each margin and an icon button to make all values equal.

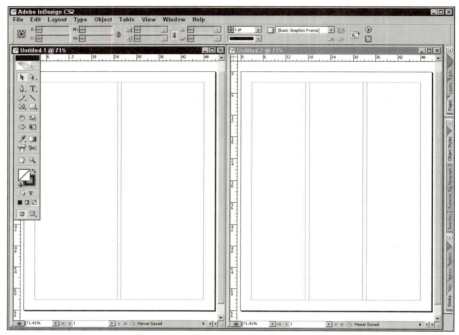

Figure 26-3: Columns split the page into several different areas.

When you create a new page, several guides denote the various page-layout settings. These guides are color-coordinated, with the margins represented by pink-colored guides, the columns and gutters represented by purple guides, the Bleed areas represented by red guides, and the Slug area represented by light-blue guides. The page edges are displayed as black guides. Figure 26-4 shows the various guides.

Creating a document preset

If you find yourself changing the default layout options every time you create a new document, you may benefit from a document preset. When you make the setting changes, click Save Preset and a simple dialog box appears where you can name the new preset.

After it's saved, the new preset is available for selection from the Document Preset list at the top of the dialog box. Selecting the preset name changes all the settings automatically. Saved presets are also available by choosing File ⇨ Document Presets.

Tip   Holding down the Shift key while selecting a preset from the File ⇨ Document Presets menu command creates a new document without opening the New Document dialog box.

Choosing File ⇨ Document Presets ⇨ Define opens the Document Presets dialog box, shown in Figure 26-5, where you can manage all the various presets. Selecting a preset from the list of presets displays all the settings associated with this preset in the lower text pane. Clicking Edit opens the settings within a dialog box that is identical to the New Document dialog box, where you can edit the settings. The New button lets you create a new document preset, and the Delete button deletes the selected preset.

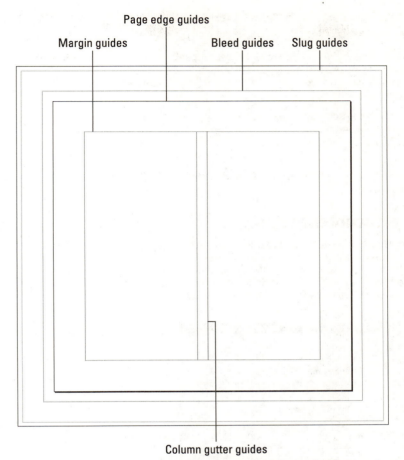

Figure 26-4: The layout of each new document is denoted with color-coded guides.

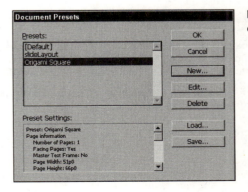

Figure 26-5: You can create and manage document presets here.

> ### Changing the default layout settings
>
> When you first create a new document, the default layout settings are used. You can alter these default settings by changing the settings in the Document Setup dialog (choose File ⇨ Document Setup) and/or the Margins and Columns dialog box (choose Layout ⇨ Margins and Columns) when you have no documents open.
>
> If you don't have any other documents opened when you make changes to these dialog boxes, and you create a new document, the default layout updates.

You can save and load document presets from the hard drive. These presets are saved using the DCST extension.

Changing document settings

If you discover that you need to change one of the layout settings for the entire document, you can revisit most of the same settings in the New Document dialog box by opening the Document Setup dialog box. Choosing File ⇨ Document Setup (Alt+Ctrl+P on Windows; Option+⌘+P on the Mac) opens, shown in Figure 26-6, which includes settings for the Number of Pages, Page Size and Orientation, and Bleed and Slug.

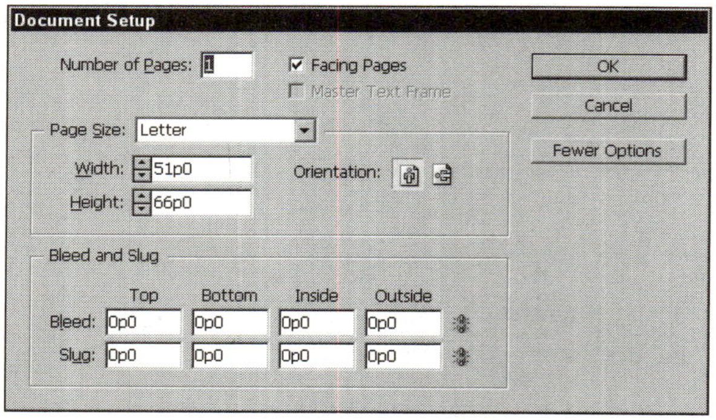

Figure 26-6: The Document Setup dialog box resets most of the New Document dialog box options.

You use the Margins and Columns dialog box to change the margins and columns settings, shown in Figure 26-7. You open this dialog box by choosing Layout ⇨ Margins and Columns. However, any changes entered into this dialog box affect only the current page or spread.

To change the margin and column settings for all pages in the document, select all pages in the Pages palette before opening the Margins and Columns dialog box.

Figure 26-7: The Margins and Columns dialog box changes only the current page or spread.

Exporting CS2 documents to CS

Layouts created with CS2 can be exported using the InDesign Interchange (INX) format and opened within CS, but you'll need to download the latest updater from the Adobe Web site at www.adobe.com. This backward compatibility enables you to work with people who haven't upgraded to the latest software version. To export a document, choose File ➪ Export and select the InDesign Interchange option in the Save as Type field. Some new CS2 features included in an exported file may not be visible when the file is opened in CS.

New Feature Backward compatibility with CS is new to CS2.

Converting Quark and PageMaker files

If you have some existing layouts created in either Quark or PageMaker, you'll be happy to know that these layouts can be opened and converted to InDesign files. Choose File ➪ Open, and InDesign can open files created in PageMaker 6.0, 6.5, and 7.0, and QuarkXPress 3.3 to 4.1.

Tip Files created using QuarkXPress 5.0 and 6.0 can be opened in InDesign by first saving them using the QuarkXPress 4.0 format and then opening them in InDesign.

When a Quark or PageMaker file is opened in InDesign, the layout elements are converted to native InDesign elements. Note that although most elements are comparable between the different systems, there are some differences that may cause problems. For example, the color profiles in Quark aren't used in InDesign and are ignored during the conversion.

Working with Pages and Spreads

After establishing a layout, you use the Pages palette to work with the different pages and/or spreads. Using this palette, you can select, target, rearrange, delete or add pages and/or spreads. The Pages palette also provides access to Master pages.

Using the Pages palette

The Pages palette, shown in Figure 26-8, provides a high-level view of all the pages in the current document. It displays each page and spread as an icon. You use it to quickly select, add and delete pages as well as to apply a Master document to specific pages. You can open the Pages palette by choosing Window ➪ Pages (or by pressing F12).

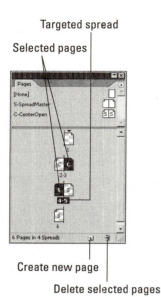

Targeted spread
Selected pages
Create new page
Delete selected pages

Figure 26-8: The Pages palette shows icons for all pages, spreads, and Masters in the current document.

You can change the size and position of icons in the Pages palette using the Palette Options palette menu command. This dialog box, shown in Figure 26-9, lets you set an icon size for Pages and Masters to be Small, Medium, Large, or Extra Large. You can also select to display the icons Vertically or Horizontally. The final option lets you place the Pages or the Masters at the top of the palette.

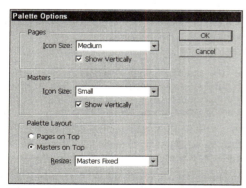

Figure 26-9: The Palette Options dialog box changes the icon size and placement within the Pages palette.

Selecting and targeting pages and spreads

You can easily select and target pages and spreads by using the following actions in the Pages palette:

- **Click:** Selects the page or spread icon.
- **Double-click:** This *targets* the page or spread or moves it to the center of the interface.
- **Holding down the Shift key while clicking on the page icons:** This selects multiple pages or spreads.

The Pages palette icons are highlighted for all selected pages. When you apply certain actions, such as applying a Master or adding page numbers, they affect all selected pages.

Targeted pages are the pages that are currently active, and they're the pages that receive any newly created objects or any object that is pasted from the Clipboard. You can also identify the targeted page because it is the page whose ruler is not dimmed. You can target only one page or spread at a time. The targeted page in the Pages palette has its page numbers highlighted.

Tip: You can also select and target pages using the Page Number drop-down list located at the bottom-left corner of the interface.

The Layout menu includes several commands for select pages and spreads:

- **Layout ⇨ First Page** selects the first page.
- **Layout ⇨ Last Page** selects the last page.
- **Layout ⇨ Previous Page/Next Page** moves between adjacent pages.
- **Layout ⇨ Previous Spread/Next Spread** moves between adjacent spreads
- **Layout ⇨ Go Back/Go Forward** moves you back and forth through pages.

Inserting and deleting and rearranging pages

You add pages to a new document using the Insert Pages palette menu command, which opens the Insert Pages dialog box, shown in Figure 26-10. This dialog box lets you add a specified number of pages to the current document. The Insert options include After Page Number, Before Page Number, At Start of Document, and At End of Document. You can also select a Master page to use.

Note: You can also add pages to the current document by entering a high value in the Number of Pages field for the Document Setup dialog box. The new pages are added onto the end of the current pages.

Figure 26-10: The Insert Pages dialog box places new pages exactly where you want them.

You can add pages to the current document by clicking on the Create New Page icon button at the bottom of the Pages palette.

In addition to inserting pages, the palette menu includes several other menu commands that are applied to the selected pages. The Duplicate Page (or Duplicate Spread, if a spread is selected) palette menu command creates a duplicate of the selected page (or spread). This duplicate also includes a duplicate of the page contents.

The Delete Page (or Spread) palette menu command removes the selected pages from the current document. If these pages contain any content, a warning dialog box appears, asking if you're sure about the deletion. You can also delete selected pages by clicking on the Delete Selected Pages icon button at the bottom of the Pages palette.

In addition to the palette menu, the Pages palette is also used to rearrange pages and spreads. By selecting and dragging the page icons in the Pages palette, you can rearrange the page order.

Creating and Using Master Pages

A Master is a page that holds all the elements that are common for several pages. It can include items such as page numbers, headers and footers, logos, and so on. All the items placed on the Master show up on the pages that the Master is applied to.

Each new document includes a single Master called the A-Master. This Master is selected from the top of the Pages palette, shown in Figure 26-11. You create and apply new Master pages to selected pages, so a document may have several Master pages applied to different pages. Each page may only have a single Master applied to it.

Tip

You can also select Master pages using the drop-down list located at the bottom-left of the Illustrator window. This drop-down list includes all pages and named Masters.

Master pages

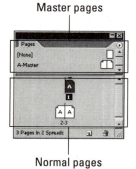

Figure 26-11: The top of the Pages palette holds the Master pages unless you change the preferences as mentioned above.

Normal pages

Creating a Master

To create a new Master page, select the New Master palette menu command. This opens the dialog box shown in Figure 26-12, which allows you to give the Master document a Prefix and a Name and to select another Master to base it on. You can also select the number of pages in the Master spread.

Tip — By basing all newly created Masters on a single main Master page, you can make changes to the main Master page, and all other Masters based on this main Master inherit the changes also.

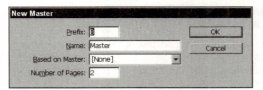

Figure 26-12: You name a new Master document with the New Master dialog box.

New Masters are also created by dragging a page or spread from the Pages palette to the Masters section at the top of the Pages palette. If the dragged page contains any objects, those objects become part of the Master page. If the dragged page has a Master applied to it, the new Master is based on the applied Master.

You can change the Master options by selecting the Master and choosing the Master Options palette menu command. This opens the Master Options dialog box again.

You can delete Master pages, like normal pages, by dragging them to the trash icon button at the bottom of the Pages palette or by selecting the Delete Master Spread palette menu command.

Applying Masters

The Pages palette makes it easy to apply Masters to different pages and spreads. Simply drag the Master that you want to apply and drop it on the icon in the Pages palette of the page or spread that you want to apply it to. Masters should only be applied to spreads with the same number of pages. The Pages palette displays the prefix for the Master applied to it, as shown in Figure 26-13.

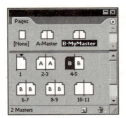

Figure 26-13: The letter on the page icon shows which Master has been applied to it.

If you select multiple pages and Option/Alt+click on a Master page, that Master page is applied to all the selected pages. You can also select the Apply Master to Pages palette menu command. This action opens a simple dialog box where you can select a Master and type in the page numbers of the pages that you want to apply the Master to. To include multiple contiguous pages, use a dash symbol (for example, 4-7).

Overriding, detaching, deleting, and hiding Master objects

If a page or a spread is selected, you typically can't edit the objects that are part of the Master. However, if you override the Master object, you can change certain attributes of the objects such as its stroke, fill, and transformations. If you need to change the Master object even more, you can detach it from the Master page. This gives you full access to the Master object on the selected page and breaks its association with the Master page.

Overriding all Master objects on the selected page is accomplished using the Override All Master Page Items (Alt+Shift+Ctrl+L on Windows, Option+Shift+⌘+L on the Mac) palette menu command. This command lets you edit all Master objects for the selected page without changing the Master.

If you want to edit only a single Master object on the selected page or spread, you can hold down the Shift+⌘/Ctrl keys while clicking on the item to change only the single Master item for the selected page without altering the other Master objects.

All Master page objects are detached using the Detach All Objects from Master palette menu command. You can also click on a single Master item while pressing Shift+⌘/Ctrl to detach a single object.

Selected pages are deleted by selecting Delete Master Page option from the palette menu, dragging the Master page to the Delete Selected Pages icon at the bottom of the palette, or by clicking on the Delete Selected Pages icon.

All page objects that are provided by a Master may be hidden or shown by choosing View ⇨ Show/Hide Master Items.

Using Layers

Document pages as well as Master pages have layers. Layers are used to organize page objects and also to control which objects appear above other objects. Objects placed on a higher layer appear on top of objects placed on a lower layer.

Cross-Reference More details on working with layers can be found in Chapter 14.

Creating new layers

All layers are displayed in the Layers palette, shown in Figure 26-14. Each layer has a name and a color associated with it. All objects are highlighted with their layer color when selected. Using the columns in the Layers palette to the left of the layer name, you can make a layer Visible or Locked.

All new documents include a single layer named Layer 1. New layers are created using the New Layer palette menu command or by clicking the Create New Layer button at the bottom of the Layers palette. The New Layer menu command opens a dialog box, shown in Figure 26-15, where you can enter a name, choose a color, and select other options.

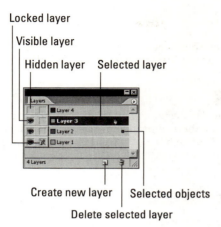

Figure 26-14: The Layers palette lists all the available layers.

Figure 26-15: The New Layer dialog box lets you name the new layer, choose its color, and set other options such as visibility and locking.

Positioning Master objects on top of document objects

Be default, all Master page objects appear behind the document objects, but you can force objects on a Master page to appear on top of the document objects by assigning a higher layer to the Master objects.

If you've already created an object on a Master page that has a lower layer number than the document object that you want to place it on top of, you can create a higher layer in the Layer palette by selecting the New Layer palette menu command or by clicking on the Create New Layer button at the bottom of the Layers palette. Then select the objects that you want to move to the new layer and drag the small square icon to the right of the layer name to the new layer. The frame edge of the object changes colors to match the new layer.

Note You can also move objects between layers by choosing Edit ➪ Cut, Edit ➪ Copy, or Edit ➪ Paste, but if you enable the Paste Remembers Layers option in the Layer palette menu, pasting an object on a new layer won't change its layer.

Adding Page Numbering

Page numbering automatically updates as you rearrange, add or delete pages from the current document. Auto page numbers may be added to a Master page or to a normal page.

Adding auto page numbering

To add auto numbering to a page, select the page or Master and drag with the Type tool to create a text object. Then type any text that you want to appear before the page number. Choose Type ➪ Insert Special Character ➪ Auto Page Number (Alt+Shift+Ctrl+N in Windows, Option+Shift+⌘+N on the Mac). The text objects are formatted using the standard formatting features found in the Character and Paragraph palettes.

Cross-Reference   For more information on formatting text, see Part IV.

By default, auto numbering calls the first page "page 1," the second page "page 2," and so on, but you can change the number formatting to Roman numerals or letters and also start with a number other than 1 using the Numbering & Section Options dialog box, shown in Figure 26-16. Open this dialog box by choosing Layout ➪ Numbering & Section Options.

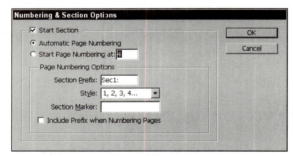

Figure 26-16: Use the Numbering & Section Options dialog box to add sections.

Defining sections

To define a section, choose the first page for the section in the Pages palette; then open the Numbering & Section Options dialog box and choose the numbering options. Enabling the Start Section option creates a new section. You can also specify a Section Prefix and a Section Marker. The Section Prefix displays along with the page number when you enable the Include Prefix When Numbering Pages option. You can add the Section Marker to the numbering text object by choosing Type ➪ Insert Special Character ➪ Section Marker.

Note   You can also use the specified numbering style in the table of contents and the index pages.

When the dialog box is closed, the Pages palette displays the page numbers using the selected numbering style and a small down-arrow icon appears above the first page of each section. Double-clicking on the section arrow icon in the Pages palette opens the Numbering & Sections dialog box. You can add several sections to the current document.

You can set InDesign to display absolute page numbers or section page numbers in the Pages palette using the Page Numbering option in the General panel of the Preferences dialog box.

Enhancing Layouts

Once you create a layout, you can enhance various elements that you want to appear consistently throughout the document. For example, you can quickly add a sidebar element to designated pages by creating a guide that identifies the placement of the element. Using rulers, grids, and guides provide an effective way to enhance a layout.

Using rulers

Rulers are positioned on the left side and above the pasteboard and are consistent to the page regardless of the amount of zooming. If you right-click on the ruler, you can change its measurement units using the pop-up menu shown in Figure 26-17. The options include Points, Picas, Inches, Inches Decimal, Millimeters, Centimeters, Ciceros, and Custom.

If the rulers aren't visible, you can make them appear by choosing View ⇨ Show/Hide Rulers (⌘/Ctrl+R).

Figure 26-17: Right-clicking on a ruler presents a pop-up menu of measurement units.

Using grids

InDesign has two different types of grids that can overlay the document. The Baseline Grid, shown in Figure 26-18, includes horizontal lines used to mark text baselines. It's confined to the page.

Figure 26-18: The Baseline Grid is displayed within the current page only.

The Document Grid type, shown in Figure 26-19, is made up of small grid squares and overlays the entire art board.

Both of these grids are made visible by choosing View ⇨ Show/Hide Baseline Grid (Alt+Ctrl+' in Windows, Option+⌘+' on the Mac) or View ⇨ Show/Hide Document Grid (Ctrl+' in Windows, ⌘+' on the Mac). You can also cause objects to snap to the Document Grid lines by enabling the View ⇨ Snap to Document Grid (Shift+Ctrl+' in Windows, Shift+⌘+' on the Mac) menu command. You configure both the Baseline Grid and the Document Grid using the Preferences ⇨ Grids panel.

Using guides

Guides are simply lines that extend from the ruler, providing a visual boundary for page objects. InDesign uses two different types of guides. Page guides are only seen within the page, and Spread guides run across the entire spread including the art board.

You create a Page guide by clicking on a ruler and dragging onto the page. Holding down the ⌘/Ctrl key while dragging from the ruler onto a page creates a Spread guide. Figure 26-20 shows each of these guide types. Choosing Layout ⇨ Ruler Guides opens a simple dialog box where you can set the View Threshold and Color for these guides.

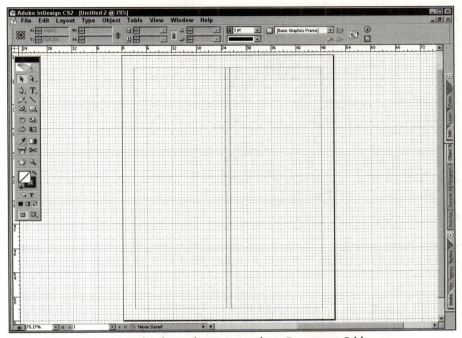

Figure 26-19: Items snap in place when you overlay a Document Grid.

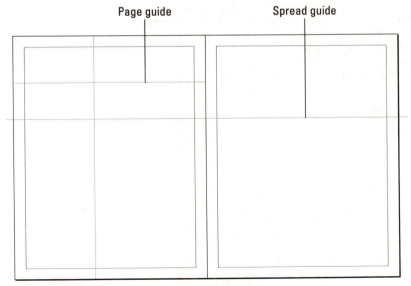

Figure 26-20: Guides are useful for positioning objects.

You create a series of consistent guides using the Create Guides dialog box, shown in Figure 26-21, which you access by choosing Layout ⇨ Create Guides. This dialog box lets you specify the number of rows and columns and the gutter between each.

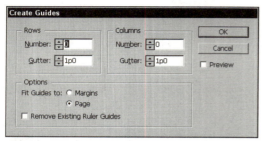

Figure 26-21: The Create Guides dialog box creates a series of evenly spaced guides.

You can select and move guides after they're created. To lock all guides so they can't be moved accidentally, choose View ⇨ Lock Guides (Option/Alt+;). All guides are hidden by choosing View ⇨ Show/Hide Guides (⌘/Ctrl+;).

Using frames

With grids and guides in place, another helpful object is a layout frame. You create frames, which act as placeholders for graphics or text, using any path or object in the Toolbox including Rectangles, Ellipses, Polygons, or any freehand drawn shape.

To create a frame, select a drawing tool in the Toolbox, such as the Rectangle Frame tool (F) and drag in the page to create a frame. With the frame selected, you can specify what type of content the frame holds by choosing Object ⇨ Content ⇨ Graphic, Object ⇨ Content ⇨ Text, or Object ⇨ Content ⇨ Unassigned.

Note You can also create text-assigned frames with the Type tool.

Graphic frames have an X through their center, and text-assigned frames have ports that thread multiple frames, as shown in Figure 26-22.

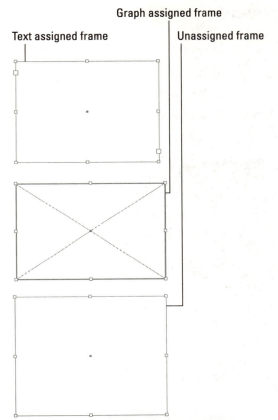

Figure 26-22: Frames create placeholders for different content types.

Importing Images and Objects

As you create a layout with frames, it's often helpful to import a stub image, which acts as a placeholder for final artwork, with the correct dimensions from Photoshop and Illustrator. After importing stub images, you can create the artwork using either Photoshop or Illustrator, and if you establish links between the two packages, the artwork can update dynamically.

Note Stub objects are frequently called FPO objects, which stands for For Placement Only.

Importing Photoshop artwork

You can import Photoshop artwork into a selected frame by choosing File ➪ Place (⌘/Ctrl+D). If you enable the Show Import Options, the Image Import Options dialog box, shown in Figure 26-23, appears after you select the image file in the file dialog box. The settings found in the Image Import Options dialog box are different depending on the type of image format that was selected.

Cross-Reference   Chapter 2 includes a good example of placing an imported file into InDesign.

Figure 26-23: The Image Import Options dialog box includes panels for selecting the Alpha Channel and Color Management profiles.

The Apply Photoshop Clipping Path and the Alpha Channel drop-down list options are enabled if the imported object includes a clipping path and/or an Alpha Channel. For imported images that include an Alpha Channel, you can select the Transparency or Graduated Transparency option.

Note   InDesign offers the option of importing an image with Graduated Transparency — a feature that isn't offered in Quark XPress.

Importing Illustrator artwork and PDF files

Artwork created in Illustrator and PDF files that are placed within a selected frame in InDesign opens the Place PDF dialog box if Show Import Options is enabled. This dialog box, shown in Figure 26-24, includes two separate panels — General and Layers. The General panel includes settings that let you place the imported artwork on the Previewed Page, All pages, or a Range of pages; and options to set a cropping option and make the background transparent. The Layers panel lets you see all the layers that are in the imported artwork. For each layer, you can select to Use PDF's Layer Visibility or to Keep Layer Visibility Overrides.

New Feature   Control over layers and the ability to place imported artwork on several pages at once is new to CS2.

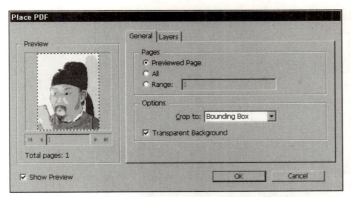

Figure 26-24: You import Illustrator's AI and PDF files into InDesign with the Place PDF dialog box options.

Dynamically updating content

You may open and edit artwork created using Photoshop and/or Illustrator in their original application by right-clicking the image and choosing Graphics ⇨ Edit Original. This causes the image to open within the original application. Any saved edits you make to the image in the original application are automatically updated within InDesign.

Tip — Holding down the Option/Alt key while double clicking on a placed source file opens the file in its native application.

Assembling a Layout

This chapter concludes with an example that takes you through the steps to create a sample layout and to add auto page numbering to a master page in InDesign.

STEPS: Creating an InDesign layout

1. **Create a new document.** Within InDesign, choose File ⇨ New ⇨ Document (⌘/Ctrl+N). In the New Document dialog box, set the Number of Pages to 6 and enable the Facing Pages option. Select the Letter Page Size, which sets the Width to 8.5 in. and the Height to 11 in. with a Portrait orientation. In the Margins and Columns section, set the Top margin to 0.5 in. and click the Make All Settings the Same button. Then set the number of Columns to 1 with a Gutter of 0.1667 in.

2. **Set the Bleed and Slug settings.** If the Bleed and Slug sections aren't visible, click More Options Set the Bleed values to 0.0 in. and click the Make All Settings the Same button. Set all Slug values to 0.0. Figure 26-25 shows the New Document dialog box with the appropriate settings. Click OK to create the new document.

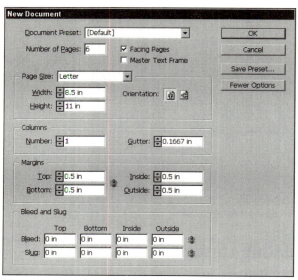

Figure 26-25: The New Document dialog box includes many initial settings for creating a layout document.

3. **Edit the Master spread.** In the Pages palette, select and target the A-Master spread by double-clicking its title. The spread icons are highlighted in the Pages palette, and the spread is centered in the interface. Select the Master Options for the A-Master palette menu command. This opens the Master Options dialog box for the A-Master spread. Change the Prefix to S and the Name to SpreadMaster. Click OK to close the dialog box.

4. **Create a New Master spread.** In the Pages palette, select the New Master palette menu command. The New Master dialog box opens, shown in Figure 26-26. Enter a Prefix value of C, enter a Name of CenterOpen, and set the spread to Based on the S-SpreadMaster Master. Click OK to close the dialog box.

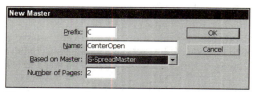

Figure 26-26: The New Master dialog box lets you name the Master spread and give it a prefix.

5. **Apply the Master spreads to the pages.** In the Pages palette, drag the Master page named None to the first page. Then drag the C-CenterOpen Master to the spread in pages 2 and 3. The remaining spreads already have the S-SpreadMaster Master applied to them.

6. **Adding content to the Master spreads.** Double-click the S-SpreadMaster to select and target it. Create the objects and position them within the Master spread. Figure 26-27 shows the Master spread with several content items added to it.

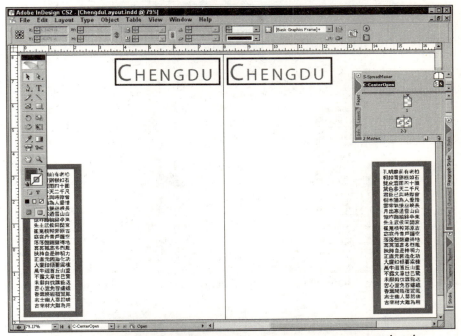

Figure 26-27: Content added to the Master spread appears on every page that the Master is applied to.

7. **Add Auto Page Numbering.** With the Type tool, drag to create a small text object in the upper-left and upper-right corners of the Master spread. With the text object selected, choose Type ➪ Insert Special Character ➪ Auto Page Number. A letter *S* appears in each text object, which is the prefix for the Master spread. Click on several of the pages in the Pages palette and see the numbering updated.

8. **Place artwork on the secondary Master.** Double-click the title for the C-CenterOpen Master in the Pages palette. This selects and targets the second Master spread. With the Secondary Master spread selected and targeted, choose File ➪ Place. In the file dialog box that opens, select the artwork pieces that you want to place within the Secondary Master spread and click OK. The artwork is added to the spread. Select the artwork and position it. Figure 26-28 shows the Secondary Master spread with some artwork added to it. Using two Master pages gives the design flexibility and power.

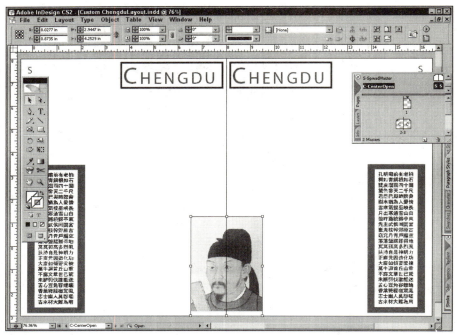

Figure 26-28: The Secondary Master can include different content from the original Master.

Summary

✦ You create Layout documents using File ➪ New ➪ Document to open a dialog box of settings including the number of pages, the page size and orientation, the margins, and the columns.

✦ You use document presets to save layout settings for reuse.

✦ You change layout settings for an existing document via the Document Setup and the Margins and Columns dialog box.

✦ Icons of all pages and spreads are viewed from within the Pages palette.

✦ The Pages palette helps you create Master pages, which hold objects that appear on all pages to which you apply the Master.

✦ The Layers palette is used to place objects on different layers.

✦ You enable Auto page numbering by adding the Auto Page Number object to a text object. When placed on a Master page, all pages based on the Master page show the page number. The document may also be divided into sections, each with a different numbering scheme.

✦ Rulers, grids, guides, and frames are useful in establishing layouts.

✦ You can import artwork created in Photoshop, Illustrator, and Acrobat into InDesign.

✦ ✦ ✦

Modifying Layouts

CHAPTER 27

In This Chapter

Using artwork versions

Working with the Links palette

Anchoring objects in InDesign

Once you create a layout, you may need to modify it. For example, embedding all the images you use in your layout in an InDesign document may result in a large, difficult-to-handle file size. However, you can place links to the larger original artwork elements within InDesign to make your file more manageable and embed smaller elements. You can also anchor graphics to a section of text so the graphic moves as the text moves.

This chapter shows you how to access links via the Links palette to see what links you need to relink, move, update or embed as well how to update edited image files. It also illustrates how to manage files with Adobe's Version Cue, which provides a file-management solution for a multiple-users environment. Finally, this chapter shows how you can edit and dynamically update images and objects within Acrobat using the original authoring software with the TouchUp Object tool.

Using Artwork Versions

When you place images in an InDesign document, the image file isn't copied into InDesign. Instead, a lower-resolution version of the image displays allowing you to position the image in the layout while maintaining a link to the original image. Using links to the original image helps keep the size of the InDesign document manageable. When you print, package, preflight, or export the document, all the links are followed and the original images are used. The original images are also used when the High Quality Display option is selected.

You place images using the File ⇨ Place (⌘/Ctrl+D) menu command. All images that you import into InDesign show up in the Links palette listing the image filename and the page it appears.

 Note Files that are smaller than 48K are actually embedded within the InDesign document, but they're still listed in the Links palette for version control.

Using the Links palette

The Links palette, shown in Figure 27-1, lists all imported images in an InDesign document. It also lists the image's location in the document. You open the Links palette by choosing Window ⇨ Links (Shift+Ctrl+D in Windows; Shift+⌘+D on the Mac).

Figure 27-1: The Links palette lists all the image files.

Depending on the state of the image file, one of the following icons may appear to the right of the image name:

- **Missing image:** Red stop sign icon indicates that the image file is missing. This means that the defined link is incorrect and that the file has been moved, renamed, or is on a network or CD-ROM that can no longer be found.
- **Modified link:** A yellow triangle icon denotes that a more up-to-date version of the image file is available and that you need to update the link.
- **Embedded link:** A gray square icon marks any embedded image files within the current document.
- **Layer Visibility Override:** This icon shows up when the Layer Visibility Override toggle is enabled for the linked image. This uses the layer visibility settings for the InDesign document instead of the native application.
- **Adobe Stock Photos Comp:** The Adobe Stock Photo Comp icon is placed beside any image that is downloaded from the Adobe Stock Photo site.

You can sort the image files listed within the Links palette by Name, Page, or Status using the commands found in the palette menu.

Editing and locating original artwork

All image files in the Links palette have links, which point to the original image-file location. The Links palette also shows which application was used to create the original image.

If you double-click on a placed image in the layout with the Option/Alt key held down, the original image opens within the application originally used to create it.

You can also open an image in its original application by selecting the Edit Original palette menu command in the Links palette or by selecting an item in the Links palette and clicking the Edit Original button at the bottom of the palette.

The Links palette is also helpful in locating images placed within InDesign. Selecting an image file in the Links palette and choosing the Go to Link palette menu command displays the page upon which the placed image is located. Alternatively, you can retrieve information by clicking the Go to Link button at the bottom of the Links palette.

Viewing link information and relinking

Double-clicking on an image name in the Links palette opens the Link Information dialog box. This dialog box, shown in Figure 27-2, shows information about the linked image file including its name, the last date it was modified, size, color space, file type, and so on. It also lists the link to the original object with a Relink button.

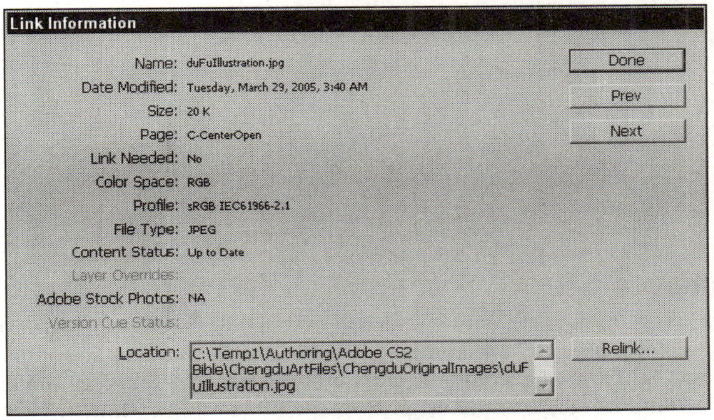

Figure 27-2: The Link Information dialog box

Clicking Relink in the Link Information dialog box opens a file dialog that points to the selected image file. If the image file displays the Missing Image icon, you can use this button to locate the original image and reestablish the link.

If you do not select objects in the Links palette, selecting the Relink palette menu option or clicking the Relink button at the bottom of the palette, causes InDesign to scan for any missing image files. When a missing image file is found, a file dialog box opens, allowing you to locate the missing file. When the image file is found or when you click the Skip button, the list is scanned again until all the missing files have been relinked.

Any out-of-date image files may be manually updated using the Update Link palette menu command or by selecting the image link in the Links palette and clicking on the Update Links button at the bottom of the palette.

STEPS: Relinking placed image files

1. **Open an InDesign document.** Choose File ⇨ Open and locate an InDesign document that includes placed images.

2. **Open the Links palette.** Choose Window ⇨ Links to make the Links palette appear, as shown in Figure 27-3. If the links are broken for any of the placed images, the Missing Image icon appears next to the image file name in the Links palette.

3. **Relink missing files.** From the palette menu, select the Relink palette menu command. InDesign scans the Links palette and presents a file dialog box, for each image file that is missing. Locate the missing file and click the Open button. Repeat this step for all missing files.

Figure 27-3: Files you need to relink are marked with a question mark and moved to the top of the palette.

Embedding linked images

To ensure that images don't end up missing, you can embed them within the InDesign document using the Embed File palette menu command from the Links palette. This action places a small gray square icon next to the image's name in the Links palette and disables the link to the original file. Any future changes made to the original image file do not update in InDesign. In addition, the InDesign file size increases to accommodate the embedded file.

You unembed embedded files using the Unembed File palette menu command or by relinking the file to its original.

Setting the display quality

For placed images, you can set the display quality of raster images, vector images, and images that include transparency. The three display options available for placed images include Fast, Typical, and High Quality. Figure 27-4 shows an example of each of these options.

Figure 27-4: Display-quality options are Fast (left), Typical (middle), and High Quality (right).

You set the Display Performance level for the selected object by choosing Object ⇨ Display Performance. The options include each of the levels along with Use View Setting. If you select the Use View Setting option, the level set in the View menu determines the Display Performance level.

For the current view, you can select each of the following settings by choosing View ⇨ Display Performance:

- **Fast**: Alt+Ctrl+O in Windows; Option+⌘+0 on the Mac.
- **Typical**: Alt+Ctrl+Z in Windows; Option+⌘+Z on the Mac.
- **High Quality:** Alt+Ctrl+H in Windows; Option+⌘+H on the Mac.

The Preserve Object-Level Display Settings option causes all placed images to use the selected Display Performance setting, except for the objects that have their own specified display level. These settings are configurable using the InDesign/Edit ⇨ Preferences ⇨ Display Performance menu command. The Display Performance panel of the Preferences dialog box, shown in Figure 27-5 lets you adjust the view settings for each of these levels. You can also enable anti-aliasing. Greeking displays text and images as a gray-shaded bar instead of individual letters. Using the Greek Type Below setting, you enable all type below a given point size to be displayed as a shaded bar. You can use the Scrolling slider to adjust the Hand tool to Greek type and images, to Greek just the images, or to have no Greeking.

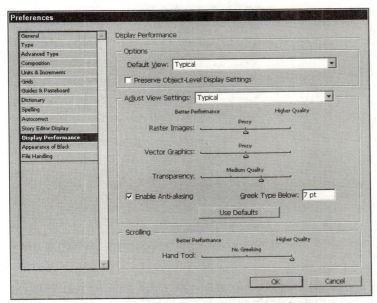

Figure 27-5: The Display Performance panel of the Preferences dialog box

Anchoring objects

Anchored objects, which can include text frames or placed graphics, are attached to a section of text. When the text frame moves, the anchored object moves with it. This is convenient for sidebars or inline graphics that highlight some text.

Anchoring objects to text is a new feature in CS2.

Anchored graphics

To create an anchored graphic, you need to select a section of text or a text position with the Type tool, then choose File ⇨ Place to place the graphic object. The anchored graphic appears as a frame within the text frame, as shown in Figure 27-6.

 An existing placed graphic can be anchored by cutting the graphic by choosing Edit ⇨ Cut and pasting it by choosing Edit ⇨ Paste after selecting the text to anchor it to with the Type tool.

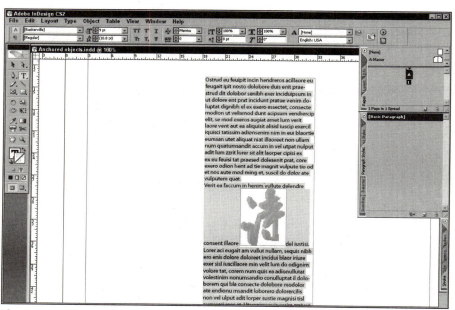

Figure 27-6: Anchored graphics are created by placing an image when a section of type is selected with the Type tool.

With the anchored graphic selected, choose Object ⇨ Anchored Object ⇨ Options to open the Anchored Object Options dialog box. The dialog box includes two Position settings — Inline or Above Line and Custom. Both of these options are shown side by side in Figure 27-7.

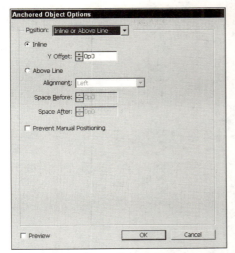 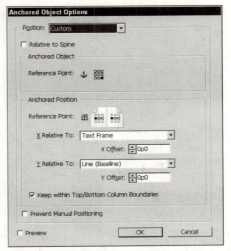

Figure 27-7: The Anchored Object Options dialog box includes different settings for setting the object's position.

For the Inline position, you can set the Y Offset and the Above Line position lets you set the Alignment to Left, Center, Right, Towards Spine, Away from Spine, or according to the Text Alignment. You can also set the Space Before and After the anchored object. The selected anchored object can be moved manually by dragging on the object if the Prevent Manual Positioning option isn't selected.

If you want even more control over the position of the anchored object, you can select the Custom Position setting, which gives you many more options.

Anchored text frames

In addition to graphics, you can also anchor text frames. Anchored text frames are created by selecting a text location with the Type tool and choosing Object ➪ Anchored Object ➪ Insert. This command opens the Insert Anchored Object dialog box shown in Figure 27-8. This dialog box includes many of the same positioning settings found in the Anchored Object Options dialog box.

The Insert Anchored Object dialog box lets you select the object type using the Content setting, which can be Text, Graphic, or Unassigned. You can also select an Object and Paragraph Style and the object Height and Width.

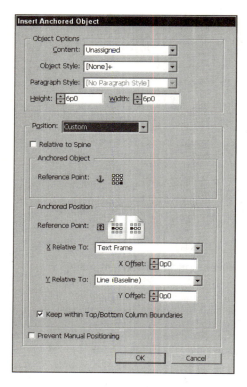

Figure 27-8: The Insert Anchored Object dialog box creates text or graphic anchored objects.

To break the link between an anchored object and its text object, select the anchored object and choose Object ➪ Anchored Object ➪ Release.

STEPS: Anchoring graphics to text

1. **Open a layout file in InDesign.** For this layout, you anchor an image of Du Fu to his bio description.

2. **Select the anchoring text.** Click the Type tool from the Toolbox and place the text cursor at the end of "Du Fu" title text, which is the anchor text for the graphic.

Don't select any text in the text frame or the placed graphic will replace the selected text.

3. **Create an Anchored Object.** With a text position selected within the anchor text frame, choose File ➪ Place. Locate and open the `DuFu.tif` file. The image gets embedded within the text frame, as shown in Figure 27-9.

4. **Set the options for the Anchored Object.** With the Selection tool, click the anchored graphic and choose Object ➪ Anchored Object ➪ Options. In the Anchored Object Options dialog box, select the Custom option from the Position drop-down list. For the Anchored Object's Reference Point, select the upper-left corner; for the Anchored Position's Reference Point, select the upper-right point. Then set the X and Y Relative options to Text Frame. Click OK. Figure 27-10 shows the resulting anchored graphic. This graphic moves with the text frame when the text frame is repositioned.

Chapter 27 ✦ Modifying Layouts 915

Figure 27-9: The placed graphic is embedded within the text frame.

Figure 27-10: The anchored graphic is positioned relative to the text frame.

5. **Reposition the Text Frame.** With the Selection tool, select and drag the text frame to the right. Notice how the anchored graphic moves along with the text frame, as shown in Figure 27-11.

Figure 27-11: The anchored graphic is automatically moved along with the text frame.

Summary

+ All images placed within an InDesign document appear in the Links palette.
+ The Links palette may be used to relink missing image files, to update changed image files, and to locate placed images within the layout.
+ InDesign's Anchoring feature let you bind images to text fields.

Document Repurposing

PART VII

In This Part

Chapter 28
Exporting Designs for Web and Screen Viewing

Chapter 29
Preparing Documents for Distribution

Chapter 30
Working with XML

Exporting Designs for Web and Screen Viewing

♦ ♦ ♦ ♦

In This Chapter

Setting up a site design

Creating Web pages in GoLive

Using Smart Objects

Working with Cascading Style Sheets

Packaging for GoLive

♦ ♦ ♦ ♦

Document repurposing deals with reusing designs for different media. In today's business climate, designs created for print are frequently reused to produce Web sites, CD-ROMs, PDF files, and video products. Repurposing designs can save a lot of time and it presents a consistent look across several products.

This chapter presents one repurposing example among many. Documents created for print in InDesign may be packaged and exported for use in GoLive to create Web sites that users can view using Web browsers, PDAs, or cell phones.

 For more information on document repurposing, see Chapter 29.

Setting Up a Site Window with the Site Wizard

Each of the applications included in the Creative Suite has its own purpose, and the purpose of GoLive is to create Web pages and manage Web sites. Web pages are much different than the layout designs found in any of the other CS2 applications, because they're constrained to conform to the Hypertext Markup Language known as HTML.

HTML is the language that Web browsers read that defines the placement of text and images on a Web page. HTML is very linear in its layout approach, with objects positioned on top of one another from the upper-left corner of the page to the bottom of the page following the left edge of the page.

Web sites are a collection of Web pages that you publish to the Web. The typical workflow for Web sites is to design the site first and then to flesh out the individual Web pages.

Using the New dialog box

When GoLive launches, a Welcome dialog box, shown in Figure 28-1, appears. This dialog box provides quick links to the new features of GoLive CS2, tutorials, and Cool Extras. It also includes icons for creating a New Document or opening an existing one. You can deselect the Show this Dialog at Startup option to make this dialog box go away.

The New dialog box has been overhauled in GoLive CS2 to include many different samples, a favorite section, and Mobile templates.

Figure 28-1: The GoLive Welcome dialog box provides all the links you need to get started.

Clicking the New Document icon in the Welcome dialog or choosing File ➪ New makes the New dialog box appear (see Figure 28-2). This dialog box includes templates for several different types of Web sites and pages. You can add new templates to the New dialog box using the Add Files palette menu command. From the palette menu, you can also select to Remove Files, Edit Description, and Add and Remove from Favorites.

Creating a new site

To create a new Web site, click the Site icon in the New dialog box. The second pane of the New dialog box lists several different templates including Web, Mobile, Scripting, Co-Author, and Further Samples. There are also options to Create Site and Connect to Site. Selecting the Create Site option begins the Site Creation Wizard, and selecting the Connect to Site option displays options where you can specify the server address, username, and password to connect to the existing site.

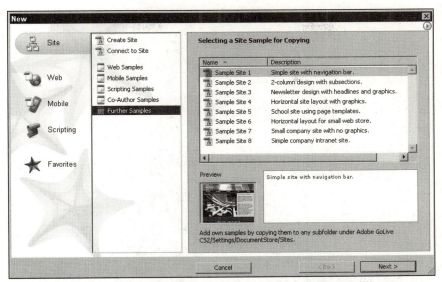

Figure 28-2: The New dialog box lets you choose from a number of different types of templates.

Selecting the Create Site option makes three choices available — Blank Site, Site from Existing Content, and Site from a Site Locator File (.aglsl). The Site Wizard creates a `project` folder that includes the project file (identified with the `.site` extension) and three folders — `web-content`, `web-data`, and `web-settings`. All the Web pages, images, and content loaded on the server are saved in the `web-content` folder. The other two folders hold configuration settings.

STEPS: Using the Site Wizard

1. **Choose File ⇨ New Site (Alt+Shift+Ctrl+N in Windows; Option+Shift+⌘+N on the Mac) to start the Site Wizard.** The first step lets choose the type of Web site template to use. Click the Site icon and then select the Create Site option in the second pane.

2. **Select the appropriate options for your site.** Select the Blank Site option in the third pane of the New dialog box, as shown in Figure 28-3. Then click Next to continue.

3. **Select a name and location.** The name is used to name the folder where you save the site content. The Advanced button opens a separate dialog box where you can specify the URL Encoding option to use. Click Next after typing a name and a location.

4. **Specify a Version Control System.** The next step in the Site Wizard lets you select and specify a Version Control System, as shown in Figure 28-4. The default Version Control choices are Version Cue, Directory in File System, FTP Server, and CVS. For this example, choose the Directory in File System option.

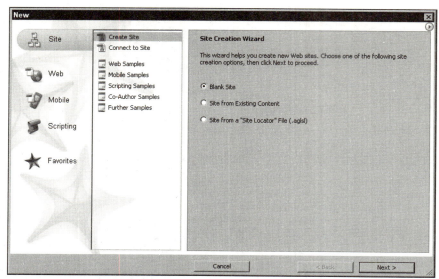

Figure 28-3: The Site Wizard lets you create sites based on imported files or on a site template.

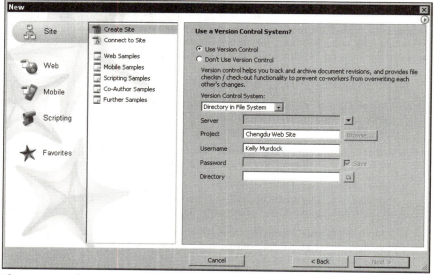

Figure 28-4: The Site Wizard lets you specify a Version Control System to use.

5. **Set Publish Server Options.** The final step of the Site Wizard lets you specify the Publish Server Options, as shown in Figure 28-5. Select the Specify Server Now option and type the information for the Web server where you plan to upload the new Web site.

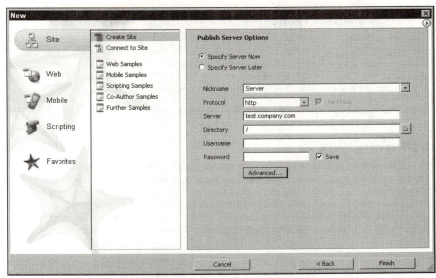

Figure 28-5: The final step of the Site Wizard lets you type the server connection information.

6. **Viewing the finished site.** When the Site Wizard is finished, a project window opens (see Figure 28-6). This window displays all the Web pages included as part of the current site in the left side of the window and all the files that have been transferred to the publish server on the right side of the window, which is a local directory for this example.

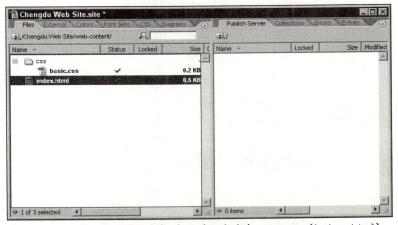

Figure 28-6: The Site Wizard displays the site's home page (index.html).

Adding pages to a site

You can add Web pages that you created before creating the site using several different methods. Right-clicking in the site window and choosing New ⇨ New HTML Page from the pop-up menu creates a new Web page and adds it to the site. You can also import an existing page by choosing File ⇨ Import ⇨ Files to Site. Finally, you can drag files from Windows Explorer (Finder) and drop them in the Site window to add them to the site.

From the site window, you can open Web pages by double-clicking them in the Files section.

Updating pages

When you add pages to a site, GoLive automatically checks the new page links to see if they are correct. If a problem occurs, the new page has a small red bug icon next to its name in the Status column, as shown in Figure 28-7. One of the most common errors is links that point to pages that don't exist. To fix bad links, locate the link on the page and change its link. To update the site file view after the incorrect links have been fixed, simply choose Update ⇨ Refresh All or Update ⇨ Refresh Selected from the right-click pop-up menu.

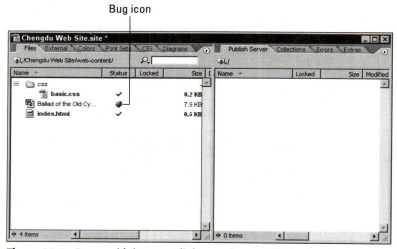

Figure 28-7: Pages with incorrect links are shown with the bug icon.

Creating Web pages in GoLive

Text on a single Web page isn't placed within a text frame like InDesign but pushes surrounding objects to fit all the text in the designated size. Images, likewise, aren't cropped or sized, but appear at their actual resolution where they rest between any text on the page.

All of these rules are understood by GoLive, but be aware that if objects don't seem to stay where you put them, HTML, not GoLive, is to blame.

Building Web pages and using views

The first place to start building Web pages is the package that you exported from InDesign. You can drag and drop Items displayed on the Package window directly on a blank Web page in the Layout Editor.

You add Web pages to a site project by choosing File ➪ New Page (⌘/Ctrl+N). Each Web page displays in its own window (Figure 28-8). You have several ways to view each page using the tabs at the top of the window:

Figure 28-8: Each Web page displays in its own window.

✦ **Layout Editor:** The default view, which displays laid-out Web-page objects, allows you to easily select and reposition objects.

✦ **Frame Editor:** Divides the Web page into frames.

✦ **Source Code Editor:** Displays the HTML code that generates the Web page, as shown in Figure 28-9.

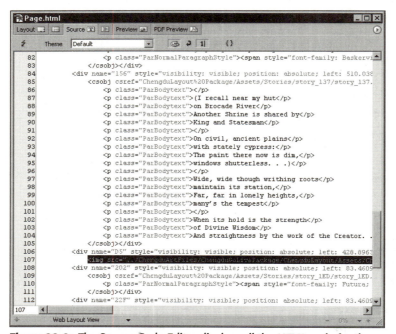

Figure 28-9: The Source Code Editor displays all the HTML code for the Web page.

✦ **Outline Editor:** This view breaks down all the HTML code into logical blocks that are easily expanded, altered, and reordered (see Figure 28-10).

✦ **Layout Preview/PDF Preview:** These views show the Web page as it would appear in a browser or saved as a PDF file.

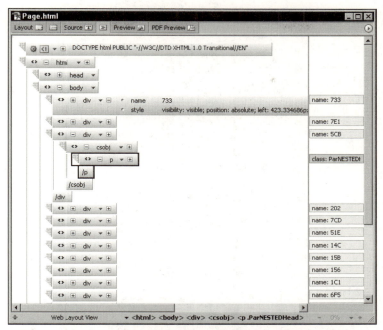

Figure 28-10: The Outline Editor offers another way to work with the HTML code in easy-to-manipulate blocks.

Using the Web page tools

At the top of the Toolbox, shown in Figure 28-11, are several tools you can use to work with the various Web page objects. These tools include the following:

- ✦ **Standard Editing tool:** Used to select objects and text.
- ✦ **Object Selection tool:** Used to select all objects except for text.
- ✦ **Layer/Grid Text Box tool:** Used to draw, move, and resize layers. The Grid Text Box tool is a flyout under the Layer Tool. It is used to draw, move, and resize text boxes on a layout grid.
- ✦ **Eyedropper tool:** Used to select a color from anywhere on your screen.
- ✦ **Hand tool:** Used to scroll the current page.
- ✦ **Zoom tool:** Used to zoom in and out of the current page.

Cross-Reference

An overview of the tools available in GoLive CS2 is found in Chapter 4.

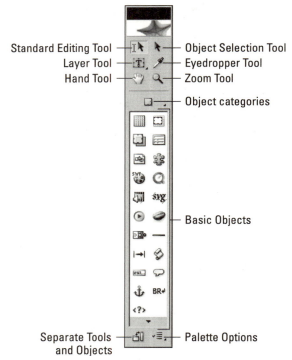

Figure 28-11: The Toolbox holds all the various Web-page objects.

Adding objects to Web pages

Beneath the tools are all the objects you can insert on a Web page. These objects are divided into separate categories, which are selected from the Object categories drop-down list. The available object categories include the following:

- **Basic:** Includes the most commonly used Web-page elements, such as Layout Grids, Layout Text Boxes, Tables, Images, and Lines.

- **Smart Objects:** Helps you add objects created in the other CS2 applications to a Web page while maintaining a link to the original authoring application. Smart Objects include easy-to-use prebuilt JavaScript functions called Actions.

- **Cascading Style Sheets:** This category includes several different CSS layout building blocks with different numbers of columns and rows.

- **Form Elements:** Includes objects found on form pages, such as buttons, labels, pop-ups, and text fields.

- **Head Elements:** Includes objects found in the head section of an HTML page, such as meta tags and keywords.

- **Frames and Framesets:** Creates frames with different formatted options.

- **Site Items:** Includes items that affect the entire site, such as the e-mail addresses, colors, and fonts.
- **Diagrams:** Includes dozens of different objects for creating site maps and wireframe walkthroughs.
- **QuickTime Elements:** This category of QuickTime-related technologies includes items like movies and sounds that you can combine into interactive multimedia presentations.
- **Movable Type 3.x:** This category includes several different text-based templates for creating text archives, calendars, category lists, comments and an entry log.
- **SMIL Elements:** Includes SMIL-related items for creating time-based media presentations using the SMIL language.
- **TypePad Blog:** Includes several objects for creating and managing blogs.

After you locate the correct object in the Toolbox, you can add it to a Web page window by dragging it from the Toolbox and dropping it on the Web page or by double clicking on an object to add it at the cursor's location.

Changing object properties

You select objects on a Web page in the Layout Editor by clicking on them with the Editing or Selection tools. A border around the object appears and the properties for the selected object appear in the Inspector palette. Figure 28-12 shows the Inspector palette when an image is selected in the Web page. The exact properties displayed in the Inspector palette depend on the object selected.

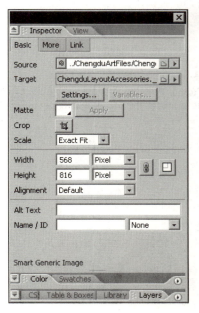

Figure 28-12: Properties for the selected Web-page object are displayed in the Inspector palette.

Adding Web page text

Text can be easily added to a Web page by simply typing on the page. The text is added at the position of the cursor. GoLive also includes basic formatting options on the Main Toolbar at the top of the interface. Formatting options include text alignment, font size, text style (strong, emphasis, and teletype), and text color. There are also options to create numbered and unnumbered lists. These text-formatting options are implemented in HTML and create markup tags for the text.

When text is added to a Web page, it flows around the other objects on the page, including headings and images. You can overlay text on top of other items using layers. Text can also be imported from other applications such as Microsoft Word using the clipboard.

Cross-Reference

Using Layers in GoLive CS2 is discussed in Chapter 14 and importing text from Word documents into GoLive is covered in Chapter 20.

Linking Web pages

You can add links, which open another Web page within a browser, to text or images within a Web page. To create a link, select the text or image you want for a link. The selected object's properties appear in the Inspector palette (see Figure 28-13). In the Inspector palette, you can click the Browse button and select the Web page or image to which you want to link. The Web page name appears in the link field. Be aware that the Browse button is tedious and error prone. The recommended method is to interactively link to pages or objects within the site with the Fetch URL icon (also known as the Point and Shoot tool). To use this tool, drag the icon to the site window, and select the Web page, image, or resource you want to link to.

Once you create links between Web pages, the Preview view lets you test the links.

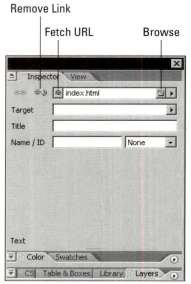

Figure 28-13: You specify the Web page or object to which you want to link at the top of the Inspector palette.

Working with Basic Objects and images

The Basic Objects category of the Toolbox includes many of the core objects that you can use to create Web pages including images, layers, tables, multimedia objects, and so on.

Cross-Reference

Creating and working with GoLive tables is covered in Chapter 22 and SWF and SVG objects are discussed in Chapter 35.

Dragging an image object onto a Web page adds a simple placeholder to the Web page. You can resize this placeholder by clicking and dragging on its corner handles or moved by dragging the center of the object to its new location. To load an image file into the image placeholder, use the Browse button found in the Inspector palette. Other Inspector palette properties include the image's size, alignment, and Alt Text, which is the text that appears when the cursor is placed over the image. Images can also have links to other Web pages.

STEPS: Building a Web page

1. **Open an existing site and add a Web page to the site.** Choose the File ➪ Open menu command and select a file with the .site extension to in the Open dialog box. This opens the site window. Right click on the left pane of the site window and choose New ➪ HTML Page from the pop-up menu. A new page is added to the site window titled, `blank.html`, as shown in Figure 28-14. Double click on the blank web page to open it for editing.

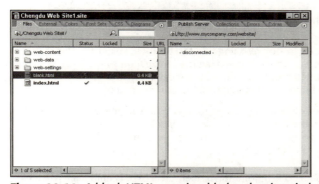

Figure 28-14: A blank HTML page is added to the site window.

2. **Add and format a heading.** At the top of the new blank Web page, type a heading for the Web page. Then select the text with the Standard Editing tool, found in the Toolbox. Click the Center Alignment button at the top of the interface to center the text and choose Type ➪ Paragraph Format ➪ Heading 1 to resize the heading.

3. **Add some more text.** At the end of the heading text, press Enter to move the cursor to the next line. Then type the main text of the Web page, as shown in Figure 28-15. Typing text here is similar to a word processor.

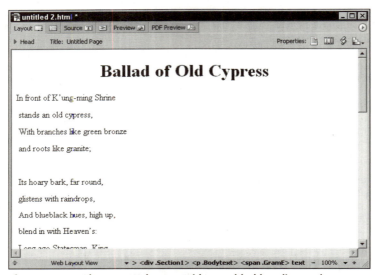

Figure 28-15: The new Web page with an added heading and text

4. **Add an image icon to the Web page.** In the toolbox, select the Basic Objects category and locate the Image object. Then drag the image icon to the Web page beneath the heading and to the left of the main text. A small icon appears. Open the Inspector palette with the Window ⇨ Inspector menu command if it isn't already open.

5. **Load an image into the image placeholder.** With the image icon selected, click the Browse button in the Inspector palette and locate an image to load into the Web page, use the Point and Shoot tool, or drag the image from the site window. The resulting Web page is shown in Figure 28-16.

If the image format is GIF, JPEG, or PNG, then the image is immediately loaded, but if it is another format such as Photoshop's PSD, an alert dialog box appears asking if you want to convert this image to a Smart Object.

6. **Correct the image alignment.** To make the text wrap around the new image, select the image object and change the Alignment value to Left in the Inspector palette. This allows the text to wrap around the image.

7. **Add some white space to the image.** To set the image off from the text, click the More tab in the Inspector palette with the image selected and change the HSpace and VSpace values to 10. This adds 10-pixel-wide margins around the image, as shown in Figure 28-17.

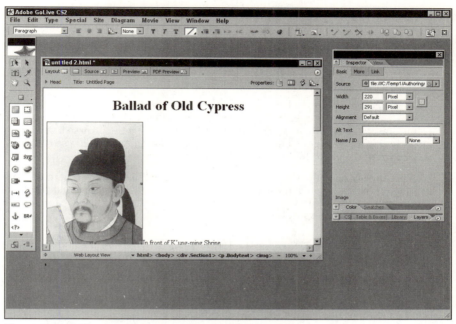

Figure 28-16: The new Web page with an added image

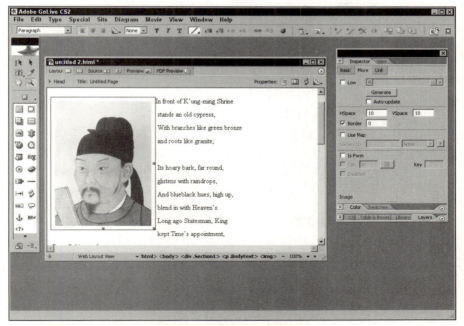

Figure 28-17: HTML text can wrap around image objects.

Using Smart Objects

Smart Objects are particularly useful in GoLive. They let you work with images created in Photoshop, Illustrator, and Acrobat without having to worry about the larger file sizes common to those applications. Smart Objects are available for Photoshop, Illustrator, Acrobat, and generic image formats such as TIFF, EPS, and BMP.

You add Smart Objects to a Web page by selecting the Smart Objects category in the Toolbox and dragging them over to the Web page. They appear initially in the Web page as simple icons. After you add them to a Web page, you can click on the Browse button in the Inspector palette (Figure 28-18) to identify the source image file. Or, you could use the Point and Shoot tool or drag the image from the site window.

A smarter way to work with Smart Objects is to place the source files into the SmartObjects folder in the Extras tab of the Site Window. From this location, you can drag and drop the source files directly into the Layout Editor. This action causes the Save for Web dialog box to appear where you can specify the optimization settings.

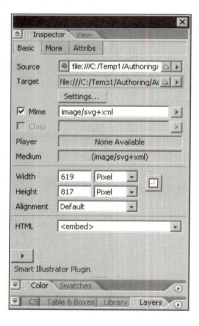

Figure 28-18: The Inspector palette for Smart Objects offers several settings.

Using the Save for Web dialog box

When you drag and drop a native source file into GoLive's Layout Editor as a Smart Object, the image file loads in the Save For Web dialog box (Figure 28-19). You use this dialog box to configure an optimized version of the source image file. The Save for Web dialog box in GoLive is identical to the one found in Photoshop and Illustrator.

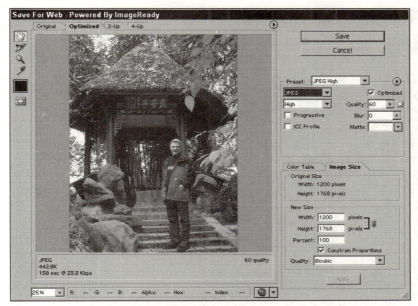

Figure 28-19: The Save For Web dialog box lets you specify how to compress a source image for viewing on a Web page.

Using this dialog box, you can select the image format, quality setting, image dimensions, and other settings. You use the tabs at the top-left corner of the dialog box to compare the selected settings between the original and optimized images. The 2-Up and 4-Up view options offer an interface where you can specify and visually compare two or four different settings before saving the Web image. Figure 28-20 shows the 4-Up display option. The settings and file size for each pane are listed under each pane.

When you're comfortable with the settings, click Save and a file dialog box appears where you may save the optimized image in the site folder. This file is called the target image file. Although it's linked to the original source file, it's a separate file.

Note   After you save and add a target image to a Web page, you can revisit the Save for Web dialog box by selecting the target image and clicking the Settings button in the Inspector palette.

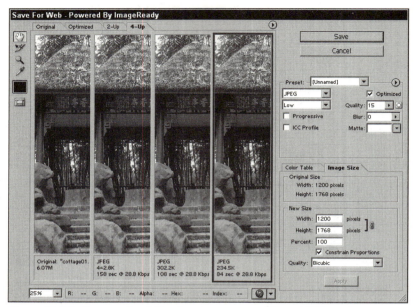

Figure 28-20: You use the 4-Up view to compare different Web settings.

Editing the Smart Objects image

To edit a source image, simply double-click on a target image within a GoLive Web page. This opens the source image in the application used to create it (for example, Photoshop, Illustrator, or Acrobat). After completing your edits, save the source file, and GoLive automatically updates the target file using the same target filename, same target file location, and same optimization settings from the Save for Web dialog box.

If you open and edit a source image in its native application, you can have GoLive check for updated images by choosing Site ➪ Update Files Dependent On ➪ Library. This automatically updates all Smart Objects and packages exported from InDesign.

Cropping Smart Objects

Another advantage of Smart Objects is that you can resize and crop them without affecting the native source files using tools in GoLive. To resize a Smart Object, just drag its borders and hold the Shift key to constrain proportions.

To crop a Smart Object, select the target image in the Layout Editor, click the Crop Image button in the Inspector palette, shown in Figure 28-21; then drag to outline the crop area in the Layout Editor. After you draw the outline, you can drag on the outline borders to resize the crop area. Double-click inside the outline area to complete the crop action.

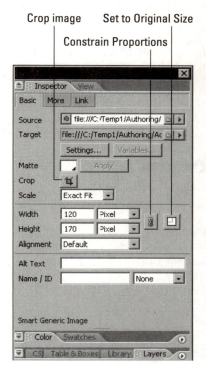

Figure 28-21: You can easily crop Smart Objects in GoLive.

Cascading Style Sheets

All text within a Web page can have formatting applied to it. These formatting styles are saved in a style sheet and may be applied to several sections of text within the Web page. If you need to change the style of text in the Web page, you can make the change to the style sheet and all text sections that use that style automatically update.

A single Web page may have several style sheets applied to it. For example, a single Web page may have an internal style sheet defined within its header that affects only the text within that Web page, but Web pages may also reference an external style sheet that governs the text styles for all the Web pages within a site. When this happens, the style that you apply to a specific text section is cascaded down according to a defined precedence.

Tip   An external style sheet makes the text styles for a whole Web site consistent, controlled, and easy to update.

Using the CSS Editor

You create Cascading Style Sheets (CSS) within GoLive using the CSS Editor. You can open this editor by choosing the Special ⇨ CSS ⇨ Open Editor (Alt+Shift+Ctrl+C in Windows; Option+Shift+⌘+C on the Mac) or by clicking on the stair-looking icon in the upper-right corner of the Web-page window. Figure 28-22 shows the CSS Editor when it's first opened. In the lower-left corner of the CSS Editor are two icons that split the editor into two panes to display the style sheet code or a preview pane.

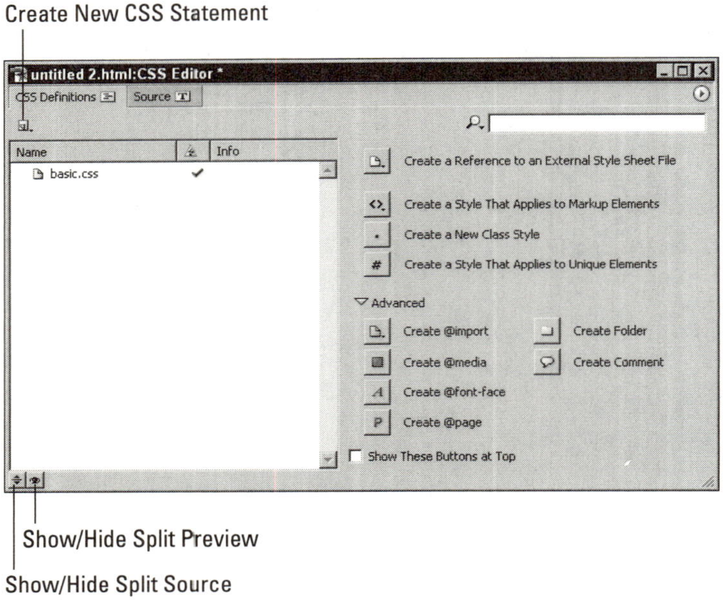

Figure 28-22: You use the CSS Editor to create style sheets and define styles.

Double-clicking a named style sheet in the CSS Editor opens it so you can see the individual styles that make up the current style sheet for editing. If you select a specific style, you can see its preview in the split pane if you enable the Show/Hide Style Preview button, as shown in Figure 28-23. Alternatively, you can see a preview within the Inspector palette if you enable the Show Inspector Panel option in the palette menu. Along the top of the right pane in the CSS Editor are several tabs that define the specifics of the selected style.

 The CSS Editor has been updated to make it easier to define and apply styles in GoLive CS2.

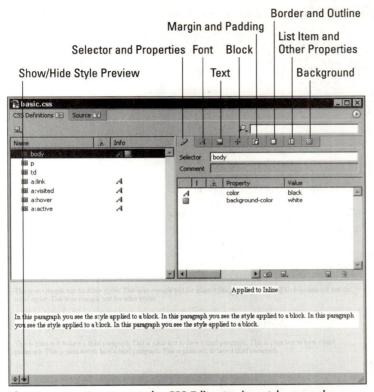

Figure 28-23: You can use the CSS Editor to view style examples.

Defining styles

You may define styles for standard HTML elements, such as h1, h2, body, p, and so on. You can also define styles using a .class definition and styles that are applied to all objects that have a specified ID. Using these tabbed panels, you may set many different properties, including Font, Text, Block, Margin, and so on. An example of the text style is displayed in the preview area under the property panels as you edit the various properties.

Applying styles

Element styles (h1, p, a, and so on) are applied automatically whenever you use the HTML element. To apply class styles, you can select the text in the Layout Editor and select the type of style to use in the CSS palette, shown in Figure 28-24, by placing check marks in the appropriate columns. This dialog can also be accessed by clicking the Apply CSS Style icon on the main toolbar. You can apply class styles to an inline section of text, an entire block of text, a spanned section, or a selected element.

Figure 28-24: You use the CSS palette to apply styles to selected text.

You apply ID styles by adding `ID="id_name"` to the HTML tag for the text item to which you want to apply the style. This is done in the Source Code Editor or the Visual Tag Editor (Shift-⌘/Control-E), or by selecting the defined CSS style from the context menu under Special ➪ CSS ➪ New.

Creating an external style sheet

When you define and apply styles to text, they're automatically added to the Web page. External style sheets are saved as a separate file. To create an external style sheet, you first need to create a reference to the external style sheet by clicking the Create a Reference to an External Style Sheet File button on the CSS Editor's initial panel. This opens a panel where you can click the Create button to locate an existing style sheet or browse to one using the Browse button.

Designing for Mobile Devices

Web browsers on personal computers have become standardized, but many mobile devices including cell phones, PDAs, and even portable game devices can connect to the Internet and view Web pages. These are as follows:

- ✦ They have small, limited viewing displays, which makes Web pages designed for the standard Web browsers incompatible.
- ✦ The bandwidth for many mobile devices is much slower than their computer counterparts.
- ✦ There is the lack of a standard language definition for displaying and viewing mobile Web devices.

The available language definitions for mobile devices include the following:

- ✦ **XHTML Basic/XHTML Mobile:** Defined and endorsed by the governing W3C organization, the XHTML Basic language definition is the standard for many mobile devices.
- ✦ **i-mode HTML:** This language definition is the standard for Japanese and European mobile device markets.

✦ **WML:** Wireless Markup Language is the standard used on WAP-enabled mobile phones and is endorsed by the OMA organization.

✦ **MMS:** Multimedia Messaging Service defines a mobile messaging standard, but it can also handle multimedia objects such as audio and images.

Despite all these problems, the good news is that GoLive supports all these various language definitions and can be used to create Web pages that users can view on a majority of mobile devices.

 Automated wizards for creating Web pages for mobile devices are new to GoLive CS2.

Creating new GoLive documents for Mobile Devices

Templates for each of these mobile device standards can be selected from the New dialog box by choosing File ⇨ New and selecting Mobile from the left pane, as shown in Figure 28-25.

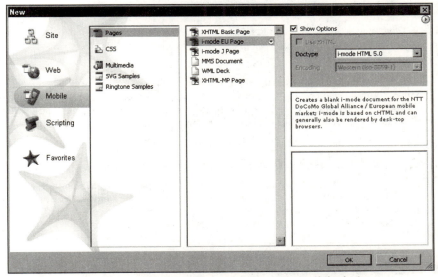

Figure 28-25: The New dialog box creates Web pages for mobile devices.

When you select any of the mobile templates from the New dialog box, the Layout Editor view is automatically set to Mobile View. You can manually set this view by choosing View ⇨ View Configuration ⇨ Mobile View. The Mobile View reduces the width of the layout space, as shown in Figure 28-26.

In addition to changing the view mode, GoLive automatically disables the features that aren't available with the selected mobile language definition. For example, if the XHTML Basic mobile template is selected, the Type Size options are disabled.

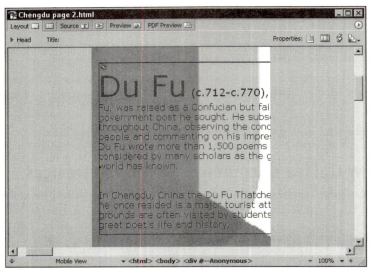

Figure 28-26: Mobile View displays a smaller Web page width.

 Tip Although the tools and objects in the Toolbox aren't disabled when a new mobile template is opened, you can customize the Toolbox to match the selected mobile template by clicking on the Palette Options button at the bottom of the toolbox, selecting the Customize pop-up menu option, and choosing the mobile template definition that matches the current Web page.

Converting existing documents to XHTML Mobile

The New dialog box works well, but many times you'll have an existing Web site that has already been designed that you simply need to convert to a specific mobile standard. To convert an existing Web page to a mobile standard, choose Special ⇨ Convert ⇨ To XHTML Mobile. This menu command opens the Convert to XHTML Mobile dialog box, as shown in Figure 28-27.

Figure 28-27: You can easily convert Web pages to the XHTML Mobile standard.

Using this dialog box, you can downscale images, define the width of the mobile display, remove named images, and strip CSS Styles and BR tags.

Previewing mobile content

Once you create or design a Web page for a mobile device, you'll want to view it using that device. This may present some difficulty because you probably don't own one of every type of mobile device. The solution to this problem is emulation. Mobile device manufacturers have created simple executables that emulate the actual device using a computer program. You can download emulators from the various mobile device companies and add them to GoLive using the Preference dialog box.

To add a new mobile device emulator to GoLive, open the Preferences dialog box by choosing Edit ⇨ Preferences or select the Edit option from the Preview in Browser button on the main toolbar. Within the Preferences dialog box, select the Browsers panel, shown in Figure 28-28, and click Add. This opens a file dialog box where you can select the emulator you want to use. All emulators marked Active appear in the Preview in Browser button.

Most emulators use the arrow keys to navigate the Web page simulating the device's buttons.

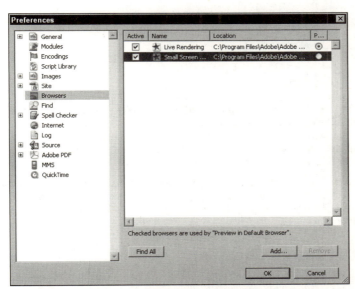

Figure 28-28: You can add emulators, which help you view mobile designed Web pages, to GoLive.

To immediately see the changes to an updated Web page, you can choose File ⇨ Preview In ⇨ Live Rendering or click the Preview in Browser button. This provides immediate feedback on your changes without waiting for a Web browser to load the current page. If you select the Auto Update option from the palette menu, any changes you make to the Web page are automatically updated in the Live Rendering window.

For Web pages designed for mobile devices, you can click the SSR button in the upper-right corner of the Live Rendering window, shown in Figure 28-29. This enables Small Screen Rendering, which simulates most mobile devices.

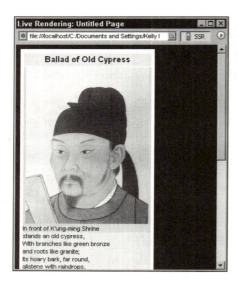

Figure 28-29: Small Screen Rendering in the Live Rendering window is a generic view for mobile devices.

Packaging for GoLive

One common design-repurposing path is to move layouts created in InDesign to the Web. To facilitate this process, InDesign includes a feature that enables you to quickly move a print design to GoLive and the Web. Choose File ➪ Package for GoLive. This compiles all graphics and text in the current document and places them in a neat little folder where you can open and manipulate them in GoLive.

The packaging process converts each InDesign story to a separate XML file. The formatting for this text is converted to a Cascading Style Sheet (CSS). All other images and objects are converted to either the JPEG or GIF formats or packaged in their native format for more controlled optimization later in GoLive.

Packaging an InDesign document

To package an InDesign document for use in GoLive, open the document in InDesign and choose File ➪ Package for GoLive. This opens a file dialog box where you can give the package a name and specify a location. After clicking Package, the Package for GoLive dialog box appears (see Figure 28-30).

 If any linked image files are missing from the InDesign document, a warning dialog box appears, informing you that if you continue, the missing images are packaged with low-resolution versions of themselves.

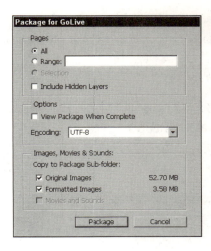

Figure 28-30: The Package for GoLive dialog box lets you open the package in GoLive.

The Package for GoLive dialog box includes options that let you package the complete document, or only a specific Range or Selection. You can also choose to Include Hidden Layers, which is very convenient if the InDesign document contains some assets that aren't included in the print material, but that may be appropriate for the Web. Selecting the View Package When Complete option opens the package in GoLive when the packaging is complete. The Encoding field lets you choose the encoding type for the text in the package.

New Feature The ability to specify a range of pages to package and to include hidden layers is new to InDesign CS2.

The Images, Movies & Sounds section lets you specify which assets to include in the package. The size to include in each type is also displayed. All images contained within the InDesign document are copied to a separate `Images` folder located within the `Package` folder. Selecting the Original Images check box moves a copy of the original images to the `Images` folder. Selecting the Formatted Images check box converts the image to a TIFF image. Formatted images are images that have been cropped or scaled within InDesign. These images have `_fmt` added to their filenames.

Note If you make changes to the InDesign document after creating a package, you can choose File ⇨ Package for GoLive again to repackage the InDesign document using the same package folder.

Examining package contents

If you look into the package folder created by InDesign after an InDesign document has been packaged for GoLive, you'll find several files, including the following:

✦ A package.PDF file that is used as a preview of the InDesign document

✦ A `package.idpk` file that is the XML document for the entire package

✦ An Assets folder that includes all the Images and Stories in two separate folders

- ✦ All images files, each within its own folder and all in a folder named `Images`
- ✦ All story files converted to XML, each within its own folder and all in a folder named `Stories`
- ✦ Any other movie or sound files included in the original InDesign document

Viewing the package in GoLive

If the View Package When Complete option in the Package for GoLive dialog box is selected, then the package opens automatically within GoLive. Figure 28-31 shows a package that has been opened in GoLive. The most noticeable aspect of an exported package is the PDF preview that appears in its own window within GoLive.

Figure 28-31: Packages opened within GoLive show the PDF preview page.

If you select the View Package When Complete option, you can open the package in GoLive by opening the `package.idpk` file or by choosing File ⇨ Import ⇨ From InDesign within GoLive.

STEPS: Packaging an InDesign document for GoLive

1. **Open the print document within InDesign.** Open InDesign and choose File ➪ Open to access a file dialog box. Select the file to open and click the Open button. The file opens within InDesign.

2. **Package the document for GoLive.** Choose File ➪ Package for GoLive. This opens the Package Publication for GoLive dialog box. Type a name for the package folder and click the Package button, which opens the Package for GoLive dialog box. Select the All pages and View Package When Complete options and select the Formatted Images option and deselect the Original Images option. Then click Package.

   After the packaging process is complete, a warning dialog box appears stating that this package isn't part of a GoLive Site. It offers you a chance to specify a destination for any generated assets. If you click Yes, you'll get a chance to select where the accessories folder is located. The packaged document preview is then opened and viewed in GoLive, as shown in Figure 28-32.

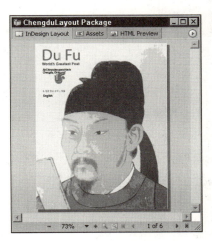

Figure 28-32: Packaged InDesign documents automatically open in GoLive.

Dragging and dropping package assets

You can drag and drop items from the package preview window into an open web page with the Layout Editor showing. HTML page easily. Moving the mouse over the top of an existing package item highlights the item. Dragging the selected item and dropping it on the Web page places the item at the point where it is dropped.

At the bottom of the package preview window are several buttons that enable you to move forward and backward through the available layout pages, as shown in Figure 28-33. You can also zoom within the package preview window using the Zoom tools.

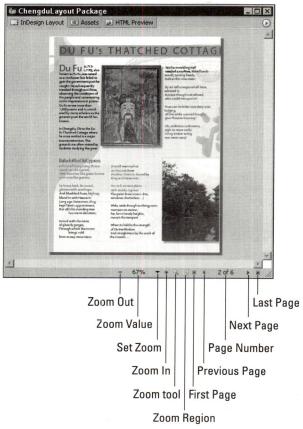

Figure 28-33: You can navigate and zoom in the package preview window.

Along the top edge of the package preview window are three tabs — InDesign Layout, Assets, and HTML Preview. The InDesign Layout tab shows what the page looks like in InDesign, the Assets tab displays a list of individual stories and images, as shown in Figure 28-34, and the HTML Preview tab shows what the layout looks like within a Web browser. Using the icons at the bottom of the window, you can switch the Assets tab between a Details and Thumbnails view. Items can be dragged and dropped from the Assets tab to a Web page also.

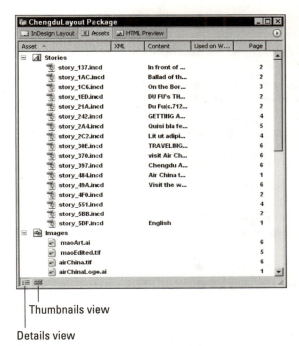

Figure 28-34: The Assets tab of the package preview window lists all the items in the layout.

Exporting to HTML

Right-clicking a selected item in the package preview reveals a pop-up menu where you can mark the selected object Include for HTML Export or to Disable Page Item. After marking the items to include, the Export as HTML palette menu command can export all the marked items to HTML. You can also select this command by choosing File ⇨ Export or from the toolbar.

After you select the filename and destination, the Export as HTML dialog box, shown in Figure 28-35, appears. With this dialog box, you can specify which pages in the original layout to export and whether or not to use a template.

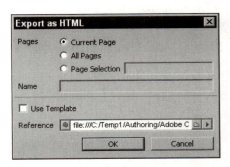

Figure 28-35: The Export as HTML dialog box specifies which layout pages are exported.

Summary

- A site project includes many Web pages. You can create site projects using GoLive's Site Wizard.
- GoLive is a robust editor for creating and designing Web pages. These Web pages can include a myriad of objects. You edit object properties using the Inspector palette.
- Smart Objects allow you to place Photoshop, Illustrator, and Acrobat source files within GoLive Web pages and create target images optimized for viewing on the Web.
- Cascading style sheets are an efficient way to apply text styles to a section of text within a Web page.
- GoLive includes templates for creating Web pages for mobile devices and features for editing and viewing mobile Web pages.
- You can repurpose documents created in InDesign for use on the Web by creating a package for GoLive. This process bundles all the necessary files into a folder that GoLive can use.

✦ ✦ ✦

Preparing Documents for Distribution

In This Chapter

Optimizing documents for various output solutions

Setting initial views

Creating search indexes

Searching index files

♦ ♦ ♦ ♦

Electronic documents are often created for one purpose and eventually modified to suit another purpose. You may initially create a design piece for print where images are optimized for high-resolution output and later want to modify the design piece for screen viewing, where image-resolution requirements are significantly less than for print. Taking a document designed for one purpose and modifying it for another purpose is known as *document repurposing*.

To prepare files for distribution electronically, via the Web, or on CD-ROM/DVDs, you may need to resample files for image resolutions appropriate for viewing, set viewing attributes suited for on-screen viewing, and create search indexes for easy access to selected files. In this chapter, we discuss preparing files for a variety of output purposes and how to optimize files for viewing.

Repurposing Documents

One of the more common needs for repurposing documents is taking a file originally designed for print and modifying it for downloading from a Web site. For high-resolution output, image files can be 300 ppi (pixels per inch) or more. For Web viewing and viewing documents on your computer monitor, you need file sizes of 72 ppi when viewing in a 100 percent view. Files with lower resolutions are smaller; when you are downloading documents from a Web server, smaller file sizes mean shorter download times.

Native files created in Illustrator, Photoshop and InDesign require much more work to modify documents originally designed for print to a file suited for Web hosting. Furthermore, you must convert files hosted on the Web to either PDF or HTML to make them easily accessible to other users.

Fortunately, if files are converted to PDF for any kind of output, you can easily repurpose a file for other types of output. There is one caveat in this notion: You can repurpose files for downward optimization only. In other words, you can take a document with high-resolution images designed for print and downsize the images to make it suitable for Web viewing, but you cannot upsize a Web-designed document and make it suitable for print.

The ideal file format for documents you want to repurpose is PDF. You can convert a page layout in InDesign to PDF while keeping all images at high resolution and send off the document to a commercial printer for high-end prepress and printing. You can then take the same PDF and *downsample* images (reduce the file sizes) for a piece to be hosted on a Web site or electronically exchanged with other users. When you're using PDFs for your output needs, you have several ways to repurpose files through Acrobat menus and commands.

Reducing file size

Reduce File Size is a menu command found in the File menu in both Acrobat Standard and Acrobat Professional. Choose File ➪ Reduce File Size and the Reduce File Size dialog box opens, shown in Figure 29-1.

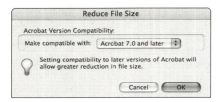

Figure 29-1: The Reduce File Size dialog box

From the pull-down menu in the Reduce File Size dialog box, you have four options for Acrobat PDF compatibility. The more recent the Acrobat compatibility, the more file-size reduction you can expect. Therefore, using Acrobat 6 or 7 compatibility reduces a PDF document size more than using either Acrobat 4 or Acrobat 5 compatibility.

The Reduce File Size command offers you a simple tool for reducing file size and offers no options choices for how much image sampling you can apply to the file-size reduction. If you're using Acrobat Standard, the Reduce File Size command is the only tool you have available in Acrobat to reduce file sizes.

After choosing Acrobat compatibility, click OK and the Save As dialog box opens. Find a folder location on your hard drive, supply a filename, and click Save. Acrobat uses an internal algorithm to downsample images and adds compression, thereby reducing file size.

If you want to examine file size after exercising the command and saving a new file, choose File ➪ Document Properties or press ⌘/Ctrl+D. The Document Properties dialog box, shown in Figure 29-2, appears. Click the Description tab, and you can see the file size noted at the bottom of the dialog box.

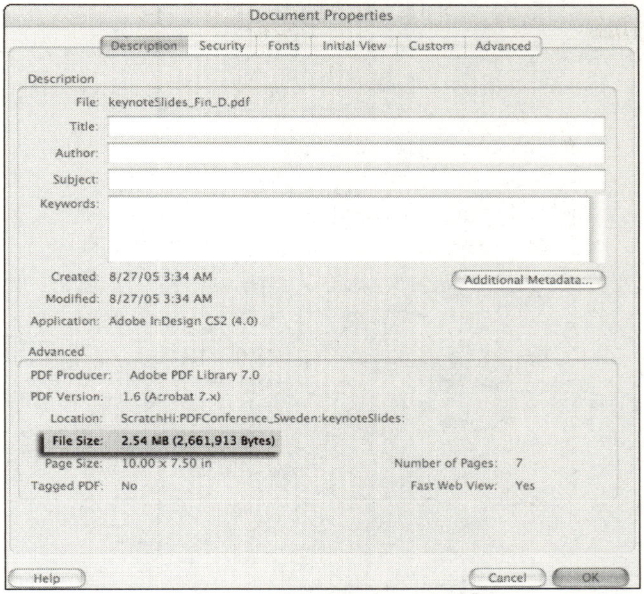

Figure 29-2: The Document Properties dialog box

Using PDF Optimizer

A much more sophisticated approach to optimizing files and reducing their size is to use the PDF Optimizer, found only in Acrobat Professional. The PDF Optimizer reduces file sizes through downsampling images according to user-specified amounts and a variety of other settings that offer options for eliminating unnecessary data. With the Reduce File Size command in the last section, you don't have user-definable settings to determine how file reduction affects data. With PDF Optimizer, you can choose different settings to determine what data is affected during optimization. The PDF Optimizer also offers you an option for analyzing a file so you can see what part of the PDF document occupies higher percentages of memory.

Auditing space usage

The first step in optimizing files with the PDF Optimizer is to analyze a file so you can see what content occupies the larger amounts of memory. You analyze a document and use the PDF Optimizer in the PDF Optimizer dialog box (Figure 29-3), which opens when you choose Advanced ⇨ PDF Optimizer.

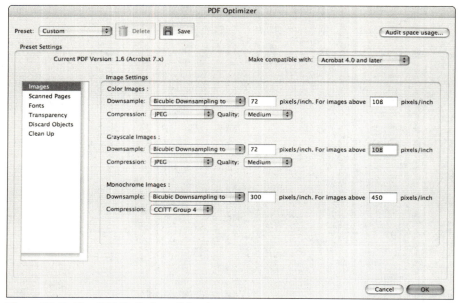

Figure 29-3: The PDF Optimizer dialog box

Click Audit space usage. Depending on the size and complexity of the document, the analysis can take a little time. When the analysis is complete, the Audit Space Usage dialog box appears, shown in Figure 29-4.

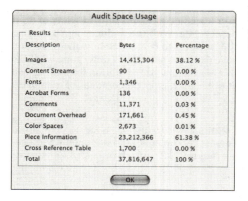

Figure 29-4: After the analysis is completed, the Audit Space Usage dialog box appears.

In the example shown in Figure 29-4, notice that over one-third of the document space is used for images. The analysis informs you that because images occupy such a large percentage of the space, you should be able to resample images at lower resolutions to reduce file size.

Optimizing files

The file analyzed in Figure 29-4 was originally created for professional printing, and the images are all sampled at 300 ppi. To repurpose the document and reduce the file size for Web hosting, the images need to be resampled at 72 ppi. Using the PDF Optimizer, you can specify image-size reductions as well as perform cleanup of content that occupies space for unnecessary items like comments, bookmarks, destinations, or other items that add to overhead in the file.

Image settings

To reduce file size with the PDF Optimizer, use the first set of options that opens in the Images tab, as shown in Figure 29-3. You can make choices for downsampling color, grayscale, and bitmap images by typing values in the field boxes for the sampling amounts desired. In our example, we edited the field boxes for color and grayscale images and chose 72 ppi as the amount of downsampling. To the right of the downsampling amount, another field box is used to identify images that are downsampled. In this box, we added 108 ppi, which instructs Acrobat to look for any image above 108 ppi and downsample the file to the amount supplied in the first field box — in this example, to 72 ppi. Note: if you type 72 ppi in the first field box, the second box defaults to 108 ppi. Other options in the PDF Optimizer dialog box include the following:

+ **Downsampling pull-down menu:** Offers choices for Retain Existing, JPEG, and Zip. Retain Existing retains the compression used when you convert the original document to PDF. JPEG is a lossy compression scheme while Zip is lossless.

+ **Quality:** Five options offer choices for image quality when using JPEG compression. Use Medium for repurposing files for Web hosting.

+ **Monochrome pull-down menu:** Monochrome images are 1-bit line art images (black and white). Monochrome images are best sampled no lower than 300 ppi for better quality displays. Use Bicubic Downsampling to for the Downsample option and CCITT4 for the best quality.

If you elect to choose Adaptive Compression Options, you may find that the file-size reduction is not as compact as choosing from the Image Settings options. Everything depends on the files and whether the images contain data that's affected when using the Adaptive Compression Options. The best way to determine what settings result in the most compact suitable files is to test compression with Image Settings controls and then again with Adaptive Compression.

Scanned Pages

This item applies only to scanned pages. Unless you scan in Acrobat, skip the settings here. If you do scan pages in Acrobat for converting text using OCR (Optical Character Recognition) you can downsample backgrounds, remove edge shadows, despeckle and descreen images, and remove halos. For more detailed information on these items, consult the Photoshop Help document in Adobe Bridge.

Fonts settings

When you click the Fonts tab in the PDF Optimizer, only fonts available for unembedding are listed. On the left side of the dialog box, fonts are listed that can be unembedded. If no fonts appear in the list, you can move on to the next tab. If fonts are listed in the left window, select the fonts to unembed and click the Move button adjacent to the right chevron.

On the right side of the dialog box are fonts listed for unembedding. If you want to keep the font embedded, select it in the right window and click the Move button adjacent to left chevron. To select multiple fonts in either window, Shift+click to select a list in a contiguous group, or ⌘/Ctrl+click to select fonts in a noncontiguous group.

Transparency settings

You can flatten transparency and save the file with the flattening adjustments made in this pane. This item is more applicable for files going to print rather than repurposing for Web hosting.

Cross-Reference For more information on transparency flattening, see Chapter 38.

Discard Objects settings

Items such as JavaScript, embedded thumbnails, hidden layers, and so on, are contained in this pane. Be careful to not select items that may render the PDF document nonfunctional. If there are JavaScript that execute actions, be certain to preserve the fields and scripts.

Clean Up settings

Click the Clean Up tab and you find a list of items checked by default that you can safely use without affecting the functionality of your document. You can enable all other items that appear unchecked, but you should have an idea of what will happen to the PDF, in terms of functionality, if you optimize the file with any additional items checked. If you check one or more of the items and return to the PDF Optimizer, the new checked items become a new set of default settings. To restore the dialog box to original defaults, click the Restore All Defaults button at the bottom of the dialog box; the check boxes return to original defaults, as shown in Figure 29-5.

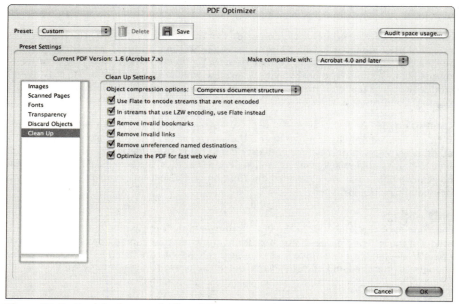

Figure 29-5: By default, a partial list of Clean Up settings is checked.

After you make your preferred settings in the PDF Optimizer, click OK and wait for the processing to finish. As a comparison between using Reduce File Size and the PDF Optimizer, using the same file with an original file size of 3.06MB, we reduced the file size with the Reduce File Size command and produced a PDF that was resampled to 454KB. The same file processed with PDF Optimizer was reduced to 285KB. The increased file reduction from PDF Optimizer was due to eliminating some document overhead and structural information.

Setting Document Open Preferences

When users acquire your PDF documents from media disks, from Web downloads, from network servers, or from documents you send via e-mail, one double-click on the file opens the PDF in a user's default Acrobat viewer. The initial view of the PDF in the Document pane is the opening view. Depending on what user preferences are set up on a given computer, the initial view conforms to the preference settings unless you specifically assign open view preferences and save them within a document.

To understand viewing preferences, choose Acrobat ⇨ Preferences (Mac) or Edit ⇨ Preferences (Windows) or press ⌘/Ctrl+K to open the Preferences dialog box. Click Page Display in the left pane, and the options choices for initial views appear in the right pane. From the pull-down menu options at the top of the dialog box, you have choices for Default page layout where you can choose what additional panes you want to display when the file is opened — items such as Page Only, Bookmarks and Page, Layers and Page, and so on are available. The Default zoom pull-down menu offers choices for several zoom magnifications as you can see in Figure 29-6.

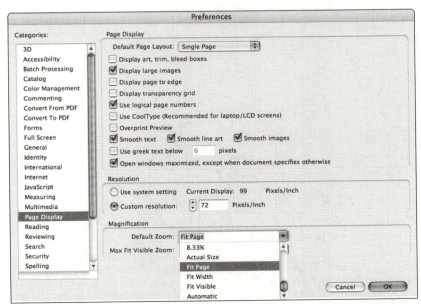

Figure 29-6: Choices for various viewing options when you first open a PDF

The preferences choices made here affect all PDF documents you open in Acrobat on your computer where no initial view has been saved inside a PDF file. For example, you can view a PDF document at a 100% view as long as Default was selected for the initial view when the file was last saved. Typically, all PDF documents exported from the CS applications save PDFs with default selections unless you specifically assign an initial view when creating the PDF.

Setting initial views

If you distribute a collection of PDF documents and use interactive buttons to open and close files for users to browse different documents, you may want to embed initial views in all your PDF documents. Because the Default view depends on settings assigned by each user, your files could conceivably be shown at different sizes depending on how a given user sets the Page Display preferences.

You can keep the viewing of your files consistent by embedding initial views in files. To set a view and save that opening view as part of the PDF, choose File ⇨ Document Properties or ⌘/Ctrl+D. In the Document Properties dialog box, click on Initial View at the top of the dialog box, and the choices available for setting initial views appear as shown in Figure 29-7.

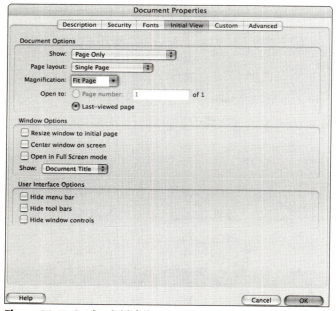

Figure 29-7: Setting initial views as part of the PDF document

In this dialog box, you make choices for the opening view and viewing magnification. When no settings have been saved with a file, the individual user preferences prevail. Acrobat provides you with many different choices for controlling the initial view of a PDF when opened in any Acrobat viewer. Settings you make here can be saved with your document. When you establish settings other than defaults, the settings saved with the file override the end user's default settings. The options available to you for controlling the initial view include the following:

✦ **Document Options:** The default opening page is the first page of a PDF document. You can change the opening page to another page, and you can control the page-layout views and magnification by selecting choices from the Document Options section. The choices include:

- **Show:** Four choices are available from the pull-down menu. Select Page Only to open the page with the Navigation Pane collapsed. Use Bookmarks Panel and Page to open the Bookmarks tab when the file opens. Use Pages Panel and Page to open the Pages tab where the thumbnails of pages are viewed. Use Attachments panel and Page to show file attachments in the Attachments pane. Use Layers Panel and Page to open the Layers tab when the file opens.

- **Page Layout:** The default for Page Layout is noted in the pull-down menu as Default. When you save a PDF file with the Default selection, the PDF opens according to the default value a user has set for page viewing on the user's computer. To override the user's default, you can set a page layout in the opening view from one of four choices. Choose Single Page to open the PDF in a single-page layout. Choose Continuous to open in a continuous page view. Choose Facing to open with facing pages or use Continuous – Facing to open with continuous facing pages.

- **Magnification:** Choose from preset magnification views from the pull-down menu. If you want the PDF document to open in a fit-in-window view, select Fit Page. Choose from other magnification options in the pull-down menu or edit the field box for a custom zoom level.

- **Open To:** You can change the opening page to another page by entering a number in the field for Page Number. You might use this setting if you wanted a user to see a contents page instead of a title page. If Last-viewed page is selected you need to open the Startup preferences and change the "Reopen Documents to Last Viewed Page" option. Select Digital Editions only from the menu choices and you can select a page to open in the Document Properties. If you select the All Files option in the Startup Preferences, options for opening to specific pages is grayed out.

✦ **Last-viewed page:** This is another option for the opening page. When enabled, the most recently viewed page opens. This setting is intended for eBooks, where you might begin reading a novel and want to mark the page like a bookmark and later return to the page where you left off. If you select All Files, any document you view in Acrobat is returned to the last page viewed after reopening it.

✦ **Window Options:** The default window for Acrobat is a full screen where the viewing area is maximized to occupy your monitor surface area. You can change the window view to size down the window to the initial page size, center a smaller window on-screen, and open a file in Full Screen mode. If you enable all three check boxes, the Full Screen mode prevails.

✦ **Show:** From the pull-down menu choose either File Name or Document Title. If File Name is selected, the title bar at the top of the Acrobat window shows the filename. If Document Title is used, the information you supply in the Document Properties dialog box for Document Title is shown in the title bar.

✦ **User Interface Options:** The Interface Options in the Initial View Document Properties dialog box have to do with user-interface items in Acrobat viewers such as menu bars, toolbars, and scrollbars. You can elect to hide these items when the PDF document opens in any Acrobat viewer. You can hide any one or a combination of the three items listed under the User Interface Options. When all three are enabled, the PDF is viewed as shown in Figure 29-8. If you elect to save files without any of the user-interface items in view, it's a good idea to create navigational buttons so users can move around your document.

Figure 29-8: Here, toolbars, the menu bar, and window controls are hidden.

The window controls you see in Figure 29-9 include the scrollbars, the status bar, and the Navigation pane. If you hide the toolbars and menu bar but elect to leave the window controls visible, users can access tools for page navigation.

If you elect to eliminate the toolbars and menu bar from view and later want to go back and edit your file, you need to use shortcut keys to get the menu bars and toolbars back. Be certain to remember the F8 and F9 keys (Windows) — F8 shows/hides the toolbars and F9 shows/hides the menu bar. On the Mac, F8 shows/hides the toolbars and Shift+Command+M shows/hides the menu bar.

Figure 29-9: With window controls visible, users can navigate with tools.

Saving the initial view

When you decide what view attributes you want assigned to your document, you can choose between one of two save options. The first option updates the file. Click on the Save tool in the Acrobat File toolbar or choose File ➪ Save. Any edits you make in the Initial View properties activates the Save command. The Save command is inactive and grayed out by default until you make any changes to your file or reset any kind of preferences that can be saved with the document.

> **Note** When using Save and Save As in Acrobat, you don't have access to the Adobe Save or Save As dialog box as you do in the other CS2 applications. For information related to using the Adobe Save and Save As dialog boxes, see Chapter 8.

The second method for updating your file uses the Save As command. When you choose File ➪ Save As, the Save As dialog box opens. The default filename is the same name as the file you opened. If you elect to save the file to the same folder where it resides, Acrobat prompts you with a warning dialog box asking whether you want to overwrite the file. Click Yes and the file is rewritten. There are many times during your Acrobat sessions that using Save As will be a benefit. As you work on documents, they retain more information than necessary to view and print the file. By using Save As and overwriting the file, you optimize it for a smaller file size. In some cases, the differences between Save and Save As can be extraordinary in terms of the file sizes. As a matter of habit, try to use the Save As command after eight to ten different saves and completely rewrite the file. If you need a backup copy of a document, you can also use Save As and supply a new name in the Save As dialog box. When you click Save, a copy of your PDF is written to disk with the new name.

After editing a file and using the Save command ten times, Acrobat asks you if you want to use the Save As command to rewrite the file and optimize it.

Using Acrobat Catalog

Regardless of whether you create PDF documents for clients for wide distribution or you use PDF documents to catalog your own files in your studio, searching through archives is a task you frequently repeat. Acrobat 6 and 7 do offer you the capability of searching collections of PDFs on CD/DVDs, on network servers, and on local hard drives without the use of a search-index file. However, the internal search capabilities in Acrobat are painfully slow and limiting compared to searching an index. As a matter of common practice, you'll want to create a search-index file when archiving or distributing large quantities of documents.

To search an index file, you must have one present on your computer, network server, or some media-storage device. Index files are files containing all the words among PDF documents that were catalogued with Acrobat Catalog. You create index files by launching Catalog from within Acrobat. Note that in earlier versions of Acrobat, Catalog was a separate executable program. In Acrobat 6 and 7, Catalog is a plug-in and requires you to first launch Acrobat before you can access Catalog.

Acrobat Catalog is available only in Acrobat Professional. All Acrobat viewers, including Adobe Reader, can use search indexes. A search index is not usable in Acrobat when hosted on Web sites.

To launch Acrobat Catalog from within Acrobat Professional, choose Tools ⇨ Catalog. Catalog is robust and provides many options for creating and modifying indexes. After a search index is created, any user can access the search index from any Acrobat viewer to find words using search criteria in the search pane. However, before you begin to work with Acrobat Catalog, you need to take some preliminary steps to be certain all your files are properly prepared and ready to be indexed.

Preparing PDFs for indexing

Preparation involves creating PDFs with all the necessary information to facilitate searches. All searchable document description information needs to be supplied in the PDF documents at the time of PDF creation or by modifying PDFs in Acrobat before you begin working with Catalog. For workgroups and multiple-user access to search indexes, this information needs to be clear and consistent. Other factors, such as naming conventions, location of files, and performance optimization should all be planned prior to creating an index file.

Note Adding document descriptions is not a requirement for creating search indexes. You can index files without any information in the document-description fields. Adding document descriptions merely adds relevant information to your PDF documents and aids users in finding search results faster.

Document descriptions (metadata)

You should supply all PDF files with document description information, which expands your search capability. Creating document descriptions and defining the field types for consistent organization allows multiple users to search documents quickly.

You supply document-summary information in the Document Properties dialog box, shown earlier in this chapter in Figure 29-2. Choose File ⇨ Document Properties or press ⌘/Ctrl+D and click on Description in the left pane. The document summary data is contained in the Title, Subject, Author, and Keywords fields. The data should be consistent and it should also follow a hierarchy consistent with a company's organizational structure and workflow.

The document-summary items should be mapped out and defined. When adding data to the Description fields, consider the following:

- **Title:** Title information is an outline — the parent statement, if you will. Use descriptive titles to help users narrow searches within specific categories. You can also use the Title field to display the title name at the top of the Acrobat window when you select viewing titles in the Initial View properties.

- **Author:** Avoid using proper names for the Author field. Personnel changes in companies and roles among employees change. Identify the author of PDF documents according to departments, workgroups, facilities, and so on.

- **Subject:** If the Title field is the parent item in an outline format, the Subject is a child item nested directly below the title. Consider subjects subsets of titles. When creating document summaries, be consistent. Don't use subject and title or subject and keyword information back and forth with different documents. If an item, such as *corporate identity*, is listed as a subject in some PDFs and then listed as titles in other documents, users will become confused with the order and searches become unnecessarily complicated.

- **Keywords:** If you have a forms identification system in place, be certain to use form numbers and identity as part of the Keywords field. You might start the Keywords field with a form number and then add additional keywords to help narrow searches. Be consistent and always start the Keywords field with forms or document numbers. If you need to have PDF author names, add them here in the Keywords field. If employees change roles or leave the company, the Author field still provides the information relative to a department.

To illustrate some examples, take a look at Table 29-1.

Table 29-1: Document Summary Examples

Title	Author	Subject	Keywords
Descriptive titles.	Department names.	Subsection of Title.	Document numbers and random identifiers.
Titles may be considered specific to workgroup tasks.	Don't use employee names in organizations; employees change, departments usually remain.	Subjects may be thought of as child outline items nested below the parent Title items — a subset of the Titles.	Forms ID numbers, internal filing numbers, and so on can be supplied in the Keyword fields. If employee names are a must for your company, add employee names in the Keywords field box. List any related words to help find the topic.
Corporate brochure	Seattle office	2004 Spring product line	CB-101, Spring brochure
FDA compliance	Quality assurance	Software validation	SOP-114, QA-182, J. Wilson, regulations, citations, eye-implant device
County fair campaign	Copy writing	1995 fair celebrity show	F-3709G, fairgrounds, talent, fair board
Receivables	Accounting	Collection policy	F-8102, M-5433, finance, collections, payments
eCommerce	Marketing	Products	M-1051, e-117A, golf clubs, sports, leisure

Tip Legacy PDF files used in an organization may have been created without a document description, or you may reorganize PDFs and want to change document summaries. You can create a batch sequence to change multiple PDF files and run the sequence. Organize PDFs in a folder where the document summaries are to be edited. In the Edit Sequence dialog box, select the items to change and edit each document summary item. Run the sequence, and an entire folder of PDFs can be updated.

Cross-Reference For more information on creating batch sequences, see Chapter 31.

Adding metadata with the Bridge

You can create a metadata template file in any one of the CS2 applications and either append or replace metadata in PDF documents. You must use one of the CS2 applications. Acrobat does not support a File Info menu command where you can add metadata and save a template. When you append or replace metadata from the Bridge to a selected group of PDF documents, the Title, Author, Subject, and Keywords fields are populated with data from corresponding fields in the template.

Cross-Reference: For a thorough description for creating metadata templates, and appending and replacing metadata, see Chapter 7.

New Feature: Creating a metadata template is a new feature in CS2.

File structure

The content, filenames, and location of PDFs to be cataloged contribute to file structure items. All the issues related to file structure must be thought out and appropriately designed for the audience that you intend to support. Among the important considerations are the following:

- **File-naming conventions:** Names provided for the PDF files are critical for distributing documents among users. If filenames get truncated, either Acrobat Search or the end user will have difficulty finding a document when performing a search. This is of special concern to Mac users who want to distribute documents across platforms. As a matter of safeguard, the best precaution to take is always use standard DOS file-naming conventions. The standard eight-character maximum filename with no more than three-character file extensions (`filename.ext`) will always work regardless of platform.

- **Folder names:** Folder names should follow the same conventions as filenames. Mac users who want to keep filenames within DOS standards should limit folder names to eight characters and no more than a three-character file extension for cross-platform compliance.

- **File- and folder-name identity:** Avoid using ASCII characters from 133 to 159 for any filename or folder name. Acrobat Catalog does support some extended characters in this range, but you may experience problems when using files across platforms. (Figure 29-10 lists the characters to avoid.)

133	à	139	ï	144	É	149	ò	154	Ü
134	å	140	î	145	æ	150	û	156	£
135	ç	141	ì	146	Æ	151	ù	157	¥
136	ê	142	Ä	147	ô	152	_	158	_
137	ë	143	Å	148	ö	153	Ö	159	ƒ
138	è								

Figure 29-10: When providing names for files and folders to be cataloged, avoid using extended characters from ASCII 133 to ASCII 159.

- **Folder organization:** Folders should have a logical hierarchy. Copy all files to a single folder or a single folder with nested folders in the same path. When nesting folders, keep the number of nested folders to a minimum. Deeply nested folders slow down searches, and path names longer than 256 characters create problems.

- **Folder locations:** For Windows users, location of folders must be contained on a local hard drive or a network server volume. Although Macintosh users can catalog information across computer workstations, creating separate indexes for files contained on separate drives would be advisable. Any files moved to different locations make searches inoperable.

✦ **PDF structure:** File and folder naming should be handled before creating links and attaching files. If filenames are changed after the PDF structure has been developed, many links become inoperable. Be certain to complete all editing in the PDF documents before cataloging files.

Optimizing performance

You can quickly perform searches if you take a little time in creating the proper structure and organization. You can avoid pitfalls, and thus slow searches, by organizing files. Consider the following:

✦ **Optimize PDF files:** Perform optimization on all PDF files as one of the last steps in your workflow. Use the Save As Optimizes for Fast Web View in the General category in the Preferences dialog box and run the PDF Optimizer located in the Advanced menu. Optimization is especially important for searches you performed from CD/DVD files.

For information on PDF Optimizer, see the section "Repurposing Documents."

✦ **Break up long PDF files:** You should break books, reports, essays, and other documents containing numerous pages into multiple PDF files. If you have books to be cataloged, break up the books into separate chapters. Acrobat Search runs much faster when finding information from several small files. It slows down when searching through long documents.

For more information on PDF interactivity and creating link buttons to open and close files, see Chapter 32.

Creating a new index file

After your files are optimized and saved in final form, it's time to create the search index. Choose Advanced ➪ Catalog to open the Catalog dialog box, shown in Figure 29-11. In the dialog box, you make choices for creating a new index file or opening an existing index file. Click New Index to create a new index file.

Managing multiple PDF documents

Books, reports, and manuals can be broken up into separate files and structured in a way that still appears to the end user as a single document. Assuming a user reads through a file in a linear fashion, you can create links to open and closed pages without user intervention. Create navigational buttons to move forward and back through document pages. On the last page of each chapter, use the navigation button to open the next chapter. Also on the last page of each chapter, create a Page Action that closes the current document when the page is closed. You can link all the chapters from a table of contents where users can open any chapter. With careful thought, your user will find browsing the contents of multiple files no different from reading a book in the analog world.

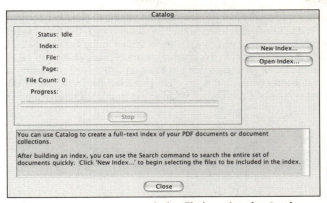

Figure 29-11: You create an index file by using the Catalog dialog box.

The New Index Definition dialog box, shown in Figure 29-12, opens where you set specific attributes for your index and determine what folder(s) are to be indexed.

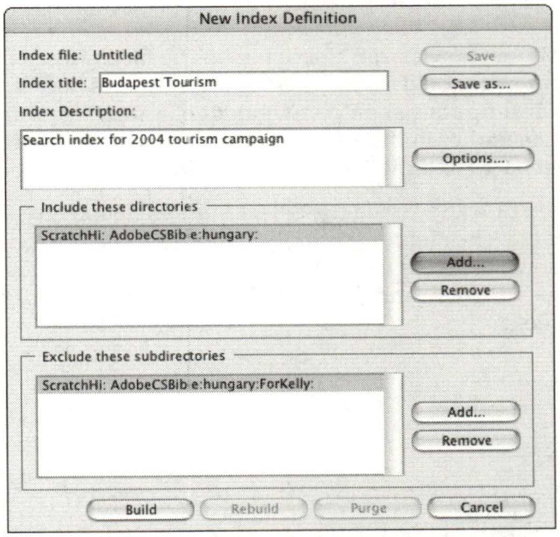

Figure 29-12: Set attributes for index files in the New Index Definition dialog box.

✦ **Index title:** The title that you place in this field is a title for the index, but not necessarily the name of the file you ultimately save. The name you enter here does not need to conform to any naming conventions because in most cases it won't be the saved filename. When you open an index file, you search your hard drive, server, or external media for a filename that ends with a PDX extension. When you visit the Search Pane and select the menu option for Select Index, the Index Selection dialog box (Figure 29-13) opens. The Index Selection dialog box lists indexes by their Index Title names. These names are derived from what you type in the Index Title field in Acrobat Catalog.

Note When you get ready to build a file, Acrobat prompts you for the index filename. By default, the text you type in the Index Title field is listed in the File Name field in the Save Index File dialog box. This dialog box opens when you click the Build button in the Catalog dialog box (see the section "Building the index" later in this chapter). In most cases where you supply a name as a description in the Index Title, you'll want to change the filename to a name consistent with standard DOS conventions (that is, an eight-character maximum with a three-character maximum extension). Make this change when you're prompted to save the file.

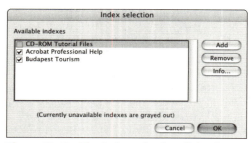

Figure 29-13: The Index selection dialog box lists all loaded indexes.

✦ **Index description:** You can supply as many as 256 characters in the Index Description field. Descriptive names and keywords should be provided so that the end user knows what each index contains. Index descriptions should be thought of as adding more information to the items mentioned earlier in this chapter regarding document descriptions. Index descriptions can help users find the index file that addresses their needs.

When an index is loaded, the index title appears in the Select Indexes dialog box. To get more information about an index file, click Info (refer to Figure 29-13). The Index Information dialog box opens, shown in Figure 29-14. The Index Information dialog box shows you the title from the Index Title field and the description added in Acrobat Catalog in the Index Description field.

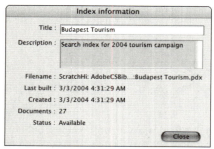

Figure 29-14: The Index information dialog box

♦ **Include these directories:** If you add nothing in this field, Catalog won't build an index because it won't know where to look for the PDF files to be included in the index. Adding the directory path(s) is essential before you begin to build the index. Notice the first Add button on the right side of the dialog box in Figure 28-15. After you click Add, a navigation dialog box opens, enabling you to identify the directory where the PDFs to be indexed are located. Many directories can be added to the Include These Directories list. These directories can be in different locations on your hard drive. When you select a given directory, all subfolders are also indexed for all directory locations unless you choose to exclude certain folders. When the directories have been identified, the directory path and folder name appear in the Include These Directories field.

♦ **Exclude these subdirectories:** If you have files in a subdirectory within the directory you're indexing and want to exclude the subdirectory, you can do so in the Exclude These Subdirectories field. The folder names and directory paths of excluded directories appear in the Exclude These Subdirectories field, as shown in Figure 29-12.

♦ **Remove:** If you decide to remove a directory from either the Include These Directories or Exclude These Subdirectories lists, select an item in the list and click Remove. You can add or delete directories in either list prior to building an index or when modifying an index.

Saving index definitions

Two buttons appear at the top-right corner of the Catalog dialog box for saving a definition. If you begin to develop an index file and supply the index title and a description and want to come back to Catalog later, you can save what you type in the Index Definition dialog box using the Save As button. The Save button does not appear active until you've saved a file with the Save As option or you're working on a file that has been built. Saving the file only saves the definition for the index. It doesn't create an index file. The Save As option enables you to prepare files for indexing and interrupt your session if you need to return later. For example, suppose you add an index title and you write an index description. If you need to quit Acrobat at this point, click Save As and save the definition to disk. You can then return later and resume creating the index by adding the directories and building the index.

After you've saved a file, you can update the file with the Save button. After a definition is saved, when you return to Acrobat Catalog, you can click Open in the Catalog dialog box and resume editing the definition file. When all the options for your search index have been determined, you click Build to actually create the index file.

Using Save As or Save is not required to create an index file. If you set all your attributes for the index and click Build, Acrobat Catalog prompts you in the Save Index File dialog box to supply a name for the index and save the definition. Essentially, Catalog is invoking the Save As command for you.

If, at any time, you click Cancel in the lower-right corner of the Index Definition dialog box, all edits are lost for the current session. If you add definition items without saving, you'll need to start over when you open the Index Definition dialog box again. If you start to work on a saved file and click Cancel without saving new edits, your file reverts to the previously saved version.

Options

To the right of the Index Description field in the New Index Definition dialog box (Figure 29-12) is a button labeled Options. Click this button and the Options dialog box appears, allowing you to choose from a number of different attributes for your index file, as shown in Figure 29-15. Some of these options are similar to Preference settings for Acrobat Catalog made in the Preferences dialog box. Any edits you make here supersede preference settings. The options in this box include the following:

For information on setting catalog preferences, see the section "Setting preferences."

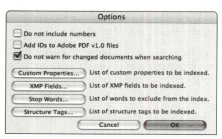

Figure 29-15: The Options dialog box assigns attributes to the index file.

✦ **Do not include numbers:** By selecting this option, you can reduce the file size, especially if data containing many numbers is part of the PDF file(s) to be indexed. Keep in mind, though, that if numbers are excluded, Search won't find numeric values.

✦ **Add IDs to Acrobat 1.0 PDF files:** Because Acrobat is now in version 6.0, it may be rare to find old PDF 1.0 files that you need to updated with IDs for Acrobat 1.0 files. If you do have legacy files saved as PDF 1.0 format, it's best to batch-process the older PDFs by saving them out of Acrobat 6.0. As software changes, many previous formats may not be supported with recent updates. To avoid this, update older documents to newer file formats.

For more information on batch processing, see Chapter 29.

If you have legacy files that haven't been updated and you want to include them in your search index, check the box. If you're not certain whether the PDFs were created with Acrobat 1.0 compatibility, check it anyway just to be safe.

✦ **Do not warn for changed documents when searching:** If you create an index file, then return to the index in Acrobat Catalog and perform some maintenance functions, save the index, and start searching the index, Acrobat notifies you in a dialog box that changes have been made and asks whether you want to proceed. To sidestep the opening of the warning dialog box, check the Do Not Warn for Changed Documents When Searching option.

✦ **Custom Properties:** This button opens a dialog box (Figure 29-16) which helps you customize Acrobat with the Acrobat Software Development Kit (SDK). This item is intended for programmers who want to add special features to Acrobat. To add a Custom Property to be indexed, you should have knowledge in programming and the PDF format.

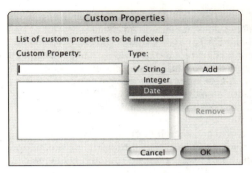

Figure 29-16: You can add custom data fields to Acrobat.

You add Custom Properties to the field box and select the type of property from the pull-down menu. You type the property values in the field box, identify the type, and click Add. The property is then listed in the window below the Custom Property field box. The types available from the pull-down menu include:

- **String:** This is any text string. If numbers are included with this option, they are treated as text.
- **Integer:** The integer field can accept values between 0 and 65,535.
- **Date:** This is a date value.

Support for programmers writing extensions, plug-ins, and working with the SDK is provided by Adobe Systems. For developers who want to use the support program, you need to become a member of the Adobe Solutions Network (ASN) Developer Program. For more information about ASN and SDK, log on to the Adobe Web site at `http://partners.adobe.com/asn/developer`.

✦ **XMP Fields:** Click XMP Fields and another dialog box opens where you add to a list of XMP fields. The dialog box is virtually identical to the Stop Words dialog box shown in Figure 29-17. Type a name in the field box and click Add. All new XMP fields are added to the list window.

✦ **Stop Words:** To optimize an index file that produces faster search results, you can add stop words. You may have words, such as *the, a, an, of,* and so on that you would typically not use in a search. You can exclude such words by typing the word in the Word field box and clicking Add in the Stop Words dialog box. Click on Stop Words in the Options dialog box to open the Stop Words dialog box (Figure 29-17). To eliminate a word after it has been added, select the word and click Remove. Keep in mind that every time you *add* a word, you're actually adding it to a list of words to be excluded.

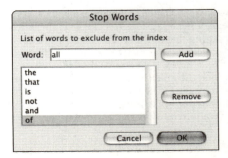

Figure 29-17: You can eliminate words from an index file.

Tip You can create an elaborate list of stop words and may want to apply the list to several index files, but Acrobat (as of this writing) does not include an ability to import or swap a list of words to be excluded from an index file. For a workaround, you can open any existing Index Definition field and change all attributes except the stop words. Add a new index title, a new index description, and select a new directory for indexing. Save the definition to a new filename and click the Build button. A new index is built using stop words created in another index. In workgroups, you can save an index definition file without adding directories and use it as a template so all index files have consistent settings for the stop words.

✦ **Tags:** If you have a Tagged PDF, you can search document tags when the tags are included in the search index. Click on Tags in the Options dialog box to open the Tags dialog box (Figure 29-18). Tagged PDFs with a tagged root and elements can have any item in the tagged logical tree marked for searching. To observe the tags in a PDF file, open the Tags palette and expand the tree. All the tags nest like a bookmark list. To mark tags for searching, type the tag name in the Tags dialog box and click Add. You remove tags from the list window by selecting a tag and clicking Remove.

Cross-Reference For more information on creating tagged PDF documents and the use of tags, see the *Adobe Acrobat 7 PDF Bible* (Wiley Publishing).

Figure 29-18: You can mark tags for searches in index files.

Building the index

After you set all the attributes for the index definition, you're ready to create the index file. Clicking the Build button in the New Index Definition dialog box (Figure 29-12) creates indexes. When you click this button, Acrobat Catalog opens the Save Index File dialog box, where you supply a filename and target a destination on your hard drive. The default file extension is PDX. Don't modify the file extension name. Acrobat recognizes these files when loading search indexes.

The location where you instruct Catalog to save your index file can be any location on your hard drive regardless of where the files being indexed reside. You can save the index file inside or outside the folder that Catalog created during the indexing. Therefore, you have an index file and a folder containing index resources. The relationship between the index file and resource folder locations is critical to the usability of the index. If you move the index file to a different location without moving the supporting folder, the index is rendered unusable. To avoid problems, create a folder either when you're in the Save Index File dialog box or before you open Catalog and save your index file to your new folder. Make the name descriptive and keep the index file together in this folder. When you want to move the index to another directory, to another computer, or to an external media cartridge or CD/DVD-ROM, copy the folder containing the index and supporting files.

Click Save in the Save Index File dialog box and Catalog closes the Index Definition dialog box, returns you to the Catalog dialog box, and begins to process all the files in the target folder(s). Depending on how many files are indexed, the time to complete the build may be considerable. Don't interrupt the processing if you want to complete the index generation. When Catalog finishes, the progress bar stops and the last line of text in the Catalog dialog box reads, "Index build successful." If the build is not successful, you can scroll the window in the Catalog dialog box and view errors reported in the list.

Stopping builds

If you want to interrupt a build, you can click the Stop button while a build is in progress. When building an index, Catalog opens a file where all the words and markers to the PDF pages are written. When you click the Stop button, Catalog saves the open file to disk and closes it with the indexed items up to the point you stopped the build. Therefore, the index is usable after stopping a build and you can search for words in the partial index. When you want to resume, you can open the file in Catalog and click Rebuild in Catalog.

Building existing indexes

When files are deleted from indexed folders and new files are added to the indexed folders, you'll want to maintain the index file and update to reflect any changes. You can open an index file and click on Build for a quick update. New files are scanned and added to the index, but the deleted files are marked for deletion without actually deleting the data. To delete data no longer valid, you need to use the Purge button. Purging can take a considerable amount of time even on small index files. Therefore, your routine maintenance might be to consistently build a file and only periodically purge data.

Building legacy index files

When you open an index file created with an Acrobat Catalog version earlier than version 6.0, a dialog box opens, as shown in Figure 29-19, informing you the index is not compatible with the current version of Acrobat. In the dialog box, you have three options: Create copy, Overwrite old index, and Cancel. Click Create copy to make a copy of the index file. A new index file is created, leaving the original index file undisturbed. You can click Overwrite old index and the file rewrites, replacing the old index. If you choose this option, your new index file won't be compatible with Acrobat viewers earlier than version 6.0. Clicking on Cancel in the dialog box returns you to the Index Selection dialog box, leaving the index file undisturbed.

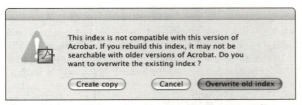

Figure 29-19: With an Acrobat Catalog version earlier than 6.0, you're informed that your index isn't compatible with the current version of Acrobat.

If you know some users won't be working with the new Acrobat viewers, be certain to make copies of your index files. Until all users have upgraded to a viewer 6.0 or higher, you may need to organize your indexes according to viewer versions.

Tip If your workflow requires having different versions of Acrobat viewers, keeping a complete installation of Acrobat 5.05 installed on a separate computer on your network is to your advantage. If you inadvertently overwrite index files or need to perform some task specifically related to Acrobat versions less than 6.0, you can use the older version to keep compatibility with other users. In addition, you can test many new files you edit in version 6.0 or higher to ensure they work with viewer versions less than 6.0. Ideally, all your colleagues, coworkers, and clients should upgrade to Acrobat 6.0. However, in a real world, we know some users are reluctant to let go of the familiar, and convincing some of your clients that upgrading Acrobat is the best solution may take some time.

Building index files from secure documents

In all earlier versions of Acrobat, you could not create index files from secure PDFs encrypted with either Acrobat Standard Security or Acrobat Self-Sign Security. Now in version 6.0 of Acrobat, you have complete access to secure files with Acrobat Catalog. Any form of encrypted file using the Acrobat-supported security features can be included in your index files. Creating an index does not compromise your security and won't affect the permissions you set forth when the files were saved.

If you have legacy files that have been secured, you can index them like other files saved in earlier PDF format compatibilities. You can only use these files, or any other files you create with Acrobat Professional, with Acrobat viewers 6.0 and later.

Cross-Reference For more information on encryption and security, see Chapter 31.

Rebuilding an index

Rebuilding index files completely re-creates a new index. You can open an Acrobat 6.0–compatible index file and click on Rebuild. The file rewrites the file you opened much like you would use a Save As menu command to rewrite a PDF document. If a substantial number of PDF documents have been deleted and new files added to the indexed folders, rebuilding the index could take less time than purging data.

Purging data

As indexes are maintained and rebuilt, you'll need to perform periodic maintenance and purge old data. A purge does not delete the index file, nor does it completely rewrite the file; it simply recovers the space used in the index for outdated information. Purging is particularly useful when you remove PDF files from a folder and the search items are no longer needed. If you've built a file several times, each build marks words for deletion. A purge eliminates the marked data and reduces the file size. With a significant number of words marked for deletion, a purge improves a search's speed. This operation might be scheduled routinely in environments where many changes occur within the indexed folders.

Tip When changing options for eliminating words and numbers from indexes or adding tags and custom properties in the Options dialog box, first open the `index.pdx` file in Catalog and purge the data. Set your new criteria in the Options dialog box and rebuild the index. Any items deleted will now be added to the index, or any items you want to eliminate will subsequently be eliminated from the index.

Setting preferences

Preference settings are contained in the Preferences dialog box. Choose Edit ➪ Preferences and click on the Catalog item in the left Pane as shown in Figure 29-20. Notice that the Index Defaults items use the same settings as found in the Options dialog box from the New Index Selection dialog box. The top three options under Indexing in Catalog Preferences are obtained only here in these preference settings.

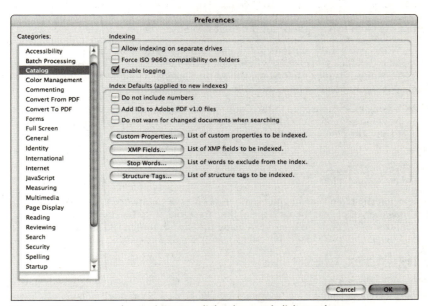

Figure 29-20: Open the Preferences dialog box and click Catalog.

- ✦ **Indexing:** The three options found in the Indexing section of the Catalog preferences include:
  - **Allow indexing on separate drives:** When creating index files where you want to include folders on network servers and/or computers on your network, select this item. The indexing option only includes indexing files on local networks. Unfortunately, you can't index files on Web servers and use indexes from within Web browsers.

- **Force ISO 9660 compatibility on folders:** This setting tells Catalog to look for any folders that aren't compliant with standard DOS conventions (eight-character maximum with three-character-maximum extensions) for folder/directory names. If Catalog encounters an unacceptable folder name, it stops the process and reports an error in the Catalog dialog box. Folder names and directory paths are listed for all incompatible names. You can review the list and manually rename folders. After changing folder names, try to create the index again.

- **Enable logging:** A log file, created during an index build, describes the processing for each indexed file. You can open the file, which is ASCII text, in any text editor or word processor. Any errors are noted in the log file, along with all documents and directory paths. If you don't want to generate a log file at the time of indexing, deselect the check box, but realize that you're prevented from analyzing problems.

✦ **Index Defaults:** These options are identical to the options you have available in the New Index Definition Options dialog box (see Figure 29-15). These default/options settings exist in two locations for different reasons:

- When you set the options in the Preferences dialog box, the options are used for all index files you create. When you elect to use the options from the New Index Selection Options dialog box, the settings are specific to the index file you create. When you create a new index file, the options return to defaults.

- If you set a preference in the Catalog Preferences and disable the option in the New Index Selection Options dialog box, the latter supersedes the former. That is to say, the New Index Selection Options dialog box settings always prevail.

Using Index Files

As stated earlier, the main reason you create index files is for speed. When you search hundreds or thousands of pages, the amount of time to return found instances for searched words is a matter of seconds compared to using the Search tool in the Search pane.

Loading index files

To search using an index file, you need to first load the index in the Search pane. Click on the Search tool or press ⌘/Control + F to open the Search pane. From the Look In pull-down menu, choose the Select Index menu option, as shown in Figure 29-21.

The Index Selection dialog box opens after making the menu selection. Click the Add button and the Open Index File dialog box opens, as shown in Figure 29-22. In this dialog box, navigate your hard drive to find the folder where your index file is located. Click on the index filename and click Open.

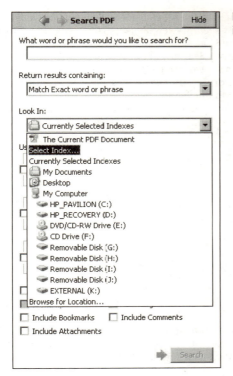

Figure 29-21: Your first step in using indexes is to load the index file(s)

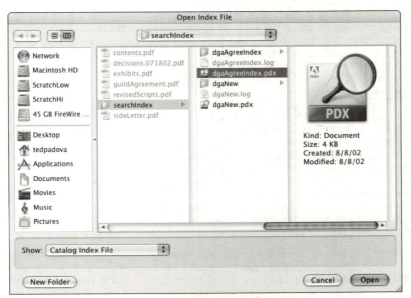

Figure 29-22: Select an index to load and click Open.

After selecting the index to load, you're returned to the Index Selection dialog box. A list of all loaded indexes appears in the dialog box. To the left of each filename is a check box. When a check mark is in view, the index file is active and can be searched. Disabled check boxes have the index file loaded, but the file remains inactive. Search will not return results from the inactive index files. If an index file is grayed out, as shown in Figure 29-23, the file path has been disrupted and Acrobat can't find the index file or the support files associated with the index. If you see a filename grayed out, select the file in the list and click Remove. Click Add and relocate the index. If the support files aren't found, an error is reported in a dialog box, indicating the index file could not be opened.

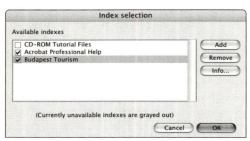

Figure 29-23: If a file is grayed out, the index is not accessible.

If you can't open a file, you need to return to the Catalog dialog box by choosing Advanced ➪ Catalog and clicking Open. Find the index file that you want to make active and rebuild the index. After rebuilding, you need to return to the Index Selection dialog box and reload it.

 If you load an index file from a CD-ROM and the CD is not inserted in your CD-ROM drive, the index-file name is grayed out in the Index Selection dialog box. After inserting the CD-ROM containing the index, the index-file name becomes active. If you know index files are loaded from CDs, don't delete them from the Index Selection dialog box. Doing so requires you to reload the index file each time you insert a CD.

Disabling indexes

If you want to eliminate an index from searches, you can deactivate the index by disabling its check box. In a later Acrobat session, you can go back and enable indexes listed in the Index Selection dialog box (open the Search pane as described in the previous section and choose Select Index from the Look In pull-down menu to open the Index Selection dialog box). You should always use this method rather than deleting an index if you intend to use it again in a later Acrobat session. However, at times, you may want to delete an index file. If you no longer intend to use the index, or you relocate your index to another drive or server, you may want to completely remove the old index. If this is the case, select the index file you want to delete and click Remove. You can enable or disable indexes before you click Remove. In either case, the index file is removed without warning.

If you inadvertently delete an index, you can always reload the index by clicking Add. Placing index files in a directory where you can easily access them is a good idea. To avoid confusion, try to keep indexes in a common directory or a directory together with the indexed PDF files.

Acrobat doesn't care where the index file is located on your hard drive or server — it just needs to know where the file is located and the file needs to keep the relative path with the support files. If you move the index file to a different directory, be certain to reestablish the connection in the Index Selection dialog box.

Index information

When a number of index files are installed on a computer or server, the names for the files may not be descriptive enough to determine which index you want to search. If more-detailed information is desired, the information provided by the Index Information dialog box may help identify the index needed for a given search. To open the Index selection dialog box click Select Index in the Look In pull-down menu. Click Info in the Index selection dialog box to display the index information.

Index information may be particularly helpful in office environments where several people in different departments create PDFs and indexes are all placed on a common server. What may be intuitive to the author of an index file in terms of index name may not be as intuitive to other users. Index information offers the capability of adding more-descriptive information that can be understood by many users.

Fortunately, you can explore more-descriptive information about an index file by clicking Info in the Index Selection dialog box. When you click Info, the Index Information dialog box opens, displaying information about the index file, as shown in Figure 29-24. Some of the information displayed requires user entry at the time the index is built. Acrobat Catalog automatically creates other information in the dialog box when the index is built. The Index information dialog box provides a description of the following:

Figure 29-24: The Index information dialog

+ **Title:** The user supplies title information at the time the index is created. Titles usually consist of several words describing the index contents. Titles can be searched so the title keywords should reflect the index content.

+ **Description:** Description can be a few words or several sentences containing information about the index. (In Figure 29-24, the description was supplied in Acrobat Catalog when the index was created.)

+ **Filename:** The directory path for the index file's location on a drive or server displays with the last item appearing as the index filename.

✦ **Last built:** If the index file is updated, the date of the last build is supplied here. If no updates have occurred, the date is the same as the date of creation.

✦ **Created:** This date reflects the time and date the index file was originally created and is, therefore, a fixed date.

✦ **Documents:** Indexes are created from one or more PDF documents. The total number of PDF files from which the index file was created appears here.

✦ **Status:** If the index file has been identified and added to the list in the Index Selection dialog box, it will be Available. Unavailable indexes appear grayed out in the list and are described as Unavailable.

Searching an index

After your index file is prepared and loaded in the Index Selection dialog box, it's ready for use. You search index files in the Advanced Search pane. From the Look In pull-down menu, select Currently Selected Indexes.

All the options discussed earlier for advanced searches are available to you. Select from the Return Results Containing pull-down menu, enter your search criteria, and select the options you want. Click Search and you'll find the search results reported much faster than using other search methods.

Index files can be created from PDF collections contained on external media where the index file can remain on your computer without the need for copying the PDF documents to your hard drive. When you insert a media disc like a CD-ROM, your search index is ready to use to search the media. To understand a little more about creating search indexes and using them with external media, follow these steps.

STEPS: Creating Index Files from Media Storage

1. **Set preferences.** Choose Edit ⇨ Preferences. Click on Catalog in the left pane. Check Allow Indexing on Separate Drives. In order to create an index file from a device other than your local hard drive(s), this preference setting must be enabled. Click OK to exit the Preferences dialog box.

2. **Open Catalog.** Choose Advanced ⇨ Catalog.

3. **Open the New Index Definition dialog box.** Click on New Index in the Catalog dialog box and the New Index Definition dialog box opens in the foreground.

4. **Add an Index title.** Click in the first field box and type a title for your index file. The example in Figure 29-25 uses "Budapest Tourist" for the title.

5. **Add an Index Description.** Type a description for the index. You can use any text you want to help remind you later what this index file is used for. An example description appears in Figure 29-25.

6. **Change Options.** Click Options to open the Options dialog box where you can make options choices. Check Do Not Warn for Changed Documents When Searching. Click OK.

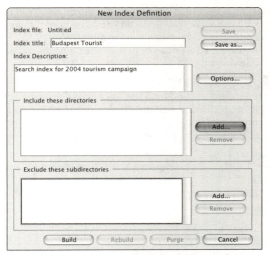

Figure 29-25: Add an index title and an index description.

7. **Add a folder to the Include These Directories list.** Click the first Add button adjacent to the list for Include These Directories. The Browse for Folder dialog box opens. If you have a folder you want to catalog, select the folder in the Browse for Folder dialog box. If you have a CD where your files are stored, click on the CD drive where the CD containing the files is located. Click OK in the Browse for Folder dialog box.

8. **Build the index.** Click the Build button in the Catalog dialog box. Acrobat prompts you with the Save Index File dialog box for the location to save your index file. Select the location on your hard drive where you want to save your file. Type a name in the File Name field. Use a short name for the file. The extension defaults to PDX. Leave the default extension and click Save.

    Acrobat Professional reads all the files on the CD-ROM and writes the Index file. Let your computer continue writing the index until it finishes the build.

9. **Examine the build results.** When Acrobat completes the build, the Catalog dialog box reports the results of the build. The last line in the results list reports the index build as successful.

10. **Quit Catalog.** Click Close to quit Catalog.

11. **Load the index file.** Click the Search button in the Acrobat File toolbar or press ⌘/Ctrl+F and select Use Advanced Search Options. Open the Look In pull-down menu and click on Select Index. The Index Selection dialog box opens. Deselect any active index files by clicking on the check boxes to remove the check mark adjacent to the index names in the list. Click Add and select your new index in the Open Index File dialog box. Click OK to return to the Index Selection dialog box. Verify that your new index is listed and the check box is enabled.

12. **Review the index information.** Select the index file in the Index Selection dialog box. Click Info to open the Index Information dialog box. Review the contents and notice the description appears as you added it in the Index Description dialog box. Click Close to return to the Index Selection dialog box. Click OK in the Index Selection dialog box to return to the Acrobat Document Pane.

13. **Search the new index file.** The index file is loaded and active. Be certain the menu option for Currently Selected Indexes is active in the Look In pull-down menu. Enter **Search AND Index Description** in the first field box. Select Boolean Query from the Return Results Containing pull-down menu. Click on Include Bookmarks and Include Attachments at the bottom of the Search pane, as shown in Figure 29-26.

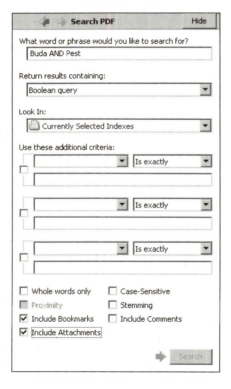

Figure 29-26: Type the words that you want to search for.

14. **Invoke the Search.** Click Search at the bottom of the Search pane. The results are reported in the list within the Search pane. Click on any text highlighted in blue to open the file and page where the results are found.

Practice searching your new index file using different options and search criteria. To compare the difference between using a search index file and using the advanced search options, you can choose the Browse for Location menu item and search the CD-ROM for the same criteria.

Go back and forth to see the differences between searching folders and searching an index file. It should be obvious that when using an index file your search results are reported much faster.

Searching external devices

A computer network server, another computer on your network, a CD-ROM, a DVD-ROM, an external hard drive, or a removable media cartridge is considered external to your local computer hard drive(s). Any of these devices can be indexed and the index file can be located on any of the devices you index. If you want to save an index file on a device different from where the PDF collection is stored, be certain to open the Preferences dialog box for the Catalog Preferences and enable the check box for Allow Indexing on Separate Drives. This preference setting enables you to index across media devices.

Note: When you want to write index files to read only media such as CD-ROMs and DVDs, you need to create the index file from PDFs stored on your hard drive. After the index file is created, copy the index file, the supporting files, and the PDFs to your media and burn the disk.

When you want to search an index, you can activate the index in the Index Selection dialog box and invoke a search, whether your external media is mounted and accessible or not. The search index returns results from the index PDX file and the IDX files without looking at the PDFs that were indexed. You can examine the results of the search in the Search pane and find the files where the search criteria match the PDF documents in the index collection.

If you want to open the link to the PDF document where a result is reported, you need to have the media mounted and accessible. If a network server or other computer contains the related files, the server/computer must be shared with appropriate permissions and visible on your desktop. If you use external media-storage devices, the media must be mounted and visible on your desktop in order to view the PDFs linked to the search results. If you attempt to view a document when the device is not mounted, Acrobat opens an error dialog box.

If you see an error dialog box, click OK in the dialog box and insert your media, connect an external hard drive, or access a computer or network server. Wait until the media is mounted, and click on a search result. Acrobat opens the linked page and you're ready to continue your search.

A search-index file created on one computer can be moved or copied to another computer. To copy an index file to another computer, be certain you copy the index file (PDX) and all supporting files in the folder created by Catalog.

You can load the index file and external media on another computer and perform the same searches as were performed where the index file was created. When you're distributing CD-ROMs and DVDs, you can copy these index files to your media and all users can access the index files. If you access an index file on a network server and the PDF collection is stored on an external device such as a CD-ROM, you cannot open files from another computer unless the CD-ROM is mounted. You may see your network server, but the associated devices with the server need to be individually mounted in order to open PDF files remotely.

Summary

- You can reduce file sizes with the Reduce File Size menu command.
- You use the PDF Optimizer, available with Acrobat Professional, to reduce file sizes and eliminate unnecessary data in PDF files. PDF Optimizer can often reduce file sizes more than when using the Reduce File Size command.
- Selecting options in the Clean Up tab in the PDF Optimizer other than the default options can interfere with the PDF functionality.
- In some cases, saving a PDF file to disk and redistilling with Acrobat Distiller can reduce file sizes.
- Users determine initial views when setting preferences for all files saved with default views. When you save initial views in PDF files, they override user preferences.
- Search index files are created in Acrobat Catalog. Searching index files returns results much faster than Acrobat built-in search tools.
- You can search document descriptions with advanced searches and via index file searches.
- Index files can be built, rebuilt, and purged with Acrobat Catalog. Old index files created with PDF formats earlier than version 6.0 need to be rebuilt with Acrobat Catalog.
- Tags and XML data can be searched with advanced searches and from index searches.
- You can copy index files to other computers, network servers, and external media-storage units.

✦ ✦ ✦

Working with XML

In This Chapter

Understanding XML

Working with XML in InDesign

Applying XML in creative workflows

Viewing and editing XML data in GoLive

Setting up an XML template

XML, or *Extensible Markup Language*, is often used as a data-transport media. As a popular format for exchanging data on the Web, many of the CS applications support XML.

InDesign, in particular, includes broad support for XML that lets you mark InDesign elements with XML tags. Exporting an InDesign document to the XML format with these tags produces an XML document that holds the content of the InDesign document. InDesign also allows you to import XML documents into the current document. Importing an XML document displays all tagged elements in the Structure pane where you can drag them into framed placeholders in the document. If you must further edit an XML document, you can use GoLive to view, edit, and create XML documents using its Outline and Source Code Editors. Acrobat also includes features to save PDF files as XML documents.

Understanding XML

To easily understand XML, consider starting with its sister technology, HTML, or *Hypertext Markup Language*. HTML is a set of syntax commands that display Web pages within a browser. If you choose View ⇨ Source in a Web browser, the HTML code for the Web page displays.

If you examine some HTML code, you'll find that it is text-based and may be created using any standard text editor. HTML code is also simplistic and fairly readable, as shown in Figure 30-1. It isn't too difficult to figure out, but the language is rigid and requires that you follow the syntax exactly to get the desired results.

HTML has a limiting problem: It describes how to place text and images on Web pages, but it doesn't know anything about the type of data it's displaying. XML addresses this concern, allowing a developer to customize the tags that are used in order to describe it. The extensible portion of XML doesn't make it stick to one particular set of tags.

For example, you use the `<img>` tag in HTML to display an image on a Web page, but in XML, you could create a `<circle>` tag with attributes such as radius and color. By endowing XML documents with tags that define different types of objects, the XML document becomes a great way to save data. Applications may then be written that use the XML document to process the data in different ways.

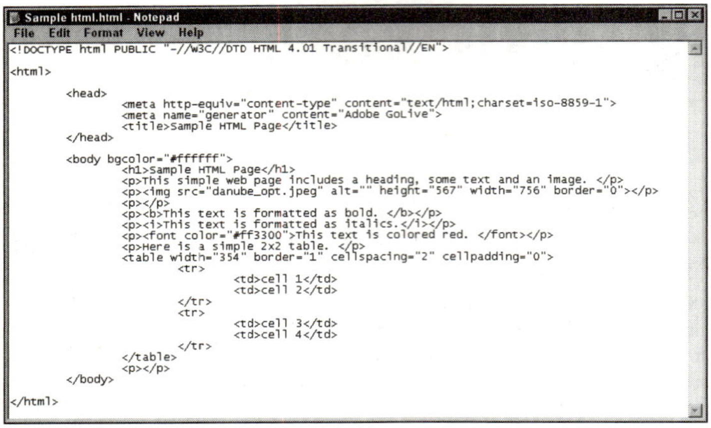
Sample html.html - Notepad

File Edit Format View Help

```
<!DOCTYPE html PUBLIC "-//W3C//DTD HTML 4.01 Transitional//EN">

<html>

	<head>
		<meta http-equiv="content-type" content="text/html;charset=iso-8859-1">
		<meta name="generator" content="Adobe GoLive">
		<title>Sample HTML Page</title>
	</head>

	<body bgcolor="#ffffff">
		<h1>Sample HTML Page</h1>
		<p>This simple web page includes a heading, some text and an image. </p>
		<p><img src="danube_opt.jpeg" alt="" height="567" width="756" border="0"></p>
		<p></p>
		<p><b>This text is formatted as bold. </b></p>
		<p><i>This text is formatted as italics.</i></p>
		<p><font color="#ff3300">This text is colored red. </font></p>
		<p>Here is a simple 2x2 table. </p>
		<table width="354" border="1" cellspacing="2" cellpadding="0">
			<tr>
				<td>cell 1</td>
				<td>cell 2</td>
			</tr>
			<tr>
				<td>cell 3</td>
				<td>cell 4</td>
			</tr>
		</table>
		<p></p>
	</body>

</html>
```

Figure 30-1: The source code for any HTML Web page is readable within a text editor.

XML tags may also include attributes. *Attributes* are additional properties embedded within the tag, further defining the tag object. Attributes are just keywords that are assigned a value.

To keep track of all the tags used in an XML document, you can create a controlling document called the *Document Type Definition* (DTD). This document lists all the different tags that are possible for the XML document that it's applied to and defines the tags, the attributes of those tags, and the overall structure of the XML.

XML and Creative Suite

So what does XML have to do with the Creative Suite applications? Several of the Creative Suite applications include support for XML and use it as a data-transport format. For example, InDesign can tag content with XML tags and import them into other documents where they may be reused. InDesign can also export XML documents. GoLive is also used to create and view XML documents.

XML and SVG

Although you can create custom XML tags to define a specific object, it would become pretty confusing if each company defined its own tags a little differently from everyone else. For example, you may need to share data sets with other companies. Several standard DTDs with broad appeal have been defined using working groups that include participants and input from many different companies.

One such DTD is used to define vector data for use on the Web called *Scalable Vector Graphic* (SVG). The SVG DTD includes all the tags to define vector graphics; using a plug-in, a Web browser is able to parse the XML document and display the vector graphics in a Web page.

If you were to open an SVG file in a text editor, you would see tags similar to HTML, like the file shown in Figure 30-2.

Cross-Reference

The SVG format is covered in Chapter 35.

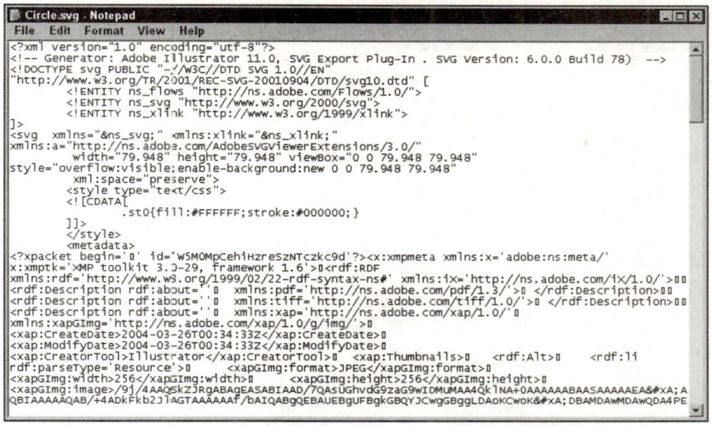

```
Circle.svg - Notepad
File Edit Format View Help
<?xml version="1.0" encoding="utf-8"?>
<!-- Generator: Adobe Illustrator 11.0, SVG Export Plug-In . SVG Version: 6.0.0 Build 78)  -->
<!DOCTYPE svg PUBLIC "-//W3C//DTD SVG 1.0//EN"
"http://www.w3.org/TR/2001/REC-SVG-20010904/DTD/svg10.dtd" [
        <!ENTITY ns_flows "http://ns.adobe.com/Flows/1.0/">
        <!ENTITY ns_svg "http://www.w3.org/2000/svg">
        <!ENTITY ns_xlink "http://www.w3.org/1999/xlink">
]>
<svg  xmlns="&ns_svg;" xmlns:xlink="&ns_xlink;"
xmlns:a="http://ns.adobe.com/AdobeSVGViewerExtensions/3.0/"
         width="79.948" height="79.948" viewBox="0 0 79.948 79.948"
style="overflow:visible;enable-background:new 0 0 79.948 79.948"
         xml:space="preserve">
        <style type="text/css">
        <![CDATA[
                .st0{fill:#FFFFFF;stroke:#000000;}
        ]]>
        </style>
        <metadata>
<?xpacket begin='' id='W5M0MpCehiHzreSzNTczkc9d'?><x:xmpmeta xmlns:x='adobe:ns:meta/'
x:xmptk='XMP toolkit 3.0-29, framework 1.6'><rdf:RDF
xmlns:rdf='http://www.w3.org/1999/02/22-rdf-syntax-ns#' xmlns:iX='http://ns.adobe.com/iX/1.0/'>
<rdf:Description rdf:about=''  xmlns:pdf='http://ns.adobe.com/pdf/1.3/'> </rdf:Description>
<rdf:Description rdf:about=''  xmlns:tiff='http://ns.adobe.com/tiff/1.0/'> </rdf:Description>
<rdf:Description rdf:about=''  xmlns:xap='http://ns.adobe.com/xap/1.0/'
xmlns:xapGImg='http://ns.adobe.com/xap/1.0/g/img/'>
<xap:CreateDate>2004-03-26T00:34:33Z</xap:CreateDate>
<xap:ModifyDate>2004-03-26T00:34:33Z</xap:ModifyDate>
<xap:CreatorTool>Illustrator</xap:CreatorTool>  <xap:Thumbnails>   <rdf:Alt>    <rdf:li
rdf:parseType='Resource'>     <xapGImg:format>JPEG</xapGImg:format>
<xapGImg:width>256</xapGImg:width>     <xapGImg:height>256</xapGImg:height>
<xapGImg:image>/9j/4AAQSkZJRgABAgEASABIAAD/7QAsUGhvdG9zaG9wIDMuMAA4QklNA+0AAAAAABAASAAAAAEA&#xA;A
QBIAAAAAQAB/+4ADkFkb2JlAGTAAAAAAf/bAIQABgQEBAUEBgUFBgkGBQYJCwgGBggLDAoKCwoK&#xA;DBAMDAwMDAwQDA4PE
```

Figure 30-2: SVG files are XML-based and, like HTML files, are also readable in a standard text editor.

Using XML in InDesign

InDesign content can be exported using the XML format. InDesign also includes features that let you mark page content with tags. Content that is exported as an XML file may be imported into the current InDesign document where all the tagged content is loaded and displayed in the Structure pane. By dragging the content from the Structure pane into the layout, you can quickly reuse any XML exported content within the new layout.

Content can be tagged using custom XML tags, but you can also import a Document Type Definition (DTD) document. When a DTD is imported, all the tags that are defined in the DTD become available for tagging content. The DTD may also be used to validate all tags before exporting the tagged content as an XML file.

Note InDesign tagged text is different from applying XML tags.

For more editing, exported XML files may also be opened and viewed within GoLive.

Tip You may find that DTDs have been created by a group or industry similar to tags and structures you use in your workflow. For a current list of registered DTDs visit `www.xml.com/pub/rg/DTD_Repositories`.

Marking elements with XML tags

You can apply XML tags to design elements using the Tags palette, shown in Figure 30-3, which you open by choosing Window ➪ Tags. To apply a tag to the selected layout element, just click on the tag name in the Tags palette. This causes the tagged element's bounding box to assume the tag's color. Conversely, when you want to create tags in an untagged document, you can import tags from an InDesign file and select content, then click on one of the imported tags.

Figure 30-3: The Tags palette has all the tags that you can apply to a document.

To remove a tag from an element, simply select the element and click the Untag button in the Tags palette. Untagging an element doesn't change the content or formatting of the element.

Tip   If you want to delete multiple tags, select all but one tag in the Tags palette and click the Trash icon. You must leave at least one tag unselected before you delete multiple tags.

Creating new XML tags

You can create new tags by selecting the New Tag tool in the Tags palette or use the New Tag menu command from a fly-out menu in the Tags palette.

Caution   Because tag names need to adhere to the XML syntax standards, they cannot contain any spaces, tabs, or special characters. Replacing spaces with the underscore (_) character is common.

New Feature   In earlier versions of InDesign, new tags were named in a dialog box. After typing a name you clicked OK and the tag was added to the Tags palette. In InDesign, CS2 tags are added directly in the Tags palette when you click the New Tag tool or select New Tag from a menu command. InDesign creates the tag and an I-beam cursor appears in a text box ready for you to type a name for the tag. In Figure 30-4 a new tag is created and the name for the tag is typed in the text box.

Figure 30-4: New tags are given a name and a color.

Creating tags from styles

If you've already invested time in defining and using custom character or paragraph styles, you can map these styles to specific tags. The Tags palette includes two palette menu commands to do this.

The Map Tags to Styles palette menu command opens a dialog box, shown in Figure 30-5. This palette lists all the available tags and allows you to select a style to map to each tag. The Map Styles to Tags palette menu command does just the opposite. It opens a dialog box that lists all the available styles and where you can select and map each tag to a style.

If the tag names match the style names, use the Map by Name button to automatically map styles and tags with the same name. You use the Load button to load tag definitions from another InDesign document.

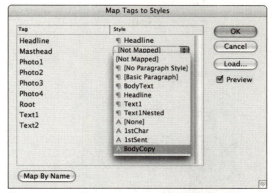

Figure 30-5: The Map Tags to Styles dialog box

Importing and viewing XML tags

You can load tags that you define in one InDesign document into the current document using the Load Tags palette menu command. This command opens a file dialog box where you may choose any InDesign or XML document. Clicking the Open button imports all the defined tags in the selected file into the Tags palette.

The color specified in the Tags palette for each tag appears as the frame color that surrounds and shades the element. These frame colors for tagged elements are shown when you choose View ⇨ Structure ⇨ Show/Hide Tagged Frames.

You can mark individual characters within an element with a separate tag. This text is surrounded with brackets that are the same color as the tag. These tags may also be hidden by choosing View ⇨ Structure ⇨ Show Tag Markers. Conversely, if the structure is visible, return to the menu and choose View ⇨ Structure ⇨ Tag Markers.

Using the Structure pane

You can view all the tags that you've applied to a document according to their hierarchal order in the Structure pane. This pane appears to the left of the document, as shown in Figure 30-6, when you choose View ⇨ Structure ⇨ Show/Hide Structure (Alt+Ctrl+1 in Windows; Option+⌘+1 on the Mac).

Tags displayed in the Structure pane also include small icons that match the type of element it is. If a tagged element isn't visible, click on the expand arrow to see all the objects underneath it in the hierarchy. All elements are under the root element, which always appears at the top of the Structure pane.

Selecting, adding, and deleting elements

The Structure pane lets you quickly select a tagged element by double-clicking its tag or by selecting the tag in the Structure pane and choosing the Go to Item pane menu command. The tag in the Structure pane that corresponds to the element that is selected in the layout is underlined in Structure pane.

If you add a new element to the layout, it doesn't appear in the Structure pane until it's tagged. After it's tagged, it appears at the bottom of the Structure pane.

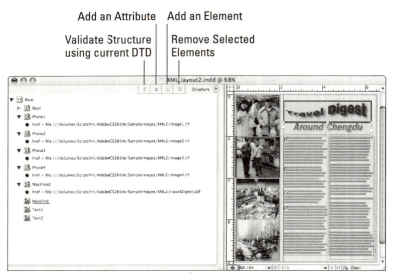

Figure 30-6: The Structure pane lists all the tagged elements.

Although most elements within the Structure pane are associated with some content in the layout, new elements may be created that act as containers for other tags. These container elements, like the root element, are identified with an icon that has brackets on it.

To create a new element, select the New Element pane menu command or click on the Add an Element button at the top of the Structure pane. This causes a simple dialog box to open, where the tag type to use for this element is selected. Note that you must select Root in the Structure pane in order to click the Add an Element button or choose the New Element menu command. If the Root tag is not selected, the button and menu command are grayed out.

To delete an element from the Structure panel, click to select it and then choose Delete from the pane menu or click on the Remove Selected Elements button at the top of the pane. A dialog box, shown in Figure 30-7, appears explaining that deleting the element also deletes the content in the layout. It also gives you a change to simply untag the content, which eliminates the tag element but keeps the content.

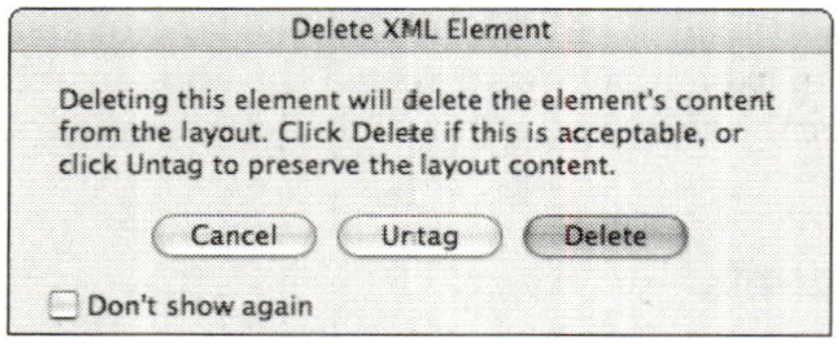

Figure 30-7: You can delete the element with its content or untag the content.

Rearranging tags

The order in which the tags are listed in the Structure pane is the same order in which the tags are listed in the exported XML file. You rearrange tags by dragging and dropping them above or below another tag. If a tag becomes highlighted when you drop a tag, the dropped tag becomes a child under the highlighted tag. Rearranging the tags and nesting them in parent/child groups is very similar to working with bookmarks in Acrobat or Layers in Illustrator.

You can also reorder tags in the Structure pane by choosing Edit ⇨ Cut, Edit ⇨ Copy, or Edit ⇨ Paste. Simply select the element to move and cut or copy it to the Clipboard; then select the tag in the Structure pane just above where you want the tag to appear and use the Paste command.

Adding information to a tag

You can add information including attributes, comments, and processing information to the selected element using the pane menu commands. This information is exported with the element tag to the XML document.

Attributes are properties and values that carry additional information about the element. A good example of this is the href attribute. This attribute is added to every image that is tagged and holds the location where the image is found. Attributes are identified in the Structure pane by a black circular bullet under the tag that it defines.

To add an attribute to an element, select the element and choose New Attribute from the pane menu or click on the Add an attribute button at the top of the pane. A dialog box, shown in Figure 30-8, appears; here, an attribute name and its value are added. To edit an attribute after its creation, simply double-click on it and a dialog box appears where you may edit its name and value.

Tip   Selecting the Hide Attributes menu command from the pane menu clears much of the Structure pane by hiding all attributes.

Figure 30-8: You name and assign values in the New Attribute dialog box.

In addition to attributes, you can also add comments and processing instructions to elements using similar pane menu commands. Comments are simple text statements that have no affect on the XML document but make it more understandable to the developer who may be reading it. Processing instructions are used by applications written to parse and use the XML document. The New Processing Instructions dialog box includes fields for entering target and data information.

Loading a DTD

The Structure pane also includes a Load DTD menu command. Loading a DTD is another way to add XML-specific tags to the Tags palette. All tags imported from a DTD file are locked in the Tags palette and cannot be changed. Figure 30-9 shows some locked tags that were imported from a DTD.

Figure 30-9: Tags imported from a DTD file are locked.

An imported DTD is identified in the Structure pane by the presence of a DOCTYPE element that appears above the root. The DOCTYPE statement is one of the first statements that appear in an XML document. It identifies the DTD that the tags in the document adhere to. Double-clicking on the DOCTYPE element in the Structure pane opens the DTD document in a text window, shown in Figure 30-10, where you can view it.

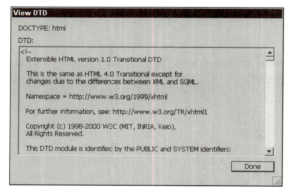

Figure 30-10: Double-clicking the DOCTYPE element opens the DTD document.

Validating structure

If a DTD is imported, clicking the Validate Structure Using Current DTD button at the top of the Structure pane compares the tagged elements to the DTD definitions and flags any elements that don't adhere to the DTD specifications. All elements with errors are marked with a yellow warning icon, and the errors are then listed in a pane below the Structure pane, as shown in Figure 30-11.

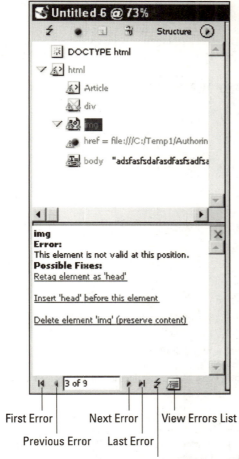

Figure 30-11: Errors and possible fixes are reported for any invalid elements.

Clicking on the warning icon displays the error for that element and also lists any possible fixes. The arrow buttons at the bottom of the Structure panel move back and forth between the errors and let you open a list of errors.

Exporting XML

You can export InDesign files to the XML format by choosing File ➪ Export (⌘/Ctrl+E). In the Save as Type field, select the XML option and name the file. After you click Save, an Export XML dialog box appears, which includes two panels — the General panel and the Images panel.

The General panel has options to include the DTD declaration; view XML using GoLive, Internet Explorer, or another selected application; export from the selected element; and specify the encoding method. The Include DTD Declaration option places a statement at the top of the XML document that lists the DTD that the document adheres to. If the document doesn't adhere to a DTD, the Include DTD Declaration is grayed out as you see in Figure 30-12.

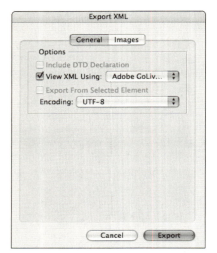

Figure 30-12: The General panel of the Export XML dialog box

Mac users cannot select Safari to view XML in the General pane in the Export XML dialog box, but XML files can be opened in Safari. To view the XML, you must follow a two-step process. When you open XML in Safari, the default view shows you formatted content. To view the XML tags, choose View ⇨ Source Code.

To view the exported XML document, you may select GoLive or Internet Explorer, or you can choose the Other option to open a file dialog box where you may select a separate application to view the XML document. If you select the Export from Selected Element, the exported XML document only includes the elements from the selected element in the Structure pane to the end of the document. The Encoding options include UTF-8, UTF-16, and Shift-JIS. Shift-JIS is used for Japanese characters.

The Images panel, shown in Figure 30-13, lets you copy the images in the document to a separate subfolder as Original Images, Optimized Original Images, or Optimized Formatted Images. If you select the Optimized Original Images option, the original images are optimized using the settings in the Images panel. However, if you select the Optimized Formatted Images option, the image retains any formatting applied in InDesign before it's optimized. This may include scaling or cropping the image.

Optimized images are copied into the subfolder with _opt appended to the end of the filename. Optimized formatted images are copied into the subfolder with _for appended to the end of the filename.

The Image Conversion option lets you select to convert the images to the GIF and JPEG formats. The Automatic option lets InDesign decide which format to use.

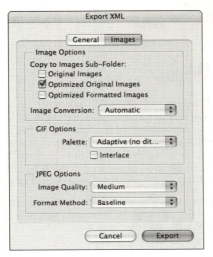

Figure 30-13: The Images panel of the Export XML dialog box

Cross-Reference More information on exporting layouts is covered in Chapter 28.

Importing XML tagged content

The typical workflow for importing XML documents is to create an InDesign document with tagged elements that match the tags used in the XML document that you want to import. Then choose File ⇨ Import XML and select a file to import. Click Open in the Import XML dialog box and the XML Import Options dialog box opens as shown in Figure 30-14. The XML Import Options dialog box includes options to have the imported content replace the existing content or append to the existing content. If you select an element in the Structure pane, you may also select to import into the selected element.

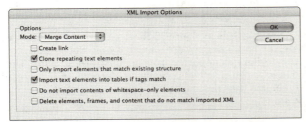

Figure 30-14: The XML Import Options dialog box lets you replace or append the contents of the XML file to the current document.

If you enable the Replace Content option, the content within the XML document loads into those tagged elements with matching tag names, but if you select the Append Content option, all the imported tags appear at the bottom of the Structure pane, where you can drag and drop them onto elements in the current document.

Note The XML document contains only content and no formatting. You apply formatting to the element placeholders in the layout using styles.

Using XML in Creative Workflows

Thus far in this chapter some of the basics of XML are described, and this description may leave you with a *so what* frame of mind. You may not completely see some benefits for using XML or lack understanding for where to start. If you work as an independent artist or in a small advertising agency, you may not have access to programming professionals who can answer questions or help you understand how you are going to use XML in your workflow. Let us back off from the programming jargon and complicated aspects of working with XML and try to bring this down to a more simple approach to help you get started with the basics.

The following steps are intended to help you to generate some ideas for how to implement XML in your work. First, you see how to Create an InDesign Layout. You next learn how to tag an InDesign document and to export files as XML. Finally, you discover how to import XML in InDesign.

Creating InDesign Layouts

Follow these steps to begin your journey through the real world XML experience:

STEPS: Create an InDesign Layout

1. **Create a layout with text and images in InDesign.** To begin your journey, start by creating a simple layout. In your layout, add some images and text frames.

   Cross-Reference For information on creating text frames, see Chapter 18. For information on designing layouts, see Chapter 26.

2. **Create style sheets.** Use placeholder text and add some character and paragraph styles to the text blocks. Adding styles is not a requirement for exporting a layout as XML, but to understand how to map content to styles, you need to have some style sheets in the layout. In Figure 30-15, you can see a layout used in the steps in this chapter.

   Several elements are added to the design in Figure 30-15. A background gradient was imported from Adobe Illustrator. Four images were imported from Photoshop files. The warped text at the top of the design was imported from an Illustrator graphic. The headline text is text added in InDesign. The two columns of placeholder text are independent elements. The left column uses nested style sheets and the right column uses a different paragraph style sheet.

   Cross-Reference For information related to adding placeholder text, creating paragraph style sheets, and nested style sheets, see Chapter 17.

3. **Save the InDesign layout.** Choose File ⇨ Save and save the document to your hard drive.

Figure 30-15: Create an InDesign layout containing text and graphics.

Tagging an InDesign Document

After you create a layout, the next step is adding XML tags to all the independent items on the document page. Using the example in Figure 30-15, tags need to be created for the background object, four different tags for the four Photoshop images, a tag for the Illustrator text, a tag for the headline, and two tags for the two text blocks. To tag the document, follow the steps below:

STEPS: Tag an InDesign Document

1. **Clear the document content.** Before you add tags to the file, delete all the content but leave the frames where the content appears. Click the Direct Selection tool and click inside each frame. Press Delete/Backspace or Num Pad Del when an item is selected. To delete text while retaining the text frames, click the Type tool inside a body of text and press Command/Ctrl+A to select all the text in the frame. Press Delete/Backspace or Num Pad Del to clear the selected text. You should be left with the placeholder frames, as shown in Figure 30-16.

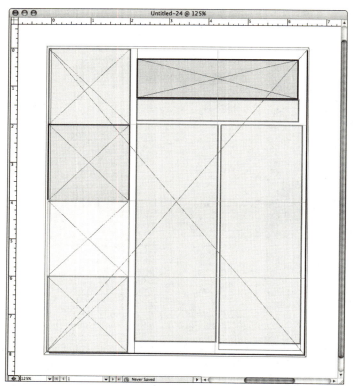

Figure 30-16: Delete all the content but leave the placeholders in the InDesign layout.

 Cross-Reference For more information related to working with frames, see Chapter 18.

2. **View the tagged markers and tagged frames.** Choose View ➪ Structure ➪ Show Tagged Markers. Return to the same menu and choose Show Tagged Frames. Inasmuch as you haven't tagged any elements yet, InDesign dynamically shows highlights on frames as you tag them. This helps you keep track of what items remain to be tagged.

3. **Open the Tags palette.** Choose Window ➪ Tags to open the Tags palette. The tags palette is where you create the XML tags.

4. **Add tag names to your document.** Click the New Tag tool at the bottom of the Tags palette or open the fly-out menu and select New tag. A tag is added to the palette and, as yet is not tagging any element. An I-beam cursor appears blinking and ready for you to add a tag name. Type text in the text box and be certain to not use spaces or special characters for your tag names. Continue adding tags for each element in the layout. In this example, Figure 30-17 shows all the tags listed in the Tags palette for the design shown earlier in Figure 30-15.

Figure 30-17: Create a new tag for each element in the layout. As yet, the frames are not tagged.

5. **Tag the layout elements.** Tagging elements in the layout is easy. First, select a frame on the document page, then click the corresponding tag name in the Tags palette.

6. **Map tags to style sheets.** Open the Tags palette fly-out menu and select Map Tags to Styles. The Map Tags to Styles dialog box opens as shown earlier in Figure 30-5. All styles are listed as [Not Mapped]. Click a text style (note, you don't have style sheets for the images and therefore do not need to map the images) to open a pull-down menu. Select the style name from the menu. As you created paragraph styles, the names you used for the style sheets appear in the pull-down menu. Click OK after mapping the tags to the style sheets.

7. **Export the tags as an XML file.** Open the Tags palette fly-out menu and select Save Tags. Using this menu command does not create an XML file you use for a layout. It merely exports the tag references in XML format. Type a descriptive name for the exported file such as TagsOnly.XML.

8. **Save the file as a template.** Choose File ⇨ Save As and select InDesign CS2 template From the Format pull-down menu. Click Save and the file is saved as a template. Close the file.

Export InDesign Files as XML

You now have two documents: the original layout and your new InDesign template with XML tags. Your next step is to export the original document as XML. You can import the XML file into the template file without using any text or image placement tools in InDesign. To create an XML file, follow the steps below:

STEPS: Export InDesign Files as XML

1. **Open the original layout.** Choose File ⇨ Open Recent ⇨ and select the original layout you created in InDesign. Note that the filename should appear in the list of recent files.

2. **Import XML tags.** When you created the layout, you didn't add the tags to the layout. You created the tags and saved the tagged file as a template. To export the file with XML tags, you need to tag all the elements in the layout file. Rather than work through the process for tagging each element, you can import the tagged XML file you exported from the template document. From the Tags palette fly-out menu select Load Tags. Locate the file you exported in Step 7 in the section "Tagging an InDesign Document."

3. **Export the layout as XML.** Choose File ➪ Export in InDesign. Type a descriptive name in the Save As text box in the Export dialog box. Be certain to use a name you can clearly distinguish from the XML tags export you saved earlier — something like XML_Layout.XML. From the Format pull-down menu select XML. Click Save and the Export XML dialog box appears.

4. **Export the images from the layout.** In the General pane of the Export XML dialog box, leave the default selection for Encoding as UTF-8 and click Images. Select the check box for the image format you want to export in the Images pane. In this example, Original Images is selected, as shown in Figure 30-18. Click Export and the layout is exported as XML along with a subfolder titled Images containing all your original images.

Figure 30-18: Select the check box for the image format used for the exported images.

Import XML in InDesign

So far, you have created a template, tagged the frame elements with XML tags, tagged style sheets, exported the tags, imported the tags in your original layout, and exported the layout file as XML. At this point, you can open your template file and import the XML. The result after importing the XML is a new file appearing exactly as your original layout. Not so exciting, is it? After all, you could just open an InDesign file and chose File ➪ Save As and save a copy of your original layout if that is what you need.

Let's take another view at using your XML file. Suppose for a moment that you have a product price list containing 100 or more pages and you have several images on each page. Your client wants an updated file for the next sales season, and the client has all new images for the next catalog. Rather than relink all the images in an InDesign document, you can use your XML file to immediately replace all the old images with new images.

To see how easy you can modify a document using XML, follow these steps:

STEPS: Import XML in InDesign

1. **Replace the image files.** Open Adobe Bridge and copy new image files from one Bridge window to the images folder created by InDesign when you exported the images. Move the original images out of the images folder.

2. **Rename the images.** The image files in the images folder were named image1, image 2, and so on, by InDesign when the images were exported with the XML file. You must use identical file names for the XML file to recognize the images and import them in a new layout. Using the Bridge, click a name and type the same names you used when you exported the XML. In Figure 30-19, new files have been copied to the images folder and file names are edited in the Bridge window.

Figure 30-19: Copy a different set of images to the images folder and rename the files to match the original filenames.

Tip

If you have a considerable number of images to change, use the Batch Rename command in Adobe Bridge.

Cross-Reference

For information regarding file and batch renaming in Adobe Bridge, see Chapter 7.

3. **Create a new layout.** Open the template file created in Step 8 in the section "Tagging an InDesign Document" earlier in this chapter. The template opens as an Untitled document.

4. **Import the XML file.** Choose File ➪ Import XML. Locate the exported file. In this example the filename is XML_Layout.XML. Select the file and click Open.

5. **Preview the results.** Choose View ➪ Structure ➪ Hide Structure to hide the Structure pane. Press W to view the document in Preview mode as shown in Figure 30-20. If you followed the steps precisely, you should see a new layout containing different images than your original design. Compare Figure 30-20 with Figure 30-15 to see how the images were changed in this example.

Figure 30-20: Press W to hide guides and frame edges to Preview the new layout.

If your XML import resulted in a problem importing the design elements, you may need to retrace your steps and try to repeat the sequences outlined here. Try a simple layout with one image and one block of text to experiment and understand more about exporting and importing XML in document templates. With a little practice, you can develop skills in using XML in your workflow without having to accumulate a lot of programming knowledge.

Tip

You can change text as well as images when creating new layouts. Open the XML file in GoLive or a text editor and make text changes as desired. Save the edited file back out as a text file, and you can import the file in an InDesign template.

Viewing and Editing XML Data in GoLive

You may open and edit XML documents within GoLive by choosing File ⇨ Open (⌘/Ctrl+O). Opened XML documents appear within GoLive's Outline Editor, as shown in Figure 30-21.

Note

Although XML is not one of the file types in the Open Document dialog box, you can open XML documents when you select the All Documents option.

Figure 30-21: XML documents opened in GoLive appear in the Outline Editor by default.

Using the Outline Editor

The Outline Editor separates all tag sets into individual bars. You can expand each of these bars by clicking on the right arrow (Macintosh) or plus-sign icon (Windows). You can select each bar by clicking on the bar (see Figure 30-21. The selected tag bar is highlighted with a black outline. The tag bars are also listed according to their hierarchy. You can move tag bars within the document by dragging on the tag-bar handle to the left of the tag bar. You can edit and add new code via a context menu (Control + Click on Macintosh or right-click in Windows). The context menu has the following options:

+ **Editing code:** The attributes and content for each tag appear when you click on the plus sign positioned to the right of the bar. Clicking on any of the attributes, content, or tag names opens a text field where you can edit the item. Existing tags may also be cut, copied, and pasted to a different location using the commands in the Edit menu.

Note: The Layout Editor also displays the document in expandable bars, but it lets you edit only the content, not the tags.

+ **Adding new code:** When the Outline Editor is selected, several icon buttons appear in the top toolbar. You can use these buttons to add new items to the XML document. Clicking on any of these buttons adds the selected item to the Outline Editor directly below the current selection where it may be edited. The Toggle Binary button is used to add or remove the closing tag from certain tags that don't need them.

Note the three tools appearing in the top-left corner of the window. Click Layout to open the Layout editor, click Source to open the Source Editor, and click the unlabeled tool appearing to the right of the Source Editor tool to open the Outline Editor.

Using the Source Code Editor

In addition to the Outline Editor, clicking on the Source Code Editor tab at the top of the document window lets you view and edit the actual text contained in the XML document. The Source Code Editor is shown in Figure 30-22.

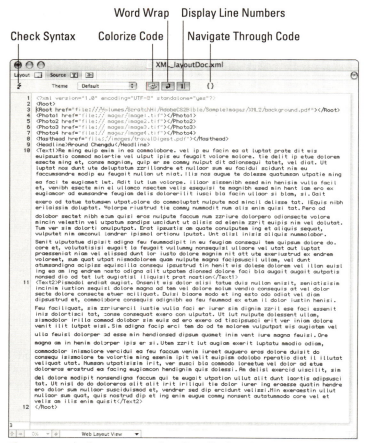

Figure 30-22: The Source Code Editor displays the actual XML text file.

The tools at the top of the editing window provide options for:

✦ **Check Syntax:** Click the tool and the Check Syntax dialog box opens. Errors and warnings are reported for all found syntax errors. This dialog box is like a debugger that helps you target problems and fix them in the editor.

✦ **Colorize Code:** By default, the code is colorized to distinguish different tags. You can turn the color off by clicking the Colorize Code tool.

♦ **Word Wrap:** By default, your data appears along a single line making it almost impossible to edit the code. Click the Word Wrap tool and all the text fits nicely in the editor window.

♦ **Display Line Numbers:** On the left side of the window appear line numbers. Click the Display Line Numbers tool to toggle line numbers off and on.

♦ **Navigate through code:** Click and hold the mouse button down to open a pop-up menu. You use the Navigate Source Code menu in the Source Code editor, the JavaScript Editor, and the CSS Source Code Editor to navigate code by function. From the menu you can select New Marker to add custom markers in the code to help easily navigate to subroutines and code sections.

Splitting the editors

When the Outline or Layout editors are selected, a small double-arrow icon appears at the bottom-left corner of the window. This button is the Show/Hide Split Source button. Clicking this button displays the Outline Editor (or Layout Editor) in the top half of the window and the Source Code Editor in the lower half of the window, as shown in Figure 30-23.

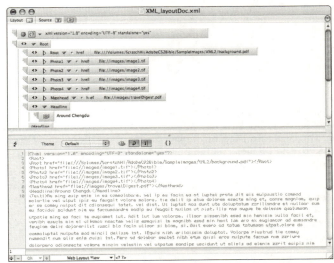

Figure 30-23: Splitting the window lets you view the Outline Editor and the Source Code Editor at the same time.

Tip   Press Option/Alt and click the split source widget and GoLive will change the orientation of the split-source view.

Saving Acrobat Files as XML Documents

You may save Acrobat PDF files as XML documents by choosing File ⇨ Save As. In the file dialog box, name the file, select XML 1.0 as the Save as Type, and click Save.

Note Exporting a PDF file to XML exports only its content. All formatting associated with the content is lost during the conversion process.

The Settings button at the bottom of the file dialog box opens the Save As XML 1.0 Settings dialog box, shown in Figure 30-24.

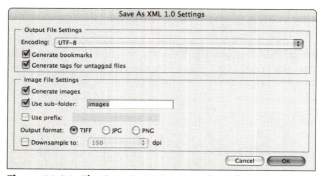

Figure 30-24: The Save As XML 1.0 Settings dialog box

The Encoding options include UTF-8, UTF-16, UCS-4, ISO-Latin-1, HTML/ASCII, and Use Mapping Table Default. The Generate Bookmarks option creates links from all the defined bookmarks in the PDF file. The Generate Tags for Untagged Files option generates tags for all files that aren't already tagged. All PDF files created before Acrobat 4.0 did not use tags; they're given tags if this option is enabled.

To have the PDF image files saved along with the XML file, select the Generate Images option and these images are placed in a designated subfolder if the Use Sub-Folder option is enabled. The Use Prefix option lets you add a prefix to the filename to distinguish it from the original image files. The Output format lets you select to convert the images to TIFF, JPG, or PNG image files. The images may also be downsampled to a specified dpi setting.

Summary

- ✦ Understanding what XML documents are and how they may be used is helpful when encountering XML features in the various CS applications.
- ✦ InDesign documents can use XML as a transport media to tag and export layout content.
- ✦ You can import XML documents into an InDesign document.
- ✦ You can use XML in design workflows to repurpose files.
- ✦ GoLive is useful for viewing, editing, and creating XML documents from scratch.

✦ ✦ ✦

Creative Suite Document Delivery Workflows

PART VIII

In This Part

Chapter 31
Understanding Digital Rights Management

Chapter 32
Creating Interactive Documents

Chapter 33
Hosting Documents on the Web

Chapter 34
Creating and Distributing PDFs on CDs and DVDs

Chapter 35
Creating SWF and SVG Files

Chapter 36
Creating Slide Presentations

Understanding Digital Rights Management

In This Chapter

Getting familiar with Digital Rights Management

Adding security to documents

Securing documents with file attachments

Digital Rights Management (DRM) is a term used to describe protecting intellectual property against unauthorized viewing, editing, reproduction, and/or distribution. As a member of a creative-design workflow, you may want to restrict document viewing to selected individuals; or you may want to share design concepts with clients so they can view your designs, although you don't want the documents printed or edited.

All the CS programs offer you a vehicle for protecting documents via export to PDF. Document security is applied to PDF files and not directly in the CS application documents. Therefore, you first need to know how to generate a PDF from the other CS applications and then apply security either at the time of PDF creation or from within Acrobat. In this chapter, you learn how to export CS application documents to PDF and secure the files against unauthorized viewing, editing, and printing.

Understanding Document Security

Securing documents created with CS applications means you ultimately get a document to PDF and apply Acrobat security either at the time of exporting a file to PDF or later, after you open a PDF in Acrobat. In either case, Acrobat security is used.

Methods of security available in Acrobat include two primary types of encryption. You can secure a file against opening and editing by applying Acrobat security at different levels of encryption, or you can secure files using certificates acquired from users when they create digital IDs. The first method should be thought of as security you might apply globally to PDFs either from within the CS programs at the time of exporting to PDF or later in Acrobat. Security added at the time of export to PDF is generally when you want the public to have a password to open your PDFs or you want to restrict editing features. This type of security is referred to as *unknown users*.

The second method of security is restrictions you want to apply for a selected group of people in your workgroup (coworkers, colleagues, or individuals with whom you have direct communication) or among your client base. This is referred to as *known users*. This method requires the use of digital IDs and Trusted Certificates.

Permissions

Permissions relate to the access you grant end users. You may restrict printing a document and, as such, you grant permission for users to view and possibly edit a file but prevent users from printing. When using the second method of security for known users, you can grant different permissions for different users all in the same document. This form of security uses digital ID identities and is discussed later in the "Securing Files with Identities" section.

Levels of encryption

Depending on the version of Acrobat compatibility you use (for example, Acrobat 4-, 5-, or 6-compatible files), the level of encryption changes according to each compatible file format. Acrobat 4 compatibility uses 40-bit encryption, Acrobat 5 and 6 use 128-bit RC4 encryption, and Acrobat 7 uses 128-bit AES (Advanced Encryption Standard) encryption. The level of encryption is not as important for you to understand as just realizing that, with each level of encryption, Acrobat offers you additional permissions. For example, with Acrobat 4 compatibility, you can grant permissions to print a document or prevent a user from printing a document. With Acrobat 5, 6, and 7 compatibility, where you use 128-bit or greater encryption, you can add to the printing permissions a restriction to only print files as low-resolution prints. This feature and others are added to encryption methods above 40-bit encryption.

 Caution Be aware that anyone using an earlier version of Acrobat cannot open a document with advanced encryption. For example, users of Acrobat 6 cannot open files secured with Acrobat 7-compatibility encryption.

Signature handlers

When you use digital IDs to encrypt files for restricting permissions, Acrobat offers you a choice for using Acrobat Certificate Authority or a signature handler you acquire from a third-party supplier. Acrobat warns you that files secured with Acrobat Certificate Authority carry no guarantee that the security cannot be compromised. For more critical Digital Rights Management, warning dialog boxes point you in the direction of third-party vendors offering signature handlers.

In normal production workflows, you're not concerned with sophisticated signature handlers from third-party vendors. When sending clients drafts of your artwork, the turnaround time is relatively short and the likelihood of a client exerting the energy and taking the time to break password security is incredibly far-fetched. Some algorithms running on powerful computers can take years to break a password.

As a matter of practice, use a minimum of 10 to 12 characters when supplying passwords to protect a file. The more characters you use, the more difficulty a software routine has in trying to break the code.

If you work with sensitive material that requires sophisticated security measures offered by third-party vendors, you can find a list of vendors offering various solutions on Adobe's Web site (www.adobe.com/security).

Securing Documents

If you create an Illustration or a layout, or you have some photos that you need to secure, you can save or export your files as PDF documents and add security at the time you create the PDF. You can also add security in Acrobat for all PDFs created without setting permissions at the time of PDF creation. Regardless of where you add permissions, the options available to you for securing PDFs are the same in all the CS2 programs.

 Because all the CS2 applications use the same Adobe PDF settings used by Acrobat and Acrobat Distiller, security is equally available to all programs including GoLive. In the first release of the CS programs, you could not apply security to PDF documents exported from GoLive.

Adding security in Acrobat

For documents converted to PDF to which you want to add security later, you add permissions in Acrobat. The options you choose are contained in the Password Security – Settings dialog box. To open the dialog box with a document currently open in the Document pane, choose File ➪ Document Properties. When the Document Properties dialog box opens, click Security in the left pane. By default, the security is turned off if you added no security when you exported the PDF or distilled it in Acrobat Distiller. From the Security pull-down menu in the Document Properties dialog box, select Password Security and the Password Security – Settings dialog box opens, shown in Figure 31-1. You can also open the same dialog box by clicking the down arrow in the Secure Task button to open the pull-down menu and select Restrict Opening and Editing.

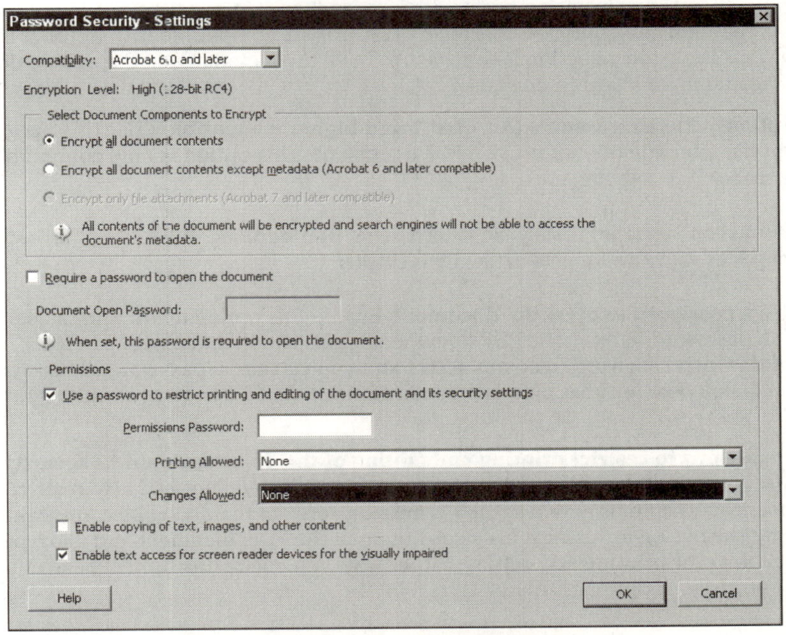

Figure 31-1: The Password Security – Settings dialog box

Note The same options for adding security exist in the PDFMaker for Microsoft Office files and in the Acrobat Distiller for PostScript files. For more information on using Distiller and applying security during distillation, refer to the *Adobe Acrobat 7 PDF Bible* (published by Wiley).

The security you add in this dialog box restricts a user from opening or changing a file's content. Users must know the password you assigned this dialog box to open a file and/or make changes. Realize that you can restrict a file from opening unless a password is supplied or you can omit a password for opening a file but limit permissions for printing and editing. You can add two passwords — one for opening a file and another for restricting editing or printing features. The options in the Password Security – Settings dialog box are:

✦ **Compatibility:** The options from this pull-down menu include Acrobat 3, Acrobat 5, Acrobat 6, and Acrobat 7 compatibility. If you select Acrobat 7 compatibility and save the PDF document, users need an Acrobat viewer of version 6 or greater to open the file. The same holds true when saving with Acrobat 5 compatibility for users who have Acrobat viewers lower than version 5.

✦ **Encryption Level:** Below the Compatibility pull-down menu Acrobat informs you what level of encryption is applied to the document based on the compatibility choice made in the pull-down menu. If you select Acrobat 3 from the Compatibility pull-down menu, the encryption level is 40-bit encryption. Acrobat 5 and Acrobat 6 compatibility are encrypted at 128-bit RCA encryption. Acrobat 7 is 128-bit AES. All the higher encryption levels offer you more options for restricting printing and editing.

✦ **Encrypt all document contents:** This option applies encryption to all document contents.

✦ **Encrypt all document contents except metadata (Acrobat 6 and later compatible):** Use this option to apply encryption to all document contents except document metadata. As the item name implies, this level of security is compatible with Acrobat 6 and above. This is a good selection if you want to have the metadata in your secure documents available for a search engine.

✦ **Encrypt only file attachments (Acrobat 7 and higher compatible):** Use this option to encrypt file attachments but not the PDF document. This option is only compatible with Acrobat 7 and above.

Cross-Reference For information regarding using file attachments and securing PDFs, see the section "Securing Files with Attachments" later in this chapter.

✦ **Require a password to open the document:** Enable this option if you want a user to supply a password to open the PDF document. Once enabled, the field box for Document Open Password becomes active and you can add a password. Before you exit the dialog box, Acrobat prompts you in another dialog box to confirm the password.

✦ **Use a password to restrict printing and editing of the document and its security settings:** You can add a password for opening the PDF document and also restrict permissions from the items active in the Permissions area of the dialog box. You can also eliminate the option for using a password to open the PDF document and make permissions choices for printing and editing. Either way, you check this box to make choices in the Permissions options.

✦ **Permissions Password:** Fill in the field box with a password. If you apply permissions options for opening the PDF and restricting permissions, the passwords must be different. Acrobat opens a dialog box and informs you to make different password choices if you attempt to use the same password for opening the file and setting permissions.

✦ **Printing Allowed:** If you use Acrobat 3 compatibility, the options are available to either enable printing or disallow printing. The choices are None and High Resolution. Although choice reads High Resolution, the result simply enables users to print your file. With Acrobat 5 and 6 compatibility, you have a third choice for enabling printing at a lower resolution (150 dpi). If you select Low Resolution (150 dpi) from the menu options, users are restricted to printing the file at the lower resolution. This choice is typically something you might use for files intended for digital prepress and high-end printing or to protect your content from being printed and then re-scanned.

✦ **Changes Allowed:** From this pull-down menu you make choices for the kinds of changes you allow users to perform on the document. Acrobat 3 compatibility offers you four choices; Acrobat 5, 6, and 7 compatibility offer five choices. These options include:

- **None:** Prevents a user from any kind of editing and content extraction.

- **Inserting, Deleting, and Rotating Pages:** This option is not available when using Acrobat 3 compatibility. Users are permitted to insert, delete, and rotate pages. If you create PDFs for eBooks, allowing users to rotate pages can be helpful when they view PDFs on tablets and portable devices.

- **Page layout, filling in forms, and signing existing signature fields (Acrobat 3 only):** Select this option to enable users to extract pages, insert pages, and also perform actions on form fields.

- **Filling in Form Fields and Signing existing signature fields:** If you create Acrobat Forms and want users to digitally sign documents, enable this check box. Forms are useless to users without the ability to fill in the form fields.

- **Commenting, filling in form fields, and signing existing signature fields:** You might use this option in a review process where you want to have users comment on a design but you don't want them to make changes in your file. You can secure the document against editing, but allow commenting and form field filling in and signing. When you enable form filling in with this option or the Filling in form fields and signing existing signature fields option, users are restricted against changing your form design and cannot make edits other than filling in the fields. A good example of using this option is when you want customers to fill out a form that includes comments that describe their selections.

- **Any Except Extracting Pages:** All the permissions are available to users except extracting pages from the document and creating separate PDFs from selected pages.

✦ **Enable copying of text, images, and other content and access for the visually impaired:** If you restrict permissions for any of the previous pull-down menu options, users aren't allowed to copy data. You can add permission for content copying by enabling this check box. This option is available to users of all Acrobat viewers version 3 and greater.

✦ **Enable text access for screen reader devices for the visually impaired:** This option is available for all versions except Acrobat 3 compatibility. As a matter of practice, selecting this check box is always a good idea because you can restrict all editing features while permitting users with screen-reading devices the ability to read your files. If the check box is not selected, screen readers cannot read the PDF document and all the options for using the View ⇨ Read Out Loud menu command are grayed out. Furthermore, users can index your files with Acrobat Professional by using Acrobat Catalog when this check box is selected, regardless of the other items you prevent users from accessing.

After making decisions for the permissions you want to restrict, you need to save the file. Choose either File ⇨ Save or File ⇨ Save As after making choices in the Password Security – Settings dialog box.

Setting permissions in the Password Security – Settings dialog box works fine for a single PDF document you want to secure, but it's a bit tedious when you want to secure a number of files. For automating the task where a common password is used in all files that need to be secured, you can use the Acrobat Batch Processing command. For a firsthand view of creating a batch sequence and applying steps in the sequence to a collection of PDF documents, follow these steps:

STEPS: Creating and Running Batch Sequences

1. **Open Batch Sequences.** Choose Advanced ⇨ Batch Processing. The Batch Sequences dialog box opens, shown in Figure 31-2.

You can only create and run batch sequences in Acrobat Professional.

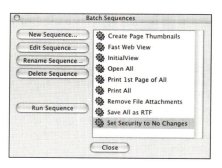

Figure 31-2: The Batch Sequences dialog box creates a new sequence.

2. **Create a new sequence.** Click New in the Batch Sequences dialog box. The Name Sequence dialog box opens. Type a name for your sequence and click OK to open the Batch Edit Sequence – *[name of your sequence]* dialog box shown in Figure 31-3. Note that the name for the dialog box in the figure is Batch Edit Sequence – Add Security. We created a new sequence and named the sequence *Add Security*; thus the name is reflected in the dialog box name. For purposes of clarity, this dialog box is henceforth referred to as the Batch Edit Sequence dialog box.

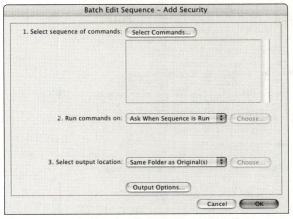

Figure 31-3: The Batch Edit Sequence dialog box

3. **Add Security to the sequence.** Click Select Commands in the Batch Edit Sequence dialog box. The Edit Sequence dialog box opens, shown in Figure 31-4. In the left pane, scroll down the window until you see Security appear at the end of the Document options. Select Security in the left pane and click Add to move Security to the right pane.

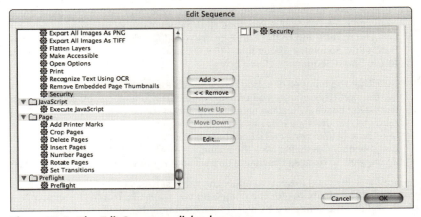

Figure 31-4: The Edit Sequence dialog box

4. **Edit the security permissions.** To set the security permissions, open the Password Security – Settings dialog box. Click on Security in the right pane and click Edit or double-click on Security in the right pane to open the Document Security dialog box. From the pull-down menu, select Password Security and click the Change Settings button to open the Password Security – Settings dialog box, shown in Figure 31-5.

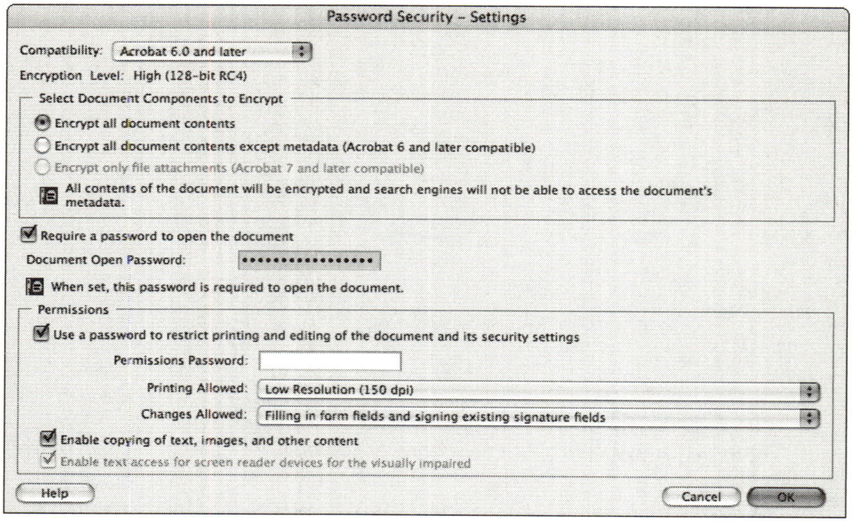

Figure 31-5: The Password Security – Settings dialog box

Edit the security items you want to use, and be certain to use passwords of ten or more characters. Click OK and a warning dialog box opens. Click OK again and the Confirm Permissions Password dialog box opens. Retype your password using the same letter case and click OK. You're returned to the Document Security dialog box. Click Close and you're returned to the Edit Sequence dialog box. Click OK and you arrive at the Batch Edit Sequence dialog box. Click OK again and you see your new sequence added to the Batch Sequences dialog box.

Note that the number of dialog boxes is extraordinary. Just keep in mind that after editing the security options, you return to the Batch Sequences by clicking OK through all the dialog boxes. When the sequence is added to the Batch Sequences dialog box you're ready to run the sequence. You can run a sequence immediately after creating it or at a later time in another Acrobat editing session. After the new sequence is added to the batch Sequences dialog box, the sequence remains there until you physically remove it. If you want to dismiss the dialog box without running a sequence, click Close.

Sequences are designed for you to apply the same settings to a collection of PDF documents. When you set the attributes for the command you want to use and the sequence has been created, you run the sequence by selecting a file, a number of files, or a folder. To run a sequence for applying security to a collection of files, follow these steps:

STEPS: Run a Sequence

1. **Edit a sequence.** Select the new sequence you created in the Batch Sequence dialog box, and click Edit Sequence. The attributes for the security permissions have been defined, but now you need to inform Acrobat where the edited files are to be saved and the file-naming convention you want to use. Note that these options can be assigned at the time you create a sequence, but it's a good idea to visit the Batch Edit Sequence dialog box whenever you run a sequence to be certain you know where your files are saved and the names given to the new files.

2. **Run a command.** In the Batch Edit Sequence dialog box, shown in Figure 31-6, open the pull-down menu for item 2. You have several options from which to choose for when a command is run. The default is Ask When Sequence is Run. When selected, this option instructs Acrobat to prompt you for what files to run a sequence. Other choices enable you to identify a specific folder location, specific files, or currently opened files. The default is set to run a sequence by asking where a navigation dialog box opens and permits you to search through your hard drive to find files you want to add to the sequence. Unless you want to run the sequence on a specific folder, leave the setting at the default.

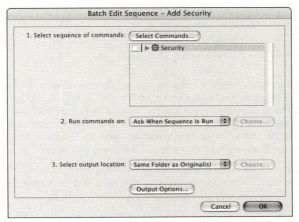

Figure 31-6: The Batch Edit Sequence – Add Security dialog box

 3. **Select an output location.** From the pull-down menu for item 3, you determine where the edited files are saved. The default is set to save files in the same folder as the original files. You also have choices for saving to a specific folder (prompting you for a folder location) or not saving changes. If you save files to the same folder, be careful about overwriting existing files. If you leave the default at Same Folder as Originals, edit the filenames in the Output Options so new files are saved with new names as opposed to overwriting files. If you make mistakes when assigning attributes in your batch sequence, you can always return to the original files.

 4. **Set output options.** Click Output Options and the Output Options dialog box, shown in Figure 31-7, opens. In this dialog box, you assign filenames. You can choose to use the default name for saving files with the same name that ultimately overwrites your existing files, or you can add to an existing name either a prefix or a suffix. If you click Add to Original Base Name(s), the field boxes for Insert Before and Insert After become active. Enter a prefix or suffix extension by typing characters in the field boxes. If you leave the default at Same As Original(s) and check the box for Do Not Overwrite Existing Files, Acrobat automatically adds to the filenames to prevent the new files from overwriting the old files. Make your choices in this dialog box and click OK to return to the Batch Edit Sequence dialog box. Click OK and you return to the original Batch Sequences dialog box.

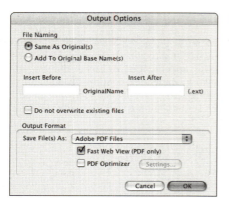

Figure 31-7: The Output Options dialog box

5. **Run a sequence.** In the Batch Sequence dialog box, click on your new sequence and click Run Sequence. If you elected to be prompted for files to select, the Select Files to Process dialog box, opens. Navigate your hard drive and open the folder where the files you want to process are located. To select files individually, ⌘/Ctrl+click to select files in a noncontiguous order. For a contiguous selection, select a file and press the Shift key to select the last file in a list. All files between the two you clicked are selected.

Click the Select button and Acrobat adds security to all the files you selected for processing. After completing the task, be certain to verify files and note the password used to protect the files.

Adding security in other CS Programs

The common denominator for securing all CS applications documents is Adobe PDF. You have two choices for securing documents. You can export the file and essentially turn it into a PDF document whereby security is applied or you can attach a native file to a PDF whereby Acrobat security is also applied. Either way, you eventually work with a PDF document.

For information on securing PDFs with file attachments, see the section "Securing PDFs with File Attachments."

When using Photoshop and Illustrator you create a PDF file by choosing File ➪ Save As and writing the file to the PDF format. When using InDesign and GoLive you create PDF documents by choosing File ➪ Export.

In all applications, you address the Adobe PDF Settings that include applying security. All the options are the same for all CS programs, regardless whether you use Save As or Export.

To understand how security settings are applied to any CS application document look over the following steps:

STEPS: Adding Security to CS2 Application Documents

1. **Launch the Bridge and double-click an image to open it in Photoshop.** You can use any CS program and follow the same steps. In this example Photoshop is used to secure image files.

2. **Open the Save As dialog box.** Choose File ⇨ Save As. The Save As dialog box appears. Select Photoshop PDF from the Format menu and click Save. The Save Adobe PDF dialog box appears.

3. **Apply security settings.** Click Security in the left pane. Select an Adobe PDF Preset from the pull-down menu at the top of the dialog box. Select a compatibility option from the Compatibility pull-down menu. Select the options you want to use for your security settings such as using an open password and/or adding editing privileges. Add a password and click Save PDF. In Figure 31-8, a password is used for opening the document.

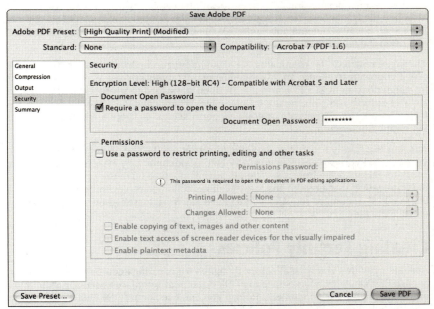

Figure 31-8: Apply security settings in the Save Adobe PDF dialog box.

4. **Confirm your password.** A second dialog box appears, prompting you to confirm the password. Type the same password used in the first dialog box and click OK. The file is saved with the settings applied for security. Note that passwords are case sensitive. Be certain to record passwords used for your files, including case sensitivity.

Note There are more options available to you for securing documents using the Adobe Policy Server and CDS partners. The scope of document security in Acrobat is enormous and is beyond the scope of this book. For an exhaustive authoritative description on Acrobat security see the *Adobe Acrobat 7 PDF Bible* (Wiley Publishing).

Securing Files with Attachments

If your workflow requires you to exchange original documents that need to be secured, obviously converting to PDF isn't a solution. With the exception of applying security to Web page designs in GoLive, the CS programs don't offer you options for securing files unless you convert to PDF. However, you can use PDF to protect native documents against unauthorized opening and viewing and you can attach any file to a PDF. If the need arises for protecting word-processing files, spreadsheets, financial documents, layouts, images, and so on, you can use PDF as the container for native files and password-protect the contents.

Note   You can attach all files to PDF documents with the exception of ZIP and EXE files on Windows. These file types are prohibited to prevent the spread of viruses.

By using file attachments in Acrobat, you use the PDF as a wrapper and secure the PDF document with open permissions. If a user doesn't have a password to open the PDF document, the attached file is inaccessible. If your clients use the Adobe Reader software, you can secure PDFs with file attachments and exchange the PDFs with Adobe Reader users who can extract and open the attachments.

There are restrictions when using file attachments compared to using PDF security. For example, if you want to secure an InDesign file against unauthorized viewing, you can embed the InDesign document in a PDF and use an open password to protect the file. However, you can't restrict editing and printing the InDesign file. When using file attachments, you prevent users from viewing the documents or grant all permissions — there are no other options for securing native documents.

Acrobat is a handy tool for exchanging files that need to be protected against unauthorized viewing, and you can easily secure any kind of document by attaching the file to a PDF. For users to extract a file from a secured PDF, they need to have the open password and the original application that created the file attachment. For example, embedding a Microsoft Word file in a PDF document requires you to have MS Word installed on your computer in order to extract the file.

Creating Security Policies

Acrobat provides you with a feature designed for creating secure PDF eEnvelopes know as Secure PDF Delivery. eEnvelopes are PDF document templates used for attaching any file and securing the PDF document. Before you can use Secure PDF Delivery, you need to create a Security Policy.

New Feature   Security Policies are a new feature in Acrobat 7 Professional.

Security Policies are like style sheets used to apply security to PDF documents. With all the attributes from which to choose for applying security to a PDF document, you need to spend some time each opening the Password Security – Settings dialog box, select options for securing a file, and apply a security password. To simplify the process you can capture all the settings used for securing a file and save the settings as a new policy. When you want to use the same policy to secure additional files, you select the policy without having to revisit the Password Security – Settings dialog box and adjust all the options choices.

You can use Security Policies with digital IDs and when you apply Acrobat Security. Creating and using digital IDs is complex and a lengthy subject. If you want to learn how to create and use digital IDs see the Acrobat Help file or the lengthy description covering the subject in the *Adobe Acrobat 7 PDF Bible* (Wiley Publishing). To create a Security Policy using Acrobat Security, follow these steps:

STEPS: Creating a Security Policy

1. **Launch Acrobat 7 Professional.** Double-click the Acrobat program icon or an alias of the program on your desktop to launch Adobe Acrobat.

2. **Open the Managing Security Policies window.** Click the Secure task button, and from the pull-down menu shown in Figure 31-9, click Manage Security Policies. The Managing Security Policies window opens.

Figure 31-9: Open the Secure task button pull-down menu and select Manage Security Policies.

3. **Open the New Security Policy wizard.** Click New in the top-left corner of the Managing Security Policies window. The New Security Policy wizard opens. Creating security polices is handled in a wizard that walks you through each step in the process.

4. **Select the type of security to use in the new policy.** You have three options in the first pane in the New Security Policy wizard. Leave the default selection for Use Passwords selected and click Next. The other options offer you choices when creating digital IDs and using the Adobe Policy Server. (See the Acrobat Help document to learn more about the other options).

5. **Add a policy name and description.** The next pane in the New Security Policy wizard provides options for adding a name and description. You can choose to discard the settings after using the policy, but if you want to reuse the same security settings when you create additional eEnvelopes, be certain the Save these settings as a policy radio button is selected. In the Policy name text box, type a name for your new policy. Below the policy name, type a description for the policy. Be certain to add descriptive information that adequately identifies your policy similar to what you see in Figure 31-10. Select the Save passwords with the policy check box. Saving the password enables you to use the same password each time the policy is used. If you leave the check box deselected, you can change the password each time the policy is applied. Click Next after setting the attributes in the General settings pane.

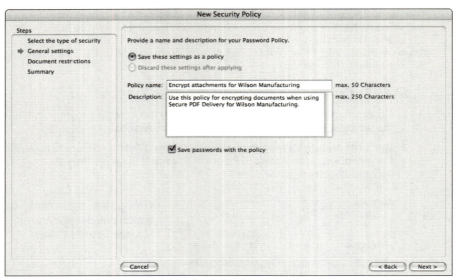

Figure 31-10: Add a name and description in the General Settings pane.

6. **Make security settings choices for the policy.** The Document restrictions pane offers you security settings options identical the to the options described in the section "Securing Documents" earlier in this chapter. Make choices for the compatibility level, the document components you want to encrypt, passwords to open and/or change the document, and the permissions you want to grant. Note that using restrictions in the Permissions section of the pane shown in Figure 31-11 applies only to PDF documents. If you want to use the policy strictly to grant permissions for accessing a file attachment, don't both making options choices in the Permissions section. Click Next when you finish adding the options choices.

7. **Confirm the password.** After clicking Next, a dialog box appears prompting you to confirm the password(s) used in the Document restrictions pane. Type the password(s) exactly the same as applied in the Document restrictions pane including case sensitivity. Be certain to record the passwords used for the policy.

8. **Review the Summary.** The next pane provides you a summary view for the settings you made for your policy (see Figure 31-12). Be certain to review the information and be certain what you see is an accurate description for the policy you want to create. If all information is correct, click Finish to complete creating the new policy. If you need to revisit a pane, click Back to make adjustments in the previous panes.

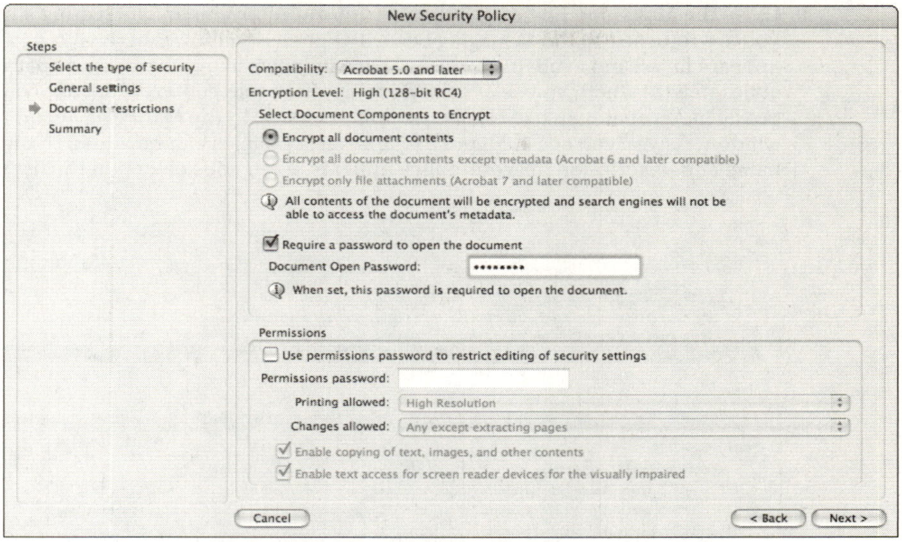

Figure 31-11: Make security choices for the new policy.

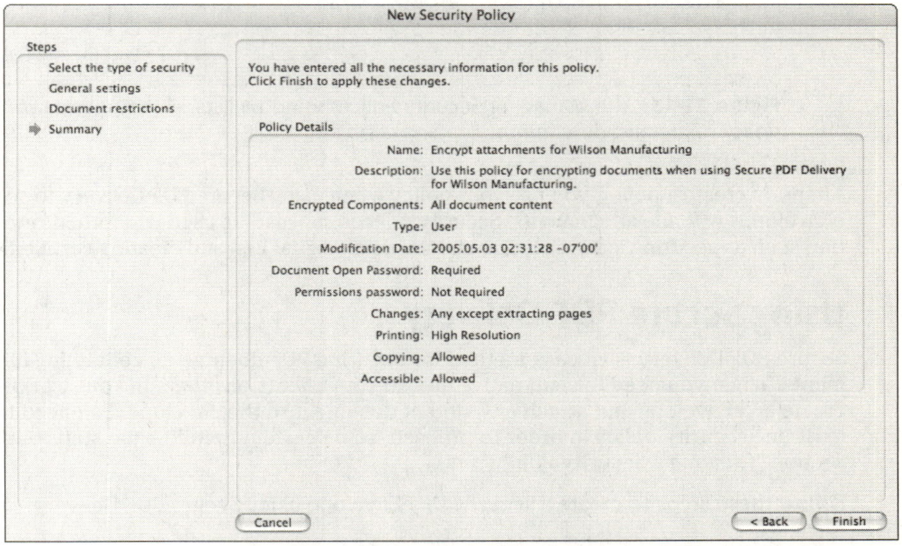

Figure 31-12: Review the Summary and click Finish if the settings accurately describe the policy choices you made.

9. **Close the Managing Security Policies window.** After you finish creating a new policy you are returned to the Managing Security Policies window where your new policy appears listed and available for use. This window is like a character or paragraph styles palette where you select a style to apply to a selection. When applying a security policy in Acrobat, you use one of the policies listed in the Managing Security Policies window. As you can see in Figure 31-13, several policies can be added to the list and the name and description for your policy appears when you select it in the list window.

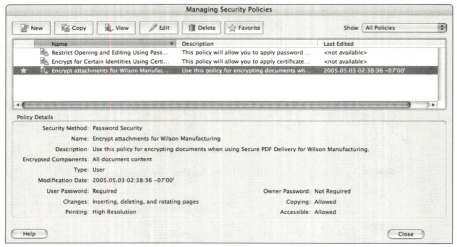

Figure 31-13: The Managing Security Polices window lists all the policies you create with policy name and description.

After you create a policy, you use your policy when using Secure PDF Delivery to secure eEnvelopes with file attachments. Security polices can also be used with other forms of encryption such as securing individual documents, using digital IDs, and creating certified documents.

Using Secure PDF Delivery

Secure PDF Delivery is an easy method for securing PDF documents containing file attachments. When you need to send native files to your clients or others in your workflow you can create an eEnvelope and attach any kind of document to the envelope. You need to have at least one security policy in order to proceed, so be certain to follow the steps outlined in the section "Creating a Security Policy."

Follow these steps to create a secure PDF eEnvelope using Secure PDF Delivery:

STEPS: Using Secure PDF Delivery

1. **Launch Acrobat.** If Acrobat is not open, double-click the program icon or an alias of the program on your desktop. When Acrobat opens, you don't need to open a file in the Document pane. Secure PDF Delivery can be used without open files in Acrobat.

2. **Open the Create Secure Envelope wizard.** Click the Secure task button and select Secure PDF Delivery (shown in Figure 31-14). The Create Secure eEnvelope wizard opens when you create an eEnvelope.

Figure 31-14: Open the Secure task button pull-down menu and select Secure PDF Delivery.

3. **Select a file to attach to the eEnvelope.** The first pane in the Creating Secure eEnvelope wizard provides an option for selecting the file you want to attach to your envelope. Any file on your hard drive can be used except a ZIP or EXE file on Windows. Click the Add file to send button below the list window. The Choose the files to enclose dialog box opens. Navigate your hard drive and select the file(s) you want to attach to the envelope. Note that you can Shift+click (Command/Control + click) to select multiple files. You can add a file and click the Add files to enclose button again when adding files from different folders. After adding files, click Next to advance to the next pane.

4. **Choose the envelope template.** The second pane offers some predesigned templates from which you can choose or an option for using your own design. If choose a custom template, the file needs to be a PDF document. Select a template from the list shown in Figure 31-15, or click Browse to locate your own custom design. In this example, template2.pdf is used. This template adds a date stamp from your system clock. After selecting a template, click Next to advance to the next pane.

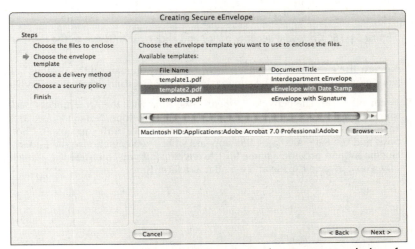

Figure 31-15: Select a template or click Browse to locate a custom design of your choice.

5. **Choose a delivery method.** The Delivery method pane offers two options. Select the Complete the eEnvelope manually option or the Email the completed eEnvelope option. If you choose the first option, you create the envelope and can save it to your hard drive for sending at a later time. If you select the second option, you save the envelope to your hard drive and the saved file is added to a new message window as an e-mail attachment in your default e-mail program. Make a choice from the options and click Next. In this example, the envelope is completed manually for emailing at a later time.

6. **Choose a Security Policy.** Select the check box for Show all policies and the list window displays the policies available to you (see Figure 31-16). You can select one of the policies you previously created or click the New Policy button and the Managing Security Policies window opens where you create a new policy as was described in the "Creating Security Policies." Select a policy or create a new one and click Next to advance to the next pane.

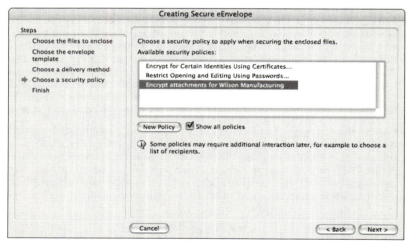

Figure 31-16: Choose a security policy and click Next to move to the last pane.

7. **Review the summary.** The last pane provides a summary of the options selected for your eEnvelope. Review the summary and click Finish to create the eEnvelope.

8. **Secure the file.** The eEnvelope opens in Acrobat with the Attachments pane open showing you the file attachments added to the envelope. Note in Figure 31-17 the document is time and date stamped. The file is not secure until you save it. Choose File ⇨ Save and the Save As dialog box appears where you can choose the folder to save the document and provide a name for the envelope. If you complete the eEnvelope manually, you can save the file and e-mail it at a later time.

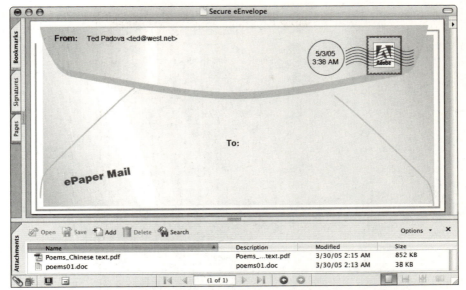

Figure 31-17: The eEnvelope is created from the template, and the Attachments pane displays the file attachments added to the envelope.

Summary

+ Different levels of security can prevent users of Acrobat viewers earlier than version 6 from opening files. It's important to know your user audience and what version of Acrobat viewers they use before securing files.

+ You can apply security to PDF documents that restrict open permissions and different levels of editing.

+ You can secure files from any CS2 application when you convert them to PDF. All the CS2 applications use the same Adobe PDF settings to convert document files to PDF.

+ PDF documents can contain file attachments from any document type except ZIP and EXE files on Windows. You can secure the PDF against unauthorized opening to prevent anyone from viewing the file attachments.

+ Security Policies are like style sheets. You can create a policy setting all the permissions attributes and reuse the policy each time you want to encrypt a file with the same permissions.

+ You use secure PDF Delivery to create eEnvelopes where you can create PDFs from templates, attach documents to the template, and secure the file with security policy permissions.

✦ ✦ ✦

Creating Interactive Documents

CHAPTER 32

In This Chapter

Working with hyperlinks

Creating animation

Adding movies and sound

Creating interactive publications

Creating document designs using JavaScript

With increasing demand for more dynamic messaging, the world of advertising and graphic design has changed greatly in recent years from the delivery of static printed matter to more interactive content. With the advent of the Web, and it's fruition in the mid-1990s, the vehicle for communication has set standards for creative professionals to meet demands for more interesting delivery of information in the form of multimedia and interactive tools that enable readers to explore information according to personal interests. Today's reader audience is becoming more familiar with information that stimulates the senses and provides for quick access to the interests of individual readers.

With the Creative Suite applications you have many tools for creating dynamic content in the form of integrating video, sound, and interactive buttons that provide readers methods for exploring information in exciting ways. In one way or another, each CS2 program provides you with opportunities to add dynamic content and/or interactive elements to your documents.

Creating Hyperlinks

Hyperlinks are nothing new to computer programs and computer systems. In the late 1980s Apple Computer introduced a program called HyperCard that might be thought of as the foundation for interactive document viewing that we now see on the Web. HyperCard was designed to provide users a tool whereby they could create links and buttons to branch out to other HyperCard pages containing information according to user interest. The premise was that we investigate and explore information in a nonlinear form according to our areas of interest. Unlike newspaper and magazine articles designed for linear viewing starting at the beginning and reading through to the end, hypertext reading enables you to navigate to a page and then branch to another page you choose from a selection of hypertext references (buttons).

Hyperlinks are obviously tools you use when viewing electronic documents and therefore require you to move away from print and look at other alternatives for deploying your creative work, such as CD/DVD-ROM, the Internet, or locally on your own computer. The CS2 programs provide you with tools to create hypertext references and enable you to explore new markets for eMagazines, eBooks, and a variety of other eContent.

When creating electronic brochures, magazines, and other content designed for interactive viewing, you have choices for creating interactive elements in the CS programs or in Adobe Acrobat. The final packaging of your content is likely to be either PDF documents or Web pages. In some cases, you may create interactive PDFs that are deployed as Web-hosted documents.

At the creation stage of your workflow, you choose either of the following paths:

✦ Add hyperlinks in a program like Adobe InDesign.

✦ Create an InDesign document without hyperlinks and convert to PDF. Then create the hyperlinks in Acrobat.

If you decide to create the links in Adobe InDesign, you can export the InDesign document to PDF and the resultant PDF recognizes the hyperlinks you added in InDesign. Where you create the links is a matter of personal choice. In some cases you may find it easier to create links in InDesign and at other times find it easier to create links in Acrobat. Therefore, it's helpful if you know a little bit about the methods in each program so you can recognize benefits and limitations of using one program or another.

Tip

Regardless of what program you work with, the process for creating links is the same. You always navigate to the destination view and then assign the link properties. In InDesign, you create a destination view, such as Page 3 at 200 percent. You then create a hyperlink where you select the destination view in the hyperlink properties. In Acrobat, you create a link or button, navigate to the destination view and then assign the link/button properties to the view. This is a consistent method regardless of whether you link to page views, layer views, or open secondary document views.

Creating links and buttons in InDesign

The most common hyperlinks are used for page and document navigation. You create a button or link with an action that opens a page view in the existing document or opens another document. InDesign supports creating these views. However, before you decide to create links in InDesign, you should be aware of the benefits and limitations of InDesign links. The primary benefit and limitation are:

✦ **Benefit:** If you intend to export to PDF, you can create interactive links in InDesign that are included in the exported document. This option eliminates a need to know more about creating links and buttons in Acrobat. When you need frequent revisions on an InDesign document, creating links in InDesign can be beneficial.

✦ **Disadvantage:** If you intend to export your InDesign file to PDF, links that you create in InDesign are converted to *Destinations* in Adobe Acrobat. Destinations are similar to bookmarks where destination views are captured. You click the link button and the action takes you to the destination. Destinations have one disadvantage over bookmarks and links in Acrobat as they carry with them a lot of unnecessary overhead resulting in larger files sizes. Therefore, when files need to be smaller for Web hosting, creating links in Acrobat will keep the files smaller.

Hyperlinks and destinations are managed in the Hyperlinks palette. Choose Window ➪ Interactive ➪ Hyperlinks to open the palette. As you create hyperlinks the hyperlink names are added to the palette. Three options exist for hyperlinks. You can create a link to a Page, a Text Anchor, and to a URL. As the links are added, the palette shows the link name with an icon representing the type of link created. In Figure 32-1 you see four links. Beginning with the top link, the icon indicates a text anchor, followed by a URL link, a page link, and the last item displays a link to an unnamed destination.

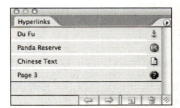

Figure 32-1: The Hyperlinks palette lists all hyperlinks for a document.

The tools at the bottom of the palette are used for navigating links. Click the left arrow to move to the previous link destination and the right arrow to move to the next link destination. The Create New Hyperlink tool is used to create a new hyperlink. The Trash icon is used to delete hyperlinks listed in the palette. The right-pointing arrow in the palette opens a palette fly-out menu where options appear for selecting hyperlink attributes such as editing names, destinations, sorting the link names, resetting links, and updating them.

Specifying a hyperlink destination

Before creating a hyperlink, it's easiest if you first to create a destination. This is the target location for the hyperlink. To create a new destination, select the New Hyperlink Destination palette menu command. This opens the dialog box shown in Figure 32-2 and presents three different destination types — Page, Text Anchor, and URL:

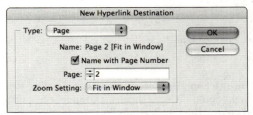

Figure 32-2: The New Hyperlink Destination dialog box helps you create destinations.

 Note If you link to a text anchor, you must first select text on a page before you create the hyperlink destination. Creating page and URL destinations doesn't require selecting any content.

A Page destination lets you create a hyperlink that jumps to a specified page, like what you'd link from in a table of contents or an index. The Name field lets you enter a name that you can select when you create the hyperlink, or you can enable the Name with Page Number option to automatically set the name to the selected page number. The Zoom Setting option lets you specify the zoom level when the page is displayed. The options include Fixed, Fit View, Fit in Window, Fit Width, Fit Height, Fit Visible, and Inherit Zoom.

The Text Anchor option makes the selected text an anchor that the hyperlink jumps to. For this anchor, you may give it a name that is used to select the anchor in the Create Hyperlink dialog box. The URL option lets you name and specify the Web address of a site on the Web.

Creating a new hyperlink

After you create and name a destination, you can select an item in the current document for use as a new hyperlink. You then create the hyperlink using the New Hyperlink palette menu command or by clicking on the Create New Hyperlink button at the bottom of the Hyperlinks palette.

This opens the New Hyperlink dialog box (Figure 32-3) where you can give the hyperlink a name, specify a destination, and determine its appearance. In the Destination section, select a document from the open documents or browse to another local document using the Browse option. The Type list includes the Page, Text Anchor, URL and All Types options, and the Name drop-down list lets you choose from the named destinations already created. There is also a None option that you may select if you have not yet created or named the destination.

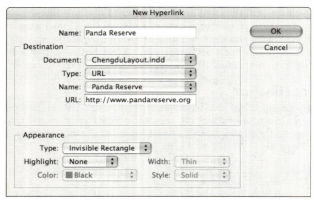

Figure 32-3: The New Hyperlink dialog box lets you specify link properties.

The Appearance section lets you define how the hyperlink looks. The Type could be Visible Rectangle or Invisible Rectangle; the Highlight could be None, Invert, Outline, or Inset; the Color could be one of many default named colors; the Width could be Thin, Medium, or Thick; and the Style could be Solid or Dashed. The Highlight appearance shows up only when the document is exported to PDF.

After the Create Hyperlink dialog box is closed, the new hyperlink appears in the Hyperlinks palette and the hyperlink content in the document is highlighted using the designated appearance settings. An icon denoting the type of hyperlink appears to the right of the hyperlink name in the Hyperlinks palette. Choose View ➪ Show/Hide Hyperlinks to hide all the hyperlinks. To edit an existing hyperlink, double-click on it in the Hyperlinks palette or select the Hyperlink Options menu command.

Testing hyperlinks

To test a hyperlink, simply select it in the Hyperlinks palette and choose the Go to Destination palette menu command. To see the hyperlink's source, select the Go to Source menu command. These commands are also available as icon buttons at the bottom of the Hyperlinks palette. If the destination is a URL, a Web browser opens and tries to load the requested URL.

Creating links and buttons in Acrobat

If your InDesign document or any other CS2 application document is designed for deployment in PDF, then Acrobat is where you want to add interactivity. Acrobat provides so many more options for adding hypertext and interactivity in a document than InDesign, you'll want to work in Acrobat without bothering to add the interactive elements in InDesign. What's more, Acrobat is a bit more intuitive and much more flexible when adding links and buttons.

Creating icon appearances

For a moment let's deviate from Acrobat and look at how you might go about creating icons that can be used for button faces in Acrobat. In order to use a button face, you need to have a PDF file or an AI file containing several pages of icons or several PDF documents you want to use for button faces. If you want to use buttons to navigate forward and back in a PDF document, you need an icon for going forward and one for moving backward. If you want a rollover appearance, you need four icons — two for the forward button and two for the back button.

To create button icons you can use Illustrator, InDesign, or Photoshop. In Illustrator CS2, you can create multipage PDF files, and Illustrator provides you with all the tools needed to create some nifty buttons. To create such a file, follow these steps:

STEPS: Creating Link Button Faces in Adobe Illustrator

1. **Create a new document in Adobe Illustrator.** Choose File ⇨ New in Illustrator. In the New Document dialog box, create an Artboard Setup of 2 inches by 2 inches. Select RGB color option, as you see in Figure 32-4.

If your unit of measure is not set to inches, press Command/Ctrl+K to open the Preferences dialog box. Select Units and Display Performance from the pull-down menu. Select Inches from the General pull-down menu and click OK. When you return to the document window, your unit of measure displays inches.

2. **Draw ruler guides.** Press Command/Ctrl+R to show rulers. Drag a guideline to the vertical and horizontal centers (the 1-inch mark on the rulers). The guidelines display four quadrants that eventually become your four pages.

Figure 32-4: Create a new custom page 2 inches square and set the color mode to RGB.

3. **Create an icon.** Choose Type ➪ Glyphs to open the Glyphs palette. Select a font from the pull-down menu at the bottom of the palette. Locate a symbol in the palette you want to use. With the Type tool, click the document page and double-click the character in the Glyphs palette. The symbol is added as type to the document page, as shown in Figure 32-5.

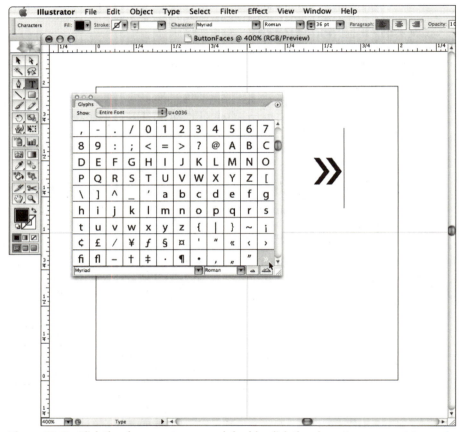

Figure 32-5: Click the document page and double-click the character you want to use in the Glyphs palette.

Cross-Reference

For more information regarding working with the Glyphs palette, see Chapter 19.

4. **Define the type attributes.** Set the type character to a size within one-eighth inch of the first quadrant. Open the Control palette and stroke and/or fill as you like.

5. **Create the rollover icon.** Duplicate the icon by pressing Option/Alt and drag to the second quadrant. Use a different color for the rollover appearance. Repeat steps 3 through 5 to create icons symbolizing moving in an opposite direction. The final image should look like something similar to the preview shown in Figure 32-6.

Figure 32-6: For a 2-inch-square art board, add 1 inch for the width and height for the Media size.

6. **Set the tile attributes.** Illustrator does not support multiple pages, but you can print tiles (divisions of a page) as separate PDF files. To set up the tiling of a document choose File ➪ Print. In the General pane, select Custom from the Media pull-down menu. Type **1** in the Width and Height text boxes. Note the values here have to be smaller than the art board size you created in step 1 in order to tile the document.

7. **Set the tile marks.** Click Setup in the left pane. Open the Tiling pull-down menu and select Tile Imageable Areas. Note the preview in the Print dialog box. You should see the page tiles represented by dashed lines, as shown in Figure 32-7.

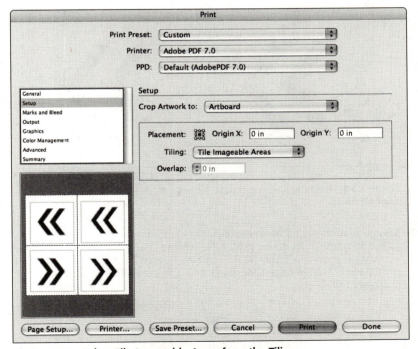

Figure 32-7: Select Tile Imageable Areas from the Tiling pull-down menu.

Cross-Reference For more information on tiling pages in Illustrator, see Chapter 36.

8. **Return to the document window.** Click Done in the Print dialog box. Note that the file does not print if you click Done. The document should appear like you see in Figure 32-8. The numbers on the four quadrants do not print. They are visible on the page to show the order of printing.

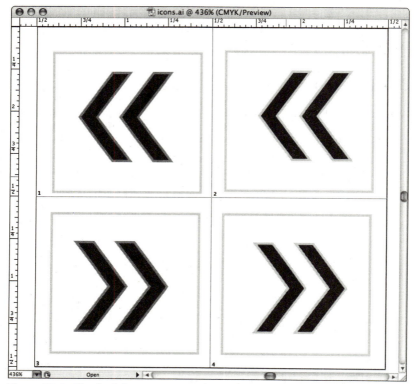

Figure 32-8: The final document page shows the tile marks and nonprinting page numbers.

9. **Save as a multi-page PDF document.** Choose File ⇨ Save As. Select Adobe PDF for the format in the Save As dialog box and click Save. The Save Adobe PDF dialog box appears, as shown in Figure 32-9. Select an Adobe PDF Preset and select the Create Multi-page PDF from Page Tiles check box. Click Save PDF and the file is saved as a four-page PDF file.

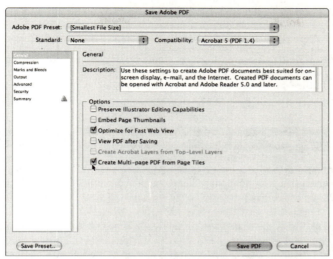

Figure 32-9: Select the Create Multi-page PDF from Page Tiles check box, and click Save PDF to create a four-page PDF document.

Adding links in Acrobat

Acrobat Professional has two tools you can use for creating links to document views and to link to secondary documents. The Link and the Button tool can be used to link to the same destinations. Where links and buttons differ is with appearances and the ability to replicate across multiple pages. Only the Button tool offers you icon representations for image appearances and the ability to duplicate the buttons across all pages in a document. As an example, you might use a button as a navigation instrument to help users move forward and back between pages while viewing PDFs in Full Screen mode. While in Full Screen view the navigation tools are hidden. If you followed the steps for Creating Link Button faces in Adobe Illustrator, you can use the PDF file to follow the steps below:

STEPS: Adding Hypertext Links in Acrobat

1. **Open a PDF document in Acrobat.** Create a design in InDesign or Illustrator and convert it to PDF. Try to use a design of multiple pages.

2. **Open the Forms toolbar.** Choose Tools ⇨ Advanced Editing ⇨ Show Forms Toolbar. The Forms toolbar opens as a floating toolbar in the Acrobat window (see Figure 32-10). Note that the Forms toolbar cannot be opened from a context menu opened from the Acrobat Toolbar Well.

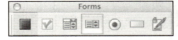

Figure 32-10: The Button tool is the first tool contained in the Forms toolbar.

3. **Create a button.** The first tool in the Forms toolbar is the Button tool. Select the tool and drag a rectangle on the first page in the document. You can draw the rectangle anywhere on the page and move it after setting the button properties.

4. **Name the button field.** After creating a rectangle on the document page the Button properties dialog box opens with the General pane in view, as shown in Figure 32-11. Type a name in the Name text box. In this example, *goNext* is the name used for the button field.

Why use type characters for button faces?

We could have created hand-drawn or scanned illustrations and saved the file as PDF. However, using type characters gives you a benefit that illustrated artwork doesn't. The type characters attributes can be changed in Acrobat. You can change the color of your icons in Acrobat even if you don't have the embedded font installed in your system.

Open a PDF document in Acrobat like the one exported to PDF in Figure 32-8. Select the TouchUp Text tool and drag across the type character. From a context menu, select Properties. The TouchUp Properties dialog box opens, as shown in the following figure. Click the Fill (or Stroke) swatch to open the pop-up color swatch palette. Select a color or click Other Color to select a custom color from your system palette. Click Close and the highlighted text changes color as defined in the swatch palette.

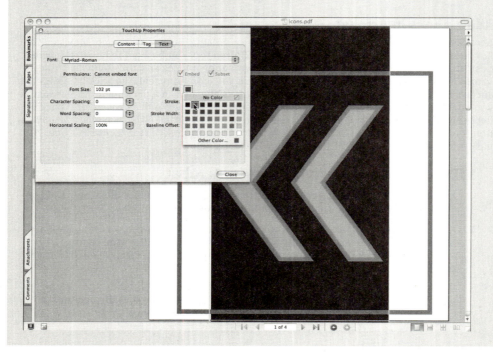

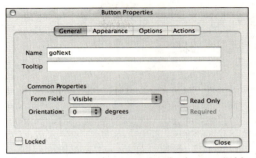

Figure 32-11: Type a name for the button field.

5. **Set the button appearance.** Click the Appearance tab to open the Appearance pane shown in Figure 32-12. Click the Border Color and Fill Color to open pop-up palettes and select No Color from the palette options.

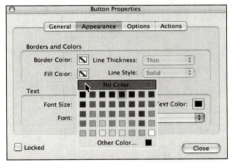

Figure 32-12: Set the appearance to no border color and no fill color.

6. **Add a button face.** Click the Options tab to open the Options pane. From the Layout pull-down menu select Icon only. Select Push from the Behavior pull-down menu. Click Up in the State window and click Choose Icon. A Select Icon dialog box appears. Click Browse and navigate your hard drive to locate a file to use as your button image. The file should be a PDF document. If using a multipage PDF document, you can scroll pages in the Select Icon dialog box by moving the scroll bar at the right side of the dialog box (see Figure 32-13).

7. **Add a rollover effect.** Click OK in the Select Icon dialog box and you return to the Button Properties. Select Rollover in the State window (Figure 32-14) and click Choose Icon. Select the icon you want to use for the rollover appearance in the Select Icon dialog box and click OK to return again to the Button Properties.

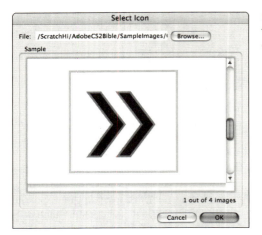

Figure 32-13: Scroll pages by dragging the scroll bar on the right side of the dialog box.

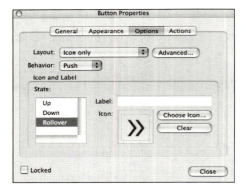

Figure 32-14: Select Rollover and click Choose Icon again to select an icon for the rollover appearance.

8. **Assign an Action.** Click the Actions tab to open the Actions pane. From the Select Action pull-down menu select Execute Menu Item. The Execute Menu Item action enables you to use all the menu commands in Acrobat as the button action. For example, if you want to open a file, you would use the Execute Menu Item and choose File ➪ Open for the menu item to execute.

9. **Define the Action.** Click Add in the Actions pane. On Windows, the Menu Item Selection dialog box appears. Select the menu item in the dialog box you want to use. In this example, choose View ➪ Go To ➪ Next Page. On the Macintosh, the Menu Item dialog box appears. You make your choices from the Acrobat top-level menu. Choose View ➪ Go To ➪ Next Page. Click OK and you should see the Execute Menu Item added to the Actions window as a Mouse Up action (see Figure 32-15). Leave the Button Properties dialog box open.

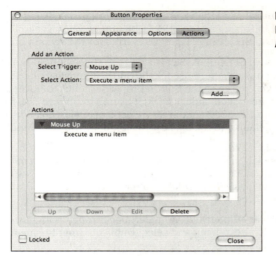

Figure 32-15: Actions added in the Button Properties are shown in the Actions window.

The advantage of using buttons in Acrobat instead of links, and the advantages for creating button links in Acrobat over InDesign are the options you have for quick and easy duplication of buttons across all pages in a document. To duplicate buttons, follow these steps:

STEPS: Duplicating Button Links

1. **Duplicate a button on a page.** To follow these steps, first complete all previous steps in the section "Adding Hypertext Links in Acrobat." Click the Select Object tool in the Acrobat Toolbar Well (selection arrow). Move the button rectangle on the page to the lower-right corner of the document page. Press Option/Ctrl, then press Shift and drag the rectangle to the left corner of the page. The button is duplicated.

Creating URL links in PDF files

When you assign actions to buttons, links, and a number of other items such as bookmarks, page actions, document actions, and so on, you can select from a number of different action types. Among the action types is Open a Web Link. If you create a button or link, you can use the Open a Web Link action and type a URL in the Edit URL dialog box that appears when you click Add in the Actions tab.

Each link or button added to a PDF document increases file size. If you duplicate buttons across all pages, the buttons can add significantly to the file size. Rather than create URL links from links or buttons in Acrobat, you can type URL text in InDesign before PDF creation. If you want to add a URL link on all pages in the document, create the URL on a master page and be certain to use the complete URL address such as `http://www.mycompany.com`. For information related to working with master pages in InDesign, see Chapter 25.

When you open PDFs in Acrobat or Adobe Reader 7, you don't need to create links or buttons for URL links. Acrobat and Adobe Reader 7 are intelligent enough to recognize URL links described in text on pages.

2. **Name the new button.** You should still have the Button Properties dialog box open. If not, double-click the new button using the Select Object tool. Click General and type a new name for this button. In this example, goPrev is used for the second button name.

3. **Change icon appearances.** Click Options. Select Up in the State window and click Choose Icon. Select the icon you want to use for the button to navigate backward in the document. Click OK, and you return to the Button Properties. Click Rollover and click Choose Icon. Select the rollover icon and click OK. If using a multipage PDF document, you don't need to search for the document in the Select Icon dialog box. The last file you visited becomes the new default and remains the default until you select another file.

4. **Edit the Action.** Click Actions. When you copied the button, all the button attributes were also copied. The last action assigned to the button was Execute Menu Item. Select Execute Menu Item in the Actions list window and click Edit. Visit the View menu and choose View ➪ Go To ➪ Previous Page. Click OK to return to the Button Properties and click Close to dismiss the dialog box.

5. **Duplicate the buttons across all pages.** Draw a marquee through both buttons with the Select Object tool. Open a context menu and select Duplicate from the menu commands, as shown in Figure 32-16.

Figure 32-16: Open a context menu on the selected buttons and choose Duplicate.

6. **Specify the page range.** The Duplicate Field dialog box opens after selecting the Duplicate command. Select All in the Duplicate Field dialog box (see Figure 32-17) to duplicate the button across all pages. Click OK and the button is duplicated.

Figure 32-17: Select All and click OK to duplicate the buttons across all pages.

7. **Remove nonfunctional buttons.** The first page *goPrev* button doesn't have a page to open and the last page *goNext* button doesn't have a page to open. Click each of these buttons with the Select Object tool and press Delete/Backspace or Num Pad Del to remove the buttons. To test the actions, click the Hand tool in the Toolbar Well and click the buttons to navigate pages. As you move the cursor over a button, you should see the button appearances change with the rollover effects.

Working with Animation

All CS2 programs work with animations in one way or another. You can create animations in some programs while other programs offer options for viewing animations. None of the CS2 programs is intended to be animation editors, but simple animation effects can be created and viewed in the programs.

Animation and Adobe Illustrator

Adobe Illustrator supports exporting files as Macromedia (Adobe) Flash files (SWF). You can create layers in Illustrator and export the layered Illustrator document as SWF.

Cross-Reference   For a complete description on exporting to SWF format from Adobe Illustrator, see Chapter 35.

Animation and Adobe Photoshop

Examination of new features in Photoshop provides you a clue as to what we may see in future versions of the program. With the introduction of the Animation palette (Window ➪ Animation) you can speculate a little about where Photoshop is headed and where ImageReady falls in Adobe's product line. The animation effects introduced in Photoshop were previously reserved for ImageReady. As more ImageReady tools are introduced in Photoshop, you can anticipate the end of life for ImageReady while Photoshop takes in the ImageReady features. We anticipate that the ImageReady CS2 program is to be the last version of ImageReady and future upgrades to the Creative Suite are likely to discontinue the product. Don't hold us to it; it's just a guess.

The Animation palette in Photoshop is used to create animation sequences from layered Photoshop files. You create the animation in the Animation palette and export the Photoshop file as an animated GIF or SWF file that can be viewed in GoLive and used in Web page designs.

The first step in creating an animation is to create a layered Photoshop file, as you see in Figure 32-18. Each layer should contain an image that is transformed in one way or another different from the previous layer. For example, if you want to rotate an object so the animation displays a revolving icon, you rotate each layer using the transformation tools in Photoshop so each image appears with a different rotation. When the animation is played, the different layer views appear at short intervals to create the illusion of a moving object.

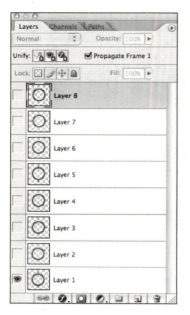

Figure 32-18: Create a layered Photoshop file with all layers containing different transformations.

 For more information about transforming images and objects, see Chapter 13.

Choose Window ⇨ Animation to open the Animation palette. The palette (see Figure 32-19) is used to identify the frames and set the frame attributes. From a fly-out palette menu you can create new frames, copy/paste frames, select frames, reverse frames, and more.

Figure 32-19: Choose Window ⇨ Animation to open the Animation pane.

You have tools in the palette to set the frame intervals and preview the animation. The frames are created by selecting New Frame from the fly-out menu or click the Duplicate Selected Frames button in the palette window. When a new frame is added, select the layer view you want for that frame by clicking the respective layer in the Layers palette. Continue adding frames and change layer views to create the animation. After previewing the animation by clicking on the right-pointing arrow in the Animation palette, and choose File ⇨ Save for Web. Be certain GIF is the format appearing in the Save For Web dialog box and click Save. The Save Optimized As dialog box opens. If you want to open the animation in GoLive, select HTML and Images from the Format pull-down menu, as shown in Figure 32-20.

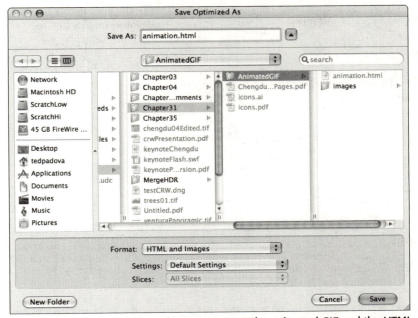

Figure 32-20: Select HTML and Images to save the animated GIF and the HTML code that creates the animation in GoLive.

 Tip If you use another form of animation other than rotating objects such as fading an object from 0 to 100% opacity or vice versa, you can create a quick transition between the layers using the Tween animation frames tool in the Animation palette. Just create two layers containing an image with different opacities and display the two layers as separate frames in the Animation palette. Click the Tween animation frames tool (to the left of the Duplicates selected frames tool. The Tween dialog box opens, where you can select parameter attributes and the number of frames to create for the transition.

The HTML export from Photoshop can be opened directly in GoLive or you can copy the code and paste it into the source code of a GoLive project. If you click the Preview tab in GoLive (see Figure 32-21), the animation plays exactly as you previewed in Photoshop.

Animation in InDesign and Acrobat

Animation files are placed in InDesign and viewed in Acrobat. You can choose to import an animation file such as SWF in InDesign or in Acrobat. Animation files are handled like other multimedia files where compatibility options and play buttons can be assigned.

 Cross-Reference For information regarding compatibility options in Acrobat, see the section "Using Multimedia in Designs."

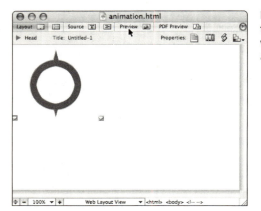

Figure 32-21: Open the HTML file and the first frame appears in a GoLive window. Click Preview to play the animation.

Acrobat has an added benefit with the ability to capture Web pages containing animation and video. You might have a client who has a Web site containing animation files and needs to repurpose documents or convert Web pages to PDF documents that you intend to integrate in a PDF collection of files to be published on CD/DVD-ROM. Once converted to PDF, the animation files can be copied and pasted into other PDF files.

You can capture Flash animation from Web sites in Acrobat, but animated GIF files are not converted with the animation effect. Captured Web pages containing animated GIF files capture the first image in the animation sequence.

There are a number of benefits in converting Web pages to PDF. You can create a Web site for a client and convert HTML files to PDF and secure the PDF documents against any unauthorized copying or editing; you can convert pages from several sources and search the PDFs locally on your hard drive using Acrobat Search; you can integrate captured Web pages in designs for display ads or brochures, and more. To understand how Acrobat is used to capture Web pages, follow these steps:

STEPS: Converting Web Pages to PDF

1. **Open a URL in Acrobat.** Launch Acrobat. From the Create PDF task button pull-down menu, select From Web page. The Create PDF from Web Page dialog box shown in Figure 32-22 opens.

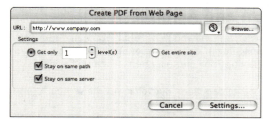

Figure 32-22: Open the Create PDF task button pull-down menu and select From Web Page to open the Create PDF from Web Page dialog box.

2. **Adjust download settings.** Add the URL for the Web site you intend to capture. Type **1** in the Get only text box to capture one level of Web pages. Select the Stay on same path and Stay on same server check boxes to be certain you are capturing Web pages from the specified URL.

3. **Adjust Web Capture Settings.** Click Settings in the Create PDF from Web Page dialog box to open the Web Capture Settings dialog box shown in Figure 32-23. Select HTML and click Settings to open the HTML Conversion Settings dialog box.

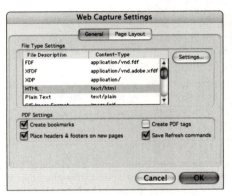

Figure 32-23: Select HTML and click Settings to adjust the conversion settings.

4. **Embed the media in the Web page.** From the Multimedia pull-down menu select Embed multimedia content when possible (Figure 32-34). Media can be either a link to a Web page or embedded in the resultant PDF document. When you embed the media, it is available locally on your hard drive and can be played when you are offline.

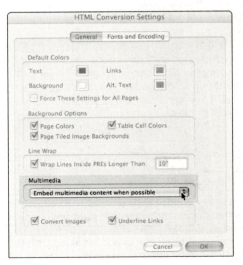

Figure 32-24: Select Embed multimedia content when possible from the Multimedia pull-down menu.

If you capture a Web page containing an animation or video clip, you can select the clip with the Select Object tool and copy it. The clip can then be pasted in another PDF document.

Note You can only paste copied media from Acrobat into PDF documents. You cannot paste the media in an InDesign file.

Using Multimedia in Designs

Of course, none of the CS2 programs is intended to be video-editing programs, so if you need to create video clips you need to work with iMovie on the Macintosh or MovieMaker on Windows for low-end video-editing programs. If you do serious video editing you need to use more professional editing tools such as Adobe Premiere Pro or Apple's Final Cut Pro.

Regardless of what application is used to create media, you can import the media in InDesign, Acrobat, and GoLive. The CS2 programs supporting media imports offer you options for creating buttons and links to control the media visibility.

Importing multimedia in InDesign

Both movies and sound files can be imported into InDesign layouts. Although InDesign supports the placing of these files in a document, they cannot actually be played until the document is exported in PDF or the document is packaged for use in GoLive. However, the media files may be previewed in InDesign by pressing and holding Option/Alt while double-clicking on the media file's frame.

The movie formats supported by InDesign include QuickTime, AVI, MPEG, and SWF movies, and WAV, AIF, and AU sound files.

Note The MPEG and SWF movie formats are only playable in Acrobat version 6 or greater or Adobe Reader version 6 or greater. QuickTime and AVI movie formats are only playable in Acrobat version 5 or later.

You add movie and sound files to the current document by choosing File ⇨ Place. The placed media file appears within a frame. Selecting the object and choosing Object ⇨ Interactive ⇨ Movie Options or Object ⇨ Interactive ⇨ Sound Options opens a dialog box where the settings for the movie or sound file are specified. If you create an empty frame, you may access either Options dialog box and select a file at a later time.

Setting movie options

The Movie Options dialog box, shown in Figure 32-25, includes a Name and a Description field. The Name appears in the object's frame; the Description appears in Acrobat when the mouse cursor is moved over the top of the object.

The Movie Options dialog box lets you either choose a file or specify a URL. Although you cannot embed movies within the InDesign document, you can embed the movie in the PDF. If you select the Embed Movie in PDF option, the movie file embeds within the PDF when it's exported. If you deselect this option, you must move the movie file along with the exported PDF file that references it. The Specify URL option lets you type the address to a media file on the Web. If a connection to the Internet is established when the media file is viewed, the movie file is downloaded into the PDF document. The Verify URL and Movie Size button checks the URL to make sure it's valid and points to a movie file.

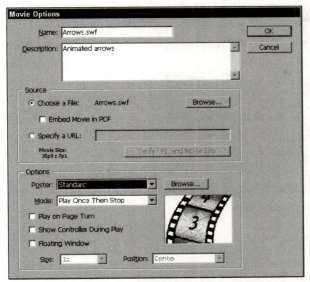

Figure 32-25: The Movie Options dialog box defines which movie file plays and when it plays.

A Poster is an image that fills the movie frame. This image appears when the movie isn't being played. There are several Poster options you can add to movie frames:

- **None:** Hides the movie file when it isn't being played.
- **Standard:** Displays the image contained in the `StandardMoviePoster.jpg` image file. This generic image displays to the right in Figure 32-25.
- **Default Poster:** Presents the poster image that is bundled with the movie file. If the movie doesn't include a poster image, the first frame of the movie is used.
- **Choose Image as Poster:** Lets you browse and load an image and display it as the movie poster.
- **Choose Movie Frame as Poster:** Lets you view the movie using the pane to the right, where you may select a single frame of the movie to use as a poster.

The Mode options define how many times the movie file plays. The options include Play Once Then Stop, Play Once Stay Open, and Repeat Play. The Play on Page Turn option causes the movie to start playing when the page that includes the movie is displayed. The Show Controller During Play option shows controls along with the movie file. These controls let the viewer play, pause, and stop the movie file. The Floating Window option displays the movie within a floating window. The size and position of the floating window are set using the fields at the bottom of the dialog box.

Setting sound options

The Sound Options dialog box, shown in Figure 32-26, includes Name and Description fields. The Name is the name that appears in the object's frame; the Description appears in Acrobat when the mouse cursor is moved over the top of the object.

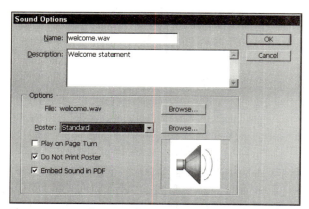

Figure 32-26: The Sound Options dialog box

The Sound Options dialog box, like the Movie Options dialog box, also lets you Browse for a new sound file. The Poster options are limited to None, Standard, and Choose Image as Poster. The Play on Page Turn option causes the sound file to play when the page that contains it is displayed. The Do Not Print Poster option ensures that the sound frame isn't printed with the rest of the document when the document is printed. The Embed Sound in PDF option causes the sound file to be embedded within the PDF, which frees you from the concern of copying the sound file along with the exported PDF, but it increases the PDF file size. Note that InDesign adds no more compression to media files to reduce their sizes.

Creating interactive multimedia buttons

You can create buttons in InDesign to jump to a page, or perform a certain action like playing a movie or sound. When you export an InDesign document containing buttons to Acrobat, the defined button and its function remain active.

 Buttons created in InDesign and exported to a PDF document are different from buttons created in Acrobat. Buttons created in InDesign are links to Destinations whereas buttons created in Acrobat are linked to target locations without defining Destinations. For more detail on learning differences between Destinations and links, see the *Adobe Acrobat 7 PDF Bible* (Wiley Publishing).

You create simple buttons in InDesign using the Button tool. You drag the tool in the layout where you want to locate the button, or you click in the document to open a simple dialog box (Figure 32-27), where you enter the Width and Height of the button. Holding down the Shift key while dragging constrains the button to a square shape. Holding down the Option/Alt key while dragging lets you drag from the button's center. If you hold down the Spacebar while dragging, you can move the button's location. Buttons are identifiable by a button icon and name that displays in the upper-left corner of the button.

In addition to regular rectangular objects created with the Button tool, you can also convert any selectable object including text objects and images to buttons by choosing Object ➪ Interactive ➪ Convert to Button.

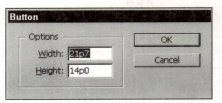

Figure 32-27: The Button dialog box lets you type precise dimensions.

Button objects may also be converted to normal objects by choosing Object ⇨ Interactive ⇨ Convert from Button.

Setting button options and behavior

You set button options using the Button Options dialog box (Figure 32-28), which appears when you choose Object ⇨ Interactive ⇨ Button Options or when you double-clicking on the button. The Button Options dialog box consists of two panels — General and Behaviors.

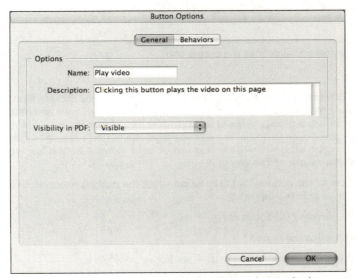

Figure 32-28: The General panel defines how a button looks and acts.

The General panel of the Button Options dialog box includes fields for naming and entering a button description. The text in the Description field appears in Acrobat when you move the mouse cursor over the button. The Visibility of the button in an exported PDF may be set to Visible, Hidden, Visible But Doesn't Print, or Hidden But Printable.

The Behavior panel of the Button Options dialog box, shown in Figure 32-29, lets you define what happens when you interact with a button. The pane on the left holds all the defined behaviors for the selected button.

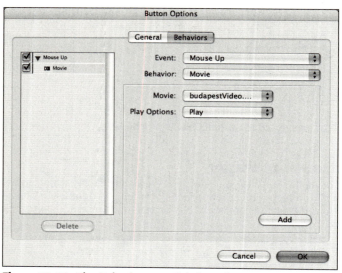

Figure 32-29: The Behaviors panel defines the events and behaviors of a button.

The Event options are different ways to interact with a button. The options include Mouse Up, Move Down, Mouse Enter, Mouse Exit, On Focus, and On Blur. The Mouse Down and Mouse Up events occur when the mouse button is pressed and released. The Mouse Enter and Mouse Exit events occur when the mouse moves over and away from the button's bounding box. The On Focus and On Blur events occur when the button has or loses focus. A button has focus when it's selected with the mouse or Tab key.

The Behavior options are all the actions that may be set when the designated event happens. The available behaviors include the following:

✦ **Close:** Closes the current PDF document.

✦ **Exit:** Causes the application to exit.

✦ **Go to Anchor:** Jumps to a specified hyperlink anchor or bookmark.

✦ **Go to First Page:** Jumps to the first page in the document.

✦ **Go to Last Page:** Jumps to the last page in the document.

✦ **Go to Next Page:** Jumps to the next page in the document.

✦ **Go to Next View:** Jumps to the next page in the view history. This behavior only becomes active after the Go to Previous View behavior is used.

✦ **Go to Previous Page:** Jumps to the previous page in the document.

✦ **Go to Previous View:** Jumps to the last viewed page in the view history.

✦ **Go to URL:** Opens a Web browser with the designated URL address loaded.

✦ **Movie:** Lets you play, pause, stop, and resume a movie.

- **Open File:** Opens another selected PDF file or opens another file type in its default application.
- **Show/Hide Fields:** Show or hide a specified form field.
- **Sound:** Lets you play, pause, stop, and resume a sound.
- **View Zoom:** Lets you designate how the current page zooms. The options include Full Screen, Zoom In, Zoom Out, Fit in Window, Actual Size, Fit Width, Fit Visible, Reflow, Single Page, Continuous, Continuous-Facing, Rotate Clockwise, and Rotate Counterclockwise.

Various settings appear under the Behavior field depending on the Behavior that you select. For example, selecting the Go to Anchor behavior displays settings for choosing the Document from the active documents, a Browse button for locating a local document, and a field for selecting an Anchor by name. The Go to URL behavior lets you type in a URL. The Movie and Sound behaviors display a field where you can select a movie or sound added to the document, as well as an option to Play, Pause, Stop, or Resume. The Open File behavior lets you browse and select a file to open. All the go to page options, plus the Go to Anchor and the View Zoom behaviors, offer a list of zoom options to use when the user jumps to the page. The Show/Hide Fields behavior presents a list of fields in the current document along with check boxes to mark which ones are visible.

After you select and define an event and a behavior, you must click the Add button to add the behavior to the pane on the right.

Setting button states

Although you can create various button states for rollovers using behaviors, button states are more easily defined using the States palette, shown in Figure 32-30. To access this palette, choose Window ⇨ Interactive ⇨ States. Each button maintains three different states:

- **Up:** The button's default state.
- **Rollover:** Occurs when the mouse cursor moves over the top of the button.
- **Down:** Occurs when a user clicks the button.

You can use the States palette to change the button's look for each of these states.

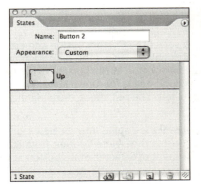

Figure 32-30: The States palette changes the button's appearance for different states.

When you first open the States palette, the name of the selected button displays in the Name field; from the Appearance field, you may select an appearance style for the selected button. Options include Bevel, Drop Shadow, Glow, Custom, and None.

The three available appearance presets automatically create new Rollover and Down states and apply a modified appearance to the button. These modified states and their appearances are visible in the States palette. Selecting one of the states in the States palette causes the document button to show the appearance for that state.

The Bevel option adds a shaded border to the edge of the button and changes the color of each button state. The Drop Shadow option adds a gradient across the face of the button along with a drop shadow. The Glow option adds a glowing gradient vertically down the face of the button, which is inverted for the Rollover state. Figure 32-31 shows each of the default states for the preset appearances.

Note Changing between the default appearance presets opens a dialog box warning you that adding the new preset will delete the appearance of any existing buttons that use the appearance preset that is being replaced.

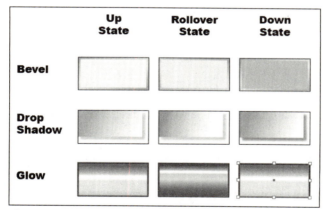

Figure 32-31: The States palette includes three different preset appearance options.

In addition to the default appearance presets, you can select the Custom option and create your own button states. To add a new state to the States palette, select the New State palette menu command or click on the Create New Optional State button at the bottom of the palette. The first state created is the Rollover state, and the second one is the Down state. You can disable either of these states using the check box to its left. The red check mark highlights the state currently displayed in the document.

When a new state is created, the original button appearance is copied into the new state. You can remove this content by selecting the state and choosing the Delete Content from State palette menu command or by clicking on the Delete Content of Selected State button at the bottom of the palette.

To replace the graphic of the selected state with another graphic file, choose the Place Content into State palette menu command or click on the Place Content into Selected State button at the bottom of the palette. This opens a file dialog box where you may select a file to place in the state.

Objects created within InDesign may be grouped and added to a button state by positioning them as they would fit in the button and then by cutting them with the Edit ⇨ Cut menu command. Select the button state and choose Edit ⇨ Paste Into.

To change the text within a button state, simply select the state in the States palette, click on the button frame with the Type tool, and start typing. To change the fill and stroke for a button state, simply select the button state and change the fill and stroke properties.

Setting tab order

One common way to navigate about documents is using the Tab key. This key moves the focus from one element to another. You can execute the element with the focus by pressing the Return/Enter key.

For InDesign documents that include several buttons, the order in which the Tab key moves between these buttons is defined using the Tab Order dialog box, shown in Figure 32-32. Open this dialog box by choosing Object ⇨ Interactive ⇨ Set Tab Order. Click on buttons and click Move Up or Move Down to change the tab order.

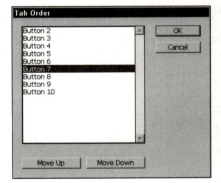

Figure 32-32: The Tab Order dialog box

Importing multimedia in Acrobat

If your ultimate display for designs containing multimedia is Acrobat PDF, you have much better solutions in Acrobat for assigning button behaviors and file linking. Acrobat provides you with a rich set of features that are expanded to almost limitless options when you consider the flexibility you have with writing JavaScripts. As an example of an impressive electronic brochure design containing interactive buttons and imported multimedia, take a look at Figure 32-33.

The Volvo brochure created by Robert Connolly of BC Pictures in Toronto, Canada (www.bcpictures.com) has interactive links at the bottom of the page. The design is originally created in InDesign and the interactive elements are added in Acrobat. The brochure opens in Full Screen mode in Adobe Acrobat or Adobe Reader. Therefore, the navigational buttons provide the reader options for moving about the brochure.

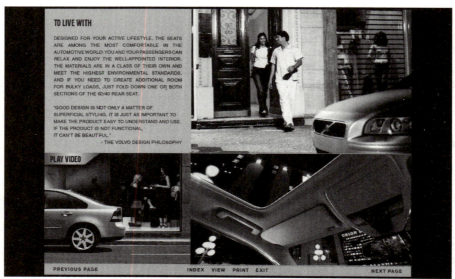

Figure 32-33: An electronic brochure created by Robert Connolly of BC Pictures in Toronto, Canada, contains interactive buttons and multimedia.

The photo in the lower-left corner contains a button that opens an embedded movie clip as a floating window. The movie frame in the lower-right corner of the page is a QuickTimeVR movie where the reader can click and move the cursor around the movie frame to view a 360-degree view of the auto interior.

On the opening page of the electronic brochure, a pop-up menu (see Figure 32-34) contains links to pages throughout the brochure. This menu is created with JavaScript in Acrobat. With the extensive list of links, the pop-up menu conveniently economizes space by serving as an alternative to a list of links on the page. When the menu is collapsed the reader sees the nicely constructed design and photo images.

Using compatibility settings

To import a movie in Acrobat, you use the Movie tool. Double-click the Movie tool and the Add Movie dialog box appears as shown in Figure 32-35. The first two radio buttons offer options for choosing the compatibility setting. These include:

- ✦ **Acrobat 6 (and later) Compatible Media:** Acrobat 6-compatible media permits you to embed media clips in the PDF file. If you choose Acrobat 6-compatible media, you have a choice for embedding the media or linking to it. Users of Acrobat 6 and above can see the media. Users of Acrobat and Adobe Reader below version 6 won't see the media.

- ✦ **Acrobat 5 (and Earlier) Compatible Media:** Selecting this option allows the user to see the media as a link to the PDF file. If you use this option, users of Acrobat/Reader prior to version 6 can see the media. The PDF and the movie file need to be copied to a CD/DVD or a Web site together for the media to play in Acrobat/Reader.

Figure 32-34: Robert Connolly created interactive links via a pop-up menu designed with Acrobat's implementation of JavaScript.

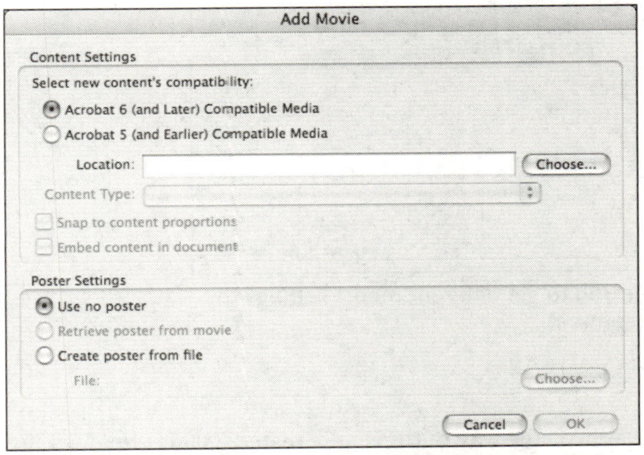

Figure 32-35: Double-click the Movie tool to open the Add Movie dialog box where you make choices for media compatibility and browsing for the media location.

Note Mac users need to upgrade to Acrobat to a version higher than version 7.03 to play Acrobat 6-compatible media on Mac OS X Tiger.

The poster options provide you the same settings as when importing media in InDesign.

Creating renditions

One of the advantages of setting media attributes in Acrobat versus InDesign is the ability to add renditions. You can add a media clip to a PDF document and specify settings for the media such as playback attributes, playback location, showing or hiding player controls, and system requirements such as download speeds. You can then create a different rendition in the same PDF document for different media attributes. For example, you may have one media setting for users with broadband Internet feeds to download movies at 384 Kbps (kilobytes per second). You can then open the media properties, create a second rendition and in the Rendition Settings dialog box specify a different download speed (see Figure 32-36).

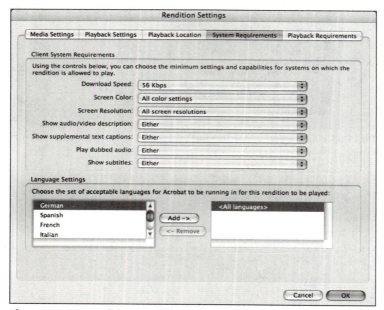

Figure 32-36: Renditions enable you to set different media settings to movie clips in the same PDF document.

Creating play buttons

You create buttons to play media the same way buttons are created as links to views. In the Actions tab you have options for selecting Acrobat 5- or Acrobat 6-compatible media. When you select the action and click Add in the Actions dialog box, the Play Media (compatibility choice) opens as shown in Figure 32-37. From the pull-down menu select the play options. You can create buttons to play, stop, resume, play from beginning, and add a custom JavaScript when selecting Acrobat 6-compatible media.

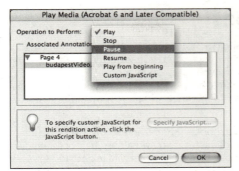

Figure 32-37: Select Play Media (Acrobat compatibility) and click Add. The Play Media dialog box opens where play actions are assigned.

In Figure 32-38, a PDF file contains buttons assigned with different play actions.

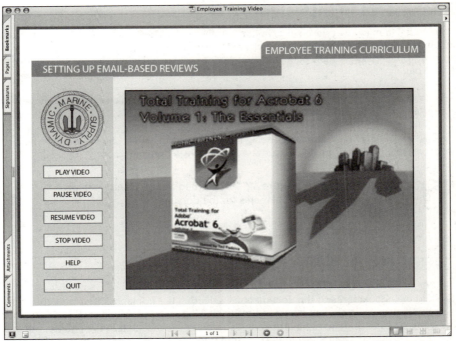

Figure 32-38: Several buttons are used in a document to control the media play actions.

Note Users of Mac OS X Tiger need to upgrade Acrobat/Adobe Reader above version 7.03 in order to see Acrobat-compatible media.

Hyperlinks and Publications

Buttons and links are items you add to InDesign or PDF pages. In order to invoke an action you need to have the button or link appear on a page when you want to initiate the action. If you have the same action assigned to a button such as opening another PDF document, it makes more sense to add the action to a bookmark. Bookmarks are visible from all pages and they add significantly less overhead to a PDF file than when creating multiple buttons or links on pages.

If you create long documents such as manuals, books, guides, and so on, your document viewing and searching information will be much faster if you break up the documents to multiple PDFs and use bookmarks to open and close files. You can organize and add interactive links to many files and create an illusion for the end user that browsing multiple files actually appears as a single file. The user is not likely to know the difference between scrolling pages in one document and opening and closing files from many documents.

Bookmarks in InDesign

Bookmarks in many ways are very similar to hyperlinks. They also mark text or images that link to places with the PDF file for quick navigation. Bookmarks are unique to PDF files and appear in the left Bookmark pane, but they aren't recognized when the layout is converted to a Web page.

Note When InDesign creates a table of contents, all entries in the table of contents are automatically added to the document as bookmarks.

You create and manage bookmarks using the Bookmarks palette, shown in Figure 32-39, which is accessed by choosing Window ➪ Interactive ➪ Bookmarks.

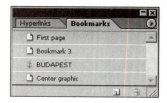

Figure 32-39: The Bookmarks palette manages all bookmarks for the document.

You add new bookmarks to the document by selecting the bookmark item and choosing the New Bookmark palette menu command or by clicking on the Create New Bookmark button at the bottom of the Bookmark palette. If no bookmarks are selected in the palette, the new bookmark is added to the bottom of the list of bookmarks. But if a bookmark is selected, the new bookmark is added as a child bookmark under the selected bookmark.

After creation, a bookmark's name appears as highlighted text, which you can edit. The bookmark's name appears in Acrobat's Bookmark pane. If some selected text is the bookmark, the selected text appears as the bookmark's name unless you change it.

The order of bookmarks within the Bookmarks palette also determines the order in which the bookmarks appear in Acrobat's bookmark pane. You can rearrange the listed bookmarks by dragging the bookmarks within the Bookmarks palette. As you're dragging a bookmark, a line appears defining where the bookmark appears when you release the mouse. If you drop a bookmark on top of an existing bookmark, the bookmark becomes a child to the highlighted bookmark.

Bookmarks in Acrobat

The most common bookmark used in Acrobat is a bookmark to a page in the existing document. Bookmarks in Acrobat are easy to create. You first navigate to the page and view you want and press Command/Ctrl+B. Alternately, you can open the Bookmarks pane and select New Bookmark from the fly-out menu in the pane. When a bookmark is created it is temporarily named Untitled. Type a name for the bookmark while Untitled is selected and you can rename the bookmark.

 If you have title headings on pages such as Chapter 1, Section 1, Part 1, and so on, you can use the Select tool and drag across the title on the pane or a section heading. When you press Command/Ctrl+B, the bookmark is created and linked to the existing view and the bookmark name appearing in the Bookmark is derived from the selected text.

Opening files using bookmarks

The real power in using bookmarks is when you add different action types to the bookmark properties. In particular, writing JavaScripts provides a limitless number of opportunities to create dynamic interactive PDF documents.

When assigning properties to bookmarks, you can create the bookmark from any given page. Bookmarks and their associated actions are accessible from any page in a PDF document. If you are organizing long publications broken into sections, bookmarks provide the ideal avenue for opening and closing the various sections. To use buttons or links requires you to add a button or link to every page so a reader can quickly explore a different section. Adding these elements increases the file size considerably. Adding bookmarks to do the job results in file size increases that are hardly noticeable.

To organize a collection of PDF documents, follow these steps:

STEPS: Navigating Files with Bookmarks

1. **Organize a collection of related documents.** If you intend to distribute documents you must be certain the file paths for all linked files remain identical within folders and nested folders. To simplify your file organization, create a folder in Adobe Bridge and add the folder as a Favorite. You can drag files to this folder from the content area. If you want to copy files, press Option/Alt and drag to your Favorite folder.

Cross-Reference For more information on creating Favorites and organizing files in Adobe Bridge, see Chapter 7.

2. **Create a blank document.** Acrobat does not have a command for you to create a new document; however, you can use one short line of JavaScript code to create a blank page that opens in the Document pane. Press Command/Ctrl+J to open the JavaScript Debugger. Click the Trash icon to clear any default code and messages in the window. Type the following code in the Console window:

```
app.newDoc();
```

The line of code is case sensitive, so be certain to type it as shown in Figure 32-40. Press the Num Pad Enter key and a new blank document opens in the Document pane. Click the Close button in the Debugger to dismiss the window.

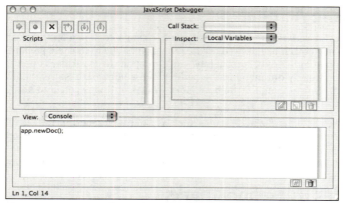

Figure 32-40: Type the code in the Console window and press the Num Pad Enter key to create a new blank document.

3. **Create a new bookmark.** Press Command/Ctrl+B. The Bookmarks pane opens and a new bookmark is created. The word untitled appears as the name and the text is highlighted.

4. **Type a name for the bookmark.** Type a name and the highlighted bookmark name is replaced with the text you type. Press the Num Pad Enter key to register the name.

5. **Open the Bookmark Properties dialog box.** Place the cursor on the bookmark name and open a context menu. Select Properties from the menu choices and the Bookmark Properties dialog box opens.

6. **Open the Actions tab.** By default, the Appearance tab is selected. Click the Actions tab in the Bookmark Properties dialog box. The Actions tab opens.

7. **Delete the existing action.** When you created the bookmark, the action was automatically set as a link to the view of the blank page in the Document pane. Delete this action by selecting the first line of text in the Actions window and click Delete. The Actions window should now appear empty.

8. **Add an Action to open a file.** Open the Select Action pull-down menu. Select Open a File from the menu options. Click Add.

9. **Select a file to open.** The Select File dialog box opens. Search your drive for the folder you created in Adobe Bridge and select the file you want to use for a contents page or opening file. Click OK in the Select File to Open dialog box.

10. **Select a window preference.** The Specify Window Preference dialog box opens. You have three choices as shown in Figure 32-41. Select Existing Window from the available choices. When you select Existing Window, the document containing this action closes as the target file opens. Click OK and you are returned to the Actions pane.

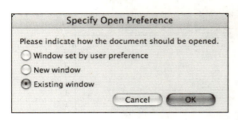

Figure 32-41: Select Existing window in the Specify Open Preference dialog box.

11. **Create another bookmark.** Follow steps 3 through 10 to add new bookmarks for additional files to open. Be certain to set the same window preference for all actions. Your bookmarks should appear listed in the bookmarks pane as shown in Figure 32-42.

Tip

You can leave the Actions pane open while creating new bookmarks.

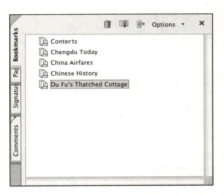

Figure 32-42: Bookmarks are listed in the order they were created in the Bookmarks pane.

12. **Specify initial view options.** Choose File ⇨ Document Properties. Click the Initial View tab. From the Show pull-down menu select Bookmarks Panel and Page. Select Single Page from the Page Layout pull-down menu and Fit Page from the Magnification menu. Select Document Title from the Show pull-down menu. The settings should look like Figure 32-43.

13. **Add metadata.** Click the Description tab. Add data common to all your files if any exist for the Author, Subject, and Keywords fields. Note that the Title field should be different for each file.

Cross-Reference

For more information about adding Initial Views and Document Descriptions, see Chapter 29.

14. **Save the file.** Choose File ⇨ Save and save the file as a temporary working document. You might want to use a name for the file like `temp.pdf` to distinguish it from your other files.

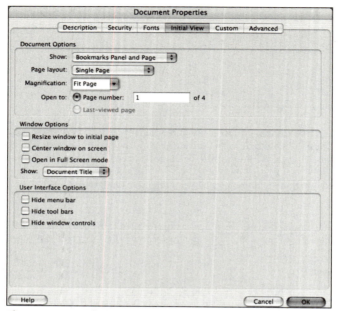

Figure 32-43: Adjust settings for the initial view that will appear each time the document opens.

15. **Import bookmarks.** You can import a file in your temp document or you can import the temp document into other files. In order to preserve the Initial View and the metadata, you should import each file in your template. To import a PDF in the open document, click the Pages tab in the Navigation pane. Open a context menu on the first page and select Insert Pages. The Select File to Insert dialog box opens. Select a file to insert and click Select.

16. **Select the location for the inserted pages.** The Insert Pages dialog box opens. Select After from the Location pull-down menu to insert pages after the selected page. Click OK to insert the pages, as shown in Figure 32-44.

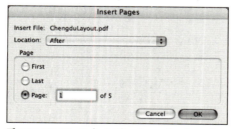

Figure 32-44: Select After from the Location pull-down menu and click OK.

17. **Delete the blank page.** The template page is contained in the document. Open a context menu on the Blank page and select Delete. Click OK in the alert dialog box.

18. **Delete the dead bookmark.** If you added bookmarks to open every file contained in your folder, the file you inserted in the open document does not need a bookmark. Select the respective bookmark in the Bookmarks pane and open a context menu. Select Delete from the menu.

19. **Edit the Title field and any unique metadata.** Open the Document Description (Command/Ctrl+D) and click Description. Edit the fields where data need to be added to uniquely describe this file.

20. **Save the file.** Choose File ➪ Save As. Be certain to provide a unique name or overwrite the file you inserted to preserve the template file.

21. **Finish the project.** Open the template file and insert the next file to modify. Follow steps 15 through 20 for each file contained in your collection. When one of the files opens, the Bookmarks pane is opened. Clicking a bookmark from any page closes the open file and opens the target file. The reader can browse your collection freely without opening several documents in the Document pane, thereby eliminating confusion when navigating documents.

Creating On Demand Documents

The power of interactivity is best exemplified in PDF documents with JavaScript routines. JavaScript provides you with a limitless opportunity to create new design looks, add more sophisticated dynamic linking, and explore a world of features not available with tools and menu commands in the other CS2 programs. As Emeril says, "It's time to kick it up a notch."

To illustrate an example for where you might use JavaScript and PDF documents, let's assume you have a document used to record ongoing progress on a campaign or design assignment. The document might be a PDF form used to fill in form data on a series of designs as they are completed by members of your workgroup. Contained within the form is the respective design piece itself. Therefore, you start with two documents. One document is a form template and the other is a design piece.

Your task is to merge the two documents for the purpose of record keeping and for your client to sign off on the final designs. Because one file contains form fields in a PDF, you can't copy and paste one document on the same page as the other in Adobe InDesign. You need some way to merge the two files together to create a single page document with the form fields.

To begin, you'll need two files that, when merged together, appear as a single page layout. You might initially lay out a document in InDesign, convert to PDF and add form fields like you see in Figure 32-45. In Adobe Acrobat, the bottom half of this design is where the merged file will eventually appear,

Working with PDF forms and adding form fields in Acrobat is not difficult, but there is a lot to it. For a more comprehensive view of creating Acrobat PDF forms, see the *Adobe Acrobat 7 PDF Bible* (Wiley Publishing).

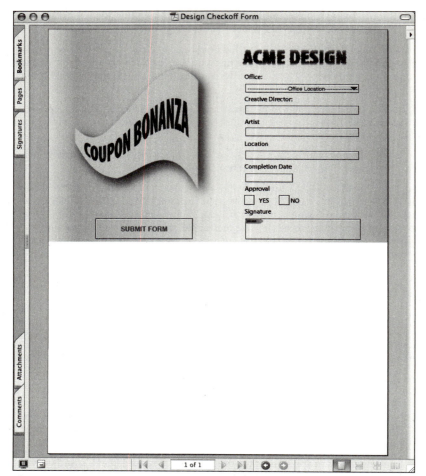

Figure 32-45: Create a layout in InDesign and convert to PDF. Add form fields in Adobe Acrobat.

To understand how to merge data in PDF documents, follow these steps:

STEPS: Dynamically Creating Content Using JavaScript

1. **Add a bookmark.** You should have two PDF documents you want to merge together. If you're not familiar with creating a PDF form, you can use any layout where two halves of a layout are converted to PDF. One layout will be used as a template. Open the file in Acrobat and press Command/Ctrl+B to create a bookmark. Name the bookmark by typing a name immediately after the bookmark is created. In this example, we use merge as the bookmark name.

2. **Add an Execute a menu item action.** Open a context menu on the bookmark name and select Properties. Click Actions. Select the existing page view action and click Delete to remove it from the Actions list. Open the Select Action pull-down menu and select Execute a menu item. Click Add and open the Document menu and select Insert Pages. Click OK, but leave the Bookmark Properties dialog box open.

Cross-Reference

For more information on creating Execute a menu item actions, see "Adding links in Acrobat" earlier in this chapter.

When the user clicks the bookmark, the Insert Pages dialog box opens. This enables the user to locate and select the file to merge with the template.

3. **Add a JavaScript.** After a page is inserted, you need to move ahead to the inserted page to follow the remaining steps. You could use another Execute a menu item action or you can add a JavaScript to accomplish the same task. Add a JavaScript here to do the job. Select Run a JavaScript from the Select Action pull-down menu, click Add and the Create and Edit JavaScripts window opens. Type the following code in the window and be certain to use the exact same letter case:

```
this.pageNum++;
```

4. **Add another Execute a menu item.** Click OK in the Create and Edit JavaScripts window and you return to the Bookmark Properties dialog box. Select Execute a menu item from the Select Action pull-down menu and choose Advanced ⇨ Forms ⇨ Page Templates. You are converting the inserted page as a PDF page template. In Acrobat, you can spawn a page from a template. The spawned page can be inserted in the PDF or it can overlay an existing page. In order to spawn a page, you first need to create a page template. When you click OK, you now have three actions shown in the Actions tab in the Bookmark properties dialog box as shown in Figure 32-46.

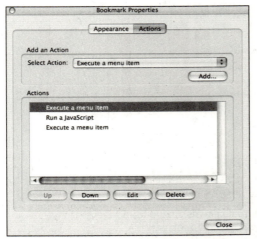

Figure 32-46: Click OK in the Execute a menu item dialog box and you can see three actions nested in the Actions list.

5. **Add another JavaScript.** Your final action is a script that you write to spawn a page from the page template, delete the page after spawning it, and delete the bookmark so a user doesn't inadvertently click it again to create another template. Select Run a JavaScript from the Select Action pull-down menu and click Add. In the Create and Edit JavaScripts window, type the following code exactly as shown here and in Figure 32-47:

```
this.pageNum--;

if(this.templates.length)
{
        var a = this.templates[this.templates.length-1];
        if(a != null)
        {
                a.spawn ({
                        nPage:this.pageNum,
                        bRename:true,
                        bOverlay:true,
                })

                this.deletePages(this.pageNum+1);

                bookmarkRoot.remove();
        }
}
```

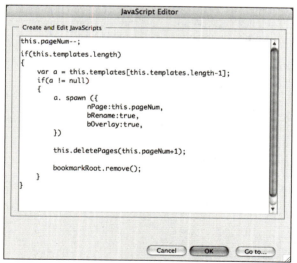

Figure 32-47: Type the code that spawns a page from the template and deletes the page and bookmark.

6. **Save the file.** Click OK in the Create and Edit JavaScripts window and Close in the Bookmark Properties dialog box. Choose File ➪ Save As and save the file with a new name.

Cross-Reference

Before saving the document, open the Initial View document properties and select Bookmarks and Page for the opening view. When a user opens the file, the bookmark is in view in the Bookmarks pane. See the section "Opening files using bookmarks."

Understanding the code

The code written in step 5 of the "Dynamically Creating Content Using JavaScripts" series of steps performs several actions. The actions specified in the script include:

- ✦ **this,pageNum–;:** The first line of code moves the user to the first page in the file and makes that page the active page.
- ✦ **if(this,templates.length) through the 5th line of code (if (a != null)):** This sets up a condition where the user can type any name for the page template name. As page templates are created, they need to be named. Rather than have the user try to remember a name, this code accepts any name for the page template.
- ✦ **a.spawn ({ through line 10 (bOverlay:true,):** This spawns the page from the template. The `bOverlay:true` statement takes the page template data and overlays it on the existing page.
- ✦ **this.deletePages(this.pageNum+1):** This deletes page 2 in the template. Since the user is currently on page 1, the `pageNum+1` portion of the statement targets the next page for deletion.
- ✦ **bookmarkRoot.remove();:** This deletes the bookmark from the document.

Running the scripts

After you add the Execute a menu item and JavaScripts actions, test the sequence of actions to be certain they work properly. Be certain you save the file before attempting to run any actions. You can always revert to the last-saved version by choosing File ➪ Revert. If your JavaScript contains an error, revert to the saved version, make an edit, and run the action. If it works properly, revert again, make the same edit and save the file.

To test your series of actions, follow these steps:

STEPS: Executing Menu Items and JavaScripts

1. **Click the bookmark.** To invoke the actions, click the bookmark with the Hand tool.
2. **Insert a page.** The first item you see after clicking the bookmark is the Select File to Insert dialog box shown in Figure 32-48. Select a file to be merged with the open template document and click Select. The Insert Pages dialog box opens next. Be certain the Location pull-down menu shows After and click OK.

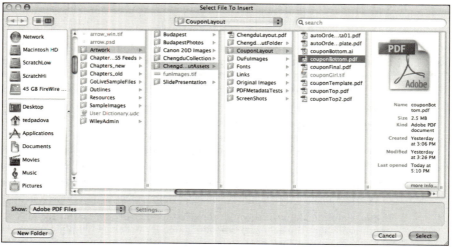

Figure 32-48: Select a file to insert and click Select.

3. **Add a template.** The next dialog box appearing is the Page Templates dialog box as shown in Figure 32-49. Type a name for the template. The name can be any text you want to add in the Name text box. In this example, we use *xyz*. Click Add and an alert dialog box opens as shown in Figure 32-50. Click Yes to continue.

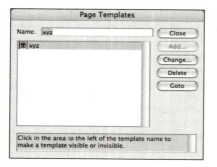

Figure 32-49: Type a name for the template and click Add and an alert dialog box opens.

4. **Close the Page Templates dialog box.** After a template name is added, the name appears in the Page Templates window, as shown in Figure 32-50. Click Close to continue.

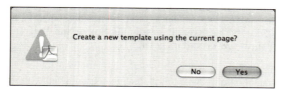

Figure 32-50: Click Yes in the alert dialog box and the template name is added in the Page Templates dialog box.

5. **Save the file.** The remaining part of the JavaScript finishes up the job. The inserted page data are overlaid on the first page, the second page is deleted, and the bookmark is deleted. If you have form fields in the document, fill in the fields. The final document is shown in Figure 32-51. Choose File ➪ Save As to save the document with a new filename.

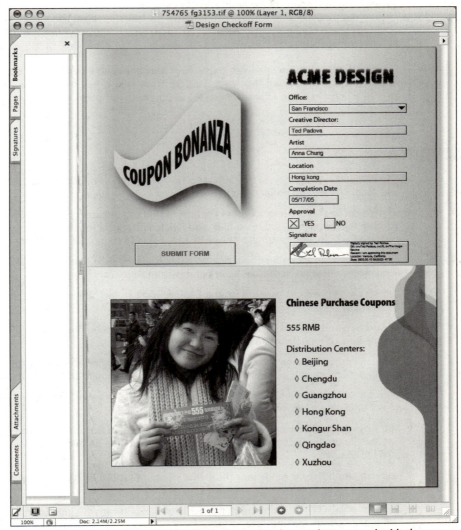

Figure 32-51: The final document shows the inserted page data merged with the template.

Spawning pages in Acrobat is a powerful tool that enables you to create pages on demand according to user needs. You might have a law firm as a client that needs to have comments added on separate pages in an arbitration agreement. Rather than adding blank pages throughout the document, you let the client create pages as needed for commenting on arbitration issues. You might have an accounting firm that needs calculation fields added to various pages in a tax organizer for auditing purposes, or you might have needs in your own design studio to merge layouts with form templates for tracking jobs. The more you become familiar with this powerful feature in Acrobat, the more you'll find solutions for your clients and your in-house needs.

For more information on spawning pages from templates and writing JavaScripts, see the Acrobat JavaScript Scripting Reference. You can download it free from Adobe's Web site at `http://partners.adobe.com/public/developer/acrobat/sdk/index_doc.html#js`.

Summary

- You can add various interactive elements including hyperlinks, bookmarks, buttons, and media files to InDesign documents and Acrobat PDF files.

- Hyperlinks can link to pages or text anchors within the document or to a URL in InDesign. You can link to page views, open files, and link to URLs in Acrobat. For URLs contained in text in a PDF file, Acrobat 7 and Adobe Reader 7 do not require adding links.

- Bookmarks in an InDesign document may link to pages, text anchors, or URLs. These bookmarks show up in the Bookmarks tab within Acrobat.

- During the PDF export process from InDesign, you can include or exclude interactive elements.

- In Acrobat, you can link to views as well as add actions to bookmark properties for executing menu commands and running JavaScripts.

- You can endow buttons with events and behaviors that define a resulting action. This action occurs when a user performs an event such as a mouse-click or a mouse-rollover.

- You can add media files, including movies and sounds, to an InDesign document and select options for playing them.

- You can add media files, including movies and sounds, in Acrobat as Acrobat 5- or Acrobat 6-compatible media. Acrobat 6-compatible media enables you to embed media files in the PDF.

- You can add different renditions for media clips in Acrobat. You can assign renditions according to end-user download speeds.

- You can create PDF documents that meet user needs for modifying files on demand using page templates and JavaScripts.

✦ ✦ ✦

Hosting Documents on the Web

In This Chapter

Preparing to publish a Web site

Publishing a Web site using GoLive

Exporting a Web site

Linking PDF documents

Understanding Digital Rights Management and document Web hosting

---

After you've completed the design for your Web site, the final step in the repurposing workflow is uploading Web content to an online server. But you must first obtain some server space from a hosting company and enter the server information within GoLive. You can then upload, download, or synchronize with the server. In addition, you can use GoLive to export the site to a local Web folder that an external FTP client can use to upload the files.

PDF files offer another common way to present designs on the Web. PDF files may include links to other Web resources and, if hosted using Adobe's Content Server, can be made secure. eBooks provide another way to distribute designs.

Preparing to Publish a Web Site

One of the key advantages of GoLive is that it's a complete Web-authoring and Web-publishing solution: It's used to design and create Web sites and also to publish those sites to a Web server. The first step in publishing Web sites is to configure GoLive so that it can access the Internet and locate the Web servers. GoLive provides two ways to upload files to a Web server:

✦ You can use the Publish Server tab of the site window.

✦ You can use the FTP Browser opened with the File ➪ Serve ➪ Connect to FTP menu command.

Setting up Internet access

The steps to configure GoLive so that it can publish to a Web site are simple, but much of the information required to configure the system comes from the Internet Service Provider (ISP) that you're using to host your site. Each ISP has different required settings, but you must follow some general guidelines.

The ISP settings within GoLive are located within the Internet panel of the Preferences dialog box, which is accessed by choosing GoLive/Edit ➪ Preferences (⌘/Ctrl+K). This panel, shown in Figure 33-1, lets you specify an FTP proxy or an HTTP proxy.

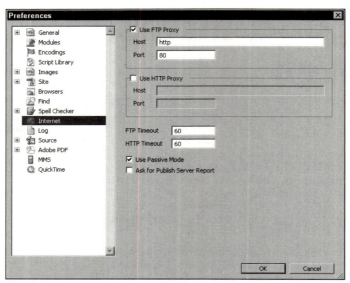

Figure 33-1: The Internet panel of the Preferences dialog box

FTP versus HTTP

Two different protocols are commonly used to transfer files on the Internet — File Transfer Protocol (FTP) and Hypertext Transfer Protocol (HTTP). FTP sites are structured like a file system with subfolders within subfolders. Understanding this directory structure helps you place files in the correct location. Web browsers use HTTP to retrieve Web pages. HTTP uses a Uniform Resource Locator (URL) to specify the location of files. The URLs are the Web addresses that request Web pages and resources.

Another key difference between the FTP and HTTP protocols is that FTP is a connection-oriented protocol and HTTP is a connectionless protocol. When you establish a connection to an FTP server, the connection usually remains open until you send a command to disconnect it. When you make a request using HTTP, the request is fulfilled and the connection is immediately released. By not holding the connection open, many HTTP requests are handled simultaneously. This can make uploading a large number of files much slower on HTTP than on FTP, because connections need to be reestablished for every file.

Another difference is the port numbers that the two protocols typically use. The Web server uses port numbers to identify the different protocols. The default port number for HTTP requests is typically 80, and the default port number for FTP requests is typically 21, but check with your ISP to confirm these port numbers.

Select the Use FTP Proxy or the Use HTTP Proxy option, if needed, and enter the host URL and its port number. Your ISP can provide you with this information.

Note Internet connections use the TCP/IP network protocols. Before you can connect to the Internet, you need to set up this networking protocol for your system.

Some Web servers require that you connect using Passive mode, especially if the Web server uses a firewall. If your ISP specifies this, enable the Use Passive Mode option. The Timeout values are the amount of time in seconds that GoLive keeps trying to connect before canceling the connection.

Note If you're having trouble connecting to a server, the server may be offline.

The Publish Server Report option causes a text report to be generated every time you connect to the server. This report includes information about every file uploaded or modified.

Specifying a publish server

Once you connect to the Internet, you can browse Web pages and get e-mail using your system. The next step in the publishing workflow for GoLive is locating the Web server to which you want to publish. GoLive can keep track of several different Web servers using its Edit Server dialog box, shown in Figure 33-2. Open this dialog box by choosing File ➪ Server ➪ Favorites.

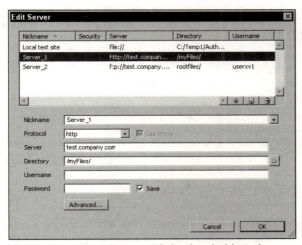

Figure 33-2: The Edit Server dialog box holds Web server information.

To enter the information for a new server, click the New button. You need to provide the following information:

- **Nickname:** This is the common name that appears in the Publish Server tab.
- **Protocol:** The available protocols for transferring the files are File, FTP, and HTTP. The File option let you publish your Web pages to a local directory. For Web servers, whether you should select FTP or HTTP depends on the type of Web server to which you're uploading the files. Most web servers use ftp access. Some Web servers require a specific transfer protocol. Check with your ISP to find out which one is required in your situation.
- **Server:** You type the URL for the Web server here.
- **Directory:** This field lets you specify a directory on the Web server that is opened when the connection is made. If you're connected to the Internet, you can click the browse button (to the right of the Directory field) to see the Web server's directory structure.
- **Username/Password:** Most servers also require a username and password.
- **Save option:** You click this check box to save the password along with the server information so you don't need to type it every time you connect to the server.

Caution If you enable the Save option, then anyone who sits at your computer has access to your hosted Web files. For security reasons, it's best *not* to enable the Save option and, instead, type in your password every time. Also, as an additional security feature, you should regularly change Web server passwords.

Adding and configuring sites

With several Web servers added to the Edit Server dialog box, you can select which one to use for a given site using the Site Settings dialog box, shown in Figure 33-3. With the site window selected, choose Site ⇨ Settings (⌘/Ctrl+Shift+Y) menu command to open the Site Settings dialog box.

Click on the Publish Server option in the left pane and the Server definition fields appear, providing another way to enter the server information. Once the server is defined, you can use the icon buttons beneath the server list to add the defined server to the list of favorites, duplicate the current selected server, create a new server, or remove the current selected server.

The Site Settings dialog box allows you to add several different servers for a single site. However, you can only select one as the active Web server.

The Site Settings dialog box also includes a panel of options for specifying how files are uploaded or exported. In the Site Settings dialog box, opened by choosing Site ⇨ Settings, select the Upload/Export panel from the list on the right. The Upload/Export panel, shown in Figure 33-4, appears. By enabling the Site Specific Settings, you can configure the upload options for the selected site.

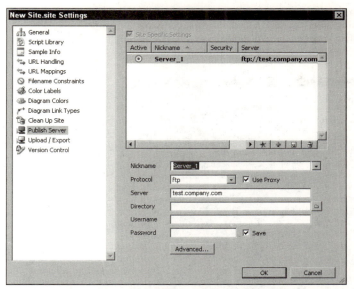

Figure 33-3: The Site Settings dialog box has all the site settings.

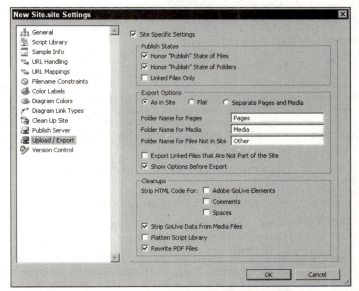

Figure 33-4: The Site Settings dialog box allows you to configure upload options.

If you want to configure the upload and export options for all sites, you find the same settings in the Preferences dialog box (Figure 33-5), which you access by choosing GoLive ⇨ Preferences (Mac) or GoLive ⇨ Edit ⇨ Preferences (Windows). Both the Site Setting dialog box and the Preference dialog box have the following configuration options.

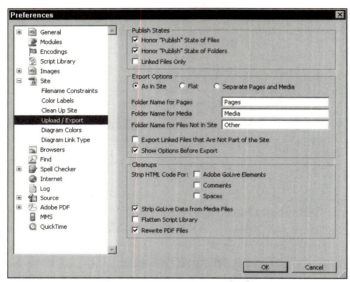

Figure 33-5: The Preferences dialog box also includes an Upload/Export panel.

- ✦ **Publish States:** Each file and/or folder can have an assigned publish state. You can designate this state as Always, Never, or If Referenced in the Inspector palette when you select a file or folder in the site window. These states are used in the Upload/Export panel with the Honor Publish State of Files and Honor Publish State of Folders options. With these options, you can select the designated states when uploading files. There is also an option to include linked files only.

- ✦ **Export Options:** This section lets you configure the file structure for the site as it's exported with the following options:

    - **As in Site:** Copies the exact file structure in the local file system to the Web server.
    - **Flat:** Copies all files in the site to a single root directory on the Web server.
    - **Separate Pages and Media:** Copies the pages and media files into separate subfolders as indicated by the Folder Name for Pages and Folder Name for Media fields.
    - **Folder options:** You can also create a separate folder for other files that are uploaded — files that aren't pages or media.
    - **Export Linked Files that Are Not Part of the Site:** Linked files that aren't part of the site typically aren't uploaded with the site, but you can export these files along with the site by enabling this option.

- **Show Options Before Export:** Displays these settings every time you choose File ➪ Export, so you can change the folder names as needed.

✦ **Cleanups:** This section optimizes your Web pages:

- **Strip HTML Code:** By stripping HTML code for Adobe GoLive elements, comments, and spaces, you reduce your Web page's file size. This decreases download time.
- **Strip GoLive Data from Media Files:** This strips GoLive data from media files to reduce their file size. This mainly applies to Photoshop Smart Objects with variables.

Caution

Stripping the GoLive elements out of Web pages makes it difficult to edit certain GoLive features such as actions, components and templates; stripping comments and spaces makes it difficult to understand the HTML code when viewed on the Web server. If you select any of these cleanup options, be careful not to download the file over the top of the local file, or it hinders your ability to make changes in GoLive.

- **Flatten Script Library:** Removes any unnecessary actions code from the site-wide JavaScript library file.
- **Rewrite PDF Files:** This likewise optimizes any PDF files.

Publishing a Web Site Using GoLive

After you configure your system to connect to a Web server, the steps involved in publishing a site are rather simple. GoLive provides two methods for actually uploading the Web-site files to the Web server. One method uses the Publish Server tab and the other uses the FTP Browser.

Connecting to a server

Before you can view a Web site on the Internet, you must transfer all the files that make up the site to the Web server. The Web server then presents the files to the user's browser upon request. You accomplish the process of moving these files using the Publish Server tab. With the site window opened in GoLive, choose Site ➪ Publish Server ➪ Connect. Once connected, the server URL or file path displays at the top of the right pane of the site window and all the uploaded files are listed, as shown in Figure 33-6.

If GoLive has any trouble connecting to the server, a warning dialog box appears with information on the problems that were encountered.

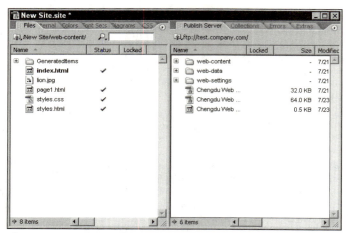

Figure 33-6: When you establish a connection to the server, files display.

Uploading, downloading, and synchronizing files

After connecting, you can upload, download, or synchronize files, depending on your situation. You upload and download files using the Upload dialog box. You synchronize files using the Synchronize dialog box. With both boxes, if you select a file in the Site column, information about the file is displayed. Icons to the right of the site filenames indicate whether a file is to be skipped, uploaded, downloaded, or deleted.

- **Uploading files:** You can upload all the files that are part of a site by choosing Site ⇨ Publish Server ⇨ Upload All. This opens the Upload dialog box (Figure 33-7), where you can confirm all the files you want to upload. When you click OK, a dialog box appears and lists the number of items to upload. The upload dialog box has two check boxes:

    - **Show Folder Structure:** This option shows the folders with the files to upload. When this option is disabled, you see a list of files regardless of location.

    - **Show Skipped Items:** This hides all files that you've marked as Skip.

When you upload files to the Web server using the Publish Server tab, GoLive copies to the server the last modification date and time for each file, not the date and time when the files were uploaded. Because of this, the local files may be synchronized with the files on the Web server.

Once you upload an entire site, you can selectively upload certain files by choosing Site ⇨ Publish Server ⇨ Upload Selection. Alternatively, you can upload only those items that you've modified since the upload by choosing Site ⇨ Publish Server ⇨ Upload Modified Files. This command causes the Upload dialog box to appear, but the Upload Selection menu command does not. You may also manually copy files to the Web server from the site window by dragging and dropping them from the left pane to the right pane.

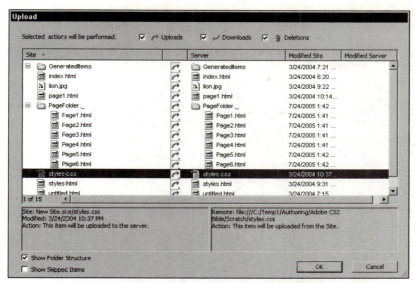

Figure 33-7: The Upload dialog box lets you confirm which files to upload.

- ✦ **Downloading Files:** Choosing Site ➪ Publish Server also offers several commands for downloading files from the Web server to your local file system. These menu commands include Download All, Download Selection, and Download Newer. Using both the Download All and Download Newer menu commands opens the Download dialog box, which is identical to the Upload dialog box, except all files or those files with a newer modification date on the Web server are marked for download.

- ✦ **Synchronizing Files:** Choose Site ➪ Publish Server ➪ Synchronize uploads and downloads files at the same time. The Synchronization dialog box — another version of the Upload and Download dialog box opens. All local files with a newer modification date and time are marked for upload, and all Web server files with a newer modification date and time are marked for download. If you've changed a file on both the local file system and the Web server, a yellow triangular Synchronization Conflict icon appears allowing you to mark these files for upload or download. If you want simply to synch the modification dates instead of moving files, you can choose Site ➪ Publish Server ➪ Sync Modification Times All or Sync Modification Times Selected.

Using the FTP Browser to view files

If you don't need to transfer the entire site or just need to transfer files that have changed, you can open an FTP Browser within GoLive to view all the files on the Web server. Then using drag and drop, you can upload or download files.

Note: Although the FTP Browser may be used to transfer files, file transfers should really take place within the Site window. Using the Site window helps keep the Web server and the local structure synchronized.

To open the FTP Browser window choose File ➪ Server ➪ Connect to FTP. From the Servers field at the top of the window, you can select the server to which that you want to connect. To open the Select Server dialog box, click the Edit Servers button. You may also browse the local file system with the Browse Local button. This opens a simple file dialog box, shown in Figure 33-8, where you can browse to a local directory. The Connect button connects to the selected server.

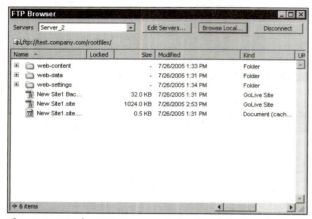

Figure 33-8: The FTP Browser dialog box lets you view files on the Web server.

Downloading a Web page

Choosing File ➪ Server ➪ Download Page (Shift+⌘/Ctrl+O), you can specify a URL for a Web page to download into GoLive. This command opens a simple dialog box, shown in Figure 33-9, where you can specify a Web page URL. If your system is connected to the Internet, GoLive then retrieves the Web page.

Figure 33-9: The Download Page dialog box lets you enter a Web page's URL.

STEPS: Publishing a Web Site

1. **Open a Web site in GoLive.** Within GoLive, choose File ➪ Open and open a Web site. With the Web site open, select the site window.

2. **Adding a Publish Server.** Choose Site ➪ Settings to open the Settings dialog box for this site. Click on the Publish Server panel in the right pane. Then click the New Server icon.

3. **Specifying the Publish Server settings.** In the Server fields that appear, shown in Figure 33-10, type a nickname for the server, select a protocol, and enter the server's URL and directory. Next, enter the username and password for the server. Uncheck the Save option for added security and click OK.

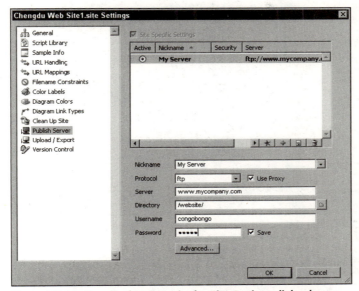

Figure 33-10: Specify the server in the Site Settings dialog box.

4. **Enable the Upload options.** In the Site Settings dialog box, select the Upload/Export panel in the right pane to display the Upload/Export panel, shown in Figure 33-11. Enable the Site Specific Settings option. Select the Honor Publish State of Files and Honor Publish State of Folders options. Then in the Cleanups section, enable all the Strip HTML Code options to reduce the file sizes of the uploaded files. Click OK to close the Site Settings dialog box.

5. **Connect to the Web server.** Make sure you're connected to the Internet and choose Site ➪ Publish Server ➪ Connect. GoLive connects to the Web server using the settings you specified. Because the Save Password option was disabled, a Connect to Server dialog box appears; here, you can enter the username and password needed to log on to the Web server.

6. **Upload files.** After connecting to the Web server, the files on the Web server display in the right pane of the site window. Choose Site ➪ Publish Server ➪ Upload All. The Upload dialog box appears with all files marked from upload. Click OK to begin the uploading. A dialog box appears, listing a count of the number of items that were uploaded.

7. **Verify the site online.** After the files upload, you can check the Web site online by entering the URL for the Web server in a browser.

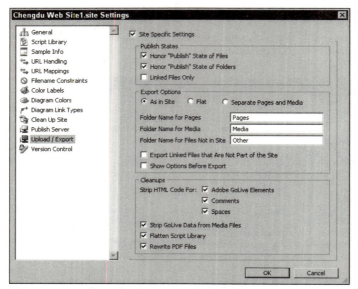

Figure 33-11: The Upload/Export panel of the Site Settings dialog box

Exporting a Web Site

If you have difficulty connecting or uploading files to a Web server using GoLive, you can always export the files to a local directory and then upload the directory using an external file-transfer program. To export a site, select the site window and choose File ➪ Export ➪ Site (⌘/Ctrl+E). If you enable the Show Options before Export option in the Upload/Export panel of the Preferences dialog box, the Export Site Options dialog box appears, shown in Figure 33-12.

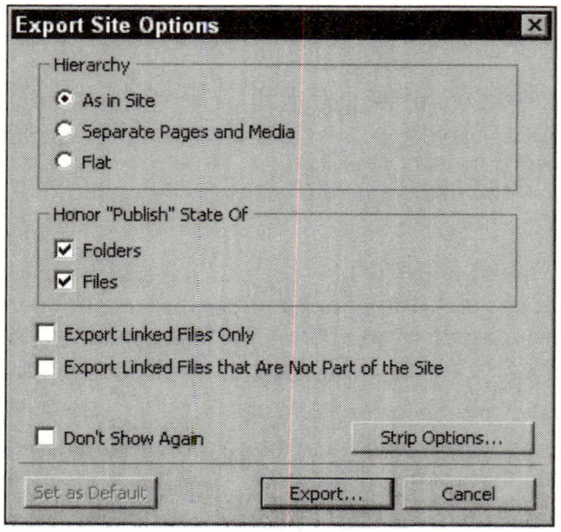

Figure 33-12: The Export Site Options dialog box

After you confirm the export options, a file dialog box opens where you can specify a folder name to which files will export. GoLive then generates a report of the exported site. This report lists all files that it couldn't find, that weren't part of the site, and that were exported but not linked to any of the Web pages. The report also lists the options you selected for the export process.

Summary

- ✦ To upload a Web site, you must configure GoLive by entering the server information in the Site Settings dialog box, which includes settings for uploading, exporting, and cleaning up files.
- ✦ After configure and connect to the Web server, you can see the files on the Web server in the site window.
- ✦ You can use the Publish Server tab in the site window to upload, download, or synchronize files between the local file system and the Web server.
- ✦ You can also use the FTP Browser to transfer files between the local file system and the Web server.
- ✦ Choose File ⇨ Export ⇨ Site to export to a local folder all the files that make up a site.

✦ ✦ ✦

Creating and Distributing PDFs on CDs/DVDs

CHAPTER 34

✦ ✦ ✦ ✦

In This Chapter

Creating PDF documents

Writing PDFs to CD-ROMs and DVDs

Securing CDs/DVDs

✦ ✦ ✦ ✦

Publishing creative works was once entirely dominated by print publishing. Today, you have a number of choices for publishing design works. Print is still a large market, but your clients may want files posted on Web sites or distributed on CDs or DVDs. Not only is CD-ROM/DVD distribution much less expensive than distribution of printed documents, but with CD-ROM/DVDs you can also include multimedia clips as part of your distributed collection. The content for your CD-ROM/DVD documents may include designs originally created for print, multimedia documents, Web documents, or other kinds of files where you can effectively display artwork.

Within the Creative Suite, you have tools that provide a simple but sophisticated means of creating files for distribution. When you need to organize files on your CD/DVDs, you can choose the Acrobat PDF file format and guarantee that anyone working on either Windows or Mac can see your files with complete document integrity, such as proper font displays and embedded images. In this chapter, you learn how to prepare PDF files for distribution on CD-ROMs and DVDs.

Preparing PDF Documents

PDF is an ideal format for distributing files because you can freely distribute the Adobe Reader installer software on the CD-ROM and make the most recent version easily accessible to your client's customers. As long as you distribute the licensing information for Acrobat, Adobe Systems grants you permission to distribute the Adobe Reader installer for Windows and Mac.

The PDF format is further beneficial in that the PDFs you produce can have all the type fonts, images, and links contained in the PDFs and displayed as you want the end user to view the files.

Cross-Reference

Font embedding presumes you're using fonts that have licensing permissions granted for embedding fonts. For more information on fonts and font embedding, see Chapter 16.

Obviously, your first step is to produce PDF documents from designs you create in other CS applications. If you designed pieces for print, you'll want to repurpose the print documents to a more suitable file for viewing from CD-ROM sources. If you include non–Adobe CS documents, you'll need to produce PDFs from other applications.

 There are many different ways to create PDFs from other programs, depending on the program and the level of support within Acrobat Professional for PDF creation. A description of the number of different programs and the ways PDFs are created from typical authoring applications is beyond the scope of this book. For a detailed look at PDF creation from the most popular computer programs, look at the *Adobe Acrobat 7 PDF Bible* (published by Wiley).

Working with Adobe PDF Settings

Adobe made it much easier to convert all CS2 programs documents to PDF. In each application, you save or export to PDF using the same Adobe PDF Settings to produce a PDF document. Illustrator and Photoshop use a Save command while InDesign and GoLive use an Export command. Both are found under the File menu and both provide the same options choices for creating PDF files.

Adobe PDF Settings are a set of options used to control how a PDF document is produced. These options have always been available with the Acrobat Distiller software that is used to convert a PostScript file to PDF. You can use one of several preset settings files to create a PDF or you can create your own custom Adobe PDF Settings file and use it with any CS program to produce a PDF. There are a number of choices when creating a new Adobe PDF Setting preset such as PDF compatibility, amount of compression to apply, downsampling images, embedding fonts, color management, and much more. When you make adjustments to settings, you can save the settings as a new preset. These preset files can be created in any CS2 application or Acrobat Distiller. When you create a preset in one program, the preset is available to all other CS2 applications as well as Acrobat Distiller.

There are many common settings used by all CS2 programs and there are some settings that uniquely apply to one program or another. For example, GoLive has options for HTML conversion that are unique to GoLive. Illustrator and InDesign uniquely support creating Adobe PDF Layers and Photoshop supports converting 16-bit images to 8-bit images. There are some other differences in settings options, but most options are common among the programs.

When you save or export to PDF you arrive at the Save (or Export) Adobe PDF dialog box. The dialog box contains several categories in a pane on the left side. Click a category and the options for that category are reflected in the right pane. In addition to the category choices and respective settings, you have some buttons and menus that remain visible regardless of the category selected in the left pane.

Common attributes

When you choose File ⇨ Save or File ⇨ Export the Save or Export dialog box opens where you can make choices for file format, filename, and location. Select PDF for the format and click Save or Export. The Adobe PDF Settings dialog box opens. In Figure 34-1, you can see the Export to Adobe PDF dialog box for InDesign.

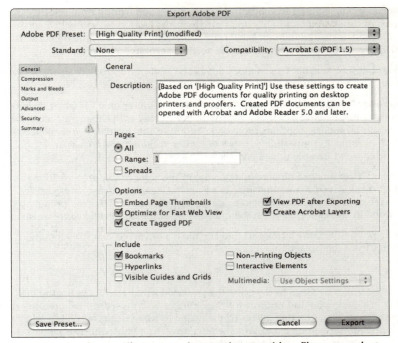

Figure 34-1: Choose File ➪ Export in InDesign. Provide a filename, select a location, and click Export to arrive at the Export Adobe PDF dialog box.

At the top and bottom of the dialog box, you have some options common to all CS2 applications. These choices include:

- **Adobe PDF Preset:** From the pull-down menu you select from several preinstalled presets or from custom presets you create in your workflow. Presets involving PDF/X are used for commercial printing. Select the Adobe PDF Preset that is suited for the output you want. For example, if preparing files for printing, use the High Quality Print setting as shown in Figure 34-1. If preparing files for Web or screen viewing, use the Smallest File Size option you can select from the Adobe PDF Preset pull-down menu.

Cross-Reference

For information on PDF/X format, see Chapter 38.

- **Standard:** The Standard pull-down menu appears in all CS2 applications except GoLive. From the menu choices you can select PDF/X for commercial printing or PDF/A for an archival format.
- **Compatibility:** Select the PDF compatibility. If you know some users work with Acrobat 5, use Acrobat 5 compatibility when distributing documents to other users. Compatibility includes:
  - **Acrobat 4.0:** If files are to be printed to high-end devices, you may want to use Acrobat 4 compatibility. Also, if your client's files need to be delivered to the largest range of users who are still using older viewers, then you might want to use this compatibility.

- **Acrobat 5.0:** Acrobat 5 compatibility offers you some additional security options over Acrobat 4 compatibility and more features related to Adobe PDF forms — especially forms containing JavaScript. Generally, most documents converted to PDF as Acrobat 5 compatible can be seen in Acrobat 4 viewers.

- **Acrobat 6.0:** Acrobat 6 uses more advanced security options than earlier formats and this version supports creating and viewing Adobe PDF layers.

- **Acrobat 7.0:** If you include the Adobe Reader installer on a CD when distributing documents, use the Acrobat 7 compatibility to stay with the most recent format. Additional security options have been added to this format. If you secure files with Acrobat 7 compatibility, users of earlier versions of Acrobat or Adobe Reader won't be able to see your files.

✦ **Save Preset:** If you make a change in any pane in the Save or Export to Adobe PDF dialog box, you can save the new settings as a Preset. Click Save Preset and you are prompted to name the preset. Provide a name and click Save. The new preset appears in the Adobe PDF Preset pull-down menu in all CS2 applications and Acrobat Distiller.

✦ **Save or Export:** Click Save or Export and the file is converted to a PDF document using the settings from the preset.

General

The General options offer settings to describe the general format attributes for the PDF document. In the General pane you find options for page ranges to convert to PDF, creating tagged documents, optimizing files, creating layers (only available when using Acrobat 6 and 7 compatibility), and preserving editing capabilities when converting Photoshop and Illustrator files. Some unique settings include: adding bookmarks, hyperlinks, interactive elements and multimedia in InDesign; and base URLs and rollover effects from GoLive. The Description field box provides you a summary of the settings used in the preinstalled presets. If you create a custom preset, you can add your own description in the text box. Wherever you see the Embed Page Thumbnails option, be sure to deselect this check box. From Acrobat 5 forward, thumbnail images are automatically created on the fly in Acrobat and Adobe Reader. Adding thumbnails adds to file sizes and are unnecessary in later Acrobat viewers.

Compression

Click the Compression item in the left pane, and the options in the right pane change, as shown later in this chapter in Figure 34-6. The Compression settings enable you to reduce file sizes by lowering resolution in raster images and compressing vector objects.

You can choose from a variety of compression options and downsampling amounts for color, grayscale, and monotone images. When using Illustrator, InDesign, and GoLive you have options for compressing text and line art. Additionally, you can crop image data to frames. This option produces PDFs at the image frame size while disregarding the page size. In Photoshop, you don't have options for text and line art compression. Photoshop does have one unique setting for converting 16-bit images to 8-bit images.

Marks and bleeds

Marks and bleeds are available in InDesign and Illustrator. Photoshop uses a different dialog box to create marks and bleeds. You first visit the Output options in Photoshop's Print with Preview dialog box and make selections for marks and bleeds before exporting the image to PDF. Unless you want to distribute PDFs for printing purposes, leave all the marks and bleed settings deselected, as shown in the InDesign Marks and Bleeds pane in Figure 34-2. If CDs are written to take a large volume of files to a print shop, you may want to submit PDFs for printing and use the marks and bleeds. If this is the case, see how these items are used in Chapter 38.

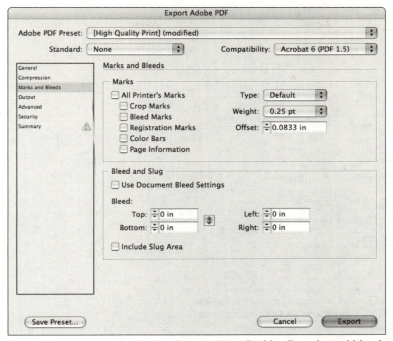

Figure 34-2: For screen viewing, be certain to disable all marks and bleeds.

The Marks and Bleeds options in Illustrator and InDesign are virtually identical. InDesign includes one more item for including the slug area.

Cross-Reference For information on printing files with Marks and Bleeds, see Chapter 38.

HTML conversions

GoLive has one pane not available in the other CS2 programs used for setting attributes for HTML conversion to PDF. As shown in Figure 34-3, you have settings options for defining page sizes, converting layouts, and color treatment. When you export to PDF from GoLive, you first need to create a PDF Preview. Click the Preview layout as Adobe PDF button at the top of the GoLive window, then choose File ⇨ Export ⇨ HTML to PDF. The Export Adobe PDF dialog box opens and enables you to address settings for GoLive exports to PDF.

Output

Output options appear in all Save Adobe PDF dialog boxes except GoLive. These options as shown later in this chapter in the InDesign Output pane in Figure 34-7 include settings for creating PDF/X files and handling color management.

Cross-Reference For information on PDF/X files see Chapter 38. For information on color management, see Chapter 6.

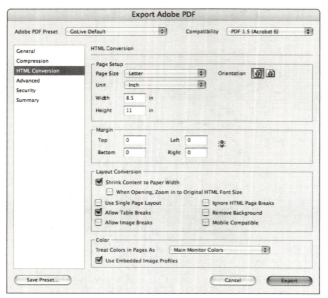

Figure 34-3: GoLive has a unique category for settings choices. Click HTML Conversion and choose options for page setup, layout conversion, and color treatment.

Advanced

Advanced settings offer options for font embedding and transparency flattening for InDesign and Illustrator. GoLive offers options for font embedding and adding document description metadata. Photoshop does not have an Advanced pane. Settings in the InDesign dialog box, shown later in this chapter in Figure 34-8, additionally include JDF job definitions.

Cross-Reference

For more information on font embedding, transparency flattening, and JDF job definitions see Chapter 38.

The Advanced settings also include an option for subsetting fonts. By default, the field box is set to 100 percent which means fonts are subset when the percentage of characters in a given font set is less than 100 percent. This makes editing the PDF possible if you need to make a quick text edit. If you have volumes of text documents you want to write to CDs, lower the value to 35 percent, and the file sizes will be a little smaller.

Security

The Security settings offer you options for file encryption. All CS2 programs support creating PDF documents with encryption. You can password-protect files against opening and/or editing and changing.

Cross-Reference

For information on applying security to PDF documents, see Chapter 31.

Summary

When you click Summary in the left pane, the right pane shows you a list of the options choices you made for all the other panes. Summaries are available for all CS2 programs. A single option exists for the Summary with the Save Summary button in all programs except Photoshop. Click this button and the summary information listed in the scrollable window shown in Figure 34-4 for Illustrator is saved to a text file.

If you want to keep a record or if you want to share your options choices in a workgroup with other users, click the Save Summary button. The Save Summary dialog box opens; here, you can provide a filename and choose a destination.

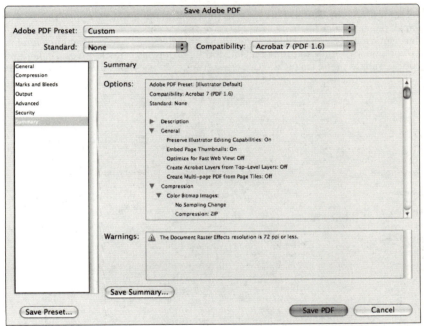

Figure 34-4: The Summary shows you a list of all the options choices you made for creating the PDF file.

There are many options from which you can choose to create PDF documents. Detailed descriptions for settings are beyond the scope of this book. For a closer look at Adobe PDF Settings and an amplified view for each setting see the *Adobe Acrobat 7 PDF Bible* (Wiley Publishing). To get a feel for creating a custom preset and converting files to PDF, follow these steps:

STEPS: Converting Documents to PDF

1. **Open a document in InDesign.** For this example, an InDesign document is used. You can use any CS2 application document, but some of the settings described here will differ a little if you use another program.

2. **Open the Adobe PDF Settings dialog box.** Choose File ⇨ Export. In the Export dialog box type a name for your exported file. From the Format pull-down menu select Adobe PDF. Navigate your hard drive to locate a folder where you want to save the file. Click Save and the Export Adobe PDF dialog box opens. By default, the General category is selected in the left pane.

3. **Select a Preset and compatibility.** Open the Adobe PDF Preset pull-down menu and select Smallest File Size. To export to PDF for CD/DVD writing, begin with this preset. From the Compatibility pull-down menu select Acrobat 7(PDF 1.6) to create Acrobat 7-compatible PDF documents. Note that when you make this menu selection, the preset name changes to [Smallest File Size] (modified). Any change to a setting automatically changes the preset name.

4. **Select options for General settings.** In the General pane, select a page range. If converting all pages, select All. Select the check boxes for Options shown in Figure 34-5. Add a description by typing in the Description text box. If you have interactive elements such as bookmarks and/or multimedia, select the appropriate check boxes. Depending on your personal preferences, the General settings should look something like Figure 34-5.

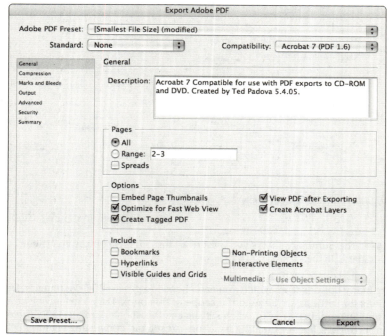

Figure 34-5: Set attributes in the General pane and click Compression to advance to the next pane.

5. **Select compression options.** If you want small image file sizes you can downsample images. The amount of downsampling is applied in the Compression pane. For the smallest file sizes that still look acceptable on-screen, type **72** in the first text box for color and grayscale images as shown in Figure 34-6. Leave the Tile Size at the default. Unless you are tiling pages in InDesign, this setting won't matter. If you are tiling pages for screen viewing set the value to 1024. The default is used for smaller tiles that might be seen on mobile devices and cell phones. Select Image Quality from the pull-down menu choices to adjust the amount of compression. Select a High Quality option for better screen viewing. Leave the remaining settings at the defaults. For screen viewing, you typically won't add marks and bleeds. Skip this pane and go directly to the Output pane.

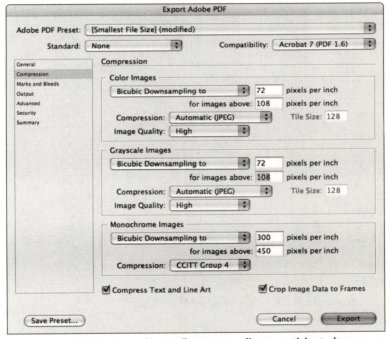

Figure 34-6: Set Compression attributes according to anticipated zoom levels.

Caution If your documents will frequently be viewed at higher zoom levels than 100 percent views, adjust the downsampling to accommodate the largest anticipated zoom level for comfortable viewing. Files at 72 ppi (pixels per inch) are intended to be viewed at 100 percent. If the pages are small and users frequently zoom to 200 percent, change the downsampling amount to 144 ppi to provide the equivalent of 72 ppi when zoomed 200 percent.

6. **Select output options.** Select Convert to Destination from the Color Conversion pull-down menu to convert colors to a different color space. For screen viewing the profile you will most commonly use is sRGB. Select sRGB IEC61966-2.1 from the Destination pull-down menu as shown in Figure 34-7. Click Advanced after making the settings in the Output pane.

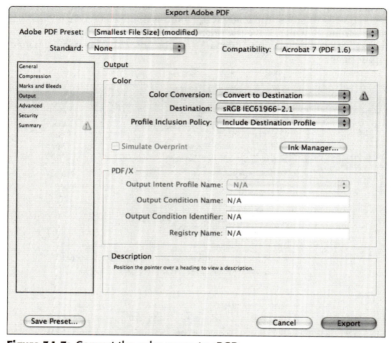

Figure 34-7: Convert the color space to sRGB.

Cross-Reference For information on profile embedding, see Chapter 6.

7. **Set font subsetting.** Reduce the amount in the Subsetting text box to 35 percent as shown in Figure 34-8. Unless your files need any editing, you can reduce the file size of the PDFs a little bit by lowering the subsetting amount.

Cross-Reference For information on font subsetting, see Chapter 16.

8. **View the summary.** Unless you want to secure the PDF documents, skip the security pane and click Summary in the left pane. Review the summary information to be certain all settings are applied as you defined them in each pane.

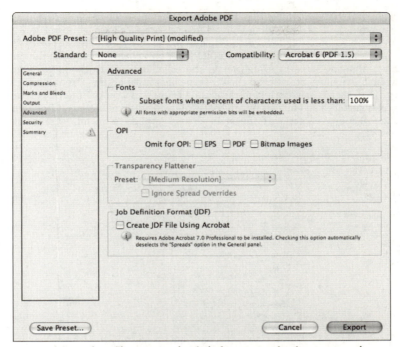

Figure 34-8: When files are used strictly for screen viewing, you can lower the font subsetting amount to slightly reduce PDF file sizes.

9. **Save a new preset.** Click Save Preset. The Save Preset dialog box shown in Figure 34-9 appears. Type a name for the preset and click OK. The preset is saved to the same folder on your hard drive where all other presets are saved. This new preset is now available to all other CS2 programs and Acrobat Distiller.

Figure 34-9: Type a descriptive name and click OK. The new preset is saved to the folder where all other presets reside.

For information on color profile embedding, see Chapter 6.

10. **Create a PDF document.** Click Export and the InDesign file is exported to PDF.

11. **Open a file from another CS2 application.** Launch Adobe Illustrator or any other application. If you have a document ready to convert, open the Bridge window and double-click on the file to launch the host application.

12. **Export to PDF.** Illustrator exports to PDF when you choose File ⇨ Save (or Save As). If you have an Illustrator document saved as a native `.ai` file, choose File ⇨ Save As. From the Format pull-down menu, select Adobe PDF (pdf). The Adobe PDF Preset dialog box appears. From the Adobe PDF Preset pull-down menu select the preset you created following Steps 1 through 11. As shown in Figure 34-10, the preset you named is available in Illustrator. Select the Preserve Illustrator editing Capabilities check box in the General pane. In both Illustrator and Photoshop, you want to be certain this check box is selected so you can return to the file and edit if necessary. Click Save PDF and the PDF file is created with the same settings applied to the InDesign export.

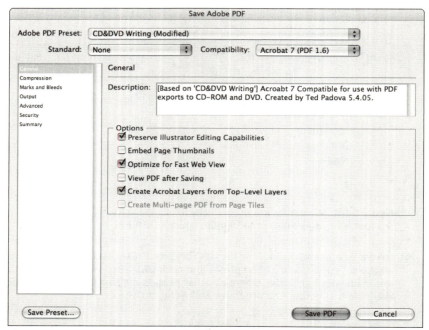

Figure 34-10: Be certain to select the Preserve Illustrator Editing Capabilities check box before saving to PDF.

Creating PDFs from Adobe Photoshop

Photoshop offers several different tools for presenting and archiving images that can be saved to the PDF format. You can use the standard-vanilla flavor of just saving a Photoshop document to the PDF format by using the same preset options as used with other CS2 programs, or you can use a little creativity in Photoshop to suit various needs before saving to Photoshop PDF.

Using Photomerge

Depending on your needs, you may want to do something other than simply saving a collection of images to individual PDFs. For example, suppose you want to write files to CD-ROM as a means of archiving jobs. You may have several Photoshop images that you want to view together and add some notes to remind you what the images were used for or perhaps some specific attributes pertaining to the job or the files used on the job. Rather than rely on the Bridge to display a folder of images, you can combine images in a single document, save as PDF, and add notes in Acrobat. A nice way of accomplishing such a task is using Photoshop's Photomerge command.

 For more information on using Adobe Bridge, see Chapter 7.

Photomerge was not designed to create a single-page document from random files. The true intent for Photomerge is to combine images taken in a panoramic view and merge them into a single file. However, Photomerge is not limited to using the command for just panoramic photos.

To merge photos into a single document, start by opening Adobe Bridge. When the files have been selected or the folder identified, choose Tools ➪ Photoshop ➪ Photomerge.

Photomerge places your images as thumbnail views along the top of the Photomerge dialog box. You can click and drag the thumbnails down to the large open window and arrange the images to your liking. In Figure 34-11, you can see images organized in the lower window while the last image is dragged down to position. If you want to view the canvas area where the images are arranged in a zoomed view, click and drag the slider in the Navigator on the right side of the dialog box.

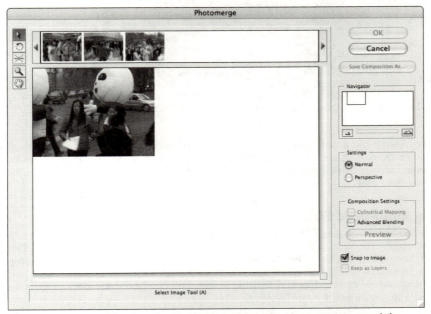

Figure 34-11: Drag the thumbnails down and position the images around the Photomerge canvas area.

When the files are arranged on the canvas, click OK. The images are then placed on a Photoshop canvas where you can save the file in Photoshop PDF format or any other format available from the Format menu in the Save or Save As dialog box. After saving the file in PDF, open the document in Adobe Acrobat. In Acrobat, you can add comments to the file using the commenting tools as shown in Figure 34-12.

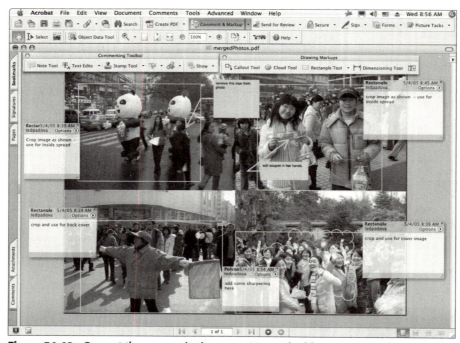

Figure 34-12: Convert the composite image to PDF and add comments in Acrobat.

Photoshop has a Note and Audio Annotation tool for adding comment notes and sound annotations. Both are visible in Acrobat when saved as PDF. If you want to add more than a note comment, add your comments in Acrobat, where you have an abundant number of comment tools.

Saving multi-page PDFs

Yet another way to display Photoshop images in a PDF file is to convert each image to a separate PDF page. Whereas the Photomerge feature in the Bridge creates a single-page document, the PDF Presentation option, also available in the Bridge, takes selected files and converts each file to separate PDF pages. A single PDF document is created with pages sized to the size of the original images saved as PDF. In other words, you can have page sizes of 3-x-5, 4-x-6, and 8-x-10 inches all in the same file.

To create a multi-page document from a collection of photo images, start by opening Adobe Bridge. In the Bridge Folders tab, navigate your folders to find the folder containing images you want to convert to PDFs. If all the photos in a given folder are to be converted, press ⌘/Ctrl+A to select all; otherwise, press ⌘/Ctrl+click to select individual files.

When you select the files in the Bridge, choose Tools ➪ Photoshop ➪ PDF Presentation.

The PDF Presentation dialog box opens, as shown in Figure 34-13. The Browse button enables you to search other folders and identify images you can add to the list of files targeted for conversion. Under Output options you have two options for the way the converted files are viewed in Acrobat. Select the radio button for Multi-Page Document. The other button, Presentation, is used for a self-running presentation.

Figure 34-13: The PDF Presentation dialog box

Cross-Reference

For information on creating PDF Presentations and setting presentation attributes, see Chapters 7 and 36.

Select the View PDF after Saving check box if you want to see the PDF document immediately after conversion. The presentation options only apply when you click the radio button for Presentation in the Output Options. Click Save and the Save dialog box appears. Supply a name, locate a folder, and click Save in the Save dialog box; the Save Adobe PDF dialog box opens.

The Adobe PDF settings are the same as the ones you have available when saving individual files as Photoshop PDF. After choosing a Preset or making choices in the Adobe PDF settings, click OK and the file opens in Acrobat if you checked the box to View PDF after Saving. If you have images of different sizes, you'll note the thumbnails in the Pages pane are all the same size, whereas the pages in the Document pane appear at different sizes.

Cross-Reference

For more information on creating PDF Presentations from Photoshop, see Chapter 7.

Converting to PDF using Acrobat

Another way to create PDFs from image files is to use Adobe Acrobat rather than the CS applications. You can convert images and a variety of non-Adobe application documents to separate PDF documents or convert a folder of images to a single PDF file. A variety of different image file formats are supported, including TIFF, PNG, JPEG, and GIF as well as AutoCAD, Microsoft programs, text files, HTML and more.

To determine what file types are supported for conversion to PDF from Acrobat, open the Preferences dialog box by pressing Command/Ctrl+K. Click Convert to PDF in the left pane and scroll the list box in the right pane. If a file format is displayed in the list box, you can drag the file to the Acrobat window or choose File ⇨ Create PDF ⇨ From File. Alternately, you can use the Create PDF task button pull-down menu and use the From File menu command. If you have multiple files to convert to PDF, use the From Multiple Files menu command. Whether you use From File or From Multiple Files, a dialog box opens where you can select the files to convert. Click Open (when using From File) or OK (when using Multiple Files). The selected files are converted to PDF using the Adobe PDF Settings you last used to produce PDF documents from your CS programs. If you want to use different settings, open Acrobat Distiller and select the setting you want to use from the Default Settings pull-down menu shown in Figure 34-14. Note that all your custom settings are listed in the menu.

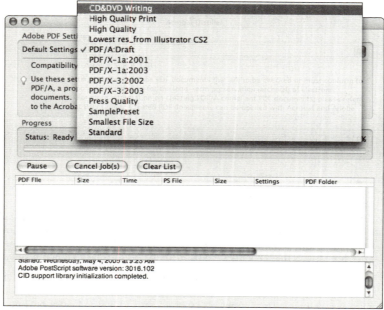

Figure 34-14: When using Acrobat to convert files to PDF, select the preset you want to use in Acrobat Distiller.

Acquiring PDFs from clients

PDF creation on your computer is something that you can control, and with the CS applications you have abundant opportunities to create PDF documents. At times you may need to acquire PDF files from your clients to integrate in a design or add to a collection of files you prepare for replication on CDs or DVDs. PDF creation at the other end is something you can't control. Quite often your clients aren't working with the CS applications and don't have the same PDF creation options.

You may need to acquire documents from dedicated accounting programs, 3-D modeling programs, engineering and scientific programs, or off-the-shelf applications like Lotus Notes. You may not even have the programs installed on your computer. In many cases your clients won't have Acrobat or a means for converting their application documents to PDF. When such cases arise, you may need to be the technical support for your clients and guide them through the process of converting files to PDF.

Obviously, if your clients have a frequent need to create and edit PDF files they should purchase Adobe Acrobat. But all too often the need arises to create a few PDF documents that wind up integrated in the designs you create. For the casual PDF creator, some solutions are available at no cost for creating PDF files.

Creating PDFs on the Macintosh

PDF creation on the Macintosh is easy and readily available to all users running OS X. PDF support was engineered by Apple at the operating system level, and Macintosh users don't need to acquire any software in addition to the operating system to create PDF files. To work through creating PDF documents on the Macintosh, follow these steps:

STEPS: Creating PDF documents using the Mac OS

1. **Open a program not supporting conversion to PDF.** Use a program like TextEdit that doesn't provide an option for saving or exporting to PDF. You can open a text document in TextEdit or create some text in the editor. Alternately, you can access the Mac Help by selecting the Help menu on the Desktop and selecting Mac Help. In Mac Help, search for an item you want to keep around for a reference document. Other options might include creating a PDF from an Email, a Web page from Safari or Internet Explorer, or a number of other programs.

2. **Open the Print dialog box.** Choose File ⇨ Print in whatever application you use to open the Print dialog box.

3. **Print to PDF.** In OS X Tiger, more support for PDF has been added to the Mac OS X upgrade. In addition to creating PDF documents like earlier versions of OS X, Tiger supports creating PDF workflows. When you open the PDF pull-down menu, as shown in Figure 34-15, you can see some preinstalled workflows added to the menu. Custom workflows can be added by clicking on the plus (+) symbol appearing below the PDF button. To convert an open document to PDF, select Save as PDF at the top of the menu.

4. **Name and save the file.** The Save dialog box opens after selecting Save as PDF. Type a name in the Save As text box and locate a folder for the saved file. Click Save and the file is saved as PDF.

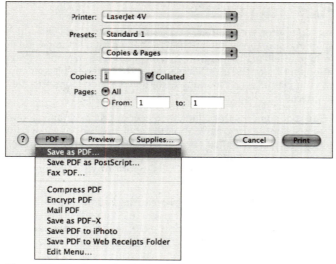

Figure 34-15: Open the PDF pull-down menu and click Save as PDF to convert the open document to a PDF file.

Creating PDFs on Windows

Quite often design professionals working on Macintoshes assume that their Windows counterparts have the same options for creating PDFs. Unfortunately, Windows doesn't have support for PDF built into the operating system. With all the noises for Longhorn (the next version of Windows) and Metro (an Acrobat-like system to be integrated in Longhorn), we most likely won't ever see PDF support built into Windows.

If your clients work on Windows and you need to have them send you PDF documents, there are some alternatives available that Windows users can easily access to create a PDF document. First, have your client search the Internet in a Web browser. Use PDF creation or PDF creator for the search criteria. The results reported in the search window will display a number of different PDF creation tools. Many of the tools are available as freeware or shareware.

Freeware tools typically get installed as a printer driver. Just like on the Mac, the Windows user can choose File ⇨ Print, select the printer driver for creating PDF documents, and click Print. The file is then saved as a PDF document.

This solution is available at no cost and may encourage people to submit PDF documents if you require some for a design campaign or when creating CDs or DVDs. Obviously, anyone needing to create and edit PDFs as a routine job function should be encouraged to purchase Acrobat.

Using plug-ins

In some cases, PDF creation needs may exceed the limitations of the simple creation tools found in an operating system or from a printer driver. Some specialized needs may be necessary for certain types of documents to be converted to PDF. For example, for map designers, a tool that takes proprietary geo-referenced GIS data formats and publishes to intelligent geo-referenced nonproprietary PDF files is just what your client wants. Such a tool is available from Layton Graphics, which produces the MAP2PDF plug-in for Acrobat (www.layton-graphics.com). In addition to converting proprietary CAD and GIS data to PDF, the resultant documents are intelligent. They contain hyperlinks and bookmarks and are searchable by attribute data, latitude/longitude, and database queries. This is but one example of specialized PDF creation tools that support intelligent PDF document creation.

As a creative professional, you may be called upon to help your clients create intelligent PDF files that are turned over to you to complete the creative work on a job or campaign. As a technical resource, you'll want to be familiar with the sources of information that can help you guide your clients. In addition to visiting Adobe's Web site for information for specialized PDF creation, you can find a list of almost every plug-in, add-on, and dedicated application that supports PDF at www.pdfstore.com. The Planet PDF Web site hosts the Planet PDF store where you can find descriptions, and in many cases, demo files for almost any workflow.

Writing PDFs to CD-ROMs and DVDs

The advantage in hosting PDFs on the Web is that you can keep them updated as they're changed. With CD/DVDs, you lose this advantage. However, CD-ROMs have their own advantages that you can't duplicate with Web-hosted documents. For example, you can eliminate any problems for users accessing your PDFs, and you can create search indexes for faster searches. You can eliminate long download times for large files and you can minimize confusion when several PDFs are interactive and need to be housed in the same directory to work properly. With some of these advantages, you may find replicating CD-ROM/DVDs a viable solution for distributing your PDFs.

If you replicate discs for distributing documents, you'll want to exercise some care in creating a master CD/DVD that works properly and provides a user with all the features you want them to enjoy.

Adding metadata to files

Before you begin organizing collections of documents, be certain you create a metadata template and populate the metadata fields that can help recipients of the files perform searches in the Bridge and in Acrobat. Be certain to add descriptions for files, locations, data about your own design firm, and any other information appropriate for the metadata.

Cross-Reference For information regarding creating metadata templates and applying metadata to files, see Chapter 7.

Organizing a collection of PDFs

When organizing your documents for CD/DVD replication, you must consider two important measures. First, you must preserve the directory path for all actions that open and close files. If you use a button, a page action, a bookmark, a link, a JavaScript, or any interactive element that opens another file, the path that Acrobat searches is absolute. If you relocate files after creating links and copy them to a disc, Acrobat won't find the linked files. The best way to prevent a potential problem is to create a single folder on your hard drive, then nest subfolders below the main folder. Create the links and test them thoroughly before creating a master used to replicate the CD/DVDs. You can copy all the files and subfolders from the main folder on your hard drive to the root location on the disc, but don't move any files from the subfolders. The folders and folder names need to be preserved.

Cross-Reference For information on linking PDF documents, see Chapter 29.

The second precaution is to ensure all filenames are preserved when copying PDFs to a CD/DVD. This issue is related to the software used to write the CD/DVD. You must use naming conventions that preserve long names. Writing media for a cross-platform audience is always best. Therefore, if you use a Mac, be sure the filenames aren't disturbed when files are viewed on a Windows machine and vice versa. As a matter of practice, using standard DOS naming conventions (an eight-character-maximum name with a three-character-maximum extension) is always successful. As a final step, you should test a CD/DVD before replication on both platforms.

Replicating CD-ROM/DVDs

If you have a limited number of CDs to copy, a personal CD/DVD-R device can satisfy your needs. These devices come with different interfaces where the write speed varies greatly according to the interface type. USB devices are extremely slow whereas FireWire drives are the top of the line. Even if your CD/DVD write needs are occasional, you'll appreciate the much faster completion time of a FireWire drive.

If your media replication involves writing many CD/DVDs, use a replication center. You can reduce the cost of replicating media to less than $1 apiece; depending on the number of discs you order. For a replication source, search the Internet and compare the costs of the services. When you find a service, send them a master disc of the PDF files you want replicated. In order to ensure the filenames and directory paths are properly specified on the destination media, thoroughly test your own CD/DVD to be certain everything works properly before submitting the files to the replication center.

Adding a Web page for updates

After you distribute a disc to clients or employees, you have no idea how long people may use the files. You might go through several updates of the same files before someone updates your disc to the latest version. To guard against obsolescence, create a folder with an HTML file to be included on the disc. For all the button and text links, make the hypertext references to the pages on your Web site where updates are routinely reported. You can add a README file or a PDF to instruct users they should frequent your Web site for updated forms. Be certain to keep the directory paths fixed on your Web site so even a user with an antiquated CD/DVD can easily access the pages without having to search your site.

Tip README files are text-only documents. On Windows use Windows WordPad or Notepad and type your help information. Save the file as text-only. On the Mac, type your help information in TextEdit and save the file as text-only.

Creating a welcome file

You can make a file that describes the CD/DVD, its contents, and a general statement about visiting your Web site into a text-only file or a PDF document. If you create a PDF file, then the user needs to have an Acrobat viewer installed on his/her computer. Any computer user can read a text file, so you may want to add both.

Unfortunately, everyone won't view the README files. Some users avoid them and jump right into your documents. If you want to ensure that every user sees your welcome file at least one time, you can add an autoplay file that automatically launches your welcome file when the media is inserted in a CD/DVD drive. Windows users can add an autoplay to a CD/DVD by writing a few lines of code and saving text as INI. Macintosh users need to use a commercial CD/DVD-writing utility.

Because authoring programs change so fast, rather than guide you to programs used for creating autoplay CD/DVDs, let us point you to the Internet, where you can search for the most recent programs that help you create autoplays. In a search engine, search for *autoplay* and you'll see many links to sites where public domain and commercial sites provide products for creating autoplay files.

Adding Adobe Reader

You should always check with Adobe's Web site for the current rules and licensing restrictions before distributing software like Adobe Reader. The distribution policy can change at any time, so what is said today may not be true tomorrow.

As of this writing, Adobe permits you to copy the Adobe Reader software installer to a media source for distribution. You must comply with the licensing policy and include all licensing information with the installer application. For specifics related to the distribution of the Acrobat Reader software, visit Adobe's Web site at www.adobe.com/products/acrobat/distribute.html for the most recent copy of Adobe Reader and the current distribution policy.

If you include the Adobe Reader installer on a disc, also create a Web page that links to the download page of the current Reader software. If your CD/DVD is in circulation for a long time, Reader may go through several versions before a user updates to your latest CD/DVD version.

Adding Security to CD-ROMs

Securing PDF documents, whether it is through Acrobat Certificate Authority or third-party signature handlers, works great for protecting content in PDF documents and protecting files from being opened when a user doesn't have access to a password. But what if you want to encrypt files against content copying, and changing, and don't want the encrypted documents circulated? Providing a user with a password to open the PDF doesn't guarantee that your documents won't be distributed along with the password to open them. eBooks are a good example of a situation in which you want to license a single copy of your content to a single user.

Contact StarForce at: www.star-force.com in San Francisco or www.star-force.ru in Moscow, Russia, for a Windows utility used for protecting CD-ROMs.

PDF Pro 1.1 is a marvelous tool for anyone who wants to license a single copy of PDF documents contained on CD-ROMs. The product was designed especially for publishers, governments, corporations, and small-business users who want to distribute eBooks, eZines, reports, statistical data, scientific, and any type of sensitive material that needs to be protected against copying, extraction, modification, and distribution.

The protection of each PDF document incorporates a unique algorithm with encryption. The end user installs the Protection plug-in that initiates the StarForce PDF protection module each time the user's Adobe Reader application is launched. Another user cannot use the plug-in module, and anyone who attempts to view any of the protected CD-ROM content is denied access. The behind-the-scenes encryption actually uses the physical parameters of the CD-ROM drive and a unique 24-byte key on each batch of licensed CD-ROMs. StarForce claims that CD-ROMs duplicated from individual users or through plant manufacturing are completely unusable.

If a user tries to access PDF files with other Acrobat viewers or applications supporting imports of PDF documents, the user is likewise denied access. The manufacturer claims the product is effective against any kind of workaround where a user may attempt to extract the content from an encrypted CD-ROM and circulate the data. If your needs include mass copy protection, this product is worth examining.

Another option for securing PDFs and CD/DVDs is to use the Adobe LiveCycle Policy Server. This option is a server side solution from Adobe Systems intended for enterprises and large organizations. It would be cost prohibitive for individual artists, but for large companies with a budget to purchase the Policy Server, Adobe provides you many sophisticated security solutions. To learn more about Adobe LiveCycle Policy Server, visit www.adobe.com/products/server/policy/main.html.

Summary

- All the Creative Suite applications export or save to the PDF format. PDF documents are a good means of hosting files on CD/DVDs, because the file integrity is preserved with font and image embedding.

- Adobe PDF Settings are used consistently with all CS2 applications. Settings created in one CS2 program are available to all other CS2 programs.

- You can copy the Adobe Reader installer to CD-ROMs as long as you comply with Adobe licensing restrictions.

- Autoplay files help you direct a user to a central navigation page. Autoplay routines are developed with CD-ROM authoring programs, script writing, or applications designed for the specific purpose of creating autoplays.

- Through the use of Adobe Policy Server or a third-party application, you can secure CD-ROMs against copying and distributing PDF documents.

✦ ✦ ✦

Creating SWF and SVG Files

In This Chapter

Creating SWF files in Illustrator

Creating SVG files in Illustrator

Using SWF and SVG in GoLive

Converting Web pages in Acrobat

The Web's popularity has seen the appearance of several new technologies that add interactivity and portability within Web pages. Of these, Flash (SWF) files and Scalable Vector Graphic (SVG) files, both vector-based image formats, create files a fraction of the size of their raster-based counterparts, making them useful for creating Web graphics and, specifically, Web animations. You can also use these formats to scale images to any size without sacrificing image quality.

You can create both Flash (SWF) files and Scalable Vector Graphics (SVG) from within Illustrator and use them in GoLive and Acrobat. You create SWF animation in Illustrator by placing the graphics for each frame of the animation on a separate layer, which you then convert to animation frames. You can also apply XML-based filters to SVG graphics and still maintains the vector nature of the file. You can also make SVG files interactive.

Creating SWF Files in Illustrator

Although you typically create SWF files using the Macromedia Flash program, Flash isn't the only application that works with vector-based images. Adobe Illustrator also creates vector-based designs, so converting a native Illustrator graphic to the SWF format is a simple conversion. You can save any Illustrator graphic as an SWF file for use on the Web. You can also use Illustrator to create SWF animations by placing each frame of the animation in a separate layer.

Saving SWF files

There are two different paths for exporting Illustrator graphics to the SWF file format. The first is choosing File ⇨ Export, and the second is choosing File ⇨ Save for Web. Both of these options offer the same options, but the Save for Web dialog box lets you preview and change options before saving the file.

Note   Keep in mind that SWF files require that you install the Flash Player browser plug-in to view files on the Web.

Exporting SWF files

Choose File ⇨ Export to open the Export dialog box. Within this dialog box, you can select Macromedia Flash (SWF) as the Save as Type. Click Save, and the Macromedia Flash (SWF) Format Options dialog box appears (see Figure 35-1). The options in this dialog box include the following:

New Feature In Illustrator CS2, the Macromedia Flash (SWF) Format Options dialog box has been endowed with several new features including expanded control over animation options, Export Text as Outlines and Compress File options, and the Background Color swatch.

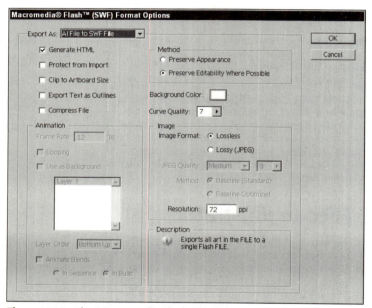

Figure 35-1: The Macromedia Flash (SWF) Format Options dialog box

✦ **The Export As:** Includes three options — AI File to SWF File, AI Layers to SWF Frames, and AI Layers to SWF Files. The AI File to SWF File option exports the Illustrator document to a single frame. The other two options convert the artwork contained on each layer to either an SWF frame or to a separate SWF file.

✦ **Generate HTML:** For a SWF file to be visible on a Web page, the Web page must include some HTML code that references the Flash plug-in. The Generate HTML option causes the export process to write this HTML code for you. The HTML code is saved to the same directory as the SWF file using the same name with an HTML extension. Figure 35-2 shows the HTML code that was generated for a simple example.

Tip Double-clicking on the generated HTML file in the Finder or in Windows Explorer causes the exported SWF artwork to open and display within the default Web browser.

Figure 35-2: The Generate HTML option generates a separate HTML file.

- **Protect from Import:** This option prevents the SWF file from being downloaded and edited, thereby protecting your design.

- **Clip to Artboard Size:** This option sets the size of the exported file to match the entire art board document, excluding any artwork outside of the art board. If this option is disabled, the exported document is set to the extents of the document objects only.

- **Export Text As Outlines:** This option converts all text to object paths as part of the export. This helps maintain the look of the text in all browsers without relying on fonts.

- **Compress File:** This option compresses the exported file to reduce its size, making it quicker to download.

Caution

Flash players prior to version 6 cannot load compressed files.

- **Method:** When the Export As setting is set to AI File to SWF File, then you can choose between the Preserve Appearance or the Preserve Editability Where Possible options. The Preserve Appearance option flattens all layers to a single layer. The Preserve Editability Where Possible option maintains all layers during exporting.

- **Background Color:** A color swatch lets you set the background color for the exported file.

- **Curve Quality:** Sets the accuracy of the Bézier curves for the artwork. Lower Curve Quality values reduce the file size by decreasing the number of points as well as the curve's quality. Higher values maintain the curve quality but increase the overall file size.

Tip

Most standard curves are adequately maintained with a Curve Quality setting of 7.

- **Image Format:** Can be set to Lossless, which keeps all the image data, resulting in large file sizes, or Lossy, which compresses the images using a JPEG format that throws away image data depending on the JPEG Quality setting. If you select Lossy, you can specify the amount quality as Low, Medium, High, or Maximum (or using a numeric value from 1 to 10). The Low setting results in the smallest file sizes at the expense of image quality, and the High setting yields a large file size but maintains the image quality. You can also select to use the Baseline (Standard) or Baseline Optimized compression method. The Baseline Optimized method provides an additional level of compression.

- **Resolution:** Lets you specify the resolution value for the SWF artwork. For SWF files that are viewed online, a setting of 72 ppi is sufficient, but if you plan to print your artwork, select a higher ppi setting. Higher resolution settings result in larger file sizes.

The Animation controls become available when the Export As option is set to All Layers to SWF Frames. The animation controls include the following:

- **Frame Rate:** This setting is the rate at which the animation frames play. Most animations on the Web are fine at 12 frames per second (fps), but if your animation includes a lot of fast-changing details, you may want to increase this value to 24 fps.

- **Looping:** Lets the animation play continuously. If disabled, the animation plays through only once.

- **Use as Background:** Selecting this option lets you choose a single layer or several layers to export along with every layer that is used as a background.

- **Layer Order:** Sets the order in which the layers are converted into frames. The options include Bottom Up and Top Down. This makes it easy to reverse an animation.

- **Animate Blends:** Allows blended objects to be animated using two different options. The In Sequence option places each object of the blend on a separate frame. The In Build option keeps the existing objects and adds a new blend to each frame, so that the final frame includes all objects that make up the blend.

Using the Save for Web window

Another way to save Illustrator artwork using the SWF format is with the Save for Web window. Open this interface by choosing File ➪ Save for Web (Alt+Shift+Ctrl+S in Windows; Option+Shift+⌘+S). The Save for Web window displays a preview of the artwork to be exported, as shown in Figure 35-3.

Tip The preview pane in the Save for Web window is convenient for viewing the changes to the artwork as a result of lowering the Curve Quality setting.

To save the artwork to the SWF format, you must select SWF from the format drop-down list located to the right. All the settings for this format type appear, including many of the same settings mentioned for the File ➪ Export process.

Note When using the Save for Web window, all image files (including the SWF file) are exported to a separate images folder when you select to save both the HTML and Image files.

Chapter 35 ✦ Creating SWF and SVG Files   1113

Figure 35-3: You can also save Illustrator artwork to the SWF format using the Save for Web window.

With the SWF format selected, the drop-down list under the Format list only includes options to save the AI file to an SWF file or to save the AI layers to SWF frames. In the Save for Web window, you cannot choose to save each layer as a different SWF file. The window also doesn't include options for setting how you save raster images, nor does it include an option to generate HTML. However, when the file dialog box appears, you can save the images only, the HTML only, or both. The Clip to Artboard option is found within the Image Size panel.

 Although the Save for Web window doesn't include any options for setting how raster images are saved, any raster images included within the artwork are saved using the last used settings specified in the Export SWF Options dialog box.

The Save for Web window does offer an option to export the layers as CSS Layers. The Export As CSS Layers option is found in the Layers panel (Figure 35-4). After the Export As CSS Layers options is enabled, you can select each layer and set it as Visible, Hidden, or Do Not Export. Layers set to Visible or Hidden are included within the HTML file where JavaScript controls which layers are visible and which are hidden.

Figure 35-4: The Layers panel in the Save for Web window

Illustrator and SWF differences

Several objects behave differently between Illustrator and Flash, which could affect the file when it's exported:

+ **Gradients and meshes:** Gradients and mesh objects that use more than eight stops convert to a raster image during export. Gradients with less than eight stops export as gradients. To keep file sizes low, only use gradients with less than eight stops for artwork exported to the SWF format.

+ **Patterns:** All patterns are rasterized and tiled when exported to the SWF format.

+ **Caps and joins:** The SWF format only supports rounded type caps and joins. Butt and Project caps and Miter and Bevel joins are converted to round caps and joins during the export process.

+ **Text and strokes:** Text and strokes that are filled with a pattern are converted to paths and then filled with a rasterized pattern during export.

+ **Text kerning, leading, and tracking:** These are not supported in exported SWF files. Instead, the text is exported as a separate text object positioned to simulate the kerning, leading, and tracking. To maintain text as a single object, enable the Convert Text to Outlines options during exporting.

Creating SWF animations with layers

You can create simple animations in Illustrator using layers. By placing each frame of an animation on a separate layer, you can then cycle through the layers to create an animated sequence. The Layers palette includes a feature that automatically creates a layer for each object in the current file and places each object in its own layer.

Before using this feature, you must create and position each object that appears in the animation. If the animation features a single moving object, you must duplicate that object for each frame of the animation. An easy way to do this is to create the object; choose Edit ⇨ Copy (⌘/Ctrl+C), then choose Edit ⇨ Paste in Front (⌘/Ctrl+F). After pasting a copy of the object, move it to its correct position.

Tip You can also duplicate the selected object by pressing and holding Option/Alt while dragging the object to a new location. Another easy way to create multiple copies along a path is to use Illustrator's Blend feature.

After you copy and position all the objects, you can select the Release to Layers (Sequence) palette menu command from the Layers palette (see Figure 35-5). This command creates a new layer for each object, placing each in its own layer.

Figure 35-5: Each frame of the animation is placed on a separate layer.

You may now export the file to the SWF format by choosing File ⇨ Export. If you select the AI Layers to SWF Frames option in the Macromedia Flash (SWF) Format Options dialog box, the animation sequence exports to the SWF file where it's viewed on a Web page.

The Layers palette also includes a Release to Layers (Build) menu command. This command is similar in that it also creates a new layer for each object, but each new object is cumulatively added to the existing objects. For example, if the original layer includes five objects, the first layer includes a single object, the second layer two objects, and the fifth layer all objects.

Using symbols

If a simple animation sequence requires a separate object for every frame of an animation, file sizes could potentially grow progressively larger as an animation sequence gets longer. However, there is a solution that keeps file sizes small — using symbols.

When you use a symbol in a SWF file, the symbol is included only once and simply referenced every other time it is used within the file. So a simple animation that includes a symbol moving across the screen would require that you duplicate the symbol multiple times and place a copy of the symbol on a separate layer for each frame of the animation, but the SWF file would include the symbol only once.

You can either use a symbol from Illustrator's Symbols palette or create your own symbol:

✦ **Using the Symbols palette:** Illustrator includes many symbols in the Symbols palette (see Figure 35-6). You can access additional symbols using the symbol libraries, which you open by choosing Window ⇨ Symbol Libraries. To use a symbol contained in the Symbols palette or in a symbol library, simply drag it onto the art board.

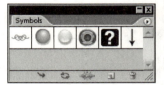

Figure 35-6: The Symbols palette holds all the symbols you need in Illustrator.

✦ **Creating your symbols:** Draw and select the artwork that you want to use as a symbol, then select the New Symbol palette menu command, or drag the artwork to the Symbols palette. If you double-click on a symbol in the Symbols palette, a dialog box appears where you can rename the symbol.

STEPS: Creating a Simple Animation Sequence and Exporting It as an SWF File

1. **Open a new file in Illustrator.** Within Illustrator, choose File ⇨ New to create a new document.
2. **Add a symbol to the document.** Choose Window ⇨ Symbol Library ⇨ 3D Symbols1 to open a symbol library of 3D objects. Drag a 3D atomic symbol to the art board. The symbol displays (Figure 35-7).

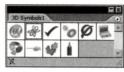

Figure 35-7: Adding symbols to a document

3. **Duplicate and position the symbol.** Hold down the Option/Alt key and drag the atomic symbol to the right. Repeat this action four times until several atomic symbols surround the original, as shown in Figure 35-8.

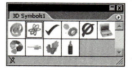

Figure 35-8: Creating duplicate copies of the object

4. **Release objects to layers.** Choose Window ⇨ Layers to open the Layers palette. Then choose the Release to Layers (Sequence) palette menu command. This creates five new sublayers under Layer 1, as shown in Figure 35-9. Each sublayer includes a single symbol object.

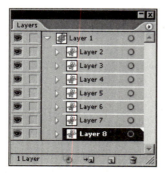

Figure 35-9: New sublayers are created for each separate layer object.

5. **Export to SWF.** Choose File ➪ Export. This opens a file dialog box. In the Save as Type drop-down list, select Macromedia Flash (*.SWF). Then type a name in the File Name field and click Save.

6. **Set export options.** Clicking Save opens the Macromedia Flash (SWF) Format Options dialog box (Figure 35-10). Within this dialog box, set the Export As option to AI Layers to SWF Frames. This makes each layer a separate SWF frame. Also enable the Generate HTML, Protect from Import, Clip to Artboard Size, and Looping options. Finally, set the Image Format to Lossless with a Resolution of 72 ppi. Then click OK.

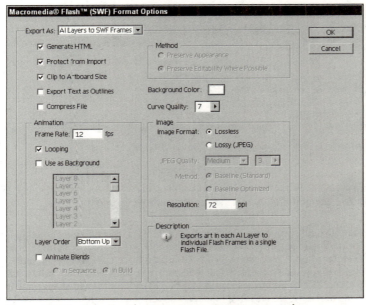

Figure 35-10: Selecting the AI Layers to SWF Frames option

7. **View the animated SWF file.** Locate the saved `Atomic Symbol animation.html` file in the Finder (Mac) or in Explorer (Windows) and double-click on it. This launches the default Web browser for your system and displays the animated SWF file.

To import the SWF file in an Acrobat PDF document, use the Movie tool and double-click in the Document pane. The Add Movie dialog box opens. Click the Choose button in the Add Movie dialog box and locate the SWF file. Click on the filename and click Select. The SWF document is added as a movie clip.

Creating SVG Files in Illustrator

Macromedia Flash (SWF) files are popular on the Web, but they aren't the only Web technology for displaying vector-based images. Another Web technology that is growing in popularity is Scalable Vector Graphics (SVG).

New Feature SVG support has been improved in CS2 with the inclusion of SVG 1.1 and SVG Tiny 1.1, which enables SVG images to be transported to wireless PDAs and phones.

SVG files have many advantages over Flash files. For one, SVG files are XML-based, meaning they're created using their own unique set of markup tags just like HTML. Thus, you can create and edit them using a standard text editor instead of a complex application. Figure 35-11 shows a simple SVG file of a circle within a text editor.

Cross-Reference An overview of XML is covered in Chapter 30.

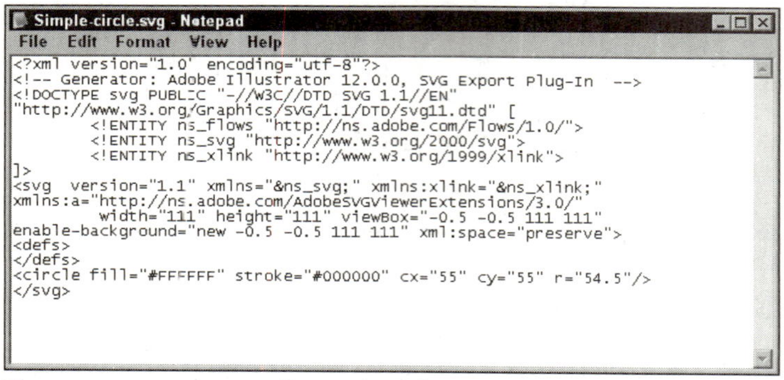


```
<?xml version="1.0" encoding="utf-8"?>
<!-- Generator: Adobe Illustrator 12.0.0, SVG Export Plug-In  -->
<!DOCTYPE svg PUBLIC "-//W3C//DTD SVG 1.1//EN"
"http://www.w3.org/Graphics/SVG/1.1/DTD/svg11.dtd" [
	<!ENTITY ns_flows "http://ns.adobe.com/Flows/1.0/">
	<!ENTITY ns_svg "http://www.w3.org/2000/svg">
	<!ENTITY ns_xlink "http://www.w3.org/1999/xlink">
]>
<svg  version="1.1" xmlns="&ns_svg;" xmlns:xlink="&ns_xlink;"
xmlns:a="http://ns.adobe.com/AdobeSVGViewerExtensions/3.0/"
	 width="111" height="111" viewBox="-0.5 -0.5 111 111"
enable-background="new -0.5 -0.5 111 111" xml:space="preserve">
<defs>
</defs>
<circle fill="#FFFFFF" stroke="#000000" cx="55" cy="55" r="54.5"/>
</svg>
```

Figure 35-11: You can edit XML-based SVG using a simple text editor.

Being XML-based also allows you to easily manipulate SVG files using a scripting language such as JavaScript. For example, you can write a simple script that lets you changes the size of a circle SVG element on a Web page. SVG objects can have special effects, called SVG effects, in Illustrator applied to them. These effects are resolution-independent and are XML-based just like the SVG file. Illustrator can enhance SVG elements with Web page interactivity in response to certain actions like clicking and rollover of a button using the SVG Interactivity palette. All interactivity added to SVG graphics are saved along with the graphics in the SVG file. Finally, the SVG format has broad industry support from many companies involved in both Web and print.

Caution Many Illustrator effects cause the object to which they're applied to rasterize when they're saved to the SVG format. These effects include Rasterize, Artistic, Blur, Brush Strokes, Distort, Pixelate, Sharpen, Sketch, Stylize, Texture, and Video. Avoid these effects for artwork that you intend to save to the SVG format. You can duplicate several of these effects using SVG filters.

Using SVG effects

SVG filters are specialized XML-based filters that perform mathematical operations on SVG objects. Illustrator includes many filters in its Effect ➪ SVG Filters menu, including several variations of the following:

✦ **AI_Alpha:** Randomly overlays alpha channel transparency.

✦ **AI_BevelShadow:** Adds a smooth beveled drop shadow.

- **AI_CoolBreeze:** Inverts the object color and moves the pixels toward the top of the document.
- **AI_Dilate:** Gradually expands all lines outwards from the object center.
- **AI_Erode:** Gradually pulls all lines inward toward the object center.
- **AI_GaussianBlur:** Adds a Gaussian blur to the entire object.
- **AI_PixelPlay:** Converts all lines to anti-aliased pixilated lines.
- **AI_Shadow:** Adds a simple drop shadow.
- **AI_Static:** Fills the object and strokes with static noise.
- **AI_Turbulence:** Adds static and random transparent lines.
- **AI_Woodgrain:** Fills the object with random wood-grain colors.

Note: Although the SVG filters are special types of filters, they're applied in Illustrator as effects, making it possible to modify and even remove the effect using the Appearance palette.

Figure 35-12 shows samples of each of these SVG filters applied to an object.

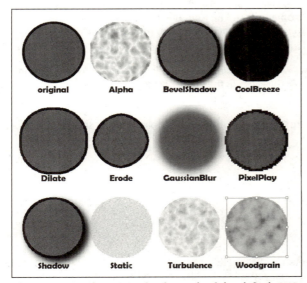

Figure 35-12: The properties for each of the default SVG filters are configurable.

To apply one of the default SVG filters to the selected object, select the filter from the Effect ⇨ SVG Filters menu. Alternatively, you can apply these SVG filters using the Apply SVG Filter dialog box (Figure 35-13), which you access via the Effect ⇨ SVG Filters ⇨ Apply SVG Filter menu command. You can import additional default SVG filters by choosing Effect ⇨ SVG Filters ⇨ Import SVG Filter.

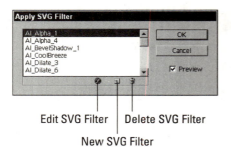

Figure 35-13: The Apply SVG Filter dialog box lists all the default SVG filters.

The Apply SVG Filter dialog box lists all the default SVG filters. To apply a filter, select it from the list and click OK. You can also preview the filter before applying it by enabling the Preview option.

 Note After you apply an SVG filter to an object, a rasterized version of the artwork displays in Illustrator, but the SVG file displays as a vector image on a Web page.

A single object may have multiple SVG filters applied to it. All SVG filters applied to an object show up in the Appearance palette, shown in Figure 35-14, when you select the object. You can delete applied filters from an object using the Remove Item palette menu command, or by selecting the filter in the Appearance palette and clicking on the trashcan icon at the bottom of the palette.

 Caution Although an object may have several filters applied to it, for SVG files, the final filter in the Appearance palette must be an SVG filter or the entire object is rasterized.

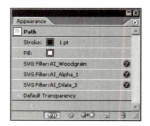

Figure 35-14: The Appearance palette holds all SVG filters.

You can edit the default SVG filters by clicking Edit SVG Filter in the Apply SVG Filter dialog box or by double-clicking on the filter you want to edit. The Edit SVG Filter dialog box (Figure 35-15) opens, listing all the XML filter commands. To edit the filter, just type the new commands or change the values within quotes.

The Apply SVG Filter dialog box also includes a New SVG Filter icon button at the bottom of the dialog box that opens a blank Edit SVG Filter dialog box where you can compose new filters.

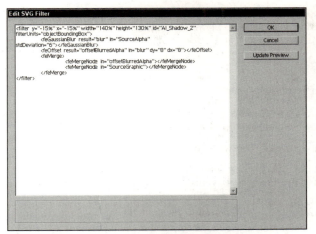

Figure 35-15: The Edit SVG Filter dialog box lets you edit XML code.

Adding interactivity

Within a Web page, you can use JavaScript to modify SVG objects. You can also use Illustrator to add some basic interactivity to objects that you want to make SVG files. The code for this interactivity is added to the SVG file automatically when you save the file. You add SVG interactivity to Illustrator objects using the SVG Interactivity palette (Figure 35-16):

+ **Event:** These are actions that take place in a Web page including onclick, onmouseover, onkeydown, onload, and so on.

+ **JavaScript:** With an event selected, you can enter a JavaScript command to execute when this event takes place in the JavaScript field. Press the Enter key to confirm the command, and the line of JavaScript is added to the palette.

Figure 35-16: The SVG Interactivity palette adds JavaScript commands.

Note   GoLive CS2 provides an easy interface for adding interactivity to SVG files.

You can also load a JavaScript file that executes when the event occurs. You do this by selecting the JavaScript Files palette menu command or by clicking on the Link JavaScript Files button at the bottom of the palette. All JavaScript statements listed in the palette are saved in the SVG file when you save the file.

Note You may open SVG files in the default browser by double-clicking on the file in the Finder (Mac) or in Explorer (Windows). An SVG Viewer is required to view SVG files within a browser. The Adobe SVG Viewer is installed automatically on systems where Illustrator is installed.

Addressing exporting issues

Although SVG is a fairly robust vector format, several aspects of the format are still different from Illustrator's native AI format, including the following:

- **Mesh objects:** These objects rasterize when you export them to SVG format.
- **Opacity:** To correctly see transparency, you adjust the Opacity for each layer object. Changing the Opacity for the entire layer causes all objects to appear opaque when saved as an SVG file.
- **Symbols:** Symbols are used effectively within SVG files. Symbols that are reused several times within a single SVG file are only included once and referenced for all other instances.
- **Objects:** Objects in each layer are converted into an SVG group. To keep objects easy to select within the SVG file, place each object on a separate layer.

Note ImageReady CS2 can export SVG files with animations.

Saving SVG files

There are also two different ways to save SVG files in Illustrator. One method is to select the SVG file type in the Save As dialog box; the other is to use the Save for Web window. If you look at the file types available in the Save As dialog box, you'll find two different SVG options — SVG and SVG Compressed with the SVGZ file extension. SVG Compressed (SVGZ) files lose their ability to be edited in a text editor. If you know you won't need to edit an SVG file, you can reduce its size even further by saving it using the SVG Compressed format.

Using the different SVG versions

As SVG matures, it has segmented into several different versions that were created for different specific purposes. The latest SVG version is 1.1, but Illustrator still supports version 1.0 for older files.

Two versions of SVG have been defined for the wireless PDA and mobile phone market. These versions, SVG Tiny 1.1 and SVG Tiny 1.1 +, are small subsets of the complete specification. These versions are optimized to be usable on smaller devices by removing many of the more complex features. SVG Tiny 1.1 doesn't support gradients, transparency, clipping, masks, symbols, or SVG effects; SVG Tiny 1.1+ is the same except it supports gradients and transparency.

Illustrator can also support SVG Basic 1.1, which is intended for handheld devices with a little more power than mobile phones. It supports only rectangular clipping and only certain SVG filter effects.

Specifying SVG Options

After you click Save in the Save As dialog box, the SVG Options dialog box opens, shown in Figure 35-17. Within this dialog box, you can select a number of options:

Several additional options are available in the SVG Options dialog box in CS2 including the ability to specify the applicable DTD, select the Font Type, and options for the <tspan> and <textPath> XML elements.

✦ **DTD:** The DTD option lets you select the Document Type Definition (DTD) to use. The selected DTD includes all the XML rules that the SVG file needs to follow. The available options include SVG 1.0, SVG 1.1, SVG Tiny 1.1, SVG Tiny 1.1+, and SVG Basic 1.1.

✦ **Font Type:** Document fonts can be specified as Adobe CEF, SVG, or Convert to Outlines. The Adobe CEF option uses font hinting, which makes small font sizes appear more clearly, but it is only supported by the Adobe SVG Viewer. The SVG option offers the broadest support working in all SVG Viewers. The Convert to Outlines option guarantees that text style is maintained by converting all text to paths, but the cost is a much larger file size.

✦ **Font Subsetting:** The options include None, which causes a user's system fonts to be used; Only Glyphs Used, which includes only those glyphs contained within the current document; Common English, which includes a set of English characters; Common Roman, which includes a set of Roman characters; and All Glyphs, which includes both English and Roman characters. There are also options to include Common English & Glyphs Used and Common Roman & Glyphs Used. These options include the given set of characters along with any characters contained in the document that aren't included in the given set.

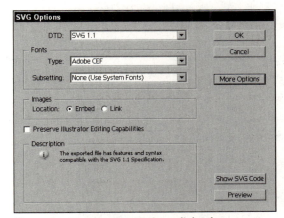

Figure 35-17: The SVG Options dialog box

Including All Glyphs increases the file size much more than including only the glyphs used. If you're certain that the text contained within the SVG file won't change, you can substantially reduce the file size by selecting the Only Glyphs Used option. If the graphic that you want to save as an SVG file includes only a small bit of text (or no text at all), you can keep the file size small by converting the text to outlines and selecting the None option for the Font Subsetting setting.

- **Images Location:** You can embed any raster images that are part of the artwork within the SVG file or link them externally. Embedding images increases the file size, but it makes the image available. If you link the image, the SVG file includes a reference to the image file.

Caution If the Illustrator document includes a Photoshop (PSD) image file (or any file type that isn't a JPEG or PNG file) and the Link option is selected as the Image Location in the SVG Options dialog box, then the image file is saved using a cryptic filename consisting of random numbers and letters, such as EA5865421.jpg.

- **Preserving editing information:** When you select this option, certain information about Illustrator is included within the SVG file. This information allows you to edit the objects in Illustrator. Enabling the Preserve Illustrator Editing Capabilities option adds around 450KB of data to your SVG file. If you save an SVG file for use on the Web, make sure this option is disabled. If you plan on editing the SVG within Illustrator in the future, save another copy of the SVG file with this option enabled or save the file using the AI format.

The SVG Options dialog box also includes buttons to Show SVG Code, which opens the XML code for the current object in a Web browser, and Preview, which displays a preview of the current object in a Web browser.

Saving with advanced SVG options

More SVG file options are available if you click on the More Options button in the SVG Options dialog (Figure 35-18).

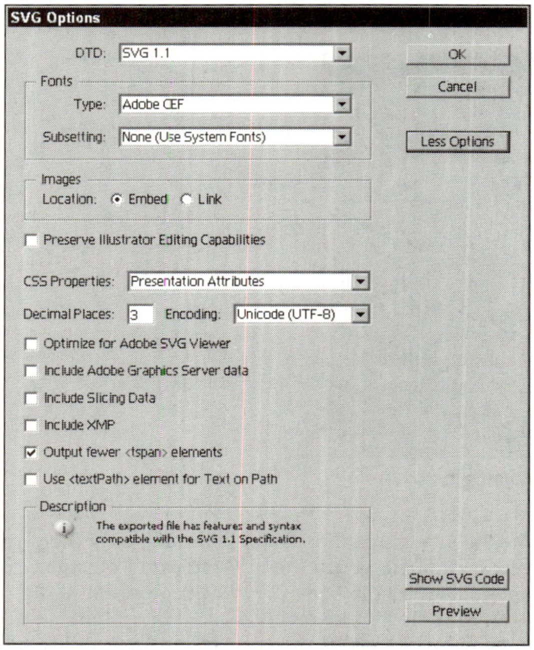

Figure 35-18: The More Options button opens a dialog box of additional options.

✦ **CSS Properties:** Lets you select the method to save the CSS properties within the SVG file. The options are Presentation Attributes, Style Attributes, Style Attributes (Entity References), and Style Elements. The first option applies the styles at the presentation level, which embeds the style within the actual objects. The Style Attributes options add CSS code to the top of the SVG file where it is easily extracted or manipulated using JavaScript. The Style Elements option applies the styles as elements that may be reused and applied to HTML elements.

✦ **Decimal Places:** Allows you to set the number of decimals to include for all data saved in the SVG file. Although values for this option can range from 1 to 7, anything over 3 is really overkill and simply increases the file size.

✦ **Encoding:** Lets you specify the encoding standard used for data saved to the SVG file. The options include ISO 8859-1, Unicode (UTF-8), and Unicode (UTF-16). The UTF-8 encoding standard includes a broad character set with Chinese, Arabic, and all European languages and is generally sufficient for most browsers.

✦ **Optimize for Adobe SVG Viewer:** Includes additional information in the SVG file that makes the SVG file render more quickly when viewed in Adobe's SVG Viewer plug-in. The extra data isn't significant enough to drastically alter the file size.

✦ **Include Adobe Graphics Server data:** Saves all variable data entered in the Variables palette within Illustrator. These variables are used to create data-driven templates.

Cross-Reference Data-Driven graphics are covered in Chapter 15.

✦ **Include Slicing Data:** Saves all slicing data in the SVG file.

✦ **Include XMP:** Adds all defined metadata to the SVG file. Metadata can be added to a file by choosing File ⇨ Info or by using the Bridge Browser. Metadata can include additional information about the file such as Description, Author, Keywords, and so on.

Cross-Reference Metadata and the Bridge Browser are covered in Chapter 7.

✦ **Output fewer <tspan> elements:** When an SVG file is saved, Illustrator applies an auto-kerning to all file text. This can result in many <tspan> elements that make the file hard to edit. Enabling this command disables the auto-kerning operation, which results in a simpler SVG file.

✦ **Use <textPath> element for Text on Path:** SVG version 1.1 includes a new <textPath> element that can be used to define text on a path, but the results may look different depending on the SVG viewer. This option lets you turn this element on and off.

Using the Save for Web window

Another way to save SVG files is with the Save for Web window. Choosing File ⇨ Save for Web (Alt+Shift+Ctrl+S in Windows; Option+Shift+⌘+S on the Mac) opens this interface, shown in Figure 35-19.

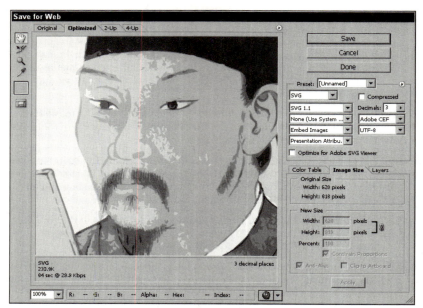

Figure 35-19: You can use the Save for Web window to save Illustrator designs as SVG files.

After you select the SVG file format, many of the same options discussed in the SVG Advanced Options dialog box appear, including SVG Version, Font Subsetting, Embedding or Linking raster images, CSS Properties, Encoding, and Decimal Places. You can also select the Compressed option to save the SVG file as an SVGZ file and the Optimize for Adobe SVG Viewer option.

STEPS: Saving an SVG File

1. **Open a new file in Illustrator.** Within Illustrator, choose File ➪ New to create a new document.

2. **Create the graphic to export.** Using the Illustrator tools, create a design to save as an SVG file. For easier manipulation, place each separate object on a separate layer.

3. **Add a Shadow SVG filter.** Select the flag objects and choose Effect ➪ SVG Filter ➪ Apply SVG Filter. The Apply SVG Filter dialog box appears. Click the Preview option and choose the AI_Shadow_1 filter from the list. Click OK to apply the filter. Figure 35-20 shows the object with the shadow filter applied.

 After the SVG filter is applied, the object is displayed as a raster object instead of as a vector object.

Figure 35-20: A simple drop shadow applied using an SVG filter

4. **Edit an SVG filter.** Select one of the flag ribbons and choose Window ➪ Appearance to open the Appearance palette. Notice that the SVG filter appears toward the bottom of the Appearance palette. Double-click on the SVG filter in the Appearance palette. This re-opens the Apply SVG Filter dialog box with the AI_Shadow_1 filter selected. Click on the Edit SVG Filter button at the bottom of the dialog box. The Edit SVG Filter dialog box opens. Change the dy and dx values within the quote marks to 2, as shown in Figure 35-21. Then click OK to close the dialog box. Figure 35-22 shows the flag with the updated SVG filter applied.

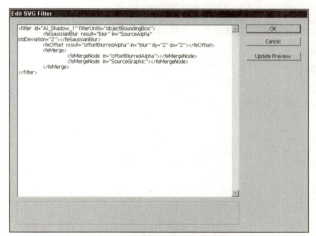

Figure 35-21: The Edit SVG Filter dialog box allows you to edit syntax.

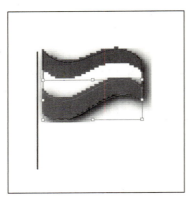

Figure 35-22: After editing the SVG filter, a smaller drop shadow appears.

5. **Save the SVG file.** Choose the File ⇨ Save As menu command. Select the SVG option from the Save as Type list; then type a name for the SVG file and click the Save button. The SVG Options dialog box opens. Because this file doesn't include any text, select None as the Font Subsetting option. Disable the Preserve Illustrator Editing Capabilities option and click OK. The SVG file is saved to the hard drive.

6. **View the saved SVG file.** Locate the HTML file for the saved SVG file on your system and double-click on it to open it within the system's default Web browser. Figure 35-23 shows the resulting flag in a Web browser.

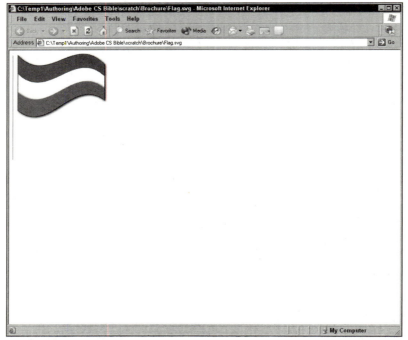

Figure 35-23: The object appears as a vector image when viewed in a Web browser.

Using SWF and SVG Files in GoLive

After you create an SWF or SVG file, you can use it to enhance a Web page in GoLive. You add SWF and SVG files to a Web page as objects by dragging them from the Basic category in the Toolbox. Alternatively, you can convert them from an Illustrator Smart Object.

Adding SWF and SVG objects to a Web page in GoLive

After you have an SWF or SVG file saved on your hard drive, you can add either to a GoLive Web page by dragging the respective SWF or SVG object icon from the Toolbox and dropping it on a Web page at the position where you want the SWF or SVG file to appear. Both SWF and SVG objects are found in the Basic Elements category in the Toolbox.

Dropping either an SWF of SVG object onto a Web page displays an object icon. These object icons are placeholders for the file and you can resize them by dragging on their borders. The properties for the selected object also display in the Inspector palette. Figure 35-24 shows a blank Web page with an SWF and an SVG object dropped onto it.

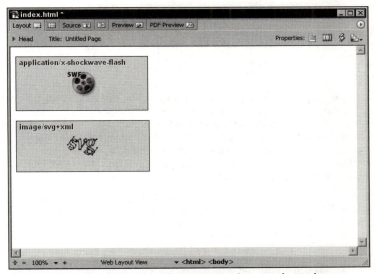

Figure 35-24: The SWF object appears as an icon on the Web page.

To load an SWF or SVG file into the respective object, click on the Browse button in the Inspector palette. This opens a file dialog box where you can select the file to use. The filename then appears in the Inspector palette, and the file loads into the Web page within the Layout Editor. The filename is also listed at the top of the object. Figure 35-25 shows a Web page with SWF and SVG files loaded.

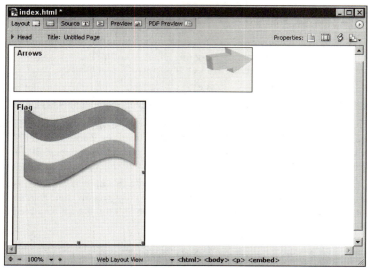

Figure 35-25: The files appear within the Web page.

When either an SWF or an SVG object is selected in the Web page, the Inspector palette includes several tabs:

- **Basic tab:** Lists the File, MIME, and Class for the object. The File field holds the path and name for the file that is loaded into the object. It includes a Fetch URL button, which lets you select files by dragging the icon to the filename in the site window, and a Browse button, which opens a file dialog box where you can select a file to open. The MIME field includes code that identifies the file type to the browser. The Class field identifies the plug-in used to view the file. For SWF and SVG files, the MIME and Class fields are filled in automatically as needed.

  The Basic panel also lets you specify the dimensions and alignment for the object. When a file is specified, the dimensions specified in the file are loaded automatically into the Width and Height fields, but you can change these values by typing new values or by dragging the object borders in the Layout Editor. Clicking the button to the right of the Width and Height fields resets the object to the dimensions specified in the file.

- **More tab:** Includes several additional properties. The Name field lets you name the element. This is the name that is used within the Web page and with JavaScript to identify the object. The Page and Code fields are used to specify a location where the information about the needed plug-in is located and the location of that plug-in. For SWF files, these fields are populated automatically. The Palette options are used to make the plug-in appear in the foreground or background. The HSpace and VSpace values define the amount of padded white space that vertically and horizontally surrounds the object. Finally, the Is Hidden option hides the object on the Web page. If the object is only used to play sound for instance, you'll want to hide the object but not its action.

- **Attribs tab:** Lists all the settings for the specific object as set in the final panel.

- **SWF tab:** With the SWF object selected in the Web page, the Inspector palette lists the SWF-specific settings in the SWF panel, shown in Figure 35-26.

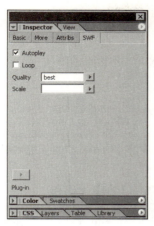

Figure 35-26: The SWF panel in the Inspector palette

- **Autoplay:** Causes any animation associated with the SWF file to begin as soon as the Web page is loaded in a browser.
- **Loop:** Causes the animation sequence to repeat again after it's finished.
- **Quality:** You can set this to Default, Best, High, Auto High, Auto Low, and Low. These settings correspond to the appearance of the animation versus the playback speed. The Default setting lets the browser player determine this setting. The Best setting shows all the details of each frame regardless of how it impacts the playback speed, and a Low setting sacrifices the quality of the animation frames in order to play back the animation at the target frame rate. The Autohigh and Autolow settings work to maintain image appearance and playback speed, respectively, while improving the other when it can.
- **Scale:** This setting determines how to handle the display of SWF files where there is a difference in the size specified on the Web page and the size of the actual SWF file. The Default setting maintains the aspect ratio of the original file within the designated Web-page area. This causes borders to appear on two sides of the SWF object. The No Border option also maintains the aspect ratio of the SWF file but crops the file so no borders appear. The Exact Fit option stretches the SWF file to fit within the given area. This may distort the SWF file.

Using Illustrator Smart Objects

Another way to add SWF and SVG objects to a Web page is using the Illustrator Smart Object. Dragging the Illustrator Smart Object from the Toolbox to the Layout Editor places an icon and loads the object's properties in the Inspector palette. Clicking on the Browse button opens a file dialog box where you can select the Illustrator (AI) file to open.

Selecting an Illustrator file to open makes the Conversion Settings dialog box appear, shown in Figure 35-27. From this dialog box, you can convert the selected Illustrator file to a bitmap format, an SVG, a compressed SVG, or an SWF file.

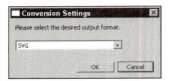

Figure 35-27: The Conversion Settings dialog box

Selecting the Bitmap Formats option opens the Save for Web window, where you can select to save the Illustrator file as an optimized GIF, JPEG, PNG, or WBMP file. The SVG, Compressed SVG, and SWF options load the file in Illustrator and open the SVG Options dialog box or the Macromedia Flash (SWF) Format Options dialog box, where you can specify the options to use to convert the file.

STEPS: Adding SWF and SVG Files to a Web Page

1. **Open a Web page in GoLive.** Within GoLive, choose File ⇨ Open to open a Web page where you want to add the SWF and SVG files, or locate and double-click on the Web page in the site window.

2. **Add SWF and SVG objects to the Web page.** With the Web page open, click on the Basic Elements category button in the Toolbox and drag both an SWF and an SVG object from the Toolbox to the Web page. The objects appear as icons, as shown in Figure 35-28.

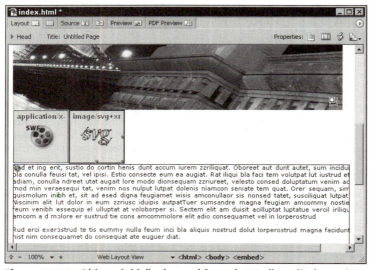

Figure 35-28: Objects initially dragged from the Toolbox display as icons.

3. **Specify the SWF and SVG files.** Select the SWF object in the Layout Editor and click on the Browse button in the Inspector palette. In the file dialog box that opens, locate an SWF file and click the Open button. Repeat for the SVG object. The selected files are loaded into the Web page. Figure 35-29 shows the Web page with the files loaded.

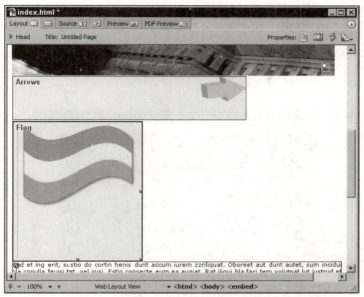

Figure 35-29: Selected SWF and SVG files load into the Web page.

4. **Resize the SVG object.** Select the SVG flag object and drag on its lower-right corner while holding down the Shift key to reduce its size until its height is equal to the SWF file. Holding down the Shift key constrains the aspect ratio of the object. Figure 35-30 shows the Web page after the SVG flag has been resized.

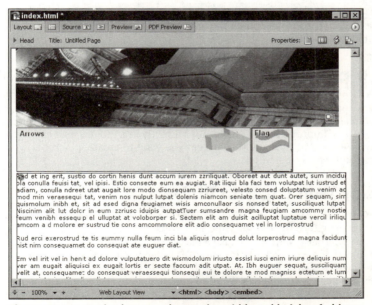

Figure 35-30: GoLive lets you change the width and height of objects.

5. **Set the SWF properties.** With the SWF object selected, click on the SWF tab in the Inspector palette. Select the Autoplay and Loop options and set the Quality setting to Autolow. This ensures that the playback speed stays constant.

6. **Preview the Web page.** To see a preview of the SWF and SVG objects added to the Web page, click the Preview tab above the Web-page window. In this view, you can see the animation sequence for the SWF file, as shown in Figure 35-31.

Figure 35-31: The Preview panel shows the Web page, as it would appear in a Web browser.

Using SWF Files in Acrobat

Acrobat offers you two interesting ways to import SWF files in PDF documents. One method is to convert animated Web pages containing SWF files to PDF documents. The other use for SWF with PDFs is to import the motion graphics directly in a PDF file as a movie-file import. Depending on your source files and the content you want to create in Acrobat, you'll find benefits using both of these methods.

Converting Web pages to PDF

You can convert Web pages to PDF using the File ➪ Create PDF ➪ From Web Page menu command in Acrobat on either the Mac or Windows. Windows users have an extra benefit when using Microsoft Internet Explorer, because a task button appears in the Explorer window that enables you to convert Web pages in view to PDF. When you create PDF documents from Web pages, all the page content is converted and the page is viewed in Acrobat viewers much like you see when the page is viewed in a Web browser, including Flash animations.

Acrobat 6 and greater viewers support two different media compatibilities. You can import a variety of media files using either the Acrobat 5 compatibility or Acrobat 6 compatibility. A few differences between the two compatibility levels are that you can embed Acrobat 6–compatible media in the PDF document and the number of media formats supported are much greater. When you convert Web pages or import SWF files, the files are imported as Acrobat 6–compatible media and either embedded or linked to a PDF file. You have no option for importing SWF files as Acrobat 5–compatible media.

To convert a Web page to a PDF document, choose File ➪ Create PDF ➪ From Web Page (Shift+Ctrl+O in Windows; Shift+⌘+O on the Mac). This opens the Create PDF from Web Page dialog box, shown in Figure 35-32. Note that Windows users can use the PDF Maker task button installed in Microsoft Internet Explorer. By default, this task button is installed in Explorer at the time of your CS Premium or Acrobat 7 installation.

Figure 35-32: The Create PDF from Web Page dialog box

The Create PDF from Web Page dialog box has the following options:

- ✦ **URL:** To select a Web site, type the URL in the URL field box or click on the Browse button to select a Web site stored locally on your hard drive or network server.

- ✦ **Settings section:** You have the following options:
  - **Get only/Get entire site:** You can select linked pages according to the number of levels contained on a Web site or you can convert the entire site to PDF. Note that if you convert more than one level or use the Get Entire Site option, you can convert an extraordinary number of pages. When converting Web sites with which you aren't familiar, be certain to gradually convert pages rather than the entire site to avoid creating PDFs of extraordinary size.
  - **Stay on same path/Stay on same server:** These options choices prevent linked Web pages from other sites and servers being converted to PDF, thereby keeping your resultant PDF smaller in size with less clutter. Obviously, if you need linked pages to be converted to PDF then you'll want to reach out to other servers and levels. You can always return to the PDF file and append more pages if needed.

Any SWF files included in the converted Web pages are added to the final PDF document. You can embed the SWF files in the PDF document or link the files to the PDF. Either way, you can select, copy, and paste them between PDF files.

Note You can embed or link multimedia files, including SWF, to a PDF file. By default, the media is embedded in the PDF during HTML-to-PDF conversion. If you want to link the files, click on Settings in the Create PDF from Web Page dialog box. In the Web Capture dialog box, scroll the list and select HTML. Click on the Settings button, and the HTML Conversion Settings dialog box opens. From the Multimedia pull-down menu, select Reference Multimedia Content by URL. The file is then linked to the PDF.

If you want to convert a Web site containing an animated page using an SWF file, convert the file and use either the Movie tool or the Select Object tool in Acrobat to select the movie frame. Copy the file by choosing Edit ⇨ Copy and paste the file into another PDF document. These steps might be helpful when working in a workflow where you want to use animated graphics from your client's Web site and don't have immediate access to the Web-site source files or a password to retrieve files from the client's Web site. In such a case, simply convert Web pages to PDF and copy and paste the movie frames as needed.

Note SWF files can be viewed in PDF documents, but SVG files are not supported in Acrobat. As of this writing, you cannot convert SVG files to PDF nor import them in existing PDFs.

Importing SWF files in PDF documents

You use the Movie tool to import SWF files in Acrobat PDFs. If you convert Web pages to PDF, you need to copy and paste SWF files using the Movie tool or the Select Object tool to select the movie frame and copy the file. However, you cannot export the frame back to an SWF file for use in HTML documents or for viewing in stand-alone SWF viewers. If you create an SWF file in either Flash or Illustrator, you can import the SWF file directly in a PDF document.

To import an SWF file, click on the Movie tool in the Advanced Editing toolbar. You can either drag open a rectangle frame or double-click the Movie tool in the Document pane. Either action opens the Add Movie dialog box, shown in Figure 35-33.

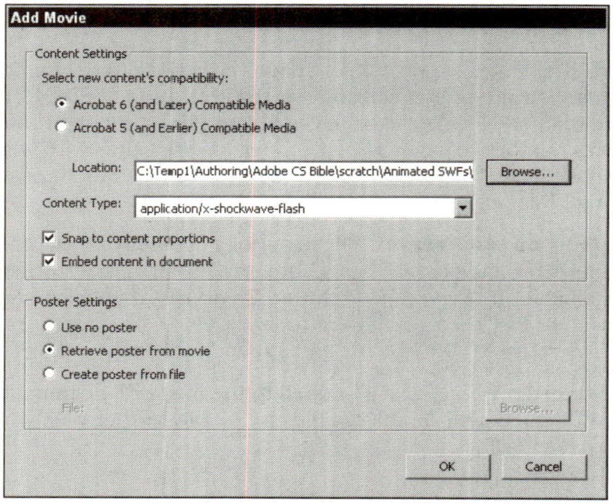

Figure 35-33: The Add Movie dialog box offers options for importing.

The options you have in this dialog box include the following:

- **Adobe Compatibility options:** The first two option choices offer you selections for choosing either Acrobat 5 or Acrobat 6 compatibility. If you select Acrobat 5 (and Earlier) Compatible Media, Acrobat won't recognize the SWF files on your computer as you try to import them in the open PDF document. You need to select Acrobat 6 Compatible Media then click on the Choose/Browse button to open the Select Movie File dialog box where movie files are identified for importing. You select the file and click on the Select button; the file is imported into the PDF document. After importing the movie file (including SWF files), you're returned to the Add Movie dialog box.

- **Snap to content proportions:** Keeps the movie frame proportional as you size it, thereby preventing distortion when playing the movie.

- **Embed content in document:** Offers an option to either embed the content (when the check box is enabled) or create a link to the file (when the check box is disabled). If you uncheck this box, the movie file needs to travel along with the PDF document as you send the file to other users.

- **Poster Settings:** These have to do with the visual contained within the movie frame known as the movie poster. You can choose to use no poster, create a poster from the first frame in the movie, or create a poster from a file. When creating posters from files, you click the Choose/Browse button to navigate your hard drive to locate the image you want to use as the poster. All files compatible with Create PDF from File can be used as a poster image. Select the file you want to use and it's converted to PDF and placed as the contents for the movie frame. As the movie plays, the poster disappears; it returns after the movie stops playing.

After using the Movie tool and importing an SWF file or other type of movie file, you can adjust various properties for the movie and the playback in Acrobat. To open the Properties dialog box, select either the Movie tool or the Select Object tool and open a context menu on the movie frame. Select Properties from the menu options, and the Multimedia Properties dialog box opens, shown in Figure 35-34.

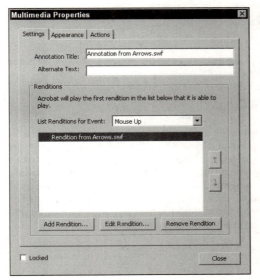

Figure 35-34: The Multimedia Properties dialog box

The default pane that appears when opening the Multimedia Properties dialog box is the Settings pane. To edit various options for the movie play, click on the Edit Rendition button. The Rendition Settings dialog box, shown in Figure 35-35, opens. In this dialog box, you have a considerable number of choices to describe attributes for playing media files.

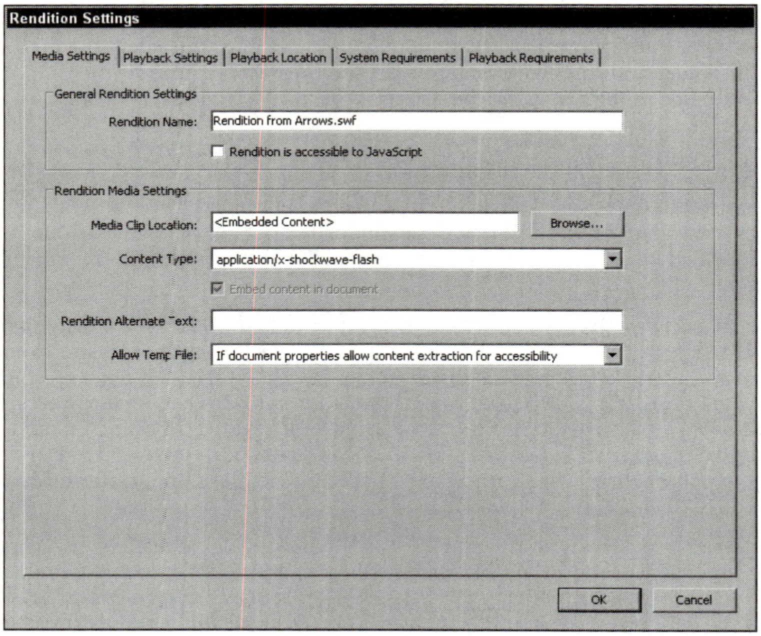

Figure 35-35: The Rendition Settings dialog box

Of particular importance to many users are the settings found in the Playback Settings pane. Click on Playback Settings at the top of the Rendition Settings dialog box, and the pane shown in Figure 35-36 opens.

If you want to show player controls where a media clip can be stopped, paused, restarted, and so on, check the box for Show Player Controls. After exiting the Renditions Settings, you'll see a player control appear at the bottom of the movie frame.

The rendition settings offer you much more than controlling the media play with player controls. You can create several renditions in the same PDF document and identify what rendition is played according to download speeds for different users. For example, users who have modem connections at 28.8 baud can receive and view a small media file, while users with DSL and cable-modem connections can view media clips of larger sizes. You can create renditions that play according to user download speeds, where Acrobat analyzes a user's connection and delivers the media defined for the respective speed. Other options in the rendition settings offer choices for where media is played within the document, embedding or linking options, associating JavaScripts with media plays, timing movie plays for a given length of time, foreign-language selections, showing subtitles, and much more.

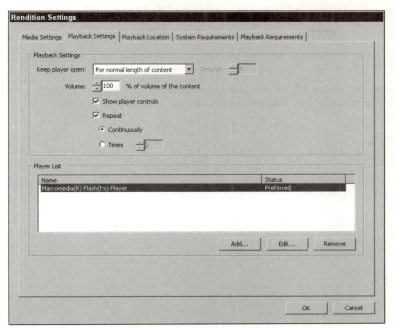

Figure 35-36: The Playback Settings pane

For a detailed review of multimedia and PDF files, refer to the *Adobe Acrobat 7 PDF Bible* (published by Wiley).

Keep in mind that the SWF files you create in Illustrator are ultimately media clips. They're handled in Acrobat and assigned properties, as any movie file would be.

Summary

✦ You use Illustrator to export graphics to SWF files.

✦ You create SWF animation sequences in Illustrator by placing the objects for each frame on a separate layer. These layers convert to frames during export.

✦ You can separate several objects included on a single layer in layers using the Layers palette's Release to Layers command.

✦ You can save objects as an SVG or as a Compressed SVG file using Illustrator's File ⇨ Save As menu command.

✦ You can apply SVG filters to objects saved as SVG files to prevent them from being rasterized.

- You attach JavaScript code to SVG objects with the SVG Interactivity palette.
- You place SWF and SVG objects within Web pages using GoLive.
- You convert Web pages containing SWF files into PDF documents using Acrobat's File ⇨ Create PDF ⇨ From Web Page menu command.
- You import SWF files into PDF documents using the Movie tool. As movie clips, you can assign SWF files a number of different play options and rendition settings.

✦ ✦ ✦

Creating Slide Presentations

CHAPTER 36

In This Chapter

Converting slide presentation files

Authoring presentations in CS programs

Using layers with presentations

Creating transitions

Using full-screen views

Slide presentations may be something you want to use in client meetings when proposing new concepts or campaigns, or your clients may ask you to create presentations they want to use at trade shows, meetings, and conferences. Whether for your own needs or your clients' needs, at one time or another design professionals periodically find a need to create slide presentations. If creating slide presentations is not something you usually do, the last thing you'll want to do is try to learn a new program to quickly assemble a presentation for yourself or your client.

Dedicated slide-creation programs like Microsoft PowerPoint and Apple's Keynote are designed specifically for creating presentations. However, if you're not up to speed with these programs and need to design a presentation quickly, you'll find working in programs you know to be much less frustrating. In this chapter, you learn how to use the CS2 programs for creating slide presentations and converting presentations from the dedicated slide-presentation applications to file formats usable with the CS2 programs.

Converting Presentation Documents to PDF

Because slide presentations may exist in a variety of different formats, you may need to convert an existing file that was created by your client to something workable with the CS2 programs. The most-popular presentation documents you'll find are Microsoft PowerPoint files — but you're not necessarily limited to PowerPoint. You may find old layouts in QuarkXPress, Adobe PageMaker, or other application documents that were once used as a presentation and now need to be updated or refined for current presentations.

In addition to converting existing documents to a format workable with the CS2 programs, you may need to integrate current files created in Illustrator, Photoshop, InDesign, and/or GoLive with older presentation documents. Assuming you're not up to speed in a program designed to create presentations, you need to convert files to a format usable as a display tool for presentations. Fortunately, you can convert all files from any authoring program to PDF, and you can use Adobe Acrobat or Adobe Reader as a presentation tool.

Acrobat is not a mere substitute for presentation programs. Acrobat can stand alone as a sophisticated presentation tool where you can add transitions, create links to documents, show multimedia film clips, display presentations in self-running modes for kiosks, add animation, and take advantage of all the other features one would expect from a presentation program. If you've begun to master the CS2 programs, you'll find creating PDF files for presentations a better solution in your workflow if you aren't familiar with creating slides in a presentation program.

Converting PowerPoint slides to PDF

The de facto standard presentation program on Windows is Microsoft PowerPoint. Microsoft Office users are so familiar with PowerPoint that they tend to create documents ranging from slide presentations to large-format display prints. If you work with corporate clients who supply files to you, you'll definitely see many PowerPoint files.

You can convert PowerPoint slides to PDF and add slide pages to an InDesign document for further development of a presentation, or convert PowerPoint slides to PDF while preserving animation effects created in PowerPoint. Any Acrobat viewer can see the animation exported with the PowerPoint slides.

Knowing you can view the files you convert to PDF in any Acrobat viewer is an important issue. You may author files in Acrobat Professional, yet you may deliver PDF documents to coworkers or clients who use either Acrobat Standard or Adobe Reader. File conversions from PowerPoint can be viewed in any Acrobat viewer, complete with transition effects.

To convert PowerPoint slides to PDF you can use the Convert to PDF from File command in Acrobat or the PDFMaker in PowerPoint. Using either method requires you to have PowerPoint installed on your computer. Therefore, if you receive PowerPoint files from your clients, be certain you own a copy of Microsoft Office, or have your clients send you a PostScript file or have them convert the PowerPoint PPT files to PDF.

The PDFMaker macro is installed automatically in Microsoft Office applications (Word, Excel, and PowerPoint) when you first install Microsoft Office and then install either Adobe Acrobat or the CS applications that include the Acrobat installation. The order of installation is no longer critical when installing Acrobat 7. MS Office can be installed before or after Acrobat. Acrobat's self-healing features can detect MS Office files and automatically install the PDF Maker.

For more information on using PDFMaker, see Part V.

Converting to PDF on the Mac

Converting PowerPoint slides to PDF on the Mac has been challenging with each release of Acrobat. In the first release of Mac OS X Tiger the complications are compounded. The PDFMaker in PowerPoint fails more often than it works. If you use other methods such as exporting to PostScript and distilling the PostScript in Acrobat Distiller, you find problems converting the proper page sizes where pages are clipped and experiencing problems with page orientation where pages are rotated. You can convert PowerPoint slides on the Mac, but the process is not intuitive and you need to avoid using PDFMaker.

Ideally, if you have access to a Windows machine, your best opportunity for PowerPoint conversion to PDF is in Windows using the PDFMaker. If you don't have access to a Windows machine and you need to convert PowerPoint files to PDF, use the following steps to do the job.

STEPS: Converting PowerPoint to PDF on the Mac

1. **Set up a custom page.** In PowerPoint, choose File ➪ Page Setup. When the Page Setup dialog box appears, click Options and a second Page Setup dialog box opens. In the second dialog box, open the Page Size pull-down menu and select Manage Custom Sizes. The Custom Page Sizes dialog box opens, as shown in Figure 36-1. In the Width and Height text boxes, add 8 inches for the Width and 10.19 inches for the Height. This is where things may begin to get confusing. You would think that a landscape page would have the width and height set to 10.19 x 8. However pages get clipped when you set the width and height at 10.19 x 8.

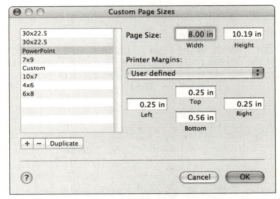

Figure 36-1: In the Custom Page Sizes dialog box set the width to 8 inches and the height to 10.19 inches.

2. **Name the custom page size.** Click the plus (+) symbol to add the page to the list of custom pages. Double-click on the default untitled name and type PowerPoint. Click OK in the Manage Page Sizes dialog box. Click OK in the Page Setup dialog boxes and your new custom page size is ready to use.

3. **Select the custom page size.** PowerPoint has a terrible time remembering the last settings made to Page Setup. Each time you covert to PDF, be certain to revisit the Page Setup dialog box. Choose File ➪ Page Setup. Click Options in the Page Setup dialog box and a second Page Setup dialog box opens. From the Paper Size pull-down menu, select the PowerPoint page size you created, as shown in Figure 36-2.

4. **Select the orientation.** The default orientation is landscape. If you print the PowerPoint slides to PostScript and distill the PostScript file, the PDF opens with all the pages rotated 90 degrees. If you export to PDF using Tiger's PDF export features, the PDF pages open in the proper page orientation. Changing the orientation to Portrait produces unsatisfactory results using either PDF conversion tool. Leave the landscape orientation at the landscape default and click OK.

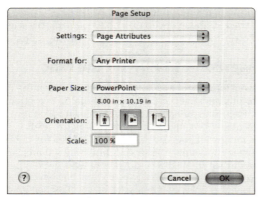

Figure 36-2: Select your new custom page size in the Page Setup dialog box.

5. **Convert to PDF.** Choose File ➪ Print. In the Print dialog box, select a PostScript printer or select Adobe PDF from the Printer pull-down menu. Open the PDF pull-down menu and select Save as PDF, as shown in Figure 36-3. The Save dialog box opens. Select a target location on your hard drive and click Save. The PowerPoint file is saved as a PDF document.

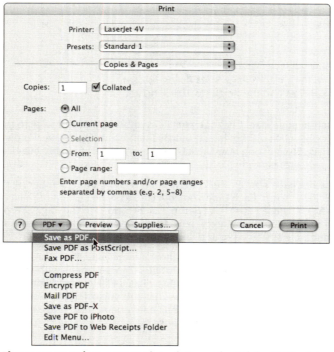

Figure 36-3: Select a PostScript printer or the Adobe PDF printer. Select Save as PDF and save the file as a PDF document.

If you select Save PDF as PostScript and distill the resultant PostScript file in Acrobat distiller, the pages are rotated. When you use the Tiger printer drive and Save as PDF, the pages in the PDF appear with the proper orientation.

Note   Using either Save as PDF or distilling a PostScript file loses all animation in the PDF file. The only way to preserve animated effects added in PowerPoint is to use the PDFMaker. Unfortunately, as of this writing the PDFMaker on the Macintosh when used with PowerPoint is unreliable.

Using PDFMaker on Windows

On Windows the PDFMaker is your tool of choice, and converting PowerPoint slides to PDF with this tool is both consistent and reliable. Additionally, you have the advantage of editing Conversion Settings from a menu command in the PowerPoint application menu. Conversion Settings offer you choices for how the PDF is created in terms of file compression, preserving various settings made in PowerPoint including transitions and effects, converting multimedia, and a host of options you have available by editing the Adobe PDF settings. To open the Adobe PDF Maker dialog box where Conversion Settings are adjusted, click on the Adobe PDF menu in PowerPoint, as shown in Figure 36-4. Select Conversion Settings from the menu options.

Figure 36-4: Select Conversion Settings from the Adobe PDF menu.

In the Adobe PDFMaker dialog box, shown in Figure 36-5, select the boxes for the items you want to enable or disable. To edit the Adobe PDF Settings that are employed with Acrobat Distiller, click the Adobe PDF Settings button. The same options you have available when adjusting the Distiller Adobe PDF Settings are available to you when you click on the Advanced Settings button. In most cases, you won't need to create custom PDF settings. Therefore, just select the conversion settings you want to use from choices in the Conversion Settings pull-down menu. By default, you should see Standard appear in the menu. Using the Standard settings generally does the job for creating slide presentations shown on-screen but not printed on commercial printing devices.

Cross-Reference   Understanding the Adobe PDF Settings (called *job options* in earlier versions of Acrobat) is an elaborate and complicated process. For almost all the PDF creation you perform with the CS programs, you won't need to adjust conversion settings and won't find a need to create custom Adobe PDF Settings. If you do find that you need to understand more and want to create your own custom settings files, see the *Adobe Acrobat 7 PDF Bible* (published by Wiley).

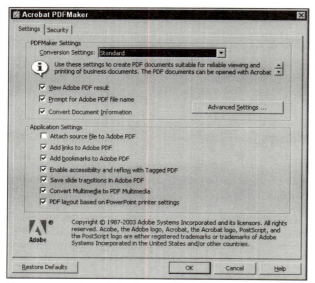

Figure 36-5: The Adobe PDFMaker dialog box offers options for creating a PDF.

Leave the default check boxes selected in the Adobe PDFMaker dialog box, and click OK to return to the PowerPoint application window. To create the PDF file, you need to select Convert to Adobe PDF from the Adobe PDF menu (Windows only) or click the Convert to Adobe PDF tool in the toolbar (Mac and Windows). PowerPoint begins to convert the open document to PDF using all the settings you made in the Print dialog box.

If you're working on a Mac, be certain to leave the Acrobat PDFMaker dialog box undisturbed until you see the View File button highlighted. After the PDF creation is completed, click View File or open the PDF from within Acrobat. If you checked the box to View PDF Result, the PDF opens automatically in your default Acrobat viewer.

Converting Apple Keynote slides to PDF (Mac)

Apple Keynote is a dedicated slide-presentation authoring application that offers a robust authoring environment with simplicity and ease in creating slide shows. The charting features in Keynote are easy to use, with intuitive palettes for editing chart types and data. Keynote supports file imports for many image formats, video and sound, and PDF imports that can be sized and scaled. The templates installed with the program are attractive and well designed.

You may not wish to choose Keynote as your application for creating slide shows, especially if you serve Windows clients. Keynote has one advantage for the Mac user beyond creating slides. You can use the program to convert existing PowerPoint files to PDF. Whereas the PDFMaker tool in PowerPoint on the Mac is unreliable and not always functional, and printing to PDF is confusing when exporting to PDF from PowerPoint, Keynote is simple to use and creates reliable PDF documents.

To convert a PowerPoint file to PDF using Keynote, choose File ➪ Open to open any PowerPoint file. Choose File ➪ Export and select PDF for the export format. Click Next in the Export window and you are prompted for a target location and filename. Provide a name for the file and click Export. The original PowerPoint file opened in Keynote is exported to PDF. There's no mess with Page Setup, selecting print attributes, or worry about producing PDFs with the wrong orientation.

Using the Mac OS to convert to PDF results in a less reliable PDF document then when using Adobe PDF creators. For slide presentations intended to be shown on-screen, exporting to PDF from Keynote is reliable. However, if you intend to print slides to a film recorder or size them up for large print output, print the files to disk and use Acrobat Distiller.

Creating Presentations in CS programs

If your comfort zone is strictly limited to the CS applications, you may not want to learn either PowerPoint or Keynote. If so, then you can use some of the CS programs as presentation-authoring tools. All the CS programs except Adobe Acrobat can be used as the authoring tool, while Acrobat is used as the display tool for showing presentations. In practicality, using Adobe GoLive is more cumbersome (unless, of course, the presentation format will be HTML), while the most likely candidate to help you create a presentation project is Adobe InDesign.

Using InDesign as a presentation-authoring tool

Creating slides in InDesign has its advantages and disadvantages. In terms of disadvantages, InDesign does not offer you dynamic outlining where you add text in an outline format that is automatically applied to individual slides. The actual creation of text on slides is much faster in a dedicated slide-creation tool. Additionally, you have no options for printing notes or handouts, adding animation to text and objects, editing charts and graphs, and a few other specific slide-creation features.

On the advantage side of using InDesign, you have much more design freedom than using dedicated slide-creation programs, including the ability to import native CS application documents; the ability to import files saved from a wider range of formats; better typographic control; more-sophisticated editing of graphic elements such as applying drop shadows, adding transparency, and feathering objects, creating layers, using style sheets and graphic styles, and all the options InDesign offers you for creating sophisticated layouts. As an example, in Figure 36-6, you can see a native Photoshop image in the lower-right corner of the slide with a graduated transparent edge on the left side of the image.

Creating bookmarks

As a final editing task, you may want to add bookmarks to your presentation. Bookmarks can help you easily return to areas of discussion when answering questions or adding information on topics as you make a presentation. You have a choice for adding bookmarks directly in InDesign and having those bookmarks exported in the PDF document or creating bookmarks in Acrobat. In some workflows, you may find a benefit in creating bookmarks in InDesign if a layout specialist is unfamiliar with Acrobat and doesn't have the full version installed on a computer.

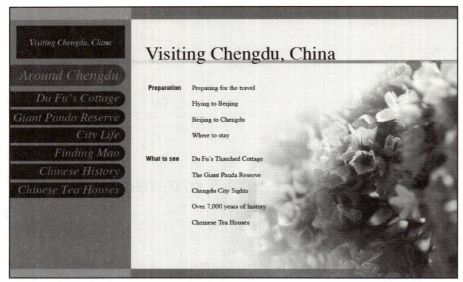

Figure 36-6: Using InDesign to create slides allows you to import native files with transparency.

Creating bookmarks: Acrobat or InDesign?

There's a big difference between bookmarks created in InDesign and bookmarks created in Acrobat. When you create bookmarks in Acrobat, the bookmark captures the view of the bookmarked page. When zooming in 400 percent and creating a bookmark, you capture the page and the zoom view. Therefore, if you are in a 100 percent view and click on a bookmark that was bookmarked at a 400 percent view, Acrobat takes you to the page bookmarked and zooms in to a 400 percent view. When you create a bookmark in InDesign, the zoom is derived from the current view. Therefore, if you zoom to 400 percent to view pages, and then click a bookmark, the bookmarked page opens at 400 percent even though the bookmark may have been created at 100 percent view. If you zoom out to a Fit Page view in the same document and continue clicking on bookmarks, the bookmark zooms inherit the current view (for example, Fit Page). Note that if the bookmarks are created in InDesign and the file is exported to PDF, viewing the bookmarked pages in Acrobat treat the zoom levels with the same inherited page views.

At first blush, you may think it more of an advantage to create bookmarks in InDesign so that all page links go to inherited zoom levels. However, there's a price to pay for having the feature. When you create bookmarks in InDesign, you add more overhead to your file because InDesign creates not only bookmarks but also Destinations. In Acrobat Destinations are similar to bookmarks where you can click on Destinations to navigate pages. However, adding Destinations to a PDF file significantly adds to the file size. For small to moderate-size presentations that are viewed from files stored on your hard drive, it shouldn't be an issue. However if you post files on the Web or use very large PDF documents, you'll want to avoid using Destinations. The added file sizes can slow down performance in Acrobat and add to the download time with Web-hosted documents.

To create bookmarks in InDesign, choose Window ➪ Interactive ➪ Bookmarks to open the Bookmarks palette. Creating bookmarks is easy in both InDesign and Acrobat. Find text on a page you want to use as a bookmark title and select the text. Click on the right-pointing arrow in the palette to open the fly-out menu, and select New Bookmark, as shown in Figure 36-7. In Acrobat, the menu command to create a new bookmark is found in the Bookmark pane Options menu.

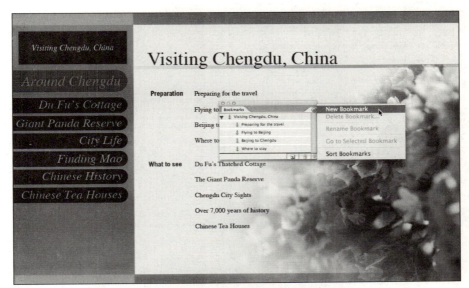

Figure 36-7: To capture the page view, select New Bookmark.

If you want to create a bookmark without capturing highlighted text as the bookmark name, don't select any text, but select New Bookmark from the fly-out palette. InDesign automatically names the bookmark simply as Bookmark. To edit the name, select Rename Bookmark in the palette menu. A dialog box opens where you edit the name.

After creating bookmarks, scroll the Bookmark palette and review the bookmark names. To check the bookmark links, double-click on a name and InDesign opens the page associated with the bookmark. Note that InDesign requires you to double-click a bookmark name to view the destination, while Acrobat requires only a single mouse click.

Cross-Reference

For more information about creating bookmarks and interactive links in InDesign, see Chapter 32.

Exporting to PDF

After you've created your slides, added bookmarks, and reviewed the document, you need to export the file as a PDF for a more-suitable file format for viewing slides. Don't attempt to use InDesign as a slide viewer, especially when you need to exchange files with clients or across platforms. Obviously, one advantage to creating PDF documents is that any user can display the slide presentation with the free Adobe Reader software. If you distribute InDesign files, every user who wants to view the presentation needs a licensed copy of InDesign.

To export the file to PDF, choose File ⇨ Export Supply a filename in the Save As field box and navigate your hard drive for a destination. Be certain Adobe PDF is selected in the Format pull-down menu and click Save.

The next dialog box that opens is the Export Adobe PDF dialog box, shown in Figure 36-8. Here, you make choices for the PDF attributes. First, select the preset you want to use from the Preset pull-down menu.

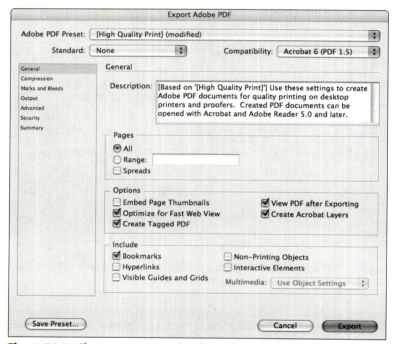

Figure 36-8: Choose a preset and make attribute choices.

New Feature In InDesign CS2 you are no longer limited to fixed presets. Any preset created in Acrobat Distiller or other CS2 application appears listed in the Adobe PDF Preset pull-down menu.

If you create bookmarks, select the box for bookmarks and any other interactive elements you may have included in the InDesign file. When you're finished with the attribute choices, click Export and the file is exported to PDF. If you selected View PDF after Exporting, the file opens in your default Acrobat viewer. In Figure 36-9, you can see a PDF exported from InDesign with bookmarks.

Cross-Reference Note that there are several categories from which to choose in the left pane in the PDF Export dialog box. The options below the General category are discussed in Chapter 38.

Chapter 36 ✦ Creating Slide Presentations 1151

Figure 36-9: The exported bookmarks should be visible in the open Bookmarks pane.

Creating notes and handouts

All the InDesign editing features you learned in Parts III, IV, and V are available to you when creating slide presentations just like other kinds of layouts. Using master pages, character and paragraph styles, tables, and so on is helpful in creating any kind of layout. Creating notes and handouts, however, is another matter. If you want to create note pages with slides on each page like you can with the slide-presentation programs, you need to export slide pages from InDesign and import them back into a template designed for creating note pages. Assuming you have a PDF document you want to use as a slide presentation, the following steps demonstrate how you can use InDesign to create note handouts:

STEPS: Creating Note Handouts in InDesign

1. **Create a new document in Adobe InDesign.** Launch Adobe InDesign and choose File ➪ New to create a new document. Set the page attributes to a letter-page size (8½ x 11 inches) and a portrait orientation. Set the margin distance to 0.5 inches for all sides, and click OK in the New Document dialog box.

   Note If you know ahead of time the number of slides in the presentation, enter the value in the Number of Pages field box. If you don't remember the exact number of pages in your PDF document, enter an approximate value and you can add or delete pages when working in the InDesign document.

2. **Create a master page.** Open the Pages palette and double-click the default A-Master master page. On the master page, draw lines for note comments, and add any graphic objects, an auto page number, a title, and other items you want to display on each note page.

Cross-Reference For information on working with master pages and adding auto page numbers, see Chapter 26.

3. **Add a graphic frame placeholder to the master page.** Select the Rectangle Frame tool in the InDesign toolbox, and click the cursor anywhere on the document page. The Rectangle dialog box opens. Enter the width and height you used in your slide presentation and click OK. Drag the frame rectangle so the top-left corner resets at the top and left guidelines. Press ⌘/Ctrl+Shift to constrain the frame size, and drag the lower-right corner to rest on the right guideline, as shown in Figure 36-10.

Tip You can use a note template for not only slides created in InDesign, but also slides you may have created in PowerPoint or Keynote. After they're exported to PDF, you have the same opportunities to design note handouts in InDesign. If you want more freedom for the way your handouts are designed, import them into an InDesign layout. If you use the standard 10-x-7½-inch slide format, enter those values in the Rectangle dialog box that opens when clicking on the Rectangle Frame tool.

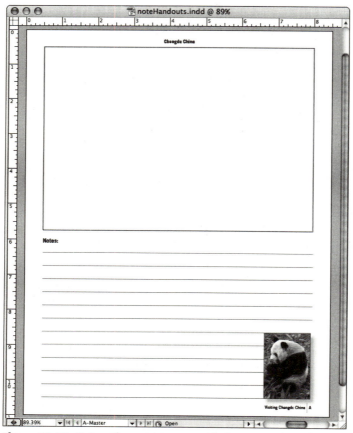
Figure 36-10: Set up the master page with the text and graphics.

Cross-Reference For more information on sizing frame rectangles, see Part III.

4. **Select the PDF file to import.** Navigate to the first page in your InDesign file and select File ⇨ Place. In the Place dialog box, navigate your hard drive and locate the PDF document to be imported. At the bottom of the Place dialog box, check the box for Show Import Options, as shown in Figure 36-11. When the Show Import Options check box is checked, the Place PDF dialog box opens, where you have options for selecting pages in the PDF document to be placed in the InDesign file.

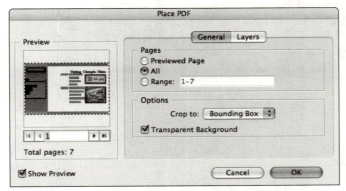

Figure 36-11: When Show Import Options is checked in the Place dialog box, the Place PDF dialog box opens.

5. **Select All pages.** Click Open in the Place dialog box, and the Place PDF dialog box opens, as shown in Figure 36-11. Select All in the dialog box to place all pages. This is a new feature in InDesign CS2.

6. **Place the first page in the rectangle frame.** Click OK in the Place PDF dialog box, and the cursor loads the graphic. Be certain to move anywhere atop the rectangle frame location on page 1 and click the cursor. The first page in the PDF file is placed inside the rectangle frame, as shown in Figure 36-12.

 New Feature If you have layers in the PDF file, you can import different layered views. Add additional layers using the Place command and click the Layers tab. Select the layer view you want to import and click OK.

7. **Size the graphic to the frame size.** Press Shift+⌘+Option+E (Shift+Ctrl+Alt+E on Windows) and the graphic image is proportionally sized to fit inside the rectangle frame. The cursor remains loaded and you can continue clicking on subsequent pages to place the remaining PDF pages. Continue to place pages from the PDF to the remaining pages in the InDesign document.

8. **Export to PDF.** If you want to send your file off to a copy shop for printing or host the note handouts on a Web site for attendees to download, convert the file to PDF. The copy shop won't need links, fonts, or a copy of InDesign CS to print the file, and those downloading your file from a Web site can use the free Adobe Reader software to view the document.

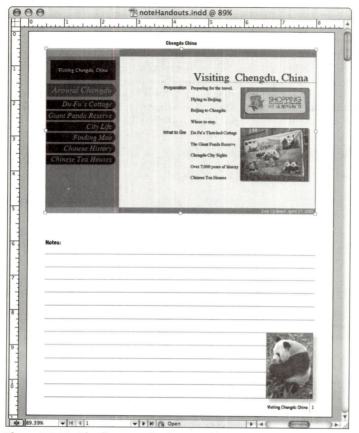

Figure 36-12: The first page in the PDF document is placed in the frame.

If you want to make edits in your note handouts, you can easily return to the master page and edit any text or images, or modify the rectangle frame. The rectangle frame in the lower right corner of Figure 36-12 was edited by adding a keyline border and drop shadow after all the PDF pages were placed in the document. The file was then exported as a PDF. Simple edits on master pages save you much time over editing each page individually.

Using Photoshop as an authoring tool

Obviously, using Photoshop to create slides is not the most practical solution. Having only one page to edit in a file at one time is certain to slow your progress, not to mention that it results in much larger files than you have using any other application. However, Photoshop does have one nice feature for creating slide presentations when creating a presentation from a collection of photos or design comps you want to display as slides: You can easily create a self-running slide show complete with transitions and add sound to the presentation if desired.

To create a slide presentation in Photoshop, start by opening the Bridge. Select the thumbnails of the images you want to convert to PDF in the Bridge content area or press ⌘/Ctrl+A to select all images in a folder.

Tip   If you have a digital camera and want to select files from your digital camera, you can open the Bridge and navigate to a camera attached to a USB or FireWire port on your computer (if such ports exist on your camera). Thumbnail images of the photos on your camera's memory card display in the Bridge window.

The PDF Presentation dialog box shown in Figure 36-13 appears.

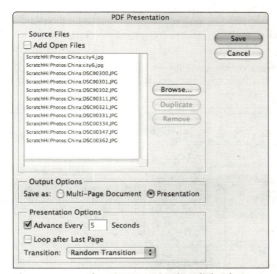

Figure 36-13: The PDF Presentation dialog box can be opened from the Bridge or from Photoshop.

You have several options for setting attributes of the resultant PDF file. If you click the check box for Add Open Files, any files open in Photoshop are added to the file exported to PDF. In the Save As area under Output Options, click the radio button for Presentation. From the Transition pull-down menu, you can choose from a variety of different transitions applied to slide wipes.

When you click Save, the image files selected in the Bridge convert to PDF and combine together in a single PDF document. The file opens in Acrobat in Full Screen mode complete with transitions as slide pages scroll automatically at the interval specified in the PDF Presentation dialog box. By default, the transition interval is 5 seconds. To bail out of Full Screen mode, press Esc or press ⌘/Ctrl+L.

Using Illustrator as an authoring tool

The last tool you should use to create a slide presentation among the CS programs is Illustrator. However, we know there are creative professionals who rely on Illustrator for everything from single-page illustrations to multipage catalogs. We don't recommend it, but we do know some artists feel so comfortable with Illustrator that they wouldn't take a second look at a layout program no matter what it had to offer.

If you're one of those die-hard Illustrator designers who wants to create some down and dirty slide presentations, follow these steps:

STEPS: Using Illustrator as a Presentation Design Tool

1. **Determine the layout size.** If you want to create 10 slides, each measuring 10 inches wide by 7 inches high, you need to create an art board 20 inches wide by 35 inches high. This art board accommodates a 2-column x 5-row layout.

2. **Create a new document in Illustrator.** Choose File ➪ New and create the page size equal to the dimensions you determined in step 1.

3. **Add guidelines.** Drag guidelines from the horizontal and vertical ruler wells to the sizes for the individual slides. Using the example in step 1, drag a vertical guideline from the vertical ruler to 10 inches and drag guides from the horizontal ruler to 7, 14, 21, and 28 inches.

4. **Create the artwork.** Create artwork on separate layers for slide. In Figure 36-14, you can see exaggerated guidelines in a layout using two columns and three rows.

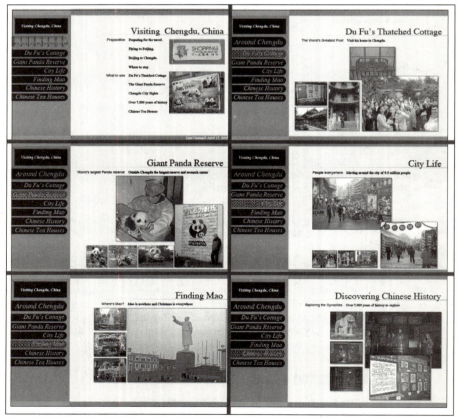

Figure 36-14: Create slides on individual layers within the guidelines.

5. **Create a PDF file.** To create a multipage PDF document use the Print command, choose File ➪ Print. In the General settings, set the page size equal to the dimensions of one slide. Click Setup in the left page and select Tile Imageable Areas from the Tiling pull-down menu. The Preview thumbnail displays the tiled pages with dashed lines as you see in Figure 36-15. Be certain to select Adobe PDF 7 as your printer and click Print. A multipage PDF document is created according to the tiling you selected in the Setup pane.

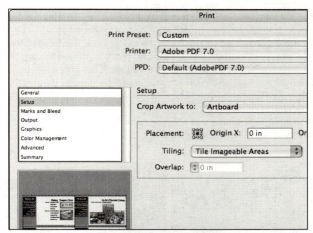

Figure 36-15: Select Tile Imageable Areas and print to the Adobe PDF 7 printer.

 Cross-Reference For more information on creating multi-page PDF documents from Adobe Illustrator, see Chapter 32.

Using Layers with Presentations

Layers offer you another dimension when creating slide presentations. Text can pop up as you cover topics in a presentation when you use layers and toggle on and off layer views. You can also use layers when you need to toggle back and forth between two slide views. Think of a slide where you want to use text and images, then move to a video, return to the text, and move to another video. Layers can handle some of these switching-back-and-forth routines as opposed to creating different slides. In many cases, changing layer views results in faster screen refreshes than changing slide pages.

To create presentations using layers, the authoring program you use needs to support two essential ingredients:

✦ Support for creating Layers

✦ Writing to the PDF 1.5 format and exporting Adobe PDF Layers

Although Photoshop and GoLive support layers, they don't export Adobe PDF Layers. InDesign and Illustrator both export layers that you can view in Acrobat with layers intact.

For an example of using layers and changing layer visibility in the Acrobat PDF, look at Figure 36-16. The default layer view is shown when the user moves to this page. You can see the Layers pane showing the Layout layer in view while the Video layer is hidden. A button in the lower-right corner has a link action that changes layer visibility to hide the Layout layer and show the Video layer. In addition, the button action plays a video that was originally imported in InDesign before exporting to PDF.

The button and button actions to show and hide layer visibility were added in Acrobat. When the user clicks the button on the default layer, the visibility changes to show the hidden layer. Notice as you look at Figure 36-17 that the background data assigned to the Background layer does not change. The elements assigned to the background are the banners at the top and bottom of the page. When you're creating layers, you can place text and images on layers common to different layer views and keep these layers visible. This eliminates a need to show/hide data that remains constant while other data is hidden and shown with different layer visibility. The result is faster screen refreshes, because some data remains in view.

Cross-Reference For more information on creating layers in CS programs and exporting Adobe PDF Layers, see Chapter 14. For information on creating buttons and interactive actions, see Chapter 32.

Figure 36-16: The default layer view changes when a user clicks a button.

Figure 36-17: Clicking the button on the default layer changes the layer visibility.

Adding Page Transitions

Page transitions are available in both Edit mode and Full Screen mode in Acrobat 7. A *page transition* is an effect such as a fade-out and fade-in applied to pages as they're turned. You can set page transitions for all pages in a file or among selected pages in the Pages palette. You might add page transitions to PDF documents for trade-show displays where you want to show slides in self-running kiosks.

To set transitions on all pages in a document, or a specified range of pages while remaining in Edit mode (as opposed to Full Screen mode), choose Document ➪ Pages ➪ Set Page Transitions. If you want to set transitions for pages in a noncontiguous order, open the Pages palette and ⌘/Ctrl+click on the individual pages where you want page transitions. After making the page selections, choose Document ➪ Pages ➪ Set Page Transitions. The Set Transitions dialog box opens, shown in Figure 36-18.

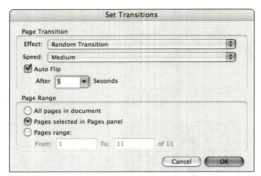

Figure 36-18: In this dialog box, select a page transition from the Effect menu.

From the Effect pull-down menu, you select the transition you want to apply to the selected pages, either from pages you selected in the Pages palette or a range of pages you specify in the Pages Range field boxes. Acrobat offers you a total of 50 different choices for different effects. One choice is to set no transition, with the remaining 49 choices being different effects.

If you check the Auto Flip check box, pages scroll at an interval automatically according to the number of seconds you select from the pull-down menu below the Auto Flip check box. Choices for the interval range from 1 to 32,767 seconds. You can select fixed interval options or type a value within the acceptable range. If you want to manually scroll pages, leave the check box disabled.

If you don't select pages in the Pages palette, you make choices for applying transitions to all pages or specify a page range in a contiguous order by clicking on the Pages range and typing in the page From and To field boxes. When you select pages in the Pages palette, the Pages Selected in the Pages Panel check box becomes active by default and the transitions are applied to the selected pages.

After setting the effects and page range, click OK and transitions apply to the pages when you scroll pages in Edit mode.

During your design phase and before you convert files to PDF you can preview a slide show in Adobe Bridge. To preview a collection of CS2 files, open a folder in the Bridge window containing your native documents. Choose View ⇨ Slide Show or press ⌘/Ctrl+L. The Bridge window changes to a full screen view like you see in Acrobat. While in slide view, press H to access settings you can use when viewing the slides.

For more information on viewing documents in slide view in Adobe Bridge, see Chapter 7.

Using Full Screen Views

The Full Screen view shows PDF pages without the presence of the Acrobat tools, title bar, menu, or palettes. Not only do Full Screen views offer you a different appearance for displaying PDF pages, but also the mode is also necessary if you want to view certain effects. PowerPoint presentations with animation, for example, can only display effects created in the original PowerPoint file while viewing a PDF in Full Screen mode.

Cross-Reference For more information on creating PDF documents from PowerPoint files, see the "Converting Presentation Documents to PDF" section, earlier in this chapter.

Viewing slides in Acrobat

If you converted PowerPoint slides containing animation effects, such as motion objects and transitions, the animation is not viewable in Edit mode. You need to change the viewing mode to Full Screen mode. Press ⌘/Ctrl+L or choose Window ➪ Full Screen View to show the PDF in Full Screen mode. Press the Page Down key, press the down-arrow key, or click the mouse button to scroll pages. As you scroll pages, any animations associated with graphics or text are visible as long as you remain in Full Screen mode.

If you prepare presentations for clients and want to make it easier for them to launch Full Screen mode, you can save the PDF file so the document always opens in Full Screen view. Choose File ➪ Document Properties while the slide presentation is open and active in the Document pane. The Document Properties dialog box opens, shown in Figure 36-19.

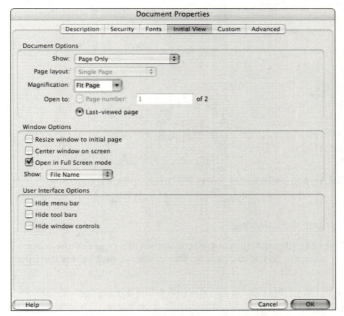

Figure 36-19: You activate Full Screen mode in the Document Properties dialog box.

In the Document Properties dialog box, click on Initial View in the left pane and check the box for Open in Full Screen mode in the right pane. Click OK and save the file. The next time you open the PDF file either by double-clicking the document icon or by choosing File ➪ Open inside Acrobat, the file opens in Full Screen mode.

Setting Full Screen preferences

If you want to set up a kiosk or workstation for viewing documents in Full Screen mode, start by making some choices in the Full Screen preferences. In the preference settings, you can control some of the viewing options. Choose Edit ⇨ Preferences on Windows or Acrobat ⇨ Preferences on the Mac. In the left pane, select Full Screen; the preference choices appear, as shown in Figure 36-20.

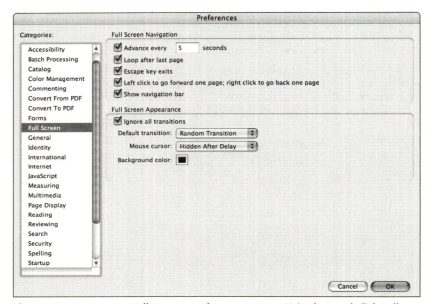

Figure 36-20: To open Full Screen preferences, press ⌘/Ctrl+K and click Full Screen in the left pane.

The preference choices include the following:

- ✦ **Advance Every:** The slide presentation automatically scrolls pages at the interval specified in the field box adjacent to the check box. The values permitted for the interval are between 1 and 60 seconds.

- ✦ **Loop after Last Page:** Using this option and the preceding setting for auto-advancing, you can set up a kiosk and have the slide presentation continue with auto repetition. After the last page, the presentation starts again.

- ✦ **Escape Key Exists:** If you want to exit Full Screen view, you can strike the Esc key when you enable this check box. Be certain to leave the check box at the default switch. If you disable the check box, remember to use ⌘/Ctrl+L to exit Full Screen view.

- ✦ **Left-Click to Go Forward One Page, Right-Click to Go Back One Page:** With this option, you can navigate pages with mouse clicks. For both Windows and Mac users who use a two-button mouse, clicking on the left or right button navigates pages in the respective direction.

- ✦ **Show Navigation Bar:** This option enables the viewer to use buttons for advancing and retracing pages.

- ✦ **Ignore All Transitions:** If you set transitions while in Edit mode and want to eliminate the transition effects while in Full Screen view, enable this option.

- ✦ **Default Transition:** From the pull-down menu, you have choices for one of the same 49 different transition effects. If you apply a transition in the Full Screen preferences, then all pages use the same transition. Selecting Random from the menu choices offers you effects that change randomly as you move through slide pages. If you want to use specific transitions that change for selected pages, set the transitions from the Document ⇨ Pages ⇨ Page Transitions menu command before opening the Preferences dialog box. Disable Ignore All Transitions and the effects you choose for page transitions applied to selected pages in the Pages palette are used when you enter Full Screen mode.

- ✦ **Mouse Cursor:** There are three choices from the pull-down menu for the mouse-cursor display while viewing slides in Full Screen mode. You can choose from Always Visible, Always Hidden, or Hidden After Delay. The Hidden After Delay menu choice shows the cursor position when you scroll pages, and then hides it after a short delay.

- ✦ **Background Color:** Click on the color swatch, and the preset color palette opens; here, you can make choices for the background color. The background color appears outside the slide pages on all pages that don't fit precisely within the monitor frame. If you want to use a custom color, click on Other Color at the bottom of the palette and select a custom color from your system palette.

Scrolling pages

To advance through slides when in Full Screen mode, you can use the preference setting and scroll pages with mouse clicks. If the preference choice for Left-Click to Go Forward One Page; Right-Click to Go Back One Page is disabled, you scroll pages with keystrokes. Strike the Page Down or Page Up keys to move forward and backward through slides. Additionally, you can use the up- or left-arrow keys to move backward and the down- or right-arrow keys to move forward. Use the Home key to move to the first page and the End key to move to the last page. If you want to move to a specific page without leaving Full Screen mode, press Shift+⌘/Ctrl+N and the Go to Page dialog box opens. Enter the page number to open in the field box and click OK.

Creating interactivity in Full Screen mode

You may have a slide presentation that doesn't require access to Acrobat menus and tools, but you want to show cross-document links. Perhaps you design a presentation about a company's financial status, economic growth, or projected growth, and your client wants to show a financial spreadsheet, another PDF document, or a scanned image of a memo or report. The slideshow created in PowerPoint with the motion objects and viewing in Full Screen mode is what you want, but you also want the flexibility for opening other files without leaving the Full Screen mode.

Creating links and buttons for cross-document linking

If you want to open a secondary document while in Full Screen mode, you can create links or form-field buttons to secondary files. When you click on the link, the link action is invoked. If opening a secondary file, the file link opens in Full Screen mode. After viewing the file, press ⌘/Ctrl+W to close the file and you're returned to the last slide view also in Full Screen mode.

To set up a file link, create a link or form-field button and create a link to open a file. Acrobat offers you options for opening a linked document in the existing window or a new window. You can create the kind of file linking and views to make things easy on your clients, and they won't need to struggle finding files located on a hard drive or launching external applications. All the file linking and activation can be created with buttons in Acrobat.

Cross-Reference For information on creating interactive links and buttons, see Chapter 32.

You can also create URL links to display a Web site while in Full Screen mode by using the Open a Web Link action. Click on the link and your Web browser opens at the specified URL. When you quit the Web browser, you're retuned to the slide presentation in Full Screen mode. If you use PowerPoint effects, the effects aren't disturbed.

Cross-Reference To learn more about setting link actions to URLs, see Chapter 33.

Tip In Acrobat 7, you do not need to create links to URLs using links or buttons. If you design your documents with URLs in text using the full URL address such as http://www.company.com before PDF creation, Acrobat 7 recognizes the text as a link to a URL. Position the cursor over the text in Acrobat and click. Your default Web browser is launched and opens the URL Web page.

Using interactive devices

Another interactivity tool that you can use with Full Screen view is a remote-control device. For about $50 to $75 you can purchase a handheld remote control. The control comes in two parts. The control device has two buttons used for moving forward and backward in the slide presentation. The companion unit is plugged into a USB port on a laptop or desktop computer. You open the slide presentation in Full Screen view and click the left or right button to navigate slides while you walk across a stage. Some devices also have a button for cursor control. You can remotely move the cursor on a slide and click on a button that opens a secondary file, Web link, or other action associated with the button or link.

When using remote devices, be certain to set your Full Screen preferences to Left-Click to Go Forward One Page; Right-Click to Go Back One Page.

Summary

- You convert PowerPoint slides to PDF with the PDFMaker macro.

- To create note handouts from PowerPoint, use the Print dialog box and print the file to the Adobe PDF Printer after making the attribute choices in the Print dialog box for the type of handouts you want to create.

- You can export Apple Keynote slides to PDF and PowerPoint formats. Keynote offers Macintosh users a robust slide-creation program with easy, intuitive palettes and tools.

- You can use layout programs such as InDesign to create slide presentations. For creating handout notes, set up a master page with objects and elements to be added to each page. Import the PDF slide presentation and convert to PDF.

- Adobe Illustrator can be used to create multipage PDF documents. Although Illustrator is not recommended as a design tool for presentations, Illustrator users can create slides and export to multiple-page PDFs.

- Layered PDFs add additional viewing options in slide presentations. To create layered PDFs use programs, such as InDesigns CS2 and Illustrator CS2, supporting layers and exporting to the PDF 1.5 format (Acrobat 6 or 7 compatibility).

- Page transitions are applied to pages individually using the Document ⇨ Pages ⇨ Set Page Transitions command in Acrobat. To apply different transitions to different pages, select pages in the Pages palette and adjust the transitions in the Set Transitions dialog box.

- When using Full Screen mode, open the Preferences dialog box and select Full Screen.

- Full Screen views support file linking with link and button actions, Microsoft PowerPoint animation, and transitions applied to pages with either the Full Screen preferences or the Set Page Transitions command.

✦ ✦ ✦

Printing and Digital Prepress

PART

In This Part

Chapter 37
Choosing Print Setups

Chapter 38
Commercial Printing

Choosing Print Setups

CHAPTER 37

In This Chapter

Choosing printers

Working with print setups

Files created for print fall into two categories — designs for composite prints and designs for color separations or commercial printing. When you design documents for composite printing, your output device might be a laser printer, a desktop inkjet printer, a large-format inkjet printer, a color copier, a film recorder, or a high-end commercial color printer. Files designed for commercial printing are typically color-separated and printed to film, direct to plate, or direct to press.

This chapter is concerned with setting print attributes for composite color that may print to your office desktop printers as well as advanced settings for commercial devices designed for printing prepress.

Selecting Desktop Printers

The first step in printing files is to select the target printer and the print attributes associated with the printer, such as paper size, paper feed, paper tray, and so on. If you work as an independent designer in a small shop, you may have only one printer on your network. After you assign your printer as the default printing device, you don't need to worry about printer selection. However, if you work in production workflows in larger shops, you may have a variety of printers attached to your network. In these environments, it's essential you make the proper printer selection before sending off a job for print. Selecting printers varies between Mac OS and Windows.

Printer selection on the Mac

One of the clear disadvantages of using the CS programs when you print a document is the inconsistency between what you see in an application document window versus what prints. The programs vary in what dialog boxes you access, whether you have access to a printing device PPD (PostScript Printer Description), how to set up custom pages, and what print attributes to use. To fully comprehend printer selection, we need to look at the CS programs individually.

InDesign

In InDesign on Mac OS, you make printer selections in the Print dialog box. Notice that you don't have a command under the File menu for Page Setup. If you choose File ➪ Document Setup, the Document Setup dialog box opens; here, the options choices are restricted to page sizes and defining bleeds and slugs. No options for printer choices or print attributes are made in the Document Setup dialog box.

To make a printer choice, choose File ➪ Print. In the Print dialog box, shown in Figure 37-1, you choose your target printer from the Printer pull-down menu. You select a printer from the menu choices and then make various print-attribute choices by clicking on the items listed in the left pane and respective choices on the right side of the dialog box.

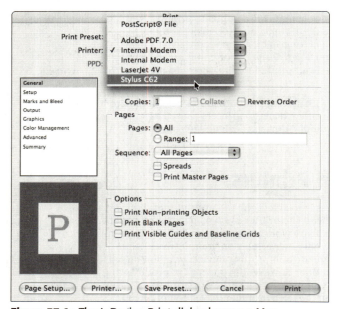

Figure 37-1: The InDesign Print dialog box on a Mac

Notice that you have a choice for accessing the Page Setup dialog box in the Print dialog box. Click on Page Setup and a warning dialog box opens, as shown in Figure 37-2. The warning informs you that settings can be made in InDesign's Print dialog box without opening the Page Setup dialog box. Be certain to use the InDesign option rather than the Page Setup dialog box. Conflicts can persist if you make choices in the Page Setup dialog box.

Figure 37-2: Clicking Page Setup opens a warning dialog box.

Illustrator

Also in the Print dialog box is a Printer pull-down menu where you select your target printer in Illustrator. Like InDesign, Illustrator has a Document Setup dialog box where no print options are selected. Additionally, no Page Setup dialog box is available in Illustrator.

To select a target printer in Illustrator, choose File ⇨ Print. The Print dialog box opens, shown in Figure 37-3. From the Printer pull-down menu, select the printer you want to use.

Note   Adobe PDF is a printer option in all applications because it's installed with Adobe Acrobat. For device output, you typically won't use the Adobe PDF printer. However, when preparing PostScript files, the Adobe PDF printer is often your best choice when a device PPD is not available.

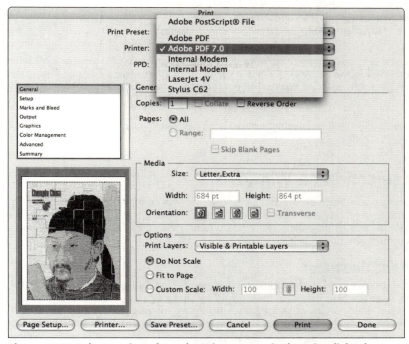

Figure 37-3: Select a printer from the Printer menu in the Print dialog box.

Photoshop, GoLive, and Acrobat

Photoshop, GoLive, and Acrobat all make use of a Page Setup dialog box. Rather than use the Print dialog box to access a printer, your first choice in these programs is the Page Setup dialog box, shown in Figure 37-4. From the Format For pull-down menu, select the printer you want to use.

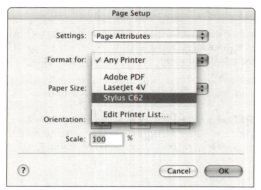

Figure 37-4: Photoshop, GoLive, and Acrobat use the Page Setup dialog box.

If you need to define custom page sizes for your output, set up the custom page by selecting Custom Paper Size in the Settings pull-down menu. After you create a custom page size, return to the Page Setup dialog box and select the new page size before moving to the Print dialog box.

For more information on creating custom page sizes, see Chapter 24.

Printer selection on Windows

Similar to printer selections on the Mac, Windows users access printers in either the Page Setup or Print dialog boxes. Also like the Mac CS applications, some programs don't have a Page Setup dialog box, while others require you to first visit a Page Setup dialog box when selecting a printer and paper size.

InDesign and Illustrator

When using Windows in InDesign and Illustrator, you make your printer selections in the Print dialog boxes. Like the Mac versions, these programs have no Page Setup dialog boxes. The Document Setup dialog boxes offer the same options as you find in the Mac counterparts. In InDesign, choose File ➪ Print and make a printer selection from the Printer drop-down list, shown in Figure 37-5.

Likewise, in Illustrator choose File ➪ Print and select your target printer from the Printer drop-down list shown in Figure 37-6. Notice that the print options available in the InDesign and Illustrator Print dialog boxes match the same options found on the Mac.

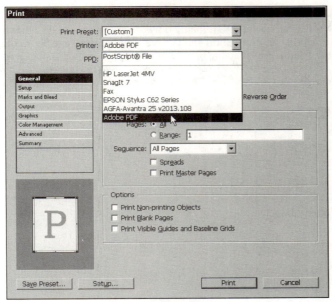

Figure 37-5: In InDesign on Windows

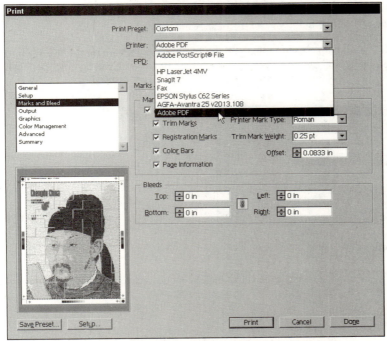

Figure 37-6: Like InDesign, Illustrator uses a Printer drop-down list.

Photoshop and GoLive

Photoshop, GoLive, and Acrobat all use different dialog boxes for printer selection than the dialog box you use for printing. In Photoshop and GoLive, you use the Page Setup dialog box; in Acrobat, you use the Printer Setup dialog box. From either Photoshop or GoLive, choose File ⇨ Page Setup and the Page Setup dialog box opens, shown in Figure 37-7. This is the first of two dialog boxes you use in these programs to make a printer selection.

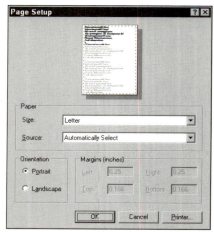

Figure 37-7: In Photoshop and GoLive, you use the Page Setup dialog box.

Printer selection is made in a second dialog box you open by clicking on the Printer button in the Page Setup dialog box. Click on Printer and another Page Setup dialog box opens, shown in Figure 37-8. From the Name drop-down list, select your target printer.

Figure 37-8: Selecting your target printer in the second Page Setup dialog box

After selecting your target printer, click OK and make a choice for the paper size in the first Page Setup dialog box (refer to Figure 37-7).

Acrobat

Acrobat treats printer selection similar to Photoshop and GoLive, but the Page Setup dialog box in Acrobat is called the Print Setup dialog box and the printer selection and paper size are both selected in the same dialog box. In Acrobat, choose File ⇨ Print Setup, and the Print Setup dialog box opens, shown in Figure 37-9.

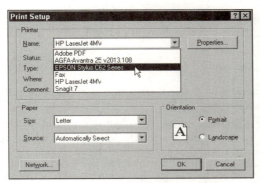

Figure 37-9: In Acrobat, select a printer in the Print Setup dialog box.

From the Name drop-down list, you make a choice for your target printer, and subsequently you make a choice for paper size in the same dialog box.

After making a printer selection, you then make choices for print attributes in the Print dialog boxes. If paper selection is handled in Page or Print Setup dialog boxes, be certain to make the proper paper choice before opening the Print dialog box.

Setting Print Options

If your task is to print composite color to desktop or large-format commercial printers, you don't need to manage many of the print attributes in the print dialog boxes. Items such as emulsion, screening, separations, and so on are used for prepress and commercial printing. In some circumstances, you must use an option designed for commercial printing when printing composite color. For example, when printing on Mylar on your desktop color printer, you must print emulsion down so the image is reversed on the back of the *substrate* (printing material). Special conditions like this require you to know all the print features in the print dialog boxes.

Although you may not use all the options available to you when printing CS application documents, an elaborate description is offered here for both composite and commercial printing. Use this information in conjunction with the material in Chapter 37 when printing to commercial printing devices. Because each program has some different attribute settings, look over the settings descriptions according to the program you use for final output.

Setting print options in Illustrator

In Illustrator, choose File ⇨ Print to open the Print dialog box, where you select your printing device. As a matter of rule, you first want to select the printing device. Items such as page sizes and PPDs (PostScript Printer Description files) are accessed after making the printer choice. A PPD contains information related to your printer when printing to PostScript devices. Such information relates to a series of fixed page sizes, color handling, screening, and similar characteristics. When you open the Print dialog box, a list of categories appears in the left pane (see Figure 37-3). Clicking an item in the left pane changes options on the right side of the dialog box.

> **Tip** PPD files are text documents. If you need to install a PPD from a Mac to a Windows machine or vice versa, you can copy the file to either platform. As text-only documents, they're completely cross-platform compliant.

General settings

The default series of settings are the General print options. When you select General in the left pane, the options choices include the following:

- **Print Preset:** At the bottom of the dialog box, notice the Save Preset button. You can change options in all the settings related to selections in the left pane and as a last option setting, click Save Preset. Illustrator opens a dialog box where you supply a name for the preset and the new preset appears in the Print Preset drop-down list. When you want to use the same print options, choose the preset name from the drop-down list, and all the settings associated with the preset are applied. The file prints according to the preset options.

- **Printer:** As discussed in the previous "Printer selection on Windows" and "Printer selection on the Mac" sections, you select the target printer from the drop-down list. You also have a selection for Adobe PostScript File. Use this option if you want to create a PostScript file that ultimately downloads to a printing device. You might use a PostScript file if you have a printer driver and PPD for a commercial printing device at your service center, but you don't have the printer online at your studio. You can create a PostScript file that your service center can download to its printer using all the attribute choices made from the PPD file.

- **PPD:** You select PostScript Printer Description file from the drop-down list. In Figure 37-10, an AGFA SelectSet Avantra 25 printer is selected in the Printer drop-down list. Like most desktop color printers, the Epson Stylus C62 is a non-PostScript printer and, therefore, does not support a PPD file. Unless your printer is a PostScript printer, you won't have an option for PPD selection. If you're using a PostScript printer, choose the associated PPD for your printer.

- **Copies:** If you're printing more than one copy, change the value in the field box to the desired number of copies. By default, 1 appears in the field box.

- **Collate/Reverse Order:** These items work when you print Illustrator documents as tiled pages. Because you don't have options for creating multiple pages with Illustrator files, the item is grayed out unless you tile pages whereby multiple pages are printed.

- **Pages:** This also only works when you print tiled pages. If you have a large drawing, you can print the document as tiled pages and then make a change in one portion of the document by selecting a page range. You can then print only the pages that have been altered since printing the original file.

- **Media:** If you're using a PostScript printer, the PPD contains all the page sizes supported by the printer and generally supports a custom page size. If the PPD supports custom pages, select Custom from the Size drop-down list and enter values in the Width and Height field boxes. If you use a non-PostScript printer, the Printer driver contains the fixed page sizes and you lose options for creating custom pages.

✦ **Orientation:** Click on one of the four icons for Portrait, Landscape, Portrait Rotated, or Landscape Rotated. Transverse rotates pages 90 degrees and is typically used on roll-fed machines to conserve paper. For example, you can rotate a portrait letter page 11 inches high so the page height is 8.5 inches high. The print is still a portrait view, but the image is rotated 90 degrees so the roll of paper uses 8.5 inches instead of 11 inches.

✦ **Options:** From the Print Layers drop-down list, you can print all visible and printable layers, only visible layers, or all layers — where layers marked for not printing are also printed. You also have controls for scaling. Do Not Scale is the default and prints the document at 100 percent. Fit to Page reduces or enlarges the illustration to the page size you print. The Custom Scale option enables you to type scaling values in the Width and Height field boxes. The chain link between Width and Height is activated by default, ensuring proportional scaling. If you click on the chain link, you can distort the drawing by typing values independently for width and height, without regard to proportional sizing.

Setup

Click the Setup category in the left pane and the Setup options appear, as shown in Figure 37-10.

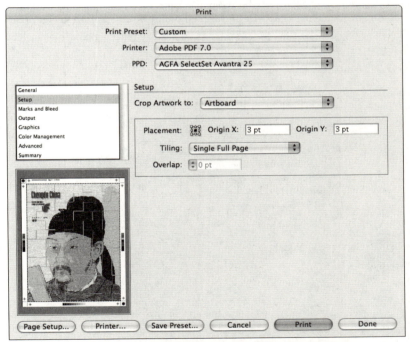

Figure 37-10: Click Setup in the left pane to open the Setup options.

✦ **Crop Artwork to:** Choices from the drop-down list include Artboard for the artwork contained within the page setup; Artboard Bounding Box, which includes all the space defined by the artwork edges, even artwork off the art board space; and Crop Area, which relates to a specific area you define as a crop region. You create a rectangle and, with the rectangle selected, choose Object ➪ Crop Area ➪ Make to define a crop area. When you select Crop Area in the Setup options, the area within the defined crop area prints.

✦ **Placement:** You can move artwork in the thumbnail image around the page area and you can target a section of a large drawing for printing on your selected page size. Click and drag in the thumbnail image on the left and the X,Y origins change values. You can also type new values in the field boxes to change the artwork position on the page and use the small Placement rectangle to select points of origin on the center, four corners, or midpoints on each side.

✦ **Tiling:** This is helpful when you print composite color on small desktop devices where you design a piece for a large display print. If you need to proof the artwork on your printer before sending it off to an imaging center, use the Tiling options for Tile Full Pages or Tile Imageable Areas. The artwork prints on several pages in sections, which you can piece together to see the full print.

Marks and bleeds

Printer's marks are essential when printing files to commercial equipment especially when printing color separations. Items such as color names, registration marks, and crop marks are needed when preparing printing plates and trimming paper. On composite color prints, you may print an image on a larger-size paper to accommodate a bleed and, therefore, need to add crop marks so you know where to trim the paper. Click on Marks and Bleed, and the options for adding printer's marks appear in the Print dialog box, as shown in Figure 37-11.

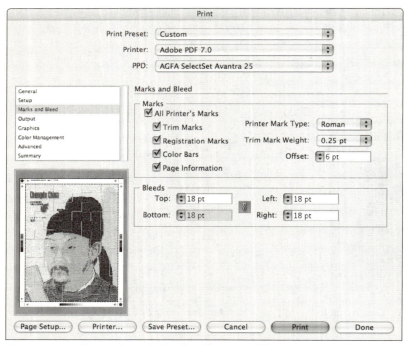

Figure 37-11: The Marks and Bleed options for adding printer's marks

- **All Printer's Marks:** When you check All Printer's Marks, the marks for (1) Trim, (2) Registration, (3) Color Bars, (4) and Page Information appear in the output and are visible in the thumbnail proof (Figure 37-11). If you want some of the available printer's marks to print, individually check those items.

- **Printer Mark Type:** Choices are Roman or Japanese. Select the type of mark from the drop-down list. To see the differences between the two marks, toggle the view by selecting from the two options in the drop-down list.

- **Trim Mark Weight:** You have choices for the stroke weight of the trim marks at 0.125, 0.25, and 0.5 stroke weights. Select the desired weight from the drop-down list.

- **Offset:** Specifying an offset amount offsets the bleed and trim marks from the artwork.

- **Bleeds:** You can specify the bleed amount uniformly on all sides or in individual distances by typing values in the Bleeds field boxes. Click the chain-link icon to toggle between uniform distances and nonuniform distances.

Tip

The chain link icon you see in the Bleeds section in Figure 37-11 appears in many dialog boxes in the CS applications, particularly in Adobe InDesign. When the icon is highlighted, a value in any one of the four text boxes is linked to the remaining text boxes. Therefore, if you type **18 pt** in one box, all other text boxes automatically add the same value. If you click the link icon to deselect it, values are uniquely added to each box individually.

Output

Output settings offer options for printing composite or separations, controlling emulsion, and screening and setting halftone frequencies. For composite color, you probably won't need separations or screening. For some composite color printers, several options are grayed out, as shown in Figure 37-12.

- **Mode:** Three choices appear for Composite, Separations (Host-Based), and In-RIP Separations. Host-based separations separate the file before it is delivered to the PostScript RIP (Raster Image Processor). In-RIP separations deliver the composite file to a PostScript 3 RIP, where the RIP separates the file.

- **Emulsion:** Choices are for Up (Right Reading) or Down (Wrong Reading). Typically, composite prints are printed positive emulsion up, while film separations are printed negative emulsion down. Upon occasion, you may need to print emulsion down for such items as iron transfers, Mylar, LexJet, and so on.

- **Image:** Choices are for Positive or Negative image. If printing a composite image the menu item is grayed out and defaults to Positive.

- **Printer Resolution:** For imagesetting and platesetting equipment at commercial print shops, you find resolution and halftone settings in the Printer Resolution drop-down list. These options are related to the PPD used for PostScript printers but are not accessible for non-PostScript printers such as desktop color printers. For printing composite color, you won't need to access any resolution/screening options.

- **Convert All Spot Colors to Process:** If your file contains spot color and the prints appear best when printing CMYK, click the check box for converting spot color to process color. Note that the option is used for spot color only and does not apply to RGB color. Also note that the conversion takes place at the printing device RIP and does not change the color in the file.

- **Overprint Black:** For files where you have black type against color backgrounds, you may want to globally overprint the black.

- **Document Ink Options:** A list of all used colors appears at the bottom of the Output settings. You can change Frequency, Angle, and/or Dot Shape by clicking in the respective column according to color and editing the value. After clicking, a field box appears where you can type new values.

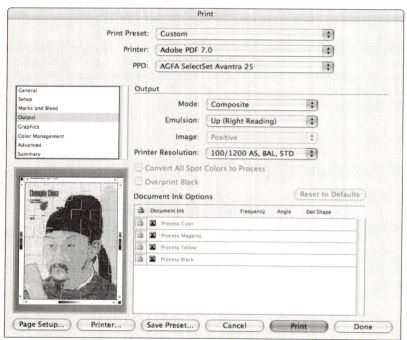

Figure 37-12: Click Output to open options for color and screening.

Graphics

The Graphics settings offer some options that help improve the ability to print complex Illustrator files on PostScript printers. For composite color printing on non-PostScript printers, the options are grayed out. Click on Graphics in the left pane, and the options shown in Figure 37-13 are available.

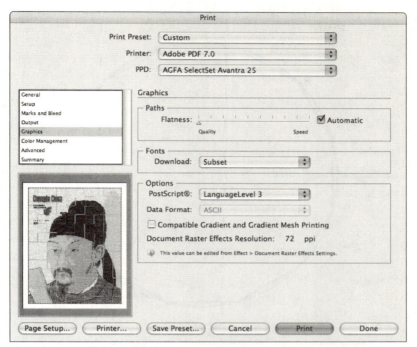

Figure 37-13: Click Graphics to open options for simplifying printing.

✦ **Paths:** Move the slider to the right to increase the flatness. Flatness breaks up complex paths to more simplified paths that make the entire drawing easier to print. If you increase the amount of flatness to the maximum, you can run the risk of distorting shapes where circles appear as polygons. In Figure 37-14, you can see how the flatness amount is measured. The original circle with an exaggerated flatness setting appears as a polygon. The flatness amount is measured by the distance between the original circle and a midpoint on a chord created with the flatness adjustment.

When you flatten transparency in the Print dialog box, transparency is flattened only at the print stream. Your file remains unaffected and the transparency in the document is preserved.

✦ **Fonts:** For PostScript printing, you can download fonts to the printer's RIP at the time a file is printed. Select None to download no fonts. Select Subset to download only font characters within font sets that are contained in the file. Select Complete to download the entire font character set.

✦ **PostScript:** Select a Language level for the PostScript printer used. In some cases, the drop-down list is grayed out and Illustrator makes an automatic selection between PostScript Level 2 and PostScript 3 depending on the printer used.

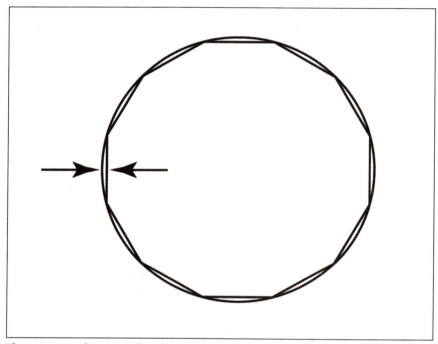

Figure 37-14: If you greatly increase flatness, circular shapes become polygons.

- ✦ **Data Format:** When printing a PostScript file, you have choices for selecting Binary or ASCII encoding. For almost all purposes, use binary encoding and the file sizes become much smaller than selecting ASCII. For other printer selections, Illustrator makes the choice for you for ASCII or Binary and grays out the drop-down list preventing you from changing the option.

- ✦ **Compatible Gradient and Gradient Mesh Printing:** Unless you experience problems printing gradients or gradient meshes on a PostScript RIP, don't select this check box. This option resolves problems when these gradients don't print.

- ✦ **Document Raster Effects Resolution:** This item is informational in the Print dialog box. It reports the current setting for document raster effects resolution. If you print to imaging equipment capable of printing at high resolutions such as 1200, 2400, or 3600 dpi, and so on, you should change the value from the default 72 ppi to a higher resolution such as 300 ppi. To make the settings adjustments you need to close the Print dialog box and choose Effect ➪ Document Raster Effects Settings. The Document Raster Effects Settings dialog box appears, as shown in Figure 37-15. Select the High option in the Resolution section, click OK, and return to the Print dialog box.

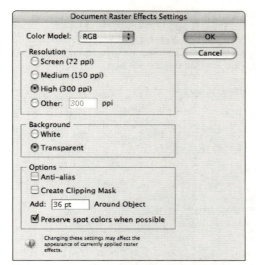

Figure 37-15: Choose Effect ➪ Document Raster Effects Settings to adjust document raster effects resolution.

Color management

For color-managed workflows, you can use ICC profiles and select your profiles from the Printer Profile drop-down list. Select a Rendering Intent from the drop-down list options for Perceptual, Saturation, Relative Colormetric, or Absolute Colormetric. The choices you make in the Color Management settings should be consistent with the color-managed workflow in your environment.

Cross-Reference

For more information on ICC profiles, managing color, and understanding the print space intent, see Chapter 6.

Advanced

Advanced options include the following:

- **Print as Bitmap:** For a quick proof print, you might use this option where all the vector art in your illustration is printed as a bitmapped image. Selecting this option prints the file as a rasterized bitmap but does not rasterize the file.

- **Overprints:** Select from options for overprinting items identified in your drawing for overprints. The options are Simulate, Preserve, or Discard. If you want to simulate an overprint on text comps, select the Simulate option. If you want to preserve overprints you identified in Illustrator, select Simulate from the drop down menu. If you want to discard all overprints, select Discard and all overprints you assigned in Illustrator are ignored.

- **Preset:** Select Low, Medium, or High for resolution related to transparency flattening and bitmap conversion. If you click Custom, the Custom Transparency Flattener Options dialog box opens as shown in Figure 37-16. In this dialog box, select the amount of transparency flattening you want by moving the slider for the Raster/Vector Balance and adjust resolution for line art and text conversion to bitmaps as well as gradients and gradient meshes. If you want to convert text and/or strokes to outlines at the time of printing, select those options. Clip Complex Regions also simplifies printing; if you have difficulty printing a file, enable this check box.

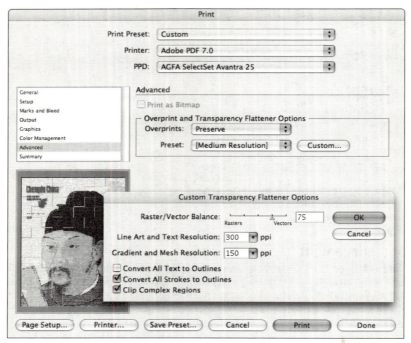

Figure 37-16: Click Advanced to move to the Advanced options. Click Custom to adjust transparency flattening.

Summary

Click on Summary and the summary options appear in the Print dialog box, as shown in Figure 37-17. The Options list displays a list of the settings you made from all the other categories. If your document contains items that won't print correctly or if you made options choices that prevent printing with optimum results, the Warnings box lists potential problems you may encounter. Read the warnings and return to either your document or the other categories and make corrections as needed.

Printing Illustrator files to non-PostScript printers

Depending on your printer and the complexity of your design, you may find rasterizing your Illustrator file in Adobe Photoshop to be the only way you can print the document. Some desktop printers do well with printing directly from Illustrator while some printers may have some difficulties for properly printing a file. In addition, some older PostScript printers may likewise have problems printing your Illustrator artwork. If you experience such problems, open the Illustrator file in Photoshop. The Import PDF dialog box opens regardless of whether you saved the file as an AI file or a PDF file. You make choices for cropping, image resolution, color mode, and bit depth. Under most circumstances you want to be certain to select the Anti-aliased check box. Click OK and the file is rasterized and opens in Photoshop.

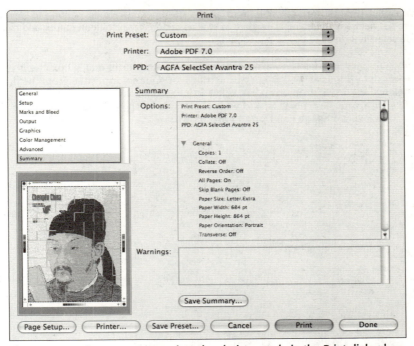

Figure 37-17: Summary summarizes the choices made in the Print dialog box.

As a Photoshop file, you can print directly from Photoshop or save the file in a format that can be downloaded directly to printers supporting direct file downloads. For example, many large-format inkjet printers support downloading TIFF files. In such cases, you would save the file from Photoshop in TIFF format.

Using device print settings

Color printers have unique attributes you select from the device printer driver. On the Mac, when you choose File ⇨ Print and make your choices for the print options you want to use, your next series of options are selected in another Print dialog box. Click on Printer in the Print dialog box, and a warning dialog box opens, as shown in Figure 37-18.

Figure 37-18: A warning to make print options choices in the Print dialog box

Note Device print settings are accessible from all the CS programs. When printing to devices where special paper handling is needed, as well as options for resolution output and color-mode selections, use the device print settings.

Click Continue to pass through the warning dialog box. Another Print dialog box opens offering a range of print options as well as specific settings for your color printer. From the drop-down list below the Presets drop-down list, select Print Settings. In this Print dialog box, you make choices for the media type, inks, and various settings for the print mode. In Figure 37-19, the options for a low-end Epson color printer are shown.

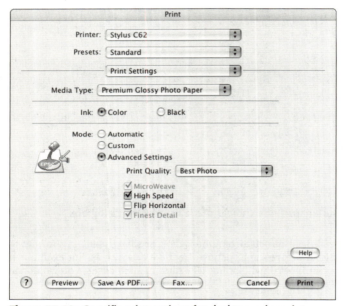

Figure 37-19: Specific print options for desktop color printers

On Windows, you make the same kinds of choices from the Page Setup dialog box. Click Printer in the Page Setup dialog box to open the Print dialog box. Select your printer from the Name drop-down list and click the Properties button. Advanced print settings are made in subsequent dialog boxes and offer options similar to those found on the Mac.

Because the range of printers is so great, discussing all the options for all printers isn't possible. For specific information related to the options choices you need to make for media type, inks, color profiles, and mode settings, consult your printer's user manual.

Setting print options in Photoshop

Printing from Photoshop is usually performed when you print composite color. For prepress and color separations, Photoshop files most often find their way into Illustrator or InDesign documents. You can print to commercial equipment from Photoshop, but most imaging technicians generally import the Photoshop files into a layout program for printing.

If you're printing composite color, you first visit the Page Setup dialog box and set the page size for the output on your printer. Be certain that when you create a custom page size in the Page Setup dialog box you return to the Page Setup dialog box and select the new custom page as was described in Chapter 23.

Note You can open the Page Setup dialog box from within the Print with Preview dialog box.

After selecting the Page Setup, choose File ⇨ Print with Preview. You'll notice that Photoshop has two menu commands for selecting a Print dialog box. If you select Print from the File menu, the print options are much more limited and don't provide you a thumbnail preview for how the document will lay down on the printed page. The Print with Preview command offers many more options with a thumbnail preview, as shown in Figure 37-20.

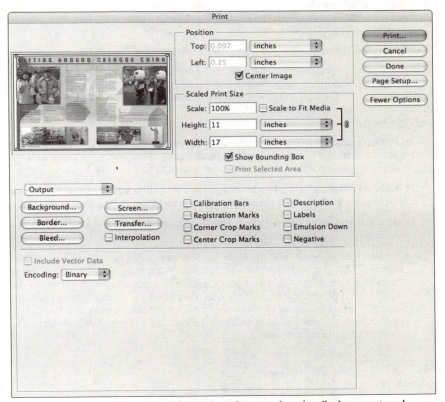

Figure 37-20: Choosing Print with Preview shows a thumbnail of your artwork.

In the Print dialog box that opens when you select Print with Preview, the following options appear:

- **Position:** If you uncheck Center Image, you can move the artwork around the page where a dynamic preview displays in the thumbnail. You can type coordinate values in the field boxes or click and drag the image in the preview box.

- **Scaled Print Size:** Use the field boxes to scale the image up or down. Be aware that, when scaling images up, you need to consider the relationship between scaling size and resolution. As a 150 ppi (pixels per inch) image is scaled up 200 percent (or twice the size) the resolution drops to 75 ppi (or one-half the resolution). You can scale by editing the Scale field box, by checking the box to scale the image to fit the media, by typing values for the height and width, or by dragging handles at one of the four corners of the bounding box.

- **Show Bounding Box:** You may have white space at one or more sides of your image or around the entire image. When you check the box for Show Bounding Box, a rectangle is displayed at the image size including the white space.

- **Print Selected Area:** Prints a selection in the image.

- **Output:** Open the pull-down menu where you see Color Management and select Output for the output options. If you select the Show More Options check box, the dialog box expands to show the options below the Show More Options check box. The first of the more-options settings is the Output. The Output section shown in Figure 37-20 provides options such as:

  - **Background:** By default, the background or area outside the image area is white. You can change the color by clicking on Background and selecting a new color in the Color Picker dialog box that opens after clicking the Background button.

  - **Border:** Border prints a border around the bounding box. You specify point size for the border in the Border dialog box that opens after clicking the Border button.

  - **Bleed:** If you want a bleed, click the Bleed button where a dialog box opens enabling you to specify the bleed amount.

  - **Screen:** Click Screen, and the Halftone Screens dialog box opens, as shown in Figure 37-21. The dialog box offers options for adding custom frequencies and screen angles, including a number of options for dot shapes. If you open the Shape drop-down list, you can choose from fixed dot shapes or the Custom option that enables you to create custom dot shapes by typing in PostScript code in the Custom Spot Function window. To use this feature, you need to be skilled at PostScript programming.

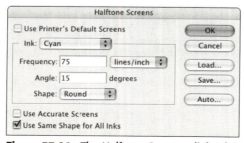

Figure 37-21: The Halftone Screens dialog box

If you edit a Photoshop file and import the image in InDesign, any custom frequencies are only preserved when you save your Photoshop file as EPS. Essentially, you embed screening attributes in the Photoshop image and preserve them whether printing directly or importing in other programs. If the need arises, you can embed one frequency in a Photoshop image that you may use as a background in an InDesign layout. You can print your InDesign file with one frequency — say, 150-line screen — while your Photoshop image has an embedded screen of something like 85 lines. In this example, the image prints at one frequency while the other document elements print at another frequency, all on the same page.

Another use for embedding frequencies is when printing spot color separations for screen printing. You may have a document with six, eight, or more colors that need to be color-separated for a silk screener. If you want to print directly from Photoshop, visit the Halftone Screens dialog box and be certain to set the screen angles apart from each other to avoid printing a moiré.

When you add custom frequencies in the Halftone Screens dialog box, you must save the settings if you want to export the file to InDesign or some other program. Click Done in the Print dialog box, and the settings apply to the document. Save the file as an EPS from Photoshop, and you can import the image in any program supporting the EPS format.

- **Transfer:** Click Transfer to open the Transfer Functions dialog box, shown in Figure 37-22. Transfer functions enable you to remap shades of gray on your final output. If an output device prints lighter or darker than the brightness values you see on your monitor, you can remap the grays to result in printing a lighter or darker image. Messing around with the transfer functions is not something you want to do before sending off a file for final print. As a creative professional, you're more likely to receive a set of transfer functions or guidelines for using them from your printer. Make adjustments according to your printer's recommendations and save the file as EPS.

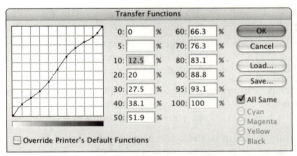

Figure 37-22: The Transfer Functions dialog box remaps the grays in your file.

Note that when you make adjustments to either the screens or transfer functions, choose File ➪ Save As, and choose the Photoshop EPS format, the EPS Options dialog box opens after you click Save. In the EPS Options dialog box, shown in Figure 37-23, you have options for Include Halftone Screen and Include Transfer Function. Check these boxes when you want to preserve any settings made for either screens or transfer functions. When you click OK and save the file, the settings are embedded in the document and normally cannot be overridden when printing from most other programs. Some programs such as Acrobat do enable you to override the settings.

Caution

Unless you want to embed screening or transfer functions, always keep the check boxes unchecked when saving Photoshop files as EPS.

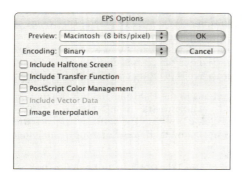

Figure 37-23: The EPS Options dialog box

- **Interpolation:** For use only with PostScript Level 2 and greater RIPs. When you check the box, the output device up sizes the image 200%, then reduces the image to its original size using bicubic interpolation. The result is low-resolution images with a less jagged appearance.

- **Calibration Bars, Registration Marks, Corner Crop Marks, Center Crop Marks, Description, Labels, Emulsion Down, and Negative:** All the check boxes on the right side of the Print dialog box offer options similar to those you find with Adobe Illustrator. Check the boxes according to marks you want printed and how you want emulsion handled.

✦ **Include Vector Data:** If your file contains vector objects or type fonts, check this box and the data is sent as vector data. Any scaling you may apply to your output scales the vector data without any visual degradation.

✦ **Encoding:** For PostScript printers, make a choice for ASCII or Binary. Almost all printers you use today are likely to perform best using binary encoding. Binary encoding prints faster and sends less data across your network than ASCII encoding.

After setting the Output options, return to the Color Management options by clicking Output and select Color Management in the pull-down menu. After setting the page size and scaling, look over the options you have for color management. The Options section in the Print dialog box is critical to the color output on your final print. Ideally you should have a color profile for your printer. Select Let Photoshop Determine Colors from the Color Handling pull-down menu and choose the color profile from the Printer Profile pull-down menu as shown in Figure 37-24.

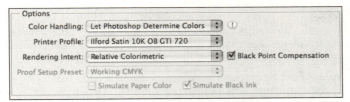

Figure 37-24: Select a color profile from the Printer Profile pull-down menu

Select the Black Point Compensation check box and click Print to print the file.

 Cross-Reference For more information on Black Point Compensation, see Chapter 6.

Setting print options in InDesign

When you print from InDesign, all the print controls are contained in the Print dialog box. Unlike Photoshop the page setup and paper size selections are made in the same dialog box where you set all the other print attributes. Select File ⇨ Print and the default General print options open, as shown in Figure 37-25.

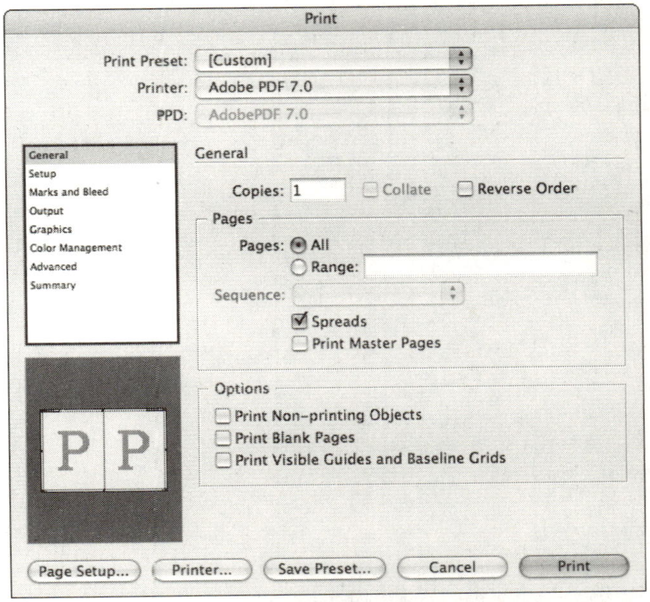

Figure 37-25: All the print options, including page size and page setup, are contained in the Print dialog box.

General print options

Items such as printer selection, page range, collating are the same in InDesign as you find in the other CS applications. As you look over the settings below, realize that what is noted here are those items *not* found in either the Illustrator or Photoshop Print dialog boxes.

- **Spreads:** Printer spreads can be output from InDesign. Spreads takes two facing pages and prints them on the same page. When you set up the page size for printing spreads, be certain to add the width dimension to accommodate both pages. Two letter portrait pages for example would be set up for 17 by 11 (2 times 8.5 inches by 11 inches high).
- **Print Master Pages:** Check this box to print the master pages.
- **Print Non-Printing Objects:** You can identify some objects and layers for nonprinting. When this option is selected, all objects targeted for nonprinting are printed.
- **Print Blank Pages:** Just as the name suggests, any blank pages contained in the file are printed.
- **Print Visible Guides and Baseline Grids:** Something that can help you in the design of a piece is to print the pages with guides and baseline grids. You can see the guide and grid lines on the printed pages and carefully look them over for alignment and formatting.

Setup print options

Click Setup in the left pane to show options for selecting paper size, scaling and tiling as shown in Figure 37-26.

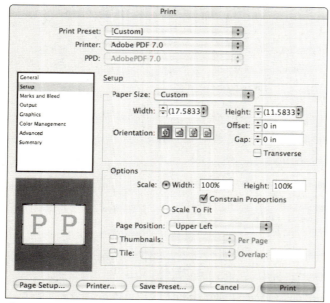

Figure 37-26: Click Setup to open options settings for selecting paper size and scaling choices.

- **Setup:** The Setup options include choices for selecting paper sizes. In InDesign you have choices for choosing fixed paper sizes from the Paper Size pull-down menu or by adding a Custom paper size and typing values in the Width and Height field boxes. The fixed sizes are derived from the PPD selected in the PPD pull-down menu. Custom sizes can be added in InDesign without going to a Page Setup dialog box and defining a custom page size. As you tab out of the Width and Height fields the thumbnail preview shows you how the page sizes appear on selected or custom page sizes.

- **Offset:** For roll fed imaging equipment, the offset offsets the printed image from the paper edge.

- **Gap:** Also on roll fed machines, the gap is the distance between printed pages.

- **Orientation and Transverse:** Same options are available in InDesign as you find in Illustrator.

- **Options:** Options settings include scaling output, page position in one of four locations, printing thumbnail images of a layout, tiling large pages that can't fit on a single paper size, and setting the overlap gap for tiled pages.

Marks and Bleeds

Marks and bleeds are similar to options you find in Illustrator and Photoshop. The items in the Marks area of the Marks and Bleed section of the Print dialog box shown in Figure 37-27 are self-descriptive. InDesign has an additional item not found in either Illustrator or Photoshop in the Bleed and Slug area of the dialog box.

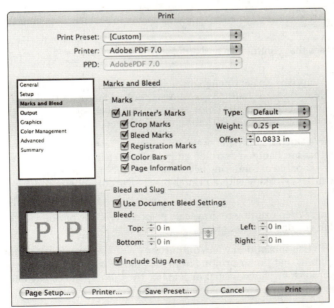

Figure 37-27: Options for setting marks, bleeds, and slugs

Output

Output options include specific settings for printing composites or separations. Color control and ink management are included in the options shown in Figure 37-28.

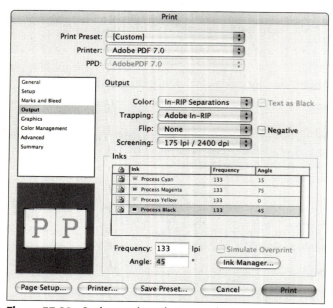

Figure 37-28: Option settings that control inks and emulsion

- **Color:** Choices are Composite Leave Unchanged, Composite Gray, Composite RGB, Composite CMYK, Separations, or In-RIP Separations. Choices made for the kind of composite print you want can affect the color, so be certain to choose the setting appropriate for your desired output. The Color choices defined include the following:
  - **Composite Leave Unchanged:** This option is intended for use where you print to color printers that are Pantone-certified and can simulate spot-color inks. Very few printers are capable of rendering accurate spot colors, so this option is one you won't use unless working with a printer that can accurately reproduce spot colors.
  - **Composite Gray:** When printing to grayscale printers, use this option. All colors are printed with varying levels of gray.
  - **Composite RGB:** Use this option when outputting for screen or when printing to inkjet color printers that prefer printing from RGB mode. Most inkjets typically use CMYK color inks, but large-format inkjets like the Colorspan DisplayMakers prefer printing RGB files.

- **Composite CMYK:** For most composite color prints, you're likely to use this option. When your inkjet printer prefers printing CMYK color, select this option from the drop-down list.

- **Separations:** Use separations when printing to RIPs using PostScript Level 2 and below or when printing to PostScript RIPs not supporting In-RIP separations. Also, if you aren't certain of the RIP PostScript level or whether In-RIP separations are supported and you're preparing PostScript files for your service center, use Separations.

- **In-RIP Separations:** A composite image is sent to the printer's RIP where the RIP separates the file. Many PostScript 3 RIPs support In-RIP separations, but not all PostScript 3 RIPs. If preparing files for imaging centers, be certain to inquire about their capabilities for printing before sending PostScript files.

✦ **Text as Black:** Check this box to print text as pure black color as opposed to printing a mix of RGB or CMYK color to produce black.

✦ **Trapping:** The drop-down list commands are made available only when Separations or In-RIP Separations are selected. Options include one of three choices. You can turn trapping off, use InDesign built-in trapping, or use In-RIP trapping. InDesign has a sophisticated built-in trapping technology, and the Adobe In-RIP Trapping engine is even more powerful. If you don't have more-powerful dedicated trapping software, either option provides you with some impressive results. Note that In-RIP Trapping is available only on PostScript 3 RIPs that support In-RIP Trapping.

✦ **Flip:** Flipping a page is available for separations as well as composite printing. If you print to Mylar, LexJet, and other substrates necessitating printing documents flipped, InDesign CS offers new options over previous versions of the program and can accommodate separation and composite printing when page flipping is needed. For printing to imagesetters and platesetters, reading and emulsion are typically handled at the writing engine or the RIP. Therefore, you most often print files emulsion up and without flipping a page.

✦ **Screening:** Derived from the selected PPD, you make fixed halftone screen selections from the drop-down list. To add a custom frequency not available from the drop-down list, you can manually adjust the inks for frequency and angle below the Inks table.

✦ **Frequency:** You can adjust the halftone frequency manually by selecting inks in the Inks table and typing values in the Frequency field box.

✦ **Angle:** The default angles for process color includes Cyan at 15°, Magenta at 75°, Yellow at 0° and Black at 45°. Spot colors all default to 45° — the same angle used for black. If you introduce spot colors, be certain that the color angles are set apart from the other color angles. For example, on a two-color job containing Black and a spot color, change the spot color to either the Cyan or Magenta angle of 15° or 75°. If you have process color and a spot color, set the spot color angle 22° apart from the other process colors — something like 22° or 37°.

Graphics

The Graphics pane includes options for how image files are printed, font handling, and PostScript level. These options are generally used for proofing when printing for high-end prepress and commercial printing. The options shown in Figure 37-29 include:

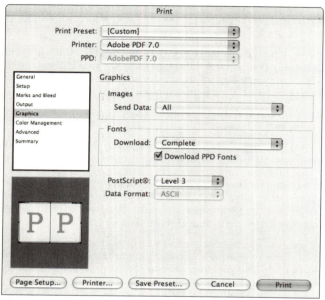

Figure 37-29: The Graphics pane has options for image and font handling as well as PostScript level.

- **Images:** From the drop-down list you have choices for what data is sent to your printer:
  - **All**: Sends all the image data to the printer and is the choice you want to use for composite color printing.
  - **Optimized Subsampling:** Sends enough data to the printer for an optimized print but downsamples images if the resolution is more than needed to output a satisfactory print.
  - **Proxy:** Sends a 72 ppi image to the printer, resulting in a faster print for proofing purposes.
  - **None:** Sends no image data for a quick print where you can examine type and layout without printing the images.
- **Fonts:** From the drop-down list you have three choices:
  - **None:** Downloads no fonts. Use this option only when you know that all the fonts in your document reside in your printer's memory or on a hard drive attached to your printer.
  - **Complete:** Downloads all fonts to your printer's memory.
  - **Subset:** Only sends the characters in a font to your printer's memory.

✦ **Download PPD Fonts:** Font lists contained in your printer's PPD are downloaded to your printer's memory. The PPD fonts are generally the fonts contained in your printer's memory. Most laser printers have the fonts Courier, Helvetica, Times, and Symbol burned into the ROM chips in the printer. The PPD for the printers list these fonts where the printer retrieves them when files containing the fonts are printed.

✦ **PostScript:** Choices are PostScript Level 2 or PostScript 3. Choose the PostScript level according to your printer if printing to a PostScript printer. If printing composite color to non-PostScript printers, don't worry about changing the default. PostScript-level choices won't have an effect on printing to non-PostScript devices.

✦ **Data Format:** Generally, the choice is made for you. By default, Binary is selected and you'll see ASCII grayed out.

Color management

Click on the Color Management item in the left pane and the Color Management options open, as shown in Figure 37-30.

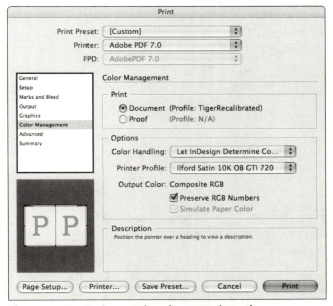

Figure 37-30: Options settings for managing color

✦ **Print:** Choose either Document, which uses the document's color space, or Proof, which uses the color space provided by the printer.

✦ **Options:** From the Color Handling drop-down menu, choose from either your PostScript printer or let InDesign determine the color handling. If using a color profile calibrated for your printer, choose Let InDesign Determine Colors. From the Printer Profile drop-down list, select a color space that InDesign uses to map the color from the document's color space to the printer's color space. If you select PostScript Color Management, you use a profile based on the CRD (color rendering dictionary) available for PostScript 3 devices that have built-in color management. Choosing the option for InDesign to handle color lets you select a profile you calibrated for your printer.

✦ **Output Color:** Check Preserve RGB Numbers to preserve the color profile in the file. If the box remains unchecked, the printer's color profile is used.

✦ **Simulate Paper Color:** This option is available if you print a Proof. Select the check box and the colors appear as when printed on specific papers, such as printing to newsprint or uncoated stock.

Advanced

Click Advanced in the left page to open options for the Advanced settings, as shown in Figure 37-31. Options such as OPI (Open Prepress Interface) management and transparency flattening are contained in this pane.

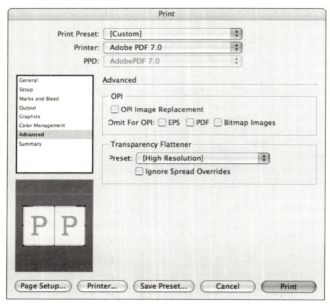

Figure 37-31: Options settings for OPI management and transparency flattening

✦ **OPI Image Replacement:** This option and the check boxes for EPS, PDF, and bitmap images relate to replacing FPO (for-position-only) low-resolution images with high-resolution images during lay out. When computers were less powerful and had less memory, OPI was used when service centers archived high-resolution images while designers used low-resolution images to create layouts. Today, with powerful computers that have plentiful RAM and hard-drive space, most people use high-resolution images for layout. For composite color printing, you're likely to never use the OPI settings.

✦ **Transparency Flattener:** On most PostScript RIPs, you need to flatten transparency to successfully print your document. Any use of the Transparency palette, applying drop shadows to objects in InDesign, applying a feather, using blending modes, or using transparency in imported images requires you to flatten the transparency. From the presets use:

• Low Resolution for quick proof prints on desktop printers

• Medium Resolution for desktop proofs on desktop color printers and copy machines, on-demand printers, and so on

- High Resolution for all files printed as separations and on high-end commercial PostScript devices

✦ **Ignore Spread Overrides:** You can flatten transparency on spreads by viewing a spread in the Document window and choosing Spread Flattening on the Pages menu. You can override spread-specific flattener settings by selecting this check box at the time of printing or export.

Summary

As in other CS applications, a summary dialog box lists all the settings made through the panes in the Print dialog box. If you want to save the summary to a text file that you can send to a service center, or that you can retain for future use, click Save Summary in the Summary pane to save a file defining all the print attributes select for a given print job.

Setting print options in Acrobat

Acrobat 7 builds on the print production tools introduced in Acrobat 6. There are more tools and commands to proof color and print to commercial printing devices. Acrobat contains all the print controls needed for high-end prepress as well as all the settings you need for printing composite color. Additionally, you can use Acrobat to print files originating in the other CS applications after converting documents to PDF. Using Acrobat as your printing tool simplifies the printing process because you need to learn only those print options from a single set of dialog boxes.

Cross-Reference For a description of all the print new tools added to Acrobat 7, see Chapter 38.

The first place to start when printing files from Acrobat is to visit the Page Setup dialog box. After selecting the proper page size and orientation or defining a custom page size, choose File ⇨ Print to open the print dialog box shown in Figure 37-32.

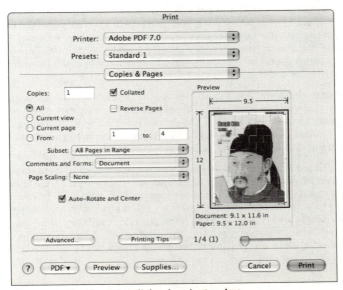

Figure 37-32: The Print dialog box in Acrobat

There are two sets of print dialog boxes in Acrobat. The default opening view is the Print dialog box. The second print dialog box is the Advanced Print Setup dialog box that opens after you click on the Advanced button; this is the place where options typically used for commercial printing are found. The Print dialog box includes the following options:

- **Copies/Collated:** Use the field box to enter the number of copies you want to print. The Collated check box collates pages when printing multiple copies.
- **All:** Prints all pages in the document.
- **Current View:** This option enables you to print a portion of a page. Zoom in to the document page and select Current View to print the page as you see it displayed on your monitor.
- **Current Page:** Navigate to the page you want to print and select Current Page. The result is a print of the page currently viewed in the Document pane.
- **Subset:** Subset contains several options in the drop-down list. Choose to print all pages in a range, odd pages only, or even pages only. Click on the Reverse Pages check box to print pages in back-to-front order.
- **Comments and Forms:** From the drop-down list, you have choices for printing the document as you might print any file. Acrobat offers additional options not available in other CS applications, such as comment notes, stamps, and form fields. The Document and Comments option prints the document and the contents of the comment notes. When you select the item, the comments on the first page, if they exist, display in the Preview area. The Form Fields Only option prints only the form fields from an Acrobat form.
- **Page Scaling:** Page Scaling offers options for None, Fit to Paper, Shrink Large Pages, Tile Large Pages, and Tile All Pages. Select the option you want from the drop-down list choices.
- **Auto-Rotate and Center:** When enabled, pages are auto-rotated and centered.
- **Preview:** A document preview shows the current page as a thumbnail in the preview box. By default, the opening page previews. If you navigate to another page, the respective page displays in the preview box. Because Acrobat accommodates pages of different sizes in the same document, you can easily check a page to see if it prints properly on the current page setup. If you select the Reverse Pages check box, the Preview shows the pages in reverse order.

For composite color printing where you don't need bleeds and printer's marks, the options in the Print dialog box are all you need to send your PDF documents to your printer. When high-end commercial prepress and printing are needed, the Advanced Print Setup dialog box is where you need to make options choices. Click the Advanced button in the Print dialog box, and the Advanced Print Setup dialog box opens, shown in Figure 37-33.

On the left side of the Advanced Print Setup dialog box, you make choices for options associated with output, marks and bleeds, transparency flattening, and PostScript. The first item available for selection is Print As Image. For composite color printing when you have difficulty printing a document to your desktop printer, use this option as a last resort. When you check the box, all vector objects and type convert to bitmaps. The results are often less than optimal but can mean the difference between printing the page or not. If you experience PostScript errors when printing a file, check the Print as Image check box.

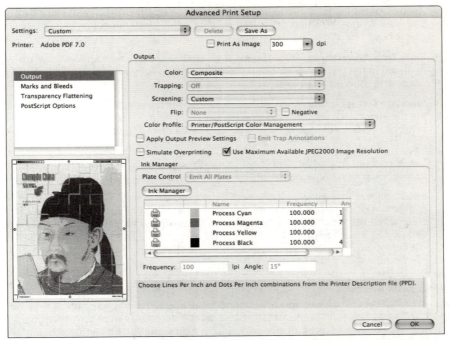

Figure 37-33: The Advanced Print Setup dialog box has commercial printing options.

The drop-down menu adjacent to the Print As Image check box provides a list of preset values for output resolution. If you want to supply a custom resolution, type a value in the text box. You can greatly improve the appearance of files printed with the Print As Image option by raising the resolution to 300 dpi or more.

Output

Output options offer choices for handling color and screening. In the Output pane, you find settings for the following:

- ✦ **Color:** The same options for composite and separations are available in Acrobat as you find in InDesign and Illustrator. See Setting print options in Illustrator and Setting print options in InDesign earlier in this chapter.

- ✦ **Trapping:** This option is available when the Color pull-down menu choice is set to In-RIP Separations. You can turn trapping off or use Adobe In-RIP trapping.

- ✦ **Screening:** Fixed values are derived from the PPD for PostScript printers. You select custom frequencies and screen angles in the Ink Manager at the bottom of the Output pane.

- ✦ **Flip/Negative.** Flip is available only when printing color separations. If you need Emulsion down on a Composite print, you need to import the PDF in InDesign and flip the page. Check the box for Negative if you want to print the file as a negative.

- **Apply Output Preview Settings:** This setting is available for composite printing only. If you want to apply settings made in the Proof Setup for a simulated print, enable the check box.

- **Emit Trap Annotations:** Only applies to documents where trap annotations are included in the file. The trap annotations are sent to RIPs when In-Rip separations are used on PostScript 3 devices.

- **Simulate Overprinting:** This option, also available for composite, prints a proof showing the effects of overprints assigned in the document. This feature emulates the overprinting previews of high-end color proofers that display overprints in composite proofs.

- **Use Maximum Available JPEG2000 Image Resolution:** When enabled, the maximum usable resolution contained in JPEG2000 images is used.

- **Ink Manager:** If your file contains spot colors or RGB colors, you can convert spot or RGB to CMYK color by clicking on the check box. The spot color converts to CMYK color when the X in the check box turns to a fill with CMYK color. To edit the frequency and angle for each plate, double-click on a color and the Edit Frequency and Angle dialog box opens. Supply the desired frequency and angle for each color by successively opening the dialog box for each color.

Marks and bleeds

Click on the Marks and Bleeds option in the left pane and the marks and bleeds options appear, shown in Figure 37-34. Acrobat behaves a little differently from the other CS applications because you don't have a document setup to define page size as in the other applications. You need to be certain that the Page Setup page size is large enough to accommodate printer's marks. However, you need to define the bleeds in the document you convert to PDF. If bleeds were not included (say, from an InDesign file), the PDF won't set a bleed outside the printer's marks. Be certain you include bleed amounts in your Illustrator and InDesign files before exporting to PDF.

Check All Marks or individually click on the check boxes below the Marks Style drop-down list. From the drop-down list options, you can choose Western Style or Eastern Style. Use Eastern Style for printing files in Far Eastern countries.

The Emit Printer Marks check box is active when printer marks were exported when the document was converted to PDF. Checking this box applies the bleed settings contained in the exported document.

Transparency flattening

Click on Transparency Flattening in the left pane to apply settings. Acrobat has a Transparency Flattener Preview where you can examine the results of applying transparency before you open the Print dialog box. The amount of flattening you determined from the Flattener Preview dialog box can be applied here. As you move the slider toward Rasters, you'll notice the preview doesn't change.

 When using the transparency flattening tools in Acrobat 7 you can apply the settings to the PDF file without printing the document.

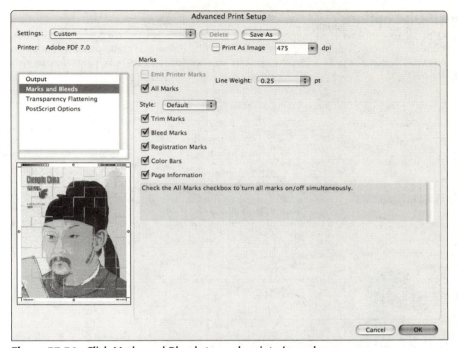

Figure 37-34: Click Marks and Bleeds to apply printer's marks.

In earlier versions of Acrobat, transparency flattening occurred only at the time a file was printed. In Acrobat 7 you can choose to flatten transparency in the Flattener Preview dialog box you access from the Print Production toolbar.

 Cross-Reference For more information on using the Flattener Preview, see Chapter 38.

Rasterizing Resolutions are similar to the options found in InDesign. For high-end printing, use 1200 ppi (pixels per inch) when flattening the transparency.

The Options choices offer you settings for converting type and strokes to outlines. As a last resort for printing stubborn fonts that you know are embedded in the PDF document, you can convert the type to outlines. As a general rule, try to avoid converting type to outlines, because the file takes longer to RIP and print than when downloading fonts to the RIP. Clicking the check box for Clip Complex Regions can reduce the amount of memory required to print a file. This can assist you in printing difficult files to PostScript devices.

PostScript options

The PostScript Options section includes a variety of settings used for preserving embedded halftone frequencies, transferring functions, handling color, and some other miscellaneous settings. Click PostScript to open the options choices for the PostScript settings, as shown in Figure 37-35.

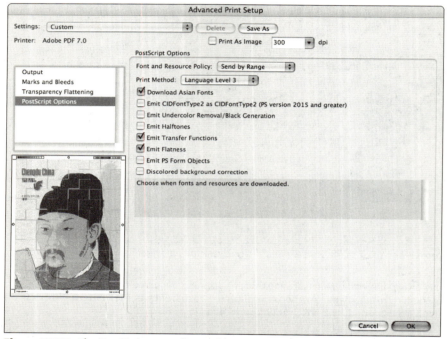

Figure 37-35: The PostScript pane has various settings for PostScript printing.

- **Font and Resource Policy:** Three options are available from the drop-down list:
  - **Send at Start:** Sends all fonts to the printer as the print job starts.
  - **Send by Range:** Sends fonts encountered on the pages as new pages print and where the fonts stay in memory until the job finishes printing.
  - **Send for Each Page:** Conserves memory where the fonts are flushed after each page prints. This option takes more time to print but can overcome problems when you experience difficulty in printing a job.
- **Print Method:** Choose from PostScript Level 2 or PostScript 3 depending on the level of PostScript used by the RIP.
- **Download Asian Fonts:** Check the box if Asian characters are in the document and not available at the RIP.

- **Emit CIDFontType2 as CDIFontType2 (PS version 2015 and greater):** Sends older CID Type 2 fonts as a newer PostScript version.

- **Emit Undercolor Removal/Black Generation:** GCR/UCR removal is only necessary if the original file contain embedded settings. Deselect the box to remove any embedded settings that you might have inadvertently added and saved in Photoshop. If you want to apply any embedded settings, checking the box to emit the settings applies them as they were embedded in the authoring program.

- **Emit Halftones:** If the PostScript file contained embedded halftones, you can preserve them here, and the frequency assigned in the Output options are used to print the file. Check the box to apply the frequency embedded in a file. You preserve halftones when you want an embedded halftone frequency in an image to print at a different frequency than the rest of the job.

- **Emit Transfer Functions:** Deselect the box to eliminate any transfer functions that might have been embedded in Photoshop images. If you know you want images to print with embedded transfer functions you may have applied according to instructions provided from a publication house, check the box to preserve the transfer functions.

- **Emit Flatness:** Applies flatness settings saved with EPS files.

- **Emit PS Form Objects:** PostScript XObjects store common information in a document — things like backgrounds, headers, and footers. When PostScript XObjects are used, the printing is faster, but it requires more memory. To speed up the printing, check the box to emit PostScript XObjects.

- **Discolored Background Correction:** Enable this option only when printing composite proofs where backgrounds print darker or with a discolored appearance like a yellow tint.

Printing PDF files to PostScript devices

For composite printing to desktop PostScript devices, you can successfully print using the Print and Advanced Print Setup dialog boxes. However, for commercial printing to imagesetters, platesetters, and direct-to-press equipment, printing direct from Acrobat can produce some unexpected results. A better option is to generate a PostScript file and download the PostScript file to your printer. When printing directly to high-end devices, you can experience problems with color handling, black type printing with tints, and PostScript errors that prevent the job from being printed.

For commercial output, choose File ➪ Save As and select PostScript as the output format. Click the Settings button where options choices identical to the Advanced Print Setup dialog box are contained. Make your options choices and save the file as PostScript. The resultant PostScript file is then downloaded to your printer. This method generally produces more-reliable output.

Cross-Reference For more information on saving files as PostScript for printing purposes, see Chapter 38.

Summary

✦ Some CS applications require you to use the Page Setup dialog box before opening the Print dialog box.

✦ Print options for screening, color handling, separations, printer's marks, and so on are found in advanced print options dialog boxes generally available through the Print dialog box.

✦ Desktop color printers often have special print options where choices for paper types and color handling are accessed via the printer's print driver.

✦ InDesign and Acrobat are the most commonly used applications for commercial printing.

✦ ✦ ✦

Commercial Printing

As a production artist, you participate in workflows with production workers and technicians at prepress houses and print shops. Your role extends beyond the creative work you do to include proper file preparation, proofing your work, checking files for potential problems, and delivering a product that has an excellent chance for successful output. The Creative Suite applications offer you many tools for diagnosing documents and reporting potential imaging problems to you. In addition, some CS applications offer you options for creating file formats optimized for high-end prepress and printing.

This chapter begins with soft-proofing color and separations on your monitor before you send files to an imaging center, and continues with the file checking process known as *preflighting*. The last part of the chapter covers packaging jobs for imaging centers. Consider the contents of this chapter as the most important aspects of your production workflow when you create documents designed for commercial printing.

Soft-Proofing Documents in the CS Programs

Soft-proofing a document is the process of viewing the file on your monitor and checking various conditions for potential printing problems. You can check issues such as overprints, proper color assignment, transparency flattening, and font problems using some of the CS applications. Your two best sources for soft-proofing documents are InDesign and Acrobat. Although InDesign has some impressive tools for soft-proofing documents, Acrobat is a more likely tool for examining files because it offers many more soft-proofing options and is a better choice for packaging documents.

Cross-Reference

For more information on packaging documents, see the section "Packaging Documents for Commercial Printing" at the end of this chapter.

In This Chapter

Proofing documents on your monitor

Using Acrobat Professional for proofing and preparing files for commercial printing

Checking jobs for potential imaging problems in the CS programs

Preparing files for prepress and printing

Printing on commercial devices

Soft-proofing files in InDesign

In InDesign, you can check files for transparency flattening and color separations. Open the Window menu and you see menu commands for Transparency Flattener and Separation Preview. Select one of the menu commands and the respective palette opens as a floating palette.

Transparency flattening

As described in Chapter 37, transparency flattener previews show you the results of applying flattening amounts. To open the Transparency Flattener, choose Window ⇨ Output Preview ⇨ Flattener. The Flattener Preview palette opens, shown in Figure 38-1.

Figure 38-1: The Flattener Preview palette

Transparency flattening occurs in InDesign and Illustrator at the time the file is printed and does not affect the document's transparency. In Acrobat, you can choose to flatten transparency at the time you print a file, which does not affect the transparency in the document, or by flattening the transparency without printing a file, which changes the document's transparency.

The Flattener Preview palette offers you various options for previewing the results of flattening transparency. You navigate to pages and see results on the page in the Document window as you apply settings and refresh the screen to update different settings options. The following options are available in the palette:

- **Rasterize Complex Regions:** From the drop-down list, the first choice is this option. From the Flattener Preview palette menu, which opens when you click the right-pointing arrow, you can show Transparency Flattener Presets in a dialog box. The dialog box contains buttons for creating new presets or editing presets you load or create. When you create or edit a preset, the Transparency Flattener Preset Options dialog box opens; here, you control the amount of transparency by moving the Raster/Vector Balance slider. The slider position in the Transparency Flattener Preset Options dialog box determines the amount of rasterizing complex regions.

- **Transparent Objects:** When you select this option from the drop-down list, transparent objects are highlighted on the page, including alpha channels in Photoshop images, objects with blending modes, and objects with opacity marks such as drop shadows applied in InDesign.

- **All Affected Objects:** Next in the drop-down list is this setting, which highlights overlapping objects where at least one of the objects contains transparency. All the highlighted objects are flattened according to the amount specified in the Transparency Flattener Preset Options dialog box.

- **Affected Graphics:** This setting highlights placed objects where transparency effects are involved.
- **Outline Strokes:** Following along in the drop-down list, this option highlights all strokes that have been marked for outlines.
- **Outline Text:** Highlights all text converted to outlines when involved with transparency.
- **Raster-Fill Text and Strokes:** You can rasterize object fills and strokes during transparency flattening. This option previews the results of rasterizing.
- **All Rasterized Regions:** Objects and intersections throughout the document are highlighted to show the results of rasterization. Photoshop files are also previewed for the results of rasterization, as are all effects that involve transparency, such as drop shadows and feathering.
- **Auto Refresh Highlight:** When you select this check box, the highlighted preview refreshes as you toggle menu commands and adjust settings.
- **Refresh:** If you want to manually refresh the preview, uncheck the Auto Refresh Highlight check box and click the Refresh button to update the preview.
- **Preset:** InDesign is installed with three presets for transparency adjustments. You can add custom presets and the new presets are added to the drop-down list. Select from the menu the preset you want to use.
- **Ignore Spread Overrides:** For individual spreads where you want to ignore spread-specific flattener presets, select the check box.
- **Apply Settings to Print:** When the preview results look appropriate for your output, click the Apply Settings to Print button to apply the transparency flattening settings to your document. When you open the Print dialog box, the results of the transparency flattening appear.

The Transparency Flattener Presets dialog box provides options for managing presets. You open the dialog box shown in Figure 38-2 by selecting Transparency Flattener Presets from the fly-out menu in the Flattener Preview palette. Options for managing presets include the following:

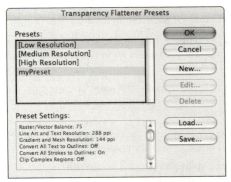

Figure 38-2: The Transparency Flattener Presets dialog box manages presets.

- **New:** Opens the Transparency Flattener Preset Options dialog box where you assign attributes for new presets.

- **Edit:** You can return to a given preset and edit it in the Transparency Flattener Presets dialog box (Figure 38-3). Select the preset to edit, then click Edit. Note that you cannot edit or delete the default presets installed with InDesign.

- **Delete:** Click a preset you want to remove and click Delete.

- **Load:** You can save a preset as a file and load it back into the Transparency Flattener Presets dialog box. In workflow environments, you can save presets and share them with colleagues so all designers use the same transparency flattening for all files for a given campaign.

- **Save:** To load a preset, you must first have a file resident on your hard drive or network server (or external media). Click Save to open the Save Transparency Flattener Presets dialog box where you can type a name for the preset and save to a folder on your hard drive.

You can define options for a transparency flattener preset in the Transparency Flattener Preset Options dialog box. When you click either the New button or the Edit button, the dialog box shown in Figure 38-3 opens. Make your adjustments in this dialog box and the collective settings are captured to the preset you create or edit.

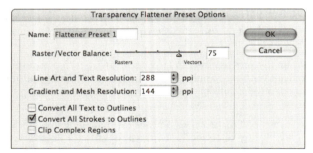

Figure 38-3: The Transparency Flattener Preset Options dialog box

The options choices you have for defining attributes for a preset include the following:

- **Name:** Type a name in the field box and the name is reflected in the Transparency Flattener Presets dialog box. Try to use descriptive names so you can easily recall a particular preset used for a given job.

- **Raster/Vector Balance:** Move the slider to apply varying amounts of flattening. As you move the slider and target a particular amount, you can return to the Flattener Preview palette and preview the transparency settings.

- **Line Art and Text Resolution:** You adjust resolution for rasterizing line art and text in the field box or by clicking on the up and down arrows to change the value.

- **Gradient and Mesh Resolution:** A separate field box is used for rasterizing gradients and meshes.

✦ **Convert All Text to Outlines:** When checking the box, you can preview the results in the Flatten Transparency dialog box by selecting Outline Text from the drop-down list.

✦ **Convert All Strokes to Outlines:** The same applies to this option as the Convert All Text to Outlines. Use the Raster-Fill and Strokes Menu command in the Flattener Preview palette to preview the flattening.

✦ **Clip Complex Regions:** Once again, the same applies to this option. Use the Flattener Transparency dialog box and choose Rasterize Complex Regions to preview the results.

Previewing separations

A nice addition to InDesign CS2 is being able to preview separations and color modes before you send a file off to the printer. If you inadvertently specify spot colors where you intend to print a process color job, the Separations Preview palette immediately shows you all process and spot color in a document to help you avoid costly errors. To open the Separations Preview palette (Figure 38-4), choose Window ➪ Output ➪ Separations Preview.

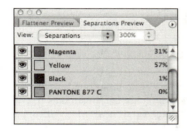

Figure 38-4: The Separations Preview palette displays all document colors.

While the Separation Preview palette is open, you can move the cursor around the document page, and ink percentages are reported in the palette for the cursor position. You can toggle each color on and off by clicking on the eye icon. Therefore, single inks or combinations of inks can be displayed in the palette and reflected in the Document window.

From the View drop-down list, you have a menu command to display ink limits. Select the menu command and the Separation Preview palette changes to the view shown in Figure 38-5. You can alter the ink coverage warning by selecting from fixed values in the drop-down list or typing values in the field box. Ink limit coverage should be assigned according to advice obtained from your printer. The ink limit is designed to keep ink limits within the capabilities of a press.

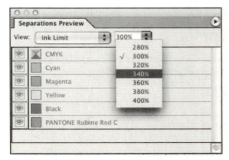

Figure 38-5: To alter ink coverage, select Ink Limit and a fixed ink-limit value.

From the palette menu, you can access the Ink Manager where you assign individual ink densities and apply spot color to process conversions. Open the palette menu by clicking the right-pointing arrow and selecting Ink Manager. The Ink Manager dialog box opens, shown in Figure 38-6.

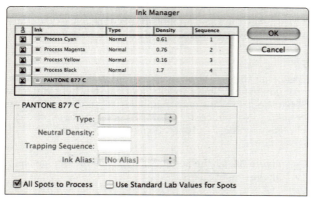

Figure 38-6: The Ink Manager dialog box

You make settings changes in this dialog box according to recommendations from your commercial printer. You can define the neutral densities, which are established as the default values upon InDesign's installation, according to the language version you use during your installation. As you use printers from other parts of the world, you might find changes in standards for neutral densities. Neutral densities are important because the trapping engine uses the values to determine precise placement of traps. You don't want to mess around with the values, until you receive precise guidelines for adjustments from your printer.

The check box for All Spots to Process is the item in this dialog box you're likely to use often. If you specify spot-color inks during a design stage, you can convert the output of spot colors to process values with this option.

In the Separations Preview palette menu, you have a menu option for displaying spot colors as black. Select Show Single Plates in Black and, when previewing the spot colors in the file without the CMYK colors previewed, each spot color displays in the Document window as black. Note that you need to turn off all the process colors to see the spot colors appear as black. When you deselect the menu command, all spot colors display in their color values when you view plates and all plates.

Soft-proofing files in Illustrator

Many of the transparency flattening preview options found in Illustrator are the same as the ones in InDesign. Open the Window menu and select Flattener Preview to open the Flattener Preview dialog box, shown in Figure 38-7.

Figure 38-7: The Flattener Preview palette has options similar to InDesign.

Transparency flattening

Those options choices that differ between Illustrator and InDesign include:

- **Affected linked EPS Files:** The preview shows all EPS files linked to the current document as they related to affected transparency.
- **Expanded Patterns:** The highlights show all patterns that will expand because they involve transparency.

From the Overprints drop-down list, you have additional options that you don't find in InDesign. The default choice is to preserve all overprints. You have other options to eliminate all overprints or to simulate overprints:

- **Discard:** Obviously discards all overprints. You might use this option when you send files to print shops that perform all the trapping on your files.
- **Simulate:** Maintains the appearance of overprinting in composite proofs. Use this when you print to composite color printers that can display the overprints.

The Presets drop-down list offers you choices for different presets installed as defaults in Illustrator and a list of all presets you save by selecting Save Transparency Flattener Preset from the palette menu. Illustrator handles saving presets differently than InDesign. When you select the menu command, the preset is automatically saved without prompting you in a Save dialog box. You can return to the Presets drop-down list, and the saved preset is listed.

Editing a preset works a bit differently in Illustrator than it does in InDesign. To change options on a preset you saved, select the preset in the Presets drop-down list. Make your new options choices, open the palette menu, and select Redefine Preset. The new attributes are assigned to the saved preset.

Managing presets

If you need to delete a preset, you won't find an option in the Flattener Preview dialog box. Instead, you must open the Edit menu and select Transparency Flattener Presets. The transparency Flattener Presets dialog box opens. Refer back to Figure 38-2 to see the dialog box with the exact same options choices as you have in InDesign. Notice that you can edit a preset in this dialog box as well as when redefining a preset as mentioned earlier, in the "Preview transparency flattening" section.

Proofing and printing in Acrobat Professional

Acrobat PDF is the best form of document format for submitting files to print shops. The ability to embed graphic images and type fonts is one of the advantages you have with PDF files. In addition to being a desirable format for delivering documents for press, Acrobat Professional also offers an abundance of soft-proofing and preflighting tools.

There are two sources for accessing features related to soft-proofing and preparing files for print in Acrobat Professional. From the Advanced menu you have commands to view color and overprinting and a command to open a rich feature set for preflighting (checking) files to be certain that they print properly.

 The Print Production toolbar is new to Acrobat 7.

The other options for proofing and preparing files exist in a set of tools in the Print Production toolbar, which neatly houses the tools creative and service professionals use to prepare files for digital prepress and printing. Some of the tools were available as menu commands in earlier versions of Acrobat, while others are completely new features added to Acrobat 7.

Soft-proofing menu commands

At the bottom of the Advanced menu, you find menu commands to show overprints in a document, check the output preview in terms of color handling, and a command to access the preflight tools. Other commands for soft-proofing color and resolving potential printing problems are contained in the Print Production toolbar.

 For information on the Print Production tools, see the section "Using the Print Production tools."

Overprint preview

You often use overprints to *trap* colors in files intended for printing separations. Trapping a color creates a color overlap that prevents gaps from appearing between colors when paper moves on a press during the printing process. You might assign an overprint to text to avoid any trapping problems where black text prints on top of a background color. In other cases, a designer might unintentionally assign an overprint to a color during the creative process. As a measure of checking overprints for those colors that you properly assign and to review a document for potential problems, you can use Acrobat's Overprint Preview to display on your monitor all the overprints created in a file. To view overprints in a PDF document, choose Advanced ➪ Overprint Preview.

Note Overprint Preview is available in Acrobat Standard and Acrobat Professional as well as Adobe Reader 7. The remaining preflighting and soft-proofing tools are available only in Acrobat Professional.

To understand what happens with overprints and knockouts, look at Figure 38-8. The composite image is created for printing two colors. These colors are printed on separate plates for two different inks. When the file is separated, the type is *knocked out* of the background, leaving holes in the background, as shown in Figure 38-9. Because the two colors butt up against each other, any slight movement of the paper creates a gap where one ink color ends and the other begins. To prevent the problem, a slight bit of overprinting is added to the type. In an exaggerated view, in Figure 38-10, you can see the stroke around the type characters. The stroke is assigned an overprint so its color, which is the foreground color, prints on top of the background color without a knockout.

Figure 38-8: Separate plates print a composite image.

Figure 38-9: The background appears with the foreground type knocked out.

Figure 38-10: The overprint area of the type color prints on top of the background color.

Designers can apply overprints in programs like Illustrator and InDesign. If a designer inadvertently makes a mistake and selects the fill color to overprint, the color of the foreground image results in a different color created by the mix of the two colors. In Figure 38-11, you view a file in Acrobat without an overprint preview. The figure shows the document as it should print. When you choose Advanced ➪ Overprint Preview, the overprints shown in Figure 38-12 appear. As you can see, the assigned overprints in the file were a mistake. Using Acrobat's Overprint Preview command, you can check for any overprint errors in illustrations.

Figure 38-11: The file as the designer intended it to print

Tip To carefully examine overprints assigned to type characters, click the Loupe tool in the Zoom toolbar. Move the cursor around the document to preview overprints on small type.

Figure 38-12: Viewing all colors in an overprint shows erroneous overprint assignments.

Output Preview

Output Preview provides options for previewing color handled in the output Preview dialog box. Choose Advanced ⇨ Output Preview and the Output Preview dialog box shown in Figure 38-13 appears. You have two categories to preview and a number of different options choices for what you want to see within each category.

Separations preview

In the Preview box in Figure 38-13, select Separations and you preview separations like the separations preview you use in InDesign.

 Cross-Reference   For more, see the section "Reviewing Separations."

If you intend to print a file in four-color process, the Separation Preview dialog box identifies any potential problems if you have spot colors in the file. Likewise, if a spot-color job contains colors that you don't intend to print, they also appear.

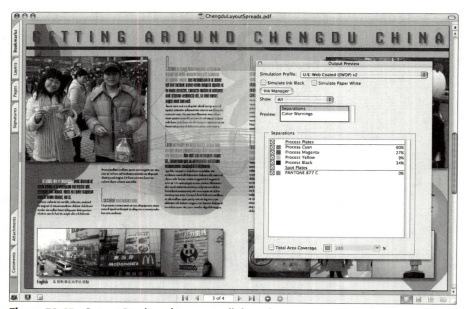

Figure 38-13: Output Preview shows you all the colors contained in a file — both process and spot.

You can selectively view individual colors by deselecting the check boxes adjacent to each color name, view selected colors only, and view spot colors converted to CMYK. Click Ink Manager and you can convert spot color to process color (see Figure 38-19 later in this chapter).

You evaluate color values by moving the cursor around the document with the Separation Preview dialog box open. Notice the percentage values on the far right side of Figure 38-13. These values represent the percent of ink at the cursor position.

Tip　　If you want to compare two documents for separation previews and inks, open both documents in Acrobat. Choose Window ⇨ Tile ⇨ Vertically (or Horizontally). Choose Advanced ⇨ Output Preview and click Separations in the Preview box. Move the cursor back and forth between the two documents. As the cursor is positioned over one document, the separations and inks are shown for that document. Moving the cursor to the other document displays readings for that document.

From the Show pull-down menu, you have several options for what you want to examine in the preview. Choose from the menu options to preview images, spot color, grays, smooth shading, and so on, and the preview dynamically shows the data you choose to view.

Select the Simulate Ink Black check box to display the dynamic range of the document's profile. Dynamic range is measured in values usually between 0 and 4, although some scanner manufacturers claim dynamic ranges of 4.1, 4.2, or higher. A dynamic range of something like 3.8 yields a wide range of grays between the white point and the black point in a scanned image. If the dynamic range is high, you see details in shadows and highlights. If the dynamic range is low, highlights can get blown out and shadows lose detail. When you select the Ink Black check box, look for the distinct tonal differences in the preview and detail in shadows and highlights.

If you select the check box for Simulate Paper White in the Output Preview dialog box, the preview shows you a particular shade of gray as simulated for the paper color by the color profile you choose. You may find that the preview looks too gray or has too much black. This preview may not be the profile used, but rather the brightness adjustment on your monitor. If your monitor is calibrated properly and the profile accurately displays the paper color, the preview should show you an accurate representation of the document as it is printed on paper.

Color Warnings

Click Color Warnings in the Preview box and the Output Preview dialog box changes as shown in Figure 38-14. Select the check boxes for Show Overprinting and Rich Black and the preview displays warnings for overprints and rich black printing in the colors appearing in the color swatches adjacent to the check boxes. If you want to display warnings in different colors, click a swatch and choose from the drop-down color palette a preset color or click Other Color to open your system color palette. In the system color palette, you can choose any color appearing in the palette to display the out-of-gamut color warnings.

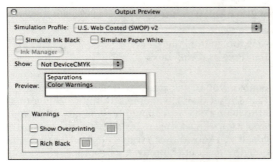

Figure 38-14: Click Color Warnings to display previews for out-of-gamut color warnings.

Soft-proofing tools

You use the third menu command in the Advanced menu for proofing and checking PDF documents for proper printing is the Preflight command. You handle preflighting a file in the Preflight dialog box, which you can open from this menu command or from the Preflight tool.

The Preflight tool appears in a toolbar along with several other tools you use for proofing and correcting potential printing problems. The tools are nested conveniently in the Print Production toolbar shown in Figure 38-15. To open the toolbar, open a context menu on the Toolbar Well and select Print Production from the menu commands. The toolbar opens as a floating toolbar in the Acrobat window. If you want to dock the toolbar in the Toolbar Well, open a context menu again and select Dock All Toolbars or drag the toolbar to the Toolbar Well.

Figure 38-15: Open the Print Production toolbar from a context menu opened from the Toolbar Well.

The Print Production tools include:

A Trap Presets: You can trap PDF files for commercial printing by applying trap presets from a selection installed as defaults or from custom trap presets you create in Acrobat. Before you trap a file, you may need to fix hairline rules. Make adjustments as needed; then click the Trap Presets tool to open the Trap Presets dialog box shown in Figure 38-16.

For more on fixing hairlines, see the section "Fix Hairlines" later in this chapter.

Figure 38-16: Click the Trap Presets tool in the Print Production toolbar to open the Trap Presets dialog box.

The first dialog box that opens enables you to select an existing preset or create a new one. Click Create, and the New Trap Preset dialog box opens as shown in Figure 38-17. In order to make adjustments in the dialog box, you should be familiar with trapping and the acceptable amounts to apply for trap widths, miter adjustments, and attributes assigned to images and thresholds. If you know how to trap a file, you'll know what settings to apply. If you don't know anything about trapping, it's best to leave the job to your commercial printer.

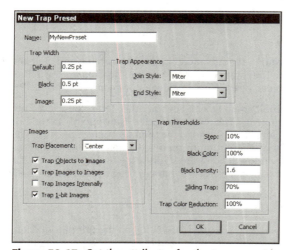

Figure 38-17: Set the attributes for the trap preset in the New Trap Preset dialog box.

Click OK after typing a name for the new preset and making the adjustments. You are then returned to the Trap Presets dialog box where your new preset is listed in the window. Click Assign and the trap values are applied to the document.

B Output Preview: This tool opens the same Output Preview dialog box as when you choose Advanced ⇨ Output Preview.

C Preflight: You can also access preflight from the Advanced menu. Clicking the tool or choosing the menu command opens the Preflight dialog box.

Cross-Reference

For information related to Output Preview see the section "Output Preview" earlier in this chapter. For information related to using the Preflight dialog box, see the section "Preflighting Documents."

D Convert Colors: Click the Convert Colors tool in the Print Production toolbar and the Convert Colors dialog box, shown in Figure 38-18, opens. In the dialog box you can convert color such as spot to process and you can map spot colors to process colors. Mapping a color results in changing the spot color angle default of 45 degrees to a process angle of either C=15, M=75, K=45, or Y = 0 degrees. Additionally you can manage color profiles for source and output intent.

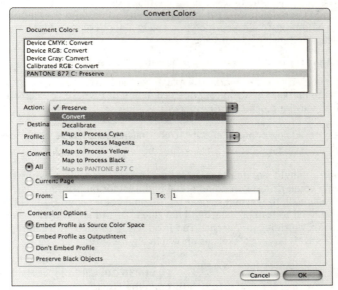

Figure 38-18: Click Convert Colors to open the Convert Colors dialog box.

E Ink Manager: The Ink Manager dialog box enables you to change ink values and convert colors. Changes you apply to the options choices aren't saved with the PDF file. If you convert spot colors to CMYK, for example, and save the document, the colors are unaffected when you reopen the file. The changes applied in the Ink Manager only take effect when you print a PDF document. To open the Ink Manager, click the Ink Manager tool in the Print Production toolbar. The Ink Manager dialog box, shown in Figure 38-19, opens.

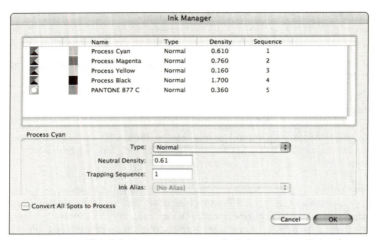

Figure 38-19: Click Ink Manager to open the Ink Manager dialog box.

Select from the pull-down menu options for changing type of color (Normal, Opaque, Transparent, and OpaqueIgnore). You change density values and the trapping sequence by editing the field box. To alias spot colors, select a spot color and map the color to the same angle and density as a process color.

- **F Add Printer Marks:** Use this tool to add printer marks to a page.
- **G Crop Pages:** If you add printer marks to a page, you need to resize the page in order to see and print the marks. The Crop tool opens a dialog box where you can size a page large enough to view and print printer marks.

 Cross-Reference For information on adding printer marks in Acrobat or for cropping pages in Acrobat, see Chapter 24.

- **H Fix Hairlines:** You might see hairlines print fine on desktop printers while they appear almost invisible when printed on commercial high-resolution printing devices. If the hairlines are too small, they won't appear on the final color separation. This is particularly true if you need to trap areas around hairlines. To add larger point sizes to hairlines, click the Fix Hairlines tool in the Print Production toolbar. You can replace narrow hairlines with larger strokes, as shown in Figure 38-20.

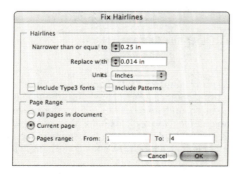

Figure 38-20: Click the Fix Hairlines tool to open the Fix Hairlines dialog box.

I **Transparency Flattening:** You have as many similar options for flattening transparency in Acrobat as you have in Adobe InDesign. Acrobat's Flattener Preview is a little more elaborate, as you can see in Figure 38-21, compared to InDesign's Flattener Preview, shown earlier in Figure 38-1.

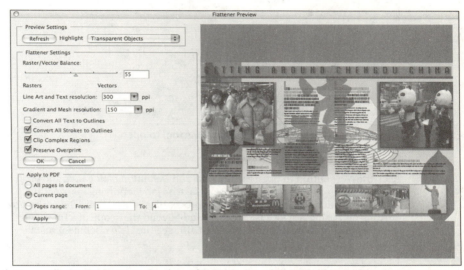

Figure 38-21: Click the Transparency Flattening tool to open the Flattener Preview dialog box.

Whereas InDesign shows you previews on the document page, Acrobat's previews are shown in the Flattener Preview dialog box. As you determine the adjustments needed to flatten transparency, click Apply. In Acrobat 7 you can apply transparency flattening and save the results when you choose File ➪ Save.

J **PDF Optimizer:** Click the tool and you open the PDF Optimizer dialog box. The same dialog box opens when you choose Advanced ➪ PDF Optimizer.

For a more detailed description of the choices in the Flattener Preview dialog box, see the section "Transparency Flattening." For information related to using the PDF Optimizer, see Chapter 29.

K **JDF Job Definitions:** You use a Job Definition File (JDF) in production workflows to include information necessary for a production process and information related to the PDF creation. You assign the information in a JDF file through a collection of dialog boxes that begin with your clicking the JDF Job Definitions tool at the far-right side of the Print Production toolbar. Click the tool and the JDF Job Definitions dialog box, shown in Figure 38-22, opens.

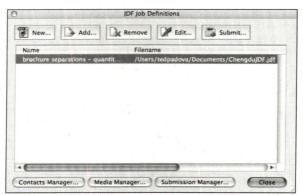

Figure 38-22: Click the JDF Job Definitions tool to open the JDF Job Definitions dialog box.

Click the New button to open the Edit JDF Job Definition dialog box, shown in Figure 38-23. You find options for adding information such as job identifying information, profile compliance, description, and printing and postprocessing information. The entire process for creating and using JDF files is extensive and beyond the scope of a thorough discussion in this chapter. For more information about JDF, see the Help document installed with Acrobat.

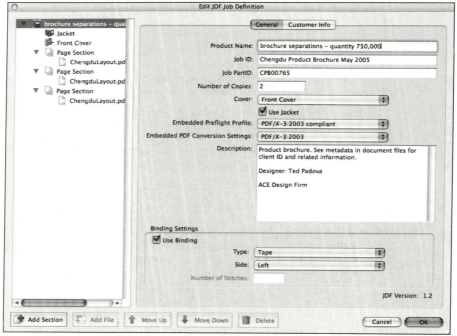

Figure 38-23: Click New in the JDF Job Definitions dialog box to add a new definition.

Preflighting PDF Files

Preflighting is a term that creative professionals and service technicians use to describe the process of analyzing a file for suitability for printing. A preflight assessment might examine a file for the proper color mode of images, for image compression, for accessibility of embedded fonts, for accessibility of fonts to the operating system, or for any number of other conditions that might interfere with successfully printing a job.

The tools preflight files might be stand-alone applications or features built in to programs specifically for printing to commercial printing equipment. Prior to Acrobat 6, you needed to preflight a file before you converted it to PDF with either a stand-alone product, which analyzed the original authoring application file prior to PDF conversion, or with a third-party plug-in for Acrobat that performed preflighting on PDF files. Preflighting PDFs from within Acrobat was introduced in Acrobat 6 and has been polished and improved in Acrobat 7.

Preflighting a file

Acrobat requires you to have a file open in the Document pane in order to run a preflight check unless you use a batch sequence (see the section "Preflighting batches of files"). To preflight a document, be certain a file is open and click the Preflight tool in the Print Production toolbar. The Preflight dialog box, shown in Figure 38-24, opens. In the top window you see a number of preinstalled profiles listed with a description for the kind of preflighting each profile performs. Use the scroll bar on the right side of the window to display additional profiles.

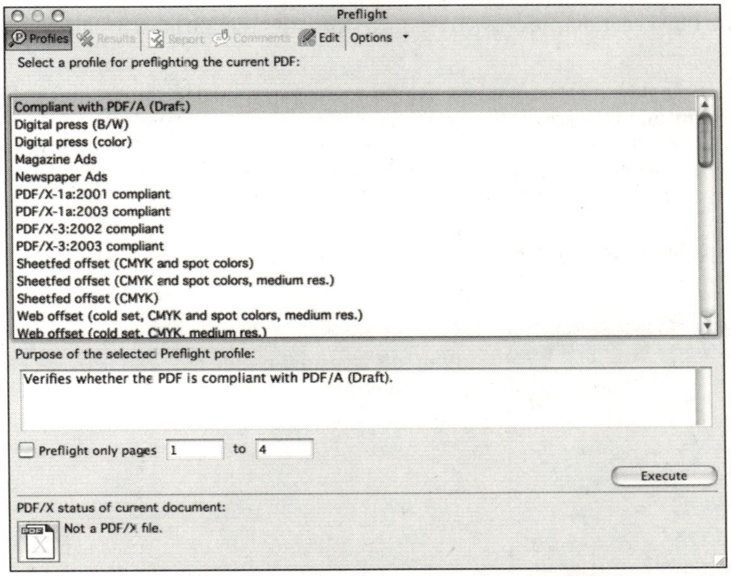

Figure 38-24: Click the Preflight tool to open the Preflight dialog box.

If a profile contains the conditions you want to check, select a profile and click Execute. If the file you preflight contains errors, a report displayed in the Preflight window after you execute the preflight. The report is listed in a hierarchy with subnotations listed under parent categories. Click the icon to the left of each category to expand the list, as shown in Figure 38-25.

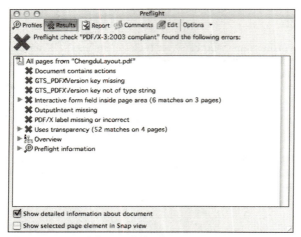

Figure 38-25: If the preflight does not match the conditions of the profile, a report lists the errors in the Preflight window.

Producing a PDF/X-compliant file

For commercial printing, you'll want to create PDF/X-compliant files. If a file is not converted to PDF/X during the PDF creation process you can postprocess the file in Acrobat to check the file for PDF/X compliance.

When the Results are displayed in the Preflight window, you can return to the profile list by clicking the Profiles button in the top of the Preflight window. To convert the open document to a PDF/X-compliant file, click the PDF/X status of current document button at the bottom of the Preflight dialog box. The Preflight: Convert to PDF/X dialog box opens as shown in Figure 38-26. In the dialog box, you make choices for the PDF/X version, output intent, and trapping key.

Cross-Reference For information about trapping, see the section "Soft-proofing tools."

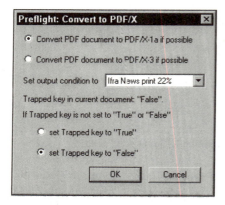

Figure 38-26: Select the PDF/X file format, output intent, and trapping key, and click OK to convert the open document to a PDF/X-compliant file.

Understanding PDF/X

PDF/X has gained acceptance among commercial printing companies for creating files suitable for printing. PDF is a reliable format for any kind of electronic file exchanges. However, files developed for Acrobat viewers, Acrobat PDF forms, Web-hosted documents, and so on carry a lot of overhead not necessary for printing on commercial printing devices. The PDF/X compliance standard was developed to streamline documents by eliminating unnecessary data and optimizing files for print. Tailoring a PDF document for print by creating a PDF/X-compliant file does not necessarily reduce file size. In many cases, file sizes grow from a standard PDF to a PDF/X file.

The PDF/X options available to you in Acrobat Distiller and the CS2 programs produce either a PDF/X-1a:2002, PDF/X-1a:2003, PDF/X-3:2002, or PDF/X-3:2003-compliant file. These file types are different versions of the PDF/X format. PDF/X-1a is designed to work well with both process and spot color, but no support is provided for color management or profile embedding. PDF/X-3 supports process and spot color and does support color-managed workflows and ICC (International Color Consortium) profile embedding.

The two distinctions between the versions for PDFX-1a:2002, and PDF/X-1a:2003 have to do with versions of the same subset. With PDF/X-1a:2002, you have compatibility with Acrobat 4. With PDF/X-1a:2003, you have compatibility with Acrobat 5. The same applies to the version 2002 and version 2003 of the PDF/X-3 subset.

When you export as PDF/X or create a PDF using Acrobat Distiller, you are checking the file for PDF/X compliance. If the file does not meet the PDF/X standard you select (that is, PDF/X-1a or PDF/X-3), a PDF is not created. If a file meets PDF/X compliance, you have much greater assurance that your PDF document will print on almost any kind of commercial printing device.

In version 2 of the CS programs, all applications support exporting to PDF/X. Other PDF producers such as PDFMaker, which you use with Microsoft Office applications, Microsoft Project, Microsoft Visio, and AutoDesk AutoCAD do not support PDF/X. If you want to print any of these files on commercial printing devices, print PostScript files and distill them with Acrobat Distiller using a PDF/X setting.

Click OK in the Preflight: Convert to PDF/X dialog box and Acrobat converts the open document to a PDF/X-compliant file. In some cases files can't be converted due to problems related to the file construction. If you cannot convert the file, you can examine the report and return to the original authoring program, where you can fix the reported problems.

After conversion, Acrobat prompts you in a Save as PDF/X dialog box. As a default name, Acrobat adds the PDF/X version extension to the file. You can accept the new filename or change it in the File name field. By default, a new filename is added to prevent you from overwriting the original file. Click Save to save the PDF/X-compliant file.

If you want to check the converted file against PDF/X compliance, you can return to the profile list in the Preflight window and select the PDF/X format used to convert the file. Click Execute and the Preflight window should display a message indicating no problems were found, as shown in Figure 38-27.

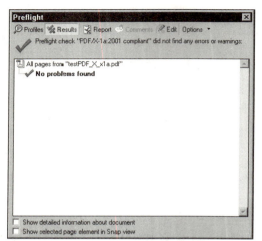

Figure 38-27: When a file meets PDF/X compliance and you run a check, the report shows no problems found.

Creating PDF/A-compliant files

Adobe has been working with international standards committees toward a goal of ensuring that the documents of today can be electronically read 10, 20, even 100 years from now. One of the fruitions of these labors is the PDF/A standard developed for archiving purposes.

PDF/A files contain essentials in terms of document structure. The necessary essentials include raster images, fonts (embedded), and vector objects. Code used in documents such as JavaScript is deemed a nonessential ingredient as well as any form of security. Therefore, you cannot create PDF/A files containing any scripts or encryption. In general you'll find PDF/A files are much leaner than other file standards such as PDF/X.

To make a PDF/A-compliant file you use a similar process as when creating PDF/X files. Select the Compliant with PDF/A (Draft) profile listed in the Preflight window and click Execute. If the file is not PDF/A compliant, review the errors reported in the Preflight window. You need to return to the document and fix the problems in order to meet PDF/A compliance.

Creating a new profile

If none of the preset profiles does the job of file checking for your workflow, you can create your own custom profiles. Acrobat offers you more than 400 different conditions that you can use in preflighting files. To create a new profile, click the Edit button in the Preflight dialog box; the Preflight: Edit Profile dialog box opens, as shown in Figure 38-28.

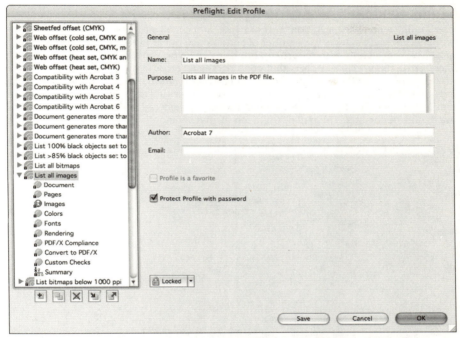

Figure 38-28: Click the Edit button in the Preflight dialog box to open the Preflight: Edit Profile dialog box.

At the bottom of the dialog box, several tools appear for creating and managing profiles. They include

- **Create a new profile.** Click the icon to create a new profile. The Preflight: Edit Profile pane changes to offer options. There are field boxes for adding a profile name, a profile description, author name, and e-mail address. Check boxes let you add a profile as a favorite, which lists the profile at the top of the Preflight window in bold type, and for password-protecting the profile. From a list of categories in the left pane you select a category and specify conditions to check.

- **Duplicate the selected profile.** Click the icon to duplicate a selected profile. Once it's duplicated you can edit the profile to change conditions.

- **Delete the selected profile.** Select a profile and click the icon to remove the profile from the list window. You cannot delete the profile if you have Locked selected in the Preflight: Edit Profile pane.

- **Import.** Click the Import tool to import a profile created by a vendor or a user in your workgroup.

- **Export.** If you are responsible for creating profiles at a service center or in a company where you want to implement a set of standards, click the Export button. The profile selected when you click this button is exported to a file that you can send to other users who in turn import the profile.

Adding conditions to a custom profile

After adding a name, description, author name, and e-mail address, select a category in the left pane. For each category, a number of conditions appear in the right pane. From pull-down menus you have choices to report conditions as an Error, Warning, Info, and Inactive. If you select Error, the preflight reports that condition as an error in the preflight report. Warnings also are reported in the preflight report. Info displays information if a condition is not true, and Inactive skips checking for the respective condition. In Figure 38-29 you can see a number of different conditions related to Document when it's selected in the left pane of the Preflight: Edit Profile dialog box. The pull-down menu displays the options for one of the subcategories.

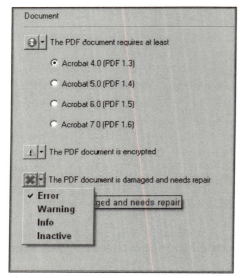

Figure 38-29: Document, one of the nine categories in the left pane, helps you choose the conditions you want checked during preflight.

By default, all conditions are ignored when you begin creating a new profile. Click the categories in the left pane and make choices in the right pane for the conditions you want to check. If you use the profile frequently, select the check box for Profile is a favorite.

Importing/exporting profiles

After creating a profile, you may want to send the profile to another user. Select the profile you want to export from the list of profiles in the Preflight: Edit Profile dialog box and click the Export icon. The Export Preflight profile dialog box opens. Find a location on your hard drive where you want to save the file and click Save. The file is saved with a default extension of .kfp.

You handle importing profiles similarly. Click Import and locate a file to import. Only .kfp files are listed in the Import Preflight Profile dialog box. Select the file to import and click Open. The imported profile is added to the list of profiles in the Preflight window.

Creating reports and comments

Additional tools for creating a report and embedding comments appear in the Preflight window. When you click the Report tool, a Save As dialog box opens. Provide a filename and click Save. The report is generated as a PDF document and opens in the Document pane. You can use the PDF file as a file attachment to send along with your job to a service center. You can save the report as PDF, XML, or TXT.

If you click the Comments tool in the Preflight window, comment notes are embedded in the file. These comments note all the conditions that were not met and the various errors. If you want to have comments appear in the document, use the Comments tool.

Preflighting batches of files

Using the Preflight command in Acrobat Professional is handy for a single file or a few files you want to preflight or save as PDF/X-compliant. If you have numerous files that need to be preflighted, you can set up a batch sequence and preflight a folder of PDF documents.

To create a batch sequence for preflighting files, choose Advanced ➪ Batch Processing. Click New Sequence in the Batch Sequence dialog box and type a name in the Name Sequence dialog box. Click OK and select Preflight in the left pane. Click Add to move the Preflight item to the right pane. Double-click Preflight in the right pane to open the Preflight: Batch Sequence Setup dialog box, as shown in Figure 38-30. From the Run Preflight check using pull-down menu you can select any profile listed in the Preflight window. If you are checking for conditions using a custom profile, select the profile from the list. For PDF/X compliance, select one of the PDF/X-compliant file types.

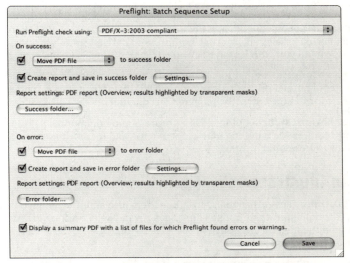

Figure 38-30: Select a profile in the Run Preflight check using pull-down menu.

Cross-Reference For a detailed description on creating and running batch sequences, see Chapter 29.

Packaging Documents for Commercial Printing

Packaging a file for printing involves collecting all the assets required for printing and gathering them on a disk, CD-ROM, or a compressed archive you intend to e-mail or FTP to your service center. With Photoshop documents, you don't need to package for printing; all assets are contained within the Photoshop document. Flatten the image and send the file off to your printer. With Illustrator and InDesign, you have issues needing attention, such as font usage and links. When you package these files, you must include all links with the active file to send to your printer.

With fonts, you're faced with some potential problems related to font licensing. Many font-manufacturer licensing restrictions prevent you from legally distributing fonts to your service provider. If your provider does not have a given font, the provider must purchase the font or you need to search for a different provider.

The complex issues related to packaging native files together with legal restrictions is reason enough to search for a better solution rather than send your native files to service providers. Fortunately, the CS applications offer you a much better alternative. Quite simply, your package utility is Acrobat PDF. When you send PDF documents to your printer, you have advantages such as:

- **Font embedding:** Not all fonts are licensed for font embedding in PDF documents. However, the more popular Adobe fonts, OpenType fonts, and many TrueType fonts carry no licensing restrictions for embedding the fonts in PDF documents. When the fonts are embedded, you don't have to worry about whether your service provider has the fonts contained in your document.

- **Image embedding:** All images are embedded in PDF documents. You don't need to worry about missing links when sending PDF files to your printer.

- **Smaller file sizes:** PDF documents occupy the least amount of space on your hard drive and are most often smaller in size than compressed native files. The results of smaller file sizes provide you with faster electronic transfer times via e-mail and FTP.

- **Optimized file types for printing:** With PDF documents, you can create PDF/X files that are optimized for commercial printing. Developing PDF/X-compliant files provides a much more reliable format for correctly imaging your documents.

Because PDF is the best file format for sending files to prepress and commercial printing, we'll skip the packaging features for bundling native documents and focus on creating PDF documents optimized for professional printing.

PDF creation in Illustrator

If you intend to print Illustrator files rather than introduce them into an InDesign layout, you can save directly to PDF from Illustrator. Choose File ➪ Save As and select Adobe PDF as the file format. After you name the file and click Save in the Save As dialog box, the Save Adobe PDF dialog box (Figure 38-31) opens.

From the Adobe PDF Preset pull-down menu, select one of the PDF/X options. Review the categories in the left pane. Add marks and bleeds, color settings, transparency flattening, and adjust the settings needed for your output.

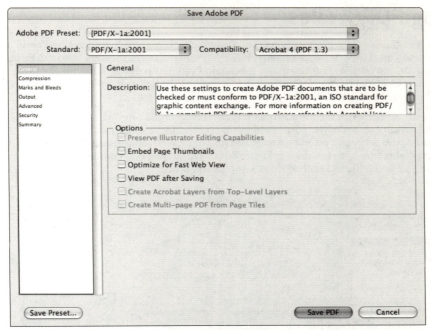

Figure 38-31: To print commercially, select a PDF/X subset from the Adobe PDF Preset pull-down menu.

All other choices are made for you when you select a PDF/X option. Look at the Summary item in the left pane. If you see a warning icon, click Summary and review the summary information. In some cases you need to return to the document and fix any problems before saving as a PDF/X file. Click Save PDF. If the file meets PDF/X compliance, the file is saved to PDF.

PDF creation in InDesign

In InDesign you might use the preflight check built into the program before exporting to PDF. InDesign enables you to completely package the file for press via an export to PDF. After preflighting, choose File ➪ Export. Provide a name for your file and be certain that you select the PDF in the Format drop-down list. Click Save, and the Export PDF dialog box opens to offer you the same options that you find with PDF exports from Adobe Illustrator.

Select a PDF/X Adobe PDF Preset and adjust the options you need to print the file, such as printing spreads, adding marks and bleeds, and so on. As with Adobe Illustrator, be certain to check the Summary and correct any errors before exporting. Click Export and the InDesign file is exported as PDF/X.

Printing PDF/X Files

All the attributes set in the Page Setup and Print dialog boxes discussed in Chapter 36 are used when you print PDF/X documents. However, rather than outputting from the Print dialog box and making options choices in the Advanced Print Setup dialog box, you can best achieve most commercial printing by exporting your PDF/X document back to PostScript and downloading the PostScript file.

To prepare a PostScript file for downloading to a commercial printing device, choose File ➪ Save As in Acrobat. From the Format drop-down list, select PostScript. When you select PostScript, the Settings button becomes active. Click the Settings button and the Save As Settings dialog box opens, shown in Figure 38-32. This dialog box contains all the print options you find in the Advanced Print Setup dialog box.

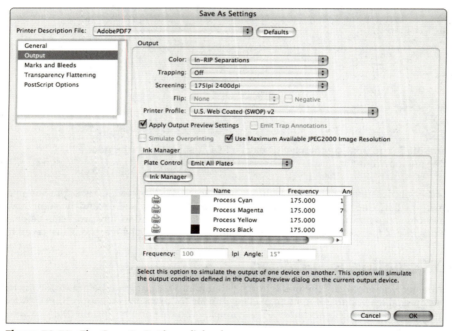

Figure 38-32: The Save As Settings dialog box

In the left pane, you make choices for the four different categories. These categories offer the same options as the Advanced Print Setup dialog box. You can use the same set of options choices as was discussed in Chapter 37, and click OK. You're returned to the Save As dialog box. Provide a name for the file, and click Save. The resultant document is a file that you can download directly to a PostScript device.

Tip   The only limitation in the Settings dialog box is the absence of a page preview. To verify that your document fits on the output, open the Print dialog box and check the thumbnail preview against the page size when printer's marks are included. If all looks fine, cancel out of the Print dialog box and return to the Save As Settings dialog box.

Summary

- InDesign, Illustrator, and Acrobat provide tools for flattening transparency.

- InDesign and Acrobat offer you tools for preflighting documents against potential printing problems and for soft-proofing files for proper color assignment.

- Acrobat offers the most sophisticated tools for preflighting and soft-proofing color. You can create or acquire preflight profiles suited to specific output equipment.

- For packaging files for prepress and printing, Acrobat PDF format offers many benefits, including font embedding, image embedding, and smaller file sizes.

- PDF/X is a subset of the PDF format and is the most desirable format for commercial prepress and printing.

- When you print PDF documents to commercial equipment, the preferable method for printing is to save the PDF to PostScript and download the PostScript file to a printer.

✦ ✦ ✦

Index

NUMERIC

3-D objects
    extruding, 497–499
    mapping artwork, 500
    revolving objects, 52–53, 500–502
    rotating objects, 502

A

Acrobat (Adobe). *See also* Organizer
    bookmarks, 1061
    described, 24–28
    documents
        converting for CD/DVD distribution, 1102
        moving with Export Menu, 754–755
    DRM, adding, 1011–1018
    keyboard shortcuts, 173–174
    layers, 511
    links and buttons
        adding, 1037–1041
        described, 1033
        duplicating, 1041–1043
        faces, creating in Illustrator, 1033–1037
        icon appearances, 1033
        type characters, 1038
        URL links, 1041–1043
    notes and form fields, 738
    objects, 317–319
    organization tool, 205
    palettes and workspaces, 153–154
    pasting Word document, 736–737
    PDF Optimizer, 71–73
    preferences, 125–126
    print setups
        color and screening output, 1201–1202
        converted Word files, 824
        dialog box, 1199–1201
        Mac desktop printer, selecting, 1171–1172
        marks and bleeds, 1202
        PostScript Options, 1204–1205
        Transparency Flattening, 1202–1203
        Windows desktop printer, selecting, 1175
    Reader, adding to CD/DVD, 1107
    review sessions
        AutoCAD, exporting comments to, 873
        Clipboard Image, pasting as Stamp tool, 858–859
        comments, moving to Word, 755–758
        Comments pane, 859–863
        comparing documents, 878–880
        described, 839
        Drawing Markup tools, 859
        e-mail-based, 866–869
        exporting selected comments, 874
        files, exporting comments to, 873–874
        filtering comments, 874–875
        note, adding to page, 851
        Note tool, 842–850
        PDFs with Reader extensions, enabling, 863–866
        preferences, 839–842
        Properties bar, viewing, 850–851
        Stamp tool, 852–858
        summaries, creating, 875–878
        Text Edit tools, 851–852
        Tracker window, 869–872
        Word, exporting comments to, 872–873
    sketch
        comments, adding, 37–39
        e-mail review, submitting, 35–37
        review comments, collecting, 39–40
        scanning, 33–35
    slide presentations
        bookmarks, creating with, 1148
        Full Screen views, 1161
    spot-proofing
        color, checking, 67–68
        PDF/X file, creating, 69–71
        transparency, flattening, 68
    SWF files
        importing in PDF documents, 1136–1139
        Web pages, converting to PDF, 1134–1136
    text, exporting to Word, 751
    tool options, 147
    trim and crops, 824–827
    user interfaces, 134–135
    XML, saving files as, 1006
Acrobat Catalog
    building index, 972–974
    definitions, saving index, 969
    downloadable documents
        described, 962
        external devices, searching, 983
        index files, 976–983
        preferences, setting, 975–976
        purging data, 974–975
    new index file, creating, 966–969
    options, 970–972
    PDFs, preparing for indexing, 962–966
administration. *See* CS2 Administration Web pages
Adobe. *See individual products listed by name*
Adobe Stock Photos, 86–87
Adobe Studio, 271
aligning
    InDesign table cell content, 778
    objects, 446–449
    Photoshop image layers, 449–451
anchoring layout objects
    described, 911
    graphics, 912–916
    text frames, 913–914
Angle effect, Illustrator, 503–504
angle, gradient, 349

animating
  GoLive layers
    enabling in Timeline, 576
    keyframes, recording, 579
    keys, creating new, 578–579
    new scene, creating, 579
    Play Animation action, 580
    previewing, 579
    steps, 580–582
  SWF files, creating in Illustrator, 1114–1115
antialiasing Type layers, 548–549
Apple Keynote slides, 1146–1147
array of objects, 426–427
ASPS stock photos
  browsing images, 242–243
  news and offers, getting, 243
  overview, 241–242
  provider libraries, 242
attachments, DRM
  Secure PDF Delivery, 1024–1027
  security policies, 1020–1024
automating tasks
  batch-processing PDF files
    creating new sequence, 608
    described, 604–605
    editing sequences, 606–608
    executing sequences, 605
    JavaScripts, 609–612
    preferences, setting, 608–609
  data-driven graphics
    data set, capturing, 604
    described, 602
    objects, binding variables to, 604
  described, 591
  InDesign corrections, 117–118
  layers, selecting with Move tool, 542
  loading fonts, 622
  Photoshop and Illustrator Actions palette
    Automate menu, 602
    batch-processing actions, 597–598
    creating new actions, 593–594
    deleting, 597
    described, 591–592
    dialog boxes, appearing, 596
    droplet, creating, 598–599
    editing, 596
    menu items, inserting, 595
    objects, selecting as part of action, 594
    paths, adding to action, 594
    playing action, 592–593
    rearranging, 596
    steps creating action, 599–600
    stop, adding with comments, 595–596
  Photoshop and Illustrator scripts, 600–602
  Photoshop Automate menu, 602
  shadows and highlights, 389–390
  text flow, 699–700
axis, Illustrator graph
  scale, 800
  value and category, 799

B

background
  GoLive layers, 49–51, 575–576
  Photoshop layers, 541
backing up projects, 294
batch processing
  documents, moving with Export Menu, 755
  PDF files
    creating new sequence, 608
    described, 604–605
    editing sequences, 606–608
    executing sequences, 605
    JavaScripts, 609–612
    preferences, setting, 608–609
  Photoshop and Illustrator actions, 597–598
  Photoshop commands with actions, 258–259
  preflighting file for commercial printing, 1231
bitmap images
  converting for printing, 1183–1184
  tracing, 48–49
black, appearance of, 98–99
bleeds
  Acrobat print setups, 1202
  Illustrator print setups, 1178–1179
  PDF documents for CD/DVD distribution, 1090–1091
blending
  editing objects in Illustrator, 375–377
  filters, Photoshop, 490
  layers, Photoshop, 553–558
  transparency modes, 357–358
blurring filters, Photoshop, 459–463
bookmarks
  Acrobat, 1061
  InDesign, 1060
  opening files, 1061–1065
  slide presentations, 1147–1149
bounding box
  Free Transform tool, 422–423
  moving, 414–415
  Reflect tool, 420–421
  Rotate tool, 418–419
  rotating, 416
  Scale tool, 419–420
  scaling and reflecting, 416–418
  Shear tool, 421–422
  snapping, 415
  steps, 423–425
break characters, inserting, 722–723
Bridge (Adobe)
  accessing project files, 58
  application commands, enabling
    Illustrator, 264
    InDesign, 264–265
    Photoshop, 257–264
  Bridge Center
    Adobe Studio, 271
    described, 265–267
    RSS Reader, 268–271
  camera raw file settings, 253–254
  color synchronization, 256–257
  described, 7–9

files and folders
    adding to Version Cue project, 57
    batch renaming, 221–223
    collections, 220–221
    context menus, 218–219
    creating new folders, 214
    deleting files, 216
    Favorites, adding, 221
    files, adding to folders, 215
    labeling files, 216–218
    moving and copying files, 215
    navigating folders, 215–216
metadata
    appending and replacing, 228–230
    deleting templates, 230
    properties, 224–226
    template, creating, 227–228
    XMP templates, 226–227
preferences
    Adobe Stock Photos, 86–87
    Advanced settings, 85–86
    described, 82–83
    File Type Associations, 84–85
    General options, 83–84
    Metadata and Labels, 84
searching
    described, 230
    documents, 231–237
    saving searches, 238
    stock photos, 238–240
slide shows, 271–272
user interfaces, 134
Version Cue versus, 56
workspace
    described, 203
    opening, 204–205
    panes, managing, 212–213
    saving custom, 210–212
    tools, 205–210
    windows, managing, 213–214
browsing
    ASPS stock photos, 242–243
    FTP files, 1081–1082
buttons
    Acrobat
        adding, 1037–1041
        described, 1033
        duplicating, 1041–1043
        faces, creating in Illustrator, 1033–1037
        icon appearances, 1033
        type characters, 1038
        URL links, 1041–1043
    cross-document linking, 1164
    InDesign
        benefits and limitations, 1030
        creating new, 1032
        destination, specifying, 1031
        managing, 1031
        testing, 1032

C

calibrating color, 190
camera. *See* digital camera
camera raw files
    described, 246
    plug-in, 248–253, 384
    preferences, setting, 246–248
    saving, 254–255
    settings, applying in Bridge, 253–254
Cascading Style Sheets. *See* CSS
Categories pane (History, My Computer, and Collections), Organizer, 298–300
category axes, Illustrator graphs, 799
CD/DVD distribution
    Acrobat, converting with, 1102
    clients, acquiring PDFs from, 1103
    Macintosh, creating PDFs on, 1103–1104
    PDF documents
        Adobe PDF Settings, 1088
        Adobe Reader, adding, 1107
        Advanced settings, 1092
        collection, organizing, 1105–1106
        common attributes, 1088–1090
        Compression settings, 1090
        format, benefits of using, 1087–1088
        General options, 1090
        HTML conversions, 1091
        Marks and Bleeds settings, 1090–1091
        metadata, adding to files, 1105
        Output options, 1091–1092
        Photoshop, creating from, 1098–1101
        replicating, 1106
        Security settings, 1092
        steps, 1093–1098
        Summary, 1093
        updates, Web page for, 1106
        welcome file, creating, 1106–1107
    plug-ins, 1104–1105
    security, 1107–1108
    Windows, creating PDFs on, 1104
character styles
    Illustrator, 665–667
    InDesign, 667–668
characters, special. *See* special type characters
charts, Illustrator
    importing Excel and Word, 812
    types, 789–792
Clean Up settings, downloadable documents, 956–957
clients, acquiring PDFs from, 1103
Clipboard
    Excel
        diagrams, transporting, 812
        Illustrator charts, transporting via, 811
        tables, importing, 769
    Image pasting as Stamp tool, 858–859
    stacking order, 446
    Word
        described, 727–728
        diagrams, transporting, 812
        document, moving to GoLive, 744

Continued

Clipboard, Word *(continued)*
  fonts, missing, 729–730
  formatting, maintaining, 728–729
  Illustrator charts, transporting via, 811
  text, exporting, 749–751
clipping mask
  editing objects in Illustrator, 377
  layers, Illustrator, 535–539
cloud effects, Photoshop, 468–470
CMYK color mode, 341
coding on demand documents, 1069
collections
  Bridge, 220–221
  creating, 220
  files, adding, 221
  PDFs for CD/DVD distribution, 1105–1106
color
  Acrobat print setups, 1201–1202
  applying to objects in Illustrator and InDesign, 325–326
  calibrating, 190
  composite, printing, 201–202
  custom, adding, 94–95
  filling and stroking objects
    CMYK mode, 341
    Color Picker, 343–344
    described, 337
    Eyedropper tools, 344–346
    gamut, 343
    Grayscale mode, 341
    hexadecimal numbers, 340
    HSB mode, 340–341
    palette, 341–343
    profiles and settings, 346–347
    RGB mode, 338, 339
    spot versus process, 342
    Web Safe mode, 338–339
  filters, Illustrator, 491–492
  management
    Illustrator print setups, 1183
    InDesign, 1197–1198
  Photoshop Eyedropper tool, 344–345
  separations, previewing
    on monitor, 1211–1212, 1217–1219
    print layout, 65–66
  settings, adjusting, 196–199
  sharp edges, Photoshop High Pass filters, 476
  spot versus process, 342
  spot-proofing Acrobat, 67–68
  synchronization, 256–257
  warnings, soft-proofing documents on monitor, 1219
Color Picker, 343–344
Color Replacement tool, 410
color-managed workflows
  CS2 applications
    adjusting, 196–199
    swapping, 200
    synchronizing, 199–200
  described, 189
  printing with profiles, 200–202
  profiling
    acquiring profiles, 191
    calibrating color, 190

described, 189–190
embedding, 192–194
mismatching, 194–196
online development resources, 192
in workflows, 190
column
  Illustrator graphs, increasing width, 796
  InDesign tables
    deleting, 774
    evenly distributing, 777
  moving in GoLive tables, 785
  Photoshop pixel selection tool, 404
  text frames, 691–695
comments
  deleting comments, 862–863
  described, 859–860
  documents, moving with Export Menu, 755–758
  editing pop-up notes, 863
  marking, 863
  navigating, 862
  objects, creating and editing in Acrobat, 319
  preferences, 839–842
  preflighting file, 1231
  printing, 862
  searching, 862
  sketch, collecting, 39–40
  sorting, 861
  status, setting, 863
  viewing, 860–861
commercial printing
  documents, packaging
    described, 1232
    Illustrator, 1232–1233
    InDesign, 1233
  file, analyzing for printing suitability
    batches, 1231
    described, 1225–1226
    new profile, creating, 1228–1230
    PDF/A-compliant file, 1228
    PDF/X-compliant file, 1226–1228, 1234
    reports and comments, 1231
  soft-proofing documents on monitor
    Acrobat Professional, 1214–1224
    described, 1207
    Illustrator, 1212–1214
    InDesign, 1208–1212
composite color, 201–202
composition
  InDesign preferences, 112
  Photoshop layers, 568–570
compound paths and shapes, 374–375
Compression settings, PDF documents, 1090
contact sheets, 260
content
  GoLive
    importing, 60–62
    packaging, examining, 945–946
  Word document, moving to GoLive
    Clipboard, using, 744
    opening text files, 745
    Paste Special command, 744

context menus
  files and folders, 218–219
  user interfaces, 158–159
contrast, adjusting image, 41–42
Control palette, InDesign type style, 657
Convert to Shapes (Rectangle, Rounded Rectangle, or Ellipse), 502
copying
  Acrobat links and buttons, 1041–1043
  Bridge files, 215
  layers, 515
  objects between layers, 514–515
  writing PDFs, CD/DVD distribution, 1106
corners
  effects, creating, 508
  filling and stroking objects in Illustrator and InDesign, 327
Creative Suite 2. *See* CS2 Administration Web pages; CS2 applications
Creative Suite, XML, 986
Crop Marks filter, Illustrator, 492–493
cropping
  images
    GoLive, 43–44
    Photoshop, 408–409
    Smart Objects in GoLive, 936–937
CS2 (Creative Suite 2) Administration Web pages
  Advanced features, 294–296
  backing up projects, 294
  creating and editing projects, 292–294
  described, 290–291
  users, adding and editing, 291–292
CS2 (Creative Suite 2) applications
  color-managed workflows
    adjusting color settings, 196–199
    swapping color settings, 200
    synchronizing color settings, 199–200
  layers
    copying objects between, 514–515
    creating, 513
    deleting, 515
    dividing document into layers, 516
    document, creating, 515–516
    duplicating, 515
    hiding and locking, 514
    merging, 515
    palette, 512
    rearranging, 514
    selecting and targeting, 513–514
  layout, InDesign, 889
  PDFs, creating, 1018–1019
  swatches, sharing, 366–367
CSS (Cascading Style Sheets)
  GoLive layers, 571
  Illustrator layers, 528–529
  Web sites, setting up
    applying styles, 939–940
    defining styles, 939
    described, 937
    editor, 938–939
    external style sheet, creating, 940
cursors, Photoshop preferences, 104–105

customizing
  character sets, working in InDesign, 718–719
  colors, Illustrator preferences, 94–95
  filters, Photoshop, 475–477
  Illustrator graphs, 809–810
  page sizes
    on Macintosh, 819–821
    in Windows, 821
  Stamp tool for review sessions, 854–856
cutting objects in Illustrator, 373

D

Dashed Line, 328–329
data
  Illustrator graphs
    changing, 796
    entering, 793
  purging from downloadable documents, 974–975
data set
  assigning to different graph type, 800
  capturing data-driven graphics, 604
data-driven graphics, automating tasks
  data set, capturing, 604
  described, 602
  objects, binding variables to, 604
  variables
    defining, 603
    saving, 604
default preferences, returning to, 81–82
defining CSS styles, 939
definitions, saving index in Catalog, 969
deleting
  actions and commands, 597
  comments, 862–863
  files in Bridge, 216
  InDesign master pages, 894
  layers, 515
  layout, InDesign, 891–892
  masking layers, 565
  rows and columns
    GoLive tables, 785
    InDesign tables, 774
  Version Cue files, 290
  Word document, 739
  XML elements, 989–990
designs
  Illustrator graphs, using, 801–807
  independent artists production workflows, modifying, 180
desktop printers
  Mac, selecting on
    described, 1169
    Illustrator, 1171
    InDesign, 1170
    Photoshop, GoLive, and Acrobat, 1171–1172
  Windows, selecting on
    Acrobat, 1175
    InDesign and Illustrator, 1172–1173
    Photoshop and GoLive, 1174
destination, specifying for InDesign links and buttons, 1031
detaching InDesign master pages, 894

device settings, Illustrator print setups, 1185–1186
diagrams, creating, 812
dialog box
    filters, Photoshop, 458–459
    InDesign tables, 775
    layers, opacity and blending mode, 553
    Photoshop and Illustrator Actions automating tasks, 596
dictionary, 116–117
digital camera
    images
        Camera Raw plug-in, 384
        Lens Correction filter, 385–386
        red eye, correcting, 385
    negatives, specifying, 384
digital negative specification, 384
Digital Rights Management. *See* DRM
Discard Objects settings, downloadable documents, 956
display
    Illustrator performance, 91–92
    InDesign
        layers, showing and hiding, 583–584
        preferences, 119–120
        quality, setting, 910–911
    Photoshop preferences, 104–105
distortion
    Illustrator filters, 493–494
    Photoshop images
        correcting, 42–43, 411
        filters, 463–465
distributing
    objects
        described, 446–447
        spacing, distributing, 447–449
    Photoshop image layers
        described, 449–450
        Smart Guides, 450–451
document repurposing. *See* repurposing documents
documents
    commercial printing, packaging
        Illustrator, 1232–1233
        InDesign, 1233
    comparing, Acrobat review sessions, 878–880
    descriptions, preparing PDFs for indexing, 963–964
    dividing into layers, 516
    layers, 515–516
    opening with Layers tab, 587
    preferences specific to, 80–81
    searching
        files for quick cleanup, 235–236
        folders, viewing files from different, 236–237
        metadata, 233–235
        options, 231–233
        saving searches, 238
    security
        Acrobat, adding, 1011–1018
        CS programs, creating PDFs from, 1018–1019
        described, 1009
        encryption levels, 1010
        permissions, 1010
        signature handlers, 1010
    tagging, 997–999
    Tracker window review sessions, viewing, 870–871
    Word, moving with Export Menu
        from Acrobat, 754–755
        batch-converting files, 755
        comments from Acrobat, 755–758
        Illustrator, 752–753
        InDesign, 753–754
    XHTML Mobile, converting to, 942–944
downloadable documents
    Acrobat Catalog
        building index, 972–974
        definitions, saving index, 969
        external devices, searching, 983
        index files, 976–983
        new index file, creating, 966–969
        options, 970–972
        PDFs, preparing for indexing, 962–966
        preferences, setting, 975–976
        purging data, 974–975
    described, 951–952
    file size, reducing, 952–953
    opening, setting preferences for
        described, 957–958
        initial views, 958–961
        saving initial view, 961–962
    PDF Optimizer
        auditing space usage, 953–954
        Clean Up settings, 956–957
        Discard Objects settings, 956
        font settings, 955–956
        image settings, 955
        scanned pages, 955
        transparency settings, 956
    PDFs, preparing for indexing
        adding metadata with Bridge, 964–965
        described, 962
        document descriptions, 963–964
        file structure, 965–966
        optimizing performance, 966
downloading
    files, GoLive Web site publishing, 1080–1081
    stock photos, 243–246
    Web pages, 1082
drag and drop text files, 734
dragging and dropping assets, GoLive, 947–949
drawing tools
    Acrobat review sessions, 859
    Illustrator, 307–308
    InDesign, 314–315
DRM (Digital Rights Management)
    attachments
        Secure PDF Delivery, 1024–1027
        security policies, creating, 1020–1024
    described, 1009
    document security
        Acrobat, adding, 1011–1018
        CS programs, creating PDFs from, 1018–1019
        encryption levels, 1010
        permissions, 1010
        signature handlers, 1010
drop shadows, 507
droplet, 598–599
DTD, loading, 992

dynamic preference adjustments, 82
dynamic text editing
   described, 758
   PDF documents, 759–763

E

editing
   actions and commands, Photoshop and Illustrator
      Actions automating tasks, 596
   artwork, Photoshop and Illustrator, 903
   CS2 Administration Web pages, 292–294
   CSS, 938–939
   images in Photoshop
      Color Replacement tool, 410
      cropping, 43–44, 408–409
      described, 40
      distortions, correcting, 42–43
      Eraser tool, 411
      Healing Brush and Patch tools, 409
      levels and contrast, adjusting, 41–42
      Spot Healing Brush, 410
      Spot Healing tool, 44–45
      Stamp tools, 409
   masking layers, 564–565
   objects in Illustrator
      blending, 375–377
      clipping mask, 377
      compound paths and shapes, 374–375
      cutting objects, 373
      Envelope distortion, 379–380
      grids, splitting into, 373
      Liquefy distortion, 377–379
      paths, 371–372
      Reshape tools, 370–371
      simplifying and cleaning up paths, 372–373
      Smooth and Erase tools, 369–370
   paths in Live Paint, 333
   pop-up notes, 863
   sequences for batch-processing PDF files, 606–608
   source image for Smart Objects in GoLive, 936
   symbols Illustrator, 361–362
   tables in InDesign
      cells, selecting, 773
      deleting rows and columns, 774
      inserting rows and columns, 773–774
      merging cells, 774
      splitting cells, 775
   text
      dynamic, 758
      PDF documents, 759–763
      Word document, 739
   XML data
      described, 1002–1003
      Outline Editor, 1003
      Outline or Layout editors, splitting, 1005
      Source Code Editor, 1004–1005
effects
   extruding objects, GoLive, 51–52
   Illustrator
      Convert to Shapes (Rectangle, Rounded
         Rectangle, or Ellipse), 502
      described, 495–496
      rasterizing, 496–497
      standard features, applying, 502
      Stylize (Feather, Scribble, and Angle), 503–504
      3-D objects, creating, 497–502
      Warp, 504–505
   InDesign
      corner effects, creating, 508
      drop shadows, 507
      feathering objects, 507
   layers, adding
      described, 558–560
      global lighting, adjusting, 560
      sample, 561–562
      scaling, 560
      turning effects into layers, 560
   3D Revolve effect, GoLive, 52–53
   type outlines and special effects (Illustrator),
      624–625
eliminating from searches, 978–979
e-mail, Acrobat review sessions, 35–37, 866–869
embedding
   color-managed workflows, 192–194
   linked images in InDesign layout, 910
encryption levels, DRM, 1010
Envelope distortion, 379–380
Erase tool, 369–370
Eraser tool, 411
Events manager, Photoshop and Illustrator scripts,
   601–602
Excel (Microsoft)
   GoLive tables, importing from, 785
   Illustrator charts, importing
      charts and diagrams, creating, 812
      creating, 811
      described, 810
      via Clipboard, 811, 812
   printing files, 834–835
   spreadsheets, using in InDesign, 778–783
   tables, importing, 769
Expand/Collapse lists in Tracker window, 871
exporting
   Acrobat review session comments
      to AutoCAD, 873
      to files, 873–874
      selected, 874
      to Word, 872–873
   data for Version Cue workspace, 277
   GoLive packaging to HTML, 949
   layers, Illustrator as CSS, 528–529
   to PDF
      InDesign slide presentations, 1149–1151
      print layout, preparing, GoLive, 66–67
   SVG files, 1122
   SWF files, 1110–1112
   Web hosting documents, 1084–1085
   Word text
      advantages, 748
      Clipboard, 749–751
      described, 731
      formatting, 749
      methods, 748
      purpose of, 747
      selecting text, 748–749
   XML files, 993–995, 999–1000

eXtensible Markup Language. *See* XML
external devices, searching, 983
external style sheet, creating, 940
Extract interface, Photoshop filters, 477–481
extracting images, Photoshop, 45–48
extruding objects
    GoLive, 51–52
    3-D objects, creating in Illustrator, 497–499
Eyedropper tools
    color, filling and stroking objects, 344–346
    Illustrator, 345
    InDesign, 346
    Photoshop, 344–345

F

faces, creating, 1033–1037
Feather effect, 503–504
feathering objects, 507
fibers filter, 468–470
file
    Bridge
        adding files to folders, 215
        batch renaming, 221–223
        collections, 220–221
        context menus, 218–219
        deleting files, 216
        Favorites, adding, 221
        labeling files, 216–218
        types, associating, 84–85
        to Version Cue, 57
    commercial printing, analyzing for suitability
        batches, 1231
        described, 1225–1226
        new profile, creating, 1228–1230
        PDF/A-compliant file, producing, 1228
        PDF/X-compliant file, producing, 1226–1228
        reports and comments, 1231
    exporting to XML, 993–995
    handling, preferences for
        Illustrator, 97–98
        InDesign, 120–123
        Photoshop, 103–104
    help, 159–161
    opening with bookmarks, 1061–1065
    Organizer pane, 300–302
    quick cleanup, documents, searching, 235–236
    size, reducing for downloadable documents, 952–953
    structure, PDFs, preparing for indexing, 965–966
    Version Cue
        adding, 288
        alternates, 288–289
        from Bridge, 57
        deleting, 290
        opening, 285–286, 290
        project, creating, 284–285
        remote projects, accessing, 285
        saving, 286–287, 290
        states, 287–288
        versions, working with, 288
    viewing from different folders, 236–237
    XML, exporting, 999–1000

File Browser. *See* Bridge
File Transfer Protocol (FTP)
    browsing files, 1081–1082
    Web hosting documents, HTTP versus, 1074
fills
    alternating table, 776
    color
        CMYK mode, 341
        Color Picker, 343–344
        described, 337
        Eyedropper tools, 344–346
        gamut, 343
        Grayscale mode, 341
        hexadecimal numbers, 340
        HSB mode, 340–341
        palette, 341–343
        profiles and settings, 346–347
        RGB mode, 338, 339
        spot versus process, 342
        Web Safe mode, 338–339
    gaps, managing, 334
    gradients
        angle, specifying, 349
        custom, creating and applying, 349–352
        meshes, creating, 352–353
        palette, 347–349
    graphic styles, 365
    Illustrator
        applying, 329–331
        colors, applying to objects, 325–326
        corners, 327
        Dashed Line, 328–329
        symbols, 360–363
        thickness inside or outside, 327–328
        weights, 326–327
    InDesign
        applying, 329–331
        colors, applying to objects, 325–326
        corners, 327
        Dashed Line, 328–329
        object styles palette, 363–364
        tables, altering, 778
        thickness inside or outside, 327–328
        weights, 326–327
    layers
        opacity and blending mode, 553
        Photoshop, 563
    libraries of content, 367–368
    Live Paint, 331–336
    patterns
        described, 353
        Illustrator, 354–355
        Photoshop, 355–356
    Photoshop
        layers, 563
        path, 337
        patterns, 355–356
        pixel selection, 336–337
        Preset Manager, 368–369
    snippets, exporting, 368
    swatches
        described, 365
        libraries, creating custom, 366

palette, 366
  sharing between CS2 applications, 366–367
transparency
  blending modes, 357–358
  objects and images, 356
  opacity, 358–360
filters
  Acrobat review session comments, 874–875
  Illustrator
    Colors, 491–492
    Crop Marks and Object Mosaic, 492–493
    described, 491
    Distort, 493–494
    Stylize, 494–495
  Photoshop
    blending, 490
    blurring, 459–463
    categories, 455
    clouds, fibers, and lighting effects (Render filters), 468–470
    custom, 475–477
    described, 453
    with dialog boxes, 458–459
    distorting images, 463–465
    Extract interface, 477–481
    gallery, 454, 456–458
    in Illustrator, 490–491
    Lighting Effects, 470–473
    Liquify interface, 482–486
    noise, adding to image, 465–466
    noise and JPEG artifacts, removing, 466–467
    Offset, 476
    Pixelate, 467–468
    Preview pane, 455
    settings, 455–456
    sharp color changing edges, 476
    sharpening images, 473–474
    Stylize, 474–475
    third-party, 477
    Video, 475
  SVG files, creating in Illustrator, 1118–1121
Flash files. *See* SWF files
flattening layers, 527, 543–544, 585–586
flipping objects, 432
flower, creating sample, 430–431
folder
  Bridge
    adding files, 215
    batch renaming, 221–223
    collections, 220–221
    context menus, 218–219
    creating new folders, 214
    Favorites, adding, 221
    navigating folders, 215–216
  Version Cue workspace, specifying, 276–277
  viewing files from different, 236–237
Font Book, Macintosh, 620
FontAgent Pro, Macintosh
  auto-loading fonts, 622
  described, 620–622
  features, 622
  testing, 622
  workspace, 623

fonts
  described, 615
  downloadable document settings, 955–956
  formats, 615–617
  installing
    in MacOS X, 618–619
    in Windows, 619
  licenses, 618
  management
    Font Book, 620
    FontAgent Pro, 620–623
  OpenType, 29–30, 617–618
  organizing, 619–620
  type, converting to outlines
    InDesign, 631–634
    Photoshop, 628–630
  type outlines and special effects, Illustrator
    converting, 624
    described, 623–624
    effects, creating, 624–625
    masks, creating, 625
    raster, converting to vector type, 626–628
  Word document, missing, 729–730
footers, InDesign tables, 772–773
formatting
  exporting Word text, 749
  GoLive table cells, 786
  tables in InDesign
    aligning cell content, 778
    alternating fills, 776
    alternating strokes, 775–776
    cell row and column dimensions, 776–777
    dialog box, 775
    evenly distributing rows and columns, 777
    strokes and fills, altering, 778
    tagged tables, exporting, 778
  Word document, maintaining, 728–729
frames
  adding to text thread, 689–690
  anchoring objects in layout, 913–914
  columns and insets, creating, 691–695
  GoLive, threading text across multiple, 63–65
  InDesign
    layout, 900–901
    tables, running between, 772
  master pages
    autoflowing text, 699–700
    described, 696–697
    manual, creating, 697–699
    modifying, 700–702
  text attributes, setting, 695–696
  threads, working with, 687–688
  unthreading, 690
Free Transform tool
  Illustrator, 422–423
  Photoshop, 441–442
freehand curves (Paintbrush and Pencil tools), 312–314
FTP (File Transfer Protocol)
  browsing files, 1081–1082
  Web hosting documents, HTTP versus, 1074

Full Screen views
   interactivity
      described, 1163–1164
      links and buttons for cross-document linking, 1164
      remote-control device, 1164
   slide presentations
      in Acrobat, 1161
      described, 1160–1161
      interactivity, 1163–1164
      preferences, setting, 1162–1163
      scrolling pages, 1163

G

gallery, Photoshop filters
   opening, 454
   using, 456–458
gamut, 105, 343
global lighting, adjusting, 560
Glyphs palette
   custom sets, working in InDesign, 718–719
   described, 715–716
   inserting into text, 716–717
GoLive (Adobe)
   described, 20–24
   HTML, exporting packaged, 75–76
   keyboard shortcuts, 172–173
   layers
      adding to Web page, 572–573
      animating, 576, 578–582
      attributes, editing, 574–575
      background, 575–576
      CSS described, 571
      described, 512
      document, opening with Layers tab, 587
      importing Photoshop images, 582–583
      initial visibility, setting, 585
      interactive buttons, adding, 587–589
      listing, 585
      merging and flattening, 585–586
      palette, 573–574
      properties, setting, 586
      showing and hiding InDesign, 583–584
      steps creating, 576–578
   Mac, desktop printers, selecting on, 1171–1172
   objects, creating, 320
   packaging
      contents, examining, 945–946
      dragging and dropping assets, 947–949
      exporting to HTML, 949
      InDesign document, 944–945
      viewing package, 946–947
      Web hosting, 73–74
   pages, creating
      adding pages and using views, 925–927
      Basic Objects and images, 931
      described, 924–925
      linking pages, 930
      objects, adding, 928–929
      properties, changing object, 929
      steps to build sample, 931–933
      text, adding, 930
      Web page tools, 927–928
   palettes and workspaces, 151–152
   preferences, 127
   SWF and SVG files
      Illustrator Smart Objects, 1131–1132
      objects, adding to Web page, 1129–1131
      steps, 1132–1134
   tables
      creating, 784
      formatting cells, 786
      importing from Word or Excel, 769, 785
      merging cells, 786–787
      moving, adding, and deleting rows and columns, 785
      populating cells, 784–785
      resizing cells, 786
      selecting cells, 785
      styles, 786
   text, exporting to Word, 749–750
   tool options, 147
   transforming objects, position and size, palette showing, 433–434
   user interfaces, 135–136
   Windows, desktop printers, selecting on, 1174
   Word
      document, moving to, 744
      tables, importing, 769
   XML, viewing and editing
      described, 1002–1003
      Outline Editor, 1003
      Outline or Layout editors, splitting, 1005
      Source Code Editor, 1004–1005
   Z-index value, stacking order, 446
gradients
   angle, specifying, 349
   custom, creating and applying, 349–352
   meshes, creating in Illustrator, 352–353
   palette, 347–349
Graph tool, 792–793
graphic styles
   Illustrator
      creating, 677–679
      described, 676–677
      filling and stroking objects, 365
   InDesign, 682–685
   Photoshop, 365, 680–681
graphics
   anchoring
      objects, 912–913
      text, 914–916
   print setups
      Illustrator, 1180–1183
      InDesign, 1196–1197
   text wraps, Illustrator, 703–706
graphs, Illustrator
   column width, increasing, 796
   creating sample, 807–809
   creating with Graph tool, 792–793
   customizing sample, 809–810
   data changes, applying, 796
   data, entering, 793
   data set, assigning to different graph type, 800
   designs, using, 801–807
   importing data, 794–795

options, changing, 797–799
parts, selecting, 801
positioning data, 795–796
shading, changing, 801
text, changing, 801
type, changing, 797
types, 789–792
value and category axes, setting, 799
Value Axis scale, changing, 800
Grayscale mode, 341
grids
    editing objects in Illustrator, 373
    Illustrator preferences, 92–94
    InDesign
        layout, 897–898
        preferences, 113
    palette layers, 574
    Photoshop preferences, 106–107
Group Selection and Magic Wand tools, selecting objects in Illustrator, 321–322
groups
    layers, creating, 542–543
    objects in Illustrator and InDesign, 324
    palettes and workspaces, 154–156
    stacking order, 446
guides
    Illustrator preferences, 92–94
    InDesign
        layers, 517
        layout, 898–900
        preferences, 114–116
    Photoshop preferences, 106–107

H

handouts, InDesign slide presentations, 1151–1154
HDR images, 262–263, 390–391
headers, InDesign tables, 772–773
Healing Brush and Patch tools, 409
help resources
    files, 159–161
    online, 162
    updates, 162
hexadecimal color numbers, 340
hiding and locking
    layers, 514
    objects in Illustrator and InDesign, 324
hiding InDesign layers, 583–584
hiding InDesign master pages, 894
High Pass filters, 476
highlights, image auto adjustments, 389–390
HSB (hue, saturation, and balance) mode, 340–341
HTML (HyperText Markup Language)
    GoLive packaging, exporting to, 949
    packaged, exporting with GoLive, 75–76
    PDF documents, converting, CD/DVD distribution, 1091
hyperlinks
    Acrobat
        adding, 1037–1041
        bookmarks, 1061
        described, 1033
        duplicating, 1041–1043

        faces, creating in Illustrator, 1033–1037
        icon appearances, 1033
        type characters, 1038
        URL links, 1041–1043
    buttons, adding to GoLive layers, 587–589
    described, 1029–1030, 1060
    Full Screen views, 1164
    InDesign
        benefits and limitations, 1030
        bookmarks, 1060
        creating new, 1032
        destination, specifying, 1031
        layout information and relinking, viewing, 909
        managing, 1031
        testing, 1032
    interactive documents, described, 1029–1030
    opening files using bookmarks, 1061–1065
HyperText Markup Language. *See* HTML
hyphenation, 96

I

icons, 1033
Illustrator (Adobe)
    Actions palette automating tasks
        batch-processing actions, 597–598
        creating and saving new action set, 593
        creating new actions, 593–594
        deleting actions and commands, 597
        described, 591–592
        dialog boxes, appearing, 596
        droplet, creating, 598–599
        editing actions and commands, 596
        menu items, inserting, 595
        objects, selecting as part of action, 594
        paths, adding to action, 594
        playing action, 592–593
        rearranging actions and commands, 596
        steps creating action, 599–600
        stop, adding with comments, 595–596
    background object, creating, 49–51
    character styles, 665–667
    chart and graph types, 789–792
    charts, importing from Excel and Word
        charts and diagrams, creating, 812
        creating, 811
        described, 810
        transporting diagrams via Clipboard, 812
        transporting via Clipboard, 811
    color, Eyedropper tools, 345
    described, 12–15
    documents
        moving with Export Menu, 752–753
        packaging for commercial printing, 1232–1233
    editing objects
        blending, 375–377
        clipping mask, 377
        compound paths and shapes, 374–375
        cutting objects, 373
        Envelope distortion, 379–380
        grids, splitting into, 373
        Liquefy distortion, 377–379

Continued

Illustrator (Adobe), editing objects *(continued)*
    paths, 371–372
        Reshape tools, 370–371
        simplifying and cleaning up paths, 372–373
        Smooth and Erase tools, 369–370
    effects
        Convert to Shapes (Rectangle, Rounded Rectangle, or Ellipse), 502
        described, 495–496
        extruding objects, 51–52
        rasterizing, 496–497
        standard features, applying, 502
        Stylize (Feather, Scribble, and Angle), 503–504
        3-D, 52–53, 497–502
        Warp, 504–505
    filling and stroking objects
        applying, 329–331
        colors, applying to objects, 325–326
        corners, 327
        Dashed Line, 328–329
        described, 360
        thickness inside or outside, 327–328
        weights, 326–327
    filters
        Colors, 491–492
        Create (Crop Marks and Object Mosaic), 492–493
        described, 491
        Distort, 493–494
        Stylize, 494–495
    fonts, described, 623–624
    gradient meshes, creating, 352–353
    graphic styles, 365, 676–679
    graphs
        column width, increasing, 796
        creating sample, 807–809
        creating with Graph tool, 792–793
        customizing sample, 809–810
        data changes, applying, 796
        data, entering, 793
        data set, assigning to different graph type, 800
        designs, using, 801–807
        importing data, 794–795
        options, changing, 797–799
        parts, selecting, 801
        positioning data, 795–796
        shading, changing, 801
        text, changing, 801
        type, changing, 797
        value and category axes, setting, 799
        Value Axis scale, changing, 800
    inserting, editing, and creating symbols, 361–362
    keyboard shortcuts, customizing, 163–164
    layers
        appearance attributes, applying, 529–531
        clipping masks, 535–539
        collecting, 527
        described, 511, 521
        exporting as CSS, 528–529
        flattening artwork, 527
        palette view, changing, 522
        Photoshop compositions, 527–528, 570–571
        printing and previewing, 523–524
        releasing items to, 527
        sublayers, 522–523
        templates, creating, 524–525
        tracing, 525–526, 531–534
    link and button faces, creating, 1033–1037
    Live Paint
        editing paths, 333
        fill gaps, managing, 334
        objects, converting to, 331–332
        paths, adding, 333
        releasing and expanding, 334
        tools, 332–333
        working with, 335–336
    Live Trace, bitmap images, tracing, 48–49
    Mac, desktop printers, selecting on, 1171
    objects, creating
        Drawing tools overview, 307–308
        freehand curves (Paintbrush and Pencil tools), 312–314
        lines and shapes (Line Segment and Rectangle tools), 311–312
        Pen tool, 308–311
        Type tool, 311
    opening and editing artwork, 903
    organizing objects
        grouping, 324
        hiding and locking, 324
        layers, adding to, 323–324
    palettes and workspaces, 149–150
    paragraph styles
        applying, 670
        new, creating, 668–670
        overrides, 670
    Pathfinder, 374–375
    patterns, 354–355
    Photoshop filters, 490–491
    placing text documents in, 732
    preferences
        black, appearance of, 98–99
        custom colors, adding, 94–95
        described, 87–88
        File Handling & Clipboard, 97–98
        General options, 88–89
        Guides and Grid, 92–94
        hyphenation, 96
        legacy files, converting, 89
        Plug-Ins and Scratch Disks, 97
        Smart Guides and Slices, 95–96
        Type, 90–91
        Units and Display Performance, 91–92
    print setups
        color management, 1183
        described, 1175–1176
        device settings, 1185–1186
        General settings, 1176–1177
        Graphics, 1180–1183
        marks and bleeds, 1178–1179
        non-PostScript printers, 1184–1185
        output, 1179–1180
        settings, summary of, 1184
        Setup, 1177–1178
        transparency flattening and bitmap conversion, 1183–1184
    raster, converting to vector type, 626–628

rasterizing objects, 396–399
scripts automating tasks
　　described, 600–601
　　Events manager, 601–602
selecting objects
　　Group Selection and Magic Wand tools, 321–322
　　Layers palette, 322
　　Select menu, 323
slide presentations, creating, 1155–1157
Smart Objects, SWF and SVG files in GoLive, 1131–1132
soft-proofing documents on monitor
　　described, 1212–1213
　　managing presets, 1214
　　transparency flattening, 1213–1214
SVG files, creating in
　　advanced options, 1124–1125
　　described, 1117–1118
　　exporting issues, 1122
　　filters, 1118–1121
　　interactivity, 1121–1122
　　options, specifying, 1123–1124
　　Save for Web window, 1125–1126
　　steps, 1126–1128
　　versions, saving with different, 1122
SWF files, creating in
　　animations with layers, 1114–1115
　　described, 1109
　　differences in files, 1114
　　exporting, 1110–1112
　　Save for Web window, 1112–1113
　　steps, 1115–1117
　　symbols, 1115
symbols, 360–363
text, exporting to Word, 749–750
text wraps
　　around images, 707–709
　　described, 702–703
　　graphic objects, 703–706
　　type objects, 706–707
3-D objects, creating
　　extruding, 497–499
　　mapping artwork, 500
　　revolving objects, 500–502
　　rotating objects, 502
tool options, 137–144
transforming objects
　　array of objects, creating, 426–427
　　described, 413–414
　　flower, creating sample, 430–431
　　Free Transform tool, 422–423
　　moving, 414–415
　　patterns, 434–435
　　position and size, palette showing, 432–433
　　Reflect tool, 420–421
　　Rotate tool, 418–419
　　rotating, 416
　　rotating patterns, 435–436
　　Scale tool, 419–420
　　scaling and reflecting, 416–418
　　Shear tool, 421–422
　　snapping, 415
　　steps, 423–425
　　Transform Each dialog box, 429–430
　　Transform menu commands, 425–426
type outlines and special effects, 624–625
user interfaces, 132–134
vector objects onto pixel images, 399–403
Windows, desktop printers, selecting on, 1172–1173
Word document, opening in, 731–732
Word tables, importing, 766–769
Image Processor, Photoshop, 260–262
images
　　aligning and distributing, layers, Photoshop, 542
　　auto adjustments, shadows and highlights, 389–390
　　digital camera
　　　　Camera Raw plug-in, 384
　　　　Lens Correction filter, 385–386
　　　　red eye, correcting, 385
　　downloadable document settings, 955
　　editing in Photoshop
　　　　Color Replacement tool, 410
　　　　cropping, 408–409
　　　　Eraser tool, 411
　　　　Healing Brush and Patch tools, 409
　　　　Spot Healing Brush, 410
　　　　Stamp tools, 409
　　HDR images, 390–391
　　Illustrator
　　　　rasterizing objects, 396–399
　　　　vector objects onto pixel images, 399–403
　　InDesign layout
　　　　importing, 901–903
　　　　viewing (Links palette), 907–908
　　levels, adjusting, 387–388
　　painting, in Photoshop, 391–395
　　pixels, selecting in Photoshop
　　　　color range, 406–407
　　　　drawn paths, converting into selections, 408
　　　　modifying selection, 407
　　　　Selection tools, 403–406
　　　　transforming selections, 408
　　scanning in Photoshop, 381–383
　　text wraps, Illustrator, 707–709
　　tonal range, adjusting with Curves dialog box, 388–389
　　transparency, 356
importing
　　content, InDesign, 60–62
　　data to Illustrator graphs, 794–795
　　document styles from Word
　　　　deleting, 739
　　　　described, 738–739
　　　　editing, 739
　　　　mapping to InDesign styles, 740
　　files layers, InDesign, 520
　　Photoshop images, layers, GoLive, 582–583
　　SWF files in PDF documents, 1136–1139
　　tables
　　　　from Excel, 769
　　　　GoLive, 769
　　　　Illustrator, 766–769
　　　　InDesign, 766, 769–770
　　　　from Word, 765–766

Continued

importing *(continued)*
  tagged XML content, 995–996
  text from Word
    drag and drop text files, 734
    formatting in Photoshop, 736
    Illustrator, opening in, 731–732
    in InDesign, 740–743
    pasting in Acrobat, 736–737
    pasting in Acrobat notes and form fields, 738
    in Photoshop, 735–736
    placing documents in InDesign, 732–734
    placing text documents in Illustrator, 732
  text wraps, InDesign, 709–711
  Word or Excel tables, 785
  XML, 1000–1002
increments, InDesign preferences, 112–113
independent artists, production workflows
  described, 178–180
  designs, modifying, 180
  extending workflow, 180–181
InDesign (Adobe)
  aligning objects, 448–449
  bookmarks, 1060
  character styles
    applying, 668
    new, creating, 667–668
  color, Eyedropper tools, 346
  content, importing, 60–62
  described, 15–19
  documents
    GoLive packaging, 944–945
    moving with Export Menu, 753–754
    packaging for commercial printing, 1233
  drawing tools overview, 314–315
  editing tables
    cells, selecting, 773
    deleting rows and columns, 774
    inserting rows and columns, 773–774
    merging cells, 774
    splitting cells, 775
  effects
    corner effects, creating, 508
    drop shadows, 507
    feathering objects, 507
  Excel
    spreadsheets, steps using, 778–783
    tables, importing, 769–770
  filling and stroking objects
    applying, 329–331
    colors, applying to objects, 325–326
    corners, 327
    Dashed Line, 328–329
    thickness inside or outside, 327–328
    weights, 326–327
  formatting tables
    aligning cell content, 778
    alternating fills, 776
    alternating strokes, 775–776
    cell row and column dimensions, 776–777
    dialog box, 775
    evenly distributing rows and columns, 777
    strokes and fills, altering, 778
    tagged tables, exporting, 778
  frame
    importing Illustrator artwork and PDF files, 902–903
    importing Photoshop artwork, 902
  graphic styles, 682–685
  keyboard shortcuts, 170–172
  layers
    described, 511
    guides, 517
    importing files, 520
    Master objects, reordering above, 518
    page numbers, displaying in front of other elements, 518–520
    palette, condensing, 517
    Photoshop compositions, 527–528, 570–571
    text wrap, suppressing on hidden layers, 517–518
    transparency and blending modes, applying, 520–521
  layout
    anchoring objects, 911–916
    CS2 documents, exporting to CS, 889
    display quality, setting, 910–911
    embedding linked images, 910
    frames, 900–901
    grids, 897–898
    guides, 898–900
    images and objects, importing, 901–903
    images, viewing (Links palette), 907–908
    inserting, deleting, and rearranging pages, 891–892
    layers, 894–895
    link information and relinking, viewing, 909
    master pages, 892–894
    new documents, creating, 883–886
    original artwork, editing and locating, 908
    Pages, viewing all, 889–890
    placed image files, relinking, 909–910
    preset document, 886–888
    Quark and PageMaker files, converting, 889
    rulers, 897
    selecting and targeting pages and spreads, 891
    settings, changing, 888–889
    steps creating sample, 58–60, 903–906
  links and buttons
    benefits and limitations, 1030
    creating new, 1032
    destination, specifying, 1031
    managing, 1031
    testing, 1032
Mac, desktop printers, selecting on, 1170
master pages, 62–63, 894
object styles palette, 363–364
organizing objects
  grouping, 324
  hiding and locking, 324
  layers, adding to, 323–324
page numbering
  automatic, 896
  sections, defining, 896–897
palettes and workspaces, 151–152
paragraph styles, 670–671
Pathfinder, 375

placing documents in, 732–734
preferences
    autocorrect, 117–118
    composition, 112
    described, 108–109
    dictionary, 116–117
    display performance, 119–120
    file handling, 120–123
    General options, 109–110
    grids, 113
    guides and pasteboard, 114–116
    path, copying and pasting text on, 123–125
    spelling, 117
    story editor display, 118–119
    type, 110–112
    units and increments, 112–113
    updates, 125
print layout, preparing, 65–67
print setups
    Color Management, 1197–1198
    dialog box, 1191
    General options, 1192
    Graphics pane, 1196–1197
    marks, 1193
    OPI management and transparency flattening, 1198–1199
    output options, 1194–1195
    paper size, scaling and tiling options, 1192–1193
    summary dialog box, 1199
rotating and flipping objects, 432
showing and hiding GoLive layers, 583–584
slide presentations, creating
    bookmarks, 1147–1149
    described, 1147
    exporting to PDF, 1149–1151
    notes and handouts, 1151–1154
soft-proofing documents on monitor
    separations, previewing, 1211–1212
    transparency flattening, 1208–1211
styles, mapping Word styles to, 740
tables, 771–773
text, exporting to Word, 751
text wraps, 709–713
threading text across multiple frames, 63–65
tool options, 144–147
Toolbox tools, selecting objects, 321
transforming objects, 428–429, 438–440
type, converting to outlines, 631–634
user interfaces, 132–134
Windows, desktop printers, selecting on, 1172–1173
XML
    described, 987–988
    DTD, loading, 992
    files, exporting, 993–995, 999–1000
    importing, 989, 1000–1002
    information, adding to tag (attributes), 991
    layouts, creating, 996–997
    new, creating, 988
    rearranging tags, 991
    selecting, adding, and deleting elements, 989–990
    styles, creating from, 988–989
    tagged content, importing, 995–996
    tagging documents, 997–999
    validating structure, 992–993
    viewing all tags (Structure pane), 989
indexing
    Acrobat Catalog, 972–974
    document descriptions (metadata), 963–964
    PDFs
        creating from media storage, 980–983
        described, 972–973
        eliminating from searches, 978–979
        existing, 973
        legacy files, 973–974
        loading files, 976–978
        names, finding, 979–980
        rebuilding, 974
        searching, 980
        from secure documents, 974
        stopping, 973
initial views, preferences for opening downloadable documents, 958–961
initial visibility, GoLive layers, 585
inline graphics, creating, 723
inserting
    pages for InDesign layout, 891–892
    rows and columns
        GoLive tables, 785
        InDesign tables, 773–774
    special characters into text, 716–717
    special typographic characters, 719–722
    symbols in Illustrator, 361–362
insets, text frame, 691–695
installing fonts
    in MacOS X, 618–619
    in Windows, 619
interactive documents
    animation
        Illustrator, 1043
        InDesign and Acrobat, 1045–1048
        Photoshop, 1043–1045
    hyperlinks
        Acrobat, 1033–1043, 1061
        described, 1029–1030, 1060
        InDesign, 1030–1032, 1060
    multimedia
        Acrobat, 1055–1059
        InDesign, 1048–1050
        interactive buttons, creating, 1050–1055
    on demand, creating
        code, understanding, 1069
        described, 1065–1066
        JavaScript content, 1066–1069
        scripts, running, 1069–1072
interactivity
    Full Screen views
        cross-document links and buttons, 1164
        described, 1163–1164
        remote-control device, 1164
        slide presentations, 1163–1164
    SVG files, creating in Illustrator, 1121–1122
interfaces. *See* user interfaces
Internet access, setting up, 1073–1074, 1075

J

JavaScript
  batch-processing PDF files, 609–612
  on demand documents, 1066–1069
JPEG artifacts, removing, 466–467

K

keyboard shortcuts
  Acrobat, 173–174
  GoLive, 172–173
  Illustrator, customizing, 163–164
  InDesign, 170–172
  Photoshop, 167–170
  workgroups, 164–167
knockout, 554, 556–558

L

labeling files, Bridge, 216–218
labels, Bridge preferences, 84
Lasso pixel selection tools, 405
layers
  Acrobat, described, 511
  CS2 applications
    copying objects between, 514–515
    creating, 513
    deleting, 515
    dividing document into layers, 516
    document, creating, 515–516
    duplicating, 515
    hiding and locking, 514
    merging, 515
    palette, described, 512
    rearranging, 514
    selecting and targeting, 513–514
  effects, adding
    described, 558–560
    global lighting, adjusting, 560
    sample, 561–562
    scaling, 560
    turning effects into layers, 560
  GoLive
    adding to Web page, 572–573
    animating, 576, 578–582
    attributes, editing, 574–575
    background, 575–576
    CSS described, 571
    described, 512
    document, opening with Layers tab, 587
    importing Photoshop images, 582–583
    initial visibility, setting, 585
    interactive buttons, adding, 587–589
    listing, 585
    merging and flattening, 585–586
    palette, 573–574
    properties, setting, 586
    showing and hiding InDesign, 583–584
    steps creating, 576–578
  Illustrator
    adding to objects, 323–324
    appearance attributes, applying, 529–531
    clipping masks, 535–539
    collecting, 527
    described, 511, 521
    exporting as CSS, 528–529
    flattening artwork, 527
    palette view, changing, 522
    Photoshop, importing, 527–528
    printing and previewing, 523–524
    releasing items to, 527
    sublayers, 522–523
    templates, creating, 524–525
    tracing, 525–526, 531–534
  InDesign
    adding to objects, 323–324
    creating new, 894–895
    described, 511
    guides, 517
    importing files, 520
    Master objects, 518, 895
    page numbers, displaying in front of other elements, 518–520
    palette, condensing, 517
    text wrap, suppressing on hidden layers, 517–518
    transparency and blending modes, applying, 520–521
  masking
    creating, 564
    editing, 564–565
    removing, 565
    steps, 565–566
    vector, creating, 565
  opacity and blending mode
    advanced options, 555–556
    dialog box, 553
    fill, setting, 553
    knockout, creating, 554, 556–558
  palette, converting to grids, 574
  Photoshop
    adjustment and fill, 563
    Auto Selecting with Move tool, 542
    background, 541
    compositions, 568–571
    described, 511, 539–540
    effects and styles palette, 506–507
    groups, creating, 542–543
    images, aligning and distributing, 542, 544–546
    linking, 543
    locking transparency, pixels, and position, 547
    logo, creating sample, 551–552
    masking, 564–566
    merging and flattening, 543–544
    multiple, selecting and controlling, 541
    opacity and blending mode, 553–558
    Shape, 550–551
    Smart objects, combining with, 566–567
    Type, 548–550
  slide presentations, 1157–1159
  stacking order, 444–445
Layers palette, 322

layout
  anchoring objects
    described, 911
    graphics, 912–913
    graphics to text, 914–916
    text frames, 913–914
  GoLive, steps, 58–60
  InDesign
    CS2 documents, exporting to CS, 889
    frames, 900–901
    grids, 897–898
    guides, 898–900
    images and objects, importing, 901–903
    inserting, deleting, and rearranging pages, 891–892
    master pages, 892–894
    new documents, creating, 883–886
    Pages, viewing all, 889–890
    preset document, 886–888
    Quark and PageMaker files, converting, 889
    rulers, 897
    selecting and targeting pages and spreads, 891
    settings, changing, 888–889
  XML, creating, 996–997
Layout Editor, XML, 1005
legacy files
  converting in Illustrator, 89
  indexing PDFs, 973–974
Lens Correction filter, 385–386
levels and contrast, adjusting image, 41–42
libraries
  ASPS stock photos, 242
  exchanging, Stamp tool for review sessions, 857–858
  filling and stroking objects, 367–368
  managing, Stamp tool for review sessions, 857
  swatches, creating custom, 366
  symbols Illustrator, accessing, 361
licenses, font, 618
lighting, adjusting global, 560
Lighting Effects filter, 470–473
lighting effects, Photoshop, 468–470
lines, drawing
  Dashed Line, 328–329
  Line Segment and Rectangle tools, 311–312
linking layers, Photoshop, 543
links. *See* hyperlinks
Liquify distortion, Illustrator, 377–379
Liquify filter, Photoshop, 482–486
listing layers, GoLive, 585
Live Paint (Adobe)
  editing paths, 333
  fill gaps, managing, 334
  objects, converting to, 331–332
  paths, adding, 333
  releasing and expanding, 334
  tools, 332–333
  working with, 335–336
Live Trace, 48–49
locking transparency, pixels, and position, 547
logo, creating sample, 551–552
low-resolution images, downloading, 243–246

M
Macintosh
  custom page sizes, creating, printing Word documents, 819–821
  desktop printers, selecting on
    described, 1169
    Illustrator, 1171
    InDesign, 1170
    Photoshop, GoLive, and Acrobat, 1171–1172
  Font Book, 620
  fonts, installing in MacOS X, 618–619
  PDFs, creating for CD/DVD distribution, 1103–1104
  PowerPoint slides, converting to PDF, 1142–1145
Magic Wand (color matching) pixel selection tool, 405
Manage Stamps command, 857
management paradigm, production workflow standards, 185–186
mapping artwork, 3-D objects, 500
marking comments, 863
marks
  Acrobat print setups, 1202
  Illustrator print setups, 1178–1179
  InDesign print setups, 1193
  PDF documents for CD/DVD distribution, 1090–1091
Marquee (Rectangle, Ellipse, Single Row, and Single Column) pixel selection tools, 404
masking layers
  creating, 564
  editing, 564–565
  removing, 565
  steps, 565–566
  vector, creating, 565
masks, type
  converting to outlines in InDesign, 631–634
  outlines and special effects in Illustrator, 625
Master objects, InDesign
  positioning on top of document objects, 895
  reordering above layers, 518
master pages
  InDesign
    described, 62–63
    layout, 892–894
    overriding, detaching, deleting, and hiding, 894
  text frames
    autoflowing text, 699–700
    described, 696–697
    manual, creating, 697–699
    modifying, 700–702
media storage, indexing PDFs, 980–983
Memory and Image Cache preferences, Photoshop, 107
menu items, Photoshop and Illustrator, 595
merging
  cells
    GoLive tables, 786–787
    InDesign tables, 774
  layers
    described, 515
    GoLive, 585–586
    Photoshop, 543–544
meshes, creating in Illustrator, 352–353

metadata
    adding and viewing, Photoshop preferences, 101–103
    Bridge
        adding to PDFs before indexing, 964–965
        appending and replacing data, 228–230
        deleting templates, 230
        preferences, 84
        properties, 224–226
        template, creating, 227–228
        XMP templates, 226–227
    documents, searching, 233–235
    PDFs, adding, 1105
Microsoft. *See* Excel; PowerPoint; Windows; Word
mobile devices
    described, 940–941
    existing documents, converting to XHTML Mobile, 942–944
    new documents, creating, 941–942
moving
    between cells, InDesign tables, 771–772
    files in Bridge, 215
    objects in Illustrator, 414–415
    rows and columns in GoLive tables, 785
multimedia
    Acrobat
        compatibility settings, 1056–1058
        described, 1055–1056
        play buttons, creating, 1058–1059
        renditions, creating, 1058
    InDesign
        described, 1048
        movie options, 1048–1049
        sound options, 1049–1050
        interactive buttons, creating
            described, 1050–1051
            options and behavior, setting, 1051–1053
            states, setting, 1053–1055
            tab order, setting, 1055
multiple layers, selecting and controlling in Photoshop, 541
multiple pages, creating PDFs from, 1100–1101

N

names, indexing PDFs, 979–980
navigating
    Bridge folders, 215–216
    comments, 862
nested styles, 671–676
new documents
    layout, InDesign, 883–886
    mobile devices, creating, 941–942
new index file, Catalog, 966–969
new profile, preflighting file, 1228–1230
news, ASPS stock photos, 243
noise, image
    adding, 465–466
    removing, 466–467
Note tool, Acrobat review session
    described, 842
    managing, 843–846
    properties, 846–851
notes, InDesign slide presentation, 1151–1154

O

Object Linking and Embedding (OLE), 751
Object Mosaic filter, Illustrator, 492–493
objects
    Acrobat Professional creating and editing
        Article, Movie, Sound, TouchUp Text, and TouchUp Object tools, 318
        commenting objects, adding, 319
        selecting, 317
    data-driven graphics, binding variables to, 604
    GoLive
        custom shapes, specifying, 316
        drawing tools overview, 307–308, 314–315
        freehand curves (Paintbrush and Pencil tools), 312–314
        lines and shapes (Line Segment and Rectangle tools), 311–312
        painting with shapes, 317
        paths, 316–317
        Pen tool, 308–311
        tools overview, 315–316
        Type tool, 311
    InDesign
        layout, importing, 901–903
        styles, filling and stroking, 363–364
    Live Paint, 331–332
    selecting as part of action, Photoshop and Illustrator Actions automating tasks, 594
    SWF and SVG files in GoLive, 1129–1131
    transparency, 356
offers, ASPS stock photos, 243
Offset filters, Photoshop, 476
OLE (Object Linking and Embedding), 751
on demand documents, creating
    code, understanding, 1069
    described, 1065–1066
    JavaScript, dynamically creating content using, 1066–1069
    scripts, running, 1069–1072
online development resources, 192
online help, 162
opacity, 358–360, 553–558
Open and Save dialog boxes, 28–29
Open dialog box, 28–29
opening
    artwork in Photoshop and Illustrator, 903
    downloadable document preferences
        described, 957–958
        initial views, 958–961
        saving initial view, 961–962
    files with bookmarks, 1061–1065
    Organizer, 297–298
    Version Cue files, 285–286, 290
    Word files and moving to GoLive, 745
OpenType fonts
    advantages of, 29–30, 617–618
    type styles, Illustrator, 643–645
OPI management, InDesign print setups, 1198–1199
Options Bar, Photoshop type styles, 650–652
organization
    Acrobat tool, 205
    fonts, 619–620

Illustrator and InDesign objects
grouping, 324
hiding and locking, 324
layers, adding to, 323–324
Organizer (Adobe)
Categories pane, 298–300
Files pane, 300–302
opening, 297–298
Pages pane, 302
Web-hosted PDFs, bookmarking, 303–304
orientation, Type layers, 548–549
Outline Editor, XML, 1003, 1005
output
Illustrator print setups, 1179–1180
InDesign print setup options, 1194–1195
PDF options, CD/DVD distribution, 1091–1092
production workflow settings, 182–184
overprint preview, Acrobat, 1215–1217
overriding InDesign master pages, 894

P

page
layout, viewing all, 889–890
numbering
automatic, 896
layers, displaying in front of other elements, 518–520
sections, defining, 896–897
review session
note, adding, 850–851
Stamp tool, 852–854
transitions in slide presentations, 1159–1160
Web site, adding, 924
PageMaker (Adobe) files, converting, 889
Pages pane in Organizer, 302
Paint Bucket tool, Photoshop, 395
painting
GoLive, 312–314
Photoshop, 317, 391–395
palette
Acrobat, 153–154
color, filling and stroking objects, 341–343
condensing, layers, InDesign, 517
described, 147
gradients, 347–349
grouping, 154–156
Illustrator, 149–150
InDesign and GoLive, 151–152
layer, 506–507, 512, 573–574
object styles in InDesign, 363–364
Photoshop, 150–151
swatches, 366
view, changing, layers, Illustrator, 522
Window menus, 148
panes, managing, 212–213. *See also individual panes listed by name*
paper size, InDesign print setups, 1192–1193
paragraph
InDesign, 670–671
and point text, converting type, 549
styles, 668–671
type styles palette, 653, 660–663

Paste Special command, Word, 744
pasteboard, InDesign, 114–116
pasting Word document in Acrobat, 736–738
path
actions, adding to Photoshop and Illustrator, 594
compound, editing in Illustrator, 374–375
editing objects in Illustrator, 371–372
filling and stroking objects in Photoshop, 337
Live Paint, adding, 333
objects, creating in Photoshop, 316–317
text, copying and pasting in InDesign, 123–125
type styles, creating on, 663–665
Pathfinder
Illustrator, 374–375
InDesign, 375
paths, simplifying and cleaning up in Illustrator, 372–373
patterns
creating with Pattern Maker, 486–487
filling and stroking objects
described, 353
Illustrator, 354–355
Photoshop, 355–356
transforming objects
Illustrator, 434–435
Photoshop, 436–438
PDF (Portable Document Format)
CD/DVD distribution
Adobe PDF Settings, 1088
Advanced settings, 1092
common attributes, 1088–1090
Compression settings, 1090
format, benefits of using, 1087–1088
General options, 1090
HTML conversions, 1091
Marks and Bleeds settings, 1090–1091
Output options, 1091–1092
Security settings, 1092
steps, 1093–1098
Summary, 1093
CS programs, creating from, 1018–1019
dynamic text editing, 759–763
exporting, InDesign slide presentations, 1149–1151
importing SWF files in, 1136–1139
indexing, preparing for
adding metadata with Bridge, 964–965
described, 962
document descriptions (metadata), 963–964
file structure, 965–966
optimizing performance, 966
nonstandard page sizes, 821–824
rasterizing in GoLive, 830–834
Reader extensions, enabling, Acrobat review sessions, 863–866
slide presentations, converting to
Apple Keynote slides, 1146–1147
described, 1141–1142
PowerPoint slides, converting to PDF, 1142–1146
standard page sizes, 816–818
Web pages, converting to, SWF files in Acrobat, 1134–1136

PDF (Portable Document Format) Optimizer
   Acrobat Professional 7, 71–73
   downloadable documents
      auditing space usage, 953–954
      Clean Up settings, 956–957
      Discard Objects settings, 956
      font settings, 955–956
      image settings, 955
      scanned pages, 955
      transparency settings, 956
   Web hosting, 71–73
PDF/A-compliant file, producing, 1228
PDFMaker on Windows, 1145–1146
PDF/X file
   commercial printing and, 1234
   producing, 1226–1228
   spot-proofing, 69–71
Pen tool, Illustrator, 308–311
Pencil tool
   GoLive, 312–314
   Photoshop, 395
permissions, DRM, 1010
perspective, controlling, 442–443
Photomerge (Adobe), 263, 1098–1100
Photoshop (Adobe)
   aligning and distributing image layers, 449–451
   application commands, enabling
      batch processing with actions, 258–259
      contact sheets, creating, 260
      HDR, merging to, 262–263
      Image Processor, 260–262
      loading actions, 259–260
      PDF Presentation, 263
      Photomerge, 263
      Picture Package, 264
      services, 257–258
      Web Photo Gallery, 264
   artwork, importing into InDesign frame, 902
   automating tasks
      Automate menu command, 602
      batch-processing actions, 597–598
      creating new actions, 593–594
      deleting actions and commands, 597
      described, 591–592
      dialog boxes, appearing, 596
      droplet, creating, 598–599
      editing actions and commands, 596
      menu items, inserting, 595
      objects, selecting as part of action, 594
      paths, adding to action, 594
      playing action, 592–593
      rearranging actions and commands, 596
      scripts, 600–602
      steps creating action, 599–600
      stop, adding with comments, 595–596
   color, Eyedropper tools, 344–345
   cropping images, 408–409
   described, 9–11
   editing images
      cropping, 43–44
      described, 40
      distortions, correcting, 42–43
      levels and contrast, adjusting, 41–42
      Spot Healing Brush, 410
      Spot Healing tool, 44–45
   extracting images, 45–48
   filling and stroking objects
      path, 337
      pixel selection, 336–337
      Preset Manager, 368–369
   filters
      blending, 490
      blurring, 459–463
      categories, 455
      clouds, fibers, and lighting effects (Render filters), 468–470
      custom, 475–477
      described, 453
      with dialog boxes, 458–459
      distorting images, 463–465
      Extract interface, 477–481
      gallery, 454, 456–458
      in Illustrator, 490–491
      Lighting Effects, 470–473
      Liquify interface, 482–486
      noise, adding to image, 465–466
      noise and JPEG artifacts, removing, 466–467
      Offset, 476
      Pixelate, 467–468
      Preview pane, 455
      settings, 455–456
      sharp color changing edges (High Pass), 476
      sharpening images, 473–474
      Stylize, 474–475
      third-party, 477
      Video, 475
   graphic styles, 365, 680–681
   Healing Brush and Patch tools, 409
   images, importing to GoLive layers, 582–583
   keyboard shortcuts, 167–170
   layers
      adjustment and fill, 563
      Auto Selecting with Move tool, 542
      background, 541
      compositions, 568–570
      described, 511, 539–540
      effects, adding, 558–562
      effects and styles palette, 506–507
      groups, creating, 542–543
      images, aligning and distributing, 542, 544–546
      importing, 527–528
      linking, 543
      locking transparency, pixels, and position, 547
      logo, creating sample, 551–552
      masking, 564–566
      merging and flattening, 543–544
      multiple, selecting and controlling, 541
      opacity and blending mode, 553–558
      Shape, 550–551
      Smart objects, combining with, 566–567
      Type, 548–550
   Mac, desktop printers, selecting on, 1171–1172
   objects, creating
      custom shapes, specifying, 316
      painting with shapes, 317

paths, 316–317
    tools overview, 315–316
opening and editing artwork, 903
painting images
    Paintbrush tool, 391–395
    Pencil and Paint Bucket tool, 395
palettes and workspaces, 150–151
patterns, 355–356, 486–487
PDFs, creating for CD/DVD distribution
    multiple pages, 1100–1101
    Photomerge, 1098–1100
pixels, selecting
    building selection, 405–406
    color range, 406–407
    described, 403–404
    drawn paths, converting into selections, 408
    Lasso tools, 405
    Magic Wand (color matching), 405
    Marquee (Rectangle, Ellipse, Single Row, and Single Column), 404
    modifying selection, 407
    transforming selection, 408
preferences
    Display & Cursors, 104–105
    File Handling, 103–104
    General options, 99–101
    Guides, Grid, and Slices, 106–107
    Memory and Image Cache, 107
    metadata, 101–103
    Plug-Ins and Scratch Disks, 107
    Transparency & Gamut, 105
    type, 107–108
    Units & Rulers, 105–106
print setups, 1186–1191
retouching images
    Color Replacement tool, 410
    distorting, 411
    Eraser tool, 411
    Healing Brush and Patch tools, 409
    Spot Healing Brush, 410
    Stamp tools, 409
rotating and flipping objects, 432
scanning images, 381–383
selecting objects, Selection and Direct Selection tools, 322
slide presentations, creating, 1154–1155
Stamp tools, 409
styles, 667
text, exporting to Word, 749–750
tool options, 144
transforming objects
    described, 440
    Free Transform, 441–442
    patterns, 436–438
    perspective, 442–443
    pixels, moving, 441
    selection, 440
    Transform menu, 442
    Warp mode, 443–444
type, converting to outlines in, 628–630
user interfaces, 132–133, 134
vanishing point, controlling, 487–490

Windows, desktop printers, selecting on, 1174
Word document, 735–736
Picture Package, enabling Photoshop commands, 264
Pixelate, filters, Photoshop, 467–468
pixels
    locking, 547
    moving in Photoshop, 441
    selecting, filling and stroking objects, 336–337
    selection tools, Photoshop
        building selection, 405–406
        color range, 406–407
        described, 403–404
        drawn paths, converting into selections, 408
        Lasso tools, 405
        Magic Wand (color matching), 405
        Marquee (Rectangle, Ellipse, Single Row, and Single Column), 404
        modifying selection, 407
        transforming selection, 408
    vector objects onto, 399–403
placed image files, relinking, 909–910
placeholder type styles, InDesign, 657–660
playing automated task, Photoshop and Illustrator, 592–593
plug-ins
    camera raw files, 248–253
    CD/DVD distribution, 1104–1105
    Illustrator preferences, 97
    Photoshop preferences, 107
point text, converting between paragraph text, 549
point type styles, Illustrator, 638–641, 645–647
populating tables
    GoLive, 784–785
    InDesign, 771
pop-up notes, editing, 863
Portable Document Format. *See* PDF; PDF Optimizer
position
    data in Illustrator graphs, 795–796
    locking, 547
    palette showing
        GoLive, 433–434
        Illustrator, 432–433
PostScript print setup, 1204–1205
PowerPoint (Microsoft)
    converting slides to PDF
        described, 1142
        on Mac, 1142–1145
        PDFMaker on Windows, 1145–1146
    printing files
        described, 827–829
        rasterizing PDFs in GoLive, 830–834
preferences
    Acrobat Professional, 125–126
    application-specific, 80
    batch-processing PDF files, 608–609
    Bridge
        Adobe Stock Photos, 86–87
        Advanced settings, 85–86
        described, 82–83
        File Type Associations, 84–85
        General options, 83–84
        Metadata and Labels, 84

Continued

preferences *(continued)*
    camera raw files, 246–248
    common attributes, described, 79–80
    default, returning to, 81–82
    document-specific, 80–81
    dynamic adjustments, 82
    GoLive, 127
    Illustrator
        black, appearance of, 98–99
        custom colors, adding, 94–95
        described, 87–88
        File Handling & Clipboard, 97–98
        General options, 88–89
        Guides and Grid, 92–94
        hyphenation, 96
        legacy files, converting, 89
        Plug-Ins and Scratch Disks, 97
        Smart Guides and Slices, 95–96
        Type, 90–91
        Units and Display Performance, 91–92
    InDesign
        autocorrect, 117–118
        composition, 112
        described, 108–109
        dictionary, 116–117
        display performance, 119–120
        file handling, 120–123
        General options, 109–110
        grids, 113
        guides and pasteboard, 114–116
        path, copying and pasting text on, 123–125
        spelling, 117
        story editor display, 118–119
        type, 110–112
        units and increments, 112–113
        updates, 125
    Photoshop
        Display & Cursors, 104–105
        File Handling, 103–104
        General options, 99–101
        Guides, Grid, and Slices, 106–107
        Memory and Image Cache, 107
        metadata, 101–103
        Plug-Ins and Scratch Disks, 107
        Transparency & Gamut, 105
        type, 107–108
        Units & Rulers, 105–106
    Version Cue workspace, setting up, 275–276
preset document layout, 886–888
Preset Manager, Photoshop, 368–369
Preview pane, Photoshop filters, 455
previewing, layers, Illustrator, 523–524
print setup
    Acrobat
        color and screening output, 1201–1202
        dialog box, 1199–1201
        marks and bleeds, 1202
        PostScript devices, 1205
        PostScript Options, 1204–1205
        Transparency Flattening, 1202–1203
    desktop printers, selecting
        Macintosh, 1169–1172
        Windows, 1172–1175
    Illustrator options
        color management, 1183
        described, 1175–1176
        device settings, 1185–1186
        General settings, 1176–1177
        Graphics, 1180–1183
        marks and bleeds, 1178–1179
        output, 1179–1180
        Print as Bitmap, Overprints, and Preset transparency flattening and bitmap conversion, 1183–1184
        printing to non-PostScript printers, 1184–1185
        settings, summary of, 1184
        Setup, 1177–1178
    InDesign
        Color Management, 1197–1198
        dialog box, 1191
        exporting layout to PDF, 66–67
        General options, 1192
        Graphics pane, 1196–1197
        marks, 1193
        OPI management and transparency flattening, 1198–1199
        output options, 1194–1195
        paper size, scaling and tiling options, 1192–1193
        separations, previewing, 65–66
        summary dialog box, 1199
    Photoshop, 1186–1191
print setups, non-PostScript printers from Illustrator, 1184–1185
printing
    comments, 862
    composite color with calibrated profiles, 201–202
    Excel files, 834–835
    layers, Illustrator, 523–524
    to non-PostScript printers, Illustrator print setups, 1184–1185
    PowerPoint files
        described, 827–829
        rasterizing PDFs in GoLive, 830–834
    transparency flattening and bitmap conversion, Illustrator, 1183–1184
    Word documents
        converted files, printing in Acrobat, 824
        custom page sizes, 819–824
        described, 815–816
        standard page sizes, 816–818
        trim and crops, applying in Acrobat, 824–827
production workflows
    described, 177–178
    document repurposing, 182–184
    independent artists
        described, 178–180
        designs, modifying, 180
        extending workflow, 180–181
    standards
        management paradigm, 185–186
        tools, 184
        training time, 185
        vendors supporting tools, 184–185
    studios and production houses, 181–182
profiling color-managed workflows
    acquiring profiles, 191

calibrating color, 190
described, 189–190
embedding, 192–194
mismatching, 194–196
online development resources, 192
in workflows, 190
project files
  Bridge, accessing in, 58
  Version Cue, 284–285
  versioning, 54–56
publications
  bookmarks
    Acrobat, 1061
    InDesign, 1060
  opening files using bookmarks, 1061–1065
publish server, Web site, 1075–1076
purging data from downloadable documents, 974–975

Q

Quark files, converting, 889

R

raster objects
  converting to vector type, 626–628
  effects, 496–497
  Illustrator, 396–399
  PDFs, 830–834
Reader, Acrobat (Adobe)
  adding to CD/DVD, 1107
  review sessions, 863–866
Really Simple Syndication (RSS)
  feeds, accessing Tracker window review sessions, 871–872
  reading, 268–271
rearranging
  actions and commands in Photoshop and Illustrator Actions automated tasks, 596
  layers, 514
  pages in InDesign layout, 891–892
  XML tags, 991
red eye, correcting, 385
Reflect tool, 420–421
reflecting, objects in Illustrator, 416–418
remote projects, accessing, 285
remote-control device, 1164
removing. *See* deleting
Render filter, 468–470
replicating. *See* copying
reports, preflighting file, 1231
repurposing documents. *See also* downloadable documents
  described, 919
  mobile devices
    described, 940–941
    existing documents, converting to XHTML Mobile, 942–944
    new documents, creating, 941–942
  production workflows, 182–184
  Web hosting
    GoLive packaging, 73–74
    HTML, packaged, exporting with GoLive, 75–76
    PDF Optimizer, 71–73

Web sites, setting up
  adding pages, 924
  creating new, 920–923
  described, 919
  GoLive, creating pages in, 924–933
  updating pages, 924
  Welcome dialog box, 920
Reshape tools, 370–371
resizing cells, GoLive tables, 786
retouching images, Photoshop
  Color Replacement tool, 410
  distorting, 411
  Eraser tool, 411
  Healing Brush and Patch tools, 409
  Spot Healing Brush, 410
  Stamp tools, 409
review sessions, Acrobat
  Clipboard Image, pasting as Stamp tool, 858–859
  comment summaries, creating, 875–878
  commenting preferences, 839–842
  Comments pane
    deleting comments, 862–863
    described, 859–860
    editing pop-up notes, 863
    marking comments, 863
    navigating comments, 862
    printing comments, 862
    searching comments, 862
    sorting comments, 861
    status, setting, 863
    viewing comments, 860–861
  comparing documents, 878–880
  described, 839
  Drawing Markup tools, 859
  e-mail, 35–37, 866–869
  exporting comments
    to AutoCAD, 873
    to files, 873–874
    to Word, 872–873
  filtering comments, 874–875
  note, adding to page, 542–851
  PDFs with Reader extensions, enabling, 863–866
  Properties bar, viewing, 850–851
  Stamp tool
    adding to page, 852–854
    custom, creating, 854–856
    libraries, 857–858
    Manage Stamps command, 857
    properties, changing, 854
    selecting, 852
  Text Edit tools, 851–852
  Tracker window
    described, 869–870
    documents, viewing, 870–871
    Expand/Collapse lists, 871
    RSS feeds, accessing, 871–872
revolving 3-D objects, 500–502
RGB color mode, 338, 339
Rotate tool, Illustrator, 418–419
rotating objects
  Illustrator, 416
  InDesign, 432

Continued

rotating objects *(continued)*
    patterns, 435–436
    Photoshop, 432
    3-D objects, 502
rows
    GoLive tables, moving, 785
    InDesign tables
        cell dimensions, 776–777
        deleting, 774
        evenly distributing, 777
    pixel selection tool, Photoshop, 404
RSS (Really Simple Syndication)
    feeds, accessing Tracker window review sessions, 871–872
    reading, 268–271
rulers, 105–106, 897

S

saving
    camera raw files, 254–255
    custom Bridge workspace, 210–212
    document searches, 238
    initial view, downloadable documents, 961–962
    new action set, Actions automating tasks, 593
    Save dialog box, 28–29
    Save for Web dialog box
        Smart Objects, 934–936
        SVG files, 1125–1126
        SWF files, 1112–1113
    SVG files with different SVG versions, 1122
    Version Cue files, 286–287, 290
    workspaces, 156–158
Scalable Vector Graphic files. *See* SVG files
scaling
    effects, adding to layers, 560
    Illustrator, 416–420
    InDesign print setups, 1192–1193
scanning
    downloadable document pages, 955
    images in Photoshop, 381–383
    sketch in Acrobat Professional, 33–35
Scratch Disks
    Illustrator preferences, 97
    Photoshop preferences, 107
screening output, Acrobat print setup, 1201–1202
Scribble effect, Illustrator, 503–504
scripts
    batch-processing PDF files, 609–612
    on demand documents
        creating, 1066–1069
        running, 1069–1072
    Photoshop and Illustrator, 600–602
scrolling pages, slide presentations, 1163
search engine
    described, 230
    documents
        files for quick cleanup, 235–236
        folders, viewing files from different, 236–237
        metadata, 233–235
        options, 231–233
        saving searches, 238

stock photos
    additional options, 240
    libraries, 238–239
    online services, 240
searching
    comments, 862
    external devices, 983
    indexing PDFs, 980
sections, InDesign page numbering, 896–897
security
    attachments
        policies, 1020–1024
        Secure PDF Delivery, 1024–1027
    CD/DVD distribution, 1092, 1107–1108
    document
        Acrobat, adding, 1011–1018
        CS programs, creating PDFs from, 1018–1019
        described, 1009
        encryption levels, 1010
        permissions, 1010
        signature handlers, 1010
    indexing PDFs, 974
selecting
    building, pixel selection tools, 405–406
    described, 320–321
    exporting Word text, 748–749
    GoLive table cells, 785
    Illustrator
        Group Selection and Magic Wand tools, 321–322
        Layers palette, 322
        Select menu, 323
    InDesign tools, 321
    layers, 513–514
    pages and spreads, 891
    Photoshop tools, 322
    Stamp tool for review sessions, 852
    transforming objects in Photoshop, 440
    XML elements, 989–990
separations, previewing
    on monitor, 1211–1212, 1217–1219
    print layout, 65–66
sequences, batch-processing PDF files, 605, 608
server, connecting to, GoLive Web site publishing, 1079–1080
services, enabling Photoshop commands, 257–258
shading, Illustrator graphs, 301
shadows, image auto adjustments, 389–390
shapes
    compound, editing objects in Illustrator, 374–375
    custom objects, creating in Photoshop, 316
    layers, Photoshop, 550–551
sharing swatches between CS2 applications, 366–367
sharp color changing edges (High Pass) filters, Photoshop, 476
sharpening images, Photoshop, 473–474
Shear tool, Illustrator, 421–422
Shockwave Flash files. *See* SWF files
showing and hiding InDesign layers, 583–584
signature handlers, DRM, 1010
size, palette showing
    GoLive, 433–434
    Illustrator, 432–433

sketch
  comments, adding, 37–39
  e-mail review, submitting, 35–37
  review comments, collecting, 39–40
  scanning, 33–35
slices
  Illustrator, 95–96
  Photoshop, 106–107
slide presentations
  Acrobat, creating with, bookmarks, 1148
  Bridge, 271–272
  converting to PDF
    Apple Keynote slides, converting, 1146–1147
    described, 1141–1142
    PowerPoint slides, converting to PDF, 1142–1146
  Full Screen views
    in Acrobat, 1161
    described, 1160–1161
    interactivity, 1163–1164
    preferences, setting, 1162–1163
    scrolling pages, 1163
  Illustrator, creating with, 1155–1157
  InDesign, creating with
    bookmarks, 1147–1149
    described, 1147
    exporting to PDF, 1149–1151
    notes and handouts, 1151–1154
  layers, 1157–1159
  page transitions, 1159–1160
  Photoshop, creating with, 1154–1155
Smart Guides
  Illustrator preferences, 95–96
  image layers, aligning and distributing, 450–451
Smart Objects
  GoLive Web sites, setting up
    cropping, 936–937
    described, 934
    editing source image, 936
    Save for Web dialog box, 934–936
  Photoshop, combining layers with, 566–567
Smooth tool, Illustrator, 369–370
snapping objects in Illustrator, 415
snippets, exporting, 368
soft-proofing documents on monitor
  Acrobat Professional
    Color Warnings, 1219
    menu commands, 1214
    overprint preview, 1215–1217
    separations preview, 1217–1219
    tools, 1219–1224
  commercial printing, 1207
  Illustrator
    described, 1212–1213
    managing presets, 1214
    transparency flattening, 1213–1214
  InDesign
    separations, previewing, 1211–1212
    transparency flattening, 1208–1211
sorting comments, 861
Source Code Editor, XML, 1004–1005
space usage, downloadable documents, 953–954
spacing, distributing objects, 447–449

special effects. *See* effects
special type characters
  break characters, inserting, 722–723
  Glyphs palette
    custom sets, working in InDesign, 718–719
    described, 715–716
    inserting into text, 716–717
  inserting, 719–722
  white space, inserting, 722
spelling, 117
splitting cells, InDesign tables, 775
Spot Healing tool, Photoshop, 44–45, 410
spot versus process color, 342
spot-proofing, Acrobat Professional
  color, checking, 67–68
  PDF/X file, creating, 69–71
  transparency, flattening, 68
stacking order
  Arrange menu, changing with, 445
  Clipboard, changing with, 446
  controlling with layers, 444–445
  GoLive Z-index value, changing, 446
  group, changing within, 446
Stamp tool
  Clipboard Image, pasting, Acrobat review sessions, 858–859
  retouching images in Photoshop, 409
  review sessions
    adding to page, 852–854
    custom, creating, 854–856
    libraries, 857–858
    Manage Stamps command, 857
    properties, changing, 854
    selecting, 852
Stamp tools in Photoshop, 409
standard page sizes, converting to PDF, 816–818
states, Version Cue files, 287–288
status, review session, 863
stock photos
  ASPS
    browsing images, 242–243
    news and offers, getting, 243
    overview, 241–242
    provider libraries, 242
  camera raw files
    described, 246
    plug-in, using, 248–253
    preferences, setting, 246–248
    saving, 254–255
    settings, applying in Bridge, 253–254
  described, 240
  libraries, 238–239
  low-resolution images, downloading (comps), 243–246
  online services, 240
  terms of service, 240–241
stop action, adding with comments, 595–596
story editor display, InDesign, 118–119
Story Editor, InDesign type styles, 654–655
strokes
  color
    CMYK mode, 341
    Color Picker, 343–344

Continued

strokes, color *(continued)*
- described, 337
- Eyedropper tools, 344–346
- gamut, 343
- Grayscale mode, 341
- hexadecimal numbers, 340
- HSB mode, 340–341
- palette, 341–343
- profiles and settings, 346–347
- RGB mode, 338, 339
- spot versus process, 342
- Web Safe mode, 338–339

gradients
- angle, specifying, 349
- custom, creating and applying, 349–352
- meshes, 352–353
- palette, 347–349

graphic styles in Illustrator and Photoshop, 365

Illustrator
- applying, 329–331
- colors, applying to objects, 325–326
- corners, 327
- Dashed Line, 328–329
- Live Paint, 331–336
- thickness inside or outside, 327–328
- weights, 326–327

InDesign
- applying, 329–331
- colors, applying to objects, 325–326
- corners, 327
- Dashed Line, 328–329
- tables, 775–776, 778
- thickness inside or outside, 327–328
- weights, 326–327

libraries of content, 367–368
object styles in InDesign, palette, 363–364

patterns
- described, 353
- Illustrator, 354–355
- Photoshop, 355–356

Photoshop
- path, 337
- pixel selection, 336–337
- Preset Manager, 368–369

snippets, exporting, 368

swatches
- described, 365
- libraries, creating custom, 366
- palette, 366
- sharing between applications, 366–367

symbols in Illustrator
- described, 360
- inserting, editing, and creating, 361–362
- libraries, accessing, 361
- tools, 362–363

transparency
- blending modes, 357–358
- objects and images, 356
- opacity, 358–360

Structure pane, XML tags, 991
studio production workflows, 181–182

styles. *See also* type styles
character
- creating in Illustrator, 667
- using in InDesign, 667–668

GoLive tables, 786

graphic
- Illustrator, 676–679
- InDesign, 682–685
- Photoshop, 680–681

nested, new, creating, 671–676

paragraph
- Illustrator, 668–670
- InDesign, 670–671

using in Photoshop, 667

Stylize
effects, Illustrator, 503–504

filters
- Illustrator, 494–495
- Photoshop, 474–475

sublayers, Illustrator, 522–523

summary
- Acrobat review sessions, 875–878
- InDesign print setups, 1199
- PDF documents for CD/DVD distribution, 1093

SVG (Scalable Vector Graphic) files
GoLive
- Illustrator Smart Objects, 1131–1132
- objects, adding to Web page, 1129–1131
- steps, 1132–1134

Illustrator, creating in
- advanced options, 1124–1125
- described, 1117–1118
- exporting issues, 1122
- filters, 1118–1121
- interactivity, 1121–1122
- options, specifying, 1123–1124
- Save for Web window, 1125–1126
- steps, 1126–1128
- versions, differing, 1122

XML, 986–987

swatches
- described, 365
- libraries, creating custom, 366
- palette, 366
- sharing between applications, 366–367

SWF (Shockwave Flash) files
Acrobat
- importing in PDF documents, 1136–1139
- Web pages, converting to PDF, 1134–1136

GoLive
- Illustrator Smart Objects, 1131–1132
- objects, adding to Web page, 1129–1131
- steps, 1132–1134

Illustrator, creating in
- animations with layers, 1114–1115
- described, 1109
- differences in files, 1114
- exporting, 1110–1112
- Save for Web window, 1112–1113
- steps, 1115–1117
- symbols, 1115

symbols
　creating, editing, and inserting, 361–362
　described, 360
　libraries, accessing, 361
　SWF files, creating, 1115
　tools, 362–363
synchronizing color settings, 199–200
synchronizing files, GoLive Web site publishing, 1080–1081

T

tables
　creating in InDesign
　　converting text to table, 772
　　frames, running table between, 772
　　headers and footers, 772–773
　　moving between cells, 771–772
　　populating, 771
　editing in InDesign
　　cells, selecting, 773
　　deleting rows and columns, 774
　　inserting rows and columns, 773–774
　　merging cells, 774
　　splitting cells, 775
　Excel spreadsheets, using in InDesign, steps, 778–783
　formatting in InDesign
　　aligning cell content, 778
　　alternating fills, 776
　　alternating strokes, 775–776
　　cell row and column dimensions, 776–777
　　dialog box, 775
　　evenly distributing rows and columns, 777
　　tagged tables, exporting, 778
　GoLive
　　creating, 784
　　formatting cells, 786
　　importing from Word or Excel, 785
　　merging cells, 786–787
　　moving, adding, and deleting rows and columns, 785
　　populating cells, 784–785
　　resizing cells, 786
　　selecting cells, 785
　　styles, 786
　importing
　　from Excel, 769
　　GoLive, using Word tables in, 769
　　Illustrator, using Word tables in, 766–769
　　InDesign, Excel tables in, 769–770
　　InDesign, Word in, 766
　　from Word, 765–766
tagging
　documents, 997–999
　InDesign tables, exporting, 778
　XML content, importing, 995–996
targeting
　layers, 513–514
　pages and spreads, layout, InDesign, 891
templates, Illustrator layers, 524–525
terms of service, stock photo, 240–241
testing InDesign links and buttons, 1032

text
　Acrobat, exporting to Word, 751
　converting to InDesign tables, 772
　GoLive, exporting to Word, 749–750
　Illustrator
　　exporting to Word, 749–750
　　graphs, changing, 801
　InDesign, exporting to Word, 751
　inline graphics, creating, 723
　inserting special characters, 716–717
　Photoshop, exporting to Word, 749–750
　thread, adding frames to, 689–690
　wrap, suppressing on hidden layers, InDesign, 517–518
Text Edit tools, Acrobat review sessions, 851–852
text frames
　adding to text thread, 689–690
　anchoring objects in layout, 913–914
　columns and insets, creating, 691–695
　master pages
　　autoflowing text, 699–700
　　described, 696–697
　　manual, creating, 697–699
　　modifying, 700–702
　text attributes, setting, 695–696
　threads, working with, 687–688
　unthreading, 690
text wraps
　Illustrator
　　around images, 707–709
　　described, 702–703
　　graphic objects, 703–706
　　type objects, 706–707
　InDesign
　　importing, 709–711
　　options, 711–713
thickness inside or outside filling and stroking objects in Illustrator and InDesign, 327–328
third-party filters, Photoshop, 477
threading text across multiple frames, InDesign, 63–65
threads, text frame, 687–688
3-D objects
　extruding, 497–499
　mapping artwork, 500
　revolving objects, 52–53, 500–502
　rotating objects, 502
tiling options, print setup, 1192–1193
Timeline, enabling animations, 576
tonal range, adjusting with Curves dialog box, 388–389
tools
　Bridge workspace, 205–210
　Live Paint, 332–333
　objects, creating in Photoshop, 315–316
　production workflow standards, 184
　symbols Illustrator, 362–363
　user interfaces
　　accessing, 136–137
　　Acrobat, 134–135, 147
　　Bridge, 134
　　described, 129–132
　　GoLive, 135–136, 147
　　Illustrator, 132–134, 137–144

Continued

tools, user interfaces *(continued)*
  InDesign, 132–134, 144–147
  Photoshop, 132–133, 134, 144
  toolboxes, 129–132
tracing layers, Illustrator, 525–526, 531–534
Tracker window
  Acrobat review sessions, 869–872
  review sessions
    described, 869–870
    documents, viewing, 870–871
    Expand/Collapse lists, 871
    RSS feeds, accessing, 871–872
transforming objects
  GoLive palette, 433–434
  Illustrator
    array of objects, creating, 426–427
    described, 413–414
    flower, creating sample, 430–431
    Free Transform tool, 422–423
    moving, 414–415
    patterns, 434–436
    position and size, palette showing, 432–433
    rotating, 416, 418–419
    scaling and reflecting, 416–421
    Shear tool, 421–422
    snapping, 415
    steps, 423–425
    Transform Each dialog box, 429–430
    Transform menu commands, 425–426
  InDesign, 428–429, 438–440
  Photoshop
    described, 440
    Free Transform, 441–442
    patterns, 436–438
    perspective, controlling, 442–443
    pixels, moving, 441
    selection, 440
    Transform menu, 442
    Warp mode, 443–444
transparency
  downloadable document settings, 956
  filling and stroking objects
    blending modes, 357–358
    objects and images, 356
    opacity, 358–360
  locking, 547
  modes, applying to InDesign layers, 520–521
  Photoshop preferences, 105
transparency flattening
  Acrobat
    print setups, 1202–1203
    spot-proofing, 68
  Illustrator
    printing, 1183–1184
    soft-proofing, 1213–1214
  InDesign
    print setups, 1198–1199
    soft-proofing, 1208–1211
type
  Acrobat link and button characters, 1038
  Illustrator graphs, changing, 797

layers
  creating, 548
  orientation and antialiasing, 548–549
  paragraph and point text, converting between, 549
  warping text, 550
outlines and special effects, Illustrator
  described, 623–624
  effects, creating, 624–625
  Illustrator, converting, 624
  masks, creating, 625
  raster, converting to vector type, 626–628
outlines, converting to, 628–634
preferences
  Illustrator, 90–91
  InDesign, 110–112
  Photoshop, 107–108
text wraps, Illustrator, 706–707
tool creating in Illustrator, 311
type styles
  described, 637
  Illustrator
    area type, creating, 641–643
    described, 638
    OpenType, 643–645
    point type, 638–641, 645–647
    updating type, 647–649
  InDesign
    Character palette, 655–657
    Control palette, 657
    described, 653
    Paragraph palette, 660–663
    placeholder, 657–660
    Story Editor, 654–655
  paths, creating on, 663–665
  Photoshop
    Character palette, 652–653
    described, 650
    Options Bar, 650–652
    Paragraph palette, 653

U

Units and Display Performance, Illustrator, 91–92
units, InDesign preferences, 112–113
Units & Rulers, Photoshop, 105–106
unthreading text frames, 690
updates
  CD/DVD, distributed, 1106
  help, 162
  InDesign preferences, 125
  type styles, Illustrator, 647–649
  Version Cue, 278–279
  Web pages, 924
uploading files, Web site, 1080–1081
URL links, 1041–1043
user interfaces
  context menus, 158–159
  help
    files, 159–161
    online, 162
    updates, 162

keyboard shortcuts
  Acrobat, 173–174
  described, 162
  GoLive, 172–173
  Illustrator, 163–164
  InDesign, 170–172
  Photoshop, 167–170
  workgroups, 164–167
palettes and workspaces
  Acrobat, 153–154
  described, 147
  grouping, 154–156
  Illustrator, 149–150
  InDesign and GoLive, 151–152
  Photoshop, 150–151
  Window menus, 148
tool options
  accessing, 136–137
  Acrobat and GoLive, 147
  Illustrator, 137–144
  InDesign, 144–147
  Photoshop, 144
tools, accessing
  Acrobat, 134–135
  Bridge, 134
  GoLive, 135–136
  Illustrator, 132–134
  InDesign, 132–134
  Photoshop, 132–134
  toolboxes, 129–132
workspaces, saving, 156–158
users, managing Web page, 291–292

V

validating XML structure, 992–993
value axis, Illustrator graph
  scale, 800
  setting, 799
vanishing point, 487–490
variables, data-driven graphics, 603–604
vector
  masking layers, 565
  objects onto pixel images, 399–403
Version Cue (Adobe)
  Adobe Dialog, 281–284
  Bridge files, adding, 57
  Bridge versus, 56
  CS2 Administration Web pages
    Advanced features, 294–296
    backing up projects, 294
    creating and editing projects, 292–294
    described, 290–291
    users, adding and editing, 291–292
  described, 28, 275
  enabling, 280
  files
    adding, 288
    alternates, 288–289
    deleting, 290
    opening, 285–286, 290
    project, creating, 284–285
    remote projects, accessing, 285
    saving, 286–287, 290

states, 287–288
versions, working with, 288
project files, versioning, 54–56
updating, 278–279
workspace, setting up
  exporting data, 277
  folders, specifying, 276–277
  preferences, 275–276
Video filter, Photoshop, 475
viewing
  comments, 860–861
  FTP files, 1081–1082
  GoLive package, 946–947
  XML tags
    described, 1002–1003
    Layout editor, 1005
    Outline Editor, 1003, 1005
    Source Code Editor, 1004–1005
    Structure pane, 989

W

Warp effect
  Illustrator, 504–505
  Photoshop, 443–444
  Type layers, 550
Web hosting documents
  adding and configuring site, 1076–1079
  exporting site, 1084–1085
  FTP versus HTTP, 1074
  GoLive packaging
    described, 73–74
    downloading Web pages, 1082
    server, connecting to, 1079–1080
    steps, 1082–1084
    uploading, downloading, and synchronizing files, 1080–1081
    viewing files with FTP Browser, 1081–1082
  HTML, packaged, exporting with GoLive, 75–76
  Internet access, setting up, 1073–1074, 1075
  PDF Optimizer, 71–73
  publish server, specifying, 1075–1076
Web page
  converting to PDF, 1046–1048, 1134–1136
  objects, adding, 1129–1131
Web Photo Gallery, 264
Web Safe mode, 338–339
Web sites
  adding pages, 924
  creating new, 920–923
  CSS
    applying styles, 939–940
    defining styles, 939
    described, 937
    editor, 938–939
    external style sheet, creating, 940
  described, 919
  GoLive, creating pages in
    adding pages and using views, 925–927
    Basic Objects and images, 931
    described, 924–925
    linking pages, 930
    objects, adding, 928–929

Continued

Web sites, GoLive, creating pages in *(continued)*
    properties, changing object, 929
    steps to build sample, 931–933
    text, adding, 930
    Web page tools, 927–928
  GoLive packaging
    contents, examining, 945–946
    dragging and dropping assets, 947–949
    exporting to HTML, 949
    InDesign document, 944–945
    viewing, 946–947
  Smart Objects in GoLive
    cropping, 936–937
    described, 934
    editing source image, 936
    Save for Web dialog box, 934–936
  updating pages, 924
  Welcome dialog box, 920
Web-hosted PDFs, bookmarking, 303–304
weights, filling and stroking objects, 326–327
Welcome dialog box, Web site, 920
white space, inserting, 722
Windows (Microsoft)
  custom page sizes, 821
  desktop printers, selecting on
    Acrobat, 1175
    InDesign and Illustrator, 1172–1173
    Photoshop and GoLive, 1174
  fonts, installing, 619
  menus, 148
  PDFs, creating, 1104
  PowerPoint slides, converting to PDF, 1145–1146
Word (Microsoft)
  Clipboard
    described, 727–728
    fonts, missing, 729–730
    formatting, 728–729
  content, moving to GoLive
    Clipboard, using, 744
    opening text files, 745
    Paste Special command, 744
  documents, moving
    from Acrobat, 754–755
    batch-converting files, 755
    comments from Acrobat, 755–758
    Illustrator, 752–753
    InDesign, 753–754
  dynamic text editing
    described, 758
    PDF documents, 759–763
  exporting text
    advantages, 748
    Clipboard, 749–751
    formatting, 749
    methods, 748
    purpose of, 747
    selecting text, 748–749
  GoLive tables, importing, 785
  Illustrator charts, importing
    charts and diagrams, 812
    creating, 811
    described, 810
    transporting via Clipboard, 811, 812

  importing styles
    deleting, 739
    described, 738–739
    editing, 739
    mapping to InDesign styles, 740
  importing tables, 765–766
  importing text
    Acrobat, 736–737, 738
    drag and drop text files, 734
    formatting in Photoshop, 736
    Illustrator, 731–732, 732
    InDesign, 732–734, 740–743
    Photoshop, 735–736
  printing
    converted files, printing in Acrobat, 824
    described, 815–816
    Macintosh custom page sizes, 819–821
    nonstandard page sizes, 821–824
    standard page sizes, converting, 816–818
    trim and crops, applying in Acrobat, 824–827
    Windows custom page sizes, 821
workflows. *See* color-managed workflows
workspaces
  Acrobat, 153–154
  described, 147
  grouping, 154–156
  Illustrator, 149–150
  InDesign and GoLive, 151–152
  Photoshop, 150–151
  user interfaces, saving, 156–158
  Window menus, 148
wrapping text. *See* text wraps

X

XHTML Mobile, 942–944
XML (eXtensible Markup Language)
  Acrobat files, saving as, 1006
  Creative Suite and, 986
  described, 985–986
  GoLive
    described, 1002–1003
    Outline Editor, 1003
    Outline or Layout editors, splitting, 1005
    Source Code Editor, 1004–1005
  InDesign
    attributes, 991
    described, 987
    DTD, loading, 992
    files, exporting, 993–995, 999–1000
    importing, 1000–1002
    layouts, creating, 996–997
    marking elements, 987–989
    rearranging tags, 991
    selecting, adding, and deleting elements, 989–990
    tagged content, importing, 995–996
    tagging documents, 997–999
    validating structure, 992–993
    viewing all tags, 989
  SVG and, 986–987